T0135257

Lecture Notes in Artificial Intelligence   13151

Subseries of Lecture Notes in Computer Science

Series Editors

Randy Goebel
University of Alberta, Edmonton, Canada

Wolfgang Wahlster
DFKI, Berlin, Germany

Zhi-Hua Zhou
Nanjing University, Nanjing, China

Founding Editor

Jörg Siekmann
DFKI and Saarland University, Saarbrücken, Germany

Guodong Long · Xinghuo Yu · Sen Wang (Eds.)

AI 2021: Advances in Artificial Intelligence

34th Australasian Joint Conference, AI 2021
Sydney, NSW, Australia, February 2–4, 2022
Proceedings

 Springer

Editors
Guodong Long ⓘ
University of Technology Sydney
Sydney, NSW, Australia

Xinghuo Yu ⓘ
RMIT University
Melbourne, SA, Australia

Sen Wang ⓘ
University of Queensland
Brisbane, QLD, Australia

ISSN 0302-9743 ISSN 1611-3349 (electronic)
Lecture Notes in Artificial Intelligence
ISBN 978-3-030-97545-6 ISBN 978-3-030-97546-3 (eBook)
https://doi.org/10.1007/978-3-030-97546-3

LNCS Sublibrary: SL7 – Artificial Intelligence

This Springer imprint is published by the registered company Springer Nature Switzerland AG
The registered company address is: Gewerbestrasse 11, 6330 Cham, Switzerland

Preface

This volume contains the papers presented at the 34th Australasian Joint Conference on Artificial Intelligence (AI 2021). Due to the COVID-19 pandemic, the conference was virtually held during February 2–4, 2022, and was hosted by the University of Technology Sydney, Australia. This annual conference is one of the longest running conferences in artificial intelligence, with the first conference held in Sydney in 1987. The conference remains the premier event for artificial intelligence in Australasia, offering a forum for researchers and practitioners across all subfields of artificial intelligence to meet and discuss recent advances.

AI 2021 received 120 submissions with 398 authors from 30 countries and more than 100 different institutions. Each submission was reviewed by at least three Program Committee (PC) members or external reviewers. After a thorough discussion and rigorous scrutiny by the reviewers and the dedicated members of the Senior Program Committee, 64 submissions were accepted for publication as full papers. Moreover, 40 papers were presented as oral presentations and 23 papers were presented as poster presentations in the conference.

AI 2021 had three keynote talks by the following distinguished scientists:

- Liz Sonenberg, University of Melbourne, Australia, on February 2, 2022.
- Jon Whittle, CSRIO's Data61, Australia, on February 3, 2022.
- Elizabeth Croft, Monash University, Australia, on February 4, 2022.

There are a number of important aspects to the AI 2021 conference worth mentioning. First, due to the impact of COVID-19, the conference date was postponed from December 2021 to February 2022 to allow for in-person gathering and networking. However, the new outbreak of the Omicron variant in December 2021 changed the conference format from hybrid to full virtual. Second, we have witnessed an overwhelming trend of deep learning that has profoundly influenced or reshaped many research and application domains; thus, many submissions in AI 2021 explored deep learning technology to redefine and solve AI problems.

We thank the authors for submitting their research papers to the conference, preparing videos, and presenting their work online to cope with the consequences of the COVID-19 pandemic. We are grateful to authors whose papers are published in this volume for their cooperation during the preparation of the final camera-ready versions of the manuscripts. We especially appreciate the work of the members of the Program Committee and the external reviewers for their expertise and tireless effort in assessing the papers within a strict timeline. We are very grateful to the members of the Organizing Committee for their efforts in the preparation, promotion, and organization of the conference, especially the general chairs for coordinating the whole event. We acknowledge the assistance provided by EasyChair for conference management.

To celebrate the diversity of talent working with, developing, and educating for emerging technology, the Women in Artificial Intelligence (WAI) committee worked in conjunction with the IEEE Women in Computational Intelligence (WCI) subcommittee and Women in Big Data (WiBD) to present three events. The panel event, Perspectives on Trust and Intelligence, brought together experts to discuss the diversity required to realize ethical and capable technology. The WAI/WCI keynote event focused on career experiences and development tips for all emerging AI/CI professionals. Finally, the WAI/WiBD event provided an opportunity for anyone within AI, CI, or data to pitch their achievements and goals, whether working in research, industry, or academia.

Lastly, we thank Springer, the National Committee for Artificial Intelligence of the Australian Computer Society, the University of Technology Sydney (UTS), the University of New South Wales (UNSW), the Royal Melbourne Institute of Technology (RMIT), CSRIO's Data61, Business Events Sydney, and Finity for their sponsorship and Springer for the professional service provided by the LNCS editorial and publishing teams.

December 2021   Guodong Long
                                                                      Xinghuo Yu
                                                                      Sen Wang

Organization

General Chairs

Mary-Anne Williams   University of New South Wales, Australia
Toby Walsh   University of New South Wales, Australia

Program Chairs

Xinghuo Yu   Royal Melbourne Institute of Technology
     University, Australia
Guodong Long   University of Technology Sydney, Australia

Organizing Committee

Local Organization Co-chairs

Jing Jiang   University of Technology Sydney, Australia
Benjamin Johnston   University of Technology Sydney, Australia
Tony Chen   University of Queensland, Australia

Tutorial Co-chairs

Wei Liu   University of Western Australia, Australia
Daswin De Silva   La Trobe University, Australia

Workshop Co-chairs

Marcus Hutter   Australian National University, Australia
Lina Yao   University of New South Wales, Australia
Stephan Chalup   University of Newcastle, Australia

Special Session Co-chairs

Tianqing Zhu   University of Technology Sydney, Australia
Shirui Pan   Monash University, Australia
Jia Wu   Macquarie University, Australia

Sponsorship Co-chairs

Andy Song	Royal Melbourne Institute of Technology University, Australia
Ian Farmer	University of Technology Sydney, Australia
Qinghua Lu	CSRIO's Data61, Australia

Publicity Co-chairs

Tongliang Liu	University of Sydney, Australia
Han Yu	Nanyang Technological University, Singapore
Xiaoying Gao	Victoria University of Wellington, New Zealand

Social Media Co-chairs

Lianhua Chi	La Trobe University, Australia
Tao Shen	Microsoft Research Asia, China

Volunteer and Virtual Co-chairs

Leah Gerrard	Commonwealth Department of Health, Australia
Lu Liu	Google, USA
Xiazhi Wang	University of Technology Sydney, Australia

Women-in-AI Chairs

Sue Keay	CSRIO's Data61, Australia
Wafa Johal	University of New South Wales, Australia

Proceedings Chair

Sen Wang	University of Queensland, Australia

Web Chair

Xueping Peng	University of Technology Sydney, Australia

Senior Program Committee

Abdul Sattar	Griffith University, Australia
Byeong-Ho Kang	University of Tasmania, Australia
Damminda Alahakoon	La Trobe University, Australia
Dongmo Zhang	Western Sydney University, Australia
Hussein Abbass	UNSW Canberra, Australia
Jiuyong Li	University of South Australia, Australia
Mark Reynolds	University of Western Australia, Australia
Mengjie Zhang	Victoria University of Wellington, New Zealand

Program Committee

Adnan Mahmood	Macquarie University, Australia
Adriana-Simona Mihaita	University of Technology Sydney, Australia
Andrea Torsello	Ca' Foscari University of Venice, Italy
Andrew Lensen	Victoria University of Wellington, New Zealand
Archie Chapman	University of Queensland, Australia
Asanka N. K. Mudiyanselage	Department of Defence, Australia
Atilla Elci	Aksaray University, Turkey
Avinash Singh	University of Technology Sydney, Australia
Bach Nguyen	Victoria University of Wellington, New Zealand
Bernhard Pfahringer	University of Waikato, New Zealand
Bing Wang	University of New South Wales, Australia
Binh Tran	Victoria University of Wellington, New Zealand
Brendon J. Woodford	University of Otago, New Zealand
Changqin Huang	Zhejiang Normal University, China
Chris Zhang	Deakin University, Australia
Daniel Le Berre	CNRS - Université d'Artois, France
Dave de Jonge	IIIA-CSIC, Spain
Dengji Zhao	ShanghaiTech University, China
Dianhui Wang	La Trobe University, Australia
Diego Molla	Macquarie University, Australia
Dilini Samarasinghe	University of New South Wales, Australia
Fangfang Zhang	Victoria University of Wellington, New Zealand
Gang Chen	Victoria University of Wellington, New Zealand
Giorgio Stefano Gnecco	IMT School for Advanced Studies Lucca, Italy
Guangyan Huang	Deakin University, Australia
Guido Governatori	CSIRO, Australia
Hannes Strass	Dresden University of Technology, Germany
Hans W. Guesgen	Massey University, New Zealand
Harisu-Abdullahi Shehu	Victoria University of Wellington, New Zealand
Harith Al-Sahaf	Victoria University of Wellington, New Zealand
Hepu Deng	RMIT University, Australia
Hongxu Chen	University of Technology Sydney, Australia
Huan Huo	University of Technology Sydney, Australia
Hui Ma	Victoria University of Wellington, New Zealand
Ickjai Lee	James Cook University, Australia
Jeffrey Chan	RMIT University, Australia
Ji Ruan	Auckland University of Technology, New Zealand
Ji Zhang	University of Southern Queensland, Australia
Jia Zhu	Zhejiang Normal University, China
Jianhua Yang	Western Sydney University, Australia

Jianlong Zhou	University of Technology Sydney, Australia
Jie Shao	University of Electronic Science and Technology of China, China
Jing Jiang	University of Technology Sydney, Australia
Jing Liu	National Laboratory of Pattern Recognition, CASIA, China
Jing Teng	North China Electric Power University, China
Jiye Liang	Shanxi University, China
Kai Qin	Swinburne University of Technology, Australia
Ke Deng	RMIT University, Australia
Kevin Wong	Murdoch University, Australia
Kun Yu	University of Technology Sydney, Australia
Laurence Park	Western Sydney University, Australia
Laurent Perrussel	IRIT - Université de Toulouse, France
Lu Liu	Google, USA
M. A. Hakim Newton	Griffith University, Australia
Mahdi Jalili	RMIT University, Australia
Manolis Gergatsoulis	Ionian University, Greece
Manqing Dong	Amazon, Shanghai, China
Maolin Tang	Queensland University of Technology, Australia
Marcello Sanguineti	University of Genova, Italy
Marcus Gallagher	University of Queensland, Australia
Marcus Randall	Bond University, Australia
Markus Wagner	University of Adelaide, Australia
Maurice Pagnucco	University of New South Wales, Australia
Miao Xu	University of Queensland, Australia
Mingyu Guo	University of Adelaide, Australia
Mohammad Reza Bonyadi	University of Adelaide, Australia
Ning Gu	University of South Australia, Australia
Oliver Obst	Western Sydney University, Australia
Peter Baumgartner	CSIRO, Australia
Qin Zhang	Shenzhen University, China
Rafal Rzepka	Hokkaido University, Japan
Richi Nayak	Queensland University of Technology, Australia
Rolf Schwitter	Macquarie University, Australia
Seyedamin Pouriyeh	Kennesaw State University, USA
Shadi Abpeikar	UNSW Canberra, Australia
Shuang Wang	Southeast University, China
Shuxiang Xu	University of Tasmania, Australia
Simone Scardapane	Sapienza University of Rome, Italy
Songcan Chen	Nanjing University of Aeronautics and Astronautics, China

Stephen Chen	York University, Canada
Sung-Bae Cho	Yonsei University, South Korea
Tao Shen	Microsoft Research Asia, China
Tao Shi	Victoria University of Wellington, New Zealand
Taotao Cai	Macquarie University, Australia
Tim French	University of Western Australia, Australia
Tim Hendtlass	Swinburne University, Australia
Tony Chen	University of Queensland, Australia
Wei Emma Zhang	University of Adelaide, Australia
Weidong Cai	University of Sydney, Australia
Weihua Li	Auckland University of Technology, New Zealand
Weitong Chen	University of Queensland, Australia
Xianzhi Wang	University of Technology Sydney, Australia
Xiaoying Gao	Victoria University of Wellington, New Zealand
Xingjun Ma	University of Melbourne, Australia
Xiu Susie Fang	Donghua University, China
Xueping Peng	University of Technology Sydney, Australia
Xuyun Zhang	Macquarie University, Australia
Yanan Sun	Sichuan University, China
Yanjun Shu	Harbin Institute of Technology, China
Yi Cai	South China University of Technology, China
Yi Guo	Western Sydney University, Australia
Yi Mei	Victoria University of Wellington, New Zealand
Yi Yang	Deakin University, Australia
Ying Bi	Victoria University of Wellington, New Zealand
Yuwei Peng	Wuhan University, China
Zehong Cao	University of South Australia, Australia
Zhihong Man	Swinburne University of Technology, Australia
Zhuoyun Ao	Defence Science and Technology Organisation, Australia
Zonghan Wu	University of Technology Sydney, Australia

Contents

Classical AI

Computer Vision and Machine Learning

Natural Language Processing and Data Mining

Network Analysis

Ethical AI

An Explanation Module for Deep Neural Networks Facing Multivariate Time Series Classification

Chao Yang[1(✉)], Xianzhi Wang[1], Lina Yao[2], Jing Jiang[3], and Guandong Xu[4]

[1] School of Computer Science, University of Technology Sydney, Ultimo, Australia
chao.yang@student.uts.edu.au
[2] School of Computer Science and Engineering, UNSW, Kensington, Australia
[3] Australian AI Institute, University of Technology Sydney, Ultimo, Australia
[4] Data Science Institute, University of Technology Sydney, Ultimo, Australia

Abstract. Deep neural networks currently achieve state-of-the-art performance in many multivariate time series classification (MTSC) tasks, which are crucial for various real-world applications. However, the black-box characteristic of deep learning models impedes humans from obtaining insights into the internal regulation and decisions made by classifiers. Existing explainability research generally requires constructing separate explanation models to work with deep learning models or process their results, thus calling for additional development efforts. We propose a novel explanation module pluggable into existing deep neural networks to explore variable importance for explaining MTSC. We evaluate our module with popular deep neural networks on both real-world and synthetic datasets to demonstrate its effectiveness in generating explanations for MTSC. Our experiments also show the module improves the classification accuracy of existing models due to the comprehensive incorporation of temporal features.

1 Introduction

The past decade has seen multivariate time series classification (MTSC) becoming one of the most critical issues in data mining [11]. MTSC finds significance in various practical tasks, such as activity recognition [40], disease diagnosis [31], and weather forecasting [25]. Currently, deep neural networks have been widely adopted for MTSC [12] and achieved state-of-the-art performance in various tasks, thanks to the ability to capture complicated, non-linear relations between inputs and outputs [29]. Generally, deep neural networks stack multiple neural layers to automate feature extraction and representation learning, and their internal mechanisms remain unrevealed to the end-user. Nevertheless, many real-world applications find the significance of gaining insights into the critical variables that impact the decisions of classifiers [37] to approach a better understanding of specific domains. For example, in aquaculture, multiple environmental conditions (e.g., light) jointly affect the creature's growth. However, although researchers can monitor environmental variables and growth of creatures [16,17]

© Springer Nature Switzerland AG 2022
G. Long et al. (Eds.): AI 2021, LNAI 13151, pp. 3–14, 2022.
https://doi.org/10.1007/978-3-030-97546-3_1

and predict the growth trend by solving a multivariate time series classification (MTSC) problem, it is more desirable to derive human-understandable interpretations of which factors play the major role in determining the classification outcomes. Various applications in other domains, e.g., healthcare and medical diagnosis [15, 32] call for explainable MTSC as well.

A deep neural network for multivariate time series classification usually consists of two components: backbone and head. The backbone is responsible for extracting temporal features and harnessing the inter-relationship of the variables to learn the representations of the input data, called feature-maps. The head can map the feature-maps to the possibility distribution of the output labels, i.e. the classes. The backbone conducts feature extraction by fusing the temporal features from different variables. While it is beneficial for the model to effectively harness the temporal features of the input time series, it leads to challenges in finding the important information from variables. For example, in convolutional neural networks, the filter in the first layer will harness all the channels' information simultaneously—the channels are fully connected for information fusion across all the channels. Hence, as the networks go deep, it is nearly impossible for the typical convolutional neural network to track the variables' importance during inference.

Although many studies have sought explanation for classification problems [1, 42], they mostly design separate architectures that are specific to certain deep neural-network types. They need to re-design the backbone architecture (following the ad-hoc approach) or propose post-hoc techniques, which lack the flexibility to be applied to different deep neural networks. Besides, the whole architecture has to be re-evaluated when task or circumstance changes, leading to extra efforts for model adaptation. All the above deficiencies call for a generic module that is pluggable into various deep neural networks for MTSC. In this regard, we propose an explanation module that can be seamlessly integrated into deep neural networks to gain the importance of variables in MTSC. We make the following contributions in this paper:

- We propose an explanation module that can be plugged into existing popular deep neural networks, such as CNN, RNN, to infer the importance of variables in MTSC automatically.
- We conducted experiments on four benchmark multivariate time series datasets using four variants of CNN and RNN to evaluate our proposed module. Our experiments on input variables with added noises validate the effectiveness of the module.
- Besides adding explainability, the experimental results show that our module enables the MTSC models to better leverage the temporal feature and achieve better accuracy.
- We provide implementation details of the proposed module and related experiments to ensure our module can be re-implemented conveniently.

The rest of this paper is organized as follows: Sect. 2 introduces some related works and techniques; Sect. 3 presents the structure of the proposed explanation module; Sect. 4 reports our experiments; finally, Sect. 5 concludes our works.

2 Related Work

2.1 Multivariate Time Series Classification

Convolutional Neural Networks (CNNs) are firstly used for image recognition [27]. Recent studies have found that 1D CNN can be used for temporal feature extraction [5,19,22], hence inspiring researchers to use CNN for time series classification [13,28,44]. For 1D CNN, the convolution computation can harness the potential temporal patterns while the information fusion across the channels is helpful to tackle the inter-relations of the variables. As CNNs focus on the information in the receptive field, it is challenging to capture a relatively long-range time series.

Recurrent Neural Network (RNN) is a structure specifically designed for temporal data [30,33]. Two most well-known variants are called Long Short-term Memory (LSTM) [21] and Recurrent Gated Unit (GRU) [8] which are widely used in dealing with time series sequences [6,36,39]. RNNs have the shortcomings of containing massive parameters. Besides, it is difficult to apply parallel computation to RNNs, which further degrades the time consumption [35].

The combination of CNN and RNN represents one effort to fix the shortcomings [3,4]. CNN and RNN are constructed in the parallel or cascade style to exploit the advantages of both CNN and RNN. This architecture is beneficial for capturing various ranges of temporal feature extraction. LSTM-FCNs [26] construct CNN and RNN in a two parallel stream style. Combining this architecture with the attention layer called Squeeze-and-Excitation Net [24] can achieve state-of-the-art performance on several benchmark multivariate time series classification datasets.

2.2 Explanation Methods

There have been several efforts exploring explanation methods for deep neural networks in various tasks. Some efforts have tried to figure out the effect of the input on the output [43]. Gradient-based methods have been used for exploring the influence of the input changes [7,38]. However, these types of methods are only feasible for convolutional neural networks.

Another explanation approach is to design a separate architecture for explanation purposes. Some studies [18,41] select a critical subset of features to figure out the most influential variables. While some work embeds attention mechanisms to evaluate the effectiveness of the input data [2,9], it may take considerable efforts to design a new architecture, not to mention the potential adverse impact of the explanation module on performance. An example is LAXCAT [23]: although it can visualize critical variables based on fully-grouped convolutions and attention mechanisms, it lacks the ability to exploit the inter-relationship among variables, resulting in suboptimal performance.

3   Our Approach

In a typical multivariate time series classification (MTSC) process (represented by blue blocks in Fig. 1), the input firstly goes through the backbone (e.g., CNN or RNN) to generate feature-maps (denoted by $\mathbf{FM}_{backbone} \in \mathbb{R}^{N \times L}$). Then, the head (usually, a fully-connected layer or 1D convolutional layer) maps feature-maps to a probability distribution of classes.

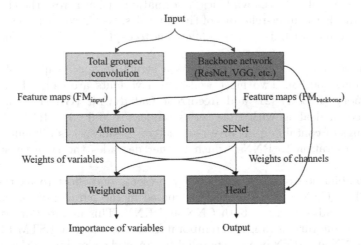

Fig. 1. The proposed module is pluggable into any existing deep learning model (i.e., *backbone network*) in a backbone-head fashion. Yellow blocks represent our proposed module and Blue ones stand for the original neural-network model. The module obtains the importance of variables by calculating attention on top of the feature-maps extracted by the backbone ($\mathbf{FM}_{backbone}$) and by the grouped convolution layers ($\mathbf{FM}_{input}$), respectively. The module updates $\mathbf{FM}_{backbone}$ twice according to the outputs of *Attention* and *SENet* to enhance the backbone network's performance. (Color figure online)

Our proposed module (represented yellow blocks in Fig. 1) aims to explore the importance of variables for pluggable explanation in MTSC. Our module works in the following steps. Given input fed to a total grouped convolution layer, the convolution filters conduct separate calculations on each variable. Normal convolution is fully connected in the channel perspective causing the information flow among the channels. Total grouped convolution splits channel of the input data and does convolutions on each channel. In this manner, the number of filters is equal to the number of the variables. Hence, during this process, the module does not consider any inter-relationship of the variables. The feature-map of each channel is the representation of each variable. The output feature-map is indicated by $\mathbf{FM}_{input} \in \mathbb{R}^{M \times L}$, where $\mathbf{M}$ is the number of variables, and $\mathbf{L}$ is the length of the feature-map. Noted, the length of the $\mathbf{FM}_{input}$ should be the same as $\mathbf{FM}_{backbone}$ for the attention calculation. Generally, the backbone downsamples the input that leads to the small length of $\mathbf{FM}_{backbone}$ than the input time series sequence. If necessary, the module will adjust the kernel size of the total grouped convolution according to the two feature-maps to ensure their lengths are equal. Typically, using a large stride for downsampling helps ensure the feature-maps' lengths meet the module's requirements. Since no information flows across variables, each channel of $\mathbf{FM}_{input}$ can be considered as the vectorized representation of the corresponding variable.

After this, the attention between the $\mathbf{FM}_{backbone}$ and $\mathbf{FM}_{input}$ is calculated. In this step, we have the importance of the variables according to the channels of $\mathbf{FM}_{backbone}$, indicated by $\mathbf{Attn}_{nm} \in \mathbb{R}^{N \times M}$, it also can be seen as the weights of the variables. Besides, $\mathbf{FM}_{backbone}$ is updated based on the results. In the next step, $\mathbf{FM}_{backbone}$ is sent to the SENet to obtain the importance of the channels or the weights of the channels. As the importance is learnt according to the inter-relationship of the channels and the importance of different channels regarding to the output, we indicate it using $\mathbf{SelfAttn}_n \in \mathbb{R}^N$, while the $\mathbf{FM}_{backbone}$ is updated the second time. Then, we have the importance of the variables regarding to the channels of the $\mathbf{FM}_{backbone}$ $\mathbf{Attn}_{nm}$ as well as the importance of the channels of the $\mathbf{FM}_{backbone}$ $\mathbf{SelfAttn}_n$. At the last step, the module does weight sum to obtain the importance of the variables as Eq. (1):

$$\text{Importance }_m = \sum_1^N \text{Attn }_{nm} \times \text{Self Attn }_n \tag{1}$$

where $\mathbf{Importance}_m \in \mathbb{R}^M$. In this way, the importance of the M variables on the decision-making process of the classifier is obtained.

As the feature-maps $\mathbf{FM}_{backbone}$ are updated twice based on the results of two attention calculation steps, the model can utilize the temporal information more effectively to achieve better performance. Specifically, the $\mathbf{FM}_{input}$ contains different granular feature-maps compared with $\mathbf{FM}_{backbone}$. Hence, the module can harness more feature-maps to achieve better classification accuracy. Besides, our module can be integrated into the classifier following a backbone-head style. It has nearly no difficulty and limitation for combining the proposed module with the existing models to figure out the importance of MTSC variables.

4   Experiments

4.1   Datasets

We conducted experiments on four carefully selected public multivariate time series datasets (Table 1), which are representative of different sizes and domains. Table 1 includes the number of the classes, number of the variables for each input sequence, the length of the sequence, and the train-test split ratio. More details are as follows:

Table 1. Experimental datasets

Dataset	Classes	Number of variables	Sequence length	Train-test ratio
AREM [10]	7	7	480	50:50
LP5 [10]	5	6	15	39:61
ArabicDigits [10]	10	13	93	75:25
Wafer [34]	5	18	214	25:75

- **AREM** [10]: AREM dataset contains time series sequences recorded by sensors placed in different positions of the body to recognize the activities. The dataset consists of six activity types: cycling, lying, sitting, standing, walking, bending1, and bending2.
- **LP5** [10]: LP5 dataset is for robot failures detection in motion. It contains five classes, including normal, bottom collision, bottom obstruction, collision in part, and collision in tool.
- **ArabicDigits** [10]: ArabicDigits is used to detect which Arabic digits the writer is writing. So it is very intuitive that the dataset contains 10 classes, including the digits ranging from 0 to 9.
- **Wafer** [34]: The wafer database comprises a collection of time-series data sets where each file contains the sequence of measurements recorded by one vacuum-chamber sensor during the etch process applied to one silicon wafer during the manufacture of semiconductor microelectronics. It contains two classes: normal or abnormal.

For each dataset, we normalized it to zero mean and unit standard deviation; we also applied zero paddings to cope with sequences with different lengths.

4.2   Baseline Methods

We select two representative variants of CNN and two representative variants of RNN to demonstrate the feasibility of plugging our proposed module into existing models. These models also serve as baseline methods for comparative experiments.

- **ResNet** [20] and **Res2Net** [14]: Popular Convolutional Neural Network-based models. We train ResNet on AREM dataset and train Res2Net on LP5 dataset. ResNet and Res2Net contain 4 convolutional layers. Each convolutional layer is 1D convolution to ensure the model is adaptable for time series data.
- **LSTM** [21] and **GRU** [8]: Popular Recurrent Neural Network-based models. We train LSTM on the ArabicDigits dataset and train GRU on the Wafer dataset. As LSTM and GRU contain 2 RNN layers, we use the last hidden state as the information vector. The vector is sent to a fully connected layer to map the information vector to the probability distribution of the classes.

4.3   Evaluation Procedure

For each model, we followed the given train-test split regulation and firstly train it on the training set. We train our model on a single GTX 3090 GPU with 24 GB memory. We apply *oversampling* to classes with fewer samples to mitigate the impact of imbalanced class distribution. Then, considering the importance of variables vary across classes, for each dataset, we select a particular class from the test set to evaluate the importance of variables produced by our module. Specifically, we select the sixth class (i.e., bending2), the third class (i.e., bottom obstruction), the first class (i.e., digit 0), and the first class (normal) from the four datasets (AREM, LP5, ArabicDigits, and Wafer), respectively, to evaluate our experimental results.

We also generate synthetic datasets by adding random noises to the original datasets to further validate the soundness of the importance of variables produced by our module. Specifically, we sample the noise data from normal distribution and add to the variables separately and text the model with the contaminated data. Intuitively, if the variable is important when adding the noise to it, it should dramatically influence the decision-making by the classifier. In other words, if the influence of the variable is significant, then the accuracy will fall significantly when the variable is affected by the noise and vice versa.

We use *accuracy* as the evaluation metric, which is commonly used as the sole performance indicator in MTSC. We tested the model for five times on the datasets and calculate the average accuracy and the standard deviation. Since we concentrate on the effectiveness of the proposed module, accuracy suffice to suggest the quality of different methods' results.

4.4   Results

Performance on Real Datasets. Tables 2, 3, 4 and 5 show our experimental results on the four datasets. Our module can be implemented to be combined with various models without much extra efforts. Through the utilization of our module, we can obtain the importance of the variables quantitatively. To make the results more convenient to understand, we execute softmax on the results. Thus, all the weights are in [0,1], and the sum is 1. We select a specific class and use the synthetic dataset and test the importance given by the module, i.e., we add noise manually to the variables separately; then, we explore the accuracy changes thanks to the noise. We present the accuracy on the specific dataset before and after adding noise to the variable separately. Intuitively, a more critical variable bears a great change in classification accuracy. Our results on the Wafer dataset (shown in Table 2) show a classification accuracy is 99.87% on the selected class. The results produced by the module indicate that the 5th and 6th variables are most important and least important, respectively. As we repeat the experiments five times, we also give the standard deviations of the average accuracy with and without the noise.

Table 2. Experimental results on Wafer dataset

Accuracy (sd) (w/o noise)	99.87% (0.68%)					
Variable id	1	2	3	4	5	6
Importance of variables	0.101	0.129	0.158	0.261	0.276	0.075
Accuracy (%) (w/noise)	99.01	96.38	96.38	96.38	94.38	99.75
Standard deviation (w/noise)	0.05	0.39	0.38	0.42	0.76	0.04
Accuracy change (Δ%)	0.86	3.49	3.49	3.49	4.9	0.12

Table 3. Experimental results on LP5 dataset

Accuracy (sd) (w/o noise)	96.15% (2.58%)					
Variable id	1	2	3	4	5	6
Importance of variables	0.225	0.157	0.186	0.082	0.148	0.202
Accuracy (%) (w/noise)	46.15	88.46	76.92	92.30	92.30	73.07
Standard deviation (%) (w/noise)	2.81	2.59	2.57	2.96	2.28	2.70
Accuracy change (Δ%)	50.00	7.69	19.23	3.85	3.85	23.08

Table 4. Experimental results on AREM dataset

Accuracy (sd) (w/o noise)	100% (0)						
Variable id	1	2	3	4	5	6	7
Importance of variables	0.215	0.150	0.060	0.115	0.174	0.229	0.057
Accuracy (%) (w/noise)	0.00	0.00	71.43	71.43	14.28	0.00	71.43
Standard deviation (%) (w/noise)	6.32	4.90	6.46	7.07	4.99	6.91	6.18
Accuracy change (Δ%)	100.00	100.00	28.57	28.57	85.71	100.00	28.57

Validating Explanation Ability. We tested adding noises to the variables manually, which results in drastic changes in the accuracy on the 5th variable while little change on the 6th variable. The results indicate that noises can influence the crucial variables, and the regulation has well-matched the hypothesis. On the other datasets, the results are similar. Hence, we can say that the importance the module obtains is convincing.

It is worth noting that the accuracy of all the datasets given in Tables 2, 3, 4 and 5 is quite high. That is because we select the specific class to evaluate our results. We have found that a satisfying performance is crucial to obtain reasonable results. Because when the classification accuracy is high, that means the model focuses on the right variables.

Impact on Performance. Besides explanation ability, our module can improve the performance of the baseline models on the respective datasets. Specifically, Fig. 2 suggests that all the selected classifiers achieve better classification accuracy on each dataset, which indicates the superiority of the proposed module. The model better harnesses the temporal features as it updates the

Table 5. Experimental results on ArabicDigits dataset

Accuracy (sd) (w/o noise)	100% (0)						
Variable id	1	2	3	4	5	6	7
Importance of variables	0.071	0.001	0.074	0.042	0.076	0.386	0.024
Accuracy (%) (w/noise)	98.83	99.10	98.83	99.10	97.54	29.24	98.83
Standard deviation (%) (w/noise)	0.35	0.21	0.25	0.24	0.34	0.33	0.36
Accuracy change (Δ%)	0.27	0.00	0.27	0.00	1.56	69.86	0.27
Variable id	8	9	10	11	12	13	
Importance of variables	0.100	0.030	0.110	0.031	0.052	0.002	
Accuracy (%) (w/noise)	85.10	98.04	61.72	98.43	98.83	98.83	
Standard deviation (%) (w/noise)	0.38	0.33	0.49	0.46	0.91	0.45	
Accuracy change (Δ%)	14.00	1.06	37.38	0.67	0.27	0.27	

Table 6. Training time consumption comparison between the model with the proposed module and without the proposed module on Wafer dataset

	Average training time (s)	Standard deviation (s)
Without the module	32.95	3.9
With the module	36.02	2.76

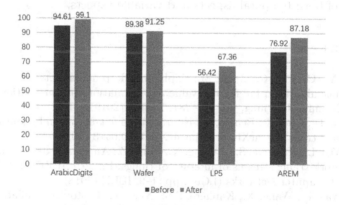

Fig. 2. Accuracy comparison between the original model and the model combined with our proposed module

feature-maps (extracted by the backbone) twice according to the self-attention of the feature-maps and the attention between feature-maps and input. The module helps the original model to fuse various levels of feature-maps and improve the classifier's performance. The accuracy given in Fig. 2 is the average accuracy of all the classes instead of a specific class. Hence the accuracy is different from the results of the tables shown in the previous contents.

Besides, the proposed module does not significantly cause extra time consumption. To indicate that, we record the training time consumption, which is shown in Table 6, on the Wafer dataset. The corresponding method we use on the Wafer dataset is the LSTM with three layers. We train the model on Intel Core i7-8550 with 16GB RAM instead of GTX 3090 GPU, because the GPU is too powerful to demonstrate the time consumption difference. In Table 6, we can see the average training time increased by 9%, thus we can say the proposed module is efficient.

5   Conclusion and Future Work

We propose an explanation module to explore the importance of the variables for multivariate time series classification. Our module can be easily plugged into the existing models and quantitatively figure out the importance of the variables for classification. Our extensive experiments demonstrate its effectiveness. Besides, the module can improve the model's performance further, as it is beneficial for leveraging the temporal information of the input. We also provide some tricks for implementing our module. However, the module is not feasible for finding the important time interval for the outcome, which leads to limitations. In the future, we plan to refine the module to make it feasible for figuring out the importance of both temporal aspects and variable aspects.

References

1. Ancona, M., Oztireli, C., Gross, M.: Explaining deep neural networks with a polynomial time algorithm for shapley value approximation. In: International Conference on Machine Learning, pp. 272–281. PMLR (2019)
2. Bahdanau, D., Cho, K., Bengio, Y.: Neural machine translation by jointly learning to align and translate. arXiv preprint arXiv:1409.0473 (2014)
3. Bai, L., Yao, L., Kanhere, S.S., Wang, X., Yang, Z.: Automatic device classification from network traffic streams of internet of things. In: 2018 IEEE 43rd Conference on Local Computer Networks (LCN), pp. 1–9. IEEE (2018)
4. Bai, L., Yao, L., Wang, X., Kanhere, S.S., Xiao, Y.: Prototype similarity learning for activity recognition. In: Lauw, H.W., Wong, R.C.-W., Ntoulas, A., Lim, E.-P., Ng, S.-K., Pan, S.J. (eds.) PAKDD 2020. LNCS (LNAI), vol. 12084, pp. 649–661. Springer, Cham (2020). https://doi.org/10.1007/978-3-030-47426-3_50
5. Borovykh, A., Bohte, S., Oosterlee, C.W.: Conditional time series forecasting with convolutional neural networks. arXiv preprint arXiv:1703.04691 (2017)
6. Cao, J., Li, Z., Li, J.: Financial time series forecasting model based on CEEMDAN and LSTM. Phys. A **519**, 127–139 (2019)
7. Chattopadhay, A., Sarkar, A., Howlader, P., Balasubramanian, V.N.: Gradcam++: generalized gradient-based visual explanations for deep convolutional networks. In: 2018 IEEE Winter Conference on Applications of Computer Vision (WACV), pp. 839–847. IEEE (2018)
8. Cho, K., et al.: Learning phrase representations using rnn encoder-decoder for statistical machine translation. arXiv preprint arXiv:1406.1078 (2014)

9. Choi, E., Bahadori, M.T., Kulas, J.A., Schuetz, A., Stewart, W.F., Sun, J.: Retain: an interpretable predictive model for healthcare using reverse time attention mechanism. arXiv preprint arXiv:1608.05745 (2016)
10. Dua, D., Graff, C.: UCI machine learning repository (2017). http://archive.ics.uci.edu/ml
11. Esling, P., Agon, C.: Time-series data mining. ACM Comput. Surv. (CSUR) **45**(1), 1–34 (2012)
12. Ismail Fawaz, H., Forestier, G., Weber, J., Idoumghar, L., Muller, P.-A.: Deep learning for time series classification: a review. Data Min. Knowl. Disc. **33**(4), 917–963 (2019). https://doi.org/10.1007/s10618-019-00619-1
13. Gamboa, J.C.B.: Deep learning for time-series analysis. arXiv preprint arXiv:1701.01887 (2017)
14. Gao, S., Cheng, M.M., Zhao, K., Zhang, X.Y., Yang, M.H., Torr, P.H.: Res2net: a new multi-scale backbone architecture. IEEE Trans. Pattern Anal. Mach. Intell. **43**(2), 652–662 (2019)
15. Goldberger, A.L., et al.: Physiobank, physiotoolkit, and physionet: components of a new research resource for complex physiologic signals. Circulation **101**(23), e215–e220 (2000)
16. Guo, B., Mu, Y., Wang, F., Dong, S.: Effect of periodic light color change on the molting frequency and growth of litopenaeus vannamei. Aquaculture **362**, 67–71 (2012)
17. Guo, B., Wang, F., Li, Y., Dong, S.: Effect of periodic light intensity change on the molting frequency and growth of litopenaeus vannamei. Aquaculture **396**, 66–70 (2013)
18. Han, M., Liu, X.: Feature selection techniques with class separability for multivariate time series. Neurocomputing **110**, 29–34 (2013)
19. Han, Z., Zhao, J., Leung, H., Ma, K.F., Wang, W.: A review of deep learning models for time series prediction. IEEE Sens. J. **21**(6), 7833–7848 (2019)
20. He, K., Zhang, X., Ren, S., Sun, J.: Deep residual learning for image recognition. In: Proceedings of the IEEE Conference on Computer Vision and Pattern Recognition, pp. 770–778 (2016)
21. Hochreiter, S., Schmidhuber, J.: Long short-term memory. Neural Comput. **9**(8), 1735–1780 (1997)
22. Hoermann, S., Bach, M., Dietmayer, K.: Dynamic occupancy grid prediction for urban autonomous driving: a deep learning approach with fully automatic labeling. In: 2018 IEEE International Conference on Robotics and Automation (ICRA), pp. 2056–2063. IEEE (2018)
23. Hsieh, T.Y., Wang, S., Sun, Y., Honavar, V.: Explainable multivariate time series classification: a deep neural network which learns to attend to important variables as well as time intervals. In: Proceedings of the 14th ACM International Conference on Web Search and Data Mining, pp. 607–615 (2021)
24. Hu, J., Shen, L., Sun, G.: Squeeze-and-excitation networks. In: Proceedings of the IEEE Conference on Computer Vision and Pattern Recognition, pp. 7132–7141 (2018)
25. Karevan, Z., Suykens, J.A.: Transductive LSTM for time-series prediction: an application to weather forecasting. Neural Netw. **125**, 1–9 (2020)
26. Karim, F., Majumdar, S., Darabi, H., Harford, S.: Multivariate LSTM-FCNS for time series classification. Neural Netw. **116**, 237–245 (2019)
27. Krizhevsky, A., Sutskever, I., Hinton, G.E.: Imagenet classification with deep convolutional neural networks. Adv. Neural. Inf. Process. Syst. **25**, 1097–1105 (2012)

28. Lea, C., Vidal, R., Reiter, A., Hager, G.D.: Temporal convolutional networks: a unified approach to action segmentation. In: Hua, G., Jégou, H. (eds.) ECCV 2016. LNCS, vol. 9915, pp. 47–54. Springer, Cham (2016). https://doi.org/10.1007/978-3-319-49409-8_7

29. LeCun, Y., Bengio, Y., Hinton, G.: Deep learning. Nature **521**(7553), 436–444 (2015)

30. Lipton, Z.C., Berkowitz, J., Elkan, C.: A critical review of recurrent neural networks for sequence learning. arXiv preprint arXiv:1506.00019 (2015)

31. Lipton, Z.C., Kale, D.C., Elkan, C., Wetzel, R.: Learning to diagnose with LSTM recurrent neural networks. arXiv preprint arXiv:1511.03677 (2015)

32. Major, P., Thiele, E.A.: Seizures in children: laboratory. Pediatr. Rev. **28**(11), 405 (2007)

33. Malhotra, P., TV, V., Vig, L., Agarwal, P., Shroff, G.: Timenet: pre-trained deep recurrent neural network for time series classification. arXiv preprint arXiv:1706.08838 (2017)

34. Olszewski, R.T.: Bobski's world (2012). http://www.cs.cmu.edu/bobski/

35. Pascanu, R., Mikolov, T., Bengio, Y.: On the difficulty of training recurrent neural networks. In: International Conference on Machine Learning, pp. 1310–1318. PMLR (2013)

36. Sagheer, A., Kotb, M.: Time series forecasting of petroleum production using deep LSTM recurrent networks. Neurocomputing **323**, 203–213 (2019)

37. Schmidhuber, J.: Deep learning in neural networks: an overview. Neural Netw. **61**, 85–117 (2015)

38. Selvaraju, R.R., Cogswell, M., Das, A., Vedantam, R., Parikh, D., Batra, D.: Grad-cam: visual explanations from deep networks via gradient-based localization. In: Proceedings of the IEEE International Conference on Computer Vision, pp. 618–626 (2017)

39. Siami-Namini, S., Tavakoli, N., Namin, A.S.: A comparison of ARIMA and LSTM in forecasting time series. In: 2018 17th IEEE International Conference on Machine Learning and Applications (ICMLA), pp. 1394–1401. IEEE (2018)

40. Yang, C., Jiang, W., Guo, Z.: Time series data classification based on dual path CNN-RNN cascade network. IEEE Access **7**, 155304–155312 (2019)

41. Yoon, H., Shahabi, C.: Feature subset selection on multivariate time series with extremely large spatial features. In: Sixth IEEE International Conference on Data Mining-Workshops (ICDMW 2006), pp. 337–342. IEEE (2006)

42. Yoon, J., Jordon, J., van der Schaar, M.: Invase: instance-wise variable selection using neural networks. In: International Conference on Learning Representations (2018)

43. Zeiler, M.D., Fergus, R.: Visualizing and understanding convolutional networks. In: Fleet, D., Pajdla, T., Schiele, B., Tuytelaars, T. (eds.) ECCV 2014. LNCS, vol. 8689, pp. 818–833. Springer, Cham (2014). https://doi.org/10.1007/978-3-319-10590-1_53

44. Zheng, Y., Liu, Q., Chen, E., Ge, Y., Zhao, J.L.: Time series classification using multi-channels deep convolutional neural networks. In: Li, F., Li, G., Hwang, S., Yao, B., Zhang, Z. (eds.) WAIM 2014. LNCS, vol. 8485, pp. 298–310. Springer, Cham (2014). https://doi.org/10.1007/978-3-319-08010-9_33

Privacy-Preserving in Double Deep-Q-Network with Differential Privacy in Continuous Spaces

Suleiman Abahussein[✉], Zishuo Cheng, Tianqing Zhu[✉], Dayong Ye, and Wanlei Zhou

School of Computer Science, University of Technology Sydney, Ultimo, Australia
suleiman.abahussein@student.uts.edu.au
{zishuo.cheng,tianqing.zhu,dayong.ye,Wanlei.Zhou}@uts.edu.au

Abstract. With extensive applications and remarkable performance, deep reinforcement learning is becoming one of the most important technologies that researchers have been focusing on. Many applications have used reinforcement learning, such as robotics, recommendation systems, and healthcare systems. These systems could collect data about the environment or users, which may contain sensitive information that posed a real risk when these data were disclosed. In this work, we aim to preserve the privacy of the data used in deep reinforcement learning with Double Deep-Q-Network in continuous space by adopting the differentially private SGD method to inject a noise to the gradient. In our experiment, we used a different amount of noise on two separate settings to demonstrate how effective of using this method.

Keywords: Differential privacy · Deep reinforcement learning · Double Deep-Q-Network · Deep Q learning

1 Introduction

Deep reinforcement learning is now witnessing much interest, which led to current advances in a wide range of algorithms. The game of deep reinforcement learning such as ATARI2600 games, receive a large part of the advancement and development. However, other applications such as health systems [2], search engines [12], recommendation systems and robotic control recently received a lot of attention and development. With the success of AlphaGo [10], the development of deep reinforcement learning has speeded up and many developers are involved in developing applications in this field. Deep reinforcement learning recently raises security and privacy issues and these issues draw full attention from researchers in the meantime. The policies of trained deep reinforcement learning could be released to the client-side, where the adversaries could infer demographic information from the policy. Furthermore, there are a lot of parameters in AI models, some of the model parameters contained sensitive information implicitly which could also be inferred by the adversary. Hence, maintaining privacy is very important. Some study shows

© Springer Nature Switzerland AG 2022
G. Long et al. (Eds.): AI 2021, LNAI 13151, pp. 15–26, 2022.
https://doi.org/10.1007/978-3-030-97546-3_2

an adversary ability to infer the sensitive information from deep reinforcement learning such as the study conducted by Pan et al. [11]. Their experiment was aimed to infer environment dynamics under various scenarios, such as when the attacker knows limited information about the training environment. The experiment demonstrates that the floor plans can successfully be inferred by the algorithm and obtain a recovery rate of 95.83%.

In this paper, we consider the Double Deep-Q-Network, which has been proposed by van Hasselt et al. [17] to solve the overestimate action values under certain conditions in Deep-Q-Network. We aim to preserve the privacy in this particular algorithm by adopting it with privacy preserving algorithm that uses differential privacy to inject gaussian noise into the gradient during the training. To the best of our knowledge, this paper is the first one that applies the privacy preservation algorithm to Double Deep-Q-Network to preserve privacy. The main contribution of this paper is the following:

1. Adopt differential privacy for Double Deep-Q-Network method to guaranty privacy level.
2. Implement extensive experiments to test the performance of our method.

Related Work: recently, there are some researches that discuss privacy-preserving approaches for reinforcement learning. Tang et al. [15] proposed a method called Heda, which is privacy-preserving for machine learning that combines of differential privacy and holomorphic cryptosystem that employs some techniques for managing privacy budget and reducing sensitivity. Balle et al. [4] proposed differentially private algorithms built on top of Monte Carlo methods for policy evaluation in the full MDP setting. Furthermore, [13,19,20] discuss preserving privacy in multi-agent system. Other research focusing on privacy-preserving approaches to protect neighboring rewards from being distinguished in bandit problems, such as Tossou and Dimitrakakis [16], by using mechanisms to add noise to the estimates of the reward distribution. Also, Ma et al. [10] proposed differentially private mechanisms for $\epsilon - greedy$ and Softmax to achieve differentially private guarantees in the K-armed bandit problem. Wang and Hegde [18] discuss privacy-preserving approaches in reinforcement learning that uses Neural Networks (DQN) in continuous space by protecting neighboring rewards. These researches did not apply the privacy-preserving in Double Deep-Q-Network method, which is proposed by van Hasselt et al. [17]. In our work, we extend the research and apply differential privacy into Double Deep-Q-Network in continuous space and inject the noise into the gradient.

2   Preliminaries

2.1   Double Deep Q Network

One of the main elements of DQN is a function approximator for the Q-function. The van Hasselt et al. [17] showed that there is an overestimate value expected return when a single estimator is used in Q-learning and DQN due to the use of the maximum action value as an approximation of the maximum expected action value [3] this could sometimes be harmful to training performance and result to have suboptimal policies [9]. In 2016 the van Hasselt et al. [17] proposed Double DQN to solve the overestimate issue in Q-learning and DQN. This is done by decoupling the evaluation from the selection. In Q-learning, the max operation uses the same values both to select and to evaluates the action. The overestimated values are more likely to be selected in case of noise or inaccuracies, which leads to getting overoptimistic value estimates. There are two different Q Networks in Double DQN, the first one is the online Q Network and the second one is the target Q Network, the propose solution is to use the online network to evaluate greedy policy and target network to estimate its value and this is based on the following:

$$y_t^{Double-DQN} = r_{t+1} + \gamma Q(s_{t+1}, \underset{a}{\mathrm{argmax}} Q(s_{t+1}, a_t; \theta_t); \theta_t^-)$$

2.2 Differential Privacy

The threats to data privacy are increased, especially with the increase of data mining and aggregation. In general, differential privacy is a mathematical model that guarantees the privacy of a statistical dataset [10]. The Dwork et al. [6,7] provides a powerful standard to preserve privacy in data analysis. Differential privacy is a common privacy model that provides privacy guarantees without knowing anything about the in trader's background knowledge [21]. We consider a finite data universe $\mathcal{X}$. Let r represents a record sampled from universe $\mathcal{X}$ with d attributes. D is an unordered set of n records from domain $\mathcal{X}$. The two datasets D and D' are neighbouring datasets if two datasets D and D' differ in only one record. The function f is query maps dataset D to an abstract range $\mathbb{R} : f : D \rightarrow \mathbb{R}$. To preserve privacy, the differential privacy aims to mask the difference of query f between the neighbouring datasets. One of the important concepts in differential privacy is sensitivity Δf which represent the maximal difference in the results of query f, this determines how much perturbation is required for the private-preserving answer. The randomization algorithm M is used to achieve this target where it accesses the database and implements some functionality. A formal definition of differential privacy is below [22].

Definition 1. A randomized mechanism $\mathcal{M} : \mathcal{D} \rightarrow \mu$ satisfies differential privacy (ϵ, δ) if for any two neighboring inputs d *and* d' and for any subset of outputs $\mathcal{Z} \subseteq \mu$ it holds that

$$\mathbb{P}(\mathcal{M}(d) \in \mathcal{Z}) \leq exp(\epsilon)\mathbb{P}(\mathcal{M}(d') \in \mathcal{Z}) + \delta$$

Definition 2 (Sensitivity) for neighboring inputs $(d, d' \in \mathcal{D})$, the mechanism M sensitivity defines as:

$$\Delta f = \underset{d,d' \in \mathcal{D}}{sup} ||f(d) - f(d')||$$

The definition of Gaussian mechanism is: $\mathcal{M}(d) \triangleq f(d) + \mathcal{N}(0, \mathcal{S}_f^2 \cdot \sigma^2)$

where the normal (Gaussian) distribution is $\mathcal{N}(0, \mathcal{S}_f^2 \cdot \sigma^2)$ with mean 0 and standard deviation $\mathcal{S}_{f\sigma}$. The Gaussian mechanism for single application to sensitivity Δf satisfies differential privacy (ε, δ) if $\delta \geq \frac{3}{4} exp(-(\sigma\varepsilon)^2/2)$ and $\varepsilon < 1$ [1].

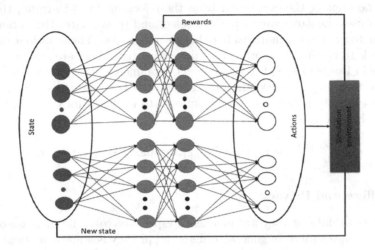

Fig. 1. Interacting Double DQN with it is environment: the Double DQN uses two neural network and aim to reduce Q-Value overestimations by splinting max operator into action selection and action evaluation

3 Differentially Private Double Deep Q Network

3.1 Overview of Our Method

Double DQN (DDQN) shows a good result on ATARI2600 games and achieving great performance in overcoming the overestimation problem that faces DQN. As the same Q function is used for both selecting and evaluating action in DQN, the overestimation of the value could occur which could lead to a decrease in the performance of DQN. The Double DQN used two neural networks in their architecture, the primary network and the target network. In our experiment, each network have three hidden layers. Figure 1 shows Double DQN and how it interacts with its environment. In our experiment the agent used epsilon-greedy method, this method gives the agent the opportunity to explore and learn from random action. To perform this, the epsilon defined to start from 1 to 0.1 with a decreased rate of 0.999. Random number generated by the code at each step, if the epsilon value is greater than generated a random number, then the action will be chosen randomly else, the model will choose the optimal action.

Algorithm 1. High level overview of Double Deep Q Network model

---
1: **Initialize:** primary network θ
2: **Initialize:** target network θ^-
3: **Initialize:** reply buffer $\mathcal{D}$ with size $\mathcal{N}$
4: **while** Training episodes not complete **do**
5:      Reset
6:      **while** not in terminal state **do**
7:          Observe state s_t
8:          With probability ε select a random action a_t
9:          Otherwise select $a_t = argmaxQ(s_t, a : \theta)$
10:          Execute action a_t and observe next state s_{t+1} , receive reward $r_t = R(s_t, a_t)$ and termination info
11:          Add (state s_t, action a_t , reward r_t , next state s_{t+1}) to reply buffer $\mathcal{D}$
12:          Sample random minibatch (s_j, a_j, r_j, s_{j+1}) from $\mathcal{D}$
13:          If episode terminates set $Y_j = r_j$ otherwise
14:          $Y_j = r_j + \gamma Q(s_{j+1}, \underset{a}{\mathrm{argmax}} Q(s_{j+1}, a_j; \theta_j); \theta_j^-)$
15:          Call DPSGD
16:          Perform a gradient descent step
17:          Every $\mathcal{C}$ step update target network parameters
18:      **end while**
19: **end while**
20: **Output** : trained DDQN

Algorithm 1 presents the high-level overview of the Double DQN model code that was used in our experiment and demonstrates the training process in the model. Firstly, lines 1–3, the primary neural network and target neural network are initialized with the random wight. The reply buffer memory $\mathcal{D}$ is initialized with a size of $\mathcal{N}$. According to the input data the neural network is trained extensively. The DDQN mode has two neural networks which play an essential role in selecting and evaluating the actions in the system, respectively. As the epsilon greedy method is used thus, the action will be selected randomly or by the model prediction based on epsilon value. Line 11, after the action is executed the action, reward, current state, and next state are stored in reply buffer. Line 12–13, the DPSGD is called to perform gradient descent with privacy-preserving by using the differential privacy technique along with a moments accountant method for tracing the privacy loss that allows the deep neural networks to train under a modest privacy budget. Line 14, after a certain number of iterations, the target network parameters are updated.

3.2   The Algorithm Design

DPSGD is a sophisticated approach aiming to protect the privacy of training data and manage the added noise to protect the data without destroying the utility. In this work, we adopt Differential privacy SGD [1] with the Double Deep-Q-Network algorithm to preserve privacy. The privacy has been achieved by adding noise into stochastic gradient descent directly with parameters θ by minimizing the empirical loss function $\mathcal{L}(\theta)$. By selecting subset of random example from the stored data of reply buffer the gradient $\nabla_\theta \mathcal{L}(\theta, x_i)$ computed at each step of SGD, for each gradient clip the ℓ_2 norm, compute the average, add noise in order to protect privacy, and take a step in the opposite direction of this average noisy gradient. At the end, the privacy loss of the mechanism needs to be computed based on the information maintained by the privacy accountant.

Norm clipping: bounding the influence of each individual example on $\widetilde{g}_t$ is required to proving and guarantee differential privacy. We clip each gradient in ℓ_2 norm since there is no a prior bound on the size of the gradient. For example, the vector $\mathbf{g}$ of the gradient is replaced by $\mathbf{g}/\max(1, \frac{\|\mathbf{g}\|_2}{C})$ for a clipping threshold C. The main purpose of this clipping is to ensure if the $\|\mathbf{g}\|_2 \leq C$, then the $\mathbf{g}$ is preserved, as it gets scaled down to be of norm C if $\|\mathbf{g}\|_2 > C$. In DPSGD consider each layer of multi-layer neural networks separately which allow to set different noise scales σ and clipping thresholds C for each layers. Furthermore, the noise and clipping parameters could be different with the number of training steps t. On group of a examples, the gradient of $\mathcal{L}$ is estimated by computing the gradient of the loss and obtaining the average. This average provides an unbiased estimator, the variance of which shrinkage rapidly with the size of the group. This group of examples is called a lot, the main purpose of gave this name is to distinguish a lot from the computational grouping that is usually called a batch. It maybe needs to set the batch size smaller than the a lot L size in order to limit memory consumption.

Privacy accounting: computing the overall privacy cost of the training important issue for differentially private SGD. Differential privacy composability allows us to perform "an accountant" procedure that calculates the privacy cost at each time use the training data and accumulates this cost during the training. The gradient is typically required in each step of training at multiple layers, and the accountant accumulates the cost that corresponds to all of them.

Moments accountant: There are many researches try to study the privacy loss for a specific noise distribution as well as the composition of privacy losses. For the gaussian noise which is used by DPSGD if we chose σ to be $\sqrt{2\log \frac{1.25}{\delta}}/\varepsilon$, with respect to the lot this will lead to be each step is (ε, δ) differentially private. As the lot is a random sample from the database, the theorem of the privacy amplification implies that each step is $(O(q\varepsilon), q\delta)$ differentially private with respect to full database where $q = L//N$ is the sampling ratio per lot and $\varepsilon \leq 1$. The DPSGD have moments accountant which is strong accounting method that let us prove that the DPSGD is differentially private $\left(O(q\varepsilon\sqrt{T}), \delta\right)$ for specific chosen settings of clipping threshold and the noise scale.

3.3   Rationale of Using DPSGD

The technique of differentially private SGD (DPSGD) allows to train deep neural networks with a modest privacy budget along with using the moments accountant method for tracing the privacy loss. The approach of differentially private versions of stochastic gradient descent is not new approach there are some previous work such as Song et al. [14], the DPSGD followed the same previous work with some number of modifications and extensions such as Moments accountant. Tracking privacy loss is a critical part of differential privacy, a new tool has come to tracking of the privacy loss in privacy is moments accountant. It permits tight automated analysis of the privacy loss of complex composite mechanisms. The DPSGD achieve high accuracy by training deep neural networks with differential privacy with a modest total privacy loss as it shows for MNIST experiments achieve 97% training accuracy and 73% accuracy for CIFAR-10 with $(8, 10^{-5})$ - differential privacy [1]. In this paper, we used DPSGD that proposed by Abadi et al. [1] as it robust and used an advanced tool such as moments accountant and showed good result in training deep neural networks with differential privacy.

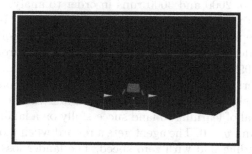

Fig. 2. The Lunar Lander environment: where Double DQN used to solve lunar lander challenge to make the ship land softly on the ground

4   Experiment

4.1   Experiment Setup

We performed our experiment on two different Double DQN application to demonstrate the ability of preserving privacy by applying differentially private SGD [1] in deep reinforcement learning that uses Double DQN. The first experiment was applied on Health System Simulations model of Double DQN [2]. This application was built as a simulation model of health systems and developed by using OpenAI Gym framework and PyTorch to build the agent. This health system intent to simulate real health system, it works to manage beds in hospital such as emergency department. The patients went to the hospital and stay for a certain time to get treatment then leave. When the patient come to the hospital the Health System Simulations check the available staffed bed and then allocate bed to this patient. There are limit number of beds available in the hospital at any time, the system has to manage the number of available staffed bed with the number of patient and try to give each patient a bed. The system has a target to make at least 5% free of the number of staffed bed in the hospital at any given time. The agent has to learn how to minimize the loss for each unoccupied bed or patient who have no bed. The reward is calculated based on the currently available bed and targeted bed and usually the reward is zero or negative. The system can request to change the number of staffed beds and this change performed after 2 days. The simulation runs for 365 days by default. The number of patients arrived at the hospital is different, the default number of arrived is 50/day. This number change as the number of arrival of patients in the weekend is 50% of average arrival numbers and the number of arrival of patients in the weekdays is 120% of average arrival numbers. The average stay of patients in the hospital is 7 days. In this experiment, four levels of noise were used to measure the effect of injected noise, the ability of the agent to learn with each different amount of noise and the ability to preserving privacy. The first time the agent run with no noise, then it runs with 10^{-10}, 10^{-5} and 10^{-3} of noise respectively. In this experiment, the agent of Double DQN have been trained for 500, 1000, 2000 and 3000 runs in order to analyze the behaviour of the agent with each noise level and different number of run. In this experiment it have been used epsilon-greedy to give the agent the opportunity to explore and learn from random action, the epsilon defined to start from 1 to 0.1 with a decreases rate of 0.999 and we use 0.9 of Moments Accountant.

The second experiment was performed on Double DQN LunarLander-v2 OpenAI Gym [8], Fig. 2 shows the Lunar Lander environment. The agent in this environment has the goal of learning to land successfully on a landing pad located at coordinates $x = 0$ and $y = 0$. The agent gets a reward when moving from the top of the screen to landing pad with zero speed. The lander loss rewards if moves away from landing pad. For each time the lander firing receives -0.03 points for each frame and the agent gets a negative reward if the lander crashes or a positive reward if the lander is able to land successfully. There are four possible action: fire left orientation engine, fire right orientation engine, fire main engine and do nothing and there is no limit for fuel. In this experiment, four levels of noise were used. The first time the agent run with no noise, then it run with 10^{-10}, 2×10^{-6} and 9×10^{-3} of noise respectively. In this experiment, the agent of Double DQN have been trained for 10000, 30000, 50000 and 80000 episodes respectively with use 0.9 of Moments Accountant and epsilon-greedy start from 1 to 0.1 with a decreases rate of 0.999.

4.2   Result and Analysis

This section will illustrate the behaviour of the Differentially Private SGD [1] algorithms on the two synthetic examples. Both two examples are MDP in continuous spaces. The implementation code is attached along with the manuscript submission.

Performance Metric 1 (Accuracy). The Figs. 3 and 4 shows the results of the Health System Simulations experiment and LunarLander-v2 experiment respectively, where x axis shows the number of run times and y axis shows the average rewards. For the Health System Simulations experiment different noise

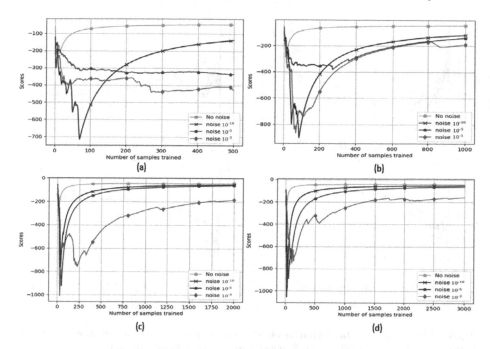

Fig. 3. The result of the Health System Simulations experiment after trained the agent for 500(a), 1000(b), 2000(c) and 3000(d) runs (Color figure online)

levels have been used with different number of run Fig. 3 shows the experiment result. In the beginning, there is very high fluctuation when the agent start specially in the first 100 of run with all levels of noise. This is due to the use of epsilon-greedy as the agent start taking action randomly for a certain time then the agent uses their prediction later to take action. This method gives the agent the opportunity to explore and learn from random action. The red line represents the performance and accuracy of the agent with no noise, as it appears that his performance increases gradually and then stabilizes to a highest level. The black and blue lines show the performance and the accuracy of the agent with a noise levels of 10^{-10} and 10^{-5} respectively. There is a slight decrease in the agent's accuracy with these noise levels and the agent is able to increase his performance over time. Even though the agent was able to improve his performance, the agent in this experiment wasn't able to reach the same level of accuracy, such as no noise even after 3000 runs. The green line shows the performance and accuracy of the agent with noise level 10^{-3} this is the highest noise level in the experiment and it demonstrates the effect of increasing noise as it shows that the agent performs with very low accuracy and far from no noise.

Figure 4 shows the result of LunarLander-v2 experiment. In all the experiments, the agent starts with very high fluctuation because of the use of epsilon-greedy method as the agent start taking the action randomly for a certain time, then the agent uses his prediction later. The red line represents the performance

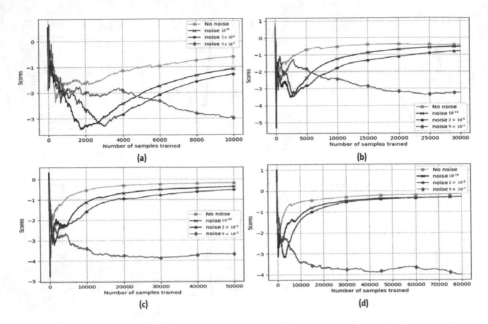

Fig. 4. The result of the LunarLander-v2 experiment after trained the agent for 10000(a), 30000(b), 50000(c) and 80000(d) runs (Color figure online)

of the agent with no noise as it shows that the performance increased steadily and shows how the agent learns over time. The black and blue lines demonstrate the performance and the accuracy of the agent with a noise level of 10^{-10} and 2×10^{-6}, where the agent starts with lower accuracy and increase over time. The agent in this two line is not able to reach the same level of accuracy such as no noise even after 80000 run. The green line represents the agent accuracy with a noise level of 9×10^{-3} the agent performs very poorly with this level of noise and shows that the accuracy drops dramatically and the agent is not able to increase his accuracy even after 80000 runs.

Performance Metric 2 (Convergent Rate/Speed). The converging is when the agent converts into optimal policy and the speed of converging is affected by different parameters such as discount factor [5]. In this section we compare the convergent rate for the agent after applying Differential privacy SGD with different amounts of noise. Figure 3 shows the performance of the Health System Simulations agent, the red line shows the agent with no noise as it able to converge and find the optimal policy very quickly after 100 samples of training. The agents in black and blue line with a low amount of noise 10^{-10} and 10^{-5} need more samples to train to reach to close level of the red line and almost they are very close to converging after 1000 samples of training. On the other hand, the agent with a higher level of noise 10^{-3} is far away from being a convert to optimal policy and still need more samples to train. Figure 4 shows the performance of LunarLander-v2, the agent in the red line with no noise is able to converges to the optimal policy after 11000 sample training. The agents in black and blue lines with a low level of noise 10^{-10} and 2×10^{-6} are very close to achieving convergence to the optimal policy after 30000 runs. On the other hand, the agent in the green line with a higher level of noise 9×10^{-3} is far away from being converged to optimal policy because of injecting high noise into the gradient by Differentially Private DPSGD.

5   Conclusion

We consider the Double DQN algorithm and preserve the privacy of the trained data from being disclosed. We adopt the Differentially Private SGD algorithm to implement the Differential Privacy method into Double DQN. In this paper, we show the result on two different experiments of Doube DQN applications. The first experiment was the Health System Simulations model this application was built to simulate real health systems, the second experiment was performed on LunarLander-v2 OpenAI Gym. For both experiments, different noise levels have been injected to demonstrate the effectiveness of the injected noise and the ability to preserve privacy. The effect of noise is very clear on the agent's performance, the noise increase leads to decreased accuracy. The agent with low noise levels needs more samples to train to almost able to converge to the optimal policy.

References

1. Abadi, M., et al.: Deep learning with differential privacy. In: Proceedings of the 2016 ACM SIGSAC Conference on Computer and Communications Security, pp. 308–318 (2016)
2. Allen, M., Monks, T.: Integrating deep reinforcement learning networks with health system simulations. arXiv preprint arXiv:2008.07434 (2020)
3. Arulkumaran, K., Deisenroth, M.P., Brundage, M., Bharath, A.A.: Deep reinforcement learning: a brief survey. IEEE Signal Process. Mag. **34**(6), 26–38 (2017)
4. Balle, B., Gomrokchi, M., Precup, D.: Differentially private policy evaluation. In: International Conference on Machine Learning, pp. 2130–2138. PMLR (2016)
5. Boufous, O.: Deep reinforcement learning for complete coverage path planning in unknown environments (2020)
6. Dwork, C., Kenthapadi, K., McSherry, F., Mironov, I., Naor, M.: Our data, ourselves: privacy via distributed noise generation. In: Vaudenay, S. (ed.) EUROCRYPT 2006. LNCS, vol. 4004, pp. 486–503. Springer, Heidelberg (2006). https://doi.org/10.1007/11761679_29
7. Dwork, C., McSherry, F., Nissim, K., Smith, A.: Calibrating noise to sensitivity in private data analysis. In: Halevi, S., Rabin, T. (eds.) TCC 2006. LNCS, vol. 3876, pp. 265–284. Springer, Heidelberg (2006). https://doi.org/10.1007/11681878_14
8. Lanham, M.: Hands-on reinforcement learning for games: implementing self-learning agents in games using artificial intelligence techniques (2020)
9. Lapan, M.: Deep Reinforcement Learning Hands-On - Second Edition. Packt Publishing Ltd (2020)

10. Ma, P., Wang, Z., Zhang, L., Wang, R., Zou, X., Yang, T.: Differentially private reinforcement learning. In: Zhou, J., Luo, X., Shen, Q., Xu, Z. (eds.) ICICS 2019. LNCS, vol. 11999, pp. 668–683. Springer, Cham (2020). https://doi.org/10.1007/978-3-030-41579-2_39
11. Pan, X., Wang, W., Zhang, X., Li, B., Yi, J., Song, D.: How you act tells a lot: privacy-leaking attack on deep reinforcement learning. In: Proceedings of the 18th International Conference on Autonomous Agents and MultiAgent Systems, pp. 368–376 (2019)
12. Rosset, C., Jose, D., Ghosh, G., Mitra, B., Tiwary, S.: Optimizing query evaluations using reinforcement learning for web search. In: The 41st International ACM SIGIR Conference on Research and Development in Information Retrieval, pp. 1193–1196 (2018)
13. Shen, S., Zhu, T., Ye, D., Wang, M., Zuo, X., Zhou, A.: A novel differentially private advising framework in cloud server environment. Concurr. Comput. Pract. Exp. e5932 (2020)
14. Song, S., Chaudhuri, K., Sarwate, A.D.: Stochastic gradient descent with differentially private updates. In: 2013 IEEE Global Conference on Signal and Information Processing, pp. 245–248. IEEE (2013)
15. Tang, X., Zhu, L., Shen, M., Du, X.: When homomorphic cryptosystem meets differential privacy: training machine learning classifier with privacy protection. arXiv preprint arXiv:1812.02292 (2018)
16. Tossou, A.C., Dimitrakakis, C.: Achieving privacy in the adversarial multi-armed bandit. arXiv preprint arXiv:1701.04222 (2017)
17. Van Hasselt, H., Guez, A., Silver, D.: Deep reinforcement learning with double q-learning. In: Proceedings of the AAAI Conference on Artificial Intelligence, vol. 30 (2016)
18. Wang, B., Hegde, N.: Privacy-preserving q-learning with functional noise in continuous spaces. In: Advances in Neural Information Processing Systems, pp. 11327–11337 (2019)
19. Ye, D., Zhu, T., Shen, S., Zhou, W., Yu, P.: Differentially private multi-agent planning for logistic-like problems. IEEE Trans. Dependable Secure Comput., 1 (2020). https://doi.org/10.1109/TDSC.2020.3017497
20. Ye, D., Zhu, T., Zhou, W., Philip, S.Y.: Differentially private malicious agent avoidance in multiagent advising learning. IEEE Trans. Cybern. 50(10), 4214–4227 (2019)
21. Zhu, T., Li, G., Zhou, W., Philip, S.Y.: Differentially private data publishing and analysis: a survey. IEEE Trans. Knowl. Data Eng. 29(8), 1619–1638 (2017)
22. Zhu, T., Philip, S.Y.: Applying differential privacy mechanism in artificial intelligence. In: 2019 IEEE 39th International Conference on Distributed Computing Systems (ICDCS), pp. 1601–1609. IEEE (2019)

HESIP: A Hybrid System for Explaining Sub-symbolic Predictions

Abdus Salam[✉], Rolf Schwitter, and Mehmet A. Orgun

Macquarie University, Sydney, Australia
{abdus.salam,rolf.schwitter,mehmet.orgun}@mq.edu.au

Abstract. Machine learning models such as neural networks have been successfully used in many application domains such as mission critical systems, digital health and autonomous vehicles. It is important to understand why particular predictions are made by a sub-symbolic machine learning (ML) model, because humans use these predictions in their decision making process. In this paper, we introduce HESIP, a hybrid system that combines symbolic and sub-symbolic representations to explain a prediction in natural language for an image prediction task. A sub-symbolic ML model makes a prediction for an image, and based on this predicted image, the system selects sample images from the dataset. Afterwards, a symbolic ML model learns probabilistic rules using the representation of positive and negative sample image instances where the decision about a positive or negative image instance comes from the sub-symbolic ML model. The prediction of an image can then be explained in natural language using the learned rules. Our evaluation shows that the probabilistic rules can be learned with high accuracy.

Keywords: Explainability · Probabilistic rule learning · Symbolic machine learning

1 Introduction

Machine learning (ML) models have been used with great success in learning tasks such as image and natural language processing [10,25]. With the growing success of these models, we can see their widespread use in different application domains, especially for classification or prediction tasks [6,24]. However, most of these models are sub-symbolic black-box models that are not easily understandable. While using a system based on a ML model to make a prediction, a user may want to know the reason why the system is making a particular prediction [11]. Most of the recently proposed explanation models try to use the features in the dataset [15,16]. For example, LIME (Local Interpretable Model-Agnostic Explanations) [15] selects super-pixels of an image as an explanation which is sometimes difficult to understand for a user who is not a domain expert. Unfortunately, very little attention has been paid to finding the relevant relation information to explain a prediction. In some problem domains such as image

© Springer Nature Switzerland AG 2022
G. Long et al. (Eds.): AI 2021, LNAI 13151, pp. 27–39, 2022.
https://doi.org/10.1007/978-3-030-97546-3_3

processing, the relation information extracted from an image makes the explanation better understandable as shown in LIME-Aleph [13]. Motivated by this observation, we propose in this paper a Hybrid Explanation System for Image Prediction (HESIP) that explains the prediction made by a ML model using the relation information for the classification task. In contrast to the LIME-Aleph system, the HESIP system uses an ontology to represent image information, generates natural language descriptions to explain predictions and is able to handle probabilistic information.

Recently, Kautz has introduced six types of artificial intelligence systems based on how symbolic and sub-symbolic models are combined in these systems [8]. According to Kautz, Type-3 systems are hybrid systems that perform one task in the sub-symbolic model and apply the symbolic model in a complementary task. Furthermore, De Raedt et al. [4] argue that the separation of the symbolic and sub-symbolic components in a hybrid system offers an opportunity to obtain the best of both worlds. In HESIP, a sub-symbolic ML model makes a prediction for an image and after that, a symbolic ML model learns probabilistic rules that are used to explain the prediction. The sub-symbolic component of HESIP decides whether a sample image is a positive or negative instance. Afterwards, the symbolic component of HESIP utilises the decision of the sub-symbolic component along with the information extracted from the sample images for rule learning. Based on this definition, our system follows the architecture of Kautz's Type-3 hybrid systems, since HESIP combines the symbolic and sub-symbolic components as system components and the output of the sub-symbolic component is employed in the symbolic component.

2   The LIME-Aleph System

Recently, Rabold et al. [13] have presented LIME-Aleph, a system that explains an image prediction with the help of learned rules. After making a prediction using a classifier F with a probability θ for an image E, LIME-Aleph finds super-pixels using LIME for the image E. LIME can explain the prediction for an instance by selecting a number of features that are considered important for making the prediction. For each super-pixel, LIME-Aleph extracts its attribute information and finds the relations between super-pixels in an image. For each relation between the super-pixels in an image E, LIME-Aleph flips the information of the super-pixels to obtain a set of perturbed images. Each perturbed image is predicted using the classifier F and if the prediction probability is greater than or equal to the probability θ, then it is a positive instance, otherwise it is a negative instance. LIME-Aleph uses Aleph to learn the rules from these perturbed instances. Aleph is an Inductive Logic Programming system implemented in Prolog that is capable of learning rules from positive and negative examples [22].

LIME-Aleph has been used on a problem domain where two objects of an image can have the following relations: left_of, right_of, top_of, bottom_of, on and under based on their positions. An image is considered as a grid and the position of an object is taken from its location in the grid. While the relations are self-explainable, the relations **on** and **under** are used when the objects are adjacent to each other. There are two learning tasks in LIME-Aleph: (1) *Single relation learning*: If an image shows a green object on the left of a blue object, then it is a positive instance, otherwise it is a negative instance (see Fig. 1); (2) *Tower concept learning*: There are three objects in an image. If the three objects in the image are stacked together on top of one another without the repetition of objects with the same colour, then the image shows a positive instance of a tower, otherwise it is a negative instance (see Fig. 1). But there is an additional constraint that the blue object needs to be at the bottom.

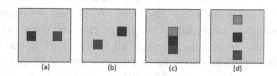

Fig. 1. (a) and (b) are positive and negative instances of single relation learning. (c) and (d) are positive and negative instances of tower concept learning.

The main weakness of the LIME-Aleph system is that it does not provide any formal way to represent image information that is used to learn a rule for explanation. That means there is no guidance to specify the predicates and their arguments for the learning program. While learning, the predicates and their arguments are specified based on the problem domain. As a result, LIME-Aleph does not use a general approach to generate verbalisations for explaining the learned rules. Instead, the authors proposed a template-based approach [21] that is highly dependent on the problem domain and on the way in which the predicates and their arguments have been specified. In contrast to the Lime-Aleph system, the HESIP system provides a common approach based on an ontology to represent the image information of the problem domain for rule learning. The learned rules do not depend on the problem domain and can be used for verbalising the explanation.

3   The HESIP System Architecture

The HESIP system (see Fig. 2) first makes a prediction P with a probability θ for an image E using a sub-symbolic ML model. Sub-symbolic ML models mostly learn functions that map the input data to the output data to find the correlations between them [7]. An artificial neural network (ANN) N [18] is used as a representative sub-symbolic ML model, but any ML model can be used.

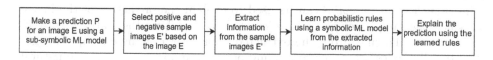

Fig. 2. Architecture of HESIP

After making a prediction for the image E, HESIP selects some sample images E' based on the image E to obtain positive and negative instances so that they can be used for learning probabilistic rules in the symbolic ML model. Symbolic ML techniques such as inductive logic programming learn rules from example instances with respect to the background knowledge [12]. HESIP goes through the dataset to find those images that are similar and dissimilar to the image E. An image that has similar features as the image E has a higher score than an image that has dissimilar features. Based on the score, some similar and dissimilar images are selected as sample images E'. The number of similar and dissimilar images is the number of positive and negative example instances that we use in the symbolic ML model for rule learning. Therefore, a prediction is made for each sample image using the ANN N. A sample image is a positive instance, if its prediction probability is greater than or equal to θ, otherwise it is a negative instance. Searching through all the images in the dataset to find sample instances is expensive if we have a large amount of images in a dataset. However, the symbolic ML model of HESIP requires only a very small number of positive and negative sample instances for learning the rules. While searching for the sample instances, HESIP keeps a record of the selected instances. Once HESIP has found the specified number of sample instances, it stops searching.

For the selected sample images E', HESIP extracts the information that will be used to explain the prediction through the learned rules. This information does not need to be based on the features that are used in making the prediction by the ANN N. This is the information that makes the explanation understandable. For example, the ANN N may use any set of features to make the prediction for the tower concept. Therefore, HESIP can extract the representation for the objects and the property and the relation information of these objects from the sample images E' that will be utilised in explanatory rule learning. For the image in Fig. 1(c), HESIP may extract the following information to be used in the explanation: (1) *Objects*: object1, object2, and object3; (2) *Properties*: object1 is pink; object2 is green; and object3 is blue. Here, pink, green, and blue represent the colour property of the objects; and (3) *Relations*: object1 is located on object2 and object2 is located on object3. Here, on represents a relation between two objects.

The rules for the explanation are learned using a symbolic ML model employing the extracted information of the sample images E'. HESIP is based on *cplint* [17], a probabilistic logic programming framework for symbolic probabilistic rule learning. A *cplint* program learns the rules from the observations provided as the data to the program with respect to the background knowledge. An ontology is used (see Sect. 4) to specify the extracted information of the images in the *cplint* program. HESIP extracts the information about the sample images, represents this information applying the ontology that is used as the data and finally employs *cplint* to learn explanatory rules using the data. The rules learned by *cplint* can be used to explain the prediction of the image E, since the sample images E' are selected by matching the features with E. *cplint* learns the rules from the extracted information of these sample images E'. HESIP applies a logic programming based grammar [5] to generate natural language explanations from the learned rules.

4   Ontology for HESIP

The ontology used in HESIP for our scenarios has four predicates: object/1, type/2, property/3 and relation/3. These predicates are employed to represent the information of an image that is later used as data in the *cplint* program for rule learning. The learned rules in *cplint* contain only these predicates. The body of a learned rule may have any of these predicates and the predicate type/2 or relation/3 are used in the head of the rule, if the prediction task consists of learning concepts or relations, respectively. If any background knowledge needs to be defined based on the extracted information of the image, then additional predicates can be employed to represent that information as data. However, these additional predicates will never appear in the rules.

After the selection of the sample images, HESIP extracts the information from the images and represents this information using the predicates of the ontology in the following way:

- the predicate object/1 is used to represent an object in an image;
- the predicate type/2 is used to represent the object type information;
- the predicate property/3 is used for the property information of an object;
- the predicate relation/3 is used for the relations between the objects.

For example, after extracting the information for the image in Fig. 1(c), HESIP uses the predicates of the ontology to represent the corresponding information: (1) *Objects*: object(object1), object(object2), object(object3); (2) *Properties*: property(object1, pink, colour), property(object2, green, colour), property(object3, blue, colour); and (3) *Relations*: relation (object1, object2, on), relation(object2, object3, on).

5   Image Information Extraction

After selecting the positive and negative sample images based on the predicted image, information is extracted from each sample image to learn the explanatory rules. For a sample image, we extract the following information: all the objects present in the image and their type information; property information about the objects; and relation information about the objects.

To detect the objects in the sample images, we have used Detectron2 [23] that comes with a pre-trained COCO model and supports state-of-the-art object detection algorithms such as Mask R-CNN [6] and Faster R-CNN [14]. We observe two types of objects: square and tower in a sample image for tower concept learning (see Fig. 1). To detect square and tower objects, we have extended the pre-trained COCO model by training it with the dataset of the tower concept. The images of the tower concept dataset are annotated with the two labels (*square* and *tower*) and after that, the dataset is employed for training. After completing the training, we employ Detectron2 to detect the objects in the sample images. In this step, we obtain all the objects present in the image along with their types and location information. The location information of a detected object is stored in the form of a box that is identified with the top-left and the bottom-right coordinates.

Once we have obtained the objects and their location information from an image, we extract the relevant property information for all the detected objects. To explain the prediction for a tower concept, we use the colour property for square objects. In the tower concept dataset, all square objects have a uniform colour: green, blue and pink. To obtain the colour information of an object, we calculate the center point of the object from the location information and pick the colour of the center point that represents the colour of the object.

To extract the relation information of the detected objects, we use the relative position information of the objects in the image. As in LIME-Aleph, we take into account six relations that may occur between two objects: left_of, right_of, top_of, bottom_of, on and under. While determining a relation between two objects, one object is assumed to be the reference object. From the reference object, we calculate the diagonal positions of the image that leads to four triangle regions: left, right, top and bottom triangle. Two objects are in a left_of relation, if the first object is located in the left triangle with respect to the position of the second (reference) object. In the same way, if the first object is located in the top, right or bottom triangle with respect to the position of the second object, then the relation between the objects is top_of, right_of or bottom_of, respectively. If an object is in the top or bottom position of another object and they are adjacent, then they are in an on or under relation. We consider an additional relation contain that exists between two objects if the position of one object is inside another object. We assume that only one relation between two objects exists. For all the detected objects, we check if a relation between two objects exists. The location information of the extracted objects is employed to identify a relation.

6   Learning Rules in *cplint*

As mentioned earlier, HESIP uses *cplint* to learn the rules from the extracted information of the selected sample images. The different parts of a *cplint* program for learning the tower (or a similar) concept are described in the following.

In the preamble part of the *cplint* program, we load and initialise the SLIP-COVER [1] library and set the necessary parameters. We use the SLIPCOVER library to learn the structure of the rules along with their probabilities. For tower concept learning, we do not have to specify any background information and this is why the background knowledge of the *cplint* program is empty. In the input-output declarations, we specify the predicate type/2 as an output predicate and all the other predicates object/1, property/3 and relation/3 are specified as input predicates. The predicates are specified in the mode declarations in such a way so that the predicate type/2 appears in the head and the other predicates appear in the body of the rule. The determination statements establish links between type/2 and all other predicates. Because of the limited space in this paper, we do not discuss the details about these different parts of a *cplint* program which can be found in the *cplint* manual [17].

The example model instances of a *cplint* program are used to represent the observed data. Listing 1.1 shows an example instance for tower concept learning which specifies that a1 is a tower; a1, b1, c1 and d1 are objects; the colour of the objects b1, c1 and d1 are blue, green and pink, respectively; and c1 is located on b1 and d1 is located on c1. The information of each sample image represents an example instance of the data. For each example instance, HESIP determines whether it is a positive or negative example instance based on the corresponding sample image prediction made by the sub-symbolic ANN N model.

Listing 1.1. An example instance in *cplint*

```
begin(model(twr1)).
  type(a1, tower).
  object(a1).  object(b1).
  object(c1).  object(d1).
  property(b1, blue, colour).
  property(c1, green, colour).
  property(d1, pink, colour).
  relation(a1, b1, contain).
  relation(a1, c1, contain).
  relation(a1, d1, contain).
  relation(c1, b1, on).
  relation(d1, c1, on).
end(model(twr1)).
```

After defining these parts of a *cplint* program, the program is ready to learn the rules. Listing 1.2 shows a rule learned by the *cplint* program for the tower concept. The rule specifies that an object A is a tower with probability 1, if all the conditions of the body are satisfied.

Listing 1.2. A sample rule learned in *cplint* for the tower concept

```
type(A, tower):1.0 :-  object(B), object(C), relation(C, B, on),
    relation(A, C, contain), relation(A, B, contain), object(A),
    property(C, green, colour), property(B, blue, colour).
```

7   Applying HESIP to a New Problem Domain

HESIP uses a more generalised approach than the LIME-Aleph system and requires less modification when applying it to a new problem domain. In this section, we discuss the steps that are required to apply HESIP to a new problem using the PASCAL-Part [3] dataset that consists of real-world images. From the PASCAL-Part dataset, we only use the images that contain potted-plants and bottles. The task is to learn the concept of a potted-plant. If an image represents a pot beneath a plant, then they together represent the potted-plant concept.

For this new task, we first build an ANN to predict the images. We have used a PyTorch-based implementation[1] of DeepLab V2 [2] that is pre-trained on the

---

[1] https://github.com/kazuto1011/deeplab-pytorch.

PASCAL-Part dataset. This DeepLab model takes an image as input, predicts the objects that occur in the image and outputs the predicted values.

No modification is required to select sample instances for the symbolic component when applying HESIP to a new problem. However, the DeepLab pre-trained model does not provide any probability while predicting objects for an image and it just predicts which objects occur in that particular image. Since our task is to learn the potted-plant concept, we consider an image as a positive example instance, if the image is predicted for the potted-plant concept; otherwise, the image is considered as a negative example instance and in our case, it will be a bottle concept.

For the image information extraction, we have trained Detectron2 with the PASCAL-Part annotated data to detect the objects and their location information. In this case, we have used the same relations as for the tower concept. After detecting the objects and their locations in an image, the relations between objects are obtained. The extracted information of an image is then represented using the ontology of the HESIP system so that the information about each image can be employed as an example instance for symbolic rule learning.

To learn an explanatory rule in the symbolic ML model, we have updated the different parts of the *cplint* program according to the requirements (as discussed in Sect. 6) for the potted-plant concept. The learned rule for the potted-plant concept is shown in Listing 1.3.

Listing 1.3. A sample rule learned in *cplint* for the potted-plant concept

```
type(A, pottedplant):1.0 :-   type(B, pot), object(B),
   type(C, plant), object(C),   relation(B, C, under),
   relation(A, C, contain), relation(A, B, contain), object(A).
```

8   Generating Explanations

The HESIP system generates natural language descriptions from the learned rules to explain the prediction in a way that is understandable by all users including those who do not understand a formal notation. To generate a natural language explanation from a rule, HESIP uses a planner that orders all the literals of the rule in a suitable order. The ordered literals are then used as input to a logic programming based bi-directional grammar to generate a natural language explanation (similar to the work by Schwitter [20]). However, it is not possible to immediately generate the explanation, since the literals of the learned rule do not follow the order of a well-defined linguistic pattern. To generate the explanation, HESIP follows a number of pre-processing steps [19]. The literals of the learned rule are first reordered according to linguistic principles, redundant information is removed using aggregation, and (potentially) ambiguous definite descriptions are resolved. The reconstructed rule is then sent to the bi-directional grammar for verbalisation. The same bi-directional grammar can reprocess the generated explanation to obtain a semantically equivalent rule. For tower concept learning, HESIP generates the following verbalisation: *"If an object A contains a green object and contains a blue object and the green object is located on the blue object then the object A is a tower."*. This example is considered as a correct explanation, since it represents all the objects and their relevant property information along with the relation information to explain the tower concept. However, there might be situations where HESIP generates a partial explanation for a concept that does not represent all the information. We consider a partial explanation as correct only if it represents the correct relation information, including the corresponding objects and their property information. The generated explanation can be modified by a human-in-the-loop if it is not correct. The modified explanation is then reprocessed by the same bi-directional grammar to produce a better explanation.

9 Experiments

The HESIP system has been evaluated on four datasets. The results of these experiments illustrate the ability of the system to generate explanations with high accuracy on these datasets.

Datasets. To evaluate HESIP, we use the following datasets: two datasets corresponding to the two tasks introduced by the LIME-Aleph system as discussed in Sect. 2; one is our own dataset related to the house concept learning task; and the PASCAL-Part dataset. The images of the PASCAL-Part dataset are real-world images while all other datasets consist of synthetic images. All the datasets, except the PASCAL-Part one, have 14000 images for training, 4000 images for validation and 2000 images for testing. Each set contains 50% positive and 50% negative examples. The images for the tower concept and the single relation consist of 32×32 pixels and the square objects consist of 4×4 pixels. In the house concept dataset, the images consist of 64×64 pixels and the square/triangle objects consist of 11×11 pixels. All the images have a fixed uniform background colour. For the tower concept dataset, a square object may have any of the three colours: green, blue or pink. However, a square object may have either blue or green as colour in the dataset for single relation learning. In the house concept dataset, the colour of the triangle and square objects are blue or green. From the PASCAL-Part dataset, we have used 382 images of potted-plants and 385 images of bottles for our experiment.

Neural Network for Prediction. As discussed in Sect. 7, a pre-tained neural network model is used for the PASCAL-Part dataset. For predicting the images of all other datasets, a convolutional neural network [9] is employed as the ANN N. The neural network consists of three convolution layers with a ReLU activation function, 16, 32 and 64 filters, and 2×2 kernels. There is a max-pooling layer after each convolution layer with a 2×2 pool size. The neural network has a flatten layer and two dense layers followed by the convolution and max-pooling layers. There are 256 and 128 neurons in the first and second dense layers with a ReLU activation function and a small dropout value. The final layer of the network uses a *sigmoid* activation function so that we can find the probability value for an image prediction. The neural network uses the loss function *binary_crossentropy* and the optimizer *rmsprop*, and is trained for 10 epochs with a batch size of 16.

Object Information of Images. A pre-trained COCO model of Detectron2 [23] is employed for detecting objects in sample images (as discussed in Sect. 5). The model is also trained with our annotated dataset so that we can detect our expected objects. After detecting objects and their types with Detectron2 for a sample image, a Python program is used to find the property information of the objects and to identify the relation between the objects.

Evaluation. From the PASCAL-Part dataset, 382 test images of potted-plants are selected and one thousand images are selected from the test data of other datasets for evaluating HESIP. Therefore, HESIP generates the explanations for the test images from the information of positive and negative example instances. HESIP employs 3 positive and 4 negative example instances for single relation learning and tower concept learning; 3 positive and 3 negative example instances for house concept learning; and 1 positive and 2 negative example instances for potted-plant concept learning. We manually go through the generated explanations to check their correctness. An explanation is considered correct based on the information discussed in Sect. 8. For single relation and tower concept learning, we found that all the explanations were correct while for house concept learning and potted-plant concept learning, 999 and 310 explanations were correct (see Table 1). Although HESIP shows high accuracy for all the datasets, we observe that the accuracy is lower for the potted-plant concept. After analysing the images of potted plants, we have found that the object detection model could not detect appropriate objects or correct location information of the objects in the images that are explained incorrectly. As a consequence, the learned rules as well as the explanations of these images were not correct. The PASCAL-Part dataset contains real-world images. The background colour, object shape and colour of these images are not uniform as in the synthetic images of the other datasets.

Table 1. Evaluation of HESIP.

Dataset	Test images	Correct explanations	Accuracy
Single relation learning	1000	1000	100%
Tower concept learning	1000	1000	100%
House concept learning	1000	999	99.9%
Potted-plant concept learning	382	310	81.15%

We cannot compare our results with the results of the LIME-Aleph system, since Rabold *et al.* [13] have only used two examples for single relation learning and one example for tower concept learning. Furthermore, the LIME-Aleph implementation is not publicly available.

10   Comparison

In comparison to the LIME-Aleph system, the HESIP system has the following advantages:

- Unlike LIME-Aleph, HESIP employs an ontology to represent the image information. A learned rule in HESIP contains only those predicates that are defined by the ontology. As a result, HESIP can apply a logic based grammar to generate explanations from learned rules for any problem domain.
- HESIP uses natural language descriptions for explanations rather than symbolic rules like those in LIME-Aleph. The explanations in HESIP are generated using a restricted form of natural language [20] that is designed in such a way that the explanations are not only human understandable but at the same time machine-processable.
- HESIP is able to handle probabilistic information by virtue of its design and architecture, since it is based on *cplint* which is a probabilistic logic programming framework for rule learning.
- LIME-Aleph depends on LIME which itself is an explanation system. For a predicted image, LIME is employed to find the super-pixels which are used to obtain the object information. One issue with this approach is that a super-pixel may identify a portion of an object instead of a whole object which will lead to incorrect explanations. It is also not possible to extract the object type information in LIME-Aleph. In contrast, HESIP applies Detectron2 and does not depend on another explanation system to obtain the object information including the object type. Since Detectron2 is a specialised system for object detection, there is only a very low chance that HESIP will miss any object information that is necessary to generate the explanation.

11   Conclusion

We have introduced the architecture of the HESIP system that can explain the prediction of an image made by a sub-symbolic ML model. After making this prediction, the HESIP system employs an ontology to represent the information of the sample images selected from the dataset based on feature similarity where the image information is extracted using Detectron2. Afterwards, the HESIP system learns probabilistic rules with the help of *cplint* and generates a natural language description from the learned rules using a logic programming based grammar to explain the prediction. The evaluation of HESIP has shown that the system is more effective than the LIME-Aleph system. The novelty of the HESIP system is that it represents image information in a formal way using an ontology and generates an explanation in a well-defined subset of natural language that does not depend on pre-defined templates. We have shown that HESIP can be used effectively for explaining the prediction of real-world images in the PASCAL-Part dataset.

References

1. Bellodi, E., Riguzzi, F.: Structure learning of probabilistic logic programs by searching the clause space. Theory Pract. Logic Program. **15**(2), 169–212 (2015)
2. Chen, L.C., Papandreou, G., Kokkinos, I., Murphy, K., Yuille, A.L.: DeepLab: semantic image segmentation with deep convolutional nets, atrous convolution, and fully connected CRFs. IEEE Trans. PAMI **40**(4), 834–848 (2017)
3. Chen, X., Mottaghi, R., Liu, X., Fidler, S., Urtasun, R., Yuille, A.: Detect what you can: detecting and representing objects using holistic models and body parts. In: Proceedings of CVPR 2014, pp. 1971–1978 (2014)
4. De Raedt, L., Manhaeve, R., Dumancic, S., Demeester, T., Kimmig, A.: Neuro-symbolic = neural + logical + probabilistic. In: NeSy'19@ IJCAI, the 14th International Workshop on Neural-Symbolic Learning and Reasoning (2019)
5. Genesereth, M., Chaudhri, V.K.: Introduction to logic programming. Synth. Lect. Artif. Intell. Mach. Learn. **14**(1), 1–219 (2020)
6. He, K., Gkioxari, G., Dollár, P., Girshick, R.: Mask R-CNN. In: 2017 IEEE International Conference on Computer Vision (ICCV), pp. 2980–2988 (2017)
7. Ilkou, E., Koutraki, M.: Symbolic vs sub-symbolic AI methods: friends or enemies? In: CIKM (Workshops) (2020)
8. Kautz, H.: The Third AI Summer, AAAI Robert S. Engelmore Memorial Lecture. AAAI 2020 (2020). https://www.cs.rochester.edu/u/kautz/talks/KautzEngelmoreLectureDirectorsCut.pdf. Accessed 17 July 2021
9. Krizhevsky, A., Sutskever, I., Hinton, G.E.: Imagenet classification with deep convolutional neural networks. In: NIPS 2012, pp. 1097–1105 (2012)
10. LeCun, Y., Bengio, Y., Hinton, G.: Deep learning. Nature **521**(7553), 436 (2015)
11. Lipton, Z.C.: The mythos of model interpretability. arXiv preprint arXiv:1606.03490 (2016)
12. Muggleton, S.: Inductive logic programming. New Gener. Comput. **8**(4), 295–318 (1991)
13. Rabold, J., Deininger, H., Siebers, M., Schmid, U.: Enriching visual with verbal explanations for relational concepts – combining LIME with aleph. In: Cellier, P., Driessens, K. (eds.) ECML PKDD 2019. CCIS, vol. 1167, pp. 180–192. Springer, Cham (2020). https://doi.org/10.1007/978-3-030-43823-4_16
14. Ren, S., He, K., Girshick, R., Sun, J.: Faster R-CNN: towards real-time object detection with region proposal networks. IEEE Trans. PAMI **39**(6), 1137–1149 (2016)
15. Ribeiro, M.T., Singh, S., Guestrin, C.: Why should I trust you?: explaining the predictions of any classifier. In: ACM SIGKDD International Conference on Knowledge Discovery and Data Mining, pp. 1135–1144. ACM (2016)
16. Ribeiro, M.T., Singh, S., Guestrin, C.: Anchors: high-precision model-agnostic explanations. In: AAAI 2018, vol. 32, no. 1, April 2018
17. Riguzzi, F., Azzolini, D.: cplint Manual. SWI-Prolog Version (2020). http://friguzzi.github.io/cplint/_build/latex/cplint.pdf. Accessed 17 July 2021
18. Russell, S., Norvig, P.: Artificial Intelligence: A Modern Approach. Pearson, London (2020)
19. Salam, A., Schwitter, R., Orgun, M.A.: Human-understandable and machine-processable explanations for sub-symbolic predictions. In: International Workshop on Controlled Natural Language (2021)
20. Schwitter, R.: Lossless semantic round-tripping in PENG^{ASP}. In: IJCAI 2020. Demonstrations Track, Yokohama, Japan, pp. 5291–5293 (2020)

21. Siebers, M., Schmid, U.: Please delete that! Why should I? KI - Künstliche Intelligenz **33**(1), 35–44 (2018). https://doi.org/10.1007/s13218-018-0565-5
22. Srinivasan, A.: The Aleph Manual (2007). http://www.cs.ox.ac.uk/activities/programinduction/Aleph/aleph.html. Accessed 17 July 2021
23. Wu, Y., Kirillov, A., Massa, F., Lo, W.Y., Girshick, R.: Detectron2 (2019). https://github.com/facebookresearch/detectron2. Accessed 17 July 2021
24. Zhang, X., Zhao, J., LeCun, Y.: Character-level convolutional networks for text classification. In: NIPS 2015, pp. 649–657 (2015)
25. Zhang, Z., Cui, P., Zhu, W.: Deep learning on graphs: a survey. IEEE Trans. KDE (2020). https://doi.org/10.1109/TKDE.2020.2981333

An Explainable Recommendation Based on Acyclic Paths in an Edge-Colored Graph

Kosuke Chinone$^{(\boxtimes)}$ and Atsuyoshi Nakamura

Graduate School of Information Science and Technology, Hokkaido University, Sapporo, Japan
{chinone,atsu}@ist.hokudai.ac.jp

Abstract. We propose a novel recommendation algorithm based on acyclic paths in an edge-colored graph. In our method, all the objects including users, items to recommend, and other things usable to recommendation are represented as vertices in an edge-colored directed graph, in which edge color represents relation between the objects of its both ends. By setting each edge weight appropriately so as to reflect how much the object corresponding to its one end is preferred by people who prefer the object corresponding to its other end, the probability of an s-t path, which is defined as the product of its component edges' weights, can be regarded as preference degree of item t (item corresponding to vertex t) by user s (user corresponding to vertex s) in the context represented by the path. Given probability threshold θ, the proposed algorithm recommends user s to item t that has high sum of the probabilities of all the acyclic s-t paths whose probability is at least θ. For item t recommended to user s, the algorithm also shows high probability color sequences of those s-t paths, from which we can know main contexts of the recommendation of item t for user s. According to our experiments using real-world datasets, the recommendation performance of our method is comparable to the non-explainable state-of-the-art recommendation methods.

Keywords: Recommender system · Explainablity · Graph algorithm

1 Introduction

Now, recommender systems are used in many web services to present items suitable for user's preference, and explainability is perceived as one of the points to be improved in them [17]. In addition to recommendation, explainable systems can also provide recommendation reasons. Explainability improves the transparency, effectiveness, trustworthiness, satisfaction, and persuasiveness of recommender systems. The classical recommendation method of user or item similarity-based collaborative filtering [1,13] can be seen as implicitly providing explanations like "the item was purchased by users whose purchase histories are similar to that of yours" or "the item was purchased by a group of users who purchased the items

© Springer Nature Switzerland AG 2022
G. Long et al. (Eds.): AI 2021, LNAI 13151, pp. 40–52, 2022.
https://doi.org/10.1007/978-3-030-97546-3_4

you bought". Recent recommendation models with high preference-prediction accuracy, such as models that learn latent factors using matrix factorization to predict items' ratings by users [9], and deep learning models [16], however, are difficult to understand the reason for recommendation intuitively.

On the other hand, there are efforts to use various relations between users, items and other related objects, to improve the accuracy and interpretability of recommendations [15]. Such relations between objects can be represented by a graph, in which objects are corresponding to vertices and relations between objects are represented by edges between vertices of corresponding objects. Considering preference-propagation degree based on each relation in the graph, items can be recommended to users by calculating estimated preference degree of items for the users. One merit of this graph-based method is that the paths most contributing to the estimated preference degree can be shown as explanation for the recommendation. In previous work, such preference degree estimation is done by calculating the stationary distribution of the Markov process with transition probability corresponding to preference-propagation degree. The approximate calculation of this method is efficiently done by repeated matrix multiplication, but contributed paths for items with high estimated preference degree can not be obtained as by-product.

In this paper, we propose a novel recommendation algorithm based on acyclic paths in an edge-colored directed graph constructed from various relations between recommendation-related objects. In an edge-colored directed graph, an edge color represents a relation between the objects that correspond to the vertices of its both ends. Given appropriate edge propagation probabilities and threshold θ, our algorithm calculates the probability sum of all the acyclic s-t paths whose probability is at least θ. On the way of the calculation, our algorithm also calculates the probability sum of each color sequence of those s-t paths. Then, high probability items t are recommended to user s accompanied by high probability color sequences of the s-t paths, from which we can know main contexts of the recommendation of item t for user s. According to our experimental results using real-world datasets, the recommendation performance of our proposed method is comparable to the non-explainable state-of-the-art recommendation methods. By checking recommendation list with the highest probability color sequences, color sequences are confirmed to be suitable for explanation of the recommendation. Furthermore, different trends are observed between the lists with different color sequences, which indicates the possibility of using color sequences to provide the recommendation lists of different trends.

Related Work

Though the term "explainable recommendation system" has only recently begun to be used [18], such recommender systems had existed before then. User-based or item-based collaborative filtering [1,8,13] can be seen as a kind of explainable recommender system because they recommend items based on user-similarity or item-similarity of ratings, and such similarities can be seen as explanation. Explicit Factor Model (EFM) [4,19] is an explainable recommendation method that is made from Latent Factor Model (LFN) [9] by modifying it so as to have explainability. Some of recent recommendation systems using deep neural networks such as CNN [14] and RNN [5] are working on automatic generation of explanations by natural language generation models [10]. It is said to be a difficult but important problem to explain the recommendation produced by latent factor and deep learning models [17].

Recent explainable recommendation systems use social information such as purchase histories, review information, and friendships between users and items [11,15]. There is one that uses tripartite graphs to represent the relationship between users, items, and aspects [7], where an aspect is a feature of an item extracted from a user's review. Knowledge graphs, which contain a wealth of information about users and items, have been used to generate intuitive and more suitable explanations for recommended items [3].

2 Preliminary

An *edge-weighted edge-colored directed graph* G is a triplet $G(V, E, p)$, where V is a set of vertices, $E \subseteq V \times V \times C$ is a set of directed colored edges with a color set C, and p is an edge weight function $p : E \to (0, \infty)$. Note that multiple edges $(u, v, c_1), (u, v, c_2) \in V \times V \times C$ are allowed if their colors c_1, c_2 are different. As for an edge weight function, we only consider the function p satisfying the probability condition that $\sum_{(v,c):(u,v,c) \in E} p((u, v, c)) = 1$ for all $u \in V$. An *acyclic s-t path* in G is defined as an edge sequence $(s, v_1, c_1)(v_1, v_2, c_2) \cdots (v_{k-1}, v_k, c_k)(v_k, t, c_{k+1})$ for some $k \leq |V|$ in which $s, v_1, v_2, \ldots, v_k, t$ must be different from each other. For an *s-t* path $(s, v_1, c_1)(v_1, v_2, c_2) \cdots (v_{k-1}, v_k, c_k)(v_k, t, c_{k+1})$, we call $c_1 c_2 \cdots c_{k+1}$ the *color sequence* of the *s-t* path, and define the *probability* of the *s-t* path as $p((s, v_1, c_1)) \times p((v_1, v_2, c_2)) \times \cdots \times p((v_{k-1}, v_k, c_k)) \times p((v_k, t, c_{k+1}))$.

3 Proposed Method

In this section, we propose an explainable recommendation model based on acyclic paths in an edge-colored graph. First, we represent the information used for recommendation as an edge-colored graph, and introduce our recommendation method based on acyclic paths. Then, we describe our recommendation explanation by color sequences.

3.1 Graph Construction

We construct an edge-weighted edge-colored directed graph $G(V, E, p)$ for recommendation using various information such as rating, tag, item attribute and so on. Let V be the set of all the objects that appear in the information used in recommendation, that is, V is composed of users, items, tags, attributes, etc. Each directed colored edge (u, v, c) is created if object u has a certain relation (that is represented by color c) with object v. For example, use color **R** for rating

---

Algorithm 1. APBRec(s, T_s)

Input: s: vertex for target user, T_s: set of recommendable items for user s
Output: $t_1, \ldots, t_k$: top-k recommended items in T_s
1: Initialization: for $v \in V$
    visited[v] $\leftarrow$ false

$$\text{recommendable}[v] \leftarrow \begin{cases} \text{true} & (v \in T_s) \\ \text{false} & (v \notin T_s) \end{cases}$$

    $P_v^\theta \leftarrow 0$
2: Cal_Path_Prob($s, 1, 0$)
3: Calculate items $t = t_1, \ldots, t_k$ with the k largest P_t^θ
4: Output item t_i as the ith recommendation
5: **for** $i = 1$ to k **do**
6:     Output color sequences $\mathbf{c} = \mathbf{c}_1, \mathbf{c}_2, \ldots, \mathbf{c}_\ell$ with ℓ largest $P_{t_i}^\theta[\mathbf{c}]$ as explanation

---

relation. Then, edge $(u, v, \mathbf{R})$ is created if user u rated item v. We are dealing with a directed graph, so we use different color for reverse relation. Thus, in the case that *rated* relation (that is represented by color $\mathbf{r}$) is considered in addition to rating relation, edge $(v, u, \mathbf{r})$ is also created. There is a case that different colored edges from u to v are created. Assume that color $\mathbf{T}$ is used for tagging relation, edge $(u, v, \mathbf{T})$ is created if user u tagged item v with some tag, which is independently done from the creation of edge $(u, v, \mathbf{R})$ for rating relation. An edge weight function $p((u, v, c))$ is set to the value that represents how much object v is preferred if object u is preferred. Such preference propagation degree depends on the relation corresponding to the color c of the edge. So, first, we construct a function $w_c : E \cap (V \times V \times \{c\}) \to (0, \infty)$ for each color c depending on its representing relation. Then, an edge weight function p is constructed by normalizing w_c for all colors c.

3.2 Acyclic-Path-Based Recommendation

We propose a recommendation method that recommends an item t to a user s based on acyclic s-t paths on an edge-colored directed graph $G(V, E, p)$. For each user s, the sum P_t of the probabilities of all the acyclic s-t paths in G is calculated for each item t, then items t with the largest P_t are recommended. One merit of this acyclic path-based recommendation, we can show high probability path information as explanation for the recommendation. As such information, we use the color sequences of high probability acyclic s-t paths, which are relation sequences because each color is corresponding to different relation. For each item t, the sum $P_t[\mathbf{c}]$ of the probabilities of all the acyclic s-t paths in G with color sequence $\mathbf{c}$ is calculated for each appearing color sequence $\mathbf{c}$, then color sequences $\mathbf{c}$ with the largest $P_t[\mathbf{c}]$ are shown as explanation for recommendation of item t.

    The largest problem of this proposed method is its high computational cost. To overcome this issue, we give up summing up the probabilities of all the acyclic s-t paths and exclude the small probability paths from the summation. Concretely, we set threshold θ and we sum up the probabilities of the acyclic s-t

---

Algorithm 2. Cal_Path_Prob(v, P, d)

Input: v: current vertex, P: probability of the current s-v path, d: current path length
1: visited$[v] \leftarrow$ true
2: **if** recommendable$[v]$ = true **then**
3:     $P_v^\theta \leftarrow P_v^\theta + P$,
4:     **if** $P_v^\theta[c[0..d-1]]$ is not registered **then**
5:         $P_v^\theta[c[0..d-1]] \leftarrow 0$
6:     $P_v^\theta[c[0..d-1]] \leftarrow P_v^\theta[c[0..d-1]] + P$
7: **for** $(v', c_d) : (v, v', c_d) \in E$ and visited$[v']$ = false **do**
8:     **if** $p((v, v', c_d)) \times P \geq \theta$ **then**
9:         c$[d] \leftarrow c_d$
10:         Cal_Path_Prob$(v', p((v, v', c_d)) \times P, d+1)$
11: visited$[v] \leftarrow$ false

---

paths whose probabilities are at least θ. If θ is small enough, the calculated probabilities are expected to be good approximations, and the ranking by such approximated probabilities is expected to be correct.

For fixed user s, probability sum P_t^θ of all the acyclic s-t path with probability at least θ can be efficiently calculated by the depth first search of G. APBRec(s, T_s), which is shown in Algorithm 1, is an algorithm that recommends the items t in T_s with the top-k P_t^θ for user s. Furthermore, for each recommended item t, the algorithm shows the color sequences c with top-ℓ probability sum $P_t^\theta[c]$ among those of the acyclic s-t paths as explanation, where $P_t^\theta[c]$ is the sum of the probabilities of all the acyclic s-t paths in G with color sequence c whose probability is at least θ. The depth first search from s can be done by executing Cal_Path_Prob$(s, 1, 0)$ at Line 2. In each recursive call of Cal_Path_Prob (Line 10), one edge is appended to the current path from s.

To prevent the current path from being cyclic, the Boolean variables visited$[v]$ are set to true for all the vertices v on the current path, and the current path is not extended to the vertices with visited$[v]$ = true (Line 7). Algorithm Cal_Path_Prob(v, P, d) is given the probability P of current s-v path, and edge (v, v', c_d) is not appended to the current path unless the probability of the path extended by the edge, which can be calculated by $p((v, v', c_d)) \times P$, is at least θ (Line 8). The color sequence of the current path is represented by a string c $= c[0]c[1]\cdots c[d-1]$, which is denoted by $c[0..d-1]$. In Algorithm Cal_Path_Prob(v, P, d), the current path probability P is added to the acyclic s-v paths' probability P_v^θ if v is a vertex corresponding to a recommendable item (Line 3). In that case, the probability P is also added to the probability $P_v^\theta[c[0..d-1]]$ of its color sequence $c[0..d-1]$ (Line 6).

3.3   Explanation by Color Sequences

As explanation for the recommendation of an item t to a user s, we use the color sequences c of s-t paths with high probabilities $P_t^\theta[c]$. Since the item t is recommended to the user u because the probability sum P_t^θ of the s-t paths

Table 1. Dataset statistics

Dataset	#users	#items	#tags	#ratings	#taggings
Movielens 20M	138493	27278	38644	20000263	465564
Food.com Recipes and Interactions	6389	197317	532	719548	2798545

is high, showing the color sequences $\mathbf{c}$ that are contributed to high P_t^θ is reasonable explanation in the context of transparency considering the fact that $P_t^\theta = \sum_{\mathbf{c}} P_t^\theta[\mathbf{c}]$. Furthermore, color sequences are relation paths from the recommended user to the recommended item, which clarifies what his/her actions (watching, rating, tagging and so on) strongly connect to the item through what other relations between objects. For example, color sequences can reveal that the recommended movie is a movie of the same genre as a movie the user has watched in the past, or a movie watched by other users who have watched the same movie as the user watched.

4 Experiments

We conduct experiments to compare the recommendation performance of our proposed algorithm APBRec with those of the state-of-the-art methods using two real-world datasets. We also check the effectiveness of high-probability color sequences as recommendation explanation.

4.1 Experimental Setup

We set the threshold θ used in Cal_Path_Prob to 10^{-7} in our experiment. Other settings are described below.

Datasets. The datasets we use in our experiments are Movielens 20M [6] and Food.com Recipes and Interactions[1], which were collected on a movie review site and a recipe aggregator site, respectively. Both the datasets are composed of rating and tagging data whose statistics are shown in Table 1. The rating scales of Movielens and Food.com[2] are 1-5 and 1-6, respectively, and every user in both the datasets has at least 20 ratings. The datasets contain tags which are words tagged to movies and recipes by users.

We randomly divide the set of ratings into 60% of the ratings for training and the other 40% for testing. We report the average results over five such random splits.

---

[1] https://www.kaggle.com/shuyangli94/food-com-recipes-and-user-interactions.

[2] The scale of the original dataset is 0-5 and it contains users who rated less than 20 recipes. We shifted the scale by one to use the same weight function and removed users who rated less than 20 recipes.

Graphs Construction. We construct the following edge-colored graph $G(V, E, p)$ from two datasets. The vertex set V is the set of all the objects, that is, users, items and tags. We abuse notation and let user u, item m, tag t represent the corresponding vertices themselves. The edge set E is constructed from ratings and taggings as follows. For each rating of item m by user u, two colored directed edges $(u, m, \mathbf{R})$ and $(m, u, \mathbf{r})$ are created. For each tagging of item m with tag t by user u, six colored directed edges $(u, m, \mathbf{T})$, $(m, u, \mathbf{t})$, $(u, t, \mathbf{U})$, $(t, u, \mathbf{u})$, $(m, t, \mathbf{M})$ and $(t, m, \mathbf{m})$ are created. So, the color set is $C = \{\mathbf{R}, \mathbf{r}, \mathbf{T}, \mathbf{t}, \mathbf{U}, \mathbf{u}, \mathbf{M}, \mathbf{m}\}$, and the relation that each color represents is shown in Table 2.

Table 2. Colored edges in $G(V, E, p)$ for the datasets, their related information that is used for determining their weight, and representing relations. We let $r_{u,m}$ denote the rating value of item m by user u, and let $t_{u,m}$ denote the set of tags to item m tagged by user u. The notation $|\cdot|$ for set '$\cdot$' means the number of elements in set '$\cdot$'.

Edge	Rel. inf.	Relation	Edge	Rel. inf.	Relation
$(u, m, \mathbf{R})$	$r_{u,m}$	User u rated item m at $r_{u,m}$	$(u, t, \mathbf{U})$	$\|\{m \mid t \in t_{u,m}\}\|$	User u tagged with tag t
$(m, u, \mathbf{r})$	$r_{u,m}$	Item m was rated at $r_{u,m}$ by user u	$(t, u, \mathbf{u})$	$\|\{m \mid t \in t_{u,m}\}\|$	With tag t user u tagged
$(u, m, \mathbf{T})$	$\|t_{u,m}\|$	User u tagged item m	$(m, t, \mathbf{M})$	$\|\{u \mid t \in t_{u,m}\}\|$	Item m was tagged with tag t
$(m, u, \mathbf{t})$	$\|t_{u,m}\|$	Item m was tagged by user u	$(t, m, \mathbf{m})$	$\|\{u \mid t \in t_{u,m}\}\|$	With tag t item m was tagged

To construct a function w_c for each color c, we apply the same normalization used for rating values in [15], which is defined as follows. Let $w_{v_1, v_2, c}$ denote the related information for edge (v_1, v_2, c) shown in the column 'Rel. inf.' of Table 2. Then, the function $w_c : E \to (0, \infty)$ for color $c \in C$ is defined as

$$w_c((v_1, v_2, c)) = \frac{w'((v_1, v_2, c))}{\text{ave}(w'((v_1, \cdot, c)))},$$

where $\text{ave}(w'((v_1, \cdot, c)))$ is the average of $w'((v_1, v, c))$ over $\{v \mid (v_1, v, c) \in E\}$, and the function w' is defined as

$$w'((v_1, v_2, c)) = w'((v_2, v_1, \bar{c})) = \frac{w_{v_1, v_2, c}}{\sqrt{\sum_{v_2' : (v_1, v_2', c) \in E} w_{v_1, v_2', c}} \sqrt{\sum_{v_1' : (v_2, v_1', \bar{c}) \in E} w_{v_1', v_2, \bar{c}}}},$$

where $\bar{c}$ is the color representing the reverse relation to the relation represented by color c, that is, $\bar{\mathbf{R}} = \mathbf{r}$, $\bar{\mathbf{T}} = \mathbf{t}$, $\bar{\mathbf{U}} = \mathbf{u}$ and $\bar{\mathbf{M}} = \mathbf{m}$. The edge weight function p is a normalized w_c so as to satisfy $\sum_{(v,c):(v_1,v,c) \in E} p((v_1, v, c)) = 1$, that is,

$$p((v_1, v_2, c)) = \frac{w_c((v_1, v_2, c))}{\sum_{(v,c):(v_1,v,c) \in E} w_c((v_1, v, c))}.$$

Evaluation Metrics. We evaluate recommendation performance by nDCG (normalized Discounted Cumulative Gain) [2], Precision, Recall and F1-measure. DCG(Discounted Cumulative Gain) for recommended item ranking $m_1, m_2, \cdots$ to user u is a ranking metric that discounts the score towards the bottom, that is,

$$DCG@n = \sum_{i=1}^{n} \frac{2^{r_{u,m_i}} - 1}{\log_2(i+1)},$$

where r_{u,m_i} is the rating value of the ith item m_i in the recommended ranking for user u, and n is the maximum rank used for the evaluation. nDCG is a normalized DCG that is the DCG divided by the IDCG (Ideal DCG), where the IDCG is the DCG for the item m ranking that is sorted in descending order of $r_{u,m}$.

Precision, Recall and F1-measure were used to measure recommendation performance for high-rated items, which are defined as the items rated at least 4 in Movielens and at least 5 in Food.com. Let M_u^{high} denote the set of items rated high by user u and let $M_u^{\text{rec}}(n)$ be the set of top n recommended items. Precision@n, Recall@n and F1@n for user u are defined as

$$\text{Precision@}n = \frac{|M_u^{\text{high}} \cap M_u^{\text{rec}}(n)|}{n}, \quad \text{Recall@}n = \frac{|M_u^{\text{high}} \cap M_u^{\text{rec}}(n)|}{|M_u^{\text{high}}|}, \text{ and}$$

$$\text{F1@}n = \frac{2\text{Precision@}n \cdot \text{Recall@}n}{\text{Precision@}n + \text{Recall@}n}.$$

They take values between 0 and 1, and the closer to 1, the better the recommendation performance is.

Comparison Methods. We compare the accuracy of the proposed method with those of baseline and state-of-the-art models. We used four models, AVE, IBCF, MRH and BPR models. AVE model is a baseline model, which ranks items by the ratings averaged over all the users who rated the item. IBCF model is an item-based collaborative filtering [13], which predicts rating $r_{u,m}$ by

$$\frac{\sum_{m' \in M_u} \text{cosine}(r_{\cdot,m}, r_{\cdot,m'}) r_{u,m}}{\sum_{m' \in M_u} \text{cosine}(r_{\cdot,m}, r_{\cdot,m'})},$$

where

$$\text{cosine}(r_{\cdot,m}, r_{\cdot,m'}) = \frac{\sum_{u \in U_m \cap U_{m'}} r_{u,m} r_{u,m'}}{\sqrt{\sum_{u \in U_m \cap U_{m'}} r_{u,m}^2} \sqrt{\sum_{u \in U_m \cap U_{m'}} r_{u,m'}^2}},$$

M_u is the set of movies rated by user u, and U_m is the set of users who rated item m. BPR (Bayesian Personalized Ranking) model is a kind of matrix factorization [12], which optimizes the posterior probability of correctly ranking item pairs for each user. We use the implementation shown at http://ethen8181.github.io/mac-hine-learning/recsys/4_bpr.html with default parameter values except the following parameters: learning_rate=0.1, n_iters=3000, n_factors=60 and batch-_size=100. MRH (Music Recommendation via Hypergraph) model is a graph-based method that uses social information to make recommendations [15]. We construct a hypergraph using rating and tagging information and make a transition matrix A for Random Walks with Restarts version of MRH model. The stationary distribution $\lim_{t \to \infty} \mathbf{f}^{(t)}$ for $\mathbf{f}^{(t+1)} = \alpha A \mathbf{f}^{(t)} + (1 - \alpha)\mathbf{y}_u$ is used for recommendation to user u, where $\mathbf{y}_u$ is a query vector for user u and whose nonzero entries are the entry corresponding to u, which is set to 1, and the entries corresponding to v that is connected to u in the graph, which are set to $A_{u,v}$. In the experiment, the restart probability $1 - \alpha$ is set to 0.04, and the stationary distribution is approximated by $\mathbf{f}^{(t)}$ for $t = 80$.

4.2   Results

Recommendation Performance. The nDCG@10, Precision@10, Recall@10 and F1@10 averaged over all users and 5 runs with 95% confidence intervals for the five methods are shown in Table 3. APBRec outperforms the baseline method AVE and has comparable performance to the other three non-explainable state-of-the-art recommendation methods.

Table 3. Recommendation performance of the five recommendation models for two datasets by nDCG@10, Precision@10, Recall@10 and F1@10. The values are averaged over all users and 5 runs and 95% confidence intervals are parenthesized. The highest values are bolded and those which are not statistically significantly different from them are italicized.

Dataset	Method	nDCG	Precision	Recall	F1
Movielens	AVE	0.4508(±0.0003)	0.3658(±0.0006)	0.3625(±0.0002)	0.3106(±0.0004)
	IBCF	**0.7667**(±0.0001)	**0.6901**(±0.0005)	**0.5239**(±0.0005)	**0.4926**(±0.0004)
	MRH	0.7354(±0.0003)	0.6478(±0.0004)	0.4991(±0.0005)	0.4657(±0.0004)
	BPR	0.6885(±0.0047)	0.6123(±0.0026)	0.4770(±0.0016)	0.4419(±0.0018)
	APBRec	0.7023(±0.0002)	0.6241(±0.0004)	0.4799(±0.0003)	0.4474(±0.0003)
Food.com	AVE	0.8328(±0.0011)	0.8587(±0.0014)	0.5673(±0.0018)	0.6094(±0.0017)
	IBCF	0.8745(±0.0012)	*0.8785*(±0.0018)	*0.5755*(±0.0016)	*0.6199*(±0.0018)
	MRH	0.8659(±0.0012)	0.8743(±0.0021)	*0.5740*(±0.0014)	*0.6179*(±0.0020)
	BPR	**0.8804**(±0.0008)	**0.8806**(±0.0018)	**0.5761**(±0.0011)	**0.6208**(±0.0015)
	APBRec	0.8735(±0.0009)	*0.8777*(±0.0019)	*0.5752*(±0.0013)	*0.6196*(±0.0018)

Explainability. Two users' top-10 recommendation lists by APBRec for Food.com dataset are shown in Table 4. As explanation of each recommended recipe, three highest-probability color sequences are shown. The color sequences give contexts of the recommendation and makes the recommendation more transparent. For example, color sequence "**RrR**" can be interpreted as "the recipes rated high by other users who highly rated your high-rating recipes". You can see tag's contribution to the recommendation lists. Color sequence "**Um**" is the highest ranked color sequence for five recipes recommended to user 231. Interpretation of "**Um**" can be "the recipes tagged with the same tag that you tagged to other recipes".

Table 4. Top-10 recommended recipes to users 133 and 231 by APBRec in Food.com dataset. The three highest probability color sequences are also shown for each recommended recipe.

User	Rank	Recipe	Color sequence ranking		
			1st(%)	2nd(%)	3rd(%)
133	1	Javanese roasted salmon and wilted spinach	**RrR**(92.3)	**TrR**(7.6)	
	2	Beer	**RrR**(91.6)	**TrR**(8.3)	
	3	Chilli beer damper	**RrR**(94.2)	**TrR**(5.7)	
	4	Meat pinwheels	**TrR**(68.4)	**RtR**(31.5)	
	5	Spicy calamari with bacon and scallions	**RrR**(86.5)	**TrR**(12.3)	**Um**(1.0)
	6	Roasted green beans with garlic and pine nuts	**RrR**(91.7)	**TrR**(5.6)	**RMm**(2.5)
	7	Bubble and squeak	**RrR**(92.5)	**TrR**(7.4)	
	8	Tamarind sauce	**TrR**(100)		
	9	Citrus morning sunrise	**TrR**(96.5)	**RrR**(3.4)	
	10	Maple sugar pumpkin pie	**TmM**(68.7)	**Um**(31.2)	
231	1	Baked sausage stuffed jumbo pasta shells	**Um**(63.2)	**TMm**(33.1)	**Uut**(1.2)
	2	Greek spinach rice balls	**RrR**(100)		
	3	Raspberry wine toaster bread	**RrR**(100)		
	4	Crunchy poppy seed chicken salad	**RrR**(100)		
	5	Salt rising bread	**RrR**(100)		
	6	Garlic lime chicken	**Um**(62.8)	**TMm**(32.8)	**RMm**(3.1)
	7	The best mexican tortilla roll ups	**RrR**(93.7)	**TrR**(5.3)	**Um**(0.9)
	8	Quick fish stew	**Um**(62.8)	**TMm**(32.8)	**RMm**(3.1)
	9	Mustard herb flank steak	**Um**(63.0)	**TMm**(32.9)	**RMm**(3.2)
	10	Caramel apple cupcakes	**Um**(63.5)	**TMm**(33.2)	**RMm**(3.2)

If the highest-probability color sequences are different, the main recommendation reasons are different. Thus, we can expect to get a different type recommendation list through filtering recommended items by the highest-probability color sequences. The recommendation list to user 1741 of Movielens dataset by APBRec in Table 5 supports this expectation. The first and last sublists are divided depending on whether the item's highest-probability color sequence is **RrR** or not. The genre distributions of the two sublists look different: genres Sci-Fi, Film-Noir, Mystery and War appear in the first sublist only while genres Children, Musical, Horror, Action, Adventure and IMAX appear in the last sublist only.

Table 5. The top 30 movies recommended to user 1741 by APBRec in Movielens dataset. The first and last sublists are divided depending on whether the item's highest-probability color sequence is **RrR** or not. The italic genres indicate sublist-uniqueness, that is, they do not appear in the other sublist.

Rank	Movie	Genres	Color sequence ranking		
			1st	2nd	3rd
1	The Man Who Wouldn't Die	Crime, Drama, Thriller	RrR	TrR	UmrR
2	Slam Dance	Thriller	RrR	TrR	UmrR
3	Shepherd	*Sci-Fi*	RrR	TrR	UmrR
9	Dragon Age	Animation, Fantasy	RrR	TrR	UmrR
16	Lady on a Train	Comedy, Crime, *Film-Noir*, *Mystery*, Romance, Thriller	RrR	TrR	UmrR
17	Long Night's Journey Into Day	Documentary	RrR	TrR	UmrR
20	Jim Jefferies Fully Functional	Comedy	RrR	TrR	UmrR
22	Napoleon	Drama, *War*	RrR	TrR	UmrR
26	Big Parade	Drama, Romance, *War*	RrR	TrR	UmrR
27	Fawlty Towers	Comedy	RrR	TrR	UmrR
4	Momo	Animation, *Children*, Fantasy	Um	TrR	UuR
5	Houseboat	Comedy, Romance	Um	TrR	RrR
6	Pina	Documentary, *Musical*	Um	TrR	UuR
7	Alvin and the Chipmunks	*Children*, Comedy	Um	RMm	TrR
8	The Wolf Brigade	Animation, Fantasy, Thriller	Um	RrR	TrR
10	My Name Is Bruce	Comedy, *Horror*	Um	TrR	RrR
11	Party Monster	Comedy, Crime, Drama, Thriller	Um	TrR	RrR
12	Out of Africa	Drama, Romance	Um	RrR	TtR
13	Shattered Glass	Crime, Drama	Um	TrR	RrR
14	Bat	*Horror*	Um	TrR	UuR
15	Children of the Corn	*Horror*	Um	TrR	UmrR
18	V.I.P.s	Drama	TrR	UmrR	TrRrR
19	A Question of Faith	Drama	Um	UmMm	TMm
21	Double Dynamite	Comedy, *Musical*	TrR	UmrR	
23	Big Fella	Drama, *Musical*	TrR	UmrR	
24	The Guardian	*Action*, Thriller	Um	TrR	UmrR
25	The Killer Whale	*Action*, Drama, *Horror*, Thriller	Um	TrR	RrR
28	Bella	Drama, Romance	Um	RrR	TrR
29	How to Train Your Dragon	*Adventure*, Animation, *Children*, Fantasy, *IMAX*	Um	TrR	UuUm
30	Art and Craft	Documentary	Um	UuR	TMm

5   Conclusion

We proposed a recommendation algorithm that shows high-probability color sequences (high-contributed relation path) as explanation for recommendation. To calculate high-probability color sequences, our algorithm does depth first search on an edge-colored directed graph that represents various relations between recommendation-related objects. The probability sum of all the above-threshold-probability acyclic s-t paths are used for the recommendation score of item t for user s. According to the experiments using real-world datasets, the recommendation performance of our proposed method is comparable to non-explainable state-of-the-art recommendation methods. Color sequences are confirmed to be useful not only for recommendation explanation but also for realizing recommendation lists of various trends.

Acknowledgments. This work was partially supported by JST CREST Grant Number JPMJCR18-K3, Japan.

References

1. Aggarwal, C.C., Wolf, J.L., Wu, K.L., Yu, P.S.: Horting hatches an egg: a new graph-theoretic approach to collaborative filtering. In: Proceedings of the Fifth ACM SIGKDD International Conference on Knowledge Discovery and Data Mining, pp. 201–212 (1999)
2. Burges, C., et al.: Learning to rank using gradient descent. In: Proceedings of the 22nd International Conference on Machine Learning, pp. 89–96 (2005)
3. Catherine, R., Mazaitis, K., Eskenazi, M., Cohen, W.: Explainable entity-based recommendations with knowledge graphs. arXiv preprint arXiv:1707.05254 (2017)
4. Chen, X., Qin, Z., Zhang, Y., Xu, T.: Learning to rank features for recommendation over multiple categories. In: Proceedings of the 39th International ACM SIGIR Conference on Research and Development in Information Retrieval, pp. 305–314 (2016)
5. Donkers, T., Loepp, B., Ziegler, J.: Sequential user-based recurrent neural network recommendations. In: Proceedings of the Eleventh ACM Conference on Recommender Systems, pp. 152–160 (2017)
6. Harper, F.M., Konstan, J.A.: The movielens datasets: history and context. ACM Trans. Interact. Intell. Syst. (TIIS) **5**(4), 1–19 (2015)
7. He, X., Chen, T., Kan, M.Y., Chen, X.: Trirank: review-aware explainable recommendation by modeling aspects. In: Proceedings of the 24th ACM International on Conference on Information and Knowledge Management, pp. 1661–1670 (2015)
8. Herlocker, J.L., Konstan, J.A., Riedl, J.: Explaining collaborative filtering recommendations. In: Proceedings of the 2000 ACM Conference on Computer Supported Cooperative Work, pp. 241–250 (2000)
9. Koren, Y.: Factorization meets the neighborhood: a multifaceted collaborative filtering model. In: Proceedings of the 14th ACM SIGKDD International Conference on Knowledge Discovery and Data Mining, pp. 426–434 (2008)
10. Li, P., Wang, Z., Ren, Z., Bing, L., Lam, W.: Neural rating regression with abstractive tips generation for recommendation. In: Proceedings of the 40th International ACM SIGIR conference on Research and Development in Information Retrieval, pp. 345–354 (2017)
11. Papadimitriou, A., Symeonidis, P., Manolopoulos, Y.: A generalized taxonomy of explanations styles for traditional and social recommender systems. Data Min Knowl. Discov. **24**(3), 555–583 (2012)
12. Rendle, S., Freudenthaler, C., Gantner, Z., Schmidt-Thieme, L.: BPR: Bayesian personalized ranking from implicit feedback. arXiv preprint arXiv:1205.2618 (2012)
13. Sarwar, B., Karypis, G., Konstan, J., Riedl, J.: Item-based collaborative filtering recommendation algorithms. In: Proceedings of the 10th International Conference on World Wide Web, pp. 285–295 (2001)
14. Seo, S., Huang, J., Yang, H., Liu, Y.: Interpretable convolutional neural networks with dual local and global attention for review rating prediction. In: Proceedings of the Eleventh ACM Conference on Recommender Systems, pp. 297–305 (2017)
15. Tan, S., et al.: Using rich social media information for music recommendation via hypergraph model. ACM Trans. Multimed. Comput. Commun. Appl. **7**(1), 22 (2011)

16. Wang, H., Wang, N., Yeung, D.Y.: Collaborative deep learning for recommender systems. In: Proceedings of the 21th ACM SIGKDD International Conference on Knowledge Discovery and Data Mining, pp. 1235–1244 (2015)
17. Zhang, Y., Chen, X.: Explainable recommendation: a survey and new perspectives. arXiv preprint arXiv:1804.11192 (2018)
18. Zhang, Y., Lai, G., Zhang, M., Zhang, Y., Liu, Y., Ma, S.: Explicit factor models for explainable recommendation based on phrase-level sentiment analysis. In: Proceedings of the 37th International ACM SIGIR Conference on Research and Development in Information Retrieval, pp. 83–92 (2014)
19. Zhang, Y., et al.: Daily-aware personalized recommendation based on feature-level time series analysis. In: Proceedings of the 24th International Conference on World Wide Web, pp. 1373–1383 (2015)

Knowledge Transfer for Deep Reinforcement Agents in General Game Playing

Cameron McEwan and Michael Thielscher[✉]

UNSW Sydney, Sydney, NSW 2052, Australia
mit@unsw.edu.au

Abstract. Learning to master new games with nothing but the rules given is a hallmark of human intelligence. This ability has recently been successfully replicated in AI systems through a combination of Knowledge Representation, Monte Carlo Tree Search and Deep Reinforcement Learning: Generalised AlphaZero [7] provides a method for building general game-playing agents that can learn any game describable in a formal specification language. We investigate how to boost the ability of deep reinforcement agents for general game playing by applying transfer learning for new game variants. Experiments show that transfer learning can significantly reduce the training time on variations of games that were previously learned, and our results further suggest that the most successful method is to train a source network that uses the guidance of multiple expert networks.

1 Introduction

In General Game Playing (GGP), agents are provided at runtime with the rules of a game they must learn [5]. Players are given formal specifications in the general Game Description Language (GDL), thereby addressing the problem that using single games for testing AI encourages niche programs that can only perform in one environment [6].

The most common algorithm employed by successful GGP agents is a variation of Monte Carlo Tree Search known as the *upper confidence bound on trees* (UCT) method [2]. UCT has been successfully combined with deep reinforcement learning in AlphaGo [16], to beat eighteen-time world champion Go player Lee Sedol, and later in AlphaZero [17], which learned to play three different board games from scratch to a superhuman level. The underlying principle of combining UCT with deep reinforcement learning was further developed to Generalised AlphaZero [7], where the two methods were further combined with knowledge representation and reasoning in order to build general game-playing agents that are capable of learning any game describable in GDL.

In both AlphaZero and Generalised AlphaZero, new games are learned from scratch. *Transfer learning* (TL) is a technique that aims to increase the efficiency of learning systems by transferring the knowledge gained from learning one task

© Springer Nature Switzerland AG 2022
G. Long et al. (Eds.): AI 2021, LNAI 13151, pp. 53–66, 2022.
https://doi.org/10.1007/978-3-030-97546-3_5

to a new but similar task [21]. Heretofore there has been limited success incorporating TL into agents for GGP [3,11,19], and no research that combines deep TL and GGP. Nevertheless, the method [3], which achieved positive transfer between completely different games, set the precedent that positive transfer in GGP is possible.

In this paper, we investigate and show how to boost the ability of deep reinforcement agents for general game playing by using transfer learning for new game variants. Our main contributions are summarised on the following page.

1. We develop a hierarchy of general game variations and strategies to best address each level by different transfer learning strategies.
2. We investigate the efficacy of two different methods of applying transfer learning in general game playing with deep reinforcement learning: using a network that has been previously trained on a single game versus a network that combines multiple expert networks, each previously trained on a different game.
3. Our analysis of the experimental results shows that guidance by multiple expert networks is the most successful of our methods to train a source network.

2   Background

General Game Playing. General game playing was developed to address the problem of niche game-playing AI programs that can only perform in certain environments [5,6]. The training process begins with players being provided with the rules of a game using the general Game Description Language GDL. Players have *startclock* seconds to perform initial training [5]. The International General Game Playing Competition typically has a 10 min *startclock* [7]. In 2014, regular competition in the related field of *General Video Game Playing* (GVGAI) was established [13]. This competition shares GGP's basic premise that agents must be able to play previously unseen games. In contrast to GGP, GVGAI focuses on video games and may require agents to interpret states from an image feed and actions from a forward network to learn to play [13].

UCT and Reinforcement Learning. The most common algorithm employed by successful GGP agents is a variation on the *upper confidence bound on trees* (UCT) method [5]. This fundamental algorithm is a modification of *Monte Carlo Tree Search* (MCTS) to improve the trade-off between exploration and exploitation, by embedding an upper confidence bound of the expected reward in each node of the tree to guide search. UCT was successfully combined with *deep reinforcement learning* (RL) in AlphaGo to beat eighteen-time world champion Go player Lee Sedol [16]. RL is a field of machine learning that is concerned with agents learning to maximise reward. *Q-learning* is a common model-free RL algorithm. Its objective is to learn the function $Q(s, a)$ which represents the total discounted reward for taking action a in state s over an infinite time horizon. *Deep Q-learning* is a deep RL method for approximating $Q(s, a)$ when the input space is too large to efficiently solve. $Q(s, a)$ is replaced by a neural network, and triples of state, action and discounted reward are gathered and sampled to train the network. Deep Q-learning is employed by most state-of-the-art GVGAI players [15].

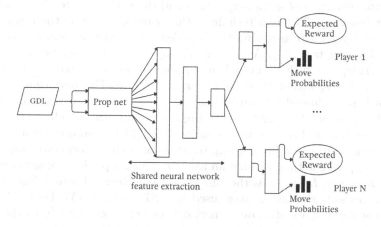

Fig. 1. Structure of a generalised AlphaZero agent.

Generalised AlphaZero. AlphaZero employed deep reinforcement learning in combination with UCT to learn to play three different board games from scratch to a superhuman level [17]. *Generalised* AlphaZero (GAZ) combines this method with a *knowledge representation and reasoning* technique to handle arbitrary games specified in the formal game description language GDL [7]. Specifically, GAZ uses *propositional networks (propnets)* [6,14] to process the GDL game rules. Moreover, various network components were adjusted to remove the assumptions of AlphaZero to make it suitable for use in the GGP environment: GAZ employs a single neural network to generate a better approximation for the UCT heuristic than MCTS alone. The network outputs an expected reward z_i and a probability distribution π_i over the action space. It then performs a number of self-play games running MCTS simulations to train the network. The MCTS simulations are conducted in the same way as standard UCT players with an adapted formula for the upper confidence bound. Upon reaching a leaf node, an option is expanded and the neural network is used to evaluate that node.

The structure of the GAZ network (shown in Fig. 1) is influenced by three factors: the size of the propnet, the number of actions each player can take and the number of players. GAZ has undergone several experimental evaluations that demonstrate it is able to perform better than a UCT benchmark in many games, but requires significant training time [7,8]. When evaluated on Connect-4, Breakthrough, Babel and Pacman, the agent was successful in thwarting a UCT benchmark agent in all games but Babel. It took the GAZ agent between one and seven hours to beat UCT and 10 to 30 h to complete a full training run on each game, significantly longer than the regular 10-min *startclock* used in GGP competitions. This training time must therefore be significantly reduced for GAZ to succeed in GGP.

Transfer Learning. The training time of a neural network is influenced by two factors, the efficiency of a training round and the learning rate of the network. *Transfer Learning* (TL) is a technique that aims to increase the efficiency of learning systems by transferring the knowledge gained from learning one task to a similar new task [21]. An important aspect is the avoidance of so-called *negative transfer*, which occurs when transferring between inappropriate tasks leads to a slower, rather than faster, training time. The performance of TL agents is best evaluated by considering the time required to train on just the new task, or *target time* [20]. Other important metrics include: (1) the time to train the new and source agents, *total time*; (2) the improvement of initial performance, *jumpstart*; (3) the improvement of final performance, *asymptotic performance*; (4) the time it takes an agent to reach a predetermined threshold, *time to threshold*. *Deep TL* is the sub-field that concerns learning agents using deep RL methods similar to those used in GAZ and GVGAI. Deep TL works by copying the weights of a source network, or networks, directly to the target network. Several decisions are then made to help mitigate negative transfer. The source network is chosen and the layers of the network adjusted with the weights either fixed, reinitialised or allowed to be retrained [1]. When setting these transfer variables it is important to consider the difference between the source and target tasks. This is particularly challenging in game playing, where goals, actions, and domains can differ significantly between games. As a result, most research on TL in game play focuses on game variants and groups of similar games.

Previous Work on Transfer Learning for General Game Playing

In GGP, so far there has been limited success incorporating TL into agents. Past research proposed using a transfer hierarchy [19] and exploiting structural similarities in the game tree [3,11] to pair source and target tasks. The transfer hierarchy only succeeded transferring between game variants and is therefore of limited use in GGP [19]. Despite this, the tiered testing methodology, which proposed to first test on simple game variants before increasing the complexity of the variations, contributed a practical methodological framework for assessing transfer in games. The more successful method [3] achieved positive transfer between completely different games. This agent did not use deep RL, however, so its heuristic method was not considered in our agent design. Nevertheless, these results were important as they set the precedent that positive transfer in GGP is possible. A missing feature of all the TL approaches to GGP so far is a way to prevent or mitigate negative transfer [9].

General Video Game Playing agents that incorporate deep TL techniques into their architectures have had more success, achieving state-of-the-art results more efficiently when playing several games. Like GGP, the variety of games in GVGAI limits TL, and the most noteworthy research addresses this by generalising from multiple source tasks to mitigate or even eliminate negative transfer [12,22]. The use of single-network transfer and experiments with fixing, retraining, or re-initialising each network layer were successfully applied to PuckWorld and Snake [1]: By allowing all layers of an expert Puckworld network to retrain, the time to learn Snake could be significantly reduced. However, these results could not be replicated training Puckworld from Snake.

Multi-network transfer methods include the Actor-Mimic Network (AMN) [12] and Policy Transfer Framework (PTF) [22]. The seminal AMN established multi-network transfer learning in video game playing trading off *total time* for resilience to negative transfer. This powerful approach distils information from *multiple* expert networks into a generic network (the mimic) that is then used as the source for transfer. Transfer with the AMN was tested by training a mimic network on 13 source games and then using the result as the basis of transfer to learn 7 new games. Performance improved learning 6 of the 7 new games. AMN not fully addressing the problem of negative transfer, PTF further extends this approach by framing TL as an option learning problem in order to facilitate the elimination of negative transfer [22]. Still, the broad, and repeated, success of AMN makes it an ideal basis for adaptation to improve GGP agents.[1]

3 Transfer Learning in Deep RL General Game-Playing Agents

Generalised AlphaZero training too slowly to compete in traditional GGP competition [7] motivates the use of transfer learning as a potential solution. Past work on GGP confirms that the barrier to successful knowledge transfer is prevention of negative transfer (cf. Sect. 2). In this section, we present a method based on the recent success of several multi-network deep Transfer Learning solutions to prevent negative transfer recent work in GVGAI [12]. We will describe two approaches and designs for deep reinforcement agents to make use Transfer Learning in General Game Playing: a *single* and a *multi-network* transfer learning method for GGP. We also distinguish between *simple* and *complex* transfer.

3.1 Simple Network Transfer in General Game Playing

Simple network transfer occurs when the source and target network have identical structures. Two Generalised AlphaZero networks (cf. Fig. 1) have identical structures when the games they are learning have the same propnet size, number of actions and number of players. Because the structure of the two networks is identical, transfer happens by way of copying the weights layer-wise without any shape transformations. Simple Network Transfer has three variables: (1) the expertise of the source network, (2) weight transformations, and (3) the number of source networks.

---

[1] Other methods in GVGAI focus on transferring learned skills about *visual* information [10,18]. Visual information is not relevant to GGP and therefore not considered in this paper.

Fully vs. Semi-trained Source Networks. We use the term *fully trained source networks* to describe expert networks that have been trained long enough to play at optimal level in a particular game. In contrast, *semi-trained networks* have only been trained for a fraction of the time, thus learning only some of the expert behaviour. Partial training could mitigate negative transfer, since the agent has less information to unlearn if all of the information in a fully trained source network is tailored to a specific game. Our agent design allows to use both fully and semi-trained agents interchangeably, with the hypothesis that fully trained agents will work best when transferring between the most similar game variants, and semi-trained agents will have better results in the least.

Weights. Weights can either be fixed; reinitialised, i.e. given random initial weights; or retrained, i.e. initialised from a pre-trained model [1]. Given the history of negative transfer in game playing and the difficultly of transferring between games, fixing weights is not an option for any layers in the agent designs. The intermediate layers are limited to retraining only, since reinitialising these layers would be equivalent to not performing transfer at all. The output layer for the move probabilities (cf. Fig. 1) can be retrained or reinitialised. This is because this layer directly impacts the chance of an agent taking a particular action based on the probability distribution. If the action layer is allowed to retrain, the network will initially repeat the behaviour of the source network but is allowed to adjust behaviour over time. This should perform well when the old and the new game have similar goals, so that good moves in one game tend to be good moves in the other game too. On the other hand, reinitialising the action layer will cause the network to choose moves randomly in its first round of training, thus encouraging exploration of the game tree. It is predicted that this will improve performance when transferring to less similar games.

Number of Source Networks. In *single* network transfer, only one expert network is used. Past research shows this approach could be vulnerable to negative transfer. *Multi-network* transfer methods were developed to address this concern, creating a source network using the guidance of multiple expert networks. To train a source network, these multi-network transfer methods employ a multi-task training method. The multitask training method developed for our proposed agent design will be detailed in Sect. 3.3 below.[2]

3.2 Complex Network Transfer

If the source and target network have different structures, then additional variables for transfer must be introduced to map the structure of the source network to the target network. The additional variables required for what we consider

---

[2] It is worth noting that many of the multitask methods in GVGAI are not directly applicable to GGP and Generalised AlphaZero because they assume specific features of the network, such as identical input shapes and action spaces, regardless of the game being played.

complex network transfer depend on the factors that vary between the two games. The variables are: (1) input transformation, (2) action transformation, and (3) player transformation.

Input transformation is necessary when the size of the propnet changes. This has a cascading effect on the size of each of the layers in the shared feature extraction. As a result, the new network must be adapted to fit the source network within its feature extraction layers. To maintain a resemblance to the structure of Generalised AlphaZero, a gradual input transformation is proposed to slowly introduce the source network to the new network. In this transformation, layers of half or double the size are added between the input of the new network and the first layer of the source network to gradually converge their size. The aim of these layers is to help learn how to convert the input from the propnet to a set of features that approximate the input of the original game. The final transformation layer is then used as the input layer to a copy of the source network.

Action transformation is necessary when the set of actions is different between the two games. In our agent designs, if the actions are completely different then the action layers are reinitialised, whereas if the games share some actions then there are two options: reinitialisation or complete action mapping. Action mapping means to map the weights of the shared actions from the source network to the new network. This is expected to be successful when takin an action in the new game that exists in the previously learned game and tends to contribute to a winning strategy there, does so in the new game too.

Finally, if there is a change in the number of players then a *player transformation* will be necessary. If the number of players increases, the new player head could be initialised with one of the existing player heads. If the number of players decreases, then one of the player heads should not be copied.

3.3 Multitask Training for General Game Playing

Our multitask method for GGP is inspired by the success of AMN [12], which trains based on a policy distillation and a scaled feature regression component. For GGP, we use only the policy distillation component since this is considered the more successful part of the network, with improvements to the AMN removing the feature regression component [4,23]. The policy distillation component trains based on the KL divergence of the multitask network compared to the expert. In the method we propose, the mimic network retains the structure of Generalised AlphaZero, but instead of training based on self-play it uses the KL divergence from the experience of a series of experts. During training, the multitask network completes N rounds of a particular game guided by the expert on that game, then moves on to the next game and expert. This process is repeated M times. Like in AMN, it is important to balance N as too many rounds of training on a particular game will over-fit the multitask network. Once trained, the multitask network is used as the source for transfer. It is important to note that this method is limited to train on games that have the same propnet size and number of actions.

4   Experimental Evaluation

4.1   Generic Agent Designs

We tested two generic agent designs based on the distinction between single network agents and those that use a network trained according to the multitask training method defined in Sect. 3.3. Each agent has a variety of settings that can be adjusted to set the variables for each type of transfer. Details of the implementation and experimental results are available at https://github.com/camronmc/transfer_ggp.

4.2   Game Variations

Our experimental evaluation of transfer learning applied to deep reinforcement GGP agents focuses on two types of game variation, namely, goal variation and environment variation. Goal variation concern the winning conditions of a game. Specifically, we investigate five such goal variations: (1) **original**; (2) **subset**, where solutions to the original game will still win the new game but there are other paths to victory; (3) **minor goal changes**, where solutions to the original game form a partial solution of the new game; (4) **superset**, where some solutions to the original game will lose the new game; and (5) **inverse goal**, where all winning states become losing states and vice versa.

Environment variations change the environment while retaining the "nature" of the original game. These could be adjustments to the board, the number of players, or new features such as obstacles on a board etc. We categorise environment variations by whether they affect the structure of a Generalised AlphaZero network. If there is no change to the input or action space, the change is considered minor, otherwise, i.e. when at least one of the two is altered, it is considered major. An example of a major change is adjusting the board size. Figure 2 ranks these variations based on similarity and maps them to the transfer variables hypothesised to perform best.

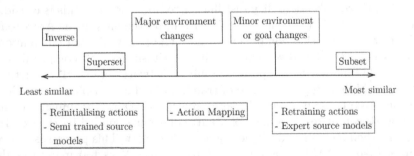

Fig. 2. Hierarchy of game variants and strategies.

4.3   Evaluation Methodology

We implemented the generic agent designs on Google Cloud's Deep Learning VM Image running Tensorflow 1, Python 3.7 and Cython 3.7.[3] The agents were evaluated by playing sets of 50 simulated games against a regular UCT agent every 50 rounds of training. Each player had a time limit of two seconds to decide their next move, and the first two moves of each game were randomised. This randomisation was necessary to ensure a spread of independent tests as all of the agents used are mostly deterministic. The randomised moves were seeded so that in each trial game all agents began with the same two moves. This allows direct comparison between agents while retaining an independent set of tests. UCT was chosen as a benchmark because it represents state-of-the-art in GGP without transfer or deep reinforcement learning [5]. The parameters of the underlying Generalised AlphaZero agent were kept constant.

Even though there are only two principled agent designs (single and multi-network), the number of combinations of variables required to run over 60 experiments on three different base games. Single network agents were tested with both semi- and fully trained source networks and with weight, action, and input transformations. Multi-network agents were tested with gradual input transformation and reinitialised move layers.

We tested variants of Connect-4 and Breakthrough along with the simple game Nim; these games were chosen due to their prominence in past GGP competitions [5]. We apply a common evaluation metric known from the literature [20], with a particular focus on *jumpstart* and *time to threshold* as the main goal of GGP is to get the best agent in limited time. A threshold was chosen for each game based on the winning score an agent without transfer converged to. Thresholds varied due to the effect of the random initial moves. Connect-4 variant thresholds ranged from 25 to 40 games, and from 40 to 45 for Breakthrough and Nim variants. As TL has no effect on the time required for each round of training, *target time* is measured in rounds rather than seconds or hours.

5   Results and Discussion

Transfer Learning proved to increase the efficiency of Generalised AlphaZero (GAZ) on most game variants. Both single and multi-network agents outperformed agents without transfer. The multi-network design had the greatest success, outperforming agents with single network transfer. Negative transfer was only experienced when complex transfer was necessary and when learning superset goal variants. Successful agents had a strong *jumpstart* and significant decrease in *time to threshold*. Consequently, the training time for these agents went down. On some occasions, the *jumpstart* of the multi-network agent outperformed a network without transfer that had trained for thousands of rounds.

---

[3] https://cloud.google.com/deep-learning-vm, accessed 01/19/21.

5.1 Single Network Agents

Although not as successful as their multi-network counterparts, single network agents still achieved positive transfer on a variety of the game variants. Experiments with subset goal variation, minor goal changes, and minor environment changes all showed positive transfer: Single network agents with tuned variables could improve *time to threshold* significantly when learning *Connect-4 Zig Zag*[4] (150 rounds to reaching the threshold with transfer, vs. 400 rounds with no transfer learning), *Connect-5* (500 vs. 2700), *Breakthrough Suicide*[5] (150 vs. 1500), and *Nim Variant-2*[6] (300 vs. 500). Even when there was no improvement to *time to threshold*, single network agents often had a strong *jumpstart*. Figure 3 shows the *jumpstart* of the single network retrain agent learning Connect-4 on a 10x8-board and Breakthrough Suicide, where the agent outperformed GAZ for more than 250 and 600 rounds, respectively. This suggests that expert networks contain good general information about the original game they train on, resulting in an initial advantage playing the new game. In GGP competitions, *jumpstart* is an advantage. If the *startclock* ends within the period of *jumpstart*, then strong initial performance would win.

Tuning the SNT variables had the expected results. Semi-trained agents gave networks a boost in *time to threshold* in the least similar games, like Connect-4 Inverse Goal, and had longer *time to threshold* in the most similar game variants, such as Connect-5. Weight transformations to the action layer also performed as expected. Retraining gave agents an advantage when learning games where behaving in the same was as you would in the source game was likely to win in the target game as well. Examples included Nim Variant-2, Connect-4 and -5 on a 10x8 board. Reinitialising yielded better results in the least similar variants, including Connect-4 Inverse Goal, Nim Inverse Goal and Connect-4 Miss-1[7].

5.2 Complex Network Transfer

Both single and multi-network agents struggled to outperform those without transfer learning when complex transfer was necessary. Gradual input transformation failed to reduce the input to a state representation similar to the input of the source network. As a result, agents encountered negative transfer at the beginning, even with small changes to the input size. The larger the change, the more negative transfer was observed. The relatively small changes in Nim were best handled with only short periods of negative transfer for the first 50–100 rounds of training. Learning Breakthrough on 5×6 and 4×7 boards, where the input changed in size by a few hundred nodes, agents experienced several hundreds of rounds of negative transfer as they had been trained to expect input in the format of the original game.

---

[4] With a "zig zag" pattern of four pieces as an additional winning condition.
[5] With inverted goal.
[6] With stacks 2,2,10,10 instead of the original 1,5,4,2.
[7] With the goal to connect 2 pieces, *miss* the third slot, and put a piece in the fourth slot.

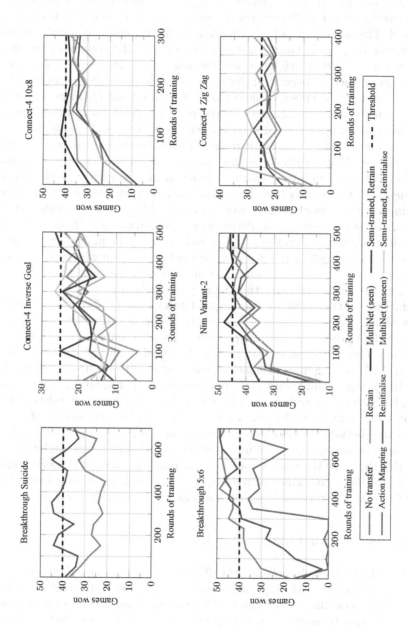

Fig. 3. Results testing transfer learning techniques and variables across Connect-4, Breakthrough and Nim variants.

5.3   Multi-network Agents

Multi-network agents mitigated negative transfer in many more game variants than single networks. They had much stronger jump starts. In Connect-4 Zig Zag the *jumpstart* (cf. Fig. 3) performed even better than the GAZ once it was fully trained. The agent typically met thresholds in 50 rounds of training when learning games they had expert knowledge in, and in 150 rounds of training learning new games. Of the 16 game variants multi-network agents were tested on, they outperformed all other transfer agents in 14 variants. Negative transfer was experienced in the superset variants Connect-4 Miss-1 and Connect-4 Inverse Goal when not been previously seen by the network. Analysis of the different variables for transfer drew the same conclusions as for the single networks.

Choosing a large number and wide range of expert networks further mitigated negative transfer. Multi-network agents trained without any inverse variants struggled to learn unseen inverse goals. Adding an inverse variant to the set of experts improved this even when there were many experts; the multi-network agent trained in variants of Nim showed no discernible negative transfer when learning variants with inverse goal. Performance also improved with more expert networks. Increasing the number of Nim variants used in multitask training worked best with the highest number of expert networks, even when the number of training rounds was kept constant. This suggests that increasing the number of varied experts is more effective than hand picking them.

The efficiency of the multitask training and its superior performance suggests that it is always better to train a multi-network agent rather than a single network one. The primary concern with multi-network agents is their increased training time. The multitask training method defined in this research is much faster than GAZ training due to its lack of self-play. As a result, the difference in training time between single and multi-network agents is negligible. If a library of buffers for each of the experts is built when they are trained, it takes just a few minutes to complete multitask training. The self-play component of GAZ takes anywhere between 20 and 80 seconds per round of training, so even when assuming optimal performance, adding a multitask network to the architecture takes roughly the same time as six rounds of training. Given that networks must train for hundreds or thousands of rounds, multitask training adds a negligible amount of time to the process but with a significant jump in performance.

6   Conclusion and Future Work

Introducing TL to the architecture of GAZ reduced the training time on game variants. The multi-network approach was the most successful method with strong results in seen and unseen games. Multi-network agents were much more resilient to negative transfer across the spectrum of variants, provided a diverse set of source games was chosen. When using single network agents, it proved prudent to consider the disparity between game variants when setting the variables for transfer. Retraining action weights assisted transfer to the most similar variants, whereas reinitialising action weights and using semi-trained source networks worked best in the least. Single and multi-network struggled to complete positive transfer between networks with different structures. Addressing this in future work is key to stable performance across a wider variety of variants.

References

1. Asawa, C., Elamri, C., Pan, D.: Using transfer learning between games to improve deep reinforcement learning performance and stability (2017). http://web. stanford.edu/class/cs234/past_projects/2017/2017_Asawa_Elamri_Pan_Transfer_ Learning_Paper.pdf
2. Auer, P.: Using confidence bounds for exploitation-exploration trade-offs. J. Mach. Learn. Res. **3**, 397–422 (2003)
3. Banerjee, B., Stone, P.: General game learning using knowledge transfer. In: Proceedings of IJCAI, pp. 672–677 (2007)
4. Czarnecki, W.M., Pascanu, R., Osindero, S., Jayakumar, S.M., Swirszcz, G., Jaderberg, M.: Distilling policy distillation. CoRR abs/1902.02186 (2019)
5. Genesereth, M., Björnsson, Y.: The international general game playing competition. AI Mag. **34**(2), 107 (2013)
6. Genesereth, M., Thielscher, M.: General Game Playing. Synthesis Lectures on Artificial Intelligence and Machine Learning. Morgan & Claypool, San Rafael (2014)
7. Goldwaser, A., Thielscher, M.: Deep reinforcement learning for general game playing. In: Proceedings of AAAI, pp. 1701–1708. AAAI Press (2020)
8. Gunawan, A., Ruan, J., Thielscher, M., Narayanan, A.: Exploring a learning architecture for general game playing. In: Gallagher, M., Moustafa, N., Lakshika, E. (eds.) AI 2020. LNCS (LNAI), vol. 12576, pp. 294–306. Springer, Cham (2020). https://doi.org/10.1007/978-3-030-64984-5_23
9. Hinrichs, T., Forbus, K.D.: Transfer learning through analogy in games. AI Mag. **32**(1), 70–83 (2011)
10. Hsu, S., Shen, I., Chen, B.: Transferring deep reinforcement learning with adversarial objective and augmentation. CoRR abs/1809.00770 (2018)
11. Kuhlmann, G., Stone, P.: Graph-based domain mapping for transfer learning in general games. In: Proceedings of ECML, pp. 188–200 (2007)
12. Parisotto, E., Ba, J., Salakhutdinov, R.: Actor-mimic: deep multitask and transfer reinforcement learning. CoRR abs/1511.06342 (2015)
13. Pérez-Liébana, D., Liu, J., Khalifa, A., Gaina, R.D., Togelius, J., Lucas, S.M.: General video game AI: a multi-track framework for evaluating agents, games and content generation algorithms. CoRR abs/1802.10363 (2018)
14. Schkufza, E., Love, N., Genesereth, M.: Propositional automata and cell automata: Representational frameworks for discrete dynamic systems. In: Proceedings of AI, pp. 56–66 (2008)
15. Shao, K., Tang, Z., Zhu, Y., Li, N., Zhao, D.: A survey of deep reinforcement learning in video games. arXiv preprint arXiv:1912.10944 (2019)
16. Silver, D., Huang, A., Maddison, C.J., Guez, A., Sifre, L., et al.: Mastering the game of go with deep neural networks and tree search. Nature **529**, 484–503 (2016)
17. Silver, D., Hubert, T., Schrittwieser, J., Antonoglou, I., Lai, M., et al.: A general reinforcement learning algorithm that masters chess, shogi, and go through self-play. Science **362**(6419), 1140–1144 (2018)

18. Sobol, D., Wolf, L., Taigman, Y.: Visual analogies between Atari games for studying transfer learning in RL. arXiv preprint arXiv:1807.11074 (2018)
19. Taylor, M.E., Kuhlmann, G., Stone, P.: Accelerating search with transferred heuristics. In: ICAPS 2007 Workshop on AI Planning and Learning (2007)
20. Taylor, M.E., Stone, P.: Cross-domain transfer for reinforcement learning. In: Proceedings of the ICML, New York, pp. 879–886 (2007)
21. Taylor, M.E., Stone, P.: Transfer learning for reinforcement learning domains: a survey. J. Mach. Learn. Res. **10**, 1633–1685 (2009)
22. Yang, T., Hao, J., Meng, Z., Zhang, Z., Wang, W., et al.: Efficient deep reinforcement learning through policy transfer. arXiv preprint arXiv:2002.08037 (2020)
23. Yin, H., Pan, S.J.: Knowledge transfer for deep reinforcement learning with hierarchical experience replay. In: Proceedings of AAAI, pp. 1640–1646. AAAI Press (2017)

GSMI: A Gradient Sign Optimization Based Model Inversion Method

Zhiyi Tian, Chenhan Zhang, Lei Cui, and Shui Yu$^{(\boxtimes)}$

School of Computer Science, FEIT, University of Technology Sydney,
Sydney, Australia
{zhiyi.tian,chenhan.zhang}@student.uts.edu.au
{lei.cui,shui.yu}@uts.edu.au

Abstract. The vulnerabilities of deep learning models on security and privacy have attracted a lot of attentions. Researchers have revealed the possibility of reconstructing training data of a target model. However, the performances of current works are highly rely on auxiliary datasets. In this paper, we investigate the model inversion problem under a strict restriction, where the adversary aims to reconstruct plausible samples of the target class without help of auxiliary information. To solve this challenge, we propose a Gradient Sign Model Inversion (GSMI) method based on the idea of adversarial examples generation. Specifically, we make three modifications on a popular adversarial examples generation method i-FGSM to generate plausible samples. 1) Increasing the number of attack iterations and 2) superposing noises to reveal more obvious features learned by target model. 3) removing subtle noises to make reconstructed samples more plausible. However, we find samples generated by GSMI still contain noisy components. Furthermore, we adopt the idea of image adjacent regions to design a two-pass components selection algorithm to generate more reasonable sample of the target class. Through experiments, we find that the inversion samples of GSMI are close to real target class samples with some fluctuations on different classes. In addition, we also provide detail analysis for reasons of limitations on the optimization-based model inversion methods.

Keywords: Deep learning · Model inversion · Adversarial example

1 Introduction

The risk of privacy leakage grows rapidly with extensive applications of deep learning on sensitive domain, such as medicine, face recognition, and many more. This has led to a class of attacks called privacy violation attacks [6–8]. One of the ultimate goals of privacy violation attack is to reconstruct training data though the information gathered from the victim model. This attack is known as model inversion attack, which was first proposed in 2014 on genomic privacy [8]. The authors inferred private genomic attributes in the training data of a linear regression model successfully.

© Springer Nature Switzerland AG 2022
G. Long et al. (Eds.): AI 2021, LNAI 13151, pp. 67–78, 2022.
https://doi.org/10.1007/978-3-030-97546-3_6

There are two main categories model inversion attacks, the optimization-based method and the training-based method. The training-based method uses auxiliary dataset to train another deep learning model to generate samples containing information of target model [22,23]. However, training-based model inversion methods need a lot of auxiliary knowledges. For example, in [23], the adversary is given an auxiliary dataset from the same domain and blurred target images to assist model inversion. The more auxiliary information required, the less practical the attack. By comparison, adversaries in optimization-based methods hold almost no auxiliary knowledge of target model [4,7,15]. Typically, they use inside information flow of the target model to optimize an objective function, such as gradient descent methods. However, the performances of existing optimization-based methods have only been demonstrated on simple models [7,8].

In this paper, we try to investigate the efficiency of optimization-based model inversion method on deep learning models. We observe that technologies used in optimization-based methods are similar to the adversarial examples generation, but the goal is different. Adversarial examples try to broaden the gap between human vision and deep learning decision criterion. Specifically, the purpose of the adversarial examples is to force the target model predicting wrongly, and no obvious abnormality perceived by human vision. However adversaries in model inversion try to generate samples that meet the decision criterion of human vision and model at the same time.

Based on observation of adversarial examples generation method, especially i-FGSM [13], we propose an optimization-based method Gradient Sign Model Inversion (GSMI). Specifically, we focus on the adversarial scenario, where an adversary is given nothing of the target class and no help from auxiliary dataset. The aim is reconstructing samples of a target class. To generate more plausible samples we make three modifications on i-FGSM: 1) Increasing the number of attack iterations. 2) Superposing noises during iterations. 3) Removing subtle noises. These modifications remove the bounds in i-FGSM and help to reveal the features learned by the target model. However, the samples generated by GSMI contain some components with negative influences on decision made by human vision. In order to make the generated samples more realistic, we design a two-pass component selection method based on the idea of adjacent region, which leverages two-pass method [10] to generate the 8-adjacent regions map of the generated sample, and then, removes the regions that have negative influences on the prediction of the target model.

We evaluate our method on MNIST dataset [14] and Fashion-MNIST dataset [21]. The experiments results show that samples generated by GSMI are close to real samples, although a few elements of the objects are lost. When dealing with complex datasets, the quality of inversion samples show some drop.

In summary, we make the following contributions in this paper.

- We design an optimization-based method GSMI. Comparing to existing works, GSMI can generate target samples without the help of auxiliary information.

- We propose a two-pass components selection algorithm to select the most representative components of the target class in samples generated by GSMI. The experiments results show that GSMI can generate samples similar to the real ones.
- We conduct a detailed analysis of the performances of GSMI, and we find that the optimization-based method is susceptible by the learned features of the target model, resulting in performances fluctuations of inverting some classes.

2   Gradient Sign Model Inversion

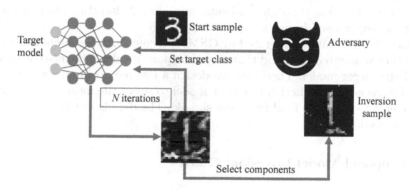

Fig. 1. Framework of GSMI. First, the adversary sets target class and the start sample to launch the optimization. Second, the optimization iterates predefined N times to generate a sample containing knowledges of the target class learned by the target model. Third, a components selection method is used to select the optimal components to form the inversion sample.

2.1   Threat model

In this paper, the target model is supervised deep learning classification model. More specifically, the target model $F_t(\mathbf{x})$ is a m-class image classification deep learning model, which predicts a vector $\mathbf{y} \in \mathbb{R}^m$ of an input $\mathbf{x} \in \mathbb{R}^n$.

The adversary tries to generate samples that can be classified as correct class both by target model and human vision. In previous literature [20,22,23] qualities of inversion samples are highly correlated with the auxiliary information. The more the adversary knows, the better the qualities of the inversion samples.

It is hard to get enough auxiliary information in the real world. Therefore, we focus on a stricter setting of auxiliary dataset. Unlike settings in training-based methods [22,23], the adversary is given a hard label of target class and no auxiliary dataset in this paper. We assume that the adversary has a white-box access of $F_t(\mathbf{x})$, which means the adversary knows precise definition of every hidden layers. He can monitor and modify the input and output of every hidden layers in $F_t(\mathbf{x})$.

2.2 Overview of the Attack

As described in Sect. 2.1, the biggest challenge in this setting is the lack of auxiliary information. All the knowledges can only be extracted from the target model. Therefore, we propose an optimization-based model inversion method called Gradient Sign Model Inversion (GSMI).

Figure 1 provides high-level overview of our model inversion attack. Our attack consists of two parts, GSMI and two-pass components selection. In GSMI, features learned by target model are extracted in each iterations by optimizing the objective function through gradients, and after N iterations the extracted feature are superposed in one sample.

However, the samples generated by GSMI still contain some components that make them look unreal. We find that these components also influence the prediction of the target model. Therefore, we design a two-pass components selection which leverages the prediction of target model to select the most representative components to form the final inversion sample. The details are discussed in the following sections.

2.3 Proposed Model Inversion: GSMI

Algorithm 1. Gradient Sign Model Inversion.
_____

Input: $\mathbf{x};\alpha;batch;N$
Output: $\mathbf{x}^{mi}$
   $\mathbf{x}_0^{mi} = \mathbf{x}$
1: **for** $i = 0;\ i < N;\ i{+}{+}$ **do**
2:    **for** $e = 0,\ \mathbf{x}_e^{mi} = \mathbf{x}_i^{mi};\ e < batch;\ e{+}{+}$ **do**
3:       $Noise\ {+}{=}\ \text{Clip}\left(\text{sign}\left(\nabla_X Loss\left(\mathbf{x}_e^{mi}, y_{true}\right)\right)\right)$ (Superposing noises)
4:    **end for**
5:    $\mathbf{x}_{i+1}^{mi} = \text{ReLUMed}(\mathbf{x}_i^{mi} + \alpha * Noise)$ (Removing subtle noises)
6: **end for**
7: $\mathbf{x}^{mi} = \mathbf{x}_{i+1}^{mi}$
8: **return** $\mathbf{x}^{mi}$

Our model inversion method is based on adversarial examples generation method i-FGSM [13]. The adversary aims to produce an adversarial example $\mathbf{x}^{adv}$ that is similar to a original image $\mathbf{x}$, but predicted as a different class. It could be denoted as following:

$$\begin{cases} \mathbf{x}_0^{adv} = \mathbf{x}, \\ \mathbf{x}_N^{adv} = \text{Clip}_{X,\epsilon}\left(\mathbf{x}_{N-1}^{adv} + \alpha\,\text{sign}\left(\nabla_X Loss\left(\mathbf{x}_{N-1}^{adv}, y\right)\right)\right), \end{cases} \tag{1}$$

where loss function $Loss(\cdot)$ is given image $\mathbf{x}$ and target class y, and then the gradients of target model are used to optimize $\mathbf{x}$. $\text{Clip}_{X,\epsilon}(\mathbf{x})$ performs per-pixel clipping of the image $\mathbf{x}$, so the result is in L_∞ ϵ-neighborhood of the source image $\mathbf{x}$. i-FGSM applies FGSM N iterations with small step size α, and finally, $\mathbf{x}^{adv}$ is similar to the original sample $\mathbf{x}$.

In adversarial examples generation, the goal of adversary is generating samples that look as similar to the original as possible while being classified by the target model as other designate class. To achieve this goal, the adversarial example is usually generated with a bound to limit the added noise. Inspired by this, we release these bounds to make the generated samples present the classification basis learned by the target model.

We design our model inversion method Gradient Sign Model Inversion (GSMI) based on i-FGSM [13] as presented in Algorithm 1. Specifically, we propose the following modifications:

1) Increasing the number of iterations. In the original method, the attack iterations number N should be $min(\epsilon + 4, 1.25\epsilon)$ as their aim is reach the edge of the ϵ max-norm ball. Instead, we try find the center of target class space. Therefore, the GSMI is designed as a dual circulation, and N is set much larger than i-FGSM. In each small iterations, GSMI performs a gradient sign optimization to generate and log the added noise. And after *batch* times small iterations, GSMI performs a denoise operation.

2) Superposing noises during iterations. In i-FGSM, the noise added on original sample is disposable, the added noise is regenerated in each iteration, while we consider that noise generated in every iteration contains information about features learned by target model. However, the noise in every iteration is so small that it almost invisible by human vision. On the basis of this observation, we gather the added noise in every iteration and superpose these noises in one samples to visualize features learned by the target model.

3) Removing subtle noises. The results of i-FGSM show that the added noises are uniformly distributed over adversarial examples, and only in this way can the added noise be imperceptible. However, in this paper, the aim is generating the main body of target class. Therefore, in order to clarify generated samples, we adopt a ReLU function to remove these subtle noises,

$$\text{ReLUMed}(a) = \begin{cases} 0, a \leq median \\ a, a > median, \end{cases} \tag{2}$$

where pixels that are less than the median of all pixels values are consider as subtle noises and are set as 0 in each iteration.

With these processes, GSMI can extract features of the target class from the target model and concentrate these features into single sample.

Algorithm 2. Two-pass Components Selection.

Input: $\mathbf{x}^{mi}; F(\mathbf{x})$
Output: $\mathbf{x}_{rp}^{mi}$
 1: $\mathbf{x}^{map} = \text{TwoPass}\left(\mathbf{x}^{mi}\right)$
 2: $\mathbf{x}_{rp}^{mi} = \text{SBS}\left(\mathbf{x}^{map}, \mathbf{x}^{mi}, F(\mathbf{x})\right)$
 3: **return** $\mathbf{x}_{rp}^{mi}$;

2.4 Two-Pass Components Selection

We find that samples generated by GSMI contains components that hinder the decision making of human vision. Therefore, in order to enhance the quality of inversion samples, we further design a two-pass components selection algorithm to form a more plausible inversion sample of the target class.

The two-pass components selection algorithm is shown in Algorithm 2. We adopt two-pass method to generate the 8-adjacent regions map $\mathbf{x}^{map}$ [10] of the inversion sample. And then we consider these adjacent regions as features that affect the decision making of the target model. The idea of feature selection could be used to select these adjacent regions. In this paper, Sequential Backward Selection (SBS) [2] is adopted. In this way, the most representative inversion sample $\mathbf{x}_{rp}^{mi}$, that meet the decision criterion of human vision and deep learning model at the same time, can be generated.

3 Performance Evaluation

3.1 Experimental Setup

We evaluate proposed GSMI over MNIST dataset [14] and Fashion-MNIST dataset [21]. There are 10 classes in these two datasets and every sample is in a $(28, 28, 1)$ shape. These two datasets contain two different object styles. In MNIST dataset, All classes are digits. Their shapes determine the class to which they belong. Classes in Fashion-MNIST datasets are more similar, and the objects have distinct boundaries and are filled inside, which can help us to comprehensively evaluate the proposed method.

All experiments are conducted on a Intel i7-7700 CPU with a single NVIDIA GeForce GTX 1080 GPU in this paper. For each target class, we random choose one sample from auxiliary dataset as the start sample. The target model is a popular CNN model adopted from [1]. All convolutions are in (3×3) kernel size applied with stride $(1, 1)$ and activation ReLU. The architecture consists of $Conv2D(32) - Conv2D(32) - MaxPooling2D() - Conv2D(64) - Conv2D(64) - MaxPooling2D() - Dense(200) - Dense(200) - Dense(10)$.

Parameter Setting: there are three tunable hyperparameters in GSMI, α, *batch* and N. All these parameters are chosen heuristically. We set $\alpha = 0.01$, *batch* = 1000 and $N = 10$. In our experiment, we find that satisfactory samples can be generated with less iteration times. Therefore, these parameters are not fixed and can be modified according to the specific situation.

3.2   Results

Target Class

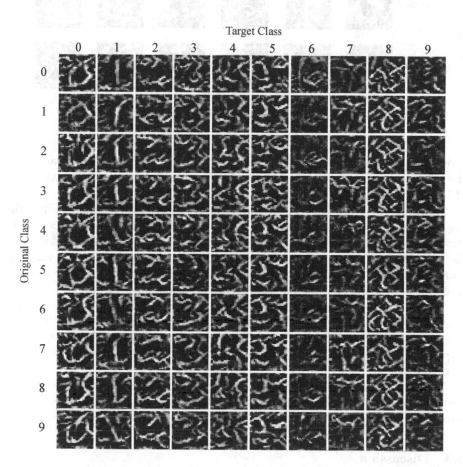

Fig. 2. Results of GSMI. Samples in each row are different target class generated with the start sample from the same original class. Samples in each column belong to the same target class generated by different start samples. All these samples are before components selection.

Samples generated by GSMI are showed in Fig. 2. In general, GSMI successfully generate the major features of target classes. And we observe that inversion samples of same target class are similar regardless of which class the original samples belong to. For example, inversion samples of the digit "0" all have a similar main component only with different noises. This demonstrates that GSMI does extract the classification criteria learned by the target model.

Then we perform two-pass components selection algorithm on these inversion samples. The results are shown in Fig. 3. After removing components that have negative impacts on the model's predictions, we observe that most classes of the

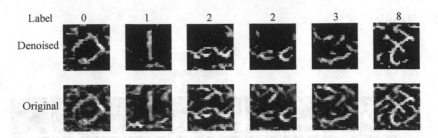

Fig. 3. Inversion samples after components selection.

generated samples can be identified visually by humans. This demonstrates that the decision criteria of the target model for most classes are consistent with that of human vision.

However, there are three obvious defects in the inversion samples. First, the inversion samples still contains some noises after denoised. These noises, unlike those in the adversarial examples, are obvious but do not flip the model's predictions. A closer look at these noises reveals that they are consistent with the features of the class to which the sample belongs. For example, in the samples of digit "8", the noises are all similar to part of the digit "8".

The second defect is that some classes of inversion samples have lost some components. For example, in the reconstructed digit "2", almost all samples lack the line in the middle of the digit "2", which leads the digit "2" separated into upper and lower parts. This phenomenon is similar to the experimental results in paper [3].

Third, the inversion ability of GSMI on different target class is fluctuating. Among inversion samples, digit "0", "1" and "8" are the most plausible. But it's hard to recognize digit "4" and "5" by human vision.

3.3   Discussion

After demonstrating the performance of our GSMI, we now seek to understand the reason behind.

Noises in Inversion Samples. We observe that some noises in the inversion samples are not removed by the two-pass components selection algorithm. This implies that the model considers these noises as positive features of the target class. The cause of these noises may be the structure of CNN. The convolution layer contains multiple filters, and different filters extract different features in model training. There are different representations of some semantic features of the target class, and the model learns all of these different representations as different features. As a result, when these features are all superimposed into single sample by gradients, it may lead to multiple similar features of the target digit class presenting at the same time.

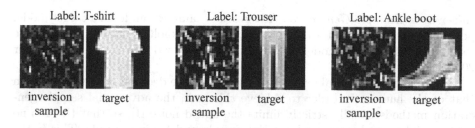

Fig. 4. Fashion-MNIST dataset target generated by GSMI. The left samples are generated by GSMI, and the right samples are samples in the training dataset.

Missing Components in Inversion Samples. Some components of the objects are missing in some inversion samples. Furthermore, as shown in Fig. 4, GSMI can only invert a very limited information on Fashion-MNIST dataset, and cannot reconstruct a complete sample. For example, the inversion sample of Trouser contains only the gap between the two trouser legs, while the heel and shoe face are features of Ankle boot revealed from the target model.

This is caused by the lack of human-like semantic knowledge of the model [3]. The decision criterion of target class is highly related to other classes in the training dataset. The features learned by the model are likely to be only part of the semantic knowledge, while ignoring the global information [18,19,24]. As a result, the generated samples lost some components of the target digit. And it is especially obvious for complex datasets. Inversion samples can contain only the features that are considered as the criteria of the target class by the target model, as shown in Fig. 4. We think the model considers the gap between the two trouser legs and the heel as decision making features, while ignoring other components of these objects.

Performance Fluctuation of GSMI. We also observe the performance fluctuation of GSMI among different classes. We relate this to the differences in the distribution of samples in these classes. For example, the common point of the digits "0" and "1" is that they have a relatively fixed writing pattern. Hence, the model can learned a fix feature about these two digits. The digits "4" and "5" have a more complex structure, so there is a greater difference in the samples in the training dataset. As a result, the feature learned by the model are also scattered leading a struggling performance of GSMI in these classes. These facts show the limitations of reconstruct satisfactory training data without the help of auxiliary dataset. Therefore, it may require more information to improve the performance of model inversion.

4 Related Work

The most related research field is adversarial examples generation and Deep learning interpretation.

Adversarial Example Generation. Adversarial examples can force a target model perform incorrectly [1,11,13,16]. For example, Eykholt *et al.* [6] attacked the road sign classification model to force it recognize road sign incorrectly in their 2018 study.

The goal of adversarial examples is deviating the decision of the model from that of the human. In order to achieve this goal, the adversarial sample generation methods usually strictly limits the added noise [1], so that there is no obvious difference between adversarial sample and benign sample. This is the biggest difference between adversarial examples and model inversion examples. The goal of model inversion is to generate as realistic samples as possible.

In this scenario, the ability of adversary could be classified as black-box setting or white-box setting. The key difference between black-box and white-box is the access of information flow inside the target model. Specifically, in a white-box setting, the adversary uses the gradient of the target model to optimize the generated sample [1,11,13]. While in a black-box setting, the adversary can only have oracle access of target model. Therefore, he need other tools to optimize the objective function, such as zeroth order optimization methods [5,12]. In this paper, our inversion method using gradients to generate samples.

Deep Learning Interpretation. Many researches have visualized the prediction process of the model to explain them [17,24]. Their experimental results reveal that models tend to make decisions only based on a part of objects, rather than the whole objects. Other researches attempt to explain the reason of the adversarial examples' existences [9,11]. They believe that the current deep learning model does not learn the real semantic features, and there are many vulnerabilities in the deep learning model due to the high-dimensional spaces of training data. In this paper, we also investigate the knowledges learned by target model.

5   Summary and Future Work

Existing model inversion works focus on how to invert a sample that looks as similar to the training data as possible. However such attacks are too restrictive and require a lot of auxiliary information to achieve. Our work, on the contrary, tries to reconstruct the most representative sample of target class. We solves this by designing an optimization-based method GSMI, which needs almost no auxiliary information. In order to extract features learned by the target model, we free some bounds of i-FGSM by increasing the number of iterations, superposing noises and removing subtle noises. And then we select the most representative components to form inversion samples. Experiments results show that GSMI can work in a relative simple scenario. We conduct a detailed analysis of our experiments results. We believe that the fundamental reason is that the model has not learned the true semantic characteristics.

The performance of GSMI shows some limitations. In the future, we will improve its performance on complex scenario. We believe that the most promising solution is introducing the auxiliary knowledges of the target model into the inversion process. We will address them in our future work.

References

1. Carlini, N., Wagner, D.A.: Towards evaluating the robustness of neural networks. In: 2017 IEEE Symposium on Security and Privacy, SP 2017, San Jose, CA, USA, 22–26 May 2017, pp. 39–57. IEEE Computer Society (2017)
2. Cotter, S.F., Kreutz-Delgado, K., Rao, B.D.: Backward sequential elimination for sparse vector subset selection. Signal Process. **81**(9), 1849–1864 (2001)
3. Dong, Y., Pang, T., Su, H., Zhu, J.: Evading defenses to transferable adversarial examples by translation-invariant attacks. In: IEEE Conference on Computer Vision and Pattern Recognition, CVPR 2019, Long Beach, CA, USA, 16–20 June 2019, pp. 4312–4321. Computer Vision Foundation/IEEE (2019)
4. Du, M., Liu, N., Song, Q., Hu, X.: Towards explanation of DNN-based prediction with guided feature inversion. In: Proceedings of the 24th ACM SIGKDD International Conference on Knowledge Discovery and Data Mining, KDD 2018, London, UK, 19–23 August 2018, pp. 1358–1367. ACM (2018)
5. Du, Y., Fang, M., Yi, J., Cheng, J., Tao, D.: Towards query efficient black-box attacks: an input-free perspective. In: Proceedings of the 11th ACM Workshop on Artificial Intelligence and Security, CCS 2018, Toronto, ON, Canada, 19 October 2018, pp. 13–24. ACM (2018)
6. Eykholt, K., et al.: Robust physical-world attacks on deep learning visual classification. In: 2018 IEEE Conference on Computer Vision and Pattern Recognition, CVPR 2018, Salt Lake City, UT, USA, 18–22 June 2018, pp. 1625–1634. IEEE Computer Society (2018)
7. Fredrikson, M., Jha, S., Ristenpart, T.: Model inversion attacks that exploit confidence information and basic countermeasures. In: Proceedings of the 22nd ACM SIGSAC Conference on Computer and Communications Security, Denver, CO, USA, 12–16 October 2015, pp. 1322–1333. ACM (2015)
8. Fredrikson, M., Lantz, E., Jha, S., Lin, S.M., Page, D., Ristenpart, T.: Privacy in pharmacogenetics: an end-to-end case study of personalized warfarin dosing. In: Proceedings of the 23rd USENIX Security Symposium, San Diego, CA, USA, 20–22 August 2014, pp. 17–32. USENIX Association (2014)
9. Gilmer, J., Ford, N., Carlini, N., Cubuk, E.D.: Adversarial examples are a natural consequence of test error in noise. In: Proceedings of the 36th International Conference on Machine Learning, ICML 2019, Long Beach, California, USA, 9–15 June 2019. Proceedings of Machine Learning Research, vol. 97, pp. 2280–2289. PMLR (2019)
10. González, R.C., Woods, R.E.: Digital Image Processing, 3rd edn. Pearson Education, London (2008)
11. Goodfellow, I.J., Shlens, J., Szegedy, C.: Explaining and harnessing adversarial examples. In: 3rd International Conference on Learning Representations, ICLR 2015, San Diego, CA, USA, 7–9 May 2015, Conference Track Proceedings (2015)
12. Ilyas, A., Engstrom, L., Athalye, A., Lin, J.: Black-box adversarial attacks with limited queries and information. In: Proceedings of the 35th International Conference on Machine Learning, ICML 2018, Stockholmsmässan, Stockholm, Sweden, 10–15 July 2018. Proceedings of Machine Learning Research, vol. 80, pp. 2142–2151. PMLR (2018)
13. Kurakin, A., Goodfellow, I.J., Bengio, S.: Adversarial examples in the physical world. In: 5th International Conference on Learning Representations, ICLR 2017, Toulon, France, 24–26 April 2017, Workshop Track Proceedings. OpenReview.net (2017)

14. Lecun, Y., Bottou, L., Bengio, Y., Haffner, P.: Gradient-based learning applied to document recognition. Proc. IEEE **86**(11), 2278–2324 (1998). https://doi.org/10.1109/5.726791
15. Mahendran, A., Vedaldi, A.: Understanding deep image representations by inverting them. In: IEEE Conference on Computer Vision and Pattern Recognition, CVPR 2015, Boston, MA, USA, 7–12 June 2015, pp. 5188–5196. IEEE Computer Society (2015)
16. Papernot, N., McDaniel, P.D., Goodfellow, I.J., Jha, S., Celik, Z.B., Swami, A.: Practical black-box attacks against machine learning. In: Proceedings of the 2017 ACM on Asia Conference on Computer and Communications Security, AsiaCCS 2017, Abu Dhabi, United Arab Emirates, 2–6 April 2017, pp. 506–519. ACM (2017)
17. Selvaraju, R.R., Cogswell, M., Das, A., Vedantam, R., Parikh, D., Batra, D.: Grad-cam: visual explanations from deep networks via gradient-based localization. In: IEEE International Conference on Computer Vision, ICCV 2017, Venice, Italy, 22–29 October 2017, pp. 618–626. IEEE Computer Society (2017)
18. Selvaraju, R.R., Cogswell, M., Das, A., Vedantam, R., Parikh, D., Batra, D.: Grad-cam: visual explanations from deep networks via gradient-based localization. Int. J. Comput. Vis. **128**(2), 336–359 (2020)
19. Szegedy, C., et al.: Intriguing properties of neural networks. In: 2nd International Conference on Learning Representations, ICLR 2014, Banff, AB, Canada, 14–16 April 2014, Conference Track Proceedings (2014)
20. Wu, X., Fredrikson, M., Jha, S., Naughton, J.F.: A methodology for formalizing model-inversion attacks. In: IEEE 29th Computer Security Foundations Symposium, CSF 2016, Lisbon, Portugal, 27 June–1 July 2016, pp. 355–370. IEEE Computer Society (2016)
21. Xiao, H., Rasul, K., Vollgraf, R.: Fashion-mnist: a novel image dataset for benchmarking machine learning algorithms (2017)
22. Yang, Z., Zhang, J., Chang, E., Liang, Z.: Neural network inversion in adversarial setting via background knowledge alignment. In: Proceedings of the 2019 ACM SIGSAC Conference on Computer and Communications Security, CCS 2019, London, UK, 11–15 November 2019, pp. 225–240. ACM (2019)
23. Zhang, Y., Jia, R., Pei, H., Wang, W., Li, B., Song, D.: The secret revealer: Generative model-inversion attacks against deep neural networks. In: 2020 IEEE/CVF Conference on Computer Vision and Pattern Recognition, CVPR 2020, Seattle, WA, USA, 13–19 June 2020, pp. 250–258. IEEE (2020)
24. Zhou, B., Khosla, A., Lapedriza, À., Oliva, A., Torralba, A.: Learning deep features for discriminative localization. In: 2016 IEEE Conference on Computer Vision and Pattern Recognition, CVPR 2016, Las Vegas, NV, USA, 27–30 June 2016, pp. 2921–2929. IEEE Computer Society (2016)

Multicollinearity Correction and Combined Feature Effect in Shapley Values

Indranil Basu[1] and Subhadip Maji[2](✉)

[1] Optum Global Solutions, Hyderabad, India
indranil.indratechie@gmail.com
[2] Optum Global Solutions, Bangalore, India
subhadipmaji.jumech@gmail.com

Abstract. Model interpretability is one of the most intriguing problems in most machine learning models, particularly for those that are mathematically sophisticated. Computing Shapley Values are one of the best approaches so far to find the importance of each feature in a model, at the instance (data point) level. In other words, Shapley values represent the importance of a feature for a particular instance or observation, especially for classification or regression problems. One of the well known limitations of Shapley values is that the estimation of Shapley values with the presence of multicollinearity among the features are not accurate as well as reliable. To address this problem, we present a unified framework to calculate accurate Shapley values with correlated features. To be more specific, we do an adjustment (matrix formulation) of the features while calculating independent Shapley values for the instances to make the features independent with each other. Our implementation of this method proves that our method is computationally efficient also, compared to the existing Shapley method.

Keywords: Model interpretation · Multicollinearity · Feature extraction · Shapley values

1 Introduction

The ability to correctly interpret a prediction model's output is extremely important. It engenders appropriate user trust, provides insight into how a model may be improved, and supports understanding of the process being modeled. Shapley values [1], a method from coalitional game theory, is a very common choice for model interpretation [6,8,9] for calculation of feature importance. Although Shapley values [5] serve this purpose to a great extent, it has the biggest limitation that in case the features (predictors) are correlated, then Shapley calculations do not consider that. If we assume that two features are correlated and we are interested to know the independent feature importance of the features for a predictive model. Shapley technique would definitely determine the feature importance, but we show that the feature importance of a feature gets

© Springer Nature Switzerland AG 2022
G. Long et al. (Eds.): AI 2021, LNAI 13151, pp. 79–90, 2022.
https://doi.org/10.1007/978-3-030-97546-3_7

reduced compared to its independent or original feature importance. To be more specific, if two features are perfectly correlated (linear correlation ≈ 1), then Shapley method calculates their feature importance as half of their original or independent importance. We try to address this issue introducing an Adjustment Factor so that the effect of correlated variables are removed while calculating the independent feature importance of features. We extend this concept and experimentation for a combination of features where one or more of the other features are correlated with this group. For example, for a given data point, if two features X_1 and X_2 with no correlation are having Shapley values s_1 and s_2, then with significant correlation, these Shapley values will definitely change. The simple reason is that, when we calculate the importance of X_1 (According to Shapley method), we remove X_1 (in a modified Shapley technique, we replace X_1 with randomized values) to find the effect on the other features including X_2. Now, if X_1 and X_2 are having a high correlation, then replacement or removal of X_1 will increase the importance of X_2. Therefore feature importance computation for X_1 would be incorrect. For this reason, we adjust X_2 with a linear modification (say X_2') so that X_2' would not have any correlation with X_1, thereby nullifying the correlation effect of X_1 while calculating the importance of X_1 by removing/replacing X_1. This method would be extended while calculating the combined importance of X_1, X_2 (or any other combination of any size).

In general, if there are m features, we present a linear adjustment based on a combination of p features on the rest of the features (i.e. rest $m - p$ features) in a matrix formulation, described in Sect. 2.2. It is to be noted that while removing or replacing a feature X_1, we shall adjust all the other features that have a non-zero correlation with X_1. Thereafter the importance of X_1 will be calculated correctly as the correlation effects of X_1 would be taken care of. Moreover, we present detailed mathematical proofs regarding how we have reached the matrix formulations while adjusting for the effect of combination $X_1, X_2, \ldots, X_p$ upon the rest of the features. It is quite intuitive that the matrix formulation representing the linear adjustment is pretty much similar to the rest of the features. A very practical assumption for this mathematical derivation is that all the correlations are linear in nature.

Some methods on handling correlation effects are mentioned in chapter 5 of the book, A Guide for Making Black Box Models Explainable by Molnar (2019) [5]. First one is to permute correlated features together and get one mutual Shapley value for them. Second one is to determine conditional sampling: features are sampled conditional on the features that are already in the data. In both the approaches, we cannot find feature importance values independent of each other. Kjersti et al. [7] also addressed the issue of calculating Shapley/SHAP [4] values with the presence of dependent variables/predictors in the model. They encountered the issue by introducing a method for aggregating individual Shapley values, such that the prediction can be explained by groups of dependent variables. Although SHAP [4] values suffers from the same multicollinearity issue, our paper is focused only on the calculation of variable importance using the original Shapley values [5].

The paper is organized as follows: Section 2 describes a novel method of calculation of Shapley Values for individual as well as combination of features with the presence of multicollinearity among the features. Section 3 contains the results of extensive experiments on multiple publicly available datasets.

2 Proposed Method

We assume, we have a dataset $(\mathbf{X}, y)$, where $\mathbf{X} \in \mathbf{R}^{n \times m}$ and $y \in \mathbf{R}^n$. Here n is number of data points and m is number of features. We also assume that two features X_j and X_k (where $j \neq k$) are linearly correlated. As, described above, presence of linear correlation does not provide expected Shapley Value outputs with the traditional Shapley Value calculation methods. Therefore, we propose a novel approach to correct the Shapley Value output of features. X_j is the j-th feature where $j = 1, 2, 3, ..., m$.

The main idea of multi-collinearity correction while calculating shapely values of feature X_j for data point i, is that while we calculate the shapley value for feature X_j, we remove the correlation effect of X_j from all of the other features X_k, where $k = 1, 2, 3, ..., m$, and $j \neq k$. We have tested this algorithm for shapely value calculation using multiple machine learning models on multiple datasets.

Unlike shapley values, as the Multi-collinearity Corrected (MCC) Shapley values are not additive, we have to calculate MCC Shapley value for specific feature combinations to get the Shapley values for that specific feature combination. We break this section into two parts, where in the first part, we discuss the calculation of MCC Shapley values for individual features, and in the following part, we discuss the same for the combination of two or more features.

2.1 MCC Shapley Values for Individual Features

Assume for a dataset the correlation of X_j with other features $X_1, X_2, ...,$ $X_{j-1}, X_{j+1}, ..., X_m$ are $c_{j1}, c_{j2}, ..., c_{j(j-1)}, c_{j(j+1)}, ..., c_{jm}$ respectively. If we are interested in calculating the shapely value of X_j, we add one Adjustment Factor (AF_k) with X_k, where $k = 1, 2, ..., j - 1, j + 1, ..., m$, while we randomize (or remove) X_j in the Shapley value calculation process so that,

$$cor(X_j, X_k + AF_k) = 0 \tag{1}$$

Putting $AF_k = aX_j$ in the above equation and solving we get,

$$AF_k = -\frac{cov(X_j, X_k)}{var(X_j)} X_j \tag{2}$$

The reason for taking AF_k as only a function of X_j, because we want to remove the correlation effect of X_k only from X_j.

2.2   MCC Shapley Values for Combination of Two or More Features

Assume for a dataset the correlation of X_i and X_j with other features X_k, where $k = 1, 2, ..., m$ and $k \notin \{i, j\}$, are c_{ik} and c_{jk} respectively. If we are interested in calculating the shapely value of the combination of X_i and X_j, we add one Adjustment Factor (AF_k) with X_k, while we randomize (or remove) X_i and X_j all together in the Shapley value calculation process so that,

$$cor(X_i, X_k + AF_k) = 0$$
$$cor(X_j, X_k + AF_k) = 0 \tag{3}$$

Putting $AF_k = aX_i + bX_j$ in the above equation and solving we get,

$$a = \frac{cov(X_i, X_k)var(X_j) - cov(X_j, X_k)cov(X_i, X_j)}{var(X_i)var(X_j) - (cov(X_i, X_j))^2}$$
$$b = \frac{cov(X_j, X_k)var(X_i) - cov(X_i, X_k)cov(X_i, X_j)}{var(X_i)var(X_j) - (cov(X_i, X_j))^2} \tag{4}$$

As we want to nullify the effect of X_k from both X_i and X_j, we have to add this adjustment factor AF_k while removing (or replacing) both $(X_i$ and $X_j)$ in order to compute the independent feature importance of the combination, X_i, and X_j. In a similar manner, the combination of two features can easily be expanded to the combination of $p+1$ $(0 \le p \le m-1)$ features. In this case Eq. 3 becomes,

$$cor(X_i, X_k + AF_k) = 0$$
$$cor(X_{i+1}, X_k + AF_k) = 0$$
$$cor(X_{i+2}, X_k + AF_k) = 0 \tag{5}$$
$$\vdots$$
$$cor(X_{i+p}, X_k + AF_k) = 0$$

Putting,

$$AF_k = a_i X_i + a_{i+1} X_{i+1} + a_{i+2} X_{i+2} + ... + a_{i+p} X_{i+p} \tag{6}$$

in the Eq. 5 and writing the p equations in matrix form we get,

$$
\begin{bmatrix}
var(X_i) & cov(X_i, X_{i+1}) & cov(X_i, X_{i+2}) & \cdots & cov(X_i, X_{i+p}) \\
cov(X_{i+1}, X_i) & var(X_{i+1}) & cov(X_{i+1}, X_{i+2}) & \cdots & cov(X_{i+1}, X_{i+p}) \\
cov(X_{i+2}, X_i) & cov(X_{i+2}, X_{i+1}) & var(X_{i+2}) & \cdots & cov(X_{i+2}, X_{i+p}) \\
\cdots & \cdots & \cdots & \cdots & \cdots \\
\cdots & \cdots & \cdots & \cdots & \cdots \\
cov(X_{i+j}, X_i) & cov(X_{i+j}, X_{i+1}) & cov(X_{i+j}, X_{i+2}) & \cdots & cov(X_{i+j}, X_{i+p}) \\
\cdots & \cdots & \cdots & \cdots & \cdots \\
\cdots & \cdots & \cdots & \cdots & \cdots \\
cov(X_{i+p}, X_i) & cov(X_{i+p}, X_{i+1}) & cov(X_{i+p}, X_{i+2}) & \cdots & var(X_{i+p})
\end{bmatrix}
\begin{bmatrix}
X_i \\ X_{i+1} \\ X_{i+2} \\ \cdots \\ \cdots \\ X_{i+j} \\ \cdots \\ \cdots \\ X_{i+p}
\end{bmatrix}
=
\begin{bmatrix}
cov(X_i, X_k) \\ cov(X_{i+1}, X_k) \\ cov(X_{i+2}, X_k) \\ \cdots \\ \cdots \\ cov(X_{i+j}, X_k) \\ \cdots \\ \cdots \\ cov(X_{i+p}, X_k)
\end{bmatrix}
\tag{7}
$$

By Cramer's rule,

$$a_{i+j} = \frac{\det A_{j+1}}{\det A} \tag{8}$$

where, $A_{j+1} =$

$$
\begin{bmatrix}
var(X_i) & \cdots & cov(X_i, X_{i+j-1}) & cov(X_i, X_k) & \cdots & cov(X_i, X_{i+p}) \\
cov(X_{i+1}, X_i) & \cdots & cov(X_{i+1}, X_{i+j-1}) & cov(X_{i+1}, X_k) & \cdots & cov(X_{i+1}, X_{i+p}) \\
cov(X_{i+2}, X_i) & \cdots & cov(X_{i+2}, X_{i+j-1}) & cov(X_{i+2}, X_k) & \cdots & cov(X_{i+2}, X_{i+p}) \\
\cdots & \cdots & \cdots & \cdots & \cdots & \cdots \\
\cdots & \cdots & \cdots & \cdots & \cdots & \cdots \\
cov(X_{i+j}, X_i) & \cdots & cov(X_{i+j}, X_{i+j-1}) & cov(X_{i+j}, X_k) & \cdots & cov(X_{i+j}, X_{i+p}) \\
\cdots & \cdots & \cdots & \cdots & \cdots & \cdots \\
\cdots & \cdots & \cdots & \cdots & \cdots & \cdots \\
cov(X_{i+p}, X_i) & \cdots & cov(X_{i+p}, X_{i+j-1}) & cov(X_{i+p}, X_k) & \cdots & var(X_{i+p})
\end{bmatrix}
$$

and, $A =$

$$
\begin{bmatrix}
var(X_i) & cov(X_i, X_{i+1}) & cov(X_i, X_{i+2}) & \cdots & cov(X_i, X_{i+p}) \\
cov(X_{i+1}, X_i) & var(X_{i+1}) & cov(X_{i+1}, X_{i+2}) & \cdots & cov(X_{i+1}, X_{i+p}) \\
cov(X_{i+2}, X_i) & cov(X_{i+2}, X_{i+1}) & var(X_{i+2}) & \cdots & cov(X_{i+2}, X_{i+p}) \\
\cdots & \cdots & \cdots & \cdots & \cdots \\
\cdots & \cdots & \cdots & \cdots & \cdots \\
cov(X_{i+j}, X_i) & cov(X_{i+j}, X_{i+1}) & cov(X_{i+j}, X_{i+2}) & \cdots & cov(X_{i+j}, X_{i+p}) \\
\cdots & \cdots & \cdots & \cdots & \cdots \\
\cdots & \cdots & \cdots & \cdots & \cdots \\
cov(X_{i+p}, X_i) & cov(X_{i+p}, X_{i+1}) & cov(X_{i+p}, X_{i+2}) & \cdots & var(X_{i+p})
\end{bmatrix}
$$

Once we calculate all the a_{i+j}, where $j = 0, 1, 2, ..., p$, those values can be put back in Eq. 6 to get the adjustment factor for feature X_j while calculating MCC Shapley values for $p + 1$ features.

2.3 Algorithm of MCC Shapley Value Calculation

For MCC Shapley value calculation we used our adjustment factor in approximate Shapley value calculation with only Monte-Carlo sampling proposed by Štrumbelj & Kononenko (2013) [2] as original Shapley value calculation is very time-consuming and practically infeasible for a large number of features. Apart from Monte-Carlo, our adjustment factor can be applied to any techniques to calculate Shapley Values. Algorithm 1 contains estimation of MCC Shapley values. This algorithm is exactly the same as the algorithm of approximate Shapley value calculation written in chapter 5 of the book by Molnar (2019) [5] except line 9 and 10, where we add our novel adjustment factors to each of the features in coalitions excluding $x_j^{(i)}$ as X_j is the feature of interest for the calculation of MCC Shapley values for $x^{(i)}$. It is to be noted that, as correlation is only restricted to numerical variables, the multi-collinearity correction is only applicable to the same. Therefore, in steps 9 and 10, X_j and the features with which we add AF must be numerical.

3 Results

We experimented on those datasets where at least two features have moderate to high correlation values between them for the MCC Shapley value calculation for

Algorithm 1. Estimation of MCC Shapley Values

1: **Output:** MCC Shapley value for the value of the j-th feature, $x_j^{(i)}$.

2: **Required:** Number of iterations M, instance of interest $x^{(i)}$, feature index j, data matrix $\mathbf{X}$, and machine learning model f

3: **for** $m \leftarrow 1, M$ **do**

4:    Draw random instance $x^{(r)}$ from the data matrix X

5:    Choose a random permutation o of the feature values

6:    Order instance $x^{(i)}$: $x_{[o]}^{(i)} \leftarrow (x_{(1)}^{(i)}, ..., x_{(j)}^{(i)}, ..., x_{(m)}^{(i)})$

7:    Order instance $x^{(r)}$: $x_{[o]}^{(r)} \leftarrow (x_{(1)}^{(r)}, ..., x_{(j)}^{(r)}, ..., x_{(m)}^{(r)})$

8:    Construct two new instances adding adjustment factors to the feature values in coalitions i.e features belongs to instance $x^{(i)}$

9:    • With feature j: $x_{+j} \leftarrow (x_{(1)}^{(i)} + AF_{(1)}, ..., x_{(j-1)}^{(i)} + AF_{(j-1)}, x_{(j)}^{(i)}, x_{(j+1)}^{(r)}, ..., x_{(m)}^{(r)})$

10:    • Without feature j: $x_{-j} \leftarrow (x_{(1)}^{(i)} + AF_{(1)}, ..., x_{(j-1)}^{(i)} + AF_{(j-1)}, x_{(j)}^{(r)}, x_{(j+1)}^{(r)}, ..., x_{(m)}^{(r)})$

11:    Compute marginal contribution: $\phi_j^m \leftarrow \hat{f}(x_{+j}) - \hat{f}(x_{-j})$

12: Compute MCC Shapley value as the average: $\phi_j(x) \leftarrow \frac{1}{M} \sum_{m=1}^{M} \phi_j^m$

---

individual features and combination of two features. The result is very intuitive to understand with the presence of strong multi-collinearity (correlation value ≈ 1) and the results are perfectly in line with what we can expect from a theoretical perspective. For example, If X_1 and X_2 are very highly correlated, then Shapely values (without the adjustment we proposed in this paper) should be almost half of their individual independent feature importances. That's exactly what we have obtained from our experiment. With the adjustment we did, the independent importance values are getting doubled compared to the original Shapley values for both the features. Thus, we can say, our method correctly determines the Independent Feature Importance Values for all features irrespective of the Correlations existing with all the other features. This statement will become clearer once we show and explain the results in this section. We mainly focused to calculate MCC Shapley values with individual and combination of two features. The other combinations can be easily calculated based on the matrix form shown in the Sect. 2.2.

3.1 Dataset - House Prices

This dataset from Kaggle [3] presents a regression problem where given the attributes of a house, the prediction of the price of the house to be predicted. We did the pre-processing which includes handling missing values and creation of dummy variables for the categorical variables to make the dataset prepared for model fitting with the final 331 predictors. The correlation plot considering only the numerical features are shown in the Fig. 1.

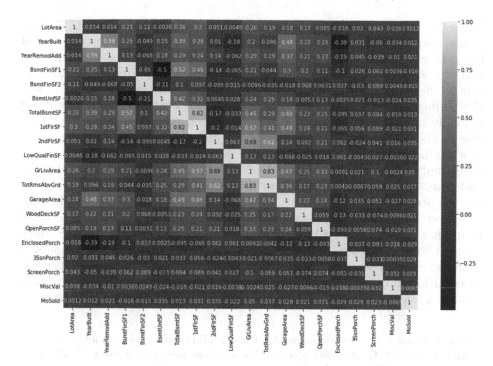

Fig. 1. Correlation plot of House Prices [3] dataset.

Results of MCC Shapley Values for Individual Features. As the dataset, with features having strong multi-collinearity (correlation ≈ 1) is hard to find, we break our results into two scenarios, in the first scenario we add one (or two) artificially created variables with correlation ≈ 1 with any one (or two) of the features to understand the effect of multi-collinearity correction. Once we understand this, in the second scenario we observe the effect of the same with two real features with high correlation. We refrain from fitting linear models as the estimate of the coefficients become unstable due to the presence of multi-collinearity. From now on we term Shapley values with and without multi-collinearity as MCC-SV and NMCC-SV respectively.

In scenario 1, we picked one numerical feature `MiscVal` as our feature of interest because `MiscVal` has a very low correlation (≈ 0) with the other numerical features. We shall explain the reason behind doing so after we show the result. We created one highly correlated variable (correlation ≈ 1) with `MiscVal` artificially and name it `MiscVal_corr`. This makes `MiscVal` and `MiscVal_corr` the equally important feature to the output feature `SalePrice`. Table 1 shows the Shapley values with and without multi-collinearity correction for a randomly picked data point for `MiscVal` feature. In the table, **Without Presence of Artificially Created Variable** and **With Presence of Artificially Created Variable** means the situations where models are trained with the original 331 predictors and 331+1 artificially created feature (`MiscVal_corr`) respectively. From

Table 1 it is seen that with the presence of `MiscVal_corr` the NMCC Shapley values have sliced to half of the NMCC Shapley values without the presence of `MiscVal_corr` for all the models. This is very intuitive because as both `MiscVal` and `MiscVal_corr` are the equally important features to the output feature and this is the reason we created the artificial feature with correlation ≈ 1. But this reduction of the Shapley values with the presence of correlated variable is highly unwanted as stated earlier, because if `MiscVal` is an important variable to the output then the importance of it reduces down due to the presence of a similar important variable. It is also seen from the table that due to our novel multi-collinearity correction the MCC Shapley values of both `MiscVal` and `MiscVal_corr` increased back to the earlier NMCC Shapley values without the presence of `MiscVal_corr`. Under **Without Presence of Artificially Created Variable** column header along with **NMCC-SV of MiscVal** there is another column **MCC-SV of MiscVal** which calculates the MCC Shapley value of `Miscval` without presence of `MiscVal_corr`. We see that the values of both the columns are almost the same because the correlation of the other features with `MiscVal` is almost 0. This is the reason we chose this type of feature to have a sanity check of the performance of our multi-collinearity correction.

Table 1. Shapley values with and without multi-collinearity correction for a randomly picked data point for `MiscVal` feature. These values are created for a Monte-Carlo simulation with 10000 iterations.

Model	Without presence of artificially created variable		With presence of artificially created variable			
	NMCC-SV of MiscVal	MCC-SV of MiscVal	NMCC-SV of MiscVal	NMCC-SV of MiscVal_corr	MCC-SV of MiscVal	MCC-SV of MiscVal_corr
Decision tree	-261.4 ± 5.3	-260.2 ± 5.3	-129.3 ± 5.1	-128.3 ± 4.8	-263.1 ± 5.4	-262.9 ± 4.7
Random forest	-210.9 ± 1.4	-209.8 ± 1.4	-107.8 ± 1.1	-102.4 ± 1.2	-213.5 ± 0.9	-210.2 ± 1.3
Gradient boosting	-273.2 ± 1.1	-272.1 ± 1.1	-138.1 ± 1.4	-137.3 ± 1.2	-276.3 ± 1.8	-275.2 ± 1.0
Extreme gradient boosting	-265.9 ± 1.2	-263.8 ± 1.2	-135.2 ± 1.2	-131.7 ± 1.3	-265.0 ± 0.9	-264.2 ± 1.1
Support vector regression	-112.6 ± 0.4	-113.9 ± 0.4	-53.4 ± 0.3	-55.6 ± 0.1	-111.0 ± 0.1	-115.7 ± 0.2

In Scenario 2, We picked feature `1stFlrSF` and we see that `1stFlrSF` has high correlation (0.82) with `TotalBsmtSF`. To understand the effect of the multi-collinearity correction, in one setting we remove highly correlated features with `1stFlrSF` and build the model to calculate the Shapley values. Then in the second setting we use all the 331 features of the dataset to build the model and compare the MCC and NMCC Shapley values. Table 2 shows Shapley values with and without Multi-collinearity Correction for a randomly picked data point for `1stFlrSF` Feature. In the first setting **Without Presence of TotalBsmtSF** we have compared between MCC and NMCC Shapley values. As we build the model removing the highly correlated features with `1stFlrSF` we see that there is not much difference between NMCC and MCC Shapley values, but there is one interesting pattern which is that the MCC Shapley values are always slightly greater than the NMCC Shapley values. Though we removed the highly correlated features while building the model there were some features (e.g. `BsmtFinSF1`, `GarageArea`, `BsmtUnfSF`, `WoodDeckSF`, etc.) having moderate/low correlation with `1stFlrSF`, thus they reduced the NMCC Shapley values to a little extent. But with the presence of the highly correlated feature `TotalBsmtSF`, we see that the NMCC Shapley values have reduced down a lot, but the reduction is not roughly 50% like scenario 1, because here the correlation between `TotalBsmtSF` and `1stFlrSF` is not 1. With the use of our multi-collinearity correction the MCC Shapley values increased and roughly matches with the MCC Shapley values calculated from the model built on **Without Presence of TotalBsmtSF** in the dataset. The match is not very close because we are comparing the Shapley values of two different models and in one of the model `TotalBsmtSF` feature is not available.

Table 2. Shapley values with and without multi-collinearity correction for a randomly picked data point for `1stFlrSF` feature. These values are created for a Monte-Carlo simulation with 10000 iterations.

Model	Without presence of TotalBsmtSF		With presence of all of 331 features	
	NMCC-SV of 1stFlrSF	MCC-SV of 1stFlrSF	NMCC-SV of 1stFlrSF	MCC-SV of 1stFlrSF
Decision tree	2721.1 ± 5.1	2832.2 ± 5.0	1932.8 ± 5.6	2841.7 ± 5.2
Random forest	2502.3 ± 1.1	2715.4 ± 1.6	1781.3 ± 1.2	2700.4 ± 1.5
Gradient boosting	2657.7 ± 0.9	2919.1 ± 1.1	1699.1 ± 0.9	2933.4 ± 1.0
Extreme gradient boosting	3356.2 ± 1.4	3612.6 ± 0.9	2134.5 ± 1.5	3597.8 ± 1.1
Support vector regression	1745.8 ± 0.5	1983.7 ± 0.4	1244.9 ± 0.7	1998.4 ± 0.8

Results of MCC Shapley Values for Combination of Two Features. For a combination of two features, for scenario 1, We picked two features `MiscVal` and `3SsnPorch` that are almost uncorrelated with the other features. We created two highly correlated artificial features and name those `MiscVal_corr` and `3SsnPorch_corr`. Table 3 shows the result of the effect of multi-collinearity correction for the combination of two features which is analogous of Table 1 for individual features. From the result, it is seen that the NMCC Shapley values sliced to half due to the presence of the perfectly correlated features, but the multi-collinearity correction factor helped those features to get back to the actual values i.e. MCC Shapley values. Also, as `MiscVal` and `3SsnPorch` are almost uncorrelated with other features, NMCC and MCC Shapley values are almost the same without the presence of artificially created variable across all the models.

For scenario 2, we just compared the Shapley values with and without multi-collinearity correction for a combination of two features i.e. `1stFlrSF` and `2ndFlrSF`. Table 4 shows the result from which it is seen that as `1stFlrSF` and

Table 3. Shapley values with and without multi-collinearity correction for a randomly picked data point for the combination of `MiscVal` and `3SsnPorch` features. These values are created for a Monte-Carlo simulation with 10000 iterations.

Model	Without presence of artificially created variable		With presence of artificially created variable	
	NMCC-SV of the combination of MiscVal and 3SsnPorch	MCC-SV of the combination of MiscVal and 3SsnPorch	NMCC-SV of the combination of MiscVal and 3SsnPorch	MCC-SV of the combination of MiscVal and 3SsnPorch
Decision tree	417.2 ± 4.9	415.6 ± 5.0	211.4 ± 5.1	419.6 ± 4.8
Random forest	323.6 ± 1.9	327.8 ± 1.8	163.8 ± 1.9	330.9 ± 2.0
Gradient boosting	374.3 ± 1.4	376.1 ± 1.7	185.0 ± 1.3	370.7 ± 1.5
Extreme gradient boosting	289.5 ± 1.1	292.5 ± 1.4	149.7 ± 1.7	289.1 ± 1.6
Support vector regression	134.5 ± 0.7	145.3 ± 0.8	67.3 ± 0.9	149.2 ± 0.6

`2ndFlrSF` have moderate to strong correlation with other features, due to correction the MCC Shapley values increase with respect to their NMCC Shapley values counter-parts.

Table 4. Shapley values with and without multi-collinearity correction for a randomly picked data point for the combination of `1stFlrSF` and `2ndFlrSF` features. These values are created for a Monte-Carlo simulation with 10000 iterations.

Model	NMCC-SV of combination of 1stFlrSF and 2ndFlrSF	MCC-SV of combination of 1stFlrSF and 2ndFlrSF
Decision tree	3321.5 ± 3.2	4610.3 ± 3.3
Random forest	2895.4 ± 1.4	3767.6 ± 1.6
Gradient boosting	3006.7 ± 1.3	4209.2 ± 1.3
Extreme gradient boosting	3209.1 ± 0.9	4479.9 ± 1.0
Support vector regression	3877.0 ± 0.7	5003.6 ± 0.9

We performed one additional experiment where we compared the execution time between the MCC and NMCC Shapley value calculation. This experiment is done in a machine with 2.6 GHz Intel Core i7 and 8 GB available RAM. Table 5 shows the comparison in execution time of the Shapley Values with and without multi-collinearity correction. This result is produced with a `Random Forest` model which is trained on default parameters and the number of iterations of Monte-Carlo simulation is 10,000. From the table, it is seen that introduction of the correlation adjustment factor has almost no effect on the execution time for calculating Shapley values.

Table 5. Comparison of shapley value calculation with and without correlation adjustment. This result is produced with `Random Forest` model and 10000 Monte-Carlo iterations.

Feature size	NMCC-SV(sec)	MCC-SV(sec)
≈ 10	0.3 ± 0.01	0.3 ± 0.03
≈ 100	0.9 ± 0.02	1.0 ± 0.03
≈ 1000	4.7 ± 0.01	4.9 ± 0.01
≈ 10000	17.3 ± 0.01	18.1 ± 0.01

4 Conclusion

This paper shows that the novel multi-collinearity correction factor with Shapley values helps to interpret individual features (and combination of features) more accurately with the presence of correlation within features in a data. Our algorithm is tested with multiple models on multiple datasets to prove it's efficacy. For better intuitive understanding we analyzed the effect of our novel multi-collinearity correction factor with the presence of both artificially created features and real features and concluded its effectiveness from different perspectives. Results are in perfect agreement with the mathematical formulation of our method. Finally, we analyzed the effect of the multi-collinearity correction factor in execution time and concluded that with the presence of multi-collinearity correction factor, the execution time is almost the same compared to the calculation of Shapley values without multi-collinearity correction factor. This definitely provides better insights on individual feature importances and a group of features, independent of their correlation effects with other features.

The obvious next step of our method is to enhance the umbrella of features to categorical ones - where classical correlation is not easily defined, rather we have to deal with ANOVA and Chi-Square values. Association values are three-fold - Numerical to Numerical (covered in this paper), Numerical to Categorical, and Categorical to Categorical. The last two will be the possible enhancement. This enhancement would build a complete framework of individual feature importance and individual group of feature importance irrespective of the feature categories. Another application is Dimensionality Reduction in terms of real features, unlike Linear (e.g. PCA) and Non-Linear combinations (Kernel PCA). It is quite obvious that the reduction of feature set to a lower value keeping the original features enhances the explainability of the predictive model, unlike the case of using an orthogonal combination of features. Besides, till now we have only considered the linear correlation between two numerical features. Consideration of non-linear correlation can be a topic of future works.

Author contributions. Both authors have contributed equally to the work.

References

1. Shapley, L.S.: A value for n-person games. Contrib. Theory Games **2**(28), 307–317 (1953)
2. Štrumbelj, E., Kononenko, I.: Explaining prediction models and individual predictions with feature contributions. Knowl. Inf. Syst. **41**(3), 647–665 (2013). https://doi.org/10.1007/s10115-013-0679-x
3. Kaggle.House Prices: Advanced Regression Techniques (2016). https://www.kaggle.com/c/house-prices-advanced-regression-techniques/
4. Lundberg, S.M., Lee, S.-I.: A unified approach to interpreting model predictions. In: Advances in Neural Information Processing Systems (2017)
5. Molnar, C.: Model-Agnostic Methods. A Guide for Making Black Box Models Explainable. Interpretable Machine Learning, Oxford (2019). Chap. 5. https://christophm.github.io/interpretable-ml-book/
6. Sundararajan, M., Najmi, A.: The many Shapley values for model explanation. arXiv preprint arXiv:1908.08474 (2019)
7. Aas, K., Jullum, M., Løland, A.: Explaining individual predictions when features are dependent: more accurate approximations to Shapley values (2019)
8. Pfannschmidt, K., Hüllermeier, E., Held, S., Neiger, R.: Evaluating tests in medical diagnosis: combining machine learning with game-theoretical concepts. In: Carvalho, J.P., Lesot, M.-J., Kaymak, U., Vieira, S., Bouchon-Meunier, B., Yager, R.R. (eds.) IPMU 2016. CCIS, vol. 610, pp. 450–461. Springer, Cham (2016). https://doi.org/10.1007/978-3-319-40596-4_38
9. Cohen, S., Dror, G., Ruppin, E.: Feature selection via coalitional game theory. Neural Comput. **19**, 1939–61 (2007). https://doi.org/10.1162/neco.2007.19.7.1939

Does a Face Mask Protect My Privacy?: Deep Learning to Predict Protected Attributes from Masked Face Images

Sachith Seneviratne[1][(✉)], Nuran Kasthuriarachchi[2], Sanka Rasnayaka[4],
Danula Hettiachchi[3], and Ridwan Shariffdeen[4]

[1] University of Melbourne, Melbourne, Australia
`sachith.seneviratne@unimelb.edu.au`
[2] University of Moratuwa, Moratuwa, Sri Lanka
`nuran.11@cse.mrt.ac.lk`
[3] RMIT University, Melbourne, Australia
`danula.hettiachchi@rmit.edu.au`
[4] National University of Singapore, Singapore, Singapore
`{sanka,ridwan}@u.nus.edu`

Abstract. Contactless and efficient systems are implemented rapidly to advocate preventive methods in the fight against the COVID-19 pandemic. Despite the positive benefits of such systems, there is potential for exploitation by invading user privacy. In this work, we analyse the privacy invasiveness of face biometric systems by predicting privacy-sensitive soft-biometrics using masked face images. We train and apply a CNN based on the ResNet-50 architecture with 20,003 synthetic masked images and measure the privacy invasiveness. Despite the popular belief of the privacy benefits of wearing a mask among people, we show that there is no significant difference to privacy invasiveness when a mask is worn. In our experiments we were able to accurately predict sex (94.7%), race (83.1%) and age (MAE 6.21 and RMSE 8.33) from masked face images. Our proposed approach can serve as a baseline utility to evaluate the privacy-invasiveness of artificial intelligence systems that make use of privacy-sensitive information. We open-source all contributions for reproducibility and broader use by the research community.

Keywords: COVID-19 · Masked faces · Privacy · Computer vision

1 Introduction

Since the outbreak of SARS-CoV-2 (COVID-19), the use of face masks has become ubiquitous around the world and has been identified as an important public health response to fight against the ongoing pandemic. The mass shift to wearing masks during the COVID-19 pandemic has radically changed the way in which many of our mundane activities are carried out. This situation demands the enablement of contactless and efficient operations, especially in retail services. Contactless technologies like face and iris based detection systems are

© Springer Nature Switzerland AG 2022
G. Long et al. (Eds.): AI 2021, LNAI 13151, pp. 91–102, 2022.
https://doi.org/10.1007/978-3-030-97546-3_8

pushed to reach newer heights, in contrast applications that rely on fingerprint recognition modalities suffer a significant loss due to the emerging requirements as an after-effect of the COVID-19 pandemic [7]. In particular, face recognition is praised as one of the efficient and contactless means of verifying identity and prior research has studied the impact and techniques to improve face-recognition systems to further advance contactless operations [6,16]. Using computer vision to enhance contactless and efficient operations has shown promise in various applications (i.e. public compliance monitoring [19]). In this work, we investigate the impact of using computer vision, specifically in face authentication systems for contactless identification and the possible implications on privacy. Despite the scalable automation it provides, face-recognition technology needs to adhere to the privacy regulations such as the General Data Protection Regulation (GDPR) and improve the perception of users to increase trust and acceptance.

Considering the advancements in surveillance and monitoring technologies in response to COVID-19, the norms of acceptable information flow may shift. For instance, users' perspectives on the use of location information (which is privacy-sensitive information), has drastically changed in times of crisis [15]. However, such temporary measures during a crisis may not prevail as a permanent and long-term acceptance because it would unnecessarily reduce a persons privacy. Although a wider acceptance of surveillance systems can be seen in the current situation, we argue that a popular misconception of, "wearing face masks will increase privacy protection" exists among most people. Therefore, we first investigate the perception of users with respect to face biometric solutions and their understanding of privacy protection. We conduct an online survey to extract the opinions of users on their privacy with face masks and we learn that generally users have higher confidence of privacy protection when using a face mask. In our study, we find that perceived privacy of wearing a mask is higher with a statistical significance ($P=0.00964 < 0.05$).

Systems that use face biometrics could potentially reveal privacy-sensitive information such as soft-biometrics, which includes but are not limited to age, sex and race. Many of the artificial intelligence systems use such privacy-sensitive information but are restricted for the intended purposes. We evaluate the possible violations of privacy-protection in such systems that use face biometrics, with the use of masked face images and quantify the privacy invasiveness of such implementations. We implement several techniques to predict privacy-sensitive soft-biometrics such as age, sex and race, and we were able to achieve an accuracy of 94.7% and 83.1% in correctly classifying the sex and race, respectively. We were also able to accurately predict the age with an RMSE score of 8.33 and MAE score of 6.21. We then analysed the privacy invasiveness in our implementation for images with mask and without mask, to understand the privacy preservation when using a face mask. We show that there is no significant difference in privacy protection by quantifying the privacy invasiveness using the Privacy Vulnerability Index (PVI) [25] for both settings, which recorded **only a 2.9% difference** that implies no significance in wearing a mask.

In this work, we make three contributions: **(1)** Quantitative analysis on privacy invasion on masked face images. To the best of our knowledge, we are the first to study the predictability of age, sex and race using masked face images. (2) Study the perception of privacy protection on wearing a face mask. Our results indicate that people consider masked faces to be less privacy invasive. In support of reproducible research, we open-source our model weights and scripts for the benefit of the research community. These models will enable future study on masked face biometric systems related to privacy protection.

2 Related Work

2.1 Biometrics and Privacy

The use of biometrics have raised various privacy concerns due to the possibility of predicting protected attributes. Many studies have evaluated the predictability of soft-biometric attributes such as age, gender and race using common biometrics such as face [14], iris [28], fingerprint [3], voice [10] and gait [25]. In this work, we go beyond than prediction and provide means of quantifying the privacy invasiveness in systems that use soft-biometric.

2.2 Face Biometric and Masks

While computer vision research has examined face recognition methods robust to partial occlusions [18,30], with increased global mask use due to COVID-19, there is a renewed interest in masked face recognition. Recent work shows that current state of the art face recognition methods trained with full face images fail in accurately recognising masked faces [12]. Although researchers have created real-world masked face datasets [6,29], there is limited work on developing specific machine learning models trained with masked images. In addition, face masks have also introduced a family of computer vision challenges such as mask detection [21]. While some prior work has implications on masked biometric analysis using masks [2], they have not used masked facial images for analysis. In particular, while biometric analysis focused around the ocular region can provide useful insights into masked facial analysis, we argue that only actual analysis on masked facial imagery provides realistic insights into masked biometric analysis. This arises from the fact that, based on the masking process used, considerable portions of the ocular region may be occluded as well. Therefore, performing end-to-end evaluation of masked facial images provides a more realistic picture of the situation corresponding to real world usage.

2.3 User Perception

User perceptions towards biometric modalities tend evolve with time [24]. State of the art face recognition methods can achieve high levels of accuracy and are widely used for different applications, including authentication and surveillance. While users are generally more familiar and comfortable with face biometric solutions [5], users also tend to resist face recognition based solutions due to privacy concerns [20]. Furthermore, wearing masks can limit the face area exposed to face recognition systems. However, there is limited literature on how people perceive the difference between masked and non-masked face recognition. This understanding could be potentially influenced by other challenges humans face when wearing masks. For instance, research shows that people find it challenging to match familiar faces, match unfamiliar faces and recognise emotions when faces are occluded with objects such as masks and sunglasses [23].

3   Methodology

Our evaluation consists of three components. First, we conducted a survey to understand the perception of users on privacy protection while wearing a mask, from the increased surveillance systems due to COVID-19. Second, we generate a synthetic face mask dataset, predict protected attributes from masked face images and compare our results with prior work that use non-masked faces. Third, we show how unmasked face images invade privacy and analyse the impact of image attributes on our predictions.

3.1   User Perception Survey

The main objective of this survey was to study the perceptions of people towards the privacy invasiveness of masked faces in comparison to unmasked face images. We aim to answer the following questions: *"Do people feel that wearing a face mask will protect their privacy?"* and *"Which is considered more private among Age, Race and Sex"*. An online survey was designed to collect this information with *Yes/No questions* comparing the privacy invasiveness of masked and unmasked face images, *Three point Likert scale questions* evaluating perceived privacy invasiveness of masked images and unmasked images and a *Sorting Activity* to sort Age, Race and Sex based on importance. The survey is conducted anonymously on a voluntary basis in June 2021. The relative ordering of the sorting activity will be used to measure the Relative Importance Index (RII) value for each of the three attributes.

3.2   Dataset and Synthetic Mask Generation

There is no openly-available large-scale mask dataset with soft-biometric labels for age, gender and race. Therefore, we select UTK faces dataset, the most commonly cited face dataset in the literature and generate a masked dataset by digitally painting a mask on top of the face image. We follow the process outlined in [22] to generate synthetic masks on the face images. This process is depicted in Fig. 1. We open-source the scripts used for this process.

UTK faces dataset has 23,542 face images with labels for age, gender and race. Following the masking process [22] we create a data-set of 23,002 masked images. We show the distributions of the attributes in Fig. 2. We bin the ages as follows, baby: 0–3 years, child: 4–12 years, teenagers: 13–19 years, young: 20–30 years, adult: 31–45 years, middle aged: 46–60 years and senior: 61 years and above, in line with the analysis in [13].

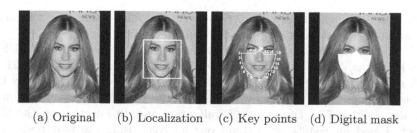

(a) Original   (b) Localization   (c) Key points   (d) Digital mask

Fig. 1. Synthetic mask creation pipeline (an example from UTK faces)

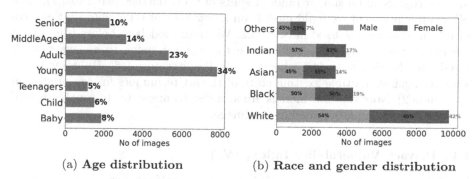

(a) **Age distribution**   (b) **Race and gender distribution**

Fig. 2. UTK faces dataset summary

3.3 Computer Vision Workflow

We use a computer vision based method with convolutional neural networks (CNN) to build models for 3 different tasks - age, sex and race prediction. Rather than building individual CNNs from scratch for each task, we build an initial facial representation within the neural network by using only the UTK facial dataset. We use a ResNet50 architecture and pre-train our representation for 3038 epochs in an unsupervised manner using the framework introduced in [17] and the projection head and augmentations from [8] using the parameters and settings described in [9]. Pre-training is carried out on a 4 GPU node with batch size set to 128. This pre-trained representation is then fine-tuned end-to-end for each specific task with a new fully connected layer incorporated past the final bottleneck layer of the pre-trained ResNet50 architecure. The size of this final output layer depends on the task. For regression the layer has a single node - as the output is a single continuous variable, while for classification we incorporate a number of nodes equal the number of classes in the problem (for instance, 2 for sex, 5 for race and 7 for age - corresponding to categorical labels). Training is carried out for 3500 epochs for each task with Stochastic Gradient Descent and learning rate 1e-3, and we isolate the single checkpoint with the best validation performance to evaluate on a holdout dataset. We evaluate the impact of additional image augmentations using RandAugment [11] with default ImageNet parameters. We open-source all contributions[1], including trained models on the different splits and dataset splits for full reproducibility.

We evaluate against an open-sourced masked-facial representation (MUFM) [27] released as part of the Masked Facial Recognition Competition 2021 [4], which claims to be a generic masked-face representation adaptable to any task on masked faces. We run this evaluation for the task of sex classification on a random split of 70% training 20% validation and 10% testing on the UTK dataset. Based on results, we extend our analysis using the best performing combination of representation and technique for the tasks of race classification and age regression on similar random splits of UTK dataset (see Table 1). As a follow up experiment we build models on a new split of UTK data that ensures a uniform split as discussed in Sect. 3.2. We train models as before (discarding previously trained models), but change the age regression to an age bracket based classification following other work in the literature [13]. By doing so we compare against multiple existing state of the art techniques for age prediction (see Table 2). Note that our models are at a disadvantage due to roughly half of the face being absent/occluded in the image.

3.4   Privacy Vulnerability Index(PVI)

The Privacy Vulnerability Index [25] is used to quantify the privacy invasiveness of a biometric modality. We use this measure to compare the privacy invasiveness of face images and masked face images. The PVI of a biometric depends on two factors, **(1) Predictability** (p_i): how well can protected attributes be predicted using the biometric modality, measured by classification accuracy. **(2) Importance** (s_i): how important is each personal attribute, measured using the RII calculated from the user perception study. The PVI value for masked and unmasked images is calculated as a weighted sum of these two values using the equation, $PVI = (\sum_i s_i * p_i)/\sum_i s_i$.

4   Evaluation Results

4.1   User Perception Study

The survey resulted in 60 complete responses. The users' responses to if the face image and masked face image could lead to privacy invasiveness is used to examine if there is a statistically significant difference in the perception towards the two modalities. We perform a the Mann-Whitney U test with a single-tail, to show that the perceived privacy of wearing a mask is higher with statistical significance ($P = 0.00964 < 0.05$). Figure 3 show the distribution of user responses.

Survey participants were asked if wearing a mask preserves privacy (compared to not wearing a mask). 50% of the participants said yes while 40% felt

---

[1] https://github.com/sachith500/MaskedFaceRepresentation.

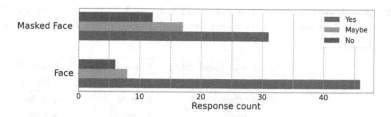

Fig. 3. User perception on privacy invasion with masked face images campared to face images.

both violated privacy equally and 10% said masked face images violates privacy more.

Relative Importance: The resulting relative ordering with the Relative Importance Index (RII) values within brackets is; 1) Age [0.3765] 2) Race [0.3353] 3) Gender [0.2882].

4.2 Prediction Accuracy

Table 1 presents the overall accuracy for models built for masked face images. Table 2 compares the results of masked and unmasked faces.

Table 1. Attribute prediction using masked face images. The first experiment (sex) was used to verify that our model performance was superior to existing masked representations.

Method	Sex	Race	Age	
	Accuracy	Accuracy	MAE	RMSE
Using representation [27] + transforms [11]	0.9374	–	–	–
Our method with transforms from [11]	**0.9401**	**0.8220**	6.2788	8.4836
Our method without complex transforms	0.9361	0.8134	**6.2168**	**8.3372**

4.3 Impact of Image Attributes

We examine whether the original user attributes (i.e., Sex, Race, Age category) influence our prediction outcome of masked faces. To this end, we select the best performing model from initial evaluation (Table 1) and evaluate sex, race and age prediction models using a new uniform test split with a balanced attribute composition. Figure 4 presents confusion matrices for each model outcome. We obtained an overall accuracy of 94.65% for sex, 83.12% for race and 67.94% for age category.

Table 2. Overall result comparison with SOTA for each protected-attribute. Models are retrained for the uniform split using **optimal parameters** from experiments in Table 1.

	Unmasked Face - SOTA	Masked Face (Random Split)	Masked Face (Uniform Split)
Sex	[13] **98.23%**	94.01%	**94.65%**
Race	[1] **91.23%**	82.20%	**83.12%**
Age (MAE) - Regression	[26] **5.44**	**6.21**	–
Age - Classification	[13] **70.1%**	–	**67.94%**

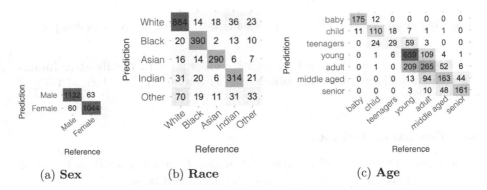

(a) **Sex**   (b) **Race**   (c) **Age**

Fig. 4. Confusion matrices for Sex, Race and Age prediction using masked images.

We conduct chi-square tests of independence to examine the relationship between different image attributes and the ability to accurately predict the them. When considering the image attribute sex there is no significant difference between prediction outcomes of sex ($\chi^2(1) = 0.006$, p = 0.936) and race ($\chi^2(1) = 0.578$, p = 0.447). However, a significant difference is noted for age category ($\chi^2(1) = 4.019$, p = 0.045 < 0.05). Furthermore, when considering race, there is a significant difference in prediction outcomes for sex ($\chi^2(4) = 12.53$, p = 0.014 < 0.05), race ($\chi^2(4) = 523.07$, p < 0.001) and age ($\chi^2(4) = 49.951$, p < 0.001) prediction. Similarly, for image attribute age, there is a significant difference for outcomes of sex ($\chi^2(6) = 164.57$, p < 0.001), race ($\chi^2(6) = 13.449$, 0.036 < 0.05) and age ($\chi^2(6) = 374.08$, p < 0.001) prediction. In summary, we note that image attributes race and age category having a significant impact on all the prediction outcomes while sex only influence age prediction. In addition, Fig. 5 provides the accuracy for each subgroup of images based on sex, race, age category of the person appearing in the image.

4.4   Privacy Invasiveness

We use the PVI equation with the SOTA for face images and our best results for masked face images to quantify the level of privacy invasiveness of both.

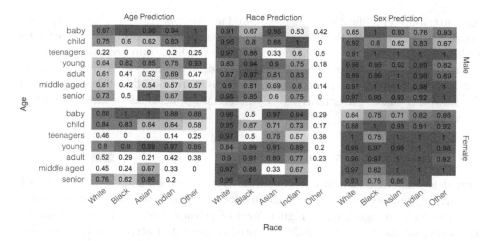

Fig. 5. Attribute prediction accuracy for each sub group

$PVI_f = 0.828, PVI_{mf} = 0.853$. The privacy invasiveness reduction by wearing a mask is only 2.9%. Which is very low compared to the 50% of people who thought that masked faces to be more private.

5 Discussion and Conclusion

5.1 Predicting Protected Attributes

Our study shows it is possible to predict sex, race, and age with a high degree of accuracy. When compared to the state of the art methods that predict these attributes for non-masked face images, we only note absolute accuracy differences of 3.58% for sex, 8.11% for race and 2.16% for age categories with nearly half the face (with key features like facial hair and lips for sex, wrinkles for age) occluded by a mask. Based on results in Table 2, we find that incorporating augmentations during training can improve sex and race prediction. During age prediction it slightly lowers accuracy. This likely stems from how predicting age is harder than race or sex (even for humans) and augmentations may create discrepancies between fine-grained features such as wrinkles which has less impact on predicting race or sex.

5.2 Biases from Image Attributes

While our models achieved high levels of overall accuracy for masked images, we observed that image attributes race and age can influence the prediction outcomes. For instance, age category prediction accuracy for teenagers (25.21%) and adults (49.71%) is low compared to the overall accuracy (67.94%). As shown in Fig. 5, prediction accuracies are consistently low across different sex and race categories as well. This is inline with results reported in prior work on biases in user attribute classification using regular face images [13]. Furthermore, when considering race prediction, we note that race prediction accuracy is lower for Other category (20.12%) with limited samples, when compared to the overall value (83.12%). We argue that biases from user attributes can greatly influence the model outcomes. Therefore, appropriate measure should be taken to account for sampling biases particularly for commercial applications of face-recognition technology.

5.3   Privacy Preservation

Our study highlights a mismatch between user perception and the reality regarding privacy preservation through face masks. Compared to regular face exposure, users perceive a significantly higher level of privacy when wearing face masks. However, we show that the ability to predict protected attributes from masked face images is not largely different from face images (Table 2) and the privacy invasiveness reduction by wearing a mask is only 2.9%. This inaccurate perceived privacy could lead to a false sense of safety for masked users, and therefore users could be targets for exploitation by malicious applications. In addition, distinct characteristics of face masks could contribute to more robust surveillance applications that users are not aware of. In the light of increased make usage, we argue that it is essential to raise user awareness and research privacy protection methods concerning face masks.

5.4   Limitations

We note a few limitations in our study. First, as there is no masked image dataset available with attributes such as sex, race and age, our evaluation is based on a synthetic mask generation process. Second, our user study is limited to 60 participants and we did not collect demographic information which may reveal interesting insights. Third, our source dataset has imbalances among classes which is reflected in our analysis.

5.5   Conclusion and Future Work

In this paper, we predict sex (94.7%), race (83.1%) and age (68.0%) on masked face images using a computer vision approach. Despite the popular belief that masks protect user privacy, we show that masks only reduce privacy invasiveness by 2.9% when compared to state of the art face recognition approaches. We further analyse the impact of image labels on the prediction ability and provide a baseline for future research by open-sourcing our models. Our research paves the way for future work that aim to study how to preserve user privacy when wearing masks while maintaining utility as a biometric modality. We open-source our contributions, including masking and inference scripts, trained models and data splits for reproducibility and broader use for both privacy and mask related research.

References

1. Ahmed, M.A., Choudhury, R.D., Kashyap, K.: Race estimation with deep networks. J. King Saud Univ.-Comput. Inf. Sci. (2020)
2. Alonso-Fernandez, F., Diaz, K.H., Ramis, S., Perales, F.J., Bigun, J.: Soft-biometrics estimation in the era of facial masks. In: 2020 International Conference of the Biometrics Special Interest Group (BIOSIG), pp. 1–6 (2020)
3. Badawi, A.M., Mahfouz, M., Tadross, R., Jantz, R.: Fingerprint-based gender classification. IPCV **6**, 41–46 (2006)
4. Boutros, F., et al.: MFR 2021: masked face recognition competition. In: 2021 IEEE International Joint Conference on Biometrics (IJCB), pp. 1–10. IEEE (2021)
5. Buckley, O., Nurse, J.R.: The language of biometrics: analysing public perceptions. J. Inf. Secur. Appl. **47**, 112–119 (2019). https://doi.org/10.1016/j.jisa.2019.05.001
6. Cabani, A., Hammoudi, K., Benhabiles, H., Melkemi, M.: MaskedFace-Net - a dataset of correctly/incorrectly masked face images in the context of COVID-19. Smart Health **19**(October 2020), 100144 (2021). https://doi.org/10.1016/j.smhl.2020.100144
7. Carlaw, S.: Impact on biometrics of COVID-19. Biom. Technol. Today **2020**(4), 8–9 (2020). https://doi.org/10.1016/S0969-4765(20)30050-3. https://www.sciencedirect.com/science/article/pii/S0969476520300503
8. Chen, T., Kornblith, S., Norouzi, M., Hinton, G.: A simple framework for contrastive learning of visual representations (2020)
9. Chen, X., Fan, H., Girshick, R., He, K.: Improved baselines with momentum contrastive learning (2020)
10. Childers, D.G., Wu, K.: Gender recognition from speech. PART II. fine analysis. J. Acoust. Soc. Am. **90**(4), 1841–1856 (1991)
11. Cubuk, E.D., Zoph, B., Shlens, J., Le, Q.V.: Randaugment: practical automated data augmentation with a reduced search space (2019)
12. Damer, N., Grebe, J.H., Chen, C., Boutros, F., Kirchbuchner, F., Kuijper, A.: The effect of wearing a mask on face recognition performance: an exploratory study. In: BIOSIG 2020 - Proceedings of the 19th International Conference of the Biometrics Special Interest Group (2020)
13. Das, A., Dantcheva, A., Bremond, F.: Mitigating bias in gender, age and ethnicity classification: a multi-task convolution neural network approach. In: Proceedings of the European Conference on Computer Vision (ECCV) Workshops (2018)
14. Guo, G., Fu, Y., Huang, T.S., Dyer, C.R.: Locally adjusted robust regression for human age estimation. In: 2008 IEEE Workshop on Applications of Computer Vision, pp. 1–6. IEEE (2008)
15. Haggag, O., Haggag, S., Grundy, J., Abdelrazek, M.: COVID-19 vs social media apps: does privacy really matter? In: 2021 IEEE/ACM 43rd International Conference on Software Engineering: Software Engineering in Society (ICSE-SEIS), pp. 48–57 (2021). https://doi.org/10.1109/ICSE-SEIS52602.2021.00014
16. Hariri, W.: Efficient Masked Face Recognition Method during the COVID-19 Pandemic (2021). https://doi.org/10.21203/rs.3.rs-39289/v1. http://arxiv.org/abs/2105.03026
17. He, K., Fan, H., Wu, Y., Xie, S., Girshick, R.: Momentum contrast for unsupervised visual representation learning (2020)
18. Kim, J., Choi, J., Yi, J., Turk, M.: Effective representation using ICA for face recognition robust to local distortion and partial occlusion. IEEE Trans. Pattern Anal. Mach. Intell. **27**(12), 1977–1981 (2005). https://doi.org/10.1109/TPAMI.2005.242

19. Ar, M.L.A., Nugraha, Y., Ernesto, A., Kanggrawan, J.I., Suherman, A.L.: A computer vision-based object detection and counting for COVID-19 protocol compliance: a case study of Jakarta. In: 2020 International Conference on ICT for Smart Society (ICISS), vol. CFP2013V-ART, pp. 1–5 (2020). https://doi.org/10.1109/ICISS50791.2020.9307594
20. Liu, Y.l., Yan, W., Hu, B.: Resistance to facial recognition payment in China: the influence of privacy-related factors. Telecommun. Policy **45**(5), 102155 (2021). https://doi.org/10.1016/j.telpol.2021.102155
21. Loey, M., Manogaran, G., Taha, M.H.N., Khalifa, N.E.M.: A hybrid deep transfer learning model with machine learning methods for face mask detection in the era of the COVID-19 pandemic. Meas.: J. Int. Meas. Confed. **167**(May 2020), 108288 (2021). https://doi.org/10.1016/j.measurement.2020.108288. https://doi.org/10.1016/j.measurement.2020.108288
22. Ngan, M.L., Grother, P.J., Hanaoka, K.K.: Ongoing face recognition vendor test (FRVT) part 6B: face recognition accuracy with face masks using post-COVID-19 algorithms (2020)
23. Noyes, E., Davis, J.P., Petrov, N., Gray, K.L., Ritchie, K.L.: The effect of face masks and sunglasses on identity and expression recognition with super-recognizers and typical observers. R. Soc. Open Sci. **8**(3), 201169 (2021). https://doi.org/10.1098/rsos.201169
24. Rasnayaka, S., Sim, T.: Who wants continuous authentication on mobile devices? In: 2018 IEEE 9th International Conference on Biometrics Theory, Applications and Systems (BTAS), pp. 1–9 (2018). https://doi.org/10.1109/BTAS.2018.8698599
25. Rasnayaka, S., Sim, T.: Your tattletale gait privacy invasiveness of IMU gait data. In: 2020 IEEE International Joint Conference on Biometrics (IJCB), pp. 1–10 (2020). https://doi.org/10.1109/IJCB48548.2020.9304922
26. Savchenko, A.V.: Efficient facial representations for age, gender and identity recognition in organizing photo albums using multi-output convnet. PeerJ Comput. Sci. **5**, e197 (2019)
27. Seneviratne, S., Kasthuriaarachchi, N., Rasnayaka, S.: Multi-dataset benchmarks for masked identification using contrastive representation learning (2021)
28. Thomas, V., Chawla, N.V., Bowyer, K.W., Flynn, P.J.: Learning to predict gender from iris images. In: 2007 First IEEE International Conference on Biometrics: Theory, Applications, and Systems, pp. 1–5. IEEE (2007)
29. Wang, Z., et al.: Masked Face Recognition Dataset and Application, pp. 1–3 (2020). http://arxiv.org/abs/2003.09093
30. Weng, R., Lu, J., Tan, Y.P.: Robust point set matching for partial face recognition. IEEE Trans. Image Process. **25**(3), 1163–1176 (2016). https://doi.org/10.1109/TIP.2016.2515987. http://ieeexplore.ieee.org/document/7377089/

Representation-Induced Algorithmic Bias

An Empirical Assessment of Behavioural Equivalence over 14 Reinforcement Learning Algorithms Across 4 Isomorphic Gameform Representations

Simon C. Stanton$^{(\boxtimes)}$ (iD), Julian Dermoudy (iD), and Robert Ollington (iD)

University of Tasmania, Hobart, Australia
simon.stanton@utas.edu.au

Abstract. In conceiving of autonomous agents able to employ adaptive cooperative behaviours we identify the need to effectively assess the equivalence of agent behavior under conditions of external change. Reinforcement learning algorithms rely on input from the environment as the sole means of informing and so reifying internal state. This paper investigates the assumption that isomorphic representations of environment will lead to equivalent behaviour. To test this *equivalence-of* assumption we analyse the variance between behavioural profiles in a set of agents using fourteen foundational reinforcement-learning algorithms across four isomorphic representations of the classical Prisoner's Dilemma gameform. A behavioural profile exists as the aggregated episode-mean distributions of the game outcomes CC, CD, DC, and DD generated from the symmetric selfplay repeated stage game across a two-axis sweep of input parameters: the principal learning rate, α, and the discount factor γ, which provides 100 observations of the frequency of the four game outcomes, per algorithm, per gameform representation. A measure of equivalence is indicated by a low variance displayed between any two behavioural profiles generated by any one single algorithm. Despite the representations being theoretically equivalent analysis reveals significant variance in the behavioural profiles of the tested algorithms at both aggregate and individual outcome scales. Given this result, we infer that the isomorphic representations tested in this study are not necessarily equivalent with respect to the induced reachable space made available to any particular algorithm, which in turn can lead to unexpected agent behaviour. Therefore, we conclude that structure-preserving operations applied to environmental reward signals may introduce a vector for algorithmic bias.

Keywords: Algorithmic Bias · Cooperative Behaviour · Game Theory

1 Introduction

An agent's relationship to its environment may change *in-situ* due to the environment being mutable, such that the process for derivation of reward signals being input *to* the agent may fluctuate. Also, an agent's internal state representation may transform as part of normal algorithmic operation. Similarly, an agent's method of utility extraction from

© Springer Nature Switzerland AG 2022
G. Long et al. (Eds.): AI 2021, LNAI 13151, pp. 103–116, 2022.
https://doi.org/10.1007/978-3-030-97546-3_9

reward signals may be altered by design, or computationally. Alternatively, an agent or algorithm may be entirely transplanted from one use case or application to another. A generalised perspective on these processes captures those occasions in everyday life that entail an implicit cast between representations, for example, whenever we (in the real-world) fix a price-point to a preference, or conversely, when compromising on features of a purchase with a known price. In other words, whenever we translate from scalar (or cardinal) values to ordinal preferences, and vice versa. This conversion impacts utility functions based in preference relations, which has relevance to how an agent may adapt to change in any external stimuli, that is, to any change in the reward signal representation as offered by the environment. This is relevant to how the agent's internal state representation of the signals received are abstracted.

The context of this research is an investigation of a computational approach to agent dynamics in a complex system by adopting the Robinson and Goforth (2005) topological classification of gameforms. Complexity is understood here as the interplay of agents and environment, as per Arthur's definition: "systems responding to the context they create" (2019, p. 186). The Robinson and Goforth (2005) classification is defined in-part topologically, with a core set of group operations that link games into regions, families, and neighbours of similar and/or aligned game-theoretic properties. Furthermore, it absorbs much previous work on game theory typologies and taxonomies such as those developed by Rapoport et al. (1976) and Brams (1994).

Ashlock and Kim (2008, p. 647) investigated the role of representation in an evolutionary computational context and found in one series of experiments that "all three representations sample the strategy space in a radically different manner", and, in another series of experiments concluded that "changing the payoff matrix, within the bounds permitted by the defining inequalities of prisoner's dilemma, yields different results" (Ashlock et al. 2010, p. 225). For various learning algorithms, Crandall et al. (2018b, pp. 8–10) note that "actual payoff values assigned to the ordinal preferences … can, and often do, impact the behaviors of some algorithms in repeated games", and in the discussion of an empirical investigation into a topological representation of Prisoner's Dilemma, Robinson and Goforth (2005, p. 156) assert that while a topology of ordinal games defines the relationships between those games, the topology "is insufficient for describing and predicting patterns of behaviour". Given that Robinson and Goforth also assert that "any ordinally equivalent game is also a Prisoner's Dilemma" (2005, p. 6) we are compelled to investigate how various reinforcement learning algorithms will perform over isomorphic representations of this canonical gameform.

The findings of this paper suggest that if differing representations induce a discrete and non-identical reachable space in respect to the values that internal agent state may take, then this will in turn circumscribe the possible behaviours that an agent can embody. Agents experiencing complex environments may display less predictable behaviour. We would regard such an outcome as a vector for *representation-induced algorithmic bias*.

Vectors for the introduction of bias—in algorithms specifically, and more generally in software—have been and are discussed widely. For example: bias via prejudice (Angwin et al. 2016; Patton et al. 2017); via both design and ethical formulations of systems (Hooker 2021; Bryson 2018; Winfield et al. 2019); through higher-order computation (Hooker et al. 2020; Waller and Waller 2021); from inferential methods (Tversky and Kahneman 1974); via our lack of understanding of animal intelligence (Herzing 2014); and, perhaps non-intuitively, via a lack of consideration to non-human machine intelligence and behaviour—a view put forward by Rahwan et al. (2019).

Therefore, we wish to investigate the role of representation in gameforms to understand the importance of representation *to* learning algorithms. To encourage parsimony and tractability we adopt the highly constrained environment of the repeated stage game Prisoner's Dilemma as the experimental domain. We regard any derivation of a scalar- or ordinal-valued gameform to an isomorphic (structure-preserving) representation as equivalent in form, subject to satisfying the four social dilemma inequalities discussed below. The response variable of interest is the *variance in the aggregated distribution of cooperative game outcomes between representations,* as observed in a symmetric selfplay paired-parameter study of the 14 foundational reinforcement learning algorithms listed in Table 1. The aggregated distribution of outcomes attained from a single gameform representation is the *behavioural profile* of the algorithm under study, for that gameform representation. We also identify the peak cooperative outcome from each behavioural profile to identify the optimal performance of each algorithm, per gameform representation.

Our initial hypothesis then, is that an algorithmic behavioural profile *will not vary between equivalent representations of the game* (environment).

Table 1. Algorithms implemented in this study and their parameters. Parameter superscript [1,2] denotes paired parameters, computed in range (0,1] with increment of 0.1 giving 100 observation sets for each algorithm, per gameform representation.

Algorithm	Parameters			
	Learning rate(s)	Discount	Trace	Action-selection
Actor/Critic	$\alpha^1, \beta = 0.9$	γ^2		*softargmax*
Actor/Critic with Eligibility Traces	$\alpha^1, \beta = 0.9$	γ^2	$\lambda = 0.9$	*softargmax*
Actor/Critic with Replacing Traces	$\alpha^1, \beta = 0.9$	γ^2	$\lambda = 0.9$	*softargmax*
Q-Learning	α^1	γ^2		$\varepsilon = 0.1$
Double Q-Learning	α^1	γ^2		$\varepsilon = 0.1$
Expected SARSA	α^1	γ^2		$\varepsilon = 0.1$
R Learning	α^1, β^2			$\varepsilon = 0.1$
SARSA	α^1	γ^2		$\varepsilon = 0.1$
SARSA Lambda	α^1	γ^2	$\lambda = 0.9$	$\varepsilon = 0.1$
SARSA Lambda, with Replacing Traces	α^1	γ^2	$\lambda = 0.9$	$\varepsilon = 0.1$

(continued)

Table 1. (*continued*)

Algorithm	Parameters			
	Learning rate(s)	Discount	Trace	Action-selection
Watkins (naïve) Q, Lambda	α^1	γ^2	$\lambda = 0.9$	$\varepsilon = 0.1$
Watkins (naïve) Q, Lambda, Replacing Traces	α^1	γ^2	$\lambda = 0.9$	$\varepsilon = 0.1$
Watkins Q, Lambda	α^1	γ^2	$\lambda = 0.9$	$\varepsilon = 0.1$
Watkins Q, Linear Function Approximation	α^1	γ^2		$\varepsilon = 0.1$

Background. This work lies at the intersection of computational learning, cooperation, and game theory. Research in computational learning ranges from learning in cellular automata (Billard 1996; Grim 1996), to applications of associative learning automata (Barto et al. 1983; Barto and Anandan 1985), and Reinforcement Learning (Sutton and Barto 1998, 2018). Furthermore, Tan's (1993) predator-prey agents using Multi-Agent Reinforcement Learning, and more recently, work by Leibo et al. (2017) on Deep Reinforcement Learning in sequential social dilemmas also inform this research. Extensive recent work by Crandall et al (2018a, 2018b) involving a variety of learning algorithms over the Robinson and Goforth topology (2005) in a tournament setting has provided invaluable insight to the problem domain in a contemporary setting.

Formal Equivalence of Representations via Inequality Rules. We examine four representations of the Prisoner's Dilemma in normal form as shown in Fig. 1. Robinson and Goforth (2005) refer to the ordinal Prisoner's Dilemma as game **g111**.

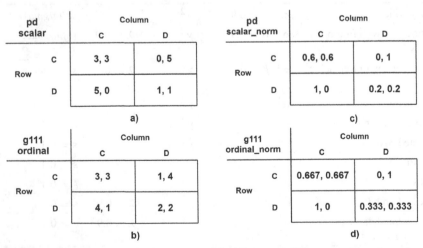

Fig. 1. Four gameform representations: a) canonical Prisoner's Dilemma with scalar values; b) scalar values are replaced by the payoff's ordinal preference; c) scalar values are normalised; d) ordinal preference values are normalised.

To assess formal equivalence, we restrict analysis in this paper to a formal definition of social dilemma inequalities as they provide a means to assert the preservation of the structure of the game representation under various transformations while retaining the meaning attributed to the dilemma. Each of the four inequalities relate to the four game outcomes as shown in Fig. 2.

Social dilemma inequalities can be found in slightly differing but effectively comparable forms in the literature (Ashlock and Kim 2008), however the form as given by Macy and Flache (2002, p. 7229) and Leibo et al. (2017) is presented here:

PD family		Column Player	
		C	D
Row Player	C	R (C,C) (R,R)	S (C,D) (S,T)
	D	T (D,C) (T,S)	P (D,D) (P, P)

Fig. 2. Semantic labels attributed to outcomes in the Prisoner's Dilemma. R (Reward), S (Sucker), T (Temptation), and P (Punishment) single-letter labels are outcomes from the perspective of the Row player. Labels in parentheses are Row, Column ordered pair where D signifies Defect and C signifies Cooperate.

$$R > P \tag{1}$$

$$R > S \tag{2}$$

$$2R > T + S \tag{3}$$

$$T > R, \, or \, P > S \tag{4}$$

We establish the formal equivalence of **pd:scalar** with the three alternative representations under examination in these experiments by observing that the social dilemma inequalities that define Prisoner's Dilemma do hold, as detailed in Table 2, illustrating that these four representations of Prisoner's Dilemma are structurally equivalent.

Table 2. Social dilemma inequalities

Inequality	Scalar	Scalar Normalised	Ordinal	Ordinal Normalised	Equivalent
(1) $R > P$	$3 > 1$	$0.6 > 0.2$	$3 > 2$	$0.667 > 0.333$	*True*
(2) $R > S$	$3 > 0$	$0.6 > 0$	$3 > 1$	$0.667 > 0$	*True*
(3) $2R > T + S$	$6 > 5 + 0$	$1.2 > 1 + 0$	$6 > 4 + 1$	$1.334 > 1 + 0$	*True*
(4) $T > R$	$5 > 3$	$1 > 0.6$	$4 > 3$	$1 > 0.667$	*True*
$P > S$	$1 > 0$	$0.2 > 0$	$2 > 1$	$0.333 > 0$	*True*

2 Methods

The experiments in this study are implemented as symmetric selfplay repeated stage games along two dimensions defined by two parameters that range from (0,1], in 0.1 increments; giving 100 observations for each algorithm. Each observation is the terminal episode-mean distribution of the four cooperative game outcomes CC, CD, DC, and DD over 500 episodes of 1000 timesteps each.

As shown in Fig. 1, this work examines four representations of the Prisoner's Dilemma gameform: *scalar*, *normalised scalar*, *ordinal*, and *normalised ordinal*. Given the infinite space of possible transformation functions, we do not examine any beyond these four common mappings.

The collection of experiments that is formed by running each algorithm in a single gameform representation gives a set of behavioural profiles. The combined grouping of two sets of behavioural profiles is referred to as *experiment groups 1* through *4* in the remainder of this work.

The 14 learning algorithms implemented are listed in Table 1. These algorithms are drawn from foundational work in Reinforcement Learning (Sutton and Barto 1998, 2018; Szepesvári 2010). Each algorithm is implemented with a representation of state by tabular data structures with the exception of Watkins Q Linear Function Approximation (Sutton and Barto 1998, 2018) where features are implemented as a mapping from the previous timestep outcome to a vector parameterised by a weight vector. For each algorithm, the parameters varied are the principal learning rate parameter α, and, in all cases except R-Learning, the discount factor parameter γ. Given that R-Learning does not use γ, we test on both learning rate parameters—α and β— instead. Fixed values for other parameters in each algorithm are as commonly found in the literature and are detailed in Table 1.

An algorithm's memory depth (history of outcomes from previous timesteps) is configured by a *memory_depth* option which is set to 1 in all algorithms (however, for Watkins Q Linear Function Approximation this is implemented as a feature vector of the outcomes from the last timestep only, plus an associated weight vector). Some algorithms incorporate *trace* data structures, which can be thought of as weights over states on longer timescales than just the immediate past. In other cases, the algorithm's data structures—such as Q-tables—are limited to handling state representation with memory of only the last timestep. This restriction on memory depth has implications for performance. However, the intent of this study is not to optimize all available parameters—nor to necessarily obtain the absolute optimal frequency of cooperation—but to examine the behaviour of the algorithms over a subset of their possible states. Implicitly, each algorithm is attempting to maximise its reward, and therefore, frequency of the CC outcome.

The data from each run is analysed in a two-stage process. The first stage takes the raw episodic data and calculates aggregated and summary statistics on episode, and timestep, actions and rewards; on game outcomes; and also extracts CPU-time and memory usage metadata. Subsequent analysis performs statistical tests on the outputs of the first pass. Each outcome distribution is tested for normality via the Shapiro-Wilk normality test, and then tested for equivalence via the Wilcoxon Signed Rank (Paired Treatment) test.

We adopt the following explicit constraints: firstly, that each episode is effectively independent, and in real-time, or *Online*; secondly, episodes have an *Infinite Horizon*, as such, $T = \infty$; thirdly, *No Signaling*, in that there is no communication between agents; and lastly, the *Environment Boundary* is everything external to the agent and the only information crossing this boundary is the reward signal.

3   Results

The results of analysis of all fourteen algorithms across each of the gameform representations are presented as a set of four experiment groups, as described in **Methods**. The aggregate distribution of each behavioural profile returns a non-normal distribution as determined by a Shapiro-Wilk Normality test; for example, the Watkins Q Linear Function Approximation algorithm's aggregated behavioural profile for the normalised ordinal representation returns a Shapiro-Wilk score of $W = 0.96486$, p-value = .00000003331).

In each experiment group we also highlight the episode-mean frequency of the peak cooperative outcome to demonstrate that where some algorithms appear to achieve near-parity in optimal behaviour between some representations, other algorithms exhibit substantial disparity.

Experiment Group One. In experiment group one the mapping between **pd:scalar** and **g111:ordinal** is assessed. Results of the Wilcoxon tests are shown in Table 3. Of the fourteen algorithms, eleven have a p-value $< .05$, which indicates that these algorithms do not exhibit equivalence of behaviour between the two representations in this experiment group. Only three algorithms—Actor/Critic, Actor/Critic with Eligibility Traces, and Watkins Q Linear Function Approximation—do not exhibit variance that can be regarded as significant.

Table 3. Exp Group One: Scalar (S) ~ Ordinal (O) Aggregated Distribution.

Algorithm	Peak % CC		Wilcoxon			
	S	O	V	p-value	CI L	CI U
Actor/Critic	32.1	30.2	35742	.07125	−0.0176	0.0006
Actor/Critic with Eligibility Traces	46.3	44.9	40978	.7047	−0.0036	0.0043
Actor/Critic with Replacing Traces	51.5	42.6	45337	.01835	0.0019	0.0200
Q-Learning	80.1	81.5	46086	.009683	0.0010	0.0061
Double Q-Learning	68.9	32.7	34431	.01428	−0.0059	−0.0006
Expected SARSA	75.7	77.3	27735	$9.08\,e-08$	−0.0185	−0.0070
R Learning	25.6	28.3	45520	.01916	0.0024	0.0177
SARSA	79.9	80.3	46848	.003545	0.0012	0.0053
SARSA Lambda	68.8	86.7	49435	$5.47\,e-05$	0.0171	0.0411
SARSA Lambda, with Replacing Traces	89.0	89	45731	.01495	0.0005	0.0057
Watkins (naïve) Q, Lambda	78.4	88.1	50043	$1.73\,e-05$	0.0270	0.0505
Watkins (naïve) Q, Lambda, Replacing Traces	76.4	89.1	49320	$6.76\,e-05$	0.0193	0.0487
Watkins Q, Lambda	87.2	87.8	49355	$6.35\,e-05$	0.0029	0.0089
Watkins Q, Linear Function Approximation	47.1	46.2	38262	.4775	−0.0013	0.0006

Experiment Group Two. Results of the Wilcoxon Signed Rank tests for experiment group two are shown in Table 4. It is apparent that of the algorithms in this experiment group, four have a p-value < .05. This indicates that these four algorithms do not exhibit equivalence between scalar and normalised scalar representations.

Table 4. Exp Group Two: Scalar (S) ~ Normalised Scalar (NS) Aggregated Distribution.

Algorithm	Peak % CC		Wilcoxon			
	S	NS	V	p-value	CI L	CI U
Actor/Critic	32.1	14.0	41239	.6227	−0.0049	0.0074
Actor/Critic with Eligibility Traces	46.3	33.7	46744	.004087	0.0026	0.0120
Actor/Critic with Replacing Traces	51.5	44.9	39599	.8286	−0.0110	0.0091
Q-Learning	80.1	80.2	40091	.9971	−0.0004	0.0004

(continued)

Table 4. (*continued*)

Algorithm	Peak % CC		Wilcoxon			
	S	NS	V	p-value	CI L	CI U
Double Q-Learning	68.9	68.5	39339	.7424	−0.0005	0.0004
Expected SARSA	75.7	75.7	37225	.214	−0.0006	0.0001
R Learning	25.6	23.7	39866	.9196	−0.0004	0.0004
SARSA	79.9	80.2	40180	.9037	−0.0003	0.0004
SARSA Lambda	68.8	86.6	49945	$2.09\,e - 05$	0.0123	0.0308
SARSA Lambda, with Replacing Traces	89.0	89.1	39177	.6901	−0.0005	0.0003
Watkins (naïve) Q, Lambda	78.4	87.2	49853	$2.50\,e - 05$	0.0273	0.0488
Watkins (naïve) Q, Lambda, Replacing Traces	76.4	89.2	48331	$2.55\,e - 05$	0.0120	0.0382
Watkins Q, Lambda	87.2	87.2	39692	.9281	−0.0005	0.0004
Watkins Q, Linear Function Approximation	47.1	24.9	39939	.9445	−0.0004	0.0004

Experiment Group Three. Results of the Wilcoxon Signed Rank tests for experiment group three are shown in Table 5. Twelve of the algorithms have p-value < .05 indicating that these algorithms do not exhibit equivalence of behaviour between the two representations in this experiment group.

Table 5. Exp Group Three: Scalar (S) ~ Normalised Ordinal (NO) Aggregated Distribution.

Algorithm	Peak % CC		Wilcoxon			
	S	NO	V	p-value	CI L	CI U
Actor/Critic	32.1	19.7	47086	.002535	0.0048	0.0195
Actor/Critic with Eligibility Traces	46.3	37.4	48229	.0003028	0.0048	0.0163
Actor/Critic with Replacing Traces	51.5	39.0	44761	.04398	0.0003	0.0253
Q-Learning	80.1	80.4	47276	.001377	0.0023	0.0075
Double Q-Learning	68.9	68.9	43233	.1758	−0.0006	0.0034
Expected SARSA	75.7	76.9	49542	$2.88\,e - 05$	0.0021	0.0049
R Learning	25.6	24.1	45745	.0147	0.0089	0.0242
SARSA	79.9	80.9	47300	.001862	0.0019	0.0068
SARSA Lambda	68.8	87.0	49205	$8.33\,e - 05$	0.0122	0.0311

(*continued*)

Table 5. (*continued*)

Algorithm	Peak % CC		Wilcoxon			
	S	NO	V	p-value	CI L	CI U
SARSA Lambda, with Replacing Traces	89.0	89.2	48050	.0005908	0.001	0.0033
Watkins (naïve) Q, Lambda	78.4	87.8	49985	$1.94\,e-05$	0.0269	0.0496
Watkins (naïve) Q, Lambda, Replacing Traces	76.4	89.1	49091	.000102	0.0154	0.0404
Watkins Q, Lambda	87.2	86.9	50420	$5.03\,e-06$	0.0020	0.0047
Watkins Q, Linear Function Approximation	47.1	46.8	38471	.4815	-0.0007	0.0004

Experiment Group Four. Results of the Wilcoxon Signed Rank tests for experiment group four are shown in Table 6. Of the fourteen algorithms, seven have p-values <.05 indicating that these algorithms do not exhibit equivalence of behaviour between the two representations in this experiment group. The set of algorithms that return significant p-values differs from those that exhibit this property in experiment groups one, two, and three, as detailed in Table 7.

Table 6. Exp Group Four: Ordinal (O) ~ Normalised Ordinal (NO) Aggregated Distribution.

Algorithm	Peak % CC		Wilcoxon			
	O	NO	V	p-value	CI L	CI U
Actor/Critic	30.2	19.7	48983	.0001235	0.0285	0.0712
Actor/Critic with Eligibility Traces	44.9	37.4	45950	.01147	0.0015	0.0147
Actor/Critic with Replacing Traces	42.6	39.0	43710	.1188	-0.0016	0.0141
Q-Learning	81.5	80.4	48454	.0003057	0.0022	0.0066
Double Q-Learning	32.7	68.9	51223	$1.53\,e-06$	0.0067	0.0140
Expected SARSA	77.3	76.9	52508	$8.21\,e-08$	0.0113	0.0248
R Learning	28.3	24.1	49944	$1.32\,e-05$	0.0011	0.0026
SARSA	80.3	80.9	49862	$2.45\,e-05$	0.0039	0.0090
SARSA Lambda	86.7	87.0	36226	.0941	-0.0036	0.0002
SARSA Lambda, with Replacing Traces	89	89.2	39935	.9431	-0.0019	0.0017
Watkins (naïve) Q, Lambda	88.1	87.8	42598	.2804	-0.0005	0.0017
Watkins (naïve) Q, Lambda, Replacing Traces	89.1	89.1	38132	.3951	-0.0020	0.0008

(*continued*)

Table 6. (*continued*)

Algorithm	Peak % CC		Wilcoxon			
	O	NO	V	p-value	CI L	CI U
Watkins Q, Lambda	87.8	86.9	35790	.07462	−0.0037	0.0001
Watkins Q, Linear Function Approximation	46.2	46.8	44057	.07136	−0.0001	0.0014

Table 7. Algorithms that do not exhibit significant variance between behavioural profiles.

Experiment Group	p-value > .05	Experiment Group	p-value > .05
One	Actor/Critic Actor/Critic with Replacing Traces **Watkins Q, Linear Function Approximation**	Three	Double Q-Learning **Watkins Q, Linear Function Approximation**
Two	Actor/Critic Actor/Critic with Replacing Traces Q-Learning Double Q-Learning Expected SARSA R Learning SARSA SARSA Lambda, with Replacing Traces Watkins Q, Lambda **Watkins Q, Linear Function Approximation**	Four	Actor/Critic with Replacing Traces SARSA Lambda SARSA Lambda, with Replacing Traces Watkins (naïve) Q, Lambda Watkins (naïve) Q, Lambda, Replacing Traces Watkins Q, Lambda **Watkins Q, Linear Function Approximation**

4   Discussion

The results of these experiments indicate that the behaviour of the algorithms studied can vary substantially as a product of the input representation of an otherwise equivalent gameform. Given the common use of semantic interpretations of repeated game outcomes the validity of the expectation that conclusions drawn over varying representations—even those that conform to the social dilemma inequalities—should be invariant with respect to behaviour is thus unclear. Rather, it may be that the domain of possible values, or reachable space, accessible to the internal state of each algorithm varies under different representations.

With regard to practical impacts on the use of learning algorithms, these results suggest that we cannot unconditionally generalise learning algorithms between representations, either *a priori*, or *in-situ*, without possibly introducing bias. Within a representation we assert that we can compare algorithms—with the proviso that the given representation may define the depth and location of local minima. In addition, we are not assured that the behaviours available to an algorithm, given the reachable space, will conform to intuitive expectations derived from a semantic interpretation of the dilemma. Furthermore, we may ask how much the variance in behaviour actually affects an algorithm—does the range of an outcome's frequency shift only slightly, or is the effect more pronounced? We assert that the character of the behavioural profile can be altered considerably, as is evident in the algorithm Watkins (naïve) Q Lambda in experiment group three, shown in Fig. 3.

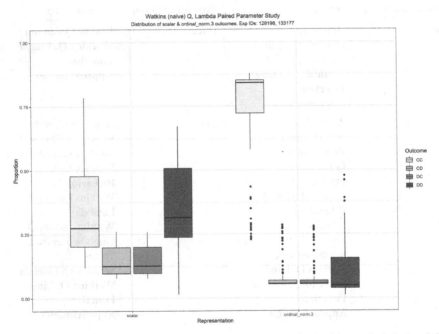

Fig. 3. Grouped boxplot of experiment group three outcomes for Watkins (naive) Q, Lambda.

We conclude that the null hypothesis—that the behavioural profile will not vary between equivalent representations of the game—is not supported for the majority of the learning algorithms, as can be seen in Table 7, where only Watkins Q Linear Function Approximation exhibits non-significant variance in all experiment groups.

The result for Watkins Q Linear Function Approximation is somewhat weak in experiment group four (V = 44057, p-value = .07136). Regardless, the ability of Watkins Q Linear Function Approximation to maintain equivalence across these four representations directs our future work in this area towards contemporary policy-gradient reinforcement learning algorithms.

Acknowledgements. We would like to acknowledge the use of the high-performance computing facilities provided by the Tasmanian Partnership for Advanced Computing (TPAC) funded and hosted by the University of Tasmania. This research is supported by an Australian Government Research Training Program (RTP) Scholarship.

Code Availability. A repository of code used in this study, and further supplementary material, is available at https://github.com/simoncstanton/equivalence_study.

References

Angwin, J., Larson, J., Mattu, S., Kirchner, L.: Machine bias. ProPublica (2016). https://www.propublica.org/article/machine-bias-risk-assessments-in-criminal-sentencing. Accessed 05 Jul 2021

Arthur, B.F.: Complexity economics: why does economics need this different approach? In: Complexity Economics: Proceedings of the Santa Fe Institute's 2019 Fall Symposium. Santa Fe Institute 2019 Fall Symposium, Santa Fe Institute (2019)

Ashlock, D., Kim, E.-Y.: Fingerprinting: visualization and automatic analysis of prisoner's dilemma strategies. IEEE Trans. Evol. Comput. **12**(5), 647–659 (2008). https://doi.org/10.1109/TEVC.2008.920675

Ashlock, D., Kim, E.-Y., Ashlock, W.: A fingerprint comparison of different Prisoner's Dilemma payoff matrices. In: Proceedings of the 2010 IEEE Conference on Computational Intelligence and Games, pp. 219–226 (2010). https://doi.org/10.1109/ITW.2010.5593352

Barto, A.G., Anandan, P.: Pattern-Recognizing Stochastic Learning Automata (1985). https://doi.org/10.1109/tsmc.1985.6313371

Barto, A.G., Sutton, R.S., Anderson, C.W.: Neuronlike adaptive elements that can solve difficult learning control problems. IEEE Trans. Syst. Man Cybern. **SMC-13**(5), 834–846 (1983). https://doi.org/10.1109/TSMC.1983.6313077

Billard, E.A.: Adaptation in a stochastic prisoner's dilemma with delayed information. Biosystems **37**(3), 211–227 (1996). https://doi.org/10.1016/0303-2647(95)01560-4

Brams, S.J.: Theory of Moves. Cambridge University Press (1994)

Bryson, J.J.: Patiency is not a virtue: the design of intelligent systems and systems of ethics. Ethics Inf. Technol. **20**(1), 15–26 (2018). https://doi.org/10.1007/s10676-018-9448-6

Crandall, J.W., et al.: Cooperating with machines. Nat. Commun. **9**(1), 233 (2018). https://doi.org/10.1038/s41467-017-02597-8

Crandall, J.W., et al.: Supplementary material—cooperating with machines. Nat. Commun. **9**(1) (2018b). https://static-content.springer.com/esm/art%3A10.1038%2Fs41467-017-02597-8/MediaObjects/41467_2017_2597_MOESM1_ESM.pdf. Accessed 07 Jan 2020

Grim, P.: Spatialization and greater generosity in the stochastic Prisoner's Dilemma. Biosystems **37**(1), 3–17 (1996). https://doi.org/10.1016/0303-2647(95)01541-8

Herzing, D.L.: Profiling nonhuman intelligence: An exercise in developing unbiased tools for describing other "types" of intelligence on earth. Acta Astronaut. **94**(2), 676–680 (2014). https://doi.org/10.1016/j.actaastro.2013.08.007

Hooker, S.: Moving beyond "algorithmic bias is a data problem". Patterns **2**(4) (2021). https://doi.org/10.1016/j.patter.2021.100241

Hooker, S., Moorosi, N., Clark, G., Bengio, S., Denton, E.: Characterising bias in compressed models (2020). https://arxiv.org/abs/2010.03058v2 Accessed 28 Jun 2021

Leibo, J.Z., Zambaldi, V., Lanctot, M., Marecki, J., Graepel, T.: Multi-agent reinforcement learning in sequential social dilemmas. In: Proceedings of the 16th International Conference on Autonomous Agents and Multiagent Systems, pp. 464–473 (2017)

Macy, M.W., Flache, A.: Learning dynamics in social dilemmas. Proc. Natl. Acad. Sci. **99**(suppl 3), 7229–7236 (2002). https://doi.org/10.1073/pnas.092080099

Patton, D.U., Brunton, D.-W., Dixon, A., Miller, R.J., Leonard, P., Hackman, R.: Stop and frisk online: theorizing everyday racism in digital policing in the use of social media for identification of criminal conduct and associations. Soc. Media + Soc. **3**(3) (2017). https://doi.org/10.1177/2056305117733344

Rahwan, I., et al.: Machine behaviour. Nature **568**(7753), 477 (2019). https://doi.org/10.1038/s41586-019-1138-y

Rapoport, A., Guyer, M., Gordon, D.G.: The 2 × 2 Game. University of Michigan Press, Ann Arbor (1976)

Robinson, D., Goforth, D.: The topology of the 2×2 games: a new periodic table. Routledge (2005). https://doi.org/10.4324/9780203340271

Sutton, R.S., Barto, A.G.: Reinforcement Learning: An Introduction (1st ed.). The MIT Press, Cambridge (1998)

Sutton, R.S., Barto, A.G.: Reinforcement Learning: An Introduction (2nd edn.). The MIT Press, Cambridge (2018)

Szepesvári, C.: Algorithms for Reinforcement Learning. Morgan and Claypool Publishers, San Rafael (2010)

Tan, M.: Multi-agent reinforcement learning: independent vs. cooperative agents. In: Proceedings of the Tenth International Conference on Machine Learning, pp. 330–337 (1993)

Tversky, A., Kahneman, D.: Judgment under uncertainty: heuristics and biases. Science **185**(4157), 1124–1131 (1974). https://doi.org/10.1126/science.185.4157.1124

Waller, R.R., Waller, R.: The machine mind: beyond transparent biases. In: Paper presented at Kinds of Intelligence Workshop Series: Cognitive Science Beyond the Human, Leverhulme Centre for the Future of Intelligence. http://lcfi.ac.uk/projects/kinds-of-intelligence/. 25 June 2021

Winfield, A.F., Michael, K., Pitt, J., Evers, V.: Machine ethics: the design and governance of ethical ai and autonomous systems. Proc. IEEE **107**(3), 509–517 (2019). https://doi.org/10.1109/JPROC.2019.2900622

Contextual Importance and Utility: A Theoretical Foundation

Kary Främling[1,2]( )

[1] Department of Computing Science, Umeå University,
Mit-huset, 901 87 Umeå, Sweden
kary.framling@umu.se
[2] Department of Computer Science, Aalto University,
Konemiehentie 1, 02150 Espoo, Finland

Abstract. This paper provides new theory to support to the eXplainable AI (XAI) method Contextual Importance and Utility (CIU). CIU arithmetic is based on the concepts of Multi-Attribute Utility Theory, which gives CIU a solid theoretical foundation. The novel concept of *contextual influence* is also defined, which makes it possible to compare CIU directly with so-called additive feature attribution (AFA) methods for model-agnostic outcome explanation. One key takeaway is that the 'influence' concept used by AFA methods is inadequate for outcome explanation purposes even for simple models to explain. Experiments with simple models show that explanations using contextual importance (CI) and contextual utility (CU) produce explanations where influence-based methods fail. It is also shown that CI and CU guarantees explanation faithfulness towards the explained model.

Keywords: Explainable AI · Contextual importance and utility · Multi-attribute utility theory · Decision theory

1 Introduction

Contextual Importance and Utility (CIU) was originally proposed by Kary Främling in 1995 in a context of Multiple Criteria Decision Making (MCDM). MCDM is a domain where mathematical models are used as Decision Support Systems (DSS) for human decision makers. No matter what model is being used for the DSS, it is crucial that the recommendations or outcome of the DSS can be presented in ways that are understandable for the decision makers, as well as for the people who might be affected by the decisions. CIU is model-agnostic and provides uniform explanation concepts for all possible DSS models, ranging from linear models such as the weighted sum, to rule-based systems, decision trees, fuzzy systems, neural networks and any machine learning-based models.

This paper solidifies and extends CIU theory and relates it to currently popular methods in the domain called eXplainable AI (XAI). In recent years, the

The work is partially supported by the Wallenberg AI, Autonomous Systems and Software Program (WASP) funded by the Knut and Alice Wallenberg Foundation.

G. Long et al. (Eds.): AI 2021, LNAI 13151, pp. 117–128, 2022.
https://doi.org/10.1007/978-3-030-97546-3_10

XAI domain has moved forward rapidly and has developed its own concepts and methods, which makes it difficult for current XAI researchers to understand and assess CIU in relation to their own work. The objectives of the paper are the following:

- Present a solid mathematical theory for CIU.
- Provide distinct definitions of the concepts *influence*, *importance* and *utility*.
- Define the new concept of *contextual influence* derived from CIU.
- Situate CIU within the latest state-of-the-art in XAI and show that it performs better than core main-stream XAI methods.

After this Introduction, Sect. 2 goes through the theoretical constructs of CIU and relates CIU to the family of additive feature attribution methods such as Shapley values and LIME. Section 3 provides empirical evidence for the theory in Sect. 2, followed by Conclusions.

2 Theory

2.1 Additive Feature Attribution Methods

We will here use notations from the paper by Lundberg and Lee [8] because it provides a unifying view on a whole family of outcome explanation methods called *additive feature attribution (AFA)* methods. Such methods use an *explanation model* g that is an interpretable approximation of the original model f. The following definition is fundamental for AFA methods [8]:

Definition 1. *AFA methods have an explanation model that is a linear function of binary variables:*

$$g(z') = \phi_0 + \sum_{i=1}^{M} \phi_i z_i', \tag{1}$$

where $z' \in \{0,1\}^M$, M is the number of simplified input features, and $\phi \in \mathbb{R}$.

Methods with explanation models g matching this definition attribute an effect ϕ_i to each input feature. Since ϕ_i is a scalar, the definition signifies that the explanation model g is linear by definition. Our interpretation of the variable ϕ_i is to call it 'influence', which has also been used by other authors. Lundberg and Lee use the word 'effect' for ϕ_i but they do also use the word 'importance' with a similar meaning in [8]. It seems like most authors use 'effect', 'influence', 'significance', 'importance', etc. interchangeably.

The *Shapley value* is an AFA method originating from cooperative game theory [13]. The concept was picked up by the XAI community [14] and has become popular for producing outcome explanations following [8], and the introduction of SHAP (SHapley Additive exPlanations). The method distributes the difference between the prediction output $f(x)$ and the *reference level*[1] ϕ_0 to the

---

[1] Called *baseline* by many authors but 'baseline' seems to be used also for other purposes. This is why we prefer using 'reference level'.

input feature influences ϕ_i according to Eq. 1. The most used ϕ_0 value is the global average predicted value for the studied output in the training data set. If $f(x) > \phi_0$, then the sum of the terms ϕ_i must be positive, and vice versa if $f(x) < \phi_0$.

Local Interpretable Model-agnostic Explanations (LIME) is a popular AFA method, which creates a linear surrogate model g that locally approximates the behaviour of the model to explain around the neighborhood of the instance being explained [12]. The sign of ϕ_i determines if the influence of the input feature i is negative or positive. The magnitude of ϕ_i expresses how great the influence is.

2.2 Decision Theory and Multi-attribute Utility Theory

In statistics, Decision Theory proposes a set of quantitative methods for reaching optimal, or at least rational, decisions. A decision problem must be capable of being formulated in terms of initial conditions and outcomes or courses of action, with their consequences. Each outcome is assigned a *utility value* based on the *preferences* of the decision maker(s). An optimal decision is one that maximizes the expected utility. It was proven already in 1947 that any individual whose preferences satisfy four axioms has a *utility function*, u, by which an individual's preferences can be represented on an interval scale [10].

If preferences over choices on attributes or *input features* $1, \ldots, n$ depend only on their marginal probability distributions, then the n-attribute utility function is additive according to:

$$u(x_1, \ldots, x_n) = \sum_{i=1}^{n} k_i u_i(x_i) \tag{2}$$

where u and the u_i are normalized to the range $[0, 1]$, and the k_i are normalization constants [1]. If the goal is to simply rank-order the available choices, then a key condition for the additive form in Eq. 2 is mutual *preference independence*. A fundamental result in utility theory is that two attributes are additive-independent if and only if their two-attribute utility function is additive and has the form:

$$u(x_1, x_2) = u(x_1) + u(x_2) \tag{3}$$

CIU respects additive-independence as long as the underlying model is linear. However, the objective of CIU is not to provide a rank-ordering but providing an explanation for the outcome of an underlying DSS model, which requires and justifies breaking the additive-independence condition given in Eq. 3, as explained in the next section.

2.3 Contextual Importance and Utility (CIU)

CIU estimates the values k_i and $u_i(y_i)$ in Eq. 2 for one or more input features $\{i\}$ in a specific context C and any black-box model f, where the context is defined by the instance or situation to be explained.

However, the use of Eq. 2 makes it necessary to map output values $y = f(x)$ into utility values u that are limited to the range $[0, 1]$. In classification tasks, the y values are usually probability values in the range $[0, 1]$ by definition, so it can be considered that $u = y$. The same is not true for regression tasks. For instance, in the well-known Boston Housing data set, the output value is the median value of owner-occupied homes in \$1000's and is in the range $[5, 50]$. A straightforward way of transforming that value into a utility value is an affine transformation $[5, 50] \mapsto [0, 1]$, assuming that the preference is to have a higher value. However, from a buyer's point of view, the preference might be for lower prices and then the transformation would rather be $[50, 5] \mapsto [0, 1]$. In this paper, we will assume that $u_j(y_j)$ is an affine transformation of the form $u_j(y_j) = Ay_j + b$, where j is the output index. In practice, $u_j(y_j)$ could have any shape as long as it produces values in the range $[0, 1]$ but that case goes beyond the scope of the current paper (and theory). This takes us to the definition of *Contextual Importance (CI)*.

Definition 2 (Contextual Importance)

$$CI_j(C, \{i\}, \{I\}) = \frac{umax_j(C, \{i\}) - umin_j(C, \{i\})}{umax_j(C, \{I\}) - umin_j(C, \{I\})}, \tag{4}$$

where $\{i\} \subseteq \{I\}$ *and* $\{I\} \subseteq \{1, \ldots, n\}$. *C is the instance/context to be explained and defines the values of input features that do not belong to* $\{i\}$ *or* $\{I\}$.

For clarity, $\{i\}$ is the set of indices studied and $\{I\}$ is the set of indices relative to which we calculate CI. When $\{I\} = \{1, \ldots, n\}$, CI is calculated relative to the output utilities u_j. For instance, $CI_j(C, \{2\}, \{1, \ldots, n\})$ is the contextual importance of input x_2, whereas $CI_j(C, \{1, 2, 3\}, \{1, \ldots, n\})$ is the **joint** contextual importance of inputs x_1, x_2, x_3 and $CI_j(C, \{1, \ldots, n\}, \{1, \ldots, n\})$ is the joint contextual importance of **all** inputs. $umin_j()$ and $umax_j()$ are the minimal and maximal utility values u_j observed for output j for all possible $x_{\{i\}}$ and $x_{\{I\}}$ values in the context C, while keeping other input values at C. Using $\{I\} \neq \{1, \ldots, n\}$ makes it possible to also use and explain *intermediate concepts* as described in [2–4].

When $u_j(y_j) = Ay_j + b$, then CI can be directly calculated as:

$$CI_j(C, \{i\}, \{I\}) = \frac{ymax_j(C, \{i\}) - ymin_j(C, \{i\})}{ymax_j(C, \{I\}) - ymin_j(C, \{I\})}, \tag{5}$$

where $ymin_j()$ and $ymax_j()$ are the minimal and maximal y_j values observed for output j. Equation 5 is identical to the CI definitions in [3,4].

The values of $umin_j$ and $umax_j$ can only be calculated exactly if the entire set of possible values for the input features $\{i\}$ is available and the corresponding u_j values can be calculated in reasonable time. For categorical input features this is feasible as long as the number of possible values doesn't grow too big. For continuous-valued input features, using a *Set of representative input vectors* $S(C, \{i\})$ is a model-agnostic approach to estimate $umin_j$ and $umax_j$.

Algorithm 1: Set of representative input vectors

Result: $N \times M$ matrix $S(C, \{i\})$

1 **begin**
2   **forall the** *categorical input features* **do**
3          $D \leftarrow$ all possible value combinations for discrete inputs $\{i\}$;
4   Randomize row order in D;
5   **if** *D has more rows than N* **then**
6 | Set N to number of rows in D;
7   **end**
8   **end**
9   **forall the** *numerical input features* **do**
10   Initialize $N \times M$ matrix R with current input values C;
11         $R \leftarrow$ two rows per continuous-valued inputs in $\{i\}$ where the current value is replaced by the values $min_{\{i\}}$ and $max_{\{i\}}$ respectively;
12         $R \leftarrow$ fill remaining rows to N with random values from intervals $[min_{\{i\}}, max_{\{i\}}]$;
13   **end**
14     $S(C, \{i\}) \leftarrow$ concatenation of C with merged D and R, where D is repeated if needed to obtain N rows;
15 **end**

Algorithm 1 shows how $S(C, \{i\})$ is constructed in the 'ciu' R package [4]. The approach taken there is to limit the range of input values to intervals $[min_{\{i\}}, max_{\{i\}}]$ for numerical input features. The studied instance C is the first sample in $S(C, \{i\})$, followed by samples with the extreme values $min_{\{i\}}$ and $max_{\{i\}}$ for numerical input features $\{i\}$. For numerical input features, the remaining samples for achieving N samples are generated randomly from the interval(s) $[min_{\{i\}}, max_{\{i\}}]$. Other sampling methods could be envisaged, including model-specific ones like the one in Främling's thesis [3] and remains a topic of future research.

When the set of input features to explain $\{i\}$ is a subset of all input features $\{1, \dots, n\}$, then we apply the *ceteris-paribus* principle, i.e. 'other things held constant' for estimating their CI value. This signifies that all input features $\neg\{i\}$ are held constant at the values given by the studied instance C while estimating $CI_j(C, \{i\})$ by varying the values of the input features $\{i\}$ according to Algorithm 1. This leads us to the following:

Lemma 1 (Contextual Importance of input feature subsets $\{i\}$). *When $\{I\} \subseteq \{1, \dots, n\}$ and $\{i\} \subseteq \{I\} \Rightarrow [umin_j(C, \{i\}), umax_j(C, \{i\})] \subseteq [umin_j (C, \{I\}), umax_j(C, \{I\})]$.*

Proof. When $\{i\} \subseteq \{I\}$, then $S(C, \{i\}) \subseteq S(C, \{I\})$ and $[umin_j(C, \{i\}), umax_j(C, \{i\})] \subseteq [umin_j(C, \{I\}), umax_j(C, \{I\})]$ when the number of samples $N \to \infty$.

When considering that $umax_j(C, \{i\}) - umin_j(C, \{i\}) \geq 0$, we get:

Theorem 1 (Maximal range of Contextual Importance). $CI_j(C, \{i\}) \in [0, 1]$ *for any set of input features* $\{i\}$.

The *Contextual Utility (CU)* corresponds to the factor $u_i(x_i)$ in Eq. 2. CU expresses to what extent the current value of a given input feature contributes to obtaining a high output utility u_j.

Definition 3 (Contextual Utility)

$$CU_j(C, \{i\}) = \frac{u_j(C) - umin_j(C, \{i\})}{umax_j(C, \{i\}) - umin_j(C, \{i\})} \tag{6}$$

When $u_j(y_j) = Ay_j + b$, this can be written as:

$$CU_j(C, \{i\}) = \left| \frac{y_j(C) - ymin_j(C, \{i\})}{ymax_j(C, \{i\}) - ymin_j(C, \{i\})} \right|, \tag{7}$$

where $yumin = ymin$ if A is positive and $yumin = ymax$ if A is negative. This definition of CU differs from CI definitions in [3, 4] by handling negative A values correctly.

Illustration of Additive Independence in CIU for Linear Model f. We will next illustrate that CIU satisfies Eqs. 2 and 3 when the input features $x_1, \ldots, x_n$ are additive-independent. For this, we use the simple function $y = x_1 + x_2$ with $x_i \in [0, 1]$. In this case we can use $u_i(x_i) = x_i$. Table 1 shows results for all the four zero-one combinations when $u(x_i) = CI(x_i) \times CU(x_i)$.

Table 1. Weighted sum input and output values, with corresponding CI and CU values.

x_1	x_2	$y = x_1 + x_2$	$CI(x_1)$	$CI(x_2)$	$CU(x_1)$	$CU(x_2)$	$u(x_1) + u(x_2)$	$u(y) = u(x_1, x_2)$
0	0	0	0.5	0.5	0	0	0	0
0	1	1	0.5	0.5	0	1	0.5	0.5
1	0	1	0.5	0.5	1	0	0.5	0.5
1	1	2	0.5	0.5	1	1	1	1

We now go to the core point of disruption of CIU with utility theory: most models f for which we would like to provide explainability are non-linear and their input features tend to be dependent on each other. Therefore, CIU proposes to abandon the requirement of additive-independence of Eq. 3. An initial assumption of CIU is indeed that both the importance and the utility function can (and usually do) depend on the values of other input features, which is the main reason for using the word *contextual* in CIU.

In order to illustrate the need and necessity to take the contextual aspects into account for outcome explanation, we will study how to explain results of

Table 2. OR function input and output values, with corresponding CI and CU values.

x_1	x_2	$y = x_1 \vee x_2$	$CI(x_1)$	$CI(x_2)$	$CU(x_1)$	$CU(x_2)$	$u(x_1) + u(x_2)$	$u(y) = u(x_1, x_2)$
0	0	0	1	1	0	0	0	0
0	1	1	0	1	NaN	1	1	1
1	0	1	1	0	1	NaN	1	1
1	1	1	0	0	NaN	NaN	0	1

Table 3. XOR function input and output values, with corresponding CI and CU values.

x_1	x_2	$y = x_1 \oplus x_2$	$CI(x_1)$	$CI(x_2)$	$CU(x_1)$	$CU(x_2)$	$u(x_1) + u(x_2)$	$u(y) = u(x_1, x_2)$
0	0	0	1	1	0	0	0	0
0	1	1	1	1	1	1	2	1
1	0	1	1	1	1	1	2	1
1	1	0	1	1	0	0	0	0

simple OR and XOR functions, where the input features are clearly dependent. The results are shown in Tables 2 and 3.

A core reason for showing these three simple examples is to emphasize that both CI and CU are **absolute** values in the range $[0, 1]$, as opposed to **relative** values used by AFA methods. $CI_j(C, \{i\}) = 0$ signifies that in the context C the input feature(s) $\{i\}$ have no effect on the utility u_j of output j. $CI_j(C, \{i\}) = 1$ signifies that changes to the values of input feature(s) $\{i\}$ can modify the value of u_j over the entire range $[0, 1]$. Similarly, $CU_j(C, \{i\}) = 0$ signifies that the value(s) of input feature(s) $\{i\}$ are the least favorable (in the sense of utility u_j) for the output j. $CU_j(C, \{i\}) = 1$ signifies that the value(s) of input feature(s) $\{i\}$ are the most favorable for the output j.

2.4   Contextual Influence

CI and CU produce explanations from any model f in a uniform way, no matter if the model is linear or not, continuous-valued or discrete, handcoded or created via machine learning. However, in order to compare CIU with AFA methods, we define *Contextual influence*. We begin by a contextual version of the term $k_i u_i(x_i)$ in Eq. 2:

$$Cinfluence_j(C, \{i\}) = CI_j(C, \{i\}) \times CU_j(C, \{i\}),$$

when $k_i = CI_j(C, \{i\})$ and $u_i = CU_j(C, \{i\})$. $Cinfluence$ can be scaled into any range $[rmin, rmax]$, which leads us to the following definition:

Definition 4 (Contextual influence)

$$\phi = (rmax - rmin) \times CI \times (CU - neutral.CU) \tag{8}$$

where '$_j(C, \{i\})$' has been omitted from all three terms ϕ, CI, and CU for easier readability.

The symbol ϕ has been chosen on purpose to signify 'influence' as for Shapley values and LIME. We use $[rmin, rmax] = [-1, 1]$ in Sect. 3. Setting $neutral.CU = 0.5$ restricts ϕ values to only negative, zero or positive, as for Shapley values and LIME.

2.5   CIU Versus Additive Feature Attribution Methods

As shown in the previous Sections, CIU makes a clear distinction between 'importance' and 'influence'. Furthermore, CIU uses the notions of 'utility function' and 'utility', which are not considered by any known AFA method. As shown by the following differences, **CIU is not an AFA method**:

- CIU does not use or create any explanation model g.
- CI and CU can be used for calculating an influence measure ϕ but it is not possible to do it the other way around.
- CI and CU provide absolute values in the range $[0, 1]$ that have precise definitions, whereas ϕ values express relative influence between input features.
- CIU is defined using utility theory and CIU explanations are entirely based on elements of that theory. CIU does not attempt to mimic or approximate the original function f in any way.
- CIU has no notion z_i' of presence or not of an input feature and should not be confused with so-called occlusion-based methods [15].

Intuitively, it might be possible to consider Contextual influence in Eq. 8 to be an AFA method, which is one reason for using the symbol ϕ for it. However, the fact that the reference level $neutral.CU$ is defined on utility values u_j and not on output values y_j as in AFA methods is a major difference. Furthermore, there's no additivity requirement on Contextual influence, even though additivity could be imposed by normalization. Still, further research on comparing Contextual influence and AFA methods is interesting and ongoing.

3   Experimental Evaluation

In this section we compare CIU, contextual influence, Shapley values and LIME for three known functions that have two input features x_1, x_2 and one output value y. The functions are linear ($y = 0.3x_1 + 0.7x_2$), rule-based and 'sombrero' ($y = \sin(\sqrt{x_1^2 + x_2^2})/\sqrt{x_1^2 + x_2^2}$), as shown in Fig. 1. The studied input values $C = (x_1, x_2)$ are indicated by the red dots in Fig. 1. Figure 2 shows how the output y changes as a function of one input feature while keeping constant the value of the other input feature, together with values and illustrations of CIU calculations.

CIU results are produced using the 'ciu' R package [4]. Shapley values are produced with the 'IML' R package [9] and LIME results are produced with the 'lime' R package [11]. All methods were run with default parameters ($N = 100$ for CIU). In Fig. 3 the order of input features is determined automatically by the respective package, so it is not necessarily the same in all bar plots.

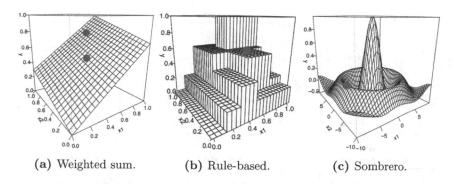

(a) Weighted sum.   (b) Rule-based.   (c) Sombrero.

Fig. 1. Linear, rule-based and non-linear models used in the study.

CIU can use the test functions directly as the model to explain and does not need a data set. Both Shapley values and LIME do require a training data set, which has been generated as a regular grid of points (x_1, x_2). A grid $x_1, x_2 \in [0, 1]$ with step size 0.05 is used for the linear and rule-based functions. For the 'sombrero' function, $x_1, x_2 \in [-10, 10]$ with step size 0.51. Table 4 and Fig. 3 show the results of the different methods. The following observations are made:

CIU consistently describes a) how much the utility ('goodness') of y can change when modifying the value of x_i from the least favorable to the most favorable, and b) how favorable the current value x_i is for the utility $u(y)$, for the current instance/context C. CIU shows complete fidelity towards the underlying model, as indicated in Table 4, which correspond exactly to the weights and input/utility values for the linear function. CI and CU values can also be 'seen' and understood directly from the graphs in Fig. 2.

Influence-based explanations are inconsistent between the different methods for the three last test cases. In particular for the linear function with $(x_1, x_2) = (0.5, 0.5)$, the influence-based explanations are in-existent because all ϕ_i values are (or should be) zero, which is indeed the case for all three influence-based methods. The slight deviations from zero are only due to numerical imprecision for contextual influence, whereas sampling leads to stochastic ϕ values that are normally distributed around zero for Shapley values and LIME.

Table 4. Results for known functions with two inputs and one output.

$f(x)$	x_1	x_2	y	CI_1	CI_2	CU_1	CU_2	ϕ_1^{ciu}	ϕ_2^{ciu}	ϕ_1^{shap}	ϕ_2^{shap}	ϕ_1^{lime}	ϕ_2^{lime}
Linear	0.7	0.8	0.77	0.3	0.7	0.7	0.8	0.12	0.42	0.065	0.208	0.040	0.331
Linear	0.5	0.5	0.5	0.3	0.7	0.5	0.5	0.0	0.0	0.007	−0.021	−0.054	−0.097
Rules	0.7	0.4	0.6	0.6	0.8	1.0	0.5	0.6	0.0	0.218	−0.046	0.285	−0.117
Sombrero	−7.5	−1.5	0.128	0.724	0.18	0.392	0.998	−0.157	0.18	0.061	0.032	−0.019	0.010

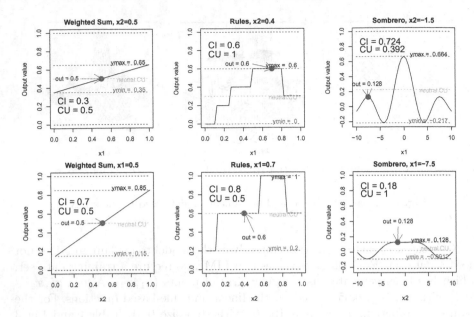

Fig. 2. Output value as a function of one variable for the test functions, with illustration of how CI and CU are calculated.

Contextual influence shows greater stability than the other influence-based methods. It also remains possible to 'read' and understand the contextual influence values directly from Fig. 2 because it corresponds to $y - neutral.CU$ relative to the $[ymin_i, ymax_i]$ range.

Shapley values distribute the difference $f(x) - \phi_0$ 'fairly' over all inputs ϕ_i. However, when that difference is zero, as for the linear function with $(x_1, x_2) = (0.5, 0.5)$, then there is nothing to distribute, at least not to input features with identical and 'average' values, so Shapley values fail in producing any explanation in this case. The corresponding bar plot in Fig. 3 gives an impression that there is a successful explanation but that is because influence values are relative, so the scale of the x-axis is extended. In practice, both ϕ values are (or should be) zero, as seen in Table 4.

LIME. For some reason, LIME's 'Explanation fit' is 0.5 for the linear function with $(x_1, x_2) = (0.7, 0.8)$ but only 0.06 with $(x_1, x_2) = (0.5, 0.5)$. It also remains unclear what is actually the reference level ϕ_0 used by LIME.

The experiments shown in this paper emphasize the theoretical difference between CIU and AFA methods, as well as the difference between the concepts of importance, utility and influence. All methods are applicable to any real-world tabular data sets and an extensive comparison between CIU, LIME and Shapley values is presented in [6]. The CIU Github site https://github.com/KaryFramling/ciu provides executable examples at least for the well-known benchmark data sets Iris, Boston, Heart Disease, UCI Cars, Diamonds, Titanic and Adult and several

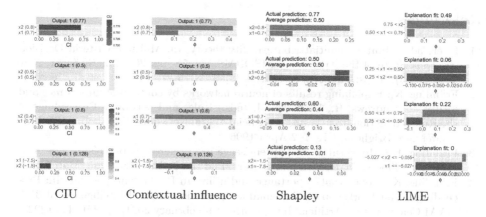

CIU   Contextual influence   Shapley   LIME

Fig. 3. Bar plots for the four methods on the four test functions.

different machine learning models. CIU is also implemented for image explanations as reported in [5,7]. The source code used in this paper is published at https://github.com/KaryFramling/AJCAI_2021.

4   Conclusion

This paper extends the theory of CIU beyond the original theory in [3] and defines the new concept of contextual influence. CIU is compared to current state-of-the-art methods, notably the family of AFA methods. As shown in the paper, CIU provides new flexibility and expressiveness by separating the notions of *importance* and *utility* from the notion of *influence* used by AFA methods. It is also illustrated why 'influence' alone lacks in explanation capability. Identified advantages of CIU compared to AFA methods are:

1. CI and CU provide absolute values in the $[0, 1]$ range that have clear definitions and interpretations
2. Separate 'importance' and 'utility' concepts allow for more fine-grained and accurate explanations than 'influence' alone.
3. CIU has only one 'tunable' parameter (the number N of samples to use), which provides robustness and simplicity of use.
4. CIU does not need access to a data set.
5. CIU is not a 'black box' in itself because CI and CU values can be 'read out' directly from input versus output graphs.
6. CIU's faithfulness/fidelity towards the model f is guaranteed because no interpretable model g is needed. CIU's faithfulness only depends on how accurately $umin$ and $umax$ can be estimated.
7. CIU has a solid and proven mathematical background and framework in multi-attribute utility theory, which puts it at least on the same level of rigor as Shapley values.

References

1. Dyer, J.S.: Maut — multiattribute utility theory. In: Multiple Criteria Decision Analysis: State of the Art Surveys. ISORMS, vol. 78, pp. 265–292. Springer, New York (2005). https://doi.org/10.1007/0-387-23081-5_7
2. Främling, K.: Explaining results of neural networks by contextual importance and utility. In: Andrews, R., Diederich, J. (eds.) Rules and networks: Proceedings of the Rule Extraction from Trained Artificial Neural Networks Workshop, AISB 1996 Conference, Brighton, UK, 1–2 April 1996
3. Främling, K.: Modélisation et apprentissage des préférences par réseaux de neurones pour l'aide à la décision multicritère. Phd thesis, INSA de Lyon, March 1996
4. Främling, K.: Contextual importance and utility in R: the 'ciu' package. In: Proceedings of 1st Workshop on Explainable Agency in Artificial Intelligence, at 35th AAAI Conference on Artificial Intelligence, 2–9 February 2021, pp. 110–114 (2021)
5. Främling, K., Knapič, S., Malhi, A.: ciu.image: an R package for explaining image classification with contextual importance and utility. In: Calvaresi, D., Najjar, A., Winikoff, M., Främling, K. (eds.) EXTRAAMAS 2021. LNCS (LNAI), vol. 12688, pp. 55–62. Springer, Cham (2021). https://doi.org/10.1007/978-3-030-82017-6_4
6. Främling, K., Westberg, M., Jullum, M., Madhikermi, M., Malhi, A.: Comparison of contextual importance and utility with lime and Shapley values. In: Calvaresi, D., Najjar, A., Winikoff, M., Främling, K. (eds.) Explainable and Transparent AI and Multi-Agent Systems - 3rd International Workshop, EXTRAAMAS 2021, pp. 39–54. Lecture Notes in Computer Science, Springer, Germany (2021)
7. Knapič, S., Malhi, A., Saluja, R., Främling, K.: Explainable artificial intelligence for human decision support system in the medical domain. Mach. Learn. Knowl. Extr. 3(3), 740–770 (2021)
8. Lundberg, S.M., Lee, S.I.: A unified approach to interpreting model predictions. In: Guyon, I., et al. (eds.) Advances in Neural Information Processing Systems, vol. 30, pp. 4765–4774. Curran Associates, Inc. (2017)
9. Molnar, C., Casalicchio, G., Bischl, B.: iml: an R package for interpretable machine learning. J. Open Source Softw. 3(26), 786 (2018)
10. von Neumann, J., Morgenstern, O.: Theory of Games and Economic Behavior. Princeton University Press (1947)
11. Pedersen, T.L., Benesty, M.: lime: local interpretable model-agnostic explanations (2019). https://CRAN.R-project.org/package=lime. r package version 0.5.1
12. Ribeiro, M.T., Singh, S., Guestrin, C.: " why should i trust you?" Explaining the predictions of any classifier. In: Proceedings of the 22nd ACM SIGKDD International Conference on Knowledge Discovery and Data Mining, pp. 1135–1144 (2016)
13. Shapley, L.: A value for n-person games. In: Kuhn, H., Tucker, A. (eds.) Contributions to the Theory of Games, vol. II, Annals of Mathematics Studies, vol. 28, pp. 307–317. Princeton University Press, Princeton (1953)
14. Štrumbelj, E., Kononenko, I.: An efficient explanation of individual classifications using game theory. J. Mach. Learn. Res. 11, 1–18 (2010)
15. Zeiler, M.D., Fergus, R.: Visualizing and understanding convolutional networks. In: Fleet, D., Pajdla, T., Schiele, B., Tuytelaars, T. (eds.) ECCV 2014. LNCS, vol. 8689, pp. 818–833. Springer, Cham (2014). https://doi.org/10.1007/978-3-319-10590-1_53

Deeper Insights into Neural Nets with Random Weights

Ming Li[1]([✉])[ID], Giorgio Gnecco[2][ID], and Marcello Sanguineti[3][ID]

[1] Key Laboratory of Intelligent Education Technology and Application of Zhejiang
Province, Zhejiang Normal University, Jinhua 321004, China
mingli@zjnu.edu.cn
[2] AXES Research Unit, IMT School for Advanced Studies, 55100 Lucca, Italy
giorgio.gnecco@imtlucca.it
[3] Department of Informatics, Bioengineering, Robotics and Systems Engineering,
University of Genoa, 16145 Genova, Italy
marcello.sanguineti@unige.it

Abstract. In this work, the "effective dimension" of the output of the hidden layer of a one-hidden-layer neural network with random inner weights of its computational units is investigated. To do this, a polynomial approximation of the sigmoidal activation function of each computational unit is used, whose degree is chosen based both on a desired upper bound on the approximation error and on an estimate of the range of the input to that computational unit. This estimate of the range is parameterized by the number of inputs to the network and by an upper bound both on the size of the random inner weights of the network and on the size of its inputs. The results show that the Root Mean Square Error (RMSE) on the training set is influenced by the effective dimension and by the quality of the features associated with the output of the hidden layer.

Keywords: Neural networks with random weights · Hyperbolic tangent · Polynomial approximation · Effective dimension · Approximate rank

1 Introduction

This work analyzes the "effective dimension" of the output of the hidden layer of a random neural network based on a sigmoidal activation function $\sigma : \mathbb{R} \to \mathbb{R}$. Such a network computes a function $g : X \subset \mathbb{R}^D \to \mathbb{R}$ of the form

G. Gnecco and M. Sanguineti are members of INdAM. G. Gnecco and M. Li acknowledge financial support from the research program ICTP-INdAM Research in Pairs in Mathematics 2020, for the project "On the Expressive Power of Neural Nets with Random Weights". The work of G. Gnecco was supported in part by the Italian Project ARTES 4.0 – Advanced Robotics and enabling digital TEchnology & Systems 4.0, funded by the Italian Ministry of Economic Development (MISE). The work of M. Li was supported in part by the National Natural Science Foundation of China under Grant 62172370.

G. Long et al. (Eds.): AI 2021, LNAI 13151, pp. 129–140, 2022.
https://doi.org/10.1007/978-3-030-97546-3_11

$$g(\mathbf{x}) := \sum_{m=1}^{M} c_m \sigma \left(\mathbf{a}_m \cdot \mathbf{x} - b_m \right), \tag{1}$$

where $\cdot$ denotes the dot product, $\mathbf{x} \in X \subset \mathbb{R}^D$, the weights $c_1, \dots, c_M$ are optimizable (e.g., using ordinary least squares), whereas the other weight vectors $\mathbf{a}_1, \dots, \mathbf{a}_M \in \mathbb{R}^D$ and the biases $b_1, \dots, b_M \in \mathbb{R}$ are randomly extracted before training (i.e., they are nonoptimizable during the training of the network).

The motivation for this study is as follows. Although [6] characterized the approximation power of neural networks with random weights, its main theoretical result (i.e., a sufficient condition for universal approximation[1] by random neural networks in a probabilistic sense) is based on the assumption that there exist some "ideal" support ranges/distributions for randomly assigning the hidden parameters of such networks. Hence, universal approximation is not guaranteed for every random assignment of such parameters, and some key issues are still unsolved [8]: e.g., what are the limitations of neural networks with random weights to approximate certain classes of target functions? For instance, the random parameters of the random neural network are typically extracted from the same interval $[-\lambda, \lambda]$, for some $\lambda > 0$. The choice of λ clearly has an influence on the resulting approximation capability, as partially discussed in [10].

In this paper, we shed some further light on this issue by considering the case of a target function defined on the hypercube $[0,1]^D$ and belonging to the function family $\Gamma_{[0,1]^D,1,C}$ (see [5] for a precise definition of this family), i.e., loosely speaking, a function whose actual dependence is only on one of its variables, and the index of this variable is not known a-priori by the network. Our analysis is based on a polynomial approximation of the sigmoidal activation function (here, the hyperbolic tangent), where the degree of that approximation is chosen implicitly as a function of λ and D, as the "effective domain" of the activation function (the domain on which its input actually ranges) depends on these choices, for each hidden unit. So, by varying λ and D, the "effective dimension" of the output of the hidden layer of the random neural network is expected to change typically (as confirmed by our numerical results). Moreover, we show that by increasing D, an increasingly larger percentage of the hidden features computed by the network is expected to be unrelated to the only variable on which a target function belonging to $\Gamma_{[0,1]^D,1,C}$ depends. This may help to explain, for this choice of the target function, the quite large RMSE error achieved on the training set for large D.

2   Literature Review on Polynomial Approximations of Activation Functions

The idea of approximating a sigmoidal activation function through a polynomial with a suitable degree is quite natural and has been investigated in previous

---

[1] This refers to the approximation of continuous functions on compact sets with arbitrary accuracy, using elements of the specific family of neural networks.

works (with various research objectives). A comparison of the approximation capability of feedforward neural networks with sigmoidal and polynomial activation functions was made in [2] (see this reference for a precise statements of results). Of the other findings, it was proved that, under mild conditions, the two kinds of networks are equivalent in the sense that, if it is possible to approximate a Lipschitz-continuous function with a suitable Lipschitz constant by one kind of network with an error (in the supremum norm) smaller than a properly defined threshold and a suitable bound on the Lipschitz constant of its neural network approximation, then it is also possible to do the same using the other kind of network, possibly by increasing its size, its number of layers, and the bound on the Lipschitz constant of the corresponding neural network approximation. Feedforward neural networks with polynomial activation functions are also of practical interest because of their suitability to digital implementation, based, e.g., on lookup tables [9]. A drawback, however, is that they do not satisfy the universal approximation property [1]; indeed, according to [7], a one-hidden-layer feedforward neural network can approximate any continuous function defined on a compact set up to any degree of accuracy (with respect to the supremum norm) if and only if its activation functions are not given polynomials. A final remark has to be made on how the coefficients of the polynomial approximation of an activation function can be obtained in practice. While a Taylor approximation appears to be suitable in the case in which only a local approximation is needed (provided the original activation function is locally smooth enough), either a least-squares approximation or a Chebyshev approximation is more suitable to a global approximation (e.g., on a closed and bounded interval).

3 Analysis

In this work, focus is given to the rank (but also to a sort of "approximate rank", based on the distribution of singular values, as discussed later in this paper) of the hidden output matrix of a one-hidden-layer random neural network, since this can be a measure of the "effective dimension" of the feature space associated with that network.

To undertake the analysis, the following proposition, inspired by [3, Lemma 1], is used. It differs from that result because the proof of the next proposition does not allow one to conclude that the equality holds in the following Eq. (3). However, this is enough to complete the successive analysis. In the proposition, $x_1, \ldots, x_N \in \mathbb{R}^D$ refers to the elements of a training set of size N. We recall that the hidden output matrix $\mathbf{H} \in \mathbb{R}^{N \times M}$ collects in each of its N rows the M outputs of the hidden neurons of the neural network (each row being associated with a particular input vector belonging to the training set).

Proposition 1. *Let the rows of the hidden output matrix $\mathbf{H} \in \mathbb{R}^{N \times M}$ have the following form:*

$$\mathbf{r}_n = \left[\sigma_{pol}^{(P)} (\mathbf{a}_1 \cdot \mathbf{x}_n - b_1), \ldots, \sigma_{pol}^{(P)} (\mathbf{a}_M \cdot \mathbf{x}_n - b_M) \right], n = 1, \ldots, N, \quad (2)$$

where $\mathbf{a}_1, \ldots, \mathbf{a}_M, \mathbf{x}_1, \ldots, \mathbf{x}_N \in \mathbb{R}^D$ *and* $\sigma_{pol}^{(P)} : \mathbb{R} \to \mathbb{R}$ *is a given polynomial approximation (with degree P) of a sigmoidal function* $\sigma : \mathbb{R} \to \mathbb{R}$. *Then, one has*

$$\mathrm{rank}(\mathbf{H}) \leq \min\left\{M, N, \binom{D+P}{P}\right\}. \tag{3}$$

Proof. By introducing the multi-index $\boldsymbol{\mu} \in \mathbb{N}_0^D$ and the notation $|\boldsymbol{\mu}| := \sum_{d=1}^D \mu_i$, then, for $n = 1, \ldots, N$, the column vectors $\mathbf{s}_n = \{x_{n,1}^{\mu_1} \cdots x_{n,D}^{\mu_D}\}_{|\boldsymbol{\mu}| \leq P} \in \mathbb{R}^{\binom{D+P}{P}}$, and, for $m = 1, \cdots, M$, suitable vectors of coefficients $\mathbf{c}_m \in \mathbb{R}^{\binom{D+P}{P}}$ (which depend both on $\mathbf{a}_m$ and on the $P+1$ coefficients of the polynomial $\sigma_{pol}^{(P)}$), and finally, the matrix $\mathbf{C} = [\mathbf{c}_1|\ldots|\mathbf{c}_M] \in \mathbb{R}^{\binom{D+P}{P} \times M}$, one gets

$$\mathbf{r}_n = \mathbf{s}_n^\top \mathbf{C}. \tag{4}$$

Hence, by introducing the matrix $\mathbf{S} = \begin{bmatrix} \mathbf{s}_1^\top \\ \cdots \\ \mathbf{s}_N^\top \end{bmatrix} \in \mathbb{R}^{N \times \binom{D+P}{P}}$, one gets

$$\mathbf{H} = \mathbf{SC}. \tag{5}$$

Since $\mathrm{rank}(\mathbf{C}) \leq \min\{\binom{D+P}{P}, M\}$ and $\mathrm{rank}(\mathbf{S}) \leq \min\{N, \binom{D+P}{P}\}$, one gets Eq. (3). $\qquad\square$

Based on Proposition 1, we analyze different polynomial approximations of the hyperbolic tangent sigmoidal function $\sigma(z) = \frac{1}{1+\exp(-z)}$, and the effect of training random neural networks based on such approximations. The reason why a polynomial approximation is considered instead of the hyperbolic tangent itself is that the hidden output matrix corresponding to the latter has a full rank under mild conditions [4] (even though some of its positive singular values could be very small). The rank (or the "approximate" rank, as discussed in the next section) of the hidden output matrix corresponding to the use of a good polynomial approximation (i.e., having a reasonably small approximation error over the domain of interest for the analysis) is expected to be a good approximation of the number of largest singular values of the hidden output matrix (with respect to a reasonable threshold) corresponding to the use of the hyperbolic tangent.

Our polynomial approximations are constructed as follows. First, for $L > 0$, we restrict the domain of σ to $[-L, L]$. The specific choice of L is discussed later and depends on the fact that, for the random neural network architecture studied in our analysis, it is possible to find a lower and an upper bound on the inputs to its computational units, depending on the constraints on the weights of the hidden neurons, on the constraints on the components of the feature vector (which are the inputs to such a network), and on the dimension D of that feature vector. Then, for each degree P, we get the best polynomial approximation $\sigma_{pol,[-L,L]}^{(P)}$ of degree P to σ in the weighted $\mathcal{L}_2([-L, L], m_u)$ norm[2] (where m_u is the uniform probability measure on $[-L, L]$). Finally, we fix a desired upper bound $\varepsilon > 0$ on the approximation error in that norm[3], and we choose the smallest degree P° for which $\|\sigma^{(P)}_{pol,[-L,L]} - \sigma\|_{\mathcal{L}_2([-L,L],m_u)} \leq \varepsilon$. To avoid boundary effects (e.g., undesired oscillations near the boundary, see Fig. 1), the domain is further restricted – for some choice of $\Delta L \in (0, L)$ – to $[-\bar{L}, \bar{L}] := [-L + \Delta L, L - \Delta L]$. As an example, Fig. 1(a) shows the graphs of the hyperbolic tangent and of its polynomial approximation found by the procedure above on the domain $[-7, 7]$ and with tolerance $\varepsilon = 10^{-4}$. The approximation has degree $P^\circ = 8$. To avoid boundary effects, its domain is further restricted to $[-5, 5]$, having chosen $\Delta L = 2$ by trial and error. Similarly, Fig. 1(b) refers to the case $\varepsilon = 10^{-5}$, for which the optimal degree of the polynomial approximation is $P^\circ = 12$.

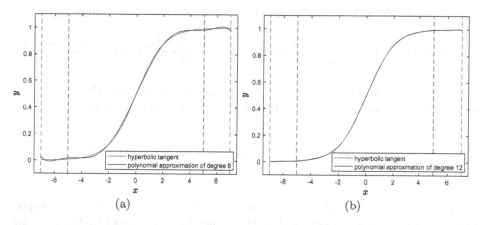

(a)   (b)

Fig. 1. (a) Polynomial approximation (with degree $P = 8$) of the hyperbolic tangent on $[-7, 7]$, and a restriction of its domain to $[-5, 5]$. (b) Polynomial approximation (with degree $P = 12$) of the hyperbolic tangent on $[-7, 7]$, and a restriction of its domain to $[-5, 5]$.

In the following section, two simulation scenarios are considered. For each such scenario and for each choice of the tolerance ε on the approximation error, a suitable value for $\bar{L}$ (and, as a consequence, one also for P°) is obtained as follows. First, an admissible range for the input $\mathbf{a}_m \cdot \mathbf{x}_n - b_m$ of each computational unit is found. Assuming that $x_{n,d} \in [0, 1]$ for each component of $\mathbf{x}_n$ and, given $\lambda > 0$, one has $a_{m,d} \in [-\lambda, \lambda]$ for each component of $\mathbf{a}_m$, and $b_m \in [-\lambda, \lambda]$, one

---

[2] In our numerical implementation, the integral in the definition of the weighted $\mathcal{L}_2([-L, L], m_u)$ norm is approximated by a finite summation on a uniform and fine grid.

[3] The error could be also measured according to the supremum norm, and Chebyshev polynomials [12] could be used to achieve this aim. However, the results obtained with the weighted $\mathcal{L}_2([-L, L], m_u)$ are already good enough, as shown in Fig. 1.

also gets $\mathbf{a}_m \cdot \mathbf{x}_n - b_m \in [-(D+1)\lambda, (D+1)\lambda]$, i.e., $\bar{L} := (D+1)\lambda$. Then, by taking, e.g., $\Delta L = 2$ as before, a possible choice for L is $L = \bar{L} + \Delta L = (D+1)\lambda + 2$.

In the next section, to further justify the use of a polynomial approximation of the hyperbolic tangent sigmoidal function, the random neural network is trained both by using the activation function, then its polynomial approximation. In both cases, the same training inputs are used. Then, to check the quality of the approximation, the results obtained in the two cases are compared on the training set, and later on the test set. For a fair comparison, the same training set is used in both cases, and later, the same test set is used to compare the generalization capabilities of the two trained models.

4   Simulations

The target function used in Simulation 1 (for which $D = 1$) is defined as

$$f(x; \theta) = 0.6 \exp\left(-\frac{(x - 0.2)^2}{\theta^2}\right) + 0.4 \exp\left(-\frac{(x - 0.5)^2}{\theta^2}\right) + \exp\left(-\frac{(x - 0.8)^2}{\theta^2}\right),$$
(6)

where $x \in [0, 1]$, and $\theta > 0$ is a scalar which directly determines the complexity of f. In the case of Simulation 2 (for which $D > 1$), it is defined as

$$f(\mathbf{x}; \theta) = 0.6 \exp\left(-\frac{(x_1 - 0.2)^2}{\theta^2}\right) + 0.4 \exp\left(-\frac{(x_1 - 0.5)^2}{\theta^2}\right) + \exp\left(-\frac{(x_1 - 0.8)^2}{\theta^2}\right),$$
(7)

where $\mathbf{x} \in [0, 1]^D$, i.e., the target function depends only on the first component x_1 of the feature vector $\mathbf{x}$ (but this is not known a-priori by the random neural network). This target function was chosen because it belongs, for $C > 0$ large enough and $D' = 1$, to the family $\Gamma_{[0,1]^D, D', C}$ of D-variable functions on the hypercube $[0, 1]^D$ whose actual dependence is only on D' of such variables (whose identity is not known a-priori by the network), and which satisfies a suitable smoothness condition, related to the choice of C (see [5] for the precise definition). In the previous work [5], it was proved that (one-hidden-layer) non-random neural networks (i.e., having optimizable inner parameters of their computational units) have a better approximation capability of functions belonging to $\Gamma_{[0,1]^D, D', C}$ than linear combinations of fixed basis functions. This holds, loosely speaking, because the computational units of such neural networks are flexible enough to be matched each time to the specific subset of D' variables associated with every element of $\Gamma_{[0,1]^D, D', C}$, via suitable choices of their inner parameters. Nevertheless, this flexibility disappears when a random neural network is considered, since the inner parameters of its computational units are fixed once they have been randomly extracted, hence they are not optimizable.

Simulation 1: One-Dimensional Function Approximation. We set $\theta = 0.05$ and sample 1000 instances $\{x_i, f(x_i)\}_{i=1}^{1000}$ based on a regularly spaced grid on [0,1], then randomly (and uniformly) select $N = 500$ samples as the training set, whereas the remaining samples are used for test.

Case 1: Using the Hyperbolic Tangent Sigmoidal Function. We test the performance of two random models with $\lambda = 1$ and $\lambda = 10$, respectively, with different numbers of M of hidden neurons. For all the simulations, the sigmoidal activation function $\sigma(z) = \frac{1}{1+\exp(-z)}$ is used. Figure 2 shows the training and test approximation results for four different learner models, as reported respectively in (a) and (b) for the model built with $\lambda = 1, M = 100$, in (c) and (d) for the model built with $\lambda = 1, M = 500$, in (e) and (f) for the model built with $\lambda = 1, M = 10000$, and in (g) and (h) for the model built with $\lambda = 10, M = 200$. It is clear that $\lambda = 1$ does *not* work at all for this simple function approximation problem, even when the number of hidden nodes is sufficiently large. In contrast, the model built with $\lambda = 100$ and trained with $M = 200$ shows a very good learning and generalization capability. On the other hand, based on our empirical experience, some values larger than 1, such as $\lambda = 50, 100, 150, 200$, also work favorably on this regression task, implying that the setting of λ has a strong impact on the expressive power of the resulting randomized learner model.

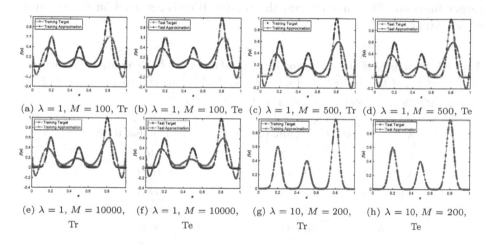

(a) $\lambda = 1, M = 100$, Tr   (b) $\lambda = 1, M = 100$, Te   (c) $\lambda = 1, M = 500$, Tr   (d) $\lambda = 1, M = 500$, Te

(e) $\lambda = 1, M = 10000$, Tr   (f) $\lambda = 1, M = 10000$, Te   (g) $\lambda = 10, M = 200$, Tr   (h) $\lambda = 10, M = 200$, Te

Fig. 2. Performance visualization for training (Tr) and testing (Te) results for random neural network models for various combinations of λ and M: (a–b) $\lambda = 1, M = 100$; (c–d) $\lambda = 1, M = 500$; (e–f) $\lambda = 1, M = 10000$; (g–h) $\lambda = 10, M = 200$.

Case 2: Using the Polynomial Approximation. We investigate the performance of two random neural network models with $\lambda = 1$ and $\lambda = 10$, respectively, where the polynomial approximation of the activation function is used for all the simulations. For simplicity, in this case, we only consider $M = 200$. As shown in Fig. 3, the training and testing performances of the random model based on the polynomial approximation of the activation function are quite similar to those of the model based on the sigmoidal activation function, confirming the good quality of the approximation constructed in line with the procedure reported in Sect. 3. Since the computation of the rank of a matrix may suffer from numerical issues, to verify Proposition 1, we calculate an "approximate" rank of $\mathbf{H}$ in MATLAB in the following way. First, we run the command $svd(\mathbf{H})$, which returns the singular values $\{v_1, v_2, \ldots, v_R\}$ of $\mathbf{H} \in \mathbb{R}^{N \times M}$, where $R \leq \min\{N, M\}$. Then, the number of "largest" singular values (hence, the approximate rank) is selected in the following way:

$$\widehat{\text{rank}}(\mathbf{H}) := \text{Cardinality}\{r|v_r > \max\{v_1, v_2, \ldots, v_R\}/S, r = 1, 2, \ldots, R\}, \quad (8)$$

where we set $S = 100$ in the simulations. Figure 4 shows an example of a singular value distribution for two random realizations of matrix $\mathbf{H}$, which clarifies the idea behind the approximation above. Table 1 shows the records of approximate rank values for the hidden output matrix $\mathbf{H}$ (for the case in which the polynomial approximation of the activation function is used), in which we can find that the simulation results are consistent with Proposition 1. In this case, it can be seen from the table that, by increasing λ, also the "effective dimension" of the feature space associated with the hidden output layer tends to increase, providing a better approximation capability of the network with respect to the target function. This may explain the smaller RMSE achieved on the training set for larger λ.

Table 1. Summary of the approximate rank values of the hidden output matrix $\mathbf{H} \in \mathbb{R}^{N \times M}$, of P°, of the upper bound $\min\left\{M, N, \binom{D+P^\circ}{P^\circ}\right\}$ on the rank of $\mathbf{H}$, and of the training RMSE: $N = 500$, $M = 200$, $L = 2\lambda + 2$, $\varepsilon = 10^{-4}$.

λ	$\widehat{\text{rank}}(\mathbf{H})$	P°	$\min\left\{M, N, \binom{D+P^\circ}{P^\circ}\right\}$	Training RMSE
$\lambda = 1$	2	6	7	0.2103
$\lambda = 3$	3	10	11	0.1609
$\lambda = 5$	3	14	15	0.0908
$\lambda = 10$	4	22	23	0.0641
$\lambda = 15$	5	30	31	0.0233
$\lambda = 20$	6	38	39	0.0170

Simulation 2: Multi-dimensional Function Approximation. To further verify our theoretical result reported in Proposition 1, we extend the 1-D regression task studied in Simulation 1 to a multi-dimensional function approximation problem (with the target function reported in Eq. (7)), via artificially including

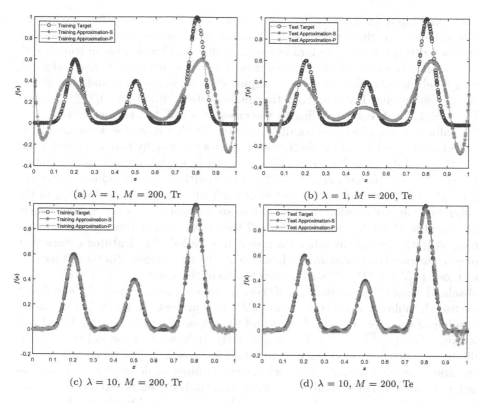

Fig. 3. Performance visualization for training (Tr) and testing (Te) results for random neural network models with $\lambda = 1$ and $\lambda = 10$, respectively, for $D = 1$ (i.e., for Simulation 1, Case 2). In the figure, "S" and "P" represent, respectively, the cases in which the hyperbolic tangent sigmoidal activation function and its polynomial approximation are used: (a–b) $\lambda = 1, M = 200, L = 4, \Delta L = 2, \varepsilon = 10^{-7}, P = 10$; (c-d) $\lambda = 10, M = 200, L = 22, \Delta L = 2, \varepsilon = 10^{-7}, P = 54$.

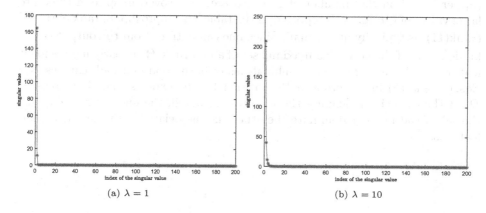

Fig. 4. Distribution of the singular values for two random realizations of $\mathbf{H}$: (a) for $\lambda = 1$; (b) for $\lambda = 10$, respectively.

additional input features. Concretely and without loss of generality, we investigate the cases in which $D = 2, 3, 4, 5$, that is, additional features are included as inputs together with the original feature x_1, while still keeping the output $f(\mathbf{x}, \theta)$ as a scalar. In other words, the additional features are only "noisy features", completely uncorrelated with the output. For simplicity, we randomly generate the additional features from the uniform distribution on $[0, 1]^{D-1}$, where $D - 1 = 1, 2, 3, 4$, corresponding to the cases $D = 2, 3, 4, 5$, respectively.

Table 2 summarizes the results obtained. In this case, the increase in the "effective dimension" of the feature spaces does not usually help in reducing the training RMSE. In order to explain the difference with respect to Simulation 1 (see the next paragraph), the following definitions are introduced. One can call "good features" those that are associated with monomials only in x_1 in the polynomial approximation (in total, there are at most $P+1$ such features, where the number $P + 1$ is obtained when all the coefficients of these monomials are nonzero), whereas all the other features can be called "bad features", since they refer to monomials containing at least one of the noisy inputs (in total, there are at most $\binom{D+P}{P} - (P + 1)$ such features, where the number $\binom{D+P}{P} - (P + 1)$ is obtained when all the coefficients of these monomials are nonzero). For simplicity, we use the abbreviations "GF" and "BF" to represent the upper bound on the number of good features ($:= P + 1$) and the upper bound on the number of bad features ($:= \binom{D+P}{P} - (P + 1)$), respectively. It is worth mentioning that this distinction between good features and bad features is highly dependent on the specific simulation scenario, in which the target function depends on one variable but not on the other variables. However, this analysis can be extended to other target functions belonging to the same class $\Gamma_{[0,1]^D, 1, C}$. Finally, in the setting considered in Case 2 of Simulation 1, one has $GF = P + 1$ and $BF = 0$, i.e., there are only good features (see Table 1 for the values assumed by the optimal P in the various cases).

Table 2 shows that, by increasing D, the ratio $\frac{GF}{GF+BF}$ is decreasing to 0, i.e., the (upper bound on the) number of bad features tends to dominate the (upper bound on the) number of good features. Moreover, in spite of the quite large values of GF and BF reported in the table, the approximate rank obtained ($\widehat{\text{rank}}(\mathbf{H})$) is typically quite small. Since one can extract from the output of the hidden layer of the network a maximal set of about $\widehat{\text{rank}}(\mathbf{H})$ linearly independent features, and these are linear combinations of both good and bad features (see Eqs. (4) and (5) in the proof of Proposition 1), one expects that by increasing D, of the coefficients defining the features extracted, the ones associated with the set of bad features dominate the other ones associated with the set of good features.

Table 2. Summary of the approximate rank values of the hidden output matrix $\mathbf{H} \in \mathbb{R}^{N \times M}$, of P°, of GF, of BF, and of the upper bound $\min\left\{M, N, \binom{D+P^\circ}{P^\circ}\right\}$ on the rank of $\mathbf{H}$. $N = 500$, $M = 200$, $\lambda = 1$, $L = (D+1)\lambda + 2$, $\Delta L = 2$, $\varepsilon = 10^{-4}$. e_1 stands for the training RMSE of the random neural network model based on the polynomial activation function, while e_2 stands for the training RMSE of the random neural network model based on the sigmoidal activation function.

D	$\widehat{\text{rank}}(\mathbf{H})$	P°	$\min\left\{M, N, \binom{D+P^\circ}{P^\circ}\right\}$	GF	BF	$\frac{GF}{GF+BF}$	e_1	e_2
$D = 2$	3	6	28	7	21	0.3333	0.1724	0.1430
$D = 3$	4	8	165	9	156	0.0577	0.1838	0.1507
$D = 4$	5	8	200	9	486	0.0185	0.1620	0.1589
$D = 5$	6	10	200	11	2992	0.0048	0.1637	0.1617

5 Conclusions

In this work, we analyzed the "effective dimension" of the output of the hidden layer of a one-hidden-layer neural network with random inner weights. Our analysis has been based on a polynomial approximation of the sigmoidal activation function of the network, whose degree has been chosen by taking into account both a desired upper bound on the approximation error, an upper bound λ both on the size of the inner weights of the network and on the size of its inputs, and the input dimension D. Our analysis is limited to explaining the behavior of the trained network on the training set, when the D-variable target function depends only on one of its inputs. As a future investigation, we plan to also explain the generalization capability of the trained neural network as a function of D and λ, and to investigate the case in which the target function depends on two or more among its inputs (whose identities are not known in advance), and the case in which its approximation is achieved by using a neural network with random inner weights having two or more hidden layers. Finally, although only the hyperbolic tangent has been used as a case study, our approach based on an optimized polynomial approximation could be applied also to other activation functions which are commonly used in the context of feedforward neural networks [11].

References

1. Cybenko, G.: Approximation by superposition of a sigmoidal function. Math. Control Sig. Syst. **2**, 303–314 (1989)
2. DasGupta, B., Schnitger, G.: The power of approximation: a comparison of activation functions. In: Advances in Neural Information Processing Systems (NIPS), pp. 615–622 (1992)
3. Fan, J., Udell, M.: Online high rank matrix completion. In: Proceedings of the IEEE/CVF Conference on Computer Vision and Pattern Recognition (CVPR), pp. 8690–8698 (2019)

4. Fu, A.M., Wang, X.Z., He, Y.L., Wang, L.S.: A study on residence error of training an extreme learning machine and its application to evolutionary algorithms. Neurocomputing **146**, 75–82 (2014)
5. Gnecco, G.: A comparison between fixed-basis and variable-basis schemes for function approximation and functional optimization. J. Appl. Math. **2012**, 17 (2012). Article ID 806945
6. Igelnik, B., Pao, Y.-H.: Stochastic choice of basis functions in adaptive function approximation and the functional-link net. IEEE Trans. Neural Netw. **6**, 1320–1329 (1995)
7. Leshno, M., Lin, V.Y., Pinkus, A., Schocken, S.: Multilayer feedforward networks with a nonpolynomial activation function can approximate any function. Neural Netw. **6**, 861–867 (1993)
8. Li, M., Wang, D.: Insights into randomized algorithms for neural networks: practical issues and common pitfalls. Inf. Sci. **382**, 170–178 (2017)
9. Piazza, F., Uncini, A., Zenobi, M.: Artificial neural networks with adaptive polynomial activation function. In: Proceedings of the International Joint Conference on Neural Networks (IJCNN), pp. 343–348 (1992)
10. Sonoda, S., Li, M., Cao, F., Huang, C., Wang, Y.G.: On the approximation lower bound for neural nets with random weights. arXiv preprint arXiv:2008.08427. https://arxiv.org/abs/2008.08427 (2020)
11. Szandała, T.: Review and comparison of commonly used activation functions for deep neural networks. In: Bhoi, A.K., Mallick, P.K., Liu, C.-M., Balas, V.E. (eds.) Bio-inspired Neurocomputing. SCI, vol. 903, pp. 203–224. Springer, Singapore (2021). https://doi.org/10.1007/978-981-15-5495-7_11
12. Vlček, M.: Chebyshev polynomial approximation for activation sigmoid function. Neural Netw. World **4**, 287–393 (2012)

Applications

De Novo Molecular Generation with Stacked Adversarial Model

Yuansan Liu[✉][iD] and James Bailey[iD]

The University of Melbourne, Melbourne, VIC, Australia
yuansanl@student.unimelb.edu.au, baileyj@unimelb.edu.au

Abstract. Generating novel drug molecules with desired biological properties is a time consuming and complex task. Conditional generative adversarial models have recently been proposed as promising approaches for de novo drug design. In this paper, we propose a new generative model which extends an existing adversarial autoencoder (AAE) based model by stacking two models together. Our stacked approach generates more valid molecules, as well as molecules that are more similar to known drugs. We break down this challenging task into two sub-problems. A first stage model to learn primitive features from the molecules and gene expression data. A second stage model then takes these features to learn properties of the molecules and refine more valid molecules. Experiments and comparison to baseline methods on the LINCS L1000 dataset demonstrate that our proposed model has promising performance for molecular generation.

Keywords: De novo · Molecule generation · Adversarial autoencoder · Stacking

1 Introduction

During recent years, there has been great pressure on the pharmaceutical industry's productivity. To address this challenge, machine learning (ML) is being widely adopted in the biomedicine area including drug generation [11]. For drug generation, researchers have focused mainly on conditional generative models, especially adversarial models like Generative Adversarial Networks (GANs) and Adversarial Autoencoders (AAE). Different from normal ones, a conditional generative model can learn a conditional distribution of a molecular structure with given properties, in order to generate molecules with specific properties. The adversarial training procedure facilitates the model to automatically learn the rules of valid structures and map them to latent representations. With such approaches, the range of candidate compounds can be narrowed down and ML generated molecule structures can be more valid.

De novo molecular generation is an iterative process which designs new molecules using the structures of receptor proteins. Several recent works have studied such generation with desired bioactivity properties by using generative adversarial models, including [17] which proposed a new AAE based model

© Springer Nature Switzerland AG 2022
G. Long et al. (Eds.): AI 2021, LNAI 13151, pp. 143–154, 2022.
https://doi.org/10.1007/978-3-030-97546-3_12

named the Bidirectional Adversarial Autoencoder(BiAAE), our main contribution in this paper is an enhancement of it, where we show how to effectively adapt the stacking method used in [22] to a new stacking method that works well for the BiAAE. By implementing this new stacking method, performance improves substantially, especially in the validity of the generation and the similarity with known compounds. Thus the generations have more likelihood to be biologically meaningful, potentially making it possible to increase the productivity of drug design.

This paper is organized as follows: Sect. 2 presents a brief literature review. In Sect. 3 we will present our proposed model. Section 4 outlines experiments to evaluate our new model and compare with baselines. Finally, Sect. 5 concludes the paper.

2   Related Works

2.1   Generative Adversarial Models

Deep learning technologies have been applied in many areas over the last decade, among them, deep generative models have shown superior performance in image and text processing. Variational autoencoders (VAE) use a Bayesian method to learn the latent representations in order to turn the classic autoencoders into generative models [6], generative adversarial networks(GAN) use an adversarial approach in the training procedure to shape the output distribution [3], adversarial autoencoders(AAE) combine the previous two models together [10]. There are also conditional extensions from these models: a conditional GAN (CGAN) concatenates label information into the generator's input noise to make GANs capable of more complex generation tasks [13], to improve the quality of generation, some researchers change the structure of the basic model: StackGAN stacked two GANs together to produce realistic images [22].

2.2   Generative Models for Drug Discovery

Successes in machine learning for graphs and text has led to new applications of generative models in the drug discovery area. Initially, several works investigated VAE like model usage on generating simplified molecular-input line-entry system (SMILES) [20] representation of molecules, the first of them being CharacterVAE [4]. Apart from VAEs, GANs have also been used for this task, LatentGAN [15] combined an autoencoder and GAN for the de novo drug design task. In recent years, conditional generative models have been used to provide guidance for molecular generation in order to generate molecules with desired properties. In [7] the authors proposed a conditional graph generative model to manage de novo molecular design, [8] developed a generative model based on conditional VAE (CVAE) for molecular generation, [12] conditioned a 3D binding pocket on the CVAE to generate 3D molecular structures for the first time.

To make the generated molecules biologically meaningful, gene expression data, which proved to be useful in identifying novel active molecules [2], roughly speaking, gene expression data records the activity (or change of activity) of genes within a cell. Researchers have thus started to condition generative models with gene expression data, e.g. in [14], a conditional WGAN is used for de novo generation of hit-like molecules from gene expression signatures.

[17] proposed an AAE based model BiAAE, which learns shared features between drug molecules and gene expression changes, to generate molecules with desired transcriptome changes. The latent codes of molecule x and gene expression change y are divided into unique part u and common part c, u represents the information that could be extracted only from x or y, and c is the information present in both x and y, hence, u is independent of c. To generate new synthetic data, the model samples unique parts u_x, u_y and common parts c independently from posterior distributions $G_x(x|c, u_x), G_y(y|c, u_y)$. Inference networks are used to predict latent codes: u_x, u_y, c and train the model: $E_x(u_x|x), E_y(u_y|y), E_x(c|x) = E_y(c|y) = E(c|x, y)$. The architecture of the BiAAE is shown in the Fig. 1, deterministic encoders E_x, E_y are used to hypothesize the latent representations of input data, and two deterministic decoders G_x, G_y rebuild x, y from their latent representations. Our model extended this work and achieved a better result, we will discuss it from next section.

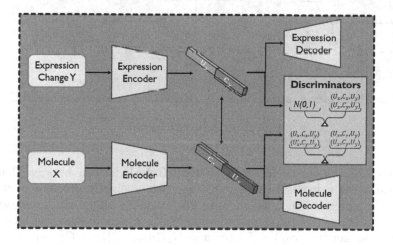

Fig. 1. BiAAE architecture

3   Stacked Bidirectional Adversarial Autoencoder

It has been shown that stacking two or more models together can facilitate generating better synthetic samples in image generation task using GAN. In molecular generation, we can also expect for a similar effect.

The targets of the adversarial training procedure are different between GAN and AAE. In GAN, the adversarial procedure is implemented over the generated samples, whereas in AAE, it is implemented over latent codes. This makes the stacking method of StackGAN inappropriate for the BiAAE. To solve this problem, we modify the original method: instead of the final output of the first stage, we use latent codes of condition y in the first stage, together with one more learning of x, we get latent codes for the second stage. Specifically, the second stage does not have an expression encoder, the latent codes of y are the ones generated by the first stage. For molecule data, we used the same learning procedure as the first stage to let it learn from molecules again to refine the learning outcome of the first stage, which is the common part of the x, y. With these modifications, we can now stack the BiAAE together to form the Stacked BiAAE (SBiAAE).

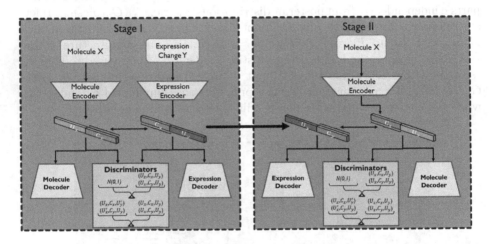

Fig. 2. SBiAAE architecture

Figure 2 shows the architecture of the SBiAAE, it can be seen that the stage one is the same as BiAAE and stage two is slightly different as it does not have a expression encoder but uses first stage's y latent codes instead. Let $E_{ix,y}, G_{ix,y}, D_i, z_{ix,y} = (u_{ix,y}, c_{ix,y})$, where $i = 1, 2$, denote each part in the ith stage, we can get:$(u_{2x}, c_{2x}) \sim E_{2x}(x), x = G_{2x}(u_{2x}, c_{2x}), y = G_{2y}(u_{1y}, c_{1y})$, and the objective function of the stacked model has two stage, the first stage contains four parts:

- **Shared Loss**: ensures the common parts extract from x and y close to each other.

$$\mathcal{L}_{1share} = \mathbb{E}_{x,y \sim p_d(x,y)} \|c_{1x} - c_{1y}\|_2^2 \tag{1}$$

- **Reconstruction Loss**: ensures the decoders can reconstruct the x, y from their latent codes: u_x, c_x, u_y, c_y. Here the model added a cross-reconstruction loss, the decoders also used the common part from another one, for example, (u_x, c_y) for G_x.

$$\mathcal{L}_{rec}^x = \mathbb{E}_{x \sim p_d(x)} l_{rec}^x(x, G_{1x}(u_{1x}, c_{1x})) + \mathbb{E}_{x,y \sim p_d(x,y)} l_{rec}^x(x, G_{1x}(u_{1x}, c_{1y})) \quad (2)$$

$$\mathcal{L}_{rec}^y = \mathbb{E}_{y \sim p_d(y)} l_{rec}^y(y, G_{1y}(u_{1y}, c_{1y})) + \mathbb{E}_{x,y \sim p_d(x,y)} l_{rec}^y(y, G_{1y}(u_{1y}, c_{1x})) \quad (3)$$

where $l_{rec}^{x,y}$ are similarity measures between original and reconstruct data.

- **Adversarial Loss:** uses a Jensen-Shannon Divergence(JSD) to guide the latent codes $z_{x,y} = (c_{x,y}, u_{x,y})$ to match an arbitrary prior distribution $\mathcal{N}(0,1)$, and encourage distributions $p(u_{x,y}), p(c_{x,y})$ to be independent.

$$\mathcal{L}_{1adv} = \mathbb{E}_{u_{1x}', c_{1x}', u_{1y}' \sim p(u_{1x}, c_{1x}, u_{1y})} log D(u_{1x}', c_{1x}', u_{1y}')$$
$$+ \mathbb{E}_{u_{1x}', c_{1y}', u_{1y}' \sim p(u_{1x}, c_{1y}, u_{1y})} log D_1(u_{1x}', c_{1y}', u_{1y}')$$
$$+ \mathbb{E}_{x,y \sim p_d(x,y)} log(1 - D_1(u_{1x}, c_{1x}, u_{1y}))$$
$$+ \mathbb{E}_{x,y \sim p_d(x,y)} log(1 - D_1(u_{1y}, c_{1y}, u_{1x})) \quad (4)$$

- **Independence Loss:** explicitly encourages the independence of u_x from (u_y, c_y) and u_y from (u_x, c_x).

$$\mathcal{L}_{ind} = \mathbb{E}_{x,y \sim p_d(x,y)} \mathbb{E}_{y' \sim p_d(y)} [log D_1(u_{1x}, c_{1x}, u_{1y}) + log(1 - D_1(u_{1x}, c_{1x}, u_{1y}'))]$$
$$+ \mathbb{E}_{x,y \sim p_d(x,y)} \mathbb{E}_{x' \sim p_d(x)} [log D_1(u_{1x}, c_{1y}, u_{1y}) + log(1 - D(u_{1x}', c_{1y}, u_{1y}))] \quad (5)$$

where u_{1x}', u_{1y}' are obtained by shuffling u_{1x}, u_{1y} in each batch.

The optimization problem is a minimax problem over the combination of (1) to (5):

$$\min_{E_{1x,y}, G_{1x,y}} \max_{D_1} \lambda_1 \mathcal{L}_{share} + \lambda_2 \mathcal{L}_{rec}^x + \lambda_3 \mathcal{L}_{rec}^y + \mathcal{L}_{adv} + \mathcal{L}_{ind}$$

The hyperparameters $\lambda_{1,2,3}$ are used to balance different objectives.

Similar to the first stage, the objective functions of the second stage model are also divided into four parts:

- **Shared Loss:**

$$\mathcal{L}_{share} = \mathbb{E}_{x,y \sim p_d(x,y)} \|c_{2x} - c_{1y}\|_2^2 \quad (6)$$

- **Reconstruction Loss:**

$$\mathcal{L}_{rec}^x = \mathbb{E}_{x \sim p_d(x)} l_{rec}^x(x, G_{2x}(u_{2x}, c_{2x})) + \mathbb{E}_{x,y \sim p_d(x,y)} l_{rec}^x(x, G_{2x}(u_{2x}, c_{1y})) \quad (7)$$

$$\mathcal{L}_{rec}^y = \mathbb{E}_{y \sim p_d(y)} l_{rec}^y(y, G_{2y}(u_{1y}, c_{1y})) + \mathbb{E}_{x,y \sim p_d(x,y)} l_{rec}^y(y, G_{2y}(u_{1y}, c_{2x})) \quad (8)$$

- **Adversarial Loss:**

$$\mathcal{L}_{adv} = \mathbb{E}_{u_{2x}', c_{2x}', u_{1y}' \sim p(u_{2x}, c_{2x}, u_{1y})} log D_2(u_{2x}', c_{2x}', u_{1y}')$$
$$+ \mathbb{E}_{u_{2x}', c_{1y}', u_{1y}' \sim p(u_{2x}, c_{1y}, u_{1y})} log D_2(u_{2x}', c_{1y}', u_{1y}')$$
$$+ \mathbb{E}_{x,y \sim p_d(x,y)} log(1 - D_2(u_{2x}, c_{2x}, u_{1y}))$$
$$+ \mathbb{E}_{x,y \sim p_d(x,y)} log(1 - D_2(u_{2x}, c_{1y}, u_{1y})) \quad (9)$$

- **Independence Loss:**

$$\mathcal{L}_{ind} = \mathbb{E}_{x,y \sim p_d(x,y)} \mathbb{E}_{y' \sim p_d(y)} [log D_2(u_{2x}, c_{2x}, u_{1y}) + log(1 - D_2(u_{2x}, c_{2x}, u_{1y}'))]$$
$$+ \mathbb{E}_{x,y \sim p_d(x,y)} \mathbb{E}_{x' \sim p_d(x)} [log D_2(u_{2x}, c_{1y}, u_{1y}) + log(1 - D_2(u_{2x}', c_{1y}, u_{1y}))] \quad (10)$$

Combine the Eqs. (6) to (10), we can get the optimization problem for the second stage:

$$\min_{E_{2x,y},G_{2x,y}} \max_{D_2} \lambda_1\mathcal{L}_{2share} + \lambda_2\mathcal{L}^x_{2rec} + \lambda_3\mathcal{L}^y_{2rec} + \mathcal{L}_{2adv} + \mathcal{L}_{2ind}$$

4 Experiments

The original BiAAE model and the modified SBiAAE model are evaluated on two different datasets. An experiment on Noisy MNIST dataset is used as a preliminary evaluation from which we can test if the model has the potential to improve the original model. We then run the experiment on the LINCS L1000 molecular database to test the model's performance when conditioned using gene expression profiles.

4.1 Dataset Description

- **Noisy MNIST**:
  The Noisy MNIST dataset was generated using the MNIST dataset [19]. In general, the images pair (x, y) contain same digit with different angles and y has strong additive noise. Thus, the only common information in (x, y) is the digit they contain, the joint distribution $p_{xy}(x, y)$ should represent this digit.
- **LINCS L1000**:
  The dataset is from the Library of Integrated Network-based Cellular Signatures (LINCS) L1000 project [18]. The dataset is organized by cell lines, times, doses, molecules, and perturbagens. For each cell, it lists the gene expressions before and after (ge_a, ge_b) it reacts with the given molecule, so we can obtain the gene expression changes for a given molecule by subtracting these two expressions.

4.2 Experimental Setup

Noisy MNIST. The whole Noisy MNIST dataset was split into three parts: 50000 training samples, 10000 validation samples and 10000 testing samples. The batch size was set to 128 with a learning rate 0.0003. The input data x, y was encoded to a 16-dimensional tensor with 12-dimensional u_x, u_y and 4-dimensional c. The same encoders for both x, y, each consisting of two convolutional layers with a 0.2 dropout rate, and rectified linear unit (ReLU) as activation function, then followed by three fully connected layers, with LeakyReLU activation function and batch normalization. The decoder has two fully connected layers with the exponential linear unit (ELU) activation function, followed by three transposed convolutional layers. The discriminator is a multilayer perceptron (MLP) with hidden layers of 1024 and 512 neurons. Balance weight $\lambda_{1,2,3}$ are set to 0.1, 10, and 1 respectively. The second stage is the same as the first one but without an encoder for y. The optimizer for the model is Adam with $\beta_1 = 0.5, \beta_2 = 0.9$ for adversarial training and $\beta_1 = 0.99, 0.999$ for others.

Gene Expression. For LINCS 1000 dataset, the training set contains experiments characterized by the control (ge_a) and perturbation (ge_b) induced gene expression profiles for each cell line. The molecules were represented by SMILES strings. The dataset was preprocessed based on Lipinski's rule of five [9] and its extensions.

The molecular encoder for X took a pretrained RNN encoder's two-layers gated recurrent unit (GRU) as an initial part, followed by an fine-tuned MLP as second part. The expression encoder for $Y = (\Delta ge, \eta)$ embedded $\Delta ge = ge_b - ge_a$ using a two-layers MLP and concatenated the resulting hidden codes with logarithm of the concentration value η, processed it to another MLP to get the final representation. The decoders for two objects were built symmetrically to the corresponding encoders. The second stage used the same structure except the expression encoder, which does not exist, and the latent codes of the gene expression Y in this stage are the results of the first stage expression encoder.

4.3   Experimental Evaluations

Metrics

- **Accuracy**:
  Accuracy is mainly used for evaluation on the Noisy MNIST experiment, the ratio between correction generation and total number generated is the accuracy of the model.
- **Mutual Information(MI)**:
  We calculated the mutual information using MINE [1], this score can represent the ability of the encoders to extract relevant information.
- **Validity**:
  Validity is the proportion between valid number and total number, it evaluates how often the model produces valid molecule.
- **Overall Similarity**:
  The similarity between generated molecules and their templates are calculated using Tanimoto similarity of their Extended Connectivity Fingerprints(ECFPs) [16]. $\frac{\sum T(A,B)}{N}, T(A,B) = \frac{A \cap B}{A+B-A \cap B}$. Where A, B are ECFPs for generated and template molecules, T is Tanimoto similarity, N is total number of valid generation.
- **Diversity**:
  $1 - \frac{1}{N} \sum_{i,j>i} T(m_i, m_j)$ for N pairs of valid generated molecules, normally $N = \binom{n}{2}$ where n is total number of valid generation.

Noisy MNIST Experiment. The experiment run over Noisy MNIST dataset is intended to test model performance on common information extraction, this ability should be reflected by the accuracy and mutual information scores. We use $MI(z_x, c_y | y)$ for mutual information score, it represents how much the c_y can indicate about z_x. The only common thing between them is c_y itself, so, higher MI score means the encoder produced more desirable latent codes. The quantitative results for several models run on the Noisy MNIST shown in the Table 1, the UniAAE is the unidirectional version of BiAAE. SAAE is conditional AAE mentioned in [10], we use $MI(z_x, c|y)$ since it cannot extract the common parts from the latent codes explicitly. Examples of some generated images from BiAAE(left) and SBiAAE(right) are shown in the Fig. 3. Comparing two figures, we can observe that samples generated by BiAAE still contain some wrong digits, whereas most of the SBiAAE generations are correct digits.

Table 1. Noisy MNIST results

Model	Accuracy	$MI(z_x, c_y|y)$	$MI(z_x, c|y)$
Stacked BiAAE	**68.06**	**1.729**	–
BiAAE	61.34	1.432	–
UniAAE	50.11	1.550	–
SAAE	45.46	–	**1.673**

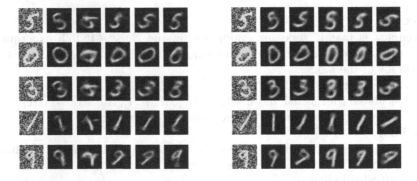

Fig. 3. Generated figures by BiAAE and SBiAAE

From the results in Table 1 and examples in Fig. 3, we can see the SBiAAE did well in extracting digits from the image pairs as intended. Based on this performance, we can draw an initial conclusion that the stacked model is better at joint distribution learning for Noisy MNIST dataset, in next part we would run the experiment on gene expression dataset to check how well the model perform for our real task.

LINCS L1000 Experiment. The results from Noisy MNIST dataset gave us enough confidence to run the model on LINCS L1000 dataset.

In modern chemistry, a pharmacophore is a part of a molecular structure which can be used to represent an abstraction of the molecular features and is capable of inferring the affected genes, since it ensures the optimal molecule interactions with a single specific biological target so that it would trigger (or block) its biological response [21]. This makes the latent representations of pharmacophore and the affected proteins similar and hence in our joint distribution learning, the common part between the given molecule x and gene expression y can be the pharmacophore in the molecule and affected protein in gene expressions.

The mutual information used in this experiment is $MI(z_x, c_y|\Delta ge, \eta)$ which calculates the relevant information between molecular latent codes and common part of gene expressions extracted by the expression encoder. Together with overall similarity, they reveal the ability of the encoders for extracting common parts from molecules and gene expressions. The validity reflects how well the decoder learnt the rules of the molecular structure. As a de novo generation task, the model is also expected to keep a good diversity in generation while raising the similarity to the templates.

The results of models for molecular generation are shown in Table 2, in this part we only list two models: BiAAE and SBiAAE for direct comparison.

Table 2. LINCS L1000 results

Model	$MI(x, s_y|\Delta ge, \eta)$	Validity	Overall similarity	Diversity
BiAAE	0.28	64.7%	0.247	0.85
SBiAAE	0.29	69.1%	0.265	0.83

Examples of generated molecules together with their templates, which are active drugs in real world, are shown in Fig. 4. Here we listed the fingerprint similarities between the generations and corresponding templates that are calculated based on their ECFPs, the target proteins are also listed for each generated molecule. The main intuition for this presentation is the models are expected to generate some biologically meaningful molecules, thus by presenting the generated molecule and its template drug, we can show that these generated molecules indeed do have bioactivity. This is due to the similarity principle which states "structurally similar molecules tend to have similar properties in both physicochemical and biological ones" [5], and the pharmacophore's application on defining the essential features of one or more molecules with the same biological activity.

From Table 2 we can see the greatest improvement that our stacked model achieves is on generation validity. The stacking method allows the model to learn more from molecular data and, as intended, it learns more rules from the valid molecules and generates more valid molecules.

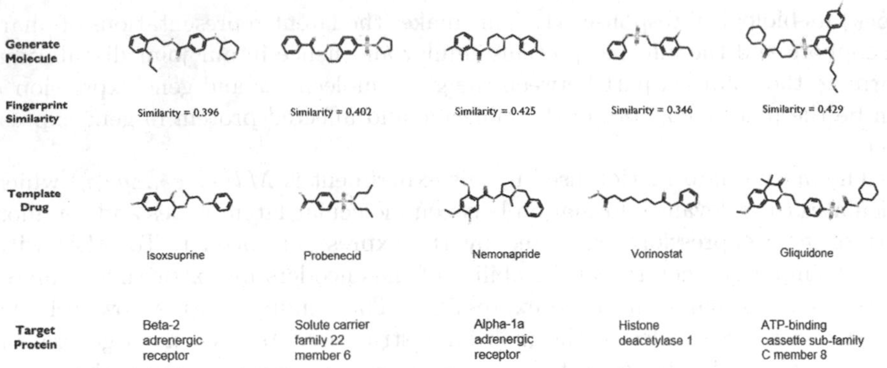

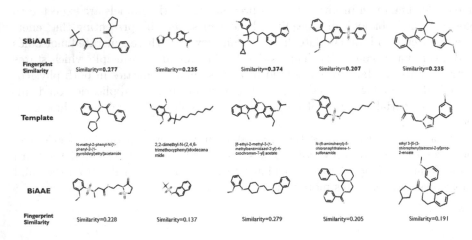

Generate Molecule					
Fingerprint Similarity	Similarity = 0.396	Similarity = 0.402	Similarity = 0.425	Similarity = 0.346	Similarity = 0.429
Template Drug	Isoxsuprine	Probenecid	Nemonapride	Vorinostat	Gliquidone
Target Protein	Beta-2 adrenergic receptor	Solute carrier family 22 member 6	Alpha-1a adrenergic receptor	Histone deacetylase 1	ATP-binding cassette sub-family C member 8

Fig. 4. Generated molecules with their drug templates

For common part extraction, the SBiAAE does improve the performance a little. The mutual information scores indicate encoders from stacked model extracted the common part slightly better than the original model, a similar result is also shown in the Overall Similarity. These two scores suggest the SBiAAE extracts something extra from the molecules and the gene expression changes, and the resulting common parts of gene expression changes contain more relevant information about the molecules, which as previously mentioned could be the pharmacophore of the molecule. In Fig. 5 we present a comparison between two models' generations, and the templates they based on. For better comparison, we also listed the similarity for each molecule. Some of the generations from SBiAAE are much more similar to the templates like the second and third columns.

Fig. 5. Generations of BiAAE and SBiAAE

In general, the stacked model SBiAAE improved the performance of the original BiAAE model, the most obvious improvement lies in the validity of the generated molecules. For common information extraction, the stacking method improved the original model, though it did not improve as much as for the Noisy MNIST experiment. Based on the generated samples, we can also say that the generated molecules might be biologically meaningful because of the improvements on the average similarity, the stacked model can have more chance to generate the bioactive molecules compared to the original model. Overall, for this dataset, we have evidence that SBiAAE performs better than BiAAE for de novo generation of desired molecules.

5 Conclusion

To conclude, in this project, we studied an existing model for de novo molecular generation named BiAAE, and investigated the machine learning technologies and biochemical knowledge related to it. Then, we developed a new stacking method derived from StackGAN to make it appropriate for the joint distribution learning task in BiAAE, with this method we stacked an other model on the original BiAAE and improved the performance of BiAAE on a molecular generation task. The main contribution of our work is the modified stacking method which made it possible for the new SBiAAE model to be more reliable for generating molecule.

References

1. Belghazi, M.I., et al.: Mine: mutual information neural estimation (2018)
2. De Wolf, H., et al.: High-throughput gene expression profiles to define drug similarity and predict compound activity. ASSAY Drug Dev. Technol. 16(3), 162–176 (2018). https://doi.org/10.1089/adt.2018.845
3. Goodfellow, I.J., et al.: Generative adversarial networks (2014)
4. Gómez-Bombarelli, R., et al.: Automatic chemical design using a data-driven continuous representation of molecules. ACS Cent. Sci. 4(2), 268–276 (2018). https://doi.org/10.1021/acscentsci.7b00572
5. Hendrickson, J.B.: Concepts and applications of molecular similarity. Science 252, 1189–1190 (1991)
6. Kingma, D.P., Welling, M.: Auto-encoding variational bayes (2013)
7. Li, Y., Zhang, L., Liu, Z.: Multi-objective de novo drug design with conditional graph generative model. J. Cheminform. 10(1), 1–24 (2018). https://doi.org/10.1186/s13321-018-0287-6
8. Lim, J., Ryu, S., Kim, J., Kim., W.Y.: Molecular generative model based on conditional variational autoencoder for de novo molecular design. J. Cheminform. 10 (2018). https://doi.org/10.1186/s13321-018-0286-7
9. Lipinski, C.A., Lombardo, F., Dominy, B.W., Feeney, P.J.: Experimental and computational approaches to estimate solubility and permeability in drug discovery and development settings. Adv. Drug Deliv. Rev. 46(1), 3–26 (2001). http://www.sciencedirect.com/science/article/pii/S0169409X00001290

10. Makhzani, A., Shlens, J., Jaitly, N., Goodfellow, I., Frey, B.: Adversarial autoencoders (2015)
11. Mamoshina, P., Vieira, A., Putin, E., Zhavoronkov, A.: Applications of deep learning in biomedicine. Mol. Pharm. **13**(5), 1445–1454 (2016). https://doi.org/10.1021/acs.molpharmaceut.5b00982. pMID: 27007977
12. Masuda, T., Ragoza, M., Koes, D.R.: Generating 3D molecular structures conditional on a receptor binding site with deep generative models (2020)
13. Mirza, M., Osindero, S.: Conditional generative adversarial nets (2014)
14. Méndez-Lucio, O., Baillif, B., Clevert, D., Rouquié, D., Wichard, J.: De novo generation of hit-like molecules from gene expression signatures using artificial intelligence. Nat. Commun. **11** (2020). https://doi.org/10.1038/s41467-019-13807-w
15. Prykhodko, O., et al.: A de novo molecular generation method using latent vector based generative adversarial network. J. Cheminform. **11**(1), 1–13 (2019). https://doi.org/10.1186/s13321-019-0397-9
16. Rogers, D., Hahn, M.: Extended-connectivity fingerprints. J. Chem. Inf. Modeling **50**(5), 742–754 (2010). https://doi.org/10.1021/ci100050t. pMID: 20426451
17. Shayakhmetov, R., et al.: Molecular generation for desired transcriptome changes with adversarial autoencoders. Frontiers Pharmacol. **11**, 269 (2020). https://www.frontiersin.org/article/10.3389/fphar.2020.00269
18. Subramanian, A., et al.: A next generation connectivity map: L1000 platform and the first 1,000,000 profiles. bioRxiv (2017). https://doi.org/10.1101/136168
19. Wang, W., Arora, R., Livescu, K., Bilmes, J.: On deep multi-view representation learning: objectives and optimization (2016)
20. Weininger, D.: Smiles, a chemical language and information system. 1. Introduction to methodology and encoding rules. J. Chem. Inf. Comput. Sci. **28**(1), 31–36 (1988). https://pubs.acs.org/doi/abs/10.1021/ci00057a005
21. Wermuth, C.G., Ganellin, C.R., Lindberg, P., Mitscher, L.A.: Glossary of terms used in medicinal chemistry (IUPAC recommendations 1998). Pure Appl. Chem. **70**(5), 1129–1143 (1998). https://doi.org/10.1351/pac199870051129
22. Zhang, H., et al.: StackGAN: text to photo-realistic image synthesis with stacked generative adversarial networks. In: 2017 IEEE International Conference on Computer Vision (ICCV), pp. 5908–5916 (2017)

Tailoring Contact Based Scoring Functions for Protein Structure Prediction

Rianon Zaman[1]([✉]), M. A. Hakim Newton[2]([✉]), Fereshteh Mataeimoghadam[1], and Abdul Sattar[1,2]

[1] School of ICT, Griffith University, Brisbane, Australia
{rianon.zaman,fereshteh.mataeimoghadam}@griffithuni.edu.au
[2] IIIS, Griffith University, Brisbane, Australia
{mahakim.newton,a.sattar}@griffith.edu.au

Abstract. Protein structure prediction (PSP) is a challenge in Bioinformatics. Given a protein's amino acid sequence, PSP involves finding its three dimensional native structure having the minimum free energy. Unfortunately, the search space is astronomical and the energy function is not known. Many PSP search algorithms develop their own proxy energy functions known as scoring functions using predicted contacts between amino acid residue pairs where two residues are said to be in contact if their distance in the native structure is within a given threshold. Scoring functions are crucial for search guidance since they allow evaluation of the generated structures. Unfortunately, existing contact based scoring functions have not been directly compared and which one among them is the best is not known. In this paper, our goal is to evaluate a number of existing contact based scoring functions within the same PSP search framework on the same set of benchmark proteins. Moreover, we also propose a number of contact based scoring function variants. Our proposed contact based scoring functions help our search algorithm to significantly outperform existing state-of-the-art PSP search algorithm, CGLFOLD that uses contact based scoring functions. We get 0.77Å average RMSD and 0.01 average GDT values improvement than CGLFOLD.

Keywords: Protein structure prediction · Search-based optimisation · Contact-based energy function

1 Introduction

Protein structure prediction (PSP) is a challenging problem in Bioinformatics. Proteins comprise amino acid (AA) sequences and fold into three dimensional structures to perform their functions. Given a protein's AA sequence, PSP involves finding its native structure that has the minimum free energy.

Energy functions have been developed based on molecular dynamics e.g. CHARMM [3]. Unfortunately, such energy functions involve all atomic details

© Springer Nature Switzerland AG 2022
G. Long et al. (Eds.): AI 2021, LNAI 13151, pp. 155–168, 2022.
https://doi.org/10.1007/978-3-030-97546-3_13

and so are computationally very expensive. Rosetta [8] is a popular energy function but involves 18 different energy components. Consequently, various other proxy energy functions known as scoring functions have been designed. In this context, contact based scoring functions have been used by many recent PSP search algorithms. Two amino acid residues of a protein are in contact if their distance in the native structure of the protein is at most 8Å. Contact based scoring functions are then developed to evaluate protein structures based on the deviations in the distances between residue pairs that are supposed to be in contact. Search algorithms then use the scoring functions to rank generated protein structures or conformations.

Machine learning algorithms such as SPOT-Contact [5], Restriplet [9], and TripletRes [10] predict contacts among residues. Search algorithms such as Pconsfold [16], CONFOLD [1], RBO Aleph [12], Unicon3D [2] and CGLFOLD [11] use contact based scoring functions. In this context, recent contact based scoring functions include modified Lorentz potential [12], soft square [1], square well [2,7], bounded potential [7], and cglfold [11]. However, these scoring functions have not been directly compared and which one among them is the best is not known.

In this paper, we evaluate the aforementioned five contact based scoring functions within the same PSP search framework on the same single set of benchmark proteins. Based on the results, we also propose four contact based scoring function variants. Our proposed contact based scoring functions help our search algorithm to significantly outperform existing state-of-the-art PSP search algorithm CGLFOLD [11] that uses a contact based scoring function.

The rest of the papers is organized as follows: Section 2 provide preliminaries of protein structures and our search framework; Sect. 3 describes existing contact based scoring functions as well as our proposed ones; Sect. 4 provides our experimental results and analyses; and Sect. 5 presents our conclusions.

2   Preliminaries

We briefly describe protein structure preliminaries and our search framework.

Protein Structures. Proteins comprise 20 types of AA and the AAs can appear in any order in any number of times. Moreover, AAs all have N, C^α, and C atoms in their main chains. Two successive AA residues in a protein are joined by a non-rotatable peptide bond formed between the C atom of the previous residue and the N atom of the next residue. The bond between N and C^α in an AA is rotatable and the rotation angle is denoted by ϕ. Similarly, the bond between C^α and C in an AA is also rotatable and the rotation angle is denoted by ψ. Both can take any value from $[-180°, +180°]$. Proteins exhibit certain local structures comprising successive residues. These local structures known as secondary structures are of three major types: helices, sheets, and coils. Among these, helices and sheets are rigid and normally have narrow ranges of ϕ and ψ values but coils are very flexible; hence, in this work, we mainly search for ϕ and ψ angles of the coil residues. Nevertheless, besides main chains, AAs have unique side chains (Glycine has no side chain) starting from C^α and having C^β as the first atom. Nevertheless, in the definition of contacts between residues, typically distances are measured between the C^β atoms (C^α for Glycine) of the two residues so that side chains are counted to some extent.

Search Framework. We use a constraint based local search (CBLS) framework to evaluate the existing and the proposed contact based energy functions. The search algorithm is implemented on top of a new python library named Koala, which draws concepts from a constraint based local search system named Kangaroo [15]. We briefly describe the steps of our search algorithm below:

1. Generate one initial conformation c using ϕ, ψ angles predicted for each residue of the protein by a machine learning algorithm.
2. Evaluate the conformation c using a contact based scoring function σ.
3. Select the residue pair $\langle i, j \rangle$ from c such that residues i and j are supposed to be in contact (as predicted by a machine learning algorithm) but their distance is the maximum in c among all such candidate residue pairs.
4. Select a residue k randomly from any coil (not helices and sheets since they are rigid) in between the selected residues i and j. Changing ϕ and ψ of the selected residue k might essentially bring residues i and j in contact.
5. Generate a number (e.g. 20) of neighbouring conformations by changing ϕ and ψ angles of the selected residue k. Consider up to $\pm\Delta$ with interval $\delta = 3$ for ϕ and ψ values where Δ is the mean absolute error of the machine learning algorithm used in Step 1 for the respective ϕ or ψ angle.
6. Evaluate the generated neigbouring conformations using the same contact based scoring function σ used in Step 2.
7. Accept the neighbouring conformation having the minimum score as the current conformation for the next iteration.
8. Return the best conformation found so far (in terms of scores) if the termination criterion is satisfied; otherwise, move to Step 3.

3   Scoring Functions

Assume d_{ij} is the distance and σ_{ij} is the score for a residue pair $\langle i, j \rangle$ in a conformation c having the score $\sigma = \sum \sigma_{ij}$. Also, assume p_{ij} be the probability that residues i and j are in contact in the native conformation.

3.1   Existing Scoring Functions

Figure 1 shows five existing contact based scoring functions. These functions are square well (sw) [2,7], bounded potential (bp) [7], modified Lorentz potential (mlp) [12], soft square (ss) [1], cglfold (cf) [11]. The parameter values used in the functions are as suggested by the respective methods using them.

From the charts of the five scoring functions in Fig. 1, notice that most of the scoring functions have a d_{ij} range with some least penalty value. Any d_{ij} below ≈ 3.8Å is highly penalised to avoid steric clash between residues. Also, any d_{ij} above ≈ 8Å is penalised to avoid not having contact while a contact is rather expected. The square well function does not penalise for steric clash ($d_{ij} \leq d_0 = 3.8$) but the other functions do. The modified Lorentz potential and the soft square functions become flat in large d_{ij} values. So these functions perhaps would not be able to provide effective search guidance when d_{ij} values are large since such values cannot be differentiated. The square well and the cglfold functions are very similar for large d_{ij} values but are different for small d_{ij} values. Moreover, both functions somewhat keep growing in the large d_{ij} values and so could provide some search guidance. The bounded potential function grows steadily

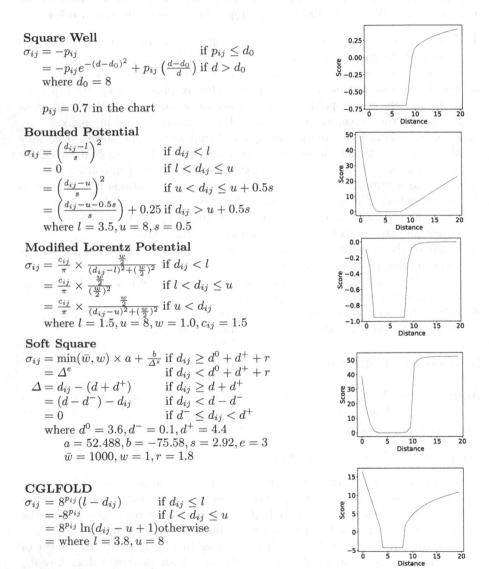

Square Well

$$\sigma_{ij} = -p_{ij} \qquad\qquad \text{if } p_{ij} \leq d_0$$
$$= -p_{ij}e^{-(d-d_0)^2} + p_{ij}\left(\frac{d-d_0}{d}\right) \text{ if } d > d_0$$
where $d_0 = 8$

$p_{ij} = 0.7$ in the chart

Bounded Potential

$$\sigma_{ij} = \left(\frac{d_{ij}-l}{s}\right)^2 \qquad\qquad \text{if } d_{ij} < l$$
$$= 0 \qquad\qquad\qquad \text{if } l < d_{ij} \leq u$$
$$= \left(\frac{d_{ij}-u}{s}\right)^2 \qquad\quad \text{if } u < d_{ij} \leq u + 0.5s$$
$$= \left(\frac{d_{ij}-u-0.5s}{s}\right) + 0.25 \text{ if } d_{ij} > u + 0.5s$$
where $l = 3.5, u = 8, s = 0.5$

Modified Lorentz Potential

$$\sigma_{ij} = \frac{c_{ij}}{\pi} \times \frac{\frac{w}{2}}{(d_{ij}-l)^2+(\frac{w}{2})^2} \text{ if } d_{ij} < l$$
$$= \frac{c_{ij}}{\pi} \times \frac{\frac{w}{2}}{(\frac{w}{2})^2} \qquad\qquad \text{if } l < d_{ij} \leq u$$
$$= \frac{c_{ij}}{\pi} \times \frac{\frac{w}{2}}{(d_{ij}-u)^2+(\frac{w}{2})^2} \text{ if } u < d_{ij}$$
where $l = 1.5, u = 8, w = 1.0, c_{ij} = 1.5$

Soft Square

$$\sigma_{ij} = \min(\bar{w}, w) \times a + \frac{b}{\Delta^s} \text{ if } d_{ij} \geq d^0 + d^+ + r$$
$$= \Delta^e \qquad\qquad\qquad \text{if } d_{ij} < d^0 + d^+ + r$$
$$\Delta = d_{ij} - (d + d^+) \qquad \text{if } d_{ij} \geq d + d^+$$
$$= (d - d^-) - d_{ij} \qquad \text{if } d_{ij} < d - d^-$$
$$= 0 \qquad\qquad\qquad \text{if } d^- \leq d_{ij} < d^+$$
where $d^0 = 3.6, d^- = 0.1, d^+ = 4.4$
$\qquad a = 52.488, b = -75.58, s = 2.92, e = 3$
$\qquad \bar{w} = 1000, w = 1, r = 1.8$

CGLFOLD

$$\sigma_{ij} = 8^{p_{ij}}(l - d_{ij}) \qquad \text{if } d_{ij} \leq l$$
$$= -8^{p_{ij}} \qquad\qquad\qquad \text{if } l < d_{ij} \leq u$$
$$= 8^{p_{ij}} \ln(d_{ij} - u + 1) \text{otherwise}$$
$$= \text{where } l = 3.8, u = 8$$

Fig. 1. Five existing contact based scoring functions

in the large d_{ij} values and is expected to provide effective search guidance as it will be able to distinguish large d_{ij} values from each other. Considering the qualitative similarity of the existing scoring functions, we choose the soft square and the bounded potential functions and create their variants. The other function like square well doesn't have any penalty value for negative distance.

3.2 Proposed Scoring Functions

Our proposed soft square moderated is a qualitative version of modified Lorentz Potential and CGLFOLD. The variants will be mainly created more based on qualitative considerations than quantitative ones, particularly changing the steepness of the transition of the function from low to high for as the d_{ij} grows. The motive behind creating these variants is to study the effect of the slope of the curve on the progress of the search towards the region with the least function values. Figure 2 shows the four proposed scoring function variants: soft square moderated (ssm), soft square steepened (sss), bounded potential

Soft Square Moderated
$$\sigma_{ij} = a + \frac{b}{\Delta} \quad \text{if } d_{ij} > u + r$$
$$= \Delta^{2.5} \quad \text{if } d_{ij} \leq u + r$$
$$\Delta = d_{ij} - u \text{ if } d_{ij} \geq u$$
$$= l - d_{ij} \text{ if } d_{ij} < l$$
$$\text{where } l = 5, u = 8, r = 1$$
$$a = 52.488, b = -75.58$$

Soft Square Steepened
$$\sigma_{ij} = a + \frac{b}{\Delta^5} \quad \text{if } d_{ij} > u + r$$
$$= \Delta^{1.3} \quad \text{if } d_{ij} \leq u + r$$
$$\Delta = d_{ij} - u \text{ if } d_{ij} \geq u$$
$$= l - d_{ij} \text{ if } d_{ij} < l$$
$$\text{where } l = 5, u = 8, r = 1$$
$$a = 10, b = -15$$

Bounded Potential Moderated
$$\sigma_{ij} = m(l - d_{ij})^2 \quad \text{if } d_{ij} < l$$
$$= s(d_{ij} - u - 0.25) + 0.25 \text{ if } d_{ij} > u$$
$$= 0 \quad \text{otherwise}$$
$$\text{where } l = 5, u = 8, m = 3, s = 3$$

Bound Potential Steepened
$$\sigma_{ij} = m(l - d_{ij})^2 \quad \text{if } d_{ij} < l$$
$$= s(d_{ij} - u - 0.25) + 0.25 \text{ if } d_{ij} > u$$
$$= 0 \quad \text{otherwise}$$
$$\text{where } l = 5, u = 8, m = 3, s = 7$$

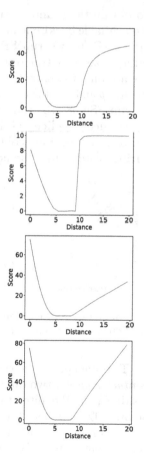

Fig. 2. Four proposed contact based scoring functions

moderated (bpm), and bounded potential steepened (bps). Also, these functions are somewhat simplified in their expressions compared to the original versions. The two soft square variants differ on the values of a and b and in the power of Δ while the two bounded potential variants differ on the value of m. From our intuition, we expect the bounded potential steepened variant to perform better than the other variants. We assume that with sharpness, it should converse faster.

4   Experiments

We describe the experimental setup, compare the contact based scoring functions, and compare our best results with the results obtained by a recent state-of-the-art PSP search algorithm that uses a contact based scoring function.

4.1   Experimental Setup

To obtain the ϕ and ψ values for the initial conformation construction, among the available backbone angle predictor methods SAP [14], OPUS-TASS [18] and SPOT-1D [6], we run SPOT-1D, since in our pilot runs, SPOT-1D predicted values lead to better results. We only consider ϕ and ψ because main angle ω has an almost constant value 180°. For SPOT-1D, the mean absolute error Δ is 16° for ϕ and 23° for ψ. To obtain secondary structure prediction of the residues, we run SSpro8 [13] and get 8-state predictions but we convert them into three states such as helices [G, H, I], sheets [B, E], and coils [C, T, U]. Note that once initial conformation is obtained, ϕ and ψ angles of the coil residues get changed during search while the helix and sheet regions remain unchanged.

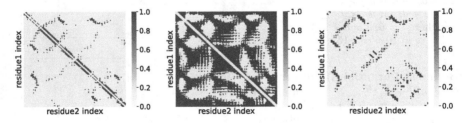

Fig. 3. Actual contact map (left), predicted contact map before filtering (middle), and predicted contact map after filtering (right) for protein 1T1J

To obtain predicted contact for the residue pairs, we run SPOT-Contact [5]. A *contact map* is a two dimensional array showing the contact probability for each residue pair. We filter the contact map discarding contacts with probabilities below 30% and also the contacts between residues that are within the same helices or sheets and so are not changed during search. Figure 3 shows the actual contact map for one protein 1T1J and the predicted one before and after filtering.

To evaluate the contact based scoring functions, we use 39 proteins that have 42 to 181 residues. Out of them, 15 are α type, 13 are β type, and 11 are α/β type. These proteins have been obtained from QUARK [17], MODE-K [4], and SPOT-1D [6]. We have used CD-HIT to check for 25% sequence similarity of these proteins with the training proteins of the machine learning algorithms SPOT-1D [6], SSPro8 [13], and SPOT-Contact [5].

4.2   Comparison of Scoring Functions

Table 1 shows the mean of root mean square deviation (RMSD) values for the 39 proteins as obtained by running each of the scoring functions with our search framework 5 times. Note there are 8000 iterations generating 20 neighbours like benchmark method CGLFOLD.

As we see the results in Fig. 1, among the existing 5 scoring functions, as expected before in their descriptions, bp achieves the best results. Among all 9 scoring functions, bps function obtains the best results. Notice that bps obtains the best mean RMSD in 13 out of 39 proteins and the second best in 12 proteins. The second best scoring function among all 9 scoring functions is bpm with the best performance in 10 and the second best performance in 9 proteins.

Since bp, bpm, and bps have no flat region for the undesired d_{ij} values, they do not loose search direction and essentially perform better than other functions. Moreover, bps is steeper than bpm which is steeper than bp for large d_{ij} values. Arguably, greater slopes essentially push the search more towards the minimum regions of the functions. Nevertheless, ssm performs better than ss but sss performs worse than ss. The reason is sss is more flat than ss which is more flat than ssm for large d_{ij} values. The more flat the function, the more loss of direction for the search. These are the explanations behind the performances.

To determine the statistical significance of the performance differences of the scoring functions at 95% confidence level, we perform Friedman test and get 5.78×10^{-11} as the p value. Then, we perform Nemenyi test and show the p values in Table 2. Notice that existing functions sw and bp are significantly different but all other pairs are not significantly different from each other. On the other hand, the proposed functions are significantly different from one another. Among other pairs, bps is significantly different from all other while bpm is not significantly different from cf. Both sss and ssm show mixed performance.

Among the 9 contact based scoring functions studied, since the bps function performs the best in RMSD values, we provide its further analysis.

Table 1. Top: comparison of mean RMSD values obtained by existing and proposed scoring functions; Bottom: the numbers of proteins for which scoring functions obtained mean RMSD values ≤ various threshold levels. The emboldened numbers are the best ones, while the underlined ones are the second-best ones among the versions.

Type	Protein	Length	sw	bp	mlp	ss	cf	ssm	sss	bpm	bps
α	5AON	48	4.12	2.91	3.97	4.06	3.56	<u>2.79</u>	3.37	**2.32**	4.23
	5B1A	58	8.66	7.88	10.04	9.03	9.63	7.57	7.85	**6.51**	<u>6.52</u>
	1SXD	91	11.13	8.66	8.81	<u>8.13</u>	8.55	10.98	10.47	8.42	**7.76**
	5B1N	59	5.14	5.41	4.31	<u>4.21</u>	4.51	4.38	4.33	4.41	**3.76**
	5COS	56	3.56	4.26	4.42	<u>3.26</u>	3.92	3.73	4.07	**3.00**	4.03
	5E5Y	61	10.15	9.24	**8.04**	9.03	9.83	8.21	8.45	8.80	<u>8.10</u>
	5FVK	82	5.40	<u>5.26</u>	5.27	5.75	5.96	6.61	8.24	6.09	**3.47**
	5EMX	54	5.94	6.08	5.08	6.07	<u>5.03</u>	5.65	6.03	**4.67**	5.37
	5TDY	42	7.18	8.61	6.81	<u>8.61</u>	9.92	7.71	6.94	7.44	**6.34**
	5HE9	56	6.34	6.44	6.39	6.58	6.29	**5.98**	6.19	<u>6.06</u>	6.68
	2O4T	90	9.38	**7.83**	10.11	9.50	<u>7.87</u>	9.25	9.11	9.41	9.07
	2O42	138	20.67	26.95	13.59	13.92	13.68	15.42	13.89	**11.51**	<u>13.52</u>
	5B5I	67	9.5	10.08	<u>9.22</u>	9.37	8.91	10.18	**8.40**	9.48	9.63
	5DIC	115	10.25	**7.19**	<u>7.84</u>	9.97	8.41	6.80	9.94	9.18	9.47
	5CKL	181	17.83	16.41	16.29	17.73	15.67	15.68	18.57	**12.83**	<u>14.63</u>
β	1R75	110	9.69	8.09	10.86	11.56	10.09	8.49	**7.49**	9.70	<u>7.57</u>
	1OKO	74	9.56	9.62	7.23	<u>6.67</u>	7.72	7.99	9.08	6.7	**6.43**
	2AXW	134	13.02	13.49	14.94	15.83	**11.79**	14.20	16.40	12.80	<u>12.22</u>
	2BT9	90	8.74	8.83	9.75	10.02	7.92	8.18	8.11	**6.23**	<u>6.22</u>
	2CHH	113	19.34	15.33	21.82	21.33	18.75	17.00	20.59	**13.74**	<u>14.42</u>
	2V33	91	9.58	<u>7.28</u>	13.76	9.34	8.59	10.59	11.82	8.02	**6.54**
	5AEJ	113	17.32	<u>14.22</u>	18.15	14.26	15.54	14.57	14.43	14.36	**14.09**
	5AOT	102	17.68	17.46	19.02	**15.16**	<u>17.15</u>	17.26	18.35	17.2	17.25
	5EZU	67	9.61	7.58	9.46	7.48	8.57	**6.65**	7.93	<u>7.21</u>	7.48
	5FUI	124	12.32	**9.08**	14.25	13.94	11.89	12.07	14.48	<u>10.13</u>	11.33
	5HDW	131	13.35	<u>11.19</u>	13.61	13.05	11.52	11.89	13.21	<u>11.19</u>	**10.47**
	7C28	58	7.74	8.04	8.66	8.20	8.19	6.96	6.72	<u>6.70</u>	**6.55**
	6WES	158	23.18	**21.15**	22.13	<u>21.72</u>	21.73	21.83	23.80	22.83	22.01
α/β	1CRN	46	5.1	**4.47**	5.42	<u>4.53</u>	5.03	5.87	4.99	5.08	5.15
	1CF7	82	8.40	7.85	8.37	5.51	5.41	<u>4.6</u>	7.38	8.48	**4.30**
	1IS7	84	8.70	<u>7.32</u>	6.85	8.37	8.30	**6.5**	8.10	8.56	7.43
	1KA8	100	12.10	11.97	11.86	10.77	11.31	10.49	11.38	**8.00**	<u>8.1</u>
	1MC2	122	10.46	10.49	11.01	12.33	12.05	12.19	10.01	**8.69**	<u>9.05</u>
	1T1J	125	9.91	7.54	9.84	7.52	8.13	7.83	6.23	<u>6.15</u>	**5.74**
	1Y71	112	8.47	9.68	11.76	9.10	13.54	9.49	10.98	<u>7.11</u>	**7.08**
	2BSE	107	14.31	10.1	14.63	11.04	11.78	11.64	9.96	**9.57**	<u>9.97</u>
	3BJO	100	10.30	9.86	**7.53**	12.42	9.92	11.47	10.47	8.78	<u>8.72</u>
	3CHB	103	12.47	**9.06**	16.49	12.85	10.61	10.58	11.93	<u>10.43</u>	10.58
	6CP8	163	13.67	<u>11.61</u>	13.81	11.84	12.21	12.22	12.28	12.69	**11.18**
Average RMSD			10.78	9.96	10.79	10.26	10.01	9.84	10.36	9.13	**8.78**
Mean RMSD ≤ 6Å			6	5	6	6	5	<u>7</u>	4	5	**8**
Mean RMSD ≤ 9Å			14	20	16	15	19	19	18	**23**	**23**
Mean RMSD ≤ 12Å			26	**32**	26	27	<u>30</u>	29	29	**32**	**32**

Table 2. Nemenyi test results for the scoring functions where $p \geq 0.05$ are emboldened

	bp	mlp	ss	cf	ssm	sss	bpm	bps
sw	0.04	**0.90**	**0.62**	**0.11**	0.01	**0.53**	0.00	0.00
bp		**0.20**	**0.90**	**0.90**	**0.09**	0.01	0.04	0.04
mlp			**0.90**	**0.39**	0.03	0.01	0.00	0.00
ss				**0.90**	**0.09**	**0.90**	0.02	0.00
cf					**0.09**	0.01	**0.22**	0.02
ssm						0.01	0.03	0.04
sss							0.02	0.00
bpm								0.00

Figure 4 shows the correlations between the bps scores and the RMSD values of the conformations generated during search for three proteins 5FVK, 2V33, and 1T1J. The Pearson correlation coefficients for these three proteins are 0.647, 0.454, and 0.661 respectively. These results give the evidence that improving the bps scores lead us to better conformations in terms of the RMSD values.

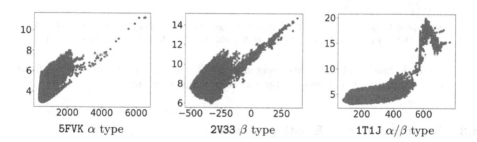

5FVK α type   2V33 β type   1T1J α/β type

Fig. 4. Scatter plots of bps contact based scores (x-axis) vs RMSD values (y-axis)

Figure 5 depicts the mean RMSD values of the initial and final conformations obtained for all proteins by using the bps function during search. Clearly, the bps function, improves the quality of the conformations.

Figure 6 shows samples of the initial and the final conformations obtained for three proteins when the bps function is used in search.

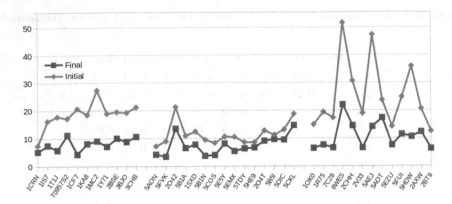

Fig. 5. Deviation in mean RMSD values of the initial conformations and the final conformations returned by the search when using the bps scoring function

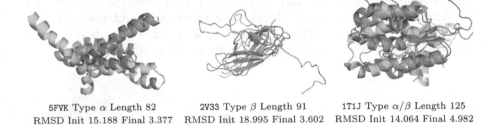

5FVK Type α Length 82   2V33 Type β Length 91   1T1J Type α/β Length 125
RMSD Init 15.188 Final 3.377   RMSD Init 18.995 Final 3.602   RMSD Init 14.064 Final 4.982

Fig. 6. Sample final conformations (magenta) obtained by scoring function bps from initial ones (cyan) w.r.t. native ones (green) (Color figure online)

4.3   Comparison with Existing Methods

We finalize the bps function along with our search framework as our final algorithm named Contact Guided PSP Search (CGPSPS). We then compare its performance with CGLFOLD [11]. We choose CGLFOLD because it uses a similar type of contact map based scoring function like ours. Also, CGLFOLD uses loop sampling and makes change to the angles in the loop residues; which is quite similar to ours. We run both CGPSPS and CGLFOLD 5 times on each protein. Each run explores 160000 conformations before termination. This is the same termination criterion used in evaluation of CGLFOLD [11]. We take the mean RMSD and Global Distance Test (GDT) scores over the 5 runs. Note that the smaller the RMSD value, the better the performance, while the larger the GDT score, the better the performance. Also, note GDT scores are in a 0–1 scale.

Table 3 shows that in terms of RMSD values, CGPSPS outperforms CGLFold in 31 out 39 proteins. CGLFold along with its contact based scoring function, also uses rosetta energy function. However, CGPSPS using only the contact based scoring function outperforms it. Table 3 also shows that in terms of mean

Table 3. Mean RMSD and GDT values obtained by our algorithm and state-of-the-art CGLFOLD algorithm. The emboldened numbers are the best ones while the underlined ones are the very close second best ones.

Type	Protein	Length	Mean RMSD		Mean GDT	
			CGPSPS	CGLFOLD	CGPSPS	CGLFOLD
α	5AON	48	**4.23**	6.41	**0.63**	0.54
	5B1A	58	**6.52**	17.14	**0.49**	0.35
	1SXD	91	**7.76**	9.06	**0.44**	0.40
	5B1N	59	**3.76**	4.43	**0.61**	0.60
	5COS	56	4.03	**3.13**	0.60	**0.72**
	5E5Y	61	8.10	**6.03**	0.39	**0.41**
	5FVK	82	**3.47**	3.57	0.59	**0.72**
	5EMX	54	**5.37**	5.54	0.56	**0.64**
	5TDY	42	**6.34**	10	**0.50**	0.35
	5HE9	56	**6.68**	8.25	0.54	**0.59**
	2O4T	90	**9.07**	10.68	**0.39**	0.24
	2O42	138	**13.52**	13.62	**0.4**	0.27
	5B5I	67	**9.63**	9.86	**0.45**	0.34
	5DIC	115	9.47	**3.33**	**0.44**	0.38
	5CKL	181	**14.63**	14.74	**0.3**	0.19
β	1R75	110	**7.57**	13.08	**0.39**	0.18
	1OKO	74	**6.43**	7.85	**0.51**	0.38
	2AXW	134	**12.22**	15.47	**0.25**	0.19
	2DTO	90	**0.22**	0.57	**0.48**	0.47
	2CHH	113	14.42	**8.57**	0.24	**0.35**
	2V33	91	**6.54**	7.38	**0.49**	0.36
	5AEJ	113	**14.09**	17.07	**0.27**	0.23
	5AOT	102	17.25	**12.23**	**0.31**	**0.31**
	5EZU	67	**7.48**	7.53	0.41	**0.45**
	5FUI	124	**11.33**	11.38	**0.30**	0.23
	5HDW	131	**10.47**	12.01	**0.26**	**0.26**
	7C28	58	**6.55**	9.26	**0.45**	0.29
	6WES	158	22.01	**19.43**	**0.12**	0.12
α/β	1CRN	46	5.15	**4.84**	0.60	**0.65**
	1CF7	82	**4.3**	4.60	0.50	**0.60**
	1IS7	84	**7.43**	7.50	0.39	**0.51**
	1KA8	100	**8.1**	8.72	0.29	**0.40**
	1MC2	122	**9.05**	10.29	0.39	**0.47**
	1T1J	125	**5.74**	6.47	**0.48**	0.47
	1Y71	112	**7.08**	7.78	**0.42**	0.42
	2BSE	107	**9.97**	10.26	0.30	**0.34**
	3BJO	100	**8.72**	9.02	**0.40**	0.33
	3CHB	103	10.58	**8.96**	0.28	**0.35**
	6CP8	163	**11.18**	13.52	**0.20**	0.15
Mean over all proteins			**8.78**	9.45	**0.41**	0.40

GDT values, in 22 out of 39 proteins, CGPSPS performs better than CGLFold. Considering protein types, CGPSPS is better than CGLFold in 9 in RMSD values and 3 in GDT values, 12 in RMSD values and 10 in GDT values, and 10 in RMSD value and 9 in GDT values in 11 α/β, 15 α and 13 β type proteins respectively. CGPSPS obtains the best performance both in RMSD and GDT values in 3, 10 and 8 proteins, respectively, in total 20 out of 39 proteins. At the bottom of Table 3, we observe that about 0.77Å average RMSD and 0.01 average GDT values improvement than CGLFOLD. We perform the Wilcoxon signed rank test with 95% confidence level and found the difference in GDT is not significant with p value 0.44 but is significant in RMSD with p value 0.02.

Table 4 shows the number of proteins in which two algorithms obtain mean RMSD values less than or equal to certain threshold values. In most of the protein types, CGPSPS outperforms CGLFold (Fig. 7).

Table 4. Numbers of proteins with mean RMSD values $\leq$ various threshold values.

Algorithm name	Mean RMSD $\leq$ 6Å				Mean RMSD $\leq$ 9Å				Mean RMSD $\leq$ 12Å			
	α	β	α/β	All	α	β	α/β	All	α	β	α/β	All
CGPSPS	5	0	3	**8**	10	6	7	**23**	13	8	11	**32**
CGLFOLD	5	0	2	7	8	5	7	20	11	7	10	28

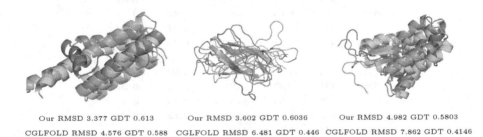

Our RMSD 3.377 GDT 0.613   Our RMSD 3.602 GDT 0.6036   Our RMSD 4.982 GDT 0.5803

CGLFOLD RMSD 4.576 GDT 0.588   CGLFOLD RMSD 6.481 GDT 0.446   CGLFOLD RMSD 7.862 GDT 0.4146

Fig. 7. Sample best conformations obtained by CGPSPS (cyan) and CGLFOLD (magenta) w.r.t. native conformations (green) (Color figure online)

5   Conclusions

Scoring functions are crucial in protein structure prediction. Contacts between residues in given proteins are predicted by machine learning algorithms. Search algorithms then design scoring functions using the predicted contacts and compare conformations generated during search using the scoring functions. There exists a number of contact based scoring functions but they have not been compared within the same search framework on the same set of benchmark proteins. We evaluate five existing and four proposed contact based scoring functions.

One of our proposed scoring function along with our search framework performs the best and significantly outperforms a similar state-of-the-art PSP search method in average root mean square distance and global distance test scores.

Acknowledgements. This research is partially supported by Australian Research Council Discovery Grant DP180102727.

References

1. Adhikari, B., Cheng, J.: CONFOLD2: improved contact-driven ab initio protein structure modeling. BMC Bioinformatics **19**(1), 1–5 (2018)
2. Bhattacharya, D., Cao, R., Cheng, J.: UniCon3D: de novo protein structure prediction using united-residue conformational search via stepwise, probabilistic sampling. Bioinformatics **32**(18), 2791–2799 (2016). https://doi.org/10.1093/bioinformatics/btw316
3. Brooks, B.R., Brooks, C.L., III., Mackerell, A.D., Jr., Nilsson, L., Petrella, R.J., Roux, B., Won, Y., Archontis, G., Bartels, C., Boresch, S., et al.: CHARMM: the biomolecular simulation program. J. Comput. Chem. **30**(10), 1545–1614 (2009)
4. Chen, X., Song, S., Ji, J., Tang, Z., Todo, Y.: Incorporating a multiobjective knowledge-based energy function into differential evolution for protein structure prediction. Information Sciences 540, 69–88 (2020)
5. Hanson, J., Paliwal, K., Litfin, T., Yang, Y., Zhou, Y.: Accurate prediction of protein contact maps by coupling residual two-dimensional bidirectional long short-term memory with convolutional neural networks. Bioinformatics 34(23), 4039–4045 (2018)
6. Hanson, J., Paliwal, K., Litfin, T., Yang, Y., Zhou, Y.: Improving prediction of protein secondary structure, backbone angles, solvent accessibility and contact numbers by using predicted contact maps and an ensemble of recurrent and residual convolutional neural networks. Bioinformatics 35(14), 2403–2410 (2018)
7. Hou, J., Wu, T., Cao, R., Cheng, J.: Protein tertiary structure modeling driven by deep learning and contact distance prediction in CASP13. Proteins Struct. Funct. Bioinf. **87**(12), 1165–1178 (2019). https://doi.org/10.1002/prot.25697
8. Leaver-Fay A, T.M., SM, L.: ROSETTA3: an object- oriented software suite for the simulation and design of macromolecules. Methods Enzymol 487, 545–574 (2011)
9. Li, Y., Zhang, C., Bell, E.W., Yu, D.-J., Zhang, Y.: Ensembling multiple raw coevolutionary features with deep residual neural networks for contact-map prediction in CASP13. Proteins Struct. Funct. Bioinf. **87**(12), 1082–1091 (2019). https://doi.org/10.1002/prot.25798
10. Li, Y., Zhang, C., Bell, E.W., Zheng, W., Zhou, X., Yu, D.J., Zhang, Y.: Deducing high-accuracy protein contact-maps from a triplet of coevolutionary matrices through deep residual convolutional networks. PLoS Comput. Biol. **17**, 1–19 (2021)
11. Liu, J., Zhou, X.G., Zhang, Y., Zhang, G.J.: CGLFold: a contact-assisted de novo protein structure prediction using global exploration and loop perturbation sampling algorithm. Bioinformatics 36(8), 2443–2450 (2020)
12. Mabrouk, M., Werner, T., Schneider, T., Putz, I., Brock, O.: Analysis of free modelling predictions by RBO aleph in casp11. Proteins **84**, 87–104 (2015)
13. Magnan, C.N., Baldi, P.: SSpro/ACCpro 5: almost perfect prediction of protein secondary structure and relative solvent accessibility using profiles, machine learning and structural similarity. Bioinformatics 30(18), 2592–2597 (2014)

14. Mataeimoghadam, F., Newton, M.H., Dehzangi, A., Karim, A., Jayaram, B., Ranganathan, S., Sattar, A.: Enhancing protein backbone angle prediction by using simpler models of deep neural networks. Sci. Rep. **10**(1), 1–12 (2020)
15. Newton, M.H., Pham, D.N., Sattar, A., Maher, M.: Kangaroo: An efficient constraint-based local search system using lazy propagation. In: International Conference on Principles and Practice of Constraint Programming. pp. 645–659. Springer (2011)
16. Skwark, M.J., Abdel-Rehim, A., Elofsson, A.: PconsC: combination of direct information methods and alignments improves contact prediction. Bioinformatics **29**(14), 1815–1816 (2013)
17. Xu, D., Zhang, Y.: Ab initio protein structure assembly using continuous structure fragments and optimized knowledge-based force field. Proteins Struct. Funct. Bioinf. **80**(7), 1715–1735 (2012). https://doi.org/10.1002/prot.24065
18. Xu, G., Wang, Q., Ma, J.: OPUS-TASS: a protein backbone torsion angles and secondary structure predictor based on ensemble neural networks. Bioinformatics **36**(20), 5021–5026 (2020)

Evaluation of Deep Learning Techniques on a Novel Hierarchical Surgical Tool Dataset

Mark Rodrigues[1]($\boxtimes$), Michael Mayo[1], and Panos Patros[2]

[1] Department of Computer Science, University of Waikato, Hamilton, New Zealand
[2] Department of Software Engineering, University of Waikato, Hamilton, New Zealand

Abstract. A new hierarchically organised dataset for artificial intelligence and machine learning research is presented, focusing on intelligent management of surgical tools. In addition to 360 surgical tool classes, we create a four level hierarchical structure for our dataset defined by 2 specialities, 12 packs and 35 sets. We employ different convolutional neural network training strategies to evaluate image classification and retrieval performance on this dataset, including the utilisation of prior information in the form of a taxonomic hierarchy tree structure. We evaluate the effects of image size and the number of images per class on model predictive performance. Experiments with the mapping of image features and class embeddings in semantic space using measures of semantic similarity between classes show that providing prior information results in a significant improvement in image retrieval performance on our dataset.

Keywords: Surgical tool dataset · Semantic similarity · Hierarchy tree · Surgery hierarchy

1 Introduction

Surgical tool management in hospitals is a difficult, time consuming and costly task; lost, misplaced or unavailable surgical tools were estimated to cost just one New Zealand hospital over NZ\$500,000 annually (Unit Manager, personal communication, Nov. 2019). Challenges faced in management of these tools included high inventory levels, multiple surgical tool set assembly errors, high staffing requirements, high costs, inconsistent availability of surgical tools, and non-functional or broken instruments being presented at surgery. Large volumes and varieties of surgical tools (Fig. 1) also pose a formidable challenge for management. According to Stockert and Langerman [21], just one institution can process over 100,000 surgical trays and 2.6 million tools every year. With an average of 38 surgical instruments present per tray, and six trays deployed on average per surgery [14], managing this volume and complexity manually under mission-critical conditions is a challenging task. Surgical tool detection and recognition through artificial intelligence (AI) and machine learning systems can provide a

© Springer Nature Switzerland AG 2022
G. Long et al. (Eds.): AI 2021, LNAI 13151, pp. 169–180, 2022.
https://doi.org/10.1007/978-3-030-97546-3_14

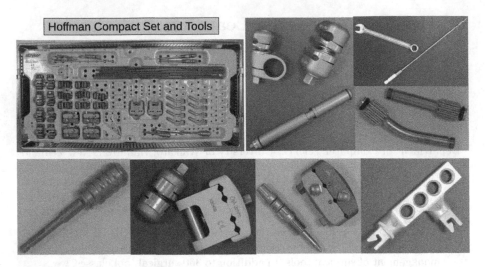

Fig. 1. Surgical set and tool examples

solution that can reduce incidents of lost or misplaced tools, improve packing accuracy, reduce errors, lower costs, and improve overall efficiencies within hospitals. Surgical tool recognition can be used in AI based hospital inventory management systems, and also in robotic and computer-assisted surgery, instrument position recognition, and in surgical monitoring, audit and training [11,18,24].

Table 1. Current tool datasets

Characteristic	CATARACTS [2]	Cholec80 [22]	EndoVis2017 [3]	ROBUST-MIS19 [16]
Size	50 videos	80 videos	10 videos	30 videos
Focus	Cataract surgeries	Cholecystectomy surgeries	Abdominal (porcine)	Varied surgeries
Use case	Detection	Detection	Segmentation	Detection
Classes	21	7	7	2
Annotations	Binary	Bounding boxes	Masks	Masks
Structure	Flat	Flat	Flat	Flat

Maier-Hein et al. [13] discussed the lack of success stories in the application of machine learning to surgery, and contrasted it to success in other medical fields, such as radiology and dermatology. This was directly attributed to the lack of quality annotated data, representative of the surgery domain, and the small size and limited representation of currently available datasets were reported to be major problems. One available labelled surgical tool dataset, while useful, provides images of only four tools [10]. Similarly, the currently available surgical tool datasets with a larger number of tools do not offer a sufficiently large range nor are they arranged hierarchically (Table 1). Kohli et al. [9] highlighted the lack of data for medical image evaluation with machine learning, and described current research as being "data starved" in this area. Current research focuses on convolutional neural networks (CNNs) trained on small medical datasets and the actual detection of less than fifty types of tools [2]; however, there are many thousands of surgical instrument types in circulation [20]. Clearly a new approach is required to handle this volume and variety of surgical tools. To help in addressing these challenges, we created a new surgical tool dataset named **HOS-PITools**, short for "**H**ierarchically **O**rganised **S**urgical **P**rocedure **I**nstruments and **Tools**". This dataset offers a wide range of tools, and we evaluate its performance with different deep learning methods and techniques.

2   Class Hierarchies and Training Strategies

Image features learned by CNNs have been used extensively to classify images, or to retrieve images that are visually similar to a query image [4]. While deep CNNs are extremely effective in object classification and recognition, classification of fine-grained classes and discrimination between classes with relatively minor differences is a challenge [19]. This is a significant problem for our work, since many surgical tools are visually similar and often differ in minor, subtle and hard to discern ways. An approach that can potentially improve classification or retrieval performance for such fine grained classes is to embed prior knowledge of the classes or class hierarchies into the model [7]. Class hierarchies share knowledge of relationships in the ground truth class label arrangements, as opposed to class labels in a flattened arrangement where every class is assumed independent and unrelated, and incorporating this information into the model can potentially lead to better classification and retrieval performance.

The main challenge, as highlighted by Narayana et al. [15], lies in mapping images and labels to a shared latent space where embeddings that correspond to a similar semantic (not just visual) concepts lie closer to each other than embeddings corresponding to different semantic concepts. They addressed this problem by first constructing a semantic embedding space based on prior domain knowledge and then projecting image embeddings onto this fixed semantic embedding space. Their model ensured that distance between image embeddings were similar to corresponding class embedding distances in the semantic embedding space [15]. Barz and Denzler [4] computed class embeddings by a deterministic algorithm based on prior domain knowledge encoded in a hierarchy of classes – this was a novel feature level approach that mapped image embeddings to semantic embeddings, and successfully incorporated class information and semantic relationships into a deep learning model. The semantic embeddings of image features were shown to result in a model that was much more invariant against superficial visual differences such as colour and shape [4], and we therefore experiment with this method for our project.

The most common loss function used in the training of CNNs is the categorical cross-entropy loss in conjunction with a softmax activation, also known as the softmax loss [4,23].

$$\mathcal{L}_{CCE} = -\sum_{i=1}^{k} c_i \log(\hat{c}_i) \tag{1}$$

In Eq. 1, $\hat{c}_i$ represents the probability score for class c_i. This training strategy separates the classes, but it may not be sufficient for fine grained classification tasks [4]. The center-loss was therefore designed to increase the separation of classes while minimizing the distances between samples from the same class, and was defined as [23]:

$$\mathcal{L}_{center-loss} = \frac{1}{2}\sum_{i=1}^{k} \|\boldsymbol{x}_i - \boldsymbol{c}_{y_i}\|_2^2 \tag{2}$$

In Eq. 2, $\boldsymbol{x}_i$ represents the center of the ith class and $\boldsymbol{c}_{y_i}$ the deep feature vectors for each class. A multiple loss training strategy was used where the center-loss was employed to pull the deep features of the same class to their centers, while the softmax loss forced the deep features of different classes apart [23]. A combination of losses was also employed by Barz and Denzler [4], who used a classification loss along with an embedding loss designed to maximise the cosine similarity or the inner product between the image features and the embeddings of their classes. This correlation or cosine loss function was defined as:

$$\mathcal{L}_{CORR} = \frac{1}{k}\sum_{i=1}^{k}\left(1 - \psi(I_i)^{\top}\varphi(c_{y_i})\right) \tag{3}$$

In Eq. 3, φ defined the class embedding function, ψ the embedding function for image I, and $^{\top}$ was the dot product. Another important distance based loss is the mean squared error (MSE) loss, defined for class c_i as:

$$\mathcal{L}_{MSE} = \frac{1}{k}\sum_{i=1}^{k}(c_i - \hat{c}_i)^2 \tag{4}$$

We evaluate our dataset with these training strategies and loss functions.

3   Methodology

In this section, we describe the HOSPITools dataset, and we experiment with different strategies to train CNNs using this dataset. We believe that this dataset can be an important resource for AI and machine learning research on surgical tool management, and we use our experience with CNN training strategies to try to improve its structure and organisation.

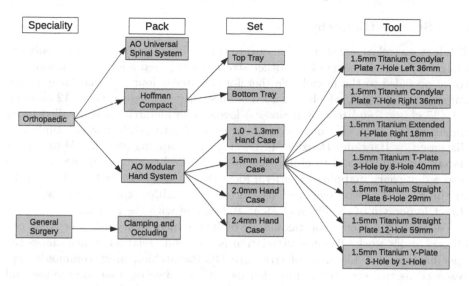

Fig. 2. Surgical tool dataset structure

3.1   Surgery Dataset

We developed our surgical dataset based on an hierarchical structure – speciality, pack, set and tool – as shown in Fig. 2. We captured RGB images of surgical tools using a DSLR camera, and manually arranged the images hierarchically in the dataset. We took these pictures on site in a major hospital, with the surgical tools currently in use. Image backgrounds were essentially flat colours, even though different backgrounds were used. Illumination sources included natural light – direct sunlight and shaded light – LED, halogen and fluorescent lighting. Distances of the camera to the object ranged from 60 to 150 cm. We focused on two specialities – Orthopaedics and General Surgery – for the initial stages of development of the dataset. The former speciality offers a wide range of instruments, implants and screws, while the latter covers the most common instruments used across all open surgery. We propose to add images of tools used in all 14 surgical specialities reported by the American College of Surgeons [1] in a phased manner as we develop this dataset. Our initial dataset consisted of 15,522 images across all hierarchies, with 11,712 images in the training set and 2,810 images in the validation set. We reserved a further 1,000 images for the test set, which the models did not see during training. While the average class size was 74 images, the range was from 139 images to as low as 10 images. This allowed us to evaluate the performance of the CNN training strategies with low class frequencies, and to explore how the dataset could be optimally structured with minimum images per class required for good performance.

3.2 Surgery Hierarchy

While it was relatively straightforward to train a baseline classifier using only the images and labels, some of our other strategies required additional information to be provided to the model. We therefore created a four level hierarchy in the surgery tool dataset, which consisted of speciality (2 classes), pack (12 classes), set (35 classes) and tool (360 classes) levels. The hierarchy was detailed in an indented tree format, which we then converted into "child-parent" tuples, as discussed by Barz and Denzler [4]. Dictionaries mapping class labels to lists of parent class labels and to child class labels in the hierarchy were created, and also a dictionary mapping hypernym identities of each element (class) to depths in the tree. We also developed lists of node identities, commencing with the direct hypernym of the given element and ending with the root node.

We only considered the taxonomic or hierarchical relationship between our classes in our work. The easiest relation is the "is-a" relation, which allows the specification of a hierarchical structure [4]. Hierarchies, most commonly represented as tree structures, provided us with an effective tool to organise and present the relationships and prior knowledge in our classes. In our tree structure, each class or node has just one parent class and distance was defined in terms of the length of the shortest path between two classes c_i, c_j. The dissimilarity of the classes $d_{\mathcal{G}}$ and the semantic similarity $s_{\mathcal{G}}$ was defined as [4]:

$$d_{\mathcal{G}} = \frac{\text{height}(\text{LCS}(c_i, c_j))}{\text{height}(\mathcal{G})}$$

$$s_{\mathcal{G}}(c_i, c_j) = 1 - d_{\mathcal{G}}(c_i, c_j)$$

(5)

In Eq. 5, LCS stands for lowest common subsumer – a class c_i was a subsumer of c_j if c_j was a descendant of c_i – and height $(\mathcal{G})$ is the height of the entire hierarchy. Using this, we obtained similarity measures in the range $(0, 1)$, where "1" represented the maximum similarity (no distance) between classes. This information can then be used to train a CNN for image classification and retrieval [6], as will be shown in the next section.

3.3 CNN Training Strategies

We used the well researched and widely used ResNet-50 [8] for all our experiments. We computed the channel mean and standard deviation of the images in the training set, and used it to normalise the data. We resized the original 6000 × 4000 pixel images to 150 × 100 pixels, and used multiple data augmentation techniques, including flipping, scale augmentation and random cropping, to add diversity to the training data [8]. We evaluated the following experiments for our image classification and retrieval tasks, including hierarchy-based semantic image embeddings, based on prior work by Barz and Denzler [4]:

Baseline Classifier: As a baseline, we used a standard ResNet-50 and the features extracted from the layer before the final classification layer of the network architecture. We used categorical cross entropy as the loss function.

Center-Loss: We used the ResNet-50 architecture and trained it with both center-loss and softmax loss, following Wen et al. [23]. We maintained the center-loss weight at 0.1 – this value was used to balance the two loss functions. Wen et al. [23] experimented with changes of this weight from 0 to 0.1; with the weight at 0, or only using softmax loss, they obtained a poor result but performance was relatively unchanged across other variations of this weight.

MDS Embeddings: We computed embeddings in 360 dimensional space so that the distances of class embeddings corresponded to their semantic dissimilarity (Eq. 5) using classical multidimensional scaling (MDS). We used the MSE loss in this distance based approach.

Sphere Embeddings: We calculated a "360-by-360" matrix specifying the distance between each pair of classes, based on the dissimilarity score of the two classes (Eq. 5). Following Barz and Denzler [4], with the first class at the origin, the second class was located at an offset along the first axis by the specified distance. We then placed all remaining classes in an iterative manner at an intersection of the hyperspheres centered at existing classes, with the radii set at the distance of the new class. We used the MSE loss in this training strategy.

Unitsphere Embeddings: The problem statement is: Given a distance matrix D, we wanted to place the set of points on a unit hypersphere which produce the same distance matrix. We used Eq. 5 to calculate similarities and the following equation to place class embeddings, where φ defined the class embedding function and $^\top$ was the dot product [4]:

$$\varphi(c_i)^\top \varphi(c_j) = s_g(c_i, c_j)$$
$$\|\varphi(c_i)\| = 1 \tag{6}$$

Equation 6 stated that the correlation of class embeddings should equal their similarity. The second function ensured that the L2-norm embeddings were on the unit hypersphere, and the dot product was then used as a substitute for the Euclidean distance [5]. The network was trained to minimise the difference between image representations and the embeddings of their respective class as per the guidelines of Barz and Denzler [4] using a combined loss $L_{CORR+CLS} = L_{CORR} + \lambda\, L_{CLS}$. Since we desired that the embedding loss L_{CORR} dominated learning, we set λ to a very low value (0.1) in our experiments (a similar value was used in the center-loss strategy).

We tried two different learning schedules for our training, a standard ResNet training schedule and Stochastic Gradient Descent with Cosine Annealing and Warm Restart (SGDR) [12]. While we tested these learning rates on each of our strategies, we only present the SGDR results since they are much better. This schedule implemented warm restarts, where in each restart the learning rate was initialized to a new value, scheduled to decrease over the cycle. The initial learning rate at the beginning of each cycle was 0.1, decreasing to a minimum of 10^{-6} using cosine annealing based on number of epochs since the last restart [12]. The first cycle was set at 12 epochs, the multiplier for cycle length was set at 2, and training was for 5 cycles or 372 epochs [4].

Table 2. Classification results

SGDR	Accuracy	Top-5 accuracy	Hierarchical accuracy	F1-score
Classifier	0.84	0.98	0.80	0.81
Center-loss	**0.88**	**1.00**	0.83	**0.86**
MDS	0.83	0.96	0.79	0.80
Spheres	0.85	0.98	0.81	0.82
Unitsphere	**0.88**	0.99	**0.84**	**0.86**

Table 3. Retrieval results (WUP)

SGDR	HP@1	HP@10	HP@50	HP@100	AHP	mAP
Classifier	0.84	0.68	0.56	0.54	0.83	0.47
Center-loss	0.91	0.81	0.65	0.60	0.84	0.76
MDS	0.90	0.87	0.87	0.87	0.95	0.73
Spheres	0.90	0.88	0.89	0.89	0.97	0.76
Unitsphere	**0.93**	**0.91**	**0.91**	**0.91**	**0.98**	**0.84**

3.4 Metrics Reported

We report the Accuracy, Top-5 Accuracy, Hierarchical Accuracy and F1-Score for the classification performance. For the retrieval tasks, we report the hierarchical precision of the nearest neighbour search performed on different image embeddings – HP@k for different k values, Average Hierarchical Precision (AHP) and Mean Average Precision (mAP). The Hierarchical Precision at k (HP@k) is a generalization of Precision@k which takes class similarities into account [7], and we report this for k at 250. This is calculated by the sum of similarities between query image class and retrieved image class over the top k retrieval results, divided by the maximum possible sum of top-k class similarities. Average Hierarchical Precision is defined by the area under the hierarchical precision curve, with the optimum normalized at 1.0. The Mean Average Precision, which does not consider class similarities, is also reported for comparison.

Class similarity is reported by the Wu-Palmer similarity metric ("WUP"), which considered the height and position of classes relative to each other in the tree – classes further from the root with a common parent tend to be more semantically similar. The WUP measure was calculated from Eq. 5.

4   Experiments and Results

Classification performance is good across the board, and there is no significant improvement in basic accuracy by including hierarchical information, as shown in Table 2. However, the biggest impact of including prior information and in the embedding strategies is found in the retrieval task, as shown in Table 3.

Table 4. Class frequency classification results

Images per class	Class	F1-score
139	Curved mayo scissors	0.96
117	7-inch metzenbaum scissors	0.94
15	0.76 mm drill bit with 10 mm stop mini QC	0.17
18	0.76 mm drill bit with 12 mm stop mini QC	0.22
13	Universal spinal system holding sleeve	1
11	Jacobs Chuck	1

Retrieval of single images is good for all models tested, but as the number of similar images retrieved increases, there is a definite advantage in terms of the embedding strategies. There is a significant drop in accuracy with increase in the k value with the Classifier and Center-loss models, but embedding with the MDS, Spheres and Unitsphere strategies demonstrates a consistent performance across different k values. Since the number of images per class is low, smaller k values retrieve images from exactly the same category as the query but as k increases, images are retrieved from outside the direct class. This is where the incorporation of semantic information excels, retrieving images from semantically similar classes even at higher k values. Semantic information significantly improves the quality of content-based image retrieval, by retrieving images that are both visually and semantically similar. Incorporating prior knowledge about class similarities by mapping class embeddings in semantic space appears to facilitate better learning by the CNN, thereby leading to better retrieval results. Organising the surgical tool dataset in the form of a hierarchical structure, and providing additional information about the taxonomic or hierarchical relationship between our classes, is therefore conclusively demonstrated to be an approach that leads to better performance, at least for the image retrieval tasks.

4.1 Does Size Matter?

The original images were captured at 6000 by 4000 pixels, on the assumption that finer detail could be captured and it would be easier to down-sample the images than to up-sample. Down-sampling was done to improve data handling, storage and processing, and we evaluated the effects of resizing images in the pre-processing pipeline on the CNN performance. We experimented with images of 600 by 400 pixels, with 300 by 200 pixels, with resizing the images to 224 by 224 with padding, and with image size of 150 by 100 pixels. There was no degradation in performance even at the smaller sizes, and so we implemented our training at an image size of 150 by 100 pixels, with random cropping of 100 by 100 pixels during augmentation. Our findings can be contrasted with the work of Sabottke and Spiele [17], who examined image resolution variations on CNN performance for radio-graphic images. While they did find some performance differences, this was relevant only when finer details needed to be captured for the diagnosis-specific tasks. For our objects of interest, image size variances do not appear to be as significant but this is a promising avenue for future work.

4.2 Class Frequencies

The class frequencies for the training set were averaged at 74 images, with a range from 10 to 139 images per class. While additional images were available, we wanted to test performance with different class frequencies. This was difficult to analyse – we obtained good classification results (Unitsphere strategy) even with 11 images per class, while much higher class frequencies did not yield the best results (Table 4). Clearly the number of images required for good performance depends on the particular tool and its distinctiveness in the dataset. An initial benchmark – at least for this dataset, for classification tasks, with the prior hierarchy information, and for these types of tools – does appear to be at least 40 images per class but this is not conclusive. As more cluttered images in realistic and messy settings are added, more images will be required to maintain accuracy and predictive performance. We will revisit this as we expand the scope and scale of our dataset.

5   Conclusions and Future Work

We developed a new surgical tool dataset – **HOSPITools** – and used it to test different CNN learning strategies. We demonstrated that the hierarchical nature of surgical tool classes could be used to make improved predictions. We also used the training to explore how the dataset should be structured and to evaluate some design parameters. This was a proof of concept for accurate recognition of surgical tools by utilising the hierarchical nature of the classes, and this solution can be used for intelligent management of surgical tools in a hospital.

We will continue to improve the dataset, with a view to making it publicly available for AI and machine learning research. We will address threats to the validity and utility of our work by adding images from more of the 14 surgical specialities, and by including greater coverage and variety in each speciality. We will include images with greater occlusions, reflections, illumination changes, the presence of blood, tissue and smoke, varied backgrounds, and from different modalities such as video, infrared and depth images. Open surgery and laparoscopic surgery images need to be sourced if possible, including live surgeries. If we can do this, then the surgery tool dataset can potentially be a valuable resource for the AI and machine learning communities.

References

1. ACS: What are the surgical specialties? (2021). https://www.facs.org/education/resources/medical-students/faq/specialties. Accessed 15 Feb 2021
2. AlHajj, H., Lamard, M., Conze, P.H., et al.: Challenge on automatic tool annotation for cataract surgery: cataracts. Med. Image Anal. **52**, 24–41 (2019). https://doi.org/10.1016/j.media.2018.11.008

3. Allan, M., Shvets, A., Kurmann, T., et al.: 2017 robotic instrument segmentation challenge. ArXiv arXiv:1902:06426 (2019)
4. Barz, B., Denzler, J.: Hierarchy-based image embeddings for semantic image retrieval. In: IEEE Winter Conference on Applications of Computer Vision (WACV) (2019). https://doi.org/10.1109/WACV.2019.00073
5. Barz, B., Denzler, J.: Deep learning on small datasets without pre-training using cosine loss. In: 2020 IEEE Winter Conference on Applications of Computer Vision (WACV) (2020). https://doi.org/10.1109/WACV45572.2020.9093286
6. Brust, C.-A., Denzler, J.: Not just a matter of semantics: the relationship between visual and semantic similarity. In: Fink, G.A., Frintrop, S., Jiang, X. (eds.) DAGM GCPR 2019. LNCS, vol. 11824, pp. 414–427. Springer, Cham (2019). https://doi.org/10.1007/978-3-030-33676-9_29
7. Deng, J., Berg, A., Fei-Fei, L.: Hierarchical semantic indexing for large scale image retrieval. In: CVPR 2011, vol. 785–792 (2011). https://doi.org/10.1109/CVPR.2011.5995516
8. He, K., Zhang, X., Ren, S., et al.: Deep residual learning for image recognition. In: IEEE Conference on Computer Vision and Pattern Recognition, Washington (DC). IEEE Computer Society (2016). https://doi.org/10.1109/CVPR.2016.90
9. Kohli, M.D., Summers, R.M., Geis, J.R.: Medical image data and datasets in the era of machine learning—whitepaper from the 2016 C-MIMI meeting dataset session. J. Digit. Imaging 30(4), 392–399 (2017). https://doi.org/10.1007/s10278-017-9976-3
10. Lavado, D.M.: Sorting surgical tools from a cluttered tray - object detection and occlusion reasoning. Master's thesis, University of Coimbra, Portugal (2018)
11. Leppanen, T., Vrzakova, H., Bednarik, R., et al.: Augmenting microsurgical training: microsurgical instrument detection using convolutional neural networks. In: IEEE 31st International Symposium on Computer-Based Medical Systems (CBMS), Karlstad, Sweden (2018). https://doi.org/10.1109/CBMS.2018.00044
12. Loshchilov, I., Hutter, F.: SGDR: stochastic gradient descent with warm restarts. In: 5th International Conference on Learning Representations (2017)
13. Maier-Hein, L., Eisenmann, M., Sarikaya, D., Marz, K., et al.: Surgical data science - from concepts to clinical translation. ArXiv arXiv:2011.02284 (2020)
14. Mhlaba, J.M., Stockert, E.W., Coronel, M., Langerman, A.J.: Surgical instrumentation: the true cost of instrument trays and a potential strategy for optimization. J. Hosp. Admin. 4, 6 (2015). https://doi.org/10.5430/jha.v4n6p82
15. Narayana, P., Pednekar, A., Krishnamoorthy, A., Sone, K., Basu, S.: HUSE: Hierarchical Universal Semantic Embeddings. ArXiv arXiv:1911.05978 (2019)
16. Ross, T., Reinke, A., Full, P.M., et al.: Robust medical instrument segmentation challenge, ArXiv preprint (2019)
17. Sabottke, C.F., Spieler, B.M.: The effect of image resolution on deep learning in radiography. Radiol. Artif. Intell. 2(1), e190015 (2020). https://doi.org/10.1148/ryai.2019190015
18. Sarikaya, D., Corso, J.J., Guru, K.A.: Detection and localization of robotic tools in robot-assisted surgery videos using deep neural networks for region proposal and detection. IEEE Trans. Med. Imaging 36(7), 1542–1549 (2017). https://doi.org/10.1109/TMI.2017.2665671
19. Setti, F.: To know and to learn - about the integration of knowledge representation and deep learning for fine-grained visual categorization. In: 13th International Joint Conference on Computer Vision, Imaging and Computer Graphics Theory and Applications (VISIGRAPP) (2018). https://doi.org/10.5220/0006651803870392

20. Sklar: Surgical instruments: the introductory guide. Sklar Instrument, West Chester, PA (2016)
21. Stockert, E.W., Langerman, A.J.: Assessing the magnitude and costs of intraoperative inefficiencies attributable to surgical instrument trays. J. Am. Coll. Surg. **219**(4), 646–655 (2014). https://doi.org/10.1016/j.jamcollsurg.2014.06.019
22. Twinanda, A.P., Shehata, S., Mutter, D., et al.: EndoNet: a deep architecture for recognition tasks on laparoscopic videos. IEEE Trans. Med. Imaging **36**, 86–97 (2017). https://doi.org/10.1109/TMI.2016.2593957
23. Wen, Y., Zhang, K., Li, Z., Qiao, Yu.: A discriminative feature learning approach for deep face recognition. In: Leibe, B., Matas, J., Sebe, N., Welling, M. (eds.) ECCV 2016. LNCS, vol. 9911, pp. 499–515. Springer, Cham (2016). https://doi.org/10.1007/978-3-319-46478-7_31
24. Zhao, Z., Voros, S., Weng, Y., Chang, F., Li, R.: Tracking-by-detection of surgical instruments in minimally invasive surgery via the convolutional neural network deep learning-based method. Comput. Assist. Surg. **22**, 26–35 (2017). https://doi.org/10.1080/24699322.2017.1378777

Feature Extraction Using Wavelet Scattering Transform Coefficients for EMG Pattern Classification

Ahmad A. Al-Taee[1]($\boxtimes$) (iD), Rami N. Khushaba[2] (iD), Tanveer Zia[1,3] (iD), and Adel Al-Jumaily[1,4] (iD)

[1] Charles Sturt University, Boorooma Street, Wagga Wagga, Australia
{AhAhmed,tzia}@csu.edu.au, adel.al-jumaily@ieee.org
[2] University of Sydney, Camperdown, Sydney, Australia
Rami.Khushaba@sydney.edu.au
[3] Naif Arab University for Security Sciences, Riyadh, Saudi Arabia
[4] Fahad Bin Sultan University, Tabuk, Saudi Arabia

Abstract. The Electromyogram (EMG) signal collected from the human muscles has been utilised for a long time to aid in diagnosing several medical conditions and for the control of external devices, including powered exoskeletons and prosthetic devices. However, there are still many challenges in analysing this signal to translate the findings into clinical and engineering applications. One of the significant challenges is the knowledge extraction part, as represented by the feature extraction stage, which is considered a vital factor in attaining the ultimate performance in EMG-driven systems. Wavelet transforms analysis is one of the several methods utilised for feature extraction with biomedical signals in the time frequency domain (TFD). Wavelet analysis-based feature extraction methods can be primarily categorised into three categories: wavelet transform (WT), wavelet packet transform (WPT), and the recently proposed deep wavelet scattering transform (WST). While many researchers utilised the first two methods to extract features from the EMG and other biomedical signals, the WST has not been appropriately investigated for feature extraction with EMG pattern recognition. This paper examines the potential benefits associated with the use of deep WST as a feature extraction method for the EMG signal and compares it with other wavelet methods. We used three well-known different EMG datasets collected with laboratory and wearable armbands hardware to provide a comprehensive performance evaluation under different settings. The new method demonstrates significant improvements in the myoelectric pattern recognition performance compared to WT and WPT, with accuracy reaching up to 96%.

Keywords: Electromyogram · Wavelet scattering transform · Feature extraction

1 Introduction

The Electromyogram (EMG) signal is traditionally used to evaluate the health of muscles and the motor neurons that control them (nerve cells). The EMG signal also provides

G. Long et al. (Eds.): AI 2021, LNAI 13151, pp. 181–189, 2022.
https://doi.org/10.1007/978-3-030-97546-3_15

valuable information about human movements and has been utilised in different medical and engineering applications to help people with upper limb deficiencies [1, 2]. When using EMG to control powered prosthetics, one of the important control strategies employed with the EMG signal is driven by a pattern recognition (PR) framework which often divided into many steps. These steps like data acquisition, data segmentation, feature extraction, classifications, and post-processing. Pattern recognition algorithms output can be used to automatically control several robotic systems and rehabilitation devices and used for patients who have suffered from transradial amputation, stroke, or spinal cord injuries. Within the EMG-PR framework, the feature extraction step is considered the essential component. The quality of the features has a significant impact on the success of the EMG-PR system, with this stage having a substantial effect on the final classification performance [1].

A wide-scale of feature extraction methods has been presented in the literature for EMG classification. Generally, there are three main groupings where these features are fallen: time, frequency, and time-frequency domains [3]. The two main characteristics in determining the feature extraction of EMG signal are the amplitude and power spectrums. In time-domain (TD) analysis, the amplitude and its associated features are frequently investigated; however, the power spectrum is typically analysed in a frequency domain (FD) analysis. Meanwhile, wavelet tools are extracted in time-frequency domain (TFD) analysis. The important parameters in each of these domains can be demonstrated in Fig. 1 [4].

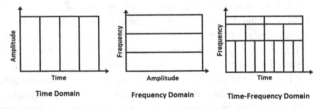

Fig. 1. Different domains of signal analysis [4]

Time-domain feature extraction methods count as most popular in pattern recognition classification, given their simplicity and low computational costs. In addition, TD driven features are usually also reported to have good robustness against noise which is desirable for real-time implementations [5]. Examples of some well-known TD feature extraction methods include (but are not limited to): the waveform length (WL), Integrated EMG (IEMG), Simple Square Integral (SSI), Variance of EMG (VAR), Root Mean Square (RMS), mean absolute value (MAV), sloop sign changes (SSC), number of zero crossings (ZC), Willison amplitude (WAMP) and Hjorth time domain parameters (HTD) [6, 7].

On the other hand, muscle fatigue and understanding the changes in motor unit (MU) recruitment are usually analysed via Frequency-domain features. These features are generally obtained from power spectral density (PSD). Spectral domain analysis has more flexibility than TD analysis, as noises and disturbances are best understood with FD analysis [8]. The main drawback of FD feature extraction is that such methods cannot predict a specific event, so the data's transient information might be lost. Examples of some well-known FD feature extraction methods used in the literature included (but were not limited to): Autoregressive (AR), Modified Median Frequency (MMDF), Modified Mean Frequency (MMNF), and Traditional median frequency (MDF) [8]. On the other hand, the Time-Frequency domain method is used to overcome the drawbacks of FD feature extraction methods. Due to the non-stationary behavior of the EMG signals, then methods like Short-Time Fourier Transform (STFT), Wavelet Transform (WT), Wavelet Packet Transform (WPT) [9] were all recommended for use for EMG PR.

Recently there has been a growing interest in applying the deep Wavelet Scattering Transform (WST) on different signal types. It enables the derivation of low-variance features from input data to be used in deep learning applications. WST can extract reliable information from the bio-signals at different scales, and it can be used to build translation invariant representations of the underlying features that are also durable to distortions and conserves class discriminability. WST was also reported as being efficient for use in biomedical signal classification [10–13]. The scattering transform is a series of multidirectional and multiscale wavelet transforms incorporated with non-linearities modulus. Although many researchers have used WT and WPT to analyse the EMG signal, WST was not used to analyse the EMG signal before. Hence, this paper suggests using WST to analyse the EMG signal, compare it with other TFD features (WT and WPT), and validate the results using three different datasets. These validation datasets are open-source and have been used by many researchers in several publications. The spectral regression feature projection method (SR) is used after extracting the feature for dimensionality reduction [14]. SR used to employ a mapping for the initial feature set from one domain into $(c - 1)$ features only as a new domain, where the number of classes is denoted by (c), this leading to a diminished computational cost. Finally, Support Vector Machines (SVM) are utilised for classification.

2 Wavelet Scattering Transform

One of the efficient tools for data descriptions and feature extractions is the WST, which is considered more advantageous than convolutional neural networks (CNN). Compared to CNN, WST can overcome the need for many model parameters, high computational costs, hyperparameters tuning, and difficulty understanding and interpreting the extracted features. WST can be considered as a deep scattering network, as it also employs convolutions, non-linearity, and pooling, just like CNN. However, unlike CNN, wavelet scattering requires no training and works perfectly with small data sizes, which is a major bottleneck for all deep neural network models. In addition, the WST can deliver reliable locally stable features to small deformations that can be combined with a deep neural network.

In WST, the time-series input of the EMG signal passes through several layers; the output of one layer is an input for the next layer. Each layer consists of three steps to perform wavelet scattering transform: convolution, non-linearity, and averaging, as shown in Fig. 2. Although the acting of wavelet scattering transform is like a convolutional neural network, it does not have any learnable parameters; therefore, it is fit for use in the low data scheme.

Fig. 2. Wavelet Scattering Transform steps

The WST develops translation-invariant as it is obtained by progressively mapping high-frequency wavelet coefficients to lower frequencies. Also, it is durable to time-warping distortion and conserves class discriminability; therefore, it has excellent efficacy for classification in real-time application. Finally, it considers an informative representation of non-stationary signals like EMG [10–12].

In this section, we will derive and explain the WST equations [11]. Let the time-series input EMG signal passes through the WST is denoted by X. To cover all the frequencies in this signal, $\varnothing$ represents the low-pass filter function, and the wavelet function is defined by ψ. A low-pass filter can achieve the local translation-invariant representation for the signal X $\varnothing_J(t)$, over a time window of size T to remove all high frequencies. Wavelet modulus transform is used to recover these high frequencies. A local translation-invariant descriptor of X can be obtained by averaging the input signal with a low-pass filter.

$$S_0 X(t) = X * \phi_J(t) \tag{1}$$

All the high frequencies will be removed by this averaging. These high frequencies can be retrieved using a wavelet modulus transform $|X * \psi_j|$. To get the first layer of scattering coefficients through averaging the output using the low pass filtering operations.

$$S_1 X(t) = \{|X * \psi_{j1}| * \phi_J(t)\}_{\forall j1} \tag{2}$$

Where wavelet scales $j1 \leq J$, to retrieve the information lost by averaging and getting the second layer scattering coefficients, this can be done by getting the complimentary high-frequency coefficients and averaging them again.

$$S_2 X(t) = \{||X * \psi_{j1}| * \psi_{j2}| * \phi_J(t)\}_{\forall j2} \tag{3}$$

By repeating this process for other layers, it will give the wavelet modulus convolutions.

$$S_m X(t) = \{||X * \psi_{j1}| * \dots |* \psi_{jm}|\}_{\forall ji} \quad i = 1, 2, \dots, m \tag{4}$$

Averaging Sm gives the mth order of scattering coefficients.

$$S_m X(t) = \{||X * \psi_{j1}| * \dots| * \psi_{jm}| * \phi_J(t)\}_{\forall ji} \quad i = 1, 2, \dots, m \tag{5}$$

The features of input signal X for $0 < m < k$, can be found via the scattering coefficients of all the orders.

$$SX(t) = \{S_m * X(t)\}_{0 < m < k} \tag{6}$$

Where k is the maximal decomposition order, we can have up to three layers, as the energy dissipates after every iteration; therefore, three layers are sufficient for nearly all applications. The process above can be illustrated in Fig. 3.

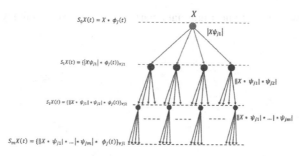

Fig. 3. Tree view for WST

3   Data Acquisition

This approach validated using three EMG datasets have been used. The first dataset is the BioPatrec [15], where the data was collected from 17 hands, intact people. Eight bipolar electrodes were used to collect the data. Ten different movements for wrist and hand were repeated three times for 3 s with the same relaxation intervals between repetitions with a sampling frequency are 2000 Hz [18]. These movements are close hand (CH), open hand (OH), extend hand (EH), pronation (PR), flex hand (FH), supination (SP), fine grip (FG), side grip (SG), a thumb up (AG), and a pointer or index extension (PT).

The second dataset is the Force dataset [16], where nine transradial amputees partic-ipated in the data collection process (seven traumatic and two congenital). The sampling frequency is 2000 Hz. The number of movements is six different hand movements, and these movements are Index Flexion (IF), Thumb Flexion (TF), Fine Pinch (FP), Hook Grip (HG), Tripod Grip (TG), and Spherical Grip (SG) [16]. There are three force levels for each of these movements: low, medium, and high. For each amputee, five to eight trials were recorded at each force level.

The third source of data is the 3DC dataset employing a wearable EMG acquisi-tion system [17]. Ten bipolar electrodes were used to collect the data. The number of movements is eleven different wrists, and hand gestures were repeated four times during 5 s with the same relaxation intervals between repetitions. The sampling frequency is 200 Hz. These movements are Radial Deviation (RD), Wrist Flexion (RF), Ulnar Devia-tion (UD), Wrist Extension (WE), Supination (S), Pronation (P), Power Grip (PG), Open Hand (OH), Chuck Grip (CG) and Pinch Grip (PG) [20].

4   Results

The extracted features were examined via the scattering transform method to show the superiority of the proposed technique while using a support vector machine (SVM) classifier to get classification error rates.

4.1   Results of BioPatrec-Database

Figure 4 shows the invariance scale by finding the inverse Fourier transform of the scaling function and centring it at 0 s. The two vertical lines represent the boundaries at −75 and

75 s. It also shows the real and imaginary parts of the lowest frequency wavelet $\phi_J(t)$ from the first filter.

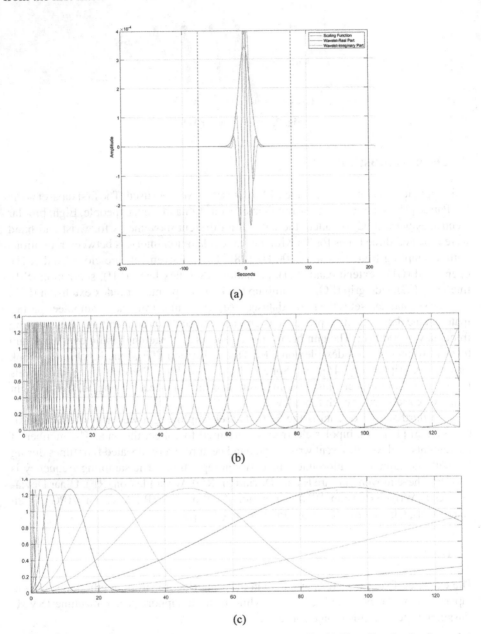

(a)

(b)

(c)

Fig. 4. (a) The coarsest-scale wavelet from the first filter bank. (b) First filter bank of wavelet filter. (c) Second filter bank of wavelet filter

The classification errors comparison between the proposed method, WT and WPT features averaged across the 17 participants of the BioPatrec database are shown in Fig. 5. As shown, the WST features have better performance than other methods, with p-value of <0.01 using the Wilcoxon signed rank test of significance.

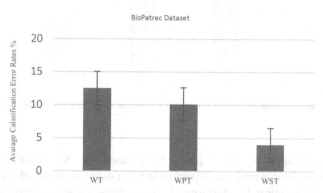

Fig. 5. Shows the effectiveness of the proposed method with different Wavelet methods for BioPatrec Dataset.

4.2 Results of Force-Database

For the transradial amputee's dataset, the results were calculated for each force level, as shown in Fig. 6. Across these results, the proposed method achieved a lower classification error with $p < 0.001$ for all tests.

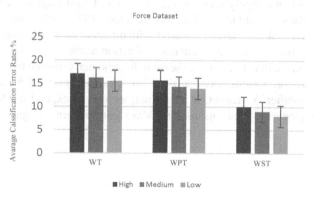

Fig. 6. Shows the effectiveness of the proposed method with different Wavelet methods for Force Dataset.

4.3 Results of 3DC-Database

Figure 7 shows the averaged classification error results across all the 22 subjects of the EMG 3DC database, following a similar trend displayed with the other two datasets.

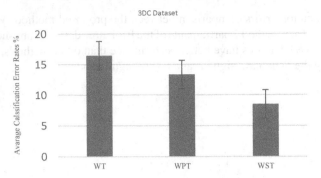

Fig. 7. Shows the effectiveness of the proposed method with different Wavelet methods for 3DC dataset.

The results of applying the proposed WST based feature extraction across three different datasets demonstrate the impact of WST in deriving more robust features that are invariant to translation. Furthermore, due to the non-stationary behavior of the EMG signals, their high variance is usually dispersed across the dimensions, then utilising the WST was beneficial to consolidate the variance in a small number of features that have very low variance.

5 Conclusion

This study discussed the analysis and classification of the EMG signals utilising the nonlinear features extracted method using the deep wavelet scattering transform (WST). This work proves that a highly accurate classification of EMG signals can be extracted using the SVM classifier and the coefficients from the WST. Furthermore, the proposed method has been tested over several datasets with different sampling frequencies, a different number of channels, and different data collection methods, proving its robustness. In our future work, we plan to improve the classification performance by getting the spatial and temporal correlations between the EMG channels using WST and then feed them into the classifier. Moreover. It is of great interest to expand the WST for real-time medical/engineering applications for EMG signal pattern recognition controlling systems.

References

1. Phinyomark, A., Quaine, F., Charbonnier, S., Serviere, C., Tarpin-Bernard, F., Laurillau, Y.: EMG feature evaluation for improving myoelectric pattern recognition robustness. Expert Syst. Appl. **40**(12), 4832–4840 (2013)
2. Phinyomark, A., Scheme, E.: EMG pattern recognition in the era of big data and deep learning. Big Data Cogn. Comput. **2**(3), 21 (2018). https://doi.org/10.3390/bdcc2030021
3. Zecca, M., Micera, S., Carrozza, M.C., Dario, P.: Control of multifunctional prosthetic hands by processing the electromyographic signal. Crit. Reviews TM Biomed. Eng. Begell House **30**, 459–485 (2002)

4. Misiti, M., Misiti, Y., Oppenheim, G., Poggi, J.: Wavelet Toolbox User's Guide. The MathWorks, Inc. (1997–2006)
5. Hu, X., Wang, Z., Ren, X.: Classification of surface EMG signal using relative wavelet packet energy. Comput. Methods Programs Biomed. **79**(3), 189–195 (2005)
6. Chan, A.D.C., Green, G.C.: Myoelectric control development toolbox. In: 30th Conference of the Canadian Medical & Biological Engineering Society, Toronto, Canada, M0100 (2007)
7. Boostani, R., Moradi, M.: Evaluation of the forearm EMG signal features for the control of a prosthetic hand. Physiol. Meas. – IOP **24**(2), 309–319 (2003)
8. Karlsson, S., Yu, J., Akay, M.: Enhancement of spectral analysis of myo-electric signals during static contractions using wavelet methods. IEEE Trans. Biomed. Eng. **46**(6), 670–684 (1999)
9. Englehart, K., Hudgins, B., Parker, P., Stevenson, M.: Classification of the myoelectric signal using time-frequency based representations. Med. Eng. Phys. **21**, 431–438 (1999)
10. Leonarduzzi, R., Liu, H., Wang, Y.: Scattering transform and sparse linear classifiers for art authentication. Signal Process. **150**, 11–19 (2018)
11. Bruna, J., Mallat, S.: Classification with scattering operators. In: Computer Vision and Pattern Recognition, pp. 1561–1566, Providence, RI, USA, June 2011
12. Andén, J., Mallat, S.: Multiscale scattering for audio classification. In: International Society for Music Information Retrieval Conference, pp. 657–662, Miami, Florida, USA (2011)
13. Andén, J., Mallat, S.: Deep scattering spectrum. IEEE Trans. Signal Process. **62**(16), 4114–4128 (2014)
14. Cai, D., He, X., Han, J.: SRDA: an efficient algorithm for large-scale discriminant analysis. IEEE Trans. Knowl. Data Eng. **20**(1), 1–12 (2008)
15. Ortiz-Catalan, M., Branemark, R., Hakansson, B.: BioPatRec: a modular research platform for the control of artificial limbs based on pattern recognition algorithms. Source Code Biol. Med. **8**(11), 12013. https://doi.org/10.1186/1751-0473-8-11
16. Al-Timemy, A.H., Khushaba, R.N., Bugmann, G., Escudero, J.: Improving the performance against force variation of EMG controlled multifunctional upper-limb prostheses for transradial amputees. IEEE Trans. Neural Syst. Rehabil. Eng. **24**(6), 650–661 (2016). https://doi.org/10.1109/TNSRE.2015.2445634
17. Côté-Allard, U., Gagnon-Turcotte, G., Laviolette, F., Gosselin, B.: A low-cost, wireless, 3-D-printed custom armband for sEMG hand gesture recognition. Sensors **19**(12) (2019). https://doi.org/10.3390/s19122811

Modelling Eye-Gaze Movement Using Gaussian Auto-regression Hidden Markov

Beinan Xu$^{(\boxtimes)}$ and Andy Song

RMIT University, Melbourne, VIC 3001, Australia

Abstract. Modelling and prediction of eye gaze movement can be highly desirable in many real-world scenarios, e.g. human-machine interaction and human behavior analysis. This challenging area largely remains unexplored. In this study we tackle this challenge and propose a method to predict eye-gaze movement of human observers. Eye gaze trajectories are separated into three components, where two of them are considered as noise or bias, which can be removed from the trajectory data. So the remaining component, principle movement, can be modelled by a proposed new method, GAR HMM, which stands for Gaussian Auto-regression Hidden Markov Model based on AR HMM. Instead of the Beta Processes in AR HMM, GAR HMM introduces a Gaussian Process. So the model can predict the probability of occurrence of eye gaze in each region over time. By joining the predicted points together as a sequence, we can generate the eye gaze movement prediction as a time series. To evaluate GAR HMM we collected eye gaze movement data from over 20 volunteers. Experiments show that good prediction can be achieved by our proposed GAR HMM method. As a groundbreaking work GAR HMM can lead to much further extension to benefit real applications.

Keywords: Eye gaze movement prediction · Hidden Markov model

1 Introduction

Predicting eye gaze movement can be very significant in many applications, such as automatic focusing for advanced cameras and eye-gaze guided targeting. However, the mechanism of human eye gaze movement is very complicated. It is not only related to the information contained in the observed target, but also by different effects of human cognitive behaviors [5]. Eye-gaze movement can be regarded as a time series, which changes over time on a two-dimensional image. In reality, it is very difficult to predict the movement because of its complex nature [7]. The main drive in eye gaze movement can be categorized into three groups, (1) the object of interest, which may change quickly due to the complex nature of the scene in front of the observer, (2) interference that often occur in real world scenarios e.g. a fly passing, a light flashing or other kinds of distractions, and (3) uncontrollable movement caused by subconscious reasons yet still to be understood by scientists. Accordingly we aim to separate eye gaze movement

© Springer Nature Switzerland AG 2022
G. Long et al. (Eds.): AI 2021, LNAI 13151, pp. 190–202, 2022.
https://doi.org/10.1007/978-3-030-97546-3_16

into three components, namely the *principle movement* (the movement behavior affected by the primary targets), *interference* and *subconscious movement*.

This study mainly focuses on the principle movement in the eye gaze movement, because the interference and subconscious movement are unpredictable and shall be considered as noise and bias. The first task is to remove the impact of interference and subconscious movement in the eye gaze data. Interference is the movement caused by something other than the intended target during the observation. Human attention will deviate from where it is under unconditioned reflex. This is a human instinct in order to respond to potential risks [17]. Subconscious movement is the manifestation of human brain's subconscious activities in eye control. In this study we found observers could not explain the motives behind such kind of movement. These movements appear as outliers in eye gaze movement data. Their patterns are unpredictable. Although eye gaze movement can be considered as time series, it is more complex than normal time series even considering multivariate time series, because eye gaze movement is spatial and temporal. Furthermore eye gaze movement is different to two dimensional time series models such as videos. Therefore a new method is needed to capture two dimensional eye-gaze movement.

In the following paper, we will introduce experiments and data (Sect. 2) and a new image transform method (Sect. 3.1). Gaussian Auto-regression Hidden Markov model (GAR HMM) is introduced in Section 3.2, which is to analyze and capture the probability of eye gaze occurrence in different regions over time. This model is base on Auto-regression Hidden Markov with Beta Processes (AR HMM) [4, 18]. We create a region based method instead of pixel based prediction as an image can be divided into different regions. Our method is to predict the eye gaze movement from region to region instead of pixel to pixel. After getting the probability of occurrence of eye-gaze movement in different regions, the predicted eye-gaze trajectory then can be obtained by joining the regions with the highest probability at different time intervals. Our experiments show the success of GAR HMM.

2 Preliminaries

2.1 Preparation for Data Collection

The experimental material of our design contains 100+ static images. In order to reduce the bias in the experiments as much as possible, 20 volunteers were invited, from different gender groups, different age groups, and different occupational backgrounds. During each experiment one volunteer is instructed to watch different pictures, each picture appearing for 5 s. The total duration of each experiment does not exceed 5 min.

Images: A collection of images are artificially created for our study. This is to reduce the so-called top-down effect as certain observers may be drawn to one particular type of object. Another consideration is visual tendency. Images have obvious visually induced tendency may skew the eye gaze data [19]. Hence each image has several variations set up as a control group, so visual tendency can be reduced as much as possible. These images in the control group have the exact same content, but flipped horizontally or vertically.

Questionnaire: In order to effectively eliminate components other than the principle movement in the eye gaze data set, a questionnaire was established. The questionnaire was not only used to investigate whether the volunteers had emotional changes before, during and after the experiment, and was also used to determine whether there were external and unrelated factors that affected the volunteers' attention during the experiment. By this way we can reduce or eliminate distracted eye-gaze and unconscious eye-gaze components, so the resulting data can be more helpful on the modelling of principle movement.

2.2 Data Collection

Eye gaze data were collected using 60 Hz Tobii II eye tracker while observers were presented with designated images. The experiment environment is an all-sealed quiet laboratory. We can collect 300 eye movement data points from one volunteer for one image. Due to the limitations of the equipment and the personal condition of the subject, e.g. level of concentration, whether wearing glasses or not, etc., each set of data has some missing data points (less than 20%).

2.3 Data Pre-processing

To further improve the data quality, K-NN and Fourier transform are used to fill the "gaps". The former is to generate missing values while the latter is to adjust the added values so they are consistent with the data distribution.

K-Nearest Neighbor: K-NN algorithm is to supplement all the missing values in the data set [11]. Suppose the data point at time p is missing, then the data from the beginning of the eye tracker reading t_{p-11} to t_{p-1} are used to form a data segment. Since eye gaze movement data includes both temporal continuity and two-dimensional scatter distribution, the optimal K value of data between t_{p-11} and t_{p-1} changes over time. For the selection of K value, considering that only 10 points in t_{p-11} to t_{p-1} and the filled missing value will be subjected by Fourier transform, so we set the K value to 3. If p is a missing value, data after p are probably missing as well. Therefore, it is more meaningful to calculate the p value using only the data before p.

Fourier Transform: Through the adjustment of K-NN algorithm, the data set is free from missing values. But these artificial data values may have a large bias comparing with the actual values [8,13]. Therefore we use two-dimensional continuous Fourier transform to adjust the data set by extracting the eigenvalue frequency of the eye gaze movement data [6]. Fourier transform filter uses the obtained feature frequency and adjusts the data points generated for the missing values. It can also adjust the outliers that caused by subconscious movement. The process is as below.

First, Fourier transformation is performed on the data set after filling the missing values to obtain a two-dimensional spectrum:

$$F(u,v) = \int_{-\infty}^{\infty} \int_{-\infty}^{\infty} f(x,y)e^{-2\pi iux+vy}dxdy \qquad (1)$$

where $F(u,v)$ is the two-dimensional frequency spectrum of $f(x,y)$. It shows the components of the signal at frequency u in the x direction and frequency v in the y direction. The component $e^{i2\pi(ux+vy)}$ can be expanded to $[cos(2\pi ux)cos(2\pi vy) - sin(2\pi ux)sin(2\pi vy)] + i[sin(2\pi ux)cos(2\pi vy) + sin(2\pi vy)cos(2\pi ux)]$. Afterwards, the obtained two-dimensional Fourier spectrum is regenerated into processed eye movement data by using Formula 2.

$$f(x,y) = \int_{-\infty}^{\infty} \int_{-\infty}^{\infty} F(u,v)e^{2\pi iux+vy}dudv \qquad (2)$$

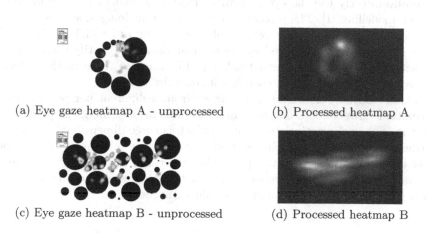

(a) Eye gaze heatmap A - unprocessed   (b) Processed heatmap A

(c) Eye gaze heatmap B - unprocessed   (d) Processed heatmap B

Fig. 1. Examples of generated eye gaze heatmap obtained after filling missing data and the Fourier transform process.

Output Examples. Figure 1 shows some examples of the output from the aforementioned process. On the left hand, there are two eye gaze heatmaps overlaying on top of their respective target images, color to signify the intensity of the gaze on a particular spot. There are a few tiny spots far apart from the rest. They are possible outliers in the data set. The right side of Fig. 1 shows the heatmaps generated on the data transformed by K-nearest Neighbor and the Fourier process. Compared to their counterparts on the left, they are much smoother and connected. Furthermore the isolated small spots are no longer present. The pre-processing discussed here can help extract two dimensional features of the eye movement data more effectively, not only by supplementing values for the missing data points, but also by eliminating the influence of subconscious eye-gaze points.

Note the purpose of this research is to find the instantaneous tendency of human eye movement and make short-term predictions. Our pre-processing although in some degrees makes modifications to the original data, but does not change the inherent characteristics of eye gaze movement contained in the data. Therefore this modification is considered to be within an acceptable range.

3   Methodology of Eye Gaze Predictive Modelling

3.1   Image Transform

A main point of eye gaze prediction is to explain some visual tendencies and find commonality since different people often have different perceptions on the same image [2,10]. We aim to unify different factors to provide an effective mechanism for subsequent modelling, analysis and prediction.

At present, the study on eye gaze and saliency related areas mainly adapt three methods. The first is to set aside the content information of the target image and directly use the eye movement rules provided by the eye movement data for modelling [1]. The second is to select content images, such as books or newspapers, that have a relatively regular or reading order [3,14]. The third is to use experimentally obtained eye movement data to quantify each region of the picture to obtain the visual tendency [15]. Each of these methods has its own scope of application, but each has its own limitations.

In this study, we address this challenge from a different perspective. Image information (gray value) contained in a two-dimensional image is quantized to form the image information distribution which is three-dimensional. This initial distribution will constantly change with the eye gaze movement. We divide a target image evenly into a $n \times n$ grid. The larger n is, the viewing behavior on the image, e.g. the eye gaze movement, can be better separated. However that means greater amount of calculation would be needed.

Fig. 2. Generating region map based on pixel information. The number of each region represents the cumulative amount level of the total gray scale of the regions (0 to 10)

For example, a target image is marked as 16 smaller regions as in Fig. 2. Each cell is assigned with a value, which represents the relative cumulative amount level of the total inverted grayscale of that region (white is 0 and black is 255). The higher the value, the higher the sum of the inverted gray values of the pixels contained in the region of the image. The value here does not represent the amount of human-identified information contained in the region, but only represents the difference between the information contained in this region relative to the information contained in other regions.

Each cumulative gray value in a cell is called the initial influence parameter of eye gaze movement. The values of all regions are normalised to generate an integer value from 0 to 10, which is the initial value of the regions of the image. It is also the up-bound of changes meaning the value in that cell will never go beyond that point. We can also obtain a value from 0 to 1, which is 1/10 of the eye gaze influence parameter. This value represents the eye gaze influence coefficient

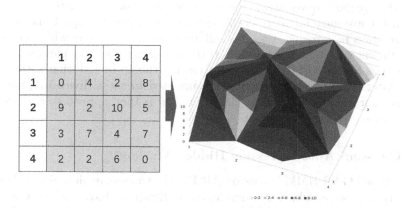

Fig. 3. Eye gaze influence parameter distribution plot base on above example. The shade of the color represents the size of the parameter. (Color figure online)

ψ of the image information in the region on the eye movement behavior. As shown in Fig. 3, by obtaining the eye gaze influence parameters in different regions, we can get a 3D distribution plot to show the image information distribution of the observed image.

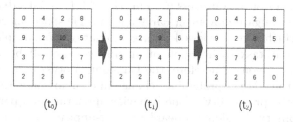

Fig. 4. First example of adjustment of the region map. When the eye gaze falls on a region, the value of that region will decrease by ψ (10 to 9). If the eye gaze stays in this region from t_0 to t_2, the region will be reduced by $2 \times \psi$ (10 to 8).

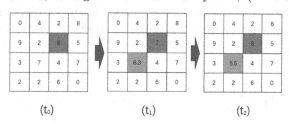

Fig. 5. Second example of adjustment of the region map. The eye gaze falls on the yellow region at time t_0. When the eye gaze moves to the blue region at t_1, the value of yellow region rises with ($\psi = 1$) per interval until its initial value 10. The value of the blue region then starts to decrease with ($\psi = 0.7$) per interval until 0 or eye gaze goes elsewhere. (Color figure online)

As the eye gaze moves along, these eye gaze influence parameters will change base on the eye gaze influence coefficient, as illustrated in Figs. 4 and 5. If the eye gaze stays in a region, the area influence parameter value will decrease by the coefficient ψ until it reaches zero. If the eye gaze leaves, the parameter value will increase by the coefficient ψ until it reaches the up-bound, that is the initial value. After all changes in eye gaze are updated in these divided regions, the Gaussian auto-regression hidden Markov model is then applied to capture and analyze these eye gaze movement.

3.2 Gaussian Auto-regression Hidden Markov

Our proposed GAR HMM is base on AR HMM, Auto-regression hidden Markov with a beta process, which was developed by Emily B. Fox, Michael I. Jordan, etc. [4]. Their approach is designed to analyze gestures which naturally contain latent dynamic behaviors that are reflected across multiple time series. In such time series data, behaviors can be modeled separately through dynamic systems. The transition between behaviors is approximately Markovian [12,16]. Examples of such Markov process include hidden Markov models, switched vector auto-regressive processes, and switched linear dynamic systems [9]. This type of modelling assumes that a time series contains data points that are dependent; different points on the time series have mutual influence to each other; and changes in behavior are recorded collectively in the time series.

Instead of the prior beta process used in AR HMM, we introduce a Gaussian process, because eye gaze movement carry out in a 2D space, more complicated than gesture, which can be viewed as a combination of multiple single-point time series. In our task each region of an image bears all behavior changes occurred in other regions. Therefore, the Gaussian process is more appropriate as it can reflect the state of probability change in comparison with beta process. It can estimate the probability of one behavior appearing in a particular region rather than a binary decision "appear" or "not-appear" in that region. With the predicted probability, one can easily work out a binary predication, "yes" or "no", by simply providing a probability threshold.

As described in Sect. 3.1, eye gaze movement data are combined with transformed image method to generate a 4×4 grid. Each cell represents a behavior that is related to other regions. Therefore for each set of eye movement data set, there are 16 behaviors at any time point. Hence we can utilize the following modelling of Auto-regression:

$$Y_t = \sum_{g=1}^{G} A_{g,z_t} Y_{t-g} + e_t(z_t) \triangleq A_{z_t} \tilde{Y} + e_t(z_t) \tag{3}$$

where $z_t \sim \pi_{z_{t-1}}$ and $e_t(z_t) \sim N(0, \sum_{z_t})$. These vector auto-regression processes with parameters A_{g,z_t} and $\sum_{z_t}$ are considered as eye gaze behaviors. Changes in the behaviors will affect y with changes in z. At the same time y will have a time lag effect. The Bayes process is used before coupling the dynamic behaviors with different objects or sequences. f_i is an indicator variable.

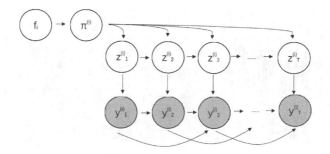

Fig. 6. Graphical model of GAR HMM, Gaussian auto-regression hidden Markov.

In the Beta process of AR HMM, f_i indicates whether the behavior k will occur. The output is either occurrence or non-occurrence. For eye gaze movement, although Beta process can be used, the eye gaze movement is very complicated, such as multiple regions have the high occurring probability of behavior k at the same time. Gaussian process hence has advantages. See the diagram of the GAR HMM model in Fig. 5, where f_i represents the probability within the acceptable range of k. A feature-constrained transition distribution $pi = pi_{z_{t-1}}$ is defined, which controls the Markov transition between its dynamic behavior sets. Figure 6 is the visual representation, while the formula is as follows:

$$\eta_{jk}|\gamma, \kappa \sim Gamma(\gamma + \kappa\delta(j, k), 1) \tag{4}$$

where $\delta(j, k)$ is the Kronecker delta function and the collection of transition variables by η_{jk}.

$$\pi_j = \frac{[\eta_{j1} \quad \eta_{j2} \quad ...] \otimes f_i}{\sum_{k|f_{ik}=1} \eta_{jk}} \tag{5}$$

Here, $\otimes$ represents the element-wise vector product. This structure defines $\pi_{z_{t-1}}$ on the entire set of positive integers, but only assigns a positive quality at index k where $f_i = 1$. The previous generation process can be well represented by the sample $\tilde{\pi}_j$ in the finite Dirichlet distribution of dimensions f_i, which contains the non-zero term of π_j. The κ hyper-parameter places additional expected quality on the $\tilde{\pi}_j$ component corresponding to the self-transition $\pi_{z_{t-1}}$.

$$\tilde{\pi}_j |f_i, \gamma, \kappa \sim Dir([\gamma, ..., \gamma, \gamma + \kappa, \gamma, ..., \gamma]) \tag{6}$$

By applying the auto-regressive hidden Markov model on 16 behaviors, the probability changes over time can be modelled. Figure 7 shows an example the probabilistic changes of eye gaze in one region. On the figure, red, green and blue three-color curves represent the three measured hidden Markov states (shown in the form of probability). The background color represents the dominant state during the time period, e.g. red, green and blue background indicate hidden state 1, 2 and 3 being dominant respectively.

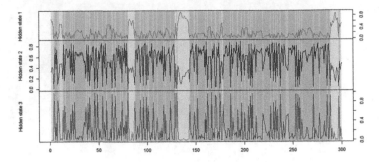

Fig. 7. Example of behavior change and and the probability change presented a graph over time. Three hidden states are presented in three colours. (Color figure online)

4   Results and Analysis

4.1   Eye Gaze Inducted Dynamic Changes

Each eye movement data set is combined with the region information of its corresponding target image, generating 300 eye-gaze behavior matrices, t_0 to t_{299} in 5 s. The value of each cell is updated over time according to eye gaze movement as shown in Figs. 4 or 5. This is the basis of our predictive GAR Hidden Markov model.

4.2   Prediction Performance

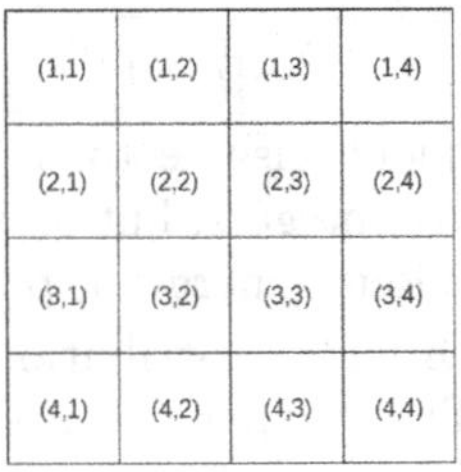

(1,1)	(1,2)	(1,3)	(1,4)
(2,1)	(2,2)	(2,3)	(2,4)
(3,1)	(3,2)	(3,3)	(3,4)
(4,1)	(4,2)	(4,3)	(4,4)

Fig. 8. The coordinate of the regions of image

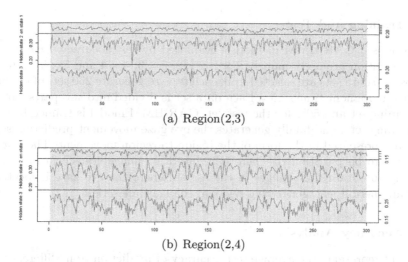

(a) Region(2,3)

(b) Region(2,4)

Fig. 9. Sample graphs of probability change in eye gaze movement behavior over a region generated by Gaussian Auto-regression Hidden Markov model.

In Fig. 8 each region represents the original data of the potential behavior of the eye-gaze movement in the image region, and this behavior will share changes with other regions. By importing the 4×4 behavior information contained in the regions of the image into GAR HMM, we can get 16 probability change curves over time, which represent the potential possibility of eye gaze movement in 16 regions of the image. Figures 9 show the probability of occurrence of the potential behavior of eye-gaze movement in two image regions as an example. Using them we can generate probability distribution, then the instantaneous tendency of the human eye is captured. The eye gaze will move toward the high probability area. When the human eye stays in a certain area for a long time, the probability of the region itself will decrease. That means the possibility of the eye moving toward other regions will increase. By selecting the region with the highest probability for each time period, we get a time series of eye gaze movement predictions by the coordinates of regions (Fig. 10).

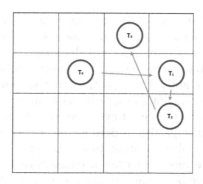

Fig. 10. Demonstration of predictive eye gaze movement over time $(t_0 : t_3)$

4.3   Training and Test

The proposed GAR HMM method is evaluated by test accuracy. Five types of image partition are used, namely 2×1, 2×2, 3×3, 4×4 and 5×5 for testing purpose. 50 data sets are selected from each type to generate 250 sets of predicted eye gaze movement time series. Each data set is divided into two parts, 50% for the training set and 50% for the test set. GAR HMM model is trained based on the training sets, and finally generates the eye gaze movement prediction series, which are presented in the form of the region to region movement. The test sets also need to be partitioned. There is no need for image transform for testing, but only to obtain the changes in the region where the eye gaze is located at each time period, e.g. generating regional change time series.

4.4   Accuracy Analysis

Figure 11 represents the average test accuracy of prediction from different types of partition. Through the results, we can see that with a 4×4 grid GAR HMM can achieve good accuracy in capturing the eye movement tendency, which is 73.7%. This shows that our hypothesis of predicting eye gaze movement is feasible and the proposed GAR HMM can obtain reason performance for this challenging task.

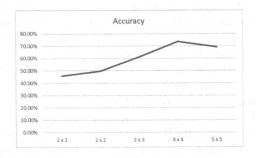

Fig. 11. Average prediction test accuracy using different types of partition

By comparing the 250 sets prediction time series from 5 types of partitions with the corresponding actual eye gaze movement time series, we can see that in general when the number of split regions of the image increases, the accuracy of the probability prediction will increase as well, except 5, where the average prediction accuracy drops slightly. If the partition is too coarse, for example 2×1, the accuracy is close to random guess, 50%. That meas two regions are insufficient to capture the characteristic of eye gaze movement. After examining the results we found that more partitions does lead to the higher accuracy although the computational cost will also dramatically increase. We hold the hypothesis that when the partitions are within a computationally feasible range, the more partitions, the more potential eye gaze movement information captured by the Gaussian auto-regression hidden Markov model, so the eye gaze movement prediction can be more accurate.

5 Conclusion

This study investigates an unexplored challenge, predicting eye gaze movement. It is important due to its potential big impact on advanced human-machine interaction applications. It is difficult because the human eye gaze movement involves influence from many complex factors. To address this challenge we proposed a filtering method to remove non-principle movement by k-Nearest Neighbor classification and Fourier transform. Our results show that the method is effective. The processed trajectories after the filtering are consistent with the underline image content. We also proposed a new method, Gaussian auto-regression hidden Markov model to predict how eye gaze moves between image regions base on the filtered eye gaze movement data. From our experiments, we show that the proposed predictive method (GAR HMM) is effective, in particular with region size of 4×4, where the test accuracy can be 73.7%. Therefore, we conclude K-Nearest Neighbor and Fourier transform are effective filters and it is possible to predict eye gaze by modelling its trajectories in two dimensional space.

References

1. Blohm, G., Optican, L.M., Lefèvre, P.: A model that integrates eye velocity commands to keep track of smooth eye displacements. J. Comput. Neurosci. **21**(1), 51–70 (2006)
2. Chen, D., Jia, T., Wu, C.: Visual saliency detection. Signal Process. Image Commun. **44**, 57–68 (2016)
3. Engbert, R., Longtin, A., Kliegl, R.: A dynamical model of saccade generation in reading based on spatially distributed lexical processing. Vis. Res. **42**(5), 621–636 (2002)
4. Fox, E., Jordan, M.I., Sudderth, E.B., Willsky, A.S.: Sharing features among dynamical systems with beta processes. In: Advances in Neural Information Processing Systems, pp. 549–557 (2009)
5. Gregory, R.L.: Eye and Brain: The Psychology of Seeing, vol. 38. Princeton University Press, Princeton (2015)
6. Harezlak, K., Kasprowski, P.: Searching for chaos evidence in eye movement signals. Entropy **20**(1), 32 (2018)
7. Judd, T., Ehinger, K., Durand, F., Torralba, A.: Learning to predict where humans look. In: 2009 IEEE 12th International Conference on Computer Vision, pp. 2106–2113. IEEE (2009)
8. Kumari, L.K., Jagadesh, B.N.: A novel approach for detection of tumors in mammographic images using Fourier descriptors and KNN. In: Kumar, A., Paprzycki, M., Gunjan, V.K. (eds.) ICDSMLA 2019. LNEE, vol. 601, pp. 1877–1884. Springer, Singapore (2020). https://doi.org/10.1007/978-981-15-1420-3_191
9. Luis, D., Michael, W., Brian, P.: BayesHMM: full Bayesian inference for hidden Markov models (2020)

10. Marchesotti, L., Cifarelli, C., Csurka, G.: A framework for visual saliency detection with applications to image thumbnailing. In: 2009 IEEE 12th International Conference on Computer Vision, pp. 2232–2239 (2009)
11. Mucherino, A., Papajorgji, P.J., Pardalos, P.M.: k-nearest neighbor classification, pp. 83–106 (2009)
12. Otsuka, K., Takemae, Y., Yamato, J.: A probabilistic inference of multiparty-conversation structure based on Markov-switching models of gaze patterns, head directions, and utterances. In: Proceedings of the 7th International Conference on Multimodal Interfaces, pp. 191–198. ACM (2005)
13. Rahman, S.A., Huang, Y., Claassen, J., Heintzman, N., Kleinberg, S.: Combining Fourier and lagged k-nearest neighbor imputation for biomedical time series data. J. Biomed. Inform. **58**, 198–207 (2015)
14. Rayner, K.: Eye movements in reading and information processing. Psychol. Bull. **85**(3), 618 (1978)
15. Ren-san, W.: Automatic zoom and eye track system based on image processing. Optical Instruments (2005)
16. Simola, J., Salojärvi, J., Kojo, I.: Using hidden Markov model to uncover processing states from eye movements in information search tasks. Cogn. Syst. Res. **9**(4), 237–251 (2008)
17. Stasi, L.D., Contreras, D., Cándido, A., Cañas, J., Catena, A.: Behavioral and eye-movement measures to track improvements in driving skills of vulnerable road users: first-time motorcycle riders. Transp. Res. Part F Traffic Psychol. Behav. **14**(1), 26–35 (2011)
18. Zhang, C., Zhou, J., Gu, X., Zhu, S., Bovik, A.C.: Eye movement pattern modeling and visual comfort viewing S3D images. In: 2018 IEEE Visual Communications and Image Processing (VCIP). pp. 1–4. IEEE (2019)
19. Zhou, Q., et al.: Learning adaptive contrast combinations for visual saliency detection. Multimedia Tools Appl. **79**(21), 14419–14447 (2020)

Strategies Improve Social Welfare: An Empirical Study of Strategic Voting in Social Networks

Xiaoxue Liu[✉], Fenghui Ren, Guoxin Su, and Minjie Zhang

School of Computing and Information Technology, University of Wollongong, Wollongong, Australia
xl018@uowmail.edu.au, {fren,guoxin,minjie}@uow.edu.au

Abstract. In utilitarian social choice settings, agents have cardinal utilities over candidates, while for many reasons they only report their ordinal rankings for candidates. One possible way is to use voting systems that have access to the ordinal rankings, to maximize the sum of utility of all agents, i.e. social welfare. However, most work does not consider strategic play when using ordinal preferences as a proxy for cardinal utilities. In this paper, we present a new decision-making model of strategic voting to map cardinal utilities to votes under incomplete information. We consider an iterative setting, where agents will update their votes based on information observed from their neighbors in a social network. We compare our model with three existing models, one is a simple heuristic model and the other two are boundedly rational models. Results from extensive simulations on both random networks and a real social network show that although the strategic play is not frequent, sometimes rare, it does improve the social welfare of selected winners. We investigate the Duverger's Law, showing that only the simple heuristic model that requires low cognitive efforts like human voters can replicate the law.

1 Introduction

Social choice theory is concerned with aggregating the preferences of multiple agents into a collective choice [8]. In a utilitarian setting of social choice, agents have cardinal preferences over candidates, by assigning a numerical value – a utility– to each of them to represent the intensity of preference [10,22,23]. In this context, the purpose of social choice is to select an outcome with the maximal sum of utility of all agents, i.e. (utilitarian) social welfare. Maximizing social welfare is particularly relevant in scenarios such as in resource allocation where social welfare serves as a criterion for quantifying the efficiency of an allocating scheme [9], or in automated design of voting rules where social welfare is a property to determine a winner [6], or in iterative elections where social welfare is used for measuring the quality of an outcome [16,17,22,23].

It is trivial to identify the sociable desired outcome if the utility profile is known. However, direct access to agents' utilities is often not feasible for various

© Springer Nature Switzerland AG 2022
G. Long et al. (Eds.): AI 2021, LNAI 13151, pp. 203–215, 2022.
https://doi.org/10.1007/978-3-030-97546-3_17

reasons, such as privacy concerns, or conveying utility function per agent requires a huge communication band, or asking each agent to report its utility is too demanding. In contrast, simple comparisons among alternatives based on some options are more easily conceivable. Thus, one possible way is to use voting, given transformed ordinal rankings as inputs, to aggregate the preferences so that the sum of utilities is maximized. Voting has been commonly used in recommender systems, product designs, and many practical domains, for its simplicity.

One straightforward way of translating cardinal utilities into ordinal preferences is to rank a candidate with the kth highest utility in the kth place. However, there are mainly two drawbacks of the direct mapping approach. One is transforming cardinal utilities into ordinal rankings leads to distortion because some information is missing during the mapping procedure. Most work in this area explores the distortion of outcomes determined by voting systems [2,3,10] through theoretical analysis, lacking empirical support. The other is direct mapping assumes that all the agents always report the true ordinal preferences, neglecting the reasoning process of how they come to their decisions. In reality, agents are self-interested and they tend to vote strategically for better outcomes by considering their utilities and the current partial vote profile [22,23].

In this work, we study the problem of maximizing social welfare from a utilitarian view and consider iterative voting, where agents are allowed to change their votes for higher utilities. We assume that agents are located in a social network and have incomplete information gained from local neighbors. We consider single-winner elections determined by the Plurality rule. At each iteration, an agent(s) updates its vote using a decision-making model, given its utility and the incomplete information as an input. We introduce a new decision-making model for agents and compares it with three existing decision-making models in terms of performance. We are interested in whether social welfare can be deteriorated or not when self-interested agents in large social networks behave strategically with limited information. Tsang et al. [22,23] also investigated a similar setting to ours, but their decision-making model requires complex computation.

The contributions of this work are as follows: 1. Most works in cardinal-based voting study the bound of the distortion of utilitarian social welfare via theoretic analysis. Different from this, we use experimental ways to approximately maximize social welfare by applying decision-making models. Results show that strategization does improve social welfare generally. Overall, the percentage of agents that change their votes is low in large networks, meaning strategic play does not happen frequently in large populations. This coincides with the fact of low percentage of strategic voters in real world elections, such as in [5]. 2. We introduce a new decision-making model in social networks and compare it with three models from the literature. The experimental results show that our model outperforms other models for bringing more social welfare. 3. We investigate the replication of a common phenomenon in politics: the Duverger's Law. Results show that the size of candidates is a contributing factor to the rule and only the simple heuristic model requiring low cognitive load conforms to it.

The remaining work is organized as follow. Section 1.1 introduces the related work. Section 2 presents decision-making models in social networks. Section 3 shows the details of experiments. Section 4 concludes this paper.

1.1   Related Work

The utilitarian perspective on social choice has many supporters in welfare economics. Procaccia and Rosenschein [20] initiated the distortion framework as the maximal ratio between the total utility of an optimal outcome and that of the outcome determined by voting rules. A series of works has continued this line of research, e.g. by Caragiannis et al. [10], who focused on embedding into voting rules that translated utility into votes, or by Anshelevich et al. [3], who studied distortion of randomized social choice algorithms and well-known voting rules under metric space. However, all these works do not consider strategic play when using ordinal rankings as a proxy. Furthermore, they are from theoretic aspects, lacking empirical evaluations. In contrast, our work uses extensive simulations to show decreased distortion when agents behave strategically.

There is a sizable literature studying voting in social networks (see a survey [15]). Wilder et al. [25] studied the problem of finding a seed of nodes (representing voters) to influence other nodes in social networks via social influence to control elections under limited budgets. Faliszewski et al. [14] investigated the computational complexity of bribery with opinion diffusion in networks where a node, a cluster of like-minded voters, adopted the majority view of its neighborhood. However, the above works consider social pressure in networks and are interested in how to react to peer pressure for revising the winner of elections, while we use networks to filter information. Baumeister et al. Wilczynski [4] used social networks as a source of information, similar to our settings, but they addressed whether a poll agency announced a plausible poll could alter the election outcomes. We emphasize that the above works study election control problems, while our focus is to improve the social welfare of the outcome.

Close related work is from Tsang et al. [22], who proposed a response model to vote strategically under an iterative setting where agents were located in social networks. Their model used observations from an agent's neighbors to infer the likely outcome. They concluded that strategization could improve social welfare via simulations, which agrees with ours. However, they focused on exploring the effect of homophily networks and did not consider real social networks. Later, a set of heuristic methods were presented by Tsang et al. [23], to reduce the computational load of the previous model. In summary, such kind of models based on maximizing expected utility, required intensive computation to assign probabilities to possible outcomes. Furthermore, they focused on one model while we compared four different decision-making models.

2   Model

2.1   Basic Notations and Definitions

Consider a scenario where a set of agents faces a problem of selecting a candidate from a set of candidates. Assume agents are located in a social network, where they get incomplete information from their neighbors. The election proceeds in rounds, in which agents are allowed to update their votes to be better off. We focus on t-dimensional Euclidean model of elections, where both agents and candidates are assumed as points in a t-dimensional space. It belongs to space model, commonly used in politics [12] and in utility-based voting [3]. Here are some definitions concerning elections.

Definition 1 (candidate). A candidate denoted by c, is represented by a vector p_c whose coordinate is $(x_1, x_2, \cdots, x_t)$ in t-dimensional Euclidean space $\mathbb{R}^t$.

Definition 2 (agent). An agent is defined as a five-tuple, $v_i = (p_{v_i}, S, u, M, b)$, where p_{v_i} is a point whose coordinate is $(y_1, y_2, \cdots, y_t)$ in t-dimensional Euclidean space $\mathbb{R}^t$ supported by v_i, S is a score vector observed by v_i over a set of candidates $C = \{c_1, c_2, \ldots, c_m\}$, e.g. $S(c)$ is the count of votes for candidate c, u is a cardinal utility function $u : C \rightarrow \mathbb{R}^+$, M is a decision-making model used by agents to decide which candidate to support in each round, which is defined as $M(u, S) :\rightarrow C$. In M, there is a superscript for the name of the decision model and a subscript for agent-specific parameters (see more details in Sects. 2.2 and 2.3). The $b \in C$ is a submitted vote by using M. If $c \in C$ is the collective choice, the utility of v_i is $u(c)$.

Definition 3 (social network). A social network is defined as an undirected graph $G = (V, E)$, where $V = \{v_1, v_2, \ldots, v_n\}$ is a set of agents, and $E = \{(v_i, v_j) | v_i, v_j \in V\}$ is a set of edges representing connections among agents.

Definition 4 (election). An election is defined as an eight-tuple, $El = (C, V, P, G, f, rd, up, t))$, where C is a set of candidates, V is a set of agents, P is a profile of votes submitted by all agents, G is a network that V is situated, f is the voting rule for deciding a winner, rd represents a total rounds that the election proceeds, up is an update order for V, and t represents a tie-breaking scheme.

In the graph G, an edge $(v_i, v_j) \in E$ indicates that agent v_i and agent v_j can observe each other's votes. Let $N(v_i) = \{v_j \in V | (v_i, v_j) \in E\}$ represent the set of agents that agent v_i can observe, i.e. $N(v_i)$ is the neighbors of v_i. We consider the iterative voting. In each round, the agent v_i chooses a candidate to support based on the decision-making model M, which is formally expressed as $M(u, S)$: $u \times \mathbb{N}^m \rightarrow C$, where $S \in \mathbb{N}^m$ is observed from $N(v_i)$, e.g. the score of candidate c is $S(c) = \sum_{v_j \in N(v_i)} |b_{v_j} = c|$. In a round, if the vote submitted by an agent v_i is the same as the previous round, we say the election converges.

In the t-dimensional Euclidean model, coordinates of points represent agents' or candidates' positions regarding some t issues. We assume that the utility of an agent v_i is inversely proportional to the distance between its favored position p_{v_i} and the advocated position p_{c^*} of the winner c^*. The utility u is formally defined as the following equation:

$$u(p_{c^*}, p_{v_i}) = \frac{1}{\sqrt[2]{\sum_{i=1}^{t} (x_i^* - y_i)^2 + 1}}, \, where \; c* = (x_1^*, x_2^*, \cdots, x_t^*). \quad (1)$$

The closer between p_{v_i} and p_{c^*}, the greater utility agent v_i can obtain. Thus, it is intuitive to interpret utility as the intensity of preference. Throughout the paper, we care about the quantitative measure of the elected outcome, i.e. the utilitarian social welfare (SW). We want to explore whether using a strategic decision-making model can improve the quantity of SW.

The social welfare (SW) in this paper is formally calculated by Eq. 2:

$$SW(V) = \sum_{v_i \in V} u_{v_i}(p_{c^*}, p_{v_i}).$$ (2)

2.2 Decision Models from the Literature

We describe three decision-making models M of strategic voting behaviors from the literature.

Local-Dominance (LD) Model: Meir et al. [17] proposed a boundedly rational model of local dominance, where agents avoided voting for locally dominated candidates. Each agent has an uncertain view on the current score vector S, which is represented by an uncertain parameter r. The set of undominant candidates $(U(u, S, r))$ for an agent v_i is characterized by Meir et al. [17] as follows: first using a threshold to define the set of possible winners (PW) whose scores are at least $\{max_{c \in C} S(c) - 2 \cdot r \cdot \sum_{c \in C} S(c)\}$, second defining $U(u, S, r)$ based on PW, where if $|PW| = 1$, $U(u, S, r) = C$, while if $|PW| > 1$, $U(u, S, r) = PW$. If there is more than one candidate in $U(u, S, r)$, the agent v_i will choose the candidate with the highest utility as the following equation:

$$M_r^{LD}(u, S) := \arg\max_{c \in U(u,S,r)} u(c).$$ (3)

Note that small r means low uncertainty level, e.g. when r is small, an agent believes in the scores and is likely to support the promising candidate.

K-Pragmatist (KP) Model: Annemieke Reijngoud [21] formalized a simple heuristic model of K-Pragmatist. When an agent v_i believes that it has enough information, v_i is optimistic to move its favorite amongst the k-currently highest-ranked candidates, denoted by $B_k(S)$, and votes for its favorite candidate in $B_k(S)$, which can be defined by $M_k^{KP}(u, S)$ by the following equations:

$$M_k^{KP}(u, S) := \arg\max_{c \in B_k(S)} u(c).$$ (4)

Attainability-Utility (AU) Model: Fairstein et al. [13] proposed the Attainability Utility model, emphasizing a trade-off between the attainability factor, proposed by Bowman et al. [7], and utility when facing an uncertain vote profile. The attainability factor of a candidate c, denoted by A_c, measures the certainty that the number of votes casting for c will reach the minimal threshold for c to be the winner, i.e. $A_c = \frac{1}{\pi} arctan(\beta \cdot (\frac{S(c)}{\sum_{c \in C} S(c)} - \frac{1}{m})) + 0.5$ by using a logit-shaped function, where β is a coefficient factor which is the same for all agents. The authors used a parameter α to represent the trade-off. The AU score of the candidate c for an agent v_i is calculated by $AU_\alpha(u, S)(c) = u(c)^\alpha \cdot (A_c)^{2-\alpha}$. An agent v_i will vote for the candidate with the maximal AU score under S calculated as the following equation:

$$M_\alpha^{AU}(u, S) := \arg\max_{c \in C} AU_\alpha(u, S)(c).$$ (5)

2.3 AU Revised Model

Although the AU model allows agents some flexibility in emphasizing trade-offs between attainability and utility, every model above treats the observed information identically in all rounds. The undifferentiated treatment lacks assessment of information, which may lead to the agents' actions failing to meet their goals. To handle this a coefficient factor $\gamma = \frac{1}{1+e^{-rd}}$ is added to the attainability factor where rd represents the round in the iterative voting. The idea is inspired by Bowman et al. [7], who used an increasing variance in attainability factor to rely more on it when more votes were displayed in referendum elections. However, the purpose of γ is slightly different here, where γ is to attribute more weight to differences in candidates' score in S. This is because γ becomes larger when elections progress, which can translate a small advantage in score to a large gap in attainability. Though γ is a somewhat arbitrary increasing function, it represents the idea of adaptive reaction to the dynamic information and allows agents to revise their strategies based on the obtained information.

To this end, we apply the idea of adaptively treating information into the AU model and call the new model as AU revised model (AURe). The AURe model works as two steps. When it is the turn for an agent v_i to reconsider its vote, v_i first calculates the AURe score of each candidate by $AU_{\alpha,\gamma}(u,S)(c) = u(c)^{\alpha} \cdot (A_c)^{2-\alpha}$, where A_c is the attainability of candidate c, i.e. $A_c = \frac{1}{\pi}arctan(\beta \cdot (1+\gamma) \cdot (\frac{S(c)}{\sum_{c \in C} S(c)} - \frac{1}{m})) + 0.5$. Then, agent v_i will support the candidate with the highest AURe score defined by the following equation:

$$M_{\alpha\gamma}^{AURe}(u,S) := \arg\max_{c \in C} AU_{\alpha,\gamma}(u,S)(c). \tag{6}$$

2.4 The Iterative Voting Process

Algorithm 1 describes the iterative voting process which has been studied in [17,18,22,23]. The election starts from an initial state where agents vote for the candidate with the highest utility (see lines 2, 3). In each round rd, an agent v_i first updates its knowledge S then may revise its votes based on the decision-making model M. The election will terminate if it converges or reaches the maximal round. Two types of update methods for agents are considered in line 6: which are synchronous and sequential updates. In the synchronous update, all the agents reconsider their votes simultaneously, while in sequential update agents take turns to revise their votes based on a pre-defined order. The difference between them is that agents using a synchronous way update their knowledge based on the previous round, while the sequential update ensures that agents get the latest information, including revised votes in the current round. Two tie-breaking schemes are used in lines 7, 11. One is a random scheme that randomly selects a candidate from the set with the same score, the other is a lexicographical scheme that selects a candidate in a fixed order.

3   Experiments

Five experiments were conducted to explore how these four decision-making models (AURe, AU, KP, LD) influenced the behavior of agents and results of elections. *Experiment 1:* investigating the effects of two update methods and two tie-breaking schemes, which are mentioned in Sect. 2.4. *Experiment 2:* studying how the graph's average degrees d affected the outcomes of elections. *Experiment 3:* exploring how the size of networks affect the elections. *Experiment 4:* reproducing the common phenomenon in political science: Duverger's Law. The rule refers to that elections under the Plurality rule will eventually develop into two front-candidate races. *Experiment 5:* test four models in a real social network.

Algorithm 1: The iterative voting process

    Input: An election instance $El = \{C, V, P, G, f, rd, up, t)\}$, $maxRound$
    Output: The winner of the election c^*

1 $c^* \leftarrow c_1$;
2 **for** $v_i \in V$ **do**
3     $b_{v_i} \leftarrow \{c \in C \mid u(c) = argmax_{c \in C}\ u(c)\}$
4 **for** $rd \leftarrow 1$ **to** $maxRound$ **do**
5   **for** $v_i \in up$ **do**
6   update S from $N(v_i)$ in G;   /* according to update methods */
7        $b_{v_i} \leftarrow M(u, S)$;   /* if $|b_{v_i}|>1$, use tie-breaking schemes */
8     $isCon \leftarrow$ check whether the election converges or not;
9   **if** $isCon = True$ **then** break;
10 update P;   /* count the number of votes for each candidate */
11 $c^* \leftarrow f(P)$;   /* if $|c^*|>1$, use tie-breaking schemes */
12 **return** c^*;

3.1   Experiment Settings

We consider two types of random graph G, which are the Erdös-Renyi (ER) graph and Barabási-Albert (BA) graph. The ER graph [19] incorporates a minimum number of assumptions. Given a probability p_r, each pair of nodes has the probability p_r to be connected. Self-loops are not allowed. Many human-generated networks, such as the Internet and Facebook, exhibit a property of scale-free where there are a few highly connected hubs and numerous sparsely connected nodes. Scale-free networks can be generated via Barabási-Albert (BA) random model [1], using preferential attachment mechanisms. Given attachment parameter m_0, new nodes are added to a network, connected with existing m_0 vertices with the probability proportional to their respective degrees.

Positions of agents and candidates are independently drawn uniformly at random from the [0, 100] interval like [22,23]. Table 1 shows the settings of four experiments. The maximal round is 25. Each agent may have different parameters of M, where r of LD, k of KP, α of AU and AURe are randomly chosen from $[0,1)$, $[1, [\frac{m}{2}] + 1]$, $(0,2)$ respectively and β is set to 4. Experiments 1-4 were performed 600 times by generating 600 instances, while Experiment 5 was performed 25 times due to the large network. The average results were shown in the following section.

3.2   Results

We defined five metrics for our results. The first one is to measure the *improvement of social welfare* (Impro), which is the ratio between social welfare of the strategic outcome and that of the outcome of the initial state. The second one is to measure the *distortion in social welfare* (Dist), defined as the ratio between social welfare of the optimal outcome and that of the strategic outcome. The third one is *the percentage of agents that cast votes different from the initial state when elections end* (Stra), i.e. the percentage of strategy. The fourth one is the *percentage of elections that converge* (PerCon). The fifth one is *the percentage of elections whose winners are different from the initial state* (PerWD).

Table 1. The settings of five experiments, where the meaning of n, m, up, t can be found in Sect. 2.1, *type* is the graph, d is the average degree of graphs, $Size = \{50, 100, 200, 300, 400, 500, 600, 700, 800\}$, $Degree = \{8, 12, 16, 20, 24, 28, 32\}$, and syn, seq, ran, and lexi represent synchronous, sequential, random, and lexicographical respectively.

Experiments	n	m	$Type$	d	Up	t
Experiment 1	169	4	$type \in \{BA, ER\}$	$d \in Degree$	$up \in \{syn, seq\}$	$t \in \{ran, lexi\}$
Experiment 2	169	4	BA	$d \in Degree$	seq	lexi
Experiment 3	$n \in Size$	4	BA	20	seq	lexi
Experiment 4	$n \in Size$	$m \in \{4, 5, 6\}$	BA	20	seq	lexi
Experiment 5	63371	5	Facebook-WOSN	25.6	seq	lexi

Results in Experiment 1: Table 2 summarizes three metrics (Impro, Dist, Stra) measured on two random graphs (BA, ER). The differences of Impro and Dist between update methods and tie-breaking schemes are much bigger than between two types of graphs. The value of Stra stays the same in four settings for all models, except for the LD model. Specifically, there is little change in the amount of the above three metrics between two graphs with the synchronous update and lexicographical tie-breaking scheme. This is the reason why we focused on synchronous update and lexicographical tie-breaking for Experiment 2–5. We concluded that the update methods and tie-breaking mechanisms had smaller impact than two types of social networks on the result of the voting process. Interestingly, Impro was greater than 1 for all settings, which shows that agents using strategic decision models can improve the social welfare of the outcome.

Results in Experiment 2: Although elections using the Plurality rule are vulnerable to strategization, from our experiments we show it improves the social welfare of elected outcomes. Throughout our 4200 trials, the average ratio of

Table 2. Effects of update methods and tie-breaking schemes on two graphs with m = 4.

up/t	Models	**Impro**	Dist	Stra (%)	Models	**Impro**	Dist	Stra(%)
	BA random graph				ER random graph			
syn/ran	AU	1.0148	1.0805	0.13	AU	1.0146	1.0807	0.13
	AURe	1.0177	1.0774	0.16	AURe	1.0170	1.0781	0.16
	LD	1.0010	1.0954	0.02	LD	1.0010	1.0954	0.02
	KP	1.0087	1.0871	0.25	KP	1.0099	1.0857	0.25
seq/ran	AU	1.0152	1.0801	0.13	AU	1.0140	1.0813	0.13
	AURe	1.0172	1.0780	0.16	AURe	1.0169	1.0782	0.16
	LD	1.0006	1.0959	0.02	LD	1.0015	1.0949	0.02
	KP	1.0085	1.0873	0.25	KP	1.0085	1.0873	0.25
syn/lexi	AU	1.0142	1.0812	0.13	AU	1.0147	1.0806	0.13
	AURe	1.0165	1.0787	0.16	AURe	1.0173	1.0778	0.16
	LD	1.0047	1.0914	0.01	LD	1.0045	1.0916	0.01
	KP	1.0064	1.0896	0.25	KP	1.0087	1.0871	0.25
seq/lexi	AU	1.0147	1.0806	0.13	AU	1.0146	1.0807	0.13
	AURe	1.0164	1.0788	0.16	AURe	1.0166	1.0786	0.16
	LD	1.0044	1.0917	0.01	LD	1.0044	1.0917	0.01
	KP	1.0058	1.0901	0.25	KP	1.0086	1.0872	0.25

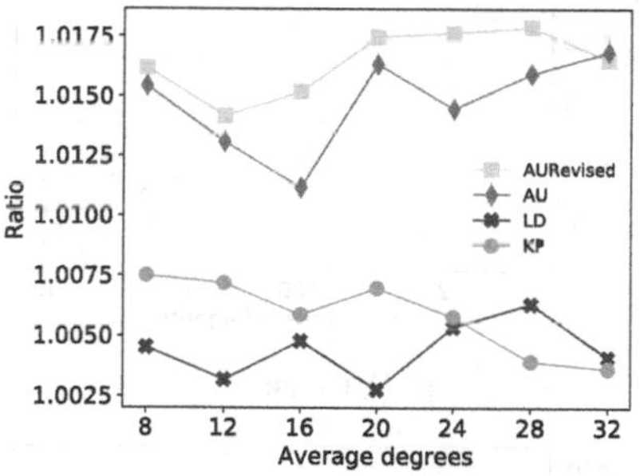

(a) Impro

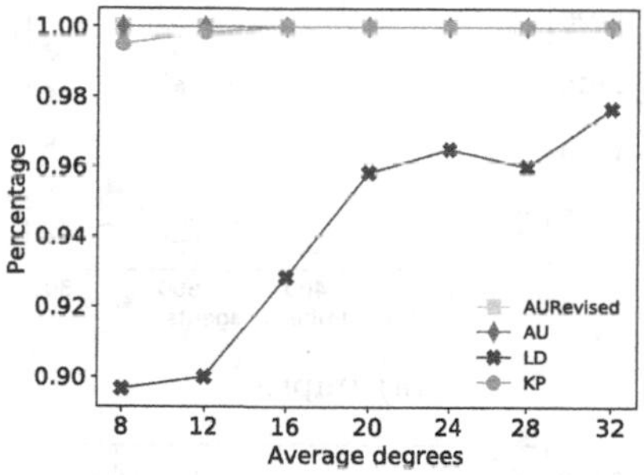

(b) PerCon

Fig. 1. Results of Experiment 2 in scenarios with n = 169, m = 4.

improvement of social welfare was consistently greater than 1 (see Fig. 1(a)), which means the winner selected by using decision models achieved higher social welfare compared with that of the initial state. When the average degree grows, there is a growing trend of improvement of social welfare and a declining trend of distortion in social welfare for all decision models of AU, AURe, and LD. It is in expectation because agents are exposed to a high level of information when the network becomes denser, while the level of information is not enough for the KP model. Specifically, decision models of AURe and AU brought the first and second amount of social welfare compared with other models for almost all settings because they required a relatively more complex calculation than KP and LD. There is a slight increase in PerCon similar to Impro. Therefore, a conclusion is made that increasing the number of neighbors slightly increased social welfare except for the KP model. More generally, when agents have a small amount of information, knowing more votes can help them make better decisions. However, the benefit of more information saturate quickly, while in this context improving the decision model will be more helpful.

Results in Experiment 3: The finding that the value of Impro was greater than 1 is consistent with that of the previous two experiments, which shows strategization can improve the social welfare in large networks. When the number of agents is largely greater than that of candidates, the average value of Impro is still greater than 1, while distortion continually drops (see Fig. 2(a), 2(b)). This means strategic play could make the selected outcome close to the optimal outcomes, even with limited information. The AURe model outperformed the other three models for bringing the highest social welfare. It is noticeable that Stra continually declines when the network becomes larger and sparser (see Fig. 2(c)) because the amount of information that agents observed became

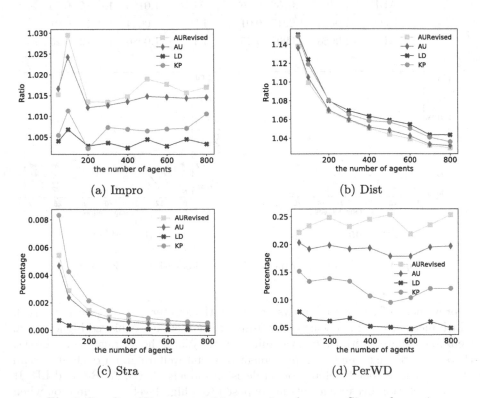

(a) Impro

(b) Dist

(c) Stra

(d) PerWD

Fig. 2. Results of Experiment 3 in scenarios where $n \in Size$ and $m = 4$.

less, which might explain why in reality the number of strategic voters is low. Figure 2(d) shows there is a small number of elections whose winners are revised when elections because a small number of changes in votes does not easily sway the winner in a large population. It also shows elections with a large population are not likely to be manipulated when agents are rational and self-interested.

Results in Experiment 4: The Duverger's Law is measured by SF Ratio, which is the ratio of support between the second- and first-runner up candidates [11]. Complete agreement with Duverger's Law is reflected by the SF Ratio of 0. From our 14400 instances, only the KP model conforms to the rule with SF Ratio staying extremely close to 0 under 4- and 5-candidate scenarios[1] (see Fig. 3(a)) because the KP model requires low cognitive effort similar to real human voters. Figure 3 shows that the more candidates are in elections, the greater the SF Ratio is, meaning that the size of candidates is a contributing factor to the rule. One possible reason is that extra candidates attract some supporters, which diminishes the absolute advantage of support for the two leading candidates, thus agents are willing to cast for other candidates. Therefore, adding some similar candidates may increase the chance for less promising candidates to win.

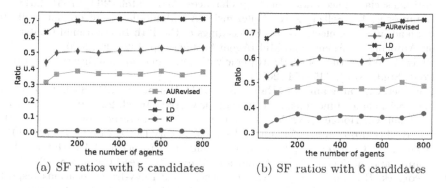

(a) SF ratios with 5 candidates   (b) SF ratios with 6 candidates

Fig. 3. Average SF Ratios of Experiment 4 under different size of populations.

Experiment 5: Finally, we tested our model on a real social network with 5 candidates. The Facebook-WOSN [24] is a sub-graph of Facebook with 63,731 nodes and average degree of 25.6401. Table 3 shows that even in real large social networks, the strategization can still improve the social welfare.

Table 3. Results of Experiment 5

Models	Impro	Dist	Stra (%)
AURe	1.0147	1.0141	4.35E−04
AU	1.0123	1.0166	3.59E−04
LD	1.0020	1.0270	1.13E−05
KP	1.0126	1.0162	7.95E−05

4   Conclusion

In this work, we introduced a strategic decision-making model into cardinal-based voting for approximately maximizing the utilitarian social welfare in an

---

[1] We obtained a smaller value of SF Ratio on m = 4 conditions than m = 5 conditions.

iterative setting where agents revised their votes successively in a social network. A conclusion that strategic play could improve social welfare was reached via simulations on both random graphs and a real social network. The act of strategic play decreased sharply when agents were situated in large sparse networks. Among these four decision-making models, our **AURe** model did well in achieving outcomes with the highest social welfare in large networks. However, our experiments were assumed in static social networks. A possible direction in our future work is to investigate a mechanism of maximizing social welfare in dynamic environments.

References

1. Albert, R., Barabási, A.L.: Statistical mechanics of complex networks. Rev. Mod. Phys. **74**(1), 47 (2002)
2. Amanatidis, G., Birmpas, G., Filos-Ratsikas, A., Voudouris, A.A.: Peeking behind the ordinal curtain: improving distortion via cardinal queries. Artif. Intell. **296**, 103488 (2021)
3. Anshelevich, E., Bhardwaj, O., Elkind, E., Postl, J., Skowron, P.: Approximating optimal social choice under metric preferences. Artif. Intell. **264**, 27–51 (2018)
4. Baumeister, D., Selker, A.K., Wilczynski, A.: Manipulation of opinion polls to influence iterative elections. In: Proceedings of the 19th International Conference on Autonomous Agents and MultiAgent Systems, pp. 132–140 (2020)
5. Blais, A.: Why is there so little strategic voting in Canadian plurality rule elections? Polit. Stud. **50**(3), 445–454 (2002)
6. Boutilier, C., Caragiannis, I., Haber, S., Lu, T., Procaccia, A.D., Sheffet, O.: Optimal social choice functions: a utilitarian view. Artif. Intell. **227**, 190–213 (2015)
7. Bowman, C., Hodge, J.K., Yu, A.: The potential of iterative voting to solve the separability problem in referendum elections. Theory Decis. **77**(1), 111–124 (2014)
8. Brandt, F., Conitzer, V., Endriss, U., Lang, J., Procaccia, A.D.: Handbook of Computational Social Choice. Cambridge University Press, Cambridge (2016)
9. Bredereck, R., Kaczmarczyk, A., Niedermeier, R.: Envy-free allocations respecting social networks. In: Proceedings of the 17th International Conference on Autonomous Agents and MultiAgent Systems. pp. 283–291 (2018)
10. Caragiannis, I., Procaccia, A.D.: Voting almost maximizes social welfare despite limited communication. Artif. Intell. **175**(9–10), 1655–1671 (2011)
11. Cox, G.W.: Making Votes Count: Strategic Coordination in the World's Electoral Systems. Cambridge University Press, Cambridge (1997)
12. Enelow, J.M., Hinich, M.J.: The Spatial Theory of Voting: An Introduction. Cambridge University Press, Cambridge (1984)
13. Fairstein, R., Lauz, A., Meir, R., Gal, K.: Modeling people's voting behavior with poll information. In: Proceedings of the 18th International Conference on Autonomous Agents and MultiAgent Systems, pp. 1422–1430 (2019)
14. Faliszewski, P., Gonen, R., Koutecký, M., Talmon, N.: Opinion diffusion and campaigning on society graphs. In: Proceedings of the 27th International Joint Conference on Artificial Intelligence, pp. 219–225 (2018)
15. Grandi, U.: Social choice and social networks. In: Trends in Computational Social Choice, pp. 169–184 (2017)
16. Meir, R.: Iterative voting. In: Trends in Computational Social Choice, pp. 69–86 (2017)

17. Meir, R., Lev, O., Rosenschein, J.S.: A local-dominance theory of voting equilibria. In: Proceedings of the Fifteenth ACM Conference on Economics and Computation, pp. 313–330 (2014)
18. Meir, R., Polukarov, M., Rosenschein, J., Jennings, N.: Convergence to equilibria in plurality voting. In: Proceedings of the AAAI Conference on Artificial Intelligence, vol. 24 (2010)
19. Paul, E., Alfréd, R.: On random graphs. I. Publicationes Mathematicae (Debrecen) **6**, 290–297 (1959)
20. Procaccia, A.D., Rosenschein, J.S.: The distortion of cardinal preferences in voting. In: Klusch, M., Rovatsos, M., Payne, T.R. (eds.) CIA 2006. LNCS (LNAI), vol. 4149, pp. 317–331. Springer, Heidelberg (2006). https://doi.org/10.1007/11839354_23
21. Reijngoud, A.: Voter response to iterated poll information (2012)
22. Tsang, A., Larson, K.: The echo chamber: strategic voting and homophily in social networks. In: Proceedings of the 2016 International Conference on Autonomous Agents & Multiagent Systems, pp. 368–375 (2016)
23. Tsang, A., Salehi-Abari, A., Larson, K.: Boundedly rational voters in large (r) networks. In: Proceedings of the 17th International Conference on Autonomous Agents and MultiAgent Systems, pp. 301–308 (2018)
24. Viswanath, B., Mislove, A., Cha, M., Gummadi, K.P.: On the evolution of user interaction in Facebook. In: Proceedings of the 2nd ACM Workshop on Online Social Networks, pp. 37–42 (2009)
25. Wilder, B., Vorobeychik, Y.: Controlling elections through social influence. In: International Conference on Autonomous Agents and Multiagent Systems (2018)

A Network-Based Rating Mechanism Against False-Name Attack

Xinyuan Lian[1,2] and Dengji Zhao[1,2(✉)]

[1] ShanghaiTech University, Shanghai, China
[2] Shanghai Engineering Research Center of Intelligent Vision and Imaging,
Shanghai, China
{lianxy,zhaodj}@shanghaitech.edu.cn

Abstract. Rating system is a commonly used approach to evaluate a product or service online. It often simply averages the ratings from all users. However, users can manipulate the rating by creating many fake ids to submit non-truthful ratings. In this paper, we propose a weighted rating system underpinned by the connections between users, where the connections can reflect their friendship. Under this rating system, we prove that a user cannot create fake ids to manipulate the evaluation towards her favor. Moreover, the system also represents all ratings, i.e., each single rating will affect the aggregated rating.

Keywords: Rating system · False-name-proof · Mechanism design

1 Introduction

E-commerce is the activity of electronically buying or selling products online. E-commerce platforms such as Amazon and Taobao allow users to report their feedback in the form of a discrete score after they buy the products. One score format is the binary rating scale since most buyers only use the extreme choices on the rating scale. Several platforms have adopted a binary rating scale where buyers rate their experience as either positive or negative. The rating result of a product is generally obtained by aggregating all buyers' report and it is an essential part of a product's competitiveness. This process encourages sellers to provide better products because higher ratings can attract more business. For example, products with higher rating are usually listed at the front by online market search engines and buyers are more keen on products with higher ratings [12]. Therefore, online sellers have strong incentives to improve their products' ratings.

The primary purpose of the rating system is to offer a way for buyers to give useful feedback on products. However, attackers may create fake accounts to increase or decrease the rating of a product. Such malicious behaviors are commonly known as *false-name attack* [13]. The false-name attack refers that an agent can gain benefits by creating multiple fake identities. This kind of attack has seriously affected the sellers' profit and the development of the e-commerce

G. Long et al. (Eds.): AI 2021, LNAI 13151, pp. 216–227, 2022.
https://doi.org/10.1007/978-3-030-97546-3_18

platforms. Furthermore, we can't avoid false-name attacks if the cost of creating fake identities is low [4,5].

Traditional solutions against false-name attack rely on trusted identity verification [2]. It limits the introduction of fake identities to ensure that the fraction of malicious nodes remains under a certain threshold. However, such verification is system-specific and it is difficult to deploy in practice. Recently, there are some studies about applying social networks to mitigate false-name attacks [3], where they proposed new algorithms for network-based reputation systems, but they did not directly address the problem on the rating system. Moreover, modern communication technologies and social media have enhanced the role of social networks in rating systems [7,8,10]. Our goal is to design a rating mechanism to avoid false-name attacks by using the properties of the social network.

In this paper, we propose a general framework based on the social network to design a rating mechanism for a binary rating system. We consider all buyers of a product form a large social network where each buyer is linked with some other buyers. The connection can reflect their friendship. After experiencing the product, they will report their feedback to the mechanism. Given the social network, the rating mechanism will output the rating of a product by considering all buyers' feedback. Attacker can bias the final rating creating many fake identities to report false feedback. Our work is to formalise the utility of attackers and design the mechanism to remove the incentives to create fake identities. Especially, we propose a weight function to identity agents' influence in the social network. Each agent's weight is related to the number of their friends and higher weight means that her feedback will have more influence on the final rating. In addition, we define the monotonicity property to ensure the result of a weighted rating mechanism is still meaningful, i.e., the result should still reflect all buyers' feedback on the products.

The techniques used in our analyses draw inspiration from the work of Grandi and Turrini [6]. They have studied a personalised rating system where a rating of a service to a user is aggregated from her friends' feedback only, which determines the probability of all individuals to use the service and thus its generated revenue. Their work focused on showing whether a network-based rating mechanism can resist the bribery, but not the false-name attack. Brill et al. [1] studied the false-name attack of finding a recommendation for an uninformed user in a social network. Machine learning can also be used to tackle the false-name attack problem by learning predictive models using features of the review texts to detect and punish fake reviews [9,11,14].

In this paper, our contributions advance the state of the art in the following ways:

- We first characterize a weighted rating mechanism for the binary rating system in a social network which is false-name-proof no matter how many fake identities the attacker creates and how they connect with each other.
- The weighted rating mechanism is monotonic to ensure the final rating of a product is sensitive to all users' ratings.

The remainder of the paper is organized as follows. The Sect. 2 defines the model and the properties of the rating mechanism in the social network. Then we propose our mechanism and give a detailed proof of the properties in Sect. 3. We conclude and discuss future work in Sect. 4.

2   The Model

We study a rating system for a product in e-commerce. The product has a binary quality, denoted by $Q = \{1, 2\}$ where 1 denotes the low quality signal or its users' dissatisfaction and 2 denotes the high quality signal or the satisfaction of its users (the quality level can also be other scales in practice). Agent i can pay a cost $c > 0$ to buy the product and has her own observation $o_i \in Q$ after experiencing the product. She will report her rating $r_i \in Q$ to the rating system. We say agent i truthfully reports her observation if $r_i = o_i$.

Let $V = \{1, 2, ..., n\}$ be the set of agents who experienced the product. We consider all the agents are connected by an undirected graph $G = (V, E)$. The edges represent trust between agents. To facilitate the analysis, we assume that graph G is connected. For an agent $i \in V$, we denote $N(i) = \{j \in V | (i, j) \in E\} \setminus \{i\}$ the neighbours of agent i. Given the graph and all agents' rating reports, we can formally define the networked rating mechanism that we are going to design.

Definition 1 (Networked Rating Mechanism). *A networked rating mechanism $\mathcal{M}$ is defined to output the final rating u according to the structure of the graph and the agents' reports, i.e. $\mathcal{M} : \mathcal{G}^V \times \mathcal{R}^V \to u \in [1, 2]$ where $\mathcal{G}^V$ is the space of all possible networks consists of V and $\mathcal{R}^V$ is the space of all possible reports by agents V.*

It is reasonable to let the final rating u be in the range of $[1, 2]$ since the quality of the product is binary. We assume that every agent wishes the final rating to be closer to her observation after reporting feedback. In many online market systems, final rating of a product can reflect its actual quality and affect the seller's profits in the long term. Hence, sellers have incentives to improve the final rating of their products and their competitors expect to decrease their ratings. In traditional rating system, one can simply change the final rating by creating many fake identities to misreport feedback. Such manipulations are known as *false-name attack*. Online social networks typically lack a proof of authenticity of agents, thus allowing agents to easily create fake identities. In this paper, an attacker can create many fake identities as her neighbours in order to increase or decrease the final rating in the graph.

Definition 2 (False-Name Attack). *Given a graph $G = (V, E)$, for any attacker $v \in V$ can perform a false-name attack by creating a set of false nodes $M_v = \{v_1, v_2, ..., v_{m_v}\}$ and choose their reports, where $m_v \in \mathbb{Z}_0^+$ denotes the number of false nodes created by the attacker v.*

An attacker can make her false nodes act as buyers and choose their reports. Due to the creation of each edge requires the consent of both agents, it's reasonable to assume that false nodes can only be connected with the attacker and themselves. We can see attacker will let her false nodes have the same report as herself since attacker desires the final rating to be biased towards her favor after the false-name attack. With the increasing number of false nodes, one's report will have a higher proportion.

Moreover, the attacker should pay $c > 0$ to buy the product if she creates one false node. Let $V^{\mathcal{A}} \subseteq V$ denote the set of all attackers in the graph. Suppose there exists a mapping function $f_c : V^{\mathcal{A}} \to \mathbb{R}^+$ for each attacker in $V^{\mathcal{A}}$. The mapping function represents the attacker's expected change on the final rating when creating a false node. Let $u^{\mathcal{A}}$ represent the final rating after the false name attack. Attacker v desires that the final rating will increase or decrease by $m_v f_c(v)$. It should be mentioned that $|u - u^{\mathcal{A}}|$ is the actual change under the attack. Then, we can define the utility of the attacker v as follows

$$u_v = \begin{cases} u - u^{\mathcal{A}} - m_v f_c(v) & \text{if } r_v = 1 \\ u^{\mathcal{A}} - u - m_v f_c(v) & \text{if } r_v = 2 \end{cases}$$

If $r_v = 1$, the attacker can be the competitor who expects to decrease the final rating and we will have $u - u^{\mathcal{A}} \geq 0$. If $r_v = 2$, the attacker can be the seller who expects to increase the final rating and we will have $u - u^{\mathcal{A}} \leq 0$. A false name attack is profitable if the attacker's utility is non-negative. It means that the actual changed amount of the final rating exceeds the expected changed amount corresponding to her payment. That is,

$$u_v = \begin{cases} u - u^{\mathcal{A}} - m_v f_c(v) \geq 0 & \text{if } r_v = 1 \\ u^{\mathcal{A}} - u - m_v f_c(v) \geq 0 & \text{if } r_v = 2. \end{cases}$$

Definition 3 (False-Name-Proof). *A networked rating mechanism $\mathcal{M}$ is false-name-proof if for all attacker $v \in V^{\mathcal{A}}$ reporting her observation truthfully and not creating any false nodes is a dominant strategy, i.e. $r_v = o_v$ and $m_v = 0$.*

According to the utility of the attacker, if the actual changed amount of the final rating $|u - u^{\mathcal{A}}|$ is smaller than the attacker's expected amount $m_v f_c(v)$, then attacker v will have no incentives to perform false-name attack i.e. $u_v < 0$.

To design a false-name-proof rating mechanism, it's easy to have a simple method that it can reverse the new agent's report i.e. the mechanism receives the opposite of her report. However, it will incentivize agents who are not fake identities to report their observation untruthfully and make the final rating meaningless. The final rating should reflect all agents' experience. We introduce the monotonicity property which means the networked rating mechanism should establish that the final rating will move towards a new agent's report when the agent is connected with the graph.

Definition 4 (Monotonicity). *Suppose a new agent $i' \notin V$ is connected with another agent in the graph and they have the same report. Let u' be the final* *rating when considering the report of i. Networked rating mechanism satisfies the monotonicity if*

$$\begin{cases} u > u' & \text{if } r_{i'} = 1 \\ u < u' & \text{if } r_{i'} = 2. \end{cases}$$

Monotonicity makes sure that each agent's report can be reflected correctly in the final rating. We aim to design the mechanism to be both false-name-proof and monotonicity. In the next section, we will propose our *weighted rating mechanism* by introducing a weight function to quantify agents' influence and show how to allocate each nodes' weight in a given social network to let the mechanism be both false-name-proof and monotonicity.

3   Weighted Rating Mechanism

Previous study [6] defined agents' weight to measure their influence on a social network. One agent's weight is proportional to the number of connections this agent has. When it comes to the false-name attack problem, attacker may have higher weight after creating many fake identities. Hence, an appropriate weight function can support us to notice such unusual weights on the social network and design a false-name-proof mechanism. Given a social network $G = (V, E)$, we introduce our weight function for each agent $i \in V$ as the following

$$w_i = \frac{1}{|N(i)| + 1} + \alpha + \sum_{j \in N(i)} \left(\frac{1}{|N(j)| + 1} - \frac{\alpha}{|N(j)|} \right) \qquad (*)$$

where $|N(i)|$ represents the number of agent i's neighbours and α is a parameter. Each agent's weight shows her influence on the network and we can set different α to change her influence. Recall that we assumed that every agent has at least one neighbour, thus w_i is well-defined for every agent. We describe our mechanism as a method to compute each agent's weight according to the structure of the social network and output the final rating u by the weighted arithmetic mean of all reports, that is,

$$u = \frac{\sum_{i \in V} w_i r_i}{n}$$

where n is the total number of agents. Then, we can formally define the weighted rating mechanism.

Definition 5 (Weighted Rating Mechanism). *Given a social network G and all agents' report on the product, the weighted rating mechanism $\mathcal{M}$ is defined to compute the weight w_i for all $i \in V$ and output the final rating $u = \frac{\sum_{i \in V} w_i r_i}{n}$.*

It can be seen that each agent's weight is related to the degree of herself and her neighbours. The sum of all agents' weight is equal to n, and the range of the final rating will be $u \in [1, 2]$. Now, the main challenge is to find the parameter α such that the weighted rating mechanism meets the desirable properties. Since the final rating should reflect agents' feedback, we begin by considering that each agent's weight is positive. To make sure $w_i > 0$, for all $i \in V$, we get that

$$\begin{cases} \frac{1}{|N(i)|+1} + \alpha > 0 \\ \frac{1}{|N(i)|+1} - \frac{\alpha}{|N(i)|} > 0 \end{cases} \Rightarrow \begin{cases} \alpha > -\frac{1}{|N(i)|+1} \\ \alpha < \frac{|N(i)|}{|N(i)|+1} \end{cases}$$

Due to the assumption that each agent has at least one neighbour, i.e. $N(i) \geq 1, \forall i \in V$, we can get $\alpha \in [0, \frac{1}{2})$ from the inequalities. Then we further refine the parameter α to make the weighted rating mechanism false-name-proof and monotonicity. We first focus on false-name-proof and show that agents will report their observations truthfully.

Lemma 1. *Agents in weighted rating mechanism will truthfully report their observations.*

Proof. Without loss of generality, we assume an agent i's observation is $o_i = 1$. If she truthfully reports $r_i = o_i = 1$, the final rating can be shown as $u_1 = \frac{w_i + \sum_{j \in V \setminus \{i\}} w_j r_j}{n}$ where n is total number of agents. If she misreport $r'_i = 2$, the final rating will be $u_2 = \frac{2w_i + \sum_{j \in V \setminus \{i\}} w_j r_j}{n}$. It can be seen that $u_2 > u_1$ and the final rating won't be closer to her observation if misreporting. It is the same that $o_i = 2$. Therefore, agents will report their observations truthfully. $\square$

An attacker can create any number of false-name nodes as her neighbours and there are two different kinds of attacker's goal: increase the final rating or decrease the final rating. For the purpose of maintaining clarity in the exposition, we first present our mechanism for the special case that the attacker creates just one false node to decrease the final rating where they are connected with each other and have the same report 1. In particular, we assume the infimum of the mapping functions, i.e. $\inf f_c$, is known to the mechanism designer.

Lemma 2. *When the attacker creates one false node to decrease the final rating, the weighted rating mechanism is false-name-proof if*

$$\alpha < \frac{(1+n)(n \times \inf f_c - 1)}{n} - 1.$$

Proof. We use u and u^A to denote the final rating before and after the false-name attack respectively. By Lemma 1, it's better for the attacker to make the false node report as herself. Assume that the attacker v has n_1 neighbours whose reports are all 1, denoted by a set N_v^1 and n_2 neighbours whose reports are all 2, denoted by a set N_v^2. For the other nodes in the graph, we use N_{-v} to denote a set of nodes who are not neighbours of attacker v. Attacker v creates a false node v' and $r_{v'} = 1$. We give a schematic diagram as Fig.1 to help understand.

Let W_1 and W_2 be the total weight of report 1 and report 2 before the false-name attack. According to the weight function, we have $W_1 + W_2 = n$ and the final rating will be $u = \frac{\sum_{i \in V} w_i r_i}{n} = \frac{W_1 + 2W_2}{n} = 1 + \frac{W_2}{n}$.

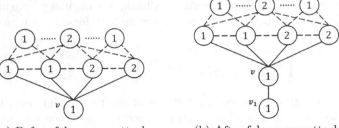

(a) Before false-name attack   (b) After false-name attack

Fig. 1. Attacker v creates a false node v_1. Solid line represents the edges between attacker and her neighbours. Dashed line represents all possible edges between all other nodes.

Similarly, let W_1' and W_2' be the total weight of report 1 and report 2 after the attacker creates a false node. Then we have $W_1' + W_2' = n + 1$ and the final rating will be $u^A = \frac{W_1' + 2W_2'}{n+1} = 1 + \frac{W_2'}{n+1}$. Therefore, the reduced rating is $u - u^A = \frac{W_2}{n} - \frac{W_2'}{n+1}$. Now the proof focuses on the total weight of report 2 and we should find the desirable α such that $\frac{W_2}{n} - \frac{W_2'}{n+1} < f_c(v)$. When the false node appears, the weight of nodes in set N_v^2 will change and the weight of nodes in set N_{-v} will stay the same with the fact that one's weight is only related to her neighbours' degree in the graph. Before the false-name attack, for a node $i \in N_v^2$, her weight w_i is $w_i = \frac{1}{|N(i)|+1} + \alpha + \sum_{j \in N(i)} \left(\frac{1}{|N(j)|+1} - \frac{\alpha}{|N(j)|} \right) = \frac{1}{|N(i)|+1} + \alpha + \frac{1}{n_1+n_2+1} - \frac{\alpha}{n_1+n_2} + \overline{w}_i$, where $\overline{w}_i = \sum_{j \in N(i) \setminus \{v\}} \left(\frac{1}{|N(j)|+1} - \frac{\alpha}{|N(j)|} \right)$. Let $\overline{W}_2$ be the total weights of the nodes in N_{-v} whose report is 2. Then we can get $W_2 = \overline{W}_2 + \sum_{i \in N_v^2} w_i = \overline{W}_2 + \sum_{i \in N_v^2} \left(\frac{1}{|N(i)|+1} + \overline{w}_i \right) + n_2 \alpha + \frac{n_2}{n_1+n_2+1} - \frac{n_2 \alpha}{n_1+n_2}$.

It should be mentioned that $\overline{w}_i$ and $\overline{W}_2$ don't change after false-name attack. However, it will increase the attacker's degree i.e. $|N(v)| = n_1 + n_2 + 1$. Then we can get $W_2' = \overline{W}_2 + \sum_{i \in N_v^2} \left(\frac{1}{|N(i)|+1} + \overline{w}_i \right) + n_2 \alpha + \frac{n_2}{n_1+n_2+2} - \frac{n_2 \alpha}{n_1+n_2+1}$. Let $T = \overline{W}_2 + \sum_{i \in N_v^2} \left(\frac{1}{|N(i)|+1} + \overline{w}_i \right) + n_2 \alpha$ which is invariant before and after false-name attack.

To make mechanism false-name-proof, we have $\frac{W_2}{n} - \frac{W_2'}{n+1} < f_c(v)$, i.e. $(n+1)W_2 - nW_2' < n(n+1)f_c(v)$. For the left-hand side (LHS), we have $(n+1)W_2 - nW_2' = T + \frac{n_2+nn_2+nn_2\alpha}{n_1+n_2+1} - \frac{n_2\alpha+nn_2\alpha}{n_1+n_2} - \frac{nn_2}{n_1+n_2+2}$. As T is a part of the W_2 in the given graph, we have $T < n$ and α is non-negative. Then the LHS will be $(n+1)W_2 - nW_2' < n + (1+n+n\alpha)\frac{n_2}{n_1+n_2+1} < n+1+n+n\alpha$. Hence, the false-name-proof inequality will be

$$(n+1)W_2 - nW_2' < n(n+1)f_c(v)$$
$$n + n\alpha < (n+1)(nf_c(v) - 1)$$
$$\alpha < \frac{(1+n)(nf_c(v) - 1)}{n} - 1$$

Since the infimum of the mapping function f_c is $\inf f_c$ for any attacker, the weighted rating mechanism is false-name-proof if $\alpha < \frac{(1+n)(n \times \inf f_c - 1)}{n} - 1$. $\quad\square$

Lemma 2 shows that mechanism can select α to satisfy false-name-proof when an attacker creates one false node to decrease the final rating. Additionally, we have $\alpha \in [0, \frac{1}{2})$ to ensure every agents' weight is positive. It is necessary to consider that the domain of parameter α in Lemma 2 should also make sure agents have positive weight i.e. $\frac{(1+n)(n \times \inf f_c - 1)}{n} - 1 > 0$ where it is equal to $\inf f_c > \frac{2}{n}$. Online e-commerce platform has many users involving in evaluating a product. n is always a large number and $\frac{2}{n}$ will close to 0 in practice. f_c is a mapping function to show all attackers' expected change on the final rating. Hence, it is reasonable to assume that $\inf f_c > \frac{2}{n}$. Now the requirement for parameter α becomes

$$\alpha \in \left[0, \min\left\{\frac{1}{2}, \frac{(1+n)(n \times \inf f_c - 1)}{n} - 1\right\}\right)$$

We have just considered the special case where the attacker creates only one false node to decrease the final rating. However, only one fake identity's malicious report may have less influence on the final rating and the attacker will create any number of false nodes. The weighted rating mechanism should also be false-name-proof when the attacker v creates $m_v \geq 1$ false nodes and choose how they connect with each other in the social network. We first consider that all the false nodes are only connected with the attacker i.e. the false nodes are not connected with each other. Then, we will extend it to the general case.

Lemma 3. *When the attacker v creates $m_v \geq 1$ false nodes to decrease the final rating and the false nodes are only connected to the attacker, the weighted rating mechanism is false-name-proof if*

$$\alpha < \frac{(1+n)(n \times \inf f_c - 1)}{n} - 1.$$

Proof. We denote the set of false nodes as $M = \{v_1, v_2, ..., v_{m_v}\}$. Let $u^{\mathcal{A}_M}$ represent the final rating after the attacker creates a set of false nodes M. According to the Lemma 2, if $\alpha < \frac{(1+n)(n \times \inf f_c - 1)}{n} - 1$, we have

$$u - u^{\mathcal{A}_{\{v_1\}}} < f_c(v)$$
$$u^{\mathcal{A}_{\{v_1\}}} - u^{\mathcal{A}_{\{v_1, v_2\}}} < f_c(v)$$
$$\vdots \qquad \vdots$$
$$u^{\mathcal{A}_{\{v_1, ..., v_{m_v} - 1\}}} - u^{\mathcal{A}_{\{v_1, ..., v_{m_v}\}}} < f_c(v)$$

Add up these inequalities and it will be

$$u - u^{A_M} < m_v f_c(v)$$

Hence, according to the Lemma 2, the weighted rating mechanism $\mathcal{M}$ is false-name-proof if $\alpha < \frac{(1+n)(n \times \inf f_c - 1)}{n} - 1$. $\square$

Theorem 1. *When the attacker v creates $m_v \geq 1$ false nodes to decrease the final rating and the false nodes have arbitrary connectivity among themselves, the weighted rating mechanism is false-name-proof if*

$$\alpha < \frac{(1 + n)(n \times \inf f_c - 1)}{n} - 1.$$

Proof. We denote the set of false nodes as $M = \{v_1, v_2, ..., v_{m_v}\}$. No matter how the false nodes connect with each other, the weight which the attacker gets from other agents remains unchanged, denoted by W_{-v}.

When all m_v false nodes are only connected with attacker, attacker v's weight is $W_v = \frac{1}{|N(v)|+1+m} + \alpha + m_v(\frac{1}{2} - \alpha) + W_{-v}$. For each false node $i \in M = \{v_1, v_2, ..., v_{m_v}\}$, its weight is $W_v = \frac{1}{|N(v)|+1+m} + \alpha + m_v(\frac{1}{2} - \alpha) + W_{-v}$. Then the total weight of attacker and false nodes is

$$W_{\mathcal{A}} = W_v + \sum_{i \in M} W_i$$

$$= \frac{m_v + 1}{|N(v)| + 1 + m_v} - \frac{m_v \alpha}{|N(v)| + m_v} + m_v + \alpha + W_{-v}$$

When all m_v false nodes can connect arbitrarily, the attacker v's weight is $W'_v = \frac{1}{|N(v)|+1+m_v} + \alpha + W_{-v} + \sum_{i \in M} \left(\frac{1}{|N(i)|+1} - \frac{\alpha}{|N(i)|} \right)$. For each false node $i \in M$, its weight is $W'_i = \frac{1}{|N(i)|+1} + \alpha + \sum_{j \in M \setminus \{i\}} \left(\frac{1}{|N(j)|+1} - \frac{\alpha}{|N(j)|} \right)$. Then the total weight of attacker and false nodes is

$$W'_{\mathcal{A}} = W'_v + \sum_{i \in M} W'_i$$

$$= W'_v + \sum_{i \in M} \left(\frac{1}{|N(i)| + 1} \right) + m_v \alpha + \sum_{i \in M} \sum_{j \in M \setminus \{i\}} \frac{1}{|N(j)| + 1} - \frac{\alpha}{|N(j)|}$$

$$= \frac{m_v + 1}{|N(v)| + 1 + m_v} - \frac{m_v \alpha}{|N(v)| + m_v} + m_v + \alpha + W_{-v}$$

We can see that $W_{\mathcal{A}} = W'_{\mathcal{A}}$ which means two forms of attack are equivalent. Then with the Lemma 3, we can show the weighted rating mechanism is false-name-proof with the same requirement on α. $\square$

It should be mentioned that the weighted rating mechanism is still false-name-proof even if the false nodes create new false nodes since our proof method can be applied on any nodes in the graph. Now, let's discuss that an attacker creates false nodes to increase the final rating. Actually, the proof is similar to the above lemmas and theorem.

Lemma 4. *When the attacker creates one false node to increase the final rating, the weighted rating mechanism is false-name-proof if $\alpha < \frac{(1+n)(n \times \inf f_c - 1)}{n} - 1$.*

Proof. By Lemma 1, the false node will give the same report as the attacker to increase the final rating. Let W_1 and W_2 be the total weight of report 1 and report 2 before the false-name attack respectively. We have $W_1 + W_2 = n$ and the final rating $u = \frac{W_1 + 2W_2}{n} = 2 - \frac{W_1}{n}$.

Similarly, let W_1' and W_2' be the total weight of report 1 and report 2 after the false-name attack respectively. We have $W_1' + W_2' = n+1$ and the final rating $u^{\mathcal{A}} = \frac{W_1' + 2W_2'}{n+1} = 2 - \frac{W_1'}{n+1}$. Then the increased rating is $u^{\mathcal{A}} - u = \frac{W_1}{n} - \frac{W_1'}{n+1}$. The rest of the proof is same as that of Lemma 2. So the requirement on α is still equivalent.   □

Theorem 2. *When the attacker creates $m_v \geq 1$ false nodes to increase the final rating and these false nodes have arbitrary connectivity among themselves, the weighted rating mechanism is false-name-proof if $\alpha < \frac{(1+n)(n \times \inf f_c - 1)}{n} - 1$.*

The proof follows from observing that multiple false nodes case can be reduced to the one false node case, like the proof of Theorem 1. In addition to the false-name-proof, the weighted rating mechanism should also satisfy the monotonicity. It reflects the value of buyers' reports and makes the final rating meaningful.

Theorem 3. *The weighted rating mechanism satisfies monotonicity if $\alpha < \frac{1}{3}$.*

Proof. Suppose agent i has a new neighbour i' who buys the product and gives a feedback. Without loss of generality, we assume $r_i = r_{i'} = 1$. the weighted rating mechanism is monotonic if $u > u'$ where u and u' are the corresponding final rating before and after new agent's participation.

Let W_1 and W_2 be the total weight of report 1 and report 2 before the new agent's participation and we have $W_1 + W_2 = n$. The final rating can be $u = 1 + \frac{W_2}{n}$. Let W_1' and W_2' be the total weight of report 1 and report 2 after the new agent's participation and we have $W_1' + W_2' = n + 1$. The final rating can be $u' = 1 + \frac{W_2'}{n+1}$. Therefore, the decreased rating is $u - u' = \frac{W_2}{n} - \frac{W_2'}{n+1}$. Then we should find α such that $\frac{W_2}{n} - \frac{W_2'}{n+1} > 0$ to show $u > u'$. It can be seen that

$$\frac{W_2}{n} - \frac{W_2'}{n+1} > \frac{W_2 - W_2'}{n+1}$$

Then we focus on the equality $W_2 - W_2' > 0$. Similar to the proof of Lemma 2, agent i has n_1 neighbours whose reports are all 1, denoted by a set N_i^1 and n_2 neighbours whose reports are all 2, denoted by a set N_i^2. For the other nodes in graph, we use N_{-i} to denote a set of nodes who are not neighbours of agent i. We can find that

$$
\begin{cases}
W_2 = T + \frac{n_2}{n_1+n_2+1} - \frac{n_2\alpha}{n_1+n_2} \\
W_2' = T + \frac{n_2}{n_1+n_2+2} - \frac{n_2\alpha}{n_1+n_2+1}
\end{cases}
$$

where $T = \overline{W}_2 + \sum_{i \in N_i^2} \left(\frac{1}{|N(i)|+1} + \overline{w}_i \right) + n_2\alpha$ and $\overline{W}_2$ is the total weights of nodes in set N_{-i} whose reports are 2. Let $x = n_1 + n_2 \geq 1$ since each agent has at least one neighbour. Therefore, we have

$$
\begin{aligned}
& W_2 - W_2' > 0 \\
\Leftrightarrow\ & (1+\alpha)(x+2)x - \alpha(x+1)(x+2) - x(x+1) > 0 \\
\Leftrightarrow\ & (1-\alpha)x - 2\alpha > 0 \\
\Leftrightarrow\ & \alpha < \frac{1}{3}
\end{aligned}
$$

We can see mechanism is monotonic when $\alpha < \frac{1}{3}$ if agent i reports 1. If agent i reports 2, we have $u' - u = \frac{W_1}{n} - \frac{W_1'}{n+1}$ and the rest of proof is same as above. Hence, we prove that the weighted rating mechanism is monotonic if $\alpha < \frac{1}{3}$. $\square$

We already have a requirement for α to let agents have positive weight and the weighted rating mechanism be false-name-proof. The following corollary is a straightforward consequence of all the results.

Corollary 1. *The weighted rating mechanism is false-name-proof and monotonicity if*

$$
\alpha \in \left[0, \min \left\{ \frac{1}{3}, \frac{(1+n)(n \times \inf f_c - 1)}{n} - 1 \right\} \right).
$$

In summary, agent's weight is determined by the network structure and the parameter α in our mechanism. We find the range of parameter α such that the weighted rating mechanism satisfies false-name-proof and monotonicity no matter how many false nodes the attacker creates and how they connect. Moreover, the weighted rating mechanism can be applied easily in practice since the final rating is calculated based on the weighted arithmetic mean.

4   Conclusion

In this paper, we introduce a novel framework to design a weighted rating mechanism for the binary rating system in a social network. The goal is to let the mechanism be robust to the false-name attack and monotonicity. We represent a weight function with a controllable parameter and give a reasonable requirement on it to satisfy the desirable properties. Under our mechanism, all agents will truthfully report their observation and the false-name attack is not profitable. Monotonicity ensures the final rating of the product can reflect all buyers' evaluation appropriately.

Considering the n-ary rating system is an interesting future work. For instance, if an attacker intends to decrease the final rating of a product, she may create many false nodes with the same report and choose to report lower rating-level. Another challenging work is to develop more generalised rating mechanisms without the prior knowledge of the infimum of the mapping functions. It is theoretically worth to considering to relax the assumption in this paper.

References

1. Brill, M., Conitzer, V., Freeman, R., Shah, N.: False-name-proof recommendations in social networks. In: Proceedings of the 2016 International Conference on Autonomous Agents & Multiagent Systems, Singapore, 9–13 May 2016, pp. 332–340. ACM (2016)
2. Castro, M., Druschel, P., Ganesh, A., Rowstron, A., Wallach, D.S.: Secure routing for structured peer-to-peer overlay networks. ACM SIGOPS Oper. Syst. Rev. **36**(SI), 299–314 (2002)
3. Cheng, A., Friedman, E.: Sybilproof reputation mechanisms. In: Proceedings of the 2005 ACM SIGCOMM Workshop on Economics of Peer-to-Peer Systems, pp. 128–132 (2005)
4. Drucker, F.A., Fleischer, L.K.: Simpler Sybil-proof mechanisms for multi-level marketing. In: Proceedings of the 13th ACM Conference on Electronic Commerce, pp. 441–458 (2012)
5. Ferrara, E., Varol, O., Davis, C., Menczer, F., Flammini, A.: The rise of social bots. Commun. ACM **59**(7), 96–104 (2016)
6. Grandi, U., Turrini, P.: A network-based rating system and its resistance to bribery. In: Proceedings of the 25th International Joint Conference on Artificial Intelligence (2016)
7. Guille, A., Hacid, H., Favre, C., Zighed, D.A.: Information diffusion in online social networks: a survey. ACM SIGMOD Rec. **42**(2), 17–28 (2013)
8. Haythornthwaite, C.: Social networks and internet connectivity effects. Inf. Commun. Soc. **8**(2), 125–147 (2005)
9. Jindal, N., Liu, B.: Opinion spam and analysis. In: Proceedings of the 2008 International Conference on Web Search and Data Mining, pp. 219–230 (2008)
10. Liberman, J.J., Trandal, D.S.: Methods and systems for identity verification in a social network using ratings. US Patent 8,850,535, September 2014
11. Mukherjee, A., et al.: Spotting opinion spammers using behavioral footprints. In: Proceedings of the 19th ACM SIGKDD International Conference on Knowledge Discovery and Data Mining, pp. 632–640 (2013)
12. Swamynathan, G., Almeroth, K.C., Zhao, B.Y.: The design of a reliable reputation system. Electron. Commer. Res. **10**(3–4), 239–270 (2010)
13. Yokoo, M., Sakurai, Y., Matsubara, S.: The effect of false-name bids in combinatorial auctions: new fraud in internet auctions. Games Econ. Behav. **46**(1), 174–188 (2004)
14. Yoo, K.H., Gretzel, U.: Comparison of deceptive and truthful travel reviews. In: ENTER, pp. 37–47 (2009)

Modular Construction Planning Using Graph Neural Network Heuristic Search

Philip Hawkins[1]([⊠]) [iD], Frederic Maire[1] [iD], Simon Denman[1] [iD],
and Mahsa Baktashmotlagh[2] [iD]

[1] School of Electrical Engineering and Robotics, Faculty of Engineering,
Queensland University of Technology, Brisbane, Australia
pa.hawkins@hdr.qut.edu.au, {f.maire,s.denman}@qut.edu.au
[2] School of Information Technology and Electrical Engineering,
University of Queensland, Brisbane, Australia
m.baktashmotlagh@uq.edu.au

Abstract. In this paper we present a framework for learning to design and assemble modular structures using a search guided by a graph neural network heuristic trained through imitation learning. We demonstrate the effectiveness of this framework through planning the construction of modular spanning truss structures of a range of shapes and sizes given simple specifications.

1 Introduction

Graphs provide a flexible and generic method of representing real-world binary relationships and structures. Generating novel structures that achieve an objective while adhering to constraints is a important problem in modelling physical, chemical and social systems. However, applying deep learning to graph generation presents a number of challenges. Among these are the discrete nature of graph structures, the fact that the same graph has many possible representations depending on the ordering of its nodes and edges, and the large solution space formed by the permutations of possible connections [5]. A number of sequential neural graph generation methods have been proposed to construct graphs by selecting the addition of new nodes and edges one step at a time [7,8,20–22].

An additional challenge arises when the objective is to achieve a discrete final outcome, rather than to optimise against a continuous metric. This requires a capacity for looking ahead to compare alternative sequences of actions to avoid converging to a local optimum. As an example of a task that requires this type of forward planning, consider a robot that is required to independently design and build a structure in situ from modular components. To plan this construction the robot must select actions that efficiently address local challenges, such as ensuring that the components are correctly supported and braced, while converging on a goal state that meets requirements such as supporting load points or enclosing a space.

© Springer Nature Switzerland AG 2022
G. Long et al. (Eds.): AI 2021, LNAI 13151, pp. 228–239, 2022.
https://doi.org/10.1007/978-3-030-97546-3_19

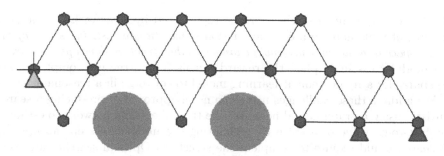

Fig. 1. The **truss structure**, generated by neural heuristic search, is composed of **hexagonal hubs** and **connecting spokes**. These are represented as nodes and edges in the state graph. The static starting points are shown as green triangles on the right, with the target point shown as the yellow triangle to the left. The two red patches indicate obstacles that the truss must avoid. Not all generated trusses are optimal. In this example the two hubs to the left extending down around the obstacles are unnecessary.

We address these challenges in training an agent to design and plan the assembly of simple modular truss structures, as illustrated in Fig. 1. The objective is for the agent to find a sequence of assembly steps that complete a truss structure that spans from a starting platform to a target support point while meeting structural constraints at each step of construction.

Following a search framework, we can consider each stage of assembly as a state in the search space. The search objective is a structure that meets the target criteria, and the construction plan is provided by the path of actions required to reach it. An optimal solution for this could theoretically be provided by an A* graph search with a consistent heuristic if the search tree is not too large [12, p. 82–83]. However in this problem, the branching factor is proportional to the perimeter of the structure, and in practice A* search time increases more than exponentially with respect to the length of the solution.

With knowledge of the dynamics involved, a hard-coded algorithmic solution could be devised. However, such a solution would be bespoke to the situation and have little to no ability to generalise. A third option, the one we consider in this paper, is to apply machine learning to develop a search strategy from observation. This provides the flexibility to adapt to variations in physical dynamics and opens the possibility of new applications, such as designing novel structures that optimise for local conditions.

Deep reinforcement learning methods that combine search and neural networks are able to benefit from both planning and learning from experience [15]. In this approach, policy networks address high branching factors by learning to predict a probability distribution over the choice of actions. These policies cannot guarantee an optimal solution, however they enable the search to look further ahead, allowing the agent to select more promising actions. In board games such as Go and Chess, the action space, though large, is bounded by the board size. The policy can therefore be represented by a network with a fixed size output that maps to a common action space. *In contrast, the shape of the action space in a modular assembly changes as the structure develops.* Moreover, in a modular assembly plan, the reward signals from structure completion are too sparse for a reinforcement learning model to converge in a reasonable time.

We address these challenges using the novel approach of producing a search heuristic using a graph neural network. We train the graph network to estimate the cost-to-go value of a state by estimating the number of steps an optimal A* search would require to complete the structure. Optimal searches are computationally expensive and provide a limited set of training data. We therefore augment this by adding synthetic data derived from states that are adjacent to the optimal paths. We demonstrate that this approach allows our building agent to extrapolate to build structures much larger than those seen in training.

2   Related work

2.1   Neural Search Based Planning

Following the success of AlphaGo [15] in defeating the Go world champion Lee Sedol, methods that combine reinforcement learning, search, and neural networks have become the focus of intense interest. Deep reinforcement learning agents have predominantly built upon Monte-Carlo Tree Search (MCTS) [3,4] and have demonstrated super-human performance in tasks ranging from poker [11] to multi-player video games [1,18].

However, problem spaces with a high branching factor and sparse rewards present difficulties for reinforcement learning. Bhardwaj et al. [2] propose Search as Imitation Learning (SAIL) which tabulates the cost-to-go values of all states in a search space using Dijkstra's algorithm, and use this as an oracle to train a policy network that can be used in a Markov Decision Process. This method however relies on the training search space being small enough to fully explore.

The task of producing symbolic programs in domain-specific languages, in common with graph generation, faces a challenge of combinatorially large problem spaces. Neural Admissible Relaxation (NEAR) [14] produces a symbolic program through an A* search by calculating a cost-to-go heuristic using gradient descent for each examined state in the expansion of a context free grammar.

2.2   Graph Generation with Neural Networks

You et al. [22] use a canonical node ordering scheme to address the problem of non-unique graph representations and propose sequential graph generation using a hierarchy of RNNs, with a *graph-level RNN* generating new nodes and an *edge-level RNN* generating edges for each new node. You et al. [21] build molecular graphs as a Markov decision process, using reinforcement learning to train a policy network to select an edge placement action at each step.

The challenge of generating a graph that satisfies a final structural objective may be classified as a problem of graph generation conditioned on semantic context [5]. Several approaches have been proposed for injecting semantic context into the generation process for molecular graphs. Li et al. [8] add a conditional context vector as an additional term in the graph convolution used in the generating decoder. Yang et al. [20] concatenate a context vector to the latent representation of each node produced in the generation process. Finally, Jonas [7] uses context in two ways. Firstly to initialise node input features and secondly to calculate an output error in order to identify the best result from multiple runs of the generating network.

3 Problem Formulation

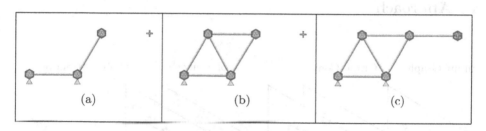

Fig. 2. A **starting platform** is shown in this sequence as a pair of pinned hexagonal hubs connected by a spoke. The '+' to the right indicates the target point. To satisfy the stability constraint, each spoke must connect to at least one stable hub. A hub is considered stable if it is part of the starting platform, or if it is directly connected to two other stable hubs. The structure in (a) has a hub that is one spoke length from the target point. Placing a spoke connecting this hub to the target would violate the stability constraint. In (b), three spokes have been added to brace the structure, making all the hubs stable. A spoke may now be placed as shown in (c).

We consider the problem of training an agent to plan a modular construction task, inspired by a related problem proposed in the control of robot swarms [10]. In our problem, we require a single agent to plan the construction in the vertical plane of a two dimensional truss structure composed of uniform hexagonal *hubs* and connecting *spokes*. The completed structure will span the distance between a static starting platform and a target point, as shown in Fig. 1.

A *plan* is composed of a sequence of spoke placement instructions. The modified structure must be adequately supported by bracing struts for an instruction to be valid. This is tested against a stability constraint requiring each spoke to connect to at least one *stable* hub. A hub is considered stable if it is part of the starting platform, or if it is directly connected to two other stable hubs. This is illustrated in Fig. 2. The goal test is that a hub at the target point is stable.

Each spoke placement action is a tuple (v, f) where v is the index of a hub in the structure and f indicates which face on the hexagonal hub the spoke attaches to. If a spoke is placed so that the end does not connect to an existing hub, a hub is automatically attached to that end of the spoke. At most, one spoke may be connected to each face of a hexagonal hub.

The truss is represented as an attributed graph $G = (V, E)$. The set $V = \{v_1, v_2, \ldots, v_{n_v}\}$ is the set of nodes where each v_i is an attribute vector representing a hub. The set $E = \{e_1, e_2, \ldots, e_{n_e}\}$ is the set of directed edges where a symmetrical pair of edges represents a spoke. Each e_i is a tuple (a_i, b_i), where a_i is the source node index, b_i is the destination node index. This model applies to a broad range of modular assemblies. In general, nodes represent the main components, while edges represent the connections or connectors between them, for example covalent bonds in the case of molecules.

4   Approach

Input Graph   Graph Conv   Graph Conv   Global Attention

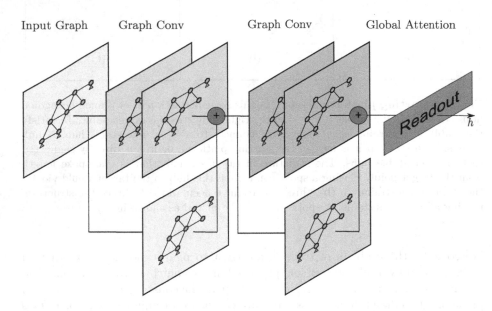

Fig. 3. Stacked residual blocks of **graph convolutions** extract latent vector representations of the local graph region for each node. The cost-to-go heuristic readout is computed from these node vectors using a global soft attention layer.

4.1   Search as Planning and Design

We approach the problem of designing and planning the assembly of a stable truss structure as a greedy best-first search, where the search space is the set of states that represent different configurations of hubs and spokes. The initial state is the starting platform and the goal conditions is a stable truss that connects starting platform to a stable node at the target point. The state transitions are made by placing spokes as illustrated in Fig. 2.

Best-first searches maintain a priority queue of the leaves of the search tree. This frontier can be visualised as a wave front that expands at each search step as nodes are expanded. The priority ranking focuses the wave-front on promising directions. This is analogous to the effect of a policy network in deepening the exploration of a Monte Carlo tree search. The key difference between sampling an action from a policy network and priority queue is that the priority queue has an unbounded cardinality that adapts to the changing action space, whereas the output dimensions of a policy network, like the one used in AlphaZero, are fixed.

In a greedy search, the accuracy of the cost-to-go heuristic, $h(x)$, determines the efficiency of the search. In the ideal case h is the true cost-to-go for any state x and selecting the lowest h value state on the frontier at each step would provide the shortest path to the goal state. In the absence of an ideal heuristic, we consider two simple but useful heuristics for baseline and training purposes.

The Manhattan distance $d(v, t)$ is the shortest path along the edge of the triangular lattice from a hub v to the target point t, the *minimum Manhattan distance heuristic* is calculated as $h(G) \stackrel{\text{def}}{=} \min_{v \in V}(d(v, t))$. If not for the stability constraint, this would equal the number of spokes required to complete the structure and would therefore be an ideal cost-to-go heuristic. However, the search is prevented from transitioning to unstable states as illustrated in Fig. 2. For the structure in Fig. 2a with $h = 1$, there is no valid action that can transition to a state with a lower h value. The search frontier must probe four levels down the search tree before it encounters the state with $h = 0$, shown in Fig. 2c.

As the structure grows, the number of valid actions for each state increases. This makes the branching factor high for large structures, leading to an increase in the rate at which the wave front expands, producing a combinatorial explosion. As shown in Table 1, a greedy search using the minimum Manhattan distance heuristic regularly exceeds 1,000 state expansions at a span distance of five spokes.

A more effective, though non-admissible, simple heuristic is the *mean Manhattan distance* calculated as $h(G) \stackrel{\text{def}}{=} \frac{1}{n} \sum_{i=1}^{n} d(v_i, t)$. This improves the efficiency of the search because it focuses attention on actions that build toward the target, regardless of whether they add a new minimum distance hub. However, the resulting structure is far from optimal and tends to spread out and consume a large number of unnecessary spokes and hubs as can be seen in Fig. 4.

We improve both the efficiency of search and material use in the structure by substituting a neural network that is trained to predict cost-to-go from the state graph as the search heuristic. The task context is injected into the graph through the node attributes. Each node holds the relative polar coordinates between the corresponding hub and the target point. The network, illustrated in Fig. 3, consists of two blocks, each with two graph convolutional operators. These produce latent vector representations of the local graph region for each node. The heuristic readout is then computed from these node vectors using a global soft attention layer [9].

Table 1. Each agent was given an identical set of 25 target points for each spanning distance and tasked to plan an assembly sequence for each target. The **mean path length** and **number of search tree nodes that were expanded** are shown for each set. Search was halted after 1000 expansions. The "Completed" column shows the rate of completion for each set due to this limit.

	span = 5			span = 10		
	Path Length	Expanded	Completed	Path length	Expanded	Completed
Search heuristic						
Min.	57.0 ± 6.0	793.5 ± 93.2	56.0%			0.0%
Mean	44.7 ± 3.1	85.7 ± 9.2	100.0%	152.0 ± 13.8	392.1 ± 50.3	100.0%
GAT	26.9 ± 1.3	26.9 ± 1.3	100.0%	68.4 ± 2.4	70.2 ± 3.1	100.0%
GIN	**22.5 ± 1.2**	**22.5 ± 1.2**	100.0%	**48.1 ± 1.5**	**48.1 ± 1.5**	100.0%

(a) **Without obstruction** between the starting platform and the target point.

	span=5			span=10		
	Path Length	Expanded	Completed	Path Length	Expanded	Completed
Search heuristic						
Min.	52.2 ± 5.2	984.6 ± 29.6	4.0%			0.0%
Mean	43.8 ± 2.2	91.1 ± 10.6	100.0%	162.7 ± 16.5	415.8 ± 56.4	100.0%
GAT	37.2 ± 2.2	84.5 ± 73.6	96.0%	64.9 ± 3.4	308.5 ± 155.1	76.0%
GIN	**36.6 ± 3.5**	**58.8 ± 27.1**	100.0%	**57.4 ± 2.3**	**60.1 ± 3.5**	100.0%

(b) With **two obstructions** as shown in Fig. 1.

4.2   Consistency of the Training Heuristic

The A* search aims at identifying a lowest cost path that connects the starting state to a target state [6]. A* ranks the priority queue by the state cost estimate function $f(G) = g(G) + h(G)$, where $f(G)$ is the estimated cost of the state represented by the graph G, $g(G)$ is the cost to reach the state and $h(G)$ is the same cost-to-go heuristic used by the greedy search. We train the neural heuristic network to imitate A*, by minimising the difference between the predicted cost-to-go for a state and the true cost-to-go that is discovered by performing an A* search.

The path found by an A* graph search is guaranteed to be the shortest path provided the cost-to-go heuristic is consistent. Using the graph representation of the state G, we calculate this heuristic $h(G)$ as the minimum Manhattan distance.

Each construction step transitions the structural state G to a successor state G' by the connection of a spoke to the structure in alignment with the underlying lattice. The transition cost of each action $c(G, G')$ is one spoke. The minimum Manhattan distance is the smallest number of spokes required to connect a structure to the target point and therefore marks the lower bound on the cost-to-go and provides an admissible heuristic.

The addition of new spokes and hubs cannot increase the minimum distance to the target. Thus, the heuristic cost of successor states will never exceed that of their predecessor state and the minimum Manhattan distance heuristic is therefore consistent.

5   Data Generation and Training

It is more difficult for A* to navigate around unstable truss states than greedy search because the cost-so-far value, g, penalises leaves that are lower in the search tree. As illustrated in Fig. 2, it is sometimes necessary to add spokes that do not reduce h to avoid instability. This weights the search toward states in the frontier that have not yet encountered instability. These low g cost states must be exhausted before A* considers the more costly states that must be traversed to avoid the instability. To ensure that data generation completes in reasonable time, we restrict the span distance of the exemplar searches.

We ran exemplar searches to determine optimal build sequences for a truss spanning to each target lattice vertex in a training range. This range was set at spans of up to three spokes from the starting platform. The A* searches require approximately 15,000 state expansions to complete the three spoke spanning targets. Each search produced an optimal path as a sequence of states $s_i \in (s_1, s_2, \ldots, s_n)$ where n is the path length and i is the path order. The true cost-to-go value for each of these states is given by the number of steps remaining to the goal state: $n - i$. Training examples were taken from each state along these optimal paths.

5.1   Data Augmentation with Adjacent States

We augment the training examples by including states that are *adjacent*, that is one spoke placement action away, from the optimal paths and calculate synthetic target values for these states. Each state s_i in an optimal plan is represented by a graph $G_i = (V_i, E_i)$ and has a set of valid actions $a_{i,j} \in A_i$ in the form of the tuples (v, f), as described in Sect. 3. Each action $a_{i,j}$ maps to a child state through the state transition function, $s_{i,j} = child(s_i, a_{i,j})$, that represents the modification of a structure by adding a component. The estimated cost-to-go for each sub-optimal child state $s_{i,j}$ is $n - i$, the known cost-to-go of the parent state. This approximates the true cost-to-go by assuming that a state that is not on a known optimal path is no closer to the goal state than a parent state that is on an optimal path.

Child (state, target) pairs are added to the training set if and only if the action $(v, f) = a_{i,j}$ that produced the child state does not map to any edge in the goal state edge set, E_n. This avoids miss-attributing sub-optimality to states that lie on the discovered optimal path, or any alternative optimal path to the same goal state. There may however exist other states that satisfy the goal condition that could be reached by an optimal path that includes the child state. In this case the calculated cost-to-go will be one greater than the true cost-to-go for that state on its optimal path. In practice these cases are rare and do not outweigh the benefit of adding this synthetic data. We demonstrate the effectiveness of this method of augmenting training data in the ablation study in Sect. 6.1.

5.2   Training

The exemplar searches generated 755 optimal path examples and 7009 synthetic examples are added through the augmentation described above. Example data was split randomly into training and validation sets with 10% of the examples going to the validation set. We trained each model using gradient descent for 2,000 epochs, where an epoch was a single pass over the training data. The network was trained to minimise the mean squared error between the prediction and target. The Adam optimiser was used in training all models. The learning rate started at 0.001 and was reduced by a factor of ten after every 100 epochs with no improvement in the validation loss.

6   Performance Evaluation

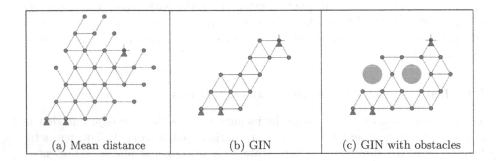

| (a) Mean distance | (b) GIN | (c) GIN with obstacles |

Fig. 4. Examples of **trusses** generated for a **five spoke span**

We evaluated the efficiency of neural heuristics against the two simple heuristic baselines described in Sect. 4.1. Neural heuristics based on the network illustrated in Fig. 3 were evaluated, comparing two graph convolutional operators: the graph attention operator (GAT) [17] and the graph isomorphism operator (GIN) [19].

We assessed the capacity of agents to plan structures larger than the maximum training spans of three spokes by evaluating target spans of five and ten spokes. Twenty-five unique target points were sampled from the set of potential vertices at each spanning distance from the starting platform. The search agent then attempted to plan an assembly for each target using each heuristic, with a limit of 1000 expansions per search. As shown in Table 1a, the minimum Manhattan distance heuristic required many expansions and was often unable to complete. The mean Manhattan distance heuristic was able to complete the trusses, however the simple strategy requires the placement of many unnecessary components as can be seen in Fig. 4a. In comparison, the neural heuristics demonstrated the capacity to plan efficient bracing as required with minimal or no additional search exploration.

In a second series of experiments we evaluated how well the heuristics adapted to obstructions in the building space without additional training. For each task, two obstructions were added midway between the starting platform and the target point, as shown in Figs. 1 and 4c. It is notable that although some unnecessary components are added, they are usually incorporated into the structural bracing by the neural search whereas the simple heuristics produce many unsupported hubs. Results of construction around obstacles are shown in Table 1b.

6.1 Ablation Evaluation for Synthetic Data Augmentation

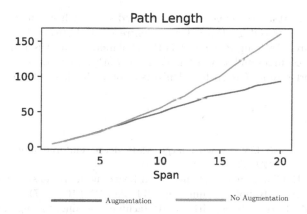

Fig. 5. Comparison of **GIN network** trained **with** and **without** synthetic targets for states adjacent to the optimal example paths

To evaluate the value of augmenting training data with adjacent states and synthetic targets, we compared the performance of a network trained with only optimal search path data with the same network trained with both optimal search path data and synthetic data. The results are shown in Fig. 5. Twenty-five runs were made with a common set of build targets for each span. These runs followed the same process as the evaluations in the previous section, however with a different sample of build targets. We observe that the use of synthetic targets reduces both the number of expansions required and the path lengths, particularly when generalising to larger spans.

7   Conclusions

In this work, we introduced a framework to learn to build modular structures. We trained a neural network to estimate the cost-to-go in a given state. Using this framework, we tasked an agent with finding an efficient action sequence to construct a modular structure under structural stability constraints and with obstacles. We showed that our approach simultaneously improved both search efficiency and material efficiency in comparison to agents using non-neural heuristics. A key factor in this improvement was the ability of the graph neural network to learn patterns from small structures at training time and during inference scale this well beyond the spatial extents of the training examples.

An avenue for future research is to remove the hard stability constraint calculation and investigate learning the constraining dynamics directly from a physical simulation. This follows a similar trajectory to the development from AlphaZero [16] to MuZero [13] in learning board game dynamics from experience. However, as previously stated, the truss assembly problem has a sparse reward. We therefore believe that imitation learning as described here will continue to be a useful strategy for pre-training the network.

Acknowledgements. We acknowledge continued support from the Queensland University of Technology (QUT) through the Centre for Robotics. The research is supported by Research Training Program (RTP) scholarship from Australian government. Computational resources and services used in this work were provided by the HPC and Research Support Group, Queensland University of Technology, Brisbane, Australia.

References

1. Berner, C., et al.: Dota 2 with large scale deep reinforcement learning. arXiv preprint arXiv:1912.06680 (2019)
2. Bhardwaj, M., Choudhury, S., Scherer, S.: Learning heuristic search via imitation. In: Conference on Robot Learning, pp. 271–280. PMLR (2017)
3. Bishop, C.M.: Pattern Recognition and Machine Learning. Springer, Cham (2006). https://doi.org/10.1007/978-1-4615-7566-5
4. Browne, C.B., et al.: A survey of Monte Carlo tree search methods. IEEE Trans. Comput. Intell. AI Games 4(1), 1–43 (2012)
5. Guo, X., Zhao, L.: A systematic survey on deep generative models for graph generation. arXiv preprint arXiv:2007.06686 (2020)
6. Hart, P.E., Nilsson, N.J., Raphael, B.: A formal basis for the heuristic determination of minimum cost paths. IEEE Trans. Syst. Sci. Cybern. 4(2), 100–107 (1968)
7. Jonas, E.: Deep imitation learning for molecular inverse problems. In: Advances in Neural Information Processing Systems, vol. 32, pp. 4990–5000 (2019)
8. Li, Y., Zhang, L., Liu, Z.: Multi-objective de novo drug design with conditional graph generative model. J. Cheminform. 10(1), 1–24 (2018). https://doi.org/10.1186/s13321-018-0287-6
9. Li, Y., Tarlow, D., Brockschmidt, M., Zemel, R.: Gated graph sequence neural networks. In: International Conference on Learning Representations 2016 (2015)

10. Melenbrink, N., Werfel, J.: Local force cues for strength and stability in a distributed robotic construction system. Swarm Intell. **12**(2), 129–153 (2017). https://doi.org/10.1007/s11721-017-0149-2
11. Moravčík, M., et al.: DeepStack: expert-level artificial intelligence in heads-up no-limit poker. Science **356**(6337), 508–513 (2017)
12. Pearl, J.: Heuristics: Intelligent Search Strategies for Computer Problem Solving. The Addison-Wesley Series in Artificial Intelligence (1985)
13. Schrittwieser, J., et al.: Mastering atari, go, chess and shogi by planning with a learned model. Nature **588**(7839), 604–609 (2020)
14. Shah, A., Zhan, E., Sun, J.J., Verma, A., Yue, Y., Chaudhuri, S.: Learning differentiable programs with admissible neural heuristics. In: Proceedings of the 34rd International Conference on Neural Information Processing Systems (2020)
15. Silver, D., et al.: Mastering the game of go with deep neural networks and tree search. Nature **529**(7587), 484–489 (2016)
16. Silver, D., et al.: A general reinforcement learning algorithm that masters chess, shogi, and go through self-play. Science **362**(6419), 1140–1144 (2018)
17. Veličković, P., Cucurull, G., Casanova, A., Romero, A., Liò, P., Bengio, Y.: Graph attention networks. In: International Conference on Learning Representations (2018)
18. Vinyals, O., et al.: Grandmaster level in StarCraft II using multi-agent reinforcement learning. Nature **575**(7782), 350–354 (2019)
19. Xu, K., Hu, W., Leskovec, J., Jegelka, S.: How powerful are graph neural networks? In: International Conference on Learning Representations (2018)
20. Yang, C., Zhuang, P., Shi, W., Luu, A., Li, P.: Conditional structure generation through graph variational generative adversarial nets. In: Proceedings of the 33rd International Conference on Neural Information Processing Systems, pp. 1340–1351 (2019)
21. You, J., Liu, B., Ying, R., Pande, V., Leskovec, J.: Graph convolutional policy network for goal-directed molecular graph generation. In: Proceedings of the 32nd International Conference on Neural Information Processing Systems, pp. 6412–6422 (2018)
22. You, J., Ying, R., Ren, X., Hamilton, W., Leskovec, J.: GraphRNN: generating realistic graphs with deep auto-regressive models. In: International Conference on Machine Learning, pp. 5708–5717. PMLR (2018)

Priority-Based Traffic Management Protocols for Autonomous Vehicles on Road Networks

Jianglin Qiao[1,2(✉)], Dongmo Zhang[1], and Dave de Jonge[2]

[1] Western Sydney University, Penrith, Australia
19469397@student.westernsydney.edu.au
[2] Artificial Intelligence Research Institute (IIIA-CSIC), Barcelona, Spain

Abstract. This paper describes a generic simulation platform for testing traffic management protocols on road networks with autonomous vehicles. Firstly, we introduce a formal model to represent a road network as a directed multigraph. We then describe traffic management protocols in terms of the priority over roads or vehicles. Based the model, we developed a system that can simulate complex road networks with traffic of autonomous vehicles under the management of different traffic control protocols in different intersections. The system was build up on the existing platform AIM4. With the simulation system, we can test a variety of properties of traffic management protocols from macro and micro perspectives of traffic network with autonomous vehicles.

Keywords: Autonomous vehicles · Intelligent traffic management protocol · Traffic modelling

1 Introduction

Self-driving cars are getting closer to our daily lives than we think and will change our lives more than we can imagine [13]. It is believed that autonomous driving technology can significantly improve driving safety by reducing road accidents, human error injuries and traffic jams [15]. In the future when all cars are autonomous, the road traffic situation can be dramatically different from what we have now thus will require different methods and infrastructures for road management and traffic control [1]. With the emergence of new technologies for vehicle-based communication and intelligent traffic control, the traditional vision-based traffic control facilities, such as traffic lights, roundabout and stop signs, are likely to be replaced by less visible but more efficient, more effective algorithmic controlled road facilities [4]. A virtual roundabout is an example of algorithmic traffic control protocol for autonomous vehicles or vehicles with vehicle-to-vehicle (V2V) or vehicle-to-infrastructure (V2I) communication [10]. With rapid growing demand and high expectation, research on autonomous driving has become extremely active in recent years. However, traffic management with autonomous vehicles on road remains almost a uncharted territory. There is a demand for in-depth research on autonomous vehicle traffic management. The existing road facilities and traffic control methods are all based on human driving. Even autonomous vehicles are trained to recognise human-oriented road signs and mimic human driving behaviours, which by no means necessary, let alone efficiency and reliability. The real-time traffic

© Springer Nature Switzerland AG 2022
G. Long et al. (Eds.): AI 2021, LNAI 13151, pp. 240–253, 2022.
https://doi.org/10.1007/978-3-030-97546-3_20

data from the traditional traffic management systems can hardly be used for the research of traffic management in the era of autonomous vehicles. In this sense, computer simulation becomes one of the most important approaches for testing, validating, and assessing performance, efficiency, and stability of traffic management systems for road networks on which vehicles are purely or dominantly self driven.

This paper describes a generic simulation platform for testing traffic management protocols on road networks with autonomous vehicles. Firstly, we introduce a graph representation for road networks. In a road graph, the vertices represent intersections of roads while the arcs that link vertices represent the roads between respective intersections. Lanes on each road are indicated by labels. We then describe traffic management protocols in terms of the priority over roads or vehicles. Based on the open source project "Autonomous Intersection Management (AIM)" conducted by the Learning Agents Research Group of the AI Laboratory in the Department of Computer Sciences at the University of Texas at Austin[1], we developed a generic simulation platform that can simulate traffics on any road network that has a graph representation of roads and a configuration of priorities among roads and vehicles[2]. With the new system, we can set the roads between any intersections with various speed limits. The vehicles can autonomously choose their routes and speeds to travel. The intersections are independently managed under different traffic control protocols based on preset priorities of roads and vehicles. Furthermore, the simulator provides a variety of data collection APIs, which allow automated data collection for different traffic scenarios.

The structure of this paper is as follows. Section 2 introduces the graph representation of road networks. Section 3 provides a formal method to represent traffic management protocols based on priority. Section 4 describes the experimental setting and shows the experimental results. Section 5 concludes the paper with a brief description of related work and future research directions.

2   Road Network Modelling

A road network is a system of interconnecting lanes and points that represents a system of streets or roads for a given area. It can be modelled in different levels of abstraction. In order to represent any complicated road network, we introduce a formal model of road network based on graph theory.

Definition 1. *A road network is a directed multi-graph with labels $G = (I, L, E)$, where I represents a set of intersections, L is a set of labels representing lanes on a road, $E \subseteq I \times I \times L$ is a set of labeled arcs representing the roads with labeled lanes that connect the intersections.*

Since a multi-graph allows the existence of parallel edges, we use labels L to indicate the uniqueness of each road lane. Thus an edge in a road network graph represent a lane of the road that links two intersections. The set of edges E represent connections and travel directions of road lanes. For each intersection $i \in I$, let $E_i^{in} \subseteq E$ denote the

---

[1] https://www.cs.utexas.edu/~aim/.

[2] Although the system can take any input of a road graph and a configuration of priorities, the capacity of roads and vehicles are limited by computer hardware and GUI setting.

set of all incoming lanes, $E_i^{out} \subseteq E$ for the set of all outgoing lanes. The following is an example a road network graph.

Example 1. *Figure 1 shows an example of a road network. It includes an intersection* (i_4) *with multiple lanes, a roundabout* (i_6), *a T-junction* (i_9), *and a merging intersection* (i_{10}). *For simplicity, we use the natural numbers as the label for lanes. For instance, with a roach with single lane in each direction, the label of the lanes is assumed to be 1, such as* $(i_2, i_6, 1)$ *and* $(i_7, i_6, 1)$. *For a road with multiple lanes in each direction, their respective labels are different natural numbers, such as* $(i_1, i_4, 1)$ *and* $(i_1, i_4, 2)$.

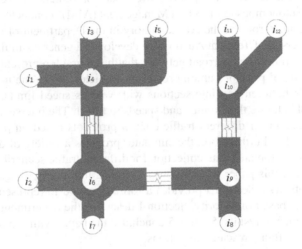

Fig. 1. Example of road network

The model of road networks can describe the relationship between intersections and road lanes. However, it cannot represent the connection and conflicts between the lanes of roads at an intersection. For instance, when a vehicle approaches an intersection, it may want to go straight, turn left or turn right. However, depending on which lane it is on, the vehicle may not allowed to travel to all directions. Therefore, we need to further specify the connections between the lanes from different road at each intersection. We call such a link "connection relation". For each intersection i of a road network, the connection relation D_i is a binary relation between incoming lanes and outgoing lanes of roads at the intersection, *i.e.*, $D_i \subseteq E_i^{in} \times E_i^{out}$. Intuitively, $(e, e') \in D_i$ means a vehicle travel on lane e is allowed to across the intersection to lane e'. Furthermore, since these road connections at the same intersection may meet thus vehicles crossing the intersection may collide if there are no rules or facilities to avoid it. For example, if a vehicle is traveling from south to north while another vehicle is going from east to west, they could collide. In order to specify traffic manage management protocols, we further introduce a relationship, called "conflict relation" on top of the connection relation. The following provides the formal definition of connection relation and conflict relation at an intersection of a road network:

Definition 2. *Given a road network $G = (I, L, E)$. For each intersection $i \in I$,*

- *a connection relation D_i of i is a binary relation between the sets of incoming lanes and outgoing lanes, i.e., $D_i \subseteq E_i^{in} \times E_i^{out}$. Each $d = (e, e') \in D_i$ is called a **link** between the lanes e and e';*
- *a conflict relation $C_i = (D_i, \mathcal{E}_i)$ is an undirected graph, where $\mathcal{E}_i \subseteq D_i \times D_i$ is a set of edges between pairs of links, which specify possibly collisions between links. If $(d, d') \in \mathcal{E}_i$, we call d and d has a conflict.*

The following is an example that explains the definition of connection relation and conflict relation of a T-junction in Fig. 1.

Example 2. *Figure 2 shows a connection relation and conflict relation for the intersection i_9 in Fig. 1. The left graph in Fig. 2 represents the connection relation $D_{i_9} = \{d_1, d_2, d_3, d_4, d_5, d_6\}$, where $d_1 = (e_1, e_2), d_2 = (e_1, e_4), d_3 = (e_3, e_4), d_4 = (e_3, e_6), d_5 = (e_5, e_2)$ and $d_6 = (e_5, e_6)$, which means that traffic from i_6 are allowed to turn left and turn right; traffic from i_{10} are allowed to go straight and turn right; traffic from i_8 are allowed to turn left and go straight. However U-turns are not allowed at i_9 from any direction. If it is allowed for the traffic from, say i_6, you may add (e_1, e_6) to D_{i_9}. The right graph in Fig. 2 shows an example of conflict relation $C_{I_9} = (D_{i_9}, \mathcal{E}_{I_9})$ at the intersection i_9, where $\mathcal{E}_{I_9} = \{(d_1, d_5), (d_5, d_1), (d_5, d_2), ..., (d_4, d_6), (d_6, d_4)\}$. In this relation, d_1 is conflict with d_5, which means that vehicles on lane e_1 turning left to lane e_2 have potential collision with vehicles on lane e_5 go straight to lane e_2.*

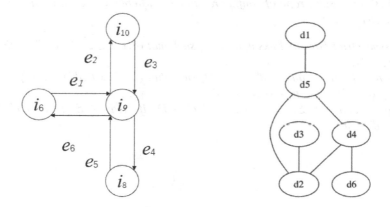

Fig. 2. Example of intersection relations

The road network and intersection relations allow us to represent complex road networks in real world. Next we will discuss traffic management protocols for autonomous vehicles based on right-of-way.

3 Priority-Based Traffic Management Protocols

Vehicles often collide with other vehicles because they're routes intersect and thus obstruct the paths of others. The general rule that determines who has the right of precedence is called *right of way*. It defines who has the right to use the conflicting portion of the route and who must wait for the other to do so. For example, in a country where driving on the left, vehicles will give way to traffic on the right whenever they app-roach an intersection, which means that the road on the right has higher priority than the road on which the vehicle is traveling. Despite major variances in traffic manage-ment methods and systems, all traffic management methods can be classified into two types of traffic management protocols: road-based priority management traffic protocol and vehicle-based priority traffic management protocol. More specific, the road-based priority management can be divided into static-priority and dynamic-priority. A more detailed explanation of traffic management protocols is given in the following subsec-tions.

3.1 Static Priority Management Protocol

The static priority management protocol is based on predefined priorities of the links at each intersection. We introduced a graph representation to describe the priority of links for each intersection based on the formal representation of the road networks and the intersection relations in the section above. For each intersection $i \in I$, we use a directed graph, which is sub-graph of the conflict relation of intersection i, to specify the priority of each links. Formally, a static-priority management protocol P_i is defined as follows:

Definition 3. *Given a road network $G = (I, L, E)$. For each intersection $i \in I$, and its connection relation D_i and conflict relation C_i, a static-priority management protocol $p_i = (D_i, \Phi_i)$ is a sub-graph of conflict relation C_i, where $\Phi_i \subseteq \mathcal{E}_i$. It must satisfy the following conditions:*

- *Anti-symmetric: For any links $d, d' \in D_i$ such that $(d, d') \in \mathcal{E}_i$. If $(d, d') \in \Phi_i$ then $(d', d) \notin \Phi_i$;*
- *Transitive: For any links $d, d', d'' \in D_i$ such that $(d, d'), (d', d''), (d, d'') \in \mathcal{E}_i$. If $(d, d'), (d', d'') \in \Phi_i$, then $(d, d'') \in \Phi_i$;*
- *Complete relative to $\mathcal{E}_i$: For any links $d, d' \in D_i$, if $(d, d') \in \mathcal{E}_i$, then $(d, d') \in \Phi_i$ or $(d', d) \in \Phi_i$.*

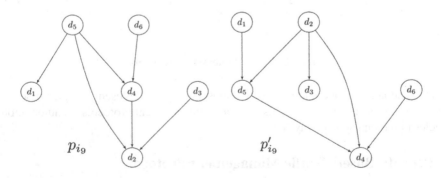

Fig. 3. Example of priority graph

The anti-symmetric and transitive conditions are able to avoid the existence of deadlock, which means that two conflicting links have the same priority, or multiple conflicting links have a priority closed loop. For example, if the two links in the directed graph meet symmetry, vehicles on the two roads will face the problem of mutual compromise due to the unclear priority. Similarly for multiple links with closed loop. Complete relative to $\mathcal{E}_i$ means that for every pair of conflicting links, one of the two must have priority over the other. If two conflicting links do not have completeness, then collision or deadlock will occur. Let P_i represent all possible priorities that satisfy with all conditions above for the intersection $i \in I$. Figure 3 left shows a simple example of priority graph for the T-junction (i_9) at Fig. 2 left. The example can be explained as a stop sign on e_1 in the real world. Vehicles on edge e_5 that turn left or go straight, and vehicles on e_4 that go straight, have highest priority. Then, vehicles on e_1 that turn left and vehicles on e_3 that turn right have second-highest priority. Last, vehicles on e_1 that turn right have lowest priority.

3.2 Dynamic Priority Management Protocol

Although the static priority protocol has certain advantages for managing unevenly distributed traffic flow, but it has certain fairness issues for relatively balanced traffic flow. For example, in the case of balanced traffic flow, vehicles on lower priority links have higher delay than vehicles on the higher priority links. As a generic assumption of this paper and a way of abstraction, we view time as a discrete variable when we specify traffic flows. In other words, time occurs at distinct separate *points in time*, throughout each non-zero region of time ("time period"), represented by natural numbers $T = \{1, \ldots, t, \ldots\}$. Based on the discrete-time distribution, we divide each time step into several phases and each phase corresponds to a priority graph. Formally, a dynamic priority management protocol is defined as follows:

Definition 4. *Given a road network $G = (I, L, E)$, connection relation D_i and conflict relation C_i for each intersection $i \in I$. A dynamic-priority management protocol $\eta_i : T \rightarrow 2^{P_i}$ is a function that maps each time period to a priority graph.*

Intuitively, a dynamic priority management protocol specifies which priority graph is used at each time period. Consider an intersection i_9 as shown in Fig. 2 left. A dynamic-priority traffic management protocol of intersection i_9 can be explained as follows:

$$\eta_{i_9}(t) = \begin{cases} p_{i_9}, & if\ 0 \leq t < l_1 \\ p'_{i_9}, & if\ l_1 \leq t < l_2 \end{cases}$$

where p_{i_9} (Fig. 3 left) and p'_{i_9} (Fig. 3 right) are two priority graph of intersection i_9, and $0 < l_1 < l_2$. The protocol specifies two time intervals in each period with length $l : [0, l_1)$ and $[l_1, l_2)$. The priority graph p_{i_9} is used in the first time interval and the priority graph p'_{i_9} is used in the second time interval.

3.3 Vehicle-Based Priority Management Protocol

The static priority and dynamic priority management protocols are based on the elaboration of the right of way. These two protocols are not only for autonomous vehicles but

---

Algorithm 1. Vehicle-based priority management protocol

Input: V_i is a set of vehicles that cross an intersection i.
Output: $CS[|V_i|]$ is cross sequence of vehicles.

1: $round = 0$;
2: $Participants(round)$: A set of first vehicles on every incoming edges of intersection i;
3: **while** $round < |V_i|$ **do**
4:     $Proposal(round) = \{t(v)|\forall v \in Participants(round)\}$;
5:     $Winner = \arg\min_{v \in Proposal(round)} arrivetime(v)$;
6:     $CS[round] = Winner$;
7:     $round = round + 1$;
8:     $Participants(round) = Participants(round) \cup \{new\_vehicle\} \setminus winner$, where $new\_vehicle$ is the vehicle behind of the winner vehicle.
9: **end while**

---

can also be used for existing traffic control. When autonomous vehicles equipped with communication facilities are implemented, vehicle-based priority management protocol can be used as one of many protocols for managing the passage of autonomous vehicles through intersections. The vehicle-based priority management protocol can be interpreted as communication between vehicles to determine the order of passing through the intersection. First-come-first-serve (FCFS) is a typical communication criterion, that is, if the vehicle arrives at the intersection first, it can pass through the intersection first. Algorithm 1 shows the vehicle-based management protocol based on the FCFS, which means that the crossing sequence of vehicles is based on the arrival time of those vehicles. Suppose V_i is a set of vehicles that cross intersection i and $t(v)$ denote the arrive time of vehicle $v \in V_i$. It can be interpreted as the sending of multiple rounds of agreement. Each round compares the arrival time of the lead vehicle entering the lane, and the winner is the vehicle that arrives at the intersection first. Then, the vehicle set for the next round is the collection of the remaining vehicles in the previous round and the vehicle after the winner's vehicle. It is worth to mention that the vehicle-based priority management protocol can not only use the arrival time as a criterion for vehicles, but also use different conditions as a criterion, such as auctions. If the arrival time in Algorithm 1 is changed to the bid of each vehicle, then the winner is determined as the vehicle with the highest bid, so that Algorithm 1 is able to represent the agreement of the auction passing right. In the rest of paper, we use the arrival time as the criterion for the vehicle-based priority management protocol.

In general, this section provides the formalization model for traffic management protocol based on priority. Next section, we introduced the simulator based on the formal models in the previous two sections and the results obtained by using the simulator to simulate traffic and analyze the data.

4   Experimental Setting and Results

The simulation code and interface are based on the AIM4 simulator [3], and it is an open source software. Different from AIM4, our implemented version can use the model of road network proposed in this paper as a basic structure and generate the expected traffic scenario to simulate the autonomous vehicles running on the virtual road network. In the experiment, we assume that all vehicles are homogeneous autonomous vehicles, so the parameters of the vehicles are the same (acceleration/deceleration, angular velocity, length and width). In this section, we first test the average delay of vehicles driving on the road network separated by different priorities. Secondly, we tested whether there is a bullwhip effect at an single intersection. Next, the average delay of vehicles managed by the different traffic management protocols mentioned above were simulated and compared. Finally, a generic delay function (latency function) is given to describe the delay of different protocols based on the testing results.

4.1 Average Delay for the Static-Priority Management Protocol

We use an intersection with one lane for each incoming direction as a simulation environment for autonomous vehicles, which means that the parallel road lanes are not contain. Figure 4 top-left shows the conflict relation of the simulation intersection which includes nine links inside of the intersection, and bot-left provides a simple priority graph of that intersection. The priority graph is separated into three hierarchies: $H_0 = \{d_1 = (e_1, e_2), d_2 = (e_1, e_4), d_3 = (e_1, e_6)\}$, $H_1 = \{d_4 = (e_3, e_4), d_5 = (e_3, e_6), d_6 = (e_3, e_8)\}$ and $H_2 = \{d_7 = (e_5, e_6), d_8 = (e_5, e_8), d_9 = (e_5, e_2)\}$, and there does allowed vehicles spawn in the incoming edge e_7 in this test. Links on H_0 have the highest priority over H_1 and H_2; it means that vehicles on the links located in the H_1 and H_2 should give the way to the vehicles on the links located on the H_0. Similarly, links on H_1 have higher priority than H_2, and links on H_2 have the lowest priority on the example priority graph.

Figure 4 right shows the average delay time for vehicles on different priority hierarchies. The X-axis is the traffic flow per hour, and Y-axis is the average delay for all vehicles in one hierarchy. It can be seen from experimental data that delay of high-priority vehicles does not increase with the increasing traffic flow. This means that the latency of vehicles traveling on high-priority links is negligible. Conversely, as the traffic flow rate increases, the delay time of the second-highest priority and lowest priority vehicles increases. When traffic flow is low, it shows a linear increase trend. As the traffic flow gradually increases, the average delay increases non-linearly.

4.2 Bullwhip Effect for the Static Priority Management Protocol

The bullwhip effect (also known as the Forrester effect) is a demand distortion that flows upstream in the supply chain from the retailer to the wholesaler and manufacturer due to order volatility that is greater than sales variance [7]. Information cannot be efficiently exchanged along the supply chain when it is conveyed from the ultimate customer to the original provider, which distorts and amplifies the information, resulting in greater and greater fluctuations in demand information. In the static-priority management protocol, the bullwhip effect is interpreted as whether the change of the standard deviation of the low priority will be affected when the standard deviation of the high priority changes, thereby affecting the delay time of the low priority.

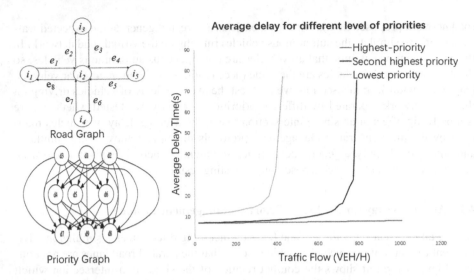

Fig. 4. Average delay for different level of priorities

In order to test the bullwhip effect on traffic scenarios, we created a new algorithm to generate vehicles as shown Algorithm 1. We use examples to explain the algorithm to make it more simple and clear. The core of this algorithm is divided into several steps. The first step is to fix the traffic flow rate and number of time intervals in an hour. Suppose traffic flow is 720 Veh/h and 40 time intervals. First, randomly generate 40 random numbers from 0–20, and then obtain the sum of the generated random numbers. The second step is to calculate the number of vehicles that need to be generated for each time interval. The calculation method is to take the random number and the total of each interval in the first step as the ratio and then multiply it by the total number of vehicles per hour. The third step is to obtain the vehicle generation time. Since there are 40 time intervals in an hour, each time interval is 90 s. It is assumed that 30 vehicles need to be generated in the first interval. The vehicle generation time is randomly generated 30 numbers from 0 s to 90 s, and each number represents the time of vehicle should be generated. The last step is to generate a vehicle when the simulator runs to the time that vehicle need to spawn. It is obvious that we can change the number of time intervals per hour to achieve the purpose of control standard deviation. As the number of time intervals increases, the randomness of vehicle generation decreases and it leads to the standard deviation decreases.

Figure 5 is the experimental results of the bullwhip effect according to different traffic flows. From the two graphs in the first row, it can be concluded that the standard deviation of the second-highest priority links increases as the standard deviation of the highest priority links increases. The second row of the graph represents the increase in the standard deviation of the second-highest priority links causing the increase in the average delay of vehicles on those links. It can be seen that the bullwhip effect exists in the static-priority management protocol. Therefore, how to eliminate the impact of the bullwhip effect on traffic will be one of the directions of future work.

Algorithm 2. Vehicle generation for Bullwhip effect

Input: Traffic flow per hour f and number of time interval N.
Output: Vehicle spawn time in an hour.

1: $Number\_of\_vehicles[N]$;
2: $sum = 0$;
3: $Time\_of\_interval = \frac{3600}{N}$;
4: **for** $i < N$ **do**
5:    $Number\_of\_vehicles[i] = Random(0, 20)$;
6:    $sum = sum + Number\_of\_vehicles[i]$;
7: **end for**
8: $sum\_real\_number = 0$;
9: **for** $i < N$ **do**
10:   $Number\_of\_vehicles[i] = \frac{Number\_of\_vehicles[i]}{sum} * f$;
11: **end for**
12: **while** $current\_time < MAX\_TEST\_TIME$ **do**
13:   $Current\_interval = Current\_time\%Time\_of\_interval$;
14:   **if** $Current\_time\%Time\_of\_interval = 0$ **then**
15:     **for** $i < Number\_of\_vehicles[i]$ **do**
16:       $Spawn\_time[i] = Random(0, Time\_of\_interval)$;
17:     **end for**
18:     Sort $Spawn\_time[]$ from smallest to largest;
19:     $Spawned\_vehicle = 0$;
20:   **end if**
21:   **if** $Current\_time = Spawn\_time[Spawned\ vehicle]$ **then**
22:     Spawn a vehicle;
23:     $Spawned\_vehicle = Spawned\_vehicle + 1$;
24:   **end if**
25: **end while**

4.3 Average Delay for Different Management Protocols

Next we compare the average delay time under different traffic management protocols. In this test, we use separate intersections and vehicles are generated from two incoming edges. This means that the dynamic priority traffic management protocol allows vehicles to pass in one incoming edge at one time interval, while the other direction is blocked. In the static-priority traffic management protocol, there are two priority levels, such as H_0 and H_1 on the Sect. 4.1. And the third protocol is vehicle-based priority management protocol, which is use the $FCFS$ as basic rules.

Figure 6 is the testing results under three different traffic management protocols proposed above. The X-axis is traffic flow ratio of two incoming edges, and the Y-axis is the average delay of all tested vehicles. For example, suppose there are 1000 vehicles per hour heading to an intersection from two incoming edges e_1 and e_2, 90 : 10 means that there are 900 vehicles heading from edge e_1 and 100 vehicles heading from edge e_2. It can be explained as extremely unbalanced traffic flow. Similarly, 50 : 50 is able to represent the balance traffic flow from two incoming edges (500 vehicles per hour for each edge). The dynamic priority management protocol exhibits symmetry. When the proportion of traffic flow is unbalanced, the delay will increase significantly. The

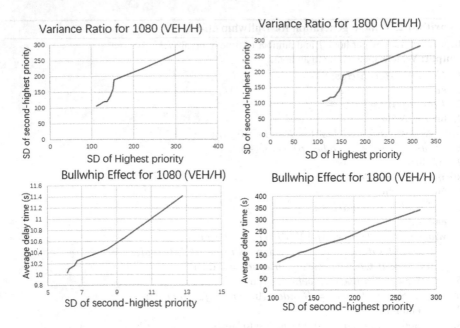

Fig. 5. Bullwhip effect with different traffic flow

last one is a static priority management protocol. When the traffic flow ratio approaches high priority, it means that the traffic flow of high priority is much larger than that of low priority. In general, vehicle-based priority management protocol and static-priority management protocols have lower delay time for vehicles.

4.4   Latency Function

Among the literature on the research of delay functions with traffic management protocols, there is a famous latency function called "Webster function" [14], which shows that the average delay, d, per vehicle on the particular direction of the intersection is:

$$d = \frac{c(1-\lambda)^2}{2(1-\lambda x)} + \frac{x^2}{2f(1-x)} \tag{1}$$

where c is the cycle time; $\lambda = \frac{g}{c}$ is the proportion of the cycle, which is effectively green for the phase under consideration, where g is the green time for the direction; f is the actual traffic flow on the direction; $x = \frac{f}{s}$ the degree of saturation, which is the ratio of the actual flow to the saturation flow s, which can be passed through the intersection per hour. But Webster function is obtained by fitting collected data, not a normalized result. After processing our collected data from the simulator, we used a composition function to fit the collected data, which is the combination of exponential function and linear function. We use regression curves to fit the experiential data to get the composition function, and obtained the coefficient of determination R^2 better than the Webster function. Formally, for each intersection $i \in I$, the latency function is:

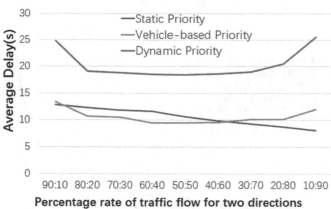

Fig. 6. Average delay of different management protocols

$$D_i = a_i e^{b_i f} + c_i f + d_i \tag{2}$$

where a_i, b_i, c_i and d_i are non-negative numbers for each intersection i, and f is traffic flow. What needs to be explained is that each intersection has an independent delay function. The input of the latency function is the traffic flow of each incoming lane, and the output is the delay time of that lane. Figure 7 shown the results of curve fitting for different priority traffic management protocols. The blue crosses, orange squares and green dots are the collected data from our simulator. The yellow line (Eq. 4) is the latency function obtained by the static-priority based management protocol using the composite function. The blue line (Eq. 5) represents the latency function of vehicle-based priority management protocol. The red line (Eq. 6) represents the latency function of the dynamic-priority based management protocol. And the black line represents the Webster function that use the same parameters as the dynamic-priority management protocol, where $c = 66, g = 30, s = 600$.

$$D_s = (4.233 \times 10^{-8})e^{0.02834f} + 0.00189f + 7.0244 \tag{3}$$

$$D_v = (1.002 \times 10^{-9})e^{0.03f} + 0.00581f + 7.24 \tag{4}$$

$$D_t = (6.34 \times 10^{-4})e^{0.01253f} + 0.000338f + 16.17 \tag{5}$$

From the Fig. 7, we can conclude that the use of a combination of linear and exponential functions can better simulate the delay at the intersection. Interestingly, our delay function can describe different traffic management protocols by changing variables, which means that our results is suit for more generic traffic scenarios. However, the different between the composite function from the simulator result and the Webster function is caused by different experimental settings, but we are not discussing it further in this paper. Finally, when there is a specific delay function, using the equation as the utility function of the multi-agent transportation network has become an important direction for the next step of research.

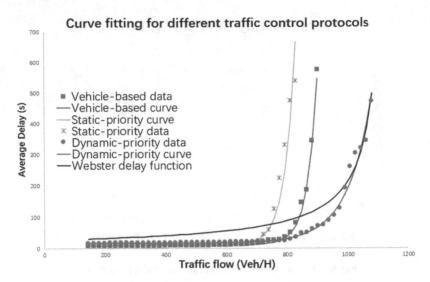

Fig. 7. Experimental results and regression for different management protocols (Color figure online)

5   Related Work and Conclusion

The graph is a set of elements and relations whose schematic expression as a set of points and lanes can be used to represent many situations where "points and connections between they have a physical or conceptual interpretation" [8]. Of most direct relevance here, graph theory has found significant application to the analysis of transport networks where there is an intuitive and obvious relationship between the links and nodes in a transport network and the edges E and vertices V in a graph G [5,9]. [11] provide a formal representation of an intersection based on the graph theory. Based on the representation, it provides time-based protocol and priority-based protocol to manage autonomous vehicles. Our main purpose is to implement the graph representation model [11] into more generic road networks.

Many simulators are designed to model true human behaviour, rather than testing custom agent algorithms. One of the most widely utilised simulation platforms in robotics and related research areas is Gazebo [6]. Different sensor types and physics engines can be added to the simulator because of its modular nature. However, Gazebo makes it tough to develop huge, complicated settings. AirSim [12] and CARLA [2] are some more notable open-source simulators for autonomous driving. When this research began, however, none gave us the ability to easily replace the mechanism by which intersections are governed. One of the important related works is the Autonomous Intersection Management (AIM) designed by Dresner and Stone [3], which could be an efficient way of handling road junction for autonomous vehicles. It is necessary to understand the basic design structure of this AIM to know the state-of-art in intersection management. However, we are unable to use this simulator in our research since the vehicles and traffic management facilities in the simulator are unable to make independent judgments and instead rely on pre-programmed tactics. As a result, more sophisticated simulators are required to mimic in a multi-agent context.

In this paper, we presents a graph representation for a road network, called a road graph. It describes the relationship between intersections and lanes. Then, the internal connection and interaction for each intersection on the road network are explained. Furthermore, we use the extended simulator to get some preliminary experimental results. This research throw up many open questions in need of further investigation. The genetic model for road network and priority-based management protocols are the first step in the research. Next, we will use game theory models to discuss some game theory properties such as Nash equilibrium, social optimal solution and price of anarchy. In addition, it is necessary to conduct an in-depth study on how to reduce the impact of the bullwhip effect on traffic. Once we have the theoretical model, the simulator will provide experimental data for our research.

References

1. Chan, C.Y.: Advancements, prospects, and impacts of automated driving systems. Int. J. Transp. Sci. Technol. **6**(3), 208–216 (2017)
2. Dosovitskiy, A., Ros, G., Codevilla, F., Lopez, A., Koltun, V.: CARLA: an open urban driving simulator. In: Proceedings of the 1st Conference on Robot Learning, pp. 1–16 (2017)
3. Dresner, K., Stone, P.: A multiagent approach to autonomous intersection management. J. Artif. Intell. Res. **31**, 591–656 (2008)
4. Gruel, W., Stanford, J.M.: Assessing the long-term effects of autonomous vehicles: a speculative approach. Transp. Res. Procedia **13**, 18–29 (2016)
5. Karimi, K.: A configurational approach to analytical urban design:'space syntax' methodology. Urban Des. Int. **17**(4), 297–318 (2012)
6. Koenig, N., Howard, A.: Design and use paradigms for Gazebo, an open-source multi-robot simulator. In: 2004 IEEE/RSJ International Conference on Intelligent Robots and Systems (IROS), vol. 3, pp. 2149–2154 (2004)
7. Lee, H.L., Padmanabhan, V., Whang, S.: The bullwhip effect in supply chains. Sloan Manage. Rev. **38**, 93–102 (1997)
8. Marshall, S.: Line structure representation for road network analysis. J. Transp. Land Use **9**(1), 29–64 (2016)
9. Porta, S., Crucitti, P., Latora, V.: The network analysis of urban streets: a dual approach. Phys. A **369**(2), 853–866 (2006)
10. Qiao, J., Zhang, D., de Jonge, D.: Virtual roundabout protocol for autonomous vehicles. In: Mitrovic, T., Xue, B., Li, X. (eds.) AI 2018. LNCS (LNAI), vol. 11320, pp. 773–782. Springer, Cham (2018). https://doi.org/10.1007/978-3-030-03991-2_70
11. Qiao, J., Zhang, D., de Jonge, D.: Graph representation of road and traffic for autonomous driving. In: Nayak, A.C., Sharma, A. (eds.) PRICAI 2019. LNCS (LNAI), vol. 11672, pp. 377–384. Springer, Cham (2019). https://doi.org/10.1007/978-3-030-29894-4_31
12. Shah, S., Dey, D., Lovett, C., Kapoor, A.: AirSim: high-fidelity visual and physical simulation for autonomous vehicles. In: Hutter, M., Siegwart, R. (eds.) Field and Service Robotics. SPAR, vol. 5, pp. 621–635. Springer, Cham (2018). https://doi.org/10.1007/978-3-319-67361-5_40
13. Thorpe, C., Herbert, M., Kanade, T., Shafer, S.: Toward autonomous driving: the CMU Navlab. I. Perception. IEEE Expert **6**(4), 31–42 (1991)
14. Webster, F.V.: Traffic signal settings. Road Research Technical report Paper No. 39, Department of Scientific and Industrial Research, London (1957)
15. Wei, Y., et al.: Dynamic programming-based multi-vehicle longitudinal trajectory optimization with simplified car following models. Transp. Res. Part B Methodol. **106**, 102–129 (2017)

Improving Traffic Load Prediction with Multi-modality
A Case Study of Brisbane

Khai Phan Tran[1]([mail])(iD), Weitong Chen[1]([mail])(iD), and Miao Xu[1,2]([mail])(iD)

[1] School of Information Technology and Electrical Engineering,
The University of Queensland, Brisbane, QLD, Australia
khai.tran@uqconnect.edu.au, {w.chen9,miao.xu}@uq.edu.au
[2] RIKEN, Wako, Japan

Abstract. Fast and accurate traffic load prediction is a pivotal component of the Intelligent Transport System. It will reduce time spent by commuters and save our environment from vehicle emissions. During the COVID-19 pandemic, people prefer to use private transportation; thus predicting the traffic load becomes more critical. In these years, researchers have developed some traffic load prediction models and have applied these models successfully on data from the US, China or Europe. However, none of these models has been applied to traffic data in Australia. Considering that Australia bears different political, geographical, and climate conditions from other countries, these models may not be suitable to predict the traffic load in Australia. In this paper, we investigate this problem and proposes a multi-modal method that is capable of using Australia-specific data to assist traffic load prediction. Specifically, we use daily social media data together with traffic data to predict the traffic load. We illustrate a protocol to pre-process raw traffic and social media data and then propose a multi-modal model, namely DM2T, which accurately make time-series prediction by using both time-series data and other media data. We validate the effectiveness of our proposed method by a case study on Brisbane city. The result shows that with the help of Australia-specific social media data, our proposed method can make more accurate traffic load prediction for Brisbane than conventional methods.

Keywords: Traffic load prediction · Deep learning · Natural Language Processing (NLP)

1 Introduction

Traffic congestion during peak hours has been placed profound consequences on human life and the economy [6]. This situation is worse during the COVID-19 pandemic as commuters are reluctant to use the public transport system, especially in Brisbane city [12]. Therefore, accurate real-time traffic load prediction

© Springer Nature Switzerland AG 2022
G. Long et al. (Eds.): AI 2021, LNAI 13151, pp. 254–266, 2022.
https://doi.org/10.1007/978-3-030-97546-3_21

is an important and urgent need for the city authority to control and plan traffic efficiently. In recent years, many efforts have been put into real-time traffic prediction, and many of them achieved satisfactory results, such as. Zhang et al. [20] used Convolutional Neural Networks (CNN) for short-term traffic flow prediction, and Poonia et al. [16] utilised Long Short-term Memory Networks (LSTM) for momentary traffic stream forecast. These models have been shown to be successful when applied to real traffic data collected from countries such as Thailand [18], Saudi Arabia [2] and the US [13]. However, none of them has been applied to predict the traffic load in Australian cities. Australia, as the world's six largest countries, is the only one of these six countries surrounded completely by water[1]. Due to its geographical nature, Australian cities have unique weather conditions, landform, and traffic laws compared to other countries. These factors may have a significant impact on traffic load prediction accuracy. For example, extreme weather can be encountered more frequently in Australia [8]. Wearing helmets while using bicycles is compulsory [10]. Considering these differences, this paper wants to investigate whether adding side information, especially about Australia, can improve the prediction accuracy of traffic load.

To collect the side information, we could collect information from local government on city planning, big events regulation, updated traffic policy; from local population about the residency distribution; from Bureau of Meteorology on weather conditions, etc. Recently, due to the popularity of social networks, people like to share news, ideas, moods, plans and activities on platforms such as Twitter. For example, the fear against a high rise of COVID-19 cases may indicate a reduction in the traffic load, and the travel guide by an internet celebrity to a particular place of interest may lead to an increase in the traffic load. In this way, social networks contain an abundant range of information covering various aspects of side information which could help a more accurate prediction of traffic load. Although there are some existing works using the information of social networks [14,17,19], these works usually prefer special information narrowed in one field, such as traffic, without considering other kinds of information that could also be helpful.

This paper proposes a multi-modal learning method, namely **Deep Multi-modal Traffic (DM2T)**, for dynamic traffic load prediction. Traffic time-series data and social media data can be different models for the learning problem. In our model, we use a Long Short-term Memory (LSTM) as the base model for time-series prediction. Social media data is used as a side input to the model to assist the forecast. To test our model on real-world traffic data, especially in Australia, we focus on the traffic of the Coronation Drive, which is one of the critical corridors of the east-west region in Brisbane. It has 70,307 vehicles per weekday on average in 2019 and is counted as one of the busiest roads in Brisbane [5]. We collected traffic data from the Brisbane Council website[2] and

---

[1] https://info.australia.gov.au/about-australia/our-country/the-australian-continent.

[2] https://www.data.brisbane.qld.gov.au/data/dataset/traffic-data-at-intersection-api.

Twitter data of all users in Brisbane area from February 20th 2021 to June 18th 2021. These raw data are pre-processed and used to test the feasibility of our proposal. The experimental results show that by using Australian local data from social media, we could improve the prediction performance of traffic load. The paper is organized as follows: Sect. 2 presents our proposed method, and the pre-processing data protocol is illustrated in Sect. 3. Section 4 shows the experimental results of our approach with different deep learning models by different experiments, followed by Sect. 5 giving a brief summary of highly related work. Finally, we conclude the paper in Sect. 6.

2 Proposed Method

Figure 1 illustrates the conceptual framework of the proposed method. We call our approach DM2T. The goal of the proposed method is to precisely predict the traffic flow in a real-time manner.

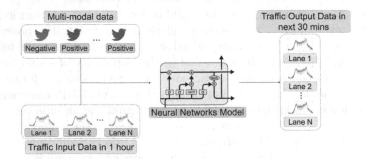

Fig. 1. The workflow of DM2T: multi-modal information and multivariate traffic information is first acquired and then fed into the LSTM model for real-time traffic prediction.

2.1 Mathematical Formulation

Traffic load prediction is to forecast the number of vehicles on the street at observation points over a time period. The problem can be formulated as: using the historical traffic data points $X_{d_{i,j}}$ which consists of timestamps from i^{th}, denoted as x_{d_i}, to j^{th}, denoted as x_{d_j}, to predict the traffic volume at $(j+1)^{th}$ timestamp, denoted as $x_{d_{j+1}}$. In this paper, the traffic volume used is the lanes' degree of saturation on the target street. For further convenience, the traffic load prediction in this paper is formulated as follow:

$$\mathbb{F}(X_{d_{i,j}}, Z) \rightarrow x_{d_{j+1}}$$

where $\mathbb{F}$ is the selected model for prediction, $X_{d_{i,j}} \in \mathbb{R}^{d_{i,j} \times k}$ is the matrix of input traffic information and Z is the multi-modal information such as images, videos or text from social media. $x_{d_{j+1}} \in \mathbb{R}^{1 \times k}$ is the traffic flow prediction from the model for a timestamp. The input traffic information has the shape of $d_{i,j} \times k$ where $d_{i,j}$ is the number of data points in the input matrix and k is the number of variables in one data point. The output x is the vector having the dimension as $d_{i,j} \times 3$ where $d_{i,j}$ is the number of timestamps we want to predict in the future and 3 is the number of lanes on the target street.

2.2 Multi-modal Method

The aim of this work is to consider sentiment information from multi-modal data for better traffic prediction. The multi-modal information m collected from social media are fed into Support Vector Machine (SVM) using RBF kernel function K for sentiment analysis [15]. The result from SVM can be divided into positive or negative. The sentiment feature extraction for multi-modal information m can be formulated as follow where sv are the support vectors from the SVM model:

$$K(m, \ sv) = e^{\gamma ||m-sv||^2} \tag{1}$$

The output of sentiment analysis s will be concatenated with the multivariate time series x traffic data under same time interval d_i, the concatenation can be described as,

$$\hat{x}_{d_i} = x_{d_i} \oplus s_{d_i} \tag{2}$$

where $\hat{x}$ is the concatenated the output. the $\hat{x}$ will be then fed into the recurrent neural network.

To improve the performance of the prediction model, we utilised the temporal information from multivariate time series traffic data and supportive information from modal data for real-time traffic prediction. In particular, LSTM [11] is used to process the sequential input by recursively applying a transaction function to its hidden vector h_i. At each time step i, an LSTM maintains a hidden vector h and a memory vector n for controlling state updates and outputs. The LSTM unit at each time step t is defined as a collection of vectors in x_{d_i}. Each LSTM unit includes v, f, o, c, v and h, which are the input gates, forget gates, output gates, memory cell, and hidden state respectively. The LSTM transition equations are defined as follows:

$$
\begin{aligned}
v_i &= \sigma(W_{\hat{x}_{d_i}v} x_i + W_{hv} h_{i-1} + W_{cv} c_{i-1} + b_v) \\
f_i &= \sigma(W_{\hat{x}_{d_i}f} x_i + W_{hf} h_{i-1} + W_{cf} c_{i-1} + b_f) \\
o_i &= \sigma(W_{\hat{x}_{d_i}o} x_i + W_{ho} h_{i-1} + W_{co} c_{i-1} + b_o) \\
c_i &= f_i c_{i-1} + i_t \tanh(W_{xc} x_i + W_{hc} h_{i-1} + b_c) \\
h_i &= o_i \tanh(c_i),
\end{aligned}
\tag{3}
$$

where x_i is the input at i time step, Ws are weights, bs are biases, and σ denotes the logistic sigmoid function.

3 Data Collection and Pre-processing

In order to evaluate the proposed method, we collected multi-modal data from Twitter and multivariate traffic data from Brisbane City Council website between February 20th 2021 and June 18th 2021 for the evaluation.

3.1 Multi-modal Data

Multi-modal data was collected from Twitter using Twitter API[3] in 4 months from February 20th 2021 to June 18th 2021. There are 126,875 tweets retrieved during this time. However, we only used text data for evaluation in this study. Therefore, we retrieved the timestamp and multimedia content of those tweets for further processing steps. Figure 2 shows some keywords from the text data collected from Twitter.

Fig. 2. Word clouds of keywords from multi-modal data collected from the Twitter between February 20th 2021 and June 18th 2021.

The raw data collected from Twitter contains much meaningless information such as URLs, user mentions and different forms of a word, making them difficult for sentiment analysis. Hence, they are pre-processed as the pipeline specified in Fig. 3.

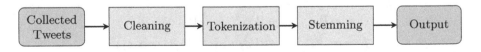

Fig. 3. Processing Twitter pipeline.

1. *Cleaning*: User mention (@user), URLs, punctuation, stopwords, number, special characters are removed. Moreover, lowercase transformation is also applied to each tweet.

---

[3] Snscrape: https://github.com/JustAnotherArchivist/snscrape.

2. *Tokenization*: Each tweet is divided into individual words that will help to build N-gram model.
3. *Stemming*: Each tweet is stemmed to achieve the core root for each word in that tweet. This process is achieved by the NLTK library in Python [4].

3.2 Traffic Data

Traffic data was collected for all streets in Brisbane city in 4 months, from February 20th 2021 to June 18th 2021, which spans from summer, fall and winter seasons. Each data point is the traffic volume at each traffic signal controller (TSC). This time period covers some special days, such as public holidays, school terms and also a short lockdown which has unique traffic volume patterns. The data was collected from the Brisbane Council Website API[4] every 5 s, in a total of 128,197 data points. Each data has 11 attributes: *'dbid'*, *'recorded'*, *'ct'*, *'link_plan'*, *'married'*, *'ss'*, *'tsc'*, *'lane'*, *'dsN'*, *'mfN'*, *'rfN'*. The *'dbid'* is the internal database identifier. The *'recorded'* is the timestamp where the traffic data point is recorded. The *'ct'* is the cycle time of the traffic signal controller (TSC). The *'link_plan'* is the linking plan at this TSC and connects to another TSC to optimize the traffic. The *'married'* attribute is the binary value indicating if the link plan is in the linked mode with the TSC. The *'ss'* attribute is the sub-system identifier to identify a group of TSC in the same region. The *'lane'* is the strategic link into the intersection. The *'dsN'*, *'mfN'* and *'rfN'* is the degree of saturation, measured flow and reconstituted flow of land N^{th} on a street. However, only six of them are relevant to the traffic flow representation including *'recorded'*, *'ss'*, *'tsc'*, *'dsN'*, *'mfN'* and *'rfN'*. Figure 4 as shown the raw data in JSON file format.

```
"dbid":2519065964,
"recorded":"2021-05-31T11:40:00",
"ct":150,
"link_plan":1,
"married":"Y",
"ss":2446,
"tsc":87,
"lane":"SA-517",
"ds1":87,
"mf1":30,
"rf1":42,
"ds2":91,
"mf2":35,
"rf2":46,
"ds3":93,
"mf3":31,
"rf3":47
```

Fig. 4. A traffic data sample: it was recorded at 11:40 AM on May 31st 2021. The recorded location is the traffic signal controller having ID as 87 in the sub-system ID 2446. This street has 3 lanes. The (ds, mf, rf) of lanes 1, 2 and 3 are (87, 30, 42), (91, 35, 46) and (93, 31, 41) respectively.

---

[4] https://www.data.brisbane.qld.gov.au/data/dataset/traffic-data-at-intersection-api.

The traffic data processing is summarized in Fig. 5. In this study, we use only data from the Coronation Drive, one of the key corridors of the east-west region in Brisbane, for evaluation.

Fig. 5. Processing traffic pipeline.

1. *Averaging*: We filter out and keep only data of TSCs which are on our targeted road - Coronation Drive in Brisbane City. The traffic volume of the whole street is the average traffic volume measured at each TSC on that street.

$$volume_{street}^t = \frac{\sum_{i=1}^{N} volume_i^t}{N}$$

where $volume_{street}^t$ is the traffic volume at time t of the Coronation Drive and $volume_i^t$ is the traffic volume at time t of the ith TSC on the street.

2. *Outliers Removal*: We remove some outliers which are days lacking significant data i.e. starting collecting traffic data at 2:00 PM because of the interruption during collecting data from API. Keeping these data will make creating datasets for training, validating and testing models become difficult.

3. *Partitioning*: We separate the traffic data into consecutive daily sequences since removing outliers creates gap between day, e.g. the next day of 03/04/2021 is 06/04/2021 in the dataset. The short lockdown from March 30th, 2021 to April 3rd, 2021 is included in the test set due to its unique characteristics shown in Fig. 6.

4. *Day type consideration*: Because the traffic is impacted by the property of the day, we also take into account if a day is a holiday, weekday or weekend and what type the following day of that day is.

5. *Smoothing and Normalizing*: The traffic data is then divided into 30-minute intervals starting from midnight and ending at 23:59. An example is shown in Table 1. We also normalize the data to prevent gradient vanishing and exploding during the training process.

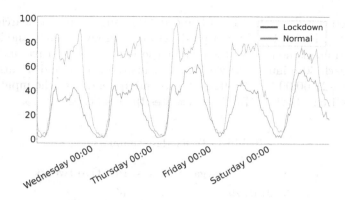

Fig. 6. Traffic volume comparison between normal days and lockdown days.
Lockdown days have traffic volume lower than normal days.

3.3 Experiment

For the performance evaluation, we conducted two experiment sets based on the collected dataset. First, we compare the DM2T with baseline deep learning methods. Secondly, to demonstrate the effectiveness of multi-modal information, an aberration study is conducted. Lastly, an evaluation of the perdition performance on time windows size is conducted. The source code and sample data are available on the GitHub[5]. In experiment, we focus on the traffic of the Coronation Drive located in the east-west region of Brisbane. In addition, we use only text data as representative of multi-modal information from collected tweets. During the experiment, 64%, 15% and 21% of total data are used for training, testing and validation.

All neural network models were implemented with TensorFlow 2.4.0 and trained on the computer with Intel(R) Core(TM) i7-9700, Nvidia GeForce RTX 2080 GPU from scratch in a fully supervised manner. To minimise the loss function, we employ the Mean Absolute Error (MAE). The parameter is optimised with 5 layers, 0.001 learning rate. The first 4 layers are LSTM layers with 0.5 dropout for each. We use the normal method [9] to initialise the biases to obtain a better result. The dimension is 64, 32, 32, 32 respectively. The output layer is the fully connected layer with size 3. The proposed model is trained with 50 epochs for each run time, and there are 50 run times in total. The loss on the testing dataset for each run time is recorded.

Multi-modal Data Analysis. We use *Sentiment 140* [7] as the dataset to pre-train the sentiment analysis model. The dataset contains 1.6M tweets which are annotated the polarity (0 = negative, 4 = positive). We shuffle and select the first 25,000 tweets. The training and testing dataset is 80% and 20% respectively. We tune hyper-parameter C with 4 different values (0.1, 1, 10 and 100) and γ

---

[5] https://github.com/khaitp/DM2T.

with 4 different values (1, 0.1, 0.01 and 0.001) using Random Search [3]. The SVM model with $C = 1$ and $\gamma = 1$ produces an accuracy of 70.4% and is selected as the pre-trained model. We then count the number of positive and negative tweets for each 30-minute interval, e.g. how many positive and negative tweets from 2021-02-21 00:00 to 2021-02-21 00:29 and append it as the input the data point at 2021-02-21 00:29. Table 1 illustrates the result.

Table 1. Traffic data summary

Interval	Negative tweets	**Positive tweets**
2021-02-21 00:29	15	14
2021-02-21 00:59	13	21
2021-02-21 01:29	16	12
2021-02-21 01:59	17	12

4 Discussion

To evaluate the effectiveness of the multi-modal data in prediction, we conduct the experiment on two different settings: with and without multi-modal data. Figure 7 shows the performance in terms of MAE for the DM2T and other baseline methods in this experiment. It is clear that the DM2T significantly improves the accuracy in predicting the performance of all models with average 2% in terms of MAE compared without using additional information. Table 2 shows the mean and standard deviation of DM2T and baseline methods to visualize more precisely the improvements.

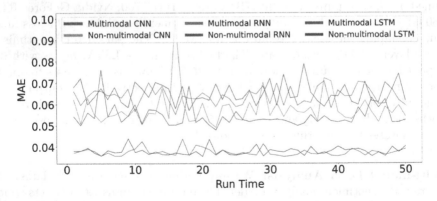

Fig. 7. Comparison in models' loss with and without multi-modal data.

Table 2. Performance summary of models in **MAE** over 50 run times.

Model	With multi-modal data	Without multi-modal data
CNN	0.0543 ± 0.0049	0.0579 ± 0.0079
RNN	0.0637 ± 0.0038	0.0651 ± 0.0048
DM2T	0.0374 ± 0.0018	0.0378 ± 0.0018

Figure 8 illustrates the performance of all methods in 50 run times measured using Mean Absolute Error (MAE) and Mean Squared Error (MSE). This figure shows that DM2T outperforms the compassion methods. In addition, to evaluate the prediction performance of the DM2T, we compare the performance of baseline methods in three different scenarios (e.g., weekday, weekend, public holiday/lockdown). From Fig. 9, it can be observed that the prediction of DM2T is nearly identical to the ground-truth and outperform the comparison methods for the lockdown period.

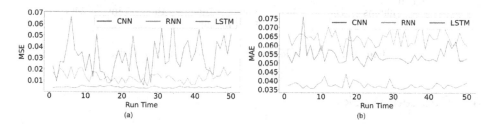

Fig. 8. Models' performance with multi-modal data in 50 run times. **(a)** MSE. **(b)** MAE.

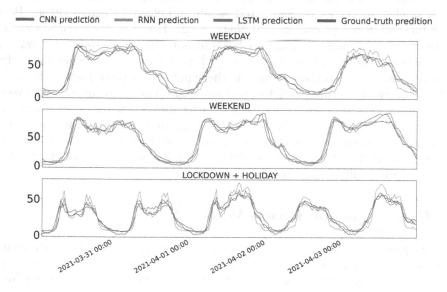

Fig. 9. Models' prediction with ground-truth data.

Prediction time window size is another factor that impacts the performance of a model. To evaluate the impact of time-window on prediction, we assess the prediction power of the DM2T on different time windows including 30 min, 1 h, 2 h, 4 h, 7 h, 11 h, 16 h, 1 day ahead and report the performance result in Fig. 10. From this figure, it can be observed that the DM2T prediction performance drops slightly with the increase of time window. This may be because of the change in the traffic condition for the long time-window.

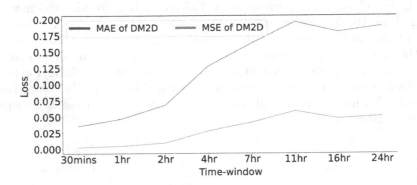

Fig. 10. DM2T's loss with different time-windows.

5   Related Works

Several studies have proposed to predict traffic accurately by considering the information from Twitter data. Alomari et al. has developed a framework for detecting traffic congestion based on sentiment analysis of Arabic tweets in Saudi Arabia. They scrape all traffic-related tweets and classify them as Strong Positive, Positive, Strong Negative and Negative [2]. However, their study was not conducted in this unique situation because not only traffic-related news can impact the traffic condition. Yao et al. [19] used Twitter to predict the traffic of early morning accurately based on the number of tweets posted the night before and early morning and the weather data. They categorized the tweets into different activities and include this Twitter incident to output the next-day morning congestion status. Alkouz et al. [1] suggested a system fusing data from multiple sources such as Twitter and Instagram in both languages, Arabic and English, to predict the traffic jam. However, similar to Alomari et al. [2], they only used the traffic-related tweets in this work.

6   Conclusion and Future Works

In this paper, we proposed a multi-modal approach called DM2T for traffic volume data prediction applied in Brisbane City using text data from Twitter to give better performance. We described how raw data is obtained from the API provided by Brisbane City Council, analyzed and incorporated with multi-modal data to predict the traffic data in 30 min in advance. The approach uses the LSTM model as the base and is evaluated with 2 different deep learning models: CNN and RNN. The experimental results show that our approach overall generates a better performance with the baseline method - LSTM, RNN and CNN. The approach shows that it can be used with simple models that do not need large time complexity and can be deployed to predict traffic volume in real-time. We also evaluated the performance of DM2T approach with different time-window and have notified that it was more challenging to predict if the time-window is larger. The future works should be carefully selecting hyper-parameters for LSTM models to have a better result for long-term traffic prediction. We also want to expand the approach for all streets in Brisbane city or other Australian cities with other deep learning-based methods that account for temporal-spatial properties, such as Graph Neural Networks, in the next step.

References

1. Alkouz, B., Al Aghbari, Z.: SNSJam: road traffic analysis and prediction by fusing data from multiple social networks. Inf. Process. Manage. **57**(1), 102139 (2020)
2. Alomari, E., Mehmood, R., Katib, I.: Sentiment analysis of Arabic tweets for road traffic congestion and event detection. In: Mehmood, R., See, S., Katib, I., Chlamtac, I. (eds.) Smart Infrastructure and Applications. EICC, pp. 37–54. Springer, Cham (2020). https://doi.org/10.1007/978-3-030-13705-2_2
3. Bergstra, J., Bengio, Y.: Random search for hyper-parameter optimization. J. Mach. Learn. Res. **13**(2), 281–305 (2012)
4. Bird, S., Klein, E., Loper, E.: Natural Language Processing with Python: Analyzing Text with the Natural Language Toolkit. O'Reilly Media, Inc., Sebastopol (2009)
5. Council, B.C.: Greater brisbane key corridors performance January June 2019. https://www.brisbane.qld.gov.au/traffic-and-transport/traffic-management/greater-brisbane-key-corridors-performance report/greater-brisbane-key-corridors-performance-january-june-2019
6. Falcocchio, J.C., Levinson, H.S.: The costs and other consequences of traffic congestion. In: Road Traffic Congestion: A Concise Guide. STTT, vol. 7, pp. 159–182. Springer, Cham (2015). https://doi.org/10.1007/978-3-319-15165-6_13
7. Go, A., Bhayani, R., Huang, L.: Twitter sentiment classification using distant supervision. CS224N project report, Stanford 1(12) (2009)
8. Guillod, B.P., et al.: Weather@ home 2: validation of an improved global-regional climate modelling system. Geoscientific Model Dev. **10**(5), 1849–1872 (2017)
9. He, K., Zhang, X., Ren, S., Sun, J.: Delving deep into rectifiers: surpassing human-level performance on ImageNet classification. In: Proceedings of the IEEE International Conference on Computer Vision, pp. 1026–1034 (2015)
10. Hirst, J.: The distinctiveness of Australian democracy. Distinctive Found. Aust. Democracy **42**, 113 (2004). https://www.aph.gov.au/binaries/senate/pubs/pops/pop42/pop42.pdf
11. Hochreiter, S., Schmidhuber, J.: Long short-term memory. Neural Comput. **9**(8), 1735–1780 (1997)

12. Hosier, P.: 'We haven't seen this in years': Brisbane roads choked with 'alarming' congestion worse than pre-covid, February 2021. https://www.abc.net.au/news/2021-02-09/coronavirus-queensland-brisbane-traffic-congestion-transport/13121108

13. Lazaris, A., Prasanna, V.K.: Deep learning models for aggregated network traffic prediction. In: 2019 15th International Conference on Network and Service Management (CNSM), pp. 1–5. IEEE (2019)

14. Lin, L., Ni, M., He, Q., Gao, J., Sadek, A.W.: Modeling the impacts of inclement weather on freeway traffic speed: exploratory study with social media data. Transp. Res. Rec. **2482**(1), 82–89 (2015)

15. Phienthrakul, T., Kijsirikul, B., Takamura, H., Okumura, M.: Sentiment classification with support vector machines and multiple Kernel functions. In: Leung, C.S., Lee, M., Chan, J.H. (eds.) ICONIP 2009. LNCS, vol. 5864, pp. 583–592. Springer, Heidelberg (2009). https://doi.org/10.1007/978-3-642-10684-2_65

16. Poonia, P., Jain, V.: Short-term traffic flow prediction: using LSTM. In: 2020 International Conference on Emerging Trends in Communication, Control and Computing (ICONC3), pp. 1–4. IEEE (2020)

17. Salas, A., Georgakis, P., Nwagboso, C., Ammari, A., Petalas, I.: Traffic event detection framework using social media. In: 2017 IEEE International Conference on Smart Grid and Smart Cities (ICSGSC), pp. 303–307. IEEE (2017)

18. Toncharoen, R., Piantanakulchai, M.: Traffic state prediction using convolutional neural network. In: 2018 15th International Joint Conference on Computer Science and Software Engineering (JCSSE), pp. 1–6. IEEE (2018)

19. Yao, W., Qian, S.: From twitter to traffic predictor: Next-day morning traffic prediction using social media data. Transp. Res. Part C Emerg. Technol. **124**, 102938 (2021)

20. Zhang, W., Yu, Y., Qi, Y., Shu, F., Wang, Y.: Short-term traffic flow prediction based on spatio-temporal analysis and CNN deep learning. Transportmetrica A Transp. Sci. **15**(2), 1688–1711 (2019)

Predicting Geological Material Types Using Ground Penetrating Radar

Oliver Fleming[✉], Adrian Ball, and Rami N. Khushaba

The Rio Tinto Centre for Mine Automation at The University of Sydney,
Sydney, Australia

Abstract. This paper presents a new machine learning feature extraction methodology for the identification of material transitions in a lateritic bauxite deposit using ground penetrating radar (GPR). This methodology allows for model results that quantitatively outperform typical feature extraction processes whilst providing qualitatively useful results. The geological domain in which this process was applied has a relatively large transition zone, which weakens the GPR characteristics that the typical feature extraction processes rely upon. While training on depth (92% accuracy), time and frequency (50–68% accuracy), wavelet decomposition (69% accuracy), and multi-signal fusion (50% accuracy) feature spaces produces results of varying quantitative success, all of them result in qualitatively poor results, often with results looking like white noise. Our proposed feature, Gaussian Ridge Extraction (GRE), achieves an accuracy of 83% while producing an estimate that is qualitatively reasonable. Combining GRE with a reduced set of features from the originally explored feature sets improves model accuracy to 87% and further strengthens the visual, qualitative estimate of the boundary transition.

Keywords: Ground penetrating radar · Classification models ·
Mineral reserve estimation · Feature extraction · Feature selection ·
Gaussian ridge extraction · Boundary estimation

1 Introduction

Mineral estimation and mine site planning are vital processes in mining operations [10]. It is the process of locating and estimating the amount of useable material in a deposit allowing assessment on the economic viability of excavation. This promotes the need for highly accurate and efficient estimation techniques.

Current mineral reserve estimation techniques rely primarily upon exploratory hole drilling which, while accurate, is time-consuming and expensive [27]. In this paper we explore the potential for an alternative estimation technique; Ground Penetrating Radar (GPR). GPR is a remote-sensing technique conducted at the surface level which, unlike exploratory drilling, is non-destructive and requires minimal setup. GPR has been used to great effect in assessing coal and iron ore deposits [11,25], and in identifying buried objects [13]. This paper seeks to mimic this success in bauxite mineral reserve estimations.

© Springer Nature Switzerland AG 2022
G. Long et al. (Eds.): AI 2021, LNAI 13151, pp. 267–278, 2022.
https://doi.org/10.1007/978-3-030-97546-3_22

In normal applications, GPR is able to estimate bauxite reserves through the identification of a boundary or transition line between the bauxite and a lower ironstone waste material [25]. This boundary is sensed by GPR as a spike in signal amplitude, the clarity of which is a function of the starkness of transition between materials [21]. At the bauxite site where data for this paper is collected from the transition line is better described as a transition zone as it is unusually indistinct and intermixed. This gradual and unclear transition results in areas of data where the transition line is particularly faint compared to other bauxite sites, and other areas where it is completely absent (Fig. 1). This lack of a visually obvious transition line is problematic and renders current estimation methods using GPR unreliable at best, and irrelevant at worst [12,30].

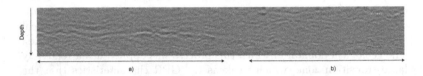

Fig. 1. An example of the GPR data used within this paper, where a) denotes a rare area with a somewhat clear transition line, and b) denotes more common data with little evidence of a transition line.

In this paper we define a novel feature extraction algorithm, Gaussian Ridge Extraction (GRE), and compare it with other established feature extraction processes. These features are used to train a random forest model that estimates the location of the material transition zone. Following this, we combine GRE with a limited set of features from the established feature sets using DEFS [17] and SHAP [20] to construct a model that performs quantitatively and qualitatively well.

The remainder of the paper is as follows: Section 2 provides an overview of GPR, the geology of the bauxite site, and the feature extraction algorithms utilised, Sect. 4 defines the methodology used in this investigation, Sect. 5 presents and discusses the results from application of our model on a bauxite deposit, and Sect. 6 concludes the paper.

2   Background

2.1   Site Geology

In this paper we investigate a method for identifying the transition zone in a bauxite deposit. At the site where data for this paper is collected, and in other sites worldwide, bauxite occurs as a flat, lateritic layer resting upon a lower ironstone deposit [12,14,26]. Bauxite is a sedimentary rock, comprised of various aluminium hydroxides which can be refined into metallic aluminium, hence its high demand [14]. Ironstone is also sedimentary and is composed of a relatively high concentration of iron and iron compounds [21]. These two materials have different electrical properties which can be identified by GPR.

This site differs from other bauxite deposits worldwide in the thickness of the transition zone [29]. At other sites worldwide the transition between bauxite and ironstone is clear and distinct, taking place over short distances. However, at this site the transition is far more indistinct and graduated, taking up to a metre to fully transition. It is this thick, gradual transition which prevents normal GPR interpretation methods from being effective.

2.2   Interaction of Site Materials and GPR

In conventional applications of GPR a pulse of radar waves are emitted at surface level which then propagate through the bauxite and reflect off of changes in electrical properties [9,21]. This reflection feedback is sensed and recorded as a function of time. When the waves reach the bauxite-ironstone transition a comparatively larger portion are reflected due to the sharp changes in dielectric permittivity, conductivity and magnetic permeability of the materials [9,10]. This increased reflectance appears as a spike in GPR signal amplitude.

At this site the normal sharp change in electrical properties between materials is diminished due to the graduated blending of materials in the thick transition zone. The expected signal spike is therefore reduced or even obscured to the point where trained geologists are unable to identify its precise location in GPR data [3]. As current interpretation processes rely upon this visual spike a new identification method is required.

2.3   Machine Learning and Feature Extraction

In this paper a number of extraction processes are utilised to generate feature spaces. Feature spaces are collections of informative variables that represent an object to be interpreted by ML models. These processes can be grouped as: depth, time & frequency domain, wavelet transform and multi-signal feature fusion. The generated features are then used to train a random forest model. We present both this model and the extraction algorithms in this section.

Depth Extraction. This process identifies the depth of a specific segment and places this information into the feature space. Due to the lateritic nature of the bauxite deposit the depth of the transition zone does not vary greatly. A depth feature was therefore expected to be a good predictor of the general depth of the transition line, resulting in high accuracies. The depth would thereby provide a baseline from which other features could improve upon.

Time and Frequency Domain Extractions. These algorithms provide time and frequency characteristic of a signal. Time domain processes often use the following algorithms: waveform length (WL) [19], root mean square (RMS) [23], zero crossing (ZC) [5], integrated absolute value (IAV) [18], mean absolute value (MAV) [1], difference absolute standard deviation value extraction (DASDV) and difference variance value extraction (DVARV) [22]. They can be extracted through Eqs. (1)–(7).

$$WL = \sum_{i=2}^{N} |x_i - x_{i-1}| \tag{1}$$

$$RMS = \sqrt{\frac{1}{N} \sum_{i=1}^{N} x_i^2} \tag{2}$$

$$ZC = \sum_{i=1}^{N-1} f_{ZC}(x_i, x_{i+1}) \tag{3}$$

$$IAV = \frac{1}{N} \sum_{i=1}^{N} |X_i| \tag{4}$$

$$MAV = \frac{1}{N} \sum_{i=1}^{N} |x_i| \tag{5}$$

$$DASDV = \sqrt{\frac{1}{N-1} \sum_{i=2}^{N} |x_i - x_{i-1}|^2} \tag{6}$$

$$DVARV = \frac{1}{N-2} \sum_{i=1}^{N} |x_i - x_{i-1}|^2 \tag{7}$$

In these equations x_i is the ith data point in the windowed segment, X_i is the ith sample in the segment of the signal $f(x)$, and:

$$f_{ZC}(x_i, x_{i+1}) = \begin{cases} 1, & \text{if } x_i > Z + T \text{ and } x_{i+1} < Z - T \\ & \text{or } x_i < Z - T \text{ and } x_{i+1} > Z + T \\ 0, & \text{otherwise,} \end{cases} \tag{8}$$

where Z is the value of the crossing point and T is the tolerance threshold.

Frequency domain processes make use of a Fourier transform and often use the following algorithms: mean absolute frequency (MAF) and median absolute frequency (MDF) [24] which are extracted through Eqs. (9) and (10).

$$MAF = \frac{\sum_{j=1}^{M} f_j P_j}{\sum_{j=1}^{M} P_j} \tag{9}$$

$$MDF = \begin{cases} X_{\frac{n}{2}}, & \text{if } n \text{ is even} \\ \frac{X_{\frac{n-1}{2}} + X_{\frac{n+1}{2}}}{2}, & \text{if } n \text{ is odd} \end{cases} \tag{10}$$

Here, X is the ordered list of values in the dataset P (the power spectrum) and n is the number of values in X.

Wavelet Decomposition Extraction. Wavelet decomposition is a time-frequency domain process, an extension upon both time and frequency domain processes. This process extracts both temporal and frequential information simultaneously resulting in more informative features than those generated through time or frequency domain processes alone. Wavelet decomposition is often applied to GPR to identify a transition line [2, 4, 31]. This algorithm uses a wavelet transform, which is similar to a Fourier Transform, except rather than decomposing signals into continuous sine and cosine waves, a wavelet transform decomposes signals into non-continuous wavelets through Eqs. (11) and (12) [28],

$$W_\varphi(j_0, k) = \frac{1}{\sqrt{M}} \sum_x f(x) \cdot \varphi_{j_0,k}(x) \tag{11}$$

$$W_\psi(j, k) = \frac{1}{\sqrt{M}} \sum_x f(x) \cdot \psi_{j,k}(x), \qquad \text{for } j \geq j_0, \tag{12}$$

where $f(x)$, $\varphi_{j_0,k}(x)$ and $\psi_{j,k}(x)$ are functions of the discrete variable x.

Multi-signal Feature Fusion Extractions. Multi-signal feature fusion is a process utilised within electromyography to remove background noise and interference when multiple nerve signals together code for one specific class. Data for a central signal is extracted by including horizontally neighbouring signal data in an applied algorithm. In this paper, due to the lateritic nature of the bauxite deposit, it was hypothesised that horizontally neighbouring segments of signals would contain data for the same material class. The fusion process could therefore remove irrelevant noise and uncover a common material-based pattern. Two fusion algorithms were adapted; waveform length fusion and root mean square fusion [16]. Equations (13) and (14) show these algorithms, respectively.

$$\text{WL}_{\text{fus}} = \frac{\sum_{i=2}^{N} ||\prod_{j=1}^{M} |k_{j,i} - k_{j,i-1}|}{\sqrt{\prod_{j=1}^{M} \sum_{i=2}^{N} (k_{j,i} - k_{j,i-1})^2}} \tag{13}$$

$$\text{RMS}_{\text{fus}} = \sqrt[M]{\sum_{j=1}^{M} \sqrt{\frac{1}{N} \sum_{i=1}^{N} k_{j,i}^2}} \tag{14}$$

Here, M is the size of the fusion window, centred on the signal for which information is extracted, k_j is a signal segment in the fusion window containing N data points, j is the horizontal position of the signal segment within the fusion window, and $k_{j,i}$ represents the ith data point in the signal segment k_j.

Random Forest Model. Random forest models are ensemble learning algorithms consisting of multiple decision trees [15]. Each tree votes for a class, resulting in a final decision on the most popular vote [7]. The trees are grown in a randomly selected area of the feature space, resulting in a more generalised model. Random forest models are therefore less likely to overfit a model than singular decision trees, performing better on unseen data [6,8,15].

3 Gaussian Ridge Extraction

The GRE algorithm is based upon observations that clusters of small amplitude spikes occur in individual GPR signals near the transition zone, even in areas of GPR line data where there is no visual transition line. By identifying these clusters and chaining them together we generate lines, or 'ridges', which act as an approximation of the transition line. These clusters were made most obvious by Eqs. (4), (11) and (12), which were a primary inspiration for the GRE. The algorithm consists of three steps (Fig. 2):

1. The identification of distinct peaks in each vertical GPR signal through a prominence function. Peaks at a depth y are ordered from most prominent to least and given a corresponding weighting, w, from a Gaussian distribution.
2. The identification of the likely location of a transition line D within each individual GPR signal via weighted voting based on prominence, through Eq. (15). This acts as an outlier removal system.

$$D = \frac{\sum_{i=1}^{n} w_i Y_i}{\sum_{i=1}^{n} w_i} \tag{15}$$

A pass of the entire GPR line is then made, with the new values of D being tested and either accepted or rejected into a circular buffer of size n (D is automatically accepted when the buffer isn't full), as seen in Eq. (16).

$$O_{buffer} = \begin{cases} \text{accept,} & \text{if } \bar{O} - \alpha\sigma \leq D_{new} \leq \bar{O} + \alpha\sigma \\ \text{reject,} & \text{otherwise} \end{cases} \tag{16}$$

Where $\bar{O}$ is the mean of the buffer contents, σ is the standard deviation of the buffer contents, and α is a constant. When the buffer is full, the average of its contents are plotted and the process is repeated for a backwards pass.

3. The identification of high/low confidence areas through comparison of forwards and backwards passes, as shown in Eq. (17), which serves to provide model input only when confident on the transition line location,

$$C_i = \begin{cases} \text{High,} & \text{if } |p_{f,i} - p_{b,i}| \leq \beta V \\ \text{Low,} & \text{otherwise} \end{cases} \tag{17}$$

where C_i is the confidence value at the ith horizontal point, $p_{f,i}$ & $p_{b,i}$ are the values of the forwards and backwards passes at i, respectively, V is the total number of vertical data points in the GPR line, and β is a constant. Each signal segment is then assigned a feature value based upon whether it is above or below an area of approximated high or low confidence.

(a) Identification of prominent peaks in each vertical GPR line. More prominent peaks are shown as a darker red.

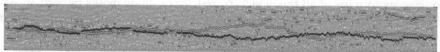

(b) The identification of the two ridge lines through Gaussian voting shown in blue and cyan, being forwards and backwards passes respectively.

(c) The identification of areas of high and low confidence, yellow and white respectively, through a comparison of forwards and backwards passes.

Fig. 2. The three steps in the Gaussian Ridge Extraction process.

4   Methodology

Two sensing modalities were utilised in this paper; GPR line data (such as Fig. 1) as well as exploration hole data. Exploration hole data was used to generate labels for the GPR data. In this section we describe the methodology applied to the datasets. First, the segmentation of GPR signals, then the extraction of features, followed by training of ML models and culminating in the presentation of performance assessment metrics.

4.1   Signal Segmentation and Classification Process

Signal segmentation is used to turn a GPR signal into segments which we then extract features from. We found that 10 segments gave the best balance of accuracy and prediction resolution. Signals near exploratory holes are labelled to train the ML model, and the remaining signals are used for classification and testing. This method, unlike more common methods, identifies a transition line indirectly through an observation on segment classification patterns.

4.2   Feature Extraction Processes

From each of the signal segments we extract features using both the algorithms presented in Sect. 2.3, as well as the GRE, presented in Sect. 3. These processes are applied to the signal segments directly, or using a sliding window technique for more focused extractions.

4.3   Training and Testing of Machine Learning Models

To test the effectiveness of the extraction processes we trained a ML model on the generated feature spaces and assessed the model predictions and performance. A random forest model with 200 decision trees was chosen as it was the strongest performing of all the models tested. To evaluate model performance we relied upon a combination of both qualitative comparisons to an approximate ground truth and average quantitative predictions on the validation dataset. The approximated ground truth is generated by interpolating a line between the bauxite-ironstone transition in each exploratory hole, as seen in Fig. 3.

(a) Interpolated transition line.   (b) Target ground truth.

Fig. 3. A ground truth is generated by a) interpolating a line between known bauxite-ironstone (blue-red) transitions. These known locations are found from exploratory hole data, denoted by the blue lines (bauxite) with red (ironstone) tips. b) Everything above the interpolated transition is defined as bauxite (green), and everything below as ironstone (blue). This interpolated transition line is shown in magenta in the qualitative output results. (Color figure online)

Using these performance assessments we proceeded to evaluate the success of the produced features. First, models were trained upon features generated by each extraction process individually, and results were compared. Next, all features were then combined into one feature space, models were trained and results were assessed. We then attempted to improve the performance of this combined feature space by reducing dimensionality using the feature selection processes DEFS and SHAP. We also augment the process by applying a horizontal majority voting convolution kernel to reduce noise.

5   Results and Discussion

5.1   Individual Feature Extraction Analysis

Quantitatively, the depth feature trained model is the best performing of all feature space trained models, with an accuracy of 91.57%. The qualitative outputs are, however, lacking, as seen in Fig. 4a. The trained model appears to simply separate the classifications with a horizontal line at whichever depth maximises classification accuracy. This is not entirely unexpected, as the feature is purely a function of the y axis and therefore has no horizontal differentiability.

The outputs of models trained on some of the time, frequency, wavelet decomposition and feature fusion extraction algorithms are shown seen in Figs. 4b through e. Each of these processes result in models with similar performance levels, with accuracy rates close to 50% and qualitative outputs which are little

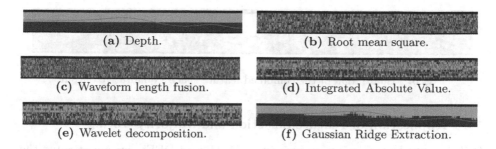

(a) Depth.

(b) Root mean square.

(c) Waveform length fusion.

(d) Integrated Absolute Value.

(e) Wavelet decomposition.

(f) Gaussian Ridge Extraction.

Fig. 4. Visualisation of the individual feature extractions' qualitative outputs. Predicted bauxite and ironstone segments are shown in green and blue respectively, whilst the target ground truth transition line is shown in magenta.

more than white noise. Only the IAV process and wavelet decomposition perform at levels above random chance with accuracy rates of 67.62% and 68.63% respectively. Qualitatively they are also noisy with only a small level of correct clustering evident. This clustering is perhaps due to the algorithms identifying a visually clear transition in the few areas in the data where it does appear.

The results of the GRE feature trained model are shown in Fig. 4f. Quantitatively, this extraction performed well at 82.83% accuracy. The qualitative results also indicate an approximately correct transition line location as, while flat, they evidence some level of correct undulation with little noise.

While the GRE model's ability to directly identify a transition line is promising, the results of the other models are not. The failure of these models indicate that there is little to no class based differentiable information contained within the GPR signals and therefore no material-based pattern to interpret. GPR signal behaviour appears largely independent of the material of propagation.

5.2   Concatenation of Features into Combined Feature Space

Following the analysis of the results of individual feature sets, we concatenated the generated individual features from each of the feature extraction processes into a single combined feature space. This was done in an attempt to increase variation and undulation generated by the GRE feature. The result of a model trained on this combined feature space is shown in Fig. 5, wherein an accuracy of 88.72% was achieved. Quantitatively this is a positive result, however, qualitatively it is clear that the combined feature space exhibits a level of negative synergy. This is evident specifically in the noise, where the otherwise clear results of the GRE and depth feature trained models appear to have been corrupted by the other time and frequency domain features. Also, while a clear transition line is generated, it lacks any predictive power being almost entirely flat. It appears that the depth feature's flat prediction is incorrectly overriding the undulation dictated by the GRE feature to achieve a higher quantitative prediction, but worse qualitative performance.

Fig. 5. Visualisation of the combined feature space's qualitative output.

5.3 Application of Feature Selection and Majority Voting

Utilising two feature selection processes, SHAP and DEFS, we investigated the relevancy of each feature thus generated. The results of the selection processes indicated that the depth feature was the most relevant, with a weighting over twice that of the second most relevant feature, the GRE feature. This is unsurprising, due to the individual quantitative superiority of a model trained upon depth, compared to GRE feature. This also indicates the usefulness of qualitative outputs in this investigation, and why they are relied upon more than quantitative outputs in assessing the predictive power of a feature, as, despite quantitative results, the GRE feature evidently has more predictive power than depth.

Utilising DEFS to identify the most synergistic feature combination, we created a new feature space with the 17 most relevant features (with depth manually removed) and trained a random forest model. To remove noise from the output we also applied a horizontal, majority voting convolution. The output of this model generated an accuracy of 86.62%, higher than the GRE alone, but lower than the previous, non-selected combined feature space. Qualitatively, however, it is much superior (Fig. 6), with a more obvious, correct undulation, although it is still slightly flat. The increased undulation is likely due to the removal of the depth feature. It is also possible that the clustering of the wavelet or IAV process contained relevant information only revealed in combination with the GRE feature. Regardless, this result indicates a level of positive synergy between features included within the space and shows the strength of feature selection in determining an ideal feature space.

Fig. 6. Visualisation of the DEFS feature selected model's qualitative output.

6 Conclusions and Future Works

In this paper we have presented and investigated a novel transition zone identification method for use in bauxite reserve estimation. This identification method and all subsequent processes are implemented within a modelling pipeline built during this investigation. In this investigation we have assessed the effectiveness of various existing feature extraction algorithms. Success was evaluated both individually and comparatively using both quantitative and qualitative performance assessment measures. We have also built and presented a novel feature extraction process, the Gaussian Ridge Extraction, which is able to approximately predict transition zone depth. Through feature selection and majority voting convolution we improved this result. The final generated models are able to predict transition zones to a reasonable degree, matching their approximate depth and undulation even in areas with no visible transition zone.

In future investigations we look to expand the capabilities of the proposed Gaussian Ridge extraction, applying it to a regression based approach. We also look to expand the modelling capabilities of the performance assessments generated. With further data we hope to generate three dimensional representations of a transition zone for more useful estimation abilities.

References

1. Altın, C., Er, O.: Comparison of different time and frequency domain feature extraction methods on elbow gesture's EMG. Eur. J. Interdisc. Stud. **2**(3), 35–44 (2016)
2. Baili, J., Lahouar, S., Hergli, M., Amimi, A., Besbes, K.: Application of the discrete wavelet transform to denoise GPR signals. In: 2nd International Symposium on Communications, Control and Signal Processing, Marrakech, Morocco, p. 11 (2006)
3. Ball, A., O'Connor, L.: Geologist in the loop: a hybrid intelligence model for identifying geological boundaries from augmented ground penetrating radar. Geosciences **11**(7), 284 (2021)
4. Bao, Q.-Z., Li, Q.-C., Chen, W.-C.: GPR data noise attenuation on the curvelet transform. Appl. Geophys. **11**(3), 301–310 (2013). https://doi.org/10.1007/s11770-014-0444-2
5. Bhattacharya, A., Sarkar, A., Basak, P.: Time domain multi-feature extraction and classification of human hand movements using surface EMG. In: 2017 4th International Conference on Advanced Computing and Communication Systems (ICACCS), pp. 1–5. IEEE (2017)
6. Breiman, L.: Bagging predictors. Mach. Learn. **24**(2), 123–140 (1996)
7. Breiman, L.: Random forests. Mach. Learn. **45**(1), 5–32 (2001)
8. Dietterich, T.G.: An experimental comparison of three methods for constructing ensembles of decision trees: bagging, boosting, and randomization. Mach. Learn. **40**(2), 139–157 (2000)
9. Erten, O., Kizil, M.S., Topal, E., McAndrew, L.: Spatial prediction of lateral variability of a laterite-type bauxite horizon using ancillary ground-penetrating radar data. Nat. Resour. Res. **22**(3), 207–227 (2013)
10. Erten, O., McAndrew, L., Kizil, M.S., Topal, E.: Incorporating fine-scale ground-penetrating radar data into the mapping of lateral variability of a laterite-type bauxite horizon. Min. Technol. **124**(1), 1–15 (2015)
11. Francke, J.: Applications of GPR in mineral resource evaluations. In: Proceedings of the XIII International Conference on Ground Penetrating Radar, pp. 1–5. IEEE (2010)
12. Francke, J.: A review of selected ground penetrating radar applications to mineral resource evaluations. J. Appl. Geophys. **81**, 29–37 (2012)

13. Frigui, H., Gader, P.: Detection and discrimination of land mines in ground-penetrating radar based on edge histogram descriptors and a possibilistic k-nearest neighbor classifier. IEEE Trans. Fuzzy Syst. **17**(1), 185–199 (2008)
14. Gow, N.N., Lozej, G.P.: Bauxite. Geoscience Canada (1993)
15. Ho, T.K.: Random decision forests. In: Proceedings of 3rd International Conference on Document Analysis and Recognition, vol. 1, pp. 278–282. IEEE (1995)
16. Khushaba, R., Phinyomark, A., Al-Timemy, A., Scheme, E.: Recursive multi-signal temporal fusions with attention mechanism improves EMG feature extraction. IEEE Trans. Artif. Intell. **1**(2), 139–150 (2020). https://doi.org/10.1109/TAI.2020.3046160
17. Khushaba, R.N., Al-Ani, A., Al-Jumaily, A.: Differential evolution based feature subset selection. In: 2008 19th International Conference on Pattern Recognition, pp. 1–4. IEEE (2008)
18. Kim, K.S., Choi, H.H., Moon, C.S., Mun, C.W.: Comparison of k-nearest neighbor, quadratic discriminant and linear discriminant analysis in classification of electromyogram signals based on the wrist-motion directions. Curr. Appl. Phys. **11**(3), 740–745 (2011)
19. Lotte, F.: A new feature and associated optimal spatial filter for EEG signal classification: waveform length. In: Proceedings of the 21st International Conference on Pattern Recognition (ICPR 2012), pp. 1302–1305. IEEE (2012)
20. Lundberg, S.M., Lee, S.I.: A unified approach to interpreting model predictions. In: Guyon, I., et al. (eds.) Advances in Neural Information Processing Systems 30, pp. 4765–4774. Curran Associates, Inc. (2017)
21. Morgan, M.: An investigation into the application of ground penetrating radar to the Weipa mining operation. Weipa, Comalco Minerals and Alumina (1995)
22. Narayan, Y., Mathew, L., Chatterji, S.: SEMG signal classification with novel feature extraction using different machine learning approaches. J. Intell. Fuzzy Syst. **35**(5), 5099–5109 (2018)
23. Negi, S., Kumar, Y., Mishra, V.: Feature extraction and classification for EMG signals using linear discriminant analysis. In: 2016 2nd International Conference on Advances in Computing, Communication, and Automation (ICACCA) (Fall), pp. 1–6. IEEE (2016)
24. Phinyomark, A., Limsakul, C., Phukpattaranont, P.: A novel feature extraction for robust EMG pattern recognition. arXiv preprint arXiv:0912.3973 (2009)
25. Ralston, J.C., Strange, A.D.: An industrial application of ground penetrating radar for coal mining horizon sensing. In: 2015 International Symposium on Antennas and Propagation (ISAP), pp. 1–4. IEEE (2015)
26. Rio Tinto Group - Pacific Operations: Changes to Rio Tinto Aluminium Pacific Operations Ore Reserve and Mineral Resource Estimates, February 2021
27. Soltani, S., Hezarkhani, A.: Determination of realistic and statistical value of the information gathered from exploratory drilling. Nat. Resour. Res. **20**(4), 207–216 (2011)
28. Talebi, S.: The wavelet transform. Towards Data Science (2020)
29. Taylor, G., Eggleton, R., Foster, L., Morgan, C.: Landscapes and regolith of Weipa, northern Australia. Aust. J. Earth Sci. **55**(S1), S3–S16 (2008)
30. Travassos, X.L., Avila, S.L., Ida, N.: Artificial neural networks and machine learning techniques applied to ground penetrating radar: a review. Appl. Comput. Inform. (2020)
31. Zhang, D.: Wavelet Transform. In: Zhang, D. (ed.) Fundamentals of Image Data Mining. TCS, pp. 35–44. Springer, Cham (2019). https://doi.org/10.1007/978-3-030-17989-2_3

A Gated Recurrent Neural Network for Electric Vehicle Detection with Imbalanced Samples

Chen Liu[1]([✉]), Hui Song[1], Mahdi Jalili[1], and Peter McTaggart[2]

[1] School of Engineering, RMIT University, Melbourne, VIC, Australia
{chen.liu3,hui.song,mahdi.jalili}@rmit.edu.au
[2] CitiPower and Powercor, Melbourne, VIC, Australia
pmctaggart@powercor.com.au

Abstract. An increasing population of electric vehicles (EVs) requests more electricity consumption to satisfy the EV charging demand. The EV charging demand should be detected and coordinated to reduces the power grid blackout risk and electricity generation cost. However, it is difficult to identify the residential EV user electricity consumption profile. In this paper, a data processing method is proposed to resample the EV charging events. Then, a multi-layer gated recurrent units (GRU) network construction is designed to train an EV user profile detection model with the resampled time series data. The proposed method is verified and tested in large-scale real-world data. The result shows the data processing method and GRU improves the EV detection model performance.

Keywords: Electric vehicle detection · Imbalanced deep learning · Gated recurrent units

1 Introduction

In the past few years, there has been a significant growth in the number of electric vehicles (EVs) being produced, and there are 10.8 million EVs on the road at the end of 2020 [16]. EV as a new generation vehicle causes less air and noise pollution than internal combustion engine vehicles. However, EV brings a serious burden to the power utilities in the power grid. To reduce the power generation problem, a part of recent studies proposed a variety of optimization approaches to coordinate EV charging strategy in public charging stations [1,10]. For the residential EV users, who charges the EV at home with a private charger, it is a challenge to detect EV charging demand distribution among the large-scale electricity customer data.

Recently, artificial neural networks (ANN) has achieved outstanding success on classification in variety applications such as anomaly detection [8,14], image recognition [9], and cyber-security [7]. In [13], a convolutional neural network (CNN) and a long short term memory (LSTM) network are combined to detect

---

Supported by organization x.

G. Long et al. (Eds.): AI 2021, LNAI 13151, pp. 279–290, 2022.
https://doi.org/10.1007/978-3-030-97546-3_23

false data injection attacks in the power grid. A two-level detector is developed by applying hybrid features. The attacks can be detected if the state vector estimator fails. In [18], a distributed anomaly detection approach is designed to detect anomaly electricity consumption activities. Stacked sparse autoencoder is used for feature extraction. An embedded semi-supervised deep learning framework is proposed in [12], to detect non-technical electricity losses in power grid. The pattern of power loss is analyzed to design a knowledge embedded sample model. Also, a regularization module, loss and training algorithm is developed to avoid overfitting problem. The ensemble deep learning method also can be applied in vehicle type classification problem [11]. This work collects vehicle images from visual traffic surveillance sensors. Then, an image classification scheme is proposed based on ensemble deep learning. The experimental result shows that the proposed method can increase the mean precision to some extent, compared with the baseline algorithms. However, most methods are developed base on balanced data. The method's classification or forecasting accuracy may be reduced if the input data is imbalanced. According to the EV annual report [5], EVs only make up a small part of the market. Thus, it is difficult to develop an EV user power load profile detection model with the imbalance of EV user and non-EV user load profiles.

In the past few years, the data resampling problem has attracted increasing attention of research communities. The existing studies can be largely classified into two groups, over-sampling and under-sampling. An synthetic minority over-sampling technique is introduced in [3]. The proposed approach generates synthetic data samples based on the minority class samples and their corresponding k-nearest neighbor (kNN) samples. A cluster-based under-sampling method is proposed in [17]. The imbalanced data is clustered first, in each cluster the new data is generated by calculating the ratio of majority to minority samples. Also the Tomek links method can be used to reduce the majority class samples in the cluster [6]. However, the over-sampling technique takes expensive computing resources and redundant samples that may reduce the classification accuracy. The under-sampling methods exclude the majority of class samples that also have the risk of reducing the model performance.

To correctly detect EV user load profile, this paper proposes an imbalanced EV user and non-EV user load data processing method based on dynamic time warping (DTW) for high efficiency while handling the imbalanced data. Then a multi-layer gated recurrent units (GRU) network with low time consumption and high performance of imbalanced EV detection is constructed.

The remaining of this paper is organized as follows. Section 2 introduces the data processing approach to balance the deep learning input data. A multi-layer neural network is presented and discussed in Sect. 3. The empirical study reports are presented in Sect. 4. Finally, the paper is concluded in Sect. 5.

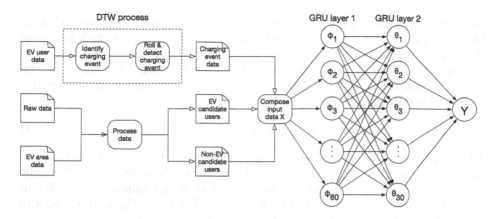

Fig. 1. The working process of EV detection problem.

2   Imbalanced Data Processing

In this section, the EV charging event data imbalance problem is introduced and solved by a DTW method. Then a GRU network is introduced in the next section applied to train the EV detection model by the time series electricity data for EV and non-EV users. The main working process is shown in Fig. 1.

2.1   Dynamic Time Warping

In the EV detection problem, a classification model is required to identify if the resident is an EV user or not by analyzing the related time series electricity consumption data. However, in the most area of the city, there are few residents have EV. The EV detection problem usually have to be addressed by using imbalanced data, which affects the classification model performance. In other words, the number of EV user data can not train the classification model to detect EV users accurately. To balance the EV user data and non-EV user data, more EV charging events should be extracted and regarded as inputs of the training model. Base on the predictable charging events distribution in a day, DTW [2] could match the time series with different length and time period. Thus, a DTW method is applied to evaluate the optimal mapping among the EV charging events. The dynamic programming is proposed to explain the similarity between the labeled time series EV charging event and unlabeled time-series data.

There are various EV brands and models in the market. The EV models implement a battery with different capacities. The charging load could be significantly different in EV users. For instance, the 2016 version of EV Nissan Leaf equip a 20 kWh capacity battery, and Tesla Model 3 is designed with up to 75 kWh battery in the 2021 version. The charging events have characteristic electricity consumption patterns in the EV models. Hence, the charging event should be compared and extracted in the same EV model groups. For a category EV users u, let $C_{u,i} = \{1, 2, \ldots, n\}$ be an labeled charging event for the resident, it includes a one-dimensional time series electricity consumption records. With the consideration of an unlabelled electricity consumption records with the same data structure $L_{u,j} = \{1, 2, \ldots, m\}$. The distance between the charging event and unlabelled data can be calculated by a $n \times m$ dimension distance matrix. The local distance between points $C_{u,t}$ and $L_{u,j}$ can be denoted as $d(i,j)$ and it is formulated as follows,

$$d(i,j) = (C_i - L_j)^2. \tag{1}$$

Euclidean distance is applied to evaluate the charging event sample and the raw data, which sums up all local distances between two data elements in the same timestamp. However, the distance can be collected and sum up with different time stamps for calculating the DTW distance. Let W be the warping path to align or map the dataset $C_{u,i}$ and $L_{u,j}$; it can be described as

$$W = (w_l(i,j)), \ k = 1, 2, \ldots, k, \tag{2}$$
$$\max(i,j) \le k \le i + j - 1, \tag{3}$$

where $w_l(i,j)$ denotes the point t in data $C_{u,i}$ is mapped with point j in $L_{u,j}$ at lth step. k is the length of the warping path. In the DTW distance calculation, the distance between two the points in the same timestamp is not considered any more. Namely, the DTW distance between $C_{u,i}$ and $L_{u,j}$ can be calculated by minimizing the all warping paths and it is explained as

$$DTW(C, L) = \min W[\sum_{k \in K} d(w_l)]. \tag{4}$$

The DTW applies dynamic programming to find the similarity between two time series by comparing the points in the two sequences reflecting the approximate states correspond to each other. In this work, the peak load timestamp point corresponds to other peak load values; the valley load values correspond to other local valley load values. The increasing trend values would not correspond to the decreasing trend values. Figure 2 shows an example of DTW distance evaluation in electricity consumption data.

2.2 DTW Constraints

The warping path W should satisfy the four constraint below [2]:

Monotonicity: The time series data must be monotonically ordered which can be formulated as

$$i' - i \ge 0, \ j' - j \ge 0, \ \forall i, \forall j \in w_{l-1}(i,j), \ \forall i', \forall j' \in w_l(i', j'). \tag{5}$$

Continuity: The time series data only compare to the same time and adjacent moment. Thus W is constrained as

$$i' - i \le 1, \ j' - j \le 1, \ \forall i, \forall j \in w_{l-1}(i,j), \ \forall i', \forall j' \in w_l(i', j'). \tag{6}$$

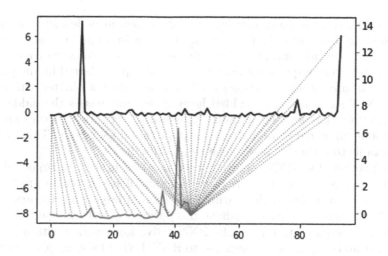

Fig. 2. DTW distance in two time series electricity load data.

Warping Window: The allowable data must fall into the given warping window,

$$|i - j| \leq \omega, \ \forall i, \forall j \in w_l(i, j). \tag{7}$$

where ω is the window width.

Boundary Conditions: The warping path W should start from $w_1(1, 1)$ to $w_l(i, j)$.

Overall, the optimal warping path of $DTW(C, L)$ can be modeled as a dynamic programming problem with the constraints:

$$DTW(C, L) = \min\{\delta(i, j)\}, \tag{8}$$

$$s.t. \ \delta(i, j) = d(i, j) + \min\{\delta(i - i, j), \delta(i - 1, j - 1), \delta(i, j - 1)\}, \tag{9}$$

$$\delta(1, 1) = d(1, 1), \tag{10}$$

$$\delta(i, 0) = \delta(0, j) = 0, \tag{11}$$

where (i, j) is the cumulative distance. Based on the continuity and monotonicity constraints, Eq. 9 identifies the point with the shortest distance to point at (i, j) from its neighbourhoods $((i - i, j), (i - 1, j - 1), (i, j - 1))$. The proposed DTW framework is applied to identify more EV charging events in each category of EV users, which balances the share of EV charging consumption data and non-EV user electricity usage data to train the EV detection model.

3   Gated Recurrent Units Network

In the next stage, the EV charging event data and non-EV user data are merged and fed to the EV detection model through an ANN. Generally speaking, the classic ANN is fully connected between the two adjacent layers. However, in the hidden layers, there is no connection among the neural nodes. In other words, the classic ANN extracts the features and the relationships from input data to output results. In this work, the electricity usage data is collected continuously. The electricity consumption value at each timestamp is affected by the previous behaviors. Recurrent neural networks (RNN) demonstrates a better performance than ANN, since it links the hidden layer nodes and passes the hidden layer node state from previous to the next. This neural network structure preserves the previous input data and output result in the hidden layer. Thus, RNN is more suitable to train the model with time series data.

On the other side, RNN could not be trained accurately in large-scale data training assignments. For the activation function of RNN courses gradient disappearance or explosion if the learning iteration is large [15]. To preserve the hidden layer state and avoid gradient disappearance or explosion, the LSTM framework is proposed to replace the RNN activation function with input gate, forget gate, and output gate. Compared to RNN, LSTM takes more computation resources on model training. The GRU network improves the training efficiency by replacing the three gates in LSTM with two gates. Simultaneously, GRU has a similar training performance to LSTM. The working process of GRU is shown in Fig. 3.

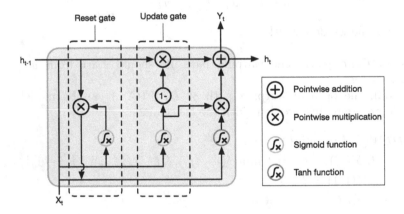

Fig. 3. The architecture of a GRU node.

As can be seen from Fig. 3, in a GRU node, x_t and h_{t-1} are the input values which denotes the input dataset and the hidden layer state at time $t-1$. y_t and h_t as the output value represent the calculation result and the current hidden layer state after the learning process. The reset gate and update gate are the major factors in the GRU. The two gates are designed as a neural network that applies sigmoid function as the activation function. Namely, both gates output values between 0 to 1. Also, there is a candidate value h_t' of hidden layer state h_t will be calculated by reset gate. The formulation of GRU learning process is listed below [4]:

$$r_t = \sigma(\mathcal{U}_r h_{t-1} + \mathcal{W}_r x_t + b_r), \tag{12}$$

$$z_t = \sigma(\mathcal{U}_z h_{t-1} + \mathcal{W}_z x_t + b_z), \tag{13}$$

$$h'_t = \tanh(\mathcal{U}_h(r_t \odot h_{t-1}) + \mathcal{W}_h x_t + b_h), \tag{14}$$

$$h_t = (1 - z_t) \odot h_{t-1} + z_t \odot h'_t. \tag{15}$$

Equation 12 represents the reset gate value at time t, where $\mathcal{U}_r$ and $\mathcal{W}_r$ are the connection weights between the gate to the last hidden layer state and input data, respectively. b_r is the bias of r_t. The reset gate applies the sigmoid function to calculate the combination of h_{t-1} and x_t with a bias. In other words, reset gate evaluates the volume of previous hidden layer state information is reserved in h'. The more information is reserved if r_t is closed to 1. Otherwise, $r_t \to 0$. Equation 13 calculates the output value of update gate at t. $\mathcal{U}_z$, $\mathcal{W}_z$, and b_z are the connection weights and bias of z_t. The function of update gate is decide the amount of h_{t-1} information is abandoned, that is the similar to forget gate and input gate in LSTM. The GRU contributes the same learning result to RNN if $r_t = 1$ and $z_t = 0$. Equation 14 and 15 show the hidden layer state update mechanism where $\odot$ is the multiplication of array elements in turn.

4   Empirical Study

In this section, we apply the large scale real world data from our industry partner Citipower/Powercor, which is a major energy distributor in Victoria Australia, to test the proposed DTW and GRU framework.

4.1   Data Preparation

EV Data. The industry partner provided two categories of EV data. The two categories of EV data collect totally different features in the same area. Namely, the two datasets cannot be merged by a common attribute. We applied the two datasets separately in the EV detection problem. One category of data contains the EV users' approximate location, which is shown as the street name and suburb name only, and the scope of the EV includes four vertexes locations by latitude and longitude. Another category data collects 93 EV user electricity consumption data for every 30 min from 01 March 2021 to 15 April 2021. Each data record includes the attributes of timestamp, the electricity consumption value, the EV brand, and the EV model. We divided the EV electricity consumption into different groups by the EV model. The number of EVs in each model is shown in Table 1. There are 7 EV models that only have one or two EVs collected in the dataset. We labeled that kind of EVs as the "Others" model. Also, 24 EVs have missing value on the EV brand and EV model attributes. We set these EVs into the same group. The 30 min electricity loads are sum up in every 24 h. We set two weeks daily electricity loads as one input data to the GRU, since we assume that an EV is charged at least once in 14 days. We labeled 3 to 5 EV charging events in each EV group. Then, we apply the proposed DTW model to calculate the distance from each labeled charging event

Table 1. The number of EVs in different models.

Brand	Model	Amount	Brand	Model	Amount
Tesla	Model 3	23	Hyundai	Kona	3
Tesla	Model S	10	Hyundai	Ioniq	3
Tesla	Model X	7	MG	ZS EV	3
Nissan	Leaf	8	Others	Others	8
Jaguar	IPace	4	Nan	Nan	24

to the remaining data in each group. If the distance is less than the threshold value, the compared data is labeled as a charging event as well.

Smart Meter Data. The smart meter data is collected from Victoria state, Australia from 01 January 2017 to 30 April 2021. Each record is in the form $< t, id, c, unit, [i_1, i_2, \ldots, i_{96}], gis, feeder >$, where t is the collection data, id is the smart meter id, $unit$ is the unit of measure for electricity consumption, $[i_1, i_2, \ldots, i_{96}]$ is the electricity consumption value in every 15 min from 00:00:00 to 23:59:59 at the day. gis is the geographic information system id of the meter. $feeder$ is the feeder id that the meter belongs to. Also, we have the feeder data in the same area, which includes the feeder id, the geographic information system id for all smart meters, the GPS (latitude and longitude) information, and the type of meter such as industrial, commercial, residential, and etc. We merge the smart meter data and feeder data by geographic information system id to find the GPS location information of smart meters. After that, we extracted all residential users with GPS locations and combined them with EV area data. A suburb of EV area data and the residential smart meter data is shown in Fig. 4. In order to anonymise the residential information, the geographical information is removed from the figure.

As can be seen from the figure, the green color square is the EV area. If the residential users are covered by the EV area, the meter data of the users are identified as EV candidate users that are shown on the map as red points. Otherwise, the meter data is recognized as non-EV users and shown as blue points. We take all EV charging events data and the non-EV users' data together in the same data structure and the same time period to train and validate the EV detection model. The output is a binary value, and it is EV users if the model outputs 1. Otherwise, it outputs 0.

4.2   The GRU Network Trianing and Validation

The balanced EV data and non-EV user data are taken into the EV detection model training and validation. The combined data is shuffled and divided to 70% for training and 30% for validation. We implement all experiments by TensorFlow (2.3.1) with Python (3.8.5). All tasks are done on a computer with Intel(R) Core(TM) @2.40 GHz 4.10 GHz, 8 GB 2133 LPDDR3 RAM, and macOS Big

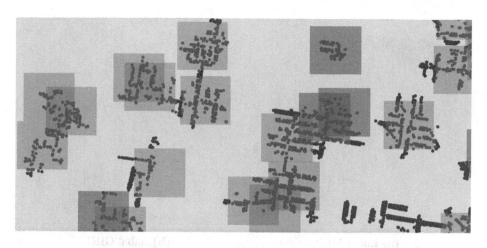

Fig. 4. A part of residential smart meter and EV area distribution. (Color figure online)

Table 2. The validation accuracy of the four methods.

	imbal-MLP	imbal-GRU	bal-MLP	bal-GRU
Accuracy	72.56%	76.99%	89.42%	95.74%

Sur 64 bit operating system. A four layers GRU network is applied that includes 14 input nodes on the input layer, 60 GRU nodes on the first hidden layer, 30 GRU nodes on the second hidden layer, and 1 output node on the output layer. The learning rate is 0.0001. The number of learning epoch is 750. The binary cross-entropy loss function is implemented to obtain the classification error, which is defined as follows:

$$Loss(y, \omega) = \begin{cases} \omega - \omega y + \log(1 + e^{-\omega}), & \text{if } \omega \geq 0, \\ -\omega y + \log(e^{\omega} + 1), & \text{if } \omega < 0. \end{cases} \tag{16}$$

To evaluate the effectiveness of the proposed framework, a multilayer perceptron (MLP) network is applied with the same structure to the proposed GRU network as the baseline method. We set the activation function for the nodes on the first hidden layer as rectified linear units (ReLU) and sigmoid function for the activation function of the second layer hidden nodes. The learning rate of MLP is the same value as GRU, and the number of learning epoch is 5000. We trained and verified the EV detection model in four methods, which are train the model by MLP with the original (imbalance) data (imbal-MLP) and balanced data (bal-MLP), and by GRU the two datasets (imbal-GRU and bal-GRU). The training and validation performances and validation accuracy of the four methods are shown in Fig. 5 and Table 2, respectively.

As can be seen from Fig. 5, with the compression between imbal-MLP and imbal-GRU, the training and validation accuracy curve of imbal-MLP is con-

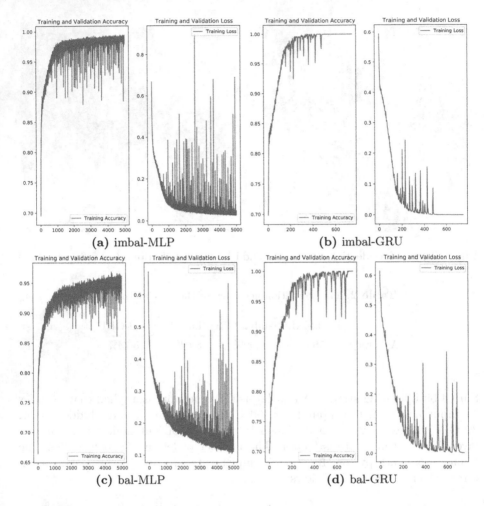

Fig. 5. The training and validation performances of the four methods.

verged between 0.95 to 1.0 after 1,000 epochs. However, the curve fluctuates significantly. The imbal-MLP accuracy is not stable even after around 4,500 epochs. On the other side, the training and validation accuracy of imbal-GRU can be converged to 1.0. Also, the training and validation accuracy is kept at 1.0 after 500 epochs. Considering balanced input data, both MLP and GRU take more training epochs to converge the accuracy and loss, for the balanced data generates more input data for EV charging events by DTW method. As a result, bal-GRU takes fewer epochs to achieve better and more stable accuracy and less than bal-MLP. Table 2 shows bal-GRU obtains the highest validation accuracy among the four proposed methods.

To evaluate the effectiveness of bal-GRU, we test the framework in the EV user candidate data (the red points in Fig. 4). The data contains 28166 residential

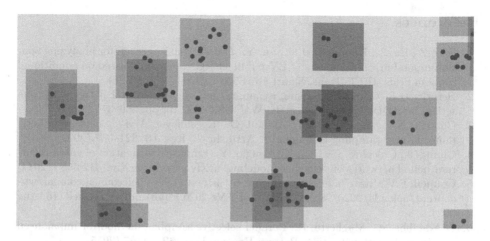

Fig. 6. A part of detected EV user distribution.

electricity customers' power load records in the metropolitan Melbourne area. We combined both training and validation data as training data. Then extracted the EV user candidate electricity load record in the same period to the training data. The trained model detected 949 (3.34%) EV users from the candidates. A part of detected EV users is shown in Fig. 6 as the red points. With the consideration of the original data, which is shown in Fig. 4, the bal-GRU labeled few customers as EV users. According to the Australia EV state report in 2020, there are 6% of vehicle users are EV users [5]. Also, the report shows 49% of EV users charge the EV by a public charger. In conclusion, the bal-GRU detected results match the realistic EV distributions.

5   Conclusion

In this paper, a novel DTW-GRU framework has been proposed to detect the EV user profiles from massive residential customer electricity load data. To improve the GRU network performance, the DTW is applied to identify more EV charging events as the extra input data by comparing the outstanding EV charging events with the EV user's other load profiles. Then, a GRU network has been proposed to train the model by the balanced data. The proposed DTW-GRU has been tested in EV and smart meter data from Victoria, Australia. The results shown DTW-GRU significantly improves the EV user classification accuracy. For further work, feature selection will be added to the proposed DTW-GRU after the data balancing process. Also, the new framework will be tested with the more complicated and larger-scale dataset.

Acknowledgements. This work was supported by the Australian Research Council under Grant No. LP180101309.

References

1. Bao, Z., Hu, Z., Kammen, D.M., Su, Y.: Data-driven approach for analyzing spatiotemporal price elasticities of EV public charging demands based on conditional random fields. IEEE Trans. Smart Grid **12**(5), 4363–4376 (2021)
2. Berndt, D.J., Clifford, J.: Using dynamic time warping to find patterns in time series. In: KDD Workshop, Seattle, WA, USA, vol. 10, pp. 359–370 (1994)
3. Chawla, N.V., Bowyer, K.W., Hall, L.O., Kegelmeyer, W.P.: Smote: synthetic minority over-sampling technique. J. Artif. Intell. Res. **16**, 321–357 (2002)
4. Chung, J., Gulcehre, C., Cho, K., Bengio, Y.: Empirical evaluation of gated recurrent neural networks on sequence modeling. arXiv preprint arXiv:1412.3555 (2014)
5. Council, E.V.: State of electric vehicles. https://electricvehiclecouncil.com.au/wp-content/uploads/2020/08/EVC-State-of-EVs-2020-report.pdf. Accessed 15 Aug 2021
6. D'Addabbo, A., Maglietta, R.: Parallel selective sampling method for imbalanced and large data classification. Pattern Recogn. Lett. **62**, 61–67 (2015)
7. Ferrag, M.A., Maglaras, L., Moschoyiannis, S., Janicke, H.: Deep learning for cyber security intrusion detection: approaches, datasets, and comparative study. J. Inf. Secur. Appl. **50**, 102419 (2020)
8. Han, S.J., Cho, S.B.: Evolutionary neural networks for anomaly detection based on the behavior of a program. IEEE Trans. Syst. Man Cybern. Part B (Cybern.) **36**(3), 559–570 (2006)
9. Koch, G., Zemel, R., Salakhutdinov, R., et al.: Siamese neural networks for one-shot image recognition. In: ICML Deep Learning Workshop, vol. 2, Lille (2015)
10. Li, C., Liu, C., Deng, K., Yu, X., Huang, T.: Data-driven charging strategy of PEVs under transformer aging risk. IEEE Trans. Control Syst. Technol. **26**(4), 1386–1399 (2017)
11. Liu, W., Zhang, M., Luo, Z., Cai, Y.: An ensemble deep learning method for vehicle type classification on visual traffic surveillance sensors. IEEE Access **5**, 24417–24425 (2017)
12. Lu, X., Zhou, Y., Wang, Z., Yi, Y., Feng, L., Wang, F.: Knowledge embedded semi-supervised deep learning for detecting non-technical losses in the smart grid. Energies **12**(18), 3452 (2019)
13. Niu, X., Li, J., Sun, J., Tomsovic, K.: Dynamic detection of false data injection attack in smart grid using deep learning. In: 2019 IEEE Power and Energy Society Innovative Smart Grid Technologies Conference (ISGT), pp. 1–6. IEEE (2019)
14. Pang, G., Shen, C., Cao, L., Hengel, A.V.D.: Deep learning for anomaly detection: a review. ACM Comput. Surv. (CSUR) **54**(2), 1–38 (2021)
15. Sak, H., Senior, A.W., Beaufays, F.: Long short-term memory recurrent neural network architectures for large scale acoustic modeling. Int. J. Speech Technol. **22**(1), 21–30 (2014)
16. Shanahan, J.: There are now more than 10 million electric vehicles on the road. https://www.zap-map.com/there-are-now-more-than-10-million-electric-vehicles-on-the-road/. Accessed 15 Aug 2021
17. Yen, S.J., Lee, Y.S.: Cluster-based under-sampling approaches for imbalanced data distributions. Expert Syst. Appl. **36**(3), 5718–5727 (2009)
18. Yuan, Y., Jia, K.: A distributed anomaly detection method of operation energy consumption using smart meter data. In: 2015 International Conference on Intelligent Information Hiding and Multimedia Signal Processing (IIH-MSP), pp. 310–313. IEEE (2015)

User-Defined Smart Contracts Using Answer Set Programming

Kevin Purnell$^{(\boxtimes)}$ and Rolf Schwitter$^{(\boxtimes)}$

Macquarie University, Sydney, Australia
kevin.purnell@hdr.mq.edu.au, rolf.schwitter@mq.edu.au

Abstract. We present a novel approach to the creation of smart contracts that takes an existing legal document and allows it to be incrementally elaborated into a tested smart contract by domain experts. Smart contracts are currently built with compiled imperative languages, and suffer from lack of agility, elevated risks from errors and security flaws, and high development costs. This paper describes a smart editor that uses a declarative language (Answer Set Programming (ASP)) to represent the business logic of legal documents. The document is incrementally elaborated in a fixed sequence of steps beginning with an ontology discovery step that identifies the explicit and implicit artefacts and applicable constraints. This information is used to generate ASP representations which provide the foundation required for modelling the legal logic. Furthermore, we have achieved the verbalisation of rules built during modelling, and have developed a method of representing artefacts visually which allows logic modelling, model validation and program verification to be visual. During these steps, the original legal document is enhanced with additional embedded information, which results in a tested executable ASP program which can then be used as a smart contract if modifications are made to the blockchain smart contract infrastructure.

Keywords: Answer Set Programming · Legal Logic · Model Validation · Ontology · Smart Contract · Verbalisation · Visualisation

1 Introduction

Agreements and arrangements between legal entities are the foundation of economic activity in most societies, and these range from agreements between individuals (e.g., leasing agreements), to financial agreements (e.g., derivatives), to complex contract sets that manage commercial activity between large organisations. The Australian Government alone issued 81,174 contracts for the supply of goods and services in 2019-20 worth AUD 53.9 Billion [1], each with significant administration and compliance costs; the implication being that even small improvements may produce significant savings. An emerging trend is the implementation of some contracts or parts of contracts as smart contracts; distributed programs embedded in a blockchain and executed according to a predefined mining protocol. The term 'smart contract' implies an underlying legal contract [2],

© Springer Nature Switzerland AG 2022
G. Long et al. (Eds.): AI 2021, LNAI 13151, pp. 291–303, 2022.
https://doi.org/10.1007/978-3-030-97546-3_24

so it is important to differentiate between legal documents and legal contracts. Smart contracts have a wider scope than legal contracts; for example, our use case, a 'Will and Testament', is not a legal contract (no offer or acceptance); however, it can be implemented as a smart contract because there is a future electronic transfer of assets controlled by logic that responds to external events. Furthermore, only some types of legal reasoning (deductive, inductive, abductive, by analogy, by principle, by precedent) can be handled by computer, implying that parts of some legal documents will not be amenable to implementation as smart contracts, and that flexible approaches that allow partial automation and 'human-in-the-loop' are preferable.

Current approaches using compiled imperative languages impede increased adoption because they require costly programmers, lack agility, and are expensive to formally verify and therefore suffer elevated risks from errors and security flaws [3]. This research investigates the potential of declarative programming to advance what can be achieved with smart contracts, as a clear opportunity exists for an application that allows domain experts to create their own smart contacts while also reducing errors and security flaws.

Such a system needs to be oriented towards low technical skills and moderate domain skills, so requires an advanced user interface. These have been graphical for decades and are now trending towards the use of English; with the feedback required by these users having similar demands. To achieve high quality testing with these users, the task needs to be broken up into digestible chunks, each of which must be exhaustively tested. Another requirement is the ability to create custom smart contracts. The current practice of using pretested code libraries, cannot respond agilely or cost-effectively in these situations [20].

Our approach starts with an existing legal document in electronic form, then seeks to understand that legal document via a guided dialogue with the domain expert (see Fig. 2). This step generates an ontology that guides the creation of representations. The recent availability of mature declarative languages in the knowledge representation and reasoning domain (e.g., Answer Set Programming - ASP) [4], provides an ability to model and reason over legal document logic using these representations. Our approach generates paired ASP and visual representations and then derives a restricted English representation from the ASP representation. We investigate using a rapid prototyping approach, and seek to demonstrate some advanced features that are difficult to achieve with the compiled imperative language approach. We have built a tool designed to allow domain experts to create, test and deploy their own smart contracts. This Smart Document Editor (SDE editor) uses clingo [8] as the solver, and is built using the HTML/CSS/JavaScript stack. It auto-generates the ASP program that becomes the smart contract.

2   Related Research

Some companies like Contract Express start with existing resources (MS Word documents) and add intelligent markup with an add-in [5]; however, this system generates smart contracts using the compiled imperative language approach

(Solidity) [16] without using an ontology discovery step [17]. Choudhury et al., [9] use a domain specific ontology to assist smart contract auto-generation; however, this ontology is supplied and not discovered. Ontology discovery from text has a long history [10] and a well-developed toolset [11]; however, discovery from dialogue with a domain expert who is being stepped through placeholders in a document, is novel. Similarly, ASP is frequently applied to difficult problems like configuration and scheduling [12], but has not been used to model smart contracts. The visualisation of ASP execution results (called answer sets) has been investigated [13], but there are few examples of attempts to visualise the modelling process, the closest being partial visual specification with ASPIDE [7]. There is some awareness of modelling approaches in legal circles [14], and an awareness that declarative languages may have advantages when applied to smart contracts [15], but few initiatives are visible.

3   Overview of the Smart Document Editor (SDE)

Traditionally, most legal documents were paper forms filled out by hand and signed. This format remains, but the medium is increasingly electronic and produced by word processors and document automation systems [5]. Our application, the SDE editor, brings the ability to model logic and to test and deploy smart contracts to this environment. As previously mentioned, the SDE editor takes an existing legal document and allows it to be incrementally developed into a smart contract. This workflow consists of a fixed sequence of steps that can be split into two main phases: 1) smart template creation; and 2) smart contract creation. Smart template creation involves three steps: i) understanding the document (ontology discovery); ii) modelling the legal logic (modelling); and iii) validating that the model matches the user's understanding of the document's legal logic (model validation). Smart contract creation involves two steps: i) entering actual data (instantiation); and ii) testing that the output is what is expected (program verification). The final product is the initial legal document completed with actual information, with a tested ASP program embedded as markup; a form of smart contract called a Ricardian contract [6].

An ASP smart contract can also be thought of as a specification, in contrast to an Ethereum smart contract which is bytecode produced by compilation [19]. Consequently, an ASP smart contract requires modified mining software, so that when a relevant transaction [22] is mined, it is converted into a matching ASP fact. The smart contract program and the new fact are merged and solved by the miner, and any answer set is converted into a new Ethereum transaction.

4   Suitability and Use of Answer Set Programming

The logic of legal documents conforms to closed world assumption (CWA) logic; that is, if something referred to by the legal document is not known to be true, then it can be considered to be false. This opens up the opportunity for using a logic programming language that implements negation as failure to represent and reason about this world. ASP combines an expressive representation language, a model-based problem specification methodology, and efficient solving tools [4]. It is based on several lines of research; including logic programming, knowledge representation and constraint satisfaction. Brewka et al. [4] note that the close connection to non-monotonic logics provides ASP with the power to model default negation, deal with incomplete information, encode domain and problem-specific knowledge, defaults, and preferences in an intuitive and natural way [4]. Furthermore, ASP exhibits 'elaboration tolerance'.

The promising pathways identified in our search for solutions to problems with current Smart Contract practise are: 1) separating logic from control code (possible 'separation of concerns' benefits), 2) a modelling and simulation development approach, 3) program code auto-generation (a given, as domain experts require a sophisticated UI). ASP facilitates all these pathways. Our investigation first modelled our use case in ASP, then worked backward to discover how to generate this ASP representation automatically from the UI. Our initial hypotheses are confirmed and a number of further advantages discovered (see Sect. 8). The current version of the SDE editor uses a restricted form of ASP which corresponds to normal logic programs that can contain aggregates in the body.

5   ASP Auto-generation

Auto-generation of Answer Set Programs requires a systematic approach that includes a representation grammar and a controlled vocabulary. The representation grammar specifies how ASP is used to represent the things, relations, events, properties or constraints referred to in a legal document (artefacts). The controlled vocabulary aligns terminology with English usage, which facilitates interpretation by domain experts, and simplifies ASP to English translation.

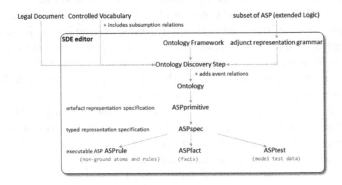

Fig. 1. The derivation of ASP representations in the SDE editor.

The grammar and the controlled vocabulary both conform to an ontology framework which is built into the SDE editor. The ontology discovery step generates five different representations for each artefact: 1) an ASP representation specification (like a class declaration); 2) an internal representation; 3) a visual representation; 4) a verbal representation; and 5) an instantiation placeholder (IPH), which embeds a specification for the data required to instantiate the artefact. The ASP representation specification (ASPspec) is used to generate the executable forms of ASP used in ASP programs (see Fig. 1). The internal representation is an indexed collection that holds the other representations in memory (e.g., icon screen co-ordinates), effectively tying all the representations together. The visual representation is displayed on screen as icons, graphics and photos, while the verbal representation is generated directly from ASP answer sets. The internal representation can be queried efficiently, providing a flexibility that enables the solving of selected parts of the ASP program, which enables incremental model validation and program verification.

5.1 Ontology Discovery

An understanding of an unprocessed legal document is acquired via an ontology discovery process which steps a user through placeholders (e.g., ____) in the document in sequential order, requesting assignment of terms (see Fig. 2). Terms are selected from smart lists supplied from a structured controlled vocabulary [23] of domain specific terms[1], or input manually. All terms are paired with icons, so both standardised text and standardised visual identifiers are assigned.

Fig. 2. An Ontology Discovery dialogue.

The top level of the ontology is a set of constructs (things, relations, events, constraints, properties, and identifiers), where: 1) 'things' are tangible objects like people; 2) 'relations' are associative tables which relate two or more 'things'; 3) 'events' are actions caused by, or impacting 'things'; 4) 'constraints' are limitations on the ASP terms that can be used in the representation of a given 'artefact'; 5) 'properties' describe features of an 'artefact'; and, 6) 'identifiers' are used to name an instance of an 'artefact' or 'property', and are assigned from the controlled vocabulary. The ASP representations for artefacts and the heads of ASP rules use a grammar built upon ASP atoms and negated atoms, and ASP bodies are largely made up of these same representations. This grammar is shown (partially) in EBNF form:

```
(1.1) thing(<thingId>[,<typeId>],<key>[,<prop>[,<prop>]])
(1.2) relation(<relationId>,<key>,<key>[,<prop>[,<prop>]])
```

---

[1] Note that the word "terms" is used in a grammatical sense, not in the ASP sense.

```
(1.3) event(<eventId>,<time>[,<agent>],<expnr>[,<modfr>][,<prop>[,<prop>]])
(1.4) ruleh(<rulehId>,[,<term>[,<term>]])
```

ASP terms have the following structure: `<termId>(<placeholderId>,<data>)`, except for terms that include text "Id" which have only one parameter. An example representation of a 'thing' is:

```
thing(thingId(legalperson), typeId(wife), key(__wife_name__, "Zoe"), birthday(.
```

The following sections describe the derivation of all ASP forms from this grammar as shown in Fig. 1. These are ASPprimitive, ASPspec, ASPrule (non-ground atoms and rules), ASPfact (ground atoms) and ASPtest. Systematic use of these uniform ASP-like representations across the system, simplifies the application.

5.2   ASP Representations

In (1.1) above, ASP term `<thingId>` identifies the type of the artefact and ASP term `<key>` identifies the instance of that type of artefact. As all ASP terms have identifiers, a unique data identifier called a placeholder identifier `<placeholderId>` can be created by concatenating the artefact and term identifiers. For example:

```
(2.1) thing(thingId(wife), key(wife_name,""), birthday(wife_birthday,""))²
```

Typing reduces the number of representations for artefacts with many varieties.

```
(3.1) thing(thingId(legalperson), typeId(wife), key(wife_name,""), birthday(..
```

Placeholder identifiers are displayed on screen and provide the binding mechanism between instantiation data and ASP representations. Because "__xxxx__" is intuitively a document placeholder for most users (see Fig. 3), the placeholder identifiers in (3.1) are simply pre- and postfixed with "__"; giving (4.1).

```
(4.1) thing(thingId(legalperson), typeId(wife), key(__wife_name__,""), ...
```

This form (ASPspec) is the output of the ontology discovery step and provides the well-defined foundation required to support logic modelling. The other production rules; (1.2) and (1.3) use foreign keys, which means that 'relations' join things, and 'events' are either caused by, or happen to 'things'. The SDE editor does not implement rules that exclude certain answer sets, but does implement restrictions via the typing mechanism. This is implemented with the untyped ASPprimitive form used to generate all the other ASP forms (see Fig. 1).

---

² 'Key' is replaced with 'name' because placeholder identifiers are exposed to the user.

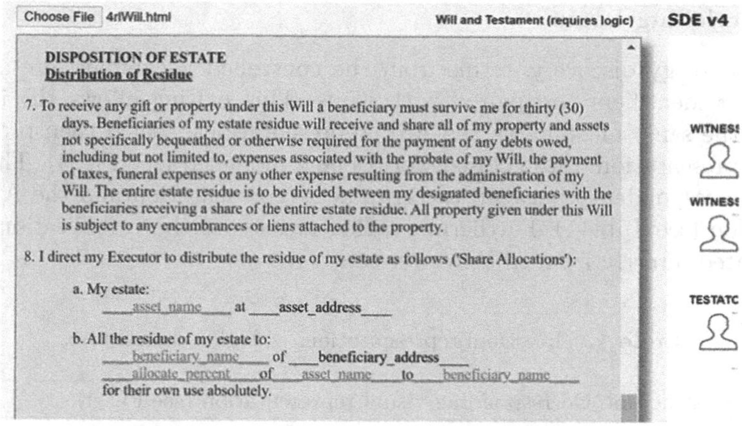

Fig. 3. Left side of the SDE editor showing use of placeholder identifiers on screen. (Color figure online)

```
(5.1) thing(thingId(legalperson), <typeId>, key(__person_name__,""), ...
(5.2) relation(..., key(__thing_name__,""), key(__thing_name__,""), ...
(5.3) event(eventId(die), time(...), experiencer(__legalperson_name__,""))
```

For example, in (5.3), the representation for the 'die' event only allows a 'legalperson' to die, whereas (5.2) allows the relating of the more general 'things'.

5.3 Generating Executable Forms of ASP

Non-ground ASP atoms and rules (ASPrule) are generated from ASPspec by a JavaScript function. For example, generating from (4.1) results in (6.1):

```
(6.1) thing(thingId(legalperson), typeId(wife), key(Wname_p,Wname_d), ...
```

This function pairs artefact identifiers with a unique string of capital letters which are then substituted to create ASP variables that are unique globally. Examples are: (wife, W), (witness, WI), and (die, D). The postfixes are: 1) "_p" for placeholder identifiers; and 2) "_d" for data. These ASP variables need to be unique in order to match the placeholder identifiers used to bind user input data to ASPfacts. ASP facts (ASPfact) are generated from the ASPspec at instantiation, when the placeholder identifier is paired with input values. For example:

```
(7.1) thing(thingId(legalperson), typeId(wife), key(__wife_name__,"Zoe"), ...
```

Test data for model testing (ASPtest) is generated via another JavaScript function which simply replaces numeric placeholder identifiers with numbers so that the arithmetic expressions can execute (see Sect. 6).

5.4 Modelling Logic

During ontology discovery, terms from the controlled vocabulary are assigned as artifact identifiers and paired with icons. This pairing allows the icons to take on the same meaning as the ASP representations, which then provides a visual representation of the closed world being modelled (see Fig. 4). There is a formal correspondence between the graphical representation and the ASP representation (see Table 1). Furthermore, this extends to the verbalisation, which is generated directly from ASP answer sets.

Table 1. The visual representations of logic constructors.

Logic constructors	Corresponding visual representation (see Fig. 4)
Rule head	Bar (can be red or green)
AND	Blue arrow meeting bar
OR[a]	2 bars with an "OR" in the centre
Expression	Blue box attached to bar
Aggregate	Blue box attached to bar + keyword ("SUM | COUNT")
NAF	Red arrow meeting bar + "NOT" (grey dash due to testing)
NOT	a "-" in front of an atom identifier
Many-to-many	The 'allocate' icon

[a] Note that this "OR" is an inclusive disjunction in the body of a rule.

Two views of the right side of the SDE editor screen are displayed in Fig. 4.

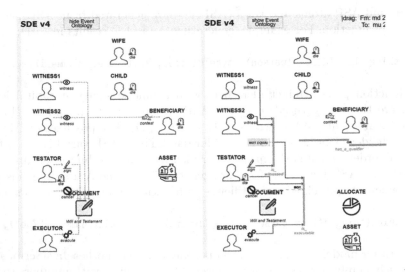

Fig. 4. SDE editor right side; 1) left: event relationships view, 2) right: logic view (Color figure online)

The left panel in Fig. 4 displays the relations between events and things, with the arrow pointing to the experiencer of the event; while the right panel removes these lines and displays the visual result of a partially complete logic modelling and testing session, where the rule 'is_executable' is being tested. In both panels, the larger icons represent 'things' and 'relations', while 'events' are displayed as smaller overlayed icons; for example, the pen (sign) overlayed on the icon representing the testator. The bars represent rule heads, with red denoting 'false' and green denoting 'true'. The arrows touching the bars represent the 'rule body' such that the rule 'is_executable' can be read as: 1) if rule 'is_witnessed' is true; and 2) the testator has died; and 3) the executor has executed the will; but 4) the testator has not cancelled the will; then rule 'is_executable' is true. This example provides a glimpse of how the SDE editor allows rules to be tested as they are built, how it allows a tree of tested rules to be built up, and how the system verbalises each rule. To record expressions and aggregates, the SDE editor uses ASP's 'built-in atom' [18] via an interface that recognises reserved words; for example, the blue rectangle with text "NOT EQUAL" in Fig. 4. Some situations require two or more things to be related at instantiation; for example, the allocation of assets to beneficiaries. The construct 'relation' embeds machinery that inserts a triple (key1,key2,property) into the auto-generated ASP code. The IPH for a 'relation' is shown in Fig. 3, starting with the string "__allocate_percent__". Our use case ("Will and Testament"), requires 15 rules to implement fully, so rule reuse, which has not been investigated, does not appear to warrant priority.

6   Model Validation

The model validation process generates its test data (ASPtest) from ASPspec via a JavaScript function, which provides a single instance for every variable. Change is generated by events, so the validation scenarios are generated by assuming all events for a rule have happened, then deleting single events one at a time. Exhaustive testing is practical because the worst case only requires the power-set of event combinations for a single rule to be tested. Testing a rule involves recursively executing constituent rules fed with their 'true' solution, (recorded when they were tested), so that the test focuses on the current rule. The solver is only called during the testing and mining steps, and mining mirrors the final solver call during the program verification step.

The four methods of user feedback can be seen in Figs. 4 and 5, and include: 1) highlighting rules that are 'true' with 'green' and rules that are 'false' with 'red'; 2) highlighting the absence of an event with a dotted grey arrow; 3) displaying the answer set; and 4) verbalising the answer set.

7   Instantiation and Program Verification

Instantiation is where the actual smart contract is generated, achieved by guiding the user through the instantiation placeholders (IPH) in the document. As

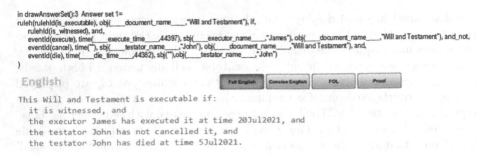

```
in drawAnswerSet():3  Answer set 1=
ruleh(rulehId(is_executable), obj(____document_name____,"Will and Testament"), if,
    rulehId(is_witnessed), and,
    eventId(execute), time(____execute_time____,44397), sbj(____executor_name____,"James"), obj(____document_name____,"Will and Testament"), and_not,
    eventId(cancel), time(""), sbj(____testator_name____,"John"), obj(____document_name____,"Will and Testament"), and,
    eventId(die), time(____die_time____,44382), sbj(""),obj(____testator_name____,"John")
)
```

English   Full English | Concise English | FOL | Proof

```
This Will and Testament is executable if:
  it is witnessed, and
  the executor James has executed it at time 20Jul2021, and
  the testator John has not cancelled it, and
  the testator John has died at time 5Jul2021.
```

Fig. 5. Verbalisation of the answer set for rule 'is_executable'.

discussed in Sect. 5, these are the smart placeholders embedded in the document by the ontology discovery step, that contain an embedded specification of the data required to instantiate the field; for example, cardinality. IPHs come in two forms, active (red underlined text in Fig. 3), and passive (olive underlined text in Fig. 3). Active IPHs are instantiated via a dialogue with the user, while passive IPHs auto-complete using data that is already known to the system (usually properties). An example of how data binding occurs is; if the user inputs "Zoe" and "1 July 2021" for __wife_name__ and __wife_birthday__, the ASPspec representation given in (4.1) is instantiated to give (7.1).

(7.1) thing(..,key(__wife_name__,"Zoe"),birthday(__wife_birthday__,"43820")).[3]

Program verification is like model validation except the focus is largely on numeric tests. Formal verification of these smart contracts relies on the Web-Assembly compile of clingo and WebAssembly itself [21] being formally verified.

8   Evaluation and Future Work

Our work demonstrates most of the requirements of a system that enables the creation of smart contracts by domain experts. We contrast this system with systems produced using the Solidity approach in Fig. 6. We have demonstrated: 1) a system usable by domain experts; 2) visual logic modelling; 3) user feedback via graphics and restricted English; 4) highly modular construction with guided exhaustive testing at individual rule level and the global level; 5) the ability for domain experts to create and test custom smart contracts; and 6) formal correspondence between graphics and the ASP program.

The advantages of our approach are most apparent in testing and in custom smart contract creation. Using a declarative language allows a model of the legal logic to be built by a domain expert. This different methodology then allows testing to be split into model validation and program verification, a simplification that makes testing more amenable for domain experts. Furthermore, we found

---

[3] Note that the date converts to days since 1/1/1900.

	Criteria	Solidity Approach	Our Approach
1	Use by domain experts (DEs)	Standard smart contracts (SCs) only	✓ DEs can build both standard and custom SCs
2	Understandability	No verbal feedback	✓ Visual and verbal feedback for each rule
3	Ease of testing	Limited decomposition	✓ DEs build & test by rule, with visual and verbal feedback
4	Agility	Custom SCs need programming	✓ DEs can build & test custom SCs
5	Free of security exploits & code errors	Formal verification is impractical	✓ A practical pathway exists to formal verification
6	Cost	Any programming is costly	✓ DEs can build custom SCs at no extra cost

Fig. 6. Evaluation of advantages.

that the visualisation of the legal logic naturally guides the creation of a tree of connected rules, providing the decomposition of the overall problem necessary to accommodate domain experts. This decomposition also allows the user to focus on creating and testing one rule at a time in a tight testing feedback loop. These two simplifications allow exhaustive testing of the logic model by domain experts, improving the quality of testing and reducing the effort required for program verification. In contrast to the imperative approach which uses a code library to speed and simplify construction, our method does not require a different approach to create a custom smart contract. In the case of Solidity, if a custom feature does not exist, it must be programmed, an aspect that limits agility and increases costs. We also see advantages in understandability, with our approach providing both visual and verbal feedback to users; the verbalisation feature being difficult to duplicate with the Solidity approach.

Future work involves: 1) applying our approach to a wider range of legal documents; 2) experimenting with different representation grammars; 3) converting more code to ASP (meta-programming in ASP); and improved verbalisation.

9 Conclusion

We have presented a novel methodology and implemented a prototype that allows domain experts to build, understand and test custom smart contracts by elaborating existing legal documents. The innovation enabling this system, is the use of a declarative language to model the ontology and the legal logic. Our prototype demonstrates features that allow domain experts to create custom smart contracts and to exhaustively test the logic models of these smart contracts, reducing validation testing to a manageable level. The advantages observed are that the system allows domain experts to perform all smart contract creation and testing activities, with further advantages in the areas of understandability, and the ability to create custom smart contracts. Furthermore, our approach has a practical pathway to achieving the formal verification of the smart contracts produced. Any practical system that allows domain experts to create, test and deploy formally verified custom smart contracts has significant economic implications. The SDEv4 prototype can be accessed at http://130.56.246.229/.

References

1. Statistics on Australian government procurement contracts (2020). www.finance. gov.au/government/procurement/statistics-australian-government-procurement-contracts
2. Working with Contracts: Practical assistance for small business managers (2019). treasury.gov.au/sites/default/files/2019-03/WorkingWithContractsGuide.pdf
3. Levi, S., Lipton, A.: An introduction to smart contracts and their potential and inherent limitations. Forum on Corporate Governance (2018). corpgov.law.harvard.edu/2018/05/26/an-introduction-to-smart-contracts-and-their-potential-and-inherent-limitations/
4. Brewka, G., Eiter, T., Truszczynski, M.: Answer set programming at a glance. Commun. ACM **54**(12), 92–103 (2011)
5. Thompson Reuters: HighQ document automation (2021). legal.thomsonreuters.com/en/products/highq/document-automation
6. Grigg, I.: The Ricardian contract. In: Proceedings of First IEEE International Workshop on Electronic Contracting, San Diego, CA, USA, pp. 25–31 (2004). https://doi.org/10.1109/WEC.2004.1319505
7. Febbraro, O., et al.: ASPIDE. Integrated Development Environment for Answer Set Programming. University of Calabria (2021). www.mat.unical.it/ricca/aspide/index.html
8. Potassco: The Potsdam answer set solving collection. Clingo and Gringo (2021). potassco.org/clingo/
9. Choudhury, O., et al.: Auto-generation of smart contracts from domain-specific ontologies and semantic rules (2018). https://doi.org/10.1109/Cybermatics_2018.2018.00183
10. Maedche, A., Staab, S.: The TEXT-TO-ONTO Ontology Learning Environment. Institute AIFB, University of Karlsruhe (2000)
11. Konys, A.: Knowledge repository of ontology learning tools from text. Procedia Comput. Sci. **159**, 1614–1628 (2019)
12. Falkner, A., et al.: Industrial applications of answer set programming. KI - Künstliche Intelligenz **32**(2–3), 165–176 (2018)
13. Kloimüllner, C., et al.: Kara: A system for visualising and visual editing of interpretations for answer set programs. In: Proceedings INAP arXiv:1109.4095 (2011)
14. Morris, J.: Modelling the World, the Law, and the Question (2021). roundtable law.medium.com/modelling-the-world-the-law-and-the-question
15. Governatori, G., Idelberger, F., Milosevic, Z., Riveret, R., Sartor, G., Xu, X.: On legal contracts, imperative and declarative smart contracts, and blockchain systems. Artif. Intell. Law **26**(4), 377–409 (2018). https://doi.org/10.1007/s10506-018-9223-3
16. Docs.openlaw.io.: Overview—OpenLaw Docs (2021). docs.openlaw.io/
17. Chainlink Blog: Embedding blockchain smart contracts into our legal system (2021). blog.chain.link/embedding-smart-contracts-into-our-legal-fabric-2/
18. Calimeri, F., et al.: ASP-Core-2 input language format. Theory Pract. Logic Program. **20**(2), 294–309 (2019)
19. Wood, G.: Ethereum: a secure decentralised generalised transaction ledger. EIP-150 Revision (2017). www.gavwood.com/paper.pdf
20. OpenZeppelin. Build secure smart contracts in solidity. openzeppelin.com/contracts/

21. Hjort, R.: Formally verifying WebAssembly with KWasm (2020). odr.chalmers.se/handle/20.500.12380/300761
22. Ethereum development documentation: Transactions (2021). ethereum.org/en/developers/docs/transactions/
23. Getty Research Institute (2021). www.getty.edu/research/publications/electronic_publications/intro_controlled_vocab/what.pdf

Predicting Financial Literacy
via Semi-supervised Learning

David Hason Rudd[1(⊠)], Huan Huo[1], and Guandong Xu[1,2]

[1] The University of Technology Sydney, 15 Broadway, Ultimo, Australia
david.hasonrudd@student.uts.edu.au, {huan.huo,guandong.xu}@uts.edu.au
[2] Advanced Analytics institute (AAi), 15 Broadway, Ultimo, Australia

Abstract. Financial literacy (FL) represents a person's ability to turn assets into income, and understanding digital currencies has been added to the modern definition. FL can be predicted by exploiting unlabelled recorded data in financial networks via semi-supervised learning (SSL). Measuring and predicting FL has not been widely studied, resulting in limited understanding of customer financial engagement consequences. Previous studies have shown that low FL increases the risk of social harm. Therefore, it is important to accurately estimate FL to allocate specific intervention programs to less financially literate groups. This will not only increase company profitability, but will also reduce government spending. Some studies considered predicting FL in classification tasks, whereas others developed FL definitions and impacts. The current paper investigated mechanisms to learn customer FL level from their financial data using sampling by synthetic minority over-sampling techniques for regression with Gaussian noise (SMOGN). We propose the SMOGN-COREG model for semi-supervised regression, applying SMOGN to deal with unbalanced datasets and a nonparametric multi-learner co-regression (COREG) algorithm for labeling. We compared the SMOGN-COREG model with six well-known regressors on five datasets to evaluate the proposed models effectiveness on unbalanced and unlabelled financial data. Experimental results confirmed that the proposed method outperformed the comparator models for unbalanced and unlabelled financial data. Therefore, SMOGN-COREG is a step towards using unlabelled data to estimate FL level.

Keywords: Financial literacy · Semi-supervised regression · Unbalanced datasets · Unlabelled data

1 Introduction

Financial literacy (FL) is an essential skill in the modern world, and is mandatory for consumers operating in an increasingly complex economic society [14]. Current economic conditions have raised significant concerns regarding Australians financial security [14], particularly for those who lack the resources and skills to withstand downswings in the economy and take advantage of upswings. Several studies have determined there is a need not only for better understanding,

© Springer Nature Switzerland AG 2022
G. Long et al. (Eds.): AI 2021, LNAI 13151, pp. 304–319, 2022.
https://doi.org/10.1007/978-3-030-97546-3_25

but also to improve FL level. Individuals are generally responsible for various financial decisions, most importantly regarding retirement preparation and house financing. Previously studies [14] confirmed the relationship between the complexity of these choices and increased stakes, and also highlights consequences from making financial decisions without sufficient FL. Therefore, effective financial management is a critical factor for any organization to achieve efficiency and success in the market [14]. Lusardi [11] surveyed FL definition and effects, evaluating FL levels by asking volunteers four questions about compound interest, inflation, time value of money, and risk diversification. He showed that risk diversification was the most challenging question, with only 9% of Australians giving the correct answer.

The current paper assessed the proposed models effectiveness on unbalanced financial network data to predict customer FL in a superannuation company. Measuring FL levels for millions of customers through a particular online survey in each financial period would be extremely time-consuming and expensive, hence SSL, which exploits a small portion of labelled data and a large amount of unlabelled data, is a smart approach. The dataset was built from customers' financial interactions data and labelled according to an online questionnaire similar to Lusardi's study [11]. To our best knowledge, no previous study exploits a large amount of unlabelled data to predict FL level. We used a baseline algorithm in the self-training method with ensemble cross-validation to justify the baseline models robustness on unbalanced dataset(s). We applied SMOGN to oversample values to enable predicting rare or uncommon data in the skewed dataset. Empirical results confirmed that the proposed SMOGN-COREG model outperformed all current models. Thus, including unlabelled examples via SSR methods improves prediction accuracy more than using only labelled data in supervised methods.

The remainder of this paper is organised as follows: Sect. 2 reviews recent related FL studies and Sect. 3 discusses sampling methods and semi-supervised learning. Section 4 discusses specific methods employed in this analysis and Sect. 5 analyses gathered data and addresses each research question in turn. Finally, Sect. 6 summarises and concludes the paper, and discusses implications for the findings in real-world applications.

2 Related Work

2.1 Financial Literacy Studies

The financial literacy literature can be categorised in two ways. The first category explains different FL survey generation, and the second concentrates on measuring FL. Most of the research makes use of surveys to evaluate and predict the FL level. Several large-scale surveys have been conducted aimed at establishing the distribution and levels of FL.

Worthington [14] examined FL across 924 individuals, largely students at 14 different colleges, and associated their scores with socioeconomic and demographic characteristics. They built a database from respondent answers to an 80 question survey covering three main areas: mathematics literacy, money management skills, and financial competence. A logit model was employed to predict FL level effectively, but their model was most precise or accurate at predicting highest and lowest FL levels with enigmatic effects on intervening cells in the model. Their model depended on density functions, producing high-accuracy results only when predicting the lowest and highest FL levels, whereas the middle 60% responses remained unpredictable [14]. Experimental results showed that students with lower FL levels were likely to live in deprived areas, were unlikely to be business majors, and did not have much work experience. Holding all other factors equivalent or constant, older, higher educated, farm owners, business owners, and university educated respondents exhibited better FL.

Observed FL levels have decreased since the early surveys, but seem to vary between demographic and socioeconomic groups [11]. Factors that influence FL level include gender, age, ethnicity, occupation, education, income, savings, and debt. FL prediction gave high scores for professional and highly educated people aged between 50 and 60; with lowest scores for unemployed females, and those who spoke English as a second language [11].

Huang [6] proposed a back propagation neural network (BPNN) to evaluate FL level. BPNNs comprising three distinct two-hidden layer networks were employed to model credit cards, loans, and superannuation on different datasets with approximately 900 examples. Their results confirmed BPNN capability to simulate FL with 92% overall performance.

Most previous FL studies collected labelled data from questionnaire surveys, whereas the current study predicted FL level on many recorded unlabelled data from customer financial activities with only a small number of labelled data acquisitions from an online questionary.

2.2   Recent Semi-supervised Learning Approaches

Semi-supervised learning uses unlabelled and labelled data in the learning process, in contrast with supervised and unsupervised learning methods, which use only labelled and unlabelled data, respectively. Having human annotators label data is prohibitively expensive and time-consuming, whereas unlabelled data acquisition for learning is easy and fast. However, although using unlabelled data via semi-supervised learning (SSL) is a good method to reduce human effort and improve model performance, some challenges make model tuning more time-consuming and critical than with other machine learning techniques. Depending on the target variable type in model output, SSL can be categorised into two main approaches: semi-supervised regression (SSR) and semi-supervised classification (SSC). SSC is used where the target variable is discrete, whereas SSR is the better choice when model output is continuous.

Different SSL methods are used to fit the structure of a problem, such as maximising expectation with generative mixture models, self-training, co-training, transductive support vector machines (SVMs), and graph based methods [5]. Ding et al. [4] proposed GraphSGAN, applying SSL on graphs with generative adversarial networks. They experimentally confirmed the proposed approach on various datasets, including labelled and unlabelled datasets, performed significantly better than other methods, such as Chebyshev [3] and graph convolutional networks (GCNs) [7], and was more sensitive to labelled data [4]. GraphSGAN generated fake nodes in the density gap, reducing node influences across the density gap. Higher curvature for learned classification function around density gaps was achieved by discriminating fake from real samples. Lin and Gao [10] proposed graph-based semi-supervised learning. They set up a shoestring framework using a typical graph based SSL, with two-layer graph convolutional neural network as a prototypical model for learning nonlinear mapping of nodes into an embedding vector, and then applied a metric learning network on the embedding vector to identify and learn pair-wise similarity between node and centroid representation in each class. The proposed method was tested on seven models and five datasets with 20 labelled data points in each class, achieving better classification performance than baseline methods.

Although the above approaches could theoretically adopt any current SSL methods, most were applied as supervised methods for classification, since real-valued target variables raise practical difficulties for SSL in regression. Motivated by these earlier studies, our methodological approach (see Sect. 4) is a mixed methodology SMOGN-COREG semi-supervised learning contribution to measuring FL.

3   Preliminary Knowledge

3.1   Sampling Techniques by SMOGN

The unbalanced learning problem is concerned with learning algorithm performance in the presence of underrepresented data and severely skewed class distributions [13]. The well-known synthetic minority oversampling technique for regression (SMOTER) extends the SMOTE algorithm for regression tasks and is commonly used in pre-processing to handle unbalanced datasets by generating synthetic samples for minority classes. Torgo and Ribeiro [12] defined a relevance function to determine normal and rare value sets and map them onto a relevance scale between 0 and 1, representing minimum and maximum relevance, respectively.

A threshold t_R was established on relevance values assigned to each user to define the rare value set as

$$D_R = \{|x, y| \in D : \phi(y) \geq t_R\}$$

and normal cases as

$$D_N = \{\langle x, y| \in D : \phi(y) < t_R\},$$

where D is a training set

$$\mathcal{D} = \{\langle \mathbf{x}_i, y_i \rangle\}_{i=1}^{N}$$

with N data points. The relevance function and t_R are used to determine D_R and D_N sets in all sampling strategies.

Branco et al. proposed SMOGN [2], combining one random under-sampling and two oversampling techniques to increase data generation diversity, which cannot be achieved using only introduced Gaussian noise. SMOGN generates new synthetic data with SMOTER, which selects k-nearest neighbors (k-NN) based on the distance between two data points or introduces Gaussian noise [1]. SMOTER uses t_R to determine whether neighbors are within safe or unsafe zones by calculating half the median distance between two data points. The main strategy is to classify important and less important cases in BinsR and BinsN partitions, and then apply oversampling and random under-sampling.

Figure 1 shows a SMOGN synthetic instance for seed cases with five nearest neighbors. Three neighbors are within the safe distance and the other two are at unsafe distance. This synthetic example shows that instances belonging to the normal bin (green) are more likely to overlap with instances associated with the relevant bin within the unsafe distance. Thus, SMOGN generates new synthetic examples and SMOTER selects K-NN or Gaussian noise based on the distance between the data points. If the neighbour is within a safe distance, it is suitable to conduct interpolation via the SMOTER method. On the other hand, if the selected neighbour is located in an unsafe zone introducing Gaussian Noise is a better selection to generate a new instance.

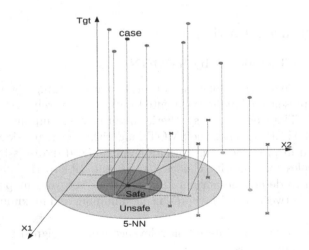

Fig. 1. Synthetic examples in SMOGN [2]

3.2 Co-regression Semi-supervised Learning

Co-regression (COREG) [15] is a nonparametric multi-view and multiple learner SSR method. The flexible COREG SSL algorithm implements two regressors, one labels unlabelled data for the other, and labeling confidence for unlabelled data is determined by the sum of the mean squared error reduction over the labelled neighborhood for that data point. Final prediction is made by averaging regression estimates generated by both regressors. COREG uses a lazy learning method including two k-NNs, which improves computational load because the lazy learner does not hold a separate training phase and refine regressors in each iteration. In contrast neural networks or regression trees require many labeling iterations, with consequently heavy computational load [15].

COREG employs two k-NNs to compute mean squared error (MSE) for each X_u to identify the most confidently labelled data by maximising

$$\Delta_{\mathbf{x}_u} = \sum_{\mathbf{x}_i \in \Omega} \left((\mathbf{y}_i - h(\mathbf{x}_i))^2 - (\mathbf{y}_i - h'(\mathbf{x}_i))^2 \right), \tag{1}$$

where h and h' are the original and refined k-NN regressors, respectively; and Ω is the set of k-NN labelled points from X_U. Information provided for regressors $(\mathbf{x}_u, \hat{\mathbf{y}}_u)$ by where $\hat{\mathbf{y}}_u$ defines with $\hat{\mathbf{y}}_u = h(\mathbf{x}_u)$.

4 Methodology

This section discusses proposed SMOGN-COREG semi-supervised learning model techniques for regression. When selecting an SSR algorithm for labeling unlabelled data, we need to consider an algorithm with low computational load and superior results on large unbalanced datasets.

4.1 Problem Statement

Depending on the model application, SSL can be categorised into inductive and transductive frameworks. Inductive semi-supervised learning can handle unseen data, whereas transductive learning only works on labelled

$$\{(\mathbf{x}_i, y_i)\}_{i=1}^{l} \overset{iid}{\sim} p(\mathbf{x}, y)$$

and unlabelled

$$\{\mathbf{x}_i\}_{i=l+1}^{l+u} \overset{id}{\sim} p(\mathbf{x})$$

training data, where L and U are labelled and unlabelled data, respectively; X is an input data point, y is a target label, $P(X, y)$ is the unknown joint distribution, $p(X)$ is marginal (typically $p(X) = l \ll u$). The transductive method is only interested in labelled data [8]

$$\{\mathbf{x}_i\}_{i=l+1}^{l+u}.$$

The proposed SSL method can be expressed as

$$X = (x_i)_{i \in [n]},$$

where n is total number of instances and x is independent predictor into labelled set $X_l = (x_1, ..., x_l)$ associated with labelled data $Y_l = (y_1, ..., y_l)$ and unlabelled instances $X_u = (x_l + 1, ..., x_{l+u})$, where labelled data are not available.

This paper focused on SSR because target value FL is continuous, and we employ SMOGN sampling on all datasets to balance target variable distributions.

4.2 SMOGN-COREG Semi-supervised Regression

We applied SMOGN for pre-processing before the learning phase to improve model performance. The SMOGN regression technique combines under-sampling the majority class (values usually found near the mean for a normal distribution in response variable y) and oversampling the minority class (rare values in a normal distribution of y, typically found at the tails). SMOGN uses a synthetic minority over-sampling technique for regression, with the additional step of using Gaussian noise to perturb interpolated values. SMOGN applies a function ϕ to the dependent variable, generating corresponding $\phi \in [0,1]$ for each value to decide whether an observation is in the majority or minority depending on t_R (defined in the arguments).

Synthetic values in categorical features are created by randomly selecting observed values contained within their respective function. After post-processing, SMOGN returns an updated data frame with under and oversampled (synthetic) observations. Figure 2 show the model process workflow comprises four main steps:

1. input data;
2. pre-processing: applied data cleansing, feature selection, and sampling;
3. labelled set data augmentation: semi-supervised regression; and
4. output.

The sampling strategies improved learning performance by increasing the small number of important rare cases.

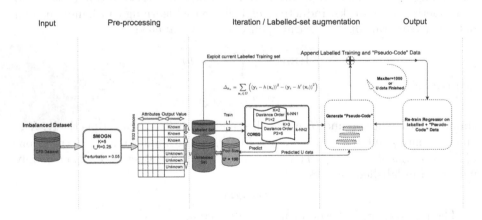

Fig. 2. Proposed SMOGN-COREG model workflow

We used COREG for different distance metrics rather than requiring sufficient and redundant views. COREG has broad applicability and can successfully use unlabelled data to boost regression predictions. Thus, combining sampling strategies with a non-parametric multi learner semi-supervised regression algorithm considerably improves performance on unbalanced datasets. Both base regressors are co-trained on the primarily labelled set with size

$$R = \frac{|L|}{|D|},\tag{2}$$

where $D = L \cup U$ is the total dataset, $|L| \ll |U|$; L is the initial training set, and U denote the initial unlabelled set.

Most focus for unbalanced domains is related to classification problems, whereas research into learning algorithms are less often explored to deal with unbalanced regression. Many important real-life applications, including the economy, crisis management, fault diagnosis, and meteorology, require predicting underrepresented data and important continuous target variables. Important rare cases often accompanied by a plethora of common values cause abnormal behavior for unbalanced learning scenarios [9].

Unbalanced datasets in regression cause more difficulty than in classification because the number of values can be practically infinite for continuous target variables. Prediction performs more poorly when important data points are poorly represented, and the target variable is distributed on unequal user preferences compared to distributions with more frequent data points [2].

5   Experimental Procedure and Results

5.1   Datasets

This study obtained five datasets obtained from a superannuation company for real-world experiments to verify the proposed models effectiveness. The various datasets including considerable skewed data due to the high cardinality ratio. We intended to use balanced datasets and hence obtain reliable evaluation results. Table 1 lists the five unbalanced datasets and their attributes. CFS_2017-2018_FL contains 68 features (54 integer and 14 real variables) and 931 instances, and the other four datasets contain with 89 features (54 integer, 16 polynomial, and 19 real variables) with approximately 900 labelled and unlabelled data points, for members holding accounts with Australian superannuation company Colonial First State (CFS). Dataset features included customer financial activities, demographics, income, account balance, marital status, age, employment, and some private features used in customer relationship management teams. We added the target variable "Financial literacy" in final dataset separately after Extract, Transform, Load (ETL) data from various sources, where FL value was derived from CFS online survey questionnaire in 2017 and 2018. However, the number of customers that participated in this survey was only approximately 5% of the whole population, i.e., approximately 5% of the data was labelled, and the rest remained unlabelled in all five datasets.

Table 1. Datasets collected

Dataset	# Attributes	# Instances	Size
CFS_201706	89	824	73336
CFS_201712	89	856	76184
CFS_201806	89	899	80011
CFS_201812	89	918	81702
CFS_2017-2018_FL	68	931	64239

5.2   Baseline and Regression Method Configuration

The regression methods were implemented using the Weka[1] platform, and we compared proposed SMOGN-COREG model performance with the following supervised and semi-supervised models.

- Linear Regression (LR) is the most popular method when there is a linear relationship between two features. We used Akaike information criterion (AIC) for model selection, and LR can deal with weighted instances.
- k-NN using Euclidean distance, where $K = k \in \{4, 7, 9\}$.
- Sequential minimization optimization (SMOreg) to implement SVM with regression using a polynomial kernel with batch size $= 100$.
- M5 Rules model tree in if-then form, with minimum instances per leaf $= 4$.
- M5 Model Trees, a well-known model tree algorithm in Weka tools, constructs multivariate linear regression trees, with minimum instances per leaf $= 4$.
- Random Forest (RF) with tree depth $=$ unlimited, and iteration and batch size $= 100$.
- Meta multi-scheme SSR algorithm (MSSRA) [5] as the baseline model. MSSRA used three k-NN base regressors (3, 7, 9 k-NN), followed by self-training to enhance the labelled set by exploiting the unlabelled set and one final random forest regressor deployed for retraining after iteration. Labels for unknown test instances were then exported. Since the algorithm uses different regressors outside the iterative process, it can be considered a diversity booster, confirmed in the experiment by its robust results.

Several more supervised regressors were utilised for comparison purposes, but we did not include them the model comparison due to their considerably unsatisfactory performance.

5.3   Experiment Setup

We initially employed cross-validation with 10 folds of the datasets, one fold for the test set and the remainder for learning. Unlabelled ratio UR $= 80\%$ was used

---

[1] Weka is a collection of machine-learning algorithms for data mining tasks in the Java SE platform, operating Windows, OSX, Linux.

to split the training set in each fold, i.e., only 20% labelled data were involved in learning. COREG maximum iterations = 100, U' pool size = 100, and always $\Delta_{x_u} > 0$ in each iteration, hence maximum labeling capacity = 50000 iterations. However, this capacity was somewhat optimistic considering the negative impact from noisy data in the L subset. Given the labeling capacity of the algorithm, all unlabelled data in the five datasets would be evaluated for labeling well before the maximum number of iterations was reached. Experimentally trading off between iterations and model runtime, we found 500 iterations and U' pool size = 100 unlabelled data was optimal and covered all confident predictions to enhance the labelled set during learning on all five datasets.

We set the distance order for the two k-NN regressors in COREG as $K = 2$ and 3, respectively; with $K = 2$ for the SMOGN algorithm oversampling, and $t_R = 0.25$. Gaussian noise introduced in SMOGN = 5%, hence perturbation = 0.05 and maximum iteration = 1000. The pool contained 100 unlabelled examples randomly selected from the unlabelled set in each iteration. The final prediction outcome is the average regression predictions for the two regressors. Average MSE was recorded for labeling most confidence instances.

We compared the proposed approach with one SSR algorithm and five widely used supervised regressors on five different datasets (see Table 1). We considered four well-known evaluation metrics to determine regression performance:

- R-squared (R^2) (3),
- Pearson correlation coefficient (PCC) (4),
- root mean squared error ($RMSE$) (5), and
- mean absolute error (MAE) (6);

Which can be expressed as

$$R^2 = 1 - \frac{RSS}{TSS}, \tag{3}$$

$$PCC = \frac{\sum_{i=1}^{n} (y_i - \bar{y})(y_i' - \bar{y}')}{\sum_{i=1}^{n} (y_i - \bar{y})^2 (y_i' - \bar{y}')^2}, \tag{4}$$

$$RMSE = \frac{1}{n} \sqrt{\sum_{i=1}^{n} (y_i - y_i')^2}, \tag{5}$$

$$MAE = \frac{1}{n} \sum_{i=1}^{n} |y_i - y_i'|, \tag{6}$$

respectively, where the dataset has n values $\{y_1, ..., y_n\}$ with y_i values are real in a multivariate linear model with

$$Y_i = \beta_0 + \sum_{j=1}^{P} \beta_j X_{i,j} + \varepsilon_i,$$

y' corresponding to the predicted value for data point x_i, $\bar{y}$ is the mean of the observed data; $\bar{y}, \bar{y}'$ are mean values for y_i and y_i', respectively. Larger PCC and R^2 and smaller MAE and $RMSE$ represent improved prediction accuracy.

5.4   Empirical Results

Based on the aim of achieving excellent results from SMOGN for tackling imbalanced regression problems, an experiment was conducted on the main dataset CFS_2017-2018_FL and its results presented in Fig. 3 show a clear pattern of the imbalanced target variable distribution, with a higher density over 0.5, and vice versa. The dark blue histogram shows that after applying SMOGN, fewer sample data points were extracted between the values of 0.6 and 0.9. In contrast, some extra samples were generated from lower than 0.5 values. Thus we can claim that the skewed data distribution was modified after applying SMOGN. On the other hand, this improvement in data distribution led to boosting the COREG learning capability to generate higher accuracy in minority samples. It concludes that the mixed methodology of oversampling and undersampling by the SMOGN and COREG is worked efficiently not only in our targeted dataset and other similar finance datasets.

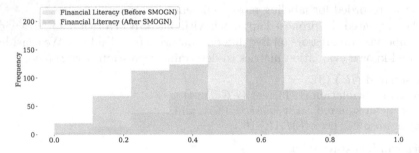

Fig. 3. Distribution of target variable before and after applying SMOGN on CFS_2017-2018_FL dataset

The experimental results on main dataset "CFS_2017-2018_FL" presented in the tables and graphs prove that the proposed model performed better than the other regression algorithms. Specific results of the aforementioned evaluation metrics on five different datasets are as follows:

- The RMSE results shown in Table 2. are in an acceptable range for the proposed model with minimum RMSE 0.1285. The M5 had the best result with the lowest RMSE at 0.1207; in contrast, the LR indicated poor performance with the highest RMSE of 1.1528. On the other hand, the data analysis in Table 2 showed that the lower fluctuation level is obtained in the proposed SMOGN-COREG and RF model with a standard deviation of 0.0051 and 0.0019, unlike the SMOreg and LR 0.023592117 and 0.459051896, respectively. This finding confirms additional evidence that although the RMSE result in the SMOGN-COREG is slightly higher than supervised models M5, SMOreg and LR because the two SMOGN-COREG regressors train on the augmented training set built by the combination of the initial labelled set

Table 2. RMSE results of supervised regressors, baseline MSSRA and proposed SMOGN-COREG model

Datasets	CFS_2017-2018_FL	CFS_201812	CFS_201806	CFS_201712	CFS_201706
MSSRA	0.1367	0.1565	0.1618	0.156	0.1549
SMOGEN-COREG	0.1356	0.1335	0.1303	0.1285	0.1416
4-NN	0.1344	0.1483	0.1581	0.1502	0.1513
7-NN	0.1306	0.1439	0.153	0.1447	0.1465
9-NN	0.1284	0.1426	0.1533	0.1448	0.1462
SMOreg	0.1317	0.1321	0.1325	0.1831	0.1263
LR	**0.1275**	0.1224	0.1304	1.1528	0.1251
M5	0.1276	**0.1214**	**0.1223**	**0.1227**	**0.1207**
M5rules	0.1277	0.1215	0.1229	0.1231	0.1208
RF	0.1317	0.1339	0.1359	0.1362	0.1361

and Pseudo-code subset increased model prediction error in SSL in compare with supervised learning methods due to the inherent limitations of SSL, the amount of noise in data generate many incorrect pseudo-labels, leading to erroneous high confidence predictions. Despite this, the SMOGN-COREG algorithm's stability is higher than the baseline SSL algorithm, and other mentioned supervised learning models in the finance datasets.

- A significant improvement in R-squared and PCC values with our proposed model demonstrates the compatibility of the two algorithms, SMOGN and COREG, on the financial dataset. Moreover, the results emphasise the importance of exploiting the sampling technique SMOGN to improve model performance on imbalanced datasets. The R-squared and PCC results in Fig. 4 and Table 3 show that the COREG algorithm achieved the lowest R-squared and PCC results at 0.4431 and 0.6656, respectively, in contrast to SMOGN-COREG, which obtains superior results of 0.7171 and 0.8468, respectively.

Table 3. PCC results of supervised regressors, baseline MSSRA and proposed SMOGN-COREG model

Dataset	CFS_2017-2018_FL	CFS_201812	CFS_201806	CFS_201712	CFS_201706
MSSRA (Base-model)	0.7922	0.7465	0.7322	0.7476	0.7501
SMOGEN-COREG	**0.8468**	**0.8384**	**0.8622**	**0.8523**	0.7454
4-NN	0.7876	0.7274	0.6837	0.7171	0.7095
7-NN	0.7988	0.7472	0.7117	0.7442	0.7325
9-NN	0.806	0.754	0.7144	0.7461	0.7365
SMOreg	0.7955	0.7919	0.7917	0.6295	0.8085
LR	0.8092	0.8249	0.8025	0.0858	0.8134
M5	0.8094	0.827	0.8259	0.8225	**0.8268**
M5rules	0.8092	0.8267	0.824	0.8214	0.8265
RF	0.7985	0.8119	0.8081	0.809	0.8053
Improved %	4.6	1.4	4.4	3.6	−8.8

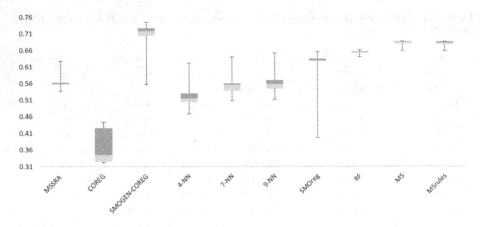

Fig. 4. The proposed SMOGN-COREG model is obtained the best R-squared.

- The MAE values represented in the boxplot graph in Fig. 5 show that M5 and M5Rules had a lower MAE than the other supervised- and semi-supervised-learning algorithms. RF had the least fluctuation in MAE, ranging from 0.102 to 0.104; however, the lowest MAE was achieved by the proposed model SMOGN-COREG, ranging from 0.0099 to 0.1091 on all datasets.

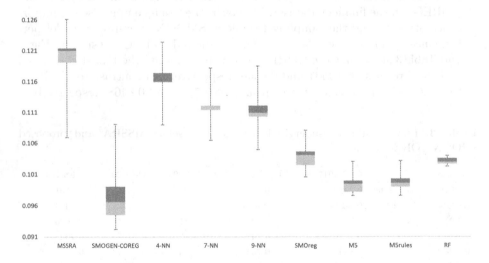

Fig. 5. The SMOGN-COREG and M5 models achieved the better MAE result.

- In addition to the above results, it should be noted that these findings cannot be extrapolated to all type of datasets structures. The max cardinality of the dataset "CFS 201706" is significantly larger than other ones. Namely, the large number of unique values led to a low strength relationship between data

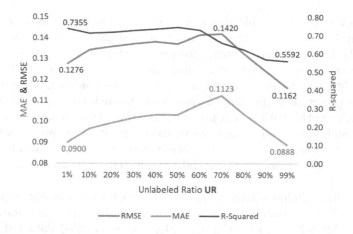

Fig. 6. The above graph shows the correlation of evaluation metrics results with UR.

points. As shown in RMSE results in Table 2. and PCC results in Table 3. the supervised model M5 performs better on the dataset "CFS 201706".

Therefore, from the final experiment, given the ability to predict the FL of customers, we can conclude two things: First, our hypothesis using a combination of sampling strategy techniques with a nonparametric multi learner SSR algorithm provides better results than other regressors on imbalanced financial network data. Second, overall, exploiting a large amount of unlabelled data via SSR methods improves prediction accuracy more than using only labelled data in supervised methods on data collected based on customer financial activities. In Fig. 5, the MAE in SMOGN-COREG improved 50% over the COREG algorithm and 7.3% over the baseline model. In Fig. 4. SMOGN-COREG improved the R-squared 67% and 18% over the COREG and baseline algorithms, respectively.

The different ratio of the size of the unlabelled dataset to the total amount of data, called Unlabelled Ratio (UR), affects the R-squared, RMSE, and MAE. Figure 6 shows that the R-squared was improved 31% by increasing the number of unlabelled data points. The MAE was worse when learning was trained with a 70% unlabelled ratio. Moreover, the RMSE value improved 9.8% with a 99% UR. Monitoring the model performance via the UR can be helpful for designers who want to simulate their own model output based on a different UR. The python implementation for the proposed model and result visualisation is available in GitHub (https://github.com/DavidHason/predicting-financial-literacy), to simplify reproducing and improving this study experiment results.

6 Conclusions

Irrational financial decisions can have irreversible impacts on quality of life. Many relevant reports and articles have shown that people with poor FL are considerably more vulnerable to social harm and financial losses, such as job loss; family loss; reduced life expectancy; mental health problems; and most importantly, low-income retirement. To prevent this, it is essential to estimate FL and hence allocate specific intervention programs and financial advice to less financially literate groups. This will not only increase company profitability but also reduce government spending. Considerable financial data is recorded in the contemporary world, with a high proportion of that data unlabelled. Therefore, it is impossible to include this massive data repository in predictive models. The primary purpose for the current study was to develop a suitable method to predict FL level using financial datasets, which often include considerable unlabelled data.

Many SSL techniques have been used for various real-world applications, including GCNs, self-training, and co-training. Empirical results confirmed that combining SMOGN and COREG algorithms on unlabelled data reduced cost and model runtime, and improved prediction accuracy beyond current supervised regression methods. Most real-world problems involving unlabelled examples analysed using SSR methods have better prediction accuracy than using only labelled data in supervised methods. Thus, this study results represent a further step towards applying SSR techniques to assist FinTech companies in narrowing their consumer financial behavior and targeted marketing campaigns.

The proposed solution was based on an offline learning process because the proposed statistical predictive method was applied to previously collected data. Future study will investigate implementing online learning on streaming data. This would provide a predictive engine to conduct more accurate and trustworthy predictions, with additional data potentially coming from other financial institutions, such as other superannuation or FinTech companies. Using an active learning algorithm in the SSR models could be a potential method to achieve this.

Acknowledgement. This work is partially supported by the Australian Research Council (ARC) under Grant No. DP200101374 and LP170100891.

References

1. Branco, P., Ribeiro, R.P., Torgo, L.: Ubl: an r package for utility-based learning. arXiv preprint arXiv:1604.08079 (2016)
2. Branco, P., Torgo, L., Ribeiro, R.P.: SMOGN: a pre-processing approach for imbalanced regression. In: Torgo, L., Krawczyk, B., Branco, P., Moniz, N. (eds.) Proceedings of the First International Workshop on Learning with Imbalanced Domains: Theory and Applications. Proceedings of Machine Learning Research, vol. 74, pp. 36–50. PMLR, ECML-PKDD, Skopje, 22 September 2017. http://proceedings.mlr.press/v74/branco17a.html
3. Defferrard, M., Bresson, X., Vandergheynst, P.: Convolutional neural networks on graphs with fast localized spectral filtering. arXiv preprint arXiv:1606.09375 (2016)

4. Ding, M., Tang, J., Zhang, J.: Semi-supervised learning on graphs with generative adversarial nets. In: Proceedings of the 27th ACM International Conference on Information and Knowledge Management, CIKM 2018, pp. 913–922. Association for Computing Machinery, New York (2018). https://doi.org/10.1145/3269206. 3271768
5. Fazakis, N., Karlos, S., Kotsiantis, S., Sgarbas, K.: A multi-scheme semi-supervised regression approach. Pattern Recogn. Lett. **125**, 758–765 (2019). https://doi.org/ 10.1016/j.patrec.2019.07.022
6. Huang, R., Tawfik, H., Samy, M., Nagar, A.: A financial literacy simulation model using neural networks: case study. In: 2007 Innovations in Information Technologies (IIT), pp. 516–520. IEEE (2007)
7. Kipf, T.N., Welling, M.: Semi-supervised classification with graph convolutional networks. arXiv preprint arXiv:1609.02907 (2016)
8. Kostopoulos, G., Karlos, S., Kotsiantis, S., Ragos, O.: Semi-supervised regression: a recent review. J. Intell. Fuzzy Syst. **35**(2), 1483–1500. https://doi.org/10.3233/ JIFS-169689
9. Krawczyk, B.: Learning from imbalanced data: open challenges and future directions. Progress Artif. Intell. **5**(4), 221–232 (2016). https://doi.org/10.1007/s13748-016-0094-0
10. Lin, W., Gao, Z., Li, B.: Shoestring: graph-based semi-supervised classification with severely limited labeled data. In: Proceedings of the IEEE/CVF Conference on Computer Vision and Pattern Recognition, pp. 4174–4182 (2020)
11. Lusardi, A., Mitchell, O.S., Curto, V.: Financial literacy among the young. J. Consum. Aff. **44**(2), 358–380 (2010). https://doi.org/10.1111/j.1745-6606.2010. 01173.x
12. Torgo, L., Ribeiro, R.: Utility-based regression. In: Kok, J.N., Koronacki, J., Lopez de Mantaras, R., Matwin, S., Mladenič, D., Skowron, A. (eds.) PKDD 2007. LNCS (LNAI), vol. 4702, pp. 597–604. Springer, Heidelberg (2007). https://doi.org/10. 1007/978-3-540-74976-9_63
13. Vluymans, S.: Learning from Imbalanced Data, pp. 81–110. Springer, Cham (2019). https://doi.org/10.1007/978-3-030-04663-74
14. Worthington, A.: Predicting financial literacy in Australia. Financ. Serv. Rev. **15**, 59–79 (2006)
15. Zhou, Z.H., Li, M.: Semi-supervised regression with co-training. In: Proceedings of the 19th International Joint Conference on Artificial Intelligence, IJCAI 2005, pp. 908–913. Morgan Kaufmann Publishers Inc., San Francisco (2005)

Machine Teaching-Based Efficient Labelling for Cross-unit Healthcare Data Modelling

Yang Wang[1,2], Xueping Peng[1(✉)], Allison Clarke[2], Clement Schlegel[2], and Jing Jiang[1]

[1] Australian AI Institute, University of Technology Sydney, Ultimo, Australia
yang.wang-17@student.uts.edu.au, {xueping.peng,jing.jiang}@uts.edu.au
[2] Health Economics and Research Division, Australian Department of Health, Canberra, Australia
{alvin.wang,allison.clarke,clement.schlegel}@health.gov.au

Abstract. A data custodian of a big organization (such as a Commonwealth Data Integrating Authority), namely teacher, can easily build an intelligent model which is well trained by comprehensive data collected from multiple sources. However, due to information security and privacy-related regulation requirements, full access to the well-trained intelligent model and the comprehensive training data is usually limited to the teacher only and not available to any unit (or branch) of that organization. Therefore, if a unit, namely student, needs an intelligent function similar to the trained intelligent model, the student has to train a similar model from scratch using the student's own dataset. Such a dataset is usually unlabelled, requiring a big workload on labelling. Inspired by the Iterative Machine Teaching, we propose a novel collaboration pipeline. It enables the teacher to iteratively guide the student to select samples that are most worth labelling from the student's own dataset, which significantly reduces the requirement for human labelling and, at the same time, prevents regulation and information security breaches. The effectiveness and efficiency of the proposed pipeline is empirically demonstrated on two publicly available healthcare datasets in comparison with baseline methods. This work has broad implications for the healthcare sector to facilitate data modelling in instances where the large labelled datasets are not accessible to each unit.

Keywords: Iterative machine teaching · Cross-units · Efficient labelling · Electronic health records

1 Introduction

The use of large-scale complex health data, including Electronic Health Records (EHR), holds immense potential to better predict patient outcomes and understand disease cohorts [23,25]. Although huge volumes of EHR are typically unlabelled and have privacy concerns, existing deep learning models [2,7,11,16,19,20]

© Springer Nature Switzerland AG 2022
G. Long et al. (Eds.): AI 2021, LNAI 13151, pp. 320–331, 2022.
https://doi.org/10.1007/978-3-030-97546-3_26

have shown great success in healthcare applications by self-supervised learning [4, 5, 15, 17, 18]. However, deep learning models typically require a large amount of labelled data for training which is not always available in real-world settings. Although data linkage and sharing can sometimes reduce the requirement for human labelling, this is often hindered due to information security and privacy-related requirements and concerns [14, 27]. Consider the below scenario that often occurs in the real world:

A large data service provider in healthcare (e.g. a Commonwealth Data Integrating Authority) may have a large amount of valuable data on a wide range of health and welfare topics (e.g. linked comprehensive dataset). Such a data service provider may have responsibility to provide end-to-end data services to ensure strong evidence available to policymakers, service planners, researchers and the community. On the other hand, an approved data recipient (e.g. a small research team in a university) may only have limited access to a specific part of the linked comprehensive dataset for approved studies. It is much easier and more achievable for the large data service provider to train a high performing machine learning model using their comprehensive dataset. However, It is difficult for the small research team to train a similar model due to the limited data access.

Let's take a more specific example here: a small research group needs to train a machine learning model to classify patient cohorts (by disease) using their approved access to a ten percent sample of patient's pharmaceutical benefits claims data. However, this would require a large number of records to be labelled by humans (i.e. label disease type on thousands of pharmaceutical benefits claim history records) to construct a sufficient training data for achieving a good machine learning classifier for this specific task. Alternatively, it would be much easier for a large data integration organization to train the same machine learning classifier, because they may already have sufficient training data. For example, the disease type on each pharmaceutical benefits claim history can be easily found from a linked comprehensive dataset that is available to the integration organization (such as the diagnosis code from the linked hospital data). Therefore, the amount of time spent on constructing the required training dataset by humans for the large data integration organization is considerably smaller. However, in this example, given the information security and privacy-related regulation requirements, the small research group is not allowed to access any extra information so the large data integration organization won't be able to directly give the researchers the trained model and/or the required training dataset.

To overcome these limitations, this paper proposes a novel collaboration pipeline, namely **Ma**chine **Te**aching-based **Labelling** (MaTe-Labelling) framework. It enables the teacher to iteratively guide the student to select samples that are most worth labelling from the student's own dataset, which significantly reduces the requirement for human labelling and, at the same time, prevents regulation and information security breaches.

More specifically, the above-mentioned large data service provider is considered to be the teacher, and the approved data recipient (i.e. the small research team) is considered to be the student. In each iteration, the teacher leverages

MaTe-Labelling to construct an optimal sample set that is selected only from the data that the student has access to. Similar to the optimization task of the Iterative Machine Teaching, the optimal sample set is carefully selected by solving an optimization task that minimizes the difficulty of the selected samples and, at the same time, maximizes their usefulness [13]. Such an optimal sample set would then be returned to the student. After being labelled by domain experts, it becomes the most efficient training set for the student model in that iteration, outperforming any training set created by labelling without teacher guidance. Given the optimal sample sets are only selected from the data that the student has access to, there is no extra information released to the student.

Our main contributions are summarized as follows:

- We propose a novel Machine Teaching-based Labelling (MaTe-Labelling) framework. It enables iterative guidance on the student to select samples that are most worth labelling, which reduces the large human efforts for labelling.
- MaTe-Labelling enables teacher to provide efficient data services and strong guidance to student without releasing any extra information, which effectively prevents regulation and information security breaches.
- Extensive experiments are conducted on two public health datasets to demonstrate effectiveness and efficiency of the proposed pipeline.

The remainder of this paper is organised as follows: Section 2 briefly reviews the related work on iterative machine teaching, interactive machine learning and active leaning. Section 3 describes the proposed model. Section 4 presents the experiments and results for EHR data from three patient cohorts and Sect. 5 concludes the paper by summarising the research.

2   Related Work

2.1   Iterative Machine Teaching

Traditional machine teaching is to solve the problem of finding an optimal (usually minimal) training set given a machine learning algorithm (the student model) and a target [28,29]. Iterative Machine Teaching was proposed afterwards and extends the traditional machine teaching from batch setting to iterative setting, enabling iterative student model to achieve faster convergence [13]. Specifically, the optimization task of the Iterative Machine Teaching is to minimize the difficulty of the selected samples and, at the same time, maximize their usefulness.

2.2   Interactive Machine Learning

Interactive machine learning has been proposed as a promising field in visual analytics [6,12,26], which couples human input with machines in the learning process. Recently, machine teaching has been combined with interactive machine learning to improve human teacher by giving teaching guidance via performing a classification task by showing examples [3]. To address the crowdsourcing problem, a model called STRICT [24] has been introduced as an efficient algorithm for selecting examples to teach crowd workers to better classify the query. These studies consider a very different setting where the learner is not iterative and does not have a particular optimization algorithm [13].

2.3   Active Learning

Active learning (also called query learning) enables the learner to choose the data from which it learns and ask an oracle for its label, which performs better with less training [21,22]. Active learning is different from machine teaching in the sense that active learners explore the optimal parameters by itself rather than being guided by the teacher. They therefore have different sample complexities [1, 13,28].

3   Methodology

This section starts with notations of several important concepts and settings in the paper. The remainder mainly focuses on details of the proposed pipeline consisting of machine teaching and example selection.

3.1   Notations and Settings

Notations. We denote an example for the teacher as (x, y) while the same example for the student as $(\widetilde{x}, \widetilde{y})$. We assume the representation spaces of $x \in \mathcal{X}$ and $\widetilde{x} \in \widetilde{\mathcal{X}}$ are the same, and $y = \widetilde{y}$. v^* and w^* are teacher's optimal model and student's optimal model, respectively. In this paper, we assume v^* is the same as w^*. The initial parameter is denoted as w_0, loss function as $\ell(f(x), y)$, learning rate as η_t over time (and initial η_0) and the trackability of the parameter as w^t, where t denotes the t-th iteration.

Settings. The paper introduces the following settings to describe the proposed model.

- **Student's Components**: The initial parameter w_0, loss function, optimization algorithm, representation, model, learning rate η_t and the trackability of the parameter w^t.
- **Model**: The teacher uses a model with parameter v^* (w^* for student's space) that is taught to the student. w and v do not necessarily lie in the same space, but in this paper, they are equivalent and interchangeably used.
- **Communication**: The teacher can only communicate with the student via examples. In this paper, the teacher provides one example x^t in the iteration t.

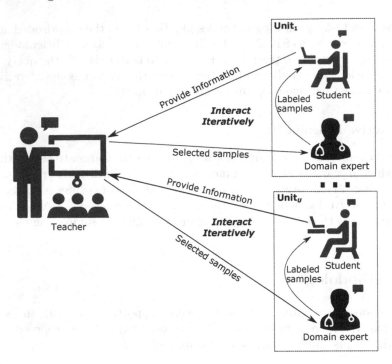

Fig. 1. The structure of the proposed model MaTe-Labelling.

- **Loss Function**: The teacher and student share the same loss function. We assume this is a convex loss function $\ell(f(x), y)$, and the best model is usually found by minimizing the expected loss below: $w^* = \arg\min_w \mathbb{E}_{(x,y)} \left[\ell(\langle w, x \rangle, y) \right]$, where the sampling distribution $(x, y) \sim \mathbb{P}(x, y)$.
- **Algorithm**: The student uses the stochastic gradient descent to optimize the model. The iterative update is $w^{t+1} = w^t - \eta_t \dfrac{\partial \ell(\langle w, x \rangle, y)}{\partial w}$.

3.2   Model Structure

As shown in Fig. 1, the whole model architecture of MaTe-Labelling consists of one Teacher and a set of Units and each Unit includes a Student and a Domain expert. In each iteration, a Student from an Unit first provides information about the Student's data access and current parameters to the Teacher. The Teacher then solves an optimization task to be able to select an optimal sample set from the data (usually unlabeled) that the Student has access to. Then the selected optimal sample set is returned to the Unit for Domain expert labelling. The labelled sample set would then be used to update the Student model in the Unit.

3.3   Machine Teaching

An teacher has access to the student's feature space, model, loss function and optimization algorithm [13]. In specific, teacher's (x, y) and student's $(\widetilde{x}, \widetilde{y})$ share the same representation space.

Teaching Algorithm. In order to make the student model converge faster with a smaller set of samples, the algorithm will start with looking into the difference between the current student parameter and the teacher parameter w^* during each iteration:

$$
\begin{aligned}
\left\|w^{t+1} - w^*\right\|_2^2 &= \left\|w^t - \eta_t \frac{\partial \ell(\langle w, x \rangle, y)}{\partial w} - w^*\right\|_2^2 \\
&= \left\|w^t - w^*\right\|_2^2 + \eta_t^2 \left\|\frac{\partial \ell(\langle w^t, x \rangle, y)}{\partial w^t}\right\|_2^2 \\
&\quad - 2\eta_t \left\langle w^t - w^*, \frac{\partial \ell(\langle w^t, x \rangle, y)}{\partial w^t}\right\rangle \\
&= \left\|w^t - w^*\right\|_2^2 + \eta_t^2 T_1(x, y|w^t) - 2\eta_t T_2(x, y|w^t)
\end{aligned}
\tag{1}
$$

where $T_1(x, y|w^t) = \left\|\frac{\partial \ell(\langle w^t, x \rangle, y)}{\partial w^t}\right\|_2^2$ and $T_2(x, y|w^t) = \left\langle w^t - w^*, \frac{\partial \ell(\langle w^t, x \rangle, y)}{\partial w^t}\right\rangle$.

Based on the decomposition of the parameter error, the teacher aims to choose a particular example (x, y) such that $\|w^{t+1} - w^*\|_2^2$ is most reduced compared to $\|w^t - w^*\|_2^2$ from the last iteration. Thus the general strategy for the teacher is to choose an example (x, y), such that $\eta_t^2 T_1 - 2\eta_t T_2$ is minimized in the t-th iteration:

$$
\underset{x \in \mathcal{X}, y \in \mathcal{Y}}{\arg\min} \; \eta_t^2 T_1(x, y|w^t) - 2\eta_t T_2(x, y|w^t).
\tag{2}
$$

The smallest value of $\eta_t^2 T_1 - 2\eta_t T_2$ is $-\|w^t - w^*\|_2^2$. If the teacher achieves this, it means that we have reached the teaching goal after this iteration. However, it usually cannot be done in just one iteration, because of the limitation of teacher's capability to provide examples. T_1 and T_2 have some nice intuitive interpretations:

Difficulty of an Example. T_1 quantifies the difficulty level of an example. The difficulty level is not related to the teacher w^*, but is based on the current parameters of the learner w^t. From another perspective, the difficulty level can also be interpreted as the information that an example carries. Essentially, a difficult example is usually more informative. In such sense, our difficulty level has similar interpretation to curriculum learning, but with different expression.

Usefulness of an Example. T_2 quantifies the usefulness of an example. Concretely, T_2 is the correlation between discrepancy $w^t - w^*$ and the information (difficulty) of an example. If the information of the example has large correlation with the discrepancy, it means that this example is very useful in this teaching iteration.

3.4   Example Selection

Teacher can access a comprehensive training set with labels generated by both domain experts and linked data that only teacher has access to. Due to information security and privacy-related regulation requirements, student from any individual unit does not have access to the same comprehensive training set that the teacher has access to. In addition, each unit is only allowed to see it's own data at all times. To this end, the optimal samples that returned by teacher to a unit are only selected from the data that the very unit has access to. There is no extra information released to any unit. We take unit u as an example to formalize example select as below,

$$
(x_u^t, y_h^t) = \underset{x_u \in \mathcal{X}_u, y_h \in \mathcal{Y}_h}{\arg\min} \quad \eta_t^2 \left\| \frac{\partial \ell(\langle w_u^t, x_u \rangle, y_h)}{\partial w_u^t} \right\|_2^2 - 2\eta_t \left\langle w_u^t - w^*, \frac{\partial \ell(\langle w_u^t, x_u \rangle, y_h)}{\partial w_u^t} \right\rangle
$$
(3)

where $\mathcal{X}_u$ denotes the set of samples collected from or available to unit u, and $\mathcal{Y}_h$ denotes corresponding labels for $\mathcal{X}_u$ that are available to the student, but not to the student, w_u^t represents the parameters of the student on unit u in the iteration t.

The optimal sample(s) selected by the teacher would be sent to the domain expert in unit u to be labelled. We set y_u^t as the label of x_u^t, thus, the student model update on unit u can be formalized as following,

$$
w_u^t = w_u^{t-1} - \eta_t \frac{\partial \ell \left(\langle w_u^{t-1}, x_u^t \rangle, y_u^t \right)}{\partial w_u^{t-1}}.
$$
(4)

The proposed MaTe-Labelling algorithm is summarized in Algorithm 1.

4   Experiments

In this section, we conduct experiments on two real world medical claim datasets to evaluate the performance of the proposed MaTe-Labelling. Compared with the baseline models, MaTe-Labelling yields better performance on different evaluation strategies.

4.1   Data Description

Dataset. We conducted comparative studies on two real-world datasets in the experiments, which are the MIMIC-III [9] and MIMIC-IV [8] databases.

- The MIMIC-III dataset [9] is an open-source, de-identified dataset of ICU patients and their EHRs between 2001 and 2012. The diagnosis codes in the dataset follow the ICD9 standard.
- The MIMIC-IV dataset [8] is an update to M-III, which incorporates contemporary data and improves on numerous aspects of M-III. The dataset consists of the medical records of 73,452 patients between 2008 and 2019.

Algorithm 1. MaTe-Labelling Algorithm

1: Randomly initialize the student and teacher parameter w^0;

2: Train teacher with comprehensive training set to get optimal teacher parameter w^*;

3: Set $t = 1$ and the maximal iteration number T, $u = 0$ and the total unit number U;

4: **while** $u < U$ **do**

5:    **while** w_u^t has not converged or $t < T$ **do**

6:       Solve the optimization (e.g., pool-based teaching):

$$(x_u^t, y_h^t) = \underset{x_u \in \mathcal{X}_u, y_h \in \mathcal{Y}_h}{\arg\min} \quad \eta_t^2 \left\| \frac{\partial \ell(\langle w_u^t, x_u \rangle, y_h)}{\partial w_u^t} \right\|_2^2$$

$$- 2\eta_t \left\langle w_u^t - w^*, \frac{\partial \ell(\langle w_u^t, x_u \rangle, y_h)}{\partial w_u^t} \right\rangle$$

7:       Domain expert labels x_u^t as y_u^t to perform the update:

$$w_u^t = w_u^{t-1} - \eta_t \frac{\partial \ell \left(\langle w_u^{t-1}, x_u^t \rangle, y_u^t \right)}{\partial w_u^{t-1}}.$$

8:      $t \leftarrow t + 1$

9:    **end while**

10:   $u \leftarrow u + 1$

11: **end while**

Cohort Identification. Patients were included in analysis if they had at least one cohort-specific International Classification of Diseases (ICD)-9 diagnosis code of 140–239 for cancer, 428 for heart failure and 249–250 for diabetes. Table 1 shows the statistical details of the three cohorts in the datasets, where the selected patients made at least two visits and the labels are identified by ICD codes in an indexed visit. If a visit includes a cohort-specific ICD-9 code (considered to be the index visit), the previous visits which represent a patient's sequential history are used as input. To evaluate the performance of the algorithm, we perform classification on the selected data and the classification is based on the original labels.

Table 1. Statistics of the datasets.

Cohort	MIMIC-III	MIMIC-IV
# of diabetes patients	943	10,640
# of heart failure patients	1,021	13,551
# of cancer patients	1,333	6,167

4.2   Experimental Setup

Performance Metric and Baseline. We evaluate the convergence performance with following metric: the average classification accuracy on testing set over U units. We compare our proposed framework to a random labelling strategy, which is teacher-free.

Implementation Details. We implement all the approaches with Pytorch 1.7.0. For the training models, we use Adam [10] with 1 patient per iteration on both MIMIC-III and MIMIC-IV. We randomly split the data into a training set and test set with ratio of 80% to 20%. The drop-out strategies (the drop-out rate is 0.1) are used for all the approaches. We set dimension $d = 200$ for all the baselines and the proposed model.

4.3   Experimental Results

Prediction Performance of Trained Student. Table 2. shows the average testing accuracy and corresponding standard deviations of the MaTe-Labelling pipeline compared with the baseline for the predictive tasks over three cohorts in the two MIMIC datasets. The results show that the proposed MaTe-Labelling pipeline outperforms baseline Random strategy on both MIMIC-III and MIMIC-IV datasets. It is obvious that the benefits of machine teaching to import global knowledge to students on individual units by selecting useful and informative samples. Specifically, the average testing accuracy of MaTe-Labelling increases by 9.2% on the task of Cancer vs. Diabetes compared to Random strategy.

Table 2. Performance comparison of classification tasks.

Dataset	Model	Testing accuracy (%)		
		Canc. vs Diab.	Canc. vs Heart.	Diab. vs Heart.
MIMIC-III	Random	65.81 ± 5.68	73.19 ± 3.81	80.63 ± 1.00
	MaTe-Labelling	$\mathbf{75.01 \pm 1.73}$	$\mathbf{74.47 \pm 3.74}$	$\mathbf{82.36 \pm 2.62}$
MIMIC-IV	Random	75.58 ± 6.41	73.10 ± 7.00	78.06 ± 4.63
	MaTe-Labelling	$\mathbf{78.99 \pm 2.49}$	$\mathbf{74.54 \pm 5.15}$	$\mathbf{79.47 \pm 5.93}$

Testing Accuracy over Iterations. Figure 2 and 3 depict the testing accuracy for all models over three prediction (Cancer vs. Diabetes, Cancer vs. Heart Failure and Diabetes vs. Heart Failure) tasks on both MIMIC datasets with iteration number varying from 1 to 200. The two figures show that MaTe-Labelling outperforms the baseline model with increasing iteration number.

The results in Fig. 2 show that the student model can converge much faster using the example provided by the teacher and labelled by domain expert, showing the effectiveness of our MaTe-Labelling pipeline. Particularly, we find that the MaTe-Labelling consistently achieves faster convergence than the random labelling over task of Cancer vs. Diabetes on MIMIC-III dataset. The results over task of Diabetes vs. Heart Failure also show that the MaTe-Labelling is much stable than random labelling.

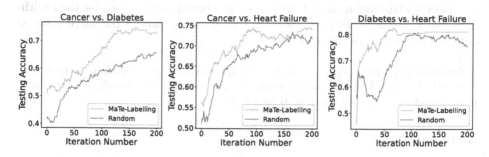

Fig. 2. Average testing accuracy on MIMIC-III with 3 units.

In contrast to the results on MIMIC-III, Fig. 3 show that the random strategy achieves better performance when the iteration number is less than 50. One possible reason is that the size of MIMIC-IV is much larger than MIMIC-III and learning ability of the student model is weak, thus, the MaTe-Laballing obtains the lower performance. However, we find that MaTe-Laballing can converge much faster with increasing iteration number when the number is larger than about 50. We also observe the similar stability issue about random strategy over task of Cancer vs. Diabetes.

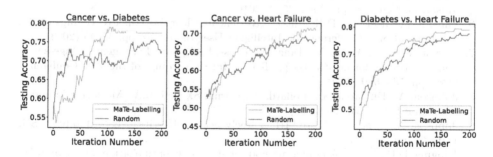

Fig. 3. Average testing accuracy on MIMIC-IV with 3 units.

5 Conclusion

In this paper, we have proposed a novel Machine Teaching-based Labelling (MaTe-Labelling) framework. It enables iterative guidance for the student to select samples that are most worth labelling, which largely reduces human efforts for labelling. On the other hand, MaTe-Labelling has also enabled teacher to provide efficient data services and strong guidance to student without releasing any extra information, which effectively prevents regulation and information security breaches. The effectiveness and efficiency of the proposed pipeline has been empirically demonstrated on two publicly available healthcare datasets in comparison with baseline methods. This work has broad implications for the healthcare sector to facilitate data modelling in instances where the large labelled datasets are not accessible to each unit.

Acknowledgements. This research is supported by an Australian Government Research Training Program Scholarship. We also thank the Australian Government Department of Health for supporting this work.

References

1. Balcan, M.F., Hanneke, S., Vaughan, J.W.: The true sample complexity of active learning. Mach. Learn. **80**(2), 111–139 (2010)
2. Baytas, I.M., Xiao, C., Zhang, X., Wang, F., Jain, A.K., Zhou, J.: Patient subtyping via time-aware LSTM networks. In: Proceedings of the 23rd ACM SIGKDD International Conference on Knowledge Discovery and Data Mining, pp. 65–74 (2017)
3. Cakmak, M., Thomaz, A.L.: Eliciting good teaching from humans for machine learners. Artif. Intell. **217**, 198–215 (2014)
4. Choi, E., Bahadori, M.T., Song, L., Stewart, W.F., Sun, J.: GRAM: graph-based attention model for healthcare representation learning. In: SIGKDD, pp. 787–795. ACM (2017)
5. Choi, E., Bahadori, M.T., Sun, J., Kulas, J., Schuetz, A., Stewart, W.: RETAIN: an interpretable predictive model for healthcare using reverse time attention mechanism. In: NeurIPS, pp. 3504–3512 (2016)
6. Fails, J.A., Olsen Jr., D.R.: Interactive machine learning. In: Proceedings of the 8th International Conference on Intelligent User Interfaces, pp. 39–45 (2003)
7. Gao, J., Xiao, C., Wang, Y., Tang, W., Glass, L.M., Sun, J.: Stagenet: Stage-aware neural networks for health risk prediction. In: Proceedings of the Web Conference 2020, pp. 530–540 (2020)
8. Johnson, A., Bulgarelli, L., Pollard, T., Horng, S., Celi, L.A., Mark, R.: Mimic-iv (version 0.4). PhysioNet (2020)
9. Johnson, A.E., et al.: MIMIC-III, a freely accessible critical care database. Sci. Data **3**, 160035 (2016)
10. Kingma, D.P., Ba, J.: Adam: a method for stochastic optimization. arXiv preprint arXiv:1412.6980 (2014)
11. Lee, D., et al.: Generating sequential electronic health records using dual adversarial autoencoder. J. Am. Med. Inform. Assoc. **27**(9), 1411–1419 (2020)
12. Liu, M., Jiang, L., Liu, J., Wang, X., Zhu, J., Liu, S.: Improving learning-from-crowds through expert validation. In: IJCAI, pp. 2329–2336 (2017)
13. Liu, W., et al.: Iterative machine teaching. In: International Conference on Machine Learning, pp. 2149–2158. PMLR (2017)
14. Long, G., Shen, T., Tan, Y., Gerrard, L., Clarke, A., Jiang, J.: Federated learning for privacy-preserving open innovation future on digital health. arXiv preprint arXiv:2108.10761 (2021)

15. Ma, F., You, Q., Xiao, H., Chitta, R., Zhou, J., Gao, J.: KAME: knowledge-based attention model for diagnosis prediction in healthcare. In: CIKM, pp. 743–752. ACM, October 2018
16. Nguyen, P., Tran, T., Wickramasinghe, N., Venkatesh, S.: Deepr: a convolutional net for medical records. IEEE J. Biomed. Health Inform. **21**(1), 22–30 (2017)
17. Peng, X., Long, G., Pan, S., Jiang, J., Niu, Z.: Attentive dual embedding for understanding medical concepts in electronic health records. In: IJCNN, pp. 1–8. IEEE (2019)
18. Peng, X., Long, G., Shen, T., Wang, S., Jiang, J., Zhang, C.: BiteNet: bidirectional temporal encoder network to predict medical outcomes. In: 2020 IEEE International Conference on Data Mining (ICDM), pp. 412–421. IEEE (2020)
19. Peng, X., Shen, T., Wang, S., Niu, Z., Zhang, C., et al.: MIMO: mutual integration of patient journey and medical ontology for healthcare representation learning. arXiv preprint arXiv:2107.09288 (2021)
20. Pham, T., Tran, T., Phung, D., Venkatesh, S.: DeepCare: a deep dynamic memory model for predictive medicine. In: Bailey, J., Khan, L., Washio, T., Dobbie, G., Huang, J.Z., Wang, R. (eds.) PAKDD 2016. LNCS (LNAI), vol. 9652, pp. 30–41. Springer, Cham (2016). https://doi.org/10.1007/978-3-319-31750-2_3
21. Settles, B.: Active learning. Synth. Lect. Artif. Intell. Mach. Learn. **6**(1), 1–114 (2012)
22. Settles, B.: Active learning literature survey (2009)
23. Shickel, B., Tighe, P.J., Bihorac, A., Rashidi, P.: Deep EHR: a survey of recent advances in deep learning techniques for electronic health record (EHR) analysis. IEEE J. Biomed. Health Inform. **22**(5), 1589–1604 (2018)
24. Singla, A., Bogunovic, I., Bartók, G., Karbasi, A., Krause, A.: Near-optimally teaching the crowd to classify. In: International Conference on Machine Learning, pp. 154–162. PMLR (2014)
25. Song, L., Cheong, C.W., Yin, K., Cheung, W.K., Cm, B.: Medical concept embedding with multiple ontological representations. In: IJCAI, pp. 4613–4619 (2019)
26. Wang, Y., Long, G., Peng, X., Clarke, A., Stevenson, R., Gerrard, L.: Interactive deep metric learning for healthcare cohort discovery. In: Le, T.D., et al. (eds.) AusDM 2019. CCIS, vol. 1127, pp. 208–221. Springer, Singapore (2019). https://doi.org/10.1007/978-981-15-1699-3_17
27. Zhao, J., Chen, Y., Zhang, W.: Differential privacy preservation in deep learning: challenges, opportunities and solutions. IEEE Access **7**, 48901–48911 (2019)
28. Zhu, X.: Machine teaching for Bayesian learners in the exponential family. In: NIPS, pp. 1905–1913 (2013)
29. Zhu, X.: Machine teaching: an inverse problem to machine learning and an approach toward optimal education. In: AAAI, vol. 29 (2015)

Predicting COVID-19 Patient Shielding: A Comprehensive Study

Vithya Yogarajan$^{(\boxtimes)}$ (iD), Jacob Montiel (iD), Tony Smith (iD), and Bernhard Pfahringer (iD)

Department of Computer Science, University of Waikato, Hamilton, New Zealand
vy1@students.waikato.ac.nz

Abstract. There are many ways machine learning and big data analytics are used in the fight against the COVID-19 pandemic, including predictions, risk management, diagnostics, and prevention. This study focuses on predicting COVID-19 patient shielding—identifying and protecting patients who are clinically extremely vulnerable from coronavirus. This study focuses on techniques used for the multi-label classification of medical text. Using the information published by the United Kingdom NHS and the World Health Organisation, we present a novel approach to predicting COVID-19 patient shielding as a multi-label classification problem. We use publicly available, de-identified ICU medical text data for our experiments. The labels are derived from the published COVID-19 patient shielding data. We present an extensive comparison across 12 multi-label classifiers from the simple binary relevance to neural networks and the most recent transformers. To the best of our knowledge this is the first comprehensive study, where such a range of multi-label classifiers for medical text are considered. We highlight the benefits of various approaches, and argue that, for the task at hand, both predictive accuracy and processing time are essential.

Keywords: COVID-19 · Multi-label · Neural networks · Transformers · Medical text

1 Introduction

The Coronavirus disease 2019 (COVID-19) pandemic has presented a considerable challenge to the world health care system, and the management of COVID-19 is an ongoing struggle. The ability to identify and protect high-risk groups is debated by the scientific community [14]. COVID-19 patient shielding refers to identifying and protecting patients who are clinically extremely vulnerable from coronavirus. Patients in these categories include those people who have been identified by health professionals before the pandemic as being clinically extremely vulnerable, and those identified through the COVID-19 Population Risk Assessment model [5]. Such patients present with co-morbidity [5] and hence the suitability of multi-label classification techniques. The clinical risk prediction model (QCOVID) [5] was developed by the United Kingdom NHS based on a

© Springer Nature Switzerland AG 2022
G. Long et al. (Eds.): AI 2021, LNAI 13151, pp. 332–343, 2022.
https://doi.org/10.1007/978-3-030-97546-3_27

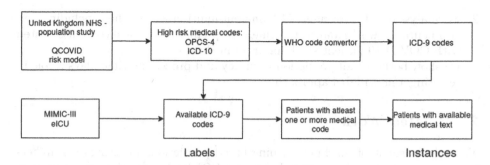

Fig. 1. Flow chat forming labels and instances for multi-label classification of predicting COVID-19 patient shielding.

cohort study of the population using data from over 6 million adults. It provides guidelines for patients who are considered high risk (clinically extremely vulnerable); for example, patients with a certain type of cancer, patients who have had organ transplants, and patients having a serious heart condition while also being pregnant.

QCOVID provides information on medical codes which can be used in hospital databases to identify patients who are at high risk and fall under the criteria of COVID-19 shielding. Due to privacy and legal issues, obtaining current patient records from hospitals is not possible [6]. However, electronic health records (EHRs) from publicly available data such as Medical Information Mart for Intensive Care (MIMIC-III) [11,15] and electronic Intensive Care Unit (eICU) [11,25] present a realistic set of EHRs obtained and de-identified from hospitals in the United States. This research presents a novel approach of considering COVID-19 patient shielding as a multi-label problem (see Fig. 1 for details). Multi-label classification assigns a set of labels to an instance. From a collection of labels, each record will be assigned relevant medical codes/labels. Using the medical codes presented in QCOVID and the code conversions presented by the WHO, we identify and predict patients with one or more high-risk medical codes associated with EHRs in MIMIC-III and eICU.

This research presents an extensive comparative study across 12 multi-label classifiers starting from the simplest binary relevance with logistic regression to neural networks and several transformers. We highlight the advantages and disadvantages of these classifiers when applied to predicting COVID-19 patient shielding. We present overall predictive accuracy as well as label F1-scores where each label is a high-risk COVID-19 medical code. We show that, in addition to the overall predictive accuracy, processing time plays a big role in decision making.[1]

The contributions of this work are:

1. we present a novel approach of considering predicting COVID-19 patient shielding as a multi-label problem;

---

[1] The code to recreate the experiments and evaluations described in this paper is accessible at: https://github.com/vithyayogarajan/COVID-19-Patient-Shielding.

2. we analyse the effectiveness of 12 different multi-label classifiers including several neural networks and transformers for predicting medical codes associated with COVID-19 patient shielding from medical text;
3. we show both overall prediction accuracy and processing time plays a role in selecting a multi-label approach;

2   Related Work

The advancement of machine learning-based predictions motivates researchers to consider ways to help in the fight against COVID-19, and there are numerous ways in which this can be achieved [1]. The year 2020 has seen many examples of machine learning approaches applied to various aspects of the COVID-19 pandemic. Some examples of machine learning approaches include:

- a hybrid machine learning technique for pandemic predictions based on data from Hungary [24]
- a deep convolutional neural network model named CoroNet for predicting COVID-19 from chest X-ray images [16]
- support vector machines for predicting radiological findings consistent with COVID-19 from radiology text reports [21]
- classifying clinical reports using logistic regression and multinomial Naive Bayes [17]
- spectrometric data analysis for a diagnosis based study [8]

These examples are only the beginning of the endless possibilities of machine learning approaches for the COVID-19 pandemic. Several machine learning methods are used for outbreak predictive studies worldwide to make decisions and enforce control measures. The systems mentioned above are only a small subset of examples of such studies. This reflects a need for extensive comparison among machine learning models, especially for predictions from medical text.
   Yogarajan et al. (2020) [30] show domain-specific skip-gram pre-trained fastText embeddings perform better that general text pre-trained embeddings. Hence, 100 and 300-dimensional domain-specific fastText pre-trained embeddings [29,30] are used for this research. A collection of neural networks and transformer models are chosen for the predictive study in this research, based on literature where such models have been used for multi-label medical code prediction and have achieved state-of-the-art results [22,23,31].

3   Data and Labels

ICD (standards for International statistical Classification of Diseases and related health problems) codes are used to classify diseases, symptoms, signs, and causes of diseases. For this research, we use ICD-9 because the available data only includes labels for ICD-9 codes. A summary of MIMIC-III and eICU, with details of number of instances and labels, label frequencies and examples of EHRs and ICD-9 codes are presented in Table 1.

Table 1. Summary of Data for COVID-19 patient shielding, for EHRs with available relevant medical codes is included. Percentage frequency of occurrences of labels for MIMIC-III and eICU is also presented.

MIMIC-III	eICU
Critical care units at the Beth Israel Deaconess Medical Center between 2001 - 2012.	The Philips eICU program. Admitted to ICUs in 2014 and 2015 across the United States.
Free-form medical text. Eg: *"59M w HepC cirrhosis c/b grade I/II esophageal varices and portal gastropathy, p/w coffee-ground"*	Semi-structured medical text. Eg: *"infectious diseases | medications | therapeutic antibacterials | cardio | inotropic agent | norepinephrine"*
35,458 hospital admissions with discharge summaries. Text length: 60 - 9500 tokens.	34,387 patients with EHRs. Text length: 50 - 1400 tokens.
42 medical codes (labels)	25 medical codes (labels)
COVID-19 Patient Shielding, MIMIC-III	COVID-19 Patient Shielding, eICU
ICD-9 code examples: Code 285 (35%) Other and unspecified anemias Code 996 (16%) Complications peculiar to certain specified procedures	ICD-9 code examples: Code 491 (40.3%) Chronic bronchitis Code 288 (17.5%) Diseases of white blood cells

4   Multi-label Classifiers

The first and simplest multi-label classification algorithm is binary relevance (BR) [10]. A separate binary classification model is created for each label, such that any text with that label is a positive instance, and all other records form the negative instances. BR models make their predictions independently. However, for multi-label problems where there is a strong correlation between labels, a model could benefit from the result of another label when making its predictions. BR models can be 'chained' together into a sequence such that the predictions made by earlier classifiers are made available as additional features for the later classifiers. Such a configuration is called a classifier chain (CC) [26]. Ensembles of classifier chains (ECC) built with diverse random chaining orders can help mitigate the effect of chaining order. In this research, logistic regression (LR) is used as the base classifier for both BR and ECC. Figure 2a provides a flow chart for BR and ECC, where document embeddings for each clinical document are used as features. Document level embeddings are computed by obtaining the vector sum of the embeddings for each word in the document and then

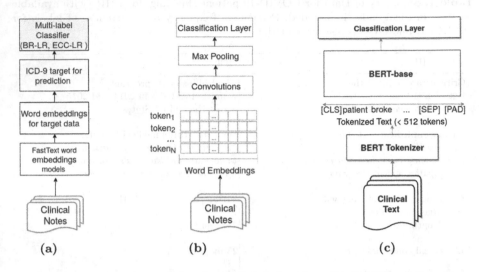

Fig. 2. (a) Flowchart for traditional multi-label classifiers; (b) CNNText [18] architecture; and (c) BERT-base model for multi-label classification.

Table 2. Summary of transformer models. Except for general text pre-trained models Longformer and TransformerXL, all other models included in this research can only handle a sequence length of at most 512 tokens. Continuous training approach would initialize with the standard BERT model, pre-trained using Wikipedia and BookCorpus. It then continues the pre-training process with masked language modelling and next sentence prediction using domain-specific data. Similarly for BioMed-RoBERTa.

Transformers	Training data	Model details
BERT [9]	Books + Wiki	12-layers with a hidden size of 768, 12 self-attention heads, 110M parameter neural network architecture
ClinicalBERT [2]	MIMIC-III	Continuous training of BERT-base
PubMedBERT [12]	PubMed	BERT-base model architecture Trained from scratch
RoBERTa-base [20]	Web crawl	Robustly optimised BERT approach improved training methodology
BioMed-RoBERTa [13]	Scientific papers	Continuous training of RoBERTa-base
TransformerXL [7]	Can handle documents with > 512 tokens. Models longer-term dependency by combining recurrence and relative positional encoding Training Data: general text including Wiki	
Longformer [3]	Can handle documents with > 512 tokens Provides computational and memory efficiency Training Data: Books + Wiki + Realnews + Stories	

normalising the sum to have length one, to ensure that documents of different lengths have representations of similar magnitudes.

CNNText [18] combines one-dimensional convolutions with a max-over-time pooling layer and a fully connected layer. Each word or token in the clinical document is mapped to its k-dimensional embeddings using the lookup table for a given pre-trained embeddings model. A new feature is produced using the convolution operation, and max-over-time pooling is applied over the feature map to capture the most important feature value. Multiple filters are used with varying window sizes. The final prediction is made by computing a weighted combination of the pooled values and applying a sigmoid function. A simple architecture of CNNText is presented in Fig. 2b.

Gated Recurrent Units (GRU) [4] are a type of recurrent neural networks which are designed to better handle vanishing gradients. Bidirectional GRU (Bi-GRU) considers both sequences from left to right and the reverse order. As with CNNText, clinical documents are mapped to their embeddings, and a sigmoid activation function is used.

Mullenbach et al. (2018) [23] present Convolutional Attention for Multi-Label classification (CAML), which achieves SOTA results for predicting ICD-9 codes from MIMIC III data [22]. CAML combines convolution networks with an attention mechanism. Simultaneously, a second module is used to learn embeddings of the descriptions of ICD-9 codes to improve the predictions of less frequent labels. A regularising objective with a trade-off hyperparameter was added to the loss function of CAML. This variant is called Description Regularized-CAML (DR-CAML) [23].

This research includes several variations of the most recent developments of NLP transformers [28]. In this paper, we perform transfer learning of pre-trained transformer models by fine tuning for predicting COVID-19 patient shielding. All parameters are fine-tuned end-to-end. A summary of Transformer models used in this research is presented in Table 2. BERT-base variations and RoBERTa-base variations can only handle a maximum sequence length of 512, whereas Longformer and TransformerXL can handle longer sequences. Continuous training of transformers refers to existing general text pre-trained models that are further trained with a masked language model and next sentence prediction using domain-specific data. The vocabulary is the same as the original BERT model, which is considered a disadvantage for domain-specific tasks [12]. Alternatively, training from scratch indicates that the models are pre-trained with domain-specific data only and the vocabulary of these models is domain-specific. Figure 2c provides an example of a BERT-base model.

5   Experimental Setup

Neural network models presented in this research are implemented using PyTorch. All evaluations were done using sklearn metrics and the transformer implementations are based on the open-source PyTorch-transformer repository. For multi-label classification MEKA [27], an open-source Java system specifically designed to support multi-label classification experiments, is used for BR and ECC. Domain-specific fastText embeddings [29,30] of 100-dimensions are used for neural networks and 300-dimensions for BR and ECC.

Transformer models were fine-tuned on all layers without freezing. Adam [19], an adaptive learning rate optimisation algorithm, is used as the optimiser for all neural networks. A non-linear sigmoid function $f(z) = \frac{1}{1+e^{-z}}$, is used as the activation function. All experiments using ECC and BR are validated through 10-fold cross-validation. Due to resource restrictions, all neural network results, including transformers, use random seed train-test hold-out set validation where the results are averaged over three runs. Experiments for neural networks and transformers were run on a 12 core Intel(R) Xeon(R) W-2133 CPU @ 3.60 GHz, and a GPU device GV100GL [Quadro GV100]. Experiments for BR and ECC were run on a 4 core Intel i7-6700K CPU @ 4.00 GHz with 64 GB of RAM.

For MIMIC-III data, discharge summaries are used as the free-form medical text and each hospital admission is treated as an instance. For ECC and BR, all available discharge summaries for each hospital admission are treated as one document, and 300 dimensional features are obtained from fastText pre-trained domain-specific embeddings. For embedding-based neural networks CNNtext, BiGRU, CAML and DRCAML, the pre-processed tokens from discharge summaries are truncated to 3,000 words. For BERT and RoBERTa based transformers, the input sequence is truncated to 512 tokens, and for Longformer and TransformerXL the input sequence is truncated to 3,000 and 3,072 tokens respectively. Discharge summaries were pre-processed by removing tokens that contain non alphabetic characters and special characters, and tokens that appear in fewer than three training documents. The extensively pre-processed eICU data was used 'as is' for all experiments.

6   Results

Table 3 presents a summary of overall micro and macro F1 scores for 12 multi-label classifiers and the total time per run of each experiment for both MIMIC-III and eICU data. Figure 3 presents critical difference plots based on the label F1 scores for MIMIC-III and eICU to help identify the statistical difference between the multi-label classifiers. Compared to the basic BR-LR, which requires the least time for experiments, there is a significant improvement in overall micro and macro F1 measures for MIMIC-III data. This observation is also reflected on the critical difference plots where BR-LR is the classifier with the worst ranking. Among transformer models, the micro and macro F1 scores of TransformerXL and Longformer are better than the scores of the BERT-base and RoBERTa-base models. One of the main reasons for this is that BERT-base and RoBERTa-base models are restricted by the maximum sequence length of 512 tokens, while TransformerXL and Longformer can handle longer sequences. Since MIMIC-III data are long with an average of 1,500 tokens, the ability to encode more extended input data improves accuracy. However, the total time required for the experiments using TransformerXL and Longformer is exceptionally high. On the CD plot, a bold line connects PubMedBERT to the above two transformers indicating no statistically significant difference in average ranking. Compared

Table 3. Comparison of micro-F1 and macro-F1 of ICD-9 codes for various multi-label classifiers for both MIMIC-III and eICU data. Time required per run is also presented. **Bold** is used to indicate the best results among the groups, and underline is used for overall best results. Results are averaged over three runs for neural networks and transformers. 10-fold cross validation is used for BR-LR and ECC-LR.

Classifiers	MIMIC-III			eICU		
	Micro-F1	Macro-F1	Total time (per run)	Micro-F1	Macro-F1	Total time (per run)
BR-LR	0.39	0.26	**12 min**	**0.54**	**0.28**	**7 min**
ECC-LR	**0.45**	**0.27**	38 min	0.51	**0.28**	34 min
CNNText	0.58	**0.42**	46 min	0.59	**0.36**	45 min
BiGRU	0.59	0.31	216 min	0.59	0.35	210 min
CAML	**0.61**	0.40	49 min	0.60	0.32	48 min
DRCAML	0.60	0.39	64 min	**0.61**	0.32	60 min
BERT-base	0.50	0.44	10 h	0.60	0.36	11 h
ClinicalBERT	0.51	0.45	16 h	0.60	0.36	11 h
BioMed-RoBERTa	0.53	0.45	12 h	0.61	0.37	11 h
PubMedBERT	0.54	0.48	16 h	<u>0.64</u>	0.39	14 h
Longformer	0.58	0.50	82 h	0.61	<u>0.40</u>	49 h
TransformerXL	<u>0.65</u>	<u>0.51</u>	206 h	0.63	<u>0.40</u>	53 h

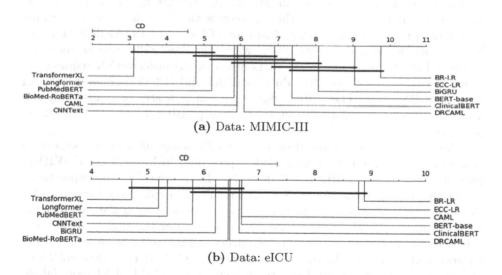

(a) Data: MIMIC-III

(b) Data: eICU

Fig. 3. Critical difference plots of label F1 scores for COVID-19 patient shielding with MIMIC-III (top) and eICU (bottom). Nemenyi post-hoc test (95% confidence level), identifying statistical differences between multi-label classifiers presented in Table 3. Critical difference is calculated for individual label F1 scores.

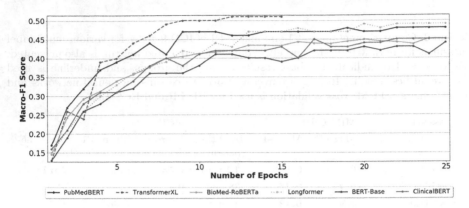

Fig. 4. Macro F1 scores of transformer models for COVID-19 patient shielding over number of epochs for MIMIC-III data. Due to resource restrictions, TransformerXL was only run for 15 epochs.

to PubMedBERT, Longformer requires 5 times more processing time and TransformerXL almost 13 times more processing time. Among the embedding-based neural networks, CNNText and CAML are the best performing models, and they require less than an hour in total for an experiment. Micro-F1 scores of embeddings-based neural networks are better than those of most transformer models, except for TransformerXL.

For eICU data, as observed in MIMIC-III, BR-LR and ECC-LR are the two worst-ranking classifiers in the CD-plot, with other classifiers performing better than ECC and BR overall. The micro-F1 score of PubMedBERT is the best among the multi-label classifiers, with a minimal difference in macro-F1 compared to the macro-F1 score of Longformer. TransformerXL requires 3.8 times more processing time than PubMedBERT and 71.6 times more processing time than CNNText. The Critical difference plot indicates no statistically significant difference between most classifiers, except BR-LR and ECC-LR (worst performers).

Figure 4 presents a comparison of macro F1 scores after each epoch for a range of 1 to 25 for transformer models presented in Table 3 for COVID-19 patient shielding using MIMIC-III data. For TransformerXL, the experiments were only performed for 15 epochs as the required computational resources for these experiments are very high. For macro-F1 scores, there is a steady increase in the number of epochs, where more are required before the model stabilise. For this research, macro-F1 scores were prioritised, as macro-F1 is an average over F1 scores of each label. In the case of predicting COVID-19 patient shielding, an increase in macro-F1 will indicate an increase in individual F1 score labels, where each label refers to a medical code associated with patient at high risk of COVID-19. The total training times presented in Table 3 are calculated for 20 epochs for all transformer models, except for TransformerXL.

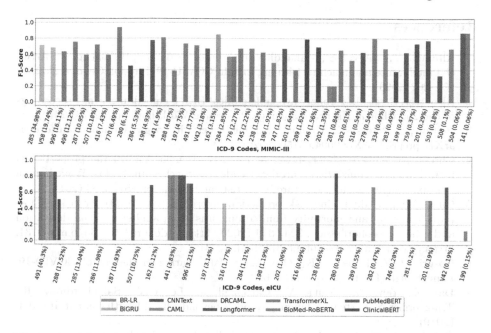

Fig. 5. Best F1 scores and corresponding multi-label classifiers for individual labels with MIMIC-III (top) and eICU (bottom). Codes 235 and 142 for MIMIC-III data and code 501 for eICU are omitted, as all models fail to predict them.

Figure 5 presents the best F1-scores for each label, and different colours are used to differentiate the corresponding classifiers. For MIMIC-III data, TransformerXL is the clear winner with the highest number of best F1 scores. For eICU data, PubMedBERT is marginally better than TransformerXL and CNNText.

7 Discussion

There are many examples of the use of machine learning approaches in the fight against COVID-19. We propose a novel multi-label approach to predicting COVID-19 patient shielding from EHRs using publicly available information on COVID-19 and publicly available data. We present an extensive study on 12 different multi-label approaches to predicting medical codes where we include simple methods such as BR and ECC, examples of traditional word embeddings based neural networks, and the most recent transformer models. If overall predictive accuracy is the only deciding factor TransformerXL is the best option. However, given pandemic situations where time is a significant factor, the predictive accuracy of models is not the only factor to consider in selecting an approach. To the best of our knowledge, this is the first study to consider such a range of multi-label text classification models to enable a better understanding of the potential to help fight against COVID-19.

References

1. Alimadadi, A., Aryal, S., Manandhar, I., Munroe, P.B., Joe, B., Cheng, X.: Artificial intelligence and machine learning to fight COVID-19. Physiol. Genomics **52**(4), 200–202 (2020)
2. Alsentzer, E., et al.: Publicly available clinical BERT embeddings. In: Proceedings of the 2nd Clinical Natural Language Processing Workshop, pp. 72–78 (2019)
3. Beltagy, I., Peters, M., Cohan, A.: Longformer: the long-document transformer. arXiv preprint arXiv:2004.05150 (2020)
4. Cho, K., van Merrienboer, B., Bahdanau, D., Bengio, Y.: On the properties of neural machine translation: encoder-decoder approaches. In: Eighth Workshop on Syntax, Semantics and Structure in Statistical Translation (SSST-8) (2014)
5. Clift, A.K., et al.: Living risk prediction algorithm (QCOVID) for risk of hospital admission and mortality from coronavirus 19 in adults: national derivation and validation cohort study. BMJ **371** (2020). https://doi.org/10.1136/bmj.m3731. https://www.bmj.com/content/371/bmj.m3731
6. Cosgriff, C.V., Ebner, D.K., Celi, L.A.: Data sharing in the era of COVID-19. Lancet Digit. Health **2**(5), e224 (2020)
7. Dai, Z., Yang, Z., Yang, Y., Carbonell, J., Le, Q.V., Salakhutdinov, R.: Transformer-XL: attentive language models beyond a fixed-length context. In: ACL (2019)
8. Delafiori, J., et al.: Covid-19 automated diagnosis and risk assessment through metabolomics and machine learning. Anal. Chem. **93**(4), 2471–2479 (2021)
9. Devlin, J., Chang, M., Lee, K., Toutanova, K.: BERT: pre-training of deep bidirectional transformers for language understanding. In: NAACL-HLT (2019)
10. Godbole, S., Sarawagi, S.: Discriminative methods for multi-labeled classification. In: Dai, H., Srikant, R., Zhang, C. (eds.) PAKDD 2004. LNCS (LNAI), vol. 3056, pp. 22–30. Springer, Heidelberg (2004). https://doi.org/10.1007/978-3-540-24775-3_5
11. Goldberger, A.L., et al.: PhysioBank, PhysioToolkit, and PhysioNet: components of a new research resource for complex physiologic signals. Circulation **101**(23), e215–e220 (2000)
12. Gu, Y., et al.: Domain-specific language model pretraining for biomedical natural language processing. arXiv preprint arXiv:2007.15779 (2020)
13. Gururangan, S., et al.: Don't stop pretraining: adapt language models to domains and tasks. In: Proceedings of ACL (2020)
14. Ioannidis, J.P.: Precision shielding for covid-19: metrics of assessment and feasibility of deployment. BMJ Glob. Health **6**(1), e004614 (2021)
15. Johnson, A.E., et al.: MIMIC-III, a freely accessible critical care database. Sci. Data **3**, 160035 (2016)
16. Khan, A.I., Shah, J.L., Bhat, M.M.: CoroNet: a deep neural network for detection and diagnosis of covid-19 from chest x-ray images. Comput. Methods Programs Biomed. **196**, 105581 (2020)
17. Khanday, A.M.U.D., Rabani, S.T., Khan, Q.R., Rouf, N., Din, M.M.U.: Machine learning based approaches for detecting covid-19 using clinical text data. Int. J. Inf. Technol. **12**(3), 731–739 (2020)
18. Kim, Y.: Convolutional neural networks for sentence classification. In: Proceedings of the 2014 Conference on Empirical Methods in Natural Language Processing (EMNLP), pp. 1746–1751. Association for Computational Linguistics (2014)

19. Kingma, D.P., Ba, J.: Adam: a method for stochastic optimization. In: International Conference on Learning Representations (ICLR) (2015)
20. Liu, Y., et al.: RoBERTa: a robustly optimized BERT pretraining approach. arXiv preprint arXiv:1907.11692 (2019)
21. López-Úbeda, P., Díaz-Galiano, M.C., Martín-Noguerol, T., Luna, A., Ureña-López, L.A., Martín-Valdivia, M.T.: Covid-19 detection in radiological text reports integrating entity recognition. Comput. Biol. Med. **127**, 104066 (2020)
22. Moons, E., Khanna, A., Akkasi, A., Moens, M.F.: A comparison of deep learning methods for ICD coding of clinical records. Appl. Sci. **10**(15), 5262 (2020)
23. Mullenbach, J., Wiegreffe, S., Duke, J., Sun, J., Eisenstein, J.: Explainable prediction of medical codes from clinical text. In: Proceedings of the 2018 Conference of the North American Chapter of the Association for Computational Linguistics: Human Language Technologies, vol. 1. ACL, New Orleans (2018)
24. Pinter, G., Felde, I., Mosavi, A., Ghamisi, P., Gloaguen, R.: Covid-19 pandemic prediction for Hungary; a hybrid machine learning approach. Mathematics **8**(6), 890 (2020)
25. Pollard, T.J., Johnson, A.E.W., Raffa, J.D., Celi, L.A., Mark, R.G., Badawi, O.: The eICU collaborative research database, a freely available multi-center database for critical care research. Sci. Data **5**, 180178 (2018)
26. Read, J., Pfahringer, B., Holmes, G., Frank, E.: Classifier chains for multi-label classification. Mach. Learn. **85**(3), 333 (2011)
27. Read, J., Reutemann, P., Pfahringer, B., Holmes, G.: MEKA: a multi-label/multi-target extension to WEKA. J. Mach. Learn. Res. **17**(21), 1–5 (2016). http://jmlr.org/papers/v17/12-164.html
28. Vaswani, A., et al.: Attention is all you need. Adv. Neural. Inf. Process. Syst. **30**, 5998–6008 (2017)
29. Yogarajan, V., Gouk, H., Smith, T., Mayo, M., Pfahringer, B.: Comparing high dimensional word embeddings trained on medical text to bag-of-words for predicting medical codes. In: Nguyen, N.T., Jearanaitanakij, K., Selamat, A., Trawiński, B., Chittayasothorn, S. (eds.) ACIIDS 2020. LNCS (LNAI), vol. 12033, pp. 97–108. Springer, Cham (2020). https://doi.org/10.1007/978-3-030-41964-6_9
30. Yogarajan, V., Montiel, J., Smith, T., Pfahringer, B.: Seeing the whole patient: using multi-label medical text classification techniques to enhance predictions of medical codes. arXiv preprint arXiv:2004.00430 (2020)
31. Yogarajan, V., Montiel, J., Smith, T., Pfahringer, B.: Transformers for multi-label classification of medical text: an empirical comparison. In: Tucker, A., Henriques Abreu, P., Cardoso, J., Pereira Rodrigues, P., Riaño, D. (eds.) AIME 2021. LNCS (LNAI), vol. 12721, pp. 114–123. Springer, Cham (2021). https://doi.org/10.1007/978-3-030-77211-6_12

Machine Learning Algorithms in Application to COVID-19 Severity Prediction in Patients

Alisher Ikramov[1]([✉])(iD), Khikmat Anvarov[2](iD), Visolat Sharipova[2](iD),
Nurbek Iskhakov[2](iD), Abdusalom Abdurakhmonov[2](iD), and Azamat Alimov[2](iD)

[1] Institute of Mathematics, Tashkent, Uzbekistan
a.ikramov@mathinst.uz
[2] Republican Scientific Center for Emergency Medicine, Tashkent, Uzbekistan

Abstract. Uzbekistan as well as the rest of the world faces the third wave of COVID-19 and uses machine learning algorithms to predict the adverse outcome during the admission of new patients. We collected the dataset of 1145 patients admitted to the Republican Center for Emergency Medicine. We use different machine learning models to predict the COVID-19 severe course. This study uses feature selection procedures based on statistical tests and the elimination of linearly dependent features. The resulting multilayer perceptron yields a ROC AUC of 86.9% on the test set outperforming other machine learning algorithms and several competing works. The model relies on easily collected features without blood laboratory testing. It increases an availability of the reliable risk prediction to developing countries.

Keywords: Multilayer perceptron · Feature elimination · COVID-19 · Machine learning · Artificial intelligence

1 Introduction

During the second wave of the COVID-19 pandemic, Uzbekistan had several hospitals designated to treat COVID-19 patients. One of those hospitals gathered data from admission, laboratory results, the course of the treatment, the changes in indicators, and the adverse outcome of hospitalization in order to form a dataset.

These clinics quickly stopped admitting new patients when the third wave started. Previously closed locations were opened again just to stop the admission in 2–3 days after opening due to overwhelming numbers of new patients. As special equipment is not widely accessible, doctors rely on artificial intelligence to predict the risk of developing a severe disease course. They redistribute new patients to the corresponding locations according to the predicted risk values.

The previous model [2] was trained on data gathered from March, 2020 to June, 2020. Then the Republican Center of Emergency Medicine has collected data on 1145 patients used in this study to develop a new version of the predictive software. Laboratory results of blood tests are available only on the second or the third day after admission in Uzbekistan due to insufficient equipment and great demand as more than 1000 new cases

© Springer Nature Switzerland AG 2022
G. Long et al. (Eds.): AI 2021, LNAI 13151, pp. 344–355, 2022.
https://doi.org/10.1007/978-3-030-97546-3_28

occur daily. Therefore, it is important to have reliable predictions based on anamnesis morbi and anamnesis vitae in the absence of lab results.

The previous study [2] dealt with highly imbalanced classes (only 8% of the patients developed severe courses) and used the anomaly detection approach to overcome the imbalance. In this study we collected a new data when asymptomatic and most of the mild patients were not admitted to the hospitals due to the overload. The same anomaly detection methods would not work on new data, therefore, this study used supervised machine learning algorithms. Furthermore, we use the linearly dependent features' elimination procedure used during the model development stage.

1.1 Related Work

Machine learning algorithms were applied to predict the severity in patients worldwide. They vary in several aspects: the accessibility of different indicators, the number of patients studied, and machine learning algorithms used. Neural Networks, Logistic Regression, and Decision Trees (including Random Forest) are the most popular methods. Logistic Regression coefficients help explain the model to medical doctors, while Neural Networks are not well interpretable models. Table 4 contains the comparison of performances and datasets of the following works.

The neural network was trained with top valuable tests (aPTT, CRP, and fibrinogen) [3] on dataset of patients admitted between February and July, 2020 in Dubai. A similar performance was achieved in [4] on comparison of Artificial neural networks, decision trees, partial least squares discriminant analysis, and K nearest neighbor algorithm models. The authors used hyperferritinaemia, hypocalcaemia, pulmonary hypoxia, hypoxemia, metabolic and respiratory acidosis, low urinary pH, and high lactate dehydrogenase levels as indicators.

A retrospective study (March-May, 2020) collected clinical and biochemical parameters at admission [5]. Using stepwise model selection by Akaike Information Criterion (AIC), the authors built the severity score Covichem. Among 26 tested variables, seven were the independent predictors of severity used in Covichem: obesity, cardiovascular conditions, plasma sodium, albumin, ferritin, LDH and CK (accuracy 0.87). The model used logistic regression to classify the patients.

Another study [6] included 116 patients with severe COVID-19. Their comorbidities, body temperature, blood laboratory test results were independent risk factors for severe disease. A nomogram was generated based on these eight variables with a predictive accuracy of 85.9% and an AUC ROC of 0.858 (95% CI, 0.823–0.893).

The model trained on test results taken on the day of admission demonstrated AUC 0.89 on external validation (N = 202, 95% CI: 0.85–0.93) in [7] (January-August, 2020). The predictive model was developed using the beta coefficients for different predictors identified from logistic regression. A risk score including the following components was derived from Cox regression: gender, age, diabetes mellitus, hypertension, atrial fibrillation, heart failure, ischemic heart disease, peripheral vascular disease, stroke, dementia, liver diseases, gastrointestinal bleeding, cancer, and blood laboratory test results.

Respiratory rate, lactate, blood pressure (diastolic and systolic), neutrophils, and oxygen saturation level were found [8] as the most significant and common parameters for the entire group of patients. The exceptional cases are venous PO_2, venous saturated O_2, and heart rate. The number of the lymphocytes decreased is correlated with the increasing severity level of the patients with COVID-19. The authors also observed the opposite scenario for neutrophil data, as in, the lymphocytes parameter increased if the patient's condition deteriorated toward a severe situation.

The transitive Sequential Pattern Mining (tSPM) along with a dimensionality reduction algorithm (MSMR) were used in [9] to predict COVID-19 adverse outcomes of over 13000 patients. The mean AUC ROC for mortality prediction was 0.91, while the prediction performance ranged between 0.80 and 0.81 for the ICU, hospitalization, and ventilation. The models that relied on both the combined demographic and clinical features resulted in the best modeling performance (as measured by AUC ROC).

Our work differs from previous research in several key aspects:

1. the use of anamnesis vitae and anamnesis morbi without laboratory blood results as the inputs to the model;
2. the large dataset consists of 1145 patients admitted to one hospital, which reduces the potential noise in data;

2   Materials and Methods

2.1   Dataset

The Republican Center for Emergency Medicine collected data on 1145 COVID-19 patients from March 2020 to December 2020 admitted only to this Center. There were 185 lethal cases, 161 mild cases, and 799 severe cases. The total number of features is 192, including laboratory test results on the first day (complete blood count, biochemical analysis, coagulation testing, c reactive protein, interleukin 1 and 6), same tests on the fifth day, results of CT scans, prescribed medicine (hydroxychloroquine, remdesevir, favipiravir, dexamethasone, antibiotics, fluconazole, aspirin, heparin, enoxaparin, diuretics, antihypertensive medications, and others), etc. The anonymized dataset is available publicly upon request.

The patients in this dataset received different treatment from the patients in the previous study as the disease has been better understood. Moreover, it has more patients treated in the same hospital with the same laboratory equipment used. The demographics of patients in the study are presented in Table 1.

Table 1. Average, standard deviation and range of age, days of admission, weight, height, BMI, and sex of admitted patients in three groups

Feature	Mild patients, n = 161		Severe patients, n = 799		Lethal outcome, n = 185	
	Average ± standard deviation	Range	Average ± standard deviation	Range	Average ± standard deviation	Range
Age	46.3 ± 18.0	1–90	55.8 ± 15.3	3–95	64.0 ± 13.8	6–90
Days of admission	4.9 ± 4.4	1–20	10.5 ± 5.7	1–38	7.8 ± 7.1	1–40
Weight	76.7 ± 20.4	11–168	82.4 ± 15.8	15–150	82.4 ± 16.1	11–125
Height	166.9 ± 14.5	75–190	169.2 ± 8.9	80–196	168.4 ± 8.8	94–188
BMI	27.2 ± 5.8	14.2–58	28.7 ± 5.2	15.5–59	29.0 ± 5.4	12.4–44
Female	50.9%		49.2%		35.7%	

2.2 Approach

To reduce the dimensionality of the classification problem we employed a feature selection procedure. We applied different statistical tests on the set to select 25 features from 192 given. The tests were Kolmogorov-Smirnov [10], Z-test [11], Kruskal-Wallis H test [12], and Mann-Whitney U test [13]. The hypothesis was that both compared groups had the same distribution. If the p-value is less than 0.01, then the hypothesis is rejected. Thus, the feature is distributed statistically different in compared groups. We use p-value of 0.01 instead of 0.05 to increase certainty in selected features. Table 5 in Supplementary materials shows the results of the statistical tests. We omitted those features for which values were unknown for more than a half of any group. The results of the statistical tests were used to select the most significant features.

The secondary feature selection procedure eliminates linearly dependent features. It uses the least squares model trained on the training set to predict one feature based on the values of other features, calculates the sum of squares of predicted values' errors, and finds the features with the smallest error. Those were considered as linearly dependent and were eliminated to form the second dataset. As all values were normalized, the comparison between the absolute values of residuals of different features was justified.

The study used classification algorithms such as Random Forest, Extra Trees, Logistic Regression, Support Vector Machines, k Nearest Neighbors, and Multilayer Perceptrons. We used the area under the curve (AUC) as the performance metric. Hyperparameter tuning was performed using the performance value on the validation set. The best model for each algorithm was then tested on the test set.

3 Results

The dataset was divided into three groups of patients: mild, severe, and lethal cases. Each group was randomly permuted and split into training (70%), validation (10%), and test (20%) sets.

Based on the results of the statistical tests and the availability of the data we primarily selected the following features:

- age,
- sex,
- cough (no/dry/wet),
- number of days of cough before the admission,
- body temperature,
- days of increased body temperature before the admission,
- weakness,
- headache,
- pain in muscles,
- loss of taste,
- loss of smell,
- diarrhea,
- vomiting,
- dyspnea,
- pain in the chest,
- comorbidities,
- height,
- weight,
- BMI,
- heart rate,
- breathing rate,
- SpO_2,
- systolic blood pressure,
- diastolic blood pressure,
- auscultation.

The size of the dataset did not change, only the number of features decreased. All values were normalized. The mean and standard deviation were calculated only on the training set and then applied to the validation and the test sets during normalization of the data.

We deal with the class imbalance using oversampling [13] by duplicating mild and lethal cases seven times and severe cases twice in the training set. The validation set and the test set are used as is without duplication.

The secondary feature elimination process used exclusion of linearly dependent features. The eliminated features included weakness, loss of smell, and weight. These three excluded features were in linear dependence with some of the remaining features. For example, loss of smell was covered by the loss of taste, while weight was covered by BMI. Different models using the same Machine Learning algorithms were built, tuned, and tested on two datasets – with 25 and 22 features.

Neural networks required altering the architecture of the network. It included the number of layers, the number of neurons in each layer, activation functions in each layer, the type of layers (fully connected linear and bilinear). The study used PyTorch[1]. The final architecture was selected based on the model performance on the validation set.

---

[1] Pytorch.org v.1.9.0.

The multilayer perceptrons (MLP) used for classification have one hidden layer with 10 units and differ only in the input dimensionality (22 and 25 units respectively). We use LeakyReLU after the first layer and Sigmoid after the last layer.

The results of the experiments are summarized in Table 2, where ROC AUC is calculated for the best models for each Machine Learning algorithm and each group of features.

Table 2. Test results of the best selected models of each studied Machine Learning algorithm using all features and set of features after elimination of linearly dependent ones

Algorithm	ROC AUC	
	25 features	22 features
Support Vector Machine	0.765	0.772
Random Forest	0.835	0.830
Extra Trees	**0.858**	0.853
k Nearest Neighbors	0.755	0.755
Logistic Regression	0.835	0.843
MLP	0.824	**0.869**

The best performing model is the MLP with 22 features input. The confusion matrix on the test set for the best model is given in Table 3. We can see that most of the cases are predicted correctly, but significant number of severe cases are predicted as mild or lethal. From the clinical perspective, it is more dangerous to underestimate severity of the illness as that could lead to unwarranted discharge of the patient. We can also see that lethal cases are predicted quite reliably with only 3% of lethal cases estimated as mild.

Table 3. Confusion matrix of the best Neural Network model with 22 input features (without linearly dependent features) on the test set

	Predicted mild	Predicted severe	Predicted lethal
True mild cases	21	9	3
True severe cases	22	126	16
True lethal cases	1	6	25

Extra Trees demonstrated promising results on a non-reduced set of features. Neural Networks supported the proven theorem and demonstrated the significance of eliminating linearly dependent features for the Neural Networks. Not all algorithms changed their performance after the applied feature selection. It can be explained by the fact that Random Forest and Extra Trees perform feature selection for each decision tree as part of the algorithm. The exclusion of linearly dependent features from ensemble algorithms decreased their probability of affecting the prediction.

The most popular machine learning algorithms for predicting severe course of COVID-19 are logistic regression and neural networks. The best model in this study outperformed models in [3, 4, 6, 9] (with ROC AUC 0.86, 0.86, 0.858, 0.80, respectfully) even without laboratory test results involved. The studies in [7] and [8] had a larger dataset and used important laboratory tests. However, their performance is only 3% higher. The study in [5] has the largest performance value, but their dataset was very small in comparison with the other research. The comparison between related work and ours is presented in Table 4. It demonstrates that our approach allowed to receive similar performance even without lab test results.

The main difference from the existing models is availability to all regions of the country regardless of their laboratory equipment. X-ray examination is more common and cheaper than CT scans in the country. The included different Machine Learning algorithms were selected as most common or previously used in other articles with the same aim as in the current research. The medical team continues to gather new data that could lead to a larger dataset with a possibility of using n-fold cross validation.

The use of the software helps to reduce the mortality rate due to early treatment of potentially severe patients using more appropriate drugs even when they are not in the severe state.

Table 4. Related retrospective studies dataset and the best model performance comparison. Feature selection methods include Kolmogorov-Smirnov (K-S), Z-test, Kruskal-Wallis H test (K-W), Mann-Whitney U test (M-W), Student T test, and Pearson's chi-squared test.

Research	Size of the dataset	ROC AUC	Used Lab tests	Used CT scans	Source of data	Feature selection
[3]	560	0.86	+	+	One hospital	M-W, K-W
[4]	557	0.86	+	+	Multiple clinics	PCA
[5]	303	0.91	+	+	Two hospitals	Pearson
[6]	582	0.858	+	+	Four hospitals	M-W
[7]	4442	0.89	+	+	Multiple hospitals	M-W
[8]	1945	0.89	+	−	External source	T test, Pearson
[9]	13000	0.81	+	+	Multiple hospitals	MSMR, iterated
Ours	1145	0.869	−	−	One hospital	M-W, K-W, K-S, Z-test

4 Conclusion

Although some previous research demonstrated the importance of laboratory blood tests for the prediction, the overload of hospitals during each wave does not allow doctors effectively collect and analyze all required information in time. Thus, the model in this work uses only data that can be easily obtained during the admission. It helps to distribute patients according to their risk levels. The primary feature selection procedure followed the results of statistical tests, the secondary feature selection procedure eliminated linearly dependent features. The dataset includes observation of 1145 admitted patients with different outcomes.

Neural networks outperformed other Machine Learning algorithms with ROC AUC 0.869. The features used in the model are extracted from anamnesis morbi and anamnesis vitae of the patients during the admission.

The resulting software is used on sites and by EMS workers to decide on the admission of patients to primary care centers or the specialized hospitals with large reanimation divisions. During the third wave, Uzbekistan faces more than 1000 new patients every day, and the software helps to admit patients according to their risk levels.

Acknowledgement. The authors would like to thank the staff of the Medical Centre involved in the study for collecting patients' data, and Maksim Bolonkin for the discussion, ideas of possible models to use, edition, and language correction.

Authors Contributions. AI built and tested all ML models; KA and NI collected the data, analyzed the results; VS, AA, AA evaluated results of statistical tests.

Funding. The study was fulfilled under project A-CC-2021–112/2 funded by Ministry of innovative development of the Republic of Uzbekistan.

Ethics and Privacy. Hospitals use the designed software to not miss the possible hard cases. If the software predicts a low risk of a hard course, but the examining doctor decides otherwise, the final decision on the admission of a patient is made by the doctor. The software does not use or disclose private information on patients. The database is available upon request but does not contain any information that can disclose the identity of the patients.

Conflict of Interests. The authors declare no conflict of interests.

Supplementary Materials

Table 5. Statistical tests to test the similarity in distributions of numerical features between mild, severe, and lethal groups. Tests are Kolmogorov-Smirnov (K-S), Z-test, Kruskal-Wallis H test (K-W), and Mann-Whitney U test (M-W)

Feature	Test	p-value		
		Mild vs Severe	Mild vs Lethal	Severe vs Lethal
Age	K-S	10^{-7}	10^{-19}	10^{-9}
	Z-test	10^{-12}	10^{-24}	10^{-11}
	K-W	10^{-10}	10^{-19}	10^{-11}
	M-W	10^{-10}	10^{-20}	10^{-12}
Days of cough before admission	K-S	10^{-3}	10^{-5}	0.46
	Z-test	10^{-5}	10^{-6}	0.09
	K-W	10^{-5}	10^{-5}	0.29
	M-W	10^{-6}	10^{-5}	0.15
Days of increased body temperature before the admission	K-S	10^{-9}	0.03	0.03
	Z-test	10^{-7}	10^{-3}	0.07
	K-W	10^{-10}	10^{-3}	10^{-3}
	M-W	10^{-11}	10^{-3}	10^{-3}
Weight	K-S	10^{-4}	0.01	0.68
	Z-test	10^{-4}	10^{-3}	0.99
	K-W	10^{-4}	10^{-3}	0.97
	M-W	10^{-5}	10^{-3}	0.48
BMI	K-S	10^{-4}	0.01	0.31
	Z-test	10^{-3}	10^{-3}	0.58
	K-W	10^{-4}	10^{-3}	0.65
	M-W	10^{-5}	10^{-4}	0.33
Breathing rate	K-S	10^{-9}	10^{-28}	10^{-18}
	Z-test	10^{-7}	10^{-16}	10^{-25}
	K-W	10^{-13}	10^{-26}	10^{-21}
	M-W	10^{-13}	10^{-26}	10^{-22}
SpO$_2$	K-S	10^{-4}	10^{-32}	10^{-35}
	Z-test	10^{-3}	10^{-27}	10^{-57}
	K-W	10^{-5}	10^{-33}	10^{-40}
	M-W	10^{-6}	10^{-33}	10^{-41}

(*continued*)

Table 5. (*continued*)

Feature	Test	p-value		
		Mild vs Severe	Mild vs Lethal	Severe vs Lethal
Heart rate	K-S	0.94	10^{-5}	10^{-6}
	Z-test	0.78	0.02	10^{-3}
	K-W	0.59	10^{-3}	10^{-4}
	M-W	0.29	10^{-3}	10^{-4}
Systolic blood pressure	K-S	10^{-6}	10^{-9}	10^{-5}
	Z-test	10^{-7}	10^{-3}	0.48
	K-W	10^{-8}	10^{-6}	0.03
	M-W	10^{-8}	10^{-6}	0.01
Diastolic blood pressure	K-S	10^{-4}	0.02	0.06
	Z-test	10^{-5}	0.35	0.02
	K-W	10^{-5}	0.01	0.94
	M-W	10^{-5}	10^{-3}	0.47
D-dimer	K-S	0.43	0.03	10^{-5}
	Z-test	0.45	0.68	0.84
	K-W	0.43	0.08	10^{-4}
	M-W	0.21	0.04	10^{-4}
Total blood protein	K-S	0.72	0.01	10^{-4}
	Z-test	0.74	0.05	10^{-3}
	K-W	0.74	0.05	0.01
	M-W	0.37	0.02	10^{-3}
Total bilirubin	K-S	0.04	10^{-3}	0.02
	Z-test	0.31	0.08	10^{-3}
	K-W	0.01	10^{-5}	0.01
	M-W	10^{-3}	10^{-5}	10^{-3}
Aspartate Aminotransferase	K-S	10^{-3}	10^{-3}	0.58
	Z-test	0.01	0.01	0.02
	K-W	10^{-3}	10^{-4}	0.16
	M-W	10^{-3}	10^{-4}	0.08

(*continued*)

Table 5. (*continued*)

Feature	Test	p-value		
		Mild vs Severe	Mild vs Lethal	Severe vs Lethal
Alanine Aminotransferase	K-S	0.02	0.02	0.74
	Z-test	0.01	10^{-3}	0.03
	K-W	10^{-3}	10^{-3}	0.35
	M-W	10^{-4}	10^{-4}	0.17
Fibrinogen	K-S	0.43	0.96	0.32
	Z-test	0.36	0.75	0.08
	K-W	0.13	0.69	0.13
	M-W	0.06	0.35	0.07
Erythrocyte sedimentation rate	K-S	0.10	0.01	0.08
	Z-test	0.03	10^{-3}	0.20
	K-W	0.10	0.01	0.04
	M-W	0.05	0.01	0.02
Thrombocytes	K-S	0.58	0.75	0.49
	Z-test	0.64	0.36	0.42
	K-W	0.99	0.64	0.31
	M-W	0.49	0.32	0.15
Erythrocytes	K-S	0.70	0.15	0.50
	Z-test	0.41	0.65	0.40
	K-W	0.48	0.42	0.73
	M-W	0.24	0.21	0.36
Hemoglobin	K-S	0.33	0.06	0.30
	Z-test	0.29	0.24	0.52
	K-W	0.33	0.13	0.31
	M-W	0.16	0.07	0.15

References

1. Robilotti, E., Babady, N., Mead, P., et al.: Determinants of COVID-19 disease severity in patients with cancer. Nat. Med. **26**, 1218–1223 (2020). https://doi.org/10.1038/s41591-020-0979-0
2. Ikramov, A., Adilova, F., Anvarov, K., Khadjibaev, A.: COVID-19 severity prediction in patients based on anomaly detection approach. In: Yang, X.-S., Sherratt, S., Dey, N., Joshi, A. (eds.) Proceedings of Sixth International Congress on Information and Communication Technology. LNNS, vol. 235, pp. 611–618. Springer, Singapore (2022). https://doi.org/10.1007/978-981-16-2377-6_56

3. Statsenko, Y., Al Zahmi, F., Habuza, T., et al.: Prediction of COVID-19 severity using laboratory findings on admission: informative values, thresholds, ML model performance. BMJ Open, **11**, e044500 (2021). https://doi.org/10.1136/bmjopen-2020-044500

4. Cobre, A., Stremel, D., Noleto, G., et al.: Diagnosis and prediction of COVID-19 severity: can biochemical tests and machine learning be used as prognostic indicators? Comput. Biol. Med. **134**, 104531 (2021). https://doi.org/10.1016/j.compbiomed.2021.104531, ISSN 0010-4825

5. Bats, M.-L., Rucheton, B., Fleur, T., et al.: Covichem: a biochemical severity risk score of COVID-19 upon hospital admission. PLoS One **16**(5), e0250956 (2021). https://doi.org/10.1371/journal.pone.0250956

6. Yuanyuan, C., Xiaolin, Z., Huadong, Y., et al.: CANPT score: a tool to predict severe COVID-19 on admission. Front. Med. **8**, 68 (2021). https://doi.org/10.3389/fmed.2021.608107

7. Zhou, J., Lee, S., Wang, X., et al.: Development of a multivariable prediction model for severe COVID-19 disease: a population-based study from Hong Kong. NPJ Digit. Med. **4**, 66 (2021). https://doi.org/10.1038/s41746-021-00433-4

8. Aktar, S., Ahamad, M.M., Rashed-Al-Mahfuz, M., et al.: Machine learning approach to predicting COVID-19 disease severity based on clinical blood test data: statistical analysis and model development. JMIR Med. Inform. **9**(4), e25884 (2021). https://doi.org/10.2196/25884

9. Estiri, H., Strasser, Z.H., Murphy, S.N.: Individualized prediction of COVID-19 adverse outcomes with MLHO. Sci. Rep. **11**, 5322 (2021). https://doi.org/10.1038/s41598-021-84781-x

10. Dimitrova, D., Kaishev, V., Tan, S.: Computing the Kolmogorov–Smirnov distribution when the underlying CDF is purely discrete, mixed or continuous. J. Stat. Softw. **95**(10), 1–42 (2020). https://doi.org/10.18637/jss.v095.i10

11. Sprinthall, R.C.: Basic Statistical Analysis, 9th edn. Pearson Education (2011). ISBN 978–0–205–05217–2

12. Daniel, W.W.: Kruskal–Wallis one-way analysis of variance by ranks. In: Applied Nonparametric Statistics, 2nd edn, pp. 226–234. PWS-Kent, Boston (1990). ISBN 0–534–91976–6

13. Chawla, N.V., Herrera, F., Garcia, S., et al.: SMOTE for learning from imbalanced data: progress and challenges, marking the 15-year anniversary. J. Artif. Intelligence Research. **61**, 863–905 (2020). https://doi.org/10.1613/jair.1.11192

Identifying the Effective Restriction and Vaccination Policies During the COVID-19 Crisis in Sydney: A Machine Learning Approach

Seunghyeon Lee(✉) [ID] and Fang Chen

Data Science Institute, University of Technology Sydney,
15 Broadway, Ultimo, NSW 2007, Australia
seunghyeon.lee@uts.edu.au

Abstract. This study identified effective COVID-19 restriction policies and the best times to deploy them to minimise locally acquired COVID-19 cases in Sydney. We normalised stringency levels of individual COVID-19 policies, usage levels of urban mobility, and vaccination rates to establish unbiased multivariate time-series features. We introduced the time-lag from 1 day to 15 d before when the governments have officially announced the number of locally acquired COVID-19 cases to the multivariate features. This time-lag dimension allows us to decide critical timings for announcing various COVID-19 related policies and vaccinations to control rapidly increasing infections. We used principal component analysis (PCA) to reduce the dimensions of the multivariate features. A Gaussian process regression (GPR) estimated the daily number of locally acquired COVID-19 cases based on the reduced dimensional features. The model outperformed diverse parametric and non-parametric models in estimating the daily number of infections. We successfully identified effective restriction policies and the best times to implement them to minimise the rate of confirmed COVID-19 cases by analysing PCA coefficients and kernel functions in GPR.

Keywords: Principal component analysis · Gaussian process regression · COVID-19

1 Introduction

Coronavirus disease 2019 (COVID-19) rapidly spread worldwide after the first confirmed case in Wuhan, China, in December 2019. In response to the outbreak, countries worldwide introduced various policies limiting mobility and accessibility; these policies have transformed diverse aspects of society and daily life. Sydney adopted diverse restriction policies to effectively control community transmission under different conditions after the first COVID-19 case in New

Supported by Data Science Institute in University of Technology Sydney.

South Wales (NSW) on March 1, 2020. The unique demographic and geographic conditions of Sydney have shaped how their policies have been implemented in response to COVID-19. The NSW government implemented restrictions on mobility within the framework of the COVID-19 guidelines offered by the Australian government for the initial year of the pandemic. Sydney announced lockdown and stay-at-home orders when additional waves of COVID-19 arrived after the initial surge. The pandemic policy-mobility-infection feedback cycles were developed to define recursive relationships between policy, mobility simultaneously, and infection before deploying national vaccination strategy [1]. After the first year of the COVID-19 era, the NSW government implemented a statewide vaccination strategy to control locally acquired COVID-19 infections from February 22, 2021. The NSW health announced that there are two COVID-19 vaccines currently available in NSW: Pfizer and AstraZeneca. Two doses of a COVID-19 vaccine will provide around 90% protection from hospitalisation and death from COVID-19.

This study aims to identify effective COVID-19 restriction policies and vaccination strategies in Sydney. Moreover, we will define the best times of the restriction policies and the vaccination strategies to deploy them to minimise locally acquired COVID-19 cases. We constructed a multi-dimensional time-series features data set including daily local COVID-19 infections, diverse levels of restriction policies, daily vaccination rates, and daily and hourly multimodal travel patterns. We designed a two-stage machine learning (ML) approach to describe relations between locally acquired COVID-19 cases, policies, mobilities, and vaccinations in Sydney.

In the first stage, we adopted principal component analysis (PCA) to identify effective restriction policies, vaccinations, mobility patterns and the most effective timings for implementing such restriction and vaccination policies to reduce the number of locally acquired COVID-19 cases. Moreover, a PCA reduces a dimension of the time-series features data set and retains uncorrelated variables for the model performance of a Gaussian process regression (GPR) model. In the second stage, we implemented a GPR model to predict locally transmitted cases, using principal components as independent variables.

The study produces two contributions:

– An integrated PCA and GPR model enables the identification of the critical timing for announcing various COVID-19-related policies and vaccination strategies to control rapidly increasing rates of infection.
– The proposed framework can be flexibly applied to predict future pandemic scenarios in other metropolitan areas

2   Literature Review

This section summarises the studies on the relations between infections, policies, vaccination, and mobility during the COVID-19 crisis and identifies the research gaps this study addresses.

2.1   COVID-19 Studies

The various policies for containing the spread of COVID-19 have led to remarkable changes in multimodal urban mobility patterns worldwide because their basic norm is to suppress the movement of people and goods. A city-based epidemic and mobility model was developed to simulate the spatiotemporal characteristics of COVID-19 [2]. Comprehensive insights were provided into the impact of COVID-19 on household travel and activities in Australia by examining infection data, policy data, and survey results [3]. They found that easing travel restrictions in Australia enabled travel activities to return slowly. The relationship between the stringency of government responses, mobility patterns, and the spread of COVID-19 cases was modelled [4]. They found that communities in Hong Kong reacted faster than implementing health interventions, whereas the government policies effectively reduced the number of infection cases. A change-point detection framework was developed to quantify the time lag effect reflected in transportation systems when authorities in New York City and Seattle announced new restriction policies in response to the COVID-19 pandemic [5].

2.2   Machine Learning

We utilised one of the most effective machine learning algorithms, a Gaussian process regression (GPR), with PCA based on a heterogeneous data set. A Gaussian process is a generalisation of the Gaussian probability distribution, which describes a finite-dimensional random variable to functions [6]. It enables simple model implementation in any area, a flexible data-driven approach, and stochastic predictions with confidence intervals. Thus, GPR is a non-parametric kernel-based probability model, one of the most powerful supervised machine learning algorithms. Moreover, it has guaranteed excellent performance in a prediction procedure with a small number of data sets. Because of its remarkable advantages, GPR has been widely used in various science and engineering areas, including transport science and engineering [7–9].

3   Data Structure

This section presented our data, including multiple data profiles and established data structures. We describe the overall framework in Fig. 1.

Our multidimensional time-series data set includes date profiles, COVID-19 related profiles, multimodal traffic and transit patronage profiles, vaccination rates, and policy profiles for Greater Sydney, Australia. The research period is 15 months from when the first infection was confirmed in Greater Sydney. In data processing, the dependent variable is the number of daily locally acquired cases, and the independent variables are the policy, vaccination, and mobility variables defined by divisions, features, and date. We normalise the independent features to numbers from 0.0 to 1.0 according to policy stringency and their ratio to pre-COVID-19 mobility behaviour. In an ML model, PCA transforms the specified

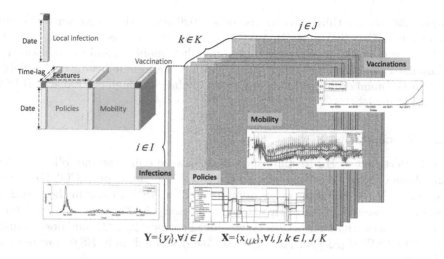

Fig. 1. Normalized multivariate time-series features with the dependent variable.

input data set to the principal component data set to reduce structural dimensions to improve the efficiency of the GPR model. The principal components are used as the independent features to estimate the number of daily locally transmitted cases in the GPR model. The specific procedures and mathematical expressions are described in the following sections.

3.1 Infections

Sydney announced locally and overseas transmitted COVID-19 cases after the first day of the COVID-19 crisis, as illustrated in Fig. 2. Figure 2 shows that overseas quarantined and locally acquired cases increased rapidly in Greater Sydney in March 2020, the initial stage of the COVID-19 crisis, after the first confirmed case.

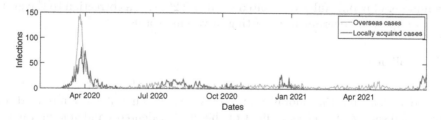

Fig. 2. Daily infections in the year after the first COVID-19 confirmed case.

Therefore, the Australian Government closed the borders to all non-residents on March 20, 2020. After the initial wave of infections, locally acquired COVID-19 did not rise above 30 cases per day in Greater Sydney in the second wave in

August 2020 or the third wave in December 2020 before the fourth wave. We used the number of locally transmitted cases in Greater Sydney as dependent variables to describe the relations between infection, policy, mobility, and vaccination. The normalised and quantified policy-related variables and mobility-related variables explain the number of infections in Greater Sydney through the integrated PCA and GPR model.

3.2 Vaccinations

The Department of Health published a nationwide daily vaccine rollout update from June 6, 2021. Moreover, the NSW health daily announced COVID-19 vaccination in NSW, including doses administered by NSW Health in the past 24 h, doses administered by NSW Health since February 22 2021, doses administered by the GP network and other providers since February 22 2021, and doses administered in NSW since February 22 2021. We described daily NSW vaccinations in Fig. 3.

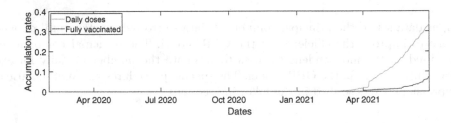

Fig. 3. Daily vaccinations in NSW.

Figure 3 illustrates the accumulation rates of total daily doses and people fully vaccinated in NSW. The accumulation rates of people fully vaccinated in NSW increased over 30%, meanwhile, that of daily doses is below ten percentages at the end of June 2021. The Government announced that the sudden jump in the number of people fully vaccinated on July 2 2021, is a correction to the graph due to improved government reporting of vaccine totals.

3.3 Policies

To control and prevent community transmission, Sydney developed and subdivided policies limiting mobility and accessibility. They flexibly modified and adjusted response strategies in light of the unprecedented pandemic and uncertainty about the nature of the virus. The Australian Federal Government also provided a framework detailing safety regulations, including the capacity of gatherings and opening of public facilities.

In May 2020, it laid out a three-step guide for responding to the outbreak in daily life settings. Step 1 was the strictest restriction level to maintain connections with friends and family in the home, while step 3 focused on reopening with social distancing. For each step, rules were laid out for gatherings and work, education and childcare, retail and sales, cafes and restaurants, entertainment and amusement venues, sport and recreation, accommodation, weddings, funerals and religious services, hair and beauty services, and domestic travel.

A stringency index (SI) was proposed in the Oxford COVID-19 Government Response Tracker to normalise and quantify the comprehensive stringency of government responses to COVID-19 in Hong Kong [4]. We modified the basic concept of the SI to identify the most effective policy and best time to impose the identified policy to decrease local transmission. For these purposes, we reversed the index table of the original SI from 0.0 (no restriction) to 1.0 (full restriction) and applied the reverse SI to the policy categories. We called this new SI "individual inverse SI" (IISI).

We categorised NSW restriction policy into 17 variables, including mask-wearing, social distancing, capacity restriction indoors, capacity restriction in a household, capacity restriction in a restaurant, capacity restriction in a pub, school restrictions, group restriction outdoors, capacity restriction for public gathering, capacity restriction in public transport, regional travel ban within NSW, interstate travel ban, international travel ban, capacity restriction for weddings, capacity restriction in hospitality, capacity restriction for funerals, and capacity restriction in worship. We constructed the IISI from 0.0 (full restriction) to 1.0 (no restriction) to normalise the stringency of an individual policy. The number of classes depended on the number of stringency levels in Fig. 4.

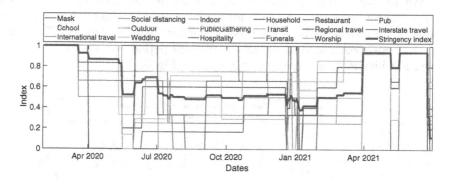

Fig. 4. Daily infections in the year after the first COVID-19 confirmed case.

Figure 4 shows the IISI for each policy in Greater Sydney. The local governments adaptively modified the stringency levels of individual policies to suppress local transmission in both areas during the initial year of the COVID-19 crisis. The inverse SIs for Greater Sydney, shown as thick red lines in Fig. 4, decreased in the year since the outbreak of COVID-19.

3.4 Mobility

TfNSW stores and provides high-quality time-series multimodal mobility data via open data web services in Greater Sydney. TfNSW provides Opal patronage data in a multimodal system, including train, bus, ferry, and light rail transit (LRT). The data framework includes the date of the trip, mode of transport, region, and the number of Opal hourly taps on and taps off in 24 h. We integrated 455 patronage files per date, including 685 rows and six columns, into one spreadsheet to construct our input data structure.

In addition to daily and hourly patterns of transit patronage, we extracted road traffic counts from the open data web services of TfNSW. TfNSW stores road traffic volume count data and traffic count station data. We used an application programming interface (API) to integrate these data into a single spreadsheet organised in 381,820 rows and 16 columns.

We divided each target area into CBD and metropolitan areas. We then aggregated hourly multimodal patronage and traffic count data sets into four groups: AM, PM, off-peak, and daily total. We categorised the patronage data into boarding and alighting groups. Finally, we divided the traffic count data into five levels of road hierarchy: arterial, distributor road, local road, motorway, primary road, and aggregated counts from all roads.

We used pre-COVID-19 mobility patterns to normalise the constructed features in the infection-mobility-policy feedback cycle. For Greater Sydney modelling, the pre-COVID-19 periods were from February 1, 2020, to February 29, 2020. We normalised mobility features by dividing by the average pre-COVID-19 values of the corresponding elements for weekdays and holidays. The normalised mobility feature denotes how much each mobility feature changed during the COVID-19 crisis compared to the pre-COVID-19 period. We illustrate the normalised mobility features for Greater Sydney in Fig. 5.

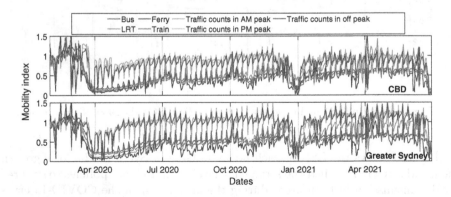

Fig. 5. Daily infections in the year after the first COVID-19 confirmed case.

Figure 5 shows that traffic counts in the CBD and metropolitan areas of Greater Sydney initially declined compared to the pre-COVID-19 period, but between waves of COVID-19 infections, they increased to over 1.0, which means larger traffic counts than during the pre-COVID-19 period. Patronage patterns mainly remained below 0.5 of mobility indicators because of the 1.5 m social distancing rules for public transport in NSW during the study period.

4   Machine Learning Approach

This section describes the mathematical formulas used to obtain the loading values in the PCA and length scales in the GPR. We integrated PCA for dimensional reductions into the GPR model because the GPR model is not efficient for high-dimensional data in a prediction process. We modified the traditional PCA mathematical framework to fit a series of formulas to the data structure proposed in this study. The defined matrix $\mathbf{X} = \{x_{i,j,k}\}$, $\forall i,j,k \in I,J,K$ has rank $\mathbf{L}$, where $\mathbf{L} \leq min\{I,J,K\}$. We integrated the number of time-lags, K, into the number of features, J, to facilitate the mathematical processes in the PCA and GPR model. First, the X columns were centred by locating the mean of each column at zero. The matrix $\mathbf{X}$ has the following singular value decomposition:

$$\mathbf{X} = \mathbf{P}\varDelta\mathbf{Q}^T \tag{1}$$

where $\mathbf{X}$ = the $I \times L$ matrix of left singular vectors, $\mathbf{Q}$ = the $J \times K \times L$ matrix of right singular vectors, and $\varDelta$ = the diagonal matrix of singular values.

$\varDelta^2$ is equal to the diagonal matrix of the eigenvalues of $\mathbf{X}^T\mathbf{X}$ and $\mathbf{XX}^T$, Λ. We define the inertia of a column, $\gamma_{j \times k}$ as follows:

$$\gamma_{j \times k}^2 = \sum_{i=1}^{I} x_{i,j \times k}^2 \tag{2}$$

We denote the sum of all $\gamma_{j \times k}^2$ as Γ, which is the total inertia of the data structure and is equal to the sum of its squared singular values. The centre of gravity of the rows, $\mathbf{g}$, is the vector of the means of each column of $\mathbf{X}$. The centre of gravity is equal to the $1 \times J$ row vector 0^T because the $\mathbf{X}$ columns are centred by locating the mean of each column at zero. The distance of the observation on date i to $\mathbf{g}$ is equal to

$$d_{i,\,\mathbf{g}}^2 = \sum_{j \times k=1}^{J \times K} x_{i,j \times k}^2 \tag{3}$$

where the sum of all $d_{i,\,\mathbf{g}}^2$ is equal to the sum of all $\gamma_{j \times k}^2$. We find the first principal component to explain the most significant part of the inertia of the data structure, i.e., the most significant possible variable. We then compute the consecutive principal components under the constraint of being orthogonal to the prior principal components and having the most significant inertia. The newly introduced variables are called factor scores, interpreted geometrically as projections of the observations onto the principal components.

We use a GPR model to predict the number of locally transmitted COVID-19 cases given the matrix of features, $\mathbf{X}$. We defined $\mathbf{Y} = \{y_i\}, \forall i \in I$ as the set of dependent variables and $\mathbf{X} = \{x_{i,j,k}\}, \forall i,j,k \in I,J,K$ as the set of independent features. For the training set $\{(x_{i,j \times k}, y_i), \forall i \in I\}$, where $x_{i,j \times k} \in \Re^d$ and $y_i \in \Re$, we formulate a general linear regression model as follows:

$$\mathbf{Y} = \mathbf{X}^T \beta + \varepsilon \tag{4}$$

where $\varepsilon \; N(0, \sigma^2)$. We introduce latent variables, $f(x_{i,j \times k}), \forall i \in I$, derived from a Gaussian process, and explicit basis functions, $\mathbf{h}$, to describe the dependent variable in the GPR model. The covariance function of the latent variables is used to present the smoothness of the dependent variables, while basis functions project x into a p-dimensional feature space. A Gaussian process is defined as a set of random variables in which any finite number of the variables have joint Gaussian distributions. The Gaussian process, $f(x)$, $x \in \Re^d$, is specified by the mean function, $\mathbf{m}(x)$, and the covariance function, $\mathbf{k}(x, x')$. Specifically, $\mathbf{E}(\mathbf{f}(x))$ and $\mathbf{Cov}[\mathbf{f}(x), \mathbf{f}(x')] = \mathbf{E}[(\mathbf{f}(x) - \mathbf{m}(x))(\mathbf{f}(x') - \mathbf{m}(x'))] = \mathbf{k}(x, x')$. Therefore, the GPR model is specified by

$$\mathbf{h}(x)^T \beta + \mathbf{f}(x) \tag{5}$$

where $\mathbf{f}(x)$ Gaussian process $(0, \mathbf{k}(x, x'))$ from a zero mean with covariance function, $\mathbf{k}(x, x')$. $\mathbf{h}(x)$ denotes a collection of basis functions projecting the vector of the original features, $x_{i,j \times k} \in \Re^d$, into the new vector of p-dimensional features, $\mathbf{h}(x)$ in $\Re^p$. β denotes a $p - by - 1$ vector of basis function coefficients. We define y_i as a form of probabilistic model,

$$\mathbf{P}(y_i | \mathbf{f}(x_{i,j \times k}), x_{i,j \times k}) \; \mathbf{N}(y_i | \mathbf{h}(x_{i,j \times k})^T \beta + \mathbf{f}(x_{i,j \times k}), \sigma^2), \tag{6}$$

where the covariance function is the squared exponential kernel function in this study,

$$textbf{k}(x, \; x' | \theta) = \sigma_f^2 exp \left[-\frac{1}{2} \sum_{m=1}^{M} \frac{(x_m - x'_m)^2}{\sigma_m^2} \right] \tag{7}$$

where σ_m and σ_f denote the length scale for predictor $m \in M$ and the signal standard deviation, respectively, with a collection of kernel parameters, $theta$. In this study, m and M are equal to $j \times k$ and $J \times K$, respectively.

5   Results

This section describes the results of the integrated PCA and GPR model. We used cross-validation methods to assess how accurately the integrated PCA and GPR model performed for the given data sets without over-fitting and selection bias concerns. To reduce their variability, we folded and shuffled the data sets from Greater Sydney five times (i.e., we used a five-fold cross-validation method).

Table 1. RMSE values of the proposed models and alternative models.

Index	Model	Vaccine	PCA	RMSE
Fine trees	Fine trees regressions	√	×	9.0459
Boosted trees	Boosted trees regression	√	√	5.991
Trilayered NN	Trilayered neural network regression	√	×	5.201
Medium NN	Medium neural network regression	√	√	5.822
GPR	Gaussian process regression	√	×	4.5628
PCA+GPR (Vac)	Gaussian process regression	√	√	4.1834
PCA+GPR (No Vac)	Gaussian process regression	×	√	4.521
Quadratic SVM	Quadratic support vector machines	√	×	4.7623
Cubic SVM	Cubic support vector machines	√	√	6.7704

This provides insight into how the proposed model can generalise future unknown data sets. We used the root-mean-square-error (RMSE) to measure the accuracy of the models.

Table 1 compares the RMSE value of the proposed model with the selected models among all possible models. The regression learner app in MATLAB R2020b was used to generate six machine-learning algorithms, including linear regression models, regression trees, support vector machines, Gaussian process regression models, ensembles of regression trees, and neural network regression models, with diverse options. In Table 1, the integrated PCA and GPR model considering vaccination rates produced the lowest RMSE values, 4.1834. The proposed model outperformed other machine learning algorithms in predicting the number of locally transmitted COVID-19 cases based on policies, mobility, and vaccination big data.

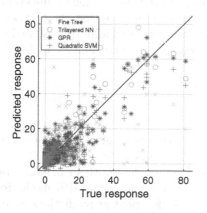

Fig. 6. Models without PCA

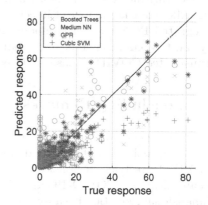

Fig. 7. Models with PCA

Figure 6 and Fig. 7 compares the performance of the four best models in two conditions, considering and do not considering dimensional reductions by PCA, respectively. Predictions of the integrated PCA and GPR model are densely distributed on the periphery of the perfect prediction lines. The predictions by the other models are widely scattered around the graphs as the size of predictions increases compared to the proposed model. Figure 8 and Fig. 9 compares the observed number of daily locally acquired COVID-19 cases with the model predictions in two conditions, considering and do not considering vaccination rates in the integrated PCA and GPR models.

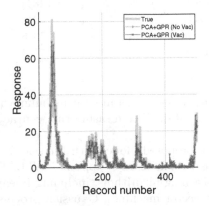
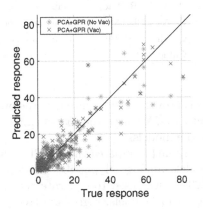

Fig. 8. PCA+GPR response   **Fig. 9.** PCA+GPR prediction

In Fig. 8 and Fig. 9, the proposed integrated PCA and GPR model explains better the large waves of infections and locally fluctuating waves during the year when considering vaccination rates. The predictions of the PCA+GPR model considering vaccination rates are almost identical to the observations of infections regardless of the number of infections. These results indicate that the proposed integrated PCA and GPR model and data structure, including policy, mobility, and vaccination indicators, can adequately predict the number of locally transmitted COVID-19 cases in Greater Sydney.

6   Concluding Remarks

We used open-source data sets to establish multivariate time-series data sets, including policy, mobility, and vaccination indicators, to identify effective COVID-19 restriction policies and the best times to deploy them to minimise locally acquired COVID-19 cases. We integrated PCA into the GPR model for dimensional reduction because the GPR model is inefficient at predictions based on a high-dimensional data structure. We adopted cross-validation methods to assess how accurately the integrated PCA and GPR model performed with the given data sets without overfitting and selection bias concerns. The integrated PCA and GPR model outperformed several different machine learning algorithms.

The proposed method paves the way for integrating machine learning algorithms to identify the best timings for imposing COVID-19 policies and the most effective policy and mobility indicators. The time-lag findings can be used to decide when and which specific restriction policies should be implemented to respond to future pandemic shocks depending on each country's policies. In addition, our study lays the foundation for predicting future infectious situations in specific policy and mobility circumstances to construct effective responses to pandemic crises. The proposed methodology can be applied to appraise and design COVID-19 policies for diverse countries.

References

1. Lee, S., Song, A.Y., Wong, S.C., Chen, F.: A data-driven approach to modelling pandemic policy-mobility-infection feedback cycles during the COVID-19 crisis case studies of Australia and South Korea. Cities Under Review (2021)
2. Wei, Y., Wang, J., Song, W., Xiu, C., Ma, L., Pei, T.: Fear, lockdown, and diversion: spread of COVID-19 in China: analysis from a city-based epidemic and mobility model. Cities 110, 103010 (2021)
3. Beck, M.J., Hensher, D.A.: Insights into the impact of COVID-19 on household travel and activities in Australia: the early days of easing restrictions. Transport Policy 99, 95–119 (2020)
4. Chan, H.Y., Chen, A., Ma, W., Sze, N.N., Liu, X.: COVID-19, community response, public policy, and travel patterns: a tale of Hong Kong. Transport Policy 106, 173–184 (2021)
5. Bian, Z., et al.: Time lag effects of COVID-19 policies on transportation systems: a comparative study of New York City and Seattle. Transp. Res. Part A Policy Practice 145, 269–283 (2021)
6. Rasmussen, C.E., Williams, C.K.: Gaussian processes for machine learning. The MIT Press, Cambridge, MA, pp. 13–16 (2006)
7. Ngoduy, D., Lee, S., Treiber, M., Keyvan-Ekbatani, M., Vu, H.L.: Langevin method for a continuous stochastic car-following model and its stability conditions. Transp. Res. Part C Emerg. Technol. 105, 599–610 (2019)
8. Lee, S., Ngoduy, D., Keyvan-Ekbatani, M.: Integrated deep learning and stochastic car-following model for traffic dynamics on multi-lane freeways. Transp. Res. Part C: Emerg. Technol. 106, 360–377 (2019)
9. Lee, S., Ryu, I., Ngoduy, D., Hoang, N.H., Choi, K.: A stochastic behaviour model of a personal mobility under heterogeneous low-carbon traffic flow. Transp. Res. Part C: Emerg. Technol. 128, 103163 (2021)

Beyond Topics: Discovering Latent Healthcare Objectives from Event Sequences

Adrian Caruana[1]($\boxtimes$), Madhushi Bandara[1], Daniel Catchpoole[1,2],
and Paul J. Kennedy[1]

[1] Australian Artificial Intelligence Institute, Faculty of Engineering and IT,
University of Technology Sydney, Sydney, Australia
{adrian.caruana,madhushi.bandara,paul.kennedy}@uts.edu.au
[2] Biospecimen Research Services, The Children's Cancer Research Unit,
The Children's Hospital at Westmead, 2145 Westmead, NSW, Australia
daniel.catchpoole@health.nsw.gov.au

Abstract. A meaningful understanding of clinical protocols and patient pathways helps improve healthcare outcomes. Electronic health records (EHR) reflect real-world treatment behaviours that are used to enhance healthcare management but present challenges; protocols and pathways are often loosely defined and with elements frequently not recorded in EHRs, complicating the enhancement. To solve this challenge, healthcare objectives associated with healthcare management activities can be indirectly observed in EHRs as latent topics. Topic models, such as Latent Dirichlet Allocation (LDA), are used to identify latent patterns in EHR data. However, they do not examine the ordered nature of EHR sequences, nor do they appraise individual events in isolation. Our novel approach, the Categorical Sequence Encoder (CaSE) addresses these shortcomings. The sequential nature of EHRs is captured by CaSE's event-level representations, revealing latent healthcare objectives. In synthetic EHR sequences, CaSE outperforms LDA by up to 37% at identifying healthcare objectives. In the real-world MIMIC-III dataset, CaSE identifies meaningful representations that could critically enhance protocol and pathway development.

Keywords: Topic modelling · Healthcare management · Healthcare representation · Sequence encoding · Electronic health records

1 Introduction

A high-level understanding of healthcare patterns is critical for management optimisation, protocol development, and resource allocation in healthcare. Healthcare patterns can provide a schematic for understanding healthcare processes, protocols, and pathways. Understanding healthcare patterns is especially relevant to population-scale healthcare management as exemplified in the studies from the United States [16], Australia [1], and Canada [6].

This work was supported by Cancer Australia in the form of a doctoral research stipend (to A. Caruana).

Population-scale healthcare management tools are typically developed manually using clinical best practice guidelines. This presents a challenge for developing further management tools for other diseases, and maintaining them to reflect new or updated guidelines. Furthermore, these tools may not accurately reflect how patients are treated in practice, since treatment patterns typically vary with demographic or geographic factors. The development of population-scale healthcare management tools should be informed by electronic health records (EHR) since they reflect actual treatment behaviour across a healthcare system.

EHRs contain sequences of treatment events, such as diagnostic activities, drug prescriptions, or surgical procedures. These events are typically recorded using a categorical coding system. The International Classification of Diseases (ICD) codes are one example of such a system, and its ninth version, ICD-9 [19], contains over 13,000 unique codes. In contrast, the clinical protocols that are used to systematise patient care typically describe a set of guidelines, procedures, or objectives. Healthcare protocols vary by region and organisation, are not standardised, and consequently are not recorded in EHRs.

This paper defines an abstraction layer, referred to as 'healthcare objective', that encapsulates reasoning behind the formation of particular EHR sequences. Healthcare objectives group and abstract individual events in EHR sequences can facilitate analysis of EHR sequences for understanding healthcare patterns. An EHR sequence may consist of many latent healthcare objectives. For example, a 'diagnostic' objective may occur before a 'treatment' objective in the treatment of a broken limb. Healthcare objectives also influence the specific events which are recorded in an EHR sequence. In the same example, the specific ICD codes that are recorded will depend on the location or severity of the injury. Treatment codes may be associated with many distinct healthcare objectives, and a patient may express many latent healthcare objectives during a treatment sequence.

Topic models can identify groups of elements within a sequence that likely occurred due to a latent theme or state. In natural language processing (NLP), topic models determine the topic of a document from the words which it contained. Topic modelling has also been used for clinical pathway analysis in healthcare [10]. Topic models use collective, unordered, macro-scale views of sequences (e.g. entire documents in NLP, or entire hospital visits in EHR). They do not appraise individual elements in isolation, nor do they consider the sequential relationship between elements. In this paper, we transcend topic modelling to consider event-level associations of treatment events in pursuit of rich representations of healthcare objectives.

The contributions of this paper are:

1. Characterisation of healthcare objectives, and prerequisites for identifying them from EHR sequences.
2. Description of a synthetic data model for modelling of healthcare objectives.
3. Introduction of Categorical Sequence Encoding (CaSE), a generalised methodology for generating representations of categorical sequences.
4. Experimental validation of healthcare objective identification in synthetic and authentic EHR data.

This paper is organised as follows: Sect. 2 outlines healthcare objective characteristics and discusses related work, Sect. 3 details our synthetic data model and CaSE, Sect. 4 applies our methodology to synthetic and authentic EHR sequences, and Sect. 5 summarises our work and discusses some limitations and future work.

2   Preliminaries and Related Work

2.1   Prerequisites for Representing Healthcare Objectives

EHR sequences contain rich, yet sometimes loosely defined concepts and information. The relationship between healthcare events and their associated healthcare objective is complex since healthcare events could be associated with multiple healthcare objectives, resulting in out-of-order healthcare events and other relational complexities. Furthermore, EHRs seldom accompany any structured information concerning healthcare objectives, so it is not possible to learn this structure in a supervised manner. Approaches that seek to represent EHR sequences to reveal healthcare objectives must: appraise individual events in EHR sequences, consider the sequential nature of the data, and learn this relationship in a unsupervised manner.

2.2   Topic Modelling in Sequence Data

Natural language is structurally similar to EHR. In each case, data is recorded as a sequence of items (tokens in NLP, and events in EHR), each drawn from a discrete sample space (dictionary in NLP, and ICD codes in EHR). Long sequences may be delineated into smaller groups (paragraphs or documents in NLP, and hospital visit or departmental segregation in EHR).

Topic models are statistical models employed to discover latent topics in documents. Topic models assume that documents are about particular topics; keywords appearing more or less frequently because of the topic being discussed in the document. A significant method for topic modelling is Latent Dirichlet Allocation (LDA) [2], and is part of a larger family of Bayesian approaches to clustering grouped data [24]. A key limitation of LDA is the modelling of topics at a document level. Relationships that occur on a more minute lexical scale (such as a sentence or paragraph) are smaller than can be perceived by the document analysis performed by LDA. Further, the positional relationships between words, sentences, and paragraphs cannot be captured through the LDA.

Clinical pathway (CP) analysis is a healthcare research approach that systemically aims to manage patient care. Bayesian approaches [10,11] have been employed to analyse EHR in pursuit of CP analysis. Like in NLP, Bayesian modelling of EHR does not directly consider the sequential nature of the data. This limits their capacity to reveal the dependencies between events in a sequence.

Sequence-based learning methods, such as long short-term memory (LSTM) [8], recurrent neural networks (RNN) [23], and most recently transformer networks [25], have shown success in several NLP tasks including topic modelling [5,9,17]. Unlike Bayesian approaches, these approaches consider the sequential nature of the data and learn item-level relationships of sequences.

Neural network-based approaches have been applied to learn representations of healthcare events. Choi *et al.* [4] learn visit-level representations in healthcare. In their approach, events in an entire sequence are aggregated into a binary vector, ignoring the sequential information carried by the healthcare sequence. Like topic models, this approach is not capable of determining patterns that occur on a finer scale than a hospital visit. Siamese networks [3] are neural networks that use the same parameters to encode pairs of inputs to the same feature space. They been used for text similarity and sentence embedding in NLP [18, 22].

We propose to observe healthcare objectives in EHR sequences. Using a synthetic data model of healthcare objectives, we hypothesise that a sequence-based approach will distinguish treatment events in EHR sequences that are expressed by distinct healthcare objectives. This model can subsequently be applied to authentic EHR sequences to observe similar structures and illustrate other natural characteristics of healthcare objectives.

3   Methodology

3.1   Latent Treatment Groups in Electronic Health Records

Observed treatment events are categorical samples from the discrete set of all possible treatment events $\mathbb{E}$. Let x be a sample in an EHR dataset where $X \in \mathbb{E}$ such that $X \sim P$ with P a discrete probability distribution over the set $\mathbb{E}$.

In practice, P is not uniformly distributed and depends on the healthcare objective being applied. Each healthcare objective will alter the distribution of observed treatment events, resulting in a 'treatment group' y. Accounting for g, the distribution of treatment events is given by $P(X, G)$, and each event is sampled based on which treatment group g is being expressed from a set of possible treatment groups $\mathbb{G}$ where $g \in \mathbb{G}$. Given many treatment event observations, we seek to construct a representation $\hat{P}$ that approximates P. The goal of this methodology is to identify areas of high local density in $\hat{P}$ to infer the existence latent treatment groups $G \in \mathbb{G}$.

Synthetic Electronic Health Records. We implement a synthetic data model defining a set of possible treatments $\mathbb{E}$, a set of treatment groups $\mathbb{G}$, and yields observations x drawn from a discrete probability distribution $P(X, G)$ where $X \in \mathbb{E}$ and $G \in \mathbb{G}$. The distribution of P for a particular treatment group g is $P(X \mid G{=}g) \sim \mathrm{Zipf}(\beta_g)$ with β_g indicating the parametrisation of the distribution. Additionally, each g corresponds to a random choice from the automorphism-group $\mathrm{Aut}(\mathbb{E})$ denoting all possible permutations over the set $\mathbb{E}$ as shown in Fig. 1. A patient sequence of $i \in [1, n]$ events is then defined as

$$x_1, \ x_2, \ x_3, \ ..., \ x_i, \ ..., \ x_n, \tag{1}$$

and at each element in the sequence the patient expresses a treatment group

$$g_1, \ g_2, \ g_3, \ ..., \ g_i, \ ..., \ g_n. \tag{2}$$

The 1st treatment group g_1 is determined by a random sample from $\mathbb{G}$ where $P(G) \sim$ Uniform over $\mathbb{G}$. The ith treatment group g_i is determined as either g_{i-1} or as a random sample from $\mathbb{G}$ where

$$P(G = g_i \mid Q = q) = \begin{cases} g \leftarrow P(G) & q < \alpha \\ g_{i-1} & q \geq \alpha \end{cases}, \tag{3}$$

where $\alpha \in [0, 1]$ and Q is a random variable following a continuous uniform distribution over the interval $[0, 1]$. α indicates the likelihood that a treatment group g changes between any two consecutive treatment events. Finally, the ith treatment event is determined by

$$x_i \leftarrow P(X \mid G = g_i). \tag{4}$$

This synthetic data model yields synthetic EHR datasets such that treatment events for patients exhibit a relationship to a latent treatment group (Eq. 4). However, the latent treatment group can at any point change to any other treatment group (Eq. 3), influencing the treatment events observed (Fig. 2). $\mathbb{E}$ is a set of categorical items, encoded as one-hot vectors $x_i \in \{0, 1\}^{|\mathbb{E}|}$.

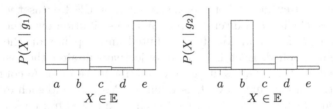

Fig. 1. The **distribution** of **treatment events** $X \in \{a, b, c, d, e\}$ given a latent **treatment group** g_i, with $|\mathbb{G}| = 2$ and $|\mathbb{E}| = 5$. Each group $G \in \mathbb{G}$ randomly permutes $\mathbb{E}$, with the distribution being Zipf.

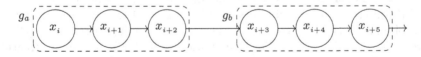

Fig. 2. The figure depicts a **sequence of observed events** x (circles), **sequence progression** (arrows), and the latent **treatment groups** g (rectangles).

MIMIC-III. The MIMIC-III dataset [12] is a large, freely-available database comprising de-identified health-related data associated with over forty thousand patients who stayed in critical care units of the Beth Israel Deaconess Medical Center between 2001 and 2012. We use sequences of ICD-9 [19] diagnosis codes of events observed by patients during hospital visits. Visits of sixteen or fewer events were removed. The dataset contains 46,520 patients, 58,976 separate hospital admissions, and 267,703 diagnosis events; from which 5,262 unique ICD-9 codes are observed. The codes form the set $\mathbb{E}$ and are encoded as one-hot vectors.

3.2   Treatment Group Representations

We propose Categorical Sequence Encoding (CaSE): a generalised method for representing sequences of categorical items. CaSE consists of a two-stage encoding process: First, a siamese network encodes categorical items. Subsequently, a transformer network generates an encoded representation of the sequence.

The siamese network learns a representation of categorical treatment events such that local neighbourhoods of events emerge. To do this, we employ a multilayer-perceptron (MLP), which we will refer to as **Cat2Vec**, that encodes an input vector $\mathbf{x}$ to a latent space vector $\mathbf{y}$ as $\mathbf{Cat2Vec}(\theta) : \mathbf{x} \rightarrow \mathbf{y}$. θ comprises the parameters fully-connected layers ℓ_1 and ℓ_2 from the input of dimension D to a hidden layer of dimension H and H to the encoding dimension N respectively. ℓ_1 may be repeated to consider multivariate categorical event data, in which case each repetition is concatenated before being passed forward to ℓ_2. ℓ_1 and ℓ_2 are activated using ReLU and sigmoid functions respectively.

To optimise the parameters θ, each training step encodes a pair of successive, one-hot encoded events $\mathbf{x}_i$ and $\mathbf{x}_{i+1}$ from a sequence to yield vectors $\mathbf{y}_i$ and $\mathbf{y}_{i+1}$. The parameters θ are optimised using Adam stochastic optimisation [13] to minimise the mean-squared error as in (5). In effect, **Cat2Vec** learns to encode sequential events closely in the latent encoding space, as shown in Fig. 3a.

$$\min_{\theta} \frac{1}{N} \sum (\mathbf{y}_i - \mathbf{y}_{i+1})^2 \tag{5}$$

The transformer architecture from Vaswani *et al.* [25] is uniquely positioned to capture event-level detail due to the attention mechanism. In a self-attention configuration, the mechanism considers the relationship between all pairs of elements from a sequence. Furthermore, the architecture's use of positional encoding is also critical as it carries positional features of the input sequence.

We use the `Transformer` Module from PyTorch [20], which implements the architecture from Vaswani *et al.* [25]. We configure it as follows: Model depth is equivalent to the encoding dimension N from **Cat2Vec**. Other parameters – the number of heads H, sequence length L, feed-forward dimension F, and number of encoder E and decoder D layers – are determined experimentally. Masking of source or target sequences is not relevant to our learning task.

The transformer model is configured in an auto-encoder fashion [7], which we will refer to as **Seq2Seq**. The architecture contains two main sections, an encoder which produces an encoding from the input sequence, followed by a decoder, which can be used to produce a resultant sequence. In the auto-encoder configuration, the model learns to reproduce the input sequence from its internal learned representation of the input sequence ω (Fig. 3b).

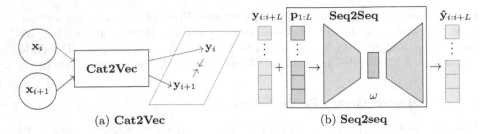

(a) Cat2Vec   (b) Seq2seq

Fig. 3. Figure 3a depicts the **siamese network**, which learns to minimises the distance (violet) between adjacent events (red and blue) encoded to the latent vector space. Figure 3b depicts the **transformer model**, which sums an input sequence **y** with a positional encoding vector **p** (blue). The model encodes (red) the sequence to produce an internal, encoded representation of the input sequence ω (green), before decoding (violet) ω to produce an output sequence $\hat{\mathbf{y}}$.(Color figure online)

Seq2Seq is trained on sequences of L consecutive events, each encoded by **Cat2Vec**, for a given patient treatment sequence. The input **y** is a sequence of length L with N features for each event. **Seq2Seq** produces an encoded representation of the sequence ω, and decodes ω to generate a resultant sequence $\hat{\mathbf{y}}$. The parameters η of **Seq2Seq** are optimised using Adam stochastic optimisation [13] such that the mean-squared error is minimised (6). Once trained, the encoder stage of **Seq2Seq** produces an encoded representation ω of the sequence, which can then be used for subsequent analytics tasks.

$$\min_{\eta} \frac{1}{N} \sum \left(\mathbf{y}_{i:i+L} - \hat{\mathbf{y}}_{i:i+L}\right)^2 \tag{6}$$

4   Experiments

4.1   Treatment Groups in Synthetic Data

First, we perform a visual experiment to demonstrate CaSE identifying latent treatment groups in synthesised EHR sequences (Sect. 3.1). We configure the synthetic data model with $|\mathbb{G}| = 6$, $|\mathbb{E}| = 100$, $\alpha = 0.03$, and $\{\beta_g = 2 \,, \forall \; g \in \mathbb{G}\}$. Figure 4 shows a 2D UMAP embedding [15] of **Cat2Vec** and **Seq2Seq** event representations. **Cat2Vec** captures the categorical nature of the $|\mathbb{E}| = 100$ events (Fig. 4a), while **Seq2Seq** groups these events into clusters of the $|\mathbb{G}| = 6$ treatment groups (Fig. 4b).

Next, we evaluate our treatment group identification approach via a clustering task. We vary the number of treatment groups $|\mathbb{G}|$ and the number of treatment events $|\mathbb{E}|$ in the synthetic data model configuration. LDA is used as a baseline. For a set of sequences, LDA yields a distribution over topics for each sequence. However, each patient treatment sequence expresses many topics throughout the sequence. A sliding window of 32 events[1] over each patient

---

[1] The sliding window length of 32 is the mean length $(1/\alpha)$ of treatment groups.

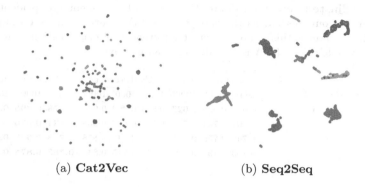

(a) **Cat2Vec**   (b) **Seq2Seq**

Fig. 4. UMAP visualisation of **events encoded from treatment sequences** in synthetic treatment data. **Points** represent treatment events, and **colours** depict the treatment group expressed by the event.

sequence is used to enable LDA to identify many treatment groups throughout a single sequence. Treatment group identification performance is first evaluated at the window-level for context, and at the event-level to compare against our method.

For CaSE, treatment groups are assigned using the HDBSCAN [14] clustering algorithm clustering with default configuration on the **Seq2Seq** encodings. A post-hoc clustering (PHC) acts on events that are classified as noise by HDB-SCAN using a consensus of a local neighbourhood of the 20 nearest events[2] in the encodings. PHC is appropriate in our case as $P(G) \sim$ Uniform, (Sect. 3.1).

Table 1 shows the treatment group identification performance quantified by the Adjusted Mutual Information score [26]. LDA performs well at the window-level as expected, but suffers at the event-level task. In contrast, CaSE with PHC exceeds the event-level performance of LDA in all experiments. The results indicate that treatment group classification suffers as $|\mathbb{E}|$ decreases. This is because the task is more difficult for small values of $|\mathbb{E}|$ due to a phenomenon we refer to as 'cross-talk'. Cross-talk is inversely proportional to $|\mathbb{E}|$, and it describes the tendency for events to occur in more than one treatment group as the sample space of possible events is restricted.

4.2   Group Representations in MIMIC-III

In Fig. 4, we observed CaSE clustering synthetic treatment events into treatment groups without prior knowledge of the treatment groups. We now observe how treatment events behave when applying CaSE to the MIMIC-III dataset

---

[2] Because HDBSCAN is nonlinear, PHC works best when the neighbourhood is small.

Table 1. Adjusted mutual information score of treatment group identification using LDA and our method as $|\mathbb{G}|$ and $|\mathbb{E}|$ vary. LDA works well in a window-level configuration, however this is not sufficient for event-level classification of healthcare objectives. Window-level LDA is included only for context.

	$|\mathbb{E}|$	LDA (window)			LDA (event)			CaSE (event)			CaSE + PHC (event)		
		100	1000	10000	100	1000	10000	100	1000	10000	100	1000	10000
	6	0.866	0.894	0.840	0.655	0.656	0.627	0.803	0.962	0.960	**0.878**	**0.995**	**0.996**
$|\mathbb{G}|$	12	0.886	0.891	0.909	0.707	0.704	0.709	0.771	0.887	0.958	**0.821**	**0.976**	**0.990**
	24	0.899	0.908	0.931	0.749	0.750	0.774	0.705	0.845	0.878	**0.788**	**0.947**	**0.966**
	48	0.880	0.925	0.931	0.763	0.795	0.796	0.655	0.775	0.844	**0.783**	**0.878**	**0.953**

(Sect. 3.1). We learn representations using events from individual patient treatment sequences, where each event contains an ICD-9 code, and the ontological information associated with the code from the Clinical Classifications Software (CCS). The multivariate event data is used to contextualise the events and is encoded via **Cat2Vec** using the method described in Sect. 3.2. We visualise the representations using a 2D UMAP embedding.

Figure 5 illustrates three findings: 1. Like the experiment depicted in Fig. 4, **Cat2Vec** captures the categorical nature of treatment events, while the **Seq2Seq** representation captures the sequential context of EHR sequences. 2. When colouring events by their level-1 CCS categorisation, the **Seq2Seq** representation separately clusters different types of treatment events indicating different treatment groups (Fig. 5a). 3. When colouring events by their position in a treatment sequence, clusters of events express a dominant colour indicating inter-treatment group dynamics (Fig. 5b). These findings demonstrate that CaSE captures the features that are characteristic of healthcare objectives as prescribed in Sect. 2.1.

4.3   Implementation Details

Cat2Vec and **Seq2Seq** were each implemented in Python 3.9 using the python package PyTorch [20] V. 1.9.0. V. 0.8.27 of the HDBSCAN [14] python package was used for clustering. V. 0.24.2 of the Scikit-learn [21] python package was used for computing the adjusted mutual information metric and implementing LDA.

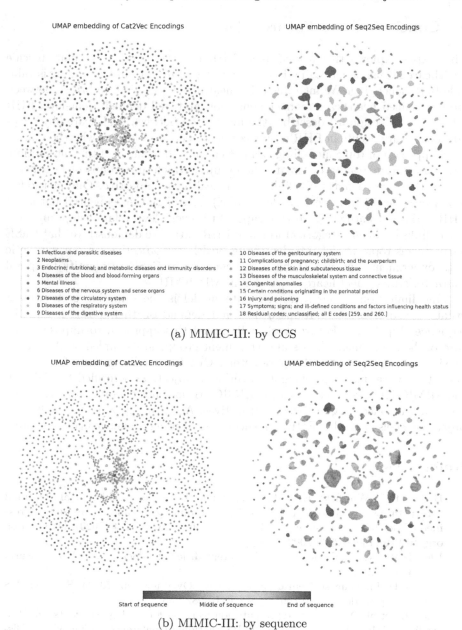

(a) MIMIC-III: by CCS

(b) MIMIC-III: by sequence

Fig. 5. UMAP visualisation of **Cat2Vec encodings** (left) and **Seq2Seq encodings** (right) of events from MIMIC-III treatment sequences. In Fig. 5a, points are events coloured by their Level 1 categorisation in CCS. In Fig. 5b, points are events coloured by their position in their source treatment sequence.

5   Conclusion and Future Work

This paper explores the task of using EHR to better inform population-scale healthcare management. Using EHR data to facilitate this understanding is valuable but challenging. We introduce the 'healthcare objective' to bridge between loosely defined healthcare management tools and well defined event-level EHR information. Section 3.1 describes the interaction between healthcare objectives and healthcare events in EHR sequences, and Sect. 3.2 outlines why the macro-scale approach of topic modelling can not capture the nuance of this interaction. This interaction results in 'treatment groups', which are groups of healthcare events that are thematically linked to a healthcare objective. Our methodology, Categorical Sequence Encoder (CaSE), considers the sequential nature of EHR and uses treatment groups to capture the event-level relationships and thematic links between categorical items in EHR data. We demonstrate that CaSE outperforms topic models at identifying healthcare objectives in our synthetic data experiment, and we establish the capacity of CaSE to identify temporal characteristics of healthcare objectives in MIMIC-III.

One limitation of our synthetic data model is the sampling of treatment events x and treatment groups g does not depend on their position i in the sequence (Eq. (3,4)). Future work will extend this approach to impose structure on how treatment events and treatment groups are sampled, and perform sensitivity analysis on model parameters. One further limitation of our work is that we were unable to evaluate healthcare objectives identified by CaSE in the MIMIC-III experiment because MIMIC-III does not contain any structured information concerning healthcare objectives. Acquiring meaningful healthcare objective labels aligned to EHR sequences is an ongoing challenge in our research.

References

1. Bergin, R.J., Whitfield, K., White, V., Milne, R.L., Emery, J.D., et al.: Optimal care pathways: a national policy to improve quality of cancer care and address inequalities in cancer outcomes. J. Cancer Policy **25**, 100254 (2020). https://doi.org/10.1016/j.jcpo.2020.100245
2. Blei, D.M., Ng, A.Y., Jordan, M.I.: Latent dirichlet allocation. J. Mach. Learn. Res. **3**, 993–1022 (2003)
3. Chicco, D. In: Siamese Neural Networks: An Overview, pp. 73–94. Springer, US (2020). https://doi.org/10.1007/978-1-0716-0826-53
4. Choi, E., et al.: Multi-layer representation learning for medical concepts. In: Proceedings of the 22nd ACM SIGKDD International Conference on Knowledge Discovery and Data Mining. ACM (2016). https://doi.org/10.1145/2939672.2939823
5. Dieng, A.B., Wang, C., Gao, J., Paisley, J.W.: Topicrnn: a recurrent neural network with long-range semantic dependency. In: ICLR (Poster) (2016)
6. Forster, K., et al.: Can concordance between actual care received and a pathway map be measured on a population level in Ontario? a pilot study. Current Oncol. **27**(1), 27–33 (2020). https://doi.org/10.3747/co.27.5349
7. Hinton, G.E.: Reducing the dimensionality of data with neural networks. Science **313**(5786), 504–507 (2006). https://doi.org/10.1126/science.1127647

8. Hochreiter, S., Schmidhuber, J.: Long short-term memory. Neural Comput. **9**(8), 1735–1780 (1997). https://doi.org/10.1162/neco.1997.9.8.1735

9. Hoyle, A.M., Goel, P., Resnik, P.: Improving neural topic models using knowledge distillation. In: Proceedings of the 2020 Conference on Empirical Methods in Natural Language Processing (EMNLP). Association for Computational Linguistics (2020). https://doi.org/10.18653/1/2020.emnlp-main.137

10. Huang, Z., Dong, W., Bath, P., Ji, L., Duan, H.: On mining latent treatment patterns from electronic medical records. Data Mining and Knowledge Discovery **29**(4), 914–949 (2014). https://doi.org/10.1007/s10618-014-0381-y

11. Huang, Z., Ge, Z., Dong, W., He, K., Duan, H.: Probabilistic modeling personalized treatment pathways using electronic health records. J. Biomed. Inf. **86**, 33–48 (2018). https://doi.org/10.1016/j.jbi.2018.08.004

12. Johnson, A., Pollard, T., Mark III, R.: Mimic-iii clinical database (version 1.4). Physio Net 10, C2XW26 (2016)

13. Kingma, D.P., Ba, J.L.: Adam: a method for stochastic optimization. In: ICLR 2015 : International Conference on Learning Representations 2015 (2015)

14. McInnes, L., Healy, J., Astels, S.: hdbscan: hierarchical density based clustering. J. Open Source Softw. **2**(11), 205 (2017). https://doi.org/10.21105/joss.00205

15. McInnes, L., Healy, J., Melville, J.: Umap: Uniform manifold approximation and projection for dimension reduction. arXiv (2018). http://arxiv.org/abs/1802.03426

16. Mohler, J.L., et al.: Prostate cancer, version 2.2019, NCCN clinical practice guidelines in oncology. J. National Comprehensive Cancer Netw. **17**(5), 479–505 (2019). https://doi.org/10.6004/jnccn.2019.0023

17. Mueller, A., Dredze, M.: Fine-tuning encoders for improved monolingual and zero-shot polylingual neural topic modeling. In: Proceedings of the 2021 Conference of the North American Chapter of the Association for Computational Linguistics: Human Language Technologies. Association for Computational Linguistics (2021). https://doi.org/10.18653/v1-2F2021.naacl-main.243

18. Neculoiu, P., Versteegh, M., Rotaru, M.: Learning text similarity with siamese recurrent networks. In: Proceedings of the 1st Workshop on Representation Learning for NLP. Association for Computational Linguistics (2016). https://doi.org/10.18653/v1/w16-1617

19. Organization, W.H.: International classification of diseases : [9th] ninth revision, basic tabulation list with alphabetic index

20. Paszke, A., et al.: Pytorch: an imperative style, high-performance deep learning library. In: Wallach, H., Larochelle, H., Beygelzimer, A., d'Alché Buc, F., Fox, E., Garnett, R. (eds.) Advances in Neural Information Processing Systems. Curran Associates Inc, vol. 32, pp. 8024–8035 (2019). papers.neurips.cc/paper/9015-pytorch-an-imperative-style-high-performance-deep-learning-library.pdf

21. Pedregosa, F., et al.: Scikit-learn: machine learning in Python. J. Mach. Learn. Res. **12**, 2825–2830 (2011)

22. Reimers, N., Gurevych, I.: Sentence-BERT: Sentence embeddings using siamese BERT-networks. Assoc. Comput. Linguist. (2019). https://doi.org/10.18653/v1/d19-1410

23. Rumelhart, D.E., Hinton, G.E., Williams, R.J.: Learning representations by back-propagating errors. Nature **323**(6088), 533–536 (1986). https://doi.org/10.1038/323533a0

24. Teh, Y.W., Jordan, M.I., Beal, M.J., Blei, D.M.: Hierarchical dirichlet processes. J. Am. Statist. Assoc. **101**(476), 1566–1581 (2006). https://doi.org/10.1198/016214506000000302

25. Vaswani, A., et al.: Attention is all you need. In: Proceedings of the 31st International Conference on Neural Information Processing Systems. vol. 30, pp. 5998–6008 (2017)
26. Vinh, N.X., Epps, J., Bailey, J.: Information theoretic measures for clusterings comparison. ACM Press (2009). https://doi.org/10.1145/1553374.1553511

Predicting Outcomes for Cancer Patients with Transformer-Based Multi-task Learning

Leah Gerrard[1,2(✉)], Xueping Peng[1(✉)], Allison Clarke[2], Clement Schlegel[2], and Jing Jiang[1]

[1] Faculty of Engineering and IT, Australian AI Institute, University of Technology Sydney, Sydney, Australia
leah.gerrard@student.uts.edu.au, {xueping.peng,jing.jiang}@uts.edu.au
[2] Health Economics and Research Division, Australian Government Department of Health, Canberra, Australia
{leah.gerrard,allison.clarke,clement.schlegel}@health.gov.au

Abstract. Cancer patients often experience numerous hospital admissions as a result of their cancer and treatment, which can negatively impact treatment progress and quality of life. Accurately predicting outcomes for cancer patients is therefore crucial in providing personalised care and improving patient outcomes. Existing models leveraging deep learning with Electronic Health Record (EHR) data to predict outcomes for cancer patients are limited, despite the demonstrated success of these approaches with cancer imaging data and non-cancer EHR applications. Additionally, current methods focus on single-task predictions, and increasing evidence suggests jointly training a model on two related tasks can improve predictive performance. To address these limitations, we propose a Transformer-based Multi-Task (TransMT) model that captures relationships between diagnosis codes and sequential hospital visits to simultaneously predict related outcomes for hospitalised cancer patients. Experiments conducted on two public datasets show the proposed model outperforms both single-task and recurrent neural network approaches in predicting future diagnosis and hospital readmission, and demonstrates the benefits of using deep learning with EHR data for cancer-related research.

Keywords: Cancer · Transformer · Multi-task learning · Healthcare · Electronic Health Record

1 Introduction

Predicting outcomes for cancer patients is an ongoing challenge due to the complexity of individuals with cancer and growing treatment options [8]. Cancer patients often experience frequent hospital admissions due to cancer symptoms and treatment, resulting in possible delays in therapy, reduced quality of life and increased financial burden [5,19]. Recent use of Electronic Health Record (EHR)

© Springer Nature Switzerland AG 2022
G. Long et al. (Eds.): AI 2021, LNAI 13151, pp. 381–392, 2022.
https://doi.org/10.1007/978-3-030-97546-3_31

data has facilitated the development of models to predict hospital readmission (usually within 30 d) and future diagnosis for admitted patients [20,23]. These outcomes are of particular importance to cancer patients who have shown an increased risk of hospital readmission [11], and are often burdened with a range of symptoms and side effects which can require hospitalisation [22]. Being able to accurately predict these outcomes for cancer patients provides opportunity for personalised treatment and care planning to improve patient outcomes.

Although EHR data has shown benefits in predicting outcomes for cancer patients, current models largely use statistical and shallow machine learning approaches [7,24], despite the recent success of deep learning. Deep learning models have been widely used in cancer prediction and prognosis with image data [6,15], and have also been used with EHR data for a range of non-cancer health applications [3,20,25,26]. Given the longitudinal nature of EHR data, many studies have leveraged recurrent neural network (RNN) approaches and their variants, which are capable of handling sequential relationships. However, the recent emergence of Transformer models has provided new state-of-the-art performance in language and health-related tasks [4,27]. While there are some examples of these models using EHR data, this research is still in its infancy, and is particularly limited for cancer use cases.

A further limitation of existing cancer-related EHR studies, is that they are primarily designed for single-task learning (STL), where only a single outcome is predicted (e.g. readmission or future diagnosis). Growing evidence indicates that multi-task learning (MTL), where multiple related outcomes are predicted simultaneously, can outperform STL in prediction tasks [6,9]. Since there are often common diagnoses for hospital readmissions [10], and up to 30% of patients are readmitted for the same diagnosis as their prior admission [1], there may be benefits to using MTL to jointly predict these patient outcomes.

To overcome the above limitations, we propose a **Trans**former-based **M**ulti-**T**ask model (called TransMT), to predict two outcomes for hospitalised patients with cancer; future diagnosis and hospital readmission. This model uses EHR data to capture inherent diagnosis and sequential visit dependencies, and applies the two predictive tasks to simultaneously learn common low-level representations and task-specific knowledge. The main contributions of this paper are: **1)** an end-to-end multi-task Transformer model that outperforms single-task and RNN baselines in predicting future diagnosis and hospital readmission, and **2)** an experimental study conducted on two public health datasets applying the proposed model to predict outcomes for cancer patients. This is, to the best of our knowledge, the first application of this type of model to a cancer-related prediction problem.

The remainder of this paper is organised as follows: Section 2 briefly reviews the related work on Transformers and multi-task learning. Section 3 describes the proposed model. Section 4 presents the experiments and results from two cancer cohorts, and Sect. 5 concludes the paper by summarising the research and presenting future directions.

2   Related Work

Transformers for EHR. There are a growing number of studies applying Transformers to healthcare data, such as the related BEHRT [16] and Med-BERT [28] models. These models both use EHR data to develop generalised pre-trained models that can be further fine-tuned for single prediction tasks. BEHRT uses a specialised code mapping to group diagnosis codes, however this approach is not well-utilised in EHR deep learning applications. BEHRT also utilises special tokens from language modelling that may lead to information loss in EHR data [28]. While Med-BERT does not use these language tokens, it does include input from multiple diagnosis classifications (International Classification of Diseases (ICD)-9 and ICD-10), and also uses a potentially unreliable diagnosis ranking strategy. Both of these aspects may have implications for learned diagnosis relationships. To address these issues, the model proposed in this paper adopts a common diagnosis grouping approach (see Sect. 4); maps all diagnoses to a single classification; and does not use diagnosis priority rankings. Furthermore, the purpose of the proposed approach differs to that of the above existing models, as it extends Transformers to enable multi-task prediction, as opposed to developing a pre-trained model. Finally, our proposed model is also related to the work of [14], who developed a Transformer model for predicting 30-day hospital readmissions using Medicare claims data. However, this paper is focused only on readmission prediction and does not explore multi-task learning.

Multi-task Learning. MTL aims to improve predictive performance by jointly training multiple related predictive tasks. It has several advantages over STL including reduced overfitting, improved generalisation and increased training sample size [30]. This makes MTL particularly relevant for health data which typically has higher dimensions and noise, but smaller size, than other data types [21]. The last few years has seen several studies exploring MTL for cancer applications with image data, such as for breast and lung cancer [6,15]. MTL has also been used in general EHR studies and has shown benefits over STL for predicting mortality and diagnosis [9,18]. None of these studies however, included both hospital readmission and future diagnosis as prediction tasks in MTL.

Of the EHR-related MTL research, only one study has compared the performance of RNNs and Transformers [21]. Interestingly, this paper found that an RNN-based model outperformed a Transformer, and MTL resulted in poorer predictions than STL. However, it is difficult to compare the two models, as they provided a reduced number of samples to the Transformer and did not use position encoding. They also included a large number of predictive tasks, some of which may not have been related, which may explain the MTL results. Nevertheless, this paper indicates a need for further exploration of MTL with Transformers for healthcare predictive tasks.

3 Methodology

This section describes the methodology of the proposed model. It starts with notations of important concepts, followed by an overview of the model. Then, the individual components of the model are explained.

3.1 Notations

We denote the set of diagnosis codes from the EHR data as $c_1, c_2, \ldots, c_{|\mathbb{C}|} \in \mathbb{C}$ and $|\mathbb{C}|$ is the number of unique diagnosis codes. A patient's EHR record can be represented by a sequence of visits $\boldsymbol{P} = \langle V_1, \ldots, V_t, \ldots, V_T \rangle$, where T is the visit number in the patient record. Each visit V_t consists of a subset of diagnosis codes ($V_t \subseteq \mathbb{C}$). For demonstration purposes, all algorithms are presented for a single patient's record. Table 1 summarises the notations used throughout the paper.

Table 1. Notations for TransMT.

Notation	Description
$\mathbb{C}$	Set of unique diagnosis codes in the dataset
$|\mathbb{C}|$	The number of unique diagnosis codes
c_i	$c_i \in \mathbb{C}$, the i-th diagnosis code in $\mathbb{C}$, $i = 1, \ldots, |\mathbb{C}|$
V^t	The t-th visit of the patient, $V^t \subseteq \mathbb{C}$
$\boldsymbol{P}$	The patient record, $\boldsymbol{P} = \langle V^1, \ldots, V^t, \ldots, V^T \rangle$
$\boldsymbol{E}_{i,:}$	Basic embedding vector of diagnosis code c_i
d	The dimension of the diagnosis code embedding

3.2 Model Overview

As illustrated in Fig. 1, TransMT is trained in an end-to-end fashion. First, an embedding layer encodes categorical diagnosis codes to dense numerical vectors. Then, an attention pooling layer compresses a set of diagnosis code embeddings from the visit into a single context-aware vector representation. Next, the position embeddings are added to the learned visit vectors, and normalized outputs are fed into the prediction tasks. The structure of the two prediction tasks are identical, using a Transformer to learn the visit relationships in the patient record. Lastly, a predictive model is used to predict the outcomes in the final hospital visit.

3.3 Common Representations

Embedding Layer. Visit $\boldsymbol{V}^t$ is denoted by a set of diagnosis codes $\boldsymbol{X}^t = [\boldsymbol{x}_{t1}, \boldsymbol{x}_{t2}, \ldots, \boldsymbol{x}_{tn}]$, where n is the number of diagnosis codes in the visit, and $\boldsymbol{x}_{ti}$

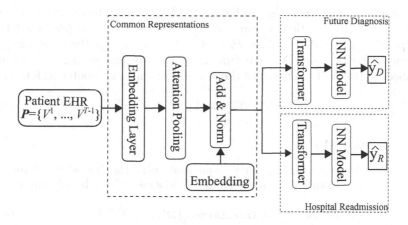

Fig. 1. The proposed TransMT model.

could be a one-hot vector whose dimension length equals the number of unique diagnosis codes $|\mathbb{C}|$. An embedding layer is applied to $\boldsymbol{X}^t$ and transforms all discrete diagnosis codes to a set of low-dimensional dense vector representations $\boldsymbol{E}^t = [\boldsymbol{e}_{t1}, \boldsymbol{e}_{t2}, ..., \boldsymbol{e}_{tn}]$ with $\boldsymbol{e}_{ti} \in \mathbb{R}^d$. This process can be formally written as $\boldsymbol{E}^t = \boldsymbol{W}^{(e)} \boldsymbol{X}^t$, where the diagnosis code embedding weight matrix $\boldsymbol{W}^{(e)} \in \mathbb{R}^{|\mathbb{C}| \times d}$ can be fine-tuned during model training.

Attention Pooling. Attention Pooling [2,17] explores the importance of each diagnosis within a visit and compresses a set of diagnosis code embeddings into a single context-aware vector representation. For simplicity, we take the embedding output $\boldsymbol{E}^t$ of the t-th visit $\boldsymbol{V}^t$ as an example. Formally, it is written as:

$$g(\boldsymbol{E}^t_{i,:}) = \boldsymbol{w}^T \sigma(\boldsymbol{W}^{(1)} \boldsymbol{E}^t_{i,:} + b^{(1)}) + b, \tag{1}$$

where $\boldsymbol{E}^t_{i,:}$ is the i-th row of $\boldsymbol{E}^t$ ($1 \leq i \leq n$), σ is ReLU function and $\boldsymbol{w}, \boldsymbol{W}^{(1)}, \boldsymbol{b}^{(1)}, \boldsymbol{b}$ are learnable parameters. The probability distribution is formalized as

$$\boldsymbol{\alpha}_t = \texttt{softmax}([g(\boldsymbol{E}^t_{i,:})]^n_{i=1}). \tag{2}$$

The final output $\boldsymbol{v}_t$ of the attention pooling is the weighted average of sampling a code according to its importance, i.e.,

$$\boldsymbol{v}_t = \sum_{i=1}^{n} \boldsymbol{\alpha}_t \odot [\boldsymbol{E}^t_{i,:}]^n_{i=1}, \tag{3}$$

where $\boldsymbol{v}_t \in \mathbb{R}^d$ ($1 \leq t \leq (T-1)$) represents the t-th visit in the patient record. The patient record in low-dimensional dense vector representations is denoted as $\boldsymbol{J} = [\boldsymbol{v}_1, \dots, \boldsymbol{v}_t, \dots, \boldsymbol{v}_{(T-1)}]$.

Position Embedding and Normalization. To incorporate information on the order of visits in a patient record, we embed each temporal position t to obtain a position embedding matrix $\boldsymbol{P}_e \in \mathbb{R}^{(T-1)\times d}$, then fuse the embeddings into a vector representation. The structure of the position embedding is identical to the embedding layer. The output of the Add&Norm layer is denoted as follows,

$$O = \texttt{LayerNorm}(\boldsymbol{J} + \boldsymbol{P}_e). \tag{4}$$

3.4 Transformer Model

To learn relationships between patients' sequential visits, the `Transformer` module is proposed to capture the inherent dependencies, which is calculated as follows:

$$\{\boldsymbol{V}^1,\dots,\boldsymbol{V}^{T-1}\} = \texttt{Transformer}(\{\boldsymbol{O}^1,\dots,\boldsymbol{O}^{T-1}\}) \tag{5}$$

The `Transformer` is identical to that of BERT [31] and [4], which has two sub-layers. The first is a multi-head attention mechanism (explained below), and the second is a position wise fully connected feed-forward network. A residual connection is employed around each of the two sub-layers, followed by layer normalization. In contrast to BERT which uses masked language modelling for the purpose of model pre-training, the proposed model is trained directly on the two prediction tasks.

Multi-head Attention. The multi-head attention mechanism relies on self-attention, where all of the keys, values and queries come from the same place. The self-attention operates on a query $\boldsymbol{Q}$, a key $\boldsymbol{K}$ and a value $\boldsymbol{V}$:

$$\text{Attention}(\boldsymbol{Q}, \boldsymbol{K}, \boldsymbol{V}) = \text{softmax}(\frac{\boldsymbol{Q}\boldsymbol{K}^T}{\sqrt{d}})\boldsymbol{V} \tag{6}$$

where $\boldsymbol{Q}$, $\boldsymbol{K}$, and $\boldsymbol{V}$ are $n \times d$ matrices, n denotes the number of diagnoses in a visit in a patient record, d denotes the embedding dimension.

The multi-head attention mechanism obtains h (i.e. one per head) different representations of $(\boldsymbol{Q}, \boldsymbol{K}, \boldsymbol{V})$, computes self-attention for each representation, and concatenates the results. This can be expressed as follow:

$$\text{head}_i = \text{Attention}(\boldsymbol{Q}\boldsymbol{W}_i^Q, \boldsymbol{K}\boldsymbol{W}_i^K, \boldsymbol{V}\boldsymbol{W}_i^V) \tag{7}$$

$$\text{MultiHead}(\boldsymbol{Q}, \boldsymbol{K}, \boldsymbol{V}) = \text{Concat}(\text{head}_1, \dots, head_h)\boldsymbol{W}^O \tag{8}$$

where the projections are parameter matrices $\boldsymbol{W}_i^Q \in \mathbb{R}^{d \times d_k}, \boldsymbol{W}_i^K \in \mathbb{R}^{d \times d_k}, \boldsymbol{W}_i^V \in \mathbb{R}^{d \times d_v}$ and $\boldsymbol{W}^O \in \mathbb{R}^{hd_v \times d}$, $d_k = d_v = d/h$.

3.5 Multi-task Learning

MTL is employed to jointly learn two prediction tasks for the final patient visit. Given a patient's record $\boldsymbol{P} = \{V^1, V^2, \dots, V^{T-1}\}$, we simultaneously predict future diagnosis and hospital readmission.

Future Diagnosis Prediction. This is a multi-class classification problem with the objective being to predict the principal diagnosis code (the diagnosis code representing the main reason for hospitalisation) in the last visit V_T, which can be expressed as follows:

$$\hat{y}_D = \text{Softmax}(W^D p_D + b^D), \tag{9}$$

$$\mathcal{L}_D = \frac{-1}{T-1} \sum_{t=1}^{T-1} \left(y_D^\mathsf{T} \log \hat{y}_D + (1 - y_D)^\mathsf{T} \log (1 - \hat{y}_D) \right), \tag{10}$$

where $p^D \in \mathbb{R}^d$ is the output of the attention pooling layer followed by Transformer to denote the representation of the patient record in the future diagnosis prediction task, and $W^D \in \mathbb{R}^{|\mathcal{C}| \times d}$ and $b^D \in \mathbb{R}^{|\mathcal{C}|}$ are learnable parameters.

Hospital Readmission Prediction. This is a binary classification problem to predict whether the patient's final visit is within 30 d of their previous hospital admission. The implementation is identical to the future diagnosis prediction task, which can be expressed as follows:

$$\hat{y}_R = \text{Softmax}(W^R p_R + b^R), \tag{11}$$

$$\mathcal{L}_R = \frac{-1}{T-1} \sum_{t=1}^{T-1} \left(y_R^\mathsf{T} \log \hat{y}_R + (1 - y_R)^\mathsf{T} \log (1 - \hat{y}_R) \right), \tag{12}$$

where $v_R \in \mathbb{R}^d$ is the output of attention pooling layer followed by Transformer to denote the representation of the patient record in the hospital readmission prediction task, and $W^R \in \mathbb{R}^{|\mathcal{C}| \times d}$ and $b^R \in \mathbb{R}^{|\mathcal{C}|}$ are the learnable parameters.

Objective Function. To allow shared information between the two predictive tasks, we jointly train the tasks using the weighted loss function below, where λ is a learnable parameter.

$$\mathcal{L} = \lambda \cdot \mathcal{L}_D + (1 - \lambda) \cdot \mathcal{L}_R. \tag{13}$$

4   Experiments

4.1   Data Description and Preprocessing

Datasets. We conduct experiments on two public real-world health datasets, the Medical Information Mart for Intensive Care (MIMIC)-III (v1.4) [13] and MIMIC-IV (v0.4) [12] datasets. Given these datasets are widely used for deep learning EHR studies, we do not explain them in detail and instead refer readers to the official sources for comprehensive information on these datasets [12,13].

Cancer Cohort Selection. Patients were included in analysis if they had at least one cancer-related ICD-9 diagnosis code (140–239) (as used elsewhere [29]). Patients with less than 2 visits were excluded and only the most recent 21 visits were used where applicable. All diagnosis codes were mapped to ICD-9 codes. A summary of the statistical information for the final cancer cohorts is included in Table 2.

Clinical Classifications Software (CCS) Mapping. To reduce the number of diagnosis code categories for model training, we used the CCS categorisation scheme[1] to group diagnosis codes into 285 mutually exclusive categories and use these categories for the future diagnosis prediction task. This scheme has been used elsewhere for similar applications [25, 26].

Table 2. Statistics of the MIMIC datasets for the two cancer cohorts.

Dataset	MIMIC-III	MIMIC-IV
# of patients	2,070	20,953
# of visits	5,552	79,177
Avg. # of visits per patient	2.68	3.78
# of unique ICD-9 codes	3,228	6,939
Avg. # of ICD-9 codes per visit	13.67	13.47
Max # of ICD-9 codes per visit	39	57
# of CCS categories	166	270

4.2 Experimental Setup

Baseline Approaches. We compare the performance of our proposed model against three baselines: two common RNN-based approaches (RETAIN and Dipole) and a single-task Transformer model. **RETAIN** [3] uses a reversed RNN with attention to capture relationships between diagnoses to perform heart failure prediction. **Dipole** [20] uses a bidirectional RNN and three attention mechanisms (location-based, general, concatenation-based) to predict future diagnosis information. We used the location-based Dipole as the baseline method. **Single-task learning (STL) model** is the proposed Transformer model trained separately for single-task prediction.

Evaluation Metrics. F1 score and ROC-AUC score are used as evaluation measures. **F1 score** is the harmonic mean of precision and recall. An F1 score close to 1 indicates high precision and recall. **ROC-AUC score** uses the Receiver Operator Characteristic (ROC) curve, which shows the relationship between true and false positive rates. The Area Under the Curve (AUC) demonstrates how well a model can distinguish between binary classes. A ROC-AUC score of 0.5 indicates a model no better than chance, with 1 indicating a perfect model.

Implementation Details. We implement all models with Pytorch 1.4.0 and run models on NVIDIA TITAN X with 12GB RAM. For training, we use Adadelta [32] with a minbatch of 16 and 32 patients on MIMIC-III and MIMIC-IV, respectively. We randomly split data into training, validation and test sets in

---

[1] https://www.hcup-us.ahrq.gov/toolssoftware/ccs/CCSUsersGuide.pdf.

ratios of 80%, 10% and 10%, respectively. The validation set is used to determine the best parameter values in the 20 training iterations for MIMIC-III and 10 iterations for MIMIC-IV. Drop-out strategies (using a drop-out rate of 0.1) are used for all approaches. We set the dimension $d = 200$ and used two Transformer layers for the proposed model and STL baseline for MIMIC-III and three Transformer layers for MIMIC-IV. All models were run three times to calculate the mean and standard deviation of performance metrics.

4.3   Results

F1 Score for Two Prediction Tasks. Table 3 shows the mean F1 scores and standard deviations of the TransMT model compared with baselines for the predictive tasks in the two MIMIC datasets. The results show that the proposed TransMT model outperforms all baselines on both MIMIC-III and MIMIC-IV datasets. This demonstrates the benefits of MTL to jointly learn the future diagnosis and hospital readmission prediction tasks. The results also show that the single-task baseline (STL) outperformed the two RNN attention-based models, RETAIN and Dipole, on both data sets, indicating the benefit of Transformers in modelling the sequential relationships in EHR data.

Table 3. Performance comparison of prediction tasks.

Dataset	Model	F1 Score (%)	
		Future diagnosis	Hospital readmission
MIMIC-III	RETAIN	12.48 ± 2.35	9.65 ± 5.67
	Dipole	10.39 ± 0.49	19.14 ± 3.85
	STL	16.19 ± 1.05	24.27 ± 4.46
	TransMT	**16.56** ± 1.34	**24.70** ± 3.95
MIMIC-IV	RETAIN	7.60 ± 0.54	35.12 ± 1.64
	Dipole	6.99 ± 0.23	38.64 ± 6.03
	STL	9.04 ± 0.19	38.97 ± 2.17
	TransMT	**9.19** ± 0.11	**41.62** ± 2.26

ROC-AUC Score for Hospital Readmission Prediction. Figure 2 depicts the ROC curve for all models on the hospital readmission task, showing that TransMT outperforms baseline models in both MIMIC datasets. In contrast to MIMIC-III data where all models show similar performance, the TransMT model outperforms the best RNN baseline by almost 15% on MIMIC-IV data. This indicates the benefit of TransMT for hospital readmission prediction, particularly with the larger and more complex MIMIC-IV data.

Relationship Between Diagnosis and Readmission. We also explored the relationship between future diagnosis and hospital readmission. Table 4 shows the proportion of patients with the same principal diagnosis and CCS category

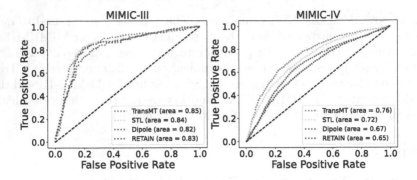

Fig. 2. ROC of hospital readmission on two datasets.

Table 4. Relationship between future diagnosis and readmission.

Dataset	Hospital readmission within 30 d	Patients with same diagnosis as previous visit (%)	Patients with same CCS category as previous visit (%)
MIMIC-III	Yes	17.76	25.68
	No	8.28	15.14
MIMIC-IV	Yes	3.94	6.71
	No	2.97	5.44

in their final visit compared with their previous visit, by hospital readmission status. Patients who were readmitted within 30 d were more likely to have the same diagnosis and CCS category in their final visit than those not readmitted within 30 d. This suggests a relationship between the two prediction tasks, and supports the results that the multi-task model produces better predictions.

5   Conclusion

In this paper, we proposed the model TransMT, which captures sequential relationships between patient visits to predict future diagnosis and hospital readmission for cancer patients. As demonstrated by the experimental results, TransMT produces better predictions than single-task and RNN-based approaches, indicating the potential for Transformer-based prediction models with EHR data to facilitate cancer-related research. Given the MIMIC datasets only capture a subset of patients in EHRs, a future direction of this work is to apply this model to other cancer datasets where patients with specific cancers and treatments can be identified. Furthermore, this paper only includes diagnosis codes as input to the model, and further work could include addition of other patient information (e.g. medications and demographics). Finally, experimentation of multi-task learning with other methods, such as pre-training approaches, will help identify where multi-task learning can be most useful in healthcare applications to further improve the performance of risk prediction models.

Acknowledgements. This research is supported by an Australian Government Research Training Program Scholarship. We also thank the Australian Government Department of Health for supporting this work.

References

1. Brunner-La Rocca, H.P., Peden, C., Soong, J., Holman, P., Bogdanovskaya, M., Barclay, L.: Reasons for readmission after hospital discharge in patients with chronic diseases-information from an international dataset. PLOS ONE **15**, e0233457 (2020)
2. Cai, X., Gao, J., Ngiam, K.Y., Ooi, B.C., Zhang, Y., Yuan, X.: Medical concept embedding with time-aware attention. In: IJCAI, pp. 3984–3990 (2018)
3. Choi, E., Bahadori, M.T., Sun, J., Kulas, J., Schuetz, A., Stewart, W.: Retain: an interpretable predictive model for healthcare using reverse time attention mechanism. In: NeurIPS, pp. 3504–3512 (2016)
4. Devlin, J., Chang, M.W., Lee, K., Toutanova, K.: Bert: pre-training of deep bidirectional transformers for language understanding. arXiv preprint arXiv:1810.04805 (2018)
5. Fadol, A., et al.: A quality improvement approach to reducing hospital readmissions in patients with cancer and heart failure. Cardio-Oncol. **5**, 5 (2019)
6. Gao, R., et al.: Deep multi-task prediction of lung cancer and cancer-free progression from censored heterogenous clinical imaging. CoRR (2019)
7. Gensheimer, M., et al.: Automated survival prediction in metastatic cancer patients using high-dimensional electronic medical record data. Ann. Oncol. **29** (2018)
8. Gupta, S., et al.: Machine-learning prediction of cancer survival: a retrospective study using electronic administrative records and a cancer registry. BMJ Open 4(3) (2014)
9. Harutyunyan, H., Khachatrian, H., Kale, D.C., Ver Steeg, G., Galstyan, A.: Multitask learning and benchmarking with clinical time series data. Sci. Data 6(1) (2019)
10. Hughes, L., Witham, M.: Causes and correlates of 30 day and 180 day readmission following discharge from a medicine for the elderly rehabilitation unit. BMC Geriatrics **18** (2018)
11. Ji, H., Abushomar, H., Chen, X.K., Qian, C., Gerson, D.: All-cause readmission to acute care for cancer patients. Healthc. Quart. Toronto Ont. **15**, 14–6 (2012)
12. Johnson, A., Bulgarelli, L., Pollard, T., Horng, S., Celi, L.A., Mark, R.: Mimic-iv (version 0.4). PhysioNet (2020)
13. Johnson, A.E., et al.: Mimic-iii, a freely accessible critical care database. Sci. Data **3**, 160035 (2016)
14. Lahlou, C., Crayton, A., Trier, C., Willett, E.: Explainable health risk predictor with transformer-based medicare claim encoder. CoRR abs/2105.09428 arxiv.org/abs/2105.09428 (2021)
15. Le, T.L.T., Thome, N., Bernard, S., Bismuth, V., Patoureaux, F.: Multitask classification and segmentation for cancer diagnosis in mammography. arXiv preprint arXiv:1909.05397 (2019)
16. Li, Y., et al.: BEHRT: transformer for electronic health records. CoRR (2019)

17. Lin, Z., Feng, M., Santos, C.N.d., Yu, M., Xiang, B., Zhou, B., Bengio, Y.: A structured self-attentive sentence embedding. arXiv:1703.03130 (2017)
18. Liu, L., et al.: Multi-task learning via adaptation to similar tasks for mortality prediction of diverse rare diseases. In: AMIA Annual Symposium Proceedings. American Medical Informatics Association, vol. 2020, p. 763 (2020)
19. Long, G., Shen, T., Tan, Y., Gerrard, L., Clarke, A., Jiang, J.: Federated learning for privacy-preserving open innovation future on digital health. arXiv preprint arXiv:2108.10761 (2021)
20. Ma, F., Chitta, R., Zhou, J., You, Q., Sun, T., Gao, J.: Dipole: diagnosis prediction in healthcare via attention-based bidirectional recurrent neural networks. In: SIGKDD, pp. 1903–1911. ACM (2017)
21. McDermott, M., et al.: A comprehensive evaluation of multi-task learning and multi-task pre-training on ehr time-series data. arXiv preprint arXiv:2007.10185 (2020)
22. Miaskowski, C., et al.: Latent class analysis reveals distinct subgroups of patients based on symptom occurrence and demographic and clinical characteristics. J. Pain Symptom Manage. **50**(1), 28–37 (2015)
23. Min, X., Yu, B., Wang, F.: Predictive modeling of the hospital readmission risk from patients' claims data using machine learning: a case study on copd. Sci. Reports **9**, 2362 (2019)
24. Parikh, R.B., et al.: Machine learning approaches to predict 6-Month mortality among patients with cancer. JAMA Netw. Open **2**(10), e1915997–e1915997 (2019)
25. Peng, X., Long, G., Shen, T., Wang, S., Jiang, J., Blumenstein, M.: Temporal self-attention network for medical concept embedding. In: ICDM, pp. 498–507. IEEE (2019)
26. Peng, X., Long, G., Shen, T., Wang, S., Jiang, J., Zhang, C.: Bitenet: bidirectional temporal encoder network to predict medical outcomes. In: ICDM, pp. 412–421. IEEE (2020)
27. Rao, S., et al.: An explainable transformer-based deep learning model for the prediction of incident heart failure. CoRR (2021)
28. Rasmy, L., Xiang, Y., Xie, Z., Tao, C., Zhi, D.: Med-bert: pretrained contextualized embeddings on large-scale structured electronic health records for disease prediction. NPJ Digital Med. **4**(1), 1–13 (2021)
29. Ruck, J., Canner, J., Smith, T., Johnston, F.: Use of inpatient palliative care by type of malignancy. J. Palliative Med. **21** (2018)
30. Ruder, S.: An overview of multi-task learning in deep neural networks. arXiv preprint arXiv:1706.05098 (2017)
31. Vaswani, A., et al.: Attention is all you need. In: NeurIPS, pp. 5998–6008 (2017)
32. Zeiler, M.D.: Adadelta: an adaptive learning rate method. arXiv preprint arXiv:1212.5701 (2012)

Deep Reinforcement Learning for Dynamic Things of Interest Recommendation in Intelligent Ambient Environment

May S. Altulyan[1,3], Chaoran Huang[1(✉)], Lina Yao[1(✉)], Xianzhi Wang[2(✉)], and Salil Kanhere[1(✉)]

[1] The University of New South Wales, Sydney 2052, Australia
{m.altulyan,chaoran.huang,lina.yao,salil.kanhere}@unsw.edu.au
[2] The University of Technology Sydney, Ultimo 2007, Australia
xianzhi.wang@uts.edu.au
[3] Prince Sattam Bin Abdulaziz University, Alkharj 11942, Saudi Arabia
m.altulayan@psau.edu.sa

Abstract. Recommender Systems for the IoT (RSIoT) aim for interactive item recommendations. Most existing methods focus on user feedback and have limitations in dealing with dynamic environments. Deep Reinforcement Learning (DRL) can deal with dynamic environments and conduct updates without waiting for user feedback. In this study, we design a Reminder Care System (RCS) to harness the advantages of deep reinforcement learning in addressing two main issues of RSIoT: capturing dynamicity patterns of human activities and system update without a focus on user feedback. The RCS is formulated based on a Deep Q-Network (DQN), which works well with the dynamic nature of human activities. We further consider harvesting the feedback automatically in the back end without requiring users to explicitly label activities. Experiments are conducted on three public datasets and have demonstrated the performance of our proposed system.

Keywords: Deep reinforcement learning · IoT · Recommender system

1 Introduction

With the rapid growth in the number of things that can be connected to the internet, Recommendation Systems for the IoT (RSIoT) have become more significant in helping a variety of applications to meet user preferences, and such applications can be smart home, smart tourism, smart parking, m-health and so on. On the one hand, RSIoT can recommend an item that users might need in situations. On the other hand, it can save time and cost by actively allocating specific IoT resources accordingly to the very situations.

We motivate RSIoT with a smart home scenario: Alice, a 79-year-old woman with dementia, lives alone in a house and is preparing a cup of coffee in her smart

G. Long et al. (Eds.): AI 2021, LNAI 13151, pp. 393–404, 2022.
https://doi.org/10.1007/978-3-030-97546-3_32

kitchen. Motion sensors monitor her every move and track each coffee-making step. If she pauses for a while, a recommender application will determine if it is too long and remind her of what to do next. If she tries to prepare a cup of coffee late at night, the system considers the time and recommends she goes back to bed instead. Later that day, Alice's son accesses the system and scans a checklist for his mother's house. He finds that his mother has taken medicine on schedule, slept, eaten regularly, and continued to manage her daily life well.

Numerous efforts have been made to develop RSIoT using different approaches. Most of the existing works adapted conventional recommender system approaches, including collaborative filtering [16], content-based [14] and hybrid-based approach [5]. However, those conventional RSIoT approaches face two main issues. The first issue is treating the recommendation procedures as statics and ignoring the dynamicity in human activity patterns. More formally, human activity patterns could be changed at any time during the day or even after a period of time. The second issue is making recommendations for users while the system must wait for user feedback to update itself. While this may provide the system with accurate labels, it can have an impact on the end-user experience. RSIoTs should able to be updated based on the recommended item status only, which means no need to hold any device or to deal with any application.

Deep Reinforcement Learning (DRL) is inherently profitable for overcoming dynamic environments and thus has been adapted in interactive recommendation systems. It has been shown the ability to learn user decision behavior by observing the user's actions and conducting accurate recommendations even from a few samples by grouping its observations. Furthermore, it considers the feedback from the environment as a reward to update the system. Significant efforts have shown the notable performance of DRL methods in conventional recommendation systems [20,21,23]. Also, there are only very few studies on RSIoT systems based on RL [7,9,10,13]. However, no previous research known to us has adapted DQN based RL for RSIoT. Inspired by [23], we design a Reminder Care System (RCS) based on DQN, which can tackle two main issues: dynamicity patterns of the human activity and the focus on the user feedback during system updates. We first formulate our system based on a Deep Q-Network (DQN), which captures the user's dynamicity pattern using three kinds of extracted features that address the first issue. Subsequently, we calculate the probabilities for items and nominate only one item with the highest probability as a recommendation. To tackle the second issue, we introduce our reward function that enables the system to receive feedback automatically without waiting for the user. Finally, we propose a new term called a Reward Delay Period which improves the evaluation for the quality of recommendations.

The main contributions of our proposed system are summarized as follows:

- We design the Reminder Care System (RCS) and formulate it based on the Deep Q-Network (DQN) which utilizes three main features: past activities features, current activities features, and item context features as an input (State).

- We formulate the reward function that helps the system to be updated automatically without needing feedback from the user by checking the status of items after a period of time.
- We conducted extensive experiments on three public datasets, and our experimental results demonstrate the feasibility and effectiveness of our system.

2 Related Work

2.1 Recommender System Approaches for the IoT

Numerous recent works provide methods and techniques for building recommender systems in several domains of the IoT. Most of the existing research falls into three categories, the same as normal recommender systems: collaborative filtering, content-based, and hybrid methods. Authors in [17,18] proposed a unified CF model based on a probabilistic matrix factorization recommender system that exploits three kinds of relations to extract the latent factors among these relations. In [6], content-based was adapted for the recommender engine in their AGILE project, which aims to improve the health conditions of users. In [8,15], authors built their recommender system engine using a hybrid recommendation algorithm. All previous categories only focus on the interaction between items and users to construct a recommendation, making them inapplicable for RSIoT.

2.2 Deep Reinforcement Learning in RSIoT

In previous studies, most approaches deal with a static recommendation process, whereas RSIoT needs to capture user's temporal intentions and to conduct recommendations in a timely manner. DRL has received significant attention in building recommender systems [12,19–22] for two main reasons; coping with dynamic environments by updating the strategies during the interactions and the ability to learn a policy that maximizes the long term reward.

Author in [21] proposed a deep recommender system framework (DEERS). It aims to exploit both negative and positive feedback to conduct recommendations in a sequential interaction environment. In [20], DRL was adapted for the page-wise recommendation. The authors in [23] proposed a novel DRL-based recommendation framework. It tackles two main issues: the dynamic nature of new features and users' preferences and the lack of information to improve the quality of recommendations. In addition, DRL has also been utilized to propose a DEAR framework for online advertising recommendations [19].

3 Reminder Care System (RCS) Framework

In this section, we introduce Reminder Care System (RCS) in detail. First, we define the problem and notations; then, we provide an overview of our framework. Finally, we describe DQN and explain the process of our agent.

3.1   Notation

Our problem is framed as follows: when extracted features of the complex activity v where $v_i \in V = \{v_1, v_2, \ldots v_m\}$ is received by the agent G (The extracted features will be explained in details in Sect. 3.2). Notice that the agent receives the extracted features of the activity that needs recommendation only as an input (state) s. Then the agent nominates an appropriate item a from a fixed candidate set of items A for the particular activity. In other words, the algorithm generates ranking list $\Gamma = <\gamma_{a_1}, \gamma_{a_2}, \ldots, \gamma_{a_l}>$, where γ_{a_i} denotes the probability of the item a_i where the user needs to finish the current activity. Unlike a conventional recommendation system that typically recommends more than one item for users each time, our agent recommends only one item with maximum probability for the activity that needs a recommendation. Table 1 summarises the notations used throughout this paper.

Table 1. System notations

Notation	Explanation
G	Agent
v, V	Activity, set of activities
s, s'	state, next state
a	action (item)
r	Reward
A	set of items
Q	Q-Network
W	Parameters of DQN parameter
Γ	Ranking list
γ_a	Probability of the item
O	Value of each item
E	Experience replay buffer

3.2   Overview

In this section, we describe our framework as shown in Fig. 1. We divided it into two main parts online and offline. In the offline part, our system will be training to deal with the activities that need a recommendation. Notice during the training, we treat each activity that needs a recommendation as a session. During the online part, the agent receives the required features as an input (state) s; then recommends an appropriate item a_i for the activity. There are three kinds of features that should be received for each activity (session) that needs a recommendation:

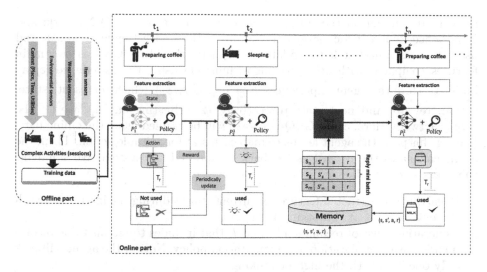

Fig. 1. The architecture of our framework, which consists of two main parts: offline and online. The offline part focuses on training our agent G using different datasets. During the online part, the agent receives each activity and extracts the required features as state s, then nominates suitable item a_i for this state. After a periodic time called reward delay period T_r, the agent will receive a reward r. Two kinds of updating will be applied for the system: periodically update after every recommendation P and the total update after a period of time using the experience replay buffer.

- Past activities features. Since each activity can have a different pattern, for each activity, the system extracts the path/sequences of items used. They enable agent G to learn different patterns of each activity.
- Current activities features. It can define where the user is stuck by reviewing all previously used items for this activity. This feature helps the agent to ignore all the used items before and to choose from the rest.
- Item context (IC). It includes information about items, such as to which activity this item belongs to, how long it could be in use, and how many times the user needs it for the current activity.

  To improve the system's recommendation accuracy, we consider all features that help our system learn the best action in a specific state. The public datasets did not meet all required features, which affect the results of our systems.

3.3   Deep Q Network for Recommendation

After the features are extracted, we apply the DQN algorithm to model our agent. It maps state and action pairs to Q-value using neural networks. It aims to maximize a cumulative future reward by recommending the correct item a_i for each activity that needs a recommendation. Three main components for the DQN are Q-Network which could be a standard neural network or regular network depending on the state; Q-Target is identical to the Q Network; and Experience Replay, which stores all the interactions with the environment and uses them as mini-batch to update the Q-network. The DQN has two main features compared with other RL algorithms: (1) using the experience replay buffer to store the agent experiences $E = \left\{ s_i, a_i, r_i, s_i' \right\}$ which represents state, action, reward, and next state respectively, (2) adjusting any update for the target network. Here, agent G (Q-network) will be trained using the offline part. During this part, the agent learns to map each stat for suitable action. Then, the agent calculates the reward as feedback to updated the system. We summary the agent roles as following:

1. Receiving the extracted features of current state s during the interaction with the environment at timestamp t.
2. Generating a list of recommendations Γ that includes top items to be recommended using exploration and exploitation policy. Notice, the agent will pick only one item with the highest ranking.
3. Calculating the reward which considers as feedback to update the system using the following equation:

$$r(a) = \frac{\sum_{t=0}^{T_r} O_{a,t}}{\sum_{a=0}^{A} \sum_{t=0}^{T_r} O_{a,t}} \tag{1}$$

   where O represents the value of each item at each time step and T_r is a Reward Delay Period.
   However, the agent G has to wait for the reward delay period T_r (will be discussed in the next part).
4. Periodically updating after every recommendation by comparing the performance of the Q-network with target network using the following loss function:

$$loss = MES(predicted\ Q - Value, Target\ Q - Value) \tag{2}$$

5. Total updating for the system to tackle the dynamicity of human activity pattern, the agent G after a period of time (it is defined to be 24 h for our system) will use the experience replay buffer to update the network Q using the following loss equation [11]:

$$L_i(\theta_i) = E_{(s,a,r,s')} \sim U(D) \left[\left(r + \gamma max_{a'} Q(s', a'; \theta_i^-) - Q(s, a; \theta_i) \right)^2 \right] \tag{3}$$

where γ is a discount factor, θ_i and θ_i^- represent the parameters of the Q-network and the target-network at iteration i respectively.

Most traditional recommender systems focus on "click" or "not click" as feedback to calculate the reward function immediately and to update the system. In contrast, our system recommends an item to the user and then waits for sufficient time to decide if the recommended item is used or not-by checking its status (on/off or moved/not moved). For example, if the system recommends a coffee machine to Alice when she is preparing a cup of coffee, whereas she wants to use it later yet not immediately. This does not mean that the recommended item is incorrect, and it is better for the system to ignore this false negative feedback this time. To facilitate the above, we introduce a Reward Delay Period T_r, which accounts for the different paces of users in carrying out activities, and we consider T_r a hyperparameter. Here, our agent acts using different policies: EpsGreedyQPolicy, GreedyQPolicy, BoltzmannGumbelQPolicy, MaxBoltzmannQPolicy. Table 2 shows details about the policies with DQN that we used for our agent and their parameters.

Table 2. Explaining policies and tuning hyperparameters for our agent.

Policies	
(1) EpsGreedyQPolicy:	It combines both exploration by taking a random action with probability epsilon and exploitation by taking the current best action with probability (1 - epsilon)
(2) GreedyQPolicy:	It focuses on exploration where it calculates the probability of choosing the action with the highest Q-value
(3) BoltzmannGumbelQPolicy:	It is an exploration rule which defines probabilities of actions based on their Q-values.
(4) MaxBoltzmannQPolicy:	It adapts the Gumbel-softmax trick to address the classic Boltzmann exploration issues
Hyperparameters	
batch_size	200
Epsilon	0.1
target_model_update	1e−3
nb_steps	50000
verbose	1

4   Experiment

In this section, we first introduce three public datasets that we used for our experiments. Next, we conduct some experiments that show the effectiveness of our proposed RCS and evaluate the performance among these datasets.

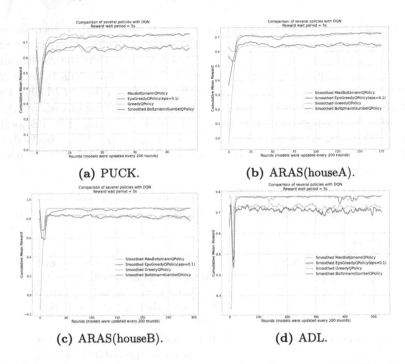

(a) PUCK.   (b) ARAS(houseA).

(c) ARAS(houseB).   (d) ADL.

Fig. 2. Performance of our system among three datasets and the $T_r = 5$.

4.1 Datasets

Our evaluation focused on the offline part, and we left the evaluation of the online part to future work. The evaluation has been applied on three public datasets: PUCK [4], ARAS [1], and ADL [3].

The PUCK dataset[1] was collected in Kyoto smart home testbed in Washington State University, and it consists of a two-story apartment with one living room, one dining area, one kitchen, one bathroom, and three bedrooms. A number of environmental sensors have been installed in this testbed. The ARAS dataset contains two houses of two residents who performed 27 daily living activities. The activity-sensory data was collected from 20 binary sensors. The ADL Normal dataset represents a public dataset published in 2010. The dataset was collected from a Kyoto smart apartment testbed in Washington State University. It includes five complex activities. The activities are performed by 20 participants. Features engineering and data processed are explained in detail in our previous work [2].

4.2 Experiments Results

We first evaluate the effectiveness of our RCS in recommending the correct item to the user in case the user's current activity needs a recommendation. The

---

[1] http://casas.wsu.edu/datasets/puck.zip.

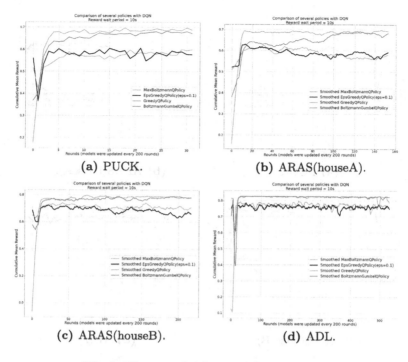

(a) PUCK. (b) ARAS(houseA).

(c) ARAS(houseB). (d) ADL.

Fig. 3. The reward delay periods $T_r - 10$ s.

agent uses all the extracted features as the state to make a recommendation of the correct item. We use the DQN model that is provided by one public available 'keras-rl' package of python for our experiments. The hyper-parameters of the DQN model are configured as follows: the number of layers in DQN is set to 6 with two Flatten layers, three Dense layers, and one Activation layer. The package provides a number of policies that help our agent to map each state with a correct action.

The performance of our system is shown in Fig. 2. As we can see, the cumulative mean reward for the three datasets; However, the two policies: GreedyQpolicy and BlotzmanngumbleQpolicy, produce the highest performance compared with another two policies. Also, the ARAS dataset for house B (see Fig. 2c) has the highest cumulative mean reward compared with other datasets. There are different reasons that could affect the results on different datasets: (1) the number of item sensors used to collect the data, (2) the time period between each reading of the sensors values, i.e., half a second for PUCK and a second for ARAS and ADL datasets, (3) the type of sensor value such as binary or continues values, (4) the number of items that are included in each activity. Moreover, all the previous datasets do not consider time as a context which is an important feature for our system. As mentioned, the Reward Delay Period parameter T_r has direct impacts on the model's performance which controls when the agent should receive the feedback as a reward. Adjusting this parameter is important,

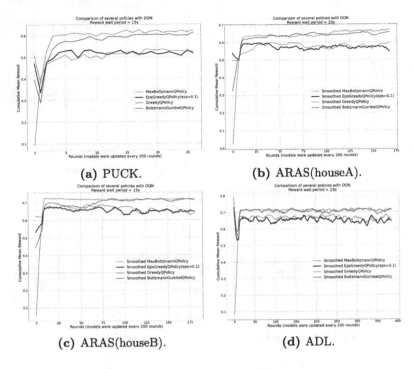

(a) PUCK.

(b) ARAS(houseA).

(c) ARAS(houseB).

(d) ADL.

Fig. 4. The reward delay periods $T_r = 15$ s.

Table 3. The cumulative mean reward of our system among three datasets using different reward delay periods.

Dataset	T_{r}	Policies			
		EpsGreedyQPolicy	GreedyQPolicy	BoltzmannGumbleQPolicy	MaxBoltzmannQPolicy
PUCK	5 s	0.65	**0.75**	**0.75**	0.67
	10 s	0.58	**0.68**	0.66	0.60
	15 s	0.51	**0.64**	0.62	0.52
ARAS house (A)	5 s	0.64	**0.72**	0.71	0.63
	10 s	0.59	**0.69**	0.68	0.57
	15 s	0.54	**0.67**	0.66	0.59
ARAS house (B)	5 s	0.77	**0.90**	**0.90**	0.83
	10 s	0.68	**0.78**	**0.78**	0.70
	15 s	0.65	**0.73**	**0.73**	0.64
ADL	5 s	0.70	**0.77**	**0.77**	0.72
	10 s	0.74	0.77	**0.82**	0.75
	15 s	0.64	0.71	**0.72**	0.65

and it is various from one activity to another depending on how much time each item consumes to be used. For example, some items take a little bit of time to be picked, and others may be a little bit longer. We assume three values of T_r: 5 s, 10 s, and 15 s, then we monitor the performance among these different values. Figure 2, Fig. 3 and, Fig. 4 show the performance of our RCS on the three datasets using three different values of T_r: 5 s, 10 s, and 15 s respectively. Table 3 summarizes all cumulative mean rewards of our system among three datasets using different reward delay periods. We can observe that our proposed system performance when the $T_r = 5$ consistently outperforms the other two values: $T_r = 10$, and $T_r = 15$ for the two datasets: PUCK, and ARAS. However, the ADL dataset demonstrates that increasing the T_r to 10 s improves the cumulative reward to be around 0.82 instead of 0.77 and 0.72 for the $T_r = 5$ and $T_r = 15$ respectively. Moreover, Table 3 shows the effectiveness of The GreedyQPolicy and BoltzmannGumbleQPolicy policies compared with the other two policies. However, among all the policies, the GreedyQPolicy performs well and is stable except in the last dataset with $T_r = 10$.

5 Conclusion

In this study, we designed a Reminder Care System (RCS) that uses deep reinforcement learning to capture dynamic patterns of human activities and update the system automatically without waiting for user feedback. The RCS uses DQN to formulate the agent and considers the reward delay period to account for the different paces of users in carrying out activities. We conducted experiments on three real-world public datasets to show that the effectiveness of our system. For future work, we will test our system on a real-time testbed that considers all features requirements for the proposed system.

References

1. Alemdar, H., Ertan, H., Incel, O.D., Ersoy, C.: Aras human activity datasets in multiple homes with multiple residents. In: 7th IEEE International Conference on Pervasive Computing Technologies for Healthcare and Workshops, pp. 232–235. IEEE (2013)
2. Altulyan, M.S., Huang, C., Yao, L., Wang, X., Kanhere, S.S.: Contextual bandit learning for activity-aware things-of-interest recommendation in an assisted living environment. In: ADC, pp. 37–49 (2021)
3. Cook, D.J., Schmitter-Edgecombe, M.: Assessing the quality of activities in a smart environment. Methods Inf. Med. **48**(05), 480–485 (2009)
4. Das, B., Cook, D.J., Schmitter-Edgecombe, M., Seelye, A.M.: PUCK: an automated prompting system for smart environments: toward achieving automated prompting–challenges involved. Pers. Ubiquitous Comput. **16**(7), 859–873 (2012)
5. De Campos, L.M., Fernández-Luna, et al.: Combining content-based and collaborative recommendations: a hybrid approach based on Bayesian networks. Int. J. Approx. Reason. **51**(7), 785–799 (2010)
6. Erdeniz, S.P., Maglogiannis, I., Menychtas, A., Felfernig, A., Tran, T.N.T.: Recommender systems for IoT enabled m-health applications. In: Iliadis, L., Maglogiannis, I., Plagianakos, V. (eds.) AIAI 2018. IAICT, vol. 520, pp. 227–237. Springer, Cham (2018). https://doi.org/10.1007/978-3-319-92016-0_21
7. Gutowski, N., Amghar, T., Camp, O., Hammoudi, S.: A framework for context-aware service recommendation for mobile users: a focus on mobility in smart cities. From Data Decis., 1–17 (2017)

8. HamlAbadi, K.G., Saghiri, A.M., Vahdati, M., TakhtFooladi, M.D., Meybodi, M.R.: A framework for cognitive recommender systems in the internet of things (IoT). In: 2017 IEEE 4th International Conference on Knowledge-Based Engineering and Innovation (KBEI), pp. 0971–0976. IEEE (2017)

9. Huang, C., Yao, L.: Active object estimation for human-robot collaborative tasks. In: Yang, H., Pasupa, K., Leung, A.C.-S., Kwok, J.T., Chan, J.H., King, I. (eds.) ICONIP 2020. LNCS, vol. 12533, pp. 750–761. Springer, Cham (2020). https://doi.org/10.1007/978-3-030-63833-7_63

10. Massimo, D.: User preference modeling and exploitation in IoT scenarios. In: 23rd International Conference on Intelligent User Interfaces, pp. 675–676 (2018)

11. Mnih, V., et al.: Human-level control through deep reinforcement learning. Nature 518(7540), 529–533 (2015)

12. Munemasa, I., Tomomatsu, Y., Hayashi, K., Takagi, T.: Deep reinforcement learning for recommender systems. In: 2018 International Conference on Information and Communications Technology (ICOIACT), pp. 226–233. IEEE (2018)

13. Oyeleke, R.O., Yu, C.Y., Chang, C.K.: Situ-centric reinforcement learning for recommendation of tasks in activities of daily living in smart homes. In: 2018 IEEE 42nd Annual Computer Software and Applications Conference (COMPSAC), vol. 2, pp. 317–322. IEEE (2018)

14. Pazzani, M.J., Billsus, D.: Content-based recommendation systems. In: Brusilovsky, P., Kobsa, A., Nejdl, W. (eds.) The Adaptive Web. LNCS, vol. 4321, pp. 325–341. Springer, Heidelberg (2007). https://doi.org/10.1007/978-3-540-72079-9_10

15. Saghiri, A.M., Vahdati, M., Gholizadeh, K., Meybodi, et al.: A framework for cognitive internet of things based on blockchain. In: 2018 4th International Conference on Web Research, pp. 138–143. IEEE (2018)

16. Sarwar, B., Karypis, G., Konstan, J., Riedl, J.: Item-based collaborative filtering recommendation algorithms. In: Proceedings of the 10th International Conference on World Wide Web, pp. 285–295 (2001)

17. Yao, L., et al.: WITS: an IoT-endowed computational framework for activity recognition in personalized smart homes. Computing 100(4), 369–385 (2018)

18. Yao, L., Wang, X., Sheng, Q.Z., Dustdar, S., Zhang, S.: Recommendations on the internet of things: requirements, challenges, and directions. IEEE Internet Comput. 23(3), 46–54 (2019)

19. Zhao, X., et al.: Dear: deep reinforcement learning for online advertising impression in recommender systems. In: Proceedings of the AAAI Conference on Artificial Intelligence, vol. 35, pp. 750–758 (2021)

20. Zhao, X., Xia, L., Zhang, L., Ding, Z., Yin, D., Tang, J.: Deep reinforcement learning for page-wise recommendations. In: Proceedings of the 12th ACM Conference on Recommender Systems, pp. 95–103. ACM (2018)

21. Zhao, X., Zhang, L., Ding, Z., Xia, L., Tang, J., Yin, D.: Recommendations with negative feedback via pairwise deep reinforcement learning. In: Proceedings of the 24th ACM SIGKDD International Conference on Knowledge Discovery & Data Mining, pp. 1040–1048. ACM (2018)

22. Zhao, Z., Chen, X., Xu, Z., Cao, L.: Tag-aware recommender system based on deep reinforcement learning. Math. Probl. Eng. 2021 (2021)

23. Zheng, G., Zhang, F., Zheng, et al.: DRN: a deep reinforcement learning framework for news recommendation. In: Proceedings of the 2018 World Wide Web Conference, pp. 167–176 (2018)

A Self-learning Approach for Beggiatoa Coverage Estimation in Aquaculture

Yanyu Chen[1(✉)], Yunjue Zhou[1], Son Tran[1], Mira Park[1], Scott Hadley[2],
Myriam Lacharite[2], and Quan Bai[1]

[1] School of Information and Communication Technology, University of Tasmania,
Hobart, Australia
{yanyu.chen,yunjuez,sn.tran,mira.park,quan.bai}@utas.edu.au
[2] Institute for Marine and Antarctic Studies, University of Tasmania,
Hobart, Australia
{s.hadley,myriam.lacharite}@utas.edu.au

Abstract. Beggiatoa is a bacterium that is associated with anoxic conditions beneath salmon aquaculture pens. Assessing the percentage coverage on the seafloor from images taken beneath a site is often undertaken as part of the environmental monitoring process. Images are assessed manually by observers with experience in identifying Beggiatoa. This is a time-consuming process and results can vary significantly between observers. Manually labelling images in order to apply visual learning techniques is also time-consuming and expensive as deep learning relies on very large data sets for training. Image segmentation techniques can automatically annotate images to release human resources and improve assessment efficiency. This paper introduces a combination method using Otsu thresholding and Fully Convolutional Networks (FCN). The self-learning method can be used to estimate coverage and generate training and testing data set for deep learning algorithms. Results showed that this combination of methods had better performance than individual methods.

Keywords: Beggiatoa coverage · Image segmentation · Self-learning

1 Introduction

Environmental sustainability is a key issue for the marine salmon aquaculture industry. The salmon waste (feed and feces) deposited on the benthic region beneath cages has the potential to shift local ecosystem function along a gradient of enrichment [7]. Beggiatoa is a bacterium that is also an anoxic and polluted environment with percentage coverage in the benthic area beneath pens used in some regions for compliance monitoring [1]. In order to do this, it is first necessary to score images or video beneath pens based on the appearance and cover of different types of Beggiatoa. To automate this scoring process, image segmentation techniques play a vital role. Image segmentation techniques divide an image into different regions based on pixel features, such as colour, texture and shape, to identify objects or boundaries. In the same region, these features

© Springer Nature Switzerland AG 2022
G. Long et al. (Eds.): AI 2021, LNAI 13151, pp. 405–416, 2022.
https://doi.org/10.1007/978-3-030-97546-3_33

show similarity regarded as a single entity, but demonstrate obvious differences between different regions [8]. Image segmentation techniques usually require a large amount of data to perform well in practice [6]. They also require an expert to annotate Beggiatoa in the training set, which is a resource intensive process in terms of time. In addition, it is a challenge to label images comprehensively and correctly, especially Beggiatoa with sparse distribution or less-obvious on the seafloor in poor light condition.

This paper studies the effectiveness of automatically annotating images and applying learning segmentation networks to underexposed small-sized datasets of Beggiatoa in footage taken beneath a salmon pen. In various image labels, automatic pixel-level image annotation is the most efficient and economical setting. The main problems is accurately assigning pixel-level labels for underexposed Beggiatoa images. To solve the problems, we propose to highlight the optical characteristic apparent in the Beggiatoa region. In practice, the highlighted regions always belong to the Beggiatoa regions. The motivation is to find the highlighted regions in an underexposed images.

To solve these issues, this paper aims to develop a new self-learning AI framework to estimate coverage, or produce mask as ground truth for next step of deep learning, based on less data application in image segmentation. This method can automatically annotate images and generate mask images. It helps aquaculture researchers and companies reduce labour costs and increase efficiency of Beggiatoa assessment, and provides practical proof of the usefulness of this technique. This technique potentially could be applied to other areas of research in benthic impacts in salmon aquaculture. Primarily however it will be put into practice for developing a bacteria assessment tool.

The paper is organized as follows. The following section shows the related works. Then, it presents the detailed introduction of this new self-learning AI framework. After that, it shows experiments and experimental results. The last part is the discussion and conclusion.

2   Related Works

There has been much kinds of research on weakly supervised methods for segmentation. For instance, FCN combined with active learning utilizing 50% data for training a model obtained similar performance when using the entire dataset [11]. Furthermore, FCN is also used to annotate images in MIL (Multiple Instance Learning) [3]. However, images annotated by experts are still needed in these models. Furthermore, self-learning methods have been proposed which have better performance than using data with training labels. For example, AlphaGo Zero becomes the expert through self-learning without using human knowledge [9]. In addition, some self-learning segmentation tasks demonstrate higher accuracy than using labelled images due to human error [5].

The self-learning strategy is to infer unlabeled data through highly confident network predictions to generate pseudo-labels, and then obtain more accurate segmentation with the self-taught supervision [10]. For example, a combination method is proposed in the medical area to segment skin lesion images automatically. It adopts Grabcut to segment the foreground and K-means to extract the lesion region [3]. After that, a two-stage deep learning model is proposed to segment images, which combines K-means and U-net to generate annotation segmentation maps [4]. Moreover, an ensemble deep learning method combined DeepLabv3 and MaskRCNN generates an accurate segmentation mask [2]. However, most previous work utilizes large datasets, which do not exist for all problems. Furthermore, small-sized datasets lead to overfitting, whereas pretraining techniques can effectively solve this issue [12].

3   Self-learning AI Framework

Data labelling is critical but labour-intensive in most deep learning applications. In Beggiatoa coverage estimation, automating coverage areas of underwater images requires significant inputs from human domain experts which is very time-consuming and thus expensive. Moreover, underwater images are normally underexposed due to poor light. Therefore, in this research, a self-learning AI framework is developed to automatically annotate and segment the Beggiatoa region from images. The overall structure of the framework is shown in Fig. 1.

There are three modules in the framework, namely the self-learning annotation, transfer-learning and coverage estimation modules. Self-learning can correctly and automatically annotate the sparsely distributed objects in the underexposed Beggiatoa images; highlight the objects to be annotated.

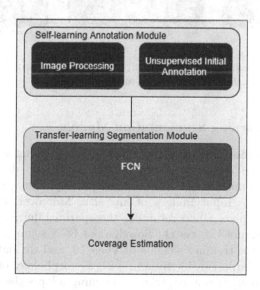

Fig. 1. Self-learning AI framework. Annotated image is generated though self-learning annotation module. This annotated image is input with original image into transfer-learning segmentation module to generate mask for coverage estimation.

3.1   Self-learning Annotation Module

Self-learning annotation module contains two parts, namely image processing and unsupervised initial annotation. Image processing aims to transfer a color image to a grey image; grey algorithm is both commonly used and effective. Otsu's threshold is used to generate initial annotation data for Beggiatoa segmentation based on the self-learning segmentation approach. Otsu's threshold solves the problem of an underexposed image with scattered distribution of Beggiatoa for automatic labelling.

Otsu's algorithm subdivides the image into two major classes, namely foreground and background. The more significant inter-class variance between target and background, the more pronounced the difference between the two parts of the image. It means if the target or background is incorrectly classified, the inter-class variance between them will become smaller. Therefore, the variance between classes is maximum, and the misclassification is minimum. A binary segmentation mask for two regions can be generated through Otsu's threshold. The flowchart of the self-learning annotation scheme is shown in Fig. 2.

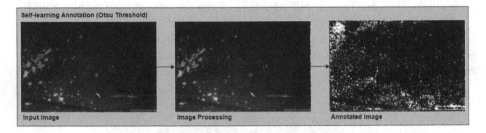

Fig. 2. Self-learning Annotation Scheme. Input a color image to generate a grey image and adopts Otsu's threshold to generate a annotated image.

3.2   Transfer-Learning Segmentation Module

Transfer-learning annotation data generated by self-learning is used by an FCN model for Beggiatoa region segmentation. In FCN, the deconvolution layer restores the feature map to the same size as the input image through upsampling and can accept input images of any size. Moreover, it can generate a prediction for each pixel while retaining the spatial information in the original input image. Figure 3 shows the flowchart of FCN segmentation. Moreover, this model adopts the training weights of VGG-16, and the dataset supplied by ImageNet. As Beggiatoa is a bacterium, with a morphology of a bacterial mat and a non-microscopic substance, transfer learning adopts the weights based on ImageNet.

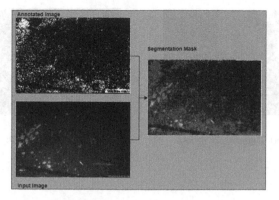

Fig. 3. Flowchart of FCN segmentation. Annotated images and original images are input into FCN to generate masks.

3.3 Coverage Percentage Module

The predicted percentage coverage of Beggiatoa in the image is calculated through the number of segmented pixels divided by the total number of pixels in the image. The total number of pixels is equal to the value of the width multiplied by the length. The function for calculating the coverage percentage is given by,

$$CoveragePercentage = \frac{number\ of\ labelled\ pixels}{width * length(px)\ of\ the\ cropped\ images} \tag{1}$$

This self-learning AI framework saves time and expertise required for manual annotation. It uses the results of unsupervised methods to effectively train segmentation techniques based on deep learning. Meanwhile, the segmented images and bounding regions labelled on the original images, will be generated when applying these segmentation methods. Moreover, the segmented results could be compared by experts to adjust the algorithms.

4   Experiments

4.1   Data Description

Beggiatoa images (see Fig. 4) were taken by a high-resolution, time-lapse camera underneath salmon pens to record benthic changes. These images may be used in understanding drivers of benthic change and eventually assist in the development of a predictive tool to aid farm management decisions. Furthermore, images with grid overlay (see Fig. 5) were annotated by an expert using a number scale to demonstrate different classes of objects.

There were five subclasses defined (see Fig. 6) in each image. These related to 'types' of beggiatoa or worm. These objects were identified within each image.

Fig. 4. Unedited Beggiatoa image.

Fig. 5. Annotated image. Grid cell where Beggiatoa is $\geq$ 50% coverage of that type.

Beggiatoa grows on the seabed and appears varying morphology and intensity. There are three classes of Beggiatoa identified in the images. Type 1 is a thick mat identified as bright white pixels packed into dense clusters. Type 2 is patchy seen as more sparse white pixels. Type 3 is a thin film which appears with a blueish hue. Beggiatoa can be distinguished from two worm species which are also typically found in this enriched environment. Type 4 is *Ophryotroca shieldsii* a grass like circular colony of very small translucent worms vertically arranged. Type 5 are *Schistomeringos lovenii* a thick pink worm which can often be seen individually or in groups. Also included is a type 6 'background' with no objects within the grid cell. In this study, 130 images were used; 80 were used for training and 50 for testing.

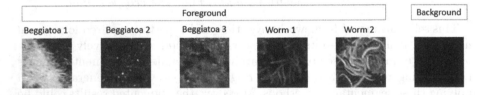

Fig. 6. Different types of objects for detection in images including Beggiatoa 1 (thick mat), Beggiatoa 2 (patchy), Beggiatoa 3 (thin film), Worm 1 (*Ophryotroca shieldsii* - thin colony), Worm 2 (*Schistomeringos lovenii* - thick worms), Background.

4.2   Self-learning Annotation Approaches Comparison

Threshold, regiongrowing and K-Means are three common methods that perform well on identifying bacteria in images. This paper will explore these three methods.

Threshold Method. Thresholding method has excellent performance on the high contrast between target and background, which is suitable for the Beggiatoa optical characteristic. It compares each pixel intensity to threshold values to classifications classified as the simple threshold, adaptive threshold and Otsu's threshold (Doxygen 2020). In this paper, the simple threshold value is set to 127 for the whole image, which is the middle of color range. The adaptive threshold value is set by calculating a small region, and different threshold values are used for different regions. Otsu's threshold value is automatically set according to the image histogram. The segmentation results could be checked by comparing mask results and original images. The same example image is processed by these three methods separately and the segmentation results are shown in Fig. 7.

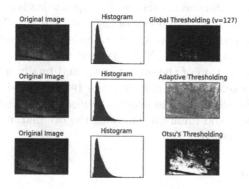

Fig. 7. Segmentation results.

According to the results, Otsu's threshold performs better than the other two methods, and labels the presence of bacteria more accurately, while the simple threshold misses a lot of targets and the adaptive threshold generates too many noises.

Region Growing. Region growing method can obtain excellent segmentation results including boundary information, when separating Beggiatoa 'regions'. The region growing method divides the image into various regions, named superpixels. Superpixels refers to clustering pixels with similar features to form large 'pixels'. According to the rapidly changing pixel intensity, the method determines the object boundary. Moreover, it can merge similar pixels around a seed pixel to determine the region [13].

K-Means. K-means adopts a clustering algorithm, and has excellent performance on large datasets. Groups of pixels sharing similar features are called clusters. 'K' represents the number of clusters. Firstly, initial clusters are randomly selected, and all pixels are assigned to a cluster. The clustering centers are generated and the distance of each pixel to the center of each cluster is calculated. Then the clusters are reassigned based on the distances. The centers of the newly formed clusters and the distances are calculated to reassign the clusters until the clusters' center does not change [13].

4.3   Transfer-Learning Approaches Comparison

Transfer-learning model can be used to test each model's performance.

FCN Model. FCN (Fully Convolutional Networks) method uses a parameter weight generated by TensorFlow VGG-16 model pretrained on ImageNet datasets, and finetuned on target images. The input image goes through the first five convolutional layers of VGG-16 with the pretrained weights, one max pooling layer and three convolutional layers using a one-dimensional vector to generate feature maps. Moreover, varying the step size leads to a change in precision. For FCN-32s, the overall step size of the feature extraction network before the transpose convolution layer was 32. One step is used to restore the predicted size to the original image size. FCN-16s is used to sample the last layer then combine with the prediction of the pool 4 layer, and finally upsample to restore the original image size. So more details could be presented through this network. As for FCN-8s, similarly, the process is upsampling first, then combining high-level information, and finally upsampling the original image size, so higher precision could be observed.

4.4   Ground Truth

The experts labelled original image with grid squares, grid squares are 4cm and to be laballed as a type with a number, must have 50%–100% or greater coverage of that type, as Fig. 5 shown. This means that when estimating % cover, a range is given. Each grid cell is classified as being Type X if it contains $\geq 50\%$ coverage of that type. So, for each specific type a total coverage percentage for an image is calculated by dividing the number of labelled grid cells of that specific type by the number of the total grids and multiplying by the range coverage within a cell (between 50% and 100%).

$$CoveragePercentage = \frac{number\ of\ labelled\ grids}{total\ grids\ number} * range\ cover\ per\ cell \quad (2)$$

4.5   Metrics

To evaluate the performance of these methods, two kinds of metrics were defined these were absolute error and precision.

Absolute Error. Absolute error is the difference between predicted coverage and the ground truth. Four absolute error (see Fig. 8) measures were compared, including: lower bound absolute error which is the difference between the predicted coverage and the lower bound value of the range; upper-bound absolute error which compared with the upper bound; center absolute error which compared with the center value of the range; and minimum absolute error generated by the previous three values. If the absolute error is lower, the method has performed better.

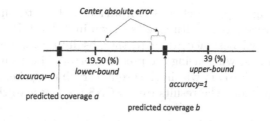

Fig. 8. Explanation of absolute error.

Precision. Precision is the ratio between the predicted result and the observations (ground truth). If the predicted coverage percentage is within the range of ground truth, the precision will be recorded as 100%, otherwise it will be divided by the nearest range value.

$$
\begin{aligned}
Precision &= \frac{TP}{TP+FP} \\
&= \frac{lower\ bound}{predicted\ coverage\ (when\ lower\ bound\ is\ nearest)} \\
&= \frac{predicted\ coverage}{upper\ bound\ (when\ lower\ bound\ is\ nearest)}
\end{aligned}
\tag{3}
$$

5   Experimental Results

To evaluate this self-learning AI framework, each model's performance was compared using absolute error and precision Results

5.1   Results

Self-learning Annotation Approaches Comparison. In this section, there are five models. Table 1 gives summary results for each model. Otsu's threshold method performs best among these methods acrossboththe absolute error or the precision measures.

Table 1. Results of self-learning annotation approaches.

	Center absolute error	Lower-bound absolute error	Upper-bound absolute error	Minimum absolute error	Precision
Otsu threshold	15.58	8.86	24.55	8.86	73.84%
Simple threshold	30.16	19.69	40.63	19.69	6.84%
Adaptive threshold	27.72	38.01	20.50	20.50	68.85%
Regional growth	15.82	8.86	25.34	8.86	72.50%
K-means	17.60	13.55	23.84	13.55	60.25%

Transfer-Learning Approaches Comparison. Due to the different step sizes, FCN has three models, with results shown in Table 2. For the FCN methods, FCN8 performed best according to the absolute error perspective, while FCN16 performed best when using the precision error. This result indicates that more results from FCN16 are within the ground truth range i.e. more images are predicted correctly, while the results from FCN8 are closer to the ground truth range.

Table 2. Results of each deep-learning method.

	Center absolute error	Lower-bound absolute error	Upper-bound absolute error	Minimum absolute error	Precision
FCN8	19.99	14.34	27.31	14.34	59.81%
FCN16	35.59	43.85	30.37	30.37	62.99%
FCN32	56.36	66.84	45.89	45.89	48.27%

Self-learning AI Framework. Model performance when combining the Ostu threshold with FCN-8 to segment the image is summarised in Table 3.

Table 3. Results of each deep-learning method.

	Center absolute error	Lower-bound absolute error	Upper-bound absolute error	Minimum absolute error	Precision
FCN + Otsu thresholding	24.46	30.60	22.84	22.84	74.35%

6   Discussion and Conclusion

This study developed a new self-learning AI framework, which was compared with existing individual methods. Overall this new method had the best performance for image recognition based on the comparison criteria. All models were evaluated by precision and absolute error through comparing the predicted cover percentage with the observed percentage. Firstly, the Otsu's thresholding method scores 73.84% for the precision and the lowest Minimum Absolute Error, which indicates its worth for future use, because of its good performance in sparsely distributed objects and objects with optical properties. It is an efficient way to segment Beggiatoa especially when the images have comparatively clear seafloor and obvious objects. Secondly, when an FCN model is trained with the predicted results from Otsu's threshold, the precision is improved by 18.03% compared to a pretrained model using another dataset. The results showcase the possibility to combine the unsupervised methods with the transfer-learning methods when trying to avoid expensive training dataset preparation. Moreover, unsupervised methods perform better than transfer-learning methods. Transfer-learning only performs well for similar objects, but unsupervised is not subject to this limitation.

There are three key limitations in this Self-learning AI Framework. The primary limitation is the Otsu's thresholding method, which is in the classification of the pixels into foreground and background in a binary way. Deep-learning models trained after the thresholding method can only deal with two labels and cannot learn more types. This is an issue for marine images, where there is noise in the data such as other types of objects like worms, macrofauna etc. Similarly, Beggiatoa is also classified into more than one type. Therefore, in order to produce more accurate coverage and segmentation, the models need to handle various labels. The other limitation is in transfer-learning segmentation module. Because weight selection and dataset similarity will influence model performance, these depend on human experience. For example, source datasets contain different kinds of animals, such as cats, birds and dogs, and target dataset only has dogs, so in transfer learning, the accuracy can be improved by artificially increasing sample weights belonging to the dog in source datasets. The last one is caused by the ground truth scope. Due the large-scale range of ground truth, the result error will increase.

In future work, the entire image could be divided into grids and each grid could be classified as a specific type, with image segmentation methods applied to small regions rather than the whole image. For each grid cell, binary classification is possible because only the corresponding (dominant) type for that cell needs to be segmented. For the whole image, the predicted results for grid of the same type could be gathered together, and the entire coverage percentage for different types could be calculated more accurately.

The testing dataset used in this study was relatively small, which may lead to coincidences and incomplete results. More data is required to improve the training process and to produce a more comprehensive result as well. Whereas to improve the precision, investigating more deep-learning techniques including ensemble deep learning should be considered. Voting ensembles helps with deciding the class of the pixels, and stacking ensembles could weight the contributions of each sub-model and combine the contributions to generate a new model.

References

1. Crawford, C., Mitchell, I., Macleod, C.: Video assessment of environmental impacts of salmon farms. ICES J. Mar. Sci. **58**(2), 445–452 (2001)
2. Goyal, M., Oakley, A., Bansal, P., Dancey, D., Yap, M.H.: Skin lesion segmentation in dermoscopic images with ensemble deep learning methods. IEEE Access **8**, 4171–4181 (2019)
3. Jaisakthi, S.M., Mirunalini, P., Aravindan, C.: Automated skin lesion segmentation of dermoscopic images using grabcut and k-means algorithms. IET Comput. Vis. **12**(8), 1088–1095 (2018)
4. Kamalakannan, A., Ganesan, S.S., Rajamanickam, G.: Self-learning AI framework for skin lesion image segmentation and classification. arXiv preprint arXiv:2001.05838 (2020)
5. Khoreva, A., Benenson, R., Hosang, J., Hein, M., Schiele, B.: Simple does it: weakly supervised instance and semantic segmentation. In: Proceedings of the IEEE Conference on Computer Vision and Pattern Recognition, pp. 876–885 (2017)

6. Knox, S.W.: Machine Learning: A Concise Introduction, vol. 285. Wiley, Hoboken (2018)
7. Pearson, T.a.: Macrobenthic succession in relation to organic enrichment and pollution of the marine environment. Oceanogr. Mar. Biol. Ann. Rev. **16**, 229–311 (1978)
8. Pratt, W.K.: Introduction to Digital Image Processing. CRC Press, Boca Raton (2013)
9. Silver, D., et al.: Mastering the game of go without human knowledge. Nature **550**(7676), 354–359 (2017)
10. Toldo, M., Maracani, A., Michieli, U., Zanuttigh, P.: Unsupervised domain adaptation in semantic segmentation: a review. Technologies **8**(2), 35 (2020)
11. Yang, L., Zhang, Y., Chen, J., Zhang, S., Chen, D.Z.: Suggestive annotation: a deep active learning framework for biomedical image segmentation. In: Descoteaux, M., Maier-Hein, L., Franz, A., Jannin, P., Collins, D.L., Duchesne, S. (eds.) MICCAI 2017. LNCS, vol. 10435, pp. 399–407. Springer, Cham (2017). https://doi.org/10.1007/978-3-319-66179-7_46
12. Yang, X., He, X., Liang, Y., Yang, Y., Zhang, S., Xie, P.: Transfer learning or self-supervised learning? A tale of two pretraining paradigms. arXiv preprint arXiv:2007.04234 (2020)
13. Yuheng, S., Hao, Y.: Image segmentation algorithms overview. arXiv preprint arXiv:1707.02051 (2017)

Real-Time Prediction of the Lane-Based Delay for Group-Based Adaptive Traffic Operations Using Long Short-Term Memory

Seunghyeon Lee[1]($\boxtimes$) ⓘ, Dong Ngoduy[2] ⓘ, and Fang Chen[1]

[1] Data Science Institute, University of Technology Sydney, 15 Broadway, Ultimo, NSW 2007, Australia
seunghyeon.lee@uts.edu.au
[2] Department of Civil Engineering, Monash University, Victoria 3800, Australia

Abstract. This study proposes a deterministic real-time lane-based control delay model for traffic operations based on Long Short-Term Memory (LSTM). Our proposed framework includes a model-based approach to compute the control delay in an individual lane for a single cycle and a data-driven approach to predict the queueing profiles and adjustment factors used in the future control delay formula. This framework not only secures an excellent performance of the proposed model under a wide range of data availability but also guarantees a lower computational burden for a real-time non-linear optimisation process in adaptive control logic. The modified deep learning method has three primary components in the proposed architecture of the lane-based control delay model cycle-by-cycle. First, the data-driven and model-based approaches are integrated to improve the reliability and the accuracy of the control delay predictive formula. Second, the novel LSTM network is constructed to predict a cycle-based control delay in an individual lane while minimising inherent errors in the algorithm. Third, the predicted queue lengths at inflection points and adjustment factors are used to construct the delay polygons in the future cycle. Numerical simulations are set up using both synthetic and real-world data to give insights into the proposed model's performance compared to the existing models.

Keywords: Incremental queue accumulations · Long short-term memory · Lane-based control delay · Queue-length estimation · Deep learning

1 Introduction

To control conflicting traffic flows at the intersection, traffic signals are installed to maximise the efficiency of the systems and minimise traffic congestion and emissions caused by unnecessary vehicular manoeuvres. In establishing an effective real-time traffic operational strategy, a control delay induced by queued vehicles is estimated as a performance index to construct optimum signal settings in both long-term and short-term analysis periods. Webster's theories [1], stochastic queueing theory [2], queued vehicular delay [3], and time-dependent delay formula [4] have laid the foundation

© Springer Nature Switzerland AG 2022
G. Long et al. (Eds.): AI 2021, LNAI 13151, pp. 417–427, 2022.
https://doi.org/10.1007/978-3-030-97546-3_34

for developing mathematical frameworks of a control delay widely used in the current adaptive traffic control systems (ATCS). The proposed real-time predictive model of the control delay in an individual lane is derived from the delay formula based on Incremental Queue Accumulations (IQAs). This has been developed in [5], which was used as the performance index in real-time non-linear optimisation method of signal timings for ATCS [6] and [7].

1.1 Delay Formula for Traffic Operations

The concept of delay formula is mainly based on the fluctuations of the queue lengths at a signalised intersection. A variety of queue lengths estimation methods are derived from the traditional techniques, containing the conservation equation [9] and the shockwave theory [10] and [11]. Various queue lengths estimation models have been developed to provide queue profiles that are as precise, time-efficient, and robust as possible for the last decades. [8] thoroughly examined from the conventional queue lengths estimation methods to the most up-to-date methods to bridge the research gap in the lane-based and real-time recursive approaches. Following the development of queue estimation methods, various deterministic and stochastic delay formulas have been developed. The delay formula has been used as an essential performance index in mathematical programs to construct fixed-time signal plans at signalised intersections and in networks.

1.2 Long Short-Term Memory Network in Transport Science

To relieve the vanishing gradient problem in the RNN, [13] suggested a new recurrent network architecture, the LSTM network. The general architecture of the LSTM consists of a memory cell, and the concept of gates, which include an input gate, an output gate, and a forget gate, for learning long-term information dependencies with back-propagation through time. Recently, the LSTM has been applied to a variety of transportation problems for predicting traffic quantities. [14] used the LSTM network to predict the traffic speed based on the remote microwave sensor data sets. In addition, [15] integrated the LSTM network with a convolutional neural network (CNN) to forecast the passenger demand under on-demand ride services. [16] used the LSTM to identify the behavioural changes among drivers. Later on, [17] applied the integrated CNN-LSTM method to estimate the probability of lane-changing (LC) manoeuvres in a stochastic multi-lane car-following model.

1.3 Research Gap and Contributions

According to the above review of the use of the control delay formula and the deep learning method in traffic operations, we found that there is plenty of room for improvements in simultaneously considering; (1) minimisation of the inherent predictive errors, (2) a lower computational burden for a real-time non-linear optimisation process in the ATCS, and (3) a detailed lane-based control delay formula for maximising flexibility in traffic controls. Therefore, our research objectives are as follows.

First, we found the inherent predictive errors in the predictive model of the lane-based control delay using the IQA in [5]. Although Lee and Wong's model has shown good performance in group-based ATCS [6] and [7], there is a possibility to improve further the model accuracy in the prediction of traffic quantities. This paper will thus extend the methods in [5] by applying a data-driven approach in the prediction process to relax the requirement of calibrating the Kalman-filter parameters in the model and to improve the effectiveness of the model performance.

Second, the lane-based control delay formula extracts queueing profiles from the lane-based queue estimation model developed in [8] to define the queue accumulated polygons by adjustment factors and queue lengths at an inflection point. It allows the real-time traffic operation strategies to use the proposed formula as a performance index in the non-linear dynamic optimisation process. The adopted LSTM network requires a relatively shorter calculation time and less computational burden than the previous method. Therefore, the proposed model will guarantee to sufficiently finish all the predictive processes for the future control delay within the designated varied cycle time from 30 s to 120 s in the ATCS.

Third, a lane-based approach allows a real-time traffic operation strategy to take full advantage of the sensor technologies to update the traffic patterns in real-time. To improve the real-time performance of the group-based approach for real-time traffic management and control, our proposed method aims to enhance the capability of a predictive process for traffic quantities, which is an integral part of the group-based ATCS.

The purposes of this study are thus to develop an architecture of the deterministic real-time lane-based control delay formula for traffic operations based on the LSTM network. The main contributions of this paper are below:

1. The LSTM is constructed to predict a cycle-based control delay in an individual lane while minimising the inherent errors in the algorithm,
2. The LSTM captures short-term arrival patterns and long-term control delay trends to improve the accuracy of the estimates of queueing profiles for the future signal cycles,
3. Predicted queue lengths at inflection points and adjustment factors are used to construct the delay polygons in the future cycle.
4. The proposed method is analysed and validated using both synthetic and real-world high-resolution detector datasets.

2 Methodology

This section shows the mathematical framework of the proposed method, including the lane-based IQAs, the architecture of the LSTM, and group-based variables for traffic operations. The definitions of the typical indices, parameters, and variables used in this study are given in [5]. They are used not only to define the modelling of the lane-based control delay using polygonal formulas in IQAs, but also to construct the architecture of the LSTM to predict a set of queueing profiles for the future cycle. The proposed data-processing framework for the integrated model-based and data-driven method of the lane-based control delay is illustrated in Fig. 1.

In the first step, ① *Real-time lane-based queue lengths second-by-second*, the real-time queue lengths in the individual lane are estimated by the lane-based queue length

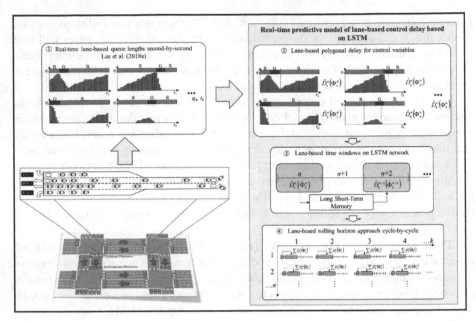

Fig. 1. Data processing method for the real-time predictive model of lane-based control delay.

estimation method developed in [8]. Queueing profiles, including temporal and spatial information of the queueing behaviours in an individual lane, are extracted from the first step to construct a real-time predictive model of the lane-based control delay using the LSTM network. In the second step, ② *Lane-based polygonal delay formula for group-based control variables*, the numbers of vehicular queues estimated in a second are aggregated in a cycle to construct a polygonal delay formula in an individual lane. Combinations of polygons in lane k on the nth cycle, $\hat{D}_k^n(\Phi_k^n)$, are specified using the queue lengths at an inflection point, adjustment factors, and group-based control variables, involving reciprocal values of cycle time, start time and duration of green signal groups. These polygons show the control delay in each lane on the nth cycle, and they are estimated through the proposed mathematical framework in [5]. In the third step, ③ *Lane-based time windows on LSTM network*, the estimates from the second step are used as input data sets in the LSTM network to predict the components of the polygons in the future cycle. The predictive processes are performed in the current cycle to predict attributes of the future control delay using trained and validated LSTM networks in each lane. The time windows in the proposed method consist of the previous cycle (e.g. n), for collecting the queueing information and establishing the polygons; the current cycle (e.g. $n + 1$) for the sufficient calculation time; and the future cycle (e.g. $n + 2$) as the target cycle of the predictive process. The proposed method only uses the queueing profiles of the control delay in the previous cycle for predictions in the next cycle with a high level of accuracy and computation efficiency. In the last step, ④ *Lane-based rolling horizon approach cycle-by-cycle*, we predict the future control delay based on the predicted temporal and spatial information of the queued vehicles in individual lanes and adjustment factors within the corresponding time windows. The total delay of the target intersection, $\sum_{k=1}^{K} \hat{D}_k^{n+1}\left(\hat{\Phi}_k^{n+1}\right)$, is computed on the nth cycle based on the data collected from the $(n - 1)$th cycle. The calculation time is provided in the current nth cycle. This data processing step is performed every cycle in each lane to estimate the future variables for predicting the future patterns of the control delay.

2.1 A Lane-Based Control Delay Formula Based on IQAs

We adopt the delay formula developed in [5] in the LSTM network for the real-time forecast of the lane-based control delay cycle-by-cycle. To design a combination of the delay polygons, a real-time estimated number of queued vehicles is used, and then, we simultaneously collect the queueing profiles in which the queue lengths change from the previous time step drastically. The x- and y-coordinates of the polygons are based on these collected data, including the queue lengths in second for spatial profiles, the group-based variables and adjustment factors for temporal profiles for the cycle delay.

2.2 LSTM Approach to Predicting the Control Parameters in IQAs

In this section, we develop an architecture of the LSTM network to predict the queue lengths at inflection points and adjustment factors for the future cycle using the queue profiles in the previous cycle. It involves the hidden layers as memory cells and can account for the autocorrelation within time series data in both long and short terms by controlling the transfer of cell states and hidden states between different cells. The predicted quantities are used to compute an amount of the control delay in an individual lane cycle-by-cycle. The current cycle is guaranteed for the calculation time for recursive predictive processes, which are carried out at the end of every cycle. We organise the related formulation with the control delay for the recursive process as the following equations and sets of variables.

$$D^n = \frac{1}{2} \sum_{k=1}^{K} \left[D_{A,k}^n\left(\Gamma^n, \Omega_k^n, \Phi_k^n\right) + D_{B,k}^n\left(\Gamma^n, \Omega_k^n, \Phi_k^n\right) + D_{B,k}^n\left(\Gamma^n, \Omega_k^n, \Phi_k^n\right) \right] \quad (1)$$

where,

$$\Gamma^n = \left\{ \zeta^n, \theta_1^n \cdots \theta_k^n, \phi_1^n \cdots \phi_k^n \right\}, \forall k \in K, \forall n \in N,$$
$$\Omega_k^n = \left\{ \alpha_k^n, \beta_k^n, \gamma_k^n, \delta_k^n \right\}, \forall k \in K, \forall n \in N,$$

$$\Psi_k^n = \left\{ \begin{array}{l} \hat{q}_k^n(\alpha_k^n), \hat{q}_k^n\left(\dfrac{\theta_k^n}{\zeta^n} + \beta_k^n\right), \hat{q}_k^n\left(\dfrac{\theta_k^n + \varphi_k^n}{\zeta^n} + \gamma_k^n\right), \\ \hat{q}_k^n\left(\dfrac{\theta_k^n + \varphi_k^n}{\zeta^n} + \gamma_k^n + \delta_k^n\right), \hat{q}_k^n\left(\dfrac{1}{\zeta^n}\right) \end{array} \right\}, \forall k \in K, \forall n \in N, \text{ and}$$

$$\Phi_k^n = \left\{ \lambda_{A,k}^n, \mu_{B,k}^n, \lambda_{C,k}^n \right\}, \forall k \in K, \forall n \in N.$$

In Eq. (1), the total delay at the target intersection for a cycle is defined with four sets of components. Γ^n is optimised based on the predicted parameters in the optimisation process. Ω_k^n is used to decide the current states of the queueing formation patterns in the current cycle. Ω_k^n and Ψ_k^n are then used as seed parameters to predict the future traffic patterns in the LSTM network. Φ_k^n includes the arrival rates before an effective green time, discharge rates, and the arrival rates after an effective green time. Φ_k^n is computed with the predicted Ω_k^n and Ψ_k^n from the LSTM network. The computed Φ_k^n and the predicted Ω_k^n are then used to estimate the future control delay in appropriate time windows with the optimised Γ^n.

To start with the LSTM network to predict Ω_k^{n+1} and Ψ_k^{n+1} in lane k for the $(n+1)$th cycle, we set Ω_k^{n-1} and Ψ_k^{n-1} in lane k for the $(n-1)$th cycle as input data for the LSTM process. Through the LSTM network, $\hat{\Omega}_k^{n+1}$ and $\hat{\Psi}_k^{n+1}$ are produced to calculate $\hat{\Phi}_k^{n+1}$ in a part of D_k^{n+1}. The LSTM contains several memory units to allow the algorithm learning both to forget the prior hidden states as well as to update the hidden states given new information. We follow the general algorithm of the LSTM provided in [13] to develop the structure of the LSTM memory for the estimates of $\hat{\Omega}_k^{n+1}$ and $\hat{\Psi}_k^{n+1}$ in this paper. Hence, the memory units are described in the following equations.

$$z^{lstm,n} = \begin{bmatrix} \alpha_k^{n-1}, \beta_k^{n-1}, \gamma_k^{n-1}, \delta_k^{n-1}, \hat{q}_k^{n-1}\left(\alpha_k^{n-1}\right), \hat{q}_k^{n-1}\left(\frac{\theta_k^{n-1}}{\zeta^{n-1}} + \beta_k^{n-1}\right), \\ \hat{q}_k^{n-1}\left(\frac{\theta_k^{n-1} + \phi_k^{n-1}}{\zeta^{n-1}} + \gamma_k^{n-1}\right), \hat{q}_k^{n-1}\left(\frac{\theta_k^{n-1} + \phi_k^{n-1}}{\zeta^{n-1}} + \gamma_k^{n-1} + \delta_k^{n-1}\right), \hat{q}_k^{n-1}\left(\frac{1}{\zeta^{n-1}}\right) \end{bmatrix} \tag{2}$$

$$i_j^l = \sigma\left(w_{X,I}^l y_j^l + w_{H,I}^l h_j^{l-1} + w_{C,I}^l c_j^{l-1} + b_I^l\right) \tag{3}$$

$$f_j^l = \sigma\left(w_{X,F}^l y_j^l + w_{H,F}^l h_j^{l-1} + w_{C,F}^l c_j^{l-1} + b_F^l\right) \tag{4}$$

$$a_j^l = \phi\left(w_{X,C}^l y_j^l + w_{H,C}^l h_j^{l-1} + b_C^l\right) \tag{5}$$

$$c_j^l = f_j^l \cdot c_j^{l-1} + i_j^l \cdot a_j^l \tag{6}$$

$$o_j^l = \sigma\left(w_{X,O}^l y_j^l + w_{H,O}^l h_j^l + w_{C,O}^l c_j^l + b_O^l\right) \tag{7}$$

$$h_j^l = o_j^l \cdot \phi\left(c_j^l\right) \tag{8}$$

In Eq. (2), the stacked LSTM updates for the lth layer given inputs for the current time step, y_j^l, including Ω_k^{n-1} and Ψ_k^{n-1} for each lane, a hidden unit at the previous layer, h_j^{l-1}, and a memory cell unit at the previous layer, c_j^{l-1}. The function $\sigma(.)$ in Eqs. (3), (4) and (7) represents the *sigmoid* non-linearity, $\sigma(x) = \left(1 + e^{-x}\right)^{-1}$, squashing real-values inputs to a $[0, 1]$ range. The function $\phi(.)$ in Eq. (5) and (8) illustrates the *hyperbolic tangent* nonlinearity, $\phi(x) = \frac{e^x - e^{-x}}{e^x + e^{-x}} = 2\sigma(2x) - 1$, which squash its inputs to a $[-1, 1]$ range.

The LSTM process can learn highly complex and long-term temporal dynamics through a series of cells around the cell state vector. In Eq. (8), the hidden unit in the lth layer, h_j^l, is defined as a combination of the output gate and a sigmoid function of c_j^l, which is the final output at time step t. The final output is the proportional lane-use of the downstream arrivals, $\hat{a}^n_{d,k}$, at the final layer $\mathbf{L}$ in the stacked LSTM.

In this paper, multiple LSTMs are stacked and temporally connected to model the complex structure of real-time predictive problems for downstream arrivals in the current cycle. The general and more detailed explanation for the LSTM formulas used in this study is illustrated in [18]. The overall process of the proposed LSTM for this study is described in the following figure.

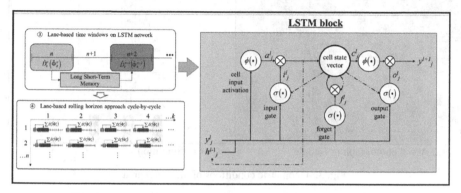

Fig. 2. The structure of the LSTM network for delay predictions.

In Fig. 2, we focus on the structure of the LSTM block, which is one sub-process of the real-time predictive model of the lane-based control delay illustrated in Fig. 1. The figure describes data flow between the cell input activation, the input gate, the forget gate, and the output gate with input data set formulated in Eqs. (2) to (8). A solid line denotes a data flow derived in the current time step, whereas a dash-double dotted line represents a recursive data flow from the previous time step. Accordingly, queueing profiles at inflection points and adjustment factors for the future cycle are predicted in the LSTM process to calculate the queue arrival and the discharge patterns in one cycle to predict the lane-based control delay at the target intersection.

3   Case Study

We apply the proposed framework to a real-life junction at Lankershim Boulevard in Los Angeles, U.S. The Federal Highway Administration's Next Generation Simulation provided a full set of required data and detailed information for deploying our proposed framework. Time-series digital images recorded by five video cameras are used to extract the vehicle trajectory data collected on June 16, 2005 from 8:28 a.m. to 9:00 a.m. The studied intersection is Lankershim Boulevard/Campo De Cahuenga Way/Universal Hollywood Drive (No. 2 intersection). An aerial photograph and the layout configuration of the target approach are shown in Figs. 3(a) and 3(b), respectively.

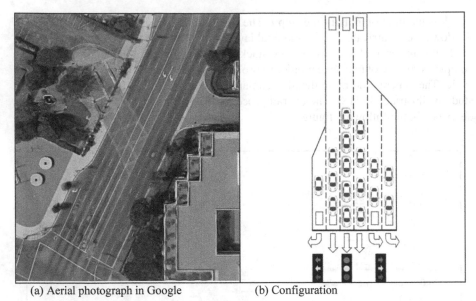

(a) Aerial photograph in Google   (b) Configuration

Fig. 3. Geometric conditions of the study area.

The recorded period has a total of 20 cycles, with a cycle length of 100 s. The trained models in the numerical results are used to validate the real data set in this case study.

3.1 Model Training and Validation

The LSTM network developed in this study is constructed using Python with Keras library to predict the queueing patterns at an inflection point and adjustment factors cycle-by-cycle. Ω_k^{n-1} and Ψ_k^{n-1} for all lanes, which are a thirty – input data set; (5 queueing patterns + 5 adjustment factors) × 3 lanes, are used in the embedded layer including 128 nodes in the first LSTM layer among the four stacked LSTM structure. The activation function is the ReLU function in all layer due to its effectiveness for predicting continuous traffic quantities. The rate of dropout is 20% in the first and the second LSTM layer. Moreover, the number of nodes gradually decrease from the first to the last layer as 128, 64, 32, and 16, respectively. For the compile process, the loss function is the mean-square-error function with the Adam optimiser. We set the total number of epochs and the size of batch to 300 and 4, respectively. The mean-absolute-error (MAE) of the training set and the validation set is 1.528 and 2.047, respectively. This means that the trained model can be installed to predict the queueing profile at an inflection point and adjust factors in the future cycle based on those in the previous cycle Meanwhile, the cycle length in the current cycle guarantees a sufficient calculation time LSTM network in all lanes. The following figures describe the result of the stacked LSTM model training and validation.

In Fig. 4(a), the mean-square-error (MSE) of training and validation sets reached 16.3558 and 21.7593, respectively, after 300 epochs. In Fig. 5(b), the estimates of Ω_k^{n+1} and Ψ_k^{n+1} are scattered around 45-degree solid line with their observed values. According

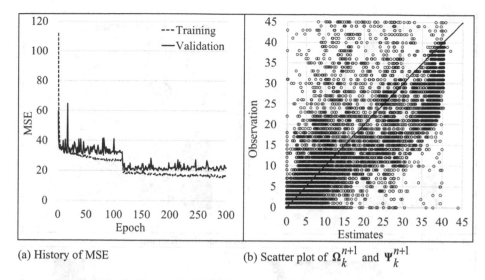

(a) History of MSE

(b) Scatter plot of Ω_k^{n+1} and Ψ_k^{n+1}

Fig. 4. The result of LSTM network training and validation.

to these results, the stacked LSTM guarantees a relatively high level of accuracy and a low level of computational burden in predicting the queueing profiles for a cycle.

The Kalman filter is applied in Models I, II, and III for the cycle-based prediction process of the lane-based control delay formula. In addition to the Kalman-based predictive process, the advanced LSTM network is used in Model III (i.e. the proposed integrated model-based and data driven method). The Kalman filter is used in Models I – III to predict the queue profiles at inflection points and adjustments factors for calculating the lane-based control delay. These models are labelled as Model I – Kalman, Model II – Kalman, and Model III – Kalman. The proposed model, which includes the LSTM network for the prediction, is defined as the **Model III – LSTM**. The performance of the LSTM network is illustrated in the previous section for forecasting Ω_k^{n+1} and Ψ_k^{n+1}. The forecasted Ω_k^{n+1} and Ψ_k^{n+1} are then used to calculate the lane-based control delay per cycle, and its performance is compared with the observed control delay per each lane per each cycle in Eq. (9).

$$\sum_{k=1}^{K} D_k^{n+1}\left(\Gamma_k^{n+1}, \Omega_k^{n+1}, \Phi_k^{n+1}\right) \approx \sum_{k=1}^{K} \hat{D}_k^{n+1}\left(\hat{\Gamma}^{n+1}, \hat{\Omega}_k^{n+1}, \hat{\Phi}_k^{n+1}\right) \tag{9}$$

The scattering plots of these four models are described with the observed control delay in each lane per cycle in Fig. 5. The LSTM network provides more accurate predictions of the control delay than the Kalman based approach in Model III. Their predictions are densely distributed on the periphery of its 45-degree line, although Model III – Kalman provides under-predicted values, and there are many outliers at the high level of vehicular delay. In other words, Model III – LSTM outperforms the other models in predicting the lane-based control delay cycle-by-cycle.

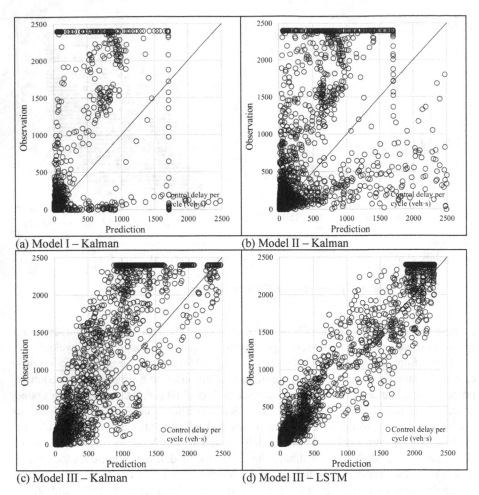

(a) Model I – Kalman

(b) Model II – Kalman

(c) Model III – Kalman

(d) Model III – LSTM

Fig. 5. Scatter plots of the four models.

4   Conclusions

We have proposed an architecture of the real-time lane-based control delay formula for traffic operations based on the LSTM method. There are a few distinctive achievements of the proposed method: (1) data-driven and model-based approaches are integrated to improve the reliability and the accuracy of the control delay predictive formula; (2) the novel LSTM is constructed to predict a cycle-based control delay in an individual lane while minimising the inherent errors in the algorithm; (3) short-term arrival patterns and long-term control delay trends are captured by the LSTM to improve the accuracy of estimates of the queueing profiles for the future signal cycles; (4) predicted queue lengths at inflection points and adjustment factors are used to construct the delay polygons in the future cycle, and (5) the proposed method paves the way for applying the deep learning to predict the control delay in real-time for lane-based ATCS.

References

1. Webster, F.V.: Traffic signal settings. Road research technical paper 39, Road Research Laboratory (1958)
2. TL Saaty 1961 Elements of Queueing Theory: With Applications McGraw-Hill New York
3. Miller, A.J.: A computer control system for traffic networks. In: Proceedings of the Second International Symposium on the Theory of Traffic Flow, London, pp. 200–220 (1963)
4. Akçelik, R.: Time-dependent expressions for delay, stop rate and queue length at traffic signals. Australian Road Research Board Melbourne, Australia (1980)
5. S Lee SC Wong 2017 Group-based approach to predictive delay model based on incremental queue accumulations for adaptive traffic control systems Transp. Res. Part B: Methodol. 98 1 20
6. S Lee SC Wong P Varaiya 2017 Group-based hierarchical adaptive traffic-signal control part I: formulation Transp. Res. Part B: Methodol. 105 1 18
7. S Lee SC Wong P Varaiya 2017 Group-based hierarchical adaptive traffic-signal control Part II: implementation Transp. Res. Part B: Methodol. 104 376 397
8. S Lee K Xie D Ngoduy M Keyvan-Ekbatani 2019 An advanced deep learning approach to real-time estimation of lane-based queue lengths at a signalised junction Transp. Res. Part C: Emerg. Technol. 109 117 136
9. Lindley, D.V.: The theory of queues with a single server. In: Mathematical Proceedings of the Cambridge Philosophical Society. Cambridge University Press, pp. 277–289 (1952)
10. Lighthill, M.J., Whitham, G.B.: On kinematic waves. I: flood movement in long rivers. II: a theory of traffic flow on long crowded roads. In: Proceedings of the Royal Society of London A: Mathematical, Physical and Engineering Sciences, London, vol. A229, pp. 281–345 (1955)
11. PI Richards 1956 Shock waves on the highway Oper. Res. 4 42 51
12. Highway Capacity Manual, TRB, National Research Council, Washington D.C. (2010)
13. S Hochreiter J Schmidhuber 1997 Long short-term memory Neural Comput. 9 1735 1780
14. X Ma Z Tao Y Wang H Yu Y Wang 2015 Long short-term memory neural network for traffic speed prediction using remote microwave sensor data Transp. Res. Part C: Emerg. Technol. 54 187 197
15. J Ke H Zheng H Yang XM Chen 2017 Short-term forecasting of passenger demand under on-demand ride services: a spatio-temporal deep learning approach Transp. Res. Part C: Emerg. Technol. 85 591 608
16. JS Wijnands J Thompson GD Aschwanden M Stevenson 2018 Identifying behavioural change among drivers using Long Short-Term Memory recurrent neural networks Transp. Res. F: Traffic Psychol. Behav. 53 34 49
17. Lee, S., Ngoduy, D., Keyvan-Ekbatani, M.S.: Integrated deep learning and stochastic car-following model for traffic dynamics on multi-lane freeways. Transp. Res. Part C: Emerg. Technol. **106**, 360–377 (2019)
18. Donahue, J., et al.: Long-term recurrent convolutional networks for visual recognition and description. In: Proceedings of the IEEE Conference on Computer Vision and Pattern Recognition, pp. 2625–2634 (2015)

Exploring Transformers for Intruder Detection in Complex Maritime Environment

Mrunalini Nalamati[✉], Muhammad Saqib, Nabin Sharma,
and Michael Blumenstein

School of Computer Science, Faculty of Engineering and Information and Technology,
University of Technology Sydney, Broadway, NSW, Australia
nalamati@student.uts.edu.au,
{muhammad.saqib,nabin.sharma,michael.blumenstein}@uts.edu.au

Abstract. The vast expanse of the coastline makes it difficult and expensive to deploy resources for monitoring it for safety from intruders or illegal activities. The advent of very sophisticated cameras and the myriad of object detection techniques applied to the surveillance photos and videos, provides new methods for automation of monitoring. In this paper we present a study on evaluating the various state-of-the-art object detection methods for identifying marine vessels for intruder detection. Particularly, a comparison of anchor-based, anchor-free and transformer-based object detection techniques is presented for intruder detection. Analysis on the suitability of transformer-based methods for intruder detection is also presented, with experiments performed on a combined marine vessels dataset. Our experiments show that CenterNet, an anchor-free, one-stage technique is still the fastest detection method and suited for online surveillance. Whereas the high accuracy of Transformer based methods, such as DETR, work best for offline video based surveillance.

Keywords: Ship detection · Deep learning · Object detection · Intruder detection · Transformer-based object detection

1 Introduction

Keeping the vast coastlines safe from illegal fishing, drug, and people smuggling is a significant challenge. There are also search and rescue operations and anti-surface and anti-submarine warfare that need to be monitored. Hence, the border security personnel need a reliable and fast way to monitor the coastline continuously. Currently, there do exist automated optical and non-optical ways for coastline monitoring [10,17]. The Synthetic Aperture Radar (SAR), Very High Radio Frequency System (VHS), and Automatic Identification System (AIS) based techniques basically require tedious processing with identification, and are prone to false detection due to ocean surface irregularities or object size limitations. Moreover, some of them require special hardware, which adds to cost and is also fallible.

© Springer Nature Switzerland AG 2022
G. Long et al. (Eds.): AI 2021, LNAI 13151, pp. 428–439, 2022.
https://doi.org/10.1007/978-3-030-97546-3_35

Fig. 1. Sample frames from SMD dataset [12], showing the (a, b) Haze conditions in which vessels are hard to detect, (c, d) clear visibility conditions with marine vessels clearly visible.

Optical image processing-based approaches such as horizon detection, pixel registration, background subtraction, foreground identification, and object tracking are sometimes dataset-specific or do not work satisfactorily with the dynamic water background. The significant challenges with using these techniques for maritime scenarios are the different weather conditions at sea, e.g., haze, rain, cloudy, very bright days, sun reflections, etc. Some of the challenges involved in maritime environment are shown in Fig. 1.

Some researchers have used combinations of pre-processing with deep learning CNN-based methods for object detection [7,27]. While these methods show improvements in detection accuracy, the step-by-step approach slows the process down.

Application of deep learning computer vision techniques to maritime surveillance needs more focus and research to find the right techniques that give results in real-time, can raise the alarms, and promptly detect intruders. Anchor-free single shot detectors such as CenterNet [4,24] have shown a promising balance between speed and accuracy. Techniques that handle scaling more smartly and show great performance in identification of objects of different sizes, such as EfficientDet [20] are also worth exploring. Furthermore, the transformer-based techniques [2,26] have been proven to be as accurate as region-proposal based methods such as Faster-RCNN [16] and are worth exploring for maritime scenarios as well.

Hence, in this paper we present a study on comparing anchor-based, anchor-free and transformer-based techniques for identifying marine vessels for intruder detection. The dataset used in this study is a combination of Singapore Maritime Database (SMD) [12] and Seaships (SS) [18]. This dataset has annotations for four classes - passenger ship, Boat, Vessel/ship, and Other. For applications needing monitoring illegal boats/immigration, the "passenger ship" category can be further broken down into appropriate classes for close monitoring. For applications related to illegal fishing detection, the focus could be on the "Boat" category. "Vessel/Ship" category can be further analysed for applications such as illegal transportation. New performance benchmarks are presented on the dataset as an outcome of the experiments.

The rest of the paper is organized as follows. Section 2 sets the background in terms of the latest work available on marine vessel detection and summarizes state-of-the-art object detection techniques. Section 3 presents the experimental settings, dataset details, results obtained from the experiments and observations. Finally, we conclude the paper with a summary in Sect. 4.

2   Related Work

In this section, we present a summary of the works available on maritime surveillance and object detection methods. At a broader level, the automated methods for sea surveillance fall into two. One category uses sensors such as thermal cameras, radio frequency messaging systems such as AIS, and radar-based systems. The second category comprises methods based on computer vision application to images and videos captured by high-range CCTV cameras, mounted onshore on towers or on-board security ships, or even passenger ships. With satellite communications becoming faster and high quality, surveillance by analyzing satellite images is also gaining popularity.

The paper [8] presents a comprehensive summary of marine vessel detection methods and datasets. Object detection methods aim to find objects in the given image, identify their type, and mark their location either as a bounding box or segmentation mask. This paper will only consider bounding box methods, as they are sufficient for this application. Firstly, we explore the latest object detection methods and then briefly cover the applications to marine vessel detection.

2.1   Object Detection Techniques

Object Detection methods started with manual feature selection to find the objects, such as edge detection, hue changes, horizon detection, and many others. The focus slowly shifted to automating feature maps with CNN-based deep learning methods. Superior and best accuracy was achieved with the Faster-RCNN [16] method. This method is composed of a region proposal network (RPN) that first scanned the image to find regions of interest, followed by detecting objects in those regions. Regression is performed for estimating bounding box co-ordinates and classes of the objects identified. In spite being a multi-step process, Faster-RCNN became a benchmark for accuracy and a foundation for the current generation of object detection methods. The one-step or single-stage methods, such as the different versions of YOLO [13] look at the entire image only once and do not rely on regions to be identified. These methods are quite fast in terms of speed, with some compromise on accuracy. Amongst the one-stage methods, there are two broad approaches. One that uses anchor boxes and the other that does not. Transformer based approaches are the latest detection methods. In this section, we review some of the most recent one-stage and transformer-based techniques.

One-Stage Anchor-Based Techniques: Anchor box based approaches localize true objects, starting with a set of predefined boxes and gradually adjust the offsets, so that the loss function with ground-truth bounding boxes is minimized. Basically, it begins with thousands of anchor boxes in the image and slowly having each box predict the offset of an object. Then removing the adjusted boxes whose overlap with the ground-truth box is less than say 50%. Different scale and number of anchor boxes could be used. In YOLO [13], a single convolutional network is applied to the entire image, only once, to predict multiple objects and locations. Anchor boxes of different sizes and aspect ratios are placed at each location, and the network predicts corrections on these anchor boxes. Not having to generate regions or process the image multiple times, makes YOLO faster than the R-CNN-based approaches. These models reach an inference speed of around 40 FPS. In YOLOv2 [14] the anchor boxes are designed specifically for the given dataset using K-means clustering. The basic YOLO model performance is improved further in YOLOv3 [15] by using multi-layer scaling with Darknet-53. In the next version, YOLO-v4 [1], Bochkovskiy et.al. have used some new features and experimented with some existing ones to get the correct combination for improved accuracy of the classifier and detector. With very fast training speed and low GPU requirements, it is a lucrative option for several applications. EfficientDet [20] is a one-stage object detection technique gaining popularity in recent years. It uses a backbone of EfficinetNet [19], which is basically based on the principle of efficiently scaling a neural network to provide the best balance between accuracy Vs. complexity. EfficientNet does scaling by balancing all network dimensions such as width, depth, and resolution e.g., number of layers in the network. A Bi-directional Feature Pyramid Network (BiFPN) helps to learn the importance of the input features in skip connections at different scales. EfficientNet followed by the BiFPN serves as the feature extractor. These fused features are then regressed through a class and bounding box network to get the predictions. EfficientDet is a family of D0–D7 object detectors based on configurations of EfficientNet from B0-B6, which is based on width and depth scaling of the BiFPN with linearly increasing depth of box/class network. The accuracy obtained by this method on the COCO dataset is up to a mean average precision (mAP) of 72.4 with speed of around 84 FPS.

One-Stage Anchor Free Techniques: Anchor-free object detection techniques have garnered a lot of research attention since 2019. These are methods such as FCOS [6], Centernet methods [4,24], Guided Anchoring [22]. For anchor-based techniques outlined in the section above, many hyper-parameters need to be carefully fine-tuned for better performance, such as the number of anchor

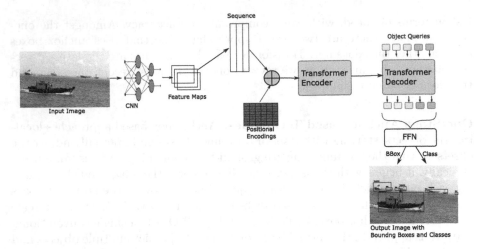

Fig. 2. Transformer-based technique pipeline [2].

boxes, sizes, and a number of regions of the image. These hyper-parameters add overhead in terms of memory and computation. The comparison techniques of the boxes with ground truth are also complicated, such as Intersection-over-Union (IoU). Taking an approach that does not need these anchor boxes makes the implementations much smaller and faster. The Centerpoint models an object as a single point at the center of the bounding box of the object with a heatmap. Key-point estimation, with a reduced negative loss method is used to find the centerpoint, and regression is performed to get the size, shape, orientation and location of the object. This is a very simple and fast approach, achieving results of 63.5 to 142 FPS depending upon the backbone used. As a backbone, the CenterNet model is presented with choices of Hourglass network (HG) [9], ResNet with Deformable Convolution Network (DCN) [25] and Deep Layer Aggregation network (DLA) [23]. The CenterNet method [4] uses the same technique, but with key-point triplets - center and two corner coordinates of the boxes. These anchor-free methods also eliminate the need for Non-Maxima-Suppression after detection. The CenterNet achieves accuracy up to 63.5 on COCO dataset and speeds up to 142 FPS. The anchor-free methods seem to be a good compromise between the single-shot detectors for speed and multi-stage detectors in terms of accuracy.

Transformer-Based Techniques: Latest transformer-based techniques largely simplify the object detection pipelines. They remove the need of special networks such as Region Proposal Networks (RPN) used by methods such as Faster RCNN [16], replacing these with Transformers. These are single-shot methods. The concept is popularly used in Natural Language Processing (NLP) to find relations in the words of a sentence. Applying it to Object detection indicates its use to find relations between pixels of an object. Transformers make use of the attention-based mechanism described in [21]. The end-to-end detection pipeline, first proposed in [2] is composed of the following steps. First, the input image is passed through a backbone CNN, generating a vector of size $H \times W \times c$. The next step is to feed the generated feature map and separately calculated position encodings to a transformer encoder. The Transformer encoder learns how to attend across each sequence for each position and outputs a vector of the same size. A set of object queries are fed to the next step of Transformer decoder, which are image-agnostic and learned separately. Inside the decoder, multi-head attention block processes these and the output vector form the encoder to generate decoded queries. These are then passed through a Feed Forward Network (FFN) to generate the predictions as a tuple of class and bounding boxes. The overall architecture is shown in Fig. 2. Each proposed bounding box is then matched to exactly one ground truth. A bipartite matching algorithm called Hungarian algorithm is used to find permutations that minimize the matching loss. For large objects the results from this pipeline are better than Faster-RCNN. However, it does not perform very well on small objects. This could be improved by reducing the stride from the default 32. However, having a single layer CNN means that it can only work with one resolution of feature map. The other drawback seen with this pipeline is slow convergence. This is mainly due to the long sequence processing that transformers need to do. The attention mass is spread thinly across the sequence and takes time to concentrate on the correct area. This mechanism is also computationally expensive due to the quadratic dependency for attention. Some of these drawbacks are overcome by the Deformable-DETR method [26]. This method introduces a Deformable Attention module for sparse spatial relationships. Instead of looking at all pixels in the row, it learns attention over K values, such that K is less that $H \times W$. This largely reduces the size of the sequence that the Transformer encoder/decoder has to process. Thus, reducing convergence time. Results from this method match the Faster-RCNN for small objects and are slightly less accurate for large objects.

2.2 Marine Vessel Detection

In this section we review recent work done for marine vessel detection. In spite of the advances in the sensor based ship detection approaches, susceptibility to intentional tampering or hardware failure and cost of implementation remain concerns. Optical image based techniques provide an alternative in these situations. Prasad et al. [11] have explored the many issues with simple image processing based approaches, such as horizon detection, pixel registration, etc. in ship datasets. Due to the multi-step approaches, they are too slow. SSD for object detection with Mobilenetv2 network is used for improving results with ship detection and classification [27]. A mean average precision of 0.92 and a speed of about 15FPS is achieved.

An improved YOLOv3 algorithm incorporating saliency features obtained by a frequency-tuned salient region algorithm is used in [3]. The detection results improve slightly to 97% mAP and speed improves to 30 FPS. This is on a private dataset of surveillance videos. In [5], Huang et al. have developed a method called Ship-YOLOv3 to improve accuracy in conditions such as fog or night and identification of small ships. Their proposed method involves pre-processing the input image using guided filtering and gray enhancement. Optimized anchor boxes are used. With this method they find that the precision is increased by 12.5% and recall by 11.5% compared to YOLO. This method is also trained and tested on a private surveillance video dataset.

3   Experimental Results

In order to see how the different methods perform on the SS-SMD dataset, we have conducted experiments using some of the discussed object detection methods. These experiments were also aimed at understanding whether the Transformer based methods perform as well as the one-stage methods. Would the Transformer methods give better results for small/medium or large objects? can they be used for real-time inference on videos?

Transformers tend to look at the whole image context and are able to establish relations between objects. Does that offer any benefit for the marine vessel detection scenario, where there are vessels of various sizes, occluding each other? Under different weather conditions such as Haze, non-ship objects could easily be mis-identified as ships, even clouds in the sky or formations in the water could appear as marine vessels. Some sample frames of such conditions are shown in Fig. 1. Would the context sensitivity of Transformer techniques help to remove such ambiguities?

Experimentation with application of CenterNet and EfficientDet models to the SS-SMD dataset were done in [8]. Expanding on that, in this paper we have further experimented with the Transformer-based techniques, DETR [2] and Deformable-DETR [26].

3.1   Dataset and Experimental Settings

Various publicly available datasets for Marine vessel detection are described in [8]. This paper uses the merged dataset of Seaships (SS) [18] and Singapore Maritime Dataset (SMD) [12] as proposed in [8]. While the SMD consists of short videos, the Seaships dataset contains images taken from the shore. The SMD has 40 videos of the marine vessels taken from onshore cameras and 11 from onboard cameras. There are 20,368 frames in the SMD dataset. The combined curated dataset of SMD and SeaShips contains 27,368 frames with 7000 frames from the SS dataset. This dataset was split as 21,908 for training, 2730 for validation, and 2730 for a test. For the training, we set up the SS-SMD dataset in COCO format, with four classes, namely - Boat, Other, passenger ship, and Vessel/ship. The category of 'Other' refers to objects in the sea, such as Bouys, people, airplanes, birds, etc. Vessel/ship refers to mostly large ships such as cargo ships, carrier ships, container ships. These are primarily large-sized objects. The class of passenger ships includes vessels such as Ferry or other smaller ships

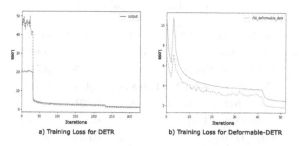

a) Training Loss for DETR   b) Training Loss for Deformable-DETR

Fig. 3. Loss curves for DETR and Deformable-DETR during training on SS-SMD dataset.

carrying passengers. The category of Boats includes vessels of small to medium sizes, such as fishing boats, speed boats, sailboats.

We trained on the Nvidia Quadro RTX 5000, with 3,072 cores, $16 \times 2G$ memory, CUDA version 11.2. Training for DETR was started with a pre-trained Resnet-50 based model on the COCO dataset. We loaded the pre-trained weights by removing the classification heads of the pre-trained model. It took more than 7 days to train the model on a single GPU system with our dataset for 300 Iterations. The use of pre-trained weights helped the model learn and converge quickly, as seen from the Loss drop around Iteration 30 in the Loss Vs. Iteration graph in Fig. 3. Without pre-trained weights, we did not see loss reduction even till Iteration 100 and would take very long to converge. The training starts with a learning rate of $1e-4$; It was dropped at the 200th iteration, with a weight decay of $1e-4$. Moreover, a slight drop in Loss at iteration 201, as can be seen in Fig. 3a. Deformable-DETR model training is even slower. However, as suggested by the author in [26], 50 iterations are enough for convergence. This took 5 days on a single GPU system. The Loss curve is seen in Fig. 3b. The training process started with a learning rate of $2e-4$; it was dropped at iteration 40 by a weight decay of $1e-4$. The corresponding drop in Loss can be seen at iteration 41. For both models, a batch size of 2 was used for training with the backbone of Resnet50. The number of queries was set to 100 with SINE for positional embedding.

3.2 Performance Evaluation and Discussion

The results from our experiments are listed in Table 1. The mAP50 is the mean Average Precision across all classes at an IoU of 50%. Random seeds were used to start the training. The other mAPs listed in the tables are for Small, Medium, and Large-sized objects averaged across IoUs of 0.5–0.95. This split is available for datasets in COCO format. These results offer a good view of how the Transformer based and Anchor-free object detection techniques have performed on our dataset.

The inference was made on the Nvidia Quadro RTX 5000, with 3,072 cores, $16 \times 2G$ memory, CUDA version 11.2. A batch size of 16 was configured, and

Table 1. Experimental results.

Type	Method and backbone	mAP50	mAP(S)	mAP(M)	mAP(L)	FPS
Transformer-based	DETR, Resnet50	**0.992**	0.707	**0.803**	**0.899**	16
	Def-DETR, Resnet50	0.985	0.613	0.717	0.837	10
Anchor-free	CenterNet, ResDCN101	0.866	0.480	0.649	0.824	29
	CenterNet, ResDCN18	0.868	0.491	0.640	0.817	**49**
	CenterNet, DLAV0	0.893	0.552	0.701	0.835	41
Anchor-based	EfficientDet-D1	0.912	0.635	–	–	23
	EfficientDet-D2	0.974	0.751	–	–	22
	EfficientDet-D3	0.981	**0.783**	–	–	13

the number of workers/parallel threads was set to 8. These were chosen as the numbers supported by our testing system. The Frames Per Second (FPS) listed in the table has the above configuration for a test size of 2730 frames.

Discussion: The outputs from 3 randomly chosen frames are shown in the image matrix in Fig. 4. For frames in rows 1 and 2, the ground truth is also shown in dark gray color. Ground-truth is not available for a frame in row 3, and it is a test-only video from SMD. For each of the methods, the detections are shown in different colors for Vessel/ship category. From the results Table 1, we can see that the performance of both the Transformer based models are similar in terms of mean Average precision at IOU of 50 (mAP50)%. Performance of anchor based, one-stage models is also in the same range above 90 mAP50. In terms of accuracy, the anchor free models fall slightly behind, giving mAP50 in high 80s. Visual analysis of DETR shows that it identifies almost all marine vessels with confidence scores close to 1.00. Deformable-DETR also identifies the vessels with average scores around 0.97, but shows many false detections and misses vessels that DETR or CenterNet identified easily. Frames in rows 1 and 3 of Fig. 4 show this. Missing identification and false detections are circled with red. Frames in row 1 are from a video captured in a haze, making it harder to identify the vessels clearly. In the output from the Deformable-DETR model in Fig. 4 row 1a, we can see that it has missed a Vessel/ship object in the haze. We see that a Boat object is missed even under clear visibility in row 3a & by CenterNet in row 3c. Though the mAP of Deformable-DETR and DETR are similar, we see many false detections with Deformable-DETR. Some are hard to explain; for example, it falsely identifies a water pattern as 'Boat' or an 'Other' object in the plain sky (row 2a). A deeper analysis needs to be done to understand the reason for this. Inference with Deformable-DETR is also slower than DETR. This is against our expectation, as the scarce matching should have resulted in faster inferences. In our experiments, with this dataset, we did not see any particular benefit of using Deformable-DETR over DETR.

The CenterNet and EfficientDet results quoted in Table 1 are from our previous work in [8] on the same dataset. We can see the output from CenterNet-

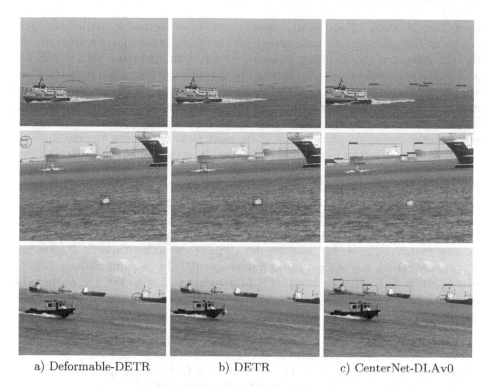

a) Deformable-DETR   b) DETR   c) CenterNet-DLAv0

Fig. 4. Outputs of the 3 models from randomly chosen frames from the SMD videos. Row 1 capture haze conditions at sea. Each column shows the output from each of the models. Ground-truth is marked in dark gray for DETR and Deformable-DETR, where annotated.

DLAv0 in column c of Fig. 4. The CenterNet is very fast compared to DETR or Deformable-DETR for inference as well as training. With CenterNet, even though it shows the least mAP of the three methods, we see that it identifies all vessels correctly, though the confidence scores of each one are lower than DETR or Deformable-DETR. It also shows very few false detections, though some minor misses are seen (e.g. row 3c). We also see from the Table 1 that EfficientDet models are best for the identification of small objects. Though, they show slightly better speeds than Transformer based models, the accuracy factor is not very different. Hence, do not offer any significant benefit over Transformer models.

4   Conclusions

Video surveillance is an effective additional tool to the already existing sensor-based technology to detect illegal marine vessels. The video surveillance provides more information than the radars, such as the type of vessel and visual analysis of the activities on the vessel. The illegal activities can be easily monitored, such as trafficking of people, illegal fishing, and inform the concerned authorities to take action in time. This paper has carried out extensive experiments with state-of-the-art object techniques using Transformer and compared them with the SSD's and region proposal-based approaches. The experiments have been performed on a dataset curated from two publicly available datasets with similar objects. The experiments show that the results obtained by Transformer based approaches are on par with the performance shown by the proposal-based approaches. However, the Transformer approaches seem to take more time in training the model. But the Transformer model can model contextual information when applied to the video and model information flow between patches taken from the large image. For our particular dataset, which contains a mix of small, medium and large objects, the Transformer model DETR gives best accuracy. However, it is slow for intruder detection from online surveillance videos. It would be best suited for offline applications. For online surveillance applications, it is most important to be able to detect the vessels, as smuggler vessels move at high speeds. If intruder alarms are raised, the system could follow up with visual confirmations, hence, even if the object detection method is as accurate as CenterNet, the purpose is achieved. Hence, in these scenarios, CenterNet models would still be best suited.

References

1. Bochkovskiy, A., Wang, C.Y., Liao, H.Y.M.: YOLOv4: optimal speed and accuracy of object detection. arXiv preprint arXiv:2004.10934 (2020)
2. Carion, N., Massa, F., Synnaeve, G., Usunier, N., Kirillov, A., Zagoruyko, S.: End-to-end object detection with transformers. In: Vedaldi, A., Bischof, H., Brox, T., Frahm, J.-M. (eds.) ECCV 2020. LNCS, vol. 12346, pp. 213–229. Springer, Cham (2020). https://doi.org/10.1007/978-3-030-58452-8_13
3. Chen, L., Li, B., Qi, L.: Improved YOLOv3 algorithm for ship target detection. In: 2020 39th Chinese Control Conference (CCC), pp. 7288–7293. IEEE
4. Duan, K., Bai, S., Xie, L., Qi, H., Huang, Q., Tian, Q.: CenterNet: keypoint triplets for object detection. In: Proceedings of the IEEE/CVF International Conference on Computer Vision, pp. 6569–6578 (2019)
5. Huang, H., Sun, D., Wang, R., Zhu, C., Liu, B.: Ship target detection based on improved YOLO network. Math. Probl. Eng. 2020 (2020)
6. Lin, T.Y., Goyal, P., Girshick, R., He, K., Dollár, P.: Focal loss for dense object detection. In: Proceedings of the IEEE International Conference on Computer Vision, pp. 2980–2988 (2017)
7. Marié, V., Béchar, I., Bouchara, F.: Real-time maritime situation awareness based on deep learning with dynamic anchors. In: 2018 15th IEEE International Conference on Advanced Video and Signal Based Surveillance (AVSS), pp. 1–6. IEEE
8. Nalamati, M., Sharma, N., Saqib, M., Blumenstein, M.: Automated monitoring in maritime video surveillance system. In: 2020 35th International Conference on Image and Vision Computing New Zealand (IVCNZ), pp. 1–6. IEEE (2020)
9. Newell, A., Yang, K., Deng, J.: Stacked hourglass networks for human pose estimation. In: Leibe, B., Matas, J., Sebe, N., Welling, M. (eds.) ECCV 2016. LNCS, vol. 9912, pp. 483–499. Springer, Cham (2016). https://doi.org/10.1007/978-3-319-46484-8_29

10. Nikolió, et al.: Multi-radar multi-target tracking algorithm for maritime surveillance at OTH distances. In: 2016 17th International Radar Symposium (IRS), pp. 1–6. IEEE

11. Prasad, D.K., Prasath, C.K., Rajan, D., Rachmawati, L., Rajabaly, E., Quek, C.: Challenges in video based object detection in maritime scenario using computer vision. arXiv preprint arXiv:1608.01079 (2016)

12. Prasad, D.K., Rajan, D., Rachmawati, L., Rajabally, E., Quek, C.: Video processing from electro-optical sensors for object detection and tracking in a maritime environment: a survey. IEEE Trans. Intell. Transp. Syst. 18(8), 1993–2016 (2017)

13. Redmon, J., Divvala, S., Girshick, R., Farhadi, A.: You only look once: unified, real-time object detection. In: Proceedings of the IEEE Conference on Computer Vision and Pattern Recognition, pp. 779–788

14. Redmon, J., Farhadi, A.: YOLO9000: better, faster, stronger. In: Proceedings of the IEEE Conference on Computer Vision and Pattern Recognition, pp. 7263–7271 (2017)

15. Redmon, J., Farhadi, A.: YOLOv3: an incremental improvement. arXiv preprint arXiv:1804.02767 (2018)

16. Ren, S., He, K., Girshick, R., Sun, J.: Faster R-CNN: towards real-time object detection with region proposal networks. In: Advances in Neural Information Processing Systems, pp. 91–99 (2015)

17. Schwehr, K.: Vessel tracking using the automatic identification system (AIS) during emergency response: lessons from the Deepwater Horizon incident. Centre for Coastal and Ocean Mapping/Joint Hydrographic Centre, p. 14 (2011)

18. Shao, Z., Wu, W., Wang, Z., Du, W., Li, C.: SeaShips: a large-scale precisely annotated dataset for ship detection. IEEE Trans. Multimedia 20(10), 2593–2604 (2018)

19. Tan, M., Le, Q.V.: EfficientNet: rethinking model scaling for convolutional neural networks. arXiv preprint arXiv:1905.11946 (2019)

20. Tan, M., Pang, R., Le, Q.V.: EfficientDet: scalable and efficient object detection. arXiv preprint arXiv:1911.09070 (2019)

21. Vaswani, A., et al.: Attention is all you need. In: Advances in Neural Information Processing Systems, pp. 5998–6008 (2017)

22. Wang, J., Chen, K., Yang, S., Loy, C.C., Lin, D.: Region proposal by guided anchoring. In: Proceedings of the IEEE/CVF Conference on Computer Vision and Pattern Recognition, pp. 2965–2974 (2019)

23. Yu, F., Wang, D., Shelhamer, E., Darrell, T.: Deep layer aggregation. In: Proceedings of the IEEE Conference on Computer Vision and Pattern Recognition, pp. 2403–2412

24. Zhou, X., Wang, D., Krähenbühl, P.: Objects as points. arXiv preprint arXiv:1904.07850 (2019)

25. Zhu, X., Hu, H., Lin, S., Dai, J.: Deformable ConvNets V2: more deformable, better results. In: Proceedings of the IEEE Conference on Computer Vision and Pattern Recognition, pp. 9308–9316

26. Zhu, X., Su, W., Lu, L., Li, B., Wang, X., Dai, J.: Deformable DETR: deformable transformers for end-to-end object detection. arXiv preprint arXiv:2010.04159 (2020)

27. Zou, Y., Zhao, L., Qin, S., Pan, M., Li, Z.: Ship target detection and identification based on SSD_MobilenetV2. In: 2020 IEEE 5th Information Technology and Mechatronics Engineering Conference (ITOEC), pp. 1676–1680. IEEE (2020)

Transfer Learning Assisted GPHH for Dynamic Multi-Workflow Scheduling in Cloud Computing

Kirita-Rose Escott[✉][ID], Hui Ma[ID], and Gang Chen

Victoria University of Wellington,
1 Kelburn Parade, Wellington, New Zealand
{kirita-rose.escott,hui.ma,aaron.chen}@ecs.vuw.ac.nz

Abstract. Dynamic Multi-Workflow Scheduling (DWS) in cloud is a challenging optimisation due to the dynamic nature of the problem. It requires complex mapping decisions to be made under unknown dynamic events. Genetic Programming Hyper-Heuristic (GPHH) has been successfully applied to generate scheduling heuristics for DWS due to its flexible representation. However, the simulation-based evaluation is computationally expensive due to calculations required by individuals to make decisions in the simulation. To improve efficiency, this paper proposes a novel Transfer Learning (TL) Assisted GPHH (TL-GPHH). Specifically, TL-GPHH is designed and compared with Non-Assisted GPHH to generate effective heuristic rules in less time. The results show that the proposed algorithm generates heuristics that can minimise makespan in more scenarios than Non-Assisted GPHH and other state-of-the-art heuristics. Moreover, the proposed algorithm can reduce the computational costs of GP without sacrificing the performance.

Keywords: Genetic Programming Hyper Heuristic · Dynamic Multi-Workflow Scheduling · Cloud computing · Transfer Learning

1 Introduction

Cloud computing is a distributed computing paradigm, which provides various resources as services. Cloud providers offer VMs, or instances, of differing type, size and cost on a pay-per-use, often hourly, basis for a fixed cost [12]. Cloud computing boasts the capacity for services to be consistently available, as well as the ability to adjust and adapt, to serve many cloud users at any given time.

Workflows are the most common way of representing complex scientific applications for modeling data and computational operations including receiving input data, data analysis and processing [2]. Workflow scheduling is a prominent issue in Cloud Computing which tries to map workflow tasks to cloud resources, i.e. Virtual Machines (VMs), driven by the goal to maximise QoS and minimise overall cost. In order to meet such requirements, several aspects, including workflow arrival time, resource availability and cost, need to be considered during workflow scheduling.

© Springer Nature Switzerland AG 2022
G. Long et al. (Eds.): AI 2021, LNAI 13151, pp. 440–451, 2022.
https://doi.org/10.1007/978-3-030-97546-3_36

Dynamic Workflow Scheduling (DWS) problems assume that information about tasks and resources, such as size and pattern of workflow, task dependencies, and available VMs, are not known apriori [7]. This is the inverse of the more commonly researched Static Workflow Scheduling (SWS) problem where information about workflows and cloud resources is known prior to scheduling. Due to complexity of dynamic scheduling problems, DWS is seldom tackled in the literature [16].

Simple man-made heuristics, such as Heterogeneous Earliest Finish Time (HEFT) [20], MINMIN [5] and MAXMIN [6], are commonly comprised of two phases, i.e., the task prioritising phase and the resource selection phase. These approaches are often designed to schedule single static workflows and are either ineffective or inapplicable to dynamic workflow scheduling problems. Therefore, there is a need to design effective heuristics for DWS.

Genetic Programming (GP) is a prominent Evolutionary Algorithm, which has been employed to design heuristics for various difficult problems [22]. Its effectiveness has been demonstrated recently to design heuristic rules for both static and dynamic workflow scheduling problems in [10,11,21,23]. However, it is challenging to design effective and efficient GP approaches. Firstly, including a wide range of features (e.g. for workflows, VMs) can help to explore and discover rules; however, it may further enlarge the search space and deteriorate GP performance [18]. Secondly, the computational costs of GP can be high as heuristic rules are evaluated by expensive computer simulation.

Transfer Learning (TL) [19] is the process by which some aspects of a machine learning model generated on a source problem is transferred to a target problem, to simplify the learning required to solve the target problem [17]. Research pertaining to the intersection of TL and GP has been scarce. Recent works have begun to explore the aforementioned intersection. However, existing research applies TL and GP to Job-Shop Scheduling [24] and Uncertain Capacitated Arc Routing [3,4] problems. The corresponding TL and GP methods cannot directly solve DWS problems.

In this paper, we aim to develop a new Transfer Learning assisted GPHH algorithm for automatically designing heuristics for workflow scheduling in cloud computing. Driven by this goal, this paper has three main research objectives:

1. Develop a new *Transfer Learning Assisted Genetic Programming Hyper Heuristic* (TL-GPHH) algorithm to automatically design scheduling heuristics for the dynamic workflow scheduling problem.
2. Conduct an extensive experimental evaluation of TL-GPHH by using the Workflowsim simulator [8] and a popular benchmark dataset with 15 different workflow applications. Scheduling heuristics designed by TL-GPHH is further compared to several existing scheduling heuristics, including GRP-HEFT, MINMIN and MAXMIN, as well as those generated by Non-Assisted GPHH.
3. Analyse the experiment results to investigate essential aspects of transfer learning with a substantial impact on the performance of designed scheduling heuristics.

It is infeasible to conduct a real-world evaluation of any scheduling heuristic designed by TL-GPHH due to high hardware and computation cost. To cope with this challenge, this paper adopts a simulated approach using WorkflowSim [8]. With the help of WorkflowSim, we can accurately evaluate any potential scheduling heuristics.

The rest of the paper is organised as follows: Sect. 2 presents previous work related to workflow scheduling in the cloud environment. Section 3 gives an overview of the DWS problem. Section 4 outlines the proposed TL-GPHH approach. Section 5 presents the experimental evaluation results and analysis. The conclusions and future work are outlined in Sect. 6.

2   Related Work

There are many existing workflow scheduling algorithms that consider single workflows and different constraints such as budget, deadline, and security level. Faragardi et al. [12] proposed a novel resource provisioning mechanism and a workflow scheduling algorithm, named Greedy Resource Provisioning and modified HEFT (GRP-HEFT), for minimising makespan of a given workflow subject to a budget constraint for the hourly-based cost model of modern IaaS clouds.

More recently, algorithms to address the scheduling of multiple workflows have emerged. Arabnejad et al. [2] proposed Dynamic Workflow Scheduling (DWS) that handles the dynamics of multiple deadline constrained workflows arriving randomly and scheduling these workflows with reduced cost in mind. Arabnejad et al. [1] proposed Multi Workflow Deadline Budget Scheduling (MW-DBS) for scheduling concurrent workflows under user-defined budget and deadline constraints. However, in these works workflows arrive at a predetermined interval, which is not reflective of cloud environment where workflows arrive randomly. Moreover, these approaches aim to maximise the Planning Success Rate (PSR), rather than minimise makespan.

Current GPHH approaches are designed for SWS, i.e. assume knowledge is know prior to scheduling. Yu et al. [23] proposed a Flexible Scheduling Genetic Programming (FSGP) approach, that employs GP to generate heuristic rules. Xiao et al. [21] proposed a Co-operative Coevolution Genetic Programming (CCGP) approach to generate two heuristic rules for scheduling. However, both approaches design heuristics that are ineffective for dynamic workflow scheduling problems. Escott et al. [10,11] explore GPHH for DWS. However, these studies found GPHH for DWS to be time-consuming, as costly cloud simulations caused GP to be computationally expensive.

Recently Transfer Learning techniques have been applied to assisting GP for combinatorial optimisation problems. Ardeh et al. [3] investigate existing GP transfer methods, such as subtree transfer, as a hyper-heuristic for Uncertain Capacitated Arc Routing Problem (UCARP). The experiments found the approach was effective for creating a better initial population. However, the approach did not scale well. Ardeh et al. [4] propose a parametric framework for GP with transfer learning fro UCARP. This work analyses different transfer learning mechanisms to understand the dynamics of knowledge transfer for UCARP.

Zhang et al. [24] propose collaborative multifidelity-based surrogate models for genetic programming in Dynamic Flexible Job Shop Scheduling (DFJSS) to reduce the computational cost of GP without sacrificing the performance. However, these approaches are not appropriate to be applied to DWS problems.

We experimentally compare with Non-Assisted GPHH, GRP-HEFT [12], MINMIN [5], MAXMIN [6], as well as First Come First Serve (FCFS), Minimum Completion Time (MCT) and Round Robin (RR) [8].

3 Preliminaries

In this section, first the overview of the problem is defined. Then, the formal definition of the dynamic workflow scheduling problem is formulated.

3.1 Problem Overview

In the workflow scheduling problem, a workflow w is commonly depicted as a directed acyclic graph $DAG([n], [e])$ where n is a set of nodes representing n dependent tasks, $[e]$ indicates the data flow dependencies between tasks. Each workflow has a task with no predecessors named *entry* task and a task with no successors names *exit* task. Considering workflows with different patterns, and tasks arriving from time to time, *dynamic workflow scheduling* allocates tasks to virtual machines with the objective of minimising the overall execution time of multiple workflows in a scenario.

In the process of allocation, the following constraints must be satisfied.

- A task can only be allocated once all its predecessors have been executed.
- Each task can be allocated to any virtual machine, which will process the task.
- Each virtual machine can only process at most one task at any given time.

3.2 Formal Definition

The following equations present the basic properties of tasks and virtual machines that will be used to formulate the dynamic workflow scheduling problem.

The execution time of task t_i on virtual machine v_k is given by Eq. (1).

$$ET_{ik} = \frac{s_i}{m_k} \tag{1}$$

ET_{ik} is obtained by dividing the size s_i of task t_i divided by the speed m_k of virtual machine v_k. The bandwidth b_k is the transmission capacity of virtual machine v_k.

A task t_i in w_j becomes ready for execution whenever all of its parents $aParent(t_i)$ have completed processing. Moreover, a workflow w_j must have arrived such that the $w_{j_{arrival}}$ must also have passed for t_i to become ready for execution. A pair p_{ik} is a mapping of ready task t_i to virtual machine v_k in set of pairs i.e. $p_{ik} \in P$, denoted by Eq. (2).

$$p_{ik} = (t_i, v_k) \tag{2}$$

The rank $r(p_{ik})$ of a pair p_{ik} is determined by the heuristic rule r. The pairs in P are ordered according to rank r_p.

Each ready task t_i can be allocated to a virtual machine v_k. The allocation time, denoted by AT_i, is given by Eq. (3).

$$AT_i = max_{p \in aParent(t_i)} FT_p \tag{3}$$

The actual start time of each task t_i, denoted by ST_i, is decided either by the time that virtual machine v_k becomes idle, or when t_i becomes a ready task t_i, whichever is later. Virtual machine v_k becomes idle when the previous task t_{prev} being executed on v_k completes processing. The actual start time is given by Eq. (4).

$$ST_i = \max\{FT_{t_{prev}}, AT_i\} \tag{4}$$

The expected completion time ECT_i of task t_i and it's children $aChild(t_i)$ is the maximum expected completion time possible and is given by Eq. (5).

$$ECT_i = total_{c \in aChild(t_i)} ET_{ik} \tag{5}$$

The makespan for all workflows, denoted MS, is the start time of the first task $ST_{t_{first}}$ in the first workflow subtracted from the finish time $FT_{t_{last}}$ of the last task in the last workflow in the Scenario Sc.

$$MS = FT_{t_{last}} - ST_{t_{first}} \tag{6}$$

The objective of the dynamic workflow scheduling problem is to minimize the overall makespan time of all the workflows in the Scenario. i.e., min MS. We aim to find a rule r, which can produce a schedule with low MS.

4   Proposed Algorithm

This paper develops a transfer-learning assisted GP to solve DWS problem. This section first describes the outline of the proposed algorithm, before discussing the key components.

4.1   Overview of Proposed Algorithm

The key idea of this paper is to solve the DWS problem by utilising the advantages of Transfer Learning to enhance the performance and efficiency of GP. Transfer Learning attempts to enhance the learning in the target problem based on the knowledge from previous solved problems [9].

We rely on the Workflow Scheduler in the WorkflowSim simulator [8] to simulate the process of dynamically arriving workflow tasks over an extensive period of time. The Workflow Scheduler obtains *ready tasks* from the Workflow Engine periodically and a task is considered a ready task when all of its predecessor tasks have finished execution. We extend this definition, such that a workflow task may not be released until the workflow is set to be executing. This allows us to simulate randomly arriving workflows as well as tasks.

This approach aims to produce a schedule of task to VM mappings that minimises the makespan or execution time of a Scenario of randomly arriving workflows of different pattern, size and arrival rate on a fixed set of VMs. This work aims to share learned knowledge to improve the efficiency of GPHH without losing quality of generated heuristic rules.

As discussed, TL-GPHH is designed to search for effective heuristics to solve DWS problem in cloud. The pseudo-code in Algorithm 1 outlines the TL-GPHH algorithm and is discussed further below.

```
Input: Source Scenario, Target Scenario
Output: Heuristic Rule
gen = 0;
maxSourceGen = g_s;
maxTargetGen = g_t;
Randomly initialise the population of rules R;
while gen < maxTargetGen do
    for a rule r in R do
        if gen < maxSourceGen then
        |   Evaluate fitness of r on Source Scenario;
        end
        else
        |   Evaluate fitness of r on Target Scenario;
        end
    end
    TournamentSelection;
    Crossover;
    Mutation;
    Reproduction;
end
Return best rule
```
Algorithm 1: TL-GPHH Algorithm

We represent a heuristic in the form of a GP tree; the aim of GP is to find the tree with the best fitness value. Standard GP contains following phases: initialisation, selection, crossover, mutation.

For TL-GPHH, the *initialisation* process is different to Non-Assisted GPHH. The final generation of individuals from the source problem is transferred as the initial population of the target problem, as seen in Algorithm 1.

The *crossover* genetic operator recombines the genetic information of two parents to create a new offspring. For example, when the left branch of Parent A is combined with the right branch of Parent B to become offspring A'. Additionally, the left branch of Parent B is combined with the right branch of Parent A to become offspring B' [11].

The *mutation* genetic operator changes the sub-tree of a tree to maintain genetic diversity from one generation to the next. For example, when the sub-tree of the parent is replaced by a new sub-tree in the child. Mutation is used to prevent instances from becoming too similar to each other, which, can lead to poor performance [23].

The *reproduction* genetic operator selects individuals from the current generation and passes the best of those individuals to the next generation as offspring.

The *Fitness* of a heuristic rule r is evaluated by the makespan MS of the workflows in a Scenario scheduled using the rule. Fitness is defined in Eq. (7).

$$fitness(r) = MS(r) \tag{7}$$

Based on the above, the goal is to find r^* such that it minimises $MS(r^*)$ over all possible rules.

The GP tree that represents a heuristic consists of function set and terminal set [14]. The function set F contains the operations of values, including arithmetic operator, mathematical function, boolean operator and conditional expression, etc. The terminal set T is composed of variables. The terminal and function sets are described in Table 1.

Table 1. The terminal and function set for the proposed TL-GPHH approach

Terminal name	Definition
TS	The total size of a task t_i
VS	The speed of a virtual machine v_j
ET	Execution time of a task t_i
EC	Execution cost of a task t_i
NC	Number of children of task t_i
ECT	Expected completion time of a task t_i
Function name	Definition
Add, Subtract, Multiply, Min, Max	Basic arithmetic operations $(+, -, \times, \text{MIN}, \text{MAX})$
Protected Division	Protected division, return 1 if the denominator is 0 (%)

As demonstrated in Table 1, the terminals used to represent important features of workflows and virtual machines, that effect the makespan of a workflow. Features such as task size, task execution time and, virtual machine speed. The function set, also described in Table 1, denotes the operators used; addition, subtraction, multiplication, and protected division. Protected division means that it will return 1 if divided by 0.

In Transfer Learning, the source problem is often simpler [9]. The target problem is often more complex and is the task to learn. For DWS, the target problem is a scenario that includes randomly arriving workflows of size small, medium and large with a fixed set of virtual machines. As it is costly to simulate all of the small medium and large workflows, we define the source problem as a scenario that includes randomly arriving workflows of size small and medium with a fixed set of virtual machines.

We can solve the target problem separately from the source problem using Non-Assisted GPHH. However, due to the difficulty of this and the relationship between the source and target problem, it is often easier if the knowledge and experiences gained in the source problem can be applied to the target problem [9]. As the source problem for DWS is simpler, we can reduce the total number of generations required for evolving GP tree, both on the source and the target.

5   Experimental Evaluation

In this section, we describe the experiments we conducted to evaluate the TL-GPHH algorithm. We perform this evaluation using the WorkflowSim simulator to simulate a real cloud environment and execute Scenarios of multiple randomly arriving workflows using our generated heuristic rule.

5.1   Dataset

Five well-known workflow patterns [13], CyberShake, Epigenomics, Inspiral, Montage, and Sipht, are used in our experiments. We use three different sizes, small, medium and large, as described in Table 2. Thus, we tested 15 workflows, with the number of tasks ranging between 25 and 100.

Table 2. Number of tasks in workflow applications

Application size	CyberShake	Epigenomics	Inspiral	Montage	SIPHT
Small	30	24	30	25	30
Medium	50	46	50	50	60
Large	100	100	100	100	100

For training and testing, a scenario of 30 workflows with different arrival rates was generated. The pattern, size and arrival rate of each workflow in the scenario were randomly generated. Moreover, we randomly generated set of 50 virtual machines ranging in size: small, medium, large and extra large. The same set of virtual machines were used in each scenario for consistency.

5.2   Baseline Algorithms

We compared our TL-GPHH approach with Non-Assisted GPHH as well as state-of-the-art scheduling algorithms. A summary of each is given below [5,6,8,12].

- Non-Assisted GPHH is standard GPHH without any knowledge transfer
- GRP-HEFT is a modified version of HEFT that considers cost while always selects the fastest available virtual machine to schedule a task to
- MINMIN takes the task with the minimum size and allocates it to the first idle virtual machine

- MAXMIN takes the task with the largest size and allocates it to the first idle virtual machine
- FCFS allocates the first ready task to the first available virtual machine
- MCT allocates a task to the virtual machine with the minimum expected completion time for that task
- RR selects the virtual machine a task is to be allocated to in a circular order

5.3   Parameter Settings

In our experiments we set the population size to 512, and the number of generations to 50. The crossover, mutation and reproduction rates are set to 85%, 10% and 5% which are common in literature [15]. The tournament size for tournament selection is 5 and the maximum depth of a tree is set to 10. Tournament selection is used to encourage the survival of effective heuristics in the population. For Non-Assisted GPHH we train 50 generations on the target problem. Contrarily, for TL-GPHH we train 30 generations on the source problem, and only 20 generations on the target problem. As the source and target are related, we transfer all the individuals from the final generation of the source problem, to generate the initial population of the target problem. For a fair comparison, we keep the total number of generations the same for both Non-Assisted GPHH and TL-GPHH. For all algorithms, we run our experiments 30 times, each with a different randomly generated scenario to verify our results.

5.4   Results

The results of our experiments show that TL-GPHH outperforms competing algorithms in the most scenarios. Table 3 demonstrates that TLGPHH achieved the best makespan in 26% of the scenarios, whereas MINMIN only achieved the best makespan in 20%. Non-Assisted GPHH performs just as well as MINMIN in that GPHH also achieved the best makespan in 20% of the scenarios. As anticipated, MCT, RR and FCFS achieve the best makespan in the least amount of scenarios, achieving the best in 6%, 3% and 0% respectively.

Table 3. Percent of performance in all scenarios

Performance	Scheduling heuristic							
	TLGPHH	GPHH	GRPHEFT	MINMIN	MAXMIN	RR	FCFS	MCT
Best	26%	20%	10%	20%	13%	3%	0%	6%
Worst	0%	10%	20%	0%	3%	26%	33%	6%

Moreover, the best performing algorithms, TL-GPHH and MINMIN, achieve the worst makespan in 0% of the scenarios. Whereas RR and FCFS consistently perform the worst, achieving the worst makespan in 26% and 33% of the scenarios respectively. Figure 1 demonstrates the makespan achieved by each algorithm per scenario. We can see that TLGPHH achieves the minimum makespan in the most individual scenarios.

5.5   Further Analysis

The aim of the TL-GPHH approach was to reduce computational costs of GP by utilising the advantages of TL to generate effective heuristics by transferring individuals from the source problem to the target problem. As discussed in Sect. 5.4, TL-GPHH was able to generate more effective heuristic rules than Non-Assisted GPHH. It can be noted that in the scenarios that Non-Assisted GPHH performed better, there were consistently more small workflows than medium and large. Moreover, Non-Assisted GPHH achieved the best results where there were more Epigenomics or Inspiral pattern. TL-GPHH is more consistent, as it was able to outperform GPHH in scenarios with large workflows, as well as small and medium. TL-GPHH is also more consistent for the patterns, performing well for scenarios with more diverse workflow patterns. Moreover, GPHH performs the worst in two scenarios where TL-GPHH performs the best. In these two scenarios there are mostly medium sized workflows that are the Epigenomics and Montage patterns.

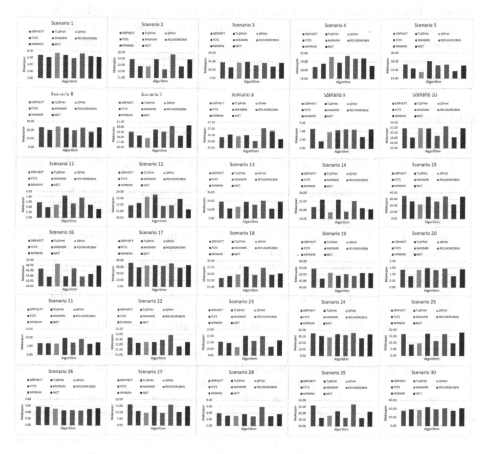

Fig. 1. Comparison of Makepsan achieved per Scenario

Furthermore, we collected the algorithm runtime for the training and testing of both TL-GPHH and GPHH. On average, TL-GPHH ran for 19 h ± 3 h, whereas GPHH ran for 25 h ± 1 h. TL-GPHH was able to obtain effective rules 20% faster than GPHH. This shows that TL-GPHH is more scalable than Non-Assisted GPHH, as smaller workflows can be used in the source problem to generate heuristic rules effective for larger workflows in the target problem, minimising the required training time therefore reducing the computational costs of GP.

6   Conclusion

In this paper, we present a TL-Assisted GPHH approach for DWS in cloud. The novelty of our paper is that our approach is able to reduce the computational cost of GP by taking advantage of TL. This makes TL-GPHH more scalable for DWS in cloud than Non-Assisted GPHH. The results show that TL-GPHH can minimise makespan in more scenarios than Non-Assisted GPHH and other state-of-the-art heuristics. Moreover, the proposed algorithm can reduce the computational costs of GP without sacrificing the performance. In the future, our proposed algorithm can be extended to consider more complex Transfer Learning methods to reduce computational cost of GP further for larger scale DWS problems.

References

1. Arabnejad, H., Barbosa, J.G.: Maximizing the completion rate of concurrent scientific applications under time and budget constraints. J. Comput. Sci. **23**, 120–129 (2017)
2. Arabnejad, V., Bubendorfer, K., Ng, B.: Dynamic multi-workflow scheduling: a deadline and cost-aware approach for commercial clouds. Future Gener. Comput. Syst. **100**, 98–108 (2019)
3. Ardeh, M.A., Mei, Y., Zhang, M.: Transfer learning in genetic programming hyper-heuristic for solving uncertain capacitated arc routing problem. In: 2019 IEEE Congress on Evolutionary Computation (CEC), pp. 49–56. IEEE (2019)
4. Ardeh, M.A., Mei, Y., Zhang, M.: A parametric framework for genetic programming with transfer learning for uncertain capacitated arc routing problem. In: Gallagher, M., Moustafa, N., Lakshika, E. (eds.) AI 2020. LNCS (LNAI), vol. 12576, pp. 150–162. Springer, Cham (2020). https://doi.org/10.1007/978-3-030-64984-5_12
5. Blythe, J., et al.: Task scheduling strategies for workflow-based applications in grids. In: IEEE International Symposium on Cluster Computing and the Grid, CCGrid 2005, vol. 2, pp. 759–767. IEEE (2005)
6. Braun, T.D., et al.: A comparison of eleven static heuristics for mapping a class of independent tasks onto heterogeneous distributed computing systems. J. Parallel Distrib. Comput. **61**(6), 810–837 (2001)
7. Chawla, Y., Bhonsle, M.: A study on scheduling methods in cloud computing. Int. J. Emerg. Trends Technol. Comput. Sci. (IJETTCS) **1**(3), 12–17 (2012)

8. Chen, W., Deelman, E.: WorkflowSim: a toolkit for simulating scientific workflows in distributed environments. In: 2012 IEEE 8th International Conference on E-Science, pp. 1–8. IEEE (2012)

9. Dinh, T.T.H., Chu, T.H., Nguyen, Q.U.: Transfer learning in genetic programming. In: 2015 IEEE Congress on Evolutionary Computation (CEC), pp. 1145–1151. IEEE (2015)

10. Escott, K.-R., Ma, H., Chen, G.: Genetic programming based hyper heuristic approach for dynamic workflow scheduling in the cloud. In: Hartmann, S., Küng, J., Kotsis, G., Tjoa, A.M., Khalil, I. (eds.) DEXA 2020. LNCS, vol. 12392, pp. 76–90. Springer, Cham (2020). https://doi.org/10.1007/978-3-030-59051-2_6

11. Escott, K.R., Ma, H., Chen, G.: A genetic programming hyper-heuristic approach to design high-level heuristics for dynamic workflow scheduling in cloud. In: 2020 IEEE Symposium Series on Computational Intelligence (SSCI), pp. 3141–3148. IEEE (2020)

12. Faragardi, H.R., Sedghpour, M.R.S., Fazliahmadi, S., Fahringer, T., Rasouli, N.: GRP-HEFT: a budget-constrained resource provisioning scheme for workflow scheduling in IaaS clouds. IEEE Trans. Parallel Distrib. Syst. **31**, 1239–1254(2019)

13. Juve, G., Chervenak, A., Deelman, E., Bharathi, S., Mehta, G., Vahi, K.: Characterizing and profiling scientific workflows. Future Gener. Comput. Syst. **29**(3), 682–692 (2013)

14. Lin, J., Zhu, L., Gao, K.: A genetic programming hyper-heuristic approach for the multi-skill resource constrained project scheduling problem. Expert Syst. Appl. **140**, 112915 (2020)

15. Masood, A., Mei, Y., Chen, G., Zhang, M.: Many-objective genetic programming for job-shop scheduling. In: 2016 IEEE Congress on Evolutionary Computation (CEC), pp. 209–216. IEEE (2016)

16. Meng, S., et al.: Security-aware dynamic scheduling for real-time optimization in cloud-based industrial applications. IEEE Trans. Ind. Inform. **17**, 4219–4228 (2020)

17. Muñoz, L., Trujillo, L., Silva, S.: Transfer learning in constructive induction with genetic programming. Genet. Program. Evolvable Mach. **21**(4), 529–569 (2020)

18. Nguyen, S., Mei, Y., Xue, B., Zhang, M.: A hybrid genetic programming algorithm for automated design of dispatching rules. Evolut. Comput. **27**(3), 467–496 (2019)

19. Pan, S.J., Yang, Q.: A survey on transfer learning. IEEE Trans. Knowl. Data Eng. **22**(10), 1345–1359 (2009)

20. Topcuoglu, H., Hariri, S., Wu, M.y.: Performance-effective and low-complexity task scheduling for heterogeneous computing. IEEE Trans. Parallel Distrib. Syst. **13**(3), 260–274 (2002)

21. Xiao, Q.z., Zhong, J., Feng, L., Luo, L., Lv, J.: A cooperative coevolution hyper-heuristic framework for workflow scheduling problem. IEEE Trans. Serv. Comput. (2019)

22. Xie, J., Mei, Y., Ernst, A.T., Li, X., Song, A.: A genetic programming-based hyper-heuristic approach for storage location assignment problem. In: 2014 IEEE congress on evolutionary computation (CEC), pp. 3000–3007. IEEE (2014)

23. Yu, Y., Feng, Y., Ma, H., Chen, A., Wang, C.: Achieving flexible scheduling of heterogeneous workflows in cloud through a genetic programming based approach. In: 2019 IEEE Congress on Evolutionary Computation (CEC), pp. 3102–3109. IEEE (2019)

24. Zhang, F., Mei, Y., Nguyen, S., Zhang, M.: Collaborative multifidelity-based surrogate models for genetic programming in dynamic flexible job shop scheduling. IEEE Trans. Cybern. (2021)

Transfer Learning and Data Augmentation in the Diagnosis of Knee MRI

John Haddadian$^{(\boxtimes)}$ and Mehala Balamurali$^{(\boxtimes)}$ (iD)

University of Sydney, Sydney, Australia
jhad4439@uni.sydney.edu.au, mehala.balamurali@sydney.edu.au

Abstract. Emergence of convolutional neural networks (CNNs) have offered better predictive performance and the possibility to replace traditional workflows with single network architecture. Recently developed MRNet CNN for the Knee MRI dataset has used AlexNet for their transfer learning implementation. This paper explores the effect of structural variations, data augmentation and various transfer learning implementations on the performance of a deep neural network in the classification task of knee MRI. Modifications of MRNet were generated by freezing the layers of the AlexNet backbone, replacing the backbone network AlexNet to other and applying the valid data augmentation techniques used on the dataset prior to input to the network. AlexNet based CNNs with layer-freezing achieved AUC for Abnormal, ACL lesion and Meniscal lesion classification of 0.913, 0.859, 0.792, an improvement over no layer freezing which had AUCs of 0.896, 0.842 and 0.773. although the result is less than that reported by Stanford's AlexNet based classifiers of 0.937, 0.965 and 0.847 AUC. ResNet18 based classifier achieved AUCs of 0.843, 0.774, 0.671. VGG16 based classifier achieved AUCs of 0.728 0.690 0.711. Using color jitter for data augmentation resulted 0.938 AUC in abnormal classification.

Keywords: Transfer learning · Data augmentation · MRI knee

1 Introduction

The leaps forward in automatic classification initiated by the success of AlexNet, and subsequent successes in the application of Convolutional Neural Networks (CNNs) has opened up the possibility of CNN application in the field of medical diagnosis. Recently, Stanford Machine Learning Group has released a dataset of labelled Knee MRI with ACL and Meniscal lesions along with a challenge to develop CNNs which attain high classification accuracy on this dataset, leading to the motivation of this paper to develop such a CNN through comparative evaluation of successful approaches to general image classification and in particular approaches which have been applied in automated diagnosis from medical images.

© Springer Nature Switzerland AG 2022
G. Long et al. (Eds.): AI 2021, LNAI 13151, pp. 452–463, 2022.
https://doi.org/10.1007/978-3-030-97546-3_37

Due to limited availability of labelled data for medical image classifiers, most deep-learning approaches must use a combination of data augmentation and transfer learning to overcome overfitting and attain the best performance possible. The MRNet CNN developed by Stanford ML for the Knee MRI dataset has used AlexNet for their transfer learning implementation, with previous research in the field suggesting that AlexNet is good for transfer learning due to its relative simplicity and fast training time allowing for fine-tuning and alteration of the network without too much time cost [1–3].

Among these are many successfully variations from AlexNet which may result in an improvement on the MRNet performance, as well as a possibility of sacrificing training time in order to achieve better performance with transfer learning networks based on deeper CNNs such as VGG.

During the training process in a transfer learning approach, parameters within the network are initialized to values achieved previously by training the network on another task, generally the classification of images from the large ImageNet database, prior to fine tuning of these parameters through training on another dataset for the required task. Previous studies have found improvements in network performance in medical image classification by freezing some layers of the network during the fine-tuning process; parameters in some of the layers are not re-trained on the new dataset and left to the values initialized by ImageNet training [4]. The application of layer freezing will yield improvements for network training time on the knee MRI classification task, and there is also likelihood for improvement in classification performance.

There may be significant differences in performance of transfer learning based neural network methods depending on the pre-trained network used as the base, with Shallu et al. [5] finding a difference as high as an area under the curve (AUC) of 95.65% for a network based on VGG-16 and AUC 79.39% for a network based on ResNet50 in a classification task on breast cancer histology [5]. There may also be improvements in performance by using model trained on data more similar to the task as the base for transfer learning. While Kim et al. [6] achieved 72% classification accuracy by transfer learning Inception v4 [6], trained on ImageNet to classify a mammography dataset, Pardamean et al. achieved a higher 90.38% accuracy by using a network trained on 112,120 X-ray images [4].

Other factors affecting performance of neural network classifiers include the choice of data augmentation techniques used on the dataset prior to input to the network. In image classification tasks, popular augmentation techniques include randomly adjusting the color of the images, cropping them, or performing affine transformations. While there have been comparative studies of different augmentation techniques performance on other datasets, the effect on performance will vary across different tasks, and such a study has not been published on knee MRI classification. Variations in data augmentation technique will have an effect on the performance of networks in classifying the Stanford MRNet dataset, and an exploration of these variations is likely to yield improved performance.

The purpose of this study is to investigate the effect of structural variations and various transfer learning implementations on the performance of a deep neural network in the classification task of knee MRI. The hypothesis is that approaches which lead to improvements on general tasks such as variations in the backbone network used from

AlexNet to more recent networks such as VGG-16 which outperform AlexNet in general tasks will yield improvements in the MRI classification task as well. Variations in data augmentation technique and the number of layers frozen in transfer learning will also allow for more optimal solutions to the classification task to be found, with higher classification performance.

2 Dataset

The dataset used has been made publicly available by Stanford Machine Learning group. Each of the 1370 Knee MRI examinations within the dataset consists of a series of MRI images with mean of 31.48 images per series, and a standard deviation of 7.97, for which the entire series has a uniform label. 1104 (80.6%) of the MRI examinations are labelled as abnormal, 319 (23.3%) have ACL lesions, and 508 (37.1%) have meniscal tears [7]. The training and validation split has been maintained as distributed by Stanford ML, having been 1130 MRI exams for the training set, and 120 MRI exams in the validation set. Stanford ML used random stratified sampling to divide the sets such that the validation set had a minimum of 50 positive samples for each of the abnormal, ACL lesion and Meniscal lesion labels. The remaining 120 exams of the total 1370 have not been used within this study as they are withheld for use in competition validation, therefore the total number of MRI exams used within this study is 1250.

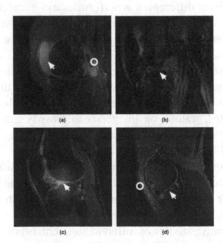

Fig. 1. Radiologist labelled Images from the MRNet Dataset [7]

Figure 1 shows examples of labelled MRI from the dataset with examples of each Abnormal, ACL tear and meniscal tear, further annotated by board-certified radiologists to aid understanding of the appearance of each class which appears in the dataset. The original MRNet was able to produce feature maps appropriate for the identification of the abnormality class such as effusions (arrow) and gastrocnemius tendon ruptures (indicated by the ring) in image (a). In images (b) and (c) the arrow indicates an ACL tear on a Sagittal T2-weighted MRI. In Image (d) the arrow indicates a meniscal tear.

3   AlexNet Based CNNs

3.1   MRNet Replication

AlexNet is widely used for classification of medical images as it is one of the simplest of the popular and high performing networks. Simplicity in this context means that the network has a relatively small depth of 8 layers, which allows for faster training times and less memory requirement compared to other networks, as well as simplifying modifications to the network and analysis of their performance. In this paper, performance of AlexNet based networks are compared to more recent and complex networks, as such several networks have been constructed for the classification of the MRI dataset with AlexNet used as the backbone for feature extraction. An attempt has been made to reproduce the CNN which was developed by Bien et al. [7] for the classification of knee MRI data; MRNet. Due to the differences in GPU hardware used for the training of the original MRNet (Nvidia GeForce GTX 8GB 1070) and the hardware used in the training of networks in this paper (Nvidia GeForce GTX 6GB 1060) we expect that there will be differences in training time, and possible differences in training result which arise from the restrictions associated with a lower available memory for training. Therefore, in order to establish a benchmark for comparison of the networks themselves without dependency of performance on differences between hardware used to train them, MRNet has been reproduced maintaining the parameters described in the original study where possible.

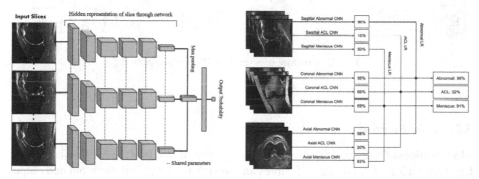

Fig. 2. (Left) Processing of a single MRI series by an MRNet; (Right) Structure of a super-MRNet [7]

Methodology

The MRNet reproduction consists of an 8-layer AlexNet feature extractor which has been initialized with parameter weights based on pre-training on the ImageNet dataset. The feature extractor returns a feature tensor of dimensions s × 256 × 7 × 7 for an input MRI series of dimensions s × 3 × 256 × 256 with s representing the number of total images in the MRI series, generally ranging in the order of 40 total images for the training dataset. The following pooling and classification layers of the original AlexNet are replaced with an average pooling layer reducing feature dimensions to s

× 256 and a maximal pooling across all images in the series resulting in a single 256 length vector to be input to a final fully connected layer. As with the original MRNet, for an input size of a single MRI series with dimensions s × 3 × 256 × 256, the 6GB of RAM available to the GPU was sufficient to train all layers of the AlexNet feature extractor and the following pooling and fully connected layers without requirement of freezing layers for training simplification. For the calculation of gradients for updating the parameter weights in training, a Binary Cross Entropy loss function is used. For the replication of the MRNet study, 9 separate MRNets reproduction (Fig. 3) networks have been produced to correspond to the 9 networks developed in the original study. Each network is a binary classifier for either Abnormalities, ACL tears and Meniscal tears from one of three views; Coronal, Sagittal, and Axial MRIs. The classifications of each exam from three views (Axial, Sagittal, Coronal) are combined through linear regression to form a total of 3 class outputs for each exam series. This method of combining 9 MRNets shall be referred to as a super-MRNet, while each individual CNN is referred to as an MRNet for clarity (Fig. 2).

As the optimizer has not been specified, an Adam optimizer was chosen as most appropriate as adaptive learning optimizers are suitable for sparse datasets. The learning rate is set to 0.0001 and the weight decay is set to 0.1.

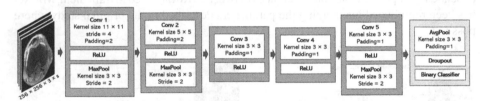

Fig. 3. Structure of a single MRNet reproduction

3.2   Layer Freezing

Modifications of MRNet were also generated by freezing layers of the AlexNet backbone. Layers which are frozen extract features and modify the input with the input and output dimensions as unfrozen layers, however during training, gradients are not required to be passed backward into the parameters of these layers, and the parameters remain with the weights generated from previous training on the ImageNet database. Thus, for the configuration in which all layers of AlexNet are frozen, the feature extractor is optimized for extracting features useful in classification of data from ImageNet, however the fully connected layer is trained to generate classifications of MRI data from these features. The motivation for training with frozen layers includes establishing an idea of the effectiveness of unmodified networks trained on ImageNet data for the classification of MRI images.

As there are significant differences between medical images and the ImageNet dataset, it is not expected that there will be a high degree of transferability between features designed for ImageNet classification and MRI classification, but deriving a numerical figure for this transferability in the form of network performance metrics such as AUC is useful for understanding of the MRI classification problem. The transferability of features derived by simple networks such as AlexNet may also be compared to the features extracted from more complex, deeper networks such as ResNet and VGG for a cross network comparison to further understanding of the classification problem. Developing several AlexNet networks each with a different number of frozen layers will also indicate the impact on performance and training time of each layer in the network.

It is expected that freezing the layers closest to the fully connected layer will have the greatest negative impact on performance accuracy as these layers extract the most abstract features which have the least transferability across different classification tasks, while the earliest layers in the network may still produce highly transferable features despite being frozen during training. A layer may be established such that the loss of performance accuracy is insignificant compared to the reduction in memory load and training time requirement by freezing the layer. With a high enough degree of transferability, such that the loss is particularly low, the increase in batch-size which is made possible by reducing the computational cost of training, the frozen layer may increase the speed with which the network can be trained, and also have an effect on the network's accuracy. Changes to batch size are not made in this study, as this would require each tensor loaded into the

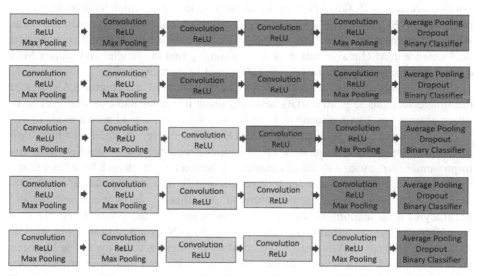

Fig. 4. Structure of Frozen Layer AlexNets. Rows1 to 5 represent FL1-AlexNet, FL2-AlexNet, FL3-AlexNet, FL4-AlexNet and FL5-AlexNet respectively by freezing the corresponding convolutional blocks in yellow. The parameters of each blocks are given in Fig. 3

batch to be of the same size, and the tensors in the dataset are of variable length due to each MRI examination having a different number of images in the series.

Methodology

An MRNet was modified by freezing the parameters in the AlexNet feature extractor. The MRNet trained on axial data have the most stable loss curves during training and validation, therefore to save time on training, rather than compiling 9 MRNets for each layer freezing configuration, we compiled only one for each of the 3 classes (Abnormal, ACL, Meniscal) with the Axial views only. These layer configurations (Fig. 4) are dubbed FL1-AlexNet, FL2-AlexNet… FL5-AlexNet where n in FLn-AlexNet represents the number of convolutional layers frozen during training. FL5-AlexNet is a simple feature extractor without any fine-tuning, such that only the classifier has been trained.

4 Variations in Network Structure: ResNet and VGG Based Classifiers

After the development of AlexNet, several networks have been developed which have had improved performance in general image classification tasks as demonstrated by performance on ImageNet database. Of note are the VGG networks which have achieved Top-5 errors of 7.3% and achieved 2nd place in the ILSVRC-2014 competition [8], which has been improved to 6.8% by the time of their paper being published. The other notable structure is Residual Networks (ResNets) as in Fig. 3, which have achieved first place in ILSVRC-2015 with 3.57% top-5 error [9]. The improvements in these networks which allow them to outperform on the ImageNet dataset should result in improved performance in MRI classification as well, assuming that the smaller and sparser MRI dataset is sufficient to train the larger ResNets and VGG networks.

VGG networks have structural changes which allow them to outperform AlexNet on the ImageNet dataset. Firstly, VGG networks make use of smaller convolutional layer filters of only 3×3 with a stride of 1, while AlexNet uses 11×11 with a stride of 4.

ResNets have been developed after AlexNet and have several changes which have allowed improvements in network classification accuracies over AlexNet. The first improvement is the use of Residual connections between layers, which have been found to increase training speed and network accuracy [10]. The introduction of batch normalization layers is a significant improvement, as it effects training speed, stability and accuracy of deep learning networks [11]. Finally, ResNets are generally deeper than AlexNet, with Pytorch offering implementations of ResNet starting from a minimum of 18 layers compared to AlexNet's 8 layers. The maximum accuracy possible has been previously found to increase with increasing network depth, although this accuracy improvement comes with a cost of a higher training data requirement.

Methodology

It is unclear whether the size of 1130 MRI examinations in the training set is large enough to sufficiently train a ResNet such that it may outperform the smaller AlexNet, even with transfer learning used to initialize the parameter weights. Therefore, choosing a relatively small 18 layer ResNet allows this issue to be minimized.

Due to limitations in memory, the entire VGG16 model was unable to be trained while taking an entire MRI series as an input. In order to train the model with 6GB of memory on the GPU, the first 7 of the total 13 Convolutional layers were required to be frozen.

All other methodology including dropout and augmentation matched that of the axial MRNets. The selection was based in order to ensure that the primary effect being studied was the difference in the backbone model used in the network, despite the ResNet study not using dropout when classifying on ImageNet [9]. For ResNet a different optimizer was tested, using an SGD with lr = 0.0001 and weight decay = 0.1.

5   Data Augmentation

In the field of classification of medical images, many studies restrict the data augmentation techniques used to a limited few, including flips and small rotations. One explanation given for this restriction is that medical images differ in nature to the general images used in other classification tasks, such as those contained within the ImageNet database, as unlike general image datasets medical images are a top-down solved problem. Further arguments are made that intensity is highly important to classification of medical images and as such color augmentations invalidate class labels.

It is clearly true that MRIs are significantly different in nature to classical images, in that the environment for taking magnetic resonance images is controlled to a much greater degree. For one orientation of the subject within the frame of the image is restricted during the imaging process. Secondly, the colors are restricted to greyscale, with white intensity of the image reflecting a portion of the organic material which has been selected for by the administering of chemical agents which embed themselves in particular tissues and cause those tissues to appear as highlighted within the MRI. However, it is also important to consider that MRI datasets are sparse and small relative to classical image datasets. In this case it may be possible that the loss of network performance resulting in decreasing the validity of some labels may be overcome with the sheer increase in data that comes from applying more transformations. With a combination of 3 forms of transformation-Rotation, Shear Mapping and Scale- Li, Hongwei and Jiang et al. [14] were able to create a 10x increase in dataset size for the purpose of brain MRI segmentation.

We investigated whether these notions on valid augmentations for medical images translate to effectiveness in the final performance of CNN networks.

Methodology
Network selection for the investigation of data augmentation is critical, as the trainable layers within the feature extractor may be a significant part of the effect of augmentation on the network. As such we selected a network which allows for finetuning on every layer of the feature extractor. A reproduction of a single Axial MRI trained MRNet with AlexNet backbone from the study by Bien et al. [7] is selected. We wish to observe the effect of augmentation on each class label therefore we trained a total of three binary classifying MRNets with each augmentation configuration.

When referring to an image as unmodified, this does not include the normalization and scaling which has been performed on all of the images in the dataset by Stanford prior to dataset release. Three variations from the data-augmentation used by Stanford in MRNet were tested, each implemented using the torch vision transform library as part of the pytorch package used to implement the models. Firstly, three MRNets (one for each classification) were trained with no data-augmentation other than the conversion of the data as parsed by the python NumPy package to a Python Image Library formatted image; an un-augmented image from the dataset as a control. Secondly, three models were trained using only the rotation affine transformation of ±25°. Finally, three models were trained using a color modification technique; Color Jitter of 0.1 for brightness and 0.1 for contrast were used, randomly adding or subtracting 10% of the brightness or contrast of the image. These latter two techniques have been to observe if a single transformation from the accepted affine transformations can outperform a single transformation of image color, which is not adopted in the MRI classifiers.

6 Results and Discussion

The results compiled from each of the previous sections is summarized and presented in the form of bar charts, compared and discussed and an overall conclusion for the study conducted in this research is provided.

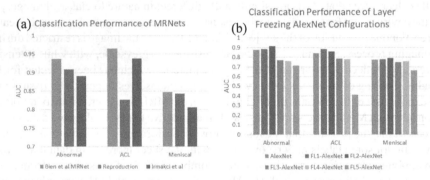

Fig. 5. (a) Reproduction of MRNet; (b) AlexNets with Layer Freezing Performance

In Fig. 5a, the results of the reproduction of Bien et al.'s [7] MRNet are presented, showing the lower network performance of the reproduction both performed in this study and in the Irmakci et al. [12] study. Due to the lack of details of the optimizer and parameters used in the actual study, as well as differences in hardware there are lower performances which must be considered. The replication trained all 9 MRNets for 50 epochs each in only 24 h, much faster than the study which claims to have required 6 h per network (54 h total). Figure 4b displays the results of layer freezing variations. As can be seen in Fig. 5b AlexNets with 1 frozen layer achieve the best ACL lesion classification, and 2 frozen layers results in the best Abnormal and Meniscal classification performances. The result that freezing the first two layers generated improvements in network AUC suggests that the features extracted by these layers are highly generalizeable across ImageNet to knee MRI classification. However, it is important to be careful with which layer is frozen such that the trade-off between performance and training time is worthwhile.

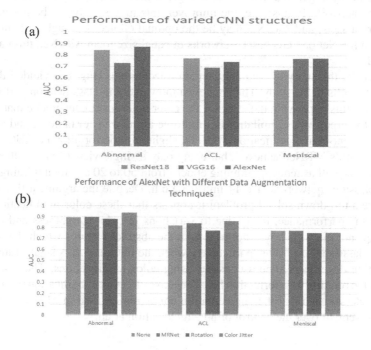

Fig. 6. (a) AlexNet, ResNet18 and VGG16 Network Performance (b) Performance of AlexNets using no data augmentation, MRNet matching data augmentation, ±25-degree affine rotation, and Color Jitter ± 10% Brightness and Saturation

As shown in Fig. 6a, the improvements of ResNet18 and VGG16 on ImageNet tasks were not transferrable to the classification of the MRNet dataset and overall these variations were the worst performing networks in any of the classification results. It is likely that the under-performance of the VGG16 based classifier when compared to the ResNet18 based classifier in the ACL and Abnormal classification can be attributed to the large number of convolutional layers which were unable to be finetuned with the limited memory available on the GPU. This is an important consideration when choosing networks for training classifiers, as VGG based networks require comparatively greater amounts of memory with similar AUC performance in cases such as training on ImageNet datasets. However, the VGG16 based classifier was able to outperform the ResNet18 based classifier on Meniscal classification is likely due to this being the most difficult classification to solve using Axial MRIs, such that the instability of the learning in the ResNet18 based model had the greatest effect on this problem, and the stability of the VGG16 classifier with frozen layers was more important in this case. Though these particular ResNet and VGG networks were unable to yield improvements over an AlexNet, but smaller variations to them may yet yield such improvements. It may also be that the batch-normalization, changes in convolutional window size, and use of residual connections to which the ImageNet improvements of these networks are attributed less significant as standalone features, and that the majority of network improvement comes simply by being larger and more complex, given that the dataset is sufficiently large to train the network. In this case, the improvements may simply not be generalizable to smaller datasets, and AlexNet may be the optimal choice, although without studies which train ResNet or VGG based networks of equal size to an AlexNet, this cannot be confirmed.

Ultimately, the study of data-augmentation techniques (Fig. 6b) yielded the most significant results in the study. The greatest improvement in classification performance was found in this paper with the effect of the color modification technique that alone is sufficient to outperform compilations of multiple affine transformations, and achieved the highest Abnormal classification of 0.938, slightly outperforming the AUC of 0.937 which Stanford's MRNet achieved, but using only a single view (Axial) rather than 3 MRI views, as well as reducing training epochs from 50 to 20 and total training time of a single classifier network to 1 h 11 min from 6 h. Despite the argument that medical images are a top-down solved problem it appears that these color modifications have improved the performance, likely due to variations in color (brightness and contrast, but perhaps not hue which was not tested) in the abstract features which the model is using for classifications. Thus, particularly when the dataset size is small, future MRI classification developers should consider using color modifications. The results also show that the rotation transformation had a negative effect on classification of knee MRI across all classes, and that the augmentation configuration used in MRNet resulted in little improvement over the control of no augmentation at all.

7 Conclusion

In conclusion the increased performances found with the deeper more complex networks such as ResNet18 and VGG16 studied in this paper were not found to generalize from the ImageNet dataset to the smaller and sparser MRI dataset when compared to a simple AlexNet classifier. Layer Freezing was able to result in great improvements to network performance both in AUC and training time for AlexNet networks. Using color augmentation techniques which have been not been considered in MRI classification literature can result in improvements to network performance, and future studies should experiment with such techniques.

References

1. Hosny, K.M, Kassem, M.A., Foaud, M.M.: Classification of skin lesions using transfer learning and augmentation with alex-net. PLOS ONE **14**, e0217293 (2019)
2. Maqsood, M., et al.: Transfer learning assisted classification and detection of alzheimer's disease stages using 3D MRI scans. Sensors **19**, 2645 (2019)
3. Choi, J.Y., Yoo, T.K., Seo, J.G., Kwak, J., Um, T.T., Rim, T.H.: Multicategorical deep learning neural network to classify retinal images: a pilot study employing small database. PLOS ONE **12**, e0187336 (2017)

4. Pardamean, B., Cenggoro, T.W., Rahutomo, R., Budiarto, A., Karuppiah, E.K.: Transfer learning from chest x-ray pre-trained convolutional neural network for learning mammogram data, Procedia Comput. Sci. **135**, 400–407, 2018. The 3rd International Conference on Computer Science and Computational Intelligence (ICCSCI 2018): Empowering Smart Technology in Digital Era for a Better Life (2018)
5. Shallu, Mehra, R.: Breast cancer histology images classification: training from scratch or transfer learning. ICT Express **4**(4), 247–254 (2018)
6. Kim, M., Zuallaert, J., De Neve W.: Towards novel methods for effective transfer learning and unsupervised deep learning for medical image analysis, pp. 32–39 (2017)
7. Bien, N., et al.: Deep-learning-assisted diagnosis for knee magnetic resonance imaging: development and retrospective validation of MRNet. PLOS Med. **15**, e1002699 (2018)
8. Simonyan, K., Zisserman, A.: Very deep convolutional networks for large-scale image recognition (2014)
9. He, K., Zhang, X., Ren, S., Sun, J.: Deep residual learning for image recognition. CoRR, abs/1512.03385 (2015)
10. Szegedy, C., Ioffe, S., Vanhoucke, V.: Inception-v4, Inception-ResNet and the impact of residual connections on learning, CoRR, abs/1602.07261 (2016)
11. Ioffe, S. Szegedy, C.: Batch normalization: accelerating deep network training by reducing internal covariate shift (2015)
12. Irmakci, I., Anwar, S.M., Torigian, D.A., Bagci, U.: Deep learning for musculoskeletal image analysis (2020)
13. Talo, M., Baloglu, U.B., Aydin, G., Acharya, U.R.: Convolutional neural networks for multi-class brain disease detection using MRI images. Comput. Med. Imag. Graph. **78**, 101673 (2019)
14. Li, H., et al.: Fully convolutional network ensembles for white matter hyperintensities segmentation in MR images. Neuroimage **183**, 650–665 (2018). https://doi.org/10.1016/j.neuroimage.2018.07.005. Epub PMID 30125711

Classical AI

Analysing Multiobjective Optimization Using Evolutionary Path Length Correlation

Daniel Herring$^{(\boxtimes)}$, Dean Pakravan, and Michael Kirley

School of Computing and Information Systems, University of Melbourne,
Melbourne, Australia
dherring@student.unimelb.edu.au

Abstract. Recently, a number of studies have attempted to characterize the interaction between objectives and decision variables in multiobjective problems. In this paper, we continue this line of research by focusing specifically on quantifying observable differences in the ease of optimizing extreme solutions (i.e. solutions on the limits of the Pareto front). We propose an evolutionary path length correlation (EPLC) measurement in the decision variable space that is computed by tracing the evolutionary history of solutions on the Pareto front. We draw on the length scale measure and extend the well-known fitness distance correlation to multiobjective optimization problems. Here, the overarching goal is to investigate the emergent dynamics of specific problem–algorithm combinations, rather than the characterization of the search landscape per se. We evaluate the efficacy of the EPLC using benchmark continuous multiobjective problems and combinatorial problems with controllable objective interactions and known Pareto optima. In some problems, observable differences in the convergence to extreme solutions in each objective can be captured using the EPLC. Our results go some way towards furthering our understanding of how specific algorithms traverse the landscape, given interactions between both decision variables and objectives.

Keywords: Multiobjective optimization · Fitness distance correlation · Length scale

1 Introduction

Understanding the relationship between the performance of algorithms and fitness landscapes of multiobjective optimization problems is a current research area in the evolutionary computation community. In single objective optimization problems, different fitness landscape features derived from *exploratory landscape analysis (ELA)* techniques are often used to help quantify problem difficulty. However, in multiobjective optimization it is often challenging to represent the landscapes, both in terms of size, dimensionality and objective correlations.

© Springer Nature Switzerland AG 2022
G. Long et al. (Eds.): AI 2021, LNAI 13151, pp. 467–479, 2022.
https://doi.org/10.1007/978-3-030-97546-3_38

In a recent paper, Liefooghe et al. [16] presented a comprehensive review of multiobjective landscape features, including clustering in decision space and correlation between features. Significantly, they also examined associations between instance features and empirical problem hardness. In this paper, we pursue a similar research direction. However, our overarching goal is to explore the dynamics of specific combinations of multiobjective optimization problems–algorithms, rather than attempting to characterize the fitness landscape as such.

Building on the *length scale* metric introduced by Morgan and Gallagher [18], we introduce an *evolutionary path length* (EPL) measure that traces the 'ancestral history' of solutions on the limits of the Pareto front for a multiobjective optimization problem. We argue that differences in the 'complexity' of specific objectives will be reflected in the corresponding EPL values. We are particularly interested in documenting difference in EPL values as the number of decision variables and/or the correlation between objectives are varied. With respect to the specific geometry over the search space that different algorithm operators impose, we introduce an extension to the well-known *fitness distance correlation* metric [13], which we call *evolutionary path length correlation* (EPLC). With this we can generate comparable estimates of problem difficulty based on differential success of algorithms on a problem's objectives.

We evaluate the efficacy of the EPL and EPLC metrics using well-known, continuous multiobjective benchmark problems [7,11,28], and combinatorial problems with controllable objective interactions and known Pareto optimal solutions [26]. Our analysis confirms observable differences in convergence of extreme solutions in each objective can be quantified in the EPL. In addition, EPLC values can describe the 'difficulty' inherent in achieving optimal solutions at the extreme of each objective in specific algorithm–problem instance combinations.

2   Background and Related Work

The factors controlling the difficulty of optimization problems for stochastic search algorithms are not fully understood. For single objective optimization problems, many papers have appeared over the last two decades describing the advantages and/or disadvantages of a given ELA technique. A survey paper by Munoz et al. [21] and subsequent work by Moser et al. [19] illustrate many examples focused predominantly on black-box continuous optimization problems. The meta-learning framework for algorithm selection introduced by Smith-Miles [24] and the recent work of Kerschke et al. [14], focused on algorithm configuration and portfolio selection spanning discrete and continuous problems, provide guidance as to problem difficulty indicators. In the multiobjective optimization domain, characterizing the fitness landscape poses many challenges. In addition to interactions between decision variables, correlations (interactions) between objective functions must also be considered.

One of the earliest studies focussed on examining fitness landscape features for multiobjective optimization was by Knowles and Corne [15]. In that work, they attempted to characterize the 'degree of difficulty' of multiobjective quadratic assignment problems. Garrett and Dasgupta [8] have used fitness land-scape analysis techniques to examine how the scaling of local optima affected multiobjective optimization problems. The idea that problem-related properties directly impact on the properties of the Pareto set and the behaviour of multi-objective optimization algorithms is now widely accepted [22].

Aguirre and Tanaka [1] have defined a number of problem features that relate to problem difficulty focusing on combinatorial space using multiobjective NK-landscapes. In a similar study, Verel et al. [26] describe how the range of features including problem dimensions, interactions between decision variables and objectives may affect the optimization process. Daolio [4] extended that work, and provided a detailed correlation analysis between the features identified.

Kerschke and others [14] have described an approach to generalize ELA meth-ods for multiobjective optimization problems. They provide characterization for a number of extracted features and report only weak correlations between some of these features as indicators of problem difficulty. More recently, Liefooghe et al. [16] have also reviewed multiobjective landscape analysis. In that work, they have documented a number of new features, including clustering and correlation between features, specifically proposed for multiobjective problems.

3 Model

Our work relates to the problem of understanding the differences in convergence speed of a given algorithm between the objectives of a problem. Whilst respect-ing the abundant algorithm-independent information obtainable from ELA, we aim to provide insights on algorithm mechanics on problems rather than a char-acterization of the problem landscape. We propose a new analysis method, the *evolutionary path length*, which we use to quantify the observable differences in the ease of optimizing extreme solutions (i.e., solutions on the limits of the Pareto front). That is, we trace the evolutionary trajectory of Pareto-optimal solutions in the evolving population for a given problem instance–algorithm combination. The intuitive 'difficulty' can then be inferred from the length of the evolutionary path. The EPL is not an exploratory landscape analysis feature, however, it does provide important information about the differential achievement of a specific algorithm mechanisms for finding solutions at the extents of the Pareto-front.

Consider a multiobjective optimization problem (definition from [5,17]).

$$
\begin{aligned}
\text{Minimise:} \quad & f(\boldsymbol{x}) = [f_1(\boldsymbol{x}), f_2(\boldsymbol{x}), \dots, f_m(\boldsymbol{x})]^T \\
\text{with:} \quad & \boldsymbol{x} = [x_1, x_2, \dots, x_n]^T \\
\text{subject to:} \quad & g_i(\boldsymbol{x}) \le 0 \ , \ i \in [1, \dots, q] \\
& h_i(\boldsymbol{x}) = 0 \ , \ i \in [1, \dots, p]
\end{aligned}
$$

where $\boldsymbol{x}$ is a vector of decision variables, g_i is an inequality constraint, and h_i is an equality constraint. $f(\boldsymbol{x})$ maps $\boldsymbol{x}$ into $\mathbb{R}^m$, where $m \ge 2$ is the number of objectives. We can think of $f(\boldsymbol{x})$ as an objective vector or point in m dimensions. The goal is to find all compromising Pareto-optimal solutions, where a solution $\boldsymbol{x}^* \in \Omega$ is Pareto-optimal if for every $\boldsymbol{x} \in \Omega$ and $I = \{1, 2 \dots k\}$ either,

$$\forall_{i \in I}(f_i(\boldsymbol{x}) = f_i(\boldsymbol{x}^*)) \tag{1}$$

or, there is at least one $i \in I$ such that

$$f_i(\boldsymbol{x}) > f_i(\boldsymbol{x}^*) \tag{2}$$

Without loss of generality, we discuss a bi-objective problem. We focus on the extreme solutions for the objectives $f_1(\boldsymbol{x})$, $f_2(\boldsymbol{x})$, as the relative ease/speed of finding the minimum values in each of the objectives may be significantly different, giving an indication of problem difficulty. We label the extreme solutions for objectives $f_1(\boldsymbol{x}) = 0$, $f_2(\boldsymbol{x}) = 0$ as $f_{1_{ex}}$ and $f_{2_{ex}}$ respectively.

Our definition of EPL was inspired in part by the *length scale* metric, introduced by Morgan and Gallagher [18] for single objective optimization problems. The length scale was based on characterization of objective function changes from the transition between two points in the search space. For the multiobjective case, we focus on the differences in the distance value derived from the evolutionary trajectory of individual Pareto-optimal solutions. That is, we compute the EPL of $f_{1_{ex}}$ and $f_{2_{ex}}$, which represents the number states generated between the initialisation and convergence of the optimization algorithm.

To calculate the evolutionary path length, we adopt the suggestion from Hart et al. [9]: we start from $f_{1_{ex}}$ and $f_{2_{ex}}$, and rewind the evolutionary process. Here, the extreme solutions correspond to a *child* solution. Then, for each of the identified *parents* of that child we select the parent with the smallest difference in the decision variable values. Consider a child c of parents p_1 & p_2 from a previous generation. Assuming the focus is on the objective function $f_1(\boldsymbol{x})$, then:

$$\boldsymbol{x}_c = \boldsymbol{x}_{f_{1_{ex}}} \tag{3}$$

$$\boldsymbol{x}_p = \min_{p_1,p_2} \sum_{i=1}^{n} |x_{c,i} - x_{p,i}| \tag{4}$$

$$\boldsymbol{x}_c = \boldsymbol{x}_p \tag{5}$$

The process is iterated across all time steps until an initial solution is reached. Thus the EPL is set to the number of iterations required to find the initial solution starting from the extreme optimal solution. It is important to note that our approach is based on identifying the parent which is closest to the child in decision space, removing the need to store every solution. It is an assumption that the nearest parent holds enough information when tracing the most optimized path and displays the behaviour of the algorithm against the problem.

The EPL provides a link between theoretical runtime and practical performance analysis. The evolutionary trajectory followed will depend upon the fitness landscape's topological features and algorithm operators. Operators impose a geometry of solution transitions in the search space and thus make comparisons of EPLs between algorithms impossible. Therefore, we propose a new metric to quantify problem difficulty, the *evolutionary path length correlation* (EPLC); an extension of the well-known *fitness distance correlation* (FDC) method [13].

The original FDC provides a measure of problem difficulty for single objective optimization problems, and has provided important insights into meta-heuristic behaviours based on global landscape structures [10,23]. One disadvantage, is it requires the global optimum to be known. This can be somewhat mediated by using the 'best known solution', however the proximity to the global optimum has a direct impact on the quality of the correlation value [10,20].

Here, the EPLC provides a comparable quantification of suitability of algorithm – problem pairings by considering the number of solutions states visited before finding the Pareto-optimal extremes of each objective.

We define the EPLC for each objective, $m \in \{1, 2\}$, using the aggregated set of solutions in a number of constructed evolutionary histories (repeats) for the Pareto-Optimal extreme solution in that objective ($f_{1_{ex}}, f_{2_{ex}}$ respectively):

$$EPLC_m = \frac{\frac{1}{N}\sum_{i=1}^{N}\left(f_{m_i} - \overline{f_m}\right)\left(EPL_{m_i} - \overline{EPL_m}\right)}{S_{f_m} S_{EPL}} \tag{6}$$

where: N is the number of solutions; $\overline{f_m}$ and $\overline{EPL_m}$ are the mean fitness in objective m and mean EPL across the set. The values S_{f_m} and S_{EPL} are standard deviations respectively for the objective values f_m and EPL values of this set.

4 Experiments

4.1 Optimization Algorithms

We employ the well-known and effective NSGA-II [6] and MOEA/D [27] optimizers. NSGA-II is dominance based, with diversity preservation based on crowding distance. MOEA/D uses decomposition into scalar sub-problems, optimized at each iteration. We rely on out-of-the-box implementations with default parameters for NSGA-II and MOEA/D in PlatEMO framework [25]. The population size is 100 and the maximum generations set to 500 (i.e. 50k function evaluations). All simulations were repeated 30 times with appropriate statistical analysis.

4.2 Test Problems

Continuous Problems: The continuous test problems are from the benchmark suites: ZDT [28], DTLZ [7] and WFG [11], implemented in PlatEMO. When running MOEA/D, appropriate decomposition methods were used for particular problems [12]: Tchebycheff with normalisation was used for ZDT1,3,6; DTLZ3,4,6; and all WFG problems; PBI was used on ZDT2,4 and DTLZ1,2,7.

In our experiments, we use default settings for all problems. For the ZDT and DTZL problems, the number of decision variables was set as increments of 5 up to 30. For the WFG problems we set $K = 4$, thus the number of decision variables was initialised at 9 and incremented by 5 up to 34, to remain consistent with the other problems. Consequently WFG2 and WFG3 were omitted from testing. We also excluded the following problems: ZDT5 as it required binary encoding and had a discrete Pareto-front; DTLZ5 and DTLZ8 as they were designed for 3+ objectives; DTLZ9 generated computational problems in PlatEMO.

Discrete Problems: We use the family of ρMNK-landscapes, introduced by Verel et al. [26]. The problem suite extends the single-objective NK-landscapes and multiobjective NK-landscapes with independent objective functions [1]. The landscape is described by four parameters: ρ (objective interaction), M (no. of objectives), N (no. of decision variables) and K (no. of epistatic interactions between decision variables). The search spaces can be enumerated and the level of interaction between objectives and decision variables can be controlled. We refer the reader to [26] for a visualization of the parameter effects. In our experiments, we vary the epistatic degree $K \in \{2, 4, 6, 8, 10\}$ and $\rho \in \{-0.9, -0.7, -0.4, -0.2, 0.0, 0.2, 0.4, 0.7, 0.9\}$ the objective correlation values. To remain consistent with the continuous problems, we set $M \in \{2\}$.

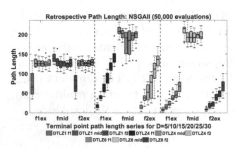

Fig. 1. ZDT problems/NSGAII

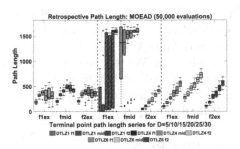

Fig. 2. ZDT problems/MOEAD

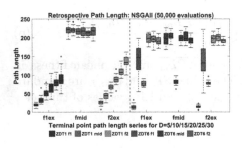

Fig. 3. DTLZ problems/NSGAII

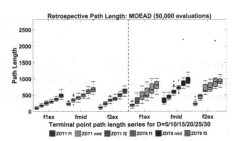

Fig. 4. DTLZ problems/MOEAD

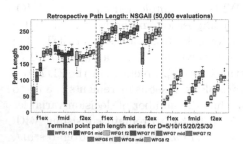

Fig. 5. WFG problems/NSGAII

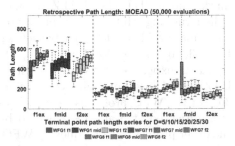

Fig. 6. WFG problems/MOEAD

5   Results

5.1   Continuous Problems

Evolutionary Path Length: Figures 1–6 present distributions of EPL values for selected problems for each of the algorithms considered.

In addition to insights gained from f_{1ex} and f_{2ex}, we include the EPL value for the midpoint f_{mid} between f_{1ex} f_{2ex}. Whilst the extrema satisfy the objective functions most differently from each other, the midpoint satisfies both objectives most differently from the extremes. The Pareto-front midpoint is the non-dominated solution closest to $y = f(x)$, where $y = x$ for all problems, except ZDT3 and WFG problems where we set $y = 0$ and $y = 2x$ respectively.

Given the underlying evolutionary operators deployed, significant differences in EPL values are to be expected between algorithms. For example, the maximum EPL is limited by the number of generations to the $\mu + \lambda$ nature of NSGA-II. In contrast, MOEA/D performs replacement in-generation within each sub-problem, meaning a parent may have been generated within the current generation, leading to inflated EPLs. This is illustrated by the difference in scale observable between the plots in Figs. 1 & 2 and highlights the need for the EPLC calculation for comparison between algorithms.

Convergence was evident for the ZDT problems and the majority of DTLZ problems. The WFG problems did not converge based on the IGD metric values (not shown), however even after 2.5 million function evaluations the minima cannot be achieved for some problems [2]. In cases where the extreme minimal solutions, f_{1ex} and f_{2ex}, were not found given the computational budget, the best solution found so far was used to construction evolutionary histories and the boxplots are patterned to indicate this.

The boxplots suggest increasing EPL values as the number of decision variables increases for both $f_{1_{ex}}$ and $f_{2_{ex}}$, with MOEA/D values being expectedly higher. In most cases, the value of the EPL for $f_{1_{ex}}$ was smaller than $f_{2_{ex}}$, with greater deviations noted in the WFG problems. In the case of ZDT6–NSGA-II, increasing the number of decision variables from 5 to 10 to 15 led to a significant increase in path length, before the value reached a plateau. An increasing median path length is evident for WGF1–NSGA-II. For DTLZ4–MOEA/D significant variation between simulation results exists for $f_{1_{ex}}$, but not $f_{2_{ex}}$. Generally, larger path lengths for f_2 than f_1 implies that finding the minimum solutions for the first objective is easier than the second; fewer solutions are visited between initialization and convergence for the f_1 extreme solution. This is expected given the documented characteristics of the problems, but provides a quantification of the commonly observable unbalanced optimization.

For all problems, the EPL value for f_{mid} is typically larger than the extreme optimal values. This is attributed to replacement mechanisms; minor changes in crowding distance selection in NSGA-II in successive generations NSGA-II and within-generation replacement for MOEA/D, inflating the EPL measurement.

However, there is significant variation in the results. For example, for NSGA-II, the f_{mid} values tended to be similar for each of the decision variable dimensions examined for the DLTZ problems, but not for the other problems where the general linear trend is evident. The outlier is ZDT6, when $D = 15$. A possible explanation is that a near-optimal solution is found relatively early in the optimization, but the minimum was not found within the evaluation limit.

The trends in the plots are generally smooth, with greatest variation occurring for the f_{mid} values in WG1-NSGA-II and WFG8–MOEA/D.

Evolutionary Path Length Correlation: Table 1 lists the EPLC values for all problems instances generated using NSGA-II and MOEA/D respectively.

As a course-grain differentiation of problem difficulty, we adopt a similar schema to the original fitness distance correlation metric [3,13]. That is, for a given minimization multiobjective optimization problem, the difficulty in terms of EPL for the extreme values can be classified as: *misleading* when EPLC $\leq$ -0.2; *difficult* when $-0.2 <$EPLC< 0.2 and *straightforward* when EPLC≥ 0.2.

For most of the DTLZ set, NSGA-II has similar EPLC values for both objectives and increases (optimizing to extremes becomes more straightforward) with the number of decision variables. DTLZ1&3 clearly show this trend. For brevity, D is used henceforth to refer to the number of decision variables in the problem. For DTLZ6 both objectives still achieve similar values, however they decrease as more decision variables are included; illustrating the notion that problems become more difficult as dimension grows.

For DTLZ2-NSGA-II we see similar EPLC values across both objectives and across D values; these values are around 0.2, indicating a difficult problem. For DTLZ4, the f_1 EPLC value maintains a value between 0.2 and 0.4 across changing D, however the f_2 EPLC increases with D. This implies counter-intuitively the f_2 objective is more difficult to optimize when D is smaller.

When using MOEA/D, we see similar trends but for different problems. This stable-f_1 and increasing-f_2 phenomenon is present for DTLZ3&6 and for DTLZ2 the stable and increasing objectives are switched. The DTLZ1-MOEA/D is similar to DTLZ2-NSGA-II but with higher EPLC values indicating an easier optimisation. For DTLZ4-MOEA/D, the respectively decreasing and increasing f_2 and f_1 EPLC values highlight the complex effects of changing D; as D increases f_2 becomes more difficult to optimize, whilst f_1 gets more straightforward.

For ZDT-NSGA-II pairings, the characteristic imbalance in Pareto-front coverage seen in real-time observation of the optimisation is represented in these EPLC values. Across the suite, f_2 EPLC values are mostly greater than 0.2 (straightforward optimization), stable across different D. The f_1 EPLC values imply difficulty for ZDT1&3 with increasing D and increasingly misleading problems for ZDT2,4&6. MOEA/D copes better with stable high EPLC values for ZDT1,4&6. The ZDT2-MOEA/D EPLC values imply straightforward optimization of f_2, but the f_1 values show no discernible trend across the range of D. Further investigation is required to glean insights from this.

NSGA-II behaviours on WFG can be described by the EPLC values obtained and presented in Table 1. Except for WFG1&8, all obtained EPLC values are close to zero, illustrating NSGA-II's poor performance. In WFG8-NSGAII the

Table 1. EPLC values for each of the continuous test problem instances when NGSA-II (left) and MOEA/D (right) were used as the optimizer.

NSGA-II		Number of decision variables (D)					MOEA/D		Number of decision variables (D)				
Problem		5	10	15	20	25	30	Problem		5	10	15	20	25	30
DTLZ1	f_1	0.13	0.27	0.32	0.38	0.40	0.45	DTLZ1	f_1	0.46	0.47	0.50	0.42	0.49	0.57
	f_2	0.17	0.28	0.33	0.38	0.42	0.44		f_2	0.43	0.45	0.42	0.38	0.48	0.53
DTLZ2	f_1	0.15	0.12	0.16	0.21	0.18	0.20	DTLZ2	f_1	−0.02	−0.04	0.30	0.17	0.33	0.42
	f_2	0.07	0.17	0.14	0.14	0.18	0.15		f_2	0.73	0.78	0.75	0.80	0.72	0.74
DTLZ3	f_1	0.14	0.30	0.32	0.36	0.41	0.42	DTLZ3	f_1	0.34	0.21	0.37	0.41	0.46	0.49
	f_2	0.14	0.28	0.35	0.35	0.42	0.41		f_2	0.18	0.11	0.43	0.38	0.48	0.45
DTLZ4	f_1	0.22	0.34	0.39	0.38	0.28	0.29	DTLZ4	f_1	0.18	0.27	0.32	0.36	0.39	0.40
	f_2	0.01	0.00	0.21	0.31	0.18	0.17		f_2	−0.15	−0.17	−0.10	−0.16	−0.10	0.04
DTLZ6	f_1	0.39	0.39	0.52	0.51	0.11	0.24	DTLZ6	f_1	0.54	0.71	0.68	0.66	0.65	0.72
	f_2	0.50	0.39	0.42	0.43	0.11	0.24		f_2	0.13	0.42	0.54	0.62	0.65	0.67
ZDT1	f_1	0.08	−0.02	−0.14	−0.15	−0.09	−0.06	ZDT1	f_1	0.65	0.63	0.48	0.60	0.61	0.42
	f_2	0.51	0.52	0.53	0.49	0.53	0.50		f_2	0.52	0.77	0.73	0.77	0.78	0.57
ZDT2	f_1	−0.13	−0.28	−0.51	−0.55	−0.60	−0.62	ZDT2	f_1	−0.26	−0.10	−0.03	0.34	−0.11	0.07
	f_2	0.46	0.53	0.49	0.52	0.49	0.50		f_2	0.58	0.53	0.70	0.53	0.69	0.44
ZDT3	f_1	−0.03	−0.03	−0.02	−0.01	−0.03	0.04	ZDT3	f_1	0.61	0.57	0.62	0.49	0.57	0.50
	f_2	0.22	0.14	0.50	0.33	0.34	0.42		f_2	−0.02	0.14	0.19	0.27	0.30	0.38
ZDT4	f_1	0.03	−0.20	−0.03	−0.39	−0.29	−0.27	ZDT4	f_1	0.32	0.51	0.42	0.63	0.53	0.27
	f_2	0.21	0.35	0.62	0.47	0.51	0.55		f_2	0.54	0.59	0.60	0.61	0.62	0.66
ZDT6	f_1	0.05	−0.21	−0.40	−0.31	−0.34	−0.39	ZDT6	f_1	0.49	0.51	0.48	0.45	0.19	0.45
	f_2	0.72	0.44	0.86	0.68	0.72	0.77		f_2	0.54	0.75	0.74	0.81	0.51	0.90
Problem		9	14	19	24	29	34	Problem		9	14	19	24	29	34
WFG1	f_1	0.15	0.44	0.48	0.35	0.48	0.45	WFG1	f_1	0.66	0.90	0.84	0.88	0.88	0.91
	f_2	0.08	0.13	0.13	0.15	0.18	0.15		f_2	0.17	−0.01	−0.14	−0.24	−0.25	−0.30
WFG4	f_1	0.00	0.05	0.03	0.06	0.03	0.02	WFG4	f_1	0.76	0.77	0.46	0.76	0.68	0.67
	f_2	0.05	0.06	0.06	0.06	0.05	0.04		f_2	0.01	0.02	0.10	0.07	0.08	0.07
WFG5	f_1	0.04	0.03	0.03	0.06	0.07	0.07	WFG5	f_1	0.87	0.85	0.79	0.84	0.83	0.75
	f_2	0.02	0.03	0.04	0.03	0.05	0.04		f_2	−0.17	−0.02	−0.11	−0.09	0.06	−0.02
WFG6	f_1	0.07	0.07	0.08	0.10	0.10	0.13	WFG6	f_1	0.75	0.31	0.22	0.69	0.79	0.72
	f_2	0.03	0.04	0.05	0.06	0.06	0.03		f_2	0.21	−0.05	−0.06	0.06	0.00	−0.04
WFG7	f_1	0.04	0.03	0.04	0.03	0.07	0.05	WFG7	f_1	0.90	0.77	0.87	0.86	0.89	0.77
	f_2	0.04	0.06	0.06	0.08	0.04	0.05		f_2	−0.10	−0.07	−0.09	−0.01	−0.30	−0.11
WFG8	f_1	0.23	0.12	0.11	0.16	0.07	0.08	WFG8	f_1	0.02	0.71	0.84	0.82	0.78	0.75
	f_2	0.34	0.16	0.16	0.11	0.10	0.07		f_2	0.18	0.19	0.31	0.11	0.26	0.13
WFG9	f_1	0.02	0.08	0.06	0.03	0.06	0.04	WFG9	f_1	0.22	0.65	0.56	0.59	0.56	0.46
	f_2	0.04	0.03	0.03	0.05	0.03	0.04		f_2	0.31	−0.02	0.01	0.00	0.21	0.14

EPLC tends towards zero for f_1 and f_2 as D increases. This confirms more decision variables increase the difficulty for NSGA-II. On WFG1, consistently low EPLC for f_2 implies difficult optimization, however the larger positive values for f_1 indicate easier optimization; in line with observable algorithm behaviours.

The suitability of the algorithms for different problems is highlighted by the EPLC obtained for MOEA/D on the WFG problems. Where most instances

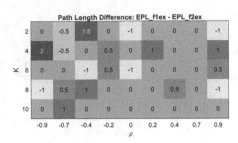

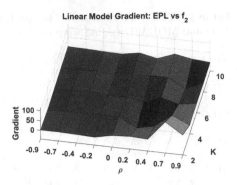

Fig. 7. Difference in EPL measurements using NSGA-II for extrema solutions in each objective across the range of discrete problem instances with different objective correlation (ρ) and epistatic interactions (K).

Fig. 8. Gradients of linear models constructed from EPL values of all Pareto-Optimal solutions against their f_1 objective values, for each combination of ρ and K parameters.

were difficult for both objectives when using NSGA-II, for MOEA/D the f_1 EPLC values indicate straightforward optimization across the values of D. The f_2 values are mostly more positive than for WFG-NSGA-II pairings, but are still close to zero, signifying the difficulty of the suite.

These results illustrate many differences in the ease of optimization for each objective when using different algorithms on a problem. Using EPLC, we can distinguish which algorithms are fit for purpose on a problem, as well as identifying the objective(s) that are hard to optimize. Whilst all function interactions cannot be captured by the EPLC, the recorded measurements of observable algorithms behaviours validates the proposed methodology.

5.2 Discrete Problems

We trace the evolutionary history and measure the EPL for every solution in the Pareto-optimal set for each of the ρMNK-landscape instances considered. The difference in EPL measurements for extreme solutions in the discrete problems are shown in the heatmap in Fig. 7. There are minimal differences in the magnitude of the EPL differences for $f_{1_{ex}}$ and $f_{2_{ex}}$ in these environments, implying that these solutions and the objectives are equally difficult for the algorithm.

To utilise the enumeration of the ρMNK-landscape, we consider the gradient of linear model constructed from the f_1 objective values for all Pareto-optimal solutions against their EPL values. This enables us to determine how the EPL changes along the Pareto Front between the extremes. The gradients are calculated across the set of discrete problems and are given in Fig. 8. Here, positive objective correlation ($\rho > 0$) results in f_1 becoming more difficult, implying the f_1 objective is more difficult than f_2, exacerbated by fewer epistatic interactions ($K = 2$). For negative objective correlation ($\rho < 0$), the gradients are closer to zero across the range of K, implying balance in difficulty between the objectives is maintained. Improvements in the efficiency of history tracking for MOEA/D will enable further comparisons using this technique. The difference in numbers of Pareto-optimal solutions as ρ changes impacts the quality of the linear model.

6   Discussion and Conclusion

Our motivation was based on the assumption that it is both the topological features of the fitness landscape and the specific meta-heuristics operators that determine the effectiveness of the optimization process. In most cases, it is very difficult to estimate the performance of an algorithm on a particular problem without retrospective evaluation. However, algorithm independent problem measurements from ELA lack the specificity for informing algorithm selection that a retrospective analysis can provide. Furthermore, the stability observed as the number of decision variables increases for some problems implies an opportunity for an easier instance of a problem to be solved by a suite of algorithms and based on the EPLC values, the best algorithm can be chosen for the harder problem. In some cases, an increase in the number of decision variables indicated declining suitability of an algorithm. The diversity observed between the examined algorithms however, may allow for the construction of ensemble methods or a hyper-heuristic approach to generate composite populations of solutions by parallelization of algorithms with differential suitability for each objective. The EPL is an indicator of stochasticity impacting on convergence speed in algorithm-problems. A large spread in EPL values indicates a high variability in the 'evolutionary route' through the solution space that the algorithm takes.

In summary, our analysis of the evolutionary history of the extreme Pareto solutions provides a quantification of the relative ease of finding the extreme value in each of the objectives, and thus providing an indication of differential difficulty between the objectives of a problem. The results from our experiments on problems covering a wide range of the structural properties illustrated that there were observable differences in the EPL corresponding to minimal values in each objective for some problems and also between the algorithms considered. The EPLC was used to evaluate problem difficulty as the number of decision variables were scaled and compare between the two examined algorithms.

Perhaps counter intuitively, our results suggest for some problems that increasing the number of decision variables, and varying the correlation between objectives does not always increase difficulty for an algorithm. This highlights the importance of quantifying and explaining differentials in algorithmic performance rather than relying on empirical inferences and observed behaviours.

Our approach is simple, highly informative and not restricted to one algorithm. Future works could explore alternative paradigms for evolutionary history construction and calculate EPL measurements across continuous Pareto-fronts. Development of evolutionary operators to balance the convergence of solutions in order achieve distributed coverage of the Pareto set is considered.

References

1. Aguirre, H.E., Tanaka, K.: Working principles, behavior, and performance of MOEAs on MNK-landscapes. Eur. J. Oper. Res. **181**(3), 1670–1690 (2007)
2. Bradstreet, L., Barone, L., While, L., Huband, S., Hingston, P.: Use of the WFG toolkit and PISA for comparison of MOEAs. In: Proceedings of the 2007 IEEE Symposium on Computational Intelligence in Multicriteria Decision Making, MCDM 2007, pp. 382–389. No. MCDM (2007)
3. Collard, P., Gaspar, A., Gaspar, A., Clergue, M., Escazut, C.: Fitness distance correlation, as statistical measure of genetic algorithm difficulty, revisited. In: Proceedings of the European Conference on Artificial Intelligence, pp. 650–654. Wiley (1998)
4. Daolio, F., Liefooghe, A., Verel, S., Aguirre, H., Tanaka, K.: Problem features versus algorithm performance on rugged multiobjective combinatorial fitness landscapes. Evol. Comput. **25**(4), 555–585 (2017)
5. Deb, K.: Multi-objective optimisation using evolutionary algorithms: an introduction. In: Wang, L., Ng, A., Deb, K. (eds.) Multi-objective Evolutionary Optimisation for Product Design and Manufacturing. Springer, London (2011). https://doi.org/10.1007/978-0-85729-652-8_1
6. Deb, K., Pratap, A., Agarwal, S., Meyarivan, T.: A fast and elitist multiobjective genetic algorithm: NSGA-II. IEEE Trans. Evol. Comput. **6**(2), 182–197 (2002)
7. Deb, K., Thiele, L., Laumanns, M., Zitzler, E.: Scalable test problems for evolutionary multiobjective optimization. In: Abraham, A., Jain, L., Goldberg, R. (eds.) Evolutionary Multiobjective Optimization. Advanced Information and Knowledge Processing. Springer, London (2005). https://doi.org/10.1007/1-84628-137-7_6
8. Garrett, D., Dasgupta, D.: Multiobjective landscape analysis and the generalized assignment problem. In: Maniezzo, V., Battiti, R., Watson, J.-P. (eds.) LION 2007. LNCS, vol. 5313, pp. 110–124. Springer, Heidelberg (2008). https://doi.org/10.1007/978-3-540-92695-5_9
9. Hart, E., Ross, P.: Gavel-a new tool for genetic algorithm visualization. IEEE Trans. Evol. Comput. **5**(4), 335–348 (2001)
10. Hoos, H.H., Stützle, T.: Stochastic local search: foundations and applications. Elsevier (2004)
11. Huband, S., Hingston, P., Barone, L.: A review of multi-objective test problems and a scalable test problem toolkit a review of multiobjective test problems and a scalable test problem toolkit. IEEE Trans. Evolution. Comput. **10**(2006), 477–506 (2006), http://ro.ecu.edu.au/ecuworks/2022
12. Jiang, S., Cai, Z., Zhang, J., Ong, Y.S.: Multiobjective optimization by decomposition with Pareto-adaptive weight vectors. In: Proceedings - 2011 7th International Conference on Natural Computation, ICNC 2011, vol. 3, pp. 1260–1264 (2011)
13. Jones, T., Forrest, S.: Fitness distance correlation as a measure of problem difficulty for genetic algorithms. In: Proceedings of the 6th International Conference on Genetic Algorithms, pp. 184–192 (1995)
14. Kerschke, P., Hoos, H.H., Neumann, F., Trautmann, H.: Automated algorithm selection: survey and perspectives. Evol. Comput. **27**(1), 3–45 (2019)
15. Knowles, J., Corne, D.: Instance generators and test suites for the multiobjective quadratic assignment problem. In: Fonseca, C.M., Fleming, P.J., Zitzler, E., Thiele, L., Deb, K. (eds.) EMO 2003. LNCS, vol. 2632, pp. 295–310. Springer, Heidelberg (2003). https://doi.org/10.1007/3-540-36970-8_21

16. Liefooghe, A., Daolio, F., Verel, S., Derbel, B., Aguirre, H., Tanaka, K.: Landscape-aware performance prediction for evolutionary multi-objective optimization. IEEE Trans. Evolution. Comput. (2019)

17. Miettinen, K.: Nonlinear multiobjective optimization. Intl. Ser. in Operations Research & Management Science: 12, Springer, New York (1998). https://doi.org/10.1007/978-1-4615-5563-6

18. Morgan, R., Gallagher, M.: Analysing and characterising optimization problems using length scale. Soft. Comput. **21**(7), 1735–1752 (2015). https://doi.org/10.1007/s00500-015-1878-z

19. Moser, I., Gheorghita, M., Aleti, A.: Identifying features of fitness landscapes and relating them to problem difficulty. Evol. Comput. **25**(3), 407–437 (2017)

20. Müller, C.L., Sbalzarini, I.F.: Global characterization of the CEC 2005 fitness landscapes using fitness-distance analysis. In: Di Chio, C., et al. (eds.) EvoApplications 2011. LNCS, vol. 6624, pp. 294–303. Springer, Heidelberg (2011). https://doi.org/10.1007/978-3-642-20525-5_30

21. Muñoz, M.A., Sun, Y., Kirley, M., Halgamuge, S.K.: Algorithm selection for black-box continuous optimization problems: a survey on methods and challenges. Inf. Sci. **317**, 224–245 (2015)

22. Paquete, L., Stützle, T.: A study of stochastic local search algorithms for the biobjective qap with correlated flow matrices. Eur. J. Oper. Res. **169**(3), 943–959 (2006)

23. Poli, R., Vanneschi, L.: Fitness-proportional negative slope coefficient as a hardness measure for genetic algorithms. In: Proceedings of the 9th Annual Conference on Genetic and Evolutionary Computation, pp. 1335–1342. ACM (2007)

24. Smith-Miles, K.A.: Cross-disciplinary perspectives on meta-learning for algorithm selection. ACM Comput. Surv. (CSUR) **41**(1), 6 (2009)

25. Tian, Y., Cheng, R., Zhang, X., Jin, Y.: Platemo: a MATlab platform for evolutionary multi-objective optimization. IEEE Comput. Intell. Mag. **12**, 73–87 (11 2017)

26. Verel, S., Liefooghe, A., Jourdan, L., Dhaenens, C.: On the structure of multiobjective combinatorial search space: MNK-landscapes with correlated objectives. Eur. J. Oper. Res. **227**(2), 331–342 (2013)

27. Zhang, Q., Li, H.: MOEA/D: a multiobjective evolutionary algorithm based on decomposition. IEEE Trans. Evol. Comput. **11**(6), 712–731 (2007)

28. Zitzler, E., Deb, K., Thiele, L.: Comparison of multiobjective evolutionary algorithms: empirical results. Evol. Comput. **8**(2), 173–195 (2000)

Decentralizing Self-organizing Maps

Md Mohiuddin Khan[✉], Kathryn Kasmarik, and Matt Garratt

School of Engineering and IT, UNSW Canberra, Canberra, Australia

Abstract. This paper presents an algorithm for a decentralized self-organizing map. With the explosion in the availability of robotics platforms, and their increasing application to multi-agent systems and robot swarms, there is a need for a new generation of machine learning algorithms that can exploit the distributed nature of sensing and processing that can be achieved using such platforms. In this paper we examine one such algorithm for decentralized pattern recognition, assuming sensors and processors are distributed across multiple agents: a decentralized self-organizing map. We examine the proposed algorithm under a range of conditions. This includes numbers of agents, communication topologies between agents and number of encounters between agents, simulating their presence in smaller or larger spaces. We demonstrate the conditions in which our decentralised self-organizing map can achieve comparable learning performance to a centralized self-organizing map on a range of synthetic datasets.

Keywords: Autonomous systems · Computational intelligence · Decentralized control · Self-organizing maps

1 Introduction

Decentralized learning in partially observed spaces is an important aspect of modern multi-robotic systems [1]. In such systems, no single robot is designed or expected to explore an entire environment, and no single robot is expected to be equipped with all sensor types. Some common examples of decentralized learning are multi-robot simultaneous localization and mapping (SLAM) [2, 3] where agents exchange information about their experiences with other agents to construct a more complete map for themselves. In contrast, traditional machine learning algorithms for tasks such as pattern recognition were designed for a single processor. Various machine learning mechanisms are utilized to make sense of data and take corresponding decisions. For example, self-organizing maps (SOMs) are a neural network proposed by Kohonen [4]. As an unsupervised algorithm, SOMs can be used to determine the number of clusters in a dataset. It has been recently shown that SOMs can be used to differentiate between structured and random behaviors of artificial swarms [5]. However, this work is currently of limited usefulness for multi-robot swarms because it requires all agents to report their experiences to a central processor. This creates a bottleneck and a single point of failure. As an alternative, this paper examines the question of whether multiple agents can come to a shared understanding of an environment under conditions where no agent senses all the data or the environment. To achieve this, we propose a decentralized SOM such that each

G. Long et al. (Eds.): AI 2021, LNAI 13151, pp. 480–493, 2022.
https://doi.org/10.1007/978-3-030-97546-3_39

agent is equipped with a SOM and learns using data it gathers from the environment and receives from other agents. Through a systematic investigation, we explore the performance of decentralized SOMs and compare that with the traditional, centralized version. The contributions of this paper are:

1. We propose design alternatives for a Decentralized SOM (DSOM) algorithm.
2. We test the performance of the DSOM through a range of synthetic environments and compare it to a centralized SOM under different conditions.
3. We demonstrate that different agents can achieve shared understanding of clusters in a dataset even though no agent directly senses all data in the environment.

The rest of the paper is organized as follows. In Sect. 2, we provide a brief introduction to SOMs and the necessity of decentralized learning algorithms. Section 3 introduces our new decentralized SOM algorithm and its assumptions. Section 4 presents the experimental results. The final section concludes the paper.

2 Background and Related Work

2.1 Self-organizing Maps (SOMs)

A SOM is an artificial neural network that has been extensively used as an automatic data analysis method. SOMs can be effectively used to transform complex, high dimensional input data into low dimensional outputs while preserving the relationships in the data. Structurally, SOMs consists of input and output layers, while every input node is connected to every output node.

The basic SOM algorithm uses a set of neurons, Y to map the M-dimensional input space. For each element x_i in the input $X \subset R^M$, we define vector $x = [x_1, x_2, \ldots, x_M]^T$. Each neuron, indexed by $c \in Y$ is also a vector $w_c(t) = \left[w_{c,1}(t), w_{c,2}(t), \ldots, w_{c,M}(t) \right]^T$, where t the index for the time step. The weight of the neurons has the same dimension as the input space. These weights are initialized either randomly or through data analysis [5] and then adjusted at each time step t while training. A randomly selected input sample, $x(t)$ from the input space is presented to the set of neurons and a winning neuron $v(t)$ for that input is computed,

$$v(t) = argmin||x(t) - w_c(t)|| \tag{1}$$

The winning neuron is calculated by measuring the distance between all the neurons and the input sample and identifying the closest neuron. After the winning neuron is found, the weights are updated using,

$$w_c(t + 1) = w_c(t) + \alpha(t)h_{c,v(t)}(t)[x(t) - w_c(t)] \tag{2}$$

$\alpha(t)$ and $h_{c,v(t)}$ are the learning rate and neighborhood function respectively. Both typically start large and decrease over time. The shape of the neighborhood determines the decay of the neighborhood. Training is usually done over a fixed number of iterations.

2.2 Decentralized Learning

Decentralized learning from partially observed spaces is an important aspect in multi-robotic systems [1]. Simultaneous localization and mapping (SLAM) extended to multiple robots [2, 6] is one active area of research. In multi-robot SLAM, one of the main areas of research is merging the map built by the individual robots. Though we take inspiration from multi-robot scenario, the problem explored in this paper is different to that of multi-robot SLAM. In this paper, we are exploring whether multiple agents equipped with SOMs can perform comparably to a centralized system.

Existing work has proposed decentralized frameworks and algorithms for multi-agent systems [7–10]. Generally, they focus on proposing a communication mechanism for specific tasks such as sweep coverage and surveillance. Another related area of research is multi-agent cooperation [11], which generally addresses coordination, resource sharing and team-performance. [12] proposed a multi-robot coordination algorithm inspired by self-organizing maps. However, this is highly specific to the information gathering problem domain. Compared to that, our investigation is how multiple agents would behave in the general case of having access to a decentralized repository of data, structured as a SOM.

Consensus of multi-agent systems [13] is another related area of research. Consensus problems deal with a network of agents with their respective "information states". Generally, it involves reaching common values through information exchange with neighboring agents. In this paper, we have a set of agents that exchange information with their neighbors, but the focus is on how effectively they can utilize a decentralized learning algorithm. In another related stream, distributed algorithms are proposed for machine learning tasks such as clustering [14, 15]. While these works are applicable to general clustering methods such as K-means or DBSCAN, our work is concerned specifically with SOMs.

3 Methodology

3.1 Decentralized Approach to a SOM

In this paper, we define the general SOM algorithm as the 'centralized' one. In this case, the SOM is fed all the data and after training, some measures of the output are generated. This output can be a visual representation, quantization error (QE), or comparison of convergence among input and neuron weights, among others. In this paper, we are not modifying the SOM algorithm, rather we are putting it in a context where the same algorithm is executed by multiple agents which have access to certain portion of the data, and must communicate that data between agents to gain a complete operating picture of their environment.

In the decentralized approach, each agent is equipped with a SOM. Unlike the centralized approach, the agents do not see the 'whole' environment, rather have a partial view. These agents complete their view through two means: (1) by communicating with other agents, and (2) by traversing and sensing the environment or dataset. They wait a certain time and then train their respective SOMs with the data gathered since the last training. The decentralized SOM algorithm is detailed in Algorithm 1.

In Algorithm 1, we first define a number of parameters that determine the interactions between decentralized agents. This includes the number of times the agents meet each other, the number of samples communicated between each other during a meeting and the number of samples taken directly from the dataset/environment. A list of these parameters is presented in Table 1. The parameter "meeting limits" controls the number of chances the agents get to "meet" and communicate with other agents. In practice this parameter may be determined by environmental factors. However, in this paper we abstract it to a parameter for testing purposes. Thus, in each iteration, agents have a chance to meet with other agents and communicate the data. The reason we restrict the number of samples to be communicated between agents is again to mimic agents operating in real conditions, which usually see communication dropout, dealing with obstacles, and noisy conditions, among other hindrances.

Table 1. Parameters for decentralized SOMs

Parameter	Symbol
Number of agents: number of SOM units	N
Meeting limits: number of times two agents meet	T
Number of samples acquired from the environment	E
Communication percentage: controls the amount of data an agent communicates to another agent with they meet	F
Probability if an agent is meeting with another agent	P_{ml}

In Algorithm 1, agent parameters are first initialized. Then a random subset of input data is assigned to each agent (line 2). This mimics environmental conditions that cause different agents to encounter different data. The main simulation loop starts from line 3. This loop executes for a certain number of iterations, denoted by meeting limits. The meeting limit is one complete cycle of the algorithm, where each agent does the following:

- Train the SOM with the current input data it has.
- Communicate with other agents. This pertains to exchanging input values subject to the communication topology. Communication is restricted by the probability P_{ml}. In addition, an agent only communicates a certain percentage of the current input dataset is has, controlled by the parameter F. The datasets for agents A_m, A_l are represented by D_m and D_l, respectively.
- Traversing the environment and gather more data. This is simulated through adding a random subset of data from the environment. This is controlled by the parameter E.

After the main loop is completed, we have N agents, each with a SOM which was trained on partially observed input dataset.

Algorithm 1: Decentralised Self-Organized Map (D-SOM)

Input:
 Input Data, D
 Number of agents, N
 Communication Percentage, F
 Environmental Percentage, E
 Meeting limit

Output:
 Individual Agents with SOMs trained on partial input

1: Initialize N Agents $(A_1, A_2, \ldots A_N)$
2: Assign each agent one random input subset
3: while (Meeting limit is not reached) **do**
4: **for** each Agent A_k **do**
5: Train SOM_k with the "most recently acquired" input
6: **end for**
7: COMMUNICATE with Other Agents:
8: **for** each neighboring pair of agents (A_l, A_m) **do**
9: if Probability, $P_{ml} \geq 0.5$ **then**
10:   A_l: Send percentage of input $(F * D_l)$ to A_m
11:   A_m: Send percentage of input $(F * D_m)$ to A_l
12: **end if**
13: **end for**
14: GATHER data from Environment:
15: **for** each agent A_k **do**
16: Add E*D samples to its own set of data
17: **end for**
18: end while

3.2 Communication Topologies

The communication topology determines how the agents supporting DSOMs can conduct the data transfer between SOM units. In practice, this will be determined by the environment. However, in this paper, we tested the decentralized approach with three common topologies: ring, mesh and star as shown in Fig. 1.

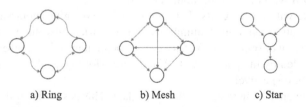

a) Ring   b) Mesh   c) Star

Fig. 1. DSOM communication topologies used in this paper.

3.3 Performance Metrics for DSOMs

Typically, QE values or convergence metrics measuring the difference between input and neuron weights [16] are used to measure the performance of a SOM. In our case, we want to compare the performance of a canonical (i.e., centralized) SOM with a set of decentralized ones. As originally claimed by Kohonen [4] and later validated by Yin and Allinson [17], the neurons of the SOM will converge on the probability distribution of the training data. Thus, we use a two-sample Kolomogorov-Smirnov (KS) test [18] to compare the inputs to the weights of the neurons of the trained maps. The two-sample KS test has the null hypothesis that two samples are drawn from the same distribution. If the corresponding p-value for a test is high, we cannot reject the null hypothesis. If the p-value is low, we can reject the null hypothesis.

4 Experimental Setup

4.1 Implementation of the DSOMs

The self-organizing maps in this paper were implemented in Python, using the MiniSom library [19]. Some modifications were made to the SOM algorithms to accommodate lifelong learning principles [20] in artificial agents. Specifically, instead of having a learning rate and neighborhood radius that reduces over time, they are kept fixed. The radius is set to 1 while the learning rate is set to 0.25. The number of neurons were determined using the heuristics $5 * \sqrt{S}$, where S is the number of samples in the dataset. The number of neurons were set to be the same in the centralized and the decentralized SOMs. A summary of the SOM parameters is listed in Table 2. These parameters are also used in all DSOMs. Additionally, a list of the DSOM specific parameter values used in the experiments in this paper is given in Table 3.

Table 2. Summary of SOM parameters and their experimental values.

Parameter	Value/Type
Number of Neurons	$5 * \sqrt{S}$, S = number of samples
Learning Rate	0.25
Neighborhood Radius	1
Network topology	Rectangular
Distance Measure	Euclidean

Table 3. Parameter values for controlling decentralized communication.

Parameter	Values Used
N	4, 10
T	4, 8
E	10% of the total available samples, with a 80–100% chance of acquiring the amount
F	10% of the current input stored in the agent
P_{ml}	0.5
Topology	Ring, Star, Mesh (all bi-directional)

4.2 Datasets

We used four datasets to test the performance of the DSOM. Two of the datasets—Hepta, and Tetra—are taken from the Fundamental Clustering Problem Suites (FCPS) [21]. The third data is RGB color data, which consists of randomly generated color values. The fourth data set is a relatively high-dimensional dataset comprised of various statistics of a list of countries. A summary of the datasets is provided in Table 4.

Table 4. Summary of the datasets

Name	Dimension	Size	Description
Hepta	3	212	Clearly defined clusters
Tetra	3	400	Almost touching clusters
Color	3	1600	Randomly generated RGB values
Country	9	167	9 columns of information for 167 countries

5 Experimental Results

For all the experiments, we use the SOM parameter values in Table 2. Each experiment consists of running the decentralized algorithm for the number of prescribed meeting limits and comparing that with the centralized SOM. We conducted each experiment 10 times and present the average p-value of the KS test between the input and the neuron weights. In describing the results, we start with 4 agents communicating through a ring topology. We do this for the first three datasets listed in Table 3. Next, we describe the results for other topologies and increased agent numbers. Finally, we describe the results for the high-dimensional data set.

5.1 Experiment 1: Comparing the Performance of SOMs and DSOMs (Ring Topology, 4 Agents, Meeting Limit of 4)

In Table 5, the average p-value for the KS test comparing the inputs to the weights for the three features are listed. Furthermore, in Table 6, we have listed the number of samples (rounded to the nearest integer) observed by the DSOMs. For Hepta, we can see that all the p-values are over 0.05, meaning that the inputs and the weights have converged in both the centralized SOM and DSOM units. This occurs even though the DSOMs had access to about 45% of the total data samples. The results are similar for the color dataset. For Tetra, we can see that both the centralized and the decentralized SOMs fail to converge for Feature 3 (which cannot be distinguished by a SOM due to overlapping ranges), whereas the performance for Feature 1 and Feature 2 are comparable. These results show that the DSOMs are achieving similar performance to that of the centralized one.

Table 5. Experiment 1: Average p-values for 2 sample KS test comparing inputs to weights for three features (f1, f2 and f3). 4 agents, meeting limit 4, ring topology

	Centralised			DSOM1			DSOM2			DSOM3			DSOM4		
	F1	F2	F3	F1	F2	F3	F1	F2	F3	F1	F2	F3	F1	F2	F3
Hepta	0.14	0.13	0.07	0.20	0.17	0.13	0.09	0.17	0.13	0.16	0.16	0.17	0.15	0.14	0.12
Tetra	0.02	0.06	0.03	0.02	0.04	0.02	0.01	0.05	0.02	0.02	0.04	0.02	0.02	0.03	0.02
Color	0.53	0.51	0.55	0.36	0.40	0.51	0.32	0.34	0.61	0.35	0.39	0.54	0.41	0.35	0.36

Table 6. Experiment 1: Number of samples seen by the SOMs: 4 agents, meeting limit 4, ring topology

	Centralised	DSOM1	DSOM2	DSOM3	DSOM4
Hepta	212	90	90	87	90
Tetra	400	169	164	169	169
Color	1600	687	700	679	669

For a further visual comparison of the SOM and DSOM approaches, we examine a case study using boxplots of inputs and the corresponding weights for the centralized and decentralized SOMs for the Hepta dataset in Fig. 2. In this case study, the data used to generate these box plots is from one single instance of the SOMs. We can see that for the centralised setting, each SOM weight has converged on the same distribution of the input data. Likewise, each DSOM weight has also converged on the distribution of the input data. The boxplots for Tetra and Color data (not included in the paper) show similar results.

5.2   Experiment 2: Examining the Impact of Communication Topology

In this experiment, we repeat the methodology of Experiment 1, but examine star and mesh topologies. The agent number and meeting limit are both set to 4. The results for the mesh topology are listed in Table 7 and Table 8. The results for star topology are listed in Table 9 and Table 10. For the star topology, we can see that the number of samples seen by the decentralized SOMs are similar to that of ring topology. This is reflected in the performance comparison as well, as the p-values are in similar ranges. In case of star topology, the first node (agent 1) works as the central node. We can see that the difference in sample numbers seen by agent 1 and the others is not large. Hence, the range of p-values are quite similar. We conclude that a difference in topology, in the given context (number of agents, dataset, and meeting limits) does not make a significant difference in the performance of the decentralized SOMs.

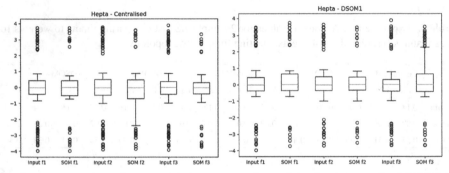

Fig. 2. Comparing input features with the corresponding weights for the centralized SOM (left) and one of the decentralised SOMs (right) for the settings in Table 2 (Hepta dataset)

Table 7. Experiment 2 Mesh Topology: Average p-values comparing inputs to weights

	Centralised			DSOM1			DSOM2			DSOM3			DSOM4		
	F1	F2	F3	F1	F2	F3	F1	F2	F3	F1	F2	F3	F1	F2	F3
Hepta	0.19	0.13	0.16	0.19	0.18	0.13	0.17	0.13	0.09	0.16	0.15	0.09	0.10	0.13	0.13
Tetra	0.02	0.06	0.02	0.01	0.06	0.02	0.01	0.05	0.02	0.02	0.04	0.01	0.01	0.05	0.01
Color	0.54	0.46	0.67	0.49	0.53	0.53	0.38	0.48	0.66	0.52	0.43	0.44	0.54	0.30	0.45

Table 8. Experiment 2 Mesh Topology: Number of samples seen by the SOMs, 4 agents, meeting limit 4

	Centralised	DSOM1	DSOM2	DSOM3	DSOM4
Hepta	212	93	95	96	96
Tetra	400	184	182	185	184
Color	1600	730	751	760	743

Table 9. Experiment 2: Star Topology: Average p-values Comparing Inputs to Weights for Each feature. 4 agents, meeting limit 4

	Centralised			DSOM1			DSOM2			DSOM3			DSOM4		
	F1	F2	F3	F1	F2	F3	F1	F2	F3	F1	F2	F3	F1	F2	F3
Hepta	0.19	0.18	0.10	0.10	0.17	0.17	0.12	0.13	0.15	0.19	0.16	0.13	0.09	0.17	0.19
Tetra	0.03	0.09	0.02	0.02	0.05	0.01	0.01	0.04	0.01	0.01	0.04	0.03	0.01	0.04	0.02
Color	0.70	0.50	0.55	0.43	0.36	0.36	0.53	0.39	0.45	0.55	0.29	0.50	0.47	0.29	0.35

Table 10. Experiment 2 Star Topology: Number of samples seen by the SOMs, 4 agents, meeting limit 4

	Centralised	DSOM1	DSOM2	DSOM3	DSOM4
Hepta	212	91	83	81	87
Tetra	400	176	158	162	161
Color	1600	732	654	655	664

5.3 Experiment 3: Increasing Number of Agents

Having shown the performance with 4 agents in a decentralized SOMs in the previous experiments, we now increase the agent number to 10. In Table 11 we show the p-values for the two-sample KS test comparing the input and the weights for the centralized SOM and the DSOMs, for the ring topology. We can see that the performance is comparable with respect to the p-values. This set of results indicates that an increase in agent numbers does not affect the performance of the DSOM approach. This makes sense because the agents observe the same number of data samples, regardless of the number of agents. The results for mesh and star topology with increased agent numbers show similar results.

Table 11. Experiment 3: Average p-values comparing inputs to the weights for each feature. N denotes the number of samples seen. 10 agents, meeting limit 4, ring topology

	Hepta				Tetra				Colour			
	F1	F2	F3	N	F1	F2	F3	N	F1	F2	F3	N
Central	0.124	0.186	0.104	212	0.028	0.052	0.027	400	0.365	0.456	0.584	1600
DSOM1	0.164	0.128	0.148	87	0.016	0.037	0.012	178	0.315	0.367	0.45	686
DSOM2	0.187	0.161	0.147	89	0.013	0.039	0.023	178	0.204	0.478	0.512	684
DSOM3	0.186	0.117	0.146	93	0.015	0.033	0.022	170	0.234	0.216	0.44	692
DSOM4	0.138	0.116	0.092	91	0.013	0.034	0.013	167	0.252	0.341	0.51	694
DSOM5	0.166	0.176	0.139	86	0.012	0.035	0.017	170	0.268	0.505	0.471	681
DSOM6	0.194	0.155	0.099	85	0.023	0.041	0.026	175	0.417	0.339	0.432	700
DSOM7	0.191	0.145	0.117	88	0.019	0.055	0.017	167	0.212	0.477	0.405	698
DSOM8	0.158	0.153	0.141	91	0.017	0.038	0.018	171	0.418	0.259	0.588	685
DSOM9	0.192	0.136	0.09	91	0.013	0.041	0.021	176	0.251	0.394	0.406	692
DSOM10	0.11	0.151	0.095	87	0.015	0.075	0.019	173	0.279	0.283	0.346	685

5.4 Experiment 4: Increasing Meeting Limit Between Agents

Having looked at increased agent numbers in Experiment 3, we revert back to our baseline scenario of 4 agents for this experiment. However, we double the possibility of agents meeting and communicating with each other. The results are shown in Table 12 and Table 13. Comparing Table 5 and Table 6, we can see an increase in the number of samples seen by the decentralized SOMs when the meeting limit is increased. The effect of this on the p-values is slight increases. We conclude that increasing the meeting limit results in increased number of samples observed by the DSOMs, and a corresponding increase in the p-value, indicative of greater convergence of the DSOMs in the presence of more data.

Table 12. Experiment 4: Average p-values comparing inputs to weights for Each feature. 4 agents, meeting limit 8, ring topology

	Centralised			DSOM1			DSOM2			DSOM3			DSOM4		
	F1	F2	F3	F1	F2	F3	F1	F2	F3	F1	F2	F3	F1	F2	F3
Hepta	0.22	0.17	0.13	0.18	0.18	0.12	0.12	0.17	0.13	0.13	0.14	0.08	0.14	0.14	0.14
Tetra	0.02	0.08	0.03	0.02	0.08	0.03	0.03	0.05	0.02	0.02	0.07	0.03	0.03	0.06	0.02
Color	0.44	0.43	0.54	0.71	0.54	0.33	0.54	0.57	0.55	0.53	0.47	0.45	0.62	0.48	0.35

Table 13. Experiment 4: Number of samples seen: 4 agents, meeting limit 8, ring topology

	Centralised	DSOM1	DSOM2	DSOM3	DSOM4
Hepta	212	141	137	139	143
Tetra	400	269	266	266	271
Colour	1600	1075	1081	1090	1090

5.5 Experiment 5: High-Dimensional Dataset

So far, the datasets we have used all have 3 features. To observe how the proposed decentralization would work in case of a dataset with higher dimensionality, we use the Country dataset. Taking cues from the previous experiments, we have opted for 4 agents, a meeting limit of 4, and chose ring topology. To accommodate the higher dimensionality, instead of a single pass, we now train the SOMs for 100 iterations.

The result for the Country dataset is shown in Table 14. We can see that with the higher dimensions, the results are a little different than what we have seen so far. In particular, only a small number of features (Feature 2 and Feature 4) appear to converge in the centralized SOM using the KS metric with alpha 0.05. This performance is not mirrored in the DSOM. All other features fail to converge in both the centralised SOM and DSOM. This means the data is inherently difficult for the traditional SOM algorithm to capture and cluster and this poor performance is reflected in the decentralized algorithms as well.

Table 14. Country Dataset: Average p-values comparing the inputs to the weights of the 9 features. 4 agents, meeting limit 4, ring topology

	F1	F2	F3	F4	F5	F6	F7	F8	F9	N
Central	0.001	0.064	0.037	0.052	0.005	0.012	0.006	0.001	0.005	167
DSOM1	0	0.014	0.004	0.016	0.001	0.006	0.001	0	0	71
DSOM2	0	0.01	0.005	0.014	0.003	0.011	0.001	0	0	70
DSOM3	0	0.012	0.007	0.02	0.001	0.011	0.002	0	0	71
DSOM4	0	0.009	0.007	0.013	0.001	0.009	0.001	0	0	70

6   Conclusion

In this paper, we explored the possibility of decentralizing one of the most popular unsupervised learning algorithms, the Self-organizing Map. We proposed an algorithm for a DSOM, and empirically investigated the performance of the decentralized SOMs for various parameters. Our results show that, for lower dimensional data, the decentralization functions comparably with the centralized algorithms. Specifically, DSOM units can converge on the same distribution as input data as a centralized SOM, even though the DSOM units see less data. The performance comparison becomes more difficult when the dimensionality of the data is increased.

These results pave the way for decentralizing machine learning algorithms for multi-agent scenarios where all the data are not readily available to the agents. Agents can be equipped with SOMs which are able to take decision under strained communication regimes and without having access to a global data repository. As future work, this proposed decentralized model can be examined under dynamic, real-life communication topologies experienced by actual multi-robot systems. Other unsupervised machine learning algorithms such as K-means, Adaptive Resonance Theory (ART) and Simplified ART networks have also been used for single agent curiosity models. These algorithms could also be decentralized using the methodology in this paper, to extend to shared memory representations in decentralized systems.

References

1. Rone, W., Ben-Tzvi, P.: Mapping, localization and motion planning in mobile multi-robotic systems. Robotica **31**(1), 1 (2013)
2. Saeedi, S., et al.: Multiple-robot simultaneous localization and mapping: a review. J. Field Robot. **33**(1), 3–46 (2016)
3. Howe, E., Novosad, J.: Extending slam to multiple robots, March 2005
4. Kohonen, T.: The self-organizing map. Proc. IEEE **78**(9), 1464–1480 (1990)
5. Khan, M.M., Kasmarik, K., Barlow, M.: Autonomous detection of collective behaviours in swarms. Swarm Evol. Comput. **57**, 100715 (2020)
6. Krinkin, K., Filatov, A., Filatov, A.: Modern multi-agent slam approaches survey. In: Proceedings of the XXth Conference of Open Innovations Association FRUCT (2017)
7. Tanner, H.G., Christodoulakis, D.K.: Decentralized cooperative control of heterogeneous vehicle groups. Robot. Auton. Syst. **55**(11), 811–823 (2007)
8. Cheng, T.M., Savkin, A.V., Javed, F.: Decentralized control of a group of mobile robots for deployment in sweep coverage. Robot. Auton. Syst. **59**(7–8), 497–507 (2011)
9. Acevedo, J.J., et al.: A decentralized algorithm for area surveillance missions using a team of aerial robots with different sensing capabilities. In: 2014 IEEE International Conference on Robotics and Automation (ICRA). IEEE (2014)
10. Jiménez, A.C., García-Díaz, V., Bolaños, S.: A decentralized framework for multi-agent robotic systems. Sensors **18**(2), 417 (2018)
11. Rizk, Y., Awad, M., Tunstel, E.W.: Cooperative heterogeneous multi-robot systems: a survey. ACM Comput. Surv. (CSUR) **52**(2), 1–31 (2019)
12. Best, G., Hollinger, G.A.: Decentralised self-organising maps for multi-robot information gathering. In: Proceeding of IEEE/RSJ IROS (2020)
13. Qin, J., et al.: Recent advances in consensus of multi-agent systems: a brief survey. IEEE Trans. Industr. Electron. **64**(6), 4972–4983 (2016)
14. Di Fatta, G., et al.: Fault tolerant decentralised k-means clustering for asynchronous large-scale networks. J. Parallel Distrib. Comput. **73**(3), 317–329 (2013)
15. Mashayekhi, H., et al.: GDCluster: a general decentralized clustering algorithm. IEEE Trans. Knowl. Data Eng. **27**(7), 1892–1905 (2015)
16. Hamel, L., Ott, B.: A population based convergence criterion for self-organizing maps. In: Proceedings of the International Conference on Data Mining (DMIN): The Steering Committee of The World Congress in Computer Science, Computer Engineering and Applied Computing (WorldComp) (2012)

17. Yin, H., Allinson, N.M.: On the distribution and convergence of feature space in self-organizing maps. Neural Comput. **7**(6), 1178–1187 (1995)
18. Berger, V.W., Zhou, Y.: Kolmogorov–smirnov test: Overview. Wiley statsref: Statistics reference online (2014)
19. Vettigli, G.: MiniSom: minimalistic and NumPy-based implementation of the Self Organizing Map (2018). https://github.com/JustGlowing/minisom/
20. Parisi, G.I., et al.: Continual lifelong learning with neural networks: a review. Neural Netw. **113**, 54–71 (2019)
21. Ultsch, A.: Clustering with SOM: U*C. In: Workshop on Self-Organizing Maps (2005)

A Heuristic Repair Algorithm for the Maximum Stable Marriage Problem with Ties and Incomplete Lists

Hoang Huu Viet[1], Nguyen Thi Uyen[1], Son Thanh Cao[1],
and TaeChoong Chung[2(✉)]

[1] School of Engineering and Technology, Vinh University, Vinh City, Vietnam
{viethh,uyennt,sonct}@vinhuni.edu.vn
[2] Department of Computer Engineering, Kyung Hee University, Yongin, South Korea
tcchung@khu.ac.kr

Abstract. This paper proposes a heuristic repair algorithm to find a maximum weakly stable matching for the stable marriage problem with ties and incomplete lists. Our algorithm is designed including a well-known Gale-Shapley algorithm to find a stable matching for the stable marriage problem with ties and incomplete lists and a heuristic repair function to improve the found stable matching in terms of maximum size. Experimental results for large randomly generated instances of the problem showed that our algorithm is efficient in terms of both execution time and solution quality for solving the problem.

Keywords: Gale-Shapley algorithm · Heuristic repair · SMTI · Stable marriage problem

1 Introduction

The stable marriage problem with ties and incomplete lists (SMTI) [13,15] is an extension of the stable marriage (SM) problem [7]. The SMTI problem is a well-known matching problem and recently, it has been attracting much attention from the research community due to its important role in a wide range of applications such as the Hospitals/Residents with Ties (HRT) problem [2,11,17], the Student-Project Allocation (SPA) problem [1,6] or the Stable Marriage and Roommates (SMR) problem [4,5].

An SMTI instance of size n comprises a set of men, denoted by $M = \{m_1, m_2, \cdots, m_n\}$, and a set of women, denoted by $W = \{w_1, w_2, \cdots, w_n\}$, in which each person has a preference list to rank some members of the opposite sex in an order of preference, meaning that a m_i's/w_i's preference list may include ties and be incomplete. If a man $m_i \in M$ is ranked by a woman $w_j \in W$ and vice versa, then m_i and w_j are called *acceptable* to each other, or (m_i, w_j) is an *acceptable* pair. We denote the rank of w_j in m_i's preference list by $r_{m_i}(w_j)$ and the rank of m_i in w_j's preference list by and $r_{w_j}(m_i)$. Thus, if (m_i, w_j) is an acceptable pair, then $r_{m_i}(w_j) > 0$ and $r_{w_j}(m_i) > 0$. If a man m_i strictly

G. Long et al. (Eds.): AI 2021, LNAI 13151, pp. 494–506, 2022.
https://doi.org/10.1007/978-3-030-97546-3_40

prefers a woman w_j to a woman w_k, then we denote by $r_{m_i}(w_j) < r_{m_i}(w_k)$. If a man m_i prefers a woman w_j and a woman w_k equally, then we denote by $r_{m_i}(w_j) = r_{m_i}(w_k)$. We use similar notations for the women' preference lists.

A matching Γ of an SMTI instance is a set of acceptable pairs (m_i, w_j), $(m_i, \varnothing)$, or $(\varnothing, w_j)$, meaning that each m_i or w_j belongs to at most one pair. If $(m_i, w_j) \in \Gamma$, then m_i and w_j are called partners in Γ, denoted by $\Gamma(m_i) = w_j$ and $\Gamma(w_j) = m_i$. If $\Gamma(m_i) = \varnothing$ or $\Gamma(w_j) = \varnothing$, then m_i or w_j is called *single* in Γ, respectively. A matching Γ is called *weakly stable* if it admits no *blocking pair*, where a pair (m_i, w_j) is blocking for Γ if (a) $r_{m_i}(w_j) > 0$ and $r_{w_j}(m_i) > 0$; (b) $\Gamma(m_i) = \varnothing$ or $r_{m_i}(w_j) < r_{m_i}(\Gamma(m_i))$; and (c) $\Gamma(w_j) = \varnothing$ or $r_{w_j}(m_i) < r_{w_j}(\Gamma(w_j))$. Otherwise, it is called *unstable*. The size of a weakly stable matching Γ, denoted by $|\Gamma|$, is the number of pairs $(m_i, w_j) \in \Gamma$. If $|\Gamma| = n$, then Γ is called *perfect*, otherwise, Γ is called *non-perfect*.

Irving et al. [12] showed that weakly stable matchings of an SMTI instance have different sizes. In order for every person paired, we need to find a matching that is not only weakly stable but also of maximum size. This problem is known as MAX-SMTI [10,15] and NP-hard [12,13] and therefore, finding an efficient algorithm to solve the problem of large sizes is a challenge for researchers.

In this paper, we call a weakly stable matching a stable matching. Accordingly, we propose an approximation algorithm to solve MAX-SMTI. Our idea is to apply the Gale-Shapley algorithm (GS) [7,14] for SMTI to find a stable matching. If the found matching is non-perfect, we propose a heuristic repair function to improve the matching by swapping the partners of men for single men in the matching, and then apply GS again. Our algorithm terminates when it finds a perfect matching or reaches a maximum number of iterations. Experiments show that our algorithm is efficient in terms of execution time and solution quality for solving MAX-SMTI of large sizes.

The rest of this paper is organized as follows: Sect. 2 describes the related work, Sect. 3 presents the proposed algorithm, Sect. 4 discusses the experiments, and Sect. 5 concludes our work.

2   Related Work

In the last few years, almost all algorithms proposed in the literature to solve MAX-SMTI are approximate since MAX-SMTI is NP-hard [12,13]. An algorithm is called r–approximation for MAX-SMTI if it always finds a stable matching Γ with $|\Gamma| \geq |\Gamma_{opt}|/r$, where Γ_{opt} is a stable matching of maximum size [14].

Several approximation algorithms have been extended from the GS [7] to solve MAX-SMTI. The general mechanism of these algorithms is to start from an empty matching and build a maximum stable matching through iterations. McDermid [16] proposed a 3/2–approximation algorithm that runs in $O(n^{3/2}m)$ time, where n is the sum of men and women, and m is the sum of lengths of the men's and women's preference lists. Király [14] modified GS [7] to achieve two approximation algorithms including a 3/2–approximation algorithm, namely GSA1, for SMTI where ties are allowed on one side only and a 5/3–approximation algorithm, namely GSA2, for the general case of SMTI. Paluch [19, 20] gave a 3/2–approximation algorithm, namely GSM, that runs in $O(m)$ time and additionally is simpler than that of McDermid [16], where m is also the sum of the lengths of the men's and women's preference lists.

Local search has been used to solve MAX-SMTI. The general mechanism of local search-based approximation algorithms is that starting from an arbitrary matching, it improves the stability of the matching by eliminating blocking pairs through iterations until it reaches a maximum stable matching. Gelain et al. [8, 9] presented a local search algorithm, namely LTIU, to deal with MAX-SMTI. Munera et al. [18] applied the adaptive search method [3], namely AS, to solve MAX-SMTI. They showed by experiments that AS outperforms LTIU in terms of execution time and solution quality. Recently, we proposed a max-conflicts-based heuristic search for MAX-SMTI [21]. Our algorithm is much more efficient than AS and LTIU in terms of execution time and solution quality for MAX-SMTI of large sizes. It should be noted that all the approaches in [8,9,18,21] used a concept of undominated blocking pair instead of blocking pair to solve MAX-SMTI. Since the computational time to determine a set of undominated blocking pairs for all men at each iteration is $O(n^2)$, these algorithms are inefficient for MAX-SMTI of large sizes.

3   Proposed Algorithm

3.1   HR Algorithm

We consider the GS given in [14] for SMTI. Given an instance I of SMTI, GS outputs a stable matching Γ_1 and we assume that Γ_1 is non-perfect, meaning that there exists some man m_i that $\Gamma_1(m_i) = \varnothing$ and m_i's preference list = {}. We consider two following cases:

Case 1: If we recover the original rank list for m_i, let m_i become active, and run GS again, then GS outputs Γ_2 which is the same as Γ_1. This is because (a) if a man $m_k \neq m_i$ and m_k was assigned to w_j in Γ_1, then m_k will keep his partner w_j in Γ_2 since there exists no man m_i such that $r_{w_j}(m_i) < r_{w_j}(m_k)$; (b) if m_i is single in Γ_1, then m_i is also single in Γ_2 since at the first run of GS, m_i was rejected by every w_j in his rank list, meaning that every w_j in m_i's rank list was assigned to some m_k or $r_{w_j}(m_k) < r_{w_j}(m_i)$ and therefore, w_j keeps her partner m_k and rejects m_i at the second run of GS.

Case 2: If we recover the original rank list for m_i, let w_j be one of the women in m_i's rank list so that either $r_{m_i}(w_j) \leq r_{m_k}(w_j)$ or $r_{w_j}(m_i) = r_{w_j}(m_k)$, where $m_k = \Gamma_1(w_j)$, then if we swap m_i for m_k in Γ_1, i.e. (a) $\Gamma_1(m_k) = \varnothing$; (b) $\Gamma_1(m_i) = w_j$; (c) delete w_j from m_k's rank list; (d) let m_k be active; and run GS again with Γ_1 as an input, then GS outputs Γ_2, in which $\Gamma_2(m_i) = w_j$ and m_k may be assigned to some woman in his rank list. If so, we have $|\Gamma_2| > |\Gamma_1|$. This is our idea to improve a stable matching in terms of maximum size.

Our heuristic repair algorithm, so called HR, to solve MAX-SMTI is shown in Algorithm 1. We call a repair(m_i, m_k) a procedure consisting of (a) $\Gamma(m_i) :=$ w_j, where $w_j = \Gamma(m_k)$, i.e. (m_i, w_j) becomes a pair; (b) $\Gamma(m_k) := \varnothing$, i.e. m_k

---

Algorithm 1: HR Algorithm

---

1. function Main(I)
2.   for ($each\ m_i \in M$) do
3. $\Gamma(m_i) := \varnothing$;
4. $a(m_i) := 1$; $\triangleright$ assign m_i to be active
5. $c(m_i) := 0$; $\triangleright$ assign a count variable of m_i to zero
6.   end
7. $iter := 1$;
8.   while $iter \leq max\_iters$ do
9. $m_i :=$ some man is active, i.e. $a(m_i) = 1$; $\triangleright$ take an active man m_i
10.   if *there exists no active man* then
11.   if Γ *is perfect* then break;
12. $iter := iter + 1$;
13. $\Gamma :=$ improve(Γ);
14.   continue;
15.   end
16.   if m_i*'s rank list is empty* then
17. $a(m_i) := 0$; $\triangleright$ assign m_i to be inactive
18. $c(m_i) := c(m_i) + 1$; $\triangleright$ increase the count variable of m_i
19.   continue;
20.   end
21.   if *there exists a single woman* w_j *to whom* m_i *prefers most* then
22. $\Gamma(m_i) := w_j$; $\triangleright$ m_i becomes engaged to w_j
23. $a(m_i) := 0$;
24.   else
25. $w_j :=$ a woman to whom m_i prefers most;
26. $m_k := \Gamma(w_j)$;
27.   if *there exists a single* w_t *that* $r_{m_k}(w_t) = r_{m_k}(w_j)$ then
28.   repair(m_i, m_k);
29.   end
30.   if $\Gamma(m_i) = \varnothing$ *and* $r_{w_j}(m_i) < r_{w_j}(m_k)$ then
31.   repair(m_i, m_k);
32. $r_{m_k}(w_j) := 0$; $\triangleright$ delete w_j from m_k's rank list
33.   else
34. $r_{m_i}(w_j) := 0$; $\triangleright$ delete w_j from m_i's rank list
35.   end
36.   end
37.   end
38.   return Γ;
39. end function

---

becomes single; (c) $a(m_i) := 0$, i.e. m_i is inactive; and (d) $a(m_k) := 1$, i.e. m_k becomes active again. At the beginning, HR creates a matching Γ of single men for each $m_i \in M$, sets each m_i to be active, and assigns a count variable for each m_i to zero (lines 2–6). At each iteration, if HR does not find any active man m_i, then it improves the matching Γ to obtain a better one in terms of maximum size (lines 10–15), otherwise, it runs GS to find a stable matching for SMTI (lines 9, 21–36). In the former case, HR checks if Γ is perfect, then it returns Γ, otherwise, it improves $|\Gamma|$ by calling Algorithm 2 and starts the next iteration. In the latter case, HR checks if m_i's rank list becomes empty (i.e. $r_{m_j}(w_j) = 0, \forall w_j \in W$), then it assigns m_i to be inactive, increases the count variable $c(m_i)$ of m_i's exhaustive search, and starts the next iteration. Otherwise, m_i proposes a single woman w_j to whom he prefers most. If there exists a such w_j, then w_j is assigned to m_i. However, if there exists no such w_j, meaning that w_j has a partner m_k. Accordingly, w_j is assigned to m_i if either m_k has a single woman w_t that $r_{m_k}(w_t) = r_{m_k}(w_j)$ or w_j prefers m_i to m_k. If w_j is assigned to m_i, then m_i becomes inactive (i.e. $a(m_i) = 0$), otherwise, m_i deletes w_j from his rank list (i.e. $r_{m_i}(w_j) = 0$). If w_j rejects m_k to be assigned to m_i, then m_k becomes active and it deletes w_j from his rank list, except m_k has a single woman w_t that $r_{m_k}(w_t) = r_{m_k}(w_j)$.

The function to improve $|\Gamma|$ is shown in Algorithm 2. For each single man $m_i \in M$, since m_i is single, meaning that it is rejected by all women in his rank list or m_i's rank list becomes empty, he first recovers his original rank list. Next, m_i finds a set of women, w_j, in his rank list such that $r_{m_i}(w_j) \leq r_{m_k}(w_j)$ or $r_{w_j}(m_i) = r_{w_j}(m_k)$, where $m_k = \Gamma(w_j)$ (lines 5–10). If there exists no such w_j, the function continues for the next single man in M. Otherwise, a woman w_j corresponding to the minimum value of $h(w_j)$ is chosen to assign to m_i and m_k, the previous partner of w_j, deletes w_j from his rank list. By doing so, m_k has opportunities to be assigned to the other women in his rank list in the next iterations of HR. It should be noted that a woman w_j is chosen such that $h(w_j)$ is minimum, meaning that (i) m_k has the maximum number of women w_t that $r_{m_k}(w_t) = r_{m_k}(w_j)$; (ii) w_j ranks m_i closest to m_k; and (iii) $c(m_k)$ is minimum.

3.2   Example

Considering an SMTI instance consists of eight men and eight women with their preference lists given in Table 1, where ties in the men's and women's preference lists are given in brackets. HR runs as follows:

(1) HR runs the first times of GS (lines 9, 21–36) and yields a stable matching $\Gamma = \{(m_1, w_3), (m_2, \varnothing), (m_3, w_8), (m_4, w_5), (m_5, w_2), (m_6, w_6), (m_7, w_1), (m_8, w_4)\}$ after 11 iterations. At the 12th iteration, since there exists no active man and $|\Gamma| = 7$, the function improve(Γ) is called to improve $|\Gamma|$. Specifically, since m_2 is single, it recovers its original rank list. Next, m_2 finds w_5 to be a candidate, since w_5 has a partner m_4, it rejects m_4 to assign to m_2 and m_4 deletes w_5 in his rank list. So, the function returns $\Gamma = \{(m_1, w_3), (m_2, w_5), (m_3, w_8), (m_4, \varnothing), (m_5, w_2), (m_6, w_6), (m_7, w_1), (m_8, w_4)\}$.

(2) HR runs the second times of GS and results in $\Gamma = \{(m_1, w_3), (m_2, w_5), (m_3, w_8), (m_4, \varnothing), (m_5, w_2), (m_6, w_6), (m_7, w_1), (m_8, w_4)\}$ at the 14th iteration. At the 15th iteration, since there exists no active man and $|\Gamma| = 7$, the function improve(Γ) is called to improve $|\Gamma|$ again. Specifically, since m_4 is single, it recovers its original rank list. Next, m_4 finds w_8 to be a candidate, since w_8 has

---

Algorithm 2: Improve a stable matching Γ

---

1. **function** Improve(Γ)
2.   **for** *each single man* $m_i \in M$ **do**
3.   recover m_i's original rank list;
4. $X := \{\}$;
5.   **for** *each* $w_j \in m_i's$ *rank list* **do**
6. $m_k := \Gamma(w_j)$;
7.   **if** $r_{m_i}(w_j) \leq r_{m_k}(w_j)$ *or* $r_{w_j}(m_i) = r_{w_j}(m_k)$ **then**
8. $X := X \cup \{w_j\}$;   ▷ w_j **is a candidate for** m_i
9.   **end**
10.   **end**
11.   **if** X *is empty* **then** continue;
12.   **for** *each* $w_j \in X$ **do**
13. $m_k := \Gamma(w_j)$;
14. $k :=$ number of w_t in m_k's rank list, where $r_{m_k}(w_t) = r_{m_k}(w_j)$;
15. $h(w_j) := 1/k + (r_{w_j}(m_i) - r_{w_j}(m_k)) \times (1 - c(m_k))$;
16.   **end**
17. $w_j := argmin(h(w_j)), \forall w_j \in X$;
18.   repair(m_i, m_k), where $m_k := \Gamma(w_j)$;
19. $r_{m_k}(w_j) := 0$;   ▷ **delete** w_j **from** m_k'**s rank list**
20.   **end**
21.   **return** Γ;
22. **end function**

Table 1. An SMTI instance of size 8

Men's preference lists	Women's preference lists
m_1: w_3 w_8 w_5 w_2 (w_1 w_7)	w_1: m_8 m_1 m_5 m_7
m_2: w_5	w_2: m_5 (m_1 m_8) m_3
m_3: w_8 (w_2 w_3 w_7) w_5 w_4	w_3: m_1 (m_4 m_7 m_8) m_3
m_4: w_8 w_5 w_3	w_4: (m_3 m_8)
m_5: (w_1 w_2 w_7)	w_5: (m_1 m_3) m_8 m_4 m_2
m_6: (w_6 w_8)	w_6: m_8 m_6
m_7: w_1 w_3 w_8 w_7	w_7: m_5 (m_3 m_7) m_1 m_8
m_8: (w_1 w_4) (w_7 w_8) (w_2 w_3 w_5 w_6)	w_8: m_8 m_7 m_6 m_1 (m_3 m_4)

a partner m_3, it rejects m_3 to assign to m_4 and m_3 deletes w_8 in his rank list. So, the function yields $\Gamma = \{(m_1, w_3), (m_2, w_5), (m_3, \varnothing), (m_4, w_8), (m_5, w_2), (m_6, w_6), (m_7, w_1), (m_8, w_4)\}$.

(*3*) HR runs the third times of GS and results in a perfect matching $\Gamma = \{(m_1, w_3), (m_2, w_5), (m_3, w_7), (m_4, w_8), (m_5, w_2), (m_6, w_6), (m_7, w_1), (m_8, w_4)\}$ of size 8 at the 17th iteration.

It should be noted that in this example, GS finds a stable matching $\Gamma = \{(m_1, w_3), (m_2, \varnothing), (m_3, w_7), (m_4, w_5), (m_5, w_2), (m_6, w_6), (m_7, w_8), (m_8, w_1)\}$ of size 7 and GSA2 finds a stable matching $\Gamma = \{(m_1, w_3), (m_2, \varnothing), (m_3, w_8),$

(m_4, w_5), (m_5, w_2), (m_6, w_6), (m_7, w_1), $(m_8, w_4)\}$ of size 7. Although GSA2 improves GS but it gets stuck at the 7th iteration, where m_2 becomes inactive forever, and so m_2 is a single man.

4 Experiments

In this section, we present experiments to evaluate the performance of our HR algorithm. To do so, we chose GSA2 [14] to compare its performance with that of HR since both GSA2 and HR are improved based on GS [14]. We implemented HR and GSA2 by Matlab R2017b software on a laptop computer with Core i7-8550U CPU 1.8 GHz and 16 GB RAM, running on Windows 10. The maximum number of iterations used in HR is 50.

Datasets. We used the random problem generator given in [10] to generate SMTI instances with three parameters (n, p_1, p_2), where n is the size, p_1 is the probability of incompleteness, and p_2 is the probability of ties. Since stable matchings of SMTI instances include acceptable pairs and singles, we generated SMTI instances that the men's and women's preference lists of each instance have only acceptable pairs.

4.1 Comparison of Solution Quality

This section presents our experimental results in comparing the percentage of perfect matchings found by HR with that found by GSA2.

Experiment 1. In this experiment, we chose $n \in \{50, 100, 150, 200\}$, let $p_1 \in \{0.1, 0.2, \cdots, 0.9\}$ and $p_2 \in \{0.0, 0.1, \cdots, 1.0\}$. For each combination of parameters (n, p_1, p_2), we generated 100 SMTI instances, ran HR and GSA2 on the generated instances. Our experimental results show that when $p_1 \in \{0.1, 0.2, \cdots, 0.5\}$ and $p_2 \in \{0.0, 0.1, \cdots, 1.0\}$, both HR and GSA2 find 100% of perfect matchings, so we do not show the experiment results here. Figure 1 shows the percentage of perfect matchings found by HR and GSA2. From the experimental results, we can give some remarks as follows:

(1) The percentage of perfect matchings found by HR is higher than that found by GSA2 for cases of (i) $n = 50$ and $p_1 \in \{0.7, 0.8, 0.9\}$; (ii) $n = 100$ and $p_1 \in \{0.8, 0.9\}$; and (iii) $n \in \{150, 200\}$ and $p_1 = 0.9$. This means when each person ranks fewer members of the opposite sex, HR is more efficient than GSA2 in finding perfect matchings for SMTI, especially for $p_1 \in \{0.8, 0.9\}$. When n increases, meaning that each person ranks many members of the opposite sex, the percentage of perfect matchings found by HR and GSA2 increases, i.e. both HR and GSA2 find easier perfect matchings.

(2) When p_1 increases, the percentage of perfect matchings found by HR and GSA2 decreases since the number of acceptable pairs in the men's and women's preference lists decreases, making more difficult for finding perfect matchings.

(3) When p_2 increases, the percentage of perfect matchings found by HR and GSA2 increases since at the same p_1 value, the number of ties in the men's and women's preference lists increases, making easier for finding perfect matchings.

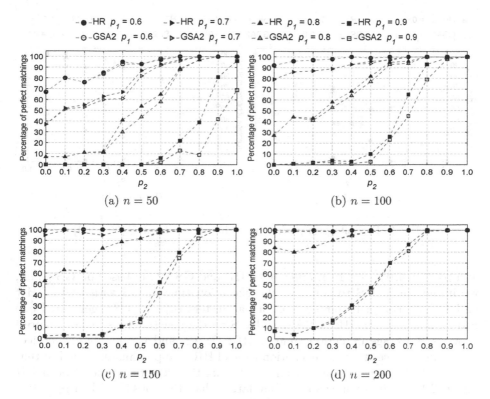

Fig. 1. Percentage of perfect matchings found for $n \in \{50, 100, 150, 200\}$

Experiment 2. In the above experiment, for $p_1 \in \{0.1, 0.2, \cdots, 0.8\}$ and when n increases, both HR and GSA2 find easy perfect matchings since the number of acceptable pairs in men's and women's rank list increases. Therefore, for example $n = 200$, the comparison of the percentage of perfect matchings found by HR and GSA2 is useless. In this experiment, we chose $n \in \{300, 400\}$, let $p_1 \in \{0.90, 0.92, \cdots, 0.98\}$ and $p_2 \in \{0.0, 0.1, \cdots, 1.0\}$. Figure 2 shows the results of this experiment. Again, we see that when p_1 increases, the percentage of perfect matchings found by HR and GSA2 decreases and when p_2 increases, the percentage of perfect matchings found by HR and GSA2 increases. However, HR outperforms GSA2 in terms of finding perfect matchings for SMTI.

4.2   Comparison of Execution Time

In the above experiments where n is small, the average execution time of HR and GSA2 is very small and almost the same and therefore, the comparison of the execution time of these algorithms is meaningless.

Experiment 3. In this experiment, to compare the execution time of HR and GSA2 more precisely, we chose $n \in \{1000, 2000\}$, let $p_1 \in \{0.1, 0.2, \cdots, 0.9\}$

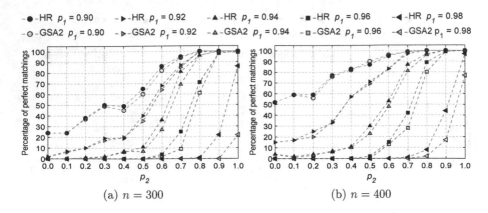

Fig. 2. Percentage of perfect matchings found for $n = \{300, 400\}$

and $p_2 \in \{0.0, 0.1, \cdots, 1.0\}$. Since both HR and GSA2 are based on GS [9,14], we implemented GS to compare the execution time of GS with that of HR and GSA2. For each combination of parameters (n, p_1, p_2), we generated one SMTI instance, ran HR, GSA2, and GS on the generated instances. Figure 3 shows the average execution time of HR, GSA2, and GS for finding perfect matchings. We see that the execution time of HR is approximately equal to that of GSA2. When p_2 increases from 0.0 to 0.8, the execution time of both HR and GSA2 is almost unchanged, but larger than that of GS. When $p_2 = 0.9$, the execution time of both HR and GSA2 significantly decreases, but that of GS slightly increases. When $p_2 = 1.0$, the execution time of HR, GSA2 and GS increases. When p_1 increases from 0.1 to 0.9, the execution time of both HR and GSA2 is almost unchanged, while that of GS significantly decreases. It should be emphasized that when $n = 2000$, SMTI has a huge search space ($2000! \simeq 10^{5735}$ matchings), but HR runs about $10^0 = 1.0$ seconds for $p_2 \leq 0.9$ and about $10^{0.3} = 1.99$ seconds for $p_2 = 1.0$.

Experiment 4. In Experiment 3, when $p_1 \in \{0.1, 0.2, \cdots, 0.9\}$, both HR and GSA2 find 100% of perfect matchings. This may result in the execution time of HR approximately equal to that of GSA2. In this experiment, we chose n and p_2 as in Experiment 3, but let $p_1 \in \{0.91, 0.92, \cdots, 0.99\}$. Figure 4 shows the average execution time of HR, GSA2, and GS for finding perfect matchings. Again, we see that the execution time of HR is approximately equal to that of GSA2. When p_2 increases from 0.0 to 1.0, the execution time of both HR and GSA2 is decreases, while that of GS increases. When p_1 increases from 0.91 to 0.99, the execution time of HR is almost unchanged, while that of GSA2 and GS decreases. It should be noted that (i) when $n = 1000$, HR and GSA2 find 72% and 67% of perfect matchings, respectively; and (ii) when $n = 2000$, HR and GSA2 find 90% and 87% of perfect matchings, respectively.

As we mentioned above, HR consists of GS to find a stable matching and a heuristic function to maximize the matching found by GS, however, when

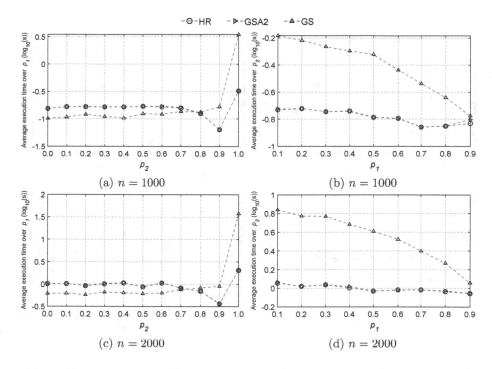

Fig. 3. Execution time for finding perfect matchings, where $p_1 \in [0.1, 0.2, \cdots, 0.9]$

$p_2 \in \{0.9, 1.0\}$ or p_1 is small, the execution time of HR is smaller than that of GS. This is because at each iteration of GS, each single man m_i proposes a woman w_j to whom he prefers most. If w_j has a partner m_k and $r_{w_j}(m_k) < r_{w_j}(m_i)$, then m_i is rejected by w_j. When $p_2 = 0.9$, each man ranks women almost equally (i.e. rarely $r_{w_j}(m_i) < r_{w_j}(m_k)$), and when $p_2 = 1.0$, each man ranks women equally (i.e. $r_{w_j}(m_i) = r_{w_j}(m_k)$), and vice versa. This means that m_i has to propose the next woman to whom he prefers most at the next iterations. If every woman w_j in m_i's preference list has a partner, then m_i has to propose every w_j and he is rejected by w_j, i.e. m_i becomes a single. In contrary, at each iteration of HR, each single man m_i proposes a woman w_j to whom he prefers most. Then, there are two cases: (i) if there exists a single woman w_j in the set of the women to whom m_i prefers equally, then w_j is assigned to m_i (lines 21–23 in HR); (ii) If w_j has a partner m_k, and if there exists a single woman w_t that $r_{m_k}(w_t) = r_{m_k}(w_j)$, then w_j is assigned to m_i (lines 27–29 in HR) and w_t has a chance to assign to m_k when m_k proposes w_t at the next some iteration. By doing so, m_i do not find the next woman to whom he prefers most at the next iterations. Obviously, when p_1 increases, each man ranks fewer women in his preference list and therefore, HR runs much faster than GS when $p_2 \in \{0.9, 1.0\}$ or p_1 is small.

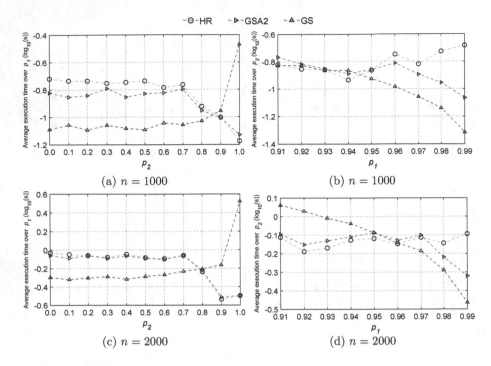

Fig. 4. Execution time for finding perfect matchings, where $p_1 \in [0.91, 0.92, \cdots, 0.99]$

5 Conclusions

This paper proposed a heuristic repair algorithm, namely HR, to solve the MAX-SMTI problem. HR is designed including a well-known GS algorithm [9,14] to find a stable matching for the SMTI problem and a heuristic repair function to improve the quality of the found stable matching in terms of maximum size. The experimental results for large randomly generated instances of SMTI showed that HR outperforms GSA2 [14] in terms of solution quality for finding perfect matchings of SMTI problem. In the future, we plan to extend the proposed approach to the Hospitals/Residents with Ties problem [11,17] and the Student-Project Allocation problem [1,6].

Acknowledgment. This research is funded by the Basic Science Research Program through the National Research Foundation of Korea under grant number NRF-2020R1F1A1050014.

References

1. Abraham, D.J., Irving, R.W., Manlove, D.F.: The student-project allocation problem. In: Ibaraki, T., Katoh, N., Ono, H. (eds.) ISAAC 2003. LNCS, vol. 2906, pp. 474–484. Springer, Heidelberg (2003). https://doi.org/10.1007/978-3-540-24587-2_49

2. Askalidis, G., Immorlica, N., Kwanashie, A., Manlove, D.F., Pountourakis, E.: Socially stable matchings in the hospitals/residents problem. In: Dehne, F., Solis-Oba, R., Sack, J.-R. (eds.) WADS 2013. LNCS, vol. 8037, pp. 85–96. Springer, Heidelberg (2013). https://doi.org/10.1007/978-3-642-40104-6_8

3. Codognet, P., Diaz, D.: Yet another local search method for constraint solving. In: Steinhöfel, K. (ed.) SAGA 2001. LNCS, vol. 2264, pp. 73–90. Springer, Heidelberg (2001). https://doi.org/10.1007/3-540-45322-9_5

4. Cseh, Á., Irving, R.W., Manlove, D.F.: The stable roommates problem with short lists. Theory Comput. Syst. **63**(1), 128–149 (2017). https://doi.org/10.1007/s00224-017-9810-9

5. Cseha, A., Manlove, D.F.: Stable marriage and roommates problems with restricted edges: complexity and approximability. Discrete Optimizat. **20**(1), 62–89 (2016)

6. Diebold, F., Bichler, M.: Matching with indifferences: a comparison of algorithms in the context of course allocation. Eur. J. Oper. Res. **260**(1), 268–282 (2017)

7. Gale, D., Shapley, L.S.: College admissions and the stability of marriage. Am. Math. Mon. **9**(1), 9–15 (1962)

8. Gelain, M., Pini, M.S., Rossi, F., Venable, K.B., Walsh, T.: Local search for stable marriage problems with ties and incomplete lists. In: Zhang, B.-T., Orgun, M.A. (eds.) PRICAI 2010. LNCS (LNAI), vol. 6230, pp. 64–75. Springer, Heidelberg (2010). https://doi.org/10.1007/978-3-642-15246-7_9

9. Gelain, M., Pini, M.S., Rossi, F., Venable, K.B., Walsh, T.: Local search approaches in stable matching problems. Algorithms **6**(4), 591–617 (2013)

10. Gent, I.P., Prosser, P.: An empirical study of the stable marriage problem with ties and incomplete lists. In: Proceedings of the 15th European Conference on Artificial Intelligence, pp. 141–145. Lyon, France, July 2002

11. Irving, R.W., Manlove, D.F.: Finding large stable matchings. J. Experiment. Algorithmics **14**(2), 1.2–1.2:30 (2009)

12. Irving, R.W., Manlove, D.F., O'Malley, G.: Stable marriage with ties and bounded length preference lists. J. Discret. Algorithms **7**(1), 213–219 (2009)

13. Iwama, K., Miyazaki, S., Morita, Y., Manlove, D.: Stable marriage with incomplete lists and ties. In: Wiedermann, J., van Emde Boas, P., Nielsen, M. (eds.) ICALP 1999. LNCS, vol. 1644, pp. 443–452. Springer, Heidelberg (1999). https://doi.org/10.1007/3-540-48523-6_41

14. Király, Z.: Linear time local approximation algorithm for maximum stable marriage. Algorithms **6**(1), 471–484 (2013)

15. Manlove, D.F., Irving, R.W., Iwama, K., Miyazaki, S., Morita, Y.: Hard variants of stable marriage. Theoret. Comput. Sci. **276**(1–2), 261–279 (2002)

16. McDermid, E.: A 3/2-approximation algorithm for general stable marriage. In: Albers, S., Marchetti-Spaccamela, A., Matias, Y., Nikoletseas, S., Thomas, W. (eds.) ICALP 2009. LNCS, vol. 5555, pp. 689–700. Springer, Heidelberg (2009). https://doi.org/10.1007/978-3-642-02927-1_57

17. Munera, D., Diaz, D., Abreu, S., Rossi, F., Saraswat, V., Codognet, P.: A local search algorithm for SMTI and its extension to HRT problems. In: Proceedings of the 3rd International Workshop on Matching Under Preferences, pp. 66–77. Glasgow, United Kingdom, April 2015

18. Munera, D., Diaz, D., Abreu, S., Rossi, F., Saraswat, V., Codognet, P.: Solving hard stable matching problems via local search and cooperative parallelization. In: Proceedings of the Twenty-Ninth AAAI Conference on Artificial Intelligence, pp. 1212–1218. Austin, Texas, January 2015

19. Paluch, K.: Faster and simpler approximation of stable matchings. In: Proceedings of the 9th International Workshop on Approximation and Online Algorithms, pp. 176–187. Saarbrucken, Germany, September 2011
20. Paluch, K.: Faster and simpler approximation of stable matchings. Algorithms **7**(2), 189–202 (2014)
21. Viet, H.H., Uyen, N.T., Lee, S.G., Chung, T.C., Trang, L.H.: A max-conflicts based heuristic search for the stable marriage problem with ties and incomplete lists. J. Heuristics **27**(3), 439–458 (2021). https://doi.org/10.1007/s10732-020-09464-8

The Hierarchical Discrete Learning Automaton Suitable for Environments with *Many* Actions and *High* Accuracy Requirements

Rebekka Olsson Omslandseter[1]([⊠]), Lei Jiao[1], Xuan Zhang[2], Anis Yazidi[3], and B. John Oommen[1,4]

[1] Department of Information and Communication Technology, University of Agder, 4879 Grimstad, Norway
{rebekka.o.omslandseter,lei.jiao}@uia.no
[2] Norwegian Research Centre (NORCE), 4879 Grimstad, Norway
[3] Oslo Metropolitan University, 0167 Oslo, Norway
[4] Carleton University, Ottawa, Canada

Abstract. Since its early beginning, the paradigm of Learning Automata (LA), has attracted much interest. Over the last decades, new concepts and various improvements have been introduced to increase the LA's speed and accuracy, including employing probability updating functions, discretizing the probability space, and implementing the "Pursuit" concept. The concept of incorporating "structure" into the ordering of the LA's actions is one of the latest advancements to the field, leading to the ϵ-optimal Hierarchical Continuous Pursuit LA (HCPA) that has superior performance to other LA variants when the number of actions is *large*. Although the previously proposed HCPA is powerful, its speed has a handicap when the required action probability of an action is approaching unity. The reason for this slow convergence is that the learning parameter operates in a multiplicative manner within the probability space, making the increment of the action probability smaller as its probability becomes close to unity. Therefore, we propose the novel Hierarchical Discrete Learning Automata (HDPA) in this paper, which does not possess the same impediment as the HCPA. The proposed machine infuse the principle of discretization into the action probability vector's updating functionality, where this type of updating is invoked recursively at every depth within a hierarchical tree structure and we pursue the best estimated action in all iterations through utilization of the Estimator phenomenon. The proposed machine is ϵ-optimal, and our experimental results demonstrate that the number of iterations required before convergence is significantly reduced for the HDPA, when compared with the HCPA.

Keywords: Reinforcement learning · Learning Automata · Hierarchical discrete pursuit LA

© Springer Nature Switzerland AG 2022
G. Long et al. (Eds.): AI 2021, LNAI 13151, pp. 507–518, 2022.
https://doi.org/10.1007/978-3-030-97546-3_41

1   Introduction

In the field of Learning Automata (LA), non-human agents, implemented through computer programs, find solutions to problems of stochastic nature through the concept of learning. One of the main advantages of this type of Machine Learning (ML) is the scheme's ability to operate adaptively. The paradigm is based on a learning agent, or Learning Automaton, referred to as a LA, that interacts with a teacher, referred to as the *Environment* [4]. The LA has several actions that often correspond to the different solutions for the given problem. Through selecting actions and getting feedback from the Environment, the LA learns which action (behavior) results in the highest probability of receiving a Reward from the Environment. Although the LA requires feedback from an Environment, it learns in a Semi-Supervised manner. Thus, the LA does not need examples of solutions to learn. They explore different actions and learn via trial-and-error. We can model the Environment in numerous ways. The reader should note that, in this paper, the shortened term LA refers to both the field of Learning Automata and the Learning Automaton according to the context where it appears.

In LA, we evaluate the schemes' performance by the number of iterations needed before convergence and the schemes' accuracy in finding the optimal solution [4]. Improvements that have enhanced the accuracy and speed in LA include using action probability vectors to decide the LA behavior (VSSA), discretizing the probability space of these vectors (Discrete LA), and deploying the "pursuit" concept. In addition, pursuing the most likely action to receive a Reward throughout the LA operation (Estimator-based LA) and ordering the LA in a hierarchical structure (Hierarchical LA) improved the LA's performance further. The structuring of the LA led to the state-of-the-art ϵ-optimal Hierarchical Continuous Pursuit LA (HCPA) [12], which can handle a large number of actions.

Although the HCPA handles a large number of actions, its convergence speed has an impediment when any action probability approaches unity. The reason for this slow convergence is that the learning parameter, and thus the updating of the probabilities operates in a multiplicative manner within the probability space. Consequently, the learning rate decreases as the probability approaches unity. In more detail, as the learning continues, the increment of action probability is less and less, making it more challenging for the LA to converge in the latter phase of learning. This drawback is even more apparent when the criterion for convergence is high, i.e., when high accuracy is required. To solve this problem, we propose the novel ϵ-optimal Hierarchical Discrete Learning Automata (HDPA) scheme in this paper. The HDPA includes all the phenomena mentioned earlier to speed up the convergence when high accuracy is required. The beauty of the HDPA is that the learning speed does not decrease as the learning continues because it operates in a step-wise manner in the probability space. Our simulation results demonstrate that the HDPA has significantly faster convergence for high accuracy requirements. Thus, the HDPA outperforms the state-of-the-art HCPA scheme presented in [12] when the accuracy requirement is high.

Our contributions are summarized as follows:

- We propose the novel HDPA that converges faster than the state-of-the-art HCPA algorithm, when the accuracy requirement is high. The advantages become more pronounced when a large number of actions exist.
- Via extensive simulations, we demonstrate how much the HDPA converged faster than the HCPA for Environments with *many* actions and high accuracy requirements.

2   Related Work

Michael Lvovitch Tsetlin pioneered the field of LA by inventing the Tsetlin Automata (TA) [10], which can be categorized as a Fixed Structure Stochastic Automata (FSSA). The FSSA has a discrete and state-based structure, where the automaton's current state determines its action. The first significant improvement in LA was achieved through the discovery/invention of Variable Structure Stochastic Automata (VSSA), where the action of the LA is selected by randomly sampling an action probability vector. The probability vector is updated through functions according to the Environment's feedback, influencing and changing the behavior of the LA (where this updating functionality can also change over time). While an FSSA needs to move through numerous states before exploring another action, VSSA can possibly explore distinct actions along consecutive iterations, speeding up the exploration of the Environment.

The earlier established variants, the Linear Reward-Penalty (L_{R-P}) scheme, the Linear Reward-Inaction (L_{R-I}) scheme, the Linear Inaction-Penalty (L_{I-P}) scheme, and the Linear Reward-ϵPenalty ($L_{R-\epsilon P}$) scheme in [1] and [4] are all examples of continuous VSSA schemes. The "linear"(L) schemes have such a categorization because the action probabilities are increased in a linear manner. The probabilities of the VSSA can also be increased in a non-linear manner [1, 2, 4]. In mathematical analyses, LA can described through Markov chains, where we have ergodic and absorbing types [1, 8].

The next quantum step in terms of speed and accuracy in LA was achieved through discretizing the action probability space [5]. In traditional VSSA, the action selection probabilities can assume any real value in the interval [0, 1], and the updating is achieved in a multiplicative manner with a learning parameter ($\lambda \in (0, 1)$). The drawback of this continuous approach is its sluggish convergence. As the action probability approach unity, the updating step becomes smaller and smaller, slowing down the algorithm's speed. To address this issue, discretizing the probability space and updating the action probabilities in constant steps was proposed, which significantly improved the convergence speed in LA. The different properties (absorbing and ergodic) of these discretized LA, and their different updating schemes were studied in [5, 6]. In addition, continuous and discretized updating mechanisms with mathematical analyzes are investigated in [7] and [13], respectively.

The invention of Estimator-based Algorithms (EAs) increased the achieved convergence speed of LA even further [9]. The EAs possessed a faster convergence than all earlier variants. These algorithms are based on VSSA, but in addition, estimates of the reward probabilities of the different actions are maintained in a separate vector. These reward estimates are employed in updating the action selection probabilities, where the LA pursues the currently estimated *best action* in terms of the reward estimates (referred to as the Pursuit paradigm). The reward estimates can be found by Maximum Likelihood, or in a Bayesian manner, investigated in [11]. Thereafter, the researchers combined dicretization and the Pursuit paradigm and introduced the family of Discrete Estimator Algorithms (DEAs) [3].

For the above mentioned LA, the convergence becomes challenging when the number of possible actions is large. Understandably, for VSSA, the action probability vector has a dimension of R (for R actions) and its elements sum up to 1. When R is large, many of the action probabilities can have very small values and may not even be chosen, thus rendering the principle behind VSSA to be void. Inclusion of structure into the field of LA solved this problem, and the HCPA constitutes the state-of-the-art [12]. Although HCPA solves the problem to a certain extent, it is always valuable if we can improve the convergence speed of the algorithm without satisfying the accuracy, leading to the proposed algorithm in this paper.

3   The Proposed Algorithm

The concept of the HDPA is to utilize VSSA, discretizing the probability space, structuring the LA instances in a hierarchical tree structure and incorporating the Estimator concept. In more detail, we organize a set of Discrete Pursuit Automata (DPA) instances in a tree structure, where each instance has a set of actions corresponding to the possible paths down the tree structure from that automaton. The probabilities of these actions are maintained through vectors that are updated in a discretized manner. At the bottom level of the tree, we have the actions that directly interact with the Environment. The HDPA maintains reward estimates of all the actions throughout the tree structure, and we pursue the action with the currently best reward estimate in all iterations according to the pursuit paradigm. The reader should note that, in reality, the reward estimates are only necessary for the actions at the leaf level. We utilize the reward estimates in this way, because the proof of the algorithm's convergence needs the reward estimates along the path[1]. A more detailed explanation of the algorithm is given in what follows.

3.1   The Structure of the HDPA

For ease of explanation of the HDPA in this paper, we utilize 2-action DP_{RI} instances as the LA in the tree structure. The reason for using Reward-Penalty

---

[1] A formal proof of the HDPA's convergence will be given in an extended version of this paper.

Inaction LA is that they have demonstrated better performance than other configurations [12]. Furthermore, we use 2-actions automatons in our explanations. Therefore, we can model the HDPA as a balanced full binary tree for a problem with 2^K actions, where K is the maximum depth of the tree. The number of actions per LA instance can be changed to another configuration. However, the reader should remember that one of the main reasons for organizing the actions in a tree structure is to mitigate a large action probability vector because of its inferior performance [12]. Therefore, the number of actions in the LA instances should, in any case, be limited. The HDPA in these explanations is, thus, configured to handle 2^K original actions. If the number of original actions is not 2^K, we consider the nearest power of 2 above the number of original actions and configure the excess number of actions with zero Reward probability. To continue our explanations in greater detail, we further formalize the levels in the tree structure as follows:

- **Hierarchical Tree Structure**: The depth of the tree is indexed by parameter k, $k \in \{0, ..., K\}$. For each level of depth, the number of nodes is indexed by $j \in \{1, ..., 2^k\}$. Note that k and j are also employed to index different LA and actions with their corresponding ranges of definition.
- **The Various LA**: The LA $j \in \{1, ..., 2^k\}$ at depth k, is referred to as $\mathcal{A}_{\{k,j\}}$, where $k \in \{0, ..., K-1\}$. The LA at the root is the one at depth 0.
- **The LA at depths from 0 to $K-1$ ($0 \le k < K-1$)**:
  - Each of the LA, $\mathcal{A}_{\{k,j\}}$, has two actions, denoted by $\alpha_{\{k+1,2j-1\}}$ and $\alpha_{\{k+1,2j\}}$, respectively.
  - Whenever the action $\alpha_{\{k+1,2j-1\}}$ is chosen, the LA, $\mathcal{A}_{\{k+1,2j-1\}}$, at the next level is activated.
  - Whenever the action $\alpha_{\{k+1,2j\}}$ is chosen, the LA, $\mathcal{A}_{\{k+1,2j\}}$, at the next level is activated.
- **The LA at depth $K-1$ ($k = K-1$)**: The LA at depth $K-1$ select the actual actions to interact with the Environment.
  - All of the LA at depth $K-1$ have two possible actions each, referred to as $\alpha_{\{K,2j-1\}}$ and $\alpha_{\{K,2j\}}$, respectively.
  - The $K-1$ depth of the tree has 2^K actions in total, referred to as $\alpha_{\{K,j\}}$ where $j \in \{1, ..., 2^K\}$.
  - The selected action denoted by: $\alpha_{\{K,j\}}$, is the child of $\mathcal{A}_{\{K-1,\lceil j/2 \rceil\}}$.
- **The actions at level K ($k = K$)**: At depth K, i.e., at leaves of the tree, we have the actions that directly interact with the Environment.
- $P_{\{k,j\}} = [p_{\{k+1,2j-1\}}, p_{\{k+1,2j\}}]$: The action probability vector of LA $\mathcal{A}_{\{k,j\}}$, where $k \in \{0, ..., K-1\}$ and $j \in \{1, ..., 2^k\}$.

Figure 1 visualizes the structure of a simple HDPA when four actions exist in the Environment. The leaves of the tree are representations of the actions that the HDPA can take and interact with the Environment. For a HDPA with 2^K actions in the leaf level, the number of LA in the tree structure is $2^K - 1$. In this example, we have three LA, i.e., $\mathcal{A}_{\{0,1\}}$, $\mathcal{A}_{\{1,1\}}$ and $\mathcal{A}_{\{1,2\}}$. As depicted, each LA in the tree has two actions. To choose an action, HDPA follows the

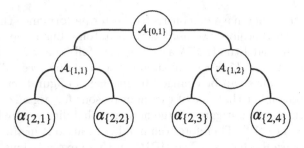

Fig. 1. A visualization of the hierarchy of the HDPA. The instances at the bottom/leaf level of the tree represent the actions that interact with the Environment.

path down the tree by sampling of these action probabilities in the vector. For example, when $\mathcal{A}_{\{0,1\}}$ has an action probability vector of [0.9, 0.1], it selects $\alpha_{\{1,1\}}$ at the root level with probability 0.9. Once $\alpha_{\{1,1\}}$ is chosen, $\mathcal{A}_{\{1,1\}}$ is selected for making the decision at level 1 for the next level (which is at the leaf level in this example), following the action probability vector that $\mathcal{A}_{\{1,1\}}$ maintains. Thereafter, if $\mathcal{A}_{\{1,1\}}$ happens to select the action $\alpha_{\{2,2\}}$, it means that the second action is chosen to interact with the Environment. Thereafter, the HDPA updates its parameters based on the feedback from the Environment. If and only if the Environment offers a Reward, following the pursuit concept, the action probabilities are updated, following the reverse path from the leaf with the current maximum reward estimate to the root. The reader should note that HDPA might reward another action than the one that is currently selected, due the inferior reward estimate in the currently selected action. Independent of whether a Reward or Penalty is received, the reward estimates in all the DPA instances are updated according to whether the action received a Reward or not. The process is detailed as follows:

Parameters:
Δ: The learning parameter, where $0 < \Delta < 1$, and its value is usually configured close to zero.
$u_{\{K,j\}}$: The number of times that action $\alpha_{\{K,j\}}$ was rewarded *when* selected, where $j \in \{1, \ldots, 2^K\}$.
$v_{\{K,j\}}$: The number of times that action $\alpha_{\{K,j\}}$ was selected, where $j \in \{1, \ldots, 2^K\}$.
$\hat{d}_{\{k,j\}}$: The estimated reward probability of action $\alpha_{\{k,j\}}$, $k \in \{1, \ldots, K\}$, $j \in \{1, \ldots, 2^k\}$. At level K, $\hat{d}_{\{K,j\}}$ is computed as $\hat{d}_{\{K,j\}} = \frac{u_{\{K,j\}}}{v_{\{K,j\}}}$, where $j \in \{1, \ldots, 2^K\}$.
β: The response from the Environment, where $\beta = 0$ corresponds to a Reward, and $\beta = 1$ to a Penalty.
T: Convergence criterion threshold.
We initialize the estimate of the reward probabilities as 0.5, i.e., $u_{\{K,j\}}(0) = 1$, $v_{\{K,j\}}(0) = 2$, thus $\hat{d}_{\{K,j\}}(0) = \frac{1}{2}$. The action probability vector is also initialized as 0.5 for all the LA, i.e., $P_{\{k,j\}}(0) = [\frac{1}{2}, \frac{1}{2}]$, where $k \in \{0, \ldots, K-1\}$ and $j \in \{1, \ldots, 2^k\}$.
Begin algorithm:
$t = 0$

Loop

1. **Depths 0 to $K - 1$:**
   - The LA $\mathcal{A}_{\{0,1\}}$ selects an action by randomly (uniformly) sampling as per its action probability vector $[p_{\{1,1\}}(t), p_{\{1,2\}}(t)]$.
   - Let $j_1(t)$ be the index of the chosen action at depth 0, where $j_1(t) \in \{1, 2\}$.
   - The next LA is activated $\mathcal{A}_{\{1,j_1(t)\}}$ which in turn chooses an action and activates the next LA at depth "2".
   - This process continues including depth $K - 1$.
2. **Depth K:**
   - Let $j_K(t)$ be the index of the chosen action at depth K where $j_K(t) \in \{1, ..., 2^K\}$.
   - Update $\hat{d}_{\{K,j_K(t)\}}(t)$ based on the response from the Environment at the leaf depth, K:
     $$u_{\{K,j_K(t)\}}(t+1) = u_{\{K,j_K(t)\}}(t) + (1 - \beta(t))$$
     $$v_{\{K,j_K(t)\}}(t+1) = v_{\{K,j_K(t)\}}(t) + 1$$
     $$\hat{d}_{\{K,j_K(t)\}}(t+1) = \frac{u_{\{K,j_K(t)\}}(t+1)}{v_{\{K,j_K(t)\}}(t+1)}.$$
   - For all other "leaf actions", where $j \in \{1, ..., 2^K\}$ and $j \neq j_K(t)$:
     $$u_{\{K,j\}}(t+1) = u_{\{K,j\}}(t)$$
     $$v_{\{K,j\}}(t+1) = v_{\{K,j\}}(t)$$
     $$\hat{d}_{\{K,j\}}(t+1) = \frac{u_{\{K,j\}}(t+1)}{v_{\{K,j\}}(t+1)}.$$
3. Define the reward estimate for all other actions along the path to the root, $k \in \{0, ..., K - 1\}$ in a recursive manner, where the LA at any one level inherits the feedback from the LA at the level below:
   $$\hat{d}_{\{k,j\}}(t) = \max\left(\hat{d}_{\{k+1,2j-1\}}(t), \hat{d}_{\{k+1,2j\}}(t)\right).$$
4. Proceed to updating the action probability vectors in the LA *along the reverse path from the leaf with the current maximum reward estimate*, as follows:
   - By definition, each LA $j \in \{1, ..., 2^k\}$ at depth k, referred to as $\mathcal{A}_{\{k,j\}}$, where $k \in \{0, ..., K - 1\}$, has two actions $\alpha_{\{k+1,2j-1\}}$ and $\alpha_{\{k+1,2j\}}$. Let $j_{k+1}^h(t) \in \{2j - 1, 2j\}$ be the index of the larger element between $\hat{d}_{\{k+1,2j-1\}}(t)$ and $\hat{d}_{\{k+1,2j\}}(t)$.
   - Let $\overline{j_{k+1}^h(t)} = \{2j - 1, 2j\} \setminus j_{k+1}^h(t)$ be the opposite action, i.e., the one that has the lower reward estimate.
   - Update $p_{\{k+1,j_{k+1}^h(t)\}}$ and $p_{\{k+1,\overline{j_{k+1}^h(t)}\}}$ using the estimates $\hat{d}_{\{k+1,2j-1\}}(t)$ and $\hat{d}_{\{k+1,2j\}}(t)$ as (for all $k \in \{0, ..., K - 1\}$):
   If $\beta(t) = 0$ Then
     $$p_{\{k+1,j_{k+1}^h(t)\}}(t+1) = \min\left(p_{\{k+1,j_{k+1}^h(t)\}}(t) + \Delta, 1\right),$$
     $$p_{\{k+1,\overline{j_{k+1}^h(t)}\}}(t+1) = 1 - p_{\{k+1,j_{k+1}^h(t)\}}(t+1).$$
   Else
     $$p_{\{k+1,\overline{j_{k+1}^h(t)}\}}(t+1) = p_{\{k+1,\overline{j_{k+1}^h(t)}\}}(t),$$
     $$p_{\{k+1,j_{k+1}^h(t)\}}(t+1) = p_{\{k+1,j_{k+1}^h(t)\}}(t).$$
   EndIf
5. For each $\mathcal{A}_{\{k,j\}}$, if either of its action probabilities $p_{\{k+1,2j-1\}}$ and $p_{\{k+1,2j\}}$ surpasses a threshold T, where T is a positive number that is close to unity, the action probabilities for the HDPA will stop updating, and *convergence* is achieved.
6. $t = t + 1$

EndLoop
End algorithm

4   Experimental Results

To demonstrate the performance of the HDPA compared with the HCPA in [12], we simulated the different schemes' performance for distinct Environments. To enhance the validity of our simulations, we increased the number of experiments and the criteria for convergence compared with the simulations in [12]. As discussed previously, the HCPA has an impediment when the action probability vector approach unity. Our simulations, which we present in more detail shortly, demonstrate the advantage of the HDPA over the HCPA as the convergence criterion is high. The reader should note that we have omitted the comparison with the traditional CPA variants in this paper due to their well-known inferior performance [12].

We conducted experiments for different Environments with *many* actions. The Environments for the 16, 32, and 64 actions were based on the benchmark action probabilities that were first established in [12]. For the 128 actions Environment, we uniformly generated 128 different probabilities between zero and unity, representing the probabilities of the LA receiving a Reward from the Environment. The 128-action Environment's reward probabilities are visualized in Fig. 2.

4.1   The Learning Parameters

From the mathematical proof in [12], and the established theory of VSSA, we understand that when the learning parameter, λ, is sufficiently small, the HCPA will most likely converge to the action that ensures it the maximum probability of obtaining a Reward. The same applies to the value of Δ [14]. In general, a smaller learning parameter results in a slower convergence but has a higher probability of finding the optimal action as its configured value approaches zero. Therefore, tuning the learning parameter is a trade-off between the system's accuracy and convergence speed. In this paper, to find the best value of λ and Δ, we utilized a top-down approach. In more detail, we decreased the value of the learning parameters in a step-wise manner with two decimals precision until their configured value made the LA achieve 100% accuracy for all the given experiments. Consequently, the value of the learning parameters that fulfilled these criteria represents the assumed "best" values of λ and Δ given the distinct Environments used in the simulations.

Although the values for λ and Δ are obtained through extensive testing, it is not entirely certain that one will achieve convergence to the correct action with the found values of λ or Δ for a certain number of consecutive experiments. The Environment and the LA's stochastic behavior over time make it impossible to determine whether the LA will surely converge correctly with a λ or Δ below a certain threshold. The reader should also note that the λ and Δ values are entirely dependent on the Environment's reward probabilities and that the best λ and Δ can vary from case to case. Therefore, we refer to the obtained values of λ and Δ as the "best" learning parameters (and not the *optimal* ones).

4.2   The Average Number of Iterations

In the field of LA, a learning scheme's performance is often measured through
the number of iterations required before the algorithm has converged. Due to
the stochastic nature of the Environments that LA operates in, we normally
measure the average number of iterations, i.e., we conduct many experiments
and report the average number of iterations required before convergence over
a number of experiments. In VSSA, the LA has achieved convergence once the
action probability of any one of the actions has reached a certain threshold.
The convergence criterion threshold is often configured close to unity. In these
simulations, we configured $T = 0.992$, and considered the average of the schemes'
performance for 600 experiments.

Table 1. HCPA performance for the different simulation Environments.

Number of actions	Mean	Standard deviation (Std.)
16	1,366.61	121.14
32	10,281.84	681.82
64	169,839.67	13,687.48
128	155,088.62	10,613.21

Table 2. HDPA performance for the different simulation Environments.

Number of actions	Mean	Standard deviation (Std.)
16	868.25	135.50
32	6,172.38	744.84
64	100,638.41	17,653.41
128	97,795.59	13,266.12

The simulations discussed in this section, the "best" learning parameters
for the Environment with 16 actions were $\lambda = 0.0043$ and $\Delta = 0.0011$. For
the Environment with 32 and 64 actions, the best learning parameters were
$\lambda = 0.00057$ and $\lambda = 3.6e-5$, and $\Delta = 0.00015$ and $\Delta = 9.9e-6$, respectively.
The "best" obtained values for the 128 action Environment were $\lambda = 3.9e-5$
and $\Delta = 9.7e-6$. The reader will observe that the learning parameters for the 64
actions and 128 actions cases are quite similar, which is because the 64 actions'
Environment's benchmark probabilities were more challenging than the generated Environment for 128 actions.

Tables 1 and 2 show results for our different simulation Environments. In
these simulations, we used the benchmark probabilities for the Environments
with 16, 32, and 64 actions. For the 128 actions Environment, we used the reward
probabilities visualized in Fig. 2. The tables include both algorithms' results and
list both the mean and the Standard Deviation (Std). Let us first consider the

16, 32, and 64 actions' Environments, where the HDPA had approximately 37%, 40%, and 41% fewer required iterations compared with the HCPA. Consequently, the benefit of HDPA over HCPA increased with the number of actions. Observing the Std, the HDPA had more variation in the number of iterations for all the three action configurations.

Considering the results obtained for the 128 actions' Environment (based on the reward probabilities visualized in Fig. 2), the HDPA converged within approximately 98,000 iterations, while the HCPA required 155,000 iterations before convergence. Comparing the algorithms' Std, the HDPA had more variation in the number of iterations before convergence than the HCPA. Thus, the HDPA was more unpredictable in its number of iterations required before convergence, but needed significantly fewer iterations on average!

Fig. 2. The action probabilities for the 128 actions Environment.

4.3   The Nature of Convergence

The nature of convergence for the HDPA compared with the HCPA is different. As explained earlier, the HDPA updates its action probability in a discretized manner. In contrast, the HCPA updates these probabilities multiplicatively, where the increase in the probability vector can take any value in the interval $[0, 1)$. In Fig. 3 and Fig. 4, we can observe the differences between the operations of the HDPA and the HCPA in greater detail. In these experiments,

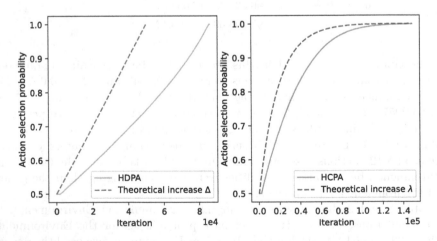

Fig. 3. The action probability of the optimal action per iteration compared to the theoretical increase in the action probability vector for the different schemes.

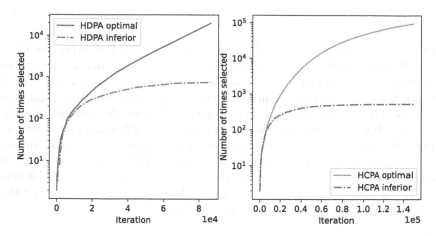

Fig. 4. The number of times that the optimal and the most inferior action were selected for the number of iterations required before convergence for the different schemes.

we increased the convergence criterion to $T = 0.999$ and used the 64 actions Environment from the benchmark probabilities. The figures depict the different schemes' operation for a single iteration. We found the "best" learning parameters through the same top-down approach as explained earlier. The "best" learning parameters were configured as $\Delta - 1e{-}5$ and $\lambda - 5.3e{-}5$, respectively.

Figure 3 depicts the action probability per iteration. As we can observe from the figure, the HDPA requires fewer iterations before convergence than the HCPA does. In addition, we observe the different nature of the two schemes. While the HDPA has a rather linear increase in the action probability, the increase of the action probability for the HCPA scheme slows down as the probability approach unity. Indeed, the HCPA has a faster increase than the HDPA in the initial iterations but suffers from slow convergence because of its behavior as the action probability increases. The reader should also observe that both schemes do not follow the theoretical increase lines in the respective plots. The theoretical increase lines show the convergences when the optimal action is chosen in each iteration, where the action probabilities of the actions in the optimal branch are monotonically increasing. Clearly, these lines depict the theoretical convergence benchmarks without any exploration and are only achievable when the optimal action is known in advance.

In Fig. 4, we observe the difference between the optimal and inferior action for the different schemes. As we observe, the inferior action (the action with the lowest probability of resulting in a Reward) is only selected in the initial phase of the schemes' operation and rarely sampled as the algorithms approach convergence. In contrast, the optimal action is selected more often as the number of iterations increases. As we observe from the figure, the HDPA required significantly fewer iterations than the HCPA. The plots also demonstrate that the inferior action is, indeed, explored throughout the LA operation.

5 Conclusion

In this paper, we proposed the HDPA scheme. The HDPA incorporates all the major phenomena within LA that have improved these algorithms over the last six decades. By implementing VSSA probability updating functionality and discretizing the probability space, utilizing the Estimator phenomenon, and structuring the LA in a hierarchical tree structure akin to the concept of binary search, the HDPA outperforms the state-of-the-art HCPA when the convergence criterion is close to unity, i.e., when the accuracy requirement is high. Our simulations demonstrated the clear advantage of the HDPA over the HCPA for different Environments with many actions. We also demonstrated the difference between the action probability updating of the schemes, and thus, why their performance and convergence speeds are different.

References

1. Lakshmivarahan, S.: Learning Algorithms Theory and Applications. Springer, New York (1981). https://doi.org/10.1007/978-1-4612-5975-6
2. Lakshmivarahan, S., Thathachar, M.A.L.: Absolutely expedient algorithms for stochastic automata. IEEE Trans. Syst. Man Cybern. **3**, 281–286 (1973)
3. Lanctot, J.K., Oommen, B.J.: Discretized estimator learning automata. IEEE Trans. Syst. Man Cybern. **22**(6), 1473–1483 (1992)
4. Narendra, K.S., Thathachar, M.A.L.: Learning automata: an introduction. Courier Corporation, December 2012
5. Oommen, B.J.: Absorbing and ergodic discretized two-action learning automata. IEEE Trans. Syst. Man Cybern. **16**(2), 282–293 (1986)
6. Oommen, B.J., Christensen, J.P.R.: ϵ-optimal discretized linear reward-penalty learning automata. IEEE Trans. Syst. Man Cybern. **18**(3), 451–458 (1988)
7. Oommen, B.J., Agache, M.: Continuous and discretized pursuit learning schemes: various algorithms and their comparison. IEEE Trans. Syst. Man Cybern. B Cybern. **31**(3), 277–287 (2001)
8. Poznyak, A.S., Najim, K.: Learning Automata and Stochastic Optimization, vol. 3. Springer, Cham (1997). https://doi.org/10.1007/BFb0015102
9. Thathachar, M.A.L., Sastry, P.S.: Estimator algorithms for learning automata. In: Proceedings of the Platinum Jubilee Conference on Systems and Signal Processing, Department of Electrical Engineering, Indian Institute of Science (1986)
10. Tsetlin, M.L.: Finite automata and the modeling of the simplest forms of behavior. Uspekhi Matem Nauk **8**, 1–26 (1963)
11. X. Zhang, B.J.O., Granmo, O.C.: The design of absorbing Bayesian pursuit algorithms and the formal analyses of their ϵ-optimality. Pattern Anal. Appl. **20**, 797–808 (2017)
12. Yazidi, A., Zhang, X., Jiao, L., Oommen, B.J.: The hierarchical continuous pursuit learning automation: a novel scheme for environments with large numbers of actions. IEEE Trans. Neural Netw. Learn. Syst. **31**(2), 512–526 (2020)
13. Zhang, X., Granmo, O.C., Oommen, B.J.: Discretized Bayesian pursuit - a new scheme for reinforcement learning. In: Proceedings of IEA-AIE, pp. 784–793. Dalian, China, June 2012
14. Zhang, X., Jiao, L., Oommen, B.J., Granmo, O.C.: A conclusive analysis of the finite-time behavior of the discretized pursuit learning automaton. IEEE Trans. Neural Netw. Learn. Syst. **31**(1), 284–294 (2020)

Hybrid Grouping Genetic Algorithm for Large-Scale Two-Level Resource Allocation of Containers in the Cloud

Taiwo Akindele$^{(\boxtimes)}$, Boxiong Tan, Yi Mei, and Hui Ma

Victoria University of Wellington, Wellington, New Zealand
{taiwo.akindele,boxiong.tan,yi.mei,hui.ma}@ecs.vuw.ac.nz

Abstract. Cloud container resource allocation aims to find container placements in cloud Virtual Machines (VM) and Physical Machines (PM) such that overall energy consumption is minimised. A resource allocation architecture where application containers are consolidated into cloud VMs in a container-VM-PM model is common practise in data centers. The VM layer may provide additional administrative or security features, but adds complexity to the optimization problem when deploying containers initially on a large scale. Research addressing this two-level resource allocation is limited, some of the recent work try to optimise consolidation of containers to VM layer separately from consolidation of VMs to PMs, which results in large portions of the search space remaining unexplored. A Grouping Genetic Algorithm (GGA) framework that can simultaneously optimize consolidation on both levels is promising. However, for large instances of the two-level optimisation, it may suffer from premature convergence and limited population diversity. In this work, we propose a new fixed-length crossover operator that is designed to improve population diversity and exploration in GGA for container resource allocation optimisation. We also propose problem-specific Best-Fit and Largest VM heuristic operators to aid local search by rearranging containers from the lower fitness PMs at the chromosome tail into existing VMs and PMs with better utilization when possible. We demonstrate that with the newly developed operators, the proposed GGA can significantly reduce energy consumption in large-scale test cases.

Keywords: Grouping genetic algorithm · Container resource allocation · Energy consumption optimisation

1 Introduction

Lowering carbon footprint and operational cost of cloud data centers are some of the motivation for research on better resource allocation optimisation approaches in the cloud [18]. Traditionally, with elastic workloads, applications were deployed with virtual machines (VM) across a cluster of shared host nodes. VMs were not very portable and used up significant overhead of the available resources since each VM ran its own operating system.

© Springer Nature Switzerland AG 2022
G. Long et al. (Eds.): AI 2021, LNAI 13151, pp. 519–530, 2022.
https://doi.org/10.1007/978-3-030-97546-3_42

Containerization provides application developers and service providers a light-weight operating system virtualization that packages software applications together with all the required system dependencies to run them in any environment. This facilitates more portable and scalable applications addressing some of the problems with traditional VM virtualisation. With the arrival of Docker [1], container virtualisation was introduced to the mainstream. Containers have been widely adopted for quick deployment of applications and microservices at scale in distributed computing environments like cloud datacenters, to the extent that all the major cloud providers have their own offerings of container services or CaaS, providing environment and services to manage containers.

For today's use-cases [7], service providers have to be able to support huge initial deployments, ranging up to thousands of containers of varying requested resources, across multiple VMs and physical machines (PM) automatically. This creates a challenge to find near optimal container placements such that utilization of PMs is as high as possible and total number of active PMs used are minimal. Poor resource allocation optimisation will keep more PMs than necessary running with low utilization, resulting in energy waste and worse carbon footprint of datacenter. This initial container placement or static resource allocation assumes that the full list of containers, their required resources, as well as the resource capacities of the available VM types and PM are all fixed and known beforehand. This optimization problem is proven to be NP-hard in literature [4,18]. Thus, exact methods are only applicable for small scale problems.

Both heuristic and meta-heuristic approaches have been applied to solve the resource allocation problem in general [4]. Many applied heuristic approaches are based on greedy search algorithms that are simple and relatively quick in execution. They may also be more prone to getting stuck at local optima in large or complex problems. Metaheuristics such as population-based or evolutionary computation approaches are popularly applied to solve complex combinatorial optimisation problems and may do better at searching for global optima in large search spaces [18]. They can also involve complex indirect representation of the resource allocation problem, such that an encoding and decoding mechanism is required to represent the problem and to interpret the solutions generated by the algorithm [2,11]. To avoid the decoding process, [17] proposed a Grouping Genetic Algorithm (GGA) framework that uses a direct representation to encode the problem solutions and designed evolutionary operators to evolve solutions while satisfying the constraints. Even though performing better than popular greedy rule-based heuristics and beating traditional GA, the GGA framework still suffered from some premature convergence in the large scale problems due to insufficient diversity in the population. The aim of this paper is to propose an effective hybrid GGA based approach to the two-level resource allocation problem, to address the diversity issue. The following are our contributions:

- We design a new Fixed-Length Crossover (FLX) operator for GGA to address premature convergence of the GGA framework [17] for large-scale container resource allocation in the cloud.

- We propose to incorporate domain-specific heuristics including Best-Fit-PM, Best-Fit-VM and Largest-VM into the GGA crossover and custom operators for improving the exploitation of GGA in large-scale container resource allocation.
- We present experiment results to demonstrate how our new algorithm performs against current state-of-the-art benchmark GGA algorithm.

The remainder of the paper is organized as follows. Section 2 gives more background and discusses related work. Section 3 covers the problem definition. Section 5 describes our algorithm in detail. In Sect. 6 we present our experiments, results and analysis, while the last section provides some conclusion and introduces future work.

2 Related Work

2.1 Container Resource Allocation Architecture

Most of the literature on resource allocation optimisation consider a single level consolidation. For example, VMs to host machines only [8], or applications to VMs or bare-metal hosts [3,6] directly. These are described as 2-tier architectures, and their solutions are not the most ideal for container-based clouds with a 3-tier container-VM-PM application environment architecture [20].

Only a few recent works have proposed solutions for the two-level optimisation problem of the 3-tier architecture. In some work [5,13,19], this has been broken down into two 2-tier stages of optimisation i.e. the container-VM tier (VM selection) is optimised separately from the VM-PM tier (VM consolidation). When initially allocating a large number of containers, e.g., hundreds or thousands at once, consolidation optimisation at each level is a NP-hard problem [18]. By breaking this problem into two, the search space for each level of optimisation is constrained by the solutions of the other level. While this helps to simplify the problem, it is not effective in finding the best possible solutions.

Experiments in [10,20] demonstrated that an approach optimising both levels of resource allocation or consolidation at the same time find better solutions than solving each allocation level separately. This is because the location of a VM chosen to place a container in, has an impact on optimising the total number of host PMs used, as well as the overall utilization or fragmentation of CPU and memory resources of those PMs.

2.2 Optimisation Approaches

In [20], an algorithm based on Best-Fit heuristics was proposed for simultaneous optimisation of the two-level resource allocation. They utilized a fitness model based on utilization of the target VM or PM. When placing a container, the algorithm selects an existing VM with the least amount of remaining resources. If the container does not fit into any existing VM, a new VM of the smallest fitting size is instantiated to place the container. Similar logic is applied when placing VMs to PMs. In [6], an Ant Colony Organisation (ACO) based algorithm was compared to Docker's native swarmkit [14] policies for a single level scheduling of containers to hosts, to demonstrate how meta-heuristic approaches can outperform greedy heuristic approaches especially when resources are nonuniform. The work in [5] combined both ACO meta-heuristic and Best-Fit heuristic approaches to two-level container resource allocation. First, BF heuristic and a fitness function based on an evaluation of the wasted resources on VMs and PMs is used to initialise a set of available VM to PM assignments. Then ACO is used to find near optimal allocation of containers to a subset of the available VMs from previous step. Similarly, a 2-step hybrid PSO approach was proposed in [13], a simple First-Fit heuristic is used to allocate containers to VMs while considering operating system requirements as a constraint. For the second step, they start from a random initialization of PM allocation for the VMs from step 1 and use PSO-based algorithm to find near optimal VM placements. However, the proposed algorithm is tested against small test cases ranging from 20 to 500.

In [16], an indirect vector-based representation using dual-chromosome GA (DGA) was proposed to solve the two-level resource allocation problem, where one chromosome represented the container-VM layer and the other was used to represent the VM-PM layer. A decoding process was required to interpret each solution which added additional complexity to the algorithm. The work in [15,17] introduced GGA for container resource allocation to address the challenge of indirect representation, making it possible to apply domain-specific heuristics to improve selection pressure of GA. GGA produced better solutions in all test cases of their experiments compared to state-of-the-art approaches including [16] and popular Bin Packing Problem heuristics tested.

As discussed above, the existing rule based methods do not consider some important problem features or are not effective for some problem instances. On the other hand, meta-heuristic approaches, in particular GGA based approaches, can directly find solutions for given problem instances but may suffer limited diversity due to evolutionary operators. Therefore, the aim of this paper is to propose a GGA-based approach with new evolutionary operators to effectively search for solutions for two-level resource allocation.

3   Problem Definition

In the *static container resource allocation* problem, a set of containers each deploying a cloud application or microservice, defined by their CPU and memory requirements, are to be initially allocated resources in the cloud. They are placed unto VMs which are in-turn consolidated into PM hosts, with the ultimate objective of minimising the total energy consumption of the utilized PMs.

Same as in [17], we assume an unlimited set of homogenous PMs defined by their CPU and Memory capacity. We also assume a pre-defined set of VM types, each defined by its CPU and memory capacity. PMs are only activated when we need to assign VMs occupied by containers, otherwise they are turned off to keep the overall energy consumption low in the data center. The following constraints are considered in this paper:

- Every container to be allocated gets assigned exactly one VM and one PM.
- The total CPU and Memory requirements of all containers allocated to a VM must not exceed the capacity of the respective VM type.
- Each VM instantiated is assigned to exactly one PM.
- The total CPU and Memory capacity of all VMs allocated to a PM must not exceed the PM's resource capacity.

Following [17], the energy consumption model for any PM, $E_{(PM)}$, is a function of its CPU utilization $cpu_{(PM)}$.

$$E_{(PM)} = E_{idle} + (E_{full} - E_{idle}) * cpu_{(PM)} \tag{1}$$

where E_{idle} and E_{full} are energy consumption when PM is idle and when PM is fully utilised respectively. This energy model is used in our algorithm to evaluate the solution fitness $E = \sum_{PM=1}^{N} E_{(PM)}$ for N number of PMs.

4   Proposed Algorithm

Algorithm 1: FLXGGA-BF/LV for **container resource allocation**

Given : a list of containers, a list of VM types, and unlimited number of PMs
Output: container allocation
1 initialise population with randomly generated solutions;
2 **while** *max generations not reached* **do**
3 | *evaluate(current_pop)*;
4 | *next_pop ← eliteindividuals*;
5 | **while** *next_gen population is incomplete* **do**
6 | | *children* = **FLX**(*tournament_selection(current_population)*);
7 | | *mutation(children)*;
8 | | *rearrangement(children)*;
9 | | **mergeLV**(*children*);
10 | | *next_pop ← children*;
11 | **end**
12 | increase generation count, *current_pop = next_pop*;
13 **end**
14 **return** container allocation

This section describes our proposed hybrid approach that uses GGA to evolve a randomly generated population of solutions, with a new crossover operator to promote more diversity and exploration, as well as new heuristic rules for the rearrangement operator used to improve local search for desirable gene characteristics. Algorithm 1 gives an overview of our proposed hybrid Grouping Genetic Algorithm, namely FLXGGA-BF/LV. The algorithm is inspired by [17], a GGA framework for container resource allocation. Section 4.1 describes the genetic representation of solutions, while subsequent sections describe the algorithm initialization, crossover as well as custom operators for mutation and local search.

Elitism is used to automatically promote individuals with the best fitness to the next generation and tournament selection determines what individuals get to pass over their genes unto offspring by crossover. The fitness function is based on the energy formula in Eq. 1.

Each individual in the GGA population is represented by a variable length chromosome as a list of PMs, where each gene in the chromosome intuitively represents an individual PM with its list of hosted containers and VMs.

4.1   Representation

This direct solution representation with GGA provides an advantage over many other evolutionary computation approaches where typically an encoding and decoding process is required in representation. It also allows us to manipulate each PM's contents individually with algorithm operators without affecting the remainder of the chromosome.

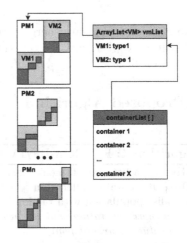

4.2   Initialization

To initialise, we generate a diverse population of solutions by randomly shuffling the container list and allocating the shuffled list to VMs using a First-

Fig. 1. GGA Direct Representation

Fit (FF) heuristic. Resulting VM list is then consolidated into PM bins with FF as well.

4.3   Fixed Length Crossover (FLX)

We introduce a new crossover approach to promote diversity in the population and exploration of the search space. Algorithm 2 illustrates the fixed-length crossover process. We employ the following specific strategies to achieve this:

- In contrast with [17] where parent genes were sorted in descending order before crossover (first by their CPU utilization when generating first child, and then by memory when generating second child), we do not sort the bins or genes of the chromosome ahead of crossover. This improves diversity in the two offspring created by two individuals especially when many of the PMs high in CPU utilization are also comparatively high in memory utilization.
- Because the GGA representation has variable length chromosomes, two parents involved in a crossover may have considerably different number of genes. This means that when we compare parent genes pair-wisely we will have a

---

Algorithm 2: Fixed Length Crossover (FLX)

   Given : 2 parent individuals: parent1, parent2
   Output: 2 child individuals
1 $child1 = nil$;
2 $child2 = nil$;
3 $l \leftarrow$ shorter PM length from either parent; /* i.e. l is the lower number of PMs from either parent */
4 **while** $x \leq l$ **do**

      /* perform pair-wise comparison of CPU & memory utilization. Copy parent gene with higher CPU utilization to child1 and parent gene with higher memory utilization to child2 (ensuring no duplicate allocation   */

5     $child1.PM[x] \leftarrow (parent1.PM[x].cpuUtil > parent2.PM[x].cpuUtil)$? $parent1.PM[x] : parent2.PM[x]$;
6     $child2.PM[x] \leftarrow (parent1.PM[x].memoryUtil > parent2.PM[x].memoryUtil)?parent1.PM[x] : parent2.PM[x]$;
7     $x = x + 1$;
8 **end**
9 $rearrangement(child1, child2)$; /* custom operator with BF/LV heuristics to place unallocated containers */
10 **return** $child1, child2$;

---

tail end of the longer parent that cannot be compared. What we do differently is, instead of simply copying over the structure of these genes to the child, we truncate these genes and apply the custom operators to reallocate the items. By truncating the tail end of the longer parent we are hoping to achieve the following. First, we are trying to increase the probability that the child will inherit the length of the shorter parent. Since shorter chromosome length means fewer PMs, this can help to guide the algorithm to a region of better fitness. Also, we are improving the diversity of the structure in the genes as we have more items displaced from the tail end of the chromosome to reallocate across the surviving bins or genes more optimally.

– Truncating the longer parent in crossover may introduce a small risk of loosing fitly packed genes that may be at the tail end, and so we introduce heuristic rules employing simple domain knowledge in the rearrangement operator to ensure that the displaced or un-allocated items are packed as optimally as possible into existing bins. A new VM will still be created or new PM will be activated when an item can not fit any of the existing bins.

4.4 Rearrangement Heuristics

To place containers that are left unallocated by GGA processes such as crossover or unpack mutation operator, we propose a Best-Fit and Largest VM heuristic approach for the rearrangement operator as discussed in the following subsections. Note that the proposed heuristics are different from [17], which use First-Fit and Random-creation (FF & RC). Considering the greedy nature of the heuristics, we never apply them across multiple individuals or genes at once since this might compromise our GGA's global search or exploration ability. Instead these are used by GGA operators to make changes to a single gene (PM) of the individual each time it is executed.

Best-Fit VM/PM (BF). Best-Fit is a Bin Packing Problem (BPP) heuristic and generally provide good approximate solutions. Like other BPP heuristics they are simple, with low computational complexity. We employ this in a few areas of our algorithm. For example, when re-allocating displaced or unallocated containers during crossover, rather than assigning this containers to the first VM they fit (FF) as done in framework algorithm, we allocate them to the Best-Fit VM. That is, from the list of all VMs that have capacity to host this container, we allocate the container to the most packed VM to promote higher resource utilization and reduce waste. Another example is when we create a new VM to allocate containers, rather than allocate them to the first fitting PM as done in framework algorithm using FF, we assign them to the highest utilised PM with sufficient capacity to accommodate the VM.

Largest VM (LV). Largest VM heuristic is a domain specific heuristic we propose based on the knowledge that choice of larger VM types when appropriate, allows us to allocate more containers into less VMs, resulting in less VM overhead and less wasted resources overall. We propose this largest VM heuristic to replace random creation heuristic in the rearrangement operator. So instead of randomly choosing any larger VM type to be created when there is no VM able to accommodate a container, our heuristic chooses to create the largest VM type that will fit the existing PM. This apparently helped us promote better PM utilisation as we are able to use more of the existing PM capacity to allocate more containers.

4.5 Mutation and Custom Operators

Custom operator referred to as *Unpack* in GGA framework algorithm performs a low probability mutation. It identifies poorly utilized PMs, so that their containers and VMs can be reallocated to reduce energy waste. Using a roulette wheel mechanism, PMs with low resource utilisation have a higher chance of being deleted (unpacked) from the solution. Containers from unpacked PMs get reallocated to existing or new bins by rearrangement heuristics described in Sect. 4.4. Also, [17] describes the custom operator *Merge* used to swap one or two small VMs with a larger one that would fit the same PM to reduce total number of VMs used. This reduces total wasted resources from VM overhead. With *Merge LV* we propose improving the exploitation of the merge custom operator for finding solutions with less VMs used and better overall resource utilisation, by choosing the largest possible VM to fit in the available PM space when replacing smaller VMs with this operator.

5   Experiments and Results

We proposed two new algorithms and compared them against benchmark GGA framework in [17]. FLXGGA is a GGA with only the proposed FLX operator. FLXGGA-BF/LV further includes new Best-Fit and Largest VM (BF/LV) heuristics in the crossover, rearrangement and merge operators of the GGA. To evaluate these algorithms for large scale resource allocation, we performed experiments based on real world datasets. Container resource requirements, VM type list and PM configuration are same as used in [17]. Container list is from AuverGrid trace [12]. We consider a homogeneous PM configuration with total CPU capacity of 13.2 GHz (8 cores) and 16 Gb ram. Energy consumption at full PM utilization is set at 540 KWh [9]. We have 2 sets of VM configurations with varying CPU and memory requirements. One set of 20 VM configurations is based on real-world legacy Amazon EC2 VM configurations, whereas the other set of 10 VM types was synthetically generated randomly [17].

5.1   Test Cases

We experimented with the algorithms on four different test case sizes (500, 1000, 1500 and 5000 containers for allocation), and for each container list size we tested on the two sets of VM types [17], making a total of 8 test cases. Unlike the VM types based on real-world, where CPU and memory capacity of the different types were proportional in comparison to each other, the randomly generated CPU and memory capacities of the synthetic VMs where more irregular. We expected this will create additional challenges for the optimization algorithm, but more importantly should reflect the performance of our algorithm in an environment where VM configurations are non-standard or variable.

5.2   GGA Parameters

All GGA algorithms where run with the same GA settings for each experiment. We set our population size to 100 for the 500 and 1000 test cases, and 200 for the larger test cases involving 1500 and 5000 containers. Elitism is set to 5 individuals. Tournament selection size is 2, and crossover rate is 70%. For our stopping criteria, we set a maximum of 100 generations for the 500 and 1000 test cases, and 200 generations for 1500 and 5000 container test cases. We ran each experiment 40 times and the results reported here are the mean and standard deviation of these 40 runs.

5.3   Experiment Results and Analysis

Our main goal is to find resource allocation with the least energy consumption. Considering that VM overhead accumulate into wasted resources, we also analyse the number of VMs used. Table 1 presents the results on energy consumption for each test-case. In addition, the algorithms are compared with each other by the Wilcoxon rank-sum test with significance level of 0.05. In Table 1, FLXGGA is compared with GGA, and its test results are shown in the column after its energy consumption column, where $+$, $-$ and $=$ indicates that FLXGGA is statistically significantly better than, worse than or comparable with GGA, respectively. FLXGGA-BF/LV is compared with GGA and FLXGGA, and the test results are shown in the last two columns. As shown in the table, both proposed algorithms significantly outperformed GGA in 5 out of 8 test instances. The difference in energy consumption for the smallest test cases involving only 500 containers was quite small between the algorithms, however, we see more significant differences in the large-scale test cases. For example, there is a energy saving of over 1900 Kwh by FLXGGA-BF/LV over the benchmark algorithm in one of our 5000 container test cases, which amounts to being able to shutdown several poorly utilized machines. FLXGGA-BF/LV is the preferred algorithm for large test cases of 1000 containers or more. However, for the smallest test cases of 500 containers, FLXGGA performed as good as GGA on average and better than FLXGGA-BF/LV.

Table 1. Energy Consumption (Kwh) - Mean, Standard Deviation

	Size	GGA	FLXGGA		FLXGGA-BF/LV		
Real world VM types	500	3844.8 ± 1.70	3843.9 ± 1.96	$+$	3850.3 ± 5.76	$-$	$-$
	1000	8035.8 ± 186.40	7838.7 ± 59.37	$+$	7817.7 ± 115.76	$+$	$=$
	1500	12072.3 ± 124.30	11388.6 ± 9.26	$+$	11391.7 ± 84.43	$+$	$=$
	5000	37850.5 ± 378.93	36587.5 ± 219.65	$+$	35935.9 ± 142.02	$+$	$+$
Synthetic VM types	500	3851.6 ± 1.03	3860.1 ± 2.60	$-$	3864.8 ± 3.75	$-$	$-$
	1000	7849.1 ± 3.19	7733.0 ± 183.29	$=$	7646.0 ± 185.16	$=$	$+$
	1500	11423.0 ± 136.02	11378.9 ± 7.78	$+$	11401.2 ± 11.85	$+$	$-$
	5000	35982.2 ± 276.3	36058.2 ± 11.14	$=$	35735.37 ± 161.38	$+$	$+$

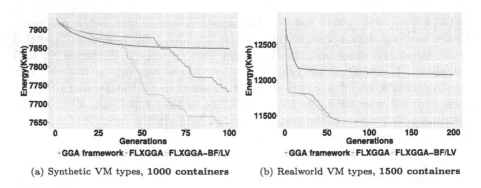

(a) Synthetic VM types, **1000 containers**   (b) Realworld VM types, **1500 containers**

Fig. 2. Convergence curve

Figure 2 presents convergence graphs from two of our test cases. We can see that the new FLX crossover operator is able to help the GGA jump out of local optima and avoid a premature convergence more effectively in both new algorithms compared to the baseline GGA.

To further investigate the performance of the proposed algorithms, we analyse the number of VMs used in the solutions. We can see that the FLXGGA-BF/LV algorithm finds solutions with more than 20% lower number of VMs on the real world data set test cases. This amounts to less wasted resources on VM overhead. Interestingly the number of VMs in use across the algorithms is much closer with the synthetic data set. Due to space constraints we highlight the number of VMs used in two of the real world test cases in Fig. 3. The *largest VM* heuristics (LV) in FLXGGA-BF/LV help with local search for genes with larger VMs, and so we consistently see solutions with lower total VMs used when compared to FLXGGA by itself.

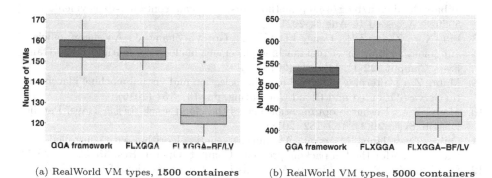

(a) RealWorld VM types, **1500 containers**   (b) RealWorld VM types, **5000 containers**

Fig. 3. Number of VMs used

6   Conclusion

In this paper we proposed a Grouping Genetic Algorithm with a fixed-length crossover designed to improve population diversity and the exploratory ability of the GGA to leap out of local optima in large problem spaces. This crossover operator is also exploitative in the sense that it favors offspring inheriting the chromosome length of the parent with fewer PM bins. The domain specific Best-Fit and Largest VM heuristics were designed to improve local search for good gene features, such as high PM utilization and use of larger VM types in the solution space. The results showed that either of the new algorithms were able to find better solutions than the benchmark algorithm in most of the test cases. For future work, we would like to consider more real world constraints such as container affinity policies, load balancing and other QoS requirements in our algorithm design for the container resource allocation problem.

References

1. Bernstein, D.: Containers and cloud: from LXC to docker to Kubernetes. IEEE Cloud Comput. **1**(3), 81–84 (2014)

2. Falkenauer, E.: A hybrid grouping genetic algorithm for bin packing. J. Heurist. **2**(1), 5–30 (1996)
3. Guerrero, C., Lera, I., Juiz, C.: Genetic algorithm for multi-objective optimization of container allocation in cloud architecture. J. Grid Comput. **16**, 113–135 (2018)
4. Helali, L., Omri, M.N.: A survey of data center consolidation in cloud computing systems. Comput. Sci. Rev. **39** (2021). https://doi.org/10.1016/j.cosrev.2021. 100366
5. Hussein, M.K., Mousa, M.H., Alqarni, M.A.: A placement architecture for a container as a service (CaaS) in a cloud environment. J. Cloud Comput. **8**(1), 1–15 (2019). https://doi.org/10.1186/s13677-019-0131-1
6. Kaewkasi, C., Chuenmuneewong, K.: Improvement of container scheduling for docker using ant colony optimization. In: 2017 9th International Conference on Knowledge and Smart Technology (KST), pp. 254–259 (2017)
7. step method for large-scale container deployment (2020). https://www. alibabacloud.com/blog/4-step-method-for-large-scale-container-deployment_ 596928. Accessed 16 August 2021
8. Liu, X.F., Zhan, Z.H., Deng, J.D., Li, Y., Gu, T., Zhang, J.: An energy efficient ant colony system for virtual machine placement in cloud computing. IEEE Trans. Evol. Comput. **22**(1), 113–128 (2018)
9. Mann, Z.Á.: Interplay of virtual machine selection and virtual machine placement. In: Service-Oriented and Cloud Computing, pp. 137–151 (2016)
10. Mann, Z.Á.: Resource optimization across the cloud stack. IEEE Trans. Parallel Distrib. Syst. **29**(1), 169–182 (2018)
11. Quiroz-Castellanos, M., et al.: A grouping genetic algorithm with controlled gene transmission for the bin packing problem. Comput. Operat. Res. **55**, 52–64 (2015)
12. Shen, S., Van Beek, V., Iosup, A.: Statistical characterization of business-critical workloads hosted in cloud datacenters. In: 15th IEEE/ACM International Symposium on Cluster, Cloud and Grid Computing, pp. 465–474 (2015)
13. Shi, T., Ma, H., Chen, G.: Energy-aware container consolidation based on PSO in cloud data centers. In: IEEE Congress on Evolutionary Computation (CEC), pp. 1–8 (2018)
14. Swarm mode overview (2021). https://docs.docker.com/engine/swarm/. Accessed 16 August 2021
15. Tan, B., Ma, H., Mei, Y.: A NSGA-ii-based approach for service resource allocation in cloud. In: 2017 IEEE Congress on Evolutionary Computation (CEC), pp. 2574–2581 (2017). https://doi.org/10.1109/CEC.2017.7969618
16. Tan, B., Ma, H., Mei, Y.: Novel genetic algorithm with dual chromosome representation for resource allocation in container-based clouds. In: IEEE International Conference on Cloud Computing (CLOUD), pp. 452–456 (2019)
17. Tan, B., Ma, H., Mei, Y.: A group genetic algorithm for resource allocation in container-based clouds. In: Paquete, L., Zarges, C. (eds.) Evolutionary Computation in Combinatorial Optimization, pp. 180–196 (2020)
18. Varasteh, A., Goudarzi, M.: Server consolidation techniques in virtualized data centers: a survey. IEEE Syst. J. **11**(2), 772–783 (2017)
19. Zhang, C., Wang, Y., Wu, H., Guo, H.: An energy-aware host resource management framework for two-tier virtualized cloud data centers. IEEE Access **9**, 3526–3544 (2021)
20. Zhang, R., Zhong, A.m., Dong, B., Tian, F., Li, R.: Container-VM-PM architecture: a novel architecture for docker container placement. In: Cloud Computing - CLOUD 2018, pp. 128–140 (2018)

Transfer Learning for Autonomous Recognition of Swarm Behaviour in UGVs

Shadi Abpeikar[(⊠)], Kathryn Kasmarik, Phi Vu Tran, and Matt Garratt

School of Engineering and IT, UNSW Canberra, Canberra, Australia
s.abpeikar@adfa.edu.au

Abstract. Recent work has developed value functions that can recognize emergent swarming behaviour and distinguish it from random behaviour. To date, this work has been done in point-mass swarm simulations. This paper proposes a transfer learning approach that can improve the performance of a value system for recognising swarming in simulated and real robots from limited data without replicating the training. A source value function is trained on human-labelled point-mass boid data. A target tree is trained on a small amount of new domain specific data. It can recognise swarm behaviour of diverse agents not used in the original training. We test the value function on homogeneous swarms of simulated and real robots. Results show that this value function can detect swarming in at least 89% of cases.

Keywords: Swarm robotics · Rule engine · Transfer learning · Unmanned ground vehicle · Decision tree

1 Introduction

Due to the increased use of autonomous robot swarms in industries, many computerised systems have been designed to work with them [1]. In future, we envisage businesses will want to roll out robot swarms from a truck and dispatch them in the environment to do their tasks of sensing, exploration, or navigation. A first step to self-positioning robots in a way they can maintain their swarm behaviour is to recognise swarm behaviour continuously. The work in this paper focuses on this fundamental aspect of automatic swarm behaviour recognition. The first computer-based system of autonomous swarms used three simple rules of cohesion, separation, and alignment [2]. This model is known as Reynolds' "boids" model, where "boid" refers to "bird androids". Extensions to Reynolds' boid model, called boid guidance algorithms (BGAs) [3], have also been introduced. BGAs contain further rules, which enable them to control unmanned ground and aerial vehicles, to stay within operating conditions boundaries, such as speed and turn rate. Recognising swarm behaviour is very challenging due to the emergent property of the behaviour, and wide variety of movement characteristics according to the physical robot type, environments, and application. To achieve this, a generic value system is required that can distinguish structured behaviour from random behaviour, without the need to precisely define swarm-specific characteristics. Various approaches have been

© Springer Nature Switzerland AG 2022
G. Long et al. (Eds.): AI 2021, LNAI 13151, pp. 531–542, 2022.
https://doi.org/10.1007/978-3-030-97546-3_43

proposed for this, including unsupervised and supervised value systems [4, 5]. However, to date, they have been applied on boid point-mass simulations. In addition, existing approaches have required up to 10 min of movement data to decide whether swarming is occurring.

This paper proposes a novel rule-based value function that can recognise swarming in homogeneous swarms of simulated and real Unmanned Ground Vehicles (UGVs) from limited data. The value function is based on a pruned decision tree classification method trained on human labelled point-mass boid data. Transfer learning is applied on this rule engine to make it applicable in a new domain. We test the value function on swarms of point-mass, simulated and real robots. UGVs have different movement properties to boid simulations as they are constrained by the manoeuvrability of the physical robot. We designed BGAs for controlling homogeneous swarms of Pioneer3DX simulated in CoppeliaSim[1], as well as swarms of real Turtlebot robots. This permits us to examine the impact of the specific control algorithm on detection performance. This value function, by the aide of transfer learning, can detect swarming in at least 89% of cases.

The remainder of this paper is organized as follows: Sect. 2 presents background and related work. Section 3 describes our approach to transfer swarm recognition learning from one domain to another. Section 4 describes our experimental setup and the results. We conclude in Sect. 5 and examine directions for future work.

2 Background and Related Work

2.1 Transfer Learning and Swarm Robotics

Intelligent systems can benefit from transfer learning (TL) because it permits a system to evolve to perform in similar situations, model manipulation and prediction of new emerging conditions [6, 7]. TL is an approach which can handle changes in operating conditions without the need and cost associated with data generation, model definition and analysis. It permits application of learning in situations similar to those on which the system was trained before [8].

With the rapid growth in systems for learning and evolving swarm behaviours, and the diversity of systems that can exhibit such behaviours, TL has a role to play. A TL approach has previously been used [9] on a Particle Swarm Optimization (PSO) to reduce the learning time for optimization of the robot's gaits over a wide variety of terrains. Also, TL on PSO was applied in groups of robots [10] to improve decision making in uncertain environments, by knowledge transferring from certain environments. Venturini et al. [11], applied TL on reinforcement learning (RL) to control a swarm of drones. Iuzzolino et al. [12] provide an approach to autonomous navigation of robots in real environments, while training is done by simulation data. Nguyen et al. [13], applied TL on RL to achieve collision-free navigation of groups of robots in an unknown indoor environment.

One common area of applying transfer learning is on decision trees [14–16]. The work in this paper applies TL to a decision-tree knowledge base to recognise swarming and not-swarming behaviour of robots. The next section provides background on the definition of swarming, and the specific BGAs used in this paper.

---

[1] https://www.coppeliarobotics.com/.

2.2 The Boid Algorithm

The basic Reynolds' boid model [2] uses three rules. Each rule of cohesion, alignment, and separation, directs movement towards the average position of neighbouring agents within a radius R_c, aligning with them in radius R_a, and avoiding collisions in radius R_s, respectively. This leads to cohesion, alignment and separation forces, as c_t^i, a_t^i, s_t^i. These forces will be applied to agents in the neighborhoods of corresponding radiuses, denoted N_c, N_a, and N_s. Finally, for a group of N agents $A^1, A^2, A^3 \ldots A^N$, each agent A^i at time t has a position point, x_t^i, and a velocity vector, v_t^i, which is updated as Eq. (1). In this equation, weights W_c, W_a and W_s strengthen or weaken the corresponding force.

$$v_{t+1}^i = v_t^i + W_c c_t^i + W_a a_t^i + W_s s_t^i \tag{1}$$

The three forces of c_t^i, a_t^i, s_t^i are also computed by Eqs. (2), (3), and (4), respectively, while x_t^k is the current position of boid k, and $k \in \{1, \ldots, N\}$.

$$\overrightarrow{C_t^i} = \frac{\sum_k x_t^k}{|(N_c)_i^t|}, \; C_t^i = \overrightarrow{C_t^i} - x_t^i \tag{2}$$

$$a_t^i = \frac{\sum_k V_t^k}{|(N_a)_i^t|} \tag{3}$$

$$\overrightarrow{S_i^i} = \frac{\sum_k x_t^k}{|(N_s)_i^t|}, \; S_i^i = x_i^i - \overrightarrow{S_i^i} \tag{4}$$

Then after updating the velocity the position of each agent is updated as:

$$x_{t+1}^i = x_t^i + v_{t+1}^i \tag{5}$$

2.3 Boid Guidance Algorithms

Simulated Swarm of Pioneer Robots. In this paper we simulate a swarm of Pioneer robots using Eq. (6). This equation extends Eq. (1) with a normal force weight of w_t^k, keeping robots away from any detected walls. w_t^k is computed the same as the separation force of Eq. (4), but based on the position of walls ($u = 4$) and robots.

$$v_{t+1}^i = v_t^i + W_c c_t^i + W_a a_t^i + W_s s_t^i + W_s \sum_u w_t^u \tag{6}$$

Then the actual wheel updates are done to change orientation, δ as in Eq. (7). In this equation θ_T is the target orientation and θ_t is the current orientation.

$$\delta = (\theta_T - \theta_t + 3\pi) mod(2\pi) - \pi \tag{7}$$

δ is then scaled by the ratio of the axel length to the wheel diameter. If the resulting δ is large (more than $\pm 90°$), only the robot's orientation is adjusted as Eq. (8). If it is small, the robot is allowed to move forward while turning as Eq. (9). Forward movement is inversely proportional to the size of δ.

$$r_{(t+1)}^{left} = -\frac{\delta}{2} \ and \ r_{(t+1)}^{left} = \frac{\delta}{2} \tag{8}$$

$$r_{(t+1)}^{left} = r_0\left(\frac{\pi - \delta}{\pi}\right) - \frac{\delta}{2} \ and \ r_{(t+1)}^{right} = r_0\left(\frac{\pi - \delta}{\pi}\right) + \frac{\delta}{2} \tag{9}$$

Real Swarm of Turtlebots. Turtlebots have a body-fixed coordinate system C_{xy} connected to an inertial Cartesian frame O_{xy}, as presented in Fig. 1. In this figure, (x_G, y_G) and (x_C, y_C) are the Cartesian coordinates of the center of mass of the robot and intersection point C in the middle of the front axle, respectively. θ indicates the rotational heading angle with respect to the O-X axis. ω_r and ω_l denote as the right and left wheel speeds, respectively. When $\omega_r = \omega_l$, the robot only moves forward following the heading direction. In contrast, when $\omega_r = -\omega_l$ are applied to the wheels, the robot only turns around the z axis. In general, the angular velocities given to the right and left wheels are different so the robot can simultaneously rotate and translate in the horizontal plane. The robot's linear and angular velocities (V, ω) can be calculated using the angular speeds of the two wheels, as in Eq. (10). In this equation, R represents the wheel radius, and d is the relative distance between point G and point H. The alignment, cohesion, and separation forces on the x and y axes were transformed into the linear and angular velocities via the Robot Operation System (ROS).

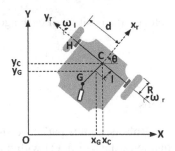

Fig. 1. Schematic of the Turtlebot configuration space

$$-\begin{bmatrix} V \\ \omega \end{bmatrix} = \begin{bmatrix} \frac{R}{2} & \frac{R}{2} \\ \frac{R}{2d} & \frac{-R}{2d} \end{bmatrix} \begin{bmatrix} \omega_r \\ \omega_l \end{bmatrix} \tag{10}$$

2.4   Swarm Recognition

Existing work has shown that various supervised learning algorithms can be used to recognise swarming [4]. In addition, these approaches require less time and less data than unsupervised approaches [5] used for the same purpose [4]. Supervised approaches suitable for swarm recognition include Decision Trees (DTs) [17], Naïve Bayes (NB) [18], Support Vector Machines (SVM) [19], Bayesian Neural Networks (BNNs) [20], Levenberg Neural Networks (LNNs) [20], and Gradient Neural Network (GNNs) [20]. Existing work has suggested that decision tree learning has the best performance for swarm recognition [4]. However, it is not clear that a trained decision tree will be fast or accurate when dealing with agents using BGAs that were not used to train the tree. This is the topic of this paper.

3 Transfer Learning for Autonomous Recognition of Swarming

This section outlines our approach of transfer learning from a supervised swarm recognition system trained on point-mass data to create a system that can better recognise real swarming robots. Our proposed approach has three steps:

(1) Train a decision tree using a large human-labelled dataset with a wide range of swarming and not-swarming behaviours.
(2) Prune the tree without loss of accuracy.
(3) Partially re-grow the tree with a small amount of labelled data from the new domain.

The decision tree of step (1) is trained with human labelled data of swarm behaviour recognition [21]. It achieves the highest accuracy in less than ten seconds comparing to neural networks, support vector machines, and Naïve Bayes, as examined in [4]. This decision tree is then pruned until the level there is no loss of accuracy, based on the pruning method which is mentioned by Utgoff et al., in [22]. Pruning aims to attain a smaller set of if-then rules. The antecedent of this rule engine works with features of $F_i \in \left[V_{x_t^i}, V_{y_t^i}, W_s.\left(s_t^i\right)_x, W_s.\left(s_t^i\right)_y, W_a.\left(a_t^i\right)_x, W_a.\left(a_t^i\right)_y, W_c.\left(c_t^i\right)_x, W_c.\left(c_t^i\right)_y, N_{ca_t^i}, N_{s_t^i} \right]$, which the consequent decides on swarming or not-swarming. To expand the ability of this rule engine in recognising swarm behaviours of agents using BGAs, a transfer learning approach is applied in step (3). In transfer learning, a new sample with features F_i extracted from BGA algorithms is fed to the source rule engine of boids. For each sample, the routes with an inconsistent decision (line 1.2 of Algorithm 1), are extended one level deeper as a partial re-grow to resolve this inconsistency [23]. To do this, each sample whose behaviour is correctly recognized by this rule will be assigned to a Matched Set, while the ones which face inconsistency will be assigned to a Not Matched Set. Consider the final node of this inconsistent route works on a specific feature F_i'. Then the maximum and minimum values of F_i' in both "Matched Set" and "Not Matched Set" are found to provide the ranges of F_i' in each of these sets (line 1.4). Then a new level will be added to the original decision tree, while the split is based on F_i' and the middle value of the intersection set of the ranges discussed above. By this approach, the updated rule engine re-grow partially, so that it is one level deeper than the source rule engine. This is called the target rule engine. An example of this one level re-growing is presented in Fig. 2.

Algorithm 1: Evolution from source to target tree for swarm recognition

Input: Pruned if-then rule engine (e.g.: as per Fig 5) as the source tree.

Output: Updated if-then rule engine as the target tree.

1.   For each scenario find the matching rule in the source tree, as rule k

   1.1.   Recognise the behaviour based on the rule k

   1.2.   If the recognised behaviour is not correct (comparing to the nature of the behaviour)

      1.2.1.   Keep this sample in the Not Matched Set "NMS"

   1.3.   Else

      1.3.1.   Keep this sample in Matched Set "MS"

   1.4.   For current feature F_i', find the upper and lower bound value of F_i' regarding to: "NMS"" as UB_{NMS_i} and LB_{NMS_i}, and "MS" as UB_{MS_i} and LB_{MS_i}

   1.5.   Find range of F_i' in $\left[LB_{MS_i}, UB_{MS_i}\right] \cap \left[LB_{NMS_i}, UB_{NMS_i}\right]$ as $[L, U]$

   1.6.   Split rule k based on the middle of the $[L, U]$, and update the source if-then rule

2.   Return the target rule engine

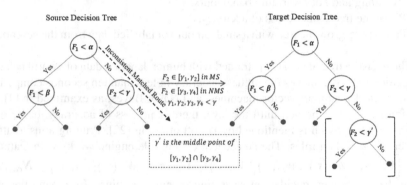

Fig. 2. An example of partially re-growing (The new level is put inside red brackets) (Color figure online)

4   Experimental Study

This section contains three experiments, which make use of the data sets of Sect. 4.1.

4.1   Data Sets

Three datasets are used in this section, (1) a point-mass boid movement data set; (2) data collected from simulated robots; and (3) data collected from real robots.

Point Mass Data. It has been generated from 16 simulations of 200 boids moving in a 2000 × 2000 pixels open area with wrap-around boundaries [5]. It is labelled by 90 participants as either swarming or not-swarming via an online survey [24]. For each simulation, the boid behavioral values were extracted in the form of Eq. (11). This results in 4, 800, 000 samples, and 10 features, available online [21].

$$\left[V_{x_t}^i, V_{y_t}^i, W_s \cdot \left(s_t^i\right)_x, W_s \cdot \left(s_t^i\right)_y, W_a \cdot \left(a_t^i\right)_x, W_a \cdot \left(a_t^i\right)_y, W_c \cdot \left(c_t^i\right)_x, W_c \cdot \left(c_t^i\right)_y, N_{ca_t}^i, N_{s_t}^i \right]$$
(11)

Simulated Swarm of Pioneer3DX Robots. Pioneer3DX robots are small two-wheeled robots simulated by equipping with 16 ultrasonic sensors to provide range and bearing information of other robots and walls. We used 8 robots in a 20×20 m open space. Two swarming and two not-swarming scenarios, designed to be as similar as possible to two of the point-mass scenarios labelled by humans. Each simulation was run for 10 min (approximately 12,000 simulation time steps). While the simulations were running, we collected the raw data shown in Eq. (11), producing datasets of size $12,000 \times 8 = 96,000$ instances for all eight robots at each simulation. The boid parameters for the simulated Pioneer3DX robots are shown in Table 1.

Real Swarm of Turtlebots. Turtlebot Burger3 is a small, affordable, programmable, intelligent, and ROS-based mobile robot platform. The swarming behaviour is generated as described in Sect. 2.3. A random behaviour is generated using only the separation rule to prevent robots colliding. All robots' behaviours are captured by the VICON Tracker system and collected in each robot every 0.02s. Each test will be run at least 4 minutes to achieve more than 12,000 data points. The boid parameter values for the Turtlebots are shown in Table 1.

Table 1. Simulated Pioneer3DX and real Turtlebot robot swarm parameters

Robots	Pioneer3DX		Turtlebot	
Parameter	Swarm	Random	Swarm	Random
Scenario	**1 2**	**1 2**	**1**	**1**
r_0	0.2 0.0	0.2 0.2	0.15	0.15
W_a	1.0 1.0	1.0 1.2	0.5	0.0
W_c	0.1 0.1	0.0 0.1	0.23	0.0
W_s	1.2 1.5	1.2 1.2	1.1	1.1
W_w	1.1 1.1	1.1 1.0	1.1	1.1
R_{ac}	2.0 2.0	2.0 2.0	1.5	1.5
R_s	1.0 1.0	1.0 2.0	0.65	0.65

4.2 Experiment 1: Recognition of Robot Swarms Using Different BGAs

The aim of this experiment is to determine the recognition performance of a supervised learner trained with point-mass data, tested on simulated and real robot data. We used the labelled point-mass data to train 6 different supervised learning algorithms. Then, the six trained classifiers were tested for recognizing swarming in three datasets of Sect. 4.1. The performance of the six classifiers on each of the datasets is presented in Fig. 3. Moreover, their speed statistics are provided in Table 2. Based on both accuracy and the processing time, we conclude that the DT appears to be the most reliable approach for detecting swarming, even in certain cases where training and testing sets are different. However, it becomes less reliable for detecting swarming in real robots controlled by a different BGA.

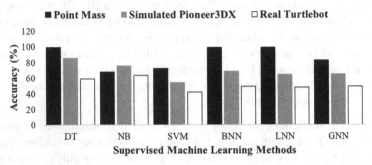

Fig. 3. Classification accuracy of supervised learning methods, trained with the Point-Mass boid data and tested for recognising Point Mass boids, and swarms of simulated and real robots

Table 2. Speed results of Fig. 3 (seconds)

	DT	NB	SVM	BNN	LNN	GNN
Point Mass	9.73	200	>300	193	38.26	37.84
Simulated Pineer3DX	1.42	>300	>300	14.33	4.22	7.84
Real Turtlebot	0.57	>300	>300	16.65	5.72	15.42

The main weakness of the DT tested above is that it results in many rules. Thus, while the fastest of the techniques examined, it is still relatively slow to accurately detect swarming (approx. 10 s). This is because the generated rule set of the DT on this dataset leads to more than 1000 rules. One way to resolve this problem is to prune the decision tree [22]. Pruning the tree means cutting a decision tree to reach a shallower tree without loss of accuracy [22]. This is examined in the next experiment.

4.3   Experiment 2: Effect of Pruning a Trained Decision Tree

The aim of this experiment is to examine whether a DT trained in swarm recognition can be pruned without loss of accuracy. To do this the accuracy of decision trees pruned at each of the 782 levels is measured. As shown in Fig. 4, the accuracy of the decision tree changes smoothly until the prune in level 758, which still has an accuracy around 96.59%. Then a significant reduction in accuracy occurs in prunes after level 758.

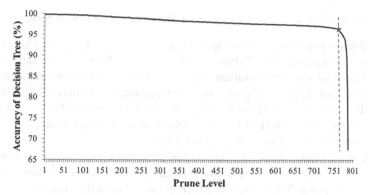

Fig. 4. Accuracy of the decision tree with different pruning levels.

The decision tree pruned at level 758 has a depth of 24, and the extracted if-then rules leads to 73 rules as presented in Fig. 5. In this rule engine, 28 rules consequence in Swarming, and 45 rules consequence in Not-Swarming.

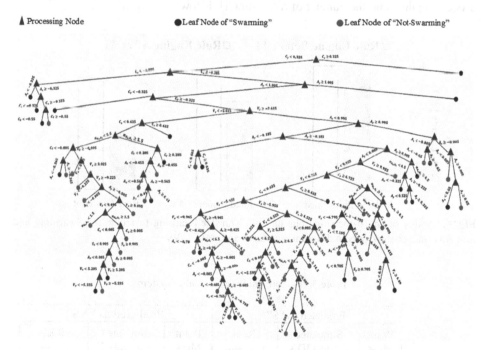

Fig. 5. Rules extracted from the pruned decision tree

4.4   Experiment 3: Transfer Learning for Recognition of Robot Swarms

The aim of this experiment is to investigate the performance of TL applied to a pruned DT trained for swarm recognition. Following Algorithm 1 in Sect. 3 the pruned DT trained on point-mass data was further trained on small amounts of simulated Pioneer3DX, and real Turtlebot data. These were then tested for recognizing swarms of these UGVs. The results of Fig. 6 shows that TL increases the accuracy of a pruned DT trained on point-mass data recognising simulated Pioneer3DX and real Turtlebots swarming. It does not affect the recognition accuracy on point mass data.

Beside these improved accuracies, one of the main concerns in designing such a value function, is when the behavior is not swarming, but the value function, predicts the behavior as swarming. This is the worst scenario as it means that useless configurations are being predicted as useful. This is called a False Positive rate in F-Score measurement. The F-Score measurements of the experiments of Fig. 6 is presented in Table 3, while the false positive rates (FP) are mentioned in bold, "S" refers to Swarming and "NS" refers to Not-Swarming. As shown in this table, the FP rate is reasonably low, which provides more confidence for the value function. Moreover, the speed statics of the rule engine after applying the transfer learning are provided in Table 4. As it is presented, processing time and the number of rules after TL is low.

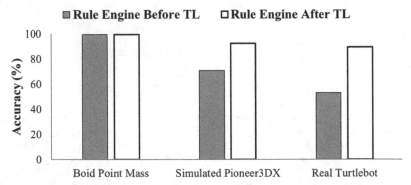

Fig. 6. Ability of the if-then rule engine with Transfer Learning to recognize Swarming and Not-Swarming behaviours in different simulated and real UGVs

Table 3. F-score values of the value system

	Predicted as "S"			Predicted as "NS"		
	Point Mass	Simulated Pioneer3DX	Real Turtlebot	Point Mass	Simulated Pioneer3DX	Real Turtlebot
Real "S"	49.25	47.01	49.12	0.75	2.99	0.78
Real "NS"	**0.01**	**4.68**	**9.86**	49.99	45.32	40.14

Table 4. Speed statistics and updated rules of transfer learning

	Time (s)	Rules no. before TL	Rules no. after TL
Boid Point Mass	0.05		73
Simulated Pioneer3DX	2.81	73	78
Real Turtlebot	2.59		86

5 Conclusion and Future Work

One of the steps of designing a system that can automatically recognise swarm behaviour, is to design a value function. In this paper a value function is designed, which works based on an if-then rule engine. This rule engine is extracted from a pruned decision tree, that was trained by human labelled point-mass flocking data. Moreover, this rule engine can recognize swarm behaviour of UGVs of Pioneer3DX and Turtlebot to a high accuracy, by the aide of transfer learning. In future, we will embed this supervised value function with the unsupervised one into an evolutionary developmental framework (such as [5]) to tune swarm behaviours on real robots, by evaluating a wider range of swarming and not-swarming behaviours. Also, we aim to experiment to achieve transfer learning of swarm behaviour recognition in different environments, and with other types of robots, in future.

References

1. Kolling, A., et al.: human interaction with robot swarms: a survey. IEEE Trans. Hum. Mach. Syst. **46**(1), 9–26 (2016)
2. Reynolds, C.W.: Flocks, herds, and schools: a distributed behavioral model. Comput. Graph. **21**(4), 25–34 (1987)
3. Clark, J.B., Jacques, D.R.: Flight test results for UAVs using boid guidance algorithms. Conf. Syst. Eng. Res. **8**, 232–238 (2012)
4. Kasmarik, K., Abpeikar, S., Khan, M.M., Khattab, N., Barlow, M., Garratt, M.: Autonomous recognition of collective behaviour in robot swarms. In: Gallagher, M., Moustafa, N., Lakshika, E. (eds.) AI 2020. LNCS (LNAI), vol. 12576, pp. 281–293. Springer, Cham (2020). https://doi.org/10.1007/978-3-030-64984-5_22
5. Khan, M.M., Kasmarik, K., Barlow, M.: Autonomous detection of collective behaviours in swarms. Swarm Evol. Comput. **57,** 100715 (2020)
6. Elgibreen, H., Aksoy, M.S.: RULES-IT: incremental transfer learning with RULES family. Front. Comp. Sci. **8**(4), 537–562 (2014). https://doi.org/10.1007/s11704-014-3297-1
7. Lu, J., et al.: Transfer learning using computational intelligence: a survey. Knowl.-Based Syst. **80**, 14–23 (2015)
8. Weiss, K., Khoshgoftaar, T.M., Wang, D.: A survey of transfer learning. J. Big Data **3**(1), 1–40 (2016). https://doi.org/10.1186/s40537-016-0043-6
9. Degrave, J., et al.: Transfer learning of gaits on a quadrupedal robot. Adapt. Behav. **23**(2), 69–82 (2015)
10. Atyabi, A., Powers, D.M.: Cooperative area extension of PSO-transfer learning vs. uncertainty in a simulated swarm robotics. In: International Conference on Informatics in Control, Automation and Robotics. SCITEPRESS (2013)

11. Venturini, F., et al.: Distributed reinforcement learning for flexible UAV swarm control with transfer learning capabilities. In: Proceedings of the 6th ACM Workshop on Micro Aerial Vehicle Networks, Systems, and Applications. Association for Computing Machinery: Toronto, Ontario, Canada. p. Article 10 (2020)

12. Iuzzolino, M.L., Walker, M.E., Szafir, D.: Virtual-to-real-world transfer learning for robots on wilderness trails. In: 2018 IEEE/RSJ International Conference on Intelligent Robots and Systems (IROS) (2018)

13. Nguyen, T.T., Hatua, A., Sung, A.H.: Cumulative training and transfer learning for multi-robots collision-free navigation problems. In: 2019 IEEE 10th Annual Ubiquitous Computing, Electronics & Mobile Communication Conference (UEMCON) (2019)

14. won Lee, J., Giraud-Carrier, C.: Transfer learning in decision trees. In: 2007 International Joint Conference on Neural Networks. IEEE (2007)

15. Minvielle, L., et al.: Transfer learning on decision tree with class imbalance. In: 2019 IEEE 31st International Conference on Tools with Artificial Intelligence (ICTAI). IEEE (2019)

16. Hlynsson, H.: Transfer learning using the minimum description length principle with a decision tree application (2007)

17. Parvin, H., MirnabiBaboli, M., Alinejad-Rokny, H.: Proposing a classifier ensemble framework based on classifier selection and decision tree. Eng. Appl. Artif. Intell. **37**, 34–42 (2015)

18. Kuncheva, L.I.: On the optimality of Naive Bayes with dependent binary features. Pattern Recogn. Lett. **27**(7), 830–837 (2006)

19. Abe, S.: Support Vector Machines for Pattern Classification, Second Edition. Support Vector Machines for Pattern Classification, Second Edition, pp. 1–471 (2010)

20. Mukherjee, I., Routroy, S.: Comparing the performance of neural networks developed by using Levenberg-Marquardt and Quasi-Newton with the gradient descent algorithm for modelling a multiple response grinding process. Expert Syst. Appl. **39**(3), 2397–2407 (2012)

21. Abpeikar, S., et al.: Swarm Behaviour Dataset on UCI Data Repository. UCI Data Repository: UCI Data Repository (2020)

22. Utgoff, P.E., Berkman, N.C., Clouse, J.A.: Decision tree induction based on efficient tree restructuring. Mach. Learn. **29**(1), 5–44 (1997)

23. Segev, N., et al.: Learn on source, refine on target: a model transfer learning framework with random forests. IEEE Trans. Pattern Anal. Mach. Intell. **39**, 1811–1824 (2017)

24. Abpeikar, S., et al.: Human Perception of Swarming (Online Survey) (2019). https://unsw-swarm-survey.netlify.com/

Multivariate Ordinal Patterns for Symmetry Approximation in Dynamic Probabilistic Relational Models

Nils Finke[1]($\boxtimes$), Ralf Möller[1], and Marisa Mohr[1,2]

[1] Institute of Information Systems, University of Lübeck, Lübeck, Germany
{finke,moeller,mohr}@ifis.uni-luebeck.de
[2] inovex GmbH, Hamburg, Germany

Abstract. Exploiting symmetries is an important topic to obtain sparse (lifted) representations, reduce complexity and achieve good performance in dynamic probabilistic relational models (DPRMs). DPRMs factorise a full joint probability distribution by encoding multivariate time series through a set of conditionally dependent random variables. As obtaining exact symmetries throughout multivariate time series is often not realistic in real-world contexts and counteracts lifted representations, we propose to approximate the multivariate time series with a symbolisation scheme that encodes the overarching trend in up and down movements. In this work, we introduce MOP4SA, an approach for the approximation of symmetries based on multivariate ordinal pattern encodings and spectral clustering. Understanding symmetrical behaviour has several benefits that we evaluate in two use cases. We use MOP4SA (a) to detect structures in model symmetries over time, and (b) to avoid model splits and groundings in DPRMs.

Keywords: Symmetry · Multivariate time series · Multivariate ordinal pattern · Relational models · Lifting

1 Introduction

Exploiting *symmetries* is key for a wide variety of different challenges in artificial intelligence in general, e.g., discussed in [1,7,21], as well as in dynamic probabilistic relational models (DPRMs[1]) in particular. Primarily in DPRMs, entities of a model that have similar or approximately similar, also called *symmetric*, behaviour, are treated together as a single entity, which is called *lifting*, to allow a sparse representation of the model while also allowing efficient inference [8]. DPRMs are usually factorised w.r.t. a full joint probability distribution by exploiting (conditional) independencies between random variables (randvars) that evolve over time. As such, DPRMs encode multivariate time series data

---

[1] Pronounced *deeper models*.

N. Finke and M. Mohr—Contributed equally to this work.

G. Long et al. (Eds.): AI 2021, LNAI 13151, pp. 543–555, 2022.
https://doi.org/10.1007/978-3-030-97546-3_44

through a set of dependent randvars. Since a DPRM encodes a probability distribution for sets of entities that all behave the same, a major challenge is to identify those sets of entities with symmetrical behaviour. Detecting such symmetrical behaviour in time series in an uncertain multivariate temporal setting is only partly solved in research yet and even more complex in DPRMs.

The notion of recurrence and symmetry of time series has indeed been discussed extensively in the literature. However, finding symmetries in time series in the context of DPRMs has particular requirements and has not yet been investigated to the necessary extent. Finding symmetries in context of DPRMs refers to finding symmetries in observations for sets of entities as realisations of a common randvar. Thus, the direct search for similarity is computationally intensive due to the high dimensionality of the time series itself, and additionally complex due to many entities represented in a lifted model. While the detection of exact symmetric behaviour, i.e., two or more entities having exactly the same behaviour, is not realistic, often approximately symmetric behaviour with a bounded error is desired, i.e., the behaviour of several entities is approximately the same over time. In this case, shape-based rather than value-based similarity measures are of interest, i.e., measures that focus on the overarching behaviour as the general up and down movements in a time series. Ordinal patterns, encoding up and downs, are the basis for symmetry approximation in DPRMs, which we introduce in [9] for the univariate case. As many real-world applications deal with multiple variables that exhibit a high degree of interdependence, the approach of the univariate case must be adapted.

In this work we use *Multivariate Ordinal Pattern* introduced by Mohr et al. [14] to extend *Symmetry Approximation* to the multivariate case, which we call MOP4SA for short. Motivated by examples from a logistics application, we show that approximating multivariate symmetries is key for different challenges in DPRMs. More specifically, we show that MOP4SA is beneficial (a) for the detection of changes in model symmetry structures, and (b) to avoid model splits caused by evidence that can slowly ground a lifted model over time.

2   Preliminaries and Related Work

This section introduces DPRMs, and describes its connection to multivariate time series and available symmetry approximation approaches.

2.1   Characteristics of Probabilistic Dynamic Relational Models

DPRMs combine relational logic with factor graphs, using logical variables (logvars) as parameters for randvars (parameterized randvar, or PRV for short) [10,18]. PRVs compactly represent sets of randvars that are considered indistinguishable without further evidence, called *lifting*. To represent independent relations, PRVs are linked by a parametric factors (parfactor) to compactly encode the full joint distribution of the DPRM. Like most dynamic model formalisms, DPRMs use two static parameterized models (PRMs) to describe how a model

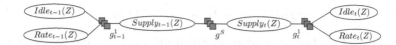

Fig. 1. Two-slice parameterized probabilistic model.

changes from one time step $t \in \{1, \ldots, T\}$ with $T \in \mathbb{N}$ to the next $t+1$. A DPRM encodes a sequential dimension by a pair of PRMs, one representing an initial time step and the other representing how the model transitions from one time step to the next. They follow the same idea as dynamic Bayesian networks with an initial model and a copy pattern for further time steps. DPRMs are based on the first-order Markov assumption, i.e., randvars from each time slice t depend only on randvars from the preceding time slice $t-1$. DPRMs model a stationary process, i.e., changes from one time step to the next follow the same distribution. Semantics of a DPRM are given by instantiating a DPRM for a given number of time steps, followed by grounding and building a full joint distribution [20].

Figure 1 shows a DPRM illustrating certain aspects of seaborne transportation. Variable nodes (ellipses) correspond to PRVs, factor nodes (boxes) to parfactors. Edges between factor and variable nodes denote relations between PRVs, encoded in parfactors. The parfactor g^S denotes a so-called inter-slice parfactor that separates the past from the present. The submodel on the left and the one on the right of this inter-slice parfactor are duplicates of each other, with the one on the left referring to time step $t-1$ and the one on the right referring to time step t. Parfactors reference time-indexed PRVs, namely $Idle_t(Z)$, $Rate_t(Z)$ and $Supply_t(Z)$ with ranges values such as $\{high, medium, low\}$, built from randvar names $\mathbf{R} = \{Idle, Rate, Supply\}$ and the logvar name $\mathbf{L} = \{Z\}$. Thus, intuitively a PRV represents multiple entities of the same type represented through the logvar, e.g., supply within zones $Z \in \{z_1, z_2, \ldots, z_n\}$. Seaborne transportation is subject to supply chain, i.e., vessels head towards zones Z with supply to load cargo. Certain zones around the globe are of greater interest due to higher freight rates ($Rate_t(Z)$), a fee per ton, paid to transport cargoes. If zones are overcrowded, idle time ($Idle_t(Z)$) can occur, affecting the overall vessel schedule. In context of the shipping application, an example query for time step $t = 10$, such as $P(Rate_{10}(z_1) \mid Supply_{10}(z_2) = high, Supply_{10}(z_3) = high)$, contains a set of observations $Supply_{10}(z_2) = high$ and $Supply_{10}(z_3) = high$ as evidence.

2.2 From DPRMs to Time Series

In an DPRM, (real-valued) random variables observed over time are considered as time series. Let Ω be a set containing all possible states of the dynamical system. A sequence of random variables, all defined on the same probability space is called a *stochastic process*. For real-valued random variables, a stochastic process is a function $X : \Omega \times \mathbb{N} \to \mathbb{R}$, where $X(\omega, t) := X_t(w)$ depending on both, coincidence and time. Over time, the individual variables $X_t(\omega)$ of this stochastic process are observed, so-called realisations. The sequence of realisations is called *time series*. With the formalism from above and fixing of some $\omega \in \Omega$, a time series is given by

$$(X_1(\omega), X_2(\omega), X_3(\omega), \dots) = (x_t)_{t \in \mathbb{N}}. \tag{1}$$

In the case $x_t \in \mathbb{R}$ the time series is called univariate, while in the case $x_t \in \mathbb{R}^m$ it is called multivariate. In the following, we focus on multivariate time series $((x_t^i)_{i=1}^m)_{t=1}^T$ as the result of observations for entities encoded through the PRVs of the model. In the context of seaborne transportation, the parfactor g_t^1 holds PRVs $Supply_t(Z)$, $Idle_t(Z)$ and $Rate_t(Z)$ for entities $z \in \mathcal{D}(Z)$, i.e., with evidence over time $t = 1, \dots, T$ the parfactor g_t^1 depicts the multivariate time series with $m = 3$ variables.

2.3   Related Work on the Symmetry Approximation in Time Series

The notion of similarity and symmetry in a set of time series has often been discussed in the literature [2,11,12]. In general, approaches for finding similarities in a set of time series are either (a) value-based, or (b) symbol-based.

Value-based approaches compare the observed values of time series. By comparing the value of each point x_t, $t = 1, \dots, T$ in a time series X with the values of each other point $y_{t'}$, $t' = 1, \dots, T'$ in another time series Y (warping), they are able to include shifts and frequencies. Popular algorithms such as dynamic time warping (DTW) [13] or matrix profile [22] are discussed, e.g., in [12]. As DPRMs encode interdependencies between multiple variables, respective multivariate procedures should be used to assess similarities. The first dependent multivariate dynamic time warping (DMDTW) approach is reported by Petitjean et al. [17], in which the authors treat a multivariate time series with all its m interdependencies as a whole. The flexibility of warping in value-based approaches leads to a high computational effort and is therefore unusable for large amounts of data. Although there are several extensions to improve runtime [19], the use of dimensionality reduction is inevitable in context of DPRMs.

For dimensionality reduction, *symbol-based* approaches encode the time series observations as sequences of symbolic abstractions that match with the shape or structure of the time series. Since DPRMs encode discrete values, depending on the degree for discretisation, symbol-based approaches are preferred as they allow for discretisation directly. As far as research is concerned, there are two general ways of symbolisation. On the one hand, *classical symbolisation* partitions the data range according to specified mapping rules in order to encode a numerical time series into a sequence of discrete symbols. A corresponding and well-know algorithm is Symbolic Aggregate ApproXimation (SAX) introduced by Chiu et al. [6]. On the other hand, as introduced by Bandt and Pompe [3] *ordinal pattern symbolisation* encodes the total order between two or more neighbours ($x < y$ or $x > y$) into so-called ordinal symbols ($(0, 1)$ or $(1, 0)$). In particular, this approach is independent of the type of time series and its data range. Further advantages of the ordinal approach compared to the classical approach are discussed in [14]. Mohr et al. [14] extend univariate ordinal patterns to the multivariate case while preserving interdependencies. Their approach to multivariate ordinal patterns is the basis of this work and is presented in detail in the next section.

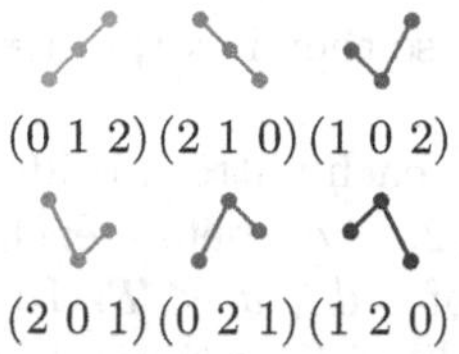

(a) All $d!$ possible univariate ordinal patterns of order $d = 3$.

$$\begin{pmatrix}0&1&2\\0&1&2\end{pmatrix}\begin{pmatrix}0&1&2\\2&1&0\end{pmatrix}\begin{pmatrix}0&1&2\\1&0&2\end{pmatrix}\cdots\begin{pmatrix}0&1&2\\1&2&0\end{pmatrix}$$
$$\begin{pmatrix}2&1&0\\0&1&2\end{pmatrix}\begin{pmatrix}2&1&0\\2&1&0\end{pmatrix}\begin{pmatrix}2&1&0\\1&0&2\end{pmatrix}\cdots\begin{pmatrix}2&1&0\\1&2&0\end{pmatrix}$$
$$\vdots \quad \vdots \quad \vdots \quad \ddots \quad \vdots$$
$$\begin{pmatrix}1&2&0\\0&1&2\end{pmatrix}\begin{pmatrix}1&2&0\\2&1&0\end{pmatrix}\begin{pmatrix}1&2&0\\1&0&2\end{pmatrix}\cdots\begin{pmatrix}1&2&0\\1&2&0\end{pmatrix}$$

(b) All $(d!)^m$ possible multivariate ordinal patterns of order $d = 3$ with $m = 2$ variables.

Fig. 2. Univariate and multivariate ordinal representations. Best viewed in colour. (Color figure online)

3 Multivariate Ordinal Pattern Symbolisation

To encode the behaviour of a time series, we use ordinal pattern symbolisation based on works from Bandt and Pompe [3]. For a better understanding, we start with univariate ordinal patterns that encode the up and downs in a time series by the total order between two or more neighbours. The encoding gives a good abstraction of the overall behaviour or generating process.

Definition 1 (Univariate Ordinal Pattern). *A vector* $(x_1, ..., x_d) \in \mathbb{R}^d$ *has ordinal pattern* $(r_1, ..., r_d) \in \mathbb{N}^d$ *of order* $d \in \mathbb{N}$ *if* $x_{r_1} \geq ... \geq x_{r_d}$ *and* $r_{l-1} > r_l$ *in the case* $x_{r_{l-1}} = x_{r_l}$.

Figure 2a shows all possible ordinal patterns of order $d = 3$ of a vector $(x_1, x_2, x_3) \in \mathbb{R}^3$. Furthermore, for a *multivariate* time series $((x_t^i)_{i=1}^m)_{t=1}^T$, each variable x^i for $i \in 1, ..., m$ depends not only on its past values but also has some dependency on other variables. To establish a total order between two time points $(x_t^i)_{i=1}^m$ and $(x_{t+1}^i)_{i=1}^m$ with m variables is only possible if $x_t^i > x_{t+1}^i$ or $x_t^i < x_{t+1}^i$ for all $i \in 1, ..., m$. An intuitive idea introduced in [14] is to store univariate ordinal patterns of all variables at a time point t together into a symbol.

Definition 2 (Multivariate Ordinal Pattern). A matrix $(x_1, ..., x_d) \in \mathbb{R}^{m \times d}$ has *multivariate ordinal pattern* (MOP) of order $d \in \mathbb{N}$

$$\begin{pmatrix} r_{11} & \cdots & r_{1d} \\ \vdots & \ddots & \vdots \\ r_{m1} & \cdots & r_{md} \end{pmatrix} \in \mathbb{N}^{m \times d} \tag{2}$$

if $x_{r_{i1}} \geq ... \geq x_{r_{id}}$ for all $i = 1, ..., m$ and $r_{il-1} > r_{il}$ in the case $x_{r_{il-1}} = x_{r_{il}}$.

Figure 2b shows all $(d!)^m$ possible MOPs of order $d = 3$ and number of variables $m = 2$. If d and m are too large, depending on the application, undersampling and a uniform distribution of ordinal patterns quickly occur [14]. This has the consequence that subsequent learning procedures can fail. Nevertheless, for a small order d and sufficiently large T the use of MOPs can lead to higher accuracy in learning tasks, e.g., classification [14] because they incorporate inter-dependence of the variables in the time series.

To symbolise a multivariate time series $X_t \in \mathbb{R}^{m \times T}$ each pattern is identified with exactly one of the *ordinal pattern symbols* $o = 1, 2, ..., d!$, before each point $t \in \{d, ..., T\}$ is assigned its ordinal pattern symbol of order $d \ll T$. To assess long-term trends, delayed behaviour is of interest, showing various details of the structure of the time series. The time delay $\tau \in \mathbb{N}_{>0}$ is the delay between successive points in the symbol sequences. In this work, we leave finding the optimal order d and delay τ as subject to hyperparameter optimisation [15].

4   MOP4SA: An Approach for Symmetry Approximation

In this section we introduce MOP4SA for the approximation of symmetries of multivariate objects in a DPRM, i.e., entities that are encoded in PRVs and linked in a parfactor. For this, we first encode the behaviour of multivariate time-dependent objects by MOPs. Then we use MOPs for the symmetry approximation by spectral clustering.

4.1   Encoding Behaviour by MOPs

To find symmetries of multivariate objects, we use evidence to encode the models entity behaviour w.r.t. a context, i.e., w.r.t. a parfactor. In particular, this means: Every PRV represents multiple entities, e.g., zones Z, of the same type. That is, for a PRV $Supply_t(Z)$, entities z are represented by a logvar Z with domain $\mathcal{D}(Z)$ and size $|\mathcal{D}(Z)|$. Note that a PRV can be parameterized with more than one logvar, but for the sake of simplicity we introduce our approach using PRVs with only one logvar. Symmetry detection for m-logvar PRVs works similarly to one-logvar PRVs, with the difference, that in symmetry detection, entity pairs, i.e., m-tuples, are used. As an example, for any 2-logvar PRV $P_t(X, Y)$, an entity pair is a 2-tuple (x_1, y_1) with $x_1 \in D(X)$ and $y_1 \in D(Y)$.

A DPRM, as introduced in Sect. 2.1, encodes temporal data by unrolling a DPRM while observing evidence for the models PRVs, e.g., the PRV $Supply_t(Z)$ encodes supply at time t in various zones Z on the globe. In addition, a DPRM exploits (conditional) in-dependencies between randvars by encoding interdependencies in parfactors. As such, parfactors describe interdependent data through its linked PRVs, e.g., the correlation between supply $Supply_t(Z)$ and freight rates $Rate_t(Z)$ within a common zone Z encoded by the parfactor g_t^1. For each entity $z_j \in D(Z)$ from the PRVs $Supply_t(Z)$ and $Rate_t(Z)$ observations are made over time, i.e., a time series $((x_t^i)_{i=1}^m)_{t=1}^T$ with $x_t^i \in \{low, mid, high\}$ is generated. In this work, the time series is to be assumed multivariate, containing interdependent variables, i.e., $m > 1$. Note that in [9] we consider the case $m = 1$. Having $|D(Z)|$ entities in Z, we consider $|D(Z)|$ samples of multivariate time series $\mathcal{X} = (((x_t^i)_{i=1}^m)_{t=1}^T)_{j=1}^{|D(Z)|} \in \mathbb{R}^{m \times T \times |D(Z)|}$, e.g., for $m = 3$ with observations $(x_t^1, x_t^2, x_t^3) = (Supply_t(z_j), Idle_t(z_j), Rate_t(z_j))$ for every $z_j \in D(Z)$ in time $t \in \{1, ..., T\}$. As such, a multivariate time series is defined for several

PRVs linked in a parfactor. Identification of entity symmetries is performed on a set of observed multivariate time series that are related to the parfactor g^1.

Now, for each time step $t = \tau(d-1) + 1, \ldots, T$ of a multivariate time series $((x_t^i)_{i=1}^m)_{t=1}^T) \in \mathcal{X}$, MOP is determined as described in Sect. 3. However, ordinal patterns are well suited to characterise an overall behaviour of time series that is independent of the data range, but the dependence on the data range can be also relevant, i.e., time series can be similar in terms of their ordinals patterns, but differ considering their y-intercept. In other words, transforming a sequence $x = (x_t^i)_{a \leq t \leq b}$ as $y = x + c$, where $c \in \mathbb{R}$ is a constant, should change y's similarity to other sequences, although the shape is the same. To address the dependence on the data range, we use the arithmetic mean $\overline{x}_t^{d,\tau} = \frac{1}{m} \sum_{i=1}^m \frac{1}{d} \sum_{k=1}^d x_{i,t-(k-1)\tau}$ of the multivariate time series' values corresponding to the ordinal pattern, where $x_{i,t-(k-1)\tau}$ is min-max normalised, as an additional characteristic or feature of behaviour. If one of the variables changes its behaviour significantly along the intercept, the arithmetic mean uncovers this. There are still other features that can be relevant. For simplicity, we only determine ordinal patterns and their means for each parfactor g^1 with, e.g., PRVs $(Supply_t(Z), Idle_t(Z), Rate_t(Z))$, yielding a new data representation

$$\mathcal{X}' = \langle o, \overline{x} \rangle^{(T-(\tau(d-1)) \times |\mathcal{D}(Z)|} \tag{3}$$

where $\langle o, \cdot \rangle_{tj} \in \mathcal{X}'$ represents the MOP and $\langle \cdot, \overline{x} \rangle_{tj} \in \mathcal{X}'$ represents the corresponding mean $\overline{x}_t^{d,\tau}$ for entity z_j at time step t. The order d and delay τ are passed in from the outside and might depend on, e.g., the frequency of the data, to capture the long-term behaviour of each entity.

4.2   MOPs for Symmetry Approximation by Spectral Clustering

Based on the derived representation in Eq. (3), we perform symmetry approximation by clustering entities. Since lifted models are specifically designed for encoding large domains, we use spectral clustering, a popular setting for handling high-dimensional data [5].

Similarity Graph. Spectral clustering is performed on a similarity graph containing nodes for each entity represented by PRVs connected within a parfactor. Specifically, the similarity graph for a parfactor g_t^1 connecting the PRVs $Supply_t(Z), Idle_t(Z)$ and $Rate_t(Z)$ contains one node for each entity $z \in \mathcal{D}(Z)$ observed in form of multivariate time series. The edges of the similarity graph represent the similarity between two nodes, or more precisely, how closely related two entities of the model are. To measure similarity, we use the symbolic representation $\mathcal{X}'$, which contains tuples of multivariate ordinal numbers and mean values that describe the behaviour of an entity. The similarity of two entities z_i and z_j is given by counts w_{ij} of equal behaviours, i.e.,

$$w_{ij} = \sum_{t \leq T} \left[\langle o, \cdot \rangle_{it} = \langle o, \cdot \rangle_{jt} \wedge |\langle \cdot, \overline{x} \rangle_{it} - \langle \cdot, \overline{x} \rangle_{jt}| < \delta \right], \tag{4}$$

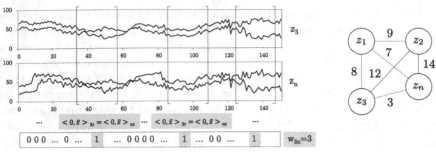

(a) Similarity counting based on MOP and means.   (b) Similarity graph $\mathcal{W}$.

Fig. 3. (a) Similarity count for w_{3n} (red) and (b) resulting similarity graph $\mathcal{W}$. (Color figure online)

where $[x] = 1$ if x and, 0 otherwise. Simply put, as visualised in Fig. 3a, one counts the time steps t at which both multivariate time series of z_i and z_j have the same MOP and the absolute difference of the mean values of the corresponding MOPs is smaller than $\delta > 0$. Finally, as shown in Fig. 3b the counts w_{ij} correspond to the weights of the edges in the similarity graph $\mathcal{W}$, where zero indicates no similarity between two entities, while the larger the count, the more similar two entities are.

Spectral Clustering. In the worst case, a similarity graph, representing the similarity of entities $z \in \mathcal{D}(Z)$, contains $\binom{|\mathcal{D}(Z)|}{2}$ fully-connected nodes. If the dimension of the similarity graph, due to the potentially large domain of a lifted model, becomes too large, classical clustering methods do not achieve good results due to the curse of dimensionality [4]. Spectral clustering involves dimensionality reduction in advance before using standard clustering methods such as k-means. For dimensionality reduction, the similarity graph $\mathcal{W}$ is transformed into the so-called graph Laplacian matrix L, which describes the relations of the nodes and edges of a graph, where the entries are defined by

$$L_{ij} := \begin{cases} \deg(z_i) & \text{if } i = j \\ -1 & \text{if } i \neq j \text{ and } w_{ij} > 0, \\ 0 & \text{else} \end{cases} \qquad (5)$$

where $\deg(z_i) = \sum_{j=1}^{|\mathcal{D}(Z)|} w_{ij}$. For decorrelation, the data in the graph Laplacian matrix L are decomposed into its sequence of eigenvalues (spectrum) and the corresponding eigenvectors. The eigenvectors form a new uncorrelated orthonormal basis and are thus suitable for standard clustering methods. The observations of the reduced data matrix whose columns contain the smallest k eigenvectors can now be clustered using k-means. An observation assigned to cluster $\mathcal{C}_i, i = 1, ..., k$ can then be traced back to its entity $z \in \mathcal{D}(Z)$ by indices. That is, entity symmetry clusters $\mathcal{C}(g_t^1) = \bigcup_{i=1}^{k} \mathcal{C}_i$ are built for parfactor g_t^i with each $\mathcal{C}_i$ containing a subset of entities $z \in \mathcal{D}(Z)$.

The usage of the learned symmetry clusters is motivated and evaluated in the next section.

5 Empirical Evaluation

Reasoning in lifted representations has a polynomial complexity in the domain of the largest logvar [16]. Thus, clustering entities which behave identically, or almost identical, is key to avoid duplicate calculations in inference since calculations can be done for one representative of similarly behaving entities only. For this reason, we evaluate two aspects for the use of MOP4SA motivating the benefits of understanding symmetries in the context of DPRMs, namely (a) *detecting structural changes* in symmetry clusters over time, and (b) using symmetry clusters to *prevent the model from grounding* to maintain a lifted solution of the model. Inference in DPRMs is performed by the lifted dynamic junction tree algorithm. Details can be found in [10].

To setup a DPRM as shown in Fig. 1, we use historical vessel movements from 2020 based on automatic identification system (AIS) data[2] provided by the Danish Maritime Authority for the Baltic Sea. Each AIS signal contains the current geo-position and the total cargo quantity of a vessel. Preprocessing for retrieving variables *Supply* and *Idle* for 367 defined *Zones* can be found on GitHub[3] or in [9]. In the experiment, we set order $d = 2$, delay $\tau = 1$ and bound $\delta - 0.1$. Symmetry clusters are learned at a fixed time $t - 15$.

Symmetries between entities can change over time. In the worst case, they can dissolve. Knowing changing symmetry structures is important when approximating symmetries in order to not compromise too much on accuracy in inference. Changes can be detected by using the similarity graph in MOP4SA. Figure 4a shows heatmaps of two symmetry clusters that relate the entities of a cluster based on their similarity count over several time steps. The heatmap at $t = 15$ shows the similarity at the time of learning clusters, while the heatmaps for all other timesteps $t > 15$ show only the difference in similarity counts to the previous time step. Thus, for $t = 20$ the heatmap is based on similarity counts between $t = 15$ and $t = 20$ only. Figure 4a (top) shows a symmetry cluster of which entities quickly drop out, but then at $t = 35$ entities behave similar again. Figure 4a (bottom) shows a symmetry cluster containing entities, which share similarities constantly over time with only a few exceptions for the relation between entities 1 and 3 and 2 and 3, which do not relate for $t = 20$ and $t = 30$. Both heatmaps indicate periodicities, while also giving insights about the validity of the cluster over time. In the context of MOP4SA, the similarity graph builds up over time and also changes over time, i.e., it can be used to detect structural changes in symmetries. If the similarity graph changes over time in a constant and balanced way, symmetry clusters stay valid. If the similarity graph changes over time in an unbalanced manner, i.e., if similarity counts change significantly, there is a

---

[2] https://www.dma.dk/SikkerhedTilSoes/Sejladsinformation/AIS/.
[3] https://github.com/FinkeNils/Processed-AIS-Data-Baltic-Sea-2020-v2.

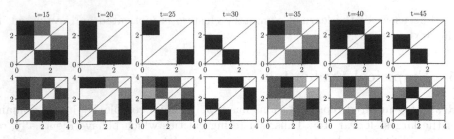

(a) Heatmap of the similarity graph for different time steps t of clusters C_1 and C_2.

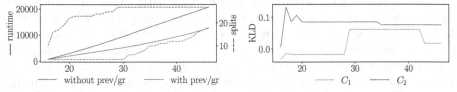

(b) Runtime [ms] and splits [#] w/ and w/o preventing groundings and KLD.

Fig. 4. Experiments for two selected clusters.

change in the structure of the symmetry clusters. Suitable metrics and their evaluations are part of future work.

Furthermore, symmetry clusters can be used to prevent the model from unnecessary groundings. Assuming a symmetry cluster contains entities z_1, z_2 and z_3, groundings occur whenever observations differ across entities in a symmetry cluster. For example, grounding occurs, if 1. The observation $(Supply_1(z_1) = high, Idle_1(z_1) = high)$ of entity z_1 differs from observations $(Supply_1(z_i) = low, Idle_1(z_i) = mid)$ of entities z_i for $i = 2, 3$, or 2. observations are only made for a subset of the entities, i.e., for entities z_2 and z_3, but not for entity z_1. In both cases, the entities z_2 and z_3 would be split off from their initial symmetry group, and are henceforth treated individually in a non lifted fashion. I.e., DPRMs dissolves into ground instances through asymmetric evidence. Entity symmetry clusters, as created in Sect. 4.2, contain entities that all behave approximately the same over time and therefore can be used to avoid model splits to some extend by applying evidence to other entities in their group. The idea is to align evidence across all entities in the cluster to prevent the model from grounding in order to preserve the runtime benefits of a lifted model, i.e., (a) if evidence is observed only for a subset of the entities, evidence is also applied to the other entities of the symmetry cluster, or (b) if evidence differs between the entities of a cluster, the most frequently observed observation is also applied to the other entities of the symmetry cluster and all contrary evidence is discarded. The complete procedure as well as an algorithm to avoid model splits is provided in previous work [9] for the univariate case. As the multivariate case differs in the symbolisation, not in the procedure itself, we refrain from repeating and focus on the evaluation in this paper.

To compare runtime and accuracy, we perform query answering given sets of evidence, i.e., we perform inference by answering for each time step $t \in \{16, \ldots, 45\}$ the prediction query $P(Supply_t(Z), Idle_t(Z))$ and obtain a marginal distribution for each entity $z \in D(Z)$. Figure 4b (left) shows runtime (solid) and number of splits (dotted) to answer queries for each time step. The two red lines, i.e., for answering queries without preventing groundings, are higher than the green ones with preventing groundings by means of MOP4SA underpinning the runtime advantage. Figure 4b (right) shows Kullback Leibler divergence (KLD) as a measure of the accuracy of the predictions, i.e., KLD compares the predicted probability distributions of the individual entities $z \in D(Z)$ respectively with and without preventing groundings. Here, the average KLD over all entities for each time step, denotes the overall accuracy for a time step. KLD close to 0 is indicative of similar distributions, thus corresponds to a small error.

6 Conclusion and Future Work

In this paper we propose MOP4SA, an approach to approximate multivariate model symmetries in DPRMs. For the determination of symmetries, this novel approach uses spectral clustering based on similarity graphs of multivariate ordinal patterns representing the up and downs in an observed multivariate time series of an entity. When using MOP4SA, the change in the similarity graph can provide information about changes in the symmetry clusters over time. By building symmetry clusters with MOP4SA, we show that groundings in a DPRM can be prevented and runtime advantages in lifted inference can be obtained while first results in accuracy are encouraging. Quantitative error bounds are yet to follow. Furthermore, this work includes a motivation for the detection of changes in symmetry clusters. Corresponding thresholds, metrics or similarity measures between graphs have to be evaluated so that explicit structures such as periodicities or interconnectivity of several variables can be identified and effectively built into the algorithm. Moreover, as the application of MOP4SA is performed on observed time series of a DPRM, the approach is suitable for the symmetry approximation of arbitrary multivariate time series. Practicality and performance in context of other models need to be evaluated in future work.

References

1. Agostini, A., Celaya, E.: Exploiting domain symmetries in reinforcement learning with continuous state and action spaces. In: 2009 International Conference on Machine Learning and Applications, Miami, FL, USA, pp. 331–336. IEEE (2009)
2. Agrawal, R., Faloutsos, C., Swami, A.: Efficient similarity search in sequence databases. In: Lomet, D.B. (ed.) FODO 1993. LNCS, vol. 730, pp. 69–84. Springer, Heidelberg (1993). https://doi.org/10.1007/3-540-57301-1_5
3. Bandt, C., Pompe, B.: Permutation entropy: a natural complexity measure for time series. Phys. Rev. Lett. 88(17), 4 (2002)
4. Bellman, R.: Adaptive Control Processes: A guided Tour. Princeton Legacy Library, Princeton University Press, Princeton (2015)

5. Bertozzi, A.L., Merkurjev, E.: Chapter 12 - Graph-based optimization approaches for machine learning, uncertainty quantification and networks. In: Kimmel, R., Tai, X.C. (eds.) Processing, Analyzing and Learning of Images, Shapes, and Forms: Part 2, Handbook of Numerical Analysis, vol. 20, pp. 503–531. Elsevier (2019)

6. Chiu, B., Keogh, E., Lonardi, S.: Probabilistic discovery of time series motifs. In: Proceedings of the Ninth ACM SIGKDD International Conference on Knowledge Discovery and Data Mining, pp. 493–498 (2003)

7. Dieleman, S., Fauw, J.D., Kavukcuoglu, K.: Exploiting cyclic symmetry in convolutional neural networks. In: Proceedings of the 33rd International Conference on Machine Learning, pp. 1889–1898 (2016)

8. Finke, N., Gehrke, M., Braun, T., Potten, T., Möller, R.: Investigating matureness of probabilistic graphical models for dry-bulk shipping. In: Proceedings of the 10th International Conference on Probabilistic Graphical Models, pp. 197–208 (2020)

9. Finke, N., Mohr, M.: A priori approximation of symmetries in dynamic probabilistic relational models. In: Edelkamp, S., Möller, R., Rueckert, E. (eds.) KI 2021. LNCS (LNAI), vol. 12873, pp. 309–323. Springer, Cham (2021). https://doi.org/10.1007/978-3-030-87626-5_23

10. Gehrke, M., Braun, T., Möller, R.: Lifted dynamic junction tree algorithm. In: Chapman, P., Endres, D., Pernelle, N. (eds.) ICCS 2018. LNCS (LNAI), vol. 10872, pp. 55–69. Springer, Cham (2018). https://doi.org/10.1007/978-3-319-91379-7_5

11. Keogh, E., Chakrabarti, K., Pazzani, M., Mehrotra, S.: Dimensionality reduction for fast similarity search in large time series databases. In: Knowledge and Information Systems, pp. 263–286 (2001). https://doi.org/10.1021/acsami.7b03579

12. Kramer, S.: A brief history of learning symbolic higher-level representations from data (and a curious look forward). In: Proceedings of the Twenty-Ninth International Joint Conference on Artificial Intelligence, IJCAI-20, pp. 4868–4876 (2020)

13. Kruskal, J.B., Liberman, M.: The symmetric time warping problem: From continuous to discrete. In: Time Warps, String Edits and Macromolecules: The Theory and Practice of Sequence Comparison. Addison-Wesley Publishing Co. (1983)

14. Mohr, M., Wilhelm, F., Hartwig, M., Möller, R., Keller, K.: New approaches in ordinal pattern representations for multivariate time series. In: Proceedings of the 33rd International Florida Artificial Intelligence Research Society Conference (2020)

15. Myers, A., Khasawneh, F.A.: On the automatic parameter selection for permutation entropy. Chaos: an Interdis. J. Nonlinear Sci. 30(3), 033130 (2020)

16. Niepert, M., Van den Broeck, G.: Tractability through exchangeability: a new perspective on efficient probabilistic inference. In: AAAI-14 Proceedings of the 28th AAAI Conference on Artificial Intelligence, pp. 2467–2475. AAAI Press (2014)

17. Petitjean, F., Inglada, J., Gancarski, P.: Satellite image time series analysis under time warping. IEEE Trans. Geosci. Remote Sens. 50(8) (2012)

18. Poole, D.: First-order probabilistic inference. In: Proceedings of the 18th International Joint Conference on Artificial Intelligence, pp. 985–991 (2003)

19. Salvador, S., Chan, P.: FastDTW: toward accurate dynamic time warping in linear time and space. In: KDD Workshop on Mining Temporal and Sequential Data, pp. 70–80 (2004)

20. Sato, T.: A Statistical learning method for logic programs with distribution semantics. In: Proceedings of the 12th International Conference on Logic Programming, pp. 715–729 (1995)

21. Satorras, V.G., Hoogeboom, E., Welling, M.: E(n) equivariant graph neural networks. In: Proceedings of the 38th ICML (2021)
22. Yeh, C.C.M., et al.: Matrix profile I: all pairs similarity joins for time series: a unifying view that includes motifs, discords and shapelets. In: 2016 IEEE 16th International Conference on Data Mining (ICDM), pp. 1317–1322 (2016)

A Hybrid Multiagent-Based Rescheduling Mechanism for Open and Stochastic Environments Concerning the Execution Stage

Yikun Yang[(✉)], Fenghui Ren, and Minjie Zhang

School of Computing and Information Technology, University of Wollongong,
Wollongong, Australia
yy048@uowmail.edu.au, {fren,minjie}@uow.edu.au

Abstract. Dynamic scheduling is a hot topic in recent years. Most existing dynamic scheduling algorithms process the rescheduling in an off-line way through the modification of created schedules in advance of further execution. However, in open and stochastic environments, such as manufacturing systems, streams of exogenous events may cause information changes inside of jobs and resources during the job execution stage, so as to increase the environmental uncertainties and rescheduling computational complexity. In such environments, the frequent occurrence of dynamic events requires scheduling methods to provide efficient and robust online rescheduling services for ensuring the success rate of jobs. This paper investigates the dynamic events during the execution stage in open and stochastic environments and proposes a multiagent-based rescheduling mechanism with the hybrid structure for such cases. Three types of agents are proposed to implement the rescheduling mechanism. The experimental results demonstrate that the proposed hybrid mechanism own higher efficiency and robustness in dealing with dynamic events in open and stochastic scheduling environments than that of existing centralized and decentralized methods.

Keywords: Rescheduling · Multi-agent system · Resource allocation

1 Introduction

Scheduling refers to the decision-making processes of planning and allocating resources for jobs over given periods and to achieve one or more optimization objectives [2]. With the development of the Internet of Things (IoT) and communication technologies, real-time data of jobs and resources becomes processable, hence the openness and uncertainty of scheduling environments increase in many industrial systems [9]. In open and stochastic environments, such as manufacturing and fog computing systems, jobs and resources are geographically distributed, and the occurrence of dynamic events (e.g., machine breakdowns) can invalidate the existing schedules [7,10].

© Springer Nature Switzerland AG 2022
G. Long et al. (Eds.): AI 2021, LNAI 13151, pp. 556–569, 2022.
https://doi.org/10.1007/978-3-030-97546-3_45

This paper investigates the rescheduling problems in the open and stochastic environment, which consists of a set of unrelated resources, and streams of jobs and dynamic events arrive over time. In such environments, new arrival jobs experience two stages to complete: (i) the pre-scheduling stage and (ii) the execution stage. In real applications, dynamic events occur in both two stages unpredictably and trigger the rescheduling process. In the pre-scheduling stage, new arrival jobs wait for the allocation decisions determined by the scheduler, as well as waiting for the beginning of the execution. In this stage, rush job arrivals, non-started job cancellations and due date changes are common dynamic events addressed in the literature [1]. The second stage is the execution of jobs by using allocated resources. This stage involves multiple dynamic events, such as machine breakdowns and requirement changes in started jobs.

Most existing rescheduling methods focus on resolving dynamic events in the pre-scheduling stage, such as periodical rescheduling [1], heuristic algorithms (e.g., genetic algorithms [14]), and predictive-reactive scheduling [13]. Since the jobs under consideration have not started execution, these methods usually assume that a schedule is generated off-line and in advance of execution. When dynamic events are detected, these methods centrally consider the attributes of remaining jobs and available resources, as well as multiple optimization objectives and constraints, to partially (e.g., right-shift method) or completely (e.g., regeneration) recover the created schedules to adapt to changes. These methods can re-generate optimal or near-optimal schedules when dynamic events occur. However, due to the centralized and off-line manner, when these methods resolve dynamic events in the execution stage, the inflexible response and long decision-making time may decrease the success rate of jobs [5,8].

This paper mainly focuses on resolving the dynamic events in the execution stage. Considering the characteristics of open and stochastic environments, three challenging issues need to be considered. (1) In the execution stage, jobs under consideration have started to execute, so deadlines of jobs are highly close. Excessive rescheduling time costs will cause time-critical jobs to fail, so as to reduce the success rate of jobs. (2) Since most resources are in use, strict resource restrictions are involved. The occurrence of dynamic events may affect the normal execution of other jobs and resources, thereby reducing the robustness of rescheduling. (3) Streams of dynamic events greatly increase the rescheduling uncertainty. The frequent modification of the created schedules may cause the scheduler to involve high computational complexity.

To address the three challenging issues mentioned above, this paper proposes a multiagent-based rescheduling mechanism with a hybrid structure for solving dynamic events. Multiagent-based approaches have demonstrated advantages in modelling complex dynamic environments [6]. The proposed hybrid mechanism takes advantages of both the decentralized and centralized structures to improve the rescheduling performance. The two contributions of the proposed mechanism are described as follows. (1) The proposed mechanism employs decentralized agents for the real-time detection of dynamic events in jobs and resources, where decentralized agents can overcome the impact of geographic distribution and own the capability to resolve dynamic events in the local range through ad-hoc communications. Ad-hoc communications distribute the rescheduling computational complexity and reduce the impact of uncertainties on the normal execution of jobs, so as to improve the rescheduling efficiency and robustness. (2) Besides, considering the time and resource restrictions, in case the dynamic events cannot be resolved in the local range, a central coordinator agent is proposed whose objective is to recommend new feasible resources for affected jobs.

The rest of this paper is organized as follows. In Sect. 2, the description of the scheduling problem is presented. In Sect. 3, the detailed design of the mechanism is given. In Sect. 4, experiments and results are discussed. In Sect. 5, related work is described and the conclusion is given in Sect. 6.

2   Problem Description

This paper considers the open and stochastic scheduling problem as follows. There are n independent jobs $J = \{j_1, j_2, ..., j_n\}$ arrive over time and Φ types of m resources $R = \{r_1, r_2, ..., r_m\}$ are consisted. A stream of dynamic events $C = \{c_1, ..., c_i\}$ appear during the execution of jobs. Three basic assumptions are considered: (i) each job can be performed by more than one resources simultaneously; (ii) each resource can only perform one job at the same time; and (iii) the execution of jobs can be interrupted by dynamic events and jobs will continue to execute after recovery, instead of restarting.

This paper considers that each job j_n has a specific arrival time ta_n and a set of resource requirements E_n. Each job can require more than one type of resources for execution, and the use of different resources can be sequential, concurrent, or hybrid. A job is formally defined as Definition 1.

Definition 1. *Job: The n-th job j_n is defined as $j_n = \langle ta_n, E_n \rangle$, where ta_n denotes the arrival time of j_n, $E_n = \{e_n^1, ..., e_n^\phi\}$ represents the resource requirements of j_n, where $e_n^\phi = [s_n^\phi, d_n^\phi, t_n^\phi]$ denotes the requirement for using the type $\phi \in \Phi$ resource, s_n^ϕ denotes the earliest time to start using the type ϕ resource, d_n^ϕ denotes the latest time to stop using the type ϕ resource, and t_n^ϕ denotes the total time of using the type ϕ resource.*

Each resource r_m has specific *resource type* ϕ (i.e., the resource can only execute the same type of resource requirements), *availability* $\alpha_m(ct)$ at current time ct and a *schedule* Sch_m. A resource is formally defined as Definition 2.

Definition 2. *Resource: The m-th resource is defined as $r_m = \langle \phi, \alpha_m(ct), Sch_m \rangle$, where $\phi \in [1, \Phi]$ denotes the resource type, $\alpha_m(ct) = \{0, 1\}$ denotes the availability of r_m at time ct, where 1 denotes r_m is available at time ct, 0 denotes r_m is unavailable, $Sch_m = \{j_m^1, ..., j_m^k\}$ is the schedule that includes waiting jobs on r_m, where $j_m^k = [\tau_1, \tau_2]$ specifies the allocated time for the k-th waiting job on r_m, τ_1 denotes the start using time and τ_2 denotes the stop using time.*

The main objective function of the scheduling problem is to minimize the completion of all jobs, i.e., to minimize the $\max\limits_{1 \leq i \leq n} CT_i$, subject to:

$$CT_i \geq ta_i + t_i^\phi, \ \phi = 1, 2, ..., \Phi, \tag{1}$$

where CT_i represents the completion time of each job j_i, and max represents the completion time of the latest job completed (i.e., the makespan). Constraint (1) gives the relationship between the completion time of j_i, the arrival time ta_i and the use time for different types of resources t_i^ϕ.

This paper considers four types of dynamic events that occur during the execution stage, including the dynamic changes from either jobs or resources. Let $C = \{c_1, ..., c_i\}$ denotes the total dynamic events during the execution stage, and c_i indicates an individual dynamic event inside a job or resource.

Type 1: Let $c_i = \{e_n^\phi\}$ indicates that a new resource requirement e_n^ϕ will be added in job j_n, or an existing e_n^ϕ in j_n will be cancelled.

Type 2: Let $c_i = \{s_n^\phi, d_n^\phi, t_n^\phi\}$ denotes the attributes of an existing e_n^ϕ change, where the earliest start using time s_n^ϕ and the latest stop using time d_n^ϕ can be advanced or delayed, and the total time of using the resource t_n^ϕ can be extended or shortened. One constraint is that the changes of attributes must satisfy $d_n^\phi - s_n^\phi > t_n^\phi$; otherwise, job j_n will fail directly.

Type 3: Let $c_i = \{\alpha_m(ct) \leftarrow 0\}$ denotes the resource r_m availability changes at time ct and the next available time of r_m is unpredictable.

Type 4: Let $c_i = \{\alpha_m(ct) \leftarrow 0, AT\}$ denotes the resource r_m availability changes at time ct and the next available time is predictable, where AT denotes the next available time.

When the stream of dynamic events occur inside of jobs or resources during the execution stage, the main consideration is to maximize the success rate of jobs, i.e., $max \dfrac{sn}{n}$, where sn represents the number of successfully finished jobs after execution, n represents the total number of jobs, and max represents the maximization of the success rate.

3 Multiagent-Based Mechanism

This section describes the *architecture* and *processes* of the proposed multi-agent based mechanism and presents the rescheduling algorithms in detail.

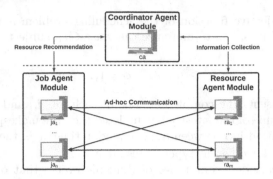

Fig. 1. Architecture of the multi-agent rescheduling mechanism

3.1   Mechanism Architecture

The hybrid mechanism includes three agent modules: (1) a *job agent module* and (2) a *resource agent module* for solving the dynamic events through decentralized ad-hoc communications, and (3) a *coordinator agent module* for the centralized resource information collections and recommendations (shown as Fig. 1).

The *job agent module* includes a set of job agents which are responsible for (1) real-time detecting dynamic events in jobs, and (2) making decisions when existing schedules are invalid. Each job agent ja_n manages one job j_n. The job agent is defined as Definition 3.

Definition 3. *Job Agent: The n-th job agent is defined as $ja_n = \langle JID_n, j_n \rangle$, where JID_n denotes the job agent ID which records the agent name and address, and j_n is the job j_n.*

The *resource agent module* includes a set of resource agents that are responsible for (1) real-time detecting dynamic events in resources, and (2) making decisions when existing schedules are invalid. Each resource agent ra_m manages one resource r_m. The resource agent is defined as Definition 4.

Definition 4. *Resource Agent: The m-th resource agent is defined as $ra_m = \langle RID_m, r_m \rangle$, where RID_m denotes the resource agent ID which records the agent name and address, and r_m is the resource r_m.*

The *coordinator agent module* includes a coordinator agent which collects resources information and recommends feasible resources for affected jobs when dynamic events cannot be solved through decentralized ad-hoc communications. In existing decentralized approaches (e.g., Guizzi et al. [4]), once dynamic events cannot be resolved by ad-hoc communications, agents will spend considerable time on the communications and negotiations for matching new resources for jobs. Some jobs fail to complete before the deadlines due to the latency issue. The coordinator agent is proposed to minimize the latency issue, so as to improve the rescheduling success rate. The coordinator agent is defined as Definition 5.

Definition 5. *Coordinator Agent: The coordinator agent ca is defined as ca =*
$\langle CID, jl, rl \rangle$, *where CID records the agent name and address,* $jl = \{ja_1, ..., ja_n\}$
is a list of job agents that have sent requests to ca, and $rl = \{ra_1, ..., ra_m\}$ *is a*
list of all available resource agents information.

3.2 Mechanism Processes

The hybrid mechanism mainly includes four processes: job and resource agents
are responsible for the decentralized (1) dynamic events detection and (2) ad-hoc
communication; and the coordinator agent is responsible for the centralized (3)
dynamic events collection and (4) feasible resource recommendation.

Step 1: Dynamic events detection: job agents and resource agents detect
the dynamic events in jobs and resources in real-time, respectively.

Step 2: Ad-hoc communication: when dynamic events are identified, relevant
job agents and resource agents will interact with each other first to try to
find feasible solutions through ad-hoc communications. If the dynamic events
can be resolved by job and resource agents themselves, then return success.
Otherwise, job and resource agents will send the unsolved dynamic events
and the current status of jobs and resources to the coordinator agent.

Step 3: Dynamic events collection: the coordinator agent receives requests
from job and resource agents in real-time and stores the information of unfinished jobs and available resources in jl and rl, respectively.

Step 4: Feasible resource recommendation: the coordinator agent analyses
the resource requirements of affected jobs in the jl based on the FCFS (First
Come, First Served) rule. The ca searches for available resources in rl and try
to recommend new feasible resources for unfinished jobs in jl. If there exist
suitable available resources for unfinished jobs in jl, the coordinator agent
will conduct relevant job and resource agents to interact with each other.
The detailed agreements on resource allocation and resource use time slots
are determined by job and resource agents themselves.

3.3 Algorithm for the Decentralized Detection and Communication

Algorithm 1 shows the rescheduling through decentralized agent detections and
ad-hoc communications. These processes are mainly implemented by job and
resource agents. The inputs of Algorithm 1 are the jobs J, resources R and
dynamic events C. The output is to resolve detected dynamic events.

Algorithm 1: Decentralized Detection and Ad-hoc Communication

> **input** : $J = \{j_1, ..., j_n\}$, $R = \{r_1, ..., r_m\}$, $C = \{c_1, ..., c_i\}$
> **output**: resolve dynamic events
> 1   job and resource agents detect C in J and R;
> 2   **while** *identify a c_i* **do**
> 3   **if** *Type 1 c_i occur in j_n* **then**
> 4 ja_n identifies the new added or cancelled e_n^ϕ;
> 5   **if** *an existing e_n^ϕ is cancelled* **then**
> 6 ja_n interacts with the relevant ra_m and ra_m deletes the $[\tau_1, \tau_2]$;
> 7   **else**
> 8 ja_n interacts with ca for resource recommendations;
>
> 9   **if** *Type 2 c_i occur in j_n* **then**
> 10 ja_n identifies the new $\left\{s_n^\phi, d_n^\phi, t_n^\phi\right\}$ and interacts with the relevant ra_m;
> 11   **if** *Sch_m satisfies the new $\left\{s_n^\phi, d_n^\phi, t_n^\phi\right\}$* **then**
> 12 ra_m modifies the Sch_m and determines the new $[\tau_1, \tau_2]$ with ja_n;
>
> 13   **if** *Type 3 c_i occur in r_m* **then**
> 14 ra_m informs relevant job agents and ca that r_m is unavailable;
> 15   job agents interact with ca for new resource recommendations;
>
> 16   **if** *Type 4 c_i occur in r_m* **then**
> 17 ra_m informs job agents and ca the AT;
> 18   **if** *ja_n decides to wait for AT* **then**
> 19 ja_n and ra_m determine the new $[\tau_1, \tau_2]$;
> 20   **else**
> 21   job agents interact with ca for new resource recommendations;

First, once a dynamic event is detected by a job or resource agent, the agent will identify the type of the c_i (Line 2). When a **Type 1** c_i is detected in job j_n, the job agent ja_n identifies the new added or cancelled resource requirement e_n^ϕ (Line 4). If an existing e_n^ϕ is cancelled, ja_n will inform the relevant resource agent ra_m the cancellation. Then ra_m will search for the schedule of resource r_m and delete the allocated time slot $[\tau_1, \tau_2]$ (Lines 5–6). If a new e_n^ϕ is added, ja_n will interact with the ca for new resources recommendations (Line 8). When a **Type 2** c_i is detected in job j_n, ja_n will interact with the relevant ra_m (Line 10). Then ra_m will search for the schedule Sch_m and check whether remaining time slots of r_m can meet the changed resource requirement. If the r_m can handle the new resource requirement, ra_m will allocate new time slot $[\tau_1, \tau_2]$ to job j_n (Lines 11–12). Otherwise, ja_n will interact with ca for new resource recommendations. When a **Type 3** c_i is detected in resource r_m, ra_m will inform all affected job agents. Because the next available time of r_m is unpredictable, all affected job agents will interact with ca directly for further rescheduling (Lines 13–15). When a **Type 4** c_i is detected in r_m, ra_m will inform all relevant job agents with the next available time AT (Line 17). Then job agents evaluate the new AT and decide whether wait for the next available time AT. If so, ra_m and ja_n

will interact with each other and determine the new time slot $[\tau_1, \tau_2]$; otherwise, affected job agents will interact with ca for further rescheduling (Line 21).

3.4 Algorithm for the Centralized Resource Recommendation

Algorithm 2 shows the resource recommendations through the coordinator agent. The inputs of Algorithm 2 are jobs J, resources R and dynamic events C. The output is to recommend new feasible resources for affected unfinished jobs.

Algorithm 2: Resource Recommendation

input : $J = \{j_1, ..., j_n\}$, $R = \{r_1, ..., r_m\}$, $C = \{c_1, ..., c_i\}$
output: recommend feasible resources for affected jobs

1 **if** *resource information changes* **then**
2 $\quad$ ca collects the information of resources $R = \{r_1, ..., r_m\}$ in real-time;
3 $\quad$ ca stores the schedules Sch of resources in rl;
4 $\quad$ ca priorities resources based on the earliest available time;

5 **while** *ca receives an unsolved c_i* **do**
6 $\quad$ ca identifies the changed e_n^ϕ and searches for schedules in rl;
7 $\quad$ **if** *exists ϕ type of resources r_m that satisfies the e_n^ϕ* **then**
8 $\quad\quad$ ca recommends the ra_m with the highest priority to ja_n;
9 $\quad\quad$ ja_n and ra_m interact with each other and determine the $[\tau_1, \tau_2]$;
10 $\quad\quad$ **if** *ja_n and ra_m reach an agreement based on CNP* **then**
11 $\quad\quad\quad$ ja_n and ra_m inform ca the time slot $[\tau_1, \tau_2]$ and return success;
12 $\quad\quad$ **else**
13 $\quad\quad\quad$ ca searches for and recommends resources for j_n again;

First, in order to recommend feasible resources for jobs, ca needs to collect the information of all resources in real-time (Line 2). The ca collects resource information in an event-driven way, where ca records each change of resource information and stores the schedule Sch of available resources in the resource list rl, and priorities resources considering their earliest available time: the earlier the available time, the higher the priority (Lines 3–4). Then ca receives dynamic events C from job and resource agents and solves them based on the FCFS rule. For each received c_i, ca will identify the unfinished requirement e_n^ϕ of j_n and search for available ϕ type of resources in the rl (Lines 5–6). If there is ϕ type of resources in the rl, ca will recommend the highest priority resource r_m with the earliest available time for ja_n (Lines 7–8). Then ja_n and ra_m interact with each other and determine the specific resource use time slot $[\tau_1, \tau_2]$ (Line 9). If ja_n and ra_m reach an agreement on the allocation based on the Contract-Net Protocol (CNP), then the c_i has been successfully solved (Lines 10–11). Otherwise, if ja_n and ra_m cannot reach an agreement, ca will continue to recommend new feasible resources for j_n (Line 13).

This paper defines four types of dynamic events that occur at the job execution stage and proposes a hybrid multiagent-based rescheduling mechanism for solving them. The proposed mechanism employs decentralized agents to perform the dynamic events detection and ad-hoc communications for distributing the computational complexity, and introduces the coordinator agent to centrally recommend feasible resources for unfinished jobs, so as to improve the speed of re-allocation. In the next section, we will evaluate the mechanism considering objective functions and compare it with two existing methods.

4   Experiment

The proposed rescheduling mechanism was implemented in Eclipse applying the JADE and a computer with an Inter(R) Core(TM) i7-7500 CPU@2.70GHz, and a 16.0 GB RAM was used. Two experiments were conducted to evaluate the proposed rescheduling mechanism. In **Experiment 1**, dynamic events occur in only jobs or resources. **Experiment 1** is to evaluate the impact of dynamic events in jobs and resources on rescheduling, respectively. In **Experiment 2**, dynamic events occur concurrently in both jobs and resources. **Experiment 2** is to observe the mutual influence between dynamic events in jobs and resources.

According to the objective functions, we evaluated the rescheduling performance in terms of *makespan* and *success rate*. *Makespan* refers to the completion time of the last job, and *success rate* refers to the proportion of jobs that are successfully executed. To verify the benefits of our proposed mechanism, a state-of-the-art decentralized multiagent-based approach proposed by Guizzi et al. [4] and a classic heuristic algorithm **min-min** [12] were selected as the two comparison models. Guizzi et al. approach has a decentralized structure where decentralized agents handle dynamic events through the Contract-Net Protocol. The min-min algorithm as a heuristic algorithm has been widely used in open and stochastic scheduling environments. Guizzi et al. approach was implemented in JADE and the min-min algorithm was coded in JAVA.

4.1   Experiment Setup

Table 1. Parameters in resource requirements

Parameter	Value(s)
Number of e	Random in $[1, 5]$
Earliest start use time s	Random in $[0, 20]$ sec after release
Latest stop use time d	Random in $[40, 70]$ sec after release
Total use time t	Random in $[10, 20]$ sec

This experiment considers allocating $\Phi = 5$ types of resources for jobs. The number of jobs and resources were set as $n = 100$ and $m = 300$ (60 resources of each type), respectively. The experiment was conducted in an open and stochastic environment, where resources are available at the release time ($\alpha_m(0) = 1$ and $Sch_m = \emptyset$), and $n = 100$ jobs arrive within 20 s ($ta \in [0, 20]$). The initial schedule of our mechanism was determined by the coordinator agent. When new jobs arrive, the coordinator agent will search for and recommend available resources for new arrival jobs according to their resource requirements E. Then four types of dynamic events occur in each job or resource with probability $\rho \in [0, 1]$ at a random time during the execution stage, where $\rho = 0$ means that there is no dynamic event that occurs in any job or resource, and $\rho = 1$ means dynamic events will occur in each job and resource. The occurrence probability ρ was set as 0%, 30%, 60% and 90%. Table 1 shows the parameters used in resource requirements E of each job.

4.2   Results and Discussions

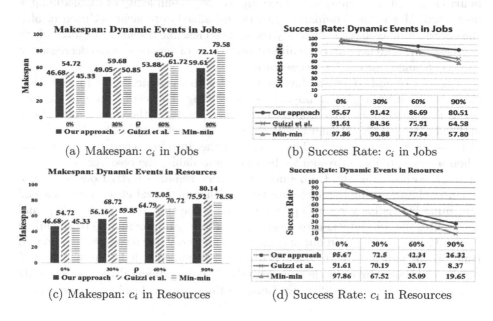

(a) Makespan: c_i in Jobs

(b) Success Rate: c_i in Jobs

(c) Makespan: c_i in Resources

(d) Success Rate: c_i in Resources

Fig. 2. Results in experiment 1

Results in Experiment 1. Figure 2 shows the comparison between three approaches concerning *makespan* and *success rate* when dynamic events occur with different probabilities ($\rho = 0\%, 30\%, 60\%, 90\%$) only in jobs (Type 1 and Type 2) and only in resources (Type 3 and Type 4), respectively. When $\rho = 0\%$, where no dynamic event happens during the execution of jobs, our approach and the min-min dispatching rule have a similar makespan (i.e. 46.68 and 45.33 s), and the makespan of Guizzi et al. approach is 54.72. The reason is that when the initial schedule is generated, the coordinator agent in our approach recommends resources for jobs with the view of all available resources. However, decentralized agents in Guizzi et al. approach only have the local view, where the agent competition and communication latency issues increase the makespan.

The performance of rescheduling from three methods when dynamic events happened only in jobs under different probabilities are shown by Fig. 2(a) and (b). From these two figures, we can see that the makespan of our approach is from 49.05 to 59.61 (59.68–72.14 of Guizzi et al. and 50.85–79.58 of min-min, respectively). Besides, our mechanism has a higher success rate than the other two approaches when dynamic events occur (from 80.51% to 91.42%). The statistics of Guizzi et al. are 64.58%–84.36% and that of min-min are 57.80%–90.88%, respectively. The reason behind is that, in our mechanism, job and resource agents will conduct the ad-hoc communication first to solve dynamics in the local range. Ad-hoc communications reduce the uncertainty in the environment caused by dynamic events and decrease the computational complexity of each agent. Compared with centralized heuristic algorithms (min-min), the computational complexity of rescheduling is decreased. Meanwhile, compared with decentralized approaches (Guizzi et al.), the coordinator agent can efficiently recommend feasible resources for jobs, which decreases the searches and communication latency of agents, so as to decrease the time costs and improve the success rate.

Figure 2(c) and (d) show that, compared with dynamic events in jobs, that in resources have a greater impact on scheduling. Especially the success rate drops dramatically in three approaches. When $\rho = 90\%$, the success rate of our approach drops to 26.32, that of Guizzi et al. approach drops to 8.37%, and that of min-min drops to 19.65%. The reason for the drop in success rate is because when a large number of resources become unavailable, the resource restrictions increase correspondingly. Even under the strict resource restrictions, our approach could have a higher success rate than that in Guizzi et al. approach and min-min. This is because our approach reduces the time costs on searches, and distributes the computations to local agents, thereby improving the rescheduling speed. Hence, more jobs in our approach can find available resources in a limited time. To be noteworthy, in real scheduling environments, it is rarely that 90% resources become unavailable concurrently. The experimental results here only discuss the performance difference between three approaches in extreme cases.

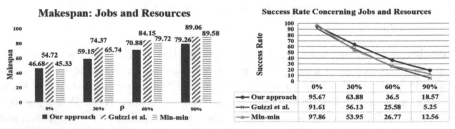

(a) Makespan: c_i in Jobs and Resources   (b) Success Rate: c_i in Jobs and Resources

Fig. 3. Results in experiment 2

Results in Experiment 2. Figure 3 shows the comparison of results between three approaches when dynamic events concurrently occur in both jobs and resources with different probabilities. When $\rho = 30\%$, our approach can handle dynamics with 63.88% success rate and the makespan is 59.15 s, and the statistics in Guizzi et al. approach are 56.13% with 74.37 s, and the success rate in min-min is 53.95% with 65.74 s. Also, due to the strict resource restrictions, when the $\rho \in [0.6, 0.9]$, the success rate in our approach decreases to 18.57%–36.50%, instead of 5.25%–25.58% in Guizzi et al. approach and 12.56%–26.77% in min-min.

Comparing with the results between Experiment 1 and 2, it can be seen that the success rate of Experiment 2 (shown as Fig. 3(b)) is approximately the product of two cases in Experiment 1 (shown as Fig. 2(b) and (d)). The reason is that the dynamic events in both jobs and resources have a mutual influence on each other. Due to occurrence of dynamic events in both jobs and resources concurrently, the computational units in three approaches need to spend considerable time on frequent modification of created schedule. However, some attempts may be in vain, because subsequent dynamics may invalidate the previous rescheduling decisions. Experimental results showed that our approach could reduce the mutual influence between dynamic events to a certain extent through the decentralized control by intelligent agents, so as to increase the rescheduling success rate and decrease the makespan.

5   Related Work

In the literature, based on the way of making (re-)scheduling decisions, dynamic scheduling approaches can be summarized as centralized and decentralized structures. Classic heuristic algorithms [7], dispatching rules [3], and learning-based scheduling algorithms [11], can be regarded own the centralized structure. For instance, Panda et al. [12] investigated the scheduling and rescheduling problems in multi-cloud systems and evaluated the min-min scheduling policy in multi-cloud systems. However, in some distributed systems, such as fog computing and manufacturing systems, resources and jobs are geographically distributed. Centralized rescheduling approaches (e.g., dispatching rules) are difficult to collect information and make decisions in a geographically distributed environment. Besides, considering the increase of uncertainties caused by the stream of dynamic events, the frequent modifications of created schedules make the computational units in centralized methods to involve considerable time on the search of scheduling space, so as to increase the computational time costs.

Decentralized agent-based approaches are considered to own higher flexibility and lower computational complexity than that of centralized approaches in open and distributed environments [2,4]. Some multiagent-based approaches were proposed to solve the scheduling and rescheduling problems. For instance, Guizzi et al. [4] proposed a decentralized agent-based approach for open scheduling problems, where resources could be allocated to jobs autonomously and dynamic events could be solved through agent interactions. However, due to decentralized agents make decisions under local view, the competition between agents and the communication latency issue decrease the scheduling efficiency.

To overcome the limits in both centralized and decentralized approaches, this paper proposed a hybrid multiagent-based rescheduling mechanism for handling dynamic events in the execution stage. Our mechanism adopts the decentralized agents to adapt to the distributed environment and to decrease the environmental uncertainty and computational complexity, and the coordinator agent is proposed to minimize the latency issues caused by the competition of agents.

6   Conclusion

This paper investigated and modeled four types of dynamic events in open and stochastic environments during the job execution stage and proposed a hybrid multiagent-based rescheduling mechanism for handling dynamic events. Experimental results show that the proposed mechanism has the higher efficiency and success rate in solving dynamic events in the execution stage than that of existing methods. In future work, we will consider introducing multiple coordinator agents with different capabilities to help decentralized agents make decisions.

References

1. Baykasoğlu, A., Karaslan, F.S.: Solving comprehensive dynamic job shop scheduling problem by using a grasp-based approach. Int. J. Prod. Res. **55**(11), 3308–3325 (2017)
2. Bittencourt, L.F., Goldman, A., Madeira, E.R., da Fonseca, N.L., Sakellariou, R.: Scheduling in distributed systems: a cloud computing perspective. Comput. Sci. Rev. **30**, 31–54 (2018)
3. Dhurasevic, M., Jakobovic, D.: A survey of dispatching rules for the dynamic unrelated machines environment. Expert Syst. Appl. **113**, 555–569 (2018)
4. Guizzi, G., Revetria, R., Vanacore, G., Vespoli, S.: On the open job-shop scheduling problem: a decentralized multi-agent approach for the manufacturing system performance optimization. Procedia CIRP **79**, 192–197 (2019)
5. Gupta, D., Maravelias, C.T., Wassick, J.M.: From rescheduling to online scheduling. Chem. Eng. Res. Des. **116**, 83–97 (2016)
6. Hsieh, F.-S.: Dynamic configuration and collaborative scheduling in supply chains based on scalable multi-agent architecture. J. Ind. Eng. Int. **15**(2), 249–269 (2018). https://doi.org/10.1007/s40092-018-0291-5
7. Huang, Z., Zhuang, Z., Cao, Q., Lu, Z., Guo, L., Qin, W.: A survey of intelligent algorithms for open shop scheduling problem. Procedia CIRP **83**, 569–574 (2019)
8. Ikonen, T.J., Heljanko, K., Harjunkoski, I.: Reinforcement learning of adaptive online rescheduling timing and computing time allocation. Comput. Chem. Eng. **141**, 106994 (2020)
9. Kan, C., Yang, H., Kumara, S.: Parallel computing and network analytics for fast industrial internet-of-things (IIOT) machine information processing and condition monitoring. J. Manuf. Syst. **46**, 282–293 (2018)

10. Kantamneni, A., Brown, L.E., Parker, G., Weaver, W.W.: Survey of multi-agent systems for microgrid control. Eng. Appl. Artif. Intell. **45**, 192–203 (2015)
11. Luo, S.: Dynamic scheduling for flexible job shop with new job insertions by deep reinforcement learning. Appl. Soft Comput. **91**, 106208 (2020)
12. Panda, S.K., Gupta, I., Jana, P.K.: Task scheduling algorithms for multi-cloud systems: allocation-aware approach. Inf. Syst. Front. **21**(2), 241–259 (2017). https://doi.org/10.1007/s10796-017-9742-6
13. Tighazoui, A., Sauvey, C., Sauer, N.: Predictive-reactive strategy for flowshop rescheduling problem: minimizing the total weighted waiting times and instability. J. Syst. Sci. Syst. Eng. **30**(3), 253–275 (2021). https://doi.org/10.1007/s11518-021-5490-8
14. Weiqing, G., Yanru, C.: Task-scheduling algorithm based on improved genetic algorithm in cloud computing environment. Recent Adv. Electr. Electron. Eng. (Formerly Recent Patents Electr. Electron. Eng.) **14**(1), 13–19 (2021)

BiES: Adaptive Policy Optimization for Model-Based Offline Reinforcement Learning

Yijun Yang[1,2], Jing Jiang[1], Zhuowei Wang[1], Qiqi Duan[2], and Yuhui Shi[2(✉)]

[1] AAII, University of Technology Sydney, Ultimo, NSW 2007, Australia
{yijun.yang-1,zhuowei.wang}@student.uts.edu.au,
jing.jiang@uts.edu.au
[2] Department of Computer Science and Engineering, Southern University of Science and Technology, Shenzhen 518055, China
11749325@mail.sustech.edu.cn, shiyh@sustech.edu.cn

Abstract. Offline reinforcement learning (RL) aims to train an agent solely using a dataset of historical interactions with the environments without any further costly or dangerous active exploration. Model-based RL (MbRL) usually achieves promising performance in offline RL due to its high sample-efficiency and compact modeling of a dynamic environment. However, it may suffer from the bias and error accumulation of the model predictions. Existing methods address this problem by adding a penalty term to the model reward but require careful hand-tuning of the penalty and its weight. Instead in this paper, we formulate the model-based offline RL as a bi-objective optimization where the first objective aims to maximize the model return and the second objective is adaptive to the learning dynamics of the RL policy. Thereby, we do not need to tune the penalty and its weight but can achieve a more advantageous trade-off between the final model return and model's uncertainty. We develop an efficient and adaptive policy optimization algorithm equipped with evolution strategy to solve the bi-objective optimization, named as BiES. The experimental results on a D4RL benchmark show that our approach sets the new state of the art and significantly outperforms existing offline RL methods on long-horizon tasks.

Keywords: Offline reinforcement learning · Multi-objective optimization · Evolution strategy

1 Introduction

Reinforcement learning (RL) encounters many obstacles when deploying an agent to real-world tasks, e.g., autonomous driving [22], robot control [21], and healthcare [27], due to costly online trial-and-error. Fortunately, it is available for these tasks to pre-collect large and diverse datasets. Hence, the research on learning high-quality policies from static datasets has promoted the development of offline RL [15].

This work is partially supported by the Shenzhen Fundamental Research Program under the Grant No. JCYJ20200109141235597.

G. Long et al. (Eds.): AI 2021, LNAI 13151, pp. 570–581, 2022.
https://doi.org/10.1007/978-3-030-97546-3_46

Since the entire learning process is carried out in a static dataset D, offline RL faces several challenging problems. (1) RL agents cannot explore environments: If D does not comprise highly rewarding demonstrations, the RL algorithms might be unable to learn a satisfying policy. Hence, the static dataset should be as large and diverse as possible [8]. (2) Another fundamental challenge is the distribution shift: The RL algorithms train a candidate policy on the distribution of data different from the distribution visited by the behavior (data collection) policy, which yields function approximation errors and results in poor performance. Several techniques have been proposed in response to the problem, such as behavior policy regularization [9] and Q-network ensembles [14]. These works in offline RL mainly focus on model-free methods. However, the recent work by [28] finds that even a vanilla model-based RL (MbRL) method can outperform model-free ones in the offline setting.

Model-based RL commonly learns an approximated dynamics model of a real Markov decision process (MDP), according to previously collected data. This paradigm benefits from powerful supervised learning techniques, allowing the learning process to leverage large-scale datasets. Moreover, once the MDP model is learned, we can employ it to generate trajectories resulting from applying a sequence of actions. As a result, MbRL algorithms have higher sample-efficiency than model-free ones. Despite these benefits, MbRL may suffer from the effect of the distribution shift issue [5] when using offline datasets. In particular, since offline datasets are unlikely to traverse all state-action pairs, the learned MDP model may not be globally accurate. Policy optimization using the model without any precautions against model inaccuracy can lead to the model exploitation issue [11], resulting in poor performance. For instance, the policy is likely to visit *risky* states where the model erroneously predicts successor states that yield higher rewards than the correct successor states obtained from the corresponding real MDP environment. One commonly-used way [28] of solving the issue is to incorporate uncertainty quantification into the model reward: $\tilde{r} = \hat{r} - \lambda u(s, a)$, which provides the agent with a penalty for visiting *risky* states.

However, it can be difficult to design a proper penalty term for complicated constraints [26]. In particular, The effort required to tune the reward penalty to a given offline RL task or repeatedly calculate it during optimization might negate any gains in the eventual model return. Conversely, in the case of a deficient penalty, a much larger region will be searched in a potentially risky policy space, resulting in an extra cost of time and unstable performance. On the other hand, recent works [11,13,28] have adopted existing RL algorithms, such as SAC [10] or NPG [19] to optimize a policy under a learned MDP model. In general, these algorithms are sample efficient due to learning the policy from every time

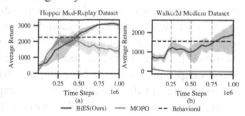

Fig. 1. A proof-of-concept experiment on two offline RL tasks from the D4RL benchmark [8]. We evaluate a SoTA offline MbRL algorithm named MOPO. The results show that it cannot achieve a higher true return than the behavior policy when using long-horizon model rollouts.

eral, these algorithms are sample efficient due to learning the policy from every time step of an episode. However, in the offline model-based setting, such a learning process may damage the performance of those algorithms since model errors rapidly accumulate with the increase of the time steps, especially when the length of the episode is long [5]. As a proof-of-concept experiment in Fig. 1, we evaluate a state-of-the-art offline MbRL algorithm named MOPO [28]. Even though MOPO applies a well-designed reward function, the results show that it cannot achieve a higher true return than the behavior policy when using long-horizon model rollouts. This finding corroborates the combination of the uncertainty penalty and RL algorithms potentially not being a panacea to the model-based offline RL tasks, which motivates two effective improvements to existing approaches in this paper. Our contributions include the following:

(1) We propose a bi-objective policy optimization algorithm where the first objective aims to maximize the model return, and the second objective synchronously calibrates the learning bias of the policy. Our method achieves more stable policy improvement on offline MbRL tasks.
(2) To the best of our knowledge, our approach is the first to adopt evolution strategy (ES) to model-based offline RL problems and solve the optimization under uncertain and long-horizon RL tasks. We also theoretically establish an upper bound for the norm of a BiES-based gradient estimation.
(3) We conduct a large-scale empirical study on offline MuJoCo locomotion tasks from the D4RL benchmark [8]. The experimental results show that our method attains state-of-the-art results compared to other offline RL algorithms.

2 Related Work

Model-Based Offline RL. Although it offers the convenience of working with large-scale datasets, the MbRL algorithm still suffers from the effects of the distribution shift, especially in the model exploitation problem [15]. Prior works in MbRL algorithms explored methods to solve this problem, such as Dyna-style algorithms [11,23], the leverage of multiple dynamics models as an ensemble [5,11], an energy-based model regularizer [2], a game-theoretic MbRL algorithm [19], meta-learning [6], policy constraints [1], and generative temporal difference learning [12]. In the offline setting, since the learned model will not be calibrated with additional data collection, it becomes crucial to prevent the policy from overly exploiting the model. Recent works propose an explicit reward penalty for this purpose [13,28]. One constructs terminating states based on a hard threshold, and the other uses a soft reward penalty associated with a user-chosen weight.

Evolution Strategy in RL. As a sub-class of the evolutionary algorithm (EA), we have seen a specific revival in evolution strategy (ES) on account of its surprising scalability and performance [20]. More particularly, recent works have applied ES to solve high-dimensional RL problems, resulting in the achievement of comparable performance to deep RL algorithms while cutting down the training time [17,20]. However, these works primarily focus on model-free tasks [4]. In the EA community, the works similar to our approach are model-based EA [3] and surrogate model-assisted EA [16], but these methods are exploited mainly in one-step black-box optimization problems rather than sequential RL tasks. Prior works showed that ES might be a more suitable choice for optimization under uncertain and long-horizon RL tasks because it learns from the result of the whole rollouts [17, 20].

3   Preliminaries

We now describe the background related to our approach, including a baseline for offline MbRL tasks and the basic concepts of evolution strategy.

3.1   Model-Based Offline Policy Optimization

A Markov Decision Process (MDP) is defined as $\mathcal{M} = \{S, A, r, p, \rho_0\}$, where S is the state space; A is the action space; r defines the reward function $S \times A \rightarrow \mathbb{R}$; p is the transition distribution $p(s_{t+1}|s_t, a_t)$; and ρ_0 is the probability distribution of the initial state s_0. The policy $\pi(a_t|s_t)$ serves as a mapping from the state space to the distribution of actions. For general RL algorithms, their goal is to search for a policy that maximizes the expected return in Eq. (1):

$$\max_{\pi} J_{\rho_0}(\pi, \mathcal{M}) = \max_{\pi} \mathbb{E}_{s_0 \sim \rho_0, \pi} \left[\sum_{t=0}^{H-1} r(s_t, a_t) \right]. \tag{1}$$

In the model-based offline setting, an approximate MDP model $\hat{\mathcal{M}} = \{\hat{S}, A, \hat{r}, \hat{p}, \rho_0\}$ is learned from a static dataset $D = \{(s_t^i, a_t^i, s_{t+1}^i, r_t^i)\}$, then $\hat{\mathcal{M}}$ is utilized to search for a policy that maximizes the expected return in the model. The transition distribution $\hat{p}$ and the reward function $\hat{r}$ can also be learned from D. Since errors accumulate rapidly when $\hat{\mathcal{M}}$ makes predictions based on its own previous outputs, offline MbRL algorithms may struggle with unstable policy learning. [11] proved that it is crucial to provide a policy with a penalty for visiting the states where the model is likely to be inaccurate. [28] suggested a practical implementation of the reward penalty, i.e., $\tilde{r} = \hat{r} - \lambda u(\hat{s}_t, a_t)$, in which $\hat{r}$ is the model reward. The penalty coefficient λ serves as a hyperparameter chosen for different tasks, and $u(\hat{s}_t, a_t)$ denotes the estimation of the model uncertainty at the state-action tuple $(\hat{s}_t, a_t)$. As such, the objective function is given as below:

$$\max_{\pi} \tilde{J}_{\rho_0}(\pi, \hat{\mathcal{M}}) = \max_{\pi} \mathbb{E}_{s_0 \sim \rho_0, \pi} \left[\sum_{t=0}^{H-1} (\hat{r}_t - \lambda u) \right]. \tag{2}$$

3.2   Evolution Strategy

It is challenging to compute accurate gradients for black-box or noisy optimization problems. Hence, as a derivative-free optimization approach, evolution strategy (ES) has seen a recent revival in the RL community. Instead of optimizing an objective function $F(x)$ directly, ES optimizes the Gaussian smoothing of F:

Algorithm 1. Bi-objective policy optimization for model-based offline RL

1: **input:** a S-MDP model with two objectives: the model return $J_\pi^{\hat{r}}$ and model uncertainty J_π^q.
2: Learn S-MDP on a static dataset.
3: Run an adaptive policy optimization algorithm on S-MDP until convergence:

$$\nabla_{\theta^\pi} J_{\rho_0} = \alpha \nabla_{\theta^\pi} J_{\rho_0}^{\hat{r}} + (1 - \alpha) \nabla_{\theta^\pi} J_{\rho_0}^q$$

Note that α exists theoretically optimal value according to Equation (4).

$F_\sigma(x) = \mathbb{E}_{\varepsilon \sim \mathcal{N}(0,I)}[F(x + \sigma\varepsilon)]$, where σ plays the role of a smoothing parameter. For $\sigma > 0$, the function $F_\sigma(x)$ is consistently differentiable, and its gradient is given by $\nabla F_\sigma(x) = (2\pi)^{-d/2} \int_{\mathbb{R}^d} F(x + \sigma\varepsilon) e^{-\frac{1}{2}\|\varepsilon\|_2^2} \varepsilon d\varepsilon$. Although the gradient is intractable, it can be estimated by a standard Monte Carlo method: $\widehat{\nabla}_N^s F_\sigma(x) = \frac{1}{N\sigma} \sum_{i=1}^N F(x + \sigma\varepsilon_i) \varepsilon_i$. The estimator is often revised to achieve unbiased estimation with reduced variance. [17] proposed an antithetic estimator: $\widehat{\nabla}_N^{at} F_\sigma(x) = \frac{1}{2N\sigma} \sum_{i=1}^N (F(x + \sigma\varepsilon_i) - F(x - \sigma\varepsilon_i)) \varepsilon_i$, where the gradient is estimated by the symmetric difference between a perturbation $\varepsilon_i \sim \mathcal{N}(0, I)$ and its antithetic counterpart $-\varepsilon_i$. Once the ES gradient is obtained, it can be equipped with popular SGD algorithms. A simple way of employing ES to optimize RL policy parameters θ is to set $F(\theta) = J_{\rho_0}(\pi_\theta, \mathcal{M}) \approx \sum_{t=0}^{H-1} r(s_t, a_t)$. Despite its simplicity, ES achieves competitive performance compared to policy gradient algorithms [4].

4   The Proposed BiES Algorithm

In this section, we first introduce a bi-objective policy optimization framework and illustrate how our method achieves an adaptive trade-off between the model return and model uncertainty. Then we propose the bi-objective evolution strategy (BiES), an efficient and stable policy optimization algorithm, by integrating ES with the framework.

Our framework consists of two steps, as presented in Algorithm 1. First, we propose a surrogate MDP (S-MDP) model and learn it on a static dataset in a supervised manner. Second, based on S-MDP, we develop a provably efficient mechanism to adjust weights between two objectives. The first objective aims to maximize the model return, and the second objective synchronously calibrates the learning bias of the policy. As a result, our approach achieves more stable policy optimization via an adaptive trade-off. More specifically, we construct the S-MDP model $\hat{\mathcal{M}} = \{\hat{S}, A, \hat{r}, q, \hat{p}, \rho_0\}$ by adding $q(\hat{s}, a)$, a guided objective for model uncertainty. We model S-MDP using a bootstrap ensemble of Gaussian dynamics models $\{\hat{\mathcal{P}}_\phi^1, \ldots, \hat{\mathcal{P}}_\phi^N\}$, in which each model of the ensemble is a multi-layer neural network parametrized by ϕ. It predicts the mean μ and covariance Σ of a Gaussian distribution over the next state and reward, $\hat{\mathcal{P}}_\phi^i(\hat{s}_{t+1}^i, \hat{r}^i | \hat{s}_t, a_t) := \mathcal{N}(\mu_\phi^i(\hat{s}_t, a_t), \Sigma_\phi^i(\hat{s}_t, a_t))$. We compute the mean of the rewards predicted by ensemble models as $\hat{r}$, and the minus ensemble difference $- \max_{i,j}(\|\mu_\phi^i(\hat{s}_t, a_t) - \mu_\phi^j(\hat{s}_t, a_t)\|^2)$ as q. Therefore, a bi-objective policy optimization problem can be formulated as:

$$\max_{\pi} \boldsymbol{J}_{\rho_0}(\pi, \hat{\mathcal{M}}) = \max_{\pi}(J_{\rho_0}^{\hat{r}}(\pi, \hat{\mathcal{M}}), J_{\rho_0}^{q}(\pi, \hat{\mathcal{M}})),$$

$$J_{\rho_0}^{\hat{r}}(s, \hat{\mathcal{M}}) = \mathbb{E}_{s_0 \sim \rho_0, \pi} \left[\sum_{t=0}^{H-1} \hat{r}(\hat{s}_t, a_t) \right],$$

$$J_{\rho_0}^{q}(s, \hat{\mathcal{M}}) = \mathbb{E}_{s_0 \sim \rho_0, \pi} \left[\sum_{t=0}^{H-1} q(\hat{s}_t, a_t) \right]. \tag{3}$$

Next, we discuss a special gradient ascent algorithm for solving the bi-objective optimization problem. For example, a general multi-objective optimization problem can be formulated as: $\max_{x \in \mathbb{R}^d} \boldsymbol{f}(x) = \max_{x \in \mathbb{R}^d}(f_1(x), f_2(x), ..., f_m(x))$, where x is a parameter vector; d represents the number of parameters; $\boldsymbol{f}(x)$ is a multi-objective function involving the m sub-objectives $f_{i=1,...,m}$. When we utilize gradient-based methods to solve the problem, the gradient of $\boldsymbol{f}(x)$ is given as follows: $\nabla_x \boldsymbol{f}(x) = \sum_{i=1}^{m} \alpha_i \nabla_x f_i(x)$, s.t. $\sum_{i=1}^{m} \alpha_i = 1, \alpha_i \geq 0$, where we achieve adaptive trade-offs between two even more objectives by automatically tuning the weight α. [7] extended the vanilla gradient descent algorithm to multi-objective optimization. His work provides a general method to calculate "optimal" α_i at each gradient update. He proved that the weight α is the optimal solution of a quadratic optimization problem. In the case of a common bi-objective optimization problem, an analytical solution exists as below:

$$\min_{\alpha \in [0,1]} \|\alpha \nabla_x f_1(x) + (1 - \alpha) \nabla_x f_2(x)\|^2$$

$$\alpha = \frac{(\nabla_x f_2(x) - \nabla_x f_1(x))^{\mathsf{T}} \nabla_x f_2(x)}{\|\nabla_x f_1(x) - \nabla_x f_2(x)\|^2} \tag{4}$$

Now moving back to Eq. (3), if we obtain the gradients of $J^{\hat{r}}$ and J^q, the our proposed optimization problem can be solved by a simple gradient method.

$$\theta_{t+1}^{\pi} = \theta_t^{\pi} + \gamma \nabla_{\theta^{\pi}} \boldsymbol{J}_{\rho_0}, \tag{5}$$

$$\nabla_{\theta^{\pi}} \boldsymbol{J}_{\rho_0} = \alpha \nabla_{\theta^{\pi}} J_{\rho_0}^{\hat{r}} + (1 - \alpha) \nabla_{\theta^{\pi}} J_{\rho_0}^{q}, \tag{6}$$

$$\alpha = \frac{\left(\nabla_{\theta^{\pi}} J_{\rho_0}^{q} - \nabla_{\theta^{\pi}} J_{\rho_0}^{\hat{r}}\right)^{\mathsf{T}} \nabla_{\theta^{\pi}} J_{\rho_0}^{q}}{\left\|\nabla_{\theta^{\pi}} J_{\rho_0}^{\hat{r}} - \nabla_{\theta^{\pi}} J_{\rho_0}^{q}\right\|^2}. \tag{7}$$

The two sub-objectives $J^{\hat{r}}$ and J^q are both uncertain and noisy functions. With that in mind, ES might be a better choice. We use the antithetic ES estimator to compute their gradients, as listed in Algorithm 2. For better performance, we propose several key improvements. First, any bi-objective optimization algorithm is likely to be stuck prematurely at a bad Pareto stationary point [7], causing no gain in the eventual policy quality. To solve this issue, BiES adopts behavior cloning initialization, which provides a relatively stable policy π_0 as the initial solution by end-to-end behavior cloning. We can intuitively understand that the method works as a regularization of

---

Algorithm 2. BiES for model-based offline RL

1: **hyperparameters:** step-size γ, number of noises N, smoothing parameter σ, b elites.
2: **inputs:** a neural network policy π_i parametrized by $\theta_i \in \mathbb{R}^d$. θ_0 is initialized by end-to-end behavior cloning, set μ, Σ to be the mean and covariance of all states in the dataset D_{env}, an initial states dataset $\rho_0 \subset D_{env}$, and $i = 0$.
3: train S-MDP $\hat{\mathcal{M}}$ on D_{env}.
4: **while** ending condition not satisfied **do**
5:   Sample $\varepsilon_1, \varepsilon_2, \ldots, \varepsilon_N$ in $\mathbb{R}^d$ from $\mathcal{N}(\mathbf{0}, \mathbf{I})$.
6:   Collect $2N$ rollouts $\{(\hat{s}_t, a_t, \hat{r}_t, q_t)|\pi_{i,k,\pm}\}_{t=0}^{H-1}$ via $\hat{\mathcal{M}}$, where $\pi_{i,k,\pm}$ uses normalized states as inputs, and initial state $s_0 \sim \rho_0$.
     $\pi_{i,k,\pm} = \theta_i \pm \sigma\varepsilon_k, k \in \mathbf{K} = \{1, 2, ..., N\}$.
7:   Compute objective functions by:
     $J^{\hat{r}} \approx \sum_{t=0}^{H-1} \hat{r}_t, J^q \approx \frac{1}{H}\sum_{t=0}^{H-1} q_t$
8:   Sort the noises ε_k for $m = \hat{r}, q$:
     $\mathbf{K}^m = \text{sort}(\mathbf{K}, \max\{J_{i,k,+}^m, J_{i,k,-}^m\})$
9:   Compute the ES gradient of J^m for $m = \hat{r}, q$:
     $g_i^m = \frac{1}{2b\sigma}\sum_{k \in \mathbf{K}^m[0:b]} \left(J_{i,k,+}^m - J_{i,k,-}^m\right)\varepsilon_k$
10: Make the update step:
     $\theta_{i+1} = \theta_i + \text{optimizer-step}(g_i, \gamma)$,
     where $g_i = \alpha g_i^{\hat{r}} + (1 - \alpha)g_i^q$, α can be computed by Eq. (7)
11:    $i \leftarrow i + 1$
12: **end while**

---

distributional shift. At the initial stage of policy optimization, behavior cloning constrains the policy to the support of training data. Second, we notice that the states of the high dimensional complex tasks take the values in a broad range, which may cause the policies only pay attention to particular features of these states. Therefore, the state normalization can make the policies more robust for multiple-scale state observations: $a_t = \pi(\text{diag}(\Sigma)^{-1/2}(\hat{s}_t - \mu))$. In the offline RL setting, a large-scale dataset is available for the learning algorithms, which means that we can set μ and Σ to be the mean and covariance of all the states in the dataset, just like the data normalization in supervised learning. Finally, BiES adopts an elite selection strategy that sorts noises ε_k in a descending order according to $\max\{J^{\hat{r}}(\pi_{i,k,+}), J^{\hat{r}}(\pi_{i,k,-})\}$ and $\max\{J^q(\pi_{i,k,+}), J^q(\pi_{i,k,-})\}$, respectively. We only choose the top-b noises for computing the gradients of two objectives. This enhancement improves the performance of BiES because it reduces the variance of gradient estimation by using more concentrated Gaussian noises.

It is proved that the optimal convex combination of $\nabla f_i(x^*)$ is equal to zero when x^* is Pareto stationary [7] (see Definition 1). However, we use the ES-based gradient estimation, which means $\mathbb{E}(\widehat{\nabla}_{ES} f_i(x^*)) = \nabla f_i(x^*)$. As such, we need to establish an upper bound for the norm of BiES-based gradient $\widehat{\nabla}_{ES} \mathbf{f}(x^*)$ when the optimal policy is Pareto stationary. Considering a general multi-objective optimization problem, the necessary conditions for a solution to be optimal are the KKT conditions. Thus each solution that satisfies these conditions is Pareto stationary [18].

Definition 1. *Let x^* be a Pareto stationary solution. Therefore, there exists non-negative scalars $\alpha_1, \ldots, \alpha_m \geq 0$ such that $\nabla \boldsymbol{f}(x^*) = \sum_{i=1}^{m} \alpha_i \nabla f_i(x^*) = 0, \sum_{i=1}^{m} \alpha_i = 1$.*

Hence, we can define an ascent direction based on the ES gradient $\widehat{\nabla}_{ES} f_i(x)$, i.e., $\widehat{\nabla}_{ES} \boldsymbol{f}(x) = \sum_{i=1}^{m} \alpha_i \widehat{\nabla}_{ES} f_i(x)$, s.t. $\sum_{i=1}^{m} \alpha_i = 1, \alpha_i \geq 0$. Suppose that we have $\widehat{\nabla}_{ES} f_i(x) = \nabla f_i(x) + \epsilon_i$, then $\|\widehat{\nabla}_{ES} f_i(x) - \nabla f_i(x)\| = \|\epsilon_i\| \leq \tilde{\epsilon}_i$. We can prove an upper bound for the norm of $\widehat{\nabla}_{ES} \boldsymbol{f}(x^*)$.

Theorem 1. *If x^* is a solution satisfying Definition 1, then $\|\widehat{\nabla}_{ES} \boldsymbol{f}(x^*)\| \leq \sum_{i=1}^{m} \alpha_i \tilde{\epsilon}_i$.*

Proof. Since x^* satisfies Definition 1, we have $\nabla \boldsymbol{f}(x^*) = 0$. Consequently,

$$\|\widehat{\nabla}_{ES} \boldsymbol{f}(x^*)\| = \| \sum_{i=1}^{m} \alpha_i \epsilon_i \| \leq \sum_{i=1}^{m} \alpha_i \tilde{\epsilon}_i.$$

5   Experiments

In this section, there are three important questions for conducting our experiments (Table 1):

Q1 Does BiES outperform other SoTA approaches on modern benchmarks?
Q2 Is our proposed BiES essential? Does a single-objective ES perform well?
Q3 How does each component affect the performance of BiES?

Note that we use the same hyper-parameters for all tasks and random seeds. In contrast, prior works, like MOPO [28] and MOReL [13], tune the hyperparameters separately for

Table 1. Hyper-parameters for BiES

Parameters	γ	σ	N	b	Policy structure
Value	0.02	0.03	30	20	MLP(32, Tanh, 32)

each benchmark problem. For **Q1**, we pick several offline RL algorithms as baselines, including the model-based and model-free approaches: Model-based policy optimization (MBPO) [11], model-based offline policy optimization (MOPO) [28], behavior regularized actor critic (BRAC) [25], bootstrapping error accumulation reduction (BEAR) [14], and batch-constrained Q-learning (BCQ) [9]. The detailed experimental results are given in Sect. 5.2. We do not pick MOReL [13] as the baseline because the author-provided implementation of MOReL achieves a lower result than their reported results[1]. Unlike MOReL, [28] argued that MOPO allows the policy to take a few risky actions due to using a soft reward penalty, leading to better exploration. For **Q2**, we compare BiES with a single-objective ES (denoted by **ES w/p**), and its objective function is given in Eq. (2). Moreover, we also evaluate a state-of-the-art multi-objective optimization approach, COMO-CMA-ES [24]. For **Q3**, we conduct a thorough ablation study.

---

[1] https://github.com/aravindr93/mjrl/issues/35

5.1 D4RL Benchmark

D4RL is a standard benchmark for evaluating offline RL algorithms [8]. It provides a variety of environments, tasks, and corresponding datasets containing samples of multiple trajectories $\{(s_i, a_i, r_i, T_i)|\pi_{bc}\}$, where T is the termination flag. We choose three MuJoCo environments (halfcheetah, hopper, walker2d) with five dataset types (random, medium, medium-replay, medium-expert, mixed) as the testbed. **Random** contains 1M samples from a random policy. **Medium** contains 1M samples from a policy trained to approximately 1/3 of the performance of the expert. **Medium-replay** contains the replay buffer of a policy trained up to the performance of the medium agent. **Medium-expert** contains a 50-50 split of medium and expert data (2M samples). **Mixed** is an aggregate of random, medium, and expert datasets (3M samples).

5.2 Experimental Results

To answer **Q1**, the experimental results are given in Table 2. BiES obtains the best mean score over 12 benchmark problems. Among the model-based methods, BiES achieves

Table 2. Experimental results for the D4RL benchmark. Each number is the normalized score $= \frac{\text{score} - \text{random score}}{\text{expert score} - \text{random score}} \times 100$ of the policy at the last iteration of training (10^6 time steps in total), $\pm$ standard deviation, k the length of model rollouts, **CMA-ES** denotes COMO-CMA-ES. We use the results reported by prior works.

Dataset	Environment	BiES (Our)		MOPO		CMA-ES	MBPO	BEAR	BRAC-v	BCQ
		k=1-1000	k=1-500	k=1-5	k=1-500					
Random	halfcheetah	**35.7** $\pm$ 6.62	24.1 $\pm$ 12.3	35.4 $\pm$ 2.5	28.2 $\pm$ 18.0	2.25 $\pm$ 0.01	30.7	25.1	31.2	2.2
	hopper	11.7 $\pm$ 1.96	**11.9** $\pm$ 0.43	11.3 $\pm$ 0.52	11.4 $\pm$ 0.47	11.6 $\pm$ 0.22	4.5	11.4	12.2	10.6
	walker2d	8.43 $\pm$ 7.49	8.91 $\pm$ 6.30	**13.6** $\pm$ 2.6	4.75 $\pm$ 1.74	5.81 $\pm$ 0.29	8.6	7.3	1.9	4.9
Medium	halfcheetah	**43.0** $\pm$ 2.63	41.2 $\pm$ 1.39	42.3 $\pm$ 1.6	2.79 $\pm$ 1.07	42.7 $\pm$ 0.79	28.3	41.7	46.3	40.7
	hopper	**90.6** $\pm$ 11.9	85.7 $\pm$ 13.5	28.0 $\pm$ 12.4	48.7 $\pm$ 11.1	76.3 $\pm$ 22.2	4.9	52.1	31.1	54.5
	walker2d	21.0 $\pm$ 12.0	20.1 $\pm$ 15.2	17.8 $\pm$ 19.3	-0.13 $\pm$ 0.01	**42.9** $\pm$ 19.5	12.7	59.1	81.1	53.1
Med-replay	halfcheetah	32.1 $\pm$ 2.27	30.7 $\pm$ 1.96	**53.1** $\pm$ 2.0	33.6 $\pm$ 7.73	32.4 $\pm$ 5.97	47.3	38.6	47.7	38.2
	hopper	**93.8** $\pm$ 2.95	93.1 $\pm$ 6.92	67.5 $\pm$ 24.7	62.3 $\pm$ 26.7	92.1 $\pm$ 2.42	49.8	33.7	0.6	33.1
	walker2d	25.2 $\pm$ 14.4	27.1 $\pm$ 17.0	**39.0** $\pm$ 9.6	17.6 $\pm$ 7.11	30.2 $\pm$ 9.62	22.2	19.2	0.9	15.0
Med-expert	halfcheetah	38.0 $\pm$ 4.30	39.2 $\pm$ 2.18	**63.3** $\pm$ 38.0	0.09 $\pm$ 0.51	42.9 $\pm$ 1.71	9.7	53.4	41.9	64.7
	hopper	**93.5** $\pm$ 11.3	92.8 $\pm$ 16.6	23.7 $\pm$ 6.0	72.8 $\pm$ 20.4	61.8 $\pm$ 18.0	56.0	96.3	0.8	110.9
	walker2d	20.7 $\pm$ 18.9	15.1 $\pm$ 20.6	**44.6** $\pm$ 12.9	2.64 $\pm$ 4.02	39.6 $\pm$ 23.9	7.6	40.1	81.6	57.5
Total mean		**42.8**	40.8	36.6	23.7	40.1	23.5	39.8	31.4	40.45

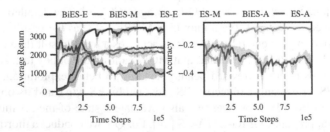

Fig. 2. Ablation study. BiES and ES w/p learning curves in the hopper environment. E: The real MDP return. M: The predicted return. A: The prediction accuracy. ES denotes ES w/p. Our BiES achieves stable and near-monotonic learning.

SoTA results in six out of the 12 problems. In particular, BiES is the strongest by a significant margin on the hopper medium and medium-replay datasets. Meanwhile, COMO-CMA-ES also achieves good results on the walker2d datasets. We hypothesize that the adaptive mechanism of COMO-CMA-ES rapidly decays the step-size when the policy reaches a near-optimal solution, preventing inaccurate update directions from degenerating the learned policy on the walker2d datasets. Such results indicate that the model-based offline policy optimization can benefit from early stopping. Moreover, we find that the larger state-action space in the walker2d environments makes it more difficult to learn a well-generalized model. Fortunately, the recent work shows a powerful γ-model that learns a more accurate state transition for MbRL [12]. Our BiES can attain better performance by being combined with stronger models. It should be pointed out that MOPO utilizes a technique named branched rollout to collect experience replay. A policy begins a rollout from the state s sampled from a static dataset and executes k steps under the learned model. Conversely, BiES learns from the result of the whole rollout $(s_0, s_1, \ldots, s_k)$. Although learning from the whole rollout may damage performance due to accumulated model errors, it will be advantageous in some scenarios where learning algorithms might not directly access the datasets. In Table 2, we compare the performance of BiES and MOPO based on different k steps. When MOPO adopts longer rollouts ($k = 1 - 500$), it performs worse on the walker2d datasets. To answer **Q2**, we pick two complex environments, hopper and walker2d, in which the policy must overcome the severe model exploitation issue. We compare BiES with a single-objective ES (**ES w/p**). The results are shown in Table 3. It is clear that BiES significantly outperforms **ES w/p**. Figure 2 records the two methods' learning curves, showing that the superiority of BiES benefits from a better trade-off between the model return and uncertainty estimation. Such results confirm the effectiveness of our method

Table 3. Ablation study. A comparison between BiES and a single-objective ES. **ES w/p** denotes a vanilla ES algorithm that adopts the reward penalty in Eq. (2) (average of five random seeds).

Environment	Dataset	BiES	ES w/p
Hopper	Random	11.5 ± 1.96	**12.5 ± 0.63**
	Medium	**90.6 ± 11.9**	33.9 ± 16.5
	Med-replay	**93.8 ± 2.95**	73.0 ± 20.3
	Med-expert	**93.5 ± 11.3**	88.2 ± 16.4
	Mixed	**72.5 ± 16.5**	47.6 ± 16.9
walker2d	Random	**8.43 ± 7.49**	−0.17 ± 0.06
	Medium	**21.0 ± 12.0**	−0.11 ± 0.01
	Med-replay	**25.2 ± 14.4**	0.21 ± 0.64
	Med-expert	**20.7 ± 18.9**	−0.14 ± 0.09
	Mixed	**35.5 ± 22.3**	−0.07 ± 0.15

Table 4. Ablation study. The effectiveness of behavior cloning initialization (average of five random seeds).

Environment	Dataset	BiES w/bc	BiES w/o bc
halfcheetah	Random	**35.7 ± 6.62**	35.0 ± 5.64
	Medium	**43.0 ± 2.63**	6.39 ± 8.86
	Med-replay	**32.1 ± 2.27**	28.1 ± 8.62
	Med-expert	**38.0 ± 4.30**	11.7 ± 17.0
	Mixed	**42.9 ± 0.72**	41.6 ± 7.23
hopper	Random	**11.5 ± 1.96**	10.5 ± 0.72
	Medium	**90.6 ± 11.9**	22.1 ± 32.8
	Med-replay	**93.8 ± 2.95**	70.7 ± 31.1
	Med-expert	**93.5 ± 11.3**	92.8 ± 19.7
	Mixed	72.5 ± 16.5	**84.1 ± 17.8**
walker2d	Random	**8.43 ± 7.49**	4.73 ± 1.76
	Medium	**21.0 ± 12.0**	12.2 ± 7.78
	Med-replay	**25.2 ± 14.4**	14.7 ± 9.27
	Med-expert	**20.7 ± 18.9**	5.49 ± 3.43
	Mixed	**35.5 ± 22.3**	6.52 ± 5.81

again. To answer **Q3**, we investigate the impact of behavior cloning initialization (**bc**) by comparing the performance of two methods: **BiES w/bc** and **BiES w/o bc**. In Table 4, we observe apparent performance degradation due to the absence of **bc**. According to [28], it is more challenging for model-based algorithms to learn a well-generalized model from the medium datasets due to the lack of action diversity. However, **BiES w/bc** obtains significant improvements on these datasets, which reflects the importance of **bc**.

6   Conclusion

This paper proposes a novel approach to address the model exploitation issue in model-based offline reinforcement learning. In contrast to adding a penalty term and user-chosen weight, we propose a bi-objective policy optimization framework where the first objective aims to maximize the model return, and the second one synchronously calibrates the learning bias of the policy. Then we integrate evolution strategy with the framework and develop BiES, an adaptive model-based offline policy optimization algorithm. Experimental results show that our approach achieves state-of-the-art performance compared to other offline RL algorithms.

References

1. Berkenkamp, F., Turchetta, M., Schoellig, A., Krause, A.: Safe model-based reinforcement learning with stability guarantees. In: NeurIPS, pp. 908–918 (2017)
2. Boney, R., Kannala, J., Ilin, A.: Regularizing model-based planning with energy-based models. In: CoRL (2019)
3. Cheng, R., He, C., Jin, Y., Yao, X.: Model-based evolutionary algorithms: a short survey. Complex Intell. Syst. **4**(4), 283–292 (2018). https://doi.org/10.1007/s40747-018-0080-1
4. Choromanski, K., et al.: Provably robust blackbox optimization for reinforcement learning. In: CoRL, pp. 683–696 (2020)
5. Chua, K., Calandra, R., McAllister, R., Levine, S.: Deep reinforcement learning in a handful of trials using probabilistic dynamics models. In: NeurIPS (2018)
6. Clavera, I., Rothfuss, J., Schulman, J., Fujita, Y., Asfour, T., Abbeel, P.: Model-based reinforcement learning via meta-policy optimization. In: CoRL (2018)
7. Désidéri, J.A.: Multiple-gradient descent algorithm (MGDA) for multiobjective optimization. C.R. Math. **350**(5), 313–318 (2012)
8. Fu, J., Kumar, A., Nachum, O., Tucker, G., Levine, S.: D4RL: datasets for deep data-driven reinforcement learning. arXiv:2004.07219 (2020)
9. Fujimoto, S., Meger, D., Precup, D.: Off-policy deep reinforcement learning without exploration. In: ICML (2019)
10. Haarnoja, T., Zhou, A., Abbeel, P., Levine, S.: Soft actor-critic: off-policy maximum entropy deep reinforcement learning with a stochastic actor. In: ICML, pp. 1861–1870 (2018)
11. Janner, M., Fu, J., Zhang, M., Levine, S.: When to trust your model: model-based policy optimization. In: NeurIPS (2019)
12. Janner, M., Mordatch, I., Levine, S.: γ-models: generative temporal difference learning for infinite-horizon prediction. arXiv:2010.14496 (2020)
13. Kidambi, R., Rajeswaran, A., Netrapalli, P., Joachims, T.: MOReL: model-based offline reinforcement learning. arXiv:2005.05951 (2020)

14. Kumar, A., Fu, J., Tucker, G., Levine, S.: Stabilizing off-policy q-learning via bootstrapping error reduction. In: NeurIPS (2019)
15. Levine, S., Kumar, A., Tucker, G., Fu, J.: Offline reinforcement learning: tutorial, review, and perspectives on open problems. arXiv:2005.01643 (2020)
16. Luo, J., Chen, L., Li, X., Zhang, Q.: Novel multitask conditional neural-network surrogate models for expensive optimization. IEEE Trans Cyber. 1–14 (2020)
17. Mania, H., Guy, A., Recht, B.: Simple random search of static linear policies is competitive for reinforcement learning. In: NeurIPS (2018)
18. Milojkovic, N., Antognini, D., Bergamin, G., Faltings, B., Musat, C.: Multi-gradient descent for multi-objective recommender systems. In: AAAI (2020)
19. Rajeswaran, A., Mordatch, I., Kumar, V.: A game theoretic framework for model based reinforcement learning. In: ICML, pp. 7953–7963 (2020)
20. Salimans, T., Ho, J., Chen, X., Sidor, S., Sutskever, I.: Evolution strategies as a scalable alternative to reinforcement learning. arXiv:1703.03864 (2017)
21. Schulman, J., Moritz, P., Levine, S., Jordan, M., Abbeel, P.: High-dimensional continuous control using generalized advantage estimation. In: ICLR (2016)
22. Shin, M., Kim, J.: Randomized adversarial imitation learning for autonomous driving. In: IJCAI, pp. 4590–4596 (2019)
23. Sutton, R.S.: Dyna, an integrated architecture for learning, planning, and reacting. ACM SIGART Bull. 2(4), 160–163 (1991)
24. Touré, C., Hansen, N., Auger, A., Brockhoff, D.: Uncrowded hypervolume improvement: COMO-CMA-ES and the sofomore framework. In: GECCO, pp. 638–646 (2019)
25. Wu, Y., Tucker, G., Nachum, O.: Behavior regularized offline reinforcement learning. arXiv:1911.11361 (2019)
26. Xu, Y., Liu, M., Lin, Q., Yang, T.: ADMM without a fixed penalty parameter: faster convergence with new adaptive penalization. In: NeurIPS, pp. 1267–1277 (2017)
27. Yu, C., Ren, G., Liu, J.: Deep inverse reinforcement learning for sepsis treatment. In: ICHI, pp. 1–3 (2019). https://doi.org/10.1109/ICHI.2019.8904645
28. Yu, T., et al.: MOPO: model-based offline policy optimization. arXiv:2005.13239 (2020)

Improvement of Arc Consistency in Asynchronous Forward Bounding Algorithm

Rachid Adrdor$^{(\boxtimes)}$ and Lahcen Koutti

Department of Computer Science, Faculty of Sciences, Ibn Zohr University,
Agadir, Morocco
rachid.adrdor@edu.uiz.ac.ma, l.koutti@uiz.ac.ma

Abstract. The AFB_BJ$^+$-AC* algorithm is one of the latest algorithms used to solve Distributed Constraint Optimization Problems known as DCOPs. It is based on soft arc consistency techniques (AC*) to speed up the process of solving a problem by permanently removing any value that doesn't belong to the optimal solution. In fact, these techniques have greatly contributed to improving the performance of the AFB_BJ$^+$ algorithm in solving DCOPs, but there are some exceptions in which they have no effect due to the limited number of deletions made. For that, we use in this paper a higher consistency level, which is a directional arc consistency (DAC*). This level makes it possible to erase more values and thus to quickly reach the optimal solution to a problem. Experiments on some benchmarks show that the new algorithm, AFB_BJ$^+$-DAC*, is better in terms of communication load and computation effort.

Keywords: DCOP · AFB_BJ$^+$ · AC* · Directional arc consistency

1 Introduction

A large number of multi-agent problems can be modeled as DCOPs such as meetings scheduling [13], sensor networks [5], and so on. Some people may say that DCOP is an outdated paradigm, especially in the age of cloud computing and wireless internet. If multiple agents need to solve a problem together, but they are physically separate, they can simply upload the problem to a remote central server and resolve it centrally. In response, we say that DCOP is one of the paradigms used in several areas of life, especially those of decision-making and the need for it increases over time for one reason which is data security. DCOP is a paradigm that deals with distributed problems, each of them is distributed among a set of agents, and allows to solve them in a distributed way, ensuring to each agent the confidentiality of its data. What does not exist in classical paradigms. In a DCOP, variables, domains, and constraints are distributed among a set of agents. Each agent has full control over a subset of variables and constraints that involve them [7]. A DCOP is solved in a distributed manner via an algorithm allowing the agents to cooperate and coordinate with each

© Springer Nature Switzerland AG 2022
G. Long et al. (Eds.): AI 2021, LNAI 13151, pp. 582–591, 2022.
https://doi.org/10.1007/978-3-030-97546-3_47

other to find a solution with a minimal cost. A solution to a DCOP is a set of value assignments, each representing the value assigned to one of the variables in that DCOP. Algorithms with various search strategies have been suggested to solve DCOPs, for example, Adopt [14], BnB-Adopt [18], BnB-Adopt$^+$ [9], SyncBB [11], AFB [7], AFB_BJ$^+$ [16], AFB_BJ$^+$-AC* [1,3], etc.

In AFB_BJ$^+$-AC*, agents synchronously develop a current partial assignment (CPA) in order to find the optimal solution to the problem to be solved. During this process, and in order to reduce the number of retries, each agent uses arc consistency (AC*) to remove any suboptimal values in its domain. But sometimes, the number of deletions generated by AC* is insufficient, which negatively affects the performance of the algorithm.

In this paper, instead of using the basic level of arc consistency (AC*), we use directional arc consistency (DAC*), which is the next higher level of AC*. DAC* allows AFB_BJ$^+$ to generate more deletions and thus quickly reach the optimal solution of a problem. The new algorithm is called AFB_BJ$^+$-DAC*. It uses DAC* to filter agent domains by performing a set of cost extensions from an agent to its neighbors, then executing AC*. Our experiments on different benchmarks show the superiority of AFB_BJ$^+$-DAC* algorithm in terms of communication load and computation effort.

This paper comprises four sections. Section 2 gives an overview of DCOPs, soft arc consistency rules, and AFB_BJ$^+$-AC* algorithm. Section 3 gives a description of AFB_BJ$^+$-DAC* algorithm. Section 4 talks about experiments fulfilled on some benchmarks. The last section gives the conclusion.

2 Background

2.1 Distributed Constraint Optimization Problem (DCOP)

A DCOP [2,6,8] is defined by 4 sets, set of agents $\mathcal{A} = \{A_1, A_2, ..., A_k\}$, set of variables $\mathcal{X} = \{x_1, x_2, ..., x_n\}$, set of domains $\mathcal{D} = \{D_1, D_2, ..., D_n\}$, where each D_i in $\mathcal{D}$ contains the possible values for its associated variable x_i in $\mathcal{X}$, and set of soft constraints $\mathcal{C} = \{c_{ij} : D_i \times D_j \to \mathbb{R}^+\} \cup \{c_i : D_i \to \mathbb{R}^+\}$. Each constraint C_{ij} is defined over the pair of variables $\{x_i, x_j\} \in \mathcal{X}$. We say that x_i and x_j are neighbors. In a DCOP, each agent is fully responsible for a subset of variables and the constraints that involve them.

For simplicity purposes, we consider a restricted version of DCOP where two variables, at most, are linked by one constraint (i.e., unary or binary constraint) and each agent is responsible for a single variable ($k = n$). Thus, we use the terms agent (A_j) and variable (x_j) interchangeably [15,16].

We consider these notations: A_j is an agent, where j is its level. (x_j, v_j) is an assignment of A_j, where $v_j \in D_j$ and $x_j \in \mathcal{X}$. C_{ij} is a binary constraint between x_i and x_j. C_{ij}^{ac} is an identical copy of the C_{ij} constraint, used in the AC* process. C_j is a unary constraint on x_j. C_ϕ is a zero-arity constraint that represents a lower bound of any problem solution. C_{ϕ_j} is the contribution value of A_j in C_ϕ. UB_j is the cost of the optimal solution reached so far and it is also the lowest unacceptable cost used for AC* process. $[A_1, A_2, ..., A_n]$ is the lexicographic ordering of agents, $\Gamma(x_j) = \{\Gamma^- : x_i \in \mathcal{X} \mid C_{ij} \in \mathcal{C}, i < j\} \cup \{\Gamma^+ : x_i \in \mathcal{X} \mid C_{ij} \in \mathcal{C}, i > j\}$ is the set of neighbors of A_j. Γ^- (resp. Γ^+) is a set of neighbors with a higher priority (resp. with a lower priority). $Y = Y^j = [(x_1, v_1), \ldots, (x_j, v_j)]$ is a current partial assignment (CPA). v_j^* is the optimal value of A_j. $lb_k[i][v_j]$ are the lower bounds of a lower neighbor A_k obtained for Y^j. GC (resp. GC^*) are the guaranteed costs of Y (resp. in AC*). $DVals$ is a list of n arrays containing deleted values, each array, $DVals[j]$, contains two elements, $listVals$ which is the list of values deleted by A_j and $UnvNbrs$ which is a counter of the A_j neighbors that have not yet processed $listVals$. $EVals$ is a list of arrays containing extension values.

The guaranteed cost of Y is the sum of c_{ij} involved in Y (1).

$$GC(Y) = \sum_{c_{ij} \in \mathcal{C}} c_{ij}(v_i, v_j) \mid \text{for all } (x_i, v_i), (x_j, v_j) \in Y \tag{1}$$

A CPA Y is said to be a complete assignment (i.e., a solution) when it comprises a value assignment for each variable of a DCOP. Solving a DCOP is to find a solution such that the sum of all the constraints involved in this solution is minimal, i.e., $Y^* = \arg\min_{Y}\{GC(Y) \mid var(Y) = \mathcal{X}\}$.

2.2   Soft Arc Consistency

Soft arc consistency techniques are used when solving a problem to delete values that are not part of the optimal solution of this problem. To apply these techniques to a problem, a set of transformations known as equivalence preserving transformations are used. They allow the exchange of costs between the constraints of the problem according to three manners that are a binary projection, a unary projection, and an extension.

The binary projection (Proc. 2) is an operation which subtracts, for a value v_i of D_i, the smallest cost α of a binary constraint C_{ij} and adds it to the unary constraint C_i. The unary projection (Proc. 1) is an operation which subtracts the smallest cost β of a unary constraint C_i and adds it to the zero-arity constraint C_ϕ. The extension (Proc. 3) is an operation which subtracts, for a value v_i of D_i, the extension value ($E[v_i]$) of v_i from a unary constraint C_i and adds it to the binary constraint C_{ij}, with $0 < E[v_i] \leq c_i(v_i)$. All of these transformations are applied to a problem under a set of conditions represented by soft arc consistency levels [12], namely:

Node Consistency (NC*): a variable x_i is NC* if each value $v_i \in D_i$ satisfies $C_\phi + c_i(v_i) < UB_i$ and there is a value $v_i \in D_i$ with $c_i(v_i) = 0$. A problem is NC* if each variable x_i of this problem is NC*.

Arc Consistency (AC*): a variable x_i is AC* with respect to its neighbor x_j if x_i is NC* and there is, for each value $v_i \in D_i$, a value $v_j \in D_j$ which satisfies $c_{ij}(v_i, v_j) = 0$. v_j is called a *simple support* of v_i. A problem is AC* if each variable x_i of this problem is AC*.

Proc. 1: ProjectUnary()

1   $\beta \leftarrow min_{v_i \in D_i} \{c_i(v_i)\}$;
2   $C_{\phi_i} \leftarrow C_{\phi_i} + \beta$;
3   **foreach** $(v_i \in D_i)$ **do**
4   $\quad\mid$ $c_i(v_i) \leftarrow c_i(v_i) - \beta$;

Proc. 2: ProjectBinary(x_i, x_j)

1   **foreach** $(v_i \in D_i)$ **do**
2   $\quad\mid$ $\alpha \leftarrow min_{v_j \in D_j} \{c_{ij}(v_i, v_j)\}$;
3   $\quad\mid$ **foreach** $(v_j \in D_j)$ **do**
4   $\quad\quad\mid$ $c_{ij}(v_i, v_j) \leftarrow c_{ij}(v_i, v_j) - \alpha$;
5   $\quad\mid$ **if** $(A_i$ *is the current agent)*
6   $\quad\quad\mid$ $c_i(v_i) \leftarrow c_i(v_i) + \alpha$;

Proc. 3: Extend(x_i, x_j, E)

1   **foreach** $(v_i \in D_i)$ **do**
2   $\quad\mid$ **foreach** $(v_j \in D_j)$ **do**
3   $\quad\quad\mid$ $c_{ij}(v_i, v_j) \leftarrow c_{ij}(v_i, v_j) + E[v_i]$;
4   $\quad\mid$ **if** $(A_i$ *is the current agent)*
5   $\quad\quad\mid$ $c_i(v_i) \leftarrow c_i(v_i) - E[v_i]$;

Proc. 4: CheckPruning()

1   **foreach** $(a \in D_j)$ **do**
2   $\quad\mid$ **if** $(c_j(a) + C_\phi \geq UB_j)$
3   $\quad\quad\mid$ $D_j \leftarrow D_j - a$;
4   $\quad\quad\mid$ $DVals[j].listVals.add(a)$;
5   **if** $(D_j$ *is changed)*
6   $\quad\mid$ $DVals[j].UnvNbrs \leftarrow A_j.Nbrs$,
7   **if** $(D_j$ *is empty)*
8   $\quad\mid$ broadcastMsg : **stp**(UB_j) ;
9   $\quad\mid$ $end \leftarrow true$;

Proc. 5: DAC*()

1   **foreach** $(A_k \in \Gamma^+)$ **do**
2   $\quad\mid$ **foreach** $(v_j \in D_j)$ **do**
3   $\quad\quad\mid$ $E[v_j] \leftarrow c_j(v_j)$
4   $\quad\mid$ Extend(x_j, x_k, E) ;
5   $\quad\mid$ $EVals[jk].put(E)$;
6   $\quad\mid$ ProjectBinary(x_k, x_j) ;

Proc. 6: ProcessPruning(msg)

1   $DVals \leftarrow msg.DVals$;
2   **foreach** $(A_k \in \Gamma)$ **do**
3   $\quad\mid$ **foreach** $(a \in DVals[k])$ **do**
4   $\quad\quad\mid$ $D_k \leftarrow D_k - a$;
5   $\quad\mid$ **if** $(D_k$ *is changed)*
6   $\quad\quad\mid$ $DVals[k].UnvNbrs.decr(-1)$;
7   $\quad\mid$ **if** $(DVals[k].UnvNbrs = 0)$
8   $\quad\quad\mid$ $DVals[k].listVals.clear$;
9   **if** $(msg.type = "Ok")$
10 $\quad\mid$ $EVals \leftarrow msg.EVals$;
11 $\quad\mid$ **foreach** $(A_k \in \Gamma^-)$ **do**
12 $\quad\quad\mid$ Extend$(x_k, x_j, EVals[kj])$;
13 $\quad\quad\mid$ $EVals[kj].clear$;
14 $\quad\quad\mid$ ProjectBinary(x_j, x_k) ;
15 $\quad\quad\mid$ ProjectUnary() ;
16 $\quad\mid$ $C_\phi \leftarrow max\{C_\phi, msg.C_\phi\} + C_{\phi_j}$;
17 $\quad\mid$ $C_{\phi_j} \leftarrow 0$;
18 **if** $(C_\phi \geq UB_j)$
19 $\quad\mid$ broadcastMsg : **stp**(UB_j) ;
20 $\quad\mid$ $end \leftarrow true$;
21 CheckPruning() ;
22 DAC*() ;
23 ExtendCPA() ;

Directional Arc Consistency (DAC*): a variable x_i is DAC* with respect to its neighbor x_j, such that $j > i$ if x_i is NC* and there is, for each value $v_i \in D_i$, a value $v_j \in D_j$ which satisfies $c_{ij}(v_i, v_j) + c_j(v_j) = 0$. v_j is called a *full support* of v_i. A problem is DAC* if each variable x_i of this problem is DAC* with its neighbors x_j, such that $j > i$.

To make a given problem DAC*, we first compute, for each variable x_i with respect to all of its neighbors x_j, such that $j > i$, the extension values appropriate to the values of its domain D_i (Proc. 5, *l.* 3). Next, we perform the extension operation (Proc. 5, *l.* 4) by subtracting the extension values from the unary constraints C_i and adding them to the binary ones C_{ij} (Proc. 3). Then, each neighbor x_j performs, successively, a binary projection (Proc. 2), a unary projection (Proc. 1), and finally a deletion of non-NC* values. These last three instructions ensure the fulfillment of arc consistency (AC*).

In a distributed case, each agent A_i performs DAC* locally and shares the value of its zero-arity constraint C_{ϕ_i} with the other agents in order to calculate the global C_ϕ (i.e., $C_\phi = \sum_{A_i \in \mathcal{A}} C_{\phi_i}$)(Proc. 6, *l.* 16). Each agent A_i keeps locally for each of its constraints C_{ij} an identical copy marked by C_{ij}^{ac} and used in DAC* procedure. During DAC*, C_{ij}^{ac} constraints are changed. To keep the symmetry of these constraints in the agents, each agent A_i applies, on its copy C_{ij}^{ac}, the same action of its neighbor A_j and vice versa (Proc. 5, *l.* 6) [10].

2.3   AFB_BJ$^+$-AC* Algorithm

Each agent A_j carries out the AFB_BJ$^+$-AC* [1] according to three phases. First, A_j initializes its data structures and performs the AC* in which it deletes permanently all suboptimal values from its domain D_j. Second, A_j chooses, for its variable x_j, a value from its previously filtered domain D_j in order to extend the CPA Y^j by its value assignment (x_j, v_j). If A_j has successfully extended the CPA, it sends an **ok?** message to the next agent asking it to continue the extension of CPA Y^j. This message loads the extended CPA Y^j, its guaranteed cost (2), its guaranteed cost in AC* (3), the C_ϕ, and the list $DVals$.

$$GC(Y^j)[j] = GC(Y^{j-1}) + \sum_{(x_i, v_i) \in Y^{j-1} \mid i < j} c_{ij}(v_i, v_j) \tag{2}$$

$$GC^*(Y^j) = GC^*(Y^{j-1}) + c_j(v_j) + \sum_{\substack{(x_i, v_i) \in Y^{j-1} \\ c_{ij}^{ac} \in C}} c_{ij}(v_i, v_j) \tag{3}$$

Otherwise, that is to say, the agent A_j fails to extend the CPA, either because it doesn't find a value that gives a valid CPA, or because all the values in its domain are exhausted, it stops the CPA extension and sends a **back** message, containing the same data structures as an **ok?** message excluding GC and GC^*, to the appropriate agent. If such an agent doesn't exist or the domain of A_j becomes empty, A_j stops its execution and informs the others via **stp** messages. A CPA Y^j is said to be valid if its lower bound (4) doesn't exceed the global upper bound UB_j, which represents the cost of the optimal solution achieved so far.

$$LB(Y^j)[i] = GC(Y^j)[i] + \sum_{A_k > A_j} LB_k(Y^j)[i] \tag{4}$$

Third, A_j evaluates the extended CPA by sending **fb?** messages, which hold the same data structures excluding C_ϕ and $DVals$, to unassigned agents asking them to evaluate the CPA and send the result of the evaluation. When an agent has completed its evaluation, it sends the result directly to the sender agent via an **lb** message. The evaluation is based on the calculation of appropriate lower bounds for the received CPA Y^i. The lower bound of Y^i (5) is the minimal lower bound over all values of D_j with respect to Y^i.

$$LB_j(Y^i)[h] = \min_{\substack{v_j \in D_j \\ (h \leq i < j)}} \left\{ \sum_{\substack{(x_k, v_k) \in Y^h \\ (k \leq h)}} c_{kj}(v_k, v_j) + \sum_{\substack{k = h+1 \\ (h < k < i)}}^{i-1} \min_{v_k \in D_k} \{c_{kj}(v_k, v_j)\} + \right.$$
$$\left. c_{ij}(v_i, v_j) + \sum_{\substack{x_k \in \Gamma^+(x_j) \\ (k > j)}} \min_{v_k \in D_k} \{c_{jk}(v_j, v_k)\} \right\} \tag{5}$$

Proc. 7: AFB_BJ$^+$-DAC*()

1 Init. of data structures
2 **foreach** $(A_k \in \Gamma^+)$ **do**
3    $lb_k[0][v_j] \leftarrow \min_{(v_j \in D_j)} \min_{v_k \in D_k} \{c_{jk}(v_j, v_k)\}$;
4 **if** $(A_j = A_1)$
5    $C_\phi \leftarrow C_\phi + C_{\phi j}; C_{\phi j} \leftarrow 0;$
6    $CheckPruning()$;
7    $DAC^*()$;
8    $ExtendCPA()$;
9 **while** $(\neg end)$ **do**
10    $msg \leftarrow getMsg()$;
11   **if** $(msg.UB < UB_j)$
12     $UB_j \leftarrow msg.UB; v_j^* \leftarrow v_j$;
13   **if** $(msg.Y$ is stronger than $Y)$
14     $Y \leftarrow msg.Y$;
15     $GC \leftarrow msg.GC$;
16   clear irrelevant $lb()$; reset D_j ;
17   **if** $(msg.type = ok?)$
18     $mustSendFB \leftarrow True$;
19     $GC^* \leftarrow msg.GC^*$;
20     $ProcessPruning(msg)$;
21   **if** $(msg.type = back)$
22     $Y \leftarrow Y^{j-1}$;
23     $ProcessPruning(msg)$;
24   **if** $(msg.type = fb?)$
25     $GC^* \leftarrow msg.GC^*$;
26   **foreach** $(v_j \in D_j)$ **do**
27      $cost \leftarrow C_\phi + GC^*(Y^{j-1}) + c_j(v_j)$;
28   **if** $(cost \geq UB_j)$
29       $D_j \leftarrow D_j - v_j$;
30   sendMsg : $\underset{\text{to } A_i}{\textbf{lb}} (lb_j(Y^i)[], msg.Y)$;
31   **if** $(msg.type = stp)$
32     $end \leftarrow true$;

---

33 **if** $(msg.type = lb)$
34    $lb_k(Y^j) \leftarrow msg.lb$;
35   **if** $(lb(Y^j) \geq UB_j)$
36     $ExtendCPA()$;

Proc. 8: ExtendCPA()

1 $v_j \leftarrow argmin_{v_j' \in D_j} \left\{ lb(Y \cup (x_j, v_j')) \right\}$;
2 **if** $(lb(Y \cup (x_j, v_j)) \geq UB_j) \vee$
    $(C_\phi + GC^*(Y^{j-1}) + c_j(v_j) \geq UB_j)$
3   **for** $i \leftarrow j - 1$ **to** 1 **do**
4   **if** $(lb(Y)[i - 1] < UB_j)$
5   sendMsg :
      $\underset{\text{to } A_i}{\textbf{back}}(Y^i, UB_j, DVals, C_\phi)$;
      return ;
6   broadcastMsg : $\textbf{stp}(UB_j)$;
7    $end \leftarrow true$;
8 **else**
9    $Y \leftarrow \{Y \cup (x_j, v_j)\}$;
10   **if** $(var(Y) = X)$
11     $UB_j \leftarrow GC(Y); v_j^* \leftarrow v_j$;
12     $Y \leftarrow Y^{j-1}$;
13     $CheckPruning()$;
14     $ExtendCPA()$;
15   **else**
16   sendMsg :
     $\underset{\text{to } A_{j+1}}{\textbf{ok?}} (Y, GC, UB_j, DVals,$
     $EVals, C_\phi, GC^*)$;
17     $EVals.clear$;
18   **if** $(mustSendFB)$
19   sendMsg :
      $\underset{\substack{\text{to } A_k \\ k>j}}{\textbf{fb?}} (Y, GC, UB_j, GC^*)$;
20     $mustSendFB \leftarrow false$;

3   The AFB_BJ$^+$-DAC* Algorithm

The AFB_BJ$^+$-DAC* algorithm uses a higher consistency level, which is a directional arc consistency (DAC*). It improves the ability of AFB_BJ$^+$-AC* algorithm to generate more deletions. It is based on executing a set of cost extensions from unary constraints to binary ones, then on executing of AC*. DAC*() (Proc. 5) is the procedure responsible for calculating the extension values (i.e., costs to be transferred) and $Extend()$ (Proc. 3) is the one that performs the extension of costs from the unary constraints towards the binary ones (§2.2). All the extension values used by an agent are stored in a list, $EVals$, and routed to its lower neighbors via an **ok?** message in order to keep the symmetry of C_{ij}^{ac} constraints in each agent and its neighbors. The list of extension values, $EVals$, is processed in the procedure $ProcessPruning()$ (Proc. 6, l. 9–13) in which DAC*() is also performed (Proc. 6, l. 22).

3.1   Description of AFB_BJ$^+$-DAC*

The AFB_BJ$^+$-DAC* (Proc. 7) is performed by each agent A_j as follows:

A_j starts with the initialization step (Proc. 7, l. 1–3). If A_j is the 1st agent (Proc. 7, l. 4), it filters its domain by calling $CheckPruning()$ (Proc. 4), then performs the appropriate extensions through DAC*() (Proc. 5), and finally calls $ExtendCPA()$ to generate a CPA Y.

Next, A_j starts processing the messages (Proc. 7, l. 9). First, it updates UB_j and v_j^* (Proc. 7, l. 12). Then, A_j updates Y and GC and erases all unrelated lower bounds if the received CPA ($msg.Y$) is fresh compared to the local one (Y) (Proc. 7, l. 13). Thereafter, A_j restores all temporarily deleted values (Proc. 7, l. 29).

When receiving an **ok?** message (Proc. 7, l. 17), A_j authorizes the sending of **fb?** messages and calls $ProcessPruning()$ (Proc. 6).

When calling $ProcessPruning()$ (Proc. 6), A_j deals initially, for **ok?** messages only, with extensions of its higher neighbors (Proc. 6, l. 9–13). Afterward, it updates its $DVals$, then its neighbors' domains separately in order to keep the same domains as these agents (Proc. 6, l. 1–4). After that, it performs the two projections fulfilling the condition of AC* (Proc. 6, l. 14–15). Next, A_j decrements the unvisited neighbors of A_k, $DVals[k].UnvNbrs$, and then checks whether it is the last visited neighbor of this agent A_k in order to reset its list of deleted values $DVals[k].listVals$ (Proc. 6, l. 5–8). Then, A_j updates its global C_ϕ (Proc. 6, l. 16). If C_ϕ exceeds the UB_j, A_j turns off its execution and notifies the others (Proc. 6, l. 18–20). Finally, A_j calls $CheckPruning()$ to prune its domain, DAC*() (Proc. 5) to make the proper extensions, and $ExtendCPA()$ to extend the received CPA (Proc. 6, l. 21–23).

When calling DAC*() (Proc. 5), A_j performs the proper extensions from C_j to each C_{ij} (Proc. 5, l. 4–5). To do that, A_j calculates, for each value v_j of D_j, its extension value (Proc. 5, l. 2–3) based on the unary cost of this value ($0 < E[v_i] \leq c_i(v_i)$). Once completed, A_j performs a binary projection to keep the symmetry of C_{ij}^{ac} constraints (Proc. 5, l. 6). It should be noted that the direction taken into account by each agent A_j for the extension of its costs is towards its lower neighbors ($\Gamma^+(x_j)$).

When calling $CheckPruning()$ (Proc. 4), A_j deletes any value from its domain for which the sum of the C_ϕ with the unary cost of this value exceeds UB_j (Proc. 4, l. 2–3). With each new deletion, A_j initializes the number of its neighbors not yet visited (Proc. 4, l. 5–6). If A_j domain becomes empty, A_j turns off its execution and notifies the others (Proc. 4, l. 7–9).

When calling $ExtendCPA()$ (Proc. 8), A_j looks for a value v_j for its variable x_j (Proc. 8, l. 1). If no value exists, A_j returns to the priority agents by sending a **back** message to the contradictory agent (Proc. 8, l. 2–5). If no agent exists, A_j turns off its execution and notifies the others via **stp** messages (Proc. 8, l. 6–7). Otherwise, A_j extends Y by adding its assignment (Proc. 8, l. 9). If A_j is the last agent (Proc. 8, l. 10) then a new solution is obtained and the UB_j is updated, which obliges A_j to call $CheckPruning()$ to filter again its domain and then $ExtendCPA()$ to proceed the search (Proc. 8, l. 11–14). Otherwise, A_j sends an **ok?** message loaded with the extended Y to the next agent (Proc. 8, l. 16) and **fb?** messages to unassigned agents (Proc. 8, l. 19).

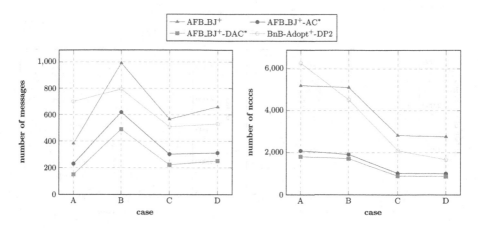

Fig. 1. Total of messages (*msgs*) sent and non-concurrent constraint checks (*ncccs*) for meetings scheduling

When A_j receives an **fb?** message, it filters its domain D_j with respect to the received Y (Proc. 7, l. 25–29), calculates the appropriate lower bounds (5), and immediately sends them to the sender via **lb** message (Proc. 7, l. 30).

When A_j receives an **lb** message, it stores the lower bounds received (Proc. 7, l. 34) and performs $ExtendCPA()$ to modify its assignment if the lower bound calculated, based on the cost of Y (4), exceeds the UB_j.

4   Experimental Results

In this section, we experimentally compare the AFB_BJ+-DAC* algorithm with its older versions [1,16] and with the BnB-Adopt+-DP2 algorithm [4], which is its famous competitor. Two benchmarks are used in these experiments: meetings scheduling and sensors network. All experiments were performed on the DisChoco 2.0 platform [17], in which agents are simulated by Java threads that communicate only through message passing.

Meetings Scheduling [13]: are defined by (m, p, ts), which are respectively the number of meetings/variables, the number of participants, and the number of time slots for each meeting. Each participant has a private schedule of meetings and each meeting takes place at a particular location and at a fixed time slot. The constraints are applied to meetings that share participants. We have evaluated 4 cases A, B, C, and D, which are different in terms of meetings/participants [13].

Sensors Network [5]: are defined by (t, s, d), which are respectively the number of targets/variables, the number of sensors, and the number of possible combinations of 3 sensors reserved for tracking each target. A sensor can only track one target at most and each combination of 3 sensors must track a target. The constraints are applied to adjacent targets. We have evaluated 4 cases A, B, C, and D, which are different in terms of targets/sensors [13].

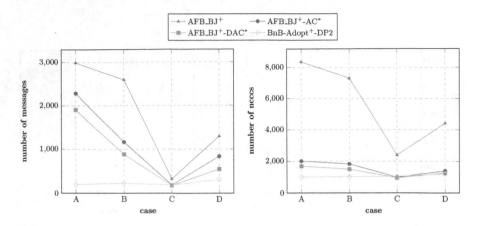

Fig. 2. Total of messages (*msgs*) sent and non-concurrent constraint checks (*ncccs*) for sensors network

To compare the algorithms, we use two metrics which are the total of messages exchanged (*msgs*) that represents the communication load and the total of non-concurrent constraint checks (*ncccs*) that represents the computation effort.

Regarding meetings scheduling problems (Fig. 1), the results show a clear improvement of the AFB_BJ⁺-DAC* compared to others, whether for *msgs* or for *ncccs*. But with regard to sensors network problems (Fig. 2), the BnB-Adopt⁺-DP2 retains the pioneering role, despite the superiority of the AFB_BJ⁺-DAC* algorithm to its older versions.

By analyzing the results, we can conclude that the AFB_BJ⁺-DAC* is better than its earlier versions, because of the existence of directional arc consistency (DAC*) which allows agents to remove more suboptimal values. This is due to a set of cost extensions applied to the problem. Regarding the superiority of the BnB-Adopt⁺-DP2 over the AFB_BJ⁺-DAC* in sensors network problems, this is mainly due to the arrangement of the pseudo-tree used by this algorithm that corresponds to the structure of these problems, as well as the existence of DP2 heuristic facilitates the proper choice of values.

5   Conclusion

In this paper, we have introduced the AFB_BJ⁺-DAC* algorithm. It is an algorithm that relies on DAC* to generate more deletions and thus quickly reach the optimal solution of a problem. DAC* mainly relies on performing a set of cost extensions in one direction from an agent to its lower priority neighbors in order to perform AC* multiple times, which increases the number of deletions made by each agent and thereby speed up the process of solving a problem. Experiments on some benchmarks show that the AFB_BJ⁺-DAC* algorithm behaves better than its older versions. As future work, we propose to exploit the change in the size of the agent domains in variable ordering heuristics.

References

1. Adrdor, R., Ezzahir, R., Koutti, L.: Connecting AFB_BJ+ with soft arc consistency. Int. J. Comput. Optim. **5**(1), 9–20 (2018). https://doi.org/10.12988/ijco.2018.857

2. Adrdor, R., Ezzahir, R., Koutti, L.: Consistance d'arc souple appliquée aux problèmes dcop. Journées d'Intelligence Artificielle Fondamentale (JIAF) 63 (2020)

3. Adrdor, R., Koutti, L.: Enhancing AFB_BJ$^+$AC* algorithm. In: 2019 International Conference of Computer Science and Renewable Energies (ICCSRE), pp. 1–7. IEEE, July 2019. https://doi.org/10.1109/ICCSRE.2019.8807711

4. Ali, S., Koenig, S., Tambe, M.: Preprocessing techniques for accelerating the DCOP algorithm ADOPT. In: Proceedings of the Fourth International Joint Conference on Autonomous Agents and Multiagent Systems, pp. 1041–1048. ACM (2005)

5. Béjar, R., et al.: Sensor networks and distributed CSP: communication, computation and complexity. Artif. Intell. **161**(1–2), 117–147 (2005)

6. Fioretto, F., Pontelli, E., Yeoh, W.: Distributed constraint optimization problems and applications: a survey. J. Artif. Intell. Res. **61**, 623–698 (2018)

7. Gershman, A., Meisels, A., Zivan, R.: Asynchronous forward bounding for distributed cops. J. Artif. Intell. Res. **34**, 61–88 (2009)

8. Grinshpoun, T., Tassa, T., Levit, V., Zivan, R.: Privacy preserving region optimal algorithms for symmetric and asymmetric DCOPs. Artif. Intell. **266**, 27–50 (2019)

9. Gutierrez, P., Meseguer, P.: Saving messages in adopt-based algorithms. In: Proceedings of 12th DCR Workshop in AAMAS 2010, pp. 53–64. Citeseer (2010)

10. Gutierrez, P., Meseguer, P.: Improving BnB-ADOPT+-AC. In: Proceedings of the 11th International Conference on Autonomous Agents and Multiagent Systems-Volume 1, pp. 273–280. International Foundation for Autonomous Agents and Multiagent Systems (2012)

11. Hirayama, K., Yokoo, M.: Distributed partial constraint satisfaction problem. In: Smolka, G. (ed.) CP 1997. LNCS, vol. 1330, pp. 222–236. Springer, Heidelberg (1997). https://doi.org/10.1007/BFb0017442

12. Larrosa, J., Schiex, T.: In the quest of the best form of local consistency for weighted CSP. In: IJCAI, vol. 3, pp. 239–244 (2003)

13. Maheswaran, R.T., Tambe, M., Bowring, E., Pearce, J.P., Varakantham, P.: Taking DCOP to the real world: efficient complete solutions for distributed multi-event scheduling. In: Proceedings of the Third International Joint Conference on Autonomous Agents and Multiagent Systems-Volume 1, pp. 310–317. IEEE Computer Society (2004)

14. Modi, P.J., Shen, W.M., Tambe, M., Yokoo, M.: Adopt: asynchronous distributed constraint optimization with quality guarantees. Artif. Intell. **161**(1–2), 149–180 (2005)

15. Nguyen, D.T., Yeoh, W., Lau, H.C., Zivan, R.: Distributed gibbs: a linear-space sampling-based DCOP algorithm. J. Artif. Intell. Res. **64**, 705–748 (2019)

16. Wahbi, M., Ezzahir, R., Bessiere, C.: Asynchronous forward bounding revisited. In: Schulte, C. (ed.) CP 2013. LNCS, vol. 8124, pp. 708–723. Springer, Heidelberg (2013). https://doi.org/10.1007/978-3-642-40627-0_52

17. Wahbi, M., Ezzahir, R., Bessiere, C., Bouyakhf, E.H.: DisChoco 2: a platform for distributed constraint reasoning. In: Proceedings of DCR 2011, pp. 112–121 (2011). http://dischoco.sourceforge.net/

18. Yeoh, W., Felner, A., Koenig, S.: BnB-adopt: an asynchronous branch-and-bound DCOP algorithm. J. Artif. Intell. Res. **38**, 85–133 (2010)

Computer Vision and Machine Learning

GAN-Assisted YUV Pixel Art Generation

Zhouyang Jiang and Penny Sweetser[✉]

The Australian National University, Canberra, ACT 2601, Australia
penny.kyburz@anu.edu.au

Abstract. Procedural Content Generation (PCG) in games has grown in popularity in recent years, with Generative Adversarial Networks (GANs) providing a promising option for applying PCG for game artistic asset generation. In this paper, we introduce a model that uses GANs and the YUV colour encoding system for automatic colouring of game assets. In this model, conditional GANs in Pix2Pix architecture are chosen as the main structure and the YUV colour encoding system is used for data preprocessing and result visualisation. We experimented with parameter settings (number of epochs, activation functions, optimisers) to optimise output. Our experimental results show that the proposed model can generate evenly coloured outputs for both small and larger datasets.

Keywords: Generative Adversarial Networks · Art generation · Video games · Procedural Content Generation · Pixel art

1 Introduction

Over the last few decades, the scale and complexity of video games have significantly increased in both technical and artistic terms. Due to advances in video game and computing technology, such as central and graphics processing, the cost of game development has rapidly grown in order to provide players with a high-quality game experience and graphics [6]. Many modern games include thousands of art assets for models, actions, rigs, and so on [2]. Moreover, the demand for amount and quality of artistic assets in games will continue to grow, driven by consumer demand and further advances in technology. To reduce the cost of development while maintaining (or improving) the quality, some of the work of generating artistic assets can be completed by artificial intelligence. In order to solve the problems of exponential growth in demand for game assets and to automate some of the tedious manual labour of asset creation, the concept of Procedural Content Generation (PCG) for games has gained increasing attention [7].

When applying PCG for game artistic asset generation, Generative Adversarial Networks (GANs) are a good option. As the assets for a specific game usually have similar features, with the help of the generator and discriminator in GANs competing with each other, the model can learn from a set of training data and generate new data with the same characteristics as the training data. Among all the procedures for producing game assets, image colourisation

© Springer Nature Switzerland AG 2022
G. Long et al. (Eds.): AI 2021, LNAI 13151, pp. 595–606, 2022.
https://doi.org/10.1007/978-3-030-97546-3_48

for game sketches is a typical tedious manual task. Using *Trajes Fatais: Suits of Fate*, a 2D pixel art fighting game [13] as an example, the time involved in making the sketch for a character is only 10 min on average. However, it takes an hour to complete the colourisation task for the sketch.

In this paper, we propose a new PCG model for automatically colouring game assets with GANs. With the help of deep learning, the aim of this project is to develop a model with GANs and Convolutional Neural Networks (CNNs) to generate 3-Channel game assets from YUV grayscale pixel art that can fit a given game theme. Specifically, the model is based on a modified version of Pix2Pix architecture [9]. The YUV colour transfer algorithm is used in data preprocessing to improve performance. After combining these two algorithms, we found that the generated outputs satisfy the requirements of generating assets that have similar characteristics and can fit the chosen game theme. Furthermore, with the help of qualitative and quantitative analysis, we optimised the parameters and model structures to provide improved performance.

2   Background

The focus of this project is on developing a model with GANs and CNNs to generate 3-Channel game assets from YUV grayscale pixel art that can fit the whole game theme. In this section, we introduce YUV colour space, GANs and Pix2Pix architecture. Additionally, a variant of the Pix2Pix architecture is also considered as a reference.

2.1   YUV Colour Encoding System (YUV Colour Space) with GANs

YUV colour space is a colour encoding system that focuses on human perception. Compared with the original RGB encoding system, it can reduce transmission errors [14]. It is not the first time that YUV colour space has been used in GANs. The YUV colour encoding system has already been added to GANs for the thin cloud removal task [15] and to transform LR SDR videos into UHD HDR format [17]. In contrast, the literature on using YUV colour space with GANs for automatic colourisation is notably scarce. There is one previous study about using DCGAN in the YUV colour encoding system for image colourisation for remote sensing images [16]. However, remote sensing images are different from game artistic assets, which are more scattered and irregular. Additionally, compared with DCGAN, Pix2Pix architecture can provide more detailed information. Therefore, investigating the use of the YUV colour encoding system in Pix2Pix GANs architecture is worthwhile.

2.2   Pix2Pix Architecture

Pix2Pix is a GAN network, developed by Isola et al. [9], which has a U-Net generator, a patch-based discriminator, and a combined objective function. Because the Pix2Pix architecture uses U-Net to improve the details of the output and a patch-based discriminator to classify small patches separately, it has been widely used for PCG of images. Lewis [8] used Pix2Pix to build an automatic pixel-art sprite generator, which generates the whole pixel-art character, combining sketch-making and colourisation together. Although this approach is more efficient for generating the game assets, the edges and shapes of assets will be blurred. There will be noise in outputs and details will be missing since there are no sketches of edges. Therefore, in our research, we focus on the colourisation task from the sketches. Compared with Lewis's research, the goal of our model is to assist game artists in performing a tedious manual task, instead of replacing the role of the artist.

2.3   Variants of the Pix2Pix Architecture

There are several variants of the Pix2Pix architecture. For colourisation tasks, Ygor et al. [13] built a modified version of the Pix2Pix architecture. To adjust the model to be suitable for colourisation tasks, they added another decoder-discriminator pair to the U-Net architecture, so that it can learn more semantic-rich features. Additionally, the original activation function for downsampling steps, LeakyReLU was changed to ELU and the original combined objective function was changed to L2 loss to converge faster and get better results. However, as Ygor's model is used to automatically colour the whole action sprites, it focused on the same characters with different actions and some modifications of that model are not suitable for our single image task. Additionally, there are also better options for parameters for our tasks, which we describe in our results and analysis section. Furthermore, among all the variants of the Pix2Pix architecture used for colourisation tasks, models that specifically colour pixel art are notably scarce. However, as there is a U-Net architecture with skip-connections in the Pix2Pix architecture, it can help to pass the location information of pixels and produce pixel-art with a clearer edge.

3   Method

Our proposed model is based on GANs and the YUV colour encoding system. We chose a conditional GAN as the main structure, as illustrated in Fig. 1. Conditional GANs [10] map grayscale inputs to coloured outputs. The discriminator, D, tries to classify between the fake outputs generated by the generator and the real original images. The generator, G, learns to synthesise outputs that are close to the real images and cannot be distinguished from the originals by the discriminator, D. The difference between unconditional GANs [3] and conditional GANs is that, for conditional GANs, both the generator and discriminator are able to receive the grayscale inputs, while, in unconditional GANs, the discriminator cannot observe the inputs. Specifically, the conditional GAN solution is built on a modified Pix2Pix architecture. The YUV colour encoding system is used for data preprocessing and results visualisation. In this section, we describe the details of our conditional GAN (Pix2Pix architecture) and the YUV colour encoding system.

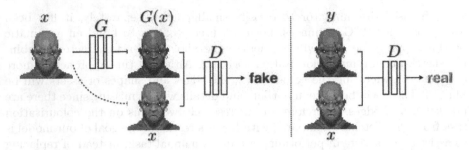

Fig. 1. Structure of conditional GAN (image based on Isola et al. [9]). Both the generator, G, and discriminator, D, are able to receive the grayscale inputs.

3.1 Datasets

In all experiments, two datasets were used: Ultimate Fantasy Sprites from Oryx Design Labs and Pokémon Images dataset from Kaggle.

Ultimate Fantasy Sprites from Oryx Design Labs. Ultimate Fantasy Sprites contain 36 PNG pixel-art portraits, which are in the same theme and suitable for RPG game making. The pixel size for each image is 48 × 48. This is a fairly small dataset that can train the model efficiently.

Pokémon Images Dataset from Kaggle. Pokémon Images dataset originally contains 1634 PNG images. However, only 870 images of the dataset are the actual characters in the Pokémon games. The remaining 764 images are gathered from fan-made games. Therefore, to ensure all the pixel-art images are in the same theme, only the actual characters were kept, while others have been removed. Each image is a front-facing battle PNG pixel art in 160 × 160 pixel size. Since this dataset is larger, the details of the outputs and the difference of using each parameter and structure can be shown more clearly.

3.2 Data Preprocessing and Results Visualisation

During data preprocessing, the YUV colour encoding system is used to convert all RGB raw image data into YUV images. Then, the Y channel is separated as the single-channel grayscale image inputs from YUV images. For results visualisation, the YUV colour encoding system is used to turn the U and V values combined with Y inputs back to RGB values that can be shown as images.

Data Preprocessing. During data preprocessing, the method of converting all RGB images into YUV images can be expressed as:

$$Y = W_R R + W_G G + W_B B = 0.299R + 0.587G + 0.114B \tag{1}$$

$$U = U_{max} \frac{B - Y}{1 - W_B} \approx 0.492(B - Y) \tag{2}$$

$$V = V_{max} \frac{R - Y}{1 - W_R} \approx 0.877(R - Y) \tag{3}$$

Where Y stands for the luma component, U is the blue projection, and V is the red projection. Y is used to indicate the value of brightness and U and V are the chrominance (colour) components. The reason why green is weighted most heavily in the Y channel is that people are more sensitive to green than other colours. After getting YUV values, the next step of data preprocessing is separating the Y channel as the single-channel grayscale image inputs from YUV images. Figure 2 shows several samples of original images and Y channel grayscale images after data preprocessing.

Fig. 2. Samples of original images and Y channel grayscale images after preprocessing.

Results Visualisation. The YUV colour encoding system is also used for results visualisation, turning YUV 3-Channel images back to RGB images. The method of converting all YUV images to RGB images can be expressed as:

$$R = Y + V \frac{1 - W_R}{V_{max}} = Y + 1.14V \tag{4}$$

$$G = Y - U \frac{W_B(1 - W_B)}{U_{max} W_G} - V \frac{W_R(1 - W_R)}{V_{max} W_G} = Y - 0.395U - 0.581V \tag{5}$$

$$B = Y + U \frac{1 - W_B}{U_{max}} = Y + 2.033U \tag{6}$$

Another task during results visualisation is to show the single Y-channel grayscale image and RGB 3-Channel image in the same whole image. The way to visualise the single-channel grayscale image in a 3-Channel structure is by copying the single Y value to all three RGB channels. Figure 3 shows several samples of visualised results.

3.3 Modified Pix2Pix Architecture

Pix2Pix is a GAN network that has a U-Net generator, a patch-based discriminator, and a combined objective function. These three parts are described in the following sections.

Fig. 3. Samples of visualised results (left-to-right: input, target, predicted).

U-Net Generator. The U-Net generator has the standard encoder-decoder architecture, except that it has skip connections between mirrored layers in the encoder and decoder stacks (see Fig. 4). The skip connection concatenates channels at the encoder layer and decoder layer. The reason why the skip connection is used is that it can provide the pixel-level information for decoder layers, from the encoder layers to reconstruct details. Specifically, in our pixel-art colourisation task, the pixel-level information that skip connections share from encoder layers to decoder layers is the location information of every edge, contour, and area in the grayscale input image.

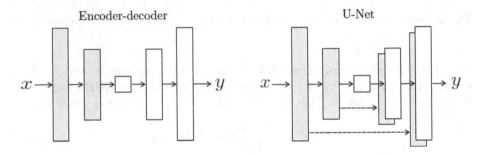

Fig. 4. Difference between the normal encoder-decoder architecture and U-Net architecture: U-Net has skip connections (image from [9]).

Patch-Based Discriminator. A patch-based discriminator is used for this modified Pix2Pix architecture. In contrast to traditional discriminators that classify the whole image as real or fake directly, the patch-based discriminator first separates the whole image into small N x N patches. Then, it tries to classify whether each patch is real or fake separately. After running this discriminator convolutionally, it will sum and average all responses to provide the output. The reason why this patch-based discriminator is beneficial is that small patches can let the training process focus on the interesting parts of the image, instead of the whole image.

Combined Objective Function. For a conditional GAN network, the objective function can be described as:

$$L_{CGAN}(G, D) = E_{x,y}[logD(x, y)] + E_{x,z}[log(1 - D(x, G(x, z)))] \tag{7}$$

However, for this modified Pix2Pix architecture, adding a traditional L1 loss to the original objective function can improve the performance [12], which can be described as:

$$L_{L1}(G) = E_{x,y,z}[||y - G(x, z)||_1] \tag{8}$$

Therefore, the final objective function can be expressed as:

$$G^* = \arg\min_G \max_D L_{CGAN}(G, D) + \lambda L_{L1}(G) \tag{9}$$

Technical Details and Parameters. To build this project in Python, the whole model was implemented with the Keras [5] framework, based on the TensorFlow [1] library. For the data preprocessing, NumPy [11] and OpenCV [4] libraries were used as the two main tools.

In our U-Net module, there are eight down sampling steps and seven up sampling steps. From previous research [9,13], ReLU and ELU are used as the activation functions for the down sampling steps. However, when testing different activation functions in our model (shown in results and analysis section), LeakyReLU provided the best performance, instead of ReLU and ELU. Therefore, LeakyReLU is chosen as the activation function for down sampling steps. As for up sampling steps, ReLU is chosen as the activation function. For the patch-based discriminator, the activation function is also LeakyReLU.

For optimisation when training the model, both the default Adam optimiser and SGD optimiser can provide good performance. The difference between the output from the two optimisers will be discussed in the results section. To get the best results, the number of epochs when using Adam as the optimiser is set to be 50, while it is 200 using SGD.

All the experiments were done on a PC with a GeForce RTX 2080 Ti GPU. With this setup, it takes around 2 to 5 h to finish training each model. The time of training is mainly related to the number of epochs and the size of the dataset.

4   Results and Analysis

Before comparing different parameters and structures of the model, Fig. 5 shows several examples of results from our model with optimised parameters for reference. We found that with increased number of epochs, the output will gain more detailed colours. Although some colours are different from the original images, the generated images can still fit the theme most of the time (Fig. 6).

Fig. 5. Examples of results with optimised parameters, trained after 10 (top-left), 25 (lower-left), 50 (top-right) and 200 (lower-right) epochs (left-to-right: input, target, predicted).

Fig. 6. From left to right, after and before using RGB colour encoding systems, after and before using YUV colour encoding systems to do the data preprocessing.

4.1   Colour Encoding Systems in Data Preprocessing

As discussed, different colour encoding systems (YUV, RGB) will lead to different data preprocessing results. In Fig. 8, the first two images are the items after and before using RGB colour encoding systems for data preprocessing. The second two images are the items after and before using YUV colour encoding systems for data preprocessing.

Compared with RGB colour encoding, we found that the results using YUV colour encoding for data preprocessing contained more detail and had a larger contrast ratio. This result is due to the Y channel combining all three RGB channels' information (Fig. 7).

Fig. 7. Sample results of using RGB colour encoding systems to inputs and outputs (left-to-right: input, target, predicted).

Fig. 8. Sample results of using YUV colour encoding systems to inputs and outputs (left-to-right: input, target, predicted).

4.2 Colour Encoding System Formats as Inputs and Outputs

We found that compared with RGB colour encoding, the YUV outputs were more detailed and evenly coloured, while some light parts in the RGB results were the same as the white background. There are two reasons that can cause this difference. First, as mentioned previously, the Y channel combines all three RGB channels' information. In the colourisation task, more information on the actual colours will provide better performance. On the other hand, when using YUV images as inputs and outputs, only U, V need to be predicted instead of the three RGB channels. Because the Y channel is always the same, which means, when using YUV colour encoding for both input and output, the colourisation task will be simplified from predicting the three RGB channels to predicting only the two U and V channels.

Fig. 9. Sample results of using ELU as activation function in down sampling steps (left-to-right: input, target, predicted).

Fig. 10. Sample results of using LeakyReLU as activation function in down sampling steps (left-to-right: input, target, predicted).

4.3 Activation Functions in Down Sampling Steps

We found that using ELU as the activation function in down sampling led to similar colours for different inputs (see Figs. 9 and 10). Specifically, all the results of using ELU as activation function in down sampling steps use orange as their main colour. However, each character has its own settings. Therefore, all the different outputs with the same colours are not acceptable. Compared with ELU, when the activation function in down sampling steps was set to be LeakyReLU, the results were improved. With LeakyReLU, the outputs were in different colours, instead of the same orange colour. The reason why ELU provided results with similar colours might be the vanishing gradient problem. Therefore, LeakyReLU was chosen as the activation function in down sampling steps.

Fig. 11. Results for Adam as optimiser, training after 50 (top) and 200 epochs.

Fig. 12. Results for SGD as optimiser, training after 50 (top) and 200 epochs.

4.4   Optimisers

We found that when using Adam as the optimiser (see Fig. 11), after 50 epochs of training, the character was given the correct blue colour as the target image. However, when using SGD as the optimiser (see Fig. 12), after 50 epochs the performance was not as good as with Adam, with very limited colour in the output. However, when we continued training the model with Adam and SGD for 200 epochs, things turn out differently. For Adam, the results after 50 epochs and results after 200 epochs were almost the same (top parts were given the correct colours). As for SGD, after 200 epochs the model gave the correct body colour for the output, which was even better than the results after 200 epochs with Adam. In summary, according to these experimental results, we concluded that both Adam and SGD were good options for this model, each with different advantages. The Adam optimiser converged faster and provided results more efficiently, while SGD needed more time to get the results, but gave more details and provide better final outputs.

5   Conclusions and Future Work

In this paper, we proposed a model using GANs and CNNs to generate 3-Channel game assets from YUV grayscale pixel art. This model uses the YUV colour encoding system for data preprocessing and result visualisation, and the Pix2Pix structure as the main GAN architecture. Based on our experiments, our model achieved the best performance when the YUV colour encoding system was applied and LeakyReLU was the activation function in down sampling steps. Both Adam and SGD can be used as the optimiser for the model and can achieve good outputs.

Although the proposed model can automatically colour game assets, it sometimes misidentified the character settings. Using Pokémon Images dataset as an example, as shown in Fig. 13, the model sometimes misidentifies the types of the characters. Specifically, the first character is a dual-type Fire/Ground character. However, the model fails to identify that correctly. On the contrary, it colours it in blue as water or ice type. The same applies to the other character. This will influence the accuracy of the final outputs. Therefore, as future work, it would be interesting and beneficial to extend this model to be able to receive the character setting information with the grayscale inputs. One of the possible solutions is to adjust the model to consider the labeled data so that the model can not only observe the image, but also gain more information from the labels.

Fig. 13. Results with misidentified types (left-to-right: input, target, predicted).

References

1. Abadi, M., et al.: Tensorflow: a system for large-scale machine learning. In: OSDI, vol. 16, pp. 265–283 (2016)
2. Baker, C., Schleser, M., Molga, K.: Aesthetics of mobile media art. J. Media Pract. **10**(2–3), 101–122 (2009)
3. Biswas, S., Rohdin, J., Drahanský, M.: Synthetic retinal images from unconditional GANs. In: 2019 41st Annual International Conference of the IEEE Engineering in Medicine and Biology Society (EMBC), pp. 2736–2739. IEEE (2019)
4. Bradski, G.: The OpenCV library. Dr. Dobb's J. Softw. Tools **25**(11), 120–123 (2000)
5. Chollet, F., et al.: Keras (2015). https://github.com/fchollet/keras
6. Folmer, E.: Component based game development – a solution to escalating costs and expanding deadlines? In: Schmidt, H.W., Crnkovic, I., Heineman, G.T., Stafford, J.A. (eds.) CBSE 2007. LNCS, vol. 4608, pp. 66–73. Springer, Heidelberg (2007). https://doi.org/10.1007/978-3-540-73551-9_5

7. Hendrikx, M., Meijer, S., Van Der Velden, J., Iosup, A.: Procedural content generation for games: a survey. ACM Trans. Multimedia Comput. Commun. Appl. (TOMM) **9**(1), 1–22 (2013)

8. Horsley, L., Perez-Liebana, D.: Building an automatic sprite generator with deep convolutional generative adversarial networks. In: 2017 IEEE Conference on Computational Intelligence and Games (CIG), pp. 134–141. IEEE (2017)

9. Isola, P., Zhu, J.Y., Zhou, T., Efros, A.A.: Image-to-image translation with conditional adversarial networks. In: Proceedings of the IEEE Conference on Computer Vision and Pattern Recognition, pp. 1125–1134 (2017)

10. Lan, H., Initiative, A.D.N., Toga, A.W., Sepehrband, F.: Three-dimensional self-attention conditional GAN with spectral normalization for multimodal neuroimaging synthesis. Magn. Reson. Med. **86**(3), 1718–1733 (2021)

11. Oliphant, T.: NumPy: A Guide to NumPy. Trelgol Publishing, USA (2006). http://www.numpy.org/. Accessed 5 Oct 2021

12. Pathak, D., Krahenbuhl, P., Donahue, J., Darrell, T., Efros, A.A.: Context encoders: feature learning by inpainting. In: Proceedings of the IEEE Conference on Computer Vision and Pattern Recognition, pp. 2536–2544 (2016)

13. Serpa, Y.R., Rodrigues, M.A.F.: Towards machine-learning assisted asset generation for games: a study on pixel art sprite sheets. In: 2019 18th Brazilian Symposium on Computer Games and Digital Entertainment (SBGames), pp. 182–191. IEEE (2019)

14. Wang, G., Fu, R., Sun, B., Lv, J., Sheng, T., Tan, Y.: Comparison of two types of color transfer algorithms in YUV and lab color spaces. In: AOPC 2017: Optical Sensing and Imaging Technology and Applications, vol. 10462, p. 104622V. International Society for Optics and Photonics (2017)

15. Wen, X., Pan, Z., Hu, Y., Liu, J.: Generative adversarial learning in YUV color space for thin cloud removal on satellite imagery. Remote Sens. **13**(6), 1079 (2021)

16. Wu, M., et al.: Remote sensing image colorization using symmetrical multi-scale DCGAN in YUV color space. Vis. Comput. **37**, 1–23 (2020)

17. Zeng, H., Zhang, X., Yu, Z., Wang, Y.: SR-ITM-GAN: learning 4K UHD HDR with a generative adversarial network. IEEE Access **8**, 182815–182827 (2020)

Investigating Active Positive-Unlabeled Learning with Deep Networks

Kun Han[1], Weitong Chen[1(✉)], and Miao Xu[1,2(✉)]

[1] University of Queensland, Brisbane, QLD 4072, Australia
kun.han@uq.net.au, {w.chen9,miao.xu}@uq.edu.au
[2] RIKEN, Tokyo 103-0027, Japan

Abstract. Positive-unlabeled (PU) learning deals with the binary classification problem when only positive (P) and unlabeled (U) data are available. Recently, many PU learning models have been proposed based on deep networks and become the SOTA of PU learning. Despite the achievements on the model aspect, theoretical analysis and empirical results have shown that the number and quality of positive data can significantly impact learning performance. Active learning is classically used in machine learning to acquire additional high-quality labelled data, however, there are only a few studies on using active learning in deep PU models. This paper investigates the use of active learning in deep PU models. Specifically, this paper studies the uncertainty query strategy for pool-based active learning and show that due to the "large-small-loss" property of deep networks, the query strategy based purely on uncertainty can achieve diversity simultaneously. Empirical results also illustrate the effectiveness of uncertainty-based queries on active PU learning with deep networks.

Keywords: PU learning · Active learning · Deep neural networks

1 Introduction

Positive-unlabeled (PU) learning deals with the binary classification problem when only positive (P) and unlabeled (U) data are available, without negative (N) data [4]. In the real world, PU learning has been applied to many different fields. For example, judging whether a bank account is legal or not is a binary classification problem. In such an example, police can provide the list of accounts already involved in financial fraud (positive data); but among the remaining accounts in the bank system, some illegal accounts are yet undetected; thus, these data should be treated as unlabeled data instead of negative.

In the last decade, many PU learning methods have been proposed. Dated back to the year 2002, [9,11] selected negative samples from unlabeled data and then did normal binary classification; [8,10] treated the unlabeled samples as negative but reweighed them with less weights. Later on, many successful PU methods based on reweighting are proposed. Among them, methods based on unbiased risk estimator [5] become dominant. Specially, nnPU [7] was proposed

© Springer Nature Switzerland AG 2022
G. Long et al. (Eds.): AI 2021, LNAI 13151, pp. 607–618, 2022.
https://doi.org/10.1007/978-3-030-97546-3_49

dealing with the problem that optimizing the PU risk directly with deep networks could easily lead to overfitting. nnPU then becomes the state-of-the-art method for PU learning, and many other PU methods [3,16,17] are built upon it.

The above methods all advance PU learning from the aspect of models. However, there is another key factor in PU learning that could dramatically impact the performance of PU learning - the number and quality of positive data. As shown in [13], the number of positive samples have larger impact on the learning performance of PU learning than PN learning. Based on the theoretical insights that the number of positive examples is important for PU learning, [17] proposed an adaptive method that selects positive samples from U data during the learning process to augment performance. However, since the positive data selected in [17] is usually high-confident, and far away from the decision boundary, they are not informative enough to dramatically improve the learning performance. Bearing the same belief that positive data is important, self-PU [3] is also proposed. Although the performance of PU has been dramatically improved by self-PU, its performance depends on a combination of many different techniques including additional labeled data to do meta-learning, and the contribution of the solely selecting P data is not clearly investigated.

The above-introduced methods try to select informative P data by the models themselves. However, another straightforward technique to improve the number and quality of positive data is active learning [15]. Active learning (AL) is an interactive learning framework that actively selects the most informative unlabeled samples and queries their true labels from the oracle [6]. Classically, AL is used in ordinal classification when both positive and negative data are available, and an essential part of AL is the query strategy. There are many query strategies proposed for AL, such as querying by uncertainty, committee, expected model change, diversity, etc. [15]. Among them, querying by uncertainty is widely used because of its simple form and low computation complexity. Later on, with the prosperity of deep learning, some deep active methods are also proposed [1]. However, these methods all assume data from all classes are available instead of only positive data. Lacking studies on active PU learning with deep models naturally raises a question: with deep networks, how can active PU learning be impacted by query strategies.

In this paper, the uncertainty query strategy is investigated, and the results provide a partial answer to this question, i.e., uncertainty querying strategy can efficiently select informative and diverse examples to boost and improve the performance of PU learning. Specifically, we are motivated by the large-small-loss trick in deep networks [2], which can be implicitly described as "deep networks memorize frequent patterns before eventually memorizing all data". Inspired by this trick, we design algorithms that use uncertainty to query examples only in the early stage of training. We also show that such query strategies could also make diverse queries. Consequently, we have tried to find the most effective uncertainty-based strategy by considering the properties of instances such as loss value, density and variance. Finally, experimental studies show that the performance achieved by the proposed query strategies can be comparable or better to the performance achieved by training with the same number of additional queried positive instances from the beginning. Our main contributions are outlined as follows:

– **Proposing an active learning framework based on the large-small loss trick** during the training process for deep learning models. Instead of adding positive samples before training, our framework actively selects, queries and updates based on the current learning model. The performance of the original deep network could be significantly improved.
– **Investigating Various Uncertainty query strategies based on confidence, variance and density** for the proposed active learning framework. We proposed several query strategies based on uncertainty, including Least Confidence (LC), Uncertainty and Density (UD), Variance Max (VM) and Window-sized Variance Max (WVM). LC aims to find the instances with more information according to their loss values. UD consider both the least confidence and density of the instance. VM and WVM focus on the changes of losses of instances in training process.

The paper is organized as follows. We introduce in Sect. 2 the formulation of the PU problem and related PU methods. In Sect. 3, we investigate uncertainty-based query strategies, followed by empirical illustration in Sect. 4. Finally, we conclude in Sect. 5.

2   Formulation and Review

Let $X \in \mathbb{R}^d$ be the input random variable and $Y \in \{-1, 1\}$ be the output random variable. In PU learning, the training set D consists of D_p and D_u, which respectively represents the positive data and unlabelled data $(D = D_p \bigcup D_u)$. We denote n_p as the number of instances in D_p and n_u as the number of instances in D_u, which respectively are sampled from $P(x|Y = +1)$ and $P(x)$. The class prior probability is denoted by $\pi_p = P(Y = +1)$. Similar to [7], this π is assumed as known throughout the paper. In practice, it can also be estimated.

Let $g : \mathbb{R}^d \to \{-1, +1\}$ be the decision function of binary classifier. θ denotes the parameters, and ℓ denotes the loss function. While we use the zero-one loss as our target, we use the sigmoid loss as the surrogate loss for zero-one loss [7]. The risk of PU learning of classifier g can be represented by

$$R_{pu}(g) = \pi E_{P(x|Y=+1)}[\ell(g(x), +1)] \\ + E_{P(x)}[\ell(g(x), -1)] - \pi E_{P(x|Y=+1)}[\ell(g(x), -1)] \tag{1}$$

and its empirical estimation would be

$$\hat{R}_{upu}(g) = \frac{\pi}{n_p} \sum_{i=1}^{n_p} \ell(g(x_i), +1) \\ + \frac{1}{n_u} \sum_{i=1}^{n_u} \ell(g(x_i), -1) - \frac{\pi}{n_p} \sum_{i=1}^{n_p} \ell(g(x_i), -1) \tag{2}$$

whose optimization leads to the uPU method [5].

The issue occurs when the uPU has been applied to deep neural networks is that the second line of Eq. (2), which should stay positive, will become negative after some iterations. To tackle this problem, nnPU [7] was proposed, which optimizes

$$
\hat{R}_{nnpu}(g) = \frac{\pi}{n_p} \sum_{i=1}^{n_p} \ell(g(x_i), +1)
$$

$$
+ \max\left(0, \frac{1}{n_u} \sum_{i=1}^{n_u} \ell(g(x_i), -1) - \frac{\pi}{n_p} \sum_{i=1}^{n_p} \ell(g(x_i), -1)\right). \tag{3}
$$

Although nnPU achieves state-of-the-art performance, researchers want to find a sample selection approach in this deep learning age. Inspired by [13], additional P data will benefit the PU learning more than PN learning. Thus, adaptive augmented PU (aaPU) [17] was proposed, which select P data as clean as they can and then estimate the new objective loss. Given the P data χ_p, U data χ_u and selected P data S, the new object function is

$$
\hat{R}_{aapu}(g) = \frac{\pi}{n_p} \sum_{x_i \in \chi_p \cup S} \ell_{log}(g(x_i), +1)
$$

$$
+ \max\left(0, \frac{1}{n_u} \sum_{x_i \in \chi_u} \ell_{log}(g(x_i), -1) - \frac{\pi}{n_p} \sum_{x_i \in \chi_p} \ell_{log}(g(x_i), -1)\right) \tag{4}
$$

where ℓ_{log} is the *logistic* function. By only considering the new positive data in the first part of the equation, aaPU has decreased the impact of biases in selected data.

Another impressive method self-PU [3], motivated by self-training, has been proposed to find the learning capacity of the model itself. The method consists of three parts, self-paced PU learning, self-Calibrated loss reweighting, and self-supervised consistency via Distillation. The self-paced partition will adaptively find confident examples and label them into positive or negative, with a hybrid loss between labelled instances and the remaining unlabeled instances. The self-Calibrated strategy is composed of loss function over instances with less confidence. The self-distillation part has guaranteed consistent regularization by the collaborative training between several teachers and students networks. The overall learning objective is

$$
\hat{R}_{self-pu} = L_{SP+Reweight} + L_{students} + L_{teachers}, \tag{5}
$$

in which

$$
L_{SP+Reweight} = \sum_{(x,y) \in D_{trust}} L_{CE}(x, y) + \sum_{x \in D_U - D_{trust}} \frac{\sum_{i=1}^{n} \ell(x)}{n} + \sum_{x \in D_P} L_{nnPU}(x) \tag{6}
$$

$$L_{students} = \sum_{x \in D - D_{trust1}} \ell(g_1, g_2, x) + \sum_{x \in D - D_{trust2}} \ell(g_1, g_2, x) \qquad (7)$$

$$L_{teachers} = \sum_{x \in D} ||f(G_1(x)) - f(g_1(x))||^2 + \sum_{x \in D} ||f(G_2(x)) - f(g_2(x))||^2. \qquad (8)$$

Among them, L_{CE} is the cross-validation loss. D_{trust} is the set of confident examples selected in self-paced partition. g_1 and g_2 are two student networks in self-distillation. G_1 and G_2 are two teacher networks. Note that in the above-introduced methods, uPU and nnPU are PU methods without sample selection, and we could use both of them as a base learner in active learning. On the other hand, aaPU and self-PU make sample selection without queries. Instead of querying the true labels from oracle, they select those samples that they believe to be positive.

3   Our Proposal

3.1   Query Strategy

The query strategy here should be combined with the training of neural networks. Note that training of neural networks is usually conducted by stochastic gradient descend (SGD), i.e., we train several epochs of the neural network, and each epoch corresponds with SGD on the whole training data. Thus, a natural way to do active learning is to select the query examples at the end of each epoch, such that the queried instances could be used in the next round of SGD training.

Considering the special case of PU learning, we plot the histogram of sigmoid loss values on unlabeled data using negative as groundtruth in Fig. 1 after training the model for one epoch, 10 epochs and 200 epochs. From the histogram, we can tell that although most of the U data can be successfully differentiated after enough epochs, there are still some "difficult" samples that cannot be differentiated at the end of training. Due to the existence of these difficult examples, the sample selection conducted by the model itself cannot result in effective learning as shown in [17]; i.e., the additional positive data found by the model itself cannot be informative enough for further performance improvement. To find the informative positive samples, we notice that some examples have a loss value around 0.5, especially in the early stage of training. These samples bear the most uncertainty by the current model and are worth querying. Moreover, most of the querying should happen in the early stage of training; otherwise, querying them will not be helpful due to these data may have already been misclassified. Note that the large-small-loss trick [2] also gives us insights to query examples from the early stage. This is due to that PU learning can be seen as positive and noisy negative learning. In the later stage of training, the model may be impacted more by noises than in the early stage of training [2].

Besides the necessary to query samples at the early stage of training, another issue here is that at the beginning of training, the model may not be good enough to catch the frequent pattern in the given training set. It may also be necessary to train several epochs without querying as warm-up. The whole process of actively

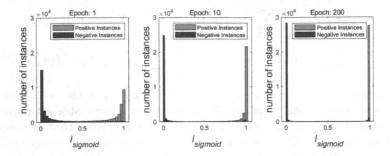

Fig. 1. Histogram of the sigmoid losses of U data using ground truth negative after Epoch 1, Epoch 10 and Epoch 200.

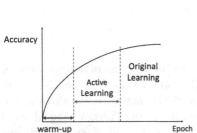

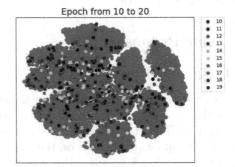

Fig. 2. Illustration of the proposed active training framework. At the first period of the training, called warm-up, the model works as the original deep learning network. After that, the model starts to actively query the most informative instances and add them to D_p. After getting enough queried data, the model will continue training.

Fig. 3. Illustration of the diversity of queries. The unlabeled data is mapped to 2-dimensional space by t-sne. All points in U are marked by grey colour. Different colours mark points queried in different epochs.

training the deep PU model with the expectation that accuracy will increase is illustrated in Fig. 2.

Figure 4, reprinted from [17] is another illustration of how the U data is distributed according to the surrogate losses. Here the positive data (+) and negative data (−) are divided by the sine function. Ranking the losses on U data in descending order, Fig. 4 shows the effect by marking the corresponding examples in the front of the ranked list to be *blue*. From it, we can also tell that examples with larger losses are further away from the decision boundary, and so it is for examples with smaller losses. Examples with loss values in the middle are more likely to be closer to the decision boundary, and contribute more to the find the decision boundary in learning.

By the above discussion, we propose four strategies for active PU learning with deep models.

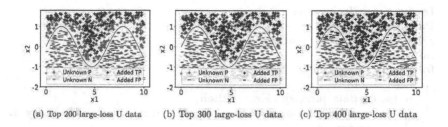

(a) Top 200 large-loss U data   (b) Top 300 large-loss U data   (c) Top 400 large-loss U data

Fig. 4. Reprinted from Figure 6 of [17]. It shows the effect by marking the U data with relatively larger losses to be *blue*, if using negative as the ground truth. (Color figure online)

Table 1. Overall query strategies

Query strategy	Selection criterion (for instances)
Least Confidence (LC)	Loss around 0.5
Uncertainty and Density (UD)	Values based on loss and density
Variance Max (VM)	Changes of loss
Window-sized Variance Max (WVM)	Changes of loss in specific range
Baseline	Loss around 1
Random sampling	Random

- Least Confidence (LC). Specifically, the informativeness of an instance can be estimated by its uncertainty, which is calculated by $0.5 - \ell_{sig}(g(x), -1)$, where ℓ_{sig} is the sigmoid loss. The queried batch is selected by

$$\text{argmin}_{D_q \subset D_u, |D_q| < budget} \quad |0.5 - \ell_{sig}(g(x), -1)|. \qquad (9)$$

The reason why we choose 0.5 here is it is the median of the range of the sigmoid loss $[0, 1]$. In other words, instances with a loss of 0.5 are much difficult to be classified for the learning model.

- Uncertainty and Density (UD). To enhance the diversity of queries, we proposed a new query strategy based on uncertainty and density. The density is defined as the proportion of the instances located in the specific bin. If the density is high, we tend to select less instances from this area. In this case, the queried batch is selected by

$$\text{argmin}_{D_q \subset D_u, |D_q| < budget} \quad | 0.5 - \ell_{sig}(g(x), -1) | \times density(x) \qquad (10)$$

- Variance Max (VM). Another strategy for defining the uncertainty of the instance is considering the changes of the loss values. This strategy assumes that the instances that are predicted with different labels in different phase of learning is uncertain by current model. Practically, we use the variance of loss values in different epochs as a measure of changes. Thus, the queried batch is selected by variance max strategy

$$\text{argmax}_{D_q \subset D_u, |D_q| < budget} \quad var(loss_1, loss_2, \ldots, loss_{current\_epoch}) \qquad (11)$$

Input   : Training data P and U
Parameters: query_size, query_epoch_range
`// set the parameters of nnPU`
Initialization;
for *epoch* < *MAX_EPOCH* **do**
  train as nnPU;
  if *epoch within query_epoch_range* **then**
    `// query_epoch_range is the set of epochs after which query is`
        `conducted`
    Select and query K instances `// K = query_size`
    Update the training P data;
  end
end

Algorithm 1: UDALPU (Uncertainty Derived Actively Labeled PU Learning)

– Window-sized Variance Max (WVM). Following the same strategy as Variance max, but considering the variance of a window instead of from the beginning, we could have the window-sized (ws) variance max strategy

$$\text{argmax}_{D_q \subset D_u, |D_q| < budget} \ var(loss_{current\_epoch-ws}, \ldots, loss_{current\_epoch}) \tag{12}$$

Additionally, we compare with the following two strategies

– Baseline. In this strategy, we do not do any querying. Instead, we select those unlabeled examples whose loss value is closest to 1 as the P data. This is the same strategy used in [17].
– Random Sampling (RS). This strategy randomly sample instances from D_u to query.

All query strategies are summarized in Table 1.

Our proposed UDALPU (Uncertainty Derived Actively Labeled PU Learning) framework is illustrated in Algorithm 1. Here we assume the oracle is only willing to provide labels for positive instances. If negative instances can also be labelled, methods such as PNU [14] may be exploited and we leave this part for future work. Finally, the objective function is the same as that of aaPU.

3.2 Diversity of Queries

Note that one of the main motivations for developing deep active learning is that uncertainty-based query, although very popular, does not select samples that are diverse [1]. In this way, these queried samples may not be that effective in improving the classification performance.

However, such a situation may not be accurate for deep PU learning. In deep PU learning, data provided are not fully labelled as in the case discussed in [1]. In this way, the large-small-loss trick can be exploited to select appropriate samples to query. Although VM and WVM cannot select the diverse instances,

LC and UD do diversely select instances in each iteration. Furthermore, these queried samples can be used to update a model and bring diversity to the model in different epochs of training. To verify this conjecture, we illustrate the distribution of the queried examples from epochs 10 to 20 in Fig. 3 using t-sne [12], which shows the distribution of all unlabeled data, and different colours mark the examples queried at different epochs. From Fig. 3, we can see that the data queried has covered the whole U data space. This result means diversity could be achieved by UDALPU with LC.

4   Empirical Illustration

The experiments are based on Python3, Pytorch 1.7 and CUDA 11.1.

4.1   Settings

Dataset. In PU learning, the most commonly used data set is MNIST, including 60,000 training examples and 10,000 test examples. For MNIST, we regard odd numbers as positive and even numbers as negative.

Baselines and Implementations. We use the SOTA nnPU as our baseline. Since we plan to query in total 1000 P data in addition to the 1000 P data provided at the beginning, we train nnPU with both 1000 P data and 2000 P data. Besides nnPU, we also compare our proposal with self-PU with 2000 P. In our implementation, we used a 6-layer *multilayer perceptron* (MLP) with logistic on MNIST. The batch size is 30000 for MNIST. For a fair comparison, we repeat each experiment ten times. The mean and standard deviations of accuracy are reported.

Parameters Settings. There are several hyper-parameters for our query, including in which epoch to start query (from $\{0, 5, 10, 20\}$ and 10 is the best), in which epoch to stop query (from $5, 10, 20, 50$ and 20 is the best), and the step size between two query epochs (from $\{1, 2, 5\}$ and 1 is the best).

4.2   Ablation Study

We demonstrate and analyse different query strategies and settings for UDALPU.

Selection of Informative Instances. Test results for different querying strategies are shown in Table 2 and Fig. 5. UDALPU (LC) is the best query strategy and even better than nnPU (2000P). UD is also better than nnPU (2000P). For VM and WVM, the performance is even worse than the original nnPU (1000P), showing that variance is not effective in active PU learning. Random Sampling can achieve comparable performance with nnPU (2000P).

Table 2. Classification accuracy (STD) for different query strategies with the tuned parameters, such as proposed UDALPU, Random Sampling, and Baseline.

Baseline	RS	LC	UD	VM	WVM
95.93 (0.86)	96.32 (0.98)	**97.27 (1.17)**	97.21 (1.16)	95.46 (0.95)	95.66 (1.09)

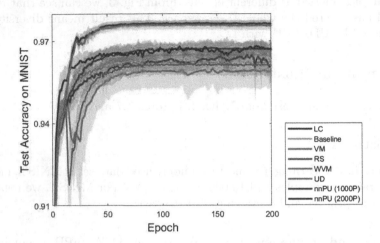

Fig. 5. Test accuracy of UDALPU strategies. The line refers to the mean value and the shadow area means the STD.

Effects of Query Settings. As shown in Table 3 and Fig. 6, comparing the test accuracy of query parameters, we found that the query strategy after warm-up and with a minor step has a better performance.

4.3   Comparing with Baselines

The experiments on MNIST are shown in Table 4 and Fig. 7. We found that most querying strategies could reach the best performed baseline nnPU* (2000), and LA and UD achieve even better results. The reason for this is that the LA and UD aim to query the most valuable instances.

Table 3. Test accuracy with different parameters, including start epoch, stop epoch and query frequency (step).

Start	0	0	0	0	0	10	10	10
Stop	1	5	10	20	45	20	30	55
Step	1	1	1	2	5	1	2	5
ACC	96.46	96.89	97.15	97.14	97.01	**97.27**	97.08	97.01
STD	0.85	0.85	0.92	1.00	1.11	**1.17**	1.17	1.25

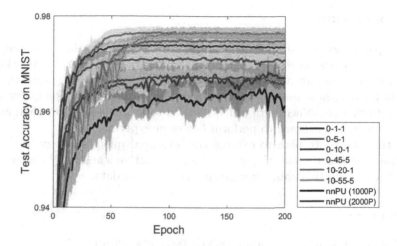

Fig. 6. Test accuracy of UDALPU (LC) based on various parameter values. The line refers to the mean value and the shadow area means the STD.

Table 4. Classification accuracy for compared methods and our proposal on MNIST. * means the experiment is trained with 2000 P initially.

Method	nnPU	nnPU*	Self-PU*	RS	UDALPU (LC)
Test accuracy	95.91 ± 0.75	96.43± 0.94	95.15 + 0.13	96.32 ± 0.98	**97.27 ± 1.17**

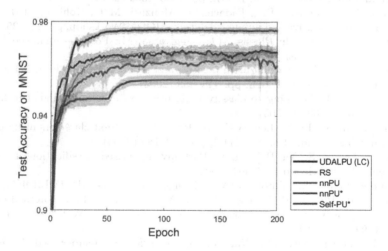

Fig. 7. Test accuracy of compared methods and our method for MNIST. Note that the line refers to the mean value and the shadow area means the STD.

5   Conclusion

In this paper, we investigate deep active learning PU methods by proposing querying strategies based on the large-small-loss trick of neural networks. The querying strategies are uncertainty based and require querying from the early stage of learning and also stop early before the training ends. The query strategies are further combined with nnPU method to form an active method and the methods have been shown to perform better in experiments.

In the future, we plan to explore the advanced query strategy further and combine it with other effective strategies to do active learning. We also plan to study the distribution shift after getting the queried data.

References

1. A survey of deep active learning. arXiv:2009.00236 (2020)
2. Arpit, D., et al.: A closer look at memorization in deep networks. In: ICML (2017)
3. Chen, X., et al.: Self-PU: self boosted and calibrated positive-unlabeled training. In: ICML, pp. 1510–1519 (2020)
4. Denis, F.Ç.: PAC learning from positive statistical queries. In: Richter, M.M., Smith, C.H., Wiehagen, R., Zeugmann, T. (eds.) ALT 1998. LNCS (LNAI), vol. 1501, pp. 112–126. Springer, Heidelberg (1998). https://doi.org/10.1007/3-540-49730-7_9
5. Du Plessis, M., Niu, G., Sugiyama, M.: Convex formulation for learning from positive and unlabeled data. In: ICML, pp. 1386–1394 (2015)
6. Ghasemi, A., Rabiee, H.R., Fadaee, M., Manzuri, M.T., Rohban, M.H.: Active learning from positive and unlabeled data. In: ICDM Workshop, pp. 244–250 (2011)
7. Kiryo, R., Niu, G., du Plessis, M.C., Sugiyama, M.: Positive-unlabeled learning with non-negative risk estimator. In: NIPS (2017)
8. Lee, W.S., Liu, B.: Learning with positive and unlabeled examples using weighted logistic regression. In: ICML, pp. 448–455 (2003)
9. Li, X., Liu, B.: Learning to classify texts using positive and unlabeled data. In: IJCAI, pp. 587–592 (2003)
10. Liu, B., Dai, Y., Li, X., Lee, W.S., Yu, P.S.: Building text classifiers using positive and unlabeled examples. In: ICDM, pp. 179–186 (2003)
11. Liu, B., Lee, W.S., Yu, P.S., Li, X.: Partially supervised classification of text documents. In: ICML, pp. 387–394 (2002)
12. Van der Maaten, L., Hinton, G.: Visualizing data using t-SNE. JMLR **9**(11) (2008)
13. Niu, G., du Plessis, M.C., Sakai, T., Ma, Y., Sugiyama, M.: Theoretical comparisons of positive-unlabeled learning against positive-negative learning. In: NIPS, pp. 1199–1207 (2016)
14. Sakai, T., du Plessis, M.C., Niu, G., Sugiyama, M.: Semi-supervised classification based on classification from positive and unlabeled data. In: ICML, pp. 2998–3006 (2017)
15. Settles, B.: Active Learning. Morgan & Claypool Publishers, San Rafael (2012)
16. Su, G., Chen, W., Xu, M.: Positive-unlabeled learning from imbalanced data. In: IJCAI, pp. 2995–3001 (2021)
17. Xu, M., Li, B., Niu, G., Han, B., Sugiyama, M.: Revisiting sample selection approach to positive-unlabeled learning: turning unlabeled data into positive rather than negative. arXiv: 1901.10155 (2019)

UFO RPN: A Region Proposal Network for Ultra Fast Object Detection

Wenkai Li[✉] and Andy Song

RMIT University, Melbourne, Australia
s3815738@student.rmit.edu.au, andy.song@rmit.edu.au

Abstract. Deep learning enables high accuracy in object detection in comparison with alternative methods. However deep learning based algorithms are often computationally expensive. That limits the use in many real world scenarios. For decades, researchers have been working on speeding up object detection. One bottleneck in current state-of-the-art methods is the region proposal generation stage as hundreds and thousands of proposed regions need to be processed before detection. Most of the regions are background areas which do not contribute to the actual detection. To improve the efficiency, we propose a region proposal network that can significantly reduce background while maintaining high accuracy. The comparison with SOTA methods shows that our network can be up to 70 times faster, since it only contains 1/15 to 1/150 parameters relative to these methods. The class IoU for MS COCO subsets achieves 40% to 70% and the inference speed on GTX 1080Ti can achieve above 1000 FPS performance. In addition, our study shows that high resolution input is not a must for high accuracy. The use of downsampled images can further reduce computation costs while retaining or even improving accuracy.

Keywords: Computer vision · Object detection · Region proposal network · Deep learning · Efficiency

1 Introduction

Object detection is of great importance both in AI research and in various industries such as surveillance and autonomous vehicles. Current state of the art of object detection are based on deep learning architectures, including Faster R-CNN [17], YOLO [15], and SSD [13]. They require both high computational cost and time to train and to inference. This is not desirable in real-world applications. Researchers have been working on improving the speed of object detection for decades. In recent deep learning based object detection algorithms, there are three major stages, namely feature extraction, region proposals, and object classification [3]. Some studies focus on reducing the complexity of the pre-trained classifier [9,14] in the third stage. Although these methods can save computation costs and boost speed, they still spend resources on unnecessary processing of

© Springer Nature Switzerland AG 2022
G. Long et al. (Eds.): AI 2021, LNAI 13151, pp. 619–631, 2022.
https://doi.org/10.1007/978-3-030-97546-3_50

a substantial proportion of non-object regions, because these images are often unbalanced, with majority of target images occupied by background [10].

Region proposal in object detection is to reduce the number of candidate object regions of interests (RoIs) sent to the detector, which speeds up object detection. R-CNN reduces region proposals from around 10^4–10^5 per image in sliding window approaches to around 2000 per image by using selective search [5]. With a Region Proposal Network (RPN) predicting regions, Faster R-CNN is able to reduce the number of region proposals to 300 per image, a significant reduction of computational cost [17]. Speed can be greatly improved by lowering the number of regions provided to the detector, but region proposals still contains large amount of background. Similarly, one-stage approaches are faster, but still slice the entire image into grids sending many "useless" regions to the classifier [9,13,15]. In contrast to the computer vision methods described above, human vision system is much more efficient since it focuses on target objects while ignoring the background [1]. The salience detection task is a mimic of human vision's selective visual attention system [6]. That would help generate region proposals on salient objects while ignoring the background. Recently, object detection based on salience map, like Saliency-based YOLO [8] and Selective convolutional network [12] have shown improvement on inference time. These studies are on the correct track but did not significantly enhance speed as they use still large networks and high-resolution inputs.

A recent research shows that salience information is preserved enough in low resolution gray scale (LG) images, according to human eye-tracking and computational modelling experiments [21]. With the inspiration from this study, we introduced low resolution image as input and proposed an efficient RPN to filter out background region. To determine the optimal resolution, we investigated the relationship between resolution and accuracy. From the benchmark MS COCO dataset, 5 subsets of various scenarios are selected, each subset containing three classes (Fig. 2). Object classes were relabeled in binary, target objects being 1 and background, including non-target objects, being 0. Our proposed UFO (Ultra Fast Object-detection) RPN adopts an efficient encoder-decoder architecture. To assess the model's performance, Intersection of Union is used. The models are trained and evaluated under six different resolutions. According to the qualitative and quantitative measure, we can see UFO RPN performed well on these object detection tasks. More importantly it is indeed ultra fast. It can achieve over 1000 FPS (Frame Per Second) on a single GTX 1080 Ti graphic card which is a rather modest setting. When compared with state-of-the-art approaches, our UFO RPN method runs 5 to 70 times faster as the network contains only 1/15 to 1/150 parameters, a tiny fraction of these large models.

This study offers two main contributions. Firstly, a fast and efficient neural network is proposed which can output regions of interest. So computational resources on areas of non-target-object area can be saved. It can be used as a regional proposal network for other object detection algorithms. Secondly, our experiment shows that high resolution input is not always necessary for high accuracy output. The use of a downsized image as input can reduce computing costs while maintaining and even improving accuracy. The optimal resolution is subject to the nature of the target objects.

2 Related Work

The generation of region proposals is an important step in object detection. It determines how the following expensive classification network is used. It is widely understood that object detection can be sped up at the cost of accuracy, if the region proposal network can generate object-only proposals more precisely [7]. Before the introduction of region proposal networks, sliding window methods are commonly used generating around 10^4–10^5 windows per image. These cut-out images are all fed into pre-trained classification detectors for object recognition [7]. To replace exhaustive window sliding, R-CNN [5] integrates convolutional neural networks (CNN) with region proposals. It applies selective search and dramatically cut down the number of region proposals to around 2000 per image. To further reduce redundant region proposals, Faster R-CNN [17] uses pre-trained CNN to generate feature map and introduces Region Proposal Network (RPN) to predict region proposals. The number of region proposal can be improved from 2000 to 300 by RPN. So RPN can save computational cost significantly. However the number of RoIs can be decreased even more because in a single image, there are usually only a couple of objects. But hundreds of region proposals are generated by current RPNs.

Inspired by the selective visual attention mechanism of human vision mechanism, saliency detection techniques can be used to generate region proposals with background areas somewhat removed [6]. Many attempts have been made to decrease region proposals using saliency-guided techniques [1,3,4,6,8,12,18,19]. M. Guo et al. uses Deformable Part Model (DPM) trained by the latent support vector machine (LSVM) to extract candidate detection area, which reduced searching area significantly without reducing accuracy [6]. However, they did not leverage convolutional network for feature extraction. Saliency-based YOLO adds a branch network on YOLO v3 to calculate salience probability for each cell of the image [8]. During training, cells with a high salience likelihood would be chosen as responsible cells. Despite the fact that it reduces computational costs, this technique is restricted to single entity recognition. Selective convolutional network uses an encoder-decoder structure to generate salience map, then only consider salience region for object detection [12]. When training salience model, their ground truth is square blocks generated from bounding box annotations, whereas we use pixel-wise ground truth to facilitate high accuracy object boundaries instead of block bounding boxes around the target.

Salience based methods can greatly save computational cost. However, apart from the points mentioned above, they are all using high resolution images as input. Salience information is preserved in low resolution gray scale (LG) images, according to human eye-tracking and computational modelling experiments [21]. Different from all other existing methods, we focus on using downsized image and lightweight network to generate region proposals that only contain objects and speed up object detection process. The exploration of the relation between accuracy and resolution is another research contribution of this study.

3 UFO RPN Architecture

The proposed UFO RPN adopts a fully convolutional encoder-decoder architecture. The encoder network consists of 4 downsampling blocks. In each encoder block, there are two 3×3 convolution layers with 1 stride following by a 2×2 max pooling layer with 2 strides for feature extracting and down-sampling. In each decoder block, there are one 2 × 2 deconvolution layers with 2 strides following by one 3 × 3 convolution layer with 1 stride for upsampling and feature extraction. The last 2 × 2 deconvolution layer with 2 strides generates the attention map and upsamples the output to the same size as the input. Figure 1 shows detailed input and output channels for each layer. The architecture is inspired by a recent work [21], which shows that salience information is preserved well in low-resolution grayscale images. These low-resolution images were used to generate salient maps with low computational cost and achieved a high speed of processing. A similar architecture is also used in video salience detection with success [20]. We reduced output channels of each convolutional layer to reduce the total size of the model.

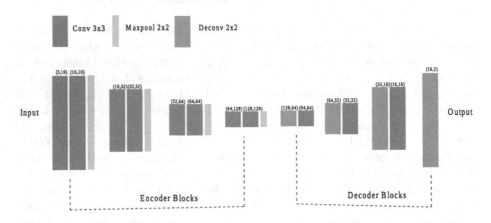

Fig. 1. Proposed region proposal network.

4 Data Set

The data set for training and evaluation is Microsoft Common Objects in Context 2017 (MS COCO 2017) [11], a benchmark for object detection. It contains 80 categories of objects with both bounding box and pixel level ground truth annotations. The original data set contains 118k images for training and 5k images for validation with corresponding ground truth annotations. Five scenarios are taken out from COCO, including 'sky', 'street', 'vehicle', 'food', and 'wildlife'. Each scenario contains three classes of objects. The ground truth we used is the original COCO annotations which are at pixel level. All images from the COCO dataset that include the target objects are utilised. We relabeled the ground truth when training for a specific object class. Pixels of the three classes of objects in each scenario are all labeled as '1', indicating that only labeled objects are of interest, while the background pixels and non-target object pixels are labeled as '0'.

The original resolution of images in COCO data set is not fixed, but often around 640 × 480. To explore the relationship between accuracy and resolution, we resized original images and labels to six variations: {16 × 16, 32 × 32, 64 × 64, 128 × 128, 256 × 256, 512 × 512} with linear interpolation. Each dataset is randomly split into training set (70%), testing set (20%) and validation set (10%). A detailed composition is shown in Fig. 2. Totally, we generated 30 subsets and trained different models on each subset. Apart from evaluating the proposed UFO RPN, another goal is to investigate the impact of different resolutions on detection accuracy, hence to discover the optimal resolution that is both small and offers high accuracy.

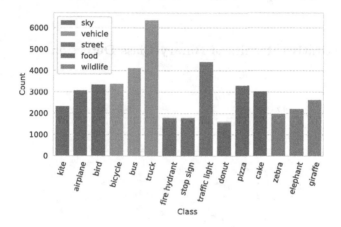

Fig. 2. Composition of datasets from COCO 2017

5   Experiments

On subsets of each resolution, we trained separate networks. All experiments were conducted on Pytorch framework with single GTX 1080 Ti graphic card. In each training, network weights were randomly initialized. The initial learning rate was set to 0.05. We used Stochastic Gradient Descent optimizer with weight decay set to 0.0001 and a momentum set to 0.9. Cross Entropy loss function was used here to compute loss for gradient descent. The batch size was set to 16. The max training epoch was set to 300 with an early stop policy to prevent overfitting. The training would stop if the validation mean IoU (mIou) does not improve after 10 epochs. The weights that generate the best mIou would be used as the final model. All training sessions were terminated before reaching the maximum epoch. We trained each model five times for each subset at each resolution to verify possible fluctuation between each training. The final result was calculated by averaging the test IoU scores across all five models.

5.1   Evaluation Metrics

Intersection over union [2] (IoU) is used for measuring the accuracy of predicted object area. It is calculated by dividing the intersection area of ground truth and the union of these two areas. The equation of IoU is as follow, where A_{gt} denotes ground truth area and A_{pr} denotes predicted area:

$$IoU = \frac{A_{gt} \cap A_{pr}}{A_{gt} \cup A_{pr}} \tag{1}$$

The predicted labels were first upsampled to the original image size before being compared to the ground truth labels to compute the IoU for a fair comparison. Mean average precision (mAP) was not adopted since we relabeled multi classes as one salience class, which could have resulted in overlapped objects in the output. We use floating point operations (FLOPs) and frames per second (FPS) to measure computational cost and speed. The FPS was averaged on 1000 inferences.

5.2   Quantitative Results of Binary-Class Detection

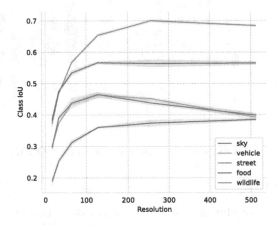

Fig. 3. IoU in relation to input resolutions

Figure 3 shows that high resolution is not a must for high accuracy. The plots are averaged on testing results of 5 repetitions. Lines represent the averaged IoU. Bands or shade represent upper and lower bounds of IoU. As can be seen the variations between each training are minor. Only the sky scenario show a slightly improved IoU at higher resolution. This is likely due to the large proportion of tiny objects in this subset. It can also be observed that resolutions under a certain level, e.g. below 32×32, would lead to low IoUs. Individual class also shows that trend as shown in Fig. 4.

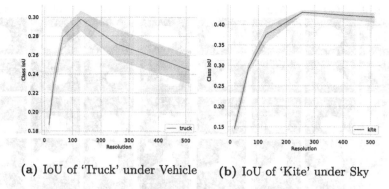

(a) IoU of 'Truck' under Vehicle   **(b)** IoU of 'Kite' under Sky

Fig. 4. IoU trained separately with binary labeling

In contrast, when resolution is high, excessive amount of information may also cause difficulty in detection. Considering the trade-off between the computing cost and accuracy, we define the optimal resolution for each subset as the lowest resolution that can generate a comparable accuracy. Although in sky subset IoU of 512×512 resolution increases by 5% (from 0.37 to 0.39) than in 128×128 resolution, FPS (Fig. 5a) drops by 63% (from 1011 to 365). So, we define 128×128 as the optimal resolution in the sky subset. For vehicle, street and food subset, the optimal resolution is 128×128, while 256×256 is the best resolution for wild life subset.

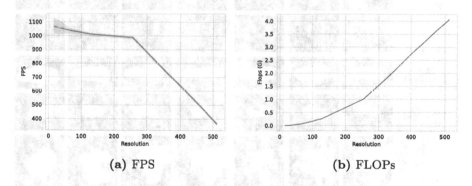

(a) FPS   **(b)** FLOPs

Fig. 5. FPS and FLOPs in relation to resolutions

5.3   Qualitative Results of Binary-Class Detection

Detection results under different resolutions are shown in Fig. 6. For each scenario, three images are selected. The optimal resolution for each scenario is highlighted with a red frame. As outputs for all resolutions are resized to original resolution, the results show that UFO RPN can achieve good detection.

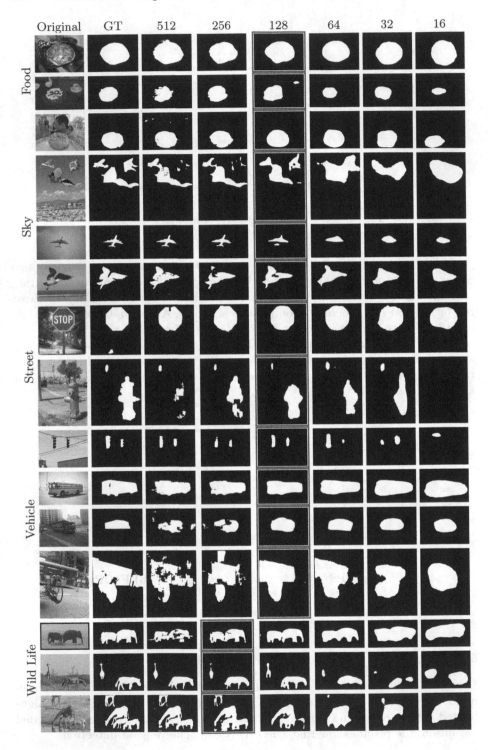

Fig. 6. Detection output from different resolutions

Similar to the trend in IoU, we can also observe that higher resolution are not always better. For example, in the outputs of the third image of Vehicle subset, prediction of 128×128 is more clear than 256×256 and 512×512. For large objects like pizza, stop sign and bus, predictions of 16×16 are as good as higher resolutions. By contrast, when resolution is lower than a certain level, the shapes of some objects are unable to recognise and some small objects are missing. For example, in the second image of street subset, when the resolution is downsized to 16×16, neither stop sign nor fire hybrid were detected. Only one traffic light was detected in the third image of street subset of 16×16 resolution. The bounding box labeling results of optimal resolution are shown in Fig. 7.

Food   Sky   Street   Vehicle   Wildlife

Fig. 7. Bounding box labeling of subsets

5.4   Results of Multi-class Detection

With UFO RPN, binary-class detection can be easily extended to multi-class detection. Figure 8 shows the relation between IoU with resolution under multi-class setting, e.g. detecting individual classes categorised from COCO. The figures show that IoU follow the same pattern as that in binary-class detection. The optimal resolutions for each subset are the same as in binary-class detection. For most of the classes, when the resolution is greater than 256×256, the IoU starts to drop.

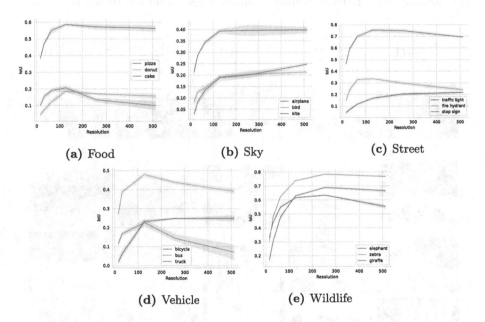

(a) Food   (b) Sky   (c) Street

(d) Vehicle   (e) Wildlife

Fig. 8. Multi-class IoU in relation to resolution

One observation from the experiment is the IoU of truck in vehicle subset (Fig. 8d) decreased significantly when resolution is higher than 128×128. So we trained it separately to detect just truck which is a binary task. We used all images from MS COCO dataset that contains trucks labeling truck pixels as '1' and others '0'. Figure 4a is actually from that training which also repeated 5 times. So we can see 128×128 is an optimal resolution for either binary or multiple classes involving truck. This finding further supports our hypothesis that the best resolution is determined by the attributes of the target.

5.5   Comparison of Speed and Computing Cost

To further evaluate UFO RPN, we compared with state-of-the-art models on number of parameters, FLOPs and FPS (Table 1). FPS is averaged on 1000 inferences on GTX 1080 Ti. Only the inference time of the model is considered when calculating FPS. Models with pre-trained backbone require fixed input resolutions, while input size of our model is flexible. We put 128×128 and 256×256 into the comparison as they are the optimal resolutions appeared in our experiments. Comparison with state-of-the-art methods shows that our network is 5 to 70 times faster and only has 1/15 to 1/150 parameters.

Table 1. Comparison with SOTA models

Model	Backbone	Parameters (M)	FLOPs (G)	FPS
SSD [13]	VGG16	26	31	82
RetinaNet [10]	Resnet50	38	78	35
YOLOV4-tiny [9]	Darknet53 tiny	6	2	238
YOLOV3 [16]	Darknet53	62	33	62
Faster R-CNN [17]	Resnet50	28	52	14
UFO-RPN (256×256)	–	**0.38**	**1**	**988**
UFO-RPN (128×128)	–	**0.38**	**0.3**	**1011**

6   Conclusions

In this study we proposed a selective attention based regional proposal network for object detection, namely UFO RPN. It can greatly reduces computational cost by ignoring large proportion of non-valuable regions, e.g. background and non targets. Hence it can significantly improve inference speed without sacrificing detection accuracy. This advantage makes possible to deploy object detection algorithm on edge devices where the computation resources are very limited. In terms of computing cost and inference speed, a comparison of FPS and FLOPs shows that our network significantly outperforms state-of-the-art approaches by two to three orders of magnitude. In addition, our finding suggests that higher resolution is not necessarily the recipe for better accuracy. It is possible to achieve optimal performance at a lower resolution. The actual best resolution is likely task dependent and determined by the nature of the target object.

This work is the first stage of our study on ultra fast object detection. There are plenty of future work awaiting, for example the full-scale comparison with SOTA on large scale. Also we will examine the relation between the object and the optimal resolution so further improvement could be achieved.

References

1. Duan, L., Gu, J., Yang, Z., Miao, J., Ma, W., Wu, C.: Bio-inspired visual attention model and saliency guided object segmentation. In: Pan, J.-S., Krömer, P., Snášel, V. (eds.) Genetic and Evolutionary Computing, pp. 291–298. Springer International Publishing, Cham (2014). https://doi.org/10.1007/978-3-319-01796-9_31
2. Everingham, M., Van Gool, L., Williams, C., Winn, J., Zisserman, A.: The pascal visual object classes challenge 2012 (voc2012) results (2012). http://www.pascal-network.org/challenges/VOC/voc2011/workshop/index.html
3. Fattal, A.K., Karg, M., Scharfenberger, C., Adamy, J.: Saliency-guided region proposal network for CNN based object detection. In: 2017 IEEE 20th International Conference on Intelligent Transportation Systems (ITSC), pp. 1–8. IEEE (2017)
4. Feng, J., Wei, Y., Tao, L., Zhang, C., Sun, J.: Salient object detection by composition. In: 2011 International Conference on Computer Vision, pp. 1028–1035. IEEE (2011)
5. Girshick, R., Donahue, J., Darrell, T., Malik, J.: Rich feature hierarchies for accurate object detection and semantic segmentation. In: Proceedings of the IEEE Conference on Computer Vision and Pattern Recognition, pp. 580–587 (2014)
6. Guo, M., Zhao, Y., Zhang, C., Chen, Z.: Fast object detection based on selective visual attention. Neurocomputing **144**, 184–197 (2014)
7. Hosang, J., Benenson, R., Dollár, P., Schiele, B.: What makes for effective detection proposals? IEEE Trans. Pattern Anal. Mach. Intell. **38**(4), 814–830 (2015)
8. Hu, J.Y., Shi, C.J.R., Zhang, J.S.: Saliency-based yolo for single target detection. Knowl. Inf. Syst. **63**(3), 717–732 (2021)
9. Jiang, Z., Zhao, L., Li, S., Jia, Y.: Real-time object detection method based on improved yolov4-tiny. arXiv preprint arXiv:2011.04244 (2020)
10. Lin, T.Y., Goyal, P., Girshick, R., He, K., Dollár, P.: Focal loss for dense object detection. In: Proceedings of the IEEE International Conference on Computer Vision, pp. 2980–2988 (2017)
11. Lin, T.-Y., et al.: Microsoft COCO: common objects in context. In: Fleet, D., Pajdla, T., Schiele, B., Tuytelaars, T. (eds.) ECCV 2014. LNCS, vol. 8693, pp. 740–755. Springer, Cham (2014). https://doi.org/10.1007/978-3-319-10602-1_48
12. Ling, H., Qin, Y., Zhang, L., Shi, Y., Li, P.: Selective convolutional network: an efficient object detector with ignoring background. In: ICASSP 2020–2020 IEEE International Conference on Acoustics, Speech and Signal Processing (ICASSP), pp. 4462–4466. IEEE (2020)
13. Liu, W., et al.: SSD: single shot MultiBox detector. In: Leibe, B., Matas, J., Sebe, N., Welling, M. (eds.) ECCV 2016. LNCS, vol. 9905, pp. 21–37. Springer, Cham (2016). https://doi.org/10.1007/978-3-319-46448-0_2
14. Long, X., et al.: PP-YOLO: an effective and efficient implementation of object detector. arXiv preprint arXiv:2007.12099 (2020)
15. Redmon, J., Divvala, S., Girshick, R., Farhadi, A.: You only look once: unified, real-time object detection. In: Proceedings of the IEEE Conference on Computer Vision and Pattern Recognition, pp. 779–788 (2016)
16. Redmon, J., Farhadi, A.: YOLOv3: an incremental improvement. arXiv preprint arXiv:1804.02767 (2018)
17. Ren, S., He, K., Girshick, R., Sun, J.: Faster R-CNN: towards real-time object detection with region proposal networks. arXiv preprint arXiv:1506.01497 (2015)
18. Ren, Z., Gao, S., Chia, L.T., Tsang, I.W.H.: Region-based saliency detection and its application in object recognition. IEEE Trans. Circuits Syst. Video Technol. **24**(5), 769–779 (2013)

19. Uijlings, J.R., Van De Sande, K.E., Gevers, T., Smeulders, A.W.: Selective search for object recognition. Int. J. Comput. Vision **104**(2), 154–171 (2013)
20. Wang, W., Shen, J., Shao, L.: Video salient object detection via fully convolutional networks. IEEE Trans. Image Process. **27**(1), 38–49 (2017)
21. Yohanandan, S., Song, A., Dyer, A.G., Tao, D.: Saliency preservation in low-resolution grayscale images. In: Ferrari, V., Hebert, M., Sminchisescu, C., Weiss, Y. (eds.) ECCV 2018. LNCS, vol. 11210, pp. 237–254. Springer, Cham (2018). https://doi.org/10.1007/978-3-030-01231-1_15

Accurate New Zealand Wildlife Image Classification-Deep Learning Approach

Benjamin Curran, Seyed Mohammad Nekooei[(✉)], and Gang Chen

Victoria University of Wellington, Wellington, New Zealand
curranbenj1@myvuw.ac.nz, {mohammad.nekooei,aaron.chen}@ecs.vuw.ac.nz

Abstract. Image classification is a major machine learning problem that has a wide range of applications in the real world. The Wellington Wildlife Camera Trap dataset contains images taken from vibration triggered cameras in sequences of three. State-of-the-art deep convolutional neural network (CNN) models, such as DenseNet-121 and ResNet-50, are unable to achieve the required accuracy of classification on this dataset. This research aims to improve the performance in multi-class classification tasks on the Wellington Dataset through a newly developed dual-input channel neural network. Our experiment results provide clear evidence that the new CNN model can achieve high accuracy and confidence on this challenging and scientifically important dataset. It is able to significantly reduce the amount of time required to manually classify wildlife images for conservation research in New Zealand.

Keywords: Convolutional neural network · Image classification · Wellington camera trap dataset

1 Introduction

New Zealand is home to a unique, diverse and vulnerable native wildlife. The introduced mammals that currently live within the New Zealand ecosystem are generally seen as pests and a danger to the conservation of our native biodiversity. To help conserve this native biodiversity [1] a high number of vibration triggered cameras are installed to capture images of wildlife in urban areas of Wellington, New Zealand. The images from these camera traps have been labelled in a time-intensive process relying solely on manual processes [2][1], which is laborious and error prone.

On top of the manual classification issues, these cameras have a high rate of false-positive triggers. As a result of these false-positives, the dataset contains 75% percentage of images with no animals [16]. Accurate classification allows us to drastically reduce the amount of time spent classifying this data by removing all classes of non-interesting images or drawing attention to the interesting images [1,16].

---

[1] Wellington Camera Trap dataset - http://lila.science/datasets/wellingtoncamera traps.

© Springer Nature Switzerland AG 2022
G. Long et al. (Eds.): AI 2021, LNAI 13151, pp. 632–644, 2022.
https://doi.org/10.1007/978-3-030-97546-3_51

In the past decade, there have been significant improvements within the field of computer vision [11]. These have resulted in deep convolutional neural network (CNN) models being able to perform tasks like image classification to a degree that rivals the human visual system [3,5,16,21]. CNNs has been widely considered as a favoured deep learning technique for the past decade due to their consistent ability to classify image data with state-of-the-art accuracy. There have been numerous highly successful, well researched CNN models, including ResNet [8], VGG [18], GoogLeNet [20] and DenseNet [9].

Despite the existence of numerous high performing models, our experiments show that these models do not provide high, out of the box accuracy, on our dataset. To address this issue, we design a new dual-input channel deep convolution neural network architecture in this paper that is capable of producing high confidence classification predictions on the Wellington Camera Trap dataset, noticeably outperforming several state-of-the-art CNN models, including ResNet-50, DenseNet-121, or VGG16.

The Wellington camera trap dataset is made up of image sequences. The camera traps, when triggered, take a burst of three images with a half-second delay between photos [1]. In view of the sequential nature of captured images in the dataset, we have developed a preprocessing pipeline that produces images artefacts based on sequential differences and enables our new CNN model to load and process data at a high speed, consuming significantly less time than the baseline models tested. Overall, our newly proposed CNN model can significantly reduce the number of human hours spent on manual classification.

Finally, although limited by hardware considerations, this research provides evidence that predictions with high confidence and accuracy are possible on unique, difficult and native animal classification tasks.

The remainder of this paper is organised as follows. Section 2 provides a quick overview of related works. Section 3 introduces the architecture of the final system. Section 4 describes all the major experiments and results in detail. Finally, we conclude this paper and highlight future works in Sect. 5.

2   Related works

The use of machine learning for animal research, surveillance, and management have increased drastically over the past decade [5,6]. Despite the wide range of applications of machine learning, they generally share a common goal - species recognition. The interest in developing automated methods for image classification is a result of the expensive and time consuming nature of manual classification.

The largest existing open-source animal dataset, Snapshot Serengeti, contains over 7 million images [19]. Studies on this dataset and other similar camera trap datasets have shown that generally 75% of images collected by camera traps contain no animal at all [16]. There is evidence that the use of a pipeline stage that removes these images will lead to improvements in later classification due a better distribution of classes [4,16]. The data collected from these camera traps is noticeably different from the Wellington Camera Traps, including that the images are rarely completely saturated by a flash, the animals in the Serengeti are significantly larger than in the Wellington dataset and that the images contain the horizon in the background. These factors potentially aid in the ability to differentiate an animal from the background.

The research of deep learning for image classification tasks has rapidly lead to a large number of high accuracy models in the past decade. However, a majority of such research works focused on neural network architecture rather than the design of the entire system [11]. This research aims to introduce a classifications system that can produce high confidence classification predictions on the Wellington Camera Trap dataset.

Since the inception of automated pattern recognition, one of the biggest difficulties has been how to extract important features from a background containing irrelevant information [17]. Besides automated feature extraction techniques based on CNNs [8,11,13], there exist numerous other ways to extract image features. Some examples of traditional preprocessing techniques include linear filtering, pixel subtraction, and distribution linearisation [7]. In 2004, Wang *et al.* [22] proposed an algorithm for detecting distortion between an original image and an edited image. This algorithm can be utilized in practice as a structural similarity index. It took into account numerous features from the images including luminosity, contrast, and structural pixel difference [22], instead of comparing images through a naive pixel subtraction or other similar techniques. We adopt this structural similarity algorithm to process sequential images captured in the Wellington dataset, in order to detect distortion in an image based on movement from an animal by treating the static background as the original image.

3   Design a Dual-Input Convolutional Neural Network

The classification system in this research utilised a two-step process. The first step focuses on preprocessing the Wellington Camera Trap dataset and creating two streams of data. The second step of this system uses these two streams as input vectors for the dual-input channel CNN for image classification so as to determine whether any given image sequence contains wildlife of interest. A diagram for the system architecture can be found in Fig. 1.

3.1   Preprocessing

Being able to effectively and reliably extract information from sequences was a major milestone for this research. One major concern is that the images were not labelled independently in the Wellington dataset. In fact, if an animal is present in any image of a sequence, then all the images in that sequence are labelled as that animal. For example, in Fig. 2, we see a bird that is present in the first image, but not in either of the following two images. In this case, all three of those images are given the "bird" label. This is problematic for the training of any machine learning task. If we supplied the system with the third image in the

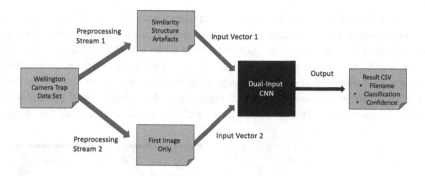

Fig. 1. An overview of the image classification system.

sequence from Fig. 2 and labelled it as a bird, we would be training our model using mislabelled data. The experiments reported in Sect. 4.1 suggest that there is a significant number of such images sequences in the dataset, confirming that we cannot train CNNs using a large amount of mislabeled data.

Furthermore, by using only the first image in each sequence, our baseline models (ResNet, VGG, and DenseNet) all predict at a higher accuracy when compared to using the entire dataset. Given this, we decided to only use the first image in a sequence when training and testing our models.

Fig. 2. Images captured sequentially in the Wellington wildlife camera trap dataset.

In the preprocessing step, the first stream applies the structural similarity algorithm to produce artefacts. The second stream of data selects all sequences that passed the acceptance criterion from the first stream. The dual-input channel CNN requires these images to align with an associated similarity artefact.

Preprocessing Stream 1: In the preprocessing step, the first stream applies the structural similarity algorithm to produce artefacts based on the differences between the images. The camera traps are set up so that the camera is pointed at a fixed position. Given this, a majority of the background across the entire sequence of images should be relatively static. However, if an animal were to appear within the frame, they will highly likely change their position across all three images. On top of this, there would be the greatest amount of difference between image 1 and 3 in a sequence as more time had passed. Unfortunately, for a substantial portion of the image sequences, the third image suffers from some degree of pixel shift. This impact is visually minor, but without complicated corrective measures our image preprocessing step may fail. Figure 3 shows the first and third images from a sequence, where a slightly downshift on the pixel is present on the third image. As a result, the artefact may produce a meaningless collection of noise (as shown in Image B from Fig. 4). Thus, we have instead chosen to apply our image difference techniques to the first and second images within a sequence, as they produce more reliable results across all the data.

A   B

Fig. 3. Pixel shift issue with first verses third image

Here we implement the structural similarity algorithm [22] as a way to compare two images beyond just pixel value. This algorithm allows us to treat the background of the images as the source of truth, and then search for distortion across the sequence. In most cases, with a static background, we are able to reveal the outline of an animal moving across the scene. For example, Image A in Fig. 4 showcases an ideal example using this algorithm. The algorithm takes into account luminance and contrast between two images and generates a result based on the combination of these measures. The result is a float similarity value between 0 and 1, and an image artefact highlighting the structural differences between the two images.

In line with our decision to use the first and second images from every sequence, we found through experiments that a low percentage (<5%) of artefacts produced by the structural similarity algorithm contain a significant amount of noise. A major reason is because the pixel shift that we observed in the third image of some sequences also occurs in the first and second images of a small number of sequences in the Wellington dataset. An example of pixel shift between images can be found in Fig. 3, and the resulting artefact is found in Image B from Fig. 4. Meanwhile, environmental factors such as wind or sudden exposure changes may also result in a shift in background. Considering this, we define an approval policy based on the similarity score obtained from the structural similarity algorithm (i.e., the similarity score must be greater than 0.45) and decide to exclude any images that violate the policy. We then save all the artefact images that obeys the policy, which helps to remove overall <3% of all image sequences in the dataset.

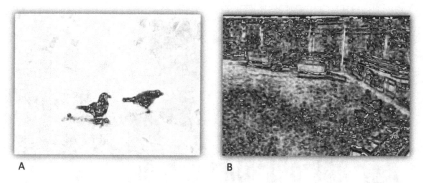

Fig. 4. Structural similarity artefacts. Image A is an artefact produced by a static background. Image B is an artefact that failed our pipeline's acceptance criteria.

Preprocessing Stream 2: The second stream of data selects all sequences that agree with the approval policy discussed above. The dual-input channel CNN requires these images to align with an associated similarity artefact. Each image has information including the time each image was taken and the camera brand. As this information has no relevance toward the image classification task, we have decided to cropped the bottom 8% of all the images. We also resized all the images down from 3264×2448 to closer match the input shape required for the CNN. By reducing the resolution of the image we reduced the amount of memory needed to load all the images into memory. However, instead of reducing down to exactly 224×224, we decided to only resize down to 600×500 to keep the resolution high enough that we could manually verify them when needed. It also allowed us to potentially experiment with variation in input shape without having to re-run the entire preprocessing pipeline. By reducing the image resolution down in a one time preprocessing pipeline, our images loaded into the model at 400 images a second rather than the original 6 images per second.

Once we had a reference to validate the sequences, we prune away the second and third images to help reduce error from non-independently labelled data. After these pre-processing steps have been completed, our dual-input channel CNN can use this data to either train or provide classification.

3.2 Model Architecture

The dual-input channel CNN architecture is designed to lean on various representations of the same data instance in multiple forms. This design draws inspiration from ensemble learning techniques and domain adaptation research. It concatenates the outputs of several parallel models into a fully connected layer which learns how to handle the input data. This provides potential benefits over ensemble techniques which often rely on naive polling to produce an output.

Our dual-input channel CNN Architecture is depicted in Fig. 5. Both parallel input channels are created using the same architecture. The input channel uses a (224, 224, 1) shaped imaged. These channels are made up of five blocks each

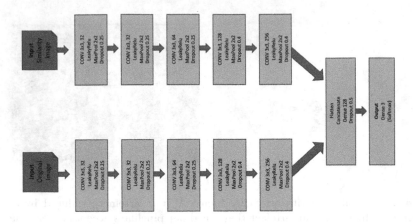

Fig. 5. The dual-input channel CNN architecture

containing a convolution layer. The decision to use five layers with sizes of 32, 32, 64, 128, and 256 was a combination of hardware limitations and norms set by the ResNet architecture. Each set of convolution layers uses LeakyReLU [14] as their activation function, and pass through max-pooling. To ensure the image dimensions remain the same, these convolution layers all use the same padding mode and a stride of 1×1. The size of the kernels is limited to 3×3 in all convolution layer [9,13].

Finally, to reduce overfitting, each convolution layer is exposed to dropout ranging from 25–40%. Once each channel reaches the end of their convolution sections the dual inputs are flattened and concatenated together. This concatenation passes through one dense layer consisting of 128 nodes, and then finally through a 3 node dense layer which produces a softmax output. The classification is then determined by the class with the highest probability outputted by the softmax function. The size versus accuracy performance of this model is one of its greatest strengths. The final model contained only 4,005,955 trainable parameters. This is a significant reduction compared to ResNet-50's 23,540,739, VGG16's 134,272,835 trainable parameters. The reduced number of trainable parameters helps this model achieve a significantly quicker training time when compared to these baseline models.

3.3 Primary Design Decisions

This research aims to provide high confidence classification while being able to operate in limited hardware environments. All design decisions made in this research considered these limitation and were a compromise between classification performance and model size.

Input Shape: The first major decision was the input image shape. Our preliminary experiments revealed that the use of three colour channels (RGB) did not lead to desirable performance. Furthermore, the ResNet architecture provided evidence that image classification does not necessarily benefit from using images larger than 224×224 resolution. As a result of this, it was decided to load images in a greyscale state and reduce their resolution down from 3264×2448 to 224×244. This resolution reduction not only leads to significantly quicker training times but also allowed for more equal comparison against the baseline models.

Layer Design: The number of layers and shape of those layers were heavily impacted by hardware limitations. Originally, given the classification performance of ResNet, we intend to replicate that structure for both of the two channels of the dual-input channel CNN. However, this resulted in a model that was too large to load into the memory of commodity computers available for this research. Given this, we instead looked at VGG16 [18], a model with significantly fewer layers. VGG16 is comprised of 5 blocks of convolution layers, where each block is separated by a pooling layer. The convolution layers are brought together with 3 dense layers and classified using a softmax function. Despite containing fewer layers, the block design and kernel size in VGG means there are approximately 6 times more trainable parameters than ResNet (134 million versus 23 million). To help reduce this, we kept the blocks, but stripped out one of the extra convolution layers in each block, and kept the kernel size to 3×3.

This model was significantly smaller but was once again too large to load into the available computer memory. To further reduce the model size, we halved all the starting convolution layer sizes down. This resulted in our first layer having a size of 32, and our final convolution layer using 256. In addition to meeting our hardware restrictions, we found that by only using one input channel, our model would not have significantly reduced performance by reducing these layer sizes. Further alterations were made to the model which resulted in the final design only having one convolution layer per block. These decisions were ultimately made to strike a desirable balance among performance, model complexity and training time. The reduction in convolution layers did not significantly affect classification accuracy, but did significantly reduce training time.

4 Experiment

This section reports the classification performance of our dual-input channel CNN model and provides comparisons with several baseline models. We use Bird, Mammal, and Not Interesting labels for this data set. We present our findings and evaluate them against their uses for real-world conservation research. In the experiment, we use Adam optimisation [12] with a learning rate of 0.001. As displayed in Fig. 3, the dropout ratio varied between 0.25 and 0.5 depending on the layer. The batch size for training was set to 32. We used a relatively small batch size in accordance with existing research suggesting a large batch can led to degraded performance [10]. 80% of the total data is used for training, and the other 20% is reserved for testing the created model. In total, the model was trained in 120 epochs. We also have 10 independent runs for statistical analysis.

4.1 Baseline Experiments

Performance of Existing CNN Models: We trained several state-of-the-art CNN models (i.e. ResNet-50, VGG-16, and DenseNet-121) using different subsets of the Wellington dataset. As shown in Table 1, The results from these experiments revealed that none of these models were able to produce high accuracy results on the dataset [4,15,16]. The best accuracy we achieved was 43.31%, which is not a large improvement over random guessing.

Table 1. Performance of existing CNN models.

Model name	Data used	Test mean	Approx. training time
DenseNet	Full sequence	$39.68 \pm 0.68\%$	150 s
ResNet	Full sequence	$38.75 \pm 0.92\%$	40 s
VGG	Full sequence	$33.33 \pm 0.00\%$	200 s
DenseNet	First image	$43.31 \pm 0.93\%$	150 s
ResNet	First image	$43.16 \pm 1.45\%$	40 s
VGG	First image	$33.33 \pm 0.00\%$	200 s
DenseNet	Greyscale	$42.75 \pm 0.37\%$	150 s
ResNet	Greyscale	$42.83 \pm 1.03\%$	40 s

Since using single-channel greyscale images does not have a noticeable impact on the classification performance. When factoring for both efficiency and classification accuracy, the experiment results obtained on greyscale images provide evidence that ResNet-50 has achieved the best classification accuracy, when compared to DenseNet and VGG. However, none of these models were able to produce a performance that would be useful for real-world classification tasks. The low accuracy compared to similar studies which have used these models [4,5,16] helps suggest that the wildlife images captured in the Wellington dataset presents a significantly difficult problem for computer vision. This experiment also helped prove that there is a large amount of mislabelled data due to non-independent labels. As discussed above, we can potentially address this problem by only using the first image from each sequence.

Classification Performance on Similarity Structure Artefacts: Similarity structure images can provide clear evidence where and when movement is present in a sequence. Given this, a CNN may be able to differentiate between the animal present labels (e.g., birds and mammals) and the not interesting label (i.e., no wildlife of interest is present in the image sequence).

Table 2. Performance of ResNet-50 on different image types

Model name	Data used	Test mean	Approx. training time
ResNet	First image	$43.16 \pm 1.45\%$	40 s
ResNet	Greyscale	$42.83 \pm 1.03\%$	40 s
ResNet	Similarity	$44.99 \pm 2.09\%$	40 s

While performing image classification based on the similarity structure images, the testing accuracy obtained by us is clearly greater than random guessing (33%). This suggests that similarity structure images does provide vital information that helps CNN distinguish images with different class labels. In particular, the results in Table 2 reveal that ResNet achieved slightly better classification accuracy upon using the similarity structure images. This experiment provides evidence that the use of similarity structure artefacts can improve the classification performance of CNNs. However, we cannot build a sufficiently accurate classification system using these image artefacts alone to substantially reduce human efforts involved manually classifying wildlife images for conservation research in New Zealand. The final experiment results provided below show that our dual-input channel CNN model can be used to achieve high confidence classification.

4.2 Performance of Dual-Input Channel CNN

The performance obtained on our dual-input channel CNN model shows significant improvement against all of the baseline models explored in this research. The testing accuracy is significantly higher than the next best model (75.62% versus 44.89%). The time per epoch needed for training was also significantly quicker than the baseline set by ResNet-50 (18 s verses 40 s per epoch). These results are shown in Table 3. An existing study [1] shows that citizen scientists can achieve an overall classification accuracy of 87.8% on the Wellington dataset. However, as shown in related wildlife research [4,16], there is benefit in reducing and simplifying a dataset by creating subsets of data. These subsets can enable quicker processing and classifications for later tasks.

Table 3. Performance comparison between dual-input channel CNN and ResNet-50

Model name	Data used	Test mean	Approx. training time
Dual Input	Combination	$75.62 \pm 1.26\%$	18 s
ResNet	First image	$43.16 \pm 1.45\%$	40 s
ResNet	Greyscale	$42.83 \pm 1.03\%$	40 s
ResNet	Similarity	$44.99 \pm 2.09\%$	40 s

Table 4. Classification accuracy when factoring model confidence.

Model confidence	Classification accuracy	Percentage of total data
1	99.08%	9.40%
0.99	96.01%	21.00%
0.95	91.55%	34.07%
0.90	89.36%	43.28%
0.80	84.97%	57.48%
0.70	83.20%	72.55%

The Pearson correlation coefficient for confidence and correct prediction reveals a positive correlation value of 0.356. This provides some evidence that the model is more accurate in cases where it is more confident in its predictions. A breakdown of confidence values versus the accuracy of predictions is shown in Table 4. At each confidence level, we report on the accuracy of all those predictions, and what total percentage of the data this included. It is clearly evident that, on a large subset of images of the Wellington dataset, the final model is highly accurate. For example, approximately 43% of the images in the dataset is classified with an accuracy of 90%. This implies that the new dual-input channel CNN model can potentially reduce human efforts by 43% during practical use.

5   Conclusions

In this research, a new dual-input channel CNN model has been developed to produce high confidence classification predictions on the Wellington Camera Trap dataset. Along with this CNN architecture, we have created a preprocessing pipeline which produces images artefacts based on sequence differences, and enables models to load and process data with high efficiency. These designs were the result of large amounts of experimentation work with proven high performing CNN designs, and comparisons to similar wildlife studies.

There were numerous times through this research where we were forced into design decisions based on hardware limitations. It would be interesting to determine how well a significantly larger neural network can handle the Wellington dataset. However, in view of the normal computation facilities available for wildlife conservation researchers, it is essential for us to strike a proper balance between efficiency and effectiveness, making our dual-input channel CNN model potentially useful for many future conservation research activities.

References

1. Anton, V., Hartley, S., Geldenhuis, A., Wittmer, H.U.: Monitoring the mammalian fauna of urban areas using remote cameras and citizen science. J. Urban Ecol. **4**(1), juy002 (2018)
2. Anton, V., Hartley, S., Wittmer, H.U.: Evaluation of remote cameras for monitoring multiple invasive mammals in New Zealand. N. Z. J. Ecol. **42**(1), 74–79 (2018)
3. Chen, G., Han, T.X., He, Z., Kays, R., Forrester, T.: Deep convolutional neural network based species recognition for wild animal monitoring. In: 2014 IEEE International Conference on Image Processing (ICIP), pp. 858–862. IEEE (2014)
4. Chen, R., Little, R., Mihaylova, L., Delahay, R., Cox, R.: Wildlife surveillance using deep learning methods. Ecol. Evol. **9**(17), 9453–9466 (2019)
5. Favorskaya, M., Pakhirka, A.: Animal species recognition in the wildlife based on muzzle and shape features using joint CNN. Procedia Comput. Sci. **159**, 933–942 (2019)
6. Gomes, H.M., Barddal, J.P., Enembreck, F., Bifet, A.: A survey on ensemble learning for data stream classification. ACM Comput. Surv. (CSUR) **50**(2), 1–36 (2017)
7. Hall, E.L., Kruger, R.P., Dwyer, S.J., Hall, D.L., Mclaren, R.W., Lodwick, G.S.: A survey of preprocessing and feature extraction techniques for radiographic images. IEEE Trans. Comput. **100**(9), 1032–1044 (1971)
8. He, K., Zhang, X., Ren, S., Sun, J.: Deep residual learning for image recognition. In: Proceedings of the IEEE Conference on Computer Vision and Pattern Recognition, pp. 770–778 (2016)
9. Huang, G., Liu, Z., Van Der Maaten, L., Weinberger, K.Q.: Densely connected convolutional networks. In: Proceedings of the IEEE Conference on Computer Vision and Pattern Recognition, pp. 4700–4708 (2017)
10. Keskar, N.S., Mudigere, D., Nocedal, J., Smelyanskiy, M., Tang, P.T.P.: On large-batch training for deep learning: generalization gap and sharp minima. arXiv preprint arXiv:1609.04836 (2016)
11. Khan, A., Sohail, A., Zahoora, U., Qureshi, A.S.: A survey of the recent architectures of deep convolutional neural networks. arXiv preprint arXiv:1901.06032 (2019)
12. Kingma, D.P., Ba, J.: Adam: a method for stochastic optimization. arXiv preprint arXiv:1412.6980 (2014)
13. Krizhevsky, A., Sutskever, I., Hinton, G.E.: ImageNet classification with deep convolutional neural networks. In: Advances in Neural Information Processing Systems, pp. 1097–1105 (2012)
14. Maas, A.L., Hannun, A.Y., Ng, A.Y.: Rectifier nonlinearities improve neural network acoustic models. In: Proceedings ICML, vol. 30, p. 3 (2013)
15. Mou, L., Ghamisi, P., Zhu, X.X.: Deep recurrent neural networks for hyperspectral image classification. IEEE Trans. Geosci. Remote Sens. **55**(7), 3639–3655 (2017)
16. Norouzzadeh, M.S., et al.: Automatically identifying, counting, and describing wild animals in camera-trap images with deep learning. Proc. Natl. Acad. Sci. **115**(25), E5716–E5725 (2018)
17. Selfridge, O.G.: Pattern recognition and modern computers. In: Proceedings of the Western Joint Computer Conference, 1–3 March 1955, pp. 91–93 (1955)
18. Simonyan, K., Zisserman, A.: Very deep convolutional networks for large-scale image recognition. arXiv preprint arXiv:1409.1556 (2014)
19. Swanson, A., Kosmala, M., Lintott, C., Simpson, R., Smith, A., Packer, C.: Snapshot Serengeti, high-frequency annotated camera trap images of 40 mammalian species in an African savanna. Sci. data **2**, 150026 (2015)

20. Szegedy, C., et al.: Going deeper with convolutions. In: Proceedings of the IEEE Conference on Computer Vision and Pattern Recognition, pp. 1–9 (2015)
21. Verma, G.K., Gupta, P.: Wild animal detection using deep convolutional neural network. In: Chaudhuri, B.B., Kankanhalli, M.S., Raman, B. (eds.) Proceedings of 2nd International Conference on Computer Vision & Image Processing. AISC, vol. 704, pp. 327–338. Springer, Singapore (2018). https://doi.org/10.1007/978-981-10-7898-9_27
22. Wang, Z., Bovik, A.C., Sheikh, H.R., Simoncelli, E.P.: Image quality assessment: from error visibility to structural similarity. IEEE Trans. Image Process. 13(4), 600–612 (2004)

Better Self-training for Image Classification Through Self-supervision

Attaullah Sahito$^{(\boxtimes)}$, Eibe Frank$^{(\boxtimes)}$, and Bernhard Pfahringer$^{(\boxtimes)}$

Department of Computer Science, University of Waikato, Hamilton, New Zealand
a19@students.waikato.ac.nz, {eibe,bernhard}@waikato.ac.nz

Abstract. Self-training is a simple semi-supervised learning approach: Unlabelled examples that attract high-confidence predictions are labelled with their predictions and added to the training set, with this process being repeated multiple times. Recently, self-supervision—learning without manual supervision by solving an automatically-generated pretext task—has gained prominence in deep learning. This paper investigates three different ways of incorporating self-supervision into self-training to improve accuracy in image classification: self-supervision as pretraining only, self-supervision performed exclusively in the first iteration of self-training, and self-supervision added to every iteration of self-training. Empirical results on the SVHN, CIFAR-10, and PlantVillage datasets, using both training from scratch, and Imagenet-pretrained weights, show that applying self-supervision only in the first iteration of self-training can greatly improve accuracy, for a modest increase in computation time.

Keywords: Self-supervised learning · Self-training · Rotational loss

1 Introduction

Contemporary machine learning based on deep neural networks achieves state-of-the-art results on many tasks, including visual understanding, language modelling, and speech recognition, but often requires a large amount of human-labelled data for such performance. Collecting large amounts of labelled data is expensive and time-consuming. Hence, there is significant interest in algorithms that can harness the benefits of unlabelled data—which is usually plentiful—in addition to the scarce labelled data. Semi-supervised learning (SSL) algorithms are designed for this scenario. Their input comprises labelled examples $L = \{(x_1, y_1), (x_2, y_2), ..., (x_{|L|}, y_{|L|})\}$ and unlabelled examples $U = \{x_1', x_2', ..., x_{|U|}'\}$, where $x_i, x_j' \in X$, with $i = 1, 2, ..., |L|$ and $j = 1, 2, ..., |U|$, and y_i are the labels of x_i, with $y_i \in \{1, 2, 3, ..., c\}$ and c being the number of classes.

Various approaches have been proposed for semi-supervised learning based on pseudo-labelling [10], autoencoders [16], and generative adversarial networks (GANs) [19]. Self-training is a simple and intuitive generic semi-supervised learning approach. First, a classifier is trained on labelled examples. Then, the trained model is used to predict labels for unlabelled examples—these labels are called

© Springer Nature Switzerland AG 2022
G. Long et al. (Eds.): AI 2021, LNAI 13151, pp. 645–657, 2022.
https://doi.org/10.1007/978-3-030-97546-3_52

"pseudo-labels" as they are not actual ground-truth labels in the original data. Finally, the unlabelled data with its pseudo-labels are merged with the initially labelled data, and the model is retrained on the merged data. The prediction-retraining loop is normally iterated multiple times. Early work on self-training, for word sense disambiguation in text documents, can be found in [21].

In contrast, self-supervised learning [9] is a fairly recent development in the literature on deep learning. Self-supervised learning is a form of unsupervised learning that works by creating an artificial supervised learning problem based on unlabelled data—a so-called "pretext" or "auxiliary" task—for instance, detecting whether an image has been rotated or not.

In this paper, we empirically compare three different ways of integrating self-supervised learning with self-training. In addition to testing them in a setting with random initial weights and training with cross-entropy loss, we also consider the effect of metric learning losses and transfer learning, as they have shown promise in self-training [15,17,18].

2   Background

Semi-supervised learning approaches have been developed since the 1970s [12], and self-training, in particular, has continued to attract interest. In the deep learning setting, PseudoLabel [10] is an instance of the most basic and straight-forward self-training approach, where a neural network model is iteratively trained on initially labelled and pseudo-labelled examples. Although self-training is an appealing and widely-used process, it is worth noting that Arazo et al. [1] found that it can overfit incorrect pseudo-labels, resulting in confirmation bias. Using MixUp [22] and enforcing a minimum number of initially labelled examples to be included in each mini-batch was proposed to reduce this bias.

In contrast, self-supervised learning is a more recent development. It is an unsupervised learning method that trains a model in a supervised fashion on an artificial supervised learning task generated without any human labelling effort. The following papers all define such tasks for image recognition:

- ExemplarCNN [5]: N different classes are generated by applying transformations on random image patches, and the network is trained to predict the correct class of a given patch.
- RotNet [7]: Geometric transformations such as rotations by 0, 90, 180, and 270 degrees are applied to an image, and the neural network is trained to predict the rotation applied to an image.
- Jigsaw Puzzles [13]: For a given image, nine patches are generated, and the network is trained to predict the correct permutation order of the patches for that image.
- Contrastive learning: The network is trained to differentiate between positive and negative samples, where an image and its augmentations are the positive examples, and all other images are the negative ones [2,3].

Algorithm 1. Self-training using Combined Training.

```
1: Input: Labelled examples (x_L, y_L), unlabelled examples x_U, neural network f_θ
      with parameters θ, weight of self-supervised loss λ_u, and selection percentage p.
2: for each meta-iteration do
3:     for each epoch over x_U ∪ x_L do
4:         b_L = sample(x_L, y_L)
5:         b_U = geometric-transform(sample(x_U ∪ x_L))
6:         for each mini-batch do
7:             L = L_SUPER(f_θ(b_L)) + λ_u L_SELF(f_θ(b_U))
8:             θ = θ − ∇_θ L
9:         end for
10:     end for
11:     labels_U, dist_U = assign_labels(f_θ, x_U, x_L, y_L)
12:     x_new, y_new = select_top(dist_U, labels_U, p)
13:     x_L, y_L = concat((x_L, y_L), (x_new, y_new))
14:     x_U = delete_from(x_U, x_new)
15: end for
```

---

3   Self-training using Self-supervised Learning

Three ways of injecting self-supervision into self-training are proposed below. The specific self-supervision task we use in our experiments is to learn to predict one of six possible geometrical transformations: rotations by 0, 90, 180, or 270 degrees respectively, and horizontal or vertical flips. To investigate the effect of the underlying basic loss function in the different variants of self-training algorithms we consider, we evaluate both cross-entropy loss and triplet loss [20]. When selecting the most confidently predicted examples in self-training, the highest predicted probability is used as confidence when cross-entropy is applied. Triplet loss, being a metric loss, needs a more complex setup based on a nearest-neighbour classifier applied to embeddings generated by the penultimate network layer. The inverse of the distance to the nearest neighbour is used as confidence.

3.1   Combined Training

Combined training (CT) is the most expensive approach we consider: whenever a model is trained in self-training, we jointly train it on both the primary classification task as well as the pretext task, using a combination of self-supervised loss and supervised loss. The supervised and self-supervised branches of the model share the same core convolutional neural network, with only the final layers being different. The loss is a weighted sum of supervised and self-supervised loss:

$$\mathcal{L} = \mathcal{L}_{SUPER}(x_L, y_L) + \lambda_u \mathcal{L}_{SELF}(x_U, y_U), \tag{1}$$

where the hyperparameter $\lambda_u \in [0, 1]$ controls the weight of self-supervised loss.

Algorithm 1 shows pseudocode for each self-training iteration using combined training (CT). For each epoch, all available training examples, i.e., labelled and

---

Algorithm 2. Self-training using Self-supervised Pretraining.

1: **Input:** Labelled examples (x_L, y_L), unlabelled examples x_U, neural network f_θ with parameters θ, and selection percentage p
2: **for** each epoch over x_U **do**
3:     $b_U = \text{geometric-transform}(\text{sample}(x_U \cup x_L))$
4:     **for** each mini-batch in $x_U \cup x_L$ **do**
5:         $\mathcal{L} = \mathcal{L}_{SELF}(f_\theta(b_U))$
6:         $\theta = \theta - \nabla_\theta \mathcal{L}$
7:     **end for**
8: **end for**
9: **for** each meta-iteration **do**
10:     $f_\theta = \text{train\_network}(x_L, y_L)$
11:     $labels_U, dist_U = \text{assign\_labels}(f_\theta, x_U, x_L, y_L)$
12:     $x_{new}, y_{new} = \text{select\_top}(dist_U, labels_U, p)$
13:     $x_L, y_L = \text{concat}((x_L, y_L), (x_{new}, y_{new}))$
14:     $x_U = \text{delete\_from}(x_U, x_{new})$
15: **end for**

---

unlabelled examples, are employed for self-supervised loss estimation, whereas only the labelled and pseudo-labelled examples are used for supervised loss estimation. The network model is used to assign labels to unlabelled examples, and the top $p\%$ most confidently predicted pseudo-labelled examples are selected and merged with the labelled examples for retraining.

3.2 Self-supervised Pretraining

Pretraining is a common strategy in deep learning: rather than starting with randomly initialised network parameters, we start with parameters obtained by training on a related task. The motivation for pretraining is that the model will learn features that may be useful for the target task. This can be of great importance in semi-supervised learning, where a few labelled and many unlabelled examples are available. It has also been shown that unsupervised pretraining helps neural networks achieve better generalisation [6]. Motivated by this, we consider self-supervision for pretraining on unlabelled examples followed by standard self-training.

Algorithm 2 presents the training procedure for the proposed self-training approach using self-supervised pretraining (SS-Pretrain). At the start of training, the network model is pretrained on all training examples, i.e., labelled and unlabelled examples using self-supervised loss.[1] Following that, simple self-training is applied using supervised loss only on labelled and pseudo-labelled examples.

3.3 Self-training using Single-Step Combined Training

In combined training (see Sect. 3.1), self-supervised training is applied in each epoch during all self-training iterations. This is rather expensive. Moreover, it

---

[1] Note that the original labels are ignored in this step.

Algorithm 3. Self-training using Single-step Combined Training.

1: **Input:** Labelled examples (x_L, y_L), unlabelled examples x_U, neural network f_θ with parameters θ, weight of self-supervised loss λ_u, and selection percentage p.

2: **for** each epoch over x_U **do**

3:     $b_L = \text{sample}(x_L, y_L)$

4:     $b_U = \text{geometric-transform}(\text{sample}(x_U \cup x_L))$

5:     **for** each mini-batch in x_U **do**

6:         $\mathcal{L} = \mathcal{L}_{SUPER}(f_\theta(b_L)) + \lambda_u \mathcal{L}_{SELF}(f_\theta(b_U))$

7:         $\theta = \theta - \nabla_\theta \mathcal{L}$

8:     **end for**

9: **end for**

10: **for** each meta-iteration **do**

11:     $f_\theta = \text{train\_network}(x_L, y_L)$

12:     $labels_U, dist_U = \text{assign\_labels}(f_\theta, x_U, x_L, y_L)$

13:     $x_{new}, y_{new} = \text{select\_top}(dist_U, labels_U, p)$

14:     $x_L, y_L = \text{concat}((x_L, y_L), (x_{new}, y_{new}))$

15:     $x_U = \text{delete\_from}(x_U, x_{new})$

16: **end for**

---

is conceivable that self-training is no longer beneficial once the model has been sufficiently adapted to the primary task: it may destroy features that are finely tuned to the primary task at hand. Therefore, we also investigate using self-supervision only in the first iteration of self-training. Algorithm 3 shows this self-training approach using single-step combined training (STSSC).

4   Empirical Evaluation

To evaluate the effect of self-supervised learning in self-training, we conduct an extensive comparison using standard benchmark datasets. We always report three different test accuracies: (a) after training on the initially labelled examples, (b) after full self-training, and (c) after training on all labelled training examples available for the benchmark problem. Results obtained for (a) and (c) act as empirical lower and upper bounds for self-training. All results are averaged over three runs with a random selection of initially labelled examples.

4.1   Datasets

We use three benchmark datasets: Street View House Numbers (SVHN), CIFAR-10, and PlantVillage [8]. PlantVillage images have been resized to 96 by 96, 64 by 64, and 32 by 32^2, respectively, to create three datasets.

Following standard semi-supervised learning practice, a small class-balanced subset of labelled examples is chosen randomly for each dataset. All remaining training examples are used as unlabelled examples. The number of initially labelled examples is 1000 for SVHN, 4000 for CIFAR-10, and 380 for PlantVillage.

---

[2] https://github.com/attaullah/downsampled-plant-disease-dataset.

4.2   Convolutional Architecture

A wide residual network with depth 28 and width 2 (WRN-28-2) is a common choice in semi-supervised classification tasks [14]. In our experiments, we add a fully connected layer at the end of the WRN-28-2 model to produce 64-dimensional embeddings. For all results, to obtain insight into the effect of standard ImageNet pretraining on the outcome of semi-supervised learning, we report test accuracy obtained by running our algorithms by starting with a) randomly initialised network weights and b) ImageNet pretrained weights. For pretraining, downsampled ImageNet [4] images with sizes 32 by 32 are used.

4.3   Algorithm Configurations

For SVHN and CIFAR-10, a mini-batch size of 100 is used, while PlantVillage uses a batch size of 64. Adam is used as the optimiser for updating the network parameters with a learning rate of 10^{-3} for randomly initialised weights and 10^{-4} for ImageNet pretrained weights. After the first iteration of self-training, the learning rate is further reduced by a factor of 0.1. Triplet loss is estimated using $l2$-normalised embeddings and a margin value of 1. A 1-nearest-neighbour classifier is employed on the embeddings to compute test accuracy. Self-training is applied for 25 meta-iterations[3]. For SVHN and CIFAR-10, $p = 5\%$ pseudo-labels are selected from unlabelled examples in each meta-iteration, while PlantVillage uses $p = 2\%$. For self-supervised loss, the weight parameter λ_u is set to 1 to avoid tuning it separately for every single dataset.

4.4   Results: Detailed Evaluation of the Three Algorithms

Table 1 shows test accuracy for CIFAR-10, SVHN, and the three PlantVillage datasets for the WRN-28-2 network using random and pretrained (ImageNet) weights based on combined training (see Sect. 3.1). Cross-entropy loss is used for the self-supervised component of the combined loss in Eq. 1, but we consider both cross-entropy loss and triplet loss for the supervised component. Values in bold highlight the best test accuracy for each dataset for (a) the empirical lower bound provided by training on initial labels ("N-Labelled"), (b) self-training using combined training, and (c) the upper bound provided by training with all labels ("All-Labelled"), across the two loss function configurations and network initialisations considered. Results for triplet loss are obtained by applying a 1-nearest-neighbour classifier to the learned embeddings.

Excluding the results obtained for the lower and upper bounds based on purely supervised training on the CIFAR-10 data with ImageNet pretraining, it is clear that there is no benefit to be had by using metric learning with triplet loss. The results also show that self-training using cross-entropy provides consistent improvements compared to the lower bound, but there is a large gap compared to the results for the upper bound. We can also see that it is generally

---

[3] https://github.com/attaullah/Self-training/blob/master/Self_supervised.md.

Table 1. Test accuracy on WRN-28-2 using random and ImageNet pretrained weights for Combined Training (CT).

	Weights	N-Labelled		Self-training		All-Labelled	
		Cross-entropy	Triplet	Cross-entropy	Triplet	Cross-entropy	Triplet
SVHN	Random	86.37 ± 3.57	89.38 ± 1.69	88.10 ± 3.02	79.47 ± 0.82	$\mathbf{95.74 \pm 0.02}$	95.07 ± 0.15
	ImageNet	$\mathbf{89.62 \pm 1.22}$	88.98 ± 2.14	$\mathbf{90.83 \pm 1.67}$	81.96 ± 3.24	95.16 ± 0.16	94.65 ± 0.35
CIFAR-10	Random	80.67 ± 2.95	81.25 ± 1.77	86.04 ± 0.60	81.51 ± 0.73	91.38 ± 0.39	86.97 ± 3.47
	ImageNet	87.00 ± 1.97	$\mathbf{90.04 \pm 1.22}$	$\mathbf{89.19 \pm 0.65}$	89.11 ± 2.33	93.47 ± 0.08	$\mathbf{93.92 \pm 0.09}$
PLANT32	Random	67.46 ± 3.39	55.27 ± 3.77	72.91 ± 3.68	50.99 ± 1.21	97.97 ± 0.64	91.23 ± 0.86
	ImageNet	$\mathbf{77.96 \pm 0.58}$	73.38 ± 1.28	$\mathbf{78.18 \pm 0.09}$	66.67 ± 0.60	$\mathbf{98.38 \pm 0.08}$	96.58 ± 0.48
PLANT64	Random	72.52 ± 3.86	63.86 ± 0.94	83.52 ± 1.84	59.84 ± 0.38	98.52 ± 0.34	91.99 ± 0.30
	ImageNet	$\mathbf{78.39 \pm 0.87}$	76.65 ± 1.06	$\mathbf{84.98 \pm 0.68}$	69.26 ± 6.11	$\mathbf{99.08 \pm 0.10}$	94.67 ± 0.52
PLANT96	Random	75.12 ± 3.91	65.94 ± 1.43	79.94 ± 1.75	44.55 ± 1.70	98.08 ± 0.65	89.47 ± 0.99
	ImageNet	$\mathbf{79.07 \pm 0.68}$	79.04 ± 0.67	$\mathbf{84.48 \pm 1.30}$	76.26 ± 1.40	$\mathbf{99.15 \pm 0.12}$	95.60 ± 1.27

Table 2. Test accuracy on WRN-28-2 using random and ImageNet pretrained weights for SS-Pretrain.

	Weights	N-Labelled		Self-training		All-Labelled	
		Cross-entropy	Triplet	Cross-entropy	Triplet	Cross-entropy	Triplet
SVHN	Random	89.51 ± 0.74	86.48 ± 2.00	$\mathbf{89.72 \pm 0.57}$	83.73 ± 2.46	95.63 ± 0.46	95.05 ± 0.06
	ImageNet	89.90 ± 0.40	$\mathbf{90.08 \pm 0.60}$	89.67 ± 0.10	86.05 ± 0.44	$\mathbf{95.90 \pm 0.05}$	95.30 ± 0.16
CIFAR-10	Random	72.02 ± 0.50	75.76 ± 2.11	85.50 ± 0.41	75.51 ± 1.88	90.32 ± 0.94	89.11 ± 0.68
	ImageNet	84.83 ± 1.99	$\mathbf{86.98 \pm 0.84}$	$\mathbf{91.06 \pm 0.47}$	90.18 ± 0.87	93.48 ± 0.09	92.64 ± 0.70
PLANT32	Random	69.80 ± 1.07	72.03 ± 1.51	68.72 ± 0.30	65.04 ± 1.19	97.14 ± 0.08	96.04 ± 0.07
	ImageNet	72.38 ± 1.22	$\mathbf{72.46 \pm 1.07}$	$\mathbf{75.21 \pm 1.34}$	69.96 ± 0.05	$\mathbf{99.24 \pm 0.12}$	97.77 ± 0.77
PLANT64	Random	73.35 ± 1.76	71.10 ± 1.16	73.45 ± 3.32	67.06 ± 1.42	97.94 ± 0.48	87.76 ± 0.96
	ImageNet	75.64 ± 0.54	$\mathbf{77.51 \pm 1.05}$	$\mathbf{75.50 \pm 0.93}$	68.37 ± 1.43	$\mathbf{99.06 \pm 0.27}$	89.48 ± 0.56
PLANT96	Random	73.29 ± 0.72	70.61 ± 0.83	75.19 ± 0.88	67.18 ± 1.81	98.43 ± 0.05	90.54 ± 1.18
	ImageNet	78.37 ± 1.19	$\mathbf{78.74 \pm 0.22}$	$\mathbf{79.11 \pm 1.24}$	74.97 ± 0.57	$\mathbf{99.47 \pm 0.12}$	93.32 ± 1.35

highly beneficial to use ImageNet weights instead of randomly initialised weights, regardless of dataset, loss function, and learning algorithm. The few observed drops in accuracy for the SVHN data are very small.

Table 2 shows test accuracy for CIFAR-10, SVHN, and PlantVillage32, 64, 96 on WRN-28-2 using random and ImageNet weights after applying SS-Pretrain (see Sect. 3.2). To apply pretraining based on self-supervision, we run it on all training examples—those that exhibit a ground-truth label as well as those missing one—for 120 epochs. After that, we run 200 epochs of fine-tuning on only the labelled training data, followed by standard self-training with 25 meta-iterations, using either cross-entropy or triplet loss. To provide a fair comparison, we also apply self-supervision in the same manner to obtain initial weights for the upper and lower bounds obtained by purely supervised training.

Values in bold highlight the best test accuracy for each dataset obtained by performing self-supervised pretraining for (a) the empirical lower bound provided by training on initial ground-truth labels ("N-Labelled"), (b) self-training, and (c) the upper bound provided by training with all ground-truth labels ("All-Labelled"), across the two loss function configurations and network initialisations considered.

Table 3. Self-training test accuracy on WRN-28-2 using random and ImageNet pretrained weights for STSSC.

	Weights	Cross-entropy	Triplet
SVHN	Random	**95.27 ± 0.20**	83.62 ± 0.03
	ImageNet	95.12 ± 0.32	83.47 ± 0.98
CIFAR-10	Random	87.24 ± 0.67	79.36 ± 1.02
	ImageNet	**91.64 ± 0.38**	90.75 ± 1.48
PLANT32	Random	77.39 ± 1.32	54.44 ± 3.72
	ImageNet	**86.72 ± 1.10**	65.14 ± 1.85
PLANT64	Random	86.13 ± 0.46	56.23 ± 2.01
	ImageNet	**89.48 ± 0.37**	74.29 ± 1.27
PLANT96	Random	84.71 ± 1.89	58.14 ± 0.82
	ImageNet	**89.95 ± 0.37**	74.41 ± 3.75

Interestingly, metric learning using triplet loss now often achieves better accuracy than applying cross-entropy loss when using only the initially labelled examples. However, cross-entropy consistently achieves higher test accuracy than metric learning when performing self-training and when training using all labelled examples. Comparing self-training to the lower bound, we see improvements when using cross-entropy, but self-training reduces accuracy most of the time when considering metric learning. Networks initialised with ImageNet weights generally perform better than those with randomly initialised weights.

Table 3 shows test accuracy of self-training with STSSC (see Sect. 3.3) for CIFAR-10, SVHN, and PlantVillage32, 64, 96 on WRN-28-2 using random and ImageNet pretrained weights. The reported results are obtained after one iteration of combined training and a further 24 iterations of regular self-training, using either cross-entropy or triplet loss. Values in bold highlight the best test accuracy for each dataset across the two loss function configurations and network initialisations considered. For the corresponding empirical lower and upper bounds, please consult the results in Table 1. Self-training using cross-entropy outperforms metric learning for all five datasets for both randomly initialised and ImageNet pretrained weights. Moreover, in the majority of the cases, using ImageNet weights achieves higher test accuracy than using random weights. Notably, for the one dataset where random weights yield higher accuracy, the difference in performance is very small.

To further illustrate the effect of starting the training process with ImageNet weights rather than random weights, Fig. 1 plots the test accuracy for STSSC over the meta-iterations across three different runs using a) randomly initialised weights and b) ImageNet weights on CIFAR-10 using 4000 labelled examples initially. Cross-entropy loss is used as the loss function throughout. The accuracy curves show definite improvements as more meta-iterations are performed, for both weight initialisations, but the ImageNet version starts from a higher initial accuracy and retains this advantage over the 25 meta-iterations of self-training.

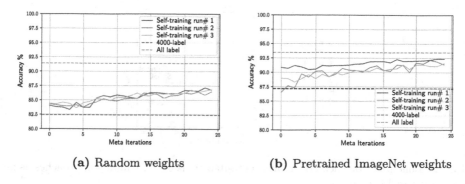

(a) Random weights   (b) Pretrained ImageNet weights

Fig. 1. Comparison of self-training using STSSC on WRN-28-2 for CIFAR-10 using cross-entropy loss.

Table 4. Test accuracy after self-training on WRN-28-2 using various self-supervised settings.

	SVHN	CIFAR-10	PLANT32	PLANT64	PLANT96
Random weights					
Simple	94.28 ± 0.45	83.05 ± 0.99	68.24 ± 2.44	69.36 ± 1.80	76.09 ± 2.35
CT	88.10 ± 3.02	86.04 ± 0.60	72.91 ± 3.68	83.52 ± 1.84	79.24 ± 1.45
SS-Pretrain	89.72 ± 0.57	85.50 ± 0.41	68.72 ± 0.30	73.45 ± 3.32	75.19 ± 0.88
STSSC	$\mathbf{95.27 \pm 0.20}$	$\mathbf{87.08 \pm 0.66}$	$\mathbf{77.39 \pm 1.32}$	$\mathbf{80.13 \pm 0.40}$	$\mathbf{84.71 \pm 1.89}$
ImageNet weights					
Simple	90.84 ± 0.48	91.62 ± 0.58	$\mathbf{87.48 \pm 0.84}$	$\mathbf{92.60 \pm 1.03}$	89.65 ± 0.88
CT	90.83 ± 1.67	89.19 ± 0.65	78.18 ± 0.09	84.60 ± 0.77	84.48 ± 1.30
SS-Pretrain	89.67 ± 0.10	91.06 ± 0.47	75.21 ± 1.34	75.50 ± 0.93	79.11 ± 1.24
STSSC	$\mathbf{95.12 \pm 0.32}$	$\mathbf{91.65 \pm 0.43}$	86.72 ± 1.10	89.48 ± 0.37	$\mathbf{89.95 \pm 0.37}$

4.5 Comparing Self-training Approaches

Table 4 presents a summary view and comparison of the three approaches to integrating self-supervision into self-training, and, importantly, reports results for self-training without using any self-supervised learning—denoted by the name "Simple" in the table. Cross-entropy loss is used for both supervised and self-supervised loss estimation throughout. The results show that STSSC performs best overall, demonstrating the importance of applying self-supervised learning in a judicious manner when combining it with self-training: applying it in all meta-iterations is generally better than simply using it for pretraining, but among the three algorithm variants considered, it is clearly best to only apply it in the first meta-iteration. Compared to the simple self-training baseline without self-supervision, STSSC performs substantially better when starting with randomly initialised weights. However, while the performance also generally improves when using ImageNet weights, and substantially so for the SVHN data, STSSC only wins in three cases, with the simple approach performing best for the two smaller-sized versions of the PlantVillage datasets.

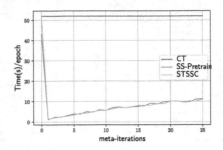

Fig. 2. Time spent on each epoch over meta-iterations of self-training approaches using self-supervised learning.

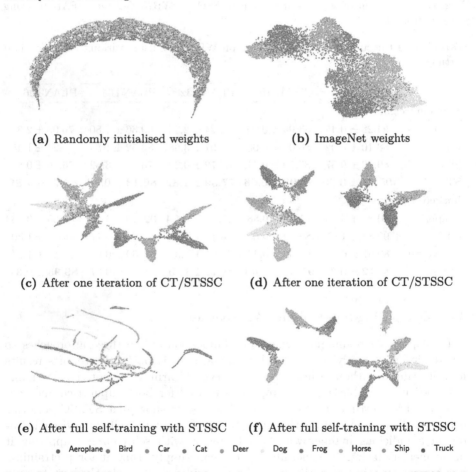

(a) Randomly initialised weights

(b) ImageNet weights

(c) After one iteration of CT/STSSC

(d) After one iteration of CT/STSSC

(e) After full self-training with STSSC

(f) After full self-training with STSSC

● Aeroplane ● Bird ● Car ● Cat ● Deer ● Dog ● Frog ● Horse ● Ship ● Truck

Fig. 3. UMAP visualisation of CIFAR10 test set embeddings obtained from WRN-28-2 using random weights [left: (a), (c), (e)] and ImageNet weights [right: (b), (d), (f)] by applying STSSC training.

Figure 2 compares the time needed for each epoch over the self-training meta-iterations for all three self-supervision-based self-training approaches, i.e., CT, SS-Pretrain, and STSSC. To estimate time, WRN-28-2 is trained on CIFAR-10 with 4000-labelled examples initially for 25 meta-iterations of self-training. Time spent by each epoch for CT is constant and higher than for SS-Pretrain and STSSC. After the first iteration, SS-Pretrain and STSSC need very little time compared to CT.

4.6 Visualising Embeddings

Embeddings generated for CIFAR-10 by STSSC are visualised in Fig. 3, using UMAP [11] to produce two-dimensional projections. The embeddings are obtained at the start of training: (a) and (b); after one meta-iteration: (c) and (d); and after 25 meta-iterations of self-training: (e) and (f). Configurations (a), (c), and (e) use randomly initialised weights, (b), (d), and (f) use ImageNet weights. Self-training clearly generates well-separated clusters.

5 Conclusion

In this paper, we have shown that self-supervision can substantially improve self-training for image classification problems. Self-supervision was applied in three different ways. The best performance was achieved by using self-supervision only in the first iteration of self-training, with cross-entropy loss and initial weights obtained from ImageNet. There are a number of directions for future research, including more complex scenarios such as self-supervised pretraining followed by a limited number of combined training meta-iterations, followed by further regular self-training. Alternatively, one could consider the use of different and potentially more challenging self-supervision tasks.

References

1. Arazo, E., Ortego, D., Albert, P., O'Connor, N.E., McGuinness, K.: Pseudo-labelling and confirmation bias in deep semi-supervised learning. In: 2020 International Joint Conference on Neural Networks (IJCNN), pp. 1–8. IEEE (2020)
2. Chen, T., Kornblith, S., Norouzi, M., Hinton, G.: A simple framework for contrastive learning of visual representations. In: International Conference on Machine Learning, pp. 1597–1607. PMLR (2020)
3. Chen, T., Kornblith, S., Swersky, K., Norouzi, M., Hinton, G.E.: Big self-supervised models are strong semi-supervised learners. In: Larochelle, H., Ranzato, M., Hadsell, R., Balcan, M., Lin, H. (eds.) Advances in Neural Information Processing Systems, 6–12 December 2020, Virtual (2020)
4. Chrabaszcz, P., Loshchilov, I., Hutter, F.: A downsampled variant of ImageNet as an alternative to the CIFAR datasets. arXiv preprint arXiv:1707.08819 (2017)

5. Dosovitskiy, A., Fischer, P., Springenberg, J.T., Riedmiller, M., Brox, T.: Discriminative unsupervised feature learning with exemplar convolutional neural networks. IEEE Trans. Pattern Anal. Mach. Intell. **38**(9), 1734–1747 (2015)

6. Erhan, D., Courville, A., Bengio, Y., Vincent, P.: Why does unsupervised pretraining help deep learning? In: Proceedings of the 13th International Conference on Artificial Intelligence and Statistics, pp. 201–208. JMLR Workshop and Conference Proceedings (2010)

7. Gidaris, S., Singh, P., Komodakis, N.: Unsupervised representation learning by predicting image rotations. In: International Conference on Learning Representations (2018)

8. Hughes, D.P., Salathé, M.: An open access repository of images on plant health to enable the development of mobile disease diagnostics through machine learning and crowdsourcing. CoRR (2015). http://arxiv.org/abs/1511.08060

9. Jing, L., Tian, Y.: Self-supervised visual feature learning with deep neural networks: a survey. IEEE Trans. Pattern Anal. Mach. Intell. **43**, 4037–4058 (2020)

10. Lee, D.H.: Pseudo-label: the simple and efficient semi-supervised learning method for deep neural networks. In: Workshop on Challenges in Representation Learning, ICML, vol. 3, p. 2 (2013)

11. McInnes, L., Healy, J., Saul, N., Großberger, L.: UMAP: uniform manifold approximation and projection. J. Open Source Softw. **3**(29), 861 (2018)

12. McLachlan, G.J.: Iterative reclassification procedure for constructing an asymptotically optimal rule of allocation in discriminant analysis. J. Am. Stat. Assoc. **70**(350), 365–369 (1975)

13. Noroozi, M., Favaro, P.: Unsupervised learning of visual representations by solving Jigsaw puzzles. In: Leibe, B., Matas, J., Sebe, N., Welling, M. (eds.) ECCV 2016. LNCS, vol. 9910, pp. 69–84. Springer, Cham (2016). https://doi.org/10.1007/978-3-319-46466-4_5

14. Oliver, A., Odena, A., Raffel, C., Cubuk, E.D., Goodfellow, I.J.: Realistic evaluation of deep semi-supervised learning algorithms. In: Proceedings of the 32nd International Conference on Neural Information Processing Systems, pp. 3239–3250 (2018)

15. Oquab, M., Bottou, L., Laptev, I., Sivic, J.: Learning and transferring mid-level image representations using convolutional neural networks. In: Proceedings of the IEEE Conference on Computer Vision and Pattern Recognition, pp. 1717–1724 (2014)

16. Rasmus, A., Berglund, M., Honkala, M., Valpola, H., Raiko, T.: Semi-supervised learning with ladder networks. In: Advances in Neural Information Processing Systems, pp. 3546–3554 (2015)

17. Sahito, A., Frank, E., Pfahringer, B.: Semi-supervised learning using Siamese networks. In: Liu, J., Bailey, J. (eds.) AI 2019. LNCS (LNAI), vol. 11919, pp. 586–597. Springer, Cham (2019). https://doi.org/10.1007/978-3-030-35288-2_47

18. Sahito, A., Frank, E., Pfahringer, B.: Transfer of pretrained model weights substantially improves semi-supervised image classification. In: Gallagher, M., Moustafa, N., Lakshika, E. (eds.) AI 2020. LNCS (LNAI), vol. 12576, pp. 433–444. Springer, Cham (2020). https://doi.org/10.1007/978-3-030-64984-5_34

19. Salimans, T., Goodfellow, I., Zaremba, W., Cheung, V., Radford, A., Chen, X.: Improved techniques for training GANs. In: Advances in Neural Information Processing Systems, pp. 2234–2242 (2016)

20. Schroff, F., Kalenichenko, D., Philbin, J.: FaceNet: a unified embedding for face recognition and clustering. In: Proceedings of the IEEE Conference on Computer Vision and Pattern Recognition, pp. 815–823 (2015)

21. Yarowsky, D.: Unsupervised word sense disambiguation rivalling supervised methods. In: 33rd Annual Meeting of the Association for Computational Linguistics, pp. 189–196 (1995)
22. Zhang, H., Cisse, M., Dauphin, Y.N., Lopez-Paz, D.: mixup: beyond empirical risk minimisation. In: International Conference on Learning Representations (2018)

Video-Based Student Engagement Estimation via Time Convolution Neural Networks for Remote Learning

Khaled Saleh$^{(\boxtimes)}$, Kun Yu, and Fang Chen

Data Science Institute, University of Technology Sydney, Ultimo, NSW, Australia
{khaled.aboufarw,kun.yu,fang.chen}@uts.edu.au

Abstract. Given the recent outbreak of COVID-19 pandemic globally, most of the schools and universities have adapted many of the learning materials and lectures to be delivered online. As a result, the necessity to have some quantifiable measures of how the students are perceiving and interacting with this 'new normal' way of education became inevitable. In this work, we are focusing on the engagement metric which was shown in the literature to be a strong indicator of how students are dealing with the information and the knowledge being presented to them. In this regard, we have proposed a novel data-driven approach based on a special variant of convolutional neural networks that can predict the students' engagement levels from a video feed of students' faces. Our proposed framework has achieved a promising mean-squared error (MSE) score of only 0.07 when evaluated on a real dataset of students taking an online course. Moreover, the proposed framework has achieved superior results when compared with two baseline models that are commonly utilised in the literature for tackling this problem.

Keywords: Engagement prediction · Time-series ConvNet · Behaviour understanding

1 Introduction

The implication of the COVID-19 pandemic on the education systems globally is dramatic. Massive school/university closures have already happened all over the world. As a result, the shift from physical face-to-face learning to remote E-learning became inevitable and has been widely adopted by many countries. Over the past few years, the remote and E-learning domain has witnessed a number of advancements when it comes to the quality and the richness of the information that could be delivered, specially with the emergent of Massive Open Online Courses (MOOCs) platforms such as: Coursera, Udacity and edx [14,18]. That being said, the current remote and E-learning systems are still lacking some of the key capabilities that account for more effective learning systems. One challenging example of such capabilities is the ability to quantify the engagement

© Springer Nature Switzerland AG 2022
G. Long et al. (Eds.): AI 2021, LNAI 13151, pp. 658–667, 2022.
https://doi.org/10.1007/978-3-030-97546-3_53

levels of students during remote and E-learning sessions and understand students behaviours that is commonly deduced by teachers in physical classrooms.

Researchers have put an enormous efforts in conceptualizing student engagement, or academic engagement, as a complex multi-dimensional construct that captures a diverse range of states, such as behavioural, cognitive and emotional states [19]. In the literature, the approaches that have been introduced to tackle the problem of measurement of student engagement levels can be categorised into two main approaches: the manual measurement approach [8,24] and the automatic measurement approach [2,5]. Manual measurement approaches rely either on surveys/questionnaires requested from students or human observations made by teachers or subject-matter experts. On the other hand, automatic measurement approaches rely mainly on sensors that monitors the behaviour of students during the learning process, these sensor could be remote non-intrusive ones such as cameras and eye tracking equipment [2,20] or physiological ones such as EEG and ECG [5,17]. Given the constraints of manual measurement approaches and their scalability shortcomings when it comes to remote and E-learning [9], in this paper we will be pursuing the automatic measurement approach.

More specifically, in this work we are introducing a novel data-driven approach based on deep convolutional neural networks, that can automatically predict continuous engagement levels of students in remote and E-learning setup based solely on video feed of their faces. The rest of the paper will be organised as follows, in Sect. 2, an overview of the recent related work on automatic measurement of student engagement based on visual analytics will be covered. In Sect. 3, the proposed methodology for the student engagement levels estimation will be introduced. In Sect. 4, we will present the experimental results we have conducted to evaluate the performance of the proposed methodology. Finally, in Sect. 5, we conclude our paper.

2 Related Work

The problem of automatic measurement of student engagement in remote and E-learning context has got some momentum over the past few years. Various number of sensor modalities have been utilised in the literature to tackle this problem, which can be classified based on the type of sensors into two classes. The first class of techniques relied on intrusive/wearable sensors that continuously monitor physiological signals of students while learning. In [17], one example of such technique was introduced, where they used a combination of EEG, blood pressure and skin conductance sensors in order to quantify students engagement during E-learning sessions. Despite the promising results they achieved in their pilot study, the applicability of this technique in real-life scenarios of nowadays E-learning is questionable. One of the main reasons for that is the complexity of the sensor setup as well as their high cost. Thus, the second class of techniques based on non-intrusive/remote sensors started to emerge such as cameras and commercial eye trackers. In these techniques unlike the intrusive sensors techniques, can monitor students while they are freely and naturally behaving and interacting during the E-learning sessions.

In [2], a method that relied on a commercial binocular eye tracker was introduced in order to characterise students engagements when different animations cues are presented within the learning materials.

More recently, Kaur et al. [10], collected a publicly available dataset of students during taking an MOOC and they captured videos of their upper bodies and faces. The dataset had total 195 videos which spanned 78 subjects and were captured in the wild with different scenes in background and each captured video lasts for almost 5 min. long. The dataset was annotated with four levels of engagement. Additionally, they proposed a baseline approach that relied on manually extracting facial features from a sequence of cropped faces of students using Local Binary Patterns from Three Orthogonal Planes (LBP-TOP) [27], and used a deep neural network to predict the engagement level. Similarly, Yang et al. [23], proposed another deep multi-instance neural network with more input features such as upper body pose in conjunction with LSTM model to estimate the student engagement intensity.

Motivated by the promising results of data-driven approaches based on deep neural networks that were presented in [10,23], a similar method will be adopted in this study. However, in our proposed framework, instead of relying on LSTM architecture to model the temporal dependency between the sequential input features, we will be proposing a novel time-series ConvNet model for this task. The rationale behind this, is to reduce the complexity of parallelisation and scaling LSTM models computationally. Additionally, LSTM architecture are faced with number of challenges when trained on longer sequences such as the vanishing gradients where the LSTM model is unable to propagate important gradient information from the output layer to the first input layers [15].

3   Methodology

In this section, we firstly start with our formulation for the student engagement estimation problem and an overview of our proposed framework. Then, a thorough description of the building blocks of our proposed approach will be presented.

3.1   Proposed Framework

We tackle the problem of automatic student engagement estimation using a data-driven approach based on convolutional neural network (ConvNet) [13]. We formulate the problem as a regression task, where given an input sequence of video frames of students, we model the spatio-temporal dynamics between these frames using a ConvNet-based framework. The framework output is an estimate of a continuous value represents the students engagement during that window of input video frames. Internally, the proposed framework (shown in Fig. 1) contains two main modules. The first is the spatial feature extractor. The spatial feature extractor is responsible for capturing and acquiring a frame-wise spatial representations of each frame from the input sequence. Since interpersonal features such as head pose, facial landmarks, eye gaze and facial action units

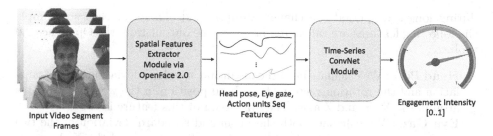

Fig. 1. Our proposed framework for student engagement estimation. The input to our framework is an input video frame sequence. The output is the predicted engagement intensity normalised between (0,1).

were shown to be an effective and discriminative features for the task of student engagement estimation [21,23], we similarly will capture these features as part of the spatial feature extractor. More specifically, we will be relying on one of state-of-the-art facial behaviour analysis toolkit, OpenFace 2.0 [1] as our spatial feature extractor module.

The second module of our framework, the temporal modelling module, processes the sequence of spatial features as input, and hence models and captures the temporal dependency between the input features sequence. In this module, we are adopting a network architecture based on ConvNet [26] that can model multivariate correlated time series data such as the time-series sequential interpersonal spatial features extracted from the first module. Detailed construction and function of the modules will be discussed in the following sections.

3.2   Spatial Features Extractor Module

As we mentioned above, we will be utilising the OpenFace 2.0 toolbox in order to extract the interpersonal spatial features of student subjects in a given input sequence video. OpenFace 2.0 provides a plethora of features related to head, face, and eyes of human subjects. In our framework, we will only rely on three categories of features, namely head pose translation and rotation of students in 3D, eye gaze vectors and angles in 3D and facial action units presence and intensity. The rationale behind choosing these specific features, is that the movement of head and eyes of students have strong correlation with the engagement of the students [7,25]. For example if a student is distracted or not fully engaged in the content being presented their gaze direction and head pose will be jumping between different areas on the screen. Additionally, as most teachers intuitively rely on reading the facial expressions of their students in classrooms in order to assess their engagement levels, the facial action units features could potentially help in discriminating between different levels of students' engagement. As a consequence, the student engagement is examined via the video of their head and face.

Given a long sequence v of video frames (roughly 5 min. long), we sample it into N sub-samples to account for the fact that students engagement intensity during long time period can change abruptly [22]. Then, for each sub-sample the following features are calculated based on the output from the OpenFace 2.0 toolbox:

- **Head Pose:** We calculate both the mean and standard deviation of the translation and the rotation vectors of the head position in the world coordinates around the X, Y and Z axis. The dimension of this feature is 12.
- **Eye Gaze:** We calculate both the mean and standard deviation of the two eyes' gaze direction vector in the world coordinates around the X, Y and Z axis. Additionally, we calculate the mean and standard deviation of the eye gaze direction in radians in the world coordinates which is the average of the two eyes. The dimension of this feature is 16.
- **Facial Action Units:** As we mentioned earlier facial action units are a mechanism to encode human facial movements based on their appearance on the face. OpenFace 2.0 toolbox can recognise the intensity levels of 17 action units. For this feature, we calculated both the mean and standard deviation of the 17 actions units which resulted in a total of 34 features.

3.3   Time-Series ConvNet Module

Modelling sequential temporal data has been approached in the literature using various techniques. One of the famous recent architectures utilised is the Recurrent Neural Networks (RNN) [11,16]. This architecture and more specifically its special variant, Long Short Term Memory networks (LSTMs), has achieved resilient results in many sequential-based tasks such as the tasks of natural language processing (NLP) [6]. That being said, we found that it won't be suitable for our task in modelling our sequential processed spatial features due to the following reasons. RNNs were designed originally for giving predictions for each time-step in its input sequential data such as the case in language translation tasks. Additionally, RNNs are not performing as good as expected when it comes to modelling long sequences because of the vanishing gradient problem when training them. Finally, the training of RNNs is complex to parallelise and scale computationally.

Thus, in order to model the temporal dependency within the sequential input features in our proposed framework, we rely on a data-driven approach based on a special variant of ConvNets, called Time-Series ConvNet [26]. As the name implies, this architecture was first introduced by Zhao et al. [26] for multivariate time-series classification tasks. Unlike traditional ConvNet architectures used in computer vision tasks which work on 2D images, in the time-series ConvNet architecture, it works by sliding a convolution filter over the input time series. In return, the time-series ConvNet preserves the integrity of the temporal dimension of the input time series instead of the spatial dimensions of 2D images in case of 2D ConvNet architecture. Time-series ConvNet architecture consists of two types of layers, one type is the convolution layers and the other is the local pooling layer. The convolution layer in time-series ConvNet, can be viewed as a non-linear transformation operation over the input sequential data. Each convolution

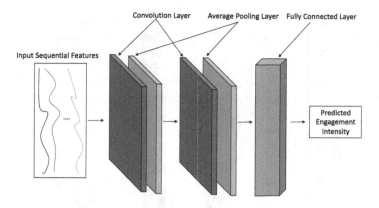

Fig. 2. The architecture of our Time-Series ConvNet Module.

layer in time-series ConvNet contains r filters, a stride of s and filter size of $k \times l$, where k is the number of input sequential features and l is the filters' length. More formally, the output of the convolution layer operation at a time-step t for feature map m is calculated as follows:

$$C_m(t) = f\left(\sum_{i=1}^{l}\sum_{j=1}^{k} z(i + s(t-1), j)\omega_m(i,j) + b(m)\right) \tag{1}$$

where $z \in \mathbf{R}^{N \times k}$ is the input sequential data to the convolution layer, $C_m(t)$ is the t-th element of feature map m, $\omega_m \in \mathbf{R}^{l \times k}$ are the weights of the m-th convolution filter and $b(m)$ is the bias of the m-th convolution filter. The f function denotes a non-linear activation function that is responsible for the non-linear transformation operation of the convolution layer, and in time-series ConvNet this is the sigmoid activation function that is calculated according to the following:

$$f(x) = \frac{1}{1 + e^{-x}} \tag{2}$$

On the other hand, the pooling layer in time-series ConvNet architecture is used for down-sampling its input feature maps into M samples and for each sample the average value is calculated. Thus it is called the average pooling layer in time-series ConvNet architecture. The output of the average pooling layer is calculated as follows:

$$P_m(t) = Avg\left(C_m((t-1)l+1), C_m((t-1)l+2), \ldots, C_m(tl)\right) \tag{3}$$

Our adapted Time-series ConvNet module (shown in Fig. 2) is comprised of two convolution layers, where each one of them is followed by an average polling layer. The final output layer in our module is the fully connected layer which has only 1 neuron that represents the students' engagement level. The initial number of filters r in the first convolution layer is 6 and 12 in the second convolution layer. The initial filter size is 7 for the two convolution layers.

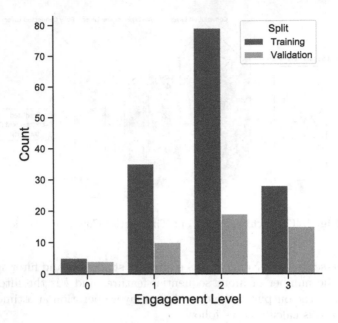

Fig. 3. Dataset distribution across the training and validations splits.

4 Experiments and Results

4.1 Dataset

In our experiments, we relied mainly on the Engagement Prediction in the Wild dataset which is part of the EmotiW 2020 challenge [4]. The dataset involves recorded videos of students who were taking MOOC and each video captures the upper body and faces of students for a duration of approximately 5 min. The dataset covers a wide variety of background environments with different wildness attributes such as varying illumination. The total number of videos in the dataset is 262, with 147 videos for training, 48 videos for validation and 67 video for testing. Each video in the dataset was holistically labelled based on four discrete labels (0, 1, 2, 3). Where '0' is the lowest level of engagement and '3' is the highest. The distribution of the labels across the train and validation splits of the dataset is shown in Fig. 3. As it can be seen, the dataset is notably imbalanced with more bias towards the engagement level 2.

4.2 Implementation Details

In our implementation of the proposed framework as described in Sect. 3, we first prepared and segmented each video from the dataset into N sub-samples in order to calculate the number of sequential feature vectors obtained from the OpenFace 2.0 toolbox. We empirically chose N to be 30 based on grid search over three possible values (15, 30, 60). Since the task of engagement estimation in the wild EmotiW 2020 challenge was casted as a regression problem, the labels of the dataset were mapped to continuous values between (0,1) as follows {0 ⇒ 0.0, 1 ⇒ 0.33, 2 ⇒ 0.66, 3 ⇒ 1.0}. Consequently, when training our Time-series ConvNet model we used the mean squared error (MSE) as our loss function which is calculated as follows:

$$\text{MSE} = \frac{1}{n} \sum_{i=1}^{n} (y_i - \tilde{y}_i)^2 \tag{4}$$

where n is total number of training samples (i.e., 147), y_i is the ground truth label for the i-th sample and $\tilde{y}_i$ is the predicted engagement level value. Furthermore, we trained our Time-series ConvNet model for 200 epochs using Adam [12] as our optimiser with an initial starting learning rate of 0.01.

4.3 Framework Evaluation

In order to evaluate the performance of our proposed framework, we tested our trained model on the testing split of the EmotiW 2020 challenge dataset. The model was evaluated against the MSE score. In Table 1, we report the MSE score of our model on the testing split. Additionally, we also compare our model against two baseline models based on LSTM architecture in order to show the capability of the proposed times-series ConvNet model in modelling temporal data. The first baseline model we refer as "Baseline" which was trained by the EmotiW 2020 challenge team in [10]. The baseline model consists of one LSTM layer and three consecutive fully connected layers and a final average pooling layer. They utilised also the OpenFace toolbox to get a statistical feature vectors based on the input sub-sampled frames from each video in the dataset. Unlike our proposed framework, they relied only on the head pose and the eye gaze information provided by the OpenFace toolbox. The second baseline model, another LSTM model named 'LSTM(Face+Body)' in Table 1. This model is similar to the baseline model but as the name implies it uses an additional input features besides the ones from OpenFace which is the full upper-body pose key-points. The models consists of two consecutive LSTM layers and each layer contains 62 neurons followed by a final fully connected layer of 1 neuron. The input features to the model is the same as the ones we utilised in our proposed framework according to the description in Sect. 3. As it can be shown from Table 1, our proposed Time-Series ConvNet model achieved the best MSE score of the two compared baseline approaches with 0.07. The closest score to our proposed model was the 'LSTM(Face+Body)' model which scored 0.08 in MSE. From these scores, we can deduce that the Time-Series ConvNet was comparable (and even scored better MSE score) with the LSTM models which is well known for modelling sequential data. One of the main reasons for that, in LSTM it is assumed that there is some temporal dependency between the input sequential observations to the model. However, in our task of the students engagement estimation, this assumption does not hold because students behaviours and emotions are independent over time and can change drastically at any time throughout the observed input frames.

Table 1. Performance of our proposed time-series ConvNet model trained using the official training split over the official validation split.

Model	Testing (MSE)
Baseline	0.19
LSTM (Face+Body) [3]	0.08
Time-series ConvNet (Ours)	**0.07**

5   Conclusion

In this work, we have introduced a framework that can effectively predict the intensity of students engagement in the context of MOOCs based on video sequences. Our framework relied on data-driven approach based on convolutional neural networks (ConvNet) architecture. Our Time-Series ConvNet model achieved competitive results in terms of MSE evaluation metric with 0.07 on the EmotiW 2020 challenge dataset. Additionally, the model also achieved competitive results when compared with two baseline models based on recurrent neural networks architecture. In future work, we will explore more discriminative feature vectors that we can utilise in order to further enhance the overall performance of our prospered framework for students engagement estimation.

References

1. Baltrusaitis, T., Zadeh, A., Lim, Y.C., Morency, L.P.: OpenFace 2.0: facial behavior analysis toolkit. In: 2018 13th IEEE International Conference on Automatic Face & Gesture Recognition (FG 2018), pp. 59–66. IEEE (2018)
2. Boucheix, J.M., Lowe, R.K., Putri, D.K., Groff, J.: Cueing animations: dynamic signaling aids information extraction and comprehension. Learn. Instr. **25**, 71–84 (2013)
3. Chang, C., Zhang, C., Chen, L., Liu, Y.: An ensemble model using face and body tracking for engagement detection. In: Proceedings of the 20th ACM International Conference on Multimodal Interaction, pp. 616–622 (2018)
4. Dhall, A., Sharma, G., Goecke, R., Gedeon, T.: EmotiW 2020: driver gaze, group emotion, student engagement and physiological signal based challenges. In: 2020 International Conference on Multimodal Interaction (2020)
5. D'mello, S., Graesser, A.: Autotutor and affective autotutor: learning by talking with cognitively and emotionally intelligent computers that talk back. ACM Trans. Interact. Intell. Syst. (TiiS) **2**(4), 1–39 (2013)
6. Fernandez, A., Bunke, R.B.H., Schmiduber, J.: A novel connectionist system for improved unconstrained handwriting recognition. IEEE Trans. Pattern Anal. Mach. Intell. **31**(5), 855–868 (2009)
7. Fredricks, J.A., Blumenfeld, P.C., Paris, A.H.: School engagement: potential of the concept, state of the evidence. Rev. Educ. Res. **74**(1), 59–109 (2004)
8. Giesbers, B., Rienties, B., Tempelaar, D., Gijselaers, W.: A dynamic analysis of the interplay between asynchronous and synchronous communication in online learning: the impact of motivation. J. Comput. Assist. Learn. **30**(1), 30–50 (2014)

9. Henrie, C.R., Halverson, L.R., Graham, C.R.: Measuring student engagement in technology-mediated learning: a review. Comput. Educ. **90**, 36–53 (2015)
10. Kaur, A., Mustafa, A., Mehta, L., Dhall, A.: Prediction and localization of student engagement in the wild. In: 2018 Digital Image Computing: Techniques and Applications (DICTA), pp. 1–8. IEEE (2018)
11. Kawakami, K.: Supervised sequence labelling with recurrent neural networks. Ph.D. thesis (2008)
12. Kingma, D.P., Ba, J.: Adam: a method for stochastic optimization. arXiv preprint arXiv:1412.6980 (2014)
13. LeCun, Y., Bengio, Y., Hinton, G.: Deep learning. Nature **521**(7553), 436–444 (2015)
14. Papamitsiou, Z., Economides, A.A.: Learning analytics and educational data mining in practice: a systematic literature review of empirical evidence. J. Educ. Technol. Soc. **17**(4), 49–64 (2014)
15. Pascanu, R., Mikolov, T., Bengio, Y.: On the difficulty of training recurrent neural networks. In: International Conference on Machine Learning, pp. 1310–1318 (2013)
16. Saleh, K., Hossny, M., Nahavandi, S.: Contextual recurrent predictive model for long-term intent prediction of vulnerable road users. IEEE Trans. Intell. Transp. Syst. **21**(8), 3398–3408 (2019)
17. Shen, L., Wang, M., Shen, R.: Affective e-learning: using "emotional" data to improve learning in pervasive learning environment. J. Educ. Technol. Soc. **12**(2), 176–189 (2009)
18. Shi, L., Cristea, A.I.: In-depth exploration of engagement patterns in MOOCs. In: Hacid, H., Cellary, W., Wang, H., Paik, H.-Y., Zhou, R. (eds.) WISE 2018. LNCS, vol. 11234, pp. 395–409. Springer, Cham (2018). https://doi.org/10.1007/978-3-030-02925-8_28
19. Sinatra, G.M., Heddy, B.C., Lombardi, D.: The challenges of defining and measuring student engagement in science. Educ. Psychol. **50**(1), 1–13 (2015)
20. Thomas, C., Jayagopi, D.B.: Predicting student engagement in classrooms using facial behavioral cues. In: Proceedings of the 1st ACM SIGCHI International Workshop on Multimodal Interaction for Education, pp. 33–40 (2017)
21. Thong Huynh, V., Kim, S.H., Lee, G.S., Yang, H.J.: Engagement intensity prediction with facial behavior features. In: 2019 International Conference on Multimodal Interaction, pp. 567–571 (2019)
22. Whitehill, J., Serpell, Z., Lin, Y.C., Foster, A., Movellan, J.R.: The faces of engagement: automatic recognition of student engagement from facial expressions. IEEE Trans. Affect. Comput. **5**(1), 86–98 (2014)
23. Yang, J., Wang, K., Peng, X., Qiao, Y.: Deep recurrent multi-instance learning with spatio-temporal features for engagement intensity prediction. In: Proceedings of the 20th ACM International Conference on Multimodal Interaction, pp. 594–598 (2018)
24. Yang, Y.F.: Engaging students in an online situated language learning environment. Comput. Assist. Lang. Learn. **24**(2), 181–198 (2011)
25. Zander, S., Reichelt, M., Wetzel, S., et al.: Does personalisation promote learners' attention? An eye-tracking study. Frontline Learn. Res. **3**(4), 1–13 (2015)
26. Zhao, B., Lu, H., Chen, S., Liu, J., Wu, D.: Convolutional neural networks for time series classification. J. Syst. Eng. Electron. **28**(1), 162–169 (2017)
27. Zhao, G., Pietikainen, M.: Dynamic texture recognition using local binary patterns with an application to facial expressions. IEEE Trans. Pattern Anal. Mach. Intell. **29**(6), 915–928 (2007)

Eye Movement and Visual Target Synchronization Level Detection Using Deep Learning

Liuchun Yao(✉), Mira Park, Saurabh Grag, and Quan Bai

School of Technology, Environment and Design, University of Tasmania, Hobart, Australia
liuchun.yao@utas.edu.au

Abstract. In recent years, deep learning has been widely used in the eye-tracking area. Eye-tracking has been studied to diagnose neurological and psychological diseases early since it is a simple, non-invasive, and objective proxy measurement of cognitive function. This project aims to develop a system to automatically track the synchronisation of eye movement data and its visual target. To achieve this goal, we employ a deep learning algorithm (Points-CNN and Head-CNN) to detect the eye centre location and classify the synchronisation level of the eye movement and visual target. Moreover, we modify the *eyediap* dataset to assist with our research objective. The video data in the *eyediap* dataset is used to track the eye movement trajectory, while the visual target movement data is used to extract the direction change window. The movement feature vectors are extracted from the eye movement data and the visual target movement data with the direction change window. Euclidean distance, Cosine similarity, and Jaccard similarity coefficient are used to assist the synchronization detection of the eye and visual target movement vector. In the synchronisation detection part, K-Nearest Neighbors, Support Vector Machine, Logistic Regression are investigated.

Keywords: Deep learning · Synchronisation detection · Multi-CNN

1 Introduction

Eye-tracking is to trace the trajectory while the eye moves. Eye movement has different types, including fixation, saccadic, pro-saccade, and smooth pursuit. In [1], the studied eye movement patterns are fixation, pro-saccade, and smooth pursuit, while in [2, 3], saccadic eye movement is used. In [4, 5], the researchers do not specify the movement pattern. Other than the eye movement pattern, in [6], a broader range of oculomotor behaviour is introduced. Eye-tracking has been studied as a method for diagnosing Neurological and psychological diseases such as Autism [7, 8], Concussion [9], Dementia, Alzheimer's Disease [1, 2, 6] at an early stage since it is a simple, non-invasive, and objective proxy measurement of cognitive function [3–5]. Antisaccade task is designed for eye movement and visual target. In [6, 10], the antisaccade test is proved to be helpful for the Alzheimer's disease diagnostic work-up. An antisaccade test requires the users to move the eye based on the movement of the visual target. The accuracy and latency

G. Long et al. (Eds.): AI 2021, LNAI 13151, pp. 668–678, 2022.
https://doi.org/10.1007/978-3-030-97546-3_54

are assessed, which requires professional human resources to assess the synchronisation of eye movement and visual target. Professional human resources would raise the cost of the test. Other than the cost, a human error would be an issue for manual assessment. With the development of eye-tracking technology, the issue of manual assessment can be addressed.

Over the past few years, researchers employed neural networks into the eye-tracking technology, which achieved decent accuracy [11, 12] in different eye-tracking areas, including eye event detection [13, 14], eye gaze detection [12, 15], and eye centre detection [16, 17]. Nevertheless, the study in eye synchronisation with a visual target is not yet well studied. In order to address the issue of manual assessment in antisaccade tests, more study is needed to enhance the usability of eye-tracking technology.

Therefore, our study will focus on developing a system to enhance eye-tracking technology's usability. Our system can be divided into two parts, eye centre detection and classification. Thus, we would employ the recent eye detection model and some traditional machine learning models to train our data and improve the interpretability of the system and the output.

Our contribution is to build a system to improve the interpretability of eye movement technology which can be further used to address the issue in antisaccade tests when assessing manually. We combine deep learning-based visual object detection algorithms and traditional classification algorithms to find the best design for our system.

2 Related Work

Many researchers carry out eye detection [17–25], and synchronisation detection is widely used in various classification tasks. However, the synchronisation detection of eye movement and the visual target is not yet well studied. Therefore, the related work of eye centre detection and synchronisation detection is reviewed to assist us in finding out the best fit for our system.

2.1 Eye Movement Detection

Eye detection requires handling various head poses because eye movements are highly dependent on the movement of the head. Ranjan et al. [24] prove that the input data with head pose positively impact eye detection. Zhang et al. [26] subject multi-CNN to detect feature points, proving that the performance is superior to state-of-art Convolutional Neural Networks architecture. Ali and Kim [25] propose multi-scale Convolutional Neural Networks to detect the eye gaze. In Ali and Kim's study [25], the multi-CNN achieves a 3.64 angular error, superior to the Diff-VGG, achieving a 4.67 angular error MPIIGaze dataset. Similarly, the model proposed by Kan et al. [17] falls to a regression problem in the final layer to compute the iris centre. Meng and Zhao [27] propose a much simpler architecture, Points-CNN. Points-CNN only uses three convolutional layers and one fully connected layer to detect the eye's feature points: the inner corner, outer corner, the centre of the upper eyelid, the lower eyelid, and iris centre.

Liu et al. [28] propose a Mr-CNN model with three Convolutional layers and three fully connected layers. This multi-CNN input contains three streams: the central region stream, the surrounding region stream, and the whole image stream. Each convolutional layer comes with different max-pooling layers for each stream to ensure the feature maps feed into the fully connected layers are the same. Dropout and ReLU are applied to fully connected layer1 and layer2. Mr-CNN model achieves 72.78% accuracy in the MIT dataset, while the state-of-art algorithm, Sr-CNN, got 71.23%.

Face image is one steam input of the CNN model [29], which can help avoid the risk of over-fitting. In Ali and Kim's [25] method, the multi-stream input is the eye images with a different noise. Among the investigated multi-CNN, Points-CNN shows more superior detection accuracy, and the model structure proposed by [29] shows stronger robustness to various head poses, which is more suitable in the practical use of eye detection. Different machine learning models show various detection rates in different cases, and the parameters for the Convolutional Neural Networks are crucial for the model performance. The multi-CNN has more flexibility than the traditional Convolutional Neural Networks [24, 30] in eye detection. However, these algorithms pay less attention to practical use in the medical domain. Therefore, our proposal considers more real-world cases.

2.2 Synchronisation Detection Methods

Supervised learning is widely used in synchronisation detection in a variety of domains. Synchronisation detection problems are transformed into classification problems because the dataset is labelled as synchronized and non-synchronized.

In the psychological domain, machine learning algorithms are used for detecting synchronisation. Lahnakoski et al. [31] use K-Nearest Neighbor and Support Vector Machine classifiers to detect eye gaze and brain activity synchronisation. Wittevrongel and Van Hulle [32] use a Support Vector Machine and K-Nearest Neighbor to classifier the synchronisation of brain-computer interface data. An activation pattern is used to capture the signal-of-interest as input features of the classification model. The Support Vector Machine's detection accuracy is 75.0%, while the accuracy for K-Nearest Neighbor is 83.3%.

In the eye-tracking domain, Copeland et al. [33] use Artificial Neural Networks to classify the comprehension score of the eye movement data to detect a person is reading or not, achieving 89% classification accuracy. Compared to a K-Nearest Neighbor's accuracy, 71%, Artificial Neural Networks shows superior performance in Copeland's study [33]. In another study, 13 subjects' data are analyzed, achieving 71.6% detection accuracy [34]. Thus, dataset size is crucial to the performance accuracy of Artificial Neural Networks. A comparative study on Support Vector Machine and Artificial Neural Networks for classifying the kurtosis and amplitude of the EEG signal is conducted [35]. Support Vector Machine achieves 91.9% classification accuracy in the eye blink classification while Artificial Neural Networks is 89.3%.

Eye detection algorithm achieves decent detection accuracy, and synchronisation detection is widely used in different domains. However, detecting eye movement and visual target synchronisation is not well studied, even though eye movement synchronisation is an essential indicator of Dementia. Thus, we aim to propose a novel system to detect eye movement synchronisation to support the diagnosis of Dementia.

3   Methodology

Figure 1 demonstrates an overview of our proposed system. Video data is used to detect the eye's location, while the visual target movement data in points generate the direction change window. The direction change window is then applied to the detected eye location data to extract eye movement features. Meanwhile, the same direction change window is applied to the corresponding visual target movement to generate the movement feature. The generated eye movement feature and visual target movement feature are used for synchronisation detection. The following sections explain each process in detail.

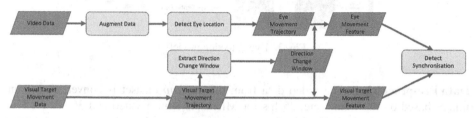

Fig. 1. Methodology overview

3.1   Dataset Augmentation

The dataset used in this paper is the *eyediap* dataset [2], which is widely used in gaze estimation and gaze detection [12, 36]. The *eyediap* dataset contains a visual target on the computer screen and a 3D floating target hanging with a thin thread. We use the visual target on the computer screen because it contains the target's location for each frame which can track the movement trajectory. The *eyediap* dataset contains 56 videos stimulated by the visual target on the computer screen, which is not enough. Augmentation is applied in two means. Firstly, the unsynchronized data is generated by flipping the videos from left to right. The number of the dataset doubled after the augmentation. Secondly, the augmented data is cut into eight pieces for each video with a randomly selected starting point, and the frames number varies from 700 to 1030. After the augmentation, the dataset increases from 112 to 896.

3.2   Eye Location Detection

We adopt two CNN models, Head-CNN [29] and Point-CNN [27], to detect the eye centre in our project for two reasons. The Head-CNN approach would provide a geometric relationship for the model to cut down the overfitting risk [29]. The eye region is tiny, and the detection target, eye centre location, is a small dot of the eye's region of interest (ROI). It will have a high risk of overfitting without the geometric information from the whole face image. Secondly, the detection system would obtain more flexibility. Figure 2 shows the overview of our eye centre location detection, which has four parts, pre-processing, Point-CNN, Head-CNN, and concatenation, which is described in the following subsections.

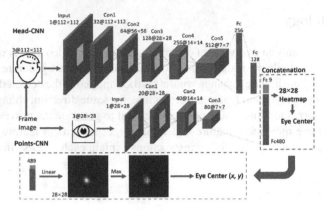

Fig. 2. Eye detection model

Data Pre-processing. The video data from the *eyediap* dataset is converted into an image based on the frame rate, 25 fps for Microsoft Kinect video and 30 fps for HD camera video. Then the ROI of the face and eye is cut from the frame image and down-scaled from three dimensions to one dimension by applying the TensorFlow grayscale function. The histogram equalization is applied to increase the contrast of the image.

Points-CNN. Points-CNN is proposed by Meng and Zhao [27], designed for webcam base video. The input of the Points-CNN is a 28×28 ROI of the eye images. In the *eyediap* dataset, the eye centre labels are annotated in pixel values (x, y) based on the video resolution. The ground truth, eye centre, is encoded into a heatmap as a 2D Gaussian centre, using equation, $G_\sigma(x, y) = \frac{1}{2\pi\sigma^2}\exp\left(-\frac{x^2+y^2}{2\sigma^2}\right)$.

Head-CNN. The Head-CNN uses the tiny-AlexNet network, similar to Zhu and Deng's study [29]. The Head-CNN requires lower computational cost because it has fewer channels than the original AlexNet. The sigmoid function is applied in the last fully connected layers to output a nine-dimensional vector, which provides the head's geometric information.

Concatenation. The Head-CNN's output and Points-CNN's output are concatenated together in the last fully connected layer. Linear activation is applied to output a 28×28 result. Then the data point in the heatmap with the maximum value is selected as the eye centre location. After the location is extracted from each frame, the eye movement trajectory is tracked. The eye movement trajectory is used to generate the direction vector.

3.3 Direction Change Window

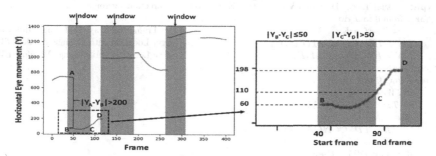

Fig. 3. Direction change window extraction

The visual target movement and the eye movement trajectory are broken into a direction change window to detect the ocular motility impairment. Dimensional reduction is applied to the eye movement data to obtain the direction change window with a better classification accuracy [37]. Because the range of the horizontal movement is much greater than the vertical, it is easier to detect synchronisation with more significant movement. Therefore, only the horizontal movement is estimated. While extracting the direction change window, the visual target's horizontal value is calculated from frame to frame. The starting frame and ending frame are defined based on the changing variance. In Fig. 3, the x-axis is the frame number, while the y-axis is the horizontal eye movement. The visual target moved from A to B, in which the variance is more significant than 200 pixels. Then, A is considered as the starting frame of a window. The accumulated changing variance will be measured starting from point B. The cumulated variance from B to C is less than 50, while from C to D is greater than 50. Thus, C is selected as the window's ending point. The output of this part is the direction change window starting frame vector S_j and the ending frame vector E_j.

3.4 Eye and Visual Target Movement Feature

Algorithm 1 explains the eye and visual target movement feature extraction. The extracted direction change windows vector (S_j and E_j) would be applied to both the visual target and the eye movement location to generate the target and eye location with the change window(TW and EW). Then, our system root through each element of TW and EW to generate the direction. If TW_l is less than TW_{l+1}, then 1 is assigned to the target movement direction vector. -1 is assigned when TW_l is greater than TW_{l+1}. Given that the subject faces the computer screen during the video recording, the eye movement direction shows an opposite trend.

Algorithm 1 Movement Feature Extraction

Input: Target Location TL_i , Eye Location EL_i, $\forall i \in \{0,...,I\}$, Start Frame S_j , End Frame E_j ,
$\forall j \in \{0,...,J\}$

Output: Visual Target Direction Vector $\overrightarrow{TD_v}$, Eye Movement Direction Vector $\overrightarrow{ED_v}$, $\forall v \in \{0,...,V\}$

1: **for** j from 0 to J **do**
2:     $sf = S_j, ef = E_j;$ ▷ Start Frame Index sf, End Frame Index ef
3:     $TW = TW \cdot CONCAT(TL_{sf})$ ▷ Target Location with Change Window TW
4:     $EW = EW \cdot CONCAT(EL_{ef})$ ▷ Eye Location with Change Window EW
5: **end for**/
6: **for** l from 0 to L **do**
7:     **if** $TW_l < TW_{l+1}$ **then**
8:         $TD = TD \cdot CONCAT(1)$
9:     **else**
10:         $TD = TD \cdot CONCAT(-1)$
11:     **end if**
12:     **if** $DW_l < DW_{l+1}$ **then**
13:         $ED = ED \cdot CONCAT(-1)$
14:     **else**
15:         $ED = ED \cdot CONCAT(1)$
16:     **end if**
17: **end for**
18: **return** $\overrightarrow{TD_v}$, $\overrightarrow{ED_v}$

3.5 Synchronisation Detection

The dataset is labelled as synchronized and unsynchronized, while the input features are the eye movement and visual target direction vectors. The synchronisation detection drops into a classification problem. Euclidean distance, cosine similarity, and Jaccard similarity coefficient are used to calculate the movement feature vectors' distance. Euclidean distance compares the shortest distance between $\overrightarrow{TD_v}$ and $\overrightarrow{ED_v}$, while cosine similarity is for the determination between $\overrightarrow{TD_v}$ and $\overrightarrow{ED_v}$. The Jaccard commonness of the overall direction change between the two corresponding vectors. After the different similarity coefficients are calculated, a comparative experiment is used to compare the performance of different classifiers, K-Nearest Neighbors, Support Vector Machine, Logistic Regression.

4 Result and Discussion

A comparative experiment is necessary to prove the final selected model and parameters. Thus, the result is displayed in different comparative experiment tests to justify selecting the used parameter in this study.

4.1 Selection of the Best Parameter

The investigated the learning-rate (0.01, 0.001, 0.0001) and dropout (0.2, 0.5) for the convolutional neural network since the selected parameters showed more promising detection performance. The data is split into three parts, 60% for training, 20% for testing, and 20% for evaluation. Learning-rate 0.001, dropout 0.5, and batch-size 128 achieves the best performance. Figure 4 shows the training and validation MAE line chart for each step. Over-fitting occurs in the 0.01 learning-rate groups. Learning-rate 0.001 achieve a smaller MAE when the dropout rate is 0.2.

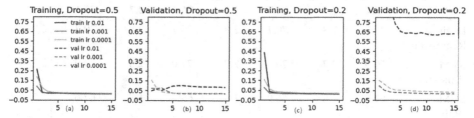

Fig. 4. Training and validation mean absolute error for different learning-rate (Batch-size 128): (a) Training MAE with Dropout 0.5, (b) Validation MAE with Dropout 0.5, (c) Training MAE with Dropout 0.2, (d) Validation MAE with Dropout 0.2

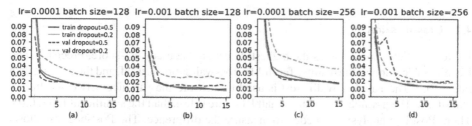

Fig. 5. Training and validation mean absolute error for different dropout group: (a) MAE for learning-rate 0.0001 Batch-Size 128, (b) MAE for learning-rate 0.001 Batch-Size 128, (c) MAE for learning-rate 0.0001 Batch-Size 256, (d) MAE for learning-rate 0.001 Batch-Size 256

Figure 5 shows the MAE of the training and validation result across different dropout groups. The generation gap for dropout 0.5 is narrower than 0.2 across different learning-rates and batch-sizes. It means skipping the neuron in the fully connected layer can prevent over-fitting effectively, and dropout 0.5 is more effective than 0.2. However, Fig. 5(d) shows a different trend. The dotted blue line (validation dropout = 0.5) fluctuates at the early stage of the training. The main reason is that the training result is not stable at the beginning. That explains the benefit of increasing the training epoch. Conclusively, the dropout rate of 0.5 is more suitable in this study.

Based on the previous analysis Kruskal-Wallis test [38] is applied to groups with learning-rate 0.001, 0.0001, and dropout 0.5 for further analysis. The null hypothesis is no significant difference between the tested groups. The results show that the P-value is 0.000, which is lower than the set significant level, 0.05. The null hypothesis is rejected. It means at least two test groups have a significant difference. Therefore, Dunn's post hoc [38] test is applied to examine the variance. The result shows that the parametric set with learning-rate 0.001, dropout 0.5, and batch-size 128 is significantly lower than any other group ($p < 0.05$).

Table 1. Kruskal-Wallis Test result in different delay time.

Method	Accuracy (%)		F1-score (%)		Precision (%)		Recall (%)	
	Avg.	Std.	Avg.	Std.	Avg.	Std.	Avg.	Std.
KNN	**75.1**	2.5	**74.7**	2.5	**76.9**	2.7	**75.1**	2.5
Logistic Regression	70.7	2.8	70.7	2.8	70.7	2.8	70.7	2.8
SVM (Linear)	70.9	2.7	70.9	2.7	71.0	2.8	70.9	2.7
SVM (Poly)	67.6	1.8	66.9	1.9	69.3	1.8	67.6	1.7
SVM (RBF)	71.0	3.0	70.9	3.0	71.1	3.0	71.0	3.0
Avg.	71.0	3.5	70.8	3.5	71.8	3.7	71.1	3.5

4.2 Classification

K-Nearest Neighbor achieves the highest detection Accuracy, F1-score, Precision, and Recall. Table 1 shows the results. Ten-folds cross-validation is used, and the training data rate is 0.9. The Kruskal-Wallis test is used to measure the variance between different classifiers. The p-value for accuracy and F1-score is less than the significant level, 0.05. Then, Post-hoc analysis is needed to measure the difference. The Post-hoc test shows that the detection Accuracy and F1 score of the KNN classifier are significantly higher than the other four classifiers ($p < 0.05$).

5 Conclusion and Discussion

We develop a system to demonstrate the synchronisation detection process to assist Dementia diagnosis, which focuses more on practicality. The video data is processed into frame images and fed into the convolutional neural network for eye location detection. Meanwhile, the visual target data is used for the direction change window extraction. The eye and visual target movement features are generated for synchronisation detection, based on the extracted direction change window. The proposed system is capable of detecting the synchronisation of eye movement and visual target automatically. Therefore, it will contribute to a more efficient way of assisting the dementia diagnosis.

Due to its efficiency and non-bias analysis, it is irresistible to boost the Dementia diagnosis process. The future working direction for this project is to include the Dementia patients' data. With the data from Dementia patients, we can find more patterns of the Dementia patients' eye movement. It is a valuable way to reduce the noise during eye movement direction detection to achieve a higher detection accuracy.

References

1. Pavisic, I.M., et al.: Eyetracking metrics in young onset Alzheimer's disease: a window into cognitive visual functions. Front. Neurol. **8**, 377 (2017)
2. Crawford, T.J., Devereaux, A., Higham, S., Kelly, C.: The disengagement of visual attention in Alzheimer's disease: a longitudinal eye-tracking study. Front. Aging Neurosci. (2015). https://doi.org/10.3389/fnagi.2015.00118
3. Wilcockson, T.D.W., et al.: Abnormalities of saccadic eye movements in dementia due to Alzheimer's disease and mild cognitive impairment. Aging (Albany NY) **11**(15), 5389–5398 (2019). https://doi.org/10.18632/aging.102118
4. Perez, A., Ratté, S.: Automatic analysis of Alzheimer's disease, evaluation of eye movements in natural conversations. In: 2020 Alzheimer's Association International Conference. ALZ (2020)
5. Nakashima, Y., Morita, K., Ishii, Y., Shouji, Y., Uchimura, N.: Characteristics of exploratory eye movements in elderly people: possibility of early diagnosis of dementia. Psychogeriatrics **10**, 124–130 (2010)
6. Lage, C., et al.: Distinctive oculomotor behaviors in Alzheimer's disease and frontotemporal dementia. Front. Aging Neurosci. **12**, 525 (2021)
7. Falck-Ytter, T., Bölte, S., Gredebäck, G.: Eye tracking in early autism research. J. Neurodev. Disord. **5**, 1–13 (2013)
8. Liu, W., Yu, X., Raj, B., Yi, L., Zou, X., Li, M.: Efficient autism spectrum disorder prediction with eye movement: A machine learning framework. In: 2015 International Conference on Affective Computing and Intelligent Interaction (ACII), pp. 649–655. IEEE (2015)
9. Maruta, J., Suh, M., Niogi, S.N., Mukherjee, P., Ghajar, J.: Visual tracking synchronization as a metric for concussion screening. J. Head Trauma Rehabil. **25**, 293–305 (2010)
10. Currie, J., Ramsden, B., McArthur, C., Maruff, P.: Validation of a clinical antisaccadic eye movement test in the assessment of dementia. Arch. Neurol. **48**, 644–648 (1991)
11. Dar, A.H., Wagner, A.S., Hanke, M.: REMoDNaV: Robust Eye-Movement Classification for Dynamic Stimulation. bioRxiv 619254 (2020)
12. Wang, X., Zhao, X., Ren, J.: A new type of eye movement model based on recurrent neural networks for simulating the gaze behavior of human reading. Complexity **2019**, 1–12 (2019)
13. Zemblys, R., Niehorster, D.C., Komogortsev, O., Holmqvist, K.: Using machine learning to detect events in eye-tracking data. Behav. Res. Methods **50**(1), 160–181 (2017). https://doi.org/10.3758/s13428-017-0860-3
14. Zemblys, R.: Eye-movement event detection meets machine learning. Biomed. Eng. **2016**, 20 (2016)
15. Lorenz, O., Thomas, U.: Real time eye gaze tracking system using CNN-based facial features for human attention measurement. In: VISIGRAPP (5: VISAPP), pp. 598–606 (2019)
16. Eivazi, S., Santini, T., Keshavarzi, A., Kübler, T., Mazzei, A.: Improving real-time CNN-based pupil detection through domain-specific data augmentation. In: Proceedings of the 11th ACM Symposium on Eye Tracking Research and Applications, pp. 1–6 (2019)
17. Kan, N., Kondo, N., Chinsatit, W., Saitoh, T.: Effectiveness of data augmentation for CNN-based pupil center point detection. In: 2018 57th Annual Conference of the Society of Instrument and Control Engineers of Japan (SICE), pp. 41–46. IEEE, (2018)
18. Ioffe, S., Szegedy, C.: Batch normalization: accelerating deep network training by reducing internal covariate shift. arXiv preprint arXiv:1502.03167 (2015)
19. He, K., Zhang, X., Ren, S., Sun, J.: Delving deep into rectifiers: surpassing human-level performance on imagenet classification. In: Proceedings of the IEEE International Conference on Computer Vision, pp. 1026–1034 (2015)

20. Colaco, S., Han, D.S.: Facial keypoint detection with convolutional neural networks. In: 2020 International Conference on Artificial Intelligence in Information and Communication (ICAIIC), pp. 671–674. IEEE (2020)
21. Hessels, R.S., Niehorster, D.C., Kemner, C., Hooge, I.T.C.: Noise-robust fixation detection in eye movement data: Identification by two-means clustering (I2MC). Behav. Res. Methods **49**(5), 1802–1823 (2016). https://doi.org/10.3758/s13428-016-0822-1
22. Chen, L.-C., Papandreou, G., Kokkinos, I., Murphy, K., Yuille, A.L.: Deeplab: semantic image segmentation with deep convolutional nets, atrous convolution, and fully connected CRFS. IEEE Trans. Pattern Anal. Mach. Intell. **40**, 834–848 (2017)
23. Long, J., Shelhamer, E., Darrell, T.: Fully convolutional networks for semantic segmentation. In: Proceedings of the IEEE Conference on Computer Vision and Pattern Recognition, pp. 3431–3440 (2015)
24. Ranjan, R., De Mello, S., Kautz, J.: Light-weight head pose invariant gaze tracking. In: Proceedings of the IEEE Conference on Computer Vision and Pattern Recognition Workshops, pp. 2156–2164 (2018)
25. Ali, A., Kim, Y.-G.: Deep fusion for 3D gaze estimation from natural face images using multi-stream CNNs. IEEE Access **8**, 69212–69221 (2020)
26. Zhang, X., Sugano, Y., Fritz, M., Bulling, A.: Appearance-based gaze estimation in the wild. In: Proceedings of the IEEE Conference on Computer Vision and Pattern Recognition, pp. 4511–4520 (2015)
27. Meng, C., Zhao, X.: Webcam-based eye movement analysis using CNN. IEEE Access **5**, 19581–19587 (2017)
28. Liu, N., Han, J., Liu, T., Li, X.: Learning to predict eye fixations via multiresolution convolutional neural networks. IEEE Trans. Neural Netw. Learn. Syst. **29**, 392–404 (2018)
29. Zhu, W., Deng, H.: Monocular free-head 3d gaze tracking with deep learning and geometry constraints. In: Proceedings of the IEEE International Conference on Computer Vision, pp. 3143–3152 (2017)
30. Stefanov, K.: Webcam-based Eye Gaze Tracking under Natural Head Movement. arXiv preprint arXiv:1803.11088 (2018)
31. Lahnakoski, J.M., et al.: Synchronous brain activity across individuals underlies shared psychological perspectives. Neuroimage **100**, 316–324 (2014)
32. Wittevrongel, B., Van Hulle, M.M.: Spatiotemporal beamforming: a transparent and unified decoding approach to synchronous visual brain-computer interfacing. Front. Neurosci. **11**, 630 (2017)
33. Copeland, L., Gedeon, T., Mendis, B.S.U.: Predicting reading comprehension scores from eye movements using artificial neural networks and fuzzy output error. Artif. Intell. Res. **3**, 35–48 (2014)
34. Chambayil, B., Singla, R., Jha, R.: EEG eye blink classification using neural network. In: Proceedings of the World Congress on Engineering, pp. 2–5 (2010)
35. Singla, R., Chambayil, B., Khosla, A., Santosh, J.: Comparison of SVM and ANN for classification of eye events in EEG. J. Biomed. Sci. Eng. **4**, 62 (2011)
36. Chatterjee, D., Gavas, R.D., Chakravarty, K., Sinha, A., Lahiri, U.: Eye movements-an early marker of cognitive dysfunctions. In: 2018 40th Annual International Conference of the IEEE Engineering in Medicine and Biology Society (EMBC), pp. 4012–4016. IEEE (2018)
37. Gruca, A., Harezlak, K., Kasprowski, P.: Application of dimensionality reduction methods for eye movement data classification. In: Gruca, A., Brachman, A., Kozielski, S., Czachórski, T. (eds.) Man–Machine Interactions 4. AISC, vol. 391, pp. 291–303. Springer, Cham (2016). https://doi.org/10.1007/978-3-319-23437-3_25
38. Ghasemi, A., Zahediasl, S.: Normality tests for statistical analysis: a guide for non-statisticians. Int. J. Endocrinol. Metab. **10**, 486–489 (2012)

Vehicle Detection Based on Cascade Deep Learning Method Using Deformed Oriented Bounding Box

Wenli Yang[1]([⊠]) [iD], Mira Park[1], Xianghui Song[2], Sun Ling[2], Yameng Li[2], and Xiaotong Gu[1]

[1] School of ICT, College of Sciences and Engineering, University of Tasmania, Hobart, Australia
`yang.wenli@utas.edu.au`
[2] National Centre of ITS Engineering and Technology, Institute of Highway Ministry of Transport, Beijing, China

Abstract. At present, the development of intelligent vehicles is a global trend, and vehicular collision estimation technology based on machine vision has become an important topic in current academic research, in which the vehicle detection problem in a general environment has attracted much attention. This paper presents a new method for vehicle detection as well as driving orientation estimation based on deformed oriented bounding box, and to predict conflict points in the vehicular surroundings based on cascade convolutional networks. Extensive experiments show that our approach provides a new solution for detecting vehicles, which could be used for further collision estimation.

Keywords: Vehicle detection · Cascade deep learning · DOBB · RCNN · Conflict points

1 Introduction

1.1 A Subsection Sample

With the development of computer technology, communication engineering, automation and other disciplines, vehicles are developing towards an intelligent direction. Intelligent driving and derivative technology can replace tedious human driving tasks to its some extent, but many problems still exist in intelligent driving under complex traffic environment [1, 2]. Research on vehicle detection can improve intelligent decisions, vehicle active control capability, and driving safety, so it has important significance and great application prospects.

Compared to active sensors, machine vision includes abundant information and is more related to human cognitive habits and has more widely application areas [3, 4]. The research on vehicle detection based on machine vision is a quite active research domain. It is the basic and the most important function in vehicular perception and can directly affect the validity of the decision and control system.

© Springer Nature Switzerland AG 2022
G. Long et al. (Eds.): AI 2021, LNAI 13151, pp. 679–690, 2022.
https://doi.org/10.1007/978-3-030-97546-3_55

In the last few years, researchers have begun to use deep learning methods to realize vehicle detection. It is because deep learning learns features and tasks directly from data instead of using traditional design features, thus have very good adaptability. The common methods of region proposal include selective search [5], edge boxes [6], etc. So far, most of deep learning methods used in vehicle detection are based on a 2D bounding box without consideration for driving direction, and the results based on 2D bounding boxes are easily influenced by vehicular body posture when predicting vehicle collisions based on detected locations between vehicles, thus it is not accurate to use existing 2D bounding box to guide the further collision estimation.

In light of the above problems, this paper presents a new method to detect vehicle and conflict points among vehicular surroundings based on deep learning method using a deformed oriented bounding box, which can efficiently predict the vehicle location realizing a minimum-area encasing box of the target and then extract conflict points based on detected boundaries. In this way, it is more accurate to detect the vehicle location using polygonal regions rather than the original 2D bounding box. Detailed experimental evaluations show that we are able to increase positioning accuracy in our designed network in the different test sets.

2   Related Work

Our approach is related to work on vehicle detection, orientation estimation, conflict points detection and collision estimation.

Vehicle Detection: is important in intelligent driving systems or Advanced Driver Assistance Systems (ADAS). Traditional vehicle detection methods include three main steps: region selection based on a sliding window, feature extraction, and classifier design. There are two main problems with traditional methods: window redundancy and poor robustness for diverse instances of the features. Deep learning [7] offers a solution in the transportation area to address these problems. For example, DNN-based vehicle detection. Chen et al. [8] presented a hybrid DNN (HDNN), which used multiple blocks of convolutional field sizes to extract multi-scale features. A more recent approach used hyper region proposal network (HRPN) to extract target objects using a combination of hierarchical feature maps [9], and it can improve the performance of R-CNN for vehicle detection [10]. However, these approaches are implemented on the bounding box located by axial position and failed to realize a minimum-area encasing box, which is very important for extracting conflict points.

Orientation Estimation. Recently, deep CNNs have been used in 2D object detection and also included several extensions such as orientation estimation. Girshick et al. [11] used R-CNN to detect objects and the resulting detected regions were passed as input to a pose estimation network. Su et al. [12] presented a similar framework that combined render-based image synthesis and CNNs to realize training data with viewpoint annotations. Poirson et al. [13] discretised the object viewpoint and train a deep convolutional network to jointly perform viewpoint estimation and 2D detection. Another related approach by Mousavian [14] proposed a new MultiBin loss for orientation prediction and an effective choice of box dimensions as regression parameters, which could estimate oriented 3D bounding boxes. Based on the above analysis, our work related to 2D orientation estimation can be also resolved by multibin orientation estimation.

Conflict Points Detection. Vehicular surroundings perception based on machine vision always focuses on conflict point extraction between vehicles, which can also be considered as key feature point detection. The evidence given by shape constraints and local component detectors showed shape constraints are important to refine key feature point detection results, and much research has been focusing on this point [3]. Among deep-learning based approaches, many deep neural networks and other deep models have been successfully used in face detection, landmark localization and corner feature points tracking [3, 4, 16, 17]. Work most related to ours is [3, 4, 16], which aims to use convolutional networks to achieve high accuracy localization. However, in these cascade structures, each local feature map was extracted by a separated convolutional network, without considering the relationship of local feature maps. In our work, we use related local feature maps to predict conflict points, which can improve positioning accuracy.

3   The Cascade Network Model

We cascade three levels of convolutional networks for conflict points prediction. At the first level, we use R-CNN regression of DOBB to realize vehicle detection and orientation estimation. Then at the second level, we combine key conflict points extracted by optimal motion corner detection based on DOBB as the input image and design a deep structure to predict key conflict points. Networks at the third level take three local ROIs from the second level as input and make small ranges to predict local conflict points including the front, body and back of the vehicle.

3.1   R-CNN Regression Using DOBB

This section describes how to design a deep neural network for vehicle detection and driving direction estimation our proposed method differs from the traditional 2D bounding box, we use RCNN regression to estimate the original bounding box and orientation, then combine these estimations to produce a DOBB which is considered as a minimum-area encasing box with the target object.

DOBB Definition. Adding bounding boxes for objects is intended to complete target detection, so as to realize accurate collision detection or prediction. The bounding boxes used in deep learning methods are always based on an axis aligned bounding box (AABB) [18] or an oriented bounding box (OBB) [19]. In an AABB each edge is parallel to axis direction as in Fig. 1(a), so it is easy to create, but its tightness is poor. Then research proposed the OBB, a minimum rectangle bounding box with one edge along the orientation of the object principal component, so it rotates along with object rotation. But it may still have a large void as in Fig. 1(b). Therefore, in order to realize accurate detection of intelligent vehicles and predict conflict points more precisely, we present a deformed oriented bounding box (DOBB) as in Fig. 2(d) to realize minimum-area encasing the target. The concrete implementation steps are explained as follows.

First, we need to determine the object principal component. We obtain an eigenvector based on the Principal Component Analysis (PCA) algorithm [20]. Then we could get the principal axis of the OBB, and the long axis is used to mark the driving direction of the vehicle.

$$A = \begin{bmatrix} cov(x, x) & cov(x, y) \\ cov(x, y) & cov(y, y) \end{bmatrix} \tag{1}$$

Where, $cov(x_i, x_j) = E[(x_i - \mu_i)(x_j - \mu_j)]$.

Secondly, the original 2D bounding box allows us to determine the DOBB's centre and half-extent lengths. If we change the orientation of short-axis to the original orientation, then we can get the long-axis OBB of the vehicle, whose shape is parallelogram as in Fig. 1(c).

Finally, the intersections of the OBB in Fig. 1(b) and the long-axis OBB in Fig. 1(c), we could get a deformed OBB in Fig. 1(d), which can obtain a minimum available area as a polygon bounding box.

a   *b*   *c*   *d*

Fig. 1. AABB, OBB and DOBB of vehicle image (a) AABB (b) OBB (c) Long-axis OBB (d) DOBB

Network Structure Selection. To realize DOBB detection, we use R-CNN networks to create DOBB. We assume that the 2D object detector has been trained to produce a bounding box that corresponds to the DOBB. The DOBB is described by its centre T = [t_x, t_y], dimensions D = [d_x, d_y] and local orientation R = [θ_x, θ_y] parameterized by azimuth θ. Assuming that the origin of the object coordinate frame is at the centre of the OBB and the dimensions D are known, the coordinates of the DOBB corners can be described simply by:

$$X_1 = \left[-d_x/2, d_y/2\right]^T, X_2 = \left[0, d_y/2\right]^T, X_3 = \left[d_x/2, d_y/2 - d_x/2\right]^T$$
$$X_4 = \left[d_x/2, -d_y/2\right]^T, X_5 = \left[0, -d_y/2\right]^T, X_6 = \left[-d_x/2, d_x/2 - d_y/2\right] \tag{2}$$

The constraints that the DOBB fits into the 2D detection window require that each point of the original 2D bounding box is related by the mapping of at least one of the DOBB points. The point-to-point correspondence constraint results in the Eq. (3):

$$\begin{cases} x_{min} = \left(K[RT]\begin{bmatrix} d_x/2 \\ -d_y/2 \end{bmatrix}\right)_x, x_{max} = \left(K[RT]\begin{bmatrix} -d_x/2 \\ d_y/2 \end{bmatrix}\right)_x \\ y_{min} = \left(K[RT]\begin{bmatrix} d_y/2 \\ -d_x/2 \end{bmatrix}\right)_y, y_{max} = \left(K[RT]\begin{bmatrix} -d_y/2 \\ d_x/2 \end{bmatrix}\right)_y \end{cases} \tag{3}$$

where (.)x and (.)y respectively refers to the x and y coordinate. In total four points of the 2D bounding box provide four constraints on the DOBB representation.

This is not enough to constrain the final DOBB. We need to add some necessary geometric properties to further constrain the DOBB. The first parameter that has an optimal effect on the DOBB is the orientation of the long axis. Apart from it, we choose to regress the box dimensions D rather than translation T because the variance of the dimension estimate is typically smaller (e.g., the same classified vehicles tend to be the same or similar size). In this paper, our approach for the DOBB box orientation and dimensions regression is shown in Fig. 2.

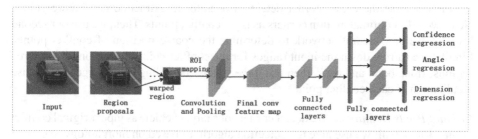

Fig. 2. Proposed architecture for orientation and dimension estimation

As shown in Fig. 2, our parameter estimation module has three branches based on multibin orientation estimation: confidence, angle and dimension regressions [14]. All the branches are derived from the same shared convolutional features and the total loss is the weighted combination of $L = \alpha \times L_{\text{dims}} + (1 - \alpha) \times L_\theta$. And we use directly the L2 distance to calculate the loss for dimension L_{dims} as:

$$L_{dims} = \frac{1}{N} \sum\nolimits_{n=1}^{N} \left\| D_n^* - \overline{D_n} \right\| \tag{4}$$

Where, D_n^* are the ground truth dimensions of the bounding box, $\overline{D_n}$ are the mean dimensions for vehicles of a certain class.

The loss function for the confidence and angle regression is shown in Eq. (5) including two branches [14]. First, we divide the orientation angle into certain pre-defined K classes, and convert the K-dimensional vector of arbitrary orientation values to another K-dimensional vector f of real values in the range [0, 1] that add up to 1. One branch for computing the confidences of classes and the other for computing the $\tan(\Delta\theta)$.

$$L_\theta = L_{\text{conf}} + \omega * L_{\text{angle}} \tag{5}$$

The confidence loss L_{conf} is the softmax loss of the confidence of each bin.

$$L_{conf} = \frac{1}{N} \sum\nolimits_{n=1}^{N} -\log\left(\frac{e^{f_n}}{\sum_{j=1}^{K} e^{f_j}} \right) \tag{6}$$

The angle L_{angle} is aimed to minimize the difference between the estimated angle and the ground truth angle,

$$L_{angle} = \frac{1}{n\theta*} \sum\nolimits_{n=1}^{n\theta*} -\log\left(\tan\left(\theta_n^* - \theta_{nc} - \delta \right) \right) \tag{7}$$

where $n_{\theta*}$ is the number of bins that cover ground truth angle θ_*, θ_{nc} is the angle of the centre of bin n, δ is the changing estimation that needs to be applied to the centre of bin n.

3.2 Multi-level CNN Regression of Conflict Points

Based on the output of the first level, we can try to extract the key features as conflict points from detected DOBB area and track these points to estimate the scale change between different frames.

First, we use the Harris corner detection operator to extract corner feature points. Next, we select optimal motion corners as input conflict points. Then, we use our second level of the deep neural network to determine the coarse position of conflict points. Finally, we narrow down the input ranges for the conflict points corresponding to three regions, front, body and back, then use three smaller bounding boxes to get the precise localization of each conflict point.

Conflict Points Definition. We detect corners of a target vehicle as input original conflict points. First of all, we use an edge detection algorithm based on morphology to extract edge points of the vehicle located in the DOBB. Then, we determine the centreline according to the detected DOBB. Finally, we use symmetry extraction based on the Harris corner detection operator to find optimal corners.

In this paper, we use cascade morphology operators C to realize vehicle edge detection as follows, because single operators such as cannot keep all the edge details.

$$\begin{cases} c_1 = (f \oplus B) \circ B - (f \oplus B) \ominus B \\ c_2 = (f \cdot B) \circ B - (f \cdot B) \ominus B \\ c_3 = (f \circ B) \oplus B - (f \circ B) \cdot B \\ c_4 = (f \ominus B) \oplus B - (f \ominus B) \cdot B \\ C = \omega_1(c_1 + c_2)/2 + \omega_2(c_3 + c_4)/2 \end{cases} \tag{8}$$

where $\oplus$, $\ominus$, $\circ$ and $\cdot$ represent dilation, erosion, opening and closing operation respectively [21], $-$ means the normal difference between the two operations.

c1 and c2: dilation and closing operation are used first to restrain strong dark noise and weak dark noise respectively, then opening and erosion operations aim to restrain bright noise and compensate edge details;

c3 and c4: erosion and opening operation are used first to restrain strong bright noise and weak bright noise respectively, then closing and dilation operations aim to restrain dark noise and guarantee bright edge against loss.

ω_1, ω_2: weight parameters, with $\omega_1 + \omega_2 = 1$, the value depends on the distribution of dark noise and bright noise in the image.

B: 3*3 structure unit including 8 directions.

Based on extracted vehicle edge and centreline of detected DOBB, we use harries detection operators to extract corners in the half side of centreline, then find the other half side corners which are nearest to symmetry points of an extracted corner based on the principal axis of detected DOBB. For example, as showed in Fig. 3, the principal axis of detected DOBB is right relative to the camera viewpoint, so we extract five corners (including two points in the front of the vehicle, one points in the body of the vehicle and two points in the back of the vehicle) located in the right side first. Harries detection operator [22] is as Eq. (9).

$$E(u, v) = \sum_{x,y} w(x, y)\big[I(x + u, y + v) - I(x, y)\big] = [u, v]M\begin{bmatrix} u \\ v \end{bmatrix} \tag{9}$$

where, $M = \sum_{x,y} w(x, y)\begin{bmatrix} I_x^2 I_x I_y \\ I_x I_y I_y^2 \end{bmatrix}$, I is image pixel matrix, w(x,y) is a Gaussian smoothing window, and Ix and Iy differences in the of x and y direction, respectively.

a   b   c

Fig. 3. The description of corner extraction method. (a) Extract five optimal corners (red) in the right side of centerline, and ten optimal corners (blue) in the left side of centerline (b) Extract symmetry points located in the left side of principal axis. (c) Find the nearest blue points to these symmetry points (Color figure online)

Shi [23] found extracted points could be considered as optimal corners when the minimal eigenvalue of M was greater than a threshold value. Thus, we select motion points as final conflict points, and delete non-motion points unrelated to vehicle collision, which can not only remove the negative effects of spurious points, but also reduce computation in our cascade networks.

Because the prediction of conflict points is not used by a single frame image, but used by a video sequence, we can delete non-motion points according to the correlation among the consecutive sequence of frames. In this paper, we extract optimal corner points as possible motion corners in three consecutive frames and save to dataset E1, E2, E3 respectively, then remove the point p does not appear in all three datasets. Figure 4 shows the results of optimal motion corners detection.

The experimental results show that the extracted optimal motion corners can cover nearly all the conflict areas of a target vehicle along the driving direction. Therefore, the detected optimal motion corners will be considered as target conflict points input into our second level convolutional network.

Network Structure Selection. The network at the second level aims to extract all the possible conflict points based on global convolutional features, and the network at the third level is used for fine adjustments according to the output of the second level, based on local convolutional features. We analyse five important factors for the choice of network structures: input, depth, layer connection, active function, and loss function.

Fig. 4. Detection of optimal motion corners in three consecutive frames.

The input of the second level is the global vehicle image including all the possible conflict points. First of all, the convolutional network at the second level should be deep. Predicting conflict points from DOBB regions is a high-level task, and the network needs to learn high-level features, which are global, while features extracted by lower layers are local due to local receptive fields. Because the location of conflict points is pixel-level calibration, and high-level features will lose a lot of spatial pixel information after multiple convolutions and pooling and make it difficult to support feature point positioning, we cascade lower layers and high layers to make up for loss spatial information. Abs (TanH) is used as the active function and L2 is used as the loss function in the second level.

The inputs of the third level include three local vehicle images: the front of the vehicle, the body of the vehicle and the back of the vehicle. We analyse three important factors for the choice of the third network structure: input, depth, and multi-objective regression. The inputs of the third level are local regions covering conflict points located in the front of the vehicle, the body of the vehicle and the back of the vehicle, respectively. Convolutional networks at the third level could be just lower levels. Because lower levels have better local features. In addition, we use multi-level regression to combine multiple convolutional networks. The output of convolution level P2 of each lower convolutional network will be combined by concatenate layer in this level, then input to the first fully connected layer to realize global non-linear conversion. The active function and loss function used are the same for the second level.

According to the feature point detection, the most common evaluation standards used recently are the mean alignment error (MAE) in Eq. (10) and Cumulative error distribution (CED):

$$e = \sum_{i=1}^{N} \left\| x_i^g - x_i^p \right\| / N \left\| x_l^g - x_r^g \right\| \tag{10}$$

where N is the total number of conflict points: x_i^g and x_i^p represent the real position and estimated position of point i. x_l^g and x_r^g represent the far-left position and the far-right position of the vehicle body. When the MAE of any point is bigger than 5%, it will be rejected as a false location.

4   Experiment Results and Analysis

The first evaluation is about our designed first level of the cascade network model. The test set consists of 1573 images, including 2990 vehicle images. Monitor cameras along the road collect all the training and test images. Images include different shooting angles and many types of vehicles. Among them, 80% are used as training images, and 20% are considered as test images. In addition, according to the target resolution and occlusion proportion, we performed our experiments on different detection difficulties, including dataset 1 with a big target size of more than 256*256 and occlusion proportion lower than 10%; dataset 2 with a medium target size between 128*128 to 256*256 and occlusion proportion between 10–20%; dataset 3 with small target size between 48*48 to 128*128 and occlusion proportion more than 20%. The number of vehicles in each dataset is respectively 550, 960 and 1480. During testing, we set the threshold of overlap between the 2D bounding box and the DOBB as 0.5. When the radio is bigger than this threshold, it is labelled as correct detection. The estimation results of OBB and DOBB based on the 2D bounding box are shown in Fig. 5.

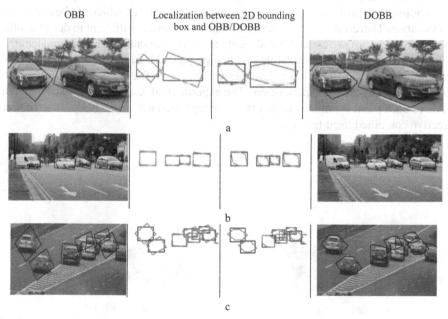

Fig. 5. OBB and DOBB detection results in different datasets. Left: OBB derived from 2D bounding box detections. Right: our DOBB improved localization. (a) Detection results based on OBB and DOBB in dataset1. (b) Detection results based on OBB and DOBB in dataset2 (c) Detection results based on OBB and DOBB in dataset3.

We can see from the bird's view of the OBB and DOBB in Fig. 5 that our DOBB can improve localization estimation over the OBB based on 2D bounding box detections (red bounding box). The DOBB can improve regional coverage of vehicles. Although sometimes it still includes some areas out of marked range, these areas are estimated according to the driving direction, so they can help us to predict conflict points more accurately. Table 1 gives the comparisons of localization estimation accuracy between OBB and DOBB. The localization estimation is defined as the ratio of target area coverage between the detected OBB or DOBB and the marked 2D bounding box.

Table 1. Comparison of the localization estimation accuracy between OBB and DOBB

Algorithm	Dataset1	Dataset2	Dataset3
OBB	89.10%	87.08%	83.68%
DOBB	96.08%	95.48%	93.65%

In addition, we also use level 2 and 3 deep networks to realize coarse to precise detection of conflict points. To test the rationality of our presented networks, we test the MAE of each level in Fig. 6. We can see that the location of each conflict point is getting closer to the real location along with the cascade structure, and the output of the third level has minor improvement over the output of the second level, which can be considered as saturation. Therefore, the three-levels cascade structure is sufficient to detect conflict points. Furthermore, we use combined local features rather than separated local features, so first we need to test the availability of feature point location after combination. We compare with the separated lower-level networks of each feature point, which have the same network structure and parameters. The experimental results in Fig. 7 show that the MAE of each point location is higher than for separated networks. It seems to be more effective combined local features.

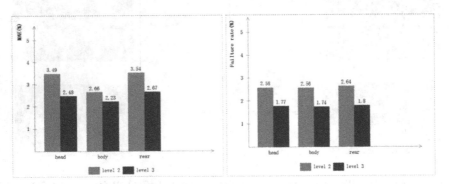

Fig. 6. Detection results of each level

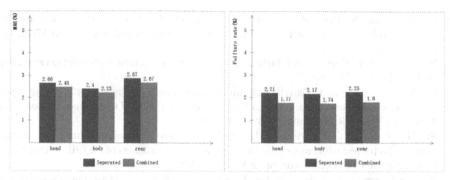

Fig. 7. The third level detection results between separated local features and combined local features

5 Conclusion

A new method for vehicle detection based on cascade deep learning is proposed. The first level of deep convolutional networks based on our presented DOBB achieves minimum area encasing of a target vehicle. Then a coarse-to-fine approach at the following two levels provides accurate location of conflict points between vehicles. The main advantage of our method is that it can eliminate the effects of vehicular body posture when predicting conflict points and improve the prediction accuracy. A lot of experiments show that our approach generalizes across different datasets and can provide fundamental information for intelligent vehicle decision and control.

Acknowledgment. The authors appreciate the Institute of highway ministry of transport's assistance in providing test images. Also, we thank Prof. Nelson Max in University of California, Davis for performing technical editing and language editing.

References

1. Gao, F., Duan, J., He, Y., Wang, Z.: A test scenario automatic generation strategy for intelligent driving systems. Math. Probl. Eng. **2019**, 1–10 (2019)
2. Cao, J., Song, C., Peng, S., Xiao, F., Song, S.: Improved traffic sign detection and recognition algorithm for intelligent vehicles. Sensors **19**(18), 4021 (2019)
3. Masaki, I.: Vision-Based Vehicle Guidance. Springer Science & Business Media (2012)
4. Wang, X., Tang, J., Niu, J., Zhao, X.: Vision-based two-step brake detection method for vehicle collision avoidance. Neurocomputing **173**, 450–461 (2016)
5. Zhang, W., et al.: Deep learning-based real-time fine-grained pedestrian recognition using stream processing. IET Intel. Transp. Syst. **12**(7), 602–609 (2018)
6. Chen, X., Xiang, S., Liu, C.L., Pan, C.H.: Vehicle detection in satellite images by hybrid deep convolutional neural networks. IEEE Geosci. Remote Sens. Lett. **11**(10), 1797–1801 (2014)
7. Zhou, Y., Nejati, H., Do, T.T., Cheung, N.M., Cheah, L.: Image-based vehicle analysis using deep neural network: a systematic study. In: 2016 IEEE International Conference on Digital Signal Processing (DSP), pp. 276–280. IEEE (2016)
8. Ren, S., He, K., Girshick, R., Sun, J.: Faster R-CNN: towards real-time object detection with region proposal networks. Adv. Neural. Inf. Process. Syst. **28**, 91–99 (2015)

9. Tang, T., Zhou, S., Deng, Z., Zou, H., Lei, L.: Vehicle detection in aerial imagesbased on region convolutional neural networks and hard negative example mining. Sensors **17**(2), 336 (2017)

10. Wang, H., Cai, Y., Chen, L.: A vehicle detection algorithm based on deep belief network. Sci. World J. **2014**, 1–7 (2014)

11. Girshick, R., Donahue, J., Darrell, T., Malik, J.: Rich feature hierarchies for ac-curate object detection and semantic segmentation. In: Proceedings of the IEEE Conference on Computer Vision and Pattern Recognition, pp. 580–587 (2014)

12. Su, H., Qi, C.R., Li, Y., Guibas, L.J.: Render for CNN: viewpoint estimation in images using CNNs trained with rendered 3d model views. In: Proceedings of the IEEE International Conference on Computer Vision, pp. 2686–2694 (2015)

13. Poirson, P., Ammirato, P., Fu, C.Y., Liu, W., Kosecka, J., Berg, A.C.: Fast singleshot detection and pose estimation. In: 2016 Fourth International Conference on 3D Vision (3DV), pp. 676–684. IEEE (2016)

14. Mousavian, A., Anguelov, D., Flynn, J., Kosecka, J.: 3d bounding box estimation using deep learning and geometry. In: Proceedings of the IEEE Conference on Computer Vision and Pattern Recognition, pp. 7074–7082 (2017)

15. Belhumeur, P.N., Jacobs, D.W., Kriegman, D.J., Kumar, N.: Localizing parts of faces using a consensus of exemplars. IEEE Trans. Pattern Anal. Mach. Intell. **35**(12), 2930–2940 (2013)

16. Jazayeri, A., Cai, H., Zheng, J.Y., Tuceryan, M.: Vehicle detection and tracking in car video based on motion model. IEEE Trans. Intell. Transp. Syst. **12**(2), 583–595 (2011)

17. Zhu, X., Ramanan, D.: Face detection, pose estimation, and landmark localization in the wild. In: 2012 IEEE Conference on Computer Vision and Pattern Recognition, pp. 2879–2886. IEEE (2012)

18. Hubbard, P.M.: Approximating polyhedra with spheres for time-critical collision detection. ACM Trans. Graph. **15**(3), 179–210 (1996)

19. Gottschalk, S., Lin, M.C., Manocha, D.: Obbtree: a hierarchical structure for rapid interference detection. In: Proceedings of the 23rd Annual Conference on Computer Graphics and Interactive Techniques, pp. 171–180 (1996)

20. Wold, S., Esbensen, K., Geladi, P.: Principal component analysis. Chemom. Intell. Lab. Syst. **2**(1–3), 37–52 (1987)

21. Sarika, K.S., Sudha, P.: An analysis of edge extraction for MRI medical images through mathematical morphological operators approaches. Int. J. Comput. Appl. 9–13 (2013)

22. Harris, C., Stephens, M., et al.: A combined corner and edge detector. In: Alvey Vision Conference, vol. 15, pp. 10–5244. Citeseer (1988)

23. Shi, J.: Good features to track. In: 1994 Proceedings of IEEE Conference on Computer Vision and Pattern Recognition, pp. 593–600. IEEE (1994)

Improving Evolutionary Generative Adversarial Networks

Zheping Liu[1](✉), Nasser Sabar[2](✉), and Andy Song[1](✉)

[1] RMIT University, Melbourne, Australia
s3811732@student.rmit.edu.au, andy.song@rmit.edu.au
[2] La Trobe University, Melbourne, Australia
n.sabar@latrobe.edu.au

Abstract. Generative adversarial network (GAN) is a powerful method to reproduce the distribution of a given data set. It is widely used for generating photo-realistic images or data collections that appear real. Evolutionary GAN (E-GAN) is one of state-of-the-art GAN variations. E-GAN combines population based search and evolutionary operators from evolutionary algorithms with GAN to enhance diversity and search performance. In this study we aim to improve E-GAN by adding transfer learning and crossover which is a key evolutionary operator that is commonly used in evolutionary algorithms, but not in E-GAN.

Keywords: Generative adversarial networks · Evolutionary algorithms · Crossover

1 Introduction

GAN (Generative Adversarial Networks) is a prominent learning method that aims to learn the data distribution of given data sets. It was first proposed in [6]. Currently, GAN is widely used in image generation, image transferring, image de-noising and other nominal data generation. GAN trains two neural networks in an adversarial matter, namely a generator and a discriminator. The generator takes randomized data from a uniform or normal distribution as its input, and outputs data of the required size. The discriminator takes input from both a training data set and the fake samples generated by the generator. It learns to classify each of these input as true of false, where true means real data, e.g. from the training data set, and false means faked data, e.g. produced by the generator. The training process of GAN is similar to a minimax search in games, but rather between the generator and the discriminator. The discriminator is trained to be able to distinguish generated samples from real data as accurately as possible. In contrast, the training of the generator is to fool the discriminator, in other words, to reduce its accuracy, by producing more realistic data samples. The objective function of conventional GAN can be expressed as in Eq. 1.

$$\min_{G} \max_{D} \mathbb{E}_{x \sim p_{data}}[log D(x)] + \mathbb{E}_{z \sim p_z}[log(1 - D(G(z)))] \tag{1}$$

© Springer Nature Switzerland AG 2022
G. Long et al. (Eds.): AI 2021, LNAI 13151, pp. 691–702, 2022.
https://doi.org/10.1007/978-3-030-97546-3_56

where $D(x)$ is the output of discriminator given samples from real data distribution; $G(z)$ is the generated sample from generator given some noise distribution z. The loss function of discriminator aims to increase the probability of identifying real samples as true, while reducing the probability of identifying generated samples as true. The loss function of the generator simply the opposite, maximising the probability of its generated samples being identified as true.

Although the effectiveness of GAN is evident in a wide range of practical applications, there are two common failures exist in conventional GAN training process, vanishing gradient [1] and mode collapse [2]. Vanishing gradient occurs when the generated samples from the generator is far too different to the real data samples, in other words, the distribution of generated samples has little overlap with the distribution of the real samples. This is often the case at the early stages of a GAN training. The generated samples usually looks like total random noises at this stage. So the discriminator can easily distinguish the real samples from the generated samples. Vanishing gradient prevents the generator from improving its performance since the generator does not receive enough valuable feedback from the discriminator. Consequently the generator and the discriminator are unlikely to converge to an equilibrium. Mode collapse happens when the generator can produce samples of good quality, but most of them fall into a similar pattern. Meaning most of the samples generated by the generators are similar to each other. Although these samples can fool the discriminator, but they have little practical value in real world applications. To minimize this issue, a certain level of diversity need to be maintained onto the generator during the GAN training process. Mode collapse and vanishing gradient together can make a conventional GAN training difficult and often require repeated restarts.

To mitigate the aforementioned two problems, a range of methods have been proposed. Among them, Evolutionary GAN (E-GAN) is an outstanding candidate, which combines evolutionary algorithms with GAN training process [14]. Instead of a single generator, a population of generators are evolved by applying three different mutations and a special fitness function. E-GAN ensures both the quality and the diversity of the generators, hence the generated samples can be improved. It can achieve state-of-the-art performance in comparison with other GAN variations [14]. Nevertheless, one area that E-GAN does not touch is crossover operator. Crossover is considered as an equally important operator as mutation operator in evolutionary algorithms. Like in the natural selection process, crossover can help offspring inherits some advantageous traits from both parents and hence could gain more fitness during the search process. One of the commonly used crossover operator for evolving neural networks is n-point crossover [13]. It is a naive method that exchanges the nodes in the parent neural networks. In this paper, we have conducted a series of study on adding n-point crossover to the existing E-GAN training process. The ultimate objective we aim to achieve is to improving the final effectiveness of E-GAN by gaining evolutionary advantages from the additional crossover operator at each iteration.

The rest of the paper is organised as following. In Sect. 2, we briefly reviews existing work related to E-GAN and E-GAN with crossover. The methodology of our proposed method is detailed in Sect. 3. The experiment setup and results are presented in Sect. 4. Section 5 elaborates our discussions and findings through this study. Finally, we conclude this investigation and lay out our future works in Sect. 6.

2 Related Works

2.1 Evolutionary GAN

Evolutionary approach is introduced into GAN to mitigate the challenges in GAN, namely Vanishing Gradient and Mode Collapse. That is known as E-GAN [14]. The foundation of evolutionary approach is search strategy that simulates the survival-of-the-fittest hypothesis in biological world. Instead of an individual solution for a particular problem, a group of potential solutions are produced, which is called a population. Every solution is assigned with a fitness value, which is the performance measure of each individual in terms of solving the particular task. In the context of GAN, the fitness is two-fold, (1) the loss function of the discriminator which is to be maximised, and (2) the loss function of the generator which is to minimised. Individuals which have a fitness measure better than others in the population would have higher chance to participate in the reproduction of the new generation. The solutions in the next generation can be direct copy of solutions from the parent generation, or solutions generated by mutation or crossover of the selected parent solutions.

E-GAN follows the same principle, meaning generators are produced repetitively using the cycle of evaluation, selection and reproduction. The key step is the reproduction phase, where new generators are produced by three types of mutation operators. They are Minimax mutation, Heuristic mutation and Least Square mutation. Their respective expressions are presented below in Eqs. 2–4.

$$\mathcal{M}_G^{minimax} = \frac{1}{2}\mathbb{E}_{z\sim p_z}[log(1 - D(G(z)))] \tag{2}$$

$$\mathcal{M}_G^{heuristic} = -\frac{1}{2}\mathbb{E}_{z\sim p_z}[log(D(G(z)))] \tag{3}$$

$$\mathcal{M}_G^{least-square} = \mathbb{E}_{z\sim p_z}[(D(G(z) - 1)^2] \tag{4}$$

The fitness of each generator is computed at the evaluation phase. In E-GAN, the fitness is the higher the better. Generators with higher fitness score will more likely to be selected to be the base for the next generation. E-GAN's fitness measure considers both quality and diversity of the generated samples, hence it has two components. Firstly there is a quality measure $\mathcal{F}_q$ expressed in Eq. 5. It computes the expected outcome of the discriminator ∇_D given samples generated by different offspring. The output will be a probability $[0 \sim 1]$ of how likely the samples are from the real data distribution. Secondly, there is a diversity measure $\mathcal{F}_d$ expressed in Eq. 6. These two parts are combined as a fitness as shown in Eq. 7, where the γ in front of $\mathcal{F}_d$ is a coefficient that can adjust the influence of the diversity factor on the overall fitness of the individual generator.

$$\mathcal{F}_q = \mathbb{E}_z[D(G(z))] \tag{5}$$

$$\mathcal{F}_d = -log||\nabla_D - \mathbb{E}_x[logD(x)] - \mathbb{E}_z[log(1 - D(G(z)]|| \tag{6}$$

$$\mathcal{F} = \mathcal{F}_q + \gamma \times \mathcal{F}_d \tag{7}$$

E-GAN can show its effectiveness on benchmark datasets including CIFAR-10 [9], CelebA [10] and LSUN [15], both in terms of minimising vanishing gradient and minimising mode collapse. However, because of the population based approach, E-GAN requires more computational cost and may slow down the search. In some scenario the efficiency of E-GAN can be a concern.

3   Methodology

In this study we propose adding n-point crossover into E-GAN. N-point crossover is naive but effective crossover operator, and this is often applied to neural networks evolution [3–5,8]. The idea of n-point crossover is straightforward. Firstly, two fittest offspring from the population will be selected as parents for this crossover operator. The selection method is by computing the fitness scores of all individuals in the population, and rank them accordingly. After two parents are selected, a given number of nodes in the neural network architectures will be randomly selected, i.e. n points will be selected, where n is an even number to enable pairing. For each pair of selected nodes, this method will exchange all nodes between them in the two parents networks. For the purpose of producing only one fittest offspring after crossover operation, the offspring will be initialized using the parameters from the fitter parent. Then those nodes are to be exchanged with the other parent which is less fit. The process of n-point crossover is displayed in Fig. 1.

In the original E-GAN, each iteration follows the process of mutation, evaluation and selection. In our proposed method, the process in each iteration is mutation, evaluation, crossover, evaluation again and selection. To be more specific, after mutation in each iteration is performed, we first evaluate all the mutated offspring by computing their fitness values. Next, two fittest offspring will be retained, and they will be parents of the crossover operator. After crossover, one crossover offspring will be produced, and its fitness score is evaluated. If its fitness score exceeds at least one of its parents, we replace the inferior parent with this crossover offspring. At the end of each iteration, we always select the fittest two offspring to proceed into next iteration. The flow of E-GAN with crossover is displayed in Fig. 2. The pseudo code is listed in Algorithm 1.

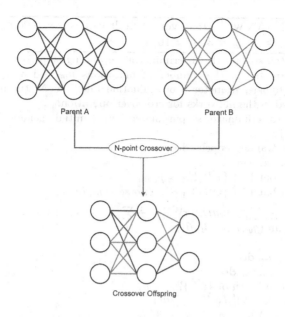

Fig. 1. n-point crossover

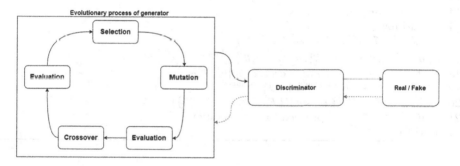

Fig. 2. Flow of E-GAN with crossover

Besides applying n-point crossover to the original E-GAN, we have conducted extra experiments on applying it to Partial Transfer training based E-GAN (PT-EGAN). PT-EGAN is a variation of E-GAN which focuses on reducing the training time.

Algorithm 1. E-GAN with crossover. Default values $\alpha = 0.0002, \beta_1 = 0.5, \beta_2 = 0.999, n_D = 2, n_p = 2, n_m = 3, m = 16, \gamma = 0.01$

Require: the batch size m; the discriminator's updating steps per iteration n_D; the number of parents n_p; the number of mutations n_m, Adam hyper-parameters α, β_1, β_2; the hyper-parameter γ of evaluation function; N, the number of nodes will be selected in the networks for crossover operation.

Require: initial discriminator's parameters w_0; initial generators' parameters $\{\theta_0^1, \theta_0^2, ...\theta_0^{n_p}\}$.

1: **for** number of training epochs **do**
2:     **for** $k = 0, ..., n_D$ **do**
3:         Sample a batch of $\{x^{(i)}\}_{i=1}^m \sim p_{data}$
4:         Sample a batch of $\{z^{(i)}\}_{i=1}^m \sim p_z(noise\ samples)$
5:         $g_w \leftarrow \nabla_w[\frac{1}{m}\sum_{i=1}^m logD_w(x^{(i)})] + \frac{1}{m}\sum_{i=1}^{\frac{m}{n_p}} log(1 - D_w(G_{\theta^j}(z^{(i)})))$
6:         $w \leftarrow$ Adam $(g_w, w, \alpha, \beta_1, \beta_2)$
7:     **end for**
8:     **for** $j = 0, ..., n_p$ **do**
9:         **for** $h = 0, ..., n_m$ **do**
10:            Sample a batch of $\{z^{(i)}\}_{i=1}^m \sim p_z$
11:            $g_{\theta^{j,h}} \leftarrow \nabla_{\theta^j}\mathcal{M}_G^h(\{z^{(i)}\}_{i=1}^m, \theta^j)$
12:            $\theta_{child}^{j,h} \leftarrow$ Adam $(g_{\theta^{j,h}}, \theta^j, \alpha, \beta_1, \beta_2)$
13:            $\mathcal{F}^{j,h} \leftarrow \mathcal{F}_q^{j,h} + \gamma\mathcal{F}_d^{j,h}$
14:         **end for**
15:     **end for**
16:     $\{\mathcal{F}^{j_1,h_1}, \mathcal{F}^{j_2,h_2}, ...\} \leftarrow sort(\{\mathcal{F}^{j,h}\})$
17:     $\theta^1, \theta^2, ..., \theta^{n_p} \leftarrow \theta_{child}^{j_1,h_1}, \theta_{child}^{j_2,h_2}, ..., \theta_{child}^{j_{n_p},h_{n_p}}$
18:     $\theta^{crossover} \leftarrow N - point - crossover\{\theta^1, \theta^2\}$
19:     $\mathcal{F}^{crossover} \leftarrow \mathcal{F}_q^{crossover} + \gamma\mathcal{F}_d^{crossover}$
20:     $\{\mathcal{F}^{best}, \mathcal{F}^{2nd\_best}\} \leftarrow sort(\{\mathcal{F}^1, \mathcal{F}^2, \mathcal{F}^{crossover}\})$
21:     $\theta^{best}, \theta^{2nd\_best}$ will proceed to next iteration
22: **end for**

---

4   Experiments

In our experiments, CIFAR-10 [9] dataset are used to train the networks. This is a relatively small dataset which only contains 50000 images in total, and these images are separated into 10 different categories, each contains 5000 images. Every image in this dataset is 32×32 pixels.

4.1   Experiment Setup

The implementation of PT-EGAN for this study is based on Pytorch. Experiments were under Python 3. The computational environment is a RTX2060, with 16 GB RAM and an AMD Ryzen 9 4900H CPU. That is consistent for all experiments presented here. For comparison purposes, the original E-GAN and PT-EGAN are also evaluated under the same computational environment using identical hyper-parameters. The evaluation metrics we used is Frechet Inception

Distance score (FID) [7], which is an improvement of the Inception Score (IS) [12]. It computes the similarity between two different sets of images by measuring their Frechet distance between each other. These data sets are treated as two multi-dimensional Gaussian distributions. The calculation follows the following formula where m and C are the mean and covariance of generated images and m_w and C_w are those of real images.

$$\mathcal{FID} = ||m - m_w||_2^2 + Tr(C + C_r - 2(CC_r)^{1/2}) \tag{8}$$

Obvious the distance between the two Gaussian distributions is the lower the better. Small FID score indicates high similarity between the generated and the real.

4.2   Experimental Results

E-GAN The experiments we obtained from our experiments is displayed in Fig. 3. The vertical axis shows the average FID obtained across several runs of the algorithms, and the horizontal axis lists the number of iterations the algorithms have been running. The scoring interval in our experiment is every 5000 iterations. The FID computation algorithm occasionally return no result at some points. To make the graph smoother, the nodes without any valid results are removed.

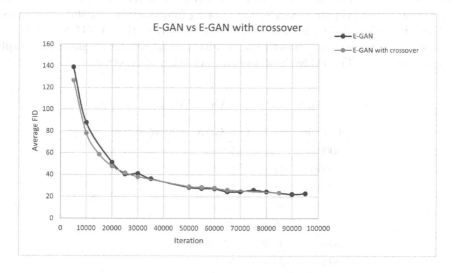

Fig. 3. Results graph - E-GAN vs E-GAN with crossover

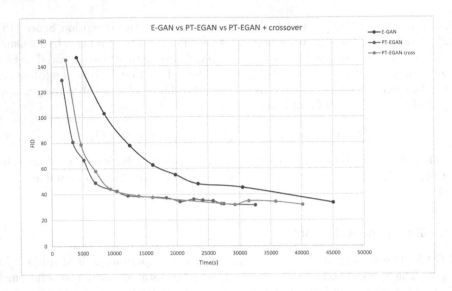

Fig. 4. Results graph - E-GAN vs PT-EGAN vs PT-EGAN with crossover

PT-EGAN. The results of applying PT-EGAN is displayed in Table 2 and Fig. 4. In the graph, the unit on the horizontal axis is replaced with training time in seconds. This is to demonstrate that PT-EGAN can reduce the training time comparing to the original E-GAN. The scoring frequency is still 5000 iterations, and in PT-EGAN, 5000 iterations will take shorter time than E-GAN. Similar to previous experiment, we removed nodes with invalid results to make the graph appear smoother. The table displays some selection of results.

Table 1. Results table - E-GAN vs E-GAN with crossover

Iteration	E-GAN	E-GAN with crossover
5000	139.03	126.64
10000	87.80	77.99
20000	51.24	47.60
25000	40.44	41.65
30000	40.92	37.97
60000	27.20	27.83
80000	24.45	N/A
85000	N/A	23.37

Table 2. Results table - E-GAN vs PT-EGAN vs PT-EGAN with crossover

Time (s)	E-GAN	Time (s)	PT-EGAN	Time (s)	PT-EGAN with crossover
4071.469	147.1291	1736.754	129.4942	2376.492	145.215
12505.7	77.73038	5167.337	66.47412	7074.22	57.81097
19800.86	55.12421	10460.14	42.2897	13867.83	38.6156
30468.96	45.21188	18316.97	37.19666	27058.16	32.73419
52072.69	32.74466	22693.84	36.13446	31477.39	34.72791
59124.92	28.19125	25790.64	34.7554	40184.41	31.81702

5 Discussion

From the above Figs. 3 and 4, it can be seen that adding n-point crossover to E-GAN and PT-EGAN did not significantly improving the performance during the training process. To find out the reason behind these insignificance, we took a more careful analysis on the results of E-GAN with crossover. We first thought this insignificance was caused by the inferiority of crossover offspring. However, from the experiment records, it turns out that the individuals participating in the crossover are actually quite fit. The Fig. 5 shows the selection rate during a particular E-GAN with crossover run through. As this graph shows, the crossover is not often selected at the very early stages. But as the training progresses, the select rate dramatically increases until finally reached around 0.48. This implies crossover offspring have very high probability being superior than other mutation offspring in later stage of the training. This do prove that crossover is having positive influence to the performance of E-GAN, nevertheless, from the evaluation results, this improvement is insignificant.

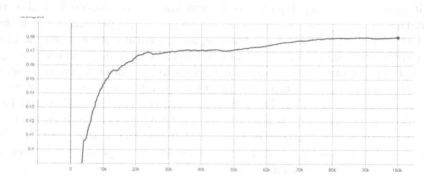

Fig. 5. Crossover offspring select rate during one training

Although adding crossover to E-GAN did not bring much boost to its effectiveness, there are valuable observation can be drawn from the different experiments conducted above. There are several hyper-parameters in the E-GAN with crossover. First one is the number of N in N-point crossover, this parameter determines how many nodes will be selected in the networks of both parents. To simplify the experiments, for each pair of nodes (all nodes between them will be exchanged), they will be picked from the same level of layer. Under this condition, we used N $\{2, 4, 6\}$. With $N = 6$, one pair of nodes in each hidden layer were selected in the networks. Similarly, with $N = 4$ and $N = 2$, we selected one pair of nodes in two or one of the hidden layers.

With higher N value, there is a generally higher probability of exchanging more nodes in the networks. Exchanging more nodes in the fitter parent from the inferior parent will make the crossover offspring more like the inferior parent. So the final performance of exchanging too much nodes is not that promising. That can bee seen from the results of our experiments. In Table 1, we can see there is a slight difference in final results between different N choices in our experiments. The difference here is quite small, but it shows a trend of decreases in the final performance as number of nodes (layers) increases (Table 3).

Table 3. Average final FID of different choices of N

N	Average FID
2	21.887
4	22.419
6	23.125

After finding out the above observation, we have done more experiments focusing on performing two-points crossover on a single layer. Rather than randomly choosing the layer where these two points are selected, we manually control it as one of the hyper-parameters. And another conclusion was observed about this hyper-parameter. In neural network area, people commonly believe that lower layers in a network is extracting more general features from the input [11]. On the other hand, higher layers are believed to handle more problem specific features. In our context, exchange nodes in the lower layers of different networks should have less impact to the final results. The results of our experiments are listed in Table 4. From these results, the correlation between layer level and final performance is not obvious. Exchanging both the high layer and low layer bring better performance than exchanging the middle layer. In addition, the differences between them are very small as it is possible that they are caused by minor errors during training.

Table 4. Average final FID of different layer

Layer	Average FID
Low	21.816
Middle	22.441
High	21.563

6 Conclusion

In this study, we aim to improve the performance of E-GAN by adding crossover operator. The crossover operator we experimented with was n-point crossover which simply exchanges an arbitrary number of nodes in parents networks. Although there are some researches supporting that adding n-point crossover can be constructive to building the neural networks, our experiments results did not show much of significance. After the analysis of experiment results, we conclude on the following points. Firstly, n-point crossover operation has been selected in the E-GAN training, and the selection rate raises gradually during the training. Secondly, the most significant hyper-parameter in this crossover operator is the number of nodes to be selected, i.e. n in the n-point crossover. As n increases, there is higher chance that more nodes will be exchanged between the parents, and brings slightly inferior results to this algorithm. Finally, exchanging nodes at different level of layers does not bring obvious differences.

References

1. Arjovsky, M., Bottou, L.: Towards principled methods for training generative adversarial networks. arXiv preprint arXiv:1701.04862 (2017)
2. Arora, S., Zhang, Y.: Do GANs actually learn the distribution? An empirical study. arXiv: abs/1706.08224 (2017)
3. Arotaritei, D.: Genetic algorithm for fuzzy neural networks using locally crossover. Int. J. Comput. Commun. Control 6(1), 8–20 (2011)
4. Foo, Y.W., Goh, C., Lim, H.C., Zhan, Z.H., Li, Y.: Evolutionary neural network based energy consumption forecast for cloud computing. In: 2015 International Conference on Cloud Computing Research and Innovation (ICCCRI), pp. 53–64. IEEE (2015)
5. García-Pedrajas, N., Ortiz-Boyer, D., Hervás-Martínez, C.: An alternative approach for neural network evolution with a genetic algorithm: crossover by combinatorial optimization. Neural Netw. 19(4), 514–528 (2006)
6. Goodfellow, I.J., et al.: Generative adversarial networks. arXiv: abs/1406.2661 (2014)
7. Heusel, M., Ramsauer, H., Unterthiner, T., Nessler, B., Hochreiter, S.: GANs trained by a two time-scale update rule converge to a local Nash equilibrium. arXiv preprint arXiv:1706.08500 (2017)
8. Kim, K.J., Cho, S.B.: Prediction of colon cancer using an evolutionary neural network. Neurocomputing 61, 361–379 (2004)

9. Krizhevsky, A., Hinton, G., et al.: Learning multiple layers of features from tiny images (2009)
10. Liu, Z., Luo, P., Wang, X., Tang, X.: Deep learning face attributes in the wild. In: Proceedings of the IEEE International Conference on Computer Vision, pp. 3730–3738 (2015)
11. Mo, S., Cho, M., Shin, J.: Freeze the discriminator: a simple baseline for fine-tuning GANs. arxiv 2020. arXiv preprint arXiv:2002.10964 (2020)
12. Salimans, T., Goodfellow, I., Zaremba, W., Cheung, V., Radford, A., Chen, X.: Improved techniques for training GANs. arXiv preprint arXiv:1606.03498 (2016)
13. Spears, W.M., Anand, V.: A study of crossover operators in genetic programming. In: Ras, Z.W., Zemankova, M. (eds.) ISMIS 1991. LNCS, vol. 542, pp. 409–418. Springer, Heidelberg (1991). https://doi.org/10.1007/3-540-54563-8_104
14. Wang, C., Xu, C., Yao, X., Tao, D.: Evolutionary generative adversarial networks. IEEE Trans. Evol. Comput. **23**, 921–934 (2019)
15. Yu, F., Seff, A., Zhang, Y., Song, S., Funkhouser, T., Xiao, J.: LSUN: construction of a large-scale image dataset using deep learning with humans in the loop. arXiv preprint arXiv:1506.03365 (2015)

Natural Language Processing and Data Mining

Focus-Based Text Summarisation with Hybrid Embeddings

Jingli Shi[1], Lui Hellesoe[1], Guan Wang[1], Weihua Li[1(✉)], and Quan Bai[2]

[1] Auckland University of Technology, Auckland, New Zealand
{jingli.shi,weihua.li}@aut.ac.nz, {mwx9073,guan.wang}@autuni.ac.nz
[2] University of Tasmania, Hobart, Australia
quan.bai@utas.edu.au

Abstract. Text summarisation has been recognised as an important Natural Language Processing task, attracting great attention from both researchers and practitioners. It has been widely adopted in various domains. For example, text summarisation of news, articles and book chapters can produce a short text, assisting the readers with grasping the main idea rapidly. In the medical domain, it is also applied to summarise the patients' questions. However, it is very challenging to control the summariser output by producing domain-specific summaries since the focus of domain-specific information may be ignored. In this paper, we propose a novel summarisation model aiming at producing summaries by focusing on the domain-specific knowledge, where hybrid embeddings, i.e., focus, domain and context embeddings, are utilised. We conduct extensive experiments to evaluate our novel model by using the MeQSum dataset. The experimental results demonstrate that our model outperforms state-of-the-art algorithms.

Keywords: Text summarisation · Hybrid embeddings · Domain-specific summarisation

1 Introduction

Grasping the main idea of a long article with less time turns out to be beneficial, especially with the huge volume of data being produced through the Internet. Text summarisation has been proved to be an effective solution, automatically filtering the foremost important information and assisting people with exploring critical content for decision-making. The research of Text Summarisation has a long history date back to the 1950s, where statistic methods were adopted [15]. It is acknowledged as one of the most important Natural Language Processing (NLP) tasks, aiming to distil the essential information and create meaningful and coherent summaries from a text. There are three major approaches, including (1) extractive methods, aiming at identifying and extracting high scoring sentences to build up a summary, (2) abstractive methods, understanding and paraphrasing the text without copying the original sentences, (3) hybrid methods, a combination of both extractive and abstractive methods. Based on these

© Springer Nature Switzerland AG 2022
G. Long et al. (Eds.): AI 2021, LNAI 13151, pp. 705–715, 2022.
https://doi.org/10.1007/978-3-030-97546-3_57

three approaches, most existing studies have been dedicated to generic text summarisation, where the domain-specific information is not taken into consideration [5, 7, 23]. In other words, many existing models are only applicable to the available domains, e.g., general news articles, where the current trendy pre-trained language models, e.g., BERT [3], are adopted. However, there are numerous domain-specific documents in the real world, e.g., biomedical reports and legislative instruments. The same term may give different meanings in different domains, and specific domains normally possess exclusive terms that are rarely seen in open domains. Thus, the general text summariser will inevitably ignore the domain-specific features and lose the focus on specialised keywords, leading to missing the critical information associated with the domain. In this sense, how to develop an effective summariser, focusing on the domain-specific features, turns out to be important [22]. A few research works are dedicated to developing text summarisers for a particular domain, e.g., medical and biomedical, with semantic-based approaches [4, 20] and deep learning models [2, 8, 12].

Domain focus (focus for short), referred to as the domain-specific information, is acknowledged as one of the main factors, significantly influencing the summary generation process and determining the desired subject of the summary. Existing research works have proved the importance of focus in decomposing consumer health questions since the focus information potentially increases the quality of summaries [21].

Motivated by this background, we propose a novel and effective focus-based model for domain-specific text summarisation in this paper. To extract the focus, we develop a module with a fine-tuned language model on the in-domain datasets. Named Entity Recognition (NER) is performed to extract the domain-specific entities of the given text automatically. Meanwhile, the hybrid embeddings strategy, including focus embeddings, domain embeddings and context embeddings, is utilised in our model. Both focus and domain context is involved as the guidance in the summarisation process. Therefore, the novel model can address the challenges of missing critical domain-specific keywords in the summary text, producing summaries relevant to the domain. We conduct extensive experiments to evaluate the performance of the proposed model. The experimental results demonstrate that our model can outperform state-of-the-art algorithms.

The rest of this paper is organised as follow. Section 2 introduces the related works and critiques the limitations, while Sect. 3 elaborates on the proposed focus-based text summarisation model. In Sect. 4, we conduct two experiments to evaluate the performance of the proposed focus-based summariser. Next, an ablation study is conducted to verify the contribution of focus embedding and domain embedding. Lastly, Sect. 5 concludes the papers and gives the future work.

2   Related Works

Summary extraction can improve the readability of long documents and the efficiency of searching information, assisting readers with obtaining more applicable information to specific domains. In recent years, deep learning has been widely adopted in text summarisation using the benchmark datasets compiled from open-domain articles, such as CNN/DailyMail [9] and XSum [18]. For example, Nallapati et al. propose a Recurrent Neural Network (RNN) based sequence model, called SummaRuNNer, for extractive summarisation of documents, where a two-layer bi-directional GRU-RNN is included [17]. Furthermore, large corpora can be utilised to obtain a better outcome using large-scale pre-trained language models. For example, the development of BERT [3] demonstrates the power of pre-trained language models with bidirectional encoding, providing more resounding synonymous words translating to shorter accurate summaries.

Most existing studies are dedicated to generic text summarisation, where only the original text is used as input, and the process mainly relies on the pre-trained language models. Even though some language models are pre-trained on an in-domain dataset, they occasionally produce generic summaries without the domain-specific keywords or information. Different from generic summarisation, domain-specific text summarisation tends to produce a short text that is highly relevant to the domain. Many studies attempt to address the text summarisation problem in specific domains, and most of them mainly focus on the biomedical domain [4, 20]. Wang et al. explore the domain shift phenomenon and prove that a model trained on one domain dataset performs poorly on another different domain [24]. Reeve et al. adopt the concepts derived from domain-specific sources and suggest using lexical chaining and frequency distribution approaches to identify the salient sentences in biomedical texts [20]. Abacha et al. introduce three summarisation tasks in the medical domain, including the consumer health question summarisation [1]. The objective is to understand the in-domain queries for a better answer retrieval performance. Similarly, Yifan et al. report the participation in the MEDIQA 2021 question summarisation task, where a re-ranker is involved in the proposed framework [8].

However, most existing studies on domain-specific text summarisation require domain experts to annotate the domain-specific documents manually. With limited resources, automatically producing abstracts from many records is a cost-effective alternative, saving both time and resources. Moreover, the focus of the domain-specific terms is ignored in the process of producing text summarisation. To tackle the challenges mentioned above, we propose a focus-based text summarisation model where the domain focus, domain context and word context are considered. We utilise the domain-specific language model, which can detect the focus and generate the domain context for summarisation. The details of the model are introduced in the following sections.

3   Focus-Based Text Summariser

The main idea of this Focus-based Text Summariser is to highlight the focus and domain information from the source text and involved them in the summarisation generation process. To achieve this, we propose a dynamic hybrid embedding strategy by fusing focus embeddings, domain embeddings and context embeddings.

Figure 1 demonstrates the overall picture of the focus-based text summariser, which consists of three major components, i.e., hybrid embeddings fusion, encoder and decoder. The details are elaborated as follows.

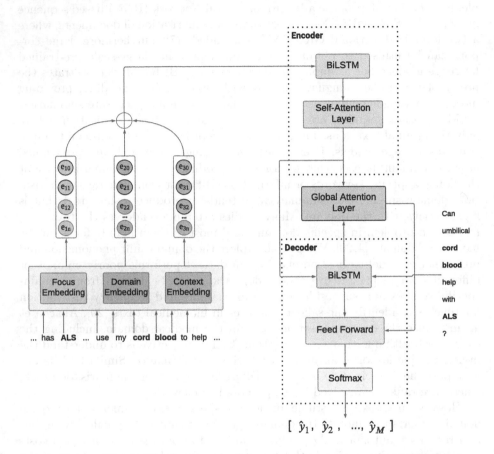

Fig. 1. The framework of focus-based text summariser

Problem Formulation. First of all, we formally define the text summarisation problem. Given a sentence, denoted by $qs = \{w_1, w_2, ..., w_N\}$, where N denotes the number of words. The objective of the text summariser is to learn the mapping $qs \rightarrow y$. $y = \{y_1, y_2, ..., y_M\}$ presents the generated summary with M words.

Hybrid Embeddings Fusion. Hybrid fusion is the critical component of the focus-based text summariser, where three types of embeddings are involved in the fusion process.

Mathematically, for each sentence qs, three continuous representations, i.e., context embedding E^c, domain embedding E^d and focus embedding E^f, are obtained via three separate embedding layers. Then, we concatenate three embeddings $E = E^c \oplus E^d \oplus E^f$ and feed the final embedding into a BiLSTM layer of the encoder to generate the hidden states in Eq. 1.

$$h^e = [\overrightarrow{LSTM}(e^c; e^d; e^f); \overleftarrow{LSTM}(e^c; e^d; e^f)] \tag{1}$$

On top of the representations generated by the BiLSTM layer, one self-attention layer is implemented to learn the long-term dependencies of the input sequence.

$$h^e_{sa} = \sigma(\frac{QK^T}{\sqrt{d_k}})V, \tag{2}$$

where Q, K and V refer to the query, key and value matrices, respectively. σ presents the activation function $Softmax$.

Given all the encoder hidden states h^e_{sa} and decoder hidden states h^d, the global attention distribution of the source sequence is calculated in Eq. 3.

$$\alpha^e_t = \frac{exp(s^e_t)}{\sum_{k=1} exp(s^e_k)}, \tag{3}$$

where $s^e_t = s(h^e_{sa}, h^d)$ denotes the alignment score, which is calculated by the content-based score function proposed in [16].

Next, we define the context vector of the source sequence for the target tokens in Eq. 4.

$$cv^e = \sum \alpha^e h^e_{sa} \tag{4}$$

Finally, the attention hidden state $\hat{h}^a$ is obtained together with the decoder hidden state h^d, and the vocabulary distribution is calculated in Eqs. 5 and 6, respectively.

$$\hat{h}^a = W_a(cv^a \oplus h^d) + b_a \tag{5}$$

$$P_{vocab} = \sigma(W_z\hat{h}^a + b_z), \tag{6}$$

where W_a and W_z are weight parameters, and b_a and b_z are bias parameters. σ refers to the activation function $Softmax$.

To train the proposed framework, we use the negative log-likelihood as the loss function formulated in Eq. 7.

$$\iota = -\sum_i p(y_i|\hat{y}_i, x, \theta), \tag{7}$$

where y_i is the reference summary, and $\hat{y}_i$ indicates the generated summary. x means the input sequence of the source text. θ presents the parameters.

4 Experiments

In this section, two experiments are conducted. The first experiment aims to evaluate the performance of the proposed focus-based text summariser, and the second experiment validates the contribution of each component.

4.1 Experiment Settings

Our experiments are implemented in PyTorch on an NVIDIA P100 GPU. The embedding dimension of context, domain and focus are 768, 768 and 30, respectively. The number of hidden units is 512. In all experiments, the batch size is set to 64. We adopt Adam optimizer with the default setting $eps = 1 \times 10^{-9}$.

4.2 Datasets

We choose MeQSum[1] as our benchmark dataset for model training and evaluation. This dataset comes from the medical domain and consists of 1,000 consumer health questions and gold standard summaries annotated professionally [1,12]. Some of the questions have been categorised into subjects describing the critical points of the question. A message with a detailed query is also available. Figure 2 demonstrates two sample records from the dataset.

However, some records have spelling and grammatical mistakes, potentially causing poor quality summaries. There are also some redundant texts and tags included in the source text. Therefore, we employ off-the-shelf services to address all the errors and remove the noise from the datasets.

4.3 Experimental Setup

Focus Detection. Since the data set adopted for the experiment comes from the medical domain. To detect the focus, BERN [10], based on BioBERT [11], is selected as the focus extractor in the experiment. A NER task is performed to capture the domain-specific entities involved in the text summarisation process.

Domain Embedding. Domain embedding can improve the performance of generating domain-related summaries [25]. In this experiment, we also fine-tune BioBERT [11] by using the data set. The hidden states from the BioBERT outputs are utilised as the domain embeddings. In terms of context embedding, BERT [3] is adopted.

4.4 Baseline Models

As the counterparts of the proposed model, the following baselines, which undergo the same experiment settings, are utilised in the experiments.

---

[1] https://github.com/abachaa/MeQSum.

Question:
SUBJECT: Blood Sugar Levels and Parkinson's
MESSAGE: I'm wondering if there is a correlation between blood sugar level's and how it may effect the presentation of Parkinson's particularly in tremors. It seems that extreme blood sugar levels would make the tremors a great deal worse and appearing none typical.

Summary: Is there a connection between blood sugar levels and symptoms of Parkinson's disease?

Question:
Can arteries in any part of the body spasm or is this only possible with coronary arteries? If so, does someone with vasospastic angina have a greater chance of developing spasms elsewhere in the body and is the treatment the same?

Summary: What are the causes of and treatment for artery spasms?

Fig. 2. Question and summary pair samples in the MeQSum dataset. Texts in red show the main focus, texts in blue refer to the clues of the domain question query, and the black relates to the context (Color figure online)

- **CopyNet** [6]. CopyNet capitalises on the sequence-to-sequence problem, noting that copied sections from the original document get chosen for the output sequence. The copying mechanism uses a sequence-to-sequence method to extract important aspects from the document, generating novel connecting words. We separately use copy mechanism and attention mechanism as our baselines.
- **T5** [19]. T5 is designed to improve downstream tasks in NLP. T5 showcases transfer learning by fine-tuning a model to predict the entire text. Using a standard encoder-decoder stack with shared parameters, T5 provides reduced computational costs, performing well on custom de-noising objectives.
- **BART** [13]. BART copies the information from the input but manipulates the information, similar to a de-noising pre-training objective for language models. BART can be fine-tuned to integrate supporting evidence found across the input document with out-of-scope background knowledge. Fine-tuning can produce highly abstractive summaries that are generally factually accurate.
- **PEGASUS** [26]. PEGASUS extracts and scores sentences directly from the source document. Excelling in low-resource environments, Pegasus incorporates sequence-to-sequence learning and principle sentence selection. The final summary combines highly prominent sentences to generate a novel abstract.

4.5 Evaluation Metrics

As ROUGE [14] is the most widely adopted measurement in the field of text summarisation, we also choose ROUGE to evaluate our model and report the results of F1 score ROUGE metrics. ROUGE_1 and ROUGE_2 refer to the overlap of uni-gram and bi-gram between the source text and the generated summary. ROUGE_L describes the longest common sub-sequence.

4.6 Experimental Results and Analysis

We conduct all the experiments through Google Colab[2]. The focus-based text summariser model is trained from scratch using 80% of the MeQSum dataset and reports the results on the rest 20% of the dataset. The experimental results are listed in Table 1. The results show that our proposed model outperforms all the baselines in terms of Rouge_2, Rouge_1 and Rouge_L.

The results prove that our hybrid embeddings mechanism can effectively improve the performance of domain-specific text summarisation even our model is light-weighted.

Table 1. Results comparison with the baseline models.

Models	Rouge_2	Rouge_1	Rouge_L
CopyNet(Attention)	0.0456	0.2619	0.2582
CopyNet(Copy)	0.0907	0.3031	0.3015
T5(base)	0.2031	0.3372	0.3216
BART(large)	0.0131	0.1214	0.0741
PEGASUS(large)	0.2409	0.3443	0.3408
Proposed	**0.2604**	**0.3583**	**0.3520**

4.7 Ablation Study

In this section, the ablation study is conducted to analyse the contributions and effects of domain embedding and focus embedding on the question text summarisation task. The experimental results on the MeQSum dataset are shown in Table 2.

As can be seen from the table, the proposed model's performance is significantly degraded when we remove the domain and focus embeddings. The generated question summary is domain-based instead of common word-based, and most of the focus words appear in the reference summary. When the domain embedding is eliminated, the performance is slightly degraded compared to removing the focus domain. This phenomenon reveals that the focus embedding contributes more to question summary than the domain embedding, especially when the focus incorporates multiple words. For example, all domain focus words 'Acute myeloblastic leukemia with minimal maturation' are included in reference summary 'Is there an ayurvedic treatment for Acute myeloblastic leukemia with minimal maturation?'.

---

[2] https://colab.research.google.com/.

Table 2. Ablation study of proposed framework. D and F denote the Domain and Focus, respectively.

Method	Rouge_2	Rouge_1	Rouge_L
−D & −F	0.1647	0.2836	0.2691
−D	0.2493	0.3283	0.3283
−F	0.1831	0.3046	0.2988
+ALL	**0.2604**	**0.3583**	**0.3520**

Based on the ablation study, we can conclude that focus and domain embeddings play essential roles in domain-specific text summarisation.

5 Conclusion and Future Works

In this paper, we propose a novel focus-based text summariser aiming at producing domain-specific text summaries with an emphasis on domain-specific information. The proposed model adopts hybrid embeddings by fusing focus, domain and context embeddings. Our extensive experiments demonstrate the effectiveness of our model and explicitly shows that it can outperform state-of-the-art algorithms. On top of that, an ablation study is conducted to validate both domain embedding and focus embedding contributions.

In the future, we plan to continue working on the hybrid embedding mechanism to improve the focus and domain context extraction process.

References

1. Abacha, A.B., M'rabet, Y., Zhang, Y., Shivade, C., Langlotz, C., Demner-Fushman, D.: Overview of the MEDIQA 2021 shared task on summarization in the medical domain. In: Proceedings of the 20th Workshop on Biomedical Language Processing, pp. 74–85 (2021)
2. Balumuri, S., Bachina, S., Kamath, S.: Sb_nitk at MEDIQA 2021: leveraging transfer learning for question summarization in medical domain. In: Proceedings of the 20th Workshop on Biomedical Language Processing, pp. 273–279 (2021)
3. Devlin, J., Chang, M.W., Lee, K., Toutanova, K.: BERT: pre-training of deep bidirectional transformers for language understanding. In: Proceedings of the 2019 Conference of the North American Chapter of the Association for Computational Linguistics: Human Language Technologies, vol. 1 (Long and Short Papers), pp. 4171–4186 (2019)
4. Fiszman, M., Rindflesch, T.C., Kilicoglu, H.: Abstraction summarization for managing the biomedical research literature. In: Proceedings of the Computational Lexical Semantics Workshop at HLT-NAACL 2004, pp. 76–83 (2004)
5. Gehrmann, S., Deng, Y., Rush, A.M.: Bottom-up abstractive summarization. In: Proceedings of the 2018 Conference on Empirical Methods in Natural Language Processing, pp. 4098–4109 (2018)

6. Gu, J., Lu, Z., Li, H., Li, V.O.: Incorporating copying mechanism in sequence-to-sequence learning. In: Proceedings of the 54th Annual Meeting of the Association for Computational Linguistics (Volume 1: Long Papers), pp. 1631–1640 (2016)

7. Guan, W., Smetannikov, I., Tianxing, M.: Survey on automatic text summarization and transformer models applicability. In: 2020 International Conference on Control, Robotics and Intelligent System, pp. 176–184 (2020)

8. He, Y., Chen, M., Huang, S.: damo_nlp at MEDIQA 2021: knowledge-based pre-processing and coverage-oriented reranking for medical question summarization. In: Proceedings of the 20th Workshop on Biomedical Language Processing, pp. 112–118 (2021)

9. Hermann, K.M., et al.: Teaching machines to read and comprehend. Adv. Neural. Inf. Process. Syst. **28**, 1693–1701 (2015)

10. Kim, D., et al.: A neural named entity recognition and multi-type normalization tool for biomedical text mining. IEEE Access **7**, 73729–73740 (2019)

11. Lee, J., et al.: BioBERT: a pre-trained biomedical language representation model for biomedical text mining. Bioinformatics **36**(4), 1234–1240 (2020)

12. Lee, J., Dang, H., Uzuner, O., Henry, S.: MNLP at MEDIQA 2021: fine-tuning Pegasus for consumer health question summarization. In: Proceedings of the 20th Workshop on Biomedical Language Processing, pp. 320–327 (2021)

13. Lewis, M., et al.: BART: denoising sequence-to-sequence pre-training for natural language generation, translation, and comprehension. arXiv preprint arXiv:1910.13461 (2019)

14. Lin, C.Y.: ROUGE: a package for automatic evaluation of summaries. In: Text Summarization Branches Out, pp. 74–81 (2004)

15. Luhn, H.P.: The automatic creation of literature abstracts. IBM J. Res. Dev. **2**(2), 159–165 (1958)

16. Luong, T., Pham, H., Manning, C.D.: Effective approaches to attention-based neural machine translation. In: EMNLP (2015)

17. Nallapati, R., Zhai, F., Zhou, B.: SummaRuNNER: a recurrent neural network based sequence model for extractive summarization of documents. In: Thirty-First AAAI Conference on Artificial Intelligence (2017)

18. Narayan, S., Cohen, S.B., Lapata, M.: Don't give me the details, just the summary! topic-aware convolutional neural networks for extreme summarization. In: Proceedings of the 2018 Conference on Empirical Methods in Natural Language Processing, pp. 1797–1807 (2018)

19. Raffel, C., et al.: Exploring the limits of transfer learning with a unified text-to-text transformer. J. Mach. Learn. Res. **21**(140), 1–67 (2020). http://jmlr.org/papers/v21/20-074.html

20. Reeve, L.H., Han, H., Brooks, A.D.: The use of domain-specific concepts in biomedical text summarization. Inf. Process. Manage. **43**(6), 1765–1776 (2007)

21. Roberts, K., Kilicoglu, H., Fiszman, M., Demner-Fushman, D.: Decomposing consumer health questions. In: Proceedings of BioNLP 2014, pp. 29–37. Association for Computational Linguistics, Baltimore, Maryland, June 2014. https://doi.org/10.3115/v1/W14-3405, https://aclanthology.org/W14-3405

22. Sarkar, K.: Using domain knowledge for text summarization in medical domain. Int. J. Recent Trends Eng. **1**(1), 200 (2009)

23. See, A., Liu, P.J., Manning, C.D.: Get to the point: summarization with pointer-generator networks. In: Proceedings of the 55th Annual Meeting of the Association for Computational Linguistics (Volume 1: Long Papers), pp. 1073–1083 (2017)

24. Wang, D., Liu, P., Zhong, M., Fu, J., Qiu, X., Huang, X.: Exploring domain shift in extractive text summarization. arXiv preprint arXiv:1908.11664 (2019)

25. Xu, H., Liu, B., Shu, L., Philip, S.Y.: Double embeddings and CNN-based sequence labeling for aspect extraction. In: Proceedings of the 56th Annual Meeting of the Association for Computational Linguistics (Volume 2: Short Papers), pp. 592–598 (2018)
26. Zhang, J., Zhao, Y., Saleh, M., Liu, P.: Pegasus: pre-training with extracted gap-sentences for abstractive summarization. In: International Conference on Machine Learning, pp. 11328–11339. PMLR (2020)

An Empirical Study of Fuzzy Decision Tree for Gradient Boosting Ensemble

Zhaoqing Liu[ID], Anjin Liu[ID], Guangquan Zhang[ID], and Jie Lu[✉][ID]

Australian Artificial Intelligence Institute, University of Technology Sydney,
Sydney, Australia
Zhaoqing.Liu-1@student.uts.edu.au,
{Anjin.Liu,Guangquan.Zhang,Jie.Lu}@uts.edu.au

Abstract. Gradient boosting has been proved to be an effective ensemble learning paradigm to combine multiple weak learners into a strong one. However, its improved performance is still limited by decision errors caused by uncertainty. Fuzzy decision trees are designed to solve the uncertainty problems caused by the collected information's limitation and incompleteness. This paper investigates whether the robustness of gradient boosting can be improved by using fuzzy decision trees even when the decision conditions and objectives are fuzzy. We first propose and implement a fuzzy decision tree (FDT) by referring to two widely cited fuzzy decision trees. Then we propose and implement a fuzzy gradient boosting decision tree (FGBDT), which integrates a set of FDTs as weak learners. Both the algorithms can be set as non-fuzzy algorithms by parameters. To study whether fuzzification can improve the proposed algorithms in classification tasks, we pair the algorithms with their non-fuzzy algorithms and run comparison experiments on UCI Repository datasets in the same settings. The experiments show that the fuzzy algorithms perform better than their non-fuzzy algorithms in many classical classification tasks. The code is available at github.com/ZhaoqingLiu/FuzzyTrees.

Keywords: Decision tree · Fuzzy system · Gradient boosting · Classification

1 Introduction

Fuzzy concepts and fuzzy objectives are ubiquitous in the process of human cognition and decision-making in real life [19]. Therefore, it is one of the hot areas of research to use fuzzy computing methods to deal with information that is not easy to be quantified. As a typical fuzzy algorithm, fuzzy decision trees [29,33] have been used in many applications, e.g., diagnosis systems [29], healthcare [1] and accounting and audit [2]. A fuzzy decision tree is an extension and improvement of traditional decision trees. A fuzzy decision tree fuzzifies training sets to fuzzy sets in the data preprocessing stage and computes splitting criteria for feature selection in the tree construction stage [33].

© Springer Nature Switzerland AG 2022
G. Long et al. (Eds.): AI 2021, LNAI 13151, pp. 716–727, 2022.
https://doi.org/10.1007/978-3-030-97546-3_58

Gradient boosting [13,22] is a primary boosting algorithm in ensemble learning. It can effectively improve a single base learning algorithm's performance [13]. The idea of gradient boosting is derived from the gradient descent method and has been widely used [20,21]. Its basic principle is to train the next weak learner according to the negative gradient of the current learner's loss function and then integrate the trained weak learner into a single strong learner in the form of an iterative combination.

Although some studies focus on fuzzy decision trees, no one compares fuzzy gradient boosting decision trees with non-fuzzy gradient boosting decision trees, and few implementations of fuzzy decision trees are based on the CART [3], which is one of the classical decision trees. In this paper, we propose a fuzzy decision tree (FDT) and fuzzy GBDT (FGBDT), which can combine the inductive capability of decision trees with the capability of fuzzy sets [34] to express uncertainty.

Unlike the fuzzy decision trees in other literature, we use the Fuzzy C-Means clustering algorithm (FCM) [9] as a feature fuzzification method in data preprocessing to improve the effectiveness of describing fuzzy concepts. We also use fuzzy Gini impurity-based metric calculation to extend the heuristic search techniques used in traditional decision trees. Compared with the fuzzy entropy [6,34] used in most existing fuzzy decision trees, the fuzzy Gini impurity used in our fuzzy feature selection technique can reduce the computation of splitting criteria and simplify the tree. For an empirical study, we develop the proposed algorithms into a software toolkit in Python. Finally, we carry out experiments, and the results show that the fuzzy trees have more advantages in solving the classification uncertainty than the non-fuzzy trees.

The contributions of this paper are summarised as follows:

- A novel fuzzy decision tree-based gradient boosting algorithm is proposed.
- A Python toolkit for FDT and FGBDT is developed.
- Extensive experiments indicate that FDT and FGBDT can achieve better accuracy in many classification tasks than non-fuzzy FDT and non-fuzzy FGBDT, respectively.

The paper is organised as follows. Section 2 introduces the related work. The details of FDT and FGBDT are presented in Sect. 3. Section 4 analyses the experimental evaluation. Conclusion and future work are discussed in Sect. 5.

2 Related Work

In this section, we review the researches on fuzzy decision trees and gradient boosting.

2.1 Fuzzy Decision Trees

As one of the most representative algorithms in machine learning, a decision tree uses a tree-like model of symbols, rules, and logic to represent knowledge and make logical inferences. A fuzzy decision tree is an extension of the classical decision tree. It is more robust in tolerating uncertainty by introducing fuzzy sets. Most of the fuzzy decision trees proposed in the literature can be regarded as the variants of the ID3 invented by Quinlan [25] and the C4.5 developed by Quinlan [26]. However, few studies involved fuzzy extensions of the CART algorithm introduced by Breiman et al. [3]. Yuan and Shaw [33] proposed a fuzzy decision tree induction method similar to the ID3 [25], except they use the classification ambiguity metric instead of entropy as the heuristic induction criterion. In the method, feature fuzzification in the data preprocessing stage is essential for constructing a fuzzy decision tree. A similar idea was also proposed in Kosko's study [16]. The author uses a simple algorithm to generate a triangular membership function to fuzzify the training sets into fuzzy membership degrees. The Fuzzy ID3 algorithm (Fuzzy ID3) proposed by Umanol et al. [29] uses fuzzy entropy first introduced by Zadeh [34], and the axiom construction of entropy of fuzzy sets was further introduced by De Luca and Termini [6]. Unlike the traditional ID3 algorithm, Fuzzy ID3 used the probability of membership degrees instead of the probability of crisp samples to calculate the metric, i.e., fuzzy entropy, when selecting the optimal splitting feature. In the literature, many other studies have extended entropy based on fuzziness in various ways.

2.2   Gradient Boosting

Gradient boosting is an ensemble learning technique and one of the most popular algorithms. Its basic idea is derived from the gradient descent method [32]. According to Schapire's proof conclusion based on Hoeffding Inequality [14] and the probably approximately correct (PAC) learning model [27], in the case that the errors of weak learners are independent of each other, the error rate of an ensemble method decreases exponentially with the increase of the number of weak learners and eventually tends to zero. Based on the proof, the gradient descent method can combine multiple weak learners in a strong learner. The regression gradient boosting algorithms developed by Freund et al. [12,13] can be used for regression and classification tasks. A more general view of functional gradient boosting was proposed by Llew et al. [22]. The basic principle of the algorithms is to train the next weak learner according to the negative gradient information of the loss function of the current model in multiple iterations, and then combine the trained weak learner into the model combination in the form of addition and finally minimise the loss function in the function space [13]. Boosting algorithms have made considerable progress in many areas of machine learning and statistics beyond regression and classification. In many current studies, the standard weak learners of gradient boosting algorithms are traditional decision trees, logistic regression classifiers, Naive Bayes, and other non-fuzzy algorithms [24].

3   Fuzzy Decision Trees for Gradient Boosting Ensemble

In this section, we detail two algorithms: FDT and FGBDT.

3.1   Framework of Fuzzy Decision Trees

The tree construction and prediction stages of FDT and its non-fuzzy FDT are similar. At the same time, there are two differences between the two algorithms. One is that the former executes additional feature fuzzification in data preprocessing, and the other is that the former uses the fuzzy sets to calculate all splitting criteria in tree construction. Specifically, the FDT calculates fuzzy metrics according to the fuzzy membership degrees obtained from the feature fuzzification rather than crisp samples.

Feature Fuzzification in Data Preprocessing. Feature Fuzzification (FF) refers to the fuzzy transformation of features in the data preprocessing stage before constructing an FDT tree. The membership function used in FF can be obtained from statistical data or determined based on the fuzzy clustering method of self-organising learning [33]. After the transformation based on the membership function, the calculated fuzzy membership degrees of the features belonging to a group of fuzzy sets are added to the samples. Considering that the Fuzzy C-Means clustering algorithm (FCM) [9] is one of the most widely used methods for feature fuzzification in fuzzy decision tree studies, we use it to cluster a group of fuzzy sets from each feature and then to calculate the fuzzy membership degrees of each feature belonging to these fuzzy sets. By calculating the membership matrix, the FCM makes the features with the maximum similarity be grouped in the same cluster, while the ones with the minimum similarity are divided into different clusters. Also, FF is a prerequisite for constructing FDTs because the metric fuzzification in the tree construction stage is based on the fuzzy membership degrees generated by FF.

Metric Fuzzification in Tree Construction. Metric fuzzification (MF) refers to the fuzzy calculation of splitting criteria for feature selection in the tree construction stage. We take the fuzzy metrics, also known as fuzzy entropy and fuzzy information gain, proposed by Umanol et al. [29] into our algorithm framework for feature selection. Specifically, assume that we have a set of samples S, where each sample has ℓ numerical features $A_1, A_2, ..., A_\ell$, and a labelled class $C = \{C_1, C_2, ..., C_n\}$ and fuzzy sets $F_{i1}, F_{i2}, ..., F_{im}$ for the feature A_i (the value of m usually varies from feature to feature). The fuzzy entropy of a fuzzy set of S is defined by:

$$I(S) = -\sum_{k=1}^{n}(p_k \log_2 p_k), \quad \text{where } p_k = \frac{|S^{C_k}|}{|S|}, \tag{1}$$

here S^{C_k} is a fuzzy subset of S, labelled as the class C_k, $|S^{C_k}|$ is the sum of the fuzzy membership degrees in S^{C_k}, and $|S|$ is the sum of the fuzzy membership degrees in a fuzzy set of S. Then, the fuzzy information gain $G(A_i, S)$ for A_i by a fuzzy set of S is defined by:

$$G(A_i, S) = I(S) - E(A_i, S), \quad \text{and} \quad E(A_i, S) = \sum_{j=1}^{m}(p_{ij}I(S_{F_{ij}})), \tag{2}$$

where

$$p_{ij} = \frac{|S_{F_{ij}}|}{\sum_{j=1}^{m} |S_{F_{ij}}|}, \tag{3}$$

$S_{F_{ij}}$ is a fuzzy subset split from a fuzzy set of S on A_i, and $|S_{F_{ij}}|$ is the sum of the fuzzy membership degrees in $S_{F_{ij}}$.

Although the fuzzy FD3 still adopts a greedy strategy to construct a tree, the two metrics used for the greedy strategy are different from the classic probability-based entropy and information gain.

- The first metric is fuzzy entropy, which is defined by Eq. 1. In Eq. 1, p_k equals the proportion of the sum of the fuzzy membership degrees in a fuzzy subset S^{C_k} of S to the sum of the fuzzy membership degrees in a fuzzy set of S. By comparison, according to Shannon [28], the classic information entropy can be given by $I(S) = -\sum_{k=1}^{n} p_k \log_2 p_k$, where S represents a set of samples with n classes; suppose $k \in \{1, 2, ..., n\}$, p_k is the probability of the samples labelled with class k in S.
- The second metric is the fuzzy information gain, which is defined by Eq. 2 and Eq. 3. In the two equations, p_{ij} equals the proportion of the sum of the fuzzy membership degrees in a fuzzy subset $S_{F_{ij}}$, which is split from a fuzzy set of S on A_i to the sum of the fuzzy membership degrees in the fuzzy set of S. In contrast, according to Quinlan [25], the classic information gain for an feature $a \in A_i$ can be given by $G(S, A_i) = I(S) - I(S|A_i) = I(S) - \sum_{a \in A_i} p(a) \sum_{i=1}^{n} -Pr(i|a) \log_2 Pr(i|a)$, where $I(S)$ represents the entropy of the parent node, $I(S|A_i)$ represents the weighted sum of the entropy of the child nodes split from S on A_i; and $Pr(i|a)$ is the conditional probability of Pr_i given a.

By analogy, we introduce two new concepts: fuzzy Gini impurity and fuzzy information gain ratio into the algorithm framework to support FDT and other fuzzy decision trees. The two concepts are the fuzzy extensions of the Gini impurity used in Breiman et al. [3] and the information gain ratio used in Quinlan [25]. Specifically, the fuzzy Gini impurity of a fuzzy set S is defined by:

$$I_G(S) = \sum_{k=1}^{n} p_k(1 - p_k), \tag{4}$$

where p_k is given by Eq. 1. Then, the fuzzy information gain ratio for the feature A_i by S is defined by:

$$GR(A_i, S) = \frac{G(A_i, S)}{IV(A_i, S)}, \tag{5}$$

where $G(A_i, S)$ is given by Eq. 2, and $IV(A_i, S)$ is the intrinsic value of A_i. That is, suppose A_i has a set of all possible values $V = \{V_1, V_2, ..., V_q\}$,

$$IV(A_i, S) = -\sum_{t=1}^{n} (p_t \log_2 p_t), \quad \text{where} \quad p_t = \frac{|A_i^{V_t}|}{|A_i|}, \tag{6}$$

here $A_i^{V_t}$ is a fuzzy subset of A_i with value V_t, $\left|A_i^{V_t}\right|$ is the sum of the fuzzy membership degrees in $A_i^{V_t}$, and $|A_i|$ is the sum of the fuzzy membership degrees in a fuzzy set of A_i.

The pseudocode for FDT is shown in Algorithm 1.

Algorithm 1. FDT algorithm.

1: **if** the current node at the level L with a fuzzy set of S satisfies: the current sample size is less than the threshold $min_{samples_{split}}$, or the tree's current depth is greater than the threshold max_{depth}, or no features available for splitting tests. **then**

2:     The current node is a leaf and is assigned a class label by majority vote calculation in classification tasks and a numerical label by mean calculation in regression tasks.

3: **else**

4:     **for** each $A_i(i = 1, 2, ...\ell)$ **do**

5:         Split S into two subsets.

6:         Calculate the information gain according to the Eq. (2), where the Eq. (1) is replaced by (4).

7:         Select the test feature A_{max} that maximises the information gain.

8:         **if** the test $best\_impurity\_gain$ is greater than the threshold $min\_impurity\_split$ **then**

9:             Generate a node according to the set of samples and the corresponding fuzzy sets containing their fuzzy membership degrees.

10:            Make the current level $L = L + 1$.

11:            Repeat recursively from Line 1 for both subsets, respectively.

12:        **end if**

13:    **end for**

14: **end if**

3.2 Implementation of Gradient Boosted Fuzzy Decision Trees

FGBDT combines multiple weak fuzzy learners into a single strong learner in an iterative fashion, then gradually approximate the optimal learner in a greedy fashion [13]. The main difference is that it integrates a set of regression FDTs instead of non-fuzzy regression trees. According to Vapnik's empirical risk minimisation principle [31], the algorithm iteratively performs the optimisation using a function gradient descent method, i.e., the steepest descent step. Specifically, the algorithm still uses the first-order derivative of the loss function to generate a set of pseudo residuals, namely the first-order Taylor polynomial in Taylor's theorem, to determine the loss function's steepest gradient descent in the current function space. Then the algorithm modifies the learner through the negative gradient direction to make it better. Algorithm 2 presents the pseudocode for the generic FGBDT for regression.

Algorithm 2. FGBDT Algorithm.

Input: Training set $\{(x_i, y_i)\}_{i=1}^{N}$; a differentiable loss function $L(y, f(x))$; number of iterations M;

1: Initialise a single learner with a constant value: $f_0(x) = \arg\min_\gamma \sum_{i=1}^{N} L(y_i, \gamma)$.
2: **for** $m = 1$ to M **do**
3:    Iteratively calculate the pseudo residuals corresponding to x:
4:    **for** $i = 1, 2, ..., N$ **do**
5:        $r_m = -\left[\frac{\partial L(y_i, f(x_i))}{\partial f(x_i)}\right]_{f(x)=f_{m-1}(x)}$.
6:    **end for**
7:    Fit a regression FDT to the pseudo residuals r_{i_m} giving disjoint regions $R_{j_m}, j = 1, 2, ..., J_m$, that is, using the training set $\{(x_i, r_i m)\}_{i=1}^{N}$.
8:    Use the fitted regression FDT to calculate the pseudo residuals by the gradient descent method: $\gamma_m = \arg\min_\gamma \sum_{i=1}^{N} L(y_i, f_{m-1}(x_i) + \gamma h_m(x_i))$.
9:    Update the learner $f_m(x) = f_{m-1}(x) + \gamma_m h_m(x)$ for the optimisation in the next iteration.
10: **end for**
Output: $\hat{f}(x) = f_M(x)$.

3.3 Time Complexity

The time complexity of the two algorithms is shown in Table 1.

Table 1. Time complexity for FDT and FGBDT.

Algorithm	Time complexity	
	Training	Prediction
FDT	$\mathcal{O}(N \log_2 NMC) \sim \mathcal{O}(N^2 MC)$	$\mathcal{O}(\log_2 N) \sim \mathcal{O}(N)$
FGBDT	$\mathcal{O}(TN \log_2 N) \sim \mathcal{O}(TN^2)$	$\mathcal{O}(T \log_2 N) \sim \mathcal{O}(TN)$

For tree training, the average depth of an FDT tree is $\log_2 N$, where N is the number of samples, and the worst-case depth is N, so the time complexity for the depth is between $O(\log_2 N)$ and $O(N)$. In a tree construction, FDT calculates the Gini impurity or entropy of the samples based on the current sample size and then calculates the information gain or information gain ratio in each iteration. So the time complexity for the tree is between $O(N \log_2 NM)$ and $O(N^2 M)$, where M is the number of features. In calculating each information gain and information gain ratio, FDT calculates the sum of membership degrees of features of the current node and the sum of membership degrees of features in each of its sub-trees. Therefore, the overall time complexity for the tree is between $O(N \log_2 NMC)$ and $O(N^2 MC)$, where C is the number of fuzzy sets (i.e., clusters) of a feature. Also, the time complexity for FGBDT is between $O(TN \log_2 N)$ and $O(TN^2)$, where T is the number of integrated trees. For prediction, the time complexity for FDT is between $O(\log_2 N)$ and $O(N)$, and that for FGBDT is between $O(T \log_2 N)$ and $O(TN)$.

According to the Master theorem, because $M \ll N$, $C \ll N$ and $T \ll N$, the time complexity for the training of both algorithms is $\mathcal{O}(N \log_2 N) \sim \mathcal{O}(N^2)$, and that for the prediction of both algorithms is $\mathcal{O}(\log_2 N) \sim \mathcal{O}(N)$.

4 Experimental Evaluation

This section empirically evaluates the proposed FDT and FGBDT.

4.1 Datasets

We consider six datasets from the UCI Machine Learning Repository [8].

- **Vehicle Silhouettes (VS)** [8]. The task is to classify a given silhouette as one of four types of vehicle, using a set of features extracted from the silhouette (846 samples, 18 features, and 4 classes).
- **German Credit (GC)** [5]. The task is to classify people described by a set of features as good or bad credit risks (1,000 samples, 24 features, and 2 classes).
- **Pima Indians Diabetes (PID)** [30]. The task is to classify the diabetes tests based on the features of a group of people (768 samples, 8 features, and 2 classes).
- **Iris** [17]. The task is to classify the types of iris plant based on the attributes of the four flowers (150 samples, 4 features, and 3 classes).
- **Wine** [18]. The task is to classify the origin of wines using the results of chemical analysis (178 samples, 13 features, and 3 classes).
- **Forest Cover Type (FCT)** [21]. The task is to classify forest cover type from cartographic variables (581,012 samples, 54 features, and 7 classes).

4.2 Baselines and Experimental Setup

We conduct four comparison experiments. The first two are to study the effect of feature fuzzification (FF) only and the combination of FF and metric fuzzification (MF) on the performance of FDT; the second is to investigate the impact of the above two types of fuzzification on the performance of FGBDT; the last one is to compare the performance of FDT with published baselines. In the first experiment, the non-fuzzy FDT (DT) without FF is the baseline of the non-fuzzy FDT with FF. In the other two experiments, the non-fuzzy FDT and non-fuzzy FGBDT are the baselines of FDT and FGBDT. In the last experiment, we compare our FDT with six representative baselines: XGBClassifier (XGBoost) [4], CatBoostClassifier (CatBoost) [7], LGBMClassifier (LightGBM) [15], HoeffdingTreeClassifier (HT) [23], HoeffdingAdaptiveTreeClassifier (HAT) [23] and SAMKNNClassifier (SAMKNN) [23].

For all datasets, categorical features are transformed into numeric features. For hyperparameters, *disable_fuzzy* for each classifier is used to specify whether to use fuzzy rules, and *max_depth* is set to 5; *learning_rate* for each pair of fuzzy and non-fuzzy FGBDT classifiers is set to 0.1, and *n_estimators* is set to 100; all other hyperparameters are left as their default values; *n_conv* for each FCM transformer is set to one of $\{3, 4, 5\}$ and 5 by default to specify the number of fuzzy sets to generate. Also, we quantify the average performance of each classifier through 10-round 10-fold cross-validation training and testing in each experiment. In the last experiment, we randomly select 1,000 samples from the dataset FCT for the training and testing of FDT and baseline classifiers. The same hyperparameters for all tree classifiers are set to identical values, except that the hyperparameters for the SAMKNN classifier are left as their default values. Our code is available on GitHub.[1]

Table 2. Results with FF ($n\_conv = 3$) and without FF.

Task	DT with FF		DT without FF	
	Acc	Std	Acc	Std
VS	**0.6963**	0.0341	0.6643	0.0305
GC	0.7080	0.0449	**0.7100**	0.0316
PID	**0.7226**	0.0478	0.7084	0.0509
Iris	**0.9333**	0.0629	**0.9333**	0.0629
Wine	0.8935	0.0676	**0.8990**	0.0742
Avg	**0.7907**	0.0515	0.7830	0.0500

Table 3. Results with FF ($n\_conv = 4$) and without FF.

Task	DT with FF		DT without FF	
	Acc	Std	Acc	Std
VS	**0.6963**	0.0341	0.6643	0.0305
GC	0.7080	0.0449	**0.7100**	0.0316
PID	**0.7226**	0.0478	0.7084	0.0509
Iris	**0.9333**	0.0629	**0.9333**	0.0629
Wine	0.8935	0.0676	**0.8990**	0.0742
Avg	**0.7907**	0.0515	0.7830	0.0500

Table 4. Results with FF ($n\_conv = 5$) and without FF.

Task	DT with FF		DT without FF	
	Acc	Std	Acc	Std
VS	**0.6963**	0.0341	0.6643	0.0305
GC	0.7080	0.0449	**0.7100**	0.0316
PID	**0.7226**	0.0478	0.7084	0.0509
Iris	**0.9333**	0.0629	**0.9333**	0.0629
Wine	0.8935	0.0676	**0.8990**	0.0742
Avg	**0.7907**	0.0515	0.7830	0.0500

Table 5. Results with FDT and non-fuzzy FDT.

Task	DT with PF		DT with non-PF	
	Acc	Std	Acc	Std
VS	**0.6915**	0.0619	0.6643	0.0305
GC	**0.7200**	0.0287	0.7100	0.0316
PID	**0.7422**	0.0389	0.7084	0.0509
Iris	**0.9333**	0.0629	**0.9333**	0.0629
Wine	**0.9108**	0.0650	0.8990	0.0742
Avg	**0.7996**	0.0515	0.7830	0.0500

---

[1] https://github.com/ZhaoqingLiu/FuzzyTrees.

Table 6. Results with FGBDT and non-fuzzy FGBDT.

Task	DT with PF		DT with non-PF	
	Acc	Std	Acc	Std
VS	**0.6832**	0.0457	0.6572	0.0223
GC	**0.6840**	0.0504	0.6790	0.0451
PID	**0.7082**	0.0465	0.7031	0.0642
Iris	**0.9400**	0.0663	0.9333	0.0629
Wine	0.8987	0.0692	**0.8990**	0.0742
Avg	**0.7828**	0.0556	0.7743	0.0537

Table 7. Comparison between FDT and baselines on dataset FCT.

Methods	Acc	Std
XGBoos t_b	0.6566	0.0395
CatBoos t_b	0.6302	0.0455
LightGB M_b	0.4880	0.0518
HT	0.5390	0.0524
HAT	0.5418	0.0510
SAMKNN	0.5533	0.0600
FDT	**0.6639**	0.0434

4.3 Experimental Results

Non-fuzzy FDT with FF vs. Non-fuzzy FDT without FF. Table 2, 3 and 4 summarise the prediction accuracy (Acc) and standard deviation (Std) of three pairs of non-fuzzy FDT trained on samples with and without FF, respectively. The results show that the average performance (Avg) of FDT with FF is better than that without FF.

FDT vs. Non-fuzzy FDT. Table 5 shows the respective Acc and Std for FDT and non-fuzzy FDT. We observe that the FDT with the combination of FF and MF outperform the non-fuzzy FDT on the average performance. In other words, using fuzzy sets to quantify fuzzy objects in classification tasks can help FDT improve performance (nearly 1.7%).

FGBDT vs. Non-fuzzy FGBDT. As shown in Table 6, the FGBDT outperforms the non-fuzzy FGBDT. We consider that FGBDT with FF and MF can further enhance the optimisation (nearly 0.9%) of gradient boosting by using the fuzzy membership degrees added to the samples as the fuzzy rules.

FDT vs. State-of-the-Art. We also compare FDT with six state-of-the-art algorithms. For a fair comparison, we only take the base learner of the ensemble algorithms for comparison. Table 7 show that FDT yields significant performance improvement compared with the six representative baselines.

5 Conclusion and Future Work

We have proposed and implemented a fuzzy gradient boosting algorithm framework with FDT and FGBDT. We have also conducted three comparison experiments to study how fuzzification affects the algorithms' performance. In conclusion, FGBDT can improve performance and enhance gradient boosting's optimisation effect in many classification tasks.

Based on the current research presented in this paper, we will further use FCM to identify the appropriate membership functions, optimise multiple ensemble learning methods based on FDT, and study how to reduce the computational overhead of the current algorithms. Furthermore, based on our observation, fuzzy sets theory does not consistently outperform the classic method. We consider this problem is caused by over fuzzification. Therefore, how to design a proper fuzzification controlling mechanism is also worth studying. Also, using transfer learning [10,11,35] to generate decision trees is an exciting challenge.

Acknowledgment. The work presented in this paper was supported by the Australian Research Council (ARC) under Discovery Project DP190101733.

References

1. Armand, S., Watelain, E., Roux, E., Mercier, M., Lepoutre, F.X.: Linking clinical measurements and kinematic gait patterns of toe-walking using fuzzy decision trees. Gait Posture **25**(3), 475–484 (2007)
2. Beynon, M.J., Peel, M.J., Tang, Y.C.: The application of fuzzy decision tree analysis in an exposition of the antecedents of audit fees. Omega **32**(3), 231–244 (2004)
3. Breiman, L., Friedman, J., Stone, C.J., Olshen, R.A.: Classification and Regression Trees. CRC Press, Boca Raton (1984)
4. Chen, T., Guestrin, C.: XGBoost: a scalable tree boosting system. In: SIGKDD, pp. 785–794. ACM (2016)
5. Chen, Z.: The application of tree-based model to unbalanced German credit data analysis. In: MATEC Web of Conferences, vol. 232, p. 01005. EDP Sciences (2018)
6. De Luca, A., Termini, S.: A definition of a nonprobabilistic entropy in the setting of fuzzy sets theory. Inf. Control **20**(4), 301–312 (1972)
7. Dorogush, A.V., Ershov, V., Gulin, A.: CatBoost: gradient boosting with categorical features support. CoRR arXiv:1810.11363 (2018)
8. Dua, D., Graff, C.: UCI machine learning repository (2017). http://archive.ics.uci.edu/ml
9. Dunn, J.C.: A fuzzy relative of the ISODATA process and its use in detecting compact well-separated clusters. J. Cybern. **3**, 32–57 (1973)
10. Fang, Z., Lu, J., Liu, F., Xuan, J., Zhang, G.: Open set domain adaptation: theoretical bound and algorithm. IEEE Trans. Neural Netw. Learn. Syst. **32**, 4309–4322 (2019)
11. Fang, Z., Lu, J., Liu, F., Zhang, G.: Unsupervised domain adaptation with sphere retracting transformation. In: IJCNN, pp. 1–8. IEEE (2019)
12. Freund, Y., Schapire, R.E.: A decision-theoretic generalization of on-line learning and an application to boosting. J. Comput. Syst. Sci. **55**(1), 119–139 (1997)
13. Friedman, J.H.: Greedy function approximation: a gradient boosting machine. Ann. Stat. **29**, 1189–1232 (2001)
14. Hoeffding, W.: Probability inequalities for sums of bounded random variables. In: The Collected Works of Wassily Hoeffding, pp. 409–426. Springer, Cham (1994). https://doi.org/10.1007/978-1-4612-0865-5_26
15. Ke, G., et al.: LightGBM: a highly efficient gradient boosting decision tree. In: NeurIPS, pp. 3146–3154 (2017)
16. Kosko, B., Burgess, J.C.: Neural networks and fuzzy systems (1998)

17. Kotsiantis, S.B., Pintelas, P.E.: Logitboost of simple Bayesian classifier. Informatica (Slovenia) **29**(1), 53–60 (2005)
18. Ledezma, A., Aler, R., Sanchis, A., Borrajo, D.: Empirical evaluation of optimized stacking configurations. In: ICTAI, pp. 49–55. IEEE Computer Society (2004)
19. Liu, A., Lu, J., Zhang, G.: Concept drift detection: dealing with missing values via fuzzy distance estimations. IEEE Trans. Fuzzy Syst. **29**, 3219–3233 (2020)
20. Liu, A., Lu, J., Zhang, G.: Concept drift detection via equal intensity k-means space partitioning. IEEE Trans. Cybern. **51**, 3198–3211 (2020)
21. Lu, J., Liu, A., Dong, F., Gu, F., Gama, J., Zhang, G.: Learning under concept drift: a review. IEEE Trans. Knowl. Data Eng. **31**(12), 2346–2363 (2018)
22. Mason, L., Baxter, J., Bartlett, P., Frean, M.: Boosting algorithms as gradient descent in function space. In: Proceedings of NIPS, vol. 12, pp. 512–518 (1999)
23. Montiel, J., Read, J., Bifet, A., Abdessalem, T.: Scikit-multiflow: a multi-output streaming framework. J. Mach. Learn. Res. **19**, 72:1–72:5 (2018)
24. Natekin, A., Knoll, A.: Gradient boosting machines, a tutorial. Front. Neurorobot. **7**, 21 (2013)
25. Quinlan, J.R.: Induction of decision trees. Mach. Learn. **1**(1), 81–106 (1986)
26. Quinlan, J.R.: C4.5: Programs for Machine Learning. Elsevier, Amsterdam (2014)
27. Schapire, R.E.: The strength of weak learnability. Mach. Learn. **5**(2), 197–227 (1990)
28. Shannon, C.E.: A mathematical theory of communication. Bell Syst. Tech. J. **27**(3), 379–423 (1948)
29. Umanol, M., et al.: Fuzzy decision trees by fuzzy ID3 algorithm and its application to diagnosis systems. In: Fuzz-IEEE, pp. 2113–2118. IEEE (1994)
30. Vaishali, R., Sasikala, R., Ramasubbareddy, S., Remya, S., Nalluri, S.: Genetic algorithm based feature selection and MOE fuzzy classification algorithm on Pima Indians diabetes dataset. In: ICCNI, pp. 1–5. IEEE (2017)
31. Vapnik, V.: Principles of risk minimization for learning theory. In: NeurIPS, pp. 831–838 (1992)
32. Wang, K., Lu, J., Liu, A., Zhang, G., Xiong, L.: Evolving gradient boost: a pruning scheme based on loss improvement ratio for learning under concept drift. IEEE Trans. Cybern. (2021)
33. Yuan, Y., Shaw, M.J.: Induction of fuzzy decision trees. Fuzzy Sets Syst. **69**(2), 125–139 (1995)
34. Zadeh, L.A.: Fuzzy sets. In: Fuzzy Sets, Fuzzy Logic, and Fuzzy Systems: Selected Papers, pp. 394–432. World Scientific (1996)
35. Zhong, L., Fang, Z., Liu, F., Lu, J., Yuan, B., Zhang, G.: How does the combined risk affect the performance of unsupervised domain adaptation approaches? In: AAAI, pp. 11079–11087. AAAI Press (2021)

SimSCL: A Simple Fully-Supervised Contrastive Learning Framework for Text Representation

Youness Moukafih[1,2(✉)], Abdelghani Ghanem[1], Karima Abidi[2], Nada Sbihi[1], Mounir Ghogho[1], and Kamel Smaili[2]

[1] TICLab, College of Engineering and Architecture,
Université Internationale de Rabat, Rabat, Morocco
{youness.moukafih,abdelghani.ghanem,nada.sbihi,mounir.ghogho}@uir.ac.ma
[2] LORIA/INRIA-Lorraine 615 rue du Jardin Botanique,
BP 101, 54600 Villers-lés-Nancy, France
{youness.moukafih,karima.abidi,kamel.smaili}@loria.fr

Abstract. During the last few years, deep supervised learning models have been shown to achieve state-of-the-art results for Natural Language Processing tasks. Most of these models are trained by minimizing the commonly used cross-entropy loss. However, the latter may suffer from several shortcomings such as sub-optimal generalization and unstable fine-tuning. Inspired by the recent works on self-supervised contrastive representation learning, we present **SimSCL**, a framework for binary text classification task that relies on two simple concepts: (i) Sampling positive and negative examples given an anchor by considering that sentences belonging to the same class as the anchor as positive examples and samples belonging to a different class as negative examples and (ii) Using a novel FULLY-SUPERVISED contrastive loss that enforces more compact clustering by leveraging label information more effectively. The experimental results show that our framework outperforms the standard cross-entropy loss in several benchmark datasets. Further experiments on Moroccan and Algerian dialects demonstrate that our framework also works well for under-resource languages.

Keywords: Natural language processing · Contrastive learning · Neural network · Supervised learning

1 Introduction

Over the last few years, deep supervised learning models have achieved tremendous success in a variety of applications across many disciplines varying from Computer Vision (CV) and Automatic Speech Recognition (ASR) to Natural Language Processing (NLP). These models are usually trained by minimizing

---

Y. Moukafih and A. Ghanem—Equal contribution.

© Springer Nature Switzerland AG 2022
G. Long et al. (Eds.): AI 2021, LNAI 13151, pp. 728–738, 2022.
https://doi.org/10.1007/978-3-030-97546-3_59

the commonly-used cross-entropy (CE) objective function. The basic concept of CE is simple and intuitive: each class is assigned a target (usually 1-hot) vector. Despite its popularity, the CE objective loss - the KL-divergence between one-hot vectors of labels and the distribution of the model's output logits - suffers from major robustness issues, which limits its use. In fact, CE suffers from adversarial robustness, as was shown in [1], which demonstrated empirically that training with a CE loss can cause the representations to spread sparsely over the representation space during training. Additionally, introducing noisy data seams to reduce the performance substantially, due to the fact that the cross entropy loss supposes that all the training labels are true, and neglects the fuzziness of noisy labels [2].

To overcome the above-mentioned challenges, many successful alternatives have been proposed to adjust the reference label distribution problems through label smoothing [3,4], Mixup [5], and knowledge distillation [6]. Recently, contrastive learning (CL) algorithms that were developed as estimators of mutual information, has led to major advances in self-supervised representation learning. These methods explicitly aim at training an encoder to learn latent representations of data instances to learn by pulling together representations of augmented views of the same data example (positive pairs), and pushing away representations of augmented views of different data examples (negative examples).

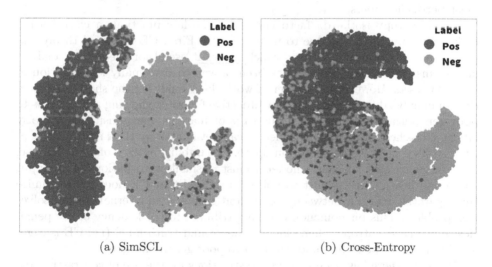

(a) SimSCL   (b) Cross-Entropy

Fig. 1. T-SNE plots of the learned sentence representations using our SimSCL framework and the common approach of using Cross-entropy on the SST-2 dataset.

Inspired by the recent works on contrastive representation learning strategy, we introduce SimSCL, a simple supervised contrastive learning framework that uses a novel contrastive loss for binary classification task by leveraging label information more effectively. In this work, we consider many positives per anchor, unlike previous works on self-supervised contrastive learning which uses only a single positive example per anchor, and many negatives. In other words, the positive points are sampled from the same class as the anchor, instead of being augmented views of the same anchor, as done in self-supervised learning. In Fig. 2, we show how we select positive examples and negative examples for each class. The use of many positives and many negatives for each anchor in our framework allows the encoder function to better maximize the inter-class and minimize the intra-class similarities (learn effective generalizable features) than the standard framework which relies on the cross-entropy loss using the same model architecture. In Fig. 1 we can clearly see that our proposed objective function enforces more compact clustering of examples within the same class.

The empirical results show that our proposed framework consistently outperforms the standard cross-entropy loss using the same model architecture on three publicly available benchmark SA datasets, namely, Yelp-2, SST-2, and Amazon-2. Further experiments on Moroccan and Algerian dialects demonstrate that our framework also works well for under-resource languages.

2   Related Work

Our research builds upon previous works in self-supervised representation learning, contrastive learning, and supervised learning. Here, we shed light on the most pertinent papers.

Cross entropy is the de facto choice for the loss function in classification tasks. This prominence is due to many reasons. First, CE has good theoretical grounding in information theory, which makes it useful for theoretical analysis of systems [7]. Second, CE loss has been proven to rival many loss function in large data-sets. However, a number of works have analyzed the shortcomings of the commonly adapted cross-entropy objective function, showing that it leads to poor generalization performance due to poor margins, and sensitivity to noisy labels. Classification models are theoretically evaluated by their ability the separate classes in the representation space. Separability is also of practical use, since large margins can make models robust to small perturbations of the input space and hence, more robust to noise. [1] showed that CE does not maximize the separating margins between classes, and proposed an alternative that solves this problem. This phenomenon can be attributed to the leniency of the penalties of the cross entropy when close to the ground truth label (i.e. CE is eager for the model to be right), and can lead to poor generalization.

Recently, there has been several investigations for the use of contrastive loss for self-supervised learning. Primarily in the computer vision (CV) field, deep Contrastive learning has been use to great effect for learning image representations. For instance, in [8] Hinton and his colleagues propose SimCLR a simple framework, for learning visual representations without specialized architectures or a memory bank, that generates anchor positive pairs by randomly augmenting the same image (e.g. random cropping and Rotation) while anchor-negative pairs are, from augmented views of different images within the same batch and minimizing a contrastive loss shown in Eq. 1 that makes augmented views of

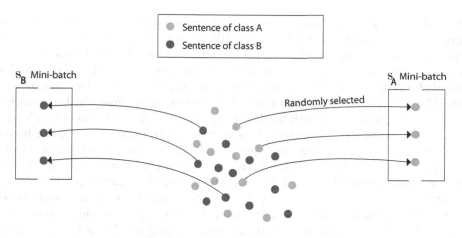

Fig. 2. Overview of the positive and negative examples construction process

the same example agree, which were shown to considerably outperform previous methods for self-supervised and semi-supervised learning on various benchmark datasets.

$$\mathcal{L}_i^{self} = -\sum_{i \in I} \log \frac{\exp(z_i.z_{j(i)}/\tau)}{\sum_{a \in A(i)} \exp(z_i.z_a/\tau)} \tag{1}$$

Where $i \in I \equiv \{1...2N\}$ is the index of an arbitrary augmented sample, $j(i)$ is the index of the other augmented sample originating from the same source sample. $A(i) \equiv I \{i\}$ is the set of all batch samples except the anchor. $P(i) \equiv \{p \in A(i) : \tilde{y}_p = \tilde{y}_i\}$ the set of indices of all positives in the multiviewed batch distinct from i. We can rewrite the set $A(i)$ as $A(i) \equiv P(i) \cup N(i)$, where $N(i) \equiv \{p \in A(i) : \tilde{y}_p \neq \tilde{y}_i\}$.

Most similar to our method is the work done by [9], in that paper the authors proposed two variants of a contrastive supervised loss named SupCon (see Eq. 2 and 3). SupCon outperforms cross entropy loss and produces state-of-the-art results on ImageNet using ResNet architecture [10] with four different implementations of data augmentation.

$$\mathcal{L}_{out,i}^{sup} = \sum_{i \in I} \frac{-1}{|P(i)|} \sum_{p \in P(i)} \log \frac{\exp(z_i.z_p/\tau)}{\sum_{a \in A(i)} \exp(z_i.z_a/\tau)} \tag{2}$$

$$\mathcal{L}_{in,i}^{sup} = \sum_{i \in I} -\log \left\{ \frac{1}{|P(i)|} \sum_{p \in P(i)} \frac{\exp(z_i.z_p/\tau)}{\sum_{a \in A(i)} \exp(z_i.z_a/\tau)} \right\} \tag{3}$$

Other researchers have extended these methods to learn representations of graph structured data [11–15]. For instance, in [15] the authors proposed GraphCL a general framework for learning node representations in a self supervised manner using a contrastive loss that aims at maximizing the similarity between the representations of two transformations of the same node's local sub-graph. In the context of NLP, in [16] Mikolov and his colleagues proposed the first contrastive-based framework for learning word-level embeddings by using co- occurring words as positive pairs and k randomly chosen negative samples words form the corpus as negative pairs. More recently, contrastive learning was used for sentence-level representations. [17] proposes a self-supervised contrastive objective by performing both masked language modeling and contrastive learning to learn a universal sentence representations by training a transformer-based encoder to minimize the distance between the embeddings of textual segments randomly sampled from nearby in the same document. More recently, in [18] the authors proposed a novel loss for fine-tuning that includes a supervised contrastive learning term $[(1 - \lambda)\mathcal{L}_{CE} + \lambda\mathcal{L}_{out}^{sup}]$ novel loss that a supervised contrastive learning objective for fine-tuning transformer-based pre-trained language models that improve performance over a strong RoBERTa-Large baseline on multiple datasets of the GLUE benchmark in the few-shot learning settings.

3   The Proposed Method

The main goal of the proposed framework is to learn representations by training an encoder network via a novel fully-supervised contrastive loss for classification task. The objective function is meant to capture the similarities between sentences of the same class while distancing the representations of sentences belonging to different classes.

First, we tackle one of the most crucial steps in any contrastive learning framework, namely, creating positive samples. In self-supervised, the common way for creating these positive samples is using various data augmentation strategies such as rotations and cropping in computer vision domain. Nevertheless, directly grafting the way of generating augmented views from the image domain is infeasible, since arbitrarily altering a sentence may change its semantics and thus its sentiment. To address this issue, we consider that sentences of the same sentiment are positive examples of each other. In Fig. 2, we show how we select positive examples and negative examples for each class.

3.1   Inter-class and Intra-class Distances

We first set up notation and describe the proposed framework for classification tasks that will be essential for the analysis. Let $\mathcal{D} = \{(x_i, y_i)\}_i$ be the dataset, where x_i represent the ith sentence of the dataset and y_i is its label. Let $\mathcal{S}_l^k = \{(x_{k_i}, y_{k_i}) | y_{k_i} = y_{k_j}, \forall i \neq j; 0 \leq i \leq l\}$ denote the set of all sentences belonging to the same class within the corpus with l being the max-length of the sentences. Let $\mathcal{B}_k \sim \mathcal{S}_l^k$ be a mini-batch of randomly sampled examples from the same class. Let $f_w(.)$ denotes the encoder operator where the sub-index w refers to the weights of the encoders to be learnt. Let $H_k = f_w(B_k) \in \mathbb{R}^{N \times d}$ be the highest level l_2 normalized representation of the encoder where N is the batch size and

d is the dimension of the embedding vector. The jth row of H_k corresponds to the embedding $h_j^{(l)}$ of sentence k. Mathematically, this can be presented as

$$H_k = \begin{bmatrix} h_1^\top \\ h_2^\top \\ \vdots \\ h_{|\mathcal{B}_k|}^\top \end{bmatrix} \in \mathbb{R}^{N \times d}$$

3.2 Contrastive Objective Function

Now that we have all the mathematical notions needed, we proceed with the formulation of the objective function of the proposed contrastive learning framework:

$$V_{(C1,C1)} = H_1 H_1^\top = f_w(\mathcal{B}_1) \times f_w(\mathcal{B}_1)^\top \in \mathbb{R}^{N_1 \times N_1} \tag{4}$$

$$V_{(C2,C2)} = H_2 H_2^\top = f_w(\mathcal{B}_2) \times f_w(\mathcal{B}_2)^\top \in \mathbb{R}^{N_2 \times N_2} \tag{5}$$

$$U_{(C1,C2)} = H_1 H_2^\top = f_w(\mathcal{B}_1) \times f_w(\mathcal{B}_2)^\top \in \mathbb{R}^{N_1 \times N_2} \tag{6}$$

$$U_{(C2,C1)} = H_2 H_1^\top = f_w(\mathcal{B}_2) \times f_w(\mathcal{B}_1)^\top \in \mathbb{R}^{N_2 \times N_1} \tag{7}$$

Where, $\mathcal{B}_1 \sim \mathcal{S}_l^1$ and $\mathcal{B}_2 \sim \mathcal{S}_l^2$. $V_{(C1,C1)}$ and $V_{(C2,C2)}$ are the distances between the positive examples, which should be minimized by the objective (inter-class similarity), and $V_{(C1,C2)}$ and $V_{(C2,C1)}$ are the distance between the representation of each batch and the representation of the other batch, which should be maximized (intra-class similarity).

Finally, we concatenate the $V_{(C1,C1)}$ with $V_{(C2,C2)}$ inter-class matrices, and $U_{(C1,C2)}$ with $U_{(C2,C1)}$ intra-class:

$$V = \begin{bmatrix} V_{(C1,C1)} \\ V_{(C2,C2)} \end{bmatrix} \qquad U = \begin{bmatrix} U_{(C1,C2)} \\ U_{(C2,C1)} \end{bmatrix}$$

In order to overcame the mismatching dimension of $V_{(C1,C1)}$ with $V_{(C2,C2)}$ and that of $U_{(C1,C2)}$ with $U_{(C2,C1)}$ we adjust the matrix of the lowest dimension (column space) to be equal to that of the highest one by adding zeros.

Given the previous calculations, we formulate our supervised contrastive objective that we call $\mathcal{L}_{concat}^{sup}$ as follows:

$$\mathcal{L}_{concat}^{sup} = -\frac{1}{N} \sum_{i=1}^{N} \log \left\{ \frac{\frac{1}{N_{C(i)}-1} \sum_{j=1,j\neq i}^{N_{C(i)}} \exp(V_{ij}/\tau)}{\frac{1}{N_{C(i)}-1} \sum_{j=1,j\neq i}^{N_{C(i)}} \exp(V_{ij}/\tau) + \frac{1}{N_{\overline{C(i)}}} \sum_{j=1}^{N_{\overline{C(i)}}} \exp(U_{ij}/\tau)} \right\} \tag{8}$$

where, $N = N_{C(i)} + N_{\overline{C(i)}}$. $N_{C(i)}$ is the number of elements of the same class as example i and $N_{\overline{C(i)}}$ the number of the elements of the other class, $\tau \in \mathbb{R}^+$ is a scalar temperature parameter, V_i and U_i are the ith elements of V and U respectively.

Note that, by minimizing the proposed supervised contrastive loss $\mathcal{L}_{concat}^{sup}$, the encoder operator adjust its weights so that representation of sentences with same class label are close to each other (high values for $[V_i]_{i=1,2...}$), while representation of sentences belonging to different classes are far from each other (low values for $[U_i]_{i=1,2...}$). Moreover, in contrast to self-supervised learning, our objective function trains the model by exploiting multiple positive examples, resulting in more compact clustering of the embedding space.

It is worth pointing out that our loss is generic, i.e., it can be used for any binary classification problem. In this paper, we only use it for text binary classification task, leaving its exploration for other classification tasks as future work.

4   Main Results

4.1   Datasets

We evaluate the effectiveness of the proposed losses on three popular datasets namely, SST-2, Yelp-2, and Amazon-2, used for benchmarking state-of-the-art sentiment classification learning methods. We also tested our proposed objective function for two other low-resource languages datasets namely, the Moroccan Sentiment Analysis Corpus (MSAC) and the Algerian Sentiment Analysis Corpus (ASAC). MSAC is a multi-domain dataset containing sentences from sport, social and politics domains. ASAC is an Algerian Sentiment Analysis Corpus, it is our own dataset that we collected and annotated taking advantage of the data available on Youtube video comments. The problem was how to extract from Youtube, only the comments concerning the Algerian dialect. As there is no standard method for this problem, we opted for the approach we had proposed in a previous work [19]. We collected data on YouTube, by selecting several hashtags or keywords used mainly by Algerians. Subsequently, all the data collected was checked and filtered and those which were not Algerian, they were excluded from the corpus. Then, we manually annotated all the comments by assigning each sentence its polarity (we didn't take into consideration neutral sentences). The constructed corpus, written in Arabic and Latin characters, is made up of 3976 positive comments and 4443 negative comments.[1] We summarize each dataset in Table 1.

---

[1] This corpus will be made public.

Table 1. Dataset statistics

Dataset	#Train	#Dev	#Test	#Classes
SST-2	60k	3.5k	3.5k	2
Yelp-P	600k	50k	38k	2
Amazon-P	3M	600k	400k	2
MSAC	1.6k	0.2k	0.2k	2
ASAC	6.8k	0.8k	0.8	2

4.2 Training Details

Our framework allows various choices of the network architecture without any constraints. However, since the aim of this work is to compare different loss functions on the same model architecture, we opt for simplicity and adopt the commonly used BiLSTM-based encoder.

For SST-2, Yelp-2, and Amazon-2 datasets, $\mathcal{L}_{concat}^{sup}$ was trained for 60 epochs using Adam optimizer with learning rate of 0.001 [20]. We initialize the input layer of the encoder with Glove pre-trained word representations of size 300 [21]. we use an encoder function of 3 hidden layers, a hidden units of 512, and a batch size of 800. We apply dropout of 0.5 on each layer. Note that the CE loss is evaluated by increasing the mini-batch size up to 1000. However, the best results are obtained using a batch size of 500.

For ASAC and MSAC datasets, similarly, the supervised $\mathcal{L}_{concat}^{sup}$ was trained for 15 epochs using Adam optimized with a learning rate of 0.003. However, for these datasets, we use an encoder with 1 hidden layer due to the number of examples that we have in the datasets, a hidden units of 128, and a batch size of 200. We apply dropout of 0.1. Similarly, we the CE is trained for a batch size up to 400, but the best results are obtained using a batch size of 64.

Following common practice, we opt for a linear evaluation of the learned sentence representations. More precisely, we use the learnt representations to train a logistic regression model to solve the text classification task. In practice, the evaluation process was performed using both a linear, and non-linear (ReLU activation) classifier. However, better results were obtained by the latter, achieving an average performance gain of 2% across all datasets.

4.3 Classification Accuracy

Here, we report the obtained results using $\mathcal{L}_{concat}^{sup}$ in different settings on 5 benchmark datasets, and those obtained by the CE and SupCon [9] losses. The results are given in terms of accuracy score measured on the same balanced test set.

Table 2. Linear evaluation of representations with different projection heads g(·) (Accuracy). The representation h (before projection) is 512-dimensional (%).

Dataset\projection	Identity	Linear	Non-linear
SST-2	93.40	93.60	**94.15**
Yelp-2	95.13	95.31	**95.45**
Amazone-2	93.23	93.61	**94.71**
MSAC	78.48	79.33	**80.10**
ASAC	79.73	80.91	**82.63**

Following common practice, we first study the importance of adding a projection head that maps representations to the space where supervised contrastive loss is applied. Similar to we tested three different MLP architecture: (1) identity mapping; (2) linear projection $z = g(h) = W^{(1)}h \in \mathcal{R}^{512}$; (3) non-linear projection with one additional hidden layer as used by several previous approaches $z = g(h) = W^{(2)} ReLU(W^{(1)}h) \in \mathcal{R}^{512}$. Similar to what have found in previous works, we observe that a non-linear is better than linear and identity functions for projection head (See Table 2). Note that, the projection head network is used only in the contrastive training phase, however, we discard it at the fine-tuning and inference phases.

Table 3. Comparison of transfer learning and fine-tuning performance (Accuracy).

Dataset	Transfer learning	Fine-tuned
SST-2	94.05	**94.15**
Yelp-2	**95.53**	95.45
Amazone-2	**94.71**	94.58
MSAC	**80.10**	78.21
ASAC	**82.63**	82.16

For the evaluation performance, we tested our supervised representation for transfer learning in two settings: (1) the (non-linear) classifier is trained on top of the frozen representation (transfer learning); (2) we train the classifier, where we allow all weights to be adjusted during training (fine-tuned). It is clear from the Table 3 that the learnt representations by our loss function are useful for the downstream tasks without adjusting them. In this paper, we provide the results that we obtained with the transfer learning strategy.

Table 4. Performance results (%)

Dataset	Classification accuracy results		
	CE	SupCon ($\mathcal{L}_{out}^{sup}$)	SimSCL ($\mathcal{L}_{concat}^{sup}$)
SST-2	91.28	93.53	**94.15**
Yelp-2	92.12	94.84	**95.45**
Amazon-2	92.94	93.98	**94.71**
MSAC	72.51	78.33	**80.10**
ASAC	78.70	82.11	**82.63**

Table 4 shows the obtained results of biLSTM-based model using our $\mathcal{L}_{concat}^{sup}$ objective function on the previously described datasets; and those obtained by the cross-entropy and SupCon losses. The results are given in terms of accuracy score measured on the same balanced test set. It is clear that in all cases, our framework provides better performance; the gain in performance is significant. Indeed, SimSCL leads to a 4.7% improvement of accuracy on SST-2, 3.6% improvement on Yelp-2, 5% improvement on Amazon, 3.9% improvement on ASAC, and 7.6% improvement on MSAC compared to CE loss. The large performance gap for MSAC dataset demonstrates that cross-entropy struggles with separating classes when dealing with small datasets. Furthermore, the results for MSAC and ASAC prove that our framework is very promising for under-resourced languages, which makes it advantageous over more sophisticated models such as transform-based models (e.g., BERT, RoBERT), which cannot be used for these languages due to the large amount of data needed for pre-training. Moreover, our experiments showed that CE overfits the MSAC dataset very quickly, with a training accuracy of 96% and only 72% accuracy on test. The overfitting problem cannot be explained by the large number of parameters of the biLTSM, since SimSCL-Obj also uses biLTSM (i.e., the same number of parameters as CE). Indeed, the problem can be explained by the fact that CE learns very poor margins between the two classes. Finally, it is worth pointing out that, similar to the cross-entropy loss, our loss function is robust to weights initialization.

5   Conclusion and Future Work

In this paper, we presented SimSCL, a simple supervised contrastive learning framework for training deep neural network for the binary classification task using a novel loss function. The latter is based on inter-class similarities (to be maximized), and intra-class similarities (to be minimized). We demonstrated, empirically, that SimSCL separates the two classes better than the encoder based on the classical cross-entropy and the SupCon losses. In the future, we plan to extend our method to other domains, such as computer vision, and graph neural network.

References

1. Pang, T., Xu, K., Dong, Y., Du, C., Chen, N., Zhu, J.: GRethinking softmax cross-entropy loss for adversarial robustness. arXiv preprint arXiv:1905.10626 (2019)
2. Zhang, T., Wu, F., Katiyar, A., Weinberger, K.Q., Artzi, Y.: Revisiting few-sample BERT fine-tuning. arXiv preprint arXiv:2006.05987 (2020)
3. Szegedy, C., Vanhoucke, V., Ioffe, S., Shlens, J., Wojna, Z.: Rethinking the inception architecture for computer vision. In: Proceedings of the IEEE Conference on Computer Vision and Pattern Recognition (2016)
4. SMüller, R., Kornblith, S., Hinton, G.: When does label smoothing help? arXiv preprint arXiv:1906.02629 (2019)
5. SZhang, H., Cisse, M., Dauphin, Y.N., Lopez-Paz, D.: mixup: beyond empirical risk minimization. arXiv preprint arXiv:1710.09412 (2017)
6. Hinton, G., Vinyals, O., Dean, J.: Distilling the knowledge in a neural network. arXiv preprint arXiv:1503.02531 (2015)
7. Andreieva, V., Shvai, N.: Generalization of cross-entropy loss function for image classification. arXiv preprint arXiv:1503.02537 (2020)
8. Chen, T., Kornblith, S., Norouzi, M., Hinton, G.: A simple framework for contrastive learning of visual representations. In: International Conference on Machine Learning (2020)
9. Khosla, P., et al.: Supervised contrastive learning. arXiv preprint arXiv:2004.11362 (2020)
10. He, K., Zhang, X., Ren, S., Sun, J.: Deep residual learning for image recognition. In: Proceedings of the IEEE Conference on Computer Vision and Pattern Recognition (2016)
11. Hassani, K., Khasahmadi, A.H.: Contrastive multi-view representation learning on graphs. In: International Conference on Machine Learning (2020)
12. Zhu, Y., Xu, Y., Yu, F., Liu, Q., Wu, S., Wang, L.: Deep graph contrastive representation learning. arXiv preprint arXiv:2006.04131 (2020)
13. Veličković, P., Fedus, W., Hamilton, W.L., Liò, P., Bengio, Y., Hjelm, R.D.: Deep graph infomax. arXiv preprint arXiv:1809.10341 (2018)
14. Qiu, J., et al.: GCC: graph contrastive coding for graph neural network pre-training. In: Proceedings of the 26th ACM SIGKDD International Conference on Knowledge Discovery & Data Mining (2020)
15. Hafidi, H., Ghogho, M., Ciblat, P., Swami, A.: GraphCL: contrastive self-supervised learning of graph representations. arXiv preprint arXiv:2007.08025 (2020)
16. Mikolov, T., Chen, K., Corrado, G., Dean, J.: Efficient estimation of word representations in vector space. arXiv preprint arXiv:1301.3781 (2013)
17. Giorgi, J.M., Nitski, O., Bader, G.D., Wang, B.: DeCLUTR: deep contrastive learning for unsupervised textual representations. arXiv preprint arXiv:2006.03659 (2020)
18. Gunel, B., Du, J., Conneau, A., Stoyanov, V.: Supervised contrastive learning for pre-trained language model fine-tuning. arXiv preprint arXiv:2011.01403 (2020)
19. Abidi, K., Menacer, M.A., Smaili, K.: CALYOU: a comparable spoken Algerian corpus harvested from YouTube. In: 18th Annual Conference of the International Communication Association (Interspeech) (2017)
20. Kingma, D.P., Ba, J.: Adam: a method for stochastic optimization. arXiv preprint arXiv:1412.6980 (2014)
21. Pennington, J., Socher, R., Manning, C.D.: GloVe: global vectors for word representation. In: Proceedings of the 2014 Conference on Empirical Methods in Natural Language Processing (2014)

KPCR: Knowledge Graph Enhanced Personalized Course Recommendation

Heeseok Jung, Yeonju Jang, Seonghun Kim, and Hyeoncheol Kim[✉]

Korea University, Seongbuk-gu, Seoul 02841, Republic of Korea
{poco2889,spring0425,ryankim0409,harrykim}@korea.ac.kr

Abstract. To handle the limitations of collaborative filtering-based recommender systems, knowledge graphs are getting attention as side information. However, there are several problems to apply the existing KG-based methods to the course recommendations of MOOCs. We propose **KPCR**, a framework for **K**nowledge graph enhanced **P**ersonalized **C**ourse **R**ecommendation. In KPCR, internal information of MOOCs and an external knowledge base are integrated through user and course related keywords. In addition, we add the level embedding module that predicts the level of students and courses. Through the experiments with the real-world datasets, we demonstrate that our knowledge graph boosts recommendation performance as side information. The results also show that the two auxiliary modules improve the recommendation performance. In addition, we evaluate the effectiveness of KPCR through the satisfaction survey of users of the real-world MOOCs platform.

Keywords: MOOCs · Personalized learning · Recommender systems

1 Introduction

Despite the growing number of users learning through Massive Open Online Courses (MOOCs), there is a big challenge that students' retention rates are less than 10% on average [1]. One of the major factors that lower retention rates are curricula that do not reflect learners' interests [7], and the content that is too difficult to follow is another main factor [26]. Meanwhile, [11] stated that providing content appropriate to the learner's level increases retention rates.

For these reasons, studies have been conducted to recommend courses to users in MOOCs in various ways [19,22], and many of them use collaborative filtering (CF). However, CF has limitations in that it has low performance in sparse data and has a cold start problem [24]. Utilizing side information has been evaluated as a good solution to solve these problems [18], and knowledge graphs (KG) are getting attention as side information [4]. Accordingly, studies have

This work was supported by Institute of Information & Communications Technology Planning & Evaluation (IITP) grant funded by the Korea government (MSIT) (No. 2020-0-00368, A Neural-Symbolic Model for Knowledge Acquisition and Inference Techniques).

© Springer Nature Switzerland AG 2022
G. Long et al. (Eds.): AI 2021, LNAI 13151, pp. 739–750, 2022.
https://doi.org/10.1007/978-3-030-97546-3_60

been conducted to utilize KG for recommendation using the embedding-based [23], the path-based [5], and the propagation-based method [8,20].

However, it is not appropriate to directly apply the existing KG-based methods to the course recommendations of MOOCs for the following reasons. First, unlike movies or books, the course itself is not included in a knowledge base such as Freebase [2], so a new way to utilize an external knowledge base is needed. Second, the existing KG-based methods usually consist of the graph embedding module and the recommendation module [4]. However, these two modules are difficult to consider the level of the students and the courses.

In this paper, we propose **KPCR**: a framework for **K**nowledge graph enhanced **P**ersonalized **C**ourse **R**ecommendation. We created a knowledge graph by integrating user-course interaction, user interests, course information, and an external knowledge base. When linking internal information in MOOCs and external knowledge bases, users and courses related keywords were used. With the external knowledge base, information related to user interests and course information (e.g., occupations, companies, or related subjects) that are not revealed in the MOOCs platform can be utilized. In addition, we created the user-course level graph containing user-course interaction and the level of users and courses. To improve the recommendation performance, we combined two additional tasks in multi-task learning: knowledge graph embedding task and node classification task, which predicts the level of courses and users.

Through the experiments with the real-world datasets, we demonstrate that our knowledge graph boosts recommendation performance as side information. The results also show that two auxiliary tasks improve the recommendation performance. In addition, we investigated the user satisfaction of KPCR's recommendations for users of real world MOOCs platforms.

2 Preliminary

2.1 Internal Knowledge Graph

A Knowledge Graph (KG) is a multi-relational graph, consisting of entities that are nodes of the graph and relations that are edges of the graph. Each instance of an edge can be expressed as a triplet (h, r, t), which means that h has some relation r with t [21].

The internal knowledge graph $KG_{internal}$ is composed of three types of entities and three types of relations. The types of entities are user, course, and keyword.

$$KG_{internal} = \{(h_{in}, r_{in}, t_{in}) \mid h_{in}, t_{in} \in \mathcal{E}_{internal}, \ r_{in} \in \mathcal{R}_{internal}\}$$
$$\mathcal{E}_{internal} = \mathcal{U} \cup \mathcal{C} \cup \mathcal{K}, \ \mathcal{U}\text{:set of users}, \mathcal{C}\text{:set of courses}, \mathcal{K}\text{:set of keywords}$$
$$\mathcal{R}_{internal} = \{enrolled\_in, \ interested\_in, \ related\_to\}$$

The keywords can be extracted from the user's interests and course descriptions provided by the MOOCs platform. A user's interests can be selected during the sign-up process or collected through the course history that the user has taken. Course-related keywords can be obtained from course descriptions such as learning topics and table of contents. Examples of keywords are '*management*', '*artificial intelligence*', and '*social science*'. In this study, the entity pairs include '*User-Course*', '*User-Keyword*', and '*Course-Keyword*'. The relation types are '*enrolled_in*', '*interested_in*', and '*related_to*'.

2.2 External Knowledge Graph

The external knowledge graph $KG_{external}$ is an external knowledge base, which is associated with the keywords mentioned in 2.1. DBpedia [14], Freebase [2], and YAGO [17] could be adopted as an external knowledge base.

$$KG_{external} = \{(h_{ext}, r_{ext}, t_{ext}) \mid h_{ext}, t_{ext} \in \mathcal{E}_{external}, \quad r_{ext} \in \mathcal{R}_{external}\}$$
$$\mathcal{E}_{external}: \text{set of entities in external knowledge base}, \mathcal{K} \subset \mathcal{E}_{external}$$
$$\mathcal{R}_{external}: \text{set of relations in external knowledge base}$$

The unified knowledge graph $KG_{unified}$ is created by integrating the internal knowledge graph and external graph through keywords. Fig. 1 shows an example of a unified knowledge graph.

$$KG_{unified} = \{(h_{uni}, r_{uni}, t_{uni}) \mid h_{uni}, t_{uni} \in \mathcal{E}_{unified}, \quad r_{uni} \in \mathcal{R}_{unified}\}$$
$$\mathcal{E}_{unified} = \mathcal{E}_{internal} \cup \mathcal{E}_{external}, \quad \mathcal{R}_{unified} = \mathcal{R}_{internal} \cup \mathcal{R}_{external}$$
$$\mathcal{E}_{external} \cap \mathcal{E}_{internal} = \mathcal{K}$$

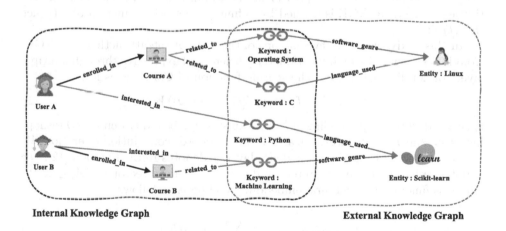

Internal Knowledge Graph   **External Knowledge Graph**

Fig. 1. Example of a unified knowledge graph.

2.3 User-Course Level Graph

To recommend appropriate courses to a user while considering the difficulty of course and the level of the user, we define the user-course level graph G_{level}. We regard the user-course bipartite graph as a homogeneous graph, and label each node with course-level and user-level. The level of user or course is defined in three stages: basic, intermediate, and advanced. The user-course level graph is used in the node classification task, which predicts the level of course or user.

$$G_{level} = \{(u, enrolled\_in, c, l_u, l_c) \mid u \in \mathcal{U}, \ c \in \mathcal{C}, \ l_u \in L_U, \ l_c \in L_C\}$$
$$L_U = \{U_{t_0-lv1}, \ U_{t_0-lv2}, \ U_{t_0-lv3}, .., \ U_{t_n-lv1}, \ U_{t_n-lv2}, \ U_{t_n-lv3}\}$$
$$L_C = \{C_{t_0-lv1}, \ C_{t_0-lv2}, \ C_{t_0-lv3}, .., \ C_{t_n-lv1}, \ C_{t_n-lv2}, \ C_{t_n-lv3}\}$$

$lv1$, $lv2$, and $lv3$ denote the basic, intermediate, and advanced level respectively. $t_k(k = 0, 1, .., n)$ means category k (e.g., *computer science*). The level of the course can be extracted from the course description. A user's level can be collected through the self-reported information entered by the users, test scores when registering, or difficulty of the courses the user has taken so far.

2.4   Task Formulation

Given the unified knowledge graph and the user-course level graph, we aim to recommend top-K courses in which each user would like to enroll.

3   Methodology

3.1   Structural Embedding

In order to get the structural embedding, we adopt the knowledge graph embedding (KGE). KGE represents the KG components (entities and relations) into low dimensional vectors while preserving the semantic meaning and their connectivities. In general, KGE is learned by defining the scoring function of a triplet (h, r, t) [21].

In this study, we use ConvE [3], one of the state-of-the-art methods for KGE. ConvE is known to be highly parameter-efficient and expressive through multiple layers of non-linear features. The scoring function of ConvE is as follows:

$$\phi(h, r, t) = f(vec(f([\bar{e}_h \parallel \bar{r}_r] * \omega))W)e_t \tag{1}$$

e_h, r_r, e_t denote the embedding of h, r, t respectively; $\bar{e}_h$ and $\bar{r}_r$ denote 2D reshaping of e_h and r_r; $\parallel$ denotes concatenation; $*$ denotes convolution operation; W denotes the weight matrix of the dense layer; f denotes ReLU function [12]; vec denotes reshaping feature map tensor $A \in \mathbb{R}^{c \times w \times h}$ into a vector $vec(A) \in \mathbb{R}^{cwh}$. The loss function of structural embedding module is as follows:

$$\mathcal{L}_{structural} = \sum_{(h,r,t) \in KG_{unified}} l(h, r, t) \tag{2}$$

$$l_{(h,r,t)} = -\frac{1}{N} \sum_i^N (y_{t_i} \cdot \ln(s_i) + (1 - y_{t_i}) \cdot \ln(1 - s_i)), s = \sigma(\phi(h, r, t)) \tag{3}$$

y_{t_i} means the label vector with dimension $\mathbb{R}^{1 \times N}$ for 1-N scoring (its elements are ones if there exists relations, otherwise zeros).

3.2 Level Embedding

Like [9], we use two-layer graph convolutional networks (GCNs) for node classification (level prediction) on the user-course level graph. The level prediction is as follows:

$$Z = f(X, A) = \text{softmax}(\hat{A}\text{ReLU}(\hat{A}XW^{(0)})W^{(1)}) \tag{4}$$

Here, $\hat{A}$ is a self-loop added and normalized adjacency matrix of the user-course level graph. $W^{(0)}$ is input-to-hidden weight matrix and $W^{(1)}$ is hidden-to-output weight matrix. X is initial node data (we used the one-hot label of the nodes' ID as X). The loss function of the level embedding module is as follows:

$$\mathcal{L}_{level} = -\sum_{l \in \mathcal{Y}_L} \sum_{f=1}^{F} Y_{lf} \ln Z_{lf} \tag{5}$$

F denotes the number of node labels, and $\mathcal{Y}_L$ is the set of node indices that have labels. We use the first hidden layer activation as the level embedding of users and courses.

3.3 Model Optimization and Prediction

Since the level and structural embedding both contain educationally important side information, we define the final embedding of the user u and the course c as follows:

$$e_u^{CF} = e_u^{level} + e_u^{structural}, e_c^{CF} = e_c^{level} + e_c^{structural} \tag{6}$$

e^{level} denotes the first hidden layer activation of the user or the course in Sect. 3.2. $e^{structural}$ denotes the representation of the user or the course from the entity embedding in Sect. 3.1.

For the final prediction, we estimate the matching score between the user u and the course c by conducting inner product of e_u^{CF} and e_c^{CF}. According to this score, we recommend top-K courses for the users.

$$p(u, c) = e_u^{CF \top} e_c^{CF} \tag{7}$$

We adopt the Bayesian Personalized Ranking (BPR) [15] as the loss function of our recommendation module. BPR assumes that the user prefers the interacted item to the other non-interacted items:

$$\mathcal{L}_{CF} = \sum_{u,c,c'} -\ln \sigma(p(u, c) - p(u, c')) \tag{8}$$

u denotes user in the train dataset; c and c' denote positive (observed) and negative (unobserved) course in the train dataset.

Our final objective function is as follows:

$$\mathcal{L}_{total} = \mathcal{L}_{CF} + \mathcal{L}_{level} + \mathcal{L}_{structural} \tag{9}$$

Specifically, we optimize $\mathcal{L}_{CF}$ and $\mathcal{L}_{structural}$ jointly (since these two tasks are similar) and optimize $\mathcal{L}_{level}$ alternatively. Figure 2 describes the training process of our model framework.

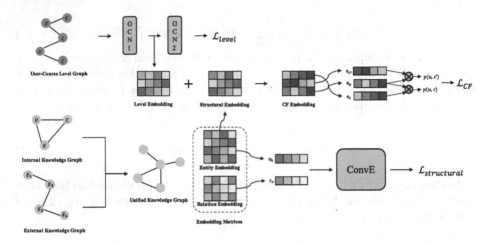

Fig. 2. Illustration of training process for our proposed KPCR.

4   Experiment 1

4.1   Datasets

We used two datasets, ESOF[1] and XuetangX,[2] to demonstrate the effectiveness of KPCR. We collected a real-world MOOCs dataset from ESOF, which is a public MOOCs platform for software education in the Republic of Korea. To verify that our method is effective on another dataset, we compared the performance using the XuetangX dataset [25]. XuetangX is one of the biggest MOOCs platforms in China.

To ensure the quality of the data, we remove users and courses with less than three interactions for both datasets. For the ESOF dataset, we conduct 3-fold cross-validation to evaluate the performance. Regarding the XuetangX dataset, we sampled about 25% of all users and randomly sampled 30% of the interactions as the test set. Also, we randomly sampled 10% of the train set as a validation set for hyper-parameter tuning. Table 1 illustrates the detailed statistics of the datasets.

---

[1] https://www.ebssw.kr/.
[2] https://www.xuetangx.com/.

Table 1. Detailed statistics of the datasets.

		ESOF	XuetangX
Internal knowledge graph	#user	3,703	10,714
	#course	276	339
	#keyword	75	5
	#user-course interaction	27,502	56,029
	#user-keyword interaction	3,355	16,621
	#course-keyword interaction	1,431	339
External knowledge graph	#entities	14,578	9,042
	#relations	310	135
	#edges	28,612	18,284

4.2 Knowledge Graph Construction

For the ESOF dataset, we extract the user-related keywords from the information entered by the user during the sign-up process. The course-related keywords are selected by the lecturers. Regarding the XuetangX dataset, since the last update of this dataset was in October 2018, we could not access the descriptions of some courses. Therefore, the course-related keywords were set as the name of the course category. The user-related keywords are the union of the course related keywords taken by each user.

Meanwhile, we used Freebase [2] as an external knowledge base to create the external knowledge graph for both datasets. Freebase is a database system composed of entities and relations in the real-world, and designed to be used as a public repository of the world's knowledge.

4.3 User-Course Level Graph Construction

For the ESOF dataset, the difficulty level of the course specified in the course description was used for the course level. The user level is set as the average level of the courses that the user has taken so far. In the case of the XuetangX dataset, we were not able to access some course descriptions. So the difficulty level of the course was determined according to the title of each course. For example, if a course title includes 'introduction', we regard the course's level as basic (level 1), and if it includes 'advanced', the course's level is set as advanced (level 3). If the title does not include difficulty information, the level of the course is set to intermediate (level 2). The user's level is set as the average level of the courses that the user has taken so far.

4.4 Experimental Settings

To investigate the effectiveness of recommendations, we opted to use Recall@K and NDCG@K [16] as evaluation metrics. Recall@K (Rec@K) is the ratio of courses selected by the user among the top-K recommended list to the total number of courses that the user enrolled in. While Recall@K equivalently considers the items ranked within the top-K, NDCG@K also considers the predicted positions. We set K in [3, 5, 10].

For both datasets, we fix the embedding size of all models to 64. For our model, we use 16 convolution filters with (3 × 3) size for ConvE. The dropout ratio of embedding, convolution feature map, and dense layer are [0.2, 0.1, 0.3]. To avoid overfitting, we also use batch-normalization [6]. The learning rate is set as 0.001. We select Adam Optimizer [8] for all models, and use the early stopping technique with 10-epoch patience according to Recall@10.

We demonstrate the performance of KPCR comparing it with the baseline models below:

BPRMF [15]: BPR-based Matrix Factorization (BPRMF) is a KG-free CF method based on pairwise preference.

CKE [23]: Collaborative Knowledge Base Embedding (CKE) is a method that utilizes textual, visual, and structural knowledge to refine item embedding. In our experiment, we only use a structural knowledge module consisting of TransR.

CKE-ConvE: A model that changed TransR to ConvE in CKE. We experiment with this model to check the efficiency of ConvE.

KGAT [20]: Knowledge Graph Attention Network (KGAT) is a propagation-based method that refines the embedding of users and items with knowledge-aware attention.

KPCR $(L + S)$: Our proposed method that uses both the level embedding module and the structural module to assist the recommendation module.

KPCR (S): A simple version of our proposed method that does not use the level embedding module.

KPCR (S_i): Another version of KPCR(S) that uses internal KG only.

4.5   Results

Table 2 shows the overall performance comparison. The experimental results showed similar trends in both datasets.

Table 2. Overall performance comparison.

	ESOF				XuetangX			
	Rec@5	Rec@10	NDCG@5	NDCG@10	Rec@5	Rec@10	NDCG@5	NDCG@10
KPCR $(L + S)$	0.633	0.728	0.628	0.659	0.503	0.609	0.450	0.489
KPCR (S)	0.618	0.712	0.618	0.648	0.498	0.595	0.448	0.483
KPCR (S_i)	0.612	0.701	0.610	0.639	0.495	0.589	0.447	0.481
KGAT	0.602	0.701	0.593	0.626	0.452	0.548	0.404	0.439
CKE-ConvE	0.527	0.617	0.510	0.542	0.368	0.446	0.326	0.355
CKE	0.450	0.544	0.433	0.467	0.347	0.423	0.306	0.335
BPRMF	0.589	0.676	0.583	0.611	0.435	0.518	0.394	0.424

Our methods (KPCR (S), KPCR (S_i), and KPCR $(L + S)$) outperforms the KG-free method (BPRMF), while some other KG-enhanced methods (CKE, CKE-ConvE) showed lower performance than BPRMF. This suggests that CKE and CKE-ConvE could not fully utilize KG [8], while our method effectively utilized the knowledge graph as side information.

CKE-ConvE is higher than that of the original CKE. This can suggest that ConvE learns expressive features better than TransR. In addition, the number of parameters of CKE is 2.5M (ESOF) and 1.9M (XuetangX), while the number of parameters of CKE-ConvE is 1.3M (ESOF) and 1.4M (XuetangX). This also suggests that ConvE is parameter efficient.

CKE-ConvE showed a lower performance compared to KPCR(S). The performance gap seems to be due to the difference in the type of KG used by the two models. Unlike CKE-ConvE, which uses KG including only item (course)-related information, KPCR (S) uses KG including user-course interactions and user-related information as well.

KPCR(S) showed a better performance than KGAT, which uses the same type of KG. There might be two reasons for this: First, KGAT uses the score function of TransR when calculating knowledge-aware attention. As mentioned earlier, TransR has limitations in learning expressive features. Second, there is a possibility that information loss occurred in the neighbor sampling process of KGAT [4].

In order to investigate whether external knowledge improves performance in educational recommendations, we compare the performance between KPCR (S_i) and KPCR (S). The former used the internal KG defined in Sect. 3.1, and the latter used the unified KG defined in Sect. 3.2. The result suggests that external knowledge was influential in the task of recommending courses.

Finally, we compare the performances of KPCR $(L + S)$ and KPCR (S). The result shows the effectiveness of using the level information in education regardless of the number of categories.

5   Experiment 2

ESOF allows authorized users to create their own homepage and load courses from ESOF. The authorized users can monitor the learning progress of the homepage members. We created a homepage and provided lists of recommended courses using KPCR and KGAT to the homepage members. Afterwards, we investigated user satisfaction for each list of recommended courses. Participants were recruited through the ESOF platform, and a total of 129 volunteers participated in the experiment. Figure 3 shows the first page of the homepage we created. The thumbnails of the courses have been blurred due to copyright issue.

5.1   Instruments

We investigated user satisfaction by measuring satisfaction with personalized services and system values. The questions were measured on a 5-point Likert scale ranging from (1) strongly disagree to (5) strongly agree. Data were statistically analyzed using SPSS 25.0, and the alpha level was set at 0.05. Separated independent sample t-tests were performed.

User satisfaction with personalized recommendations and the value of the recommender system were measured by questions adapted from the customized service part of SERVQUAL [13] and the questions used in [10]. The internal reliability of the instruments shows a Cronbach's alpha of 0.839 and 0.888 respectively.

The questions are as follows:

Q1. whether the recommender system pays attention to the user needs,
Q2. whether the recommender system captures the user's interests,
Q3. whether the system provides adaptive recommendations,
Q4. whether the recommender system is useful,
Q5. whether the recommender system finds interesting courses efficiently, and
Q6. the overall satisfaction of the recommender system.

Fig. 3. The first page of the created homepage (thumbnails have been blurred due to copyright issues).

5.2 Results

Satisfaction with personalized recommendation and value of the recommender system were analyzed using the average score of each related questions (Q1–Q3 for satisfaction with personalized recommendation, and Q4–Q6 for value of the recommender system). Recommendations using KPCR obtained high average scores in both areas. As a result of independent sample t-tests, both areas

Table 3. Results of independent sample t-tests on user satisfaction.

	Mean		t-value	Significance
	KPCR	KGAT		
Personalized recommendation	4.008	3.778	2.137	0.034*
Value of recommender system	4.191	3.876	3.165	0.002**

* Denotes p<0.05, ** denotes p<0.01.

showed statistically significant differences (personalized recommendation: p = 0.034, value of recommender system: p = 0.002). That is, KPCR showed a statistically significant higher user satisfaction than KGAT. Table 3 demonstrates the detailed results of independent sample t-tests on user satisfaction.

6 Conclusion and Future Work

In this study, we proposed KPCR, a framework for Knowledge graph enhanced Personalized Course Recommendation. KPCR creates an integrated KG through keywords, and based on this, provides recommendations that also consider the level of learners. We demonstrate that the KG we built and the two KG-related auxiliary modules improved recommendation performance through the experiments with the real-world datasets and the investigation of user satisfaction.

For future works, we can study ways to utilize more diverse educational side information, such as the learning style of the users and social interaction between users in the course.

References

1. Alraimi, K.M., Zo, H., Ciganek, A.P.: Understanding the MOOCs continuance: the role of openness and reputation. Comput. Educ. **80**, 28–38 (2015)
2. Bollacker, K., Tufts, P., Pierce, T., Cook, R.: A platform for scalable, collaborative, structured information integration. In: International Workshop on Information Integration on the Web (IIWeb 2007), pp. 22–27 (2007)
3. Dettmers, T., Minervini, P., Stenetorp, P., Riedel, S.: Convolutional 2D knowledge graph embeddings. In: Proceedings of the AAAI Conference on Artificial Intelligence, vol. 32 (2018)
4. Guo, Q., et al.: A survey on knowledge graph-based recommender systems. IEEE Trans. Knowl. Data Eng. (2020)
5. Hu, B., Shi, C., Zhao, W.X., Yu, P.S.: Leveraging meta-path based context for top-N recommendation with a neural co-attention model. In: Proceedings of the 24th ACM SIGKDD International Conference on Knowledge Discovery & Data Mining, pp. 1531–1540 (2018)
6. Ioffe, S., Szegedy, C.: Batch normalization: accelerating deep network training by reducing internal covariate shift. In: International Conference on Machine Learning, pp. 448–456. PMLR (2015)
7. Jdidou, Y., Khaldi, M.: Increasing the profitability of students in MOOCs using recommendation systems. Int. J. Knowl. Soc. Res. (IJKSR) **7**(4), 75–85 (2016)

8. Kingma, D.P., Ba, J.: Adam: a method for stochastic optimization. arXiv preprint arXiv:1412.6980 (2014)
9. Kipf, T.N., Welling, M.: Semi-supervised classification with graph convolutional networks. arXiv preprint arXiv:1609.02907 (2016)
10. Liang, T.P., Lai, H.J., Ku, Y.C.: Personalized content recommendation and user satisfaction: theoretical synthesis and empirical findings. J. Manag. Inf. Syst. **23**(3), 45–70 (2006)
11. Loyd, E., Prante, M., Messinger, L.: Evaluation of Charlotte-Mecklenburg schools personalized learning initiative-year 2 (2017)
12. Nair, V., Hinton, G.E.: Rectified linear units improve restricted Boltzmann machines. In: ICML (2010)
13. Parasuraman, A., Zeithaml, V.A., Berry, L.: SERVQUAL: a multiple-item scale for measuring consumer perceptions of service quality. J. Retail. **64**(1), 12–40 (1988)
14. Paulheim, H.: Knowledge graph refinement: a survey of approaches and evaluation methods. Semantic Web **8**(3), 489–508 (2017)
15. Rendle, S., Freudenthaler, C., Gantner, Z., Schmidt-Thieme, L.: BPR: Bayesian personalized ranking from implicit feedback. arXiv preprint arXiv:1205.2618 (2012)
16. Rodriguez, M., Posse, C., Zhang, E.: Multiple objective optimization in recommender systems. In: Proceedings of the sixth ACM Conference on Recommender Systems, pp. 11–18 (2012)
17. Suchanek, F.M., Kasneci, G., Weikum, G.: YAGO: a core of semantic knowledge. In: Proceedings of the 16th International Conference on World Wide Web, pp. 697–706 (2007)
18. Sun, Z., et al.: Research commentary on recommendations with side information: a survey and research directions. Electron. Commer. Res. Appl. **37**, 100879 (2019)
19. Symeonidis, P., Malakoudis, D.: Multi-modal matrix factorization with side information for recommending massive open online courses. Expert Syst. Appl. **118**, 261–271 (2019)
20. Wang, X., He, X., Cao, Y., Liu, M., Chua, T.S.: KGAT: knowledge graph attention network for recommendation. In: Proceedings of the 25th ACM SIGKDD International Conference on Knowledge Discovery & Data Mining, pp. 950–958 (2019)
21. Wang, Z., Zhang, J., Feng, J., Chen, Z.: Knowledge graph embedding by translating on hyperplanes. In: Proceedings of the AAAI Conference on Artificial Intelligence, vol. 28 (2014)
22. Xiaoyan, Z., Jie, B.: Research on MOOC system based on bipartite graph context collaborative filtering algorithm. In: Proceedings of the 2019 8th International Conference on Software and Computer Applications, pp. 154–158 (2019)
23. Zhang, F., Yuan, N.J., Lian, D., Xie, X., Ma, W.Y.: Collaborative knowledge base embedding for recommender systems. In: Proceedings of the 22nd ACM SIGKDD International Conference on Knowledge Discovery and Data Mining, pp. 353–362 (2016)
24. Zhang, H., Huang, T., Lv, Z., Liu, S., Yang, H.: MOOCRC: a highly accurate resource recommendation model for use in MOOC environments. Mob. Netw. Appl. **24**(1), 34–46 (2019)
25. Zhang, J., Hao, B., Chen, B., Li, C., Chen, H., Sun, J.: Hierarchical reinforcement learning for course recommendation in MOOCs. In: Proceedings of the AAAI Conference on Artificial Intelligence, vol. 33, pp. 435–442 (2019)
26. Zheng, S., Rosson, M.B., Shih, P.C., Carroll, J.M.: Understanding student motivation, behaviors and perceptions in MOOCs. In: Proceedings of the 18th ACM Conference on Computer Supported Cooperative Work & Social Computing, pp. 1882–1895 (2015)

Probabilistic Term Weighting Based on Three-Way Decisions for Class Based Feature Selection

Aisha Rashed Albqmi[1,2]([⊠]) [iD], Yuefeng Li[1] [iD], and Yue Xu[1] [iD]

[1] School of CS, Queensland University of Technology, Brisbane, QLD, Australia
{y2.li,yue.xu}@qut.edu.au
[2] Department of Computer Science, Taif University, Taif, Saudi Arabia
a.albqmi@hdr.qut.edu.au

Abstract. Selecting features that represent a specific class is important to achieve a high text classification performance. The core and critical part of any text feature selection method is the weighting function. Most term weighting methods only consider document level when calculating a term weight and do not consider the distribution of features among different classes. Such an approach does not accurately reflect the specificity of each individual term that can discriminate between the positive and negative documents in the document collection because of the numerous uncertainties in text documents. To address this problem, we propose an innovative and effective feature-weighing method based on three-way decisions to reduce uncertainties in selected features. The proposed model can assign a more discriminately accurate weight to terms based on their distribution in each class. The experimental results, based on the standard RCV1 dataset and R21578 and three popular performance measures, show that our model significantly outperforms six state-of-the-art baseline models and enhances the performance of text classifier models.

Keywords: Feature selection · Term weighting · Three-way decisions · Uncertainty · Text classification

1 Introduction

Text classification (TC) is the process of automatically classifying unlabelled text documents into a set of predefined categories (e.g., a class or label) since a labelled dataset and its labels are used to train a classifier. A fundamental step in learning a classifier is to represent text documents in a suitable format recognizable by this classifier. In the text classification process, text documents are represented mostly as vectors in the feature space (i.e., Vector Space Model). These vectors consist of weights representing the importance of each term. Since each weight describes the importance of the corresponding term in the document, term weighting is crucial for the success of TC tasks. For this purpose, term

© Springer Nature Switzerland AG 2022
G. Long et al. (Eds.): AI 2021, LNAI 13151, pp. 751–762, 2022.
https://doi.org/10.1007/978-3-030-97546-3_61

weighting algorithms have been developed to improve the terms' discriminating power for classification tasks [3,6,18]. However, recent studies [12,23,24] have highlighted the need for effective term weighting for classification purposes as an ongoing research problem.

The selected features must be relevant to the topics discussed in the collection, more discriminative and less ambiguous [10]. In real applications, however, there exist some ambiguous and uncertain objects whose relevancy to the topic/category cannot be clarified by current knowledge learning processes. They are assumed to cluster into a certain group, called uncertain documents. Thus, selecting features from such documents leads to uncertainties [1].

Traditional term weighting methods, such as the popular TF.IDF, depend on assigning weights only on the occurrences of term t in the document d and the (inverse) number of documents that include this term [19]. Such a method can lead to the loss of some relevant features, particularly those that are less frequent in the collection. The model is also sensitive to the noisy terms in the collection and cannot manage the uncertainties in relevant documents. With noisy text, the correspondence between the features of the training instances and their classes is fuzzy. Thus, in TC tasks it is important to consider how to effectively deal with imprecise and ubiquitous information.

A three-way decisions theory (TWDT) is a powerful mathematical tool introduced by Yao to deal with uncertain, vague, imprecise and incomplete information [27]. In TWDT, the training set is divided into three regions, namely, the positive (POS), boundary (BND) and negative (NEG) regions based on two thresholds. Allowing this partitioning of the training set can help to describe relevant and non-relevant information and reduce the impact of uncertainty. However, the TWDT was proposed originally to explain how to divide the training set into three independent regions. Therefore, the critical problem for this issue is how to use the benefits of the three-way decisions theory for a better term weighting scheme to reflect the discriminative power of terms in each class?

This research aims to develop an effective probabilistic term-weighting model for TC. It automatically updates the documents in positive and negative classes based on a sliding window (SW) over positive (relevant) and negative (non-relevant) ranked documents to reduce uncertainty in the relevant feature discovery. Such a method must be more informative about the relationship of the terms to the class and more discriminative in separating the relevant documents from the non-relevant documents for this class. To achieve this goal, we estimated the term probability distribution over certain POS and NEG regions rather than in a specific document. Unlike traditional supervised weighting functions, the proposed algorithm largely reduces noisy terms and uncertainties in the weighting process. Our model is supervised and starts from the strategy of partitioning the labelled training samples into three regions: two certain regions, POS and NEG and an uncertain region, BND. Based on documents in POS and NEG regions, an innovative and effective probabilistic term-weighting approach, TPR has been proposed to accurately weight the terms. This function assigns more appropriate weight to each term based on their distribution in the POS and NEG regions.

The best representation of the features of each class is then selected and used to represent documents. Therefore, two major contributions have been made in this paper to the fields of text feature selection and TC: (a) A new three-way model based on the sliding window method to identify the uncertainty in document collection and represent the certain documents in each class; (b) A new and effective supervised probabilistic weighting function that assigns a more appropriate weight to each term and, thus, increases the specificity of each individual term that can discriminate between the positive and negative documents in the document collection.

2   Related Work

In text classification, feature weighting is the main step that assigns a numerical value (usually a real number) to each feature to weight its contribution. The feature weightings are then ranked in descending order and the top-scoring features are selected [22]. A higher weight implies that this feature is more important for classification [10]. Therefore, selecting the most informative text features (e.g., terms) is an essential step to represent documents. Consequently, unsuitable numbers, inferior quality or imperfect term-weighting schemes of selected features are likely to generate a lot of noisy information that may reduce the performance of text classification [5,15]. Existing feature weighting methods derived from information retrieval include term frequency-inverse document frequency (TF-IDF) [19], mutual information (MI) [13], information gain (IG) [26], and Chi-Square (χ^2) [4]. They are term-based methods that are easy to compute, efficient and they have been developed and adopted using advanced statistical and mathematical weighting theories [10]. However, they cannot manage the uncertainties in text documents and are sensitive to noise because they do not consider the distribution of features among different classes [7,20]. Many studies including Delta tf-idf [14], relevance frequency (TF-RF) [8] and Inverse Category-Frequency based (ICF-based) [25] have been conducted to use class information for feature weighting. TF-RF is a supervised method that estimates term weightings based on their occurrences in positive and negative classes. The ICF-based model is a new supervised method developed by Wang et al. [25]. The formula of ICF is similar to that of IDF but it uses classes instead of the documents to weight terms. The two supervised models, TF-RF and ICF-based, might assign more reasonable weights to terms than IDF. This is because they consider the distribution of the documents in the positive and negative classes. However, using document frequency to calculate term weighting can generate biased term weights, especially with a small number of documents in a particular class [8]. They might also be impacted by the uncertainty of some ambiguous and uncertain documents [1,2]. Uncertainties are introduced when considering the entire training documents (containing many noisy documents) to estimate the terms' weights. The three-way decision model has been proven to be effective in describing the imprecision, vagueness and uncertainty in data analysis by identifying the uncertain region (BND) to assist in reducing uncertainties and updating the strategy to select and weight features [27].

3   The Proposed Model

To deal with the uncertainties and to improve the effectiveness of feature weighting methods for text classification task, our model aims to set the decision boundary by ranking documents according to their relevance to a given query. Document relevance ranking is established by extracting the initial features and initial weight from positive documents using the probability measure. The documents in our model are represented by a set of features (or terms) and a score is calculated to understand the relevance of documents to a given query. Given a document collection D, which consists of a relevant document set D^+, and a non-relevant document set D^-, let $T^+ = \{t_1, t_2, \ldots, t_n\}$ be a set of terms which are extracted from D^+ and $T^+ \subset T$ (T represents all terms in D). Our model selects the top-k terms by using a probabilistic model. This step first calculates $r(t)$ (the number of relevant documents containing term t) and $n(t)$ (the total number of documents containing term t), and then calculates $w(t) =$

$$\frac{(r(t) + 0.5)/(|D^+| - r(t) + 0.5)}{(n(t) - r(t) + 0.5)/(|D| - n(t) - |D^+| + r(t) + 0.5)} \tag{1}$$

where $|D^+|$ and $|D|$ denote the number of documents in D^+ and D, respectively. The constant number 0.5 is used to avoid zero-division-error. The probabilistic model is used to calculate term weight because in binary text classification we deal with uncertain information. After the weight of terms was calculated, the following rank function (i.e., score) was assigned to all $d \in D$ to decide their relevance, as follows [1,2]:

$$rank(d) = \sum_{t \in T^+} g(t) \tag{2}$$

where $g(t) = w(t)$ if $t \in d$; otherwise $g(t) = 0$. Once the weight of the documents is calculated, the documents are ranked in descending order based on their scores.

3.1   A Three-Way Decisions Model Based on SW

After ranking the training documents, the most relevant documents will be located at the top of the ranked list, while non-relevant ones will be located at the bottom, as shown in Fig. 1 (left). However, in most cases, there is a region in which relevant and non-relevant documents are mixed due to an uncertain boundary. Therefore, a SW technique and entropy are used to effectively determine the boundary region. In this paper, the size of the window was set to five documents. The model starts to slide the window from the top documents in the ranked list and then calculates the entropy value for the window. The window then slides over one document and yields a new entropy value. It continues to slide and then stops when the entropy is greater than the threshold (e.g. 95%). The same process was followed for the non-relevant documents, starting from the end of the list where we expected the negative documents to be.

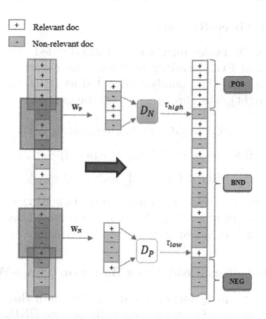

Fig. 1. Three-way decisions model based on SW.

3.2 Calculating Entropy Value

The entropy value is proposed to measures and describe the uncertainty of the documents' relevance related to the topic. The entropy value $E(W)$ in our model can be calculated based on the number of positive documents P, and negative documents N, in each window as follows:

$$E(W) = -\left(\frac{P}{|W|} \log_2 \frac{P}{|W|} + \frac{N}{|W|} \log_2 \frac{N}{|W|} \right) \qquad (3)$$

where $|W|$ is the size of sliding window. We selected two windows, W_P and W_N, with the greatest entropy value. The first window W_P, was from the top of the ranked list of documents and the second window W_N, was from the bottom of the list. For W_P, the non-relevant documents are denoted as D_N, where $D_N = \{ d \mid d \in D^- \cap W_P \}$. For W_N, relevant documents are denoted as D_P, where $D_P = \{ d \mid d \in D^+ \cap W_N \}$. We then selected the highest weighting score of non-relevant documents in D_N as a τ_{high}, and the lowest weighting score of relevant documents in D_P as a τ_{low}, as shown in Fig. 1. Thus, a pair of thresholds $(\tau_{high}, \tau_{low})$ can be defined as follows:

$$\tau_{high} = \max_{d_i \in D_N} \{ rank(d_i) \} \qquad (4)$$

$$\tau_{low} = \min_{d_i \in D_P} \{ rank(d_i) \} \qquad (5)$$

3.3   Construct Three-Regions

For a training set D, its documents $d \in D$ are divided into three regions: the positive (denoted as POS, possibly relevant), the negative (denoted as NEG, possibly irrelevant) and the boundary (denoted as BND, uncertain) regions as shown in Fig. 1 (right). The three regions can be expressed as follows:

$$POS = \{\, d \in D \mid rank(d) > \tau_{high} \,\}$$
$$BND = \{\, d \in D \mid \tau_{low} \leq rank(d) \leq \tau_{high} \,\}$$
$$NEG = \{\, d \in D \mid rank(d) < \tau_{low} \,\}$$

These three regions can help to develop a term weighting scheme to reflect the discriminative power of terms in each class (positive and negative) that lead to improvements in the predictive accuracy of the classifier.

3.4   Probabilistic Term-Weighting Based on Three-Way Decisions

In our model, the training documents are divided into three regions: two certain regions, POS and NEG, and an uncertain region, BND. Documents in the POS and NEG regions have exact class features. Thus, we can extract features from these two regions that represent each class. We present a new and effective probabilistic weighting function called Term Probability Relevance (TPR). This function assigns a more appropriate weight to each term based on their distribution in the POS and NEG regions. The best representation of the features of each class are then selected and used as inputs to the proposed classifier.

To estimate the relevance of term t in the relevant and non-relevant classes, we first calculate the probability of t in the POS region, $P(t|POS)$, and in the NEG region, $P(t|NEG)$, as follows:

$$P(t|POS) = \frac{c(t, POS)}{\sum_{d \in POS} |d_i|} \tag{6}$$

$$P(t|NEG) = \frac{c(t, NEG)}{\sum_{d \in NEG} |d_i|} \tag{7}$$

where $c(t, POS)$ and $c(t, NEG)$ are the counts of term t in the POS and NEG regions, respectively, and $|d_i|$ is the length of the document. Thus, the TPR in each class can be calculated using Eq. 6 and Eq. 7 as follows:

$$TPR^+(t) = \log\left(\frac{P(t|POS) + 0.5}{P(t|NEG) + 0.5}\right) \tag{8}$$

$$TPR^-(t) = \log\left(\frac{P(t|NEG) + 0.5}{P(t|POS) + 0.5}\right) \tag{9}$$

where $TPR^+(t)$ and $TPR^-(t)$ represent the probability that t relevance to the positive or negative class, respectively. The constant number 0.5 is added to avoid zero-division-error.

3.5   The Selection of Best Feature Representation

The value of TPR(t) in Eq. 8 and Eq. 9 represents how much the term t contributes to the class. For example, if the $TPR^+(t) > 0$, the algorithm assumes that t is more relevant to the positive class than the negative. Similarly, if the $TPR^-(t) > 0$, then the algorithm assumes that t is more relevant to the negative class. Thus, the relevance weight $w_r(t)$ for all $t \in T$ is calculated based on the maximum value among TPRs as follows:

$$w_r(t) = \max\left(TPR^+(t), TPR^-(t)\right) \qquad (10)$$

A larger TPR value means that the term is more distinctive in a specific class as it accurately estimates the relevance of the term to the class. Then, the proposed model ranks terms in descending order and uses the top words (i.e., $top - k$) to represent the documents, such that $T = \{ (t_1, w_{r1}), (t_2, w_{r2}), \ldots, (t_m, w_{rm}) \}$, where m is the size of all terms T and $k \leq m$.

4   Evaluation

To verify the proposed model, we designed two hypotheses. First, our TPR model can effectively assign a more appropriate weight to each term through the estimation of their distribution in POS and NEG regions to represent documents in each class. Second, our model, overall, is more effective in selecting the best features representation of each class than most state-of-the-art feature selection models. To support these two hypotheses, we conducted experiments and evaluated their performance.

4.1   Datasets

We used two popular datasets to test the proposed model: Reuters Corpus Volume 1 (RCV1) and Reuters-21578 (R21578). RCV1 includes 806,791 documents that are distributed over the 100 different collections. Each document is a news story in English published by Reuters [9]. Each topic has a set of training documents and a set of testing documents where all the documents have been labelled according to their relevance to the topic they describe. The first 50 collections are used in this paper due to their reliability and high quality as they were manually assessed by domain experts at the National Institute of Standards and Technology (NIST) for TREC in their filtering track.

The R21578 corpus is also widely used for text classification. The data were originally collected and labelled by the Carnegie Group, Inc. and Reuters, Ltd. in the course of developing the CONSTRUE text categorization system. In our experiments, we selected a set of 10 classes for testing, since the class distribution for documents is too skewed. According to Sebastiani's convention [21], it was called R8 because two classes *corn* and *wheat* are intimately related to the class *grain*, and they were appended to the class *grain*.

Both data collections are composed of XML-typed documents and, to eliminate bias in our experiments, all meta-data elements were ignored. All documents were treated as plain text documents by pre-processing steps, including removing a given stop-words list and stemming terms using the Porter Suffix Stripping algorithm [16].

4.2   Baseline Models

We compared the performance of our model with six different baseline models that are considered state-of-the-art. We give a brief description of all these baseline models as follows: (1) **TF-IDF** [19], which is the most popular, unsupervised term weighting scheme in IR and TC tasks. (2) **TF-RF** [8], which is a supervised state-of-the-art term-based model. This algorithm measures the distribution of a term between positive and negative classes and assigns high scores to the terms that are more concentrated in the positive class than in the negative class. (3) **BM25** [17] is one of the best term-based supervised-learning algorithms for ranking documents in IR. (4) **ICF-based** [25] is a new supervised term-based model. This model first weights terms based on their frequency in categories rf. It then combines the rf with tf to estimate the weight of terms at the document level. (5) **MI** and (6) χ^2 are two popular supervised and term-based methods for feature selection. More details about MI and χ^2 can be found in [13].

4.3   Evaluation Measures

The effectiveness of the TPR model is measured by three metrics that are well established and commonly used in the text classification tasks. These metrics are **Recall**, **Precision** and **F-score** (F_1). Readers can refer to [13] for more details. For even better analysis of the experimental results, the **Student's t-test** was used to analyse the significance of the difference between the results of the TPR and the baselines.

4.4   Experimental Design

To effectively measure the performance of our model on classification tasks, we conducted a series of experiments on the RCV1 and R21578 collections. have been carried out to prove that our evaluation hypotheses are valid. We used two known learning algorithms: Support Vector Machine (SVM) and k-Nearest Neighbours (kNN). All the experiments were based on these classifiers. This study presented research in the field of binary classification, a key type of text classification with two predefined categories, namely, relevant or non-relevant classes. However, it is important to note that we were studying the effectiveness of term weighting methods rather than the performance of the learning algorithms.

For each collection, we used the document ranking and SW technique to divide the training set into three distinct regions. Next, the TPR was used to score and rank terms using Eq. 10, and a $top - k$ feature was selected and used as input to the selected classifiers. However, determining the value of k was experimental. For every new document from the testing set, the classification task has to determine whether the new document is relevant to a given topic. A similar process was also separately applied to each baseline. If the three metrics of the model's results were significantly better than the baseline's, then we could say that our TPR model outperformed a baseline model.

4.5 Experimental Settings

The prototype of the proposed model was implemented using Java programming language as the development environment and Weka 3.8. For the SVM classifier, we used the LibSVM package run from Weka[1]. In our experiments, we used the linear kernel since it has been proven to be as powerful as other kernels when the number of features is extremely large [1,11]. We set $C = 1000$ for the RCV1 dataset and $C = 1$ for the R21578 dataset because we found that these two values achieved a higher accuracy rate in our experiments. The value of k in kNN was set to be 1, based on the settings in papers [1,11]. For the experimental parameters of the BM25, we set $k_1 = 1.2$ and $b = 0.75$ as recommended in [13].

4.6 Experimental Results

Tables 1 and 2 present the evaluation results of our model and the baselines, where the number in bold indicates the best result for each measure in all datasets. Each topic in each dataset was tested separately with the same model and the final result is the macro-average of all the tested topics. As shown in Tables 1 and 2, our model outperformed all baseline models for text classification in all measures. The performance of the TPR was consistently the best in all experiments, especially for the SVM classifier. For example, using the RCV1 dataset (Table 1), comparing TPR with the best model, namely, BM25, the minimum and maximum improvements on Precision and Recall measures were 12.72% and 52.45%, respectively. For the R21578 dataset (Table 2), the TPR also outperformed BM25 on all measures with an average improvement of 19.98%. While TF-RF scored better than BM25 on the Recall measure using the SVM classifier, TPR was significantly better than TF-RF with an average improvement of 12.78%. When using the kNN classifier, the TPR achieved the best performance for all measures. For TF-IDF, the TPR was significantly better by 15.32% and 13.32% on the F_1 score for the RCV1 and R21578 datasets, respectively. All TPR improvements were much higher than 5.0%, indicating that the TPR method is more robust than the other feature selection methods in text classification. Based on the combined results of 58 topics from RCV1 and R21578 datasets, we also used the T-test results of all performance measures to compare the p-values of the results of our model with all baseline models. From the test results in Table 3 on the 58 topics of RCV1 and R21578, the model's

---

[1] https://waikato.github.io/weka-wiki/libsvm/.

Table 1. Comparison of the proposed TPR method and baseline models on the RCV1

Classifier	Models	Recall	Precision	F_1
SVM	TPR	0.3581	0.5654	0.3883
	TF-IDF	0.2790	0.4511	0.3161
	TF-RF	0.2284	0.3729	0.2605
	BM25	0.2349	0.5016	0.3187
	ICF- based	0.2147	0.3984	0.2457
	MI	0.1383	0.3863	0.1737
	χ^2	0.2758	0.4755	0.3022
kNN	TPR	0.2845	0.5718	0.3425
	TF-IDF	0.2556	0.4473	0.2970
	TF-RF	0.1543	0.4550	0.1987
	BM25	0.1704	0.4590	0.2252
	ICF- based	0.1802	0.4291	0.2202
	MI	0.1286	0.4416	0.1696
	χ^2	0.1926	0.4927	0.2276

result is considered significantly different from other model's if the p-value is less than 0.05. Clearly, the p-value for most metrics is less than 0.05, confirming that our model's performance is significantly different from all baselines. From the obtained results on the datasets, the TPR achieved the best performance compared with the selected baselines (particularly on F_1) that best expresses the real situation in text classification.

Table 2. Comparison of the proposed TPR method and baseline models on the R21578

Classifier	Models	Recall	Precision	F_1
SVM	TPR	0.8635	0.8214	0.8341
	TF-IDF	0.5529	0.6990	0.5968
	TF-RF	0.7564	0.7358	0.7412
	BM25	0.5810	0.7701	0.7969
	ICF- based	0.6908	0.7131	0.6943
	MI	0.3503	0.6743	0.4278
	χ^2	0.7220	0.5758	0.6256
kNN	TPR	0.7192	0.8718	0.7375
	TF-IDF	0.6701	0.6573	0.6508
	TF-RF	0.5255	0.6524	0.5696
	BM25	0.5568	0.8105	0.6395
	ICF- based	0.5273	0.6024	0.5578
	MI	0.3217	0.6062	0.3893
	χ^2	0.4878	0.5817	0.5236

Table 3. T-test p-values of the baseline models in comparison with our model's on RCV1 and R21578

Classifier	Models	Recall	Precision	F_1
SVM	TF-IDF	0.000565	0.009283	0.001365
	TF-RF	5.28E-07	9.95E-06	7.37E-08
	BM25	5.82E-06	0.081185	0.000196
	ICF- based	2.06E-07	0.000105	3.49E-08
	MI	1.74E-11	0.000160	4.81E-12
	χ^2	0.001435	0.008257	0.000628
kNN	TF-IDF	0.128377	0.000617	0.035325
	TF-RF	1.95E-06	0.000281	7.25E-08
	BM25	1.49E-06	0.005169	3.94E-07
	ICF- based	8.81E-05	5.69E-05	2.2E-06
	MI	4.25E-08	0.000549	1.2E-09
	χ^2	0.000457	0.007575	3.85E-05

5 Conclusion

This paper presents TPR, innovative and supervised probabilistic weighting function. This function assigns a more accurate weight to to each term based on its distribution in the POS and NEG regions and, thus, improves the quality of the extracted features by estimating the probability of relevance of each individual term in the certain regions, effectively reflecting the distinctiveness of a term in a specific class. The best features representation of each class is then selected and used to represent the training documents that the proposed classifier will be trained on. The proposed TPR method was extensively evaluated and showed significantly better performance compared with term-weighting baseline models.

References

1. Albqmi, A.R., Li, Y., Xu, Y.: Enhancing decision boundary setting for binary text classification. In: Mitrovic, T., Xue, B., Li, X. (eds.) AI 2018. LNCS (LNAI), vol. 11320, pp. 799–811. Springer, Cham (2018). https://doi.org/10.1007/978-3-030-03991-2_72
2. Albqmi, A.R., Li, Y., Xu, Y.: A multiple SVMs classifier in three-way decisions framework for text classification. In: WI-IAT 2020, pp. 869–876. IEEE (2020)
3. Chen, K., Zhang, Z., Long, J., Zhang, H.: Turning from TF-IDF to TF-IGM for term weighting in text classification. Expert Syst. Appl. **66**, 245–60 (2016)
4. Chen, Y.-T., Chen, M.C.: Using chi-square statistics to measure similarities for text categorization. Expert Syst. Appl. **38**(4), 3085–3090 (2011)
5. Graves, K.E., Nagarajah, R.: Uncertainty estimation using fuzzy measures for multi-class classification. IEEE Trans. Neural Netw. **18**(1), 128–140 (2007)

6. Haddoud, M., Mokhtari, A., Lecroq, T., Abdeddaïm, S.: Combining supervised term-weighting metrics for SVM text classification with extended term representation. Knowl. Inf. Syst. **49**(3), 909–931 (2016). https://doi.org/10.1007/s10115-016-0924-1
7. Ko, Y.: A study of term weighting schemes using class information for text classification. In ACM SIGIR, pp. 1029–1030 (2012)
8. Lan, M., Tan, C.L., Su, J., Lu, Y.: Supervised and traditional term weighting methods for automatic text categorization. IEEE TPAMI **31**(4), 721–735 (2009)
9. Lewis, D.D., Yang, Y., Rose, T.G., Li, F.: Rcv1: A new benchmark collection for text categorization research. J. Mach. Learn. Res. **5**, 361–397 (2004)
10. Li, Y., Algarni, A., Albathan, M., Shen, Y., Bijaksana, M.A.: Relevance feature discovery for text mining. IEEE TKDE **27**(6), 1656–1669 (2015)
11. Li, Y., Zhang, L., Yue, X., Yiyu, Y., Raymond, L., Yutong, W.: Enhancing binary classification by modeling uncertain boundary in three-way decisions. IEEE Trans. Knowl. Data Eng. **29**(7), 1438–1451 (2017)
12. Maisonnave, M., Delbianco, F., Tohmé, F.A., Maguitman, A.G.: A flexible supervised term-weighting technique and its application to variable extraction and information retrieval. Inteligencia Artif. **22**(63), 61–80 (2019)
13. Manning, C.D., Raghavan, P., Schutze, H.: Introduction to information retrieval. Cambridge University Press (2008)
14. Martineau, J., Finin, T.: Delta tfidf: an improved feature space for sentiment analysis. In: AAAI Conference on Web and Social Media, pp. 258–261. San Jose, CA (2009)
15. Pipanmaekaporn, L., Li, Y.: Mining a data reasoning model for personalized text classification. IEEE Intell. Inf. Bull **12**(1), 17–24 (2011)
16. Porter, M.F.: An algorithm for suffix stripping. Program **14**(3), 130–137 (1980)
17. Robertson, S., Zaragoza, H.: The probabilistic relevance framework: BM25 and beyond. Now Publishers Inc (2009)
18. Sabbah, T., et al.: Modified frequency-based term weighting schemes for text classification. Appl. Soft Comput. **58**, 193–206 (2017)
19. Salton, G., Buckley, C.: Term-weighting approaches in automatic text retrieval. Inf. Process. Manage. **24**(5), 513–523 (1988)
20. Samant, S.S., Murthy, N.B., Malapati, A.: Improving term weighting schemes for short text classification in vector space model. IEEE Access **7**, 166578–166592 (2019)
21. Sebastiani, F.: Machine learning in automated text categorization. ACM Comput. Surveys. **34**(1), 1–47 (2002)
22. Shang, S., Shi, M., Shang, W., Hong, Z.: Improved feature weight algorithm and its application to text classification. Math. Problems Eng. **2016**, 1–12 (2016)
23. Sinoara, R.A., Camacho-Collados, J., Rossi, R.G., Navigli, R., Rezende, S.O.: Knowledge-enhanced document embeddings for text classification. Knowl. Based Syst. **163**, 955–971 (2019)
24. Tang, Z., Li, W., Li, Y.: An improved term weighting scheme for text classification. Con-currency Comput. Practice Experience **32**(9), e5604 (2020)
25. Wang, D., Zhang, H.: Inverse-Category-Frequency Based Supervised Term weighting schemes for text categorization. J. Inf. Sci. Eng. **29**(2), 209–225 (2013)
26. Yang, Y., Pedersen, J.O.: A comparative study on feature selection in text categorization. In: ICML'97, pp. 412–420, Nashville, TN, USA. Morgan Kaufmann Publishers (1997)
27. Yao, Y.: The superiority of three-way decisions in probabilistic rough set models. Inf. Sci. **181**(6), 1080–1096 (2011)

LTWNN: A Novel Approach Using Sentence Embeddings for Extracting Diverse Concepts in MOOCs

Zhijie Wu[1], Jia Zhu[2]([ID]), Shi Xu[1], Zhiwen Yan[1], and Wanying Liang[1]

[1] School of Computer Science, South China Normal University, Guangzhou, China
{2019022683,xushi,2019022686,sylvialaung}@scnu.edu.cn
[2] Zhejiang Normal University, Zhejiang, China
jiazhu@zjnu.edu.cn

Abstract. As a global online education platform, Massive Open Online Courses (MOOCs) provide high-quality learning content. It is a challenging issue to design a key course concept for students with different backgrounds. Even though much work concerned with course concept extraction in MOOC has been done, those related works simply utilize external knowledge to get the relatedness of two different candidate concepts. Furthermore, they require the input to belong to multi-document and severely rely on seed sets, in which their model shows poor performance when input is a single document. Addressing these drawbacks, we tackle concept extraction from a single document using **LTWNN**, a novel method **L**earning **t**o **W**eight with **N**eural **N**etwork for Course Concept Extraction in MOOCs. With LTWNN, we make full use of external knowledge via making relatedness between each candidate concept and document by introducing an embedding-based maximal marginal relevance (MMR), which explicitly increases diversity among selected concepts. Moreover, we combine the inner statistical information and external knowledge, in which the neural network automatically learns to allocate weight for them. Experiments on different course corpus show that our method outperforms alternative methods.

Keywords: MOOC · Course concept extraction · Learning to weight · Neural network · Diversity

1 Introduction

The rapid development of modern networks and the Internet 2.0 have spawned many online open platforms, of which Coursera and Xuetang Online are online curriculum education platforms, providing great convenience for learners within doors. Following this trend, a large amount of knowledge data are created, including course videos and their subtitles. However, it is difficult for learners to understand and analyze the knowledge from a global perspective, while course concepts

Supported by organization x.

G. Long et al. (Eds.): AI 2021, LNAI 13151, pp. 763–774, 2022.
https://doi.org/10.1007/978-3-030-97546-3_62

can describe the knowledge points contained in these classrooms or textbooks. Understanding the overall concept makes it easier to learn the subject and assist in understanding the text for learners.

Although quite a few researches [5,14,19,25] on course concepts extraction from teaching materials and course subtitles have been done, the problem of concept extraction from course subtitles in MOOCs is far from solved. Course concept extraction is non-trivial and challenging due to three reasons, including the single short context problem, the low-frequency problem, and the poor diversity of concepts.

Related research topics, including keyphrase extraction [6,12,15,21,22] and term extraction [8,11] are popular and valid in the information retrieval domain. Pan et al. [19] introduce external knowledge to explore the relationships between different concepts that have the same meanings. However, simply making use of external knowledge by using relatedness of candidates via word embedding resulting in being unable to utilize the global embedding feature. Furthermore, their work is based on multi documents, while ours is both simple and only requires the current document (single document), rather than an entire corpus. Also, their work relies heavily on seed sets, yet these seed sets are limited to acquire in some cases.

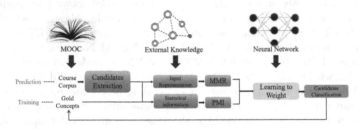

Fig. 1. Our proposed framework LTWNN. Note that we do not need extract candidates in training phase

To address the above problems, we propose learning to weight using sentence embedding with neural networks for course concept extraction in this paper, as shown in Fig. 1. The critical aspect of our idea is that it cannot only improve the diversity of extracted course concepts by introducing external knowledge but also automatically learn to weight to leverage inner statistical information and external expertise. First, we extract some keyphrases as candidates by the Part-of-speech (POS) rule template, and we introduce external knowledge to represent each document by sentence embedding model. Then, to improve the diversity of extracted concepts, we introduce the MMR algorithm and change the formula to fit our task. Next, we combine with the score of MMR and statistical information (i.e., PMI), and then our model learns to weight by neural network classifier (e.g., MLP). Finally, in the prediction phase, the MMR score and PMI score of each candidate concept will be the input of the trained model. Note that we do not care label that the model predicts, we just select the value of the maximal probability of result, as shown in Fig. 2. After the prediction of each candidate concept, we rank them by the selected maximal probability.

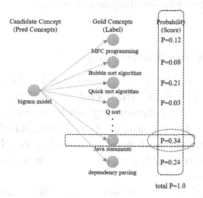

Fig. 2. For the candidate concept 'bigram model', its maximal probablity corresponding to the result of classification 'Java statements'. Here we just select the value P = 0.34 as score of concept.

The main contributions of our model are summarized as follows:

- We propose to introduce the MMR algorithm and utilize external knowledge to calculate relatedness between candidate concepts and documents, which validly solves the diversity of extracted concepts.
- We propose to combine inner statistical information and external knowledge properly, in which we apply neural networks to learn to weight for each feature information automatically.
- We propose LTWNN, which incorporates neural networks into the course concept extraction model without relying on multi-document corpus and seed sets.

2   Related Work

2.1   Course Concept Extraction (CCE)

Based on the keyphrases extraction, Pan et al. [19] compared the task with keyword extraction and designed a novel graph-based propagation process. Chen et al. [5] extended Pan's approach to upgrading the quality of candidate concepts via a novel automated phrase mining method called AutoPhrase [24]. Moreover, based on Pan's approach, Yu et al. [25] achieved course concept expansion with an interactive game.

Different from these architectures are listed above that regard CCE as a ranking problem, Lu et al. [14] applied deep learning in CCE by setting three types of tag for educational textbooks. Their proposed model mainly adopts a gated recurrent unit (GRU) network. Simultaneously, their application scenario is national curriculum standards of mathematics, which is different from ours, for that the colloquial of course data brings more difficulties for our task. All the above approaches bring valuable references for our work course concept extraction.

2.2   Word and Sentence Embeddings

We introduce external knowledge via embeddings in this paper. Next, we review the development of embeddings. Word embedding (word2vec) [16] is proposed to improve the semantic via representing words as vectors in continuous vector space. To make up for the weakness of word2vec, GloVe [20] is proposed to train the embedding model based on global vocabulary. GloVe integrated Global Matrix Factorization into word2vec, which enriches the semantic and syntax information between words.

The represent of entire sentences and documents is needed to get relatedness between two sentences. Similar to word2vec, Skip-Thought [9] provides sentence embeddings trained to predict neighbor sentences. Based on the Skip-Thought, Logeswaran et al. [13] proposed Quick-thoughts via classifying neighbor sentence, but not generating a new sentence. The Quick-thoughts features a much faster training than Skip-Thought. Different from general word vectors, Sent2Vec [18] produces words and N-gram vectors that can be integrated to form sentence vectors after special training. Additionally, experiments conducted by [1] suggest that sentence representation based on averaged word vectors is effective. This property is used in our embedding method, for the reason that it is accessible and valid.

3   LTWNN: Learning to Weight with Neural Networks

Next, we will clearly describe every procedure of the proposed method. Note that the extraction of candidates has been described in Sect. 2 and so that it will not be described in detail.

3.1   Statistical Information

Statistical information is usually regarded as an important quantization indicator for extracting keyphrases, including TFIDF [21], Log-likelihood (LL) [7], and Pointwise Mutual Information (PMI) [6]. Due to the existence of a single short document, in our paper, we adopt PMI to get enough statistical features. The basis of these methods is that if the constituents of a multi-word candidate phrase form a collocation rather than co-occurring by chance, it is more likely to be considered a phrase [10]. Specifically, for the N-gram candidate concept $P = \{c_1, c_2, ..., c_n\}$, where $N > 1$, the PMI will be calculated by

$$PMI(c_1, c_2) = \frac{2 \times freq(c_1, c_2)}{freq(c_1) + freq(c_2)} \tag{1}$$

where $freq(P)$ indicates the frequency of the candidate concept P on one document $d \in Cor$. For the candidates that belong to N-gram ($N > 2$), the PMI is defined as

$$PMI_t = max(\{PMI(P, B)\}) \tag{2}$$

where $P = \{c_1, c_2, ..., c_i\}$ and $B = \{c_{i+1}, c_{i+2}, ..., c_N\}$.

3.2 From Embedding to Candidate Concepts with MMR

The problem of low-frequency and single short context leads to some apparent weakness. For example, most candidates appear only once (i.e., the $freq(c_1 + c_2)$ = 1), which shows that the semantic relatedness between each candidate concept provided by internal statistics is limited. Therefore, we propose to represent candidates via introducing information from external knowledge.

Typical embedding methods (e.g., word, sentence and document embedding) show great performance on capturing semantic relatedness between different words within the shared vector space. Word embeddings represent each phrase and word via low-dimensional space vector, the relatedness between two phrases can be reflected by their cosine distance of their vectors. Here, we use trained word embedding $vec = \{v_{w1}, v_{w2}, ..., v_{wi}\}$, where v_{wi} is real-valued vector of each word w_i. Then, for the each candidate consist of L length, $P = \{char_1, char_2, ..., char_i\}$, we get its vectors $vp = \{v_1, v_2, ..., v_L\}$ is the corresponding word vector of $char_i$ from vec.

Getting word vector from external knowledge is helpful to improve semantic relatedness for low-frequency words, and it improves the probability of extracting the informal expression "Q sort" of "quick sort". However, it brings new problems for us. For example, we can extract the concept "bubble sort algorithm" and "heap algorithm", while another concept "algorithm methods" is also extracted just because it contains a key-word "algorithm". Pan et al.[19] called the issue "overlapping problem", they simply introduced a penalty factor to overcome the problem. In fact, the method may incorrectly filter those gold concepts containing "algorithm", for that it is hard to control the proper value of the penalty factor.

To address the problem described above, inspired by [4], we introduce Maximal Marginal Relevance (MMR), which is one of the simplest and most effective solutions to balance query-document relevance and document diversity. Next, we show how to adapt the MMR algorithm to our task course concept extraction.

The original MMR is used to improve diversity in the information retrieval and recommendation domain. Specifically, based on the all retrieved documents R, for a given input query Q, and initial set S that receives the good answer for Q in each iteration via computing MMR as described in formula (3), where Sim represent cosine similarity between two documents or query, λ is a balance factor that controls relevance and diversity of result, D_i and D_j are retrieved documents.

$$\mathbf{MMR} := \underset{D_i \in R \backslash S}{\arg\max}[\lambda \cdot Sim_1(D_i, Q) - (1 - \lambda) \underset{D_j \in S}{\max} Sim_2(D_i, D_j)] \tag{3}$$

In order to use MMR here, we change the formula to fit our task [2], as follows:

$$\mathbf{MMR} := \underset{C_i \in C \backslash K}{\arg\max} [\gamma \cdot \widehat{\cos}_{sim} (D_i, doc) - (1 - \gamma) \underset{C_j \in K}{\max} \widehat{\cos}_{sim} (D_i, D_j)] \qquad (4)$$

where C is the set of candidate concepts, K is the set of extracted concepts, doc represents full embedding of each course corpus preprocessed (it will be described as follow), D_i and D_i are embeddings of candidate concepts i and j, respectively. The γ will be set as 0.5 to ensure that the relatedness and diversity parts of the equation have equal importance. Note that $\widehat{\cos}$ is a normalized cosine similarity [17], described by the following equations.

$$\widehat{\cos} (C_i, doc) = 0.5 + \frac{n \cos_{sim} (C_i, doc) - n \cos_{sim}(C, doc)}{\sigma (n \cos_{sim}(C, doc))} \qquad (5)$$

$$n \cos_{sim}(C, doc) = \frac{\cos_{sim} (C_i, doc) - \min_{C_j \in C} \cos_{sim} (C_j, doc)}{\max_{C_j \in C} \cos_{sim} (C_j, doc)} \qquad (6)$$

To compute the cosine similarity between each candidate concept and the corresponding entire course corpus, we need to calculate the full embedding of each document (i.e., single video corpus). Compared with word embeddings, it has been proved that sentence embedding is able to retain key sentence information, which will improve semantic relatedness between one concept and corresponding corpus document.

3.3   Learn to Weight and Concepts Ranking

Learn to Weight. To properly allocate weight for each feature information, we apply a Multi-Layer Perceptron to predict concept label $y_c (i.e., 0, 1, 2, ..., n)$, where n is the total label number of gold concepts, as followed:

$$p(y_c \mid c) = MLP(c), \qquad (7)$$

where c is a candidate concept to be classified.

Concepts Ranking. At the prediction phase, $X = [PMI; MMR]$ is used as input, we get the classification probability via MLP, as followed:

$$pro = softmax(ReLU(XW_h + b_h)) \qquad (8)$$

$$score = max(pro) \qquad (9)$$

Again, we do not care classification label for each candidate but focus on maximal classification probability. Here, we get the maximal value of the function, and then select the Top-K as concepts by ranking score.

Table 1. The four datasets we use. Columns are: the domain of each dataset; the number of documents (i.e., course subtitles); the number of gold concepts; the average number of candidates per document; the average number of tokens per document; the average number of gold concepts per document.

Dataset	Domain	Documents	GoldCon	AvgCan	AvgTok	AvgCon
CSZH	Computer Science	2849	5309	27.73	804.23	1.86
CSEN	Computer Science	690	4096	85.58	1560.79	5.93
EcoZH	Economic	455	3663	133.11	2394.55	8.05
EcoEN	Economic	381	3652	72.36	896.46	9.58

4 Experiments

4.1 Dataset and Experiments Setup

We evaluate the proposed model in online MOOC datasets. The datasets[1] include two course corpus with Computer Science and Economic domains in two different languages. The statistics of the MOOC datasets are reported in Table 1. For our method, in the training phase, given gold concept as a classification result, for the extraction of statistical feature PMI, we calculate the frequency of words based on the entire document (i.e., all documents). For the concept $N = 1$ (i.e., the length of a concept is 1), we directly set PMI to 0.001. In the evaluation phase, we extract feature information on a single document separately, but not the entire corpus.

4.2 Evaluation Measure

In this paper, we select Mean Average Precision (MAP) as an evaluation metric. Considering the precision of the ranking item, we select the R-precison [26], which is also a standard information retrieval metric that is different from Recall and Precision. Specifically, given a ranking list with K candidate concepts, it computes the number of gold concepts (i.e., precision) over K highest-ranked candidates, and the real value of K will be considered in the experiment.

4.3 Comparison Method with Baseline Models

We compare the proposed method LTWNN against the following baselines:

PMI [6]: In the Point-Mutual-Information (PMI) method, we directly rank each candidate concept based on the score calculated by the method described in Sect. 3.1.

TextRank[2] [15]: TextRank is a well-known graph-based algorithm inspired by PageRank [3]. It regards each candidate as a vertex and word relatedness as an

---

[1] The source dataset is released on http://moocdata.cn/data/concept-extraction.
[2] https://github.com/boudinfl/pke.

Table 2. Comparison of proposed method with CGP on the four datasets. MAP and R-precision at K (= 5, 10, 15) are reported. Two ablation experiments about diversity are reported.

K	Method	CSZH		CSEN		EcoZH		EcoEN	
		MAP	R_p	MAP	R_p	MAP	R_p	MAP	R_p
5	CGP	0.516	0.238	0.509	0.249	**0.561**	**0.297**	0.566	**0.335**
	LTWNN	**0.705**	**0.409**	**0.547**	**0.256**	0.433	0.235	**0.632**	0.295
	W/O PMI	0.601	**0.413**	0.533	0.256	0.395	0.232	0.554	0.298
	W/O MMR	0.473	0.358	0.347	0.135	0.462	0.251	0.470	0.243
10	CGP	0.369	0.135	0.393	**0.276**	**0.398**	**0.181**	0.483	**0.254**
	LTWNN	**0.603**	**0.337**	**0.403**	0.181	0.274	0.162	**0.504**	0.216
	W/O PMI	0.506	0.336	0.388	0.181	0.276	0.158	0.450	0.223
	W/O MMR	0.399	0.311	0.182	0.140	0.326	0.159	0.314	0.191
15	CGP	0.308	0.102	0.213	0.135	**0.306**	**0.140**	0.455	**0.224**
	LTWNN	**0.581**	**0.317**	**0.341**	**0.159**	0.230	0.134	0.445	0.202
	W/O PMI	0.572	0.316	0.334	0.158	0.234	0.136	0.413	0.202
	W/O MMR	0.376	0.299	0.076	0.109	0.287	0.133	0.264	0.180

edge. As an undirected weight graph, TextRank iteratively computes the rank value of each vertex.

CGP[3] [19]: Concept Graph Propagation is the state-of-the-art method in the course concept extraction of the MOOC dataset. They construct a concept graph for each course corpus, which is similar to TextRank. Different from TextRank, they calculate concept scores with PMI and external knowledge via generalized voting scores.

4.4   Result Analysis

As shown in Table 2, at the overall level, our method LTWNN outperforms available methods on three of the four datasets in MAP and R-precision.

For the performance on English data, LTWNN outperforms other methods at the K = 5. Moreover, when the K = {10, 15}, LTWNN shows similar performance with the state-of-the-art model.

For the performance on dataset CSZH, LTWNN shows apparent robustness and effectiveness over other methods. From the information described in Table 1, we know the average number of concepts per document is only 1.86, which indicates that the phenomenon of low-frequency and poverty of diversity on the dataset is more obvious than others. Thus, the experiment suggests that LTWNN is effective in solving the problem of low-frequency and poverty of diversity on a single document.

The performance of LTWNN on dataset EcoZH shows worse than available model CGP and PMI. We conduct an experiment of diversity factor influence

---

[3] https://github.com/thukg/concept-expansion-snippet.

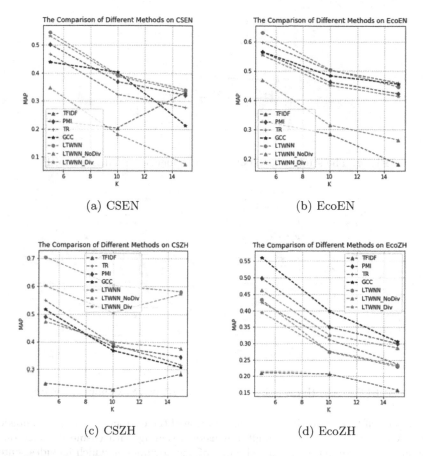

Fig. 3. Comparison of our method with baselines on the four dataset at MAP metric, these green lines are the performance of our method.

on dataset EcoEN, as shown in Fig. 4 and formulate (4), with the raise of λ (i.e., the diversity decrease), the performance of LTWNN increase continuously. As shown in experiments, the robustness and the effectiveness of Textrank in dataset CSZH is more evident than that in dataset CSEN and EcoEN, for that the average number of tokens per document in the former dataset is smaller than that in the latter.

Ablation Study. In our approach, the diversity of concepts plays a critical role in improving course concept extraction. As can be seen in Fig. 5, we show a concrete example, utilizing one 300-dimensional vector representing a single document and a 300-dimensional vector for each candidate concept. Then, We select the top-10 gold concepts out of 23 candidates, and the closer candidate is to the document vector, the higher the probability score it is a gold concept. Furthermore, as shown in Table 2 and Fig. 3, the comparison (except dataset

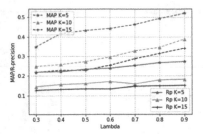

Fig. 4. The study of diversity factor influence on dataset EcoZH.

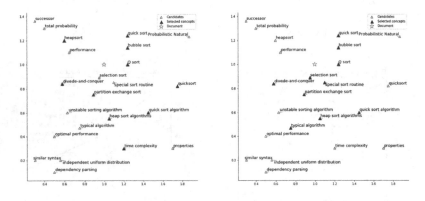

(a) LTWNN(with diversity)   (b) LTWNN(without diversity)

Fig. 5. The effect of diversity on the distribution of the extracted concepts. Embedding space (Visualization based on multidimensional scaling with cosine distance on the original Z = 300 dimensional embeddings) of one documents, which includes sentence embedding and word embedding of candidates "Q sort", "unstable sorting algorithm", and so on.

EcoZH) of LTWNN-Without-PMI and LTWNN-Without-MMR suggests that poverty of diversity hampers their performance.

5   Conclusion and Future Work

This study demonstrates how the course concept is extracted from the MOOC corpus, in which each online course may attract more than 100,000 learners [23]. Due to the attribution of open-course, the learners have diverse knowledge backgrounds. The study is aimed at extracting core knowledge for different background students. The content from MOOC courses is usually rich and complex, which is difficult for students to understand and analyze the knowledge from a global perspective. Course-related concepts represent the core knowledge, which will help students grasp the core knowledge.

Moreover, constructing educational knowledge graph based on the course concept entity is helpful for students and teachers, including makes personal education and deep knowledge tracking. And with the course concept extraction, we can build an interaction machine to help students better grasp core knowledge.

In future work, incorporating other external knowledge such as topic knowledge that classifies course knowledge into several groups is an available method to further improve the performance of course concept extraction.

Acknowledgment. This work was supported by the National Natural Science Foundation of China (No. 62077015).

References

1. Adi, Y., Kermany, E., Belinkov, Y., Lavi, O., Goldberg, Y.: Fine-grained analysis of sentence embeddings using auxiliary prediction tasks. arXiv preprint arXiv:1608.04207 (2016)
2. Bennani-Smires, K., Musat, C., Hossmann, A., Baeriswyl, M., Jaggi, M.: Simple unsupervised keyphrase extraction using sentence embeddings. arXiv preprint arXiv:1801.04470 (2018)
3. Brin, S., Page, L.: The anatomy of a large-scale hypertextual web search engine (1998)
4. Carbonell, J., Goldstein, J.: The use of MMR, diversity-based reranking for reordering documents and producing summaries. In: Proceedings of the 21st Annual International ACM SIGIR Conference on Research and Development in Information Retrieval, pp. 335–336 (1998)
5. Chen, P., Lu, Y., Zheng, V.W., Chen, X., Yang, B.: KnowEdu: a system to construct knowledge graph for education. IEEE Access **6**, 31553–31563 (2018)
6. Church, K., Hanks, P.: Word association norms, mutual information, and lexicography. Comput. Linguist. **16**(1), 22–29 (1990)
7. Dunning, T.E.: Accurate methods for the statistics of surprise and coincidence. Comput. Linguist. **19**(1), 61–74 (1993)
8. Hisamitsu, T., Niwa, Y., Tsujii, J.: A method of measuring term representativeness-baseline method using co-occurrence distribution. In: COLING 2000: The 18th International Conference on Computational Linguistics, vol. 1 (2000)
9. Kiros, R., et al.: Skip-thought vectors. In: Advances in Neural Information Processing Systems, pp. 3294–3302 (2015)
10. Korkontzelos, I., Klapaftis, I.P., Manandhar, S.: Reviewing and evaluating automatic term recognition techniques. In: Nordström, B., Ranta, A. (eds.) GoTAL 2008. LNCS (LNAI), vol. 5221, pp. 248–259. Springer, Heidelberg (2008). https://doi.org/10.1007/978-3-540-85287-2_24
11. Li, S., Li, J., Song, T., Li, W., Chang, B.: A novel topic model for automatic term extraction. In: Proceedings of the 36th International ACM SIGIR Conference on Research and Development in Information Retrieval, pp. 885–888 (2013)
12. Liu, Z., Huang, W., Zheng, Y., Sun, M.: Automatic keyphrase extraction via topic decomposition. In: Proceedings of the 2010 Conference on Empirical Methods in Natural Language Processing, pp. 366–376 (2010)
13. Logeswaran, L., Lee, H.: An efficient framework for learning sentence representations. arXiv preprint arXiv:1803.02893 (2018)

14. Lu, W., Zhou, Y., Yu, J., Jia, C.: Concept extraction and prerequisite relation learning from educational data. In: Proceedings of the AAAI Conference on Artificial Intelligence, vol. 33, pp. 9678–9685 (2019)
15. Mihalcea, R., Tarau, P.: TextRank: bringing order into text. In: Proceedings of the 2004 Conference on Empirical Methods in Natural Language Processing, pp. 404–411 (2004)
16. Mikolov, T., Chen, K., Corrado, G., Dean, J.: Efficient estimation of word representations in vector space. arXiv preprint arXiv:1301.3781 (2013)
17. Mori, T., Sasaki, T.: Information gain ratio meets maximal marginal relevance. In: les actes de National Institute of Informatics Test Collections for Information Retrieval (NTCIR) (2002)
18. Pagliardini, M., Gupta, P., Jaggi, M.: Unsupervised learning of sentence embeddings using compositional n-Gram features. arXiv preprint arXiv:1703.02507 (2017)
19. Pan, L., Wang, X., Li, C., Li, J., Tang, J.: Course concept extraction in MOOCs via embedding-based graph propagation. In: Proceedings of the Eighth International Joint Conference on Natural Language Processing (Volume 1: Long Papers), pp. 875–884 (2017)
20. Pennington, J., Socher, R., Manning, C.D.: Glove: global vectors for word representation. In: Proceedings of the 2014 Conference on Empirical Methods in Natural Language Processing (EMNLP), pp. 1532–1543 (2014)
21. Ramos, J., et al.: Using TF-IDF to determine word relevance in document queries. In: Proceedings of the First Instructional Conference on Machine Learning, vol. 242, pp. 133–142, New Jersey, USA (2003)
22. Salton, G., Buckley, C.: Term-weighting approaches in automatic text retrieval. Inf. Process. Manage. 24(5), 513–523 (1988)
23. Seaton, D.T., Bergner, Y., Chuang, I., Mitros, P., Pritchard, D.E.: Who does what in a massive open online course? Commun. ACM 57(4), 58–65 (2014)
24. Shang, J., Liu, J., Jiang, M., Ren, X., Voss, C.R., Han, J.: Automated phrase mining from massive text corpora. IEEE Trans. Knowl. Data Eng. 30(10), 1825–1837 (2018)
25. Yu, J., et al.: Course concept expansion in MOOCs with external knowledge and interactive game. arXiv preprint arXiv:1909.07739 (2019)
26. Zesch, T., Gurevych, I.: Approximate matching for evaluating keyphrase extraction. In: Proceedings of the International Conference RANLP-2009, pp. 484–489 (2009)

ETBTRank: Ranking Biterms in Paper Titles for Emerging Topic Discovery

Junfeng Wu, Guangyan Huang(✉), and Roozbeh Zarei

School of Information Technology, Deakin University, 211 Burwood Highway, Burwood, VIC 3125, Australia
guangyan.huang@deakin.edu.au

Abstract. Emerging topics, which often originate from the collaboration of two scientific subfields, can be represented by biterms (pairs of terms) where each term represents a distinct subfield. However, it is challenging to automatically find such two critical terms to represent an emerging topic exactly. First, existing term weighting models (such as TF-IDF, TextRank, RAKE, KECNW, and YAKE) may be effective for finding critical single-terms but not for critical biterms. Second, a potential biterm that may be suitable to represent the emerging topic has very low occurrences in a text (e.g., a corpus comprised of paper titles). So, even we combine two terms to generate a bag of biterms, the above term weighting models are still invalid, which will filter out these rare potential biterms. This paper proposes a novel Emerging Topic BiTerm Rank (ETBTRank) model to help automatically extract biterms for representing emerging topics, distinguishing emerging-topic biterms from unimportant biterms. In ETBTRank, we separately weigh the two terms in a biterm and find the emerging-topic biterms by a rule: if a biterm itself is rare, but each of the two terms in it has a high weight, then it is an emerging topic biterm. Experimental studies on paper title datasets demonstrate the effectiveness of the proposed model.

Keywords: Automatic biterm extraction · Automatic term extraction · Information retrieval · Emerging-topic biterm · Natural language processing

1 Introduction

Recent advances in the bag-of-biterms techniques [14,17] for biterm topic models [10,15,16] have stimulated the development of Automatic Biterm Extraction (ABE), which is a generalization of Automatic Term Extraction (ATE) [8] to extract biterms. ABE is vitally important for discovering emerging topics from paper titles because of the following two reasons.

1. Many emerging topics are either unnamed or named differently by different authors in immature terminology; therefore, they are often retrieved by backtracking their origin from two co-occurring super topics. Here, an ABE

© Springer Nature Switzerland AG 2022
G. Long et al. (Eds.): AI 2021, LNAI 13151, pp. 775–784, 2022.
https://doi.org/10.1007/978-3-030-97546-3_63

method extracts the two super topics, where each term (i.e., single-word or multi-word keyphrase) of the extracted biterm represents a distinct super-topic [7].

2. In the emerging topic discovery of academic research, using paper titles instead of full texts or abstracts allows getting satisfactory results quickly and efficiently because the terms in paper titles are usually closely related to the topics [4]. Analyzing paper titles needs short texts topic models, among which Biterm Topic Models (BTM) are popular. Advanced BTMs often require to automatically adapt to various contexts [9,18] and thus ABE is essential.

So, our insight is to develop ABE models for discovering emerging topics by ranking biterms. However, not all existing ATE models can be easily generalized to ABE using Bag of Biterms. Also, even with a feasible Bag of Biterms generalization, most ATE models rely heavily on biterm frequency (i.e., the frequency of biterm occurrences). Unfortunately, such frequency is usually useless since those biterms that can represent the emerging topics are extremely rare due to the topic's emergingness. For example, two super topics are mentioned together for the first time, where a different term mentions each. These two terms form a new (and thus rare) biterm. Furthermore, it is extraordinarily hard in a bag of multi-terms to generalize ATE models for ranking multi-terms, as an emerging topic may originate from more than two super-topics collaborations.

This paper proposes ETBTRank (Emerging Topic BiTerm Rank), a novel ABE model for ranking biterms of emerging topics. One advantage of ETB-TRank is that its direct and easy integration of any ATE model avoids difficult Bag-of-Biterms generalization of advanced ATE, enabling it easy to rank biterms based on term ranking. Another advantage is that ETBTRank does not rely on the frequency of biterm occurrences; it can identify an emerging-topic biterm (i.e., a biterm representing the emerging topic) even when the biterm's occurrence is extra rare. The third advantage is that ETBTRank can easily extend to rank multi-terms for an emerging topic that originates from more than two super-topics collaborations.

In ETBTRank, we develop a good scoring strategy for ranking emerging-topic biterms inspired by two basic observations.

- Observation 1: each emerging-topic biterm, even though rare, is usually combined by two terms with good scores assigned by the ATE models.
- Observation 2: the rarer the co-occurrence of the super-topics represented by a biterm is in a corpus, the more important the biterm often is.

The most related works are bag-of-biterms based ABE models, which are generalizations of ATE model using bag-of-biterms [14,17]. Bag-of-biterms based ABE models generate a list of biterms by combining any two terms in a document while using the minor single-term frequency as the biterm's frequency. Unlike frequency, other features are generally much harder to get, including those graph-related features used by graph-based ATE models such as in [3,5,6,11,13]. Our ETBTRank is different from the bag-of-biterms based ABE models in three aspects:

1. There is no need to generalize term features to biterm features in ETBTRank because, in ETBTRank, the ABE scores of biterms are combined by the ATE scores of terms directly;
2. ETBTRank can distinguish rare emerging-topic biterms from similarly rare but unimportant biterms because an emerging-topic biterm consists of two terms with good ATE scores.
3. Combining the ATE scores of terms into the scores of multi-terms in a similar way accomplishes an easy extension of ETBTRank to rank multi-terms, without the need to generalize term features to multi-term features.

Experimental study shows that our ETBTRank models are much more effective than the bag-of-biterms based ABE models for emerging topic discovery.

The contributions of this paper are twofold.

1. We propose a novel ABE model ETBTRank, which does not need generalization from term features to biterm features and can distinguish rare emerging-topic biterms from similarly rare but unimportant biterms.
2. We develop a general strategy for ranking emerging-topic biterms that can help further research in emerging topic discovery.

We organize the remainder of this paper as follows. Section 2 presents related work. Section 3 details our proposed ETBTRank model and discusses how to extend it to rank multi-terms that originate from the collaborations of more than two super topics. In Sect. 4, we develop a general strategy of ideal biterm ranking for emerging topics and analyze the rationale of the approximation scheme in ETBTRank to compute biterm scores without knowing the super-topic labels. In Sect. 5, our experimental study validates the accuracy of the proposed ETB-TRank on IJCAI paper-title datasets extracted from Microsoft Academic Graph. Finally, Sect. 6 concludes this paper.

2   Related Work

In this section, we present the related work for Automatic Biterm Extraction (ABE).

The only existing methods we know for ABE are the bag-of-biterms based models that generalize term features to biterm features to extend existing ATE models. However, we argue that the bag-of-biterms based models may not suit ATE for emerging topics. A disadvantage of the bag-of-biterms based models is that it is hard to implement on some recent ATE models due to the problematic generalization of term features to biterm features. Another disadvantage is that the bag-of-biterms based models yield low-frequency combinations of emerging-topic biterms. Thus those rare but critical emerging-topic biterms will usually be assigned with terrible low scores since most existing ATE models rely heavily on frequency.

We can classify most of the existing ATE models into two groups: statistic models and graph-based models. Statistic models use only term-related statistics for the computation of scores, such as TF-IDF in [12], which uses two term-related statistics, TF (term frequency) and IDF (inverse document frequency). However, bag-of-biterms based models generalize term frequency in a document to biterm frequency using the minimum single term frequency in a biterm, resulting in a bad score assigned to an emerging-topic biterm due to the rare co-occurrences of the two terms in a corpus. Graph-based models use the term-related statistics defined on the nodes of the graphs (i.e., the terms) and the statistics defined on the edges (i.e., the co-occurrence of the terms). Examples include Text Rank [11], RAKE [13], KECNW [3], and YAKE [5,6]. Aside from the issue of the extra-low frequency of important biterms, these graph-based models are also generally difficult in term-feature to biterm-feature generalization. Take the most recent model YAKE for example. YAKE uses five features to compute the scores for terms, including term frequency, term-positional weight, term-casing weight, term-relatedness to context, and the number of sentences containing the term. Among these five features, the last two are difficult to generalize. Biterm-relatedness to context is difficult due to the unease in defining the neighborhood of a biterm with two terms scattered far away. The number of sentences containing the biterm is difficult to generalize due to the necessary consistency with biterm frequency; a direct but naïve generalization will often lead to an absurd zero in such a feature in a document with positive biterm frequency. A compromised-but-better-than-wrong solution has to replace this feature with the number of documents containing the biterm to ensure consistency with biterm frequency.

ETBTRank can integrate any existing ATE models without the difficult bag-of-biterms generalization in features. More importantly, it also avoids bad scores assigning to emerging-topic biterms caused by the extra low frequency of such biterms.

3   The Proposed ETBTRank Model

This section provides an overview of ETBTRank for ABE and then discusses how to extend it to rank multi-terms that originate from the collaborations of more than two super-topics.

3.1   Overview of ETBTRank

The score of ETBTRank is defined by the following equation:

$$S_{\text{predict}}(b) = \frac{S(t_1) S(t_2)}{\text{sim}(t_1, t_2)}, \tag{1}$$

where:

- $S(t_1)$ and $S(t_2)$ are the ATE scores of the two terms t_1 and t_2 in the biterm b, computed using any chosen ATE model;
- $\text{sim}(t_1, t_2)$ is the similarity of the two terms, which can be computed easily using, for example, Jaccard Similarity that captures the overlapping ratio of their neighbor-term sets.

The relevance to topic of each term in b is denoted by the ETA scores, $S(t_1)$ and $S(t_2)$, in the equation, while the emergingness of the topic is inversely proportional to the similarity $\text{sim}(t_1, t_2)$. When the co-occurrence of the super-topics represented by these two terms is rarer, the similarity is smaller; thus, the score is higher.

3.2   An Extension of ETBTRank to Rank Multi-Terms

For emerging topics that originate from the collaborations of more than two super-topics, an extension of ETBTRank to rank multi-terms can use a similar scoring strategy:

$$S_{\text{predict}}(b) = \frac{\prod_{i=1}^{k} S(t_i)}{\prod_{1 \leq i_1 < i_2 \leq k} \text{sim}(t_{i_1}, t_{i_2})}.$$

As in ETBTRank, $S(t_i)$ $(i = 1, \ldots, k)$ denote the relevance to topic of each term, while the emergingness of the topic is inversely proportional to the product of similarities $\text{sim}(t_{i_1}, t_{i_2})$ $(1 \leq i_1 < i_2 \leq k)$.

4   Modelling the Ranking in ETBTRank

In this section, we first model the ranking of emerging-topic biterms, then deduce from this model the approximation scheme to compute biterm scores in ETB-TRank.

4.1   Modelling the Ranking of Emerging-Topic Biterms

We assume that each input title has several labels indicating the super-topics of the paper's topic. We need to know how to evaluate the importance of a biterm in representing an emerging topic. We provide the following rules:

1. Each term in the biterm should be a keyword closely related to a distinct super-topic.
2. Due to the emerging topic we try to discover, the two terms in the biterm should represent two super-topics that have rare but increasingly frequent collaborations/co-occurrences.

Therefore, Eq. (2) as follows describes the ideal importance of a biterm in representing an emerging topic:

$$S_{\text{ideal}}(b) = \text{Emergingness}(\tau_1, \tau_2) S_{\tau_1}(t_1) S_{\tau_2}(t_2), \tag{2}$$

where τ_1, τ_2 are the two underlying super-topics, $S_{\tau_1}(t_1)$ is the relevance score of term t_1 corresponding to super-topic τ_1, while $S_{\tau_2}(t_2)$ is the relevance score of term t_2 corresponding to super-topic τ_2.

Emergingness is defined as the rare but increasingly frequent co-occurrence of two super-topics. Therefore, an example emergingness function as below serves Eq. (2):

$$\text{Emergingness}\,(\tau_1, \tau_2) = (\epsilon + \text{cooccur}_{\text{before } y}\,(\tau_1, \tau_2))^{-\frac{1}{2}}\,\text{incFreq}_{\text{after } y}\,(\tau_1, \tau_2),$$

where ϵ is a small constant to avoid division by zero, $\text{cooccur}_{\text{before } y}\,(\tau_1, \tau_2)$ is the co occurrence of two super-topics τ_1, τ_2 before year y, $\text{incFreq}_{\text{after } y}\,(\tau_1, \tau_2)$ is a function predicting the increasing frequentness of the two super-topics after year y, which can be computed as the derivative of a regression function from the number of their co occurrences after year y.

The term-to-super-topic relevance functions, $S_{\tau_1}\,(t_1)$ and $S_{\tau_2}\,(t_2)$, in Eq. (2) can be computed using basic TF-IDF models, since we can group titles into documents according to super-topic labels.

4.2   Score Approximation in ETBTRank

Let's compare the proposed approximation score in Eq. (1) and the ideal score in Eq. (2). By the main result of Leap2Trend [7], we can use the shrinking distance between two terms to detect the emergingness of the topic originated from the two super-topics represented by the terms. Since distance can be represented by similarity as follows,

$$d\,(t_1, t_2) = \frac{1}{\text{sim}\,(t_1, t_2)}, \tag{3}$$

and term-to-super-topic relevance can be approximated using existing ATE models, i.e.,

$$S_{\tau_i}\,(t_i) \approx S\,(t_1), \quad i = 1, 2, \tag{4}$$

combining Eqs. (2, 3 and 4) yields the approximation of Eq. (1).

5   Experiments

Similar to ATE, ABE models require evaluations with rank correlation coefficients. Widely used rank correlation coefficients include Kendall rank coefficient [1] and Pearson correlation coefficient [2]. Our experiments adopt the Kendall rank coefficient in the computation of accuracy. Also, to guarantee the application focus, we assign weights to input samples (i.e., the paper titles) according to the sum of ideal scores over the emerging-topic biterms in the title, where we compute the ideal score using Eq. (2).

The dataset of our experiment consists of the paper titles, publication years, and references/citations' titles of IJCAI from the earliest proceeding to the proceeding of 2020. There are about 10K IJCAI paper titles, 260K reference/citation paper titles, 435K reference/citation relations, and 136K topic/super-topic labels in the dataset.

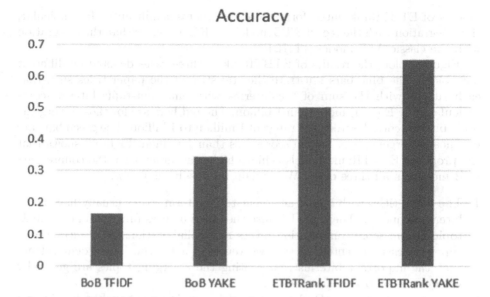

Fig. 1. Accuracy comparison.

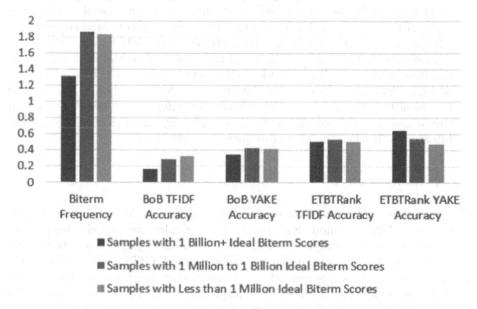

Fig. 2. Biterm frequency and accuracy on different biterm score levels. (Color figure online)

We compare our ETBTRank method with a counterpart method, BoB (bag-of-Biterms); both methods adopt two ATE models, TF-IDF and YAKE, to real-ize ABE. Figure 1 compares their accuracies and shows that the proposed ABE models of ETBTRank outperform the counterparts significantly. In particular, the integration with the recent ATE model, YAKE, is better than the integration with the classic ATE model, TF-IDF.

Figure 2 plots the results of ETBTRank in three cases denoted by different bar colors. The blue bars illustrate the statistics of the paper titles such that each title is with the sum of the biterms with emergent-topic biterm scores (calculated by Eq. (2)) more than 1 billion. The red bars are for those emergent-topic biterm scores between the range of 1 million to 1 billion. The green bars are for those emergent-topic biterm scores less than 1 million. Figure 2 shows that the proposed ETBTRank models achieve higher accuracy than the counterpart BoB models in all three cases. We explain the results as below.

1. The paper titles with higher emergent-topic biterm scores usually have lower biterm frequency. These are because the emergingness function in emergent-topic biterm score computation favors rare collaborations/co-occurrences of super-topics represented by the two terms in a biterm. These demonstrate that the important biterms representing the emerging topics are generally with extra-low occurrence frequency.
2. The counterparts, i.e., BoB based models, are inaccurate when low biterm frequency. BoB YAKE is more sensitive to biterm frequency than BoB TFIDF, probably because YAKE relies more on frequency-related features than TFIDF (in particular, the feature of biterm relatedness to context).
3. The proposed ABE models, i.e., ETBTRank using TFIDF and YAKE, outperform the BOB-based models in all three cases. It is the most obvious in the best model, i.e., ETBTRank YAKE, which performs better in the case of high ideal biterm score with low biterm frequency than in the case of low ideal biterm score with high biterm frequency. These demonstrate that the proposed model, i.e., ETBTRank, can identify the critical emerging-topic biterms, even when the biterm frequency is extra-low.

6   Conclusions

For emerging topic discovery, we have provided a novel Automatic Biterm Extraction (ABE) method, ETBTrank. In particular, we model biterm ranking scores for emerging topic discovery using topic emergingness and term-topic relevance and develop an approximate equation for ETBTRank to calculate the ranking scores. The experimental study shows that the proposed ETBTRank method achieves better accuracy of emerging topic discovery from paper titles than its counterpart, BoB, on an IJCAI conference paper title dataset. In the future, we will generalize ETBTRank to find emerging topics in any given domain with available corpus.

Acknowledgement. This work was partially supported by Australia Research Council (ARC) Discovery Project (DP190100587).

References

1. Abdi, H.: The Kendall rank correlation coefficient. In: Encyclopedia of Measurement and Statistics, pp. 508–510. Sage, Thousand Oaks (2007)
2. Benesty, J., Chen, J., Huang, Y., Cohen, I.: Pearson correlation coefficient. In: Noise Reduction in Speech Processing, pp. 1–4. Springer, Cham (2009). https://doi.org/10.1007/978-3-642-00296-0_5
3. Biswas, S.K., Bordoloi, M., Shreya, J.: A graph based keyword extraction model using collective node weight. Expert Syst. Appl. **97**, 51–59 (2018)
4. Bogomolova, A., Ryazanova, M., Balk, I.: Cluster approach to analysis of publication titles. In: Journal of Physics: Conference Series, vol. 1727, p. 012016. IOP Publishing (2021)
5. Campos, R., Mangaravite, V., Pasquali, A., Jorge, A., Nunes, C., Jatowt, A.: YAKE! Keyword extraction from single documents using multiple local features. Inf. Sci. **509**, 257–289 (2020)
6. Campos, R., Mangaravite, V., Pasquali, A., Jorge, A.M., Nunes, C., Jatowt, A.: YAKE! Collection-independent automatic keyword extractor. In: Pasi, G., Piwowarski, B., Azzopardi, L., Hanbury, A. (eds.) ECIR 2018. LNCS, vol. 10772, pp. 806–810. Springer, Cham (2018). https://doi.org/10.1007/978-3-319-76941-7_80
7. Dridi, A., Gaber, M.M., Azad, R.M.A., Bhogal, J.: Leap2Trend: a temporal word embedding approach for instant detection of emerging scientific trends. IEEE Access **7**, 176414–176428 (2019)
8. Heylen, K., De Hertog, D.: Automatic term extraction. In: Handbook of Terminology, vol. 1, no. 01 (2015)
9. Li, W., Matsukawa, T., Saigo, H., Suzuki, E.: Context-aware latent Dirichlet allocation for topic segmentation. In: Lauw, H.W., Wong, R.C.-W., Ntoulas, A., Lim, E.-P., Ng, S.-K., Pan, S.J. (eds.) PAKDD 2020. LNCS (LNAI), vol. 12084, pp. 475–486. Springer, Cham (2020). https://doi.org/10.1007/978-3-030-47426-3_37
10. Li, X., Zhang, A., Li, C., Guo, L., Wang, W., Ouyang, J.: Relational biterm topic model: short-text topic modeling using word embeddings. Comput. J. **62**(3), 359–372 (2019)
11. Mihalcea, R., Tarau, P.: TextRank: bringing order into text. In: Proceedings of the 2004 Conference on Empirical Methods in Natural Language Processing, pp. 404–411 (2004)
12. Ramos, J., et al.: Using TF-IDF to determine word relevance in document queries. In: Proceedings of the First Instructional Conference on Machine Learning, vol. 242, pp. 29–48. Citeseer (2003)
13. Rose, S., Engel, D., Cramer, N., Cowley, W.: Automatic keyword extraction from individual documents. In: Text Mining: Applications and Theory, vol. 1, pp. 1–20 (2010)
14. Tuan, A.P., Tran, B., Nguyen, T.H., Van, L.N., Than, K.: Bag of biterms modeling for short texts. Knowl. Inf. Syst. **62**(10), 4055–4090 (2020). https://doi.org/10.1007/s10115-020-01482-z
15. Wu, D., Zhang, M., Shen, C., Huang, Z., Gu, M.: BTM and GloVe similarity linear fusion-based short text clustering algorithm for microblog hot topic discovery. IEEE Access **8**, 32215–32225 (2020)
16. Yan, X., Guo, J., Lan, Y., Cheng, X.: A biterm topic model for short texts. In: Proceedings of the 22nd International Conference on World Wide Web, pp. 1445–1456 (2013)

17. Yang, S., Huang, G., Ofoghi, B.: Short text similarity measurement using context from bag of word pairs and word co-occurrence. In: He, J., et al. (eds.) ICDS 2019. CCIS, vol. 1179, pp. 221–231. Springer, Singapore (2020). https://doi.org/10.1007/978-981-15-2810-1_22
18. Yang, S., Huang, G., Ofoghi, B., Yearwood, J.: Short text similarity measurement using context-aware weighted biterms. Concurr. Comput. Pract. Exp., e5765 (2020)

Network Analysis

Inference of Geological Material Groups Using Structural Monitoring Sensors on Excavators

Liyang Liu$^{(\boxtimes)}$, Mehala Balamurali⬤, Katherine L. Silversides⬤,
and Rami N. Khushaba

Australian Centre for Field Robotics, University of Sydney, Sydney, Australia
{liyang.liu,mehala.balamurali,katherine.silversides,
rami.khushaba}@sydney.edu.au

Abstract. In mining, correctly characterising geological grades is very important as it directly relates to ore quality assessment and downstream processing. Significant effort has been placed into creating the geological block models for the mine site, through site exploration and in-lab assay analysis. Yet the blasting, digging and various processing can cause non-negligible movement of material and invalid prediction of material content due to the now obsolete model. On the other hand, it is well known to excavator operators that digging effort is closely related to the hardness or lumpiness of the material underneath, and therefore this may be exploited to indicate the material type post blasting.

This paper proposes a method that can automatically infer the geological material types of mined material during excavation at the digging location by applying machine learning methods to the force, energy and kinematic information collected from sensors mounted on the diggers. Therefore, the digging equipment is being used as a sensor for this purpose. Conversely, we also show how knowledge of material type can lead to accurate prediction of digging effort category. Further, per bucket material information can be utilised throughout the material movement pipeline. A case study was conducted in a test region at Pilbara iron ore deposit situated in the Brockman Iron Formation of the Hamersley Province, Western Australia. Initial results show strong level of inter-dependency between sensor measurements and excavated material type, demonstrating the potential of material inference at the bucket level.

Keywords: Excavator sensors · Material grouping · Machine learning

1 Introduction

Accurate geological models are important when planning and developing mines, as well as for correctly reporting the resources and reserves present in the deposit. Multiple sources of information from exploration and blast holes, such as geochemical assay data and geophysical data, are utilised to interpret geological domain boundaries and estimate 3D geological block models. Predicting material content from this model is, however,

---

L. Liu and M. Balamurali—These authors contributed equally to this work.

© Springer Nature Switzerland AG 2022
G. Long et al. (Eds.): AI 2021, LNAI 13151, pp. 787–797, 2022.
https://doi.org/10.1007/978-3-030-97546-3_64

not always successful due to the non-negligible movement of material after blasting, digging and various processing.

Post-blasting, the manually logged material types and the material density estimated from these are also available. Materials exhibit properties that characterise the lump fine split at the plant [11] due to their processing and geo metallurgical qualities. High moisture content and sticky ores can cause blockages during transportation and shipping, leading to significant delays in the downstream processes and increased production costs. Knowing the material type will aid the mitigation of many challenging problems and help ensure robust design of handling, storage, transport, and dust-suppression equipment [6].

Digging effort is closely related to the hardness or lumpiness of excavated soil properties. For example, driver actions were more aggressive for hard material, or high-magnitude force is required if the proportion of the material remains in a lump form [7]. It is therefore possible to infer information about material excavated through measurement of the physical interaction between the digger and the material. Early work in [10] investigated real-time soil parameter identification for control optimization. Recent work [6] attempted coarse gravel and rock material type classification using force measuring sensors for wheel-loaders in underground mining.

In this work, we propose an automated framework and technology that infer the material types of geology of excavated material during excavation by applying machine learning to the sensor information coming from the diggers at the given bucket dig location and thereby using equipment as a sensor for this purpose. A case study was conducted in a test region at Pilbara iron ore deposit situated in the Brockman Iron Formation of the Hamersley Province, Western Australia. We show that sensor measurements will give preliminary indication of the material type underground, and conversely knowledge of material type can help categorise digging effort, the benefit is effective resources allocation and efficient digging strategy selection, resulting in improved productivity and reduced equipment wear and tear.

2 Background

2.1 Excavator Dynamics

Early studies on excavator arm dynamics gives clue to why force and kinematic measurements may lead to material identification. The position of the excavator's bucket is determined by the joint angles formed between the three arm links, namely boom, stick and bucket, which in turn are controlled by the length of their associated hydraulic cylinders due to the heavy body weight, see Fig. 1.

The dynamic model of the arm links is given by Eq. (1) below.

$$D(\theta)\ddot{\theta} + C(\theta, \dot{\theta})\dot{\theta} + G(\theta) + B(\dot{\theta}) = \Gamma(\theta)\tau - F_L(F_n, F_t) \tag{1}$$

where θ is the set of joint angles. F_L is the forces acting on the bucket and is determined by the forces F_n and F_t due to material and bucket interaction. F_n refers to the force normal to the bucket tip surface and is closely related to material weight, i.e. payload. F_t is the force tangential to the tip, and is closely related to material property, i.e. hardness,

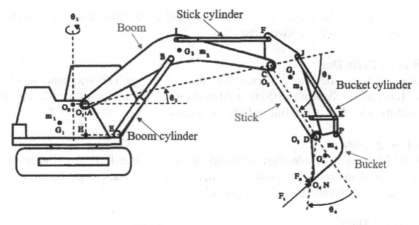

Fig. 1. Excavator dynamics [4]

lumpiness. Details of other terms such as friction $B(\theta)$, gravity $G(\theta)$, shaft torques τ, Criolix matrix $C(\theta, \theta)$ and moment arm matrix $\Gamma(\theta)$ are given in [4].

(1) shows a highly non-linear relationship between forces acting on the bucket, arm link lengths, duration of action (rate of joint angle change) and the payload. Conceivably, there is no simple mathematical model linking the magnitude of force and the material being mined. The best approach is therefore via machine learning techniques using on-board sensor measurements, such as bucket payload, digging cycle time, generic teeth force and energy.

2.2 Machine Learning Background

Different machine learning methods were applied in this work and their accuracies compared. We used implementations of these methods from scikit-learn [1]. The methods applied in this study are K-Means Clustering [1, 9], Stochastic Gradient Descent (SGD) [12], Random Forest (RF) [2, 8] and Support Vector Machine (SVM) [7, 8].

3   Data

The excavators under investigation are installed with Structural Monitoring Sensors (SMS). Data was available from 12 different mining blocks. For each block the site geologists manually logged the proportions of 21 material types that are present in the mine. Each material type represents a typical combination of minerals and hardness, e.g. a soft goethite-based ore, banded iron formation (BIF) or clay. For each blast the materials present are represented by a material group (MG). We now explain the data used in this research.

Bucket Data
Bucket data includes information collected in each bucket load cycle. Each record

includes the bucket load timestamp, the x-, y- and z-coordinates of the bucket's dig and dump locations and the swing duration.

Load-Haul Cycle Data

The load-haul cycle data are collected from the haul trucks. This was generated by the Fleet Management System (FMS) utilised in the mine, referred to as 'sites'. It includes timestamps of load start and full and MG information.

SMS Energy Data

Each SMS data point includes the timestamp, interaction time: the time of diggers engage with the ground and release from the ground, average force and energy, boom, stick and hand lengths corresponding to the diggers id.

Grade Block Data

This gives the averaged chemical grade estimation and the material type values in percentage.

Data Joining

Each digger's working blocks details were stored the load haul cycle data. This information is used to align the digger's bucket information to grade block details. The timestamp provided in the SMS cycle data and the bucket data were used to match the digger's force and energy information to the material types.

4   Methodology

4.1   Overview

We now explain how to establish the inter-dependency between SMS data and material type in this research: a two-way inference process. As seen in Fig. 2, we start with pre-processing data to form input features, we then cluster the SMS measurements into classes guided by material types and finally we perform two-way inference: a) inference of cluster type from SMS measurements, and b) reverse inference from material content to SMS cluster. The details are explained in the following sections. A successful outcome in this two-way inference can be beneficial in practical excavation application. The overall machine learning pipeline can be illustrated in the diagram below:

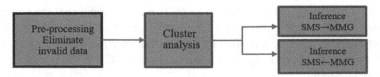

Fig. 2. Two-way Inference Pipeline to establish SMS and material type (in this case MMG) dependency

4.2 Pre-processing and Feature Formation

The pre-processing stage is for eliminating invalid samples and removing biased data clusters. The invalid data manifest in absent samples due to sensor errors or negative energy readings due to incorrect calibration. Sensor reading distribution can also appear non-uniform or form isolated clusters as a result of uncommon digging commands issued by the operators.

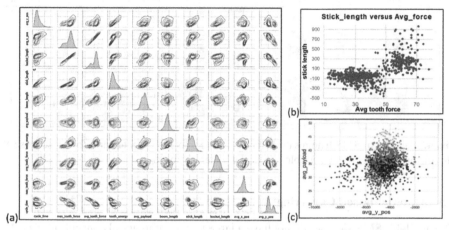

Fig. 3. Scatter plots of SMS features: (a) All feature pair plot, axis labels: cycle_time, max_tooth_force, avg_tooth_force, tooth_energy, avg_payload, boom_length, stick_length, bucket_length, avg_x_pos, avg_y_pos. (b) Close-up plot stick_length vs force reveals two clus-ters. (c) Low avg_y_pos cluster indicates digging of mug pile.

To visualize raw data distribution, we generated pair-wise scatter plots (Fig. 3a) of SMS features with crude clustering enabled. There are obvious multi-model distribution in stick length and bucket average y position (avg_y_pos). The close-up scatter plot in Fig. 3b shows two clusters: negative stick lengths with weak digging force in one cluster, and positive stick lengths with strong digging force in another cluster. This can be explained by forward kinematics (Fig. 1): extension or retraction of the stick cylinder lead to different digging poses, hence large variation in teeth force. In Fig. 3c a small cluster is formed at low vertical bucket position, a phenomenon related to a digging action known as gardening where the digger tries to fix the muck pile which consists of typically loose and light-weighted material. Since we are only interested in the effect of material type on energy consumption, samples with uncommon digging pose and action are discarded to ensure unimodal distribution.

The newly formed data is illustrated in the pair-wise scatter plot (Fig. 4a) and a close-up energy force plot (Fig. 4b). The colour-code (Fig. 4c) represents the 12 material groups involved in this research and is also used in Fig. 5. The new data shows a balanced distribution, with each MG region reasonably spotted on inspection.

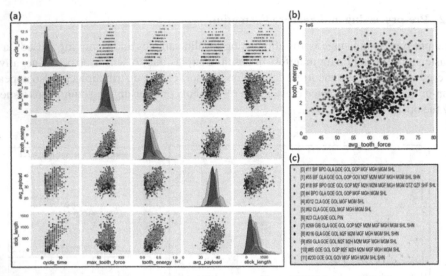

Fig. 4. Pair-plot of SMS features (a) Pair-wise scatter plots of SMS features (b) Close up scatter plot of force versus energy (c) Colour codes of material groups

4.3 Material-Based Clustering

The available SMS samples do not have a large variety of material concentrations (MC). As shown in Sect. 5.2, the distribution of the MC is not continuous but appears rather as either single concentration strip or with very few discrete levels. Therefore, any attempt to perform MC regression from SMS data or classification of MG from SMS clusters are not successful, a detailed analysis on this is given in Experiment of Sect. 5.2. On the other hand, for each of the 12 MG types, we analysed the distribution of the SMS features including force, energy, payload, cycle time and stick length (Fig. 5). Observing the similarities and differences between the feature distributions, they can be used to group the individual MG types into those with similar excavator dynamics.

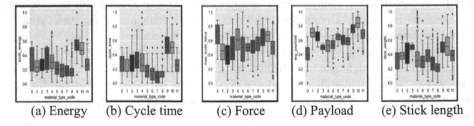

(a) Energy   (b) Cycle time   (c) Force   (d) Payload   (e) Stick length

Fig. 5. Box-plots of SMS features

We therefore propose a novel MG clustering method: instead of clustering on individual sample's physical attributes, we treat each group of excavated material (MG) as a super sample and cluster on the 12 super samples only. For each group we form the super sample's SMS attributes by averaging over the raw SMS measurements in the group. Finally, with a K-means clustering we arrive at four categories of material groups. This method of categorising the material groups helps to form a natural connection to their physical attributes. For the rest of the paper we refer the categorised material group as MMG. Details of the four MMG's are given below:

- MMG class 0: merged from MG 9 and 10
- MMG class 1: merged from MG 5, 6, 7 and 8
- MMG class 2: merged from MG 0, 3 and 4
- MMG class 3: merged from MG 1, 2, 11

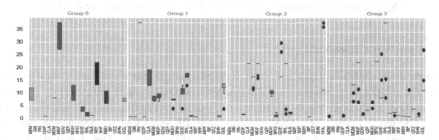

Fig. 6. Box-plots of Material Content distribution for the four merged MG's

Boxplots for material content in each MMG class is given in Fig. 6.
Each MMG occupies a different concentration band in this grouping. For example,

- MMG0 has a distinctive concentration of martite dominated ores (M2M, MGF, M2F and M2H), with some shale and goethite ores.
- MMG1 has a distinctive concentration of clay and shale, along with both martite dominated (MGM and MGF) and goethite (GOE and GOL) ores.
- MMG2 has a distinctive concentration of BPO, GOE and MGH, and represents the MG that contain some partly mineralised BIF.
- MMG3 represents the MGs with the greatest number of material types and has widest variety of material types.

We illustrate in Fig. 7 a few selected pair-wise scatterplots of SMS data color-coded with the four MMG categories. Some data separation can be observed in these plots and this may be further improved if more data are available.

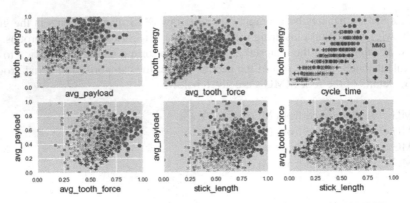

Fig. 7. Pair-wise scatter plots of SMS features, color-coded by the 4 MMGs

4.4 Two-Way Classification Test

With these four MMG categories, we performed machine learning classification to investigate the relationship between SMS and MMG. SGD classifiers are currently a popular ML method, as they are easily applied to large scale and sparse data. To test their applicability to this data they were applied, along with RF and SVM as comparison methods. We first performed classification of MMG from SMS features. The classifiers we tried in this series of experiments include RF, SVM and SGD. The next experiment was to perform classification of digging effort categories (the four MMG's) from MC. The classifiers we tried in this series of experiments include RF, SVM and SGD.

5 Results and Discussion

5.1 Two-Way Classification Results

In predicting MMG with SMS data, we found SVM to be the most accurate machine learning method out of RF, SVM and SGD. We configured the Scikit-learn tool with the RBF kernel and set the regularisation parameter to one. The results of predicting MMG using SMS data is given in Fig. 8. The accuracy of the SVM classified on the test set (267 points) was 0.72, see Fig. 8a. The accuracy of the SVM classifier on all data (1335 points) was 0.73 in Fig. 8b.

In predicting MMG with Material Content, we found RF to be the most accurate for this task out of RF, SVM and SGD. We set "n_estimators" in the Scikit-learn tool to be 15. Figure 9 contains the results when predicting digger effort (MMG) from material content (MC) data using RF. The accuracy of this classifier was 1.0 for the test data (Fig. 9b).

The above results show that we can infer from SMS features to MMG with a reasonably high accuracy. We are also able to infer material content to MMG very accurately. Considering each inference method involves 20% test data out of the total dataset, this accuracy results show that our novel strategy of material type guided SMS clustering is a viable way of grouping SMS data. Further, we may rely on the two-way inference results

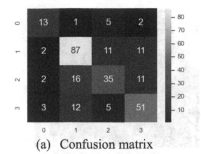

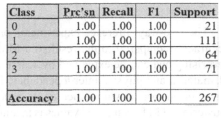

Class	Prc'sn	Recall	F1	Support
0	0.67	0.67	0.67	21
1	0.74	0.78	0.76	111
2	0.70	0.69	0.69	64
3	0.73	0.68	0.70	71
Accuracy	0.72	0.72	0.72	267

(a) Confusion matrix   (b) Accuracy results

Fig. 8. Test results of classifying for MMG categories with SMS data. Method: Linear SVM

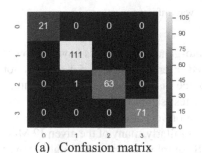

Class	Prc'sn	Recall	F1	Support
0	1.00	1.00	1.00	21
1	1.00	1.00	1.00	111
2	1.00	1.00	1.00	64
3	1.00	1.00	1.00	71
Accuracy	1.00	1.00	1.00	267

(a) Confusion matrix   (b) Material classification results

Fig. 9. Test results of classification for MMG categories with MC data. Method: Random Forest

in practical excavation applications, material inference from real-time SMS measurements and infer digging effort that corresponds to MMG. This should benefit efficient resource allocation.

5.2 Comparison with Automatic Clustering Using Force and Energy

To compare with conventional MC-based clustering, we also performed automatic clustering on SMS data using 2 clusters (Fig. 10). Similar to before we performed two-way inference experiment on the same data: classification for the auto-generated clusters from MC, and classification on the 12 MG using the SMS features. The training and test accuracies for both inferences are given in Table 1.

Table 1. Two-way classification results for auto-generated SMS cluster and Material type

	Material content -> Auto SMS cluster	SMS -> Material group
ML method	RF	SVM
Training accuracy	0.7	0.53
Test accuracy	0.67	0.47

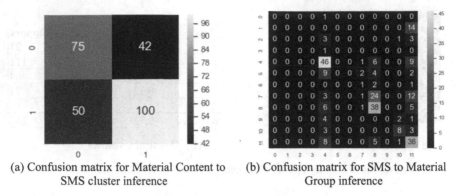

(a) Confusion matrix for Material Content to   (b) Confusion matrix for SMS to Material
SMS cluster inference   Group inference

Fig. 10. Confusion matrix for two-way inference tests

The two-way inference experiments on the auto-generated clusters have far lower accuracies compared to the results on MMG-based inference in Sect. 5.1. This is not surprising and can be explained by scarce data source distribution and complex nature of material and physics interdependency. First our test sample has a very limited MC distribution variety, with either single concentration or very few discrete levels. Naïve clustering of MT on the MC values is meaningless. Similarly, many of the given 12 MGs have similar hardness attributes. Further, the SMS samples may not thoroughly cover the underlying material physical properties. Therefore, this direct grouping of SMS and material type does not lead to significant results (Fig. 11).

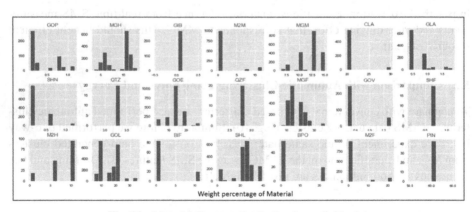

Fig. 11. Material Content distribution in available data

6 Conclusion

We presented a proof of concept study for a novel approach to infer the material group using the sensor data of diggers during mining. This is based on a common observation that the digging behaviour is related to mechanical properties of the material being dug.

We first used unsupervised k-means clustering to form four merged materials groups using their SMS features including forces, energy, payload and cycle time. We then studied two supervised classification methods to investigate relationship between SMS features and the MMG's. In the first classification method linear SVM was used on the SMS data to classify the MMG with 72% accuracy. The second approach utilized a RF method to classify the MMG class using the material content. The high accuracy is obtained in a two-way inference test using a small number of samples. The promising results suggest our approach is worth further investigation and may lead to bulk material identification at the digger level and efficient digging resource allocation.

Acknowledgements. This work has been supported by the Australian Centre for Field Robotics and the Rio Tinto Centre for Mine Automation, the University of Sydney.

References

1. Pedregosa, S., et al.: Scikit-learn: machine learning in Python. JMLR **12**, 2825–2830 (2011)
2. Breiman, L.: Random forests. Mach. Learn. **45**, 5–32 (2001). https://doi.org/10.1023/A:1010933404324
3. Cortes, C., Vapnik, V.N.: Support-vector networks (PDF). Mach. Learn. **20** (3), 273–297 (2017)
4. Koivo, J., Thoma, M., Kocaoglan, E., Andrade-Cetto, J.: Modeling and control of excavator dynamics during digging operation. J. Aerosp. Eng. **9**(1), 10–18 (1996)
5. Wikipedia. https://en.wikipedia.org/wiki/Support-vector_machine. Accessed 26 July 2021
6. Fernando, H., Marshall, J.: What lies beneath: material classification for autonomous excavators using proprioceptive force sensing and machine learning, Autom. Constr. **119** (2020). https://doi.org/10.1016/j.autcon.2020.103374
7. Dadhich, S., Bodin, U., Sandin, F., Andersson, U.: Machine learning approach to automatic bucket loading. In 24th Mediterranean Conference on Control and Automation (MED), pp. 1260–1265 (2016)
8. Bishop, C.M.: Pattern Recognition and Machine Learning (Information Science and Statistics). Springer, Heidelberg (2006)
9. Theodoridis, S., Koutroumbas, K.: Pattern Recognition, 4th edn. Academic Press Inc., Cambridge (2008)
10. Dai, J.S., Lam, H.K., Vahed. S.M.: Soil type identification for autonomous excavation based on dissipation energy. Proc. Inst. Mech. Eng. Part I J. Syst. Control Eng. **225**, 35–50 (2011)
11. Paine, M.D., Boyle, C.M.W., Lewan, A., Phuak, E.K.C., Mackenzie, P.H., Ryan, E.: Geometallurgy at Rio Tinto iron ore – a new angle on an old concept. In: Proceedings the Third AusIMM International Geometallurgy Conference (GeoMet) 2016, The Australasian Institute of Mining and Metallurgy, Melbourne, pp. 55–62 (2016)
12. Bottou, L.: Stochastic Gradient Descent - Website (2010)

Author Index

Printed in the United States
by Baker & Taylor Publisher Services